# Lecture Notes in Computer Science 16905

The series Lecture Notes in Computer Science (LNCS), including its subseries Lecture Notes in Artificial Intelligence (LNAI) and Lecture Notes in Bioinformatics (LNBI), has established itself as a medium for the publication of new developments in computer science and information technology research, teaching, and education.

LNCS enjoys close cooperation with the computer science R & D community, the series counts many renowned academics among its volume editors and paper authors, and collaborates with prestigious societies. Its mission is to serve this international community by providing an invaluable service, mainly focused on the publication of conference and workshop proceedings and postproceedings. LNCS commenced publication in 1973.

Joshua Weidlich · Irene-Angelica Chounta ·
Kairit Tammets · Tanya Nazaretsky ·
Bibeg Limbu · Fridolin Wild ·
Pablo Arnau-González
Editors

# Mindful TEL: Learning Technologies Shaped with Intention

21st European Conference on Technology Enhanced Learning, EC-TEL 2026
Valencia, Spain, September 14–18, 2026
Proceedings, Part I

Springer

*Editors*
Joshua Weidlich
University of Zurich
Zurich, Switzerland

Irene-Angelica Chounta
University of Duisburg-Essen
Essen, Germany

Kairit Tammets
Tallinn University
Tallinn, Estonia

Tanya Nazaretsky
École Polytechnique Fédérale de Lausanne
Lausanne, Switzerland

Bibeg Limbu
University of Duisburg-Essen
Essen, Germany

Fridolin Wild
The Open University
Milton Keynes, UK

Pablo Arnau-González
Universitat Politècnica de València
València, Spain

ISSN 0302-9743 ISSN 1611-3349 (electronic)
Lecture Notes in Computer Science
ISBN 978-3-032-37978-8 ISBN 978-3-032-37979-5 (eBook)
https://doi.org/10.1007/978-3-032-37979-5



This Springer imprint is published by the registered company Springer Nature Switzerland AG
The registered company address is: Gewerbestrasse 11, 6330 Cham, Switzerland

# Preface

These are the proceedings of the *21st European Conference on Technology Enhanced Learning* (ECTEL 2026), hosted by the Spanish National University of Distance Education in Valencia, Spain, September 14–18, 2026.

The theme of ECTEL 2026, *Mindful TEL: Learning Technologies Shaped with Intention*, speaks to the present moment of our field. As various digital technologies, and in particular artificial intelligence, become increasingly embedded in education, the challenge for our community is to ensure that technological innovation remains purposeful, theoretically grounded, empirically robust, and aligned with educational values. Mindful TEL therefore calls on the community to examine not only what learning technologies can do, but also what they should do, for whom, under what conditions, and with what consequences for learners, teachers, institutions, and society.

For ECTEL 2026, we received 194 submissions to the main research track, a 20% increase compared to last year. All submissions went through a double-blind review process. The individual reviews were followed by discussions and a meta-review provided by a senior member of the program committee. Each paper was reviewed by at least three reviewers, one of whom was a senior ECTEL member. As a result of this procedure, 45 papers were accepted for presentation at the conference, resulting in a 23% acceptance rate. Additionally, 50 posters, 15 demonstrations, and 3 industry papers were accepted for publication. Furthermore, the conference featured 13 workshops and a doctoral consortium as pre-conference activities held on September 14–15, 2026. The accepted contributions are published in two LNCS volumes. Volume I contains the full research papers, while Volume II includes the poster, demonstration, and practitioner and industry papers.

The papers included in these proceedings show a field that is technologically sophisticated, but also alert and reflective. Artificial Intelligence is, unsurprisingly, a major presence across this year's contributions. A wide range of AI-supported educational practices are examined: intelligent tutoring systems, LLM-based chatbots, teacher-facing AI systems, AI-supported classroom orchestration, and others. Across these studies, a recurring concern is how AI's educational value depends on design choices and pedagogical alignment, how it relates to learner agency, when it supports teacher judgement, and—crucially—the quality of the evidence used to evaluate it. These concerns resonate strongly with the conference theme, reminding us that educational technologies are never neutral, but shape the very possibilities for action, responsibility, and participation.

At the same time, the 2026 program demonstrates the continuing strength of TEL proper, including multimodal technologies, technology-supported assessment and feedback, computer-supported collaborative learning, learning analytics, and data-informed teaching practice and decision-making. Here too, we see an emphasis on mindful questions and intentionality, toward understanding how data can become meaningful for educational action: how it is interpreted, by whom, at what level of analysis, and in support of which pedagogical decisions.

A further strength of this year's proceedings is their breadth of educational contexts and learning activities. Contributions address K–12 mathematics, reading comprehension, higher education, teacher education, workforce training, public speaking, psychomotor skill acquisition, online discussion forums, collaborative programming, robots, and teacher professional learning. This breadth reflects one of ECTEL's longstanding strengths: the community does not define technology-enhanced learning by means of technology, but the learning processes it enables and enhances across various domains, contexts, and stakeholders.

We would like to thank all colleagues involved in organising, reviewing, and contributing to this year's conference. We are deeply grateful to the members of the program committee, who provided thoughtful reviews, engaged in constructive discussions, and supported the peer-review and selection process. We thank the workshop chairs, doctoral consortium chairs, proceedings chairs, communication and website chairs, practitioner and industry chairs, local organisers, steering committee representatives, and all others whose work made ECTEL 2026 possible. Most importantly, we thank all authors for sharing their excellent research with the community and all participants for contributing to the conversations that continue to shape our field of Technology Enhanced Learning. We also gratefully acknowledge the continued support of the EATEL Association, whose commitment to fostering the Technology Enhanced Learning community makes conferences such as ECTEL possible.

We also want to remember and honour those who have shaped our field over the years, among them Erik Duval, Martin Wolpers, and Ralf Klamma, whose contributions continue to inspire our work.

July 2026

Joshua Weidlich
Irene-Angelica Chounta
Kairit Tammets
Tanya Nazaretsky
Bibeg Limbu
Fridolin Wild
Pablo Arnau-González

# Organization

## General Chair

| | |
|---|---|
| Kairit Tammets | Tallinn University, Estonia |

## Program Committee Chairs

| | |
|---|---|
| Joshua Weidlich | University of Zurich, Switzerland; Zurich University of Teacher Education, Switzerland |
| Irene-Angelica Chounta | University of Duisburg-Essen, Germany |

## Poster/Demo Chairs

| | |
|---|---|
| Tanya Nazaretsky | EPFL, Switzerland |
| Bibeg Limbu | University of Duisburg-Essen, Germany |

## Practitioner and Industry Chairs

| | |
|---|---|
| Fridolin Wild | Open University, UK |
| Pablo Arnau Gonzalez | Universitat Politècnica de València, Spain |

## Workshop Chairs

| | |
|---|---|
| Justin Edwards | University of Oulu, Finland; Stockton University, USA |
| Oleksandra Poquet | Technical University of Munich, Germany |

## Doctoral Consortium Chairs

| | |
|---|---|
| Tobias Ley | University for Continuing Education Krems, Austria; Tallinn University, Estonia |
| Nikol Rummel | Center for Advanced Internet Studies and Ruhr-University Bochum, Germany |
| Paraskevi Topali | National Education Lab AI, Radboud University, Netherlands |

## Website Chair

Manisha Khulbe — Tallinn University, Estonia

## Communication Chair

Kateryna Holubinka — National Education Lab AI, Radboud University, Netherlands

## Proceedings Chairs

Edna Milena Sarmiento-Márquez — Tallinn University, Estonia, and University for Continuing Education Krems, Austria

Bhoomika Agarwal — Open University of the Netherlands, Netherlands

## Local Organization Chair

Olga C. Santos — National University of Distance Education, Spain

## Local Host Team

Alejandro Cerdá — Centro Asociado de la UNED Alzira-Valencia, Spain

Maribel Valero — Centro Asociado de la UNED Alzira-Valencia, Spain

David Torres — Centro Asociado de la UNED Alzira-Valencia, Spain

Doris García — Centro Asociado de la UNED Alzira-Valencia, Spain

María García-Pozuelo — Centro Asociado de la UNED Alzira-Valencia, Spain

Rosa Armengol — Centro Asociado de la UNED Alzira-Valencia, Spain

Josefa Doménech — Centro Asociado de la UNED Alzira-Valencia, Spain

## ECTEL Steering Committee Representative

| | |
|---|---|
| Marcus Specht | Delft University of Technology, Netherlands |

## Senior Program Committee

| | |
|---|---|
| Alejandro Ortega-Arranz | Universidad Valladolid, Spain |
| Angela Fessl | Know Center, Austria |
| Bibeg Limbu | University of Duisburg-Essen, Germany |
| Carlos Santos | University of Aveiro, Portugal |
| Danial Spikol | University of Copenhagen, Denmark |
| Davinia Hernandez-Leo | Universitat Pompeu Fabra, Spain |
| Fridolin Wild | Open University, UK |
| Irene-Angelica Chounta | University of Duisburg-Essen, Germany |
| Jelena Jovanovic | University of Belgrade, Serbia |
| Joshua Weidlich | University of Zurich; Zurich University of Education, Switzerland |
| Kairit Tammets | Tallinn University, Estonia |
| Luís Pedro | University of Aveiro, Portugal |
| Manuel Caeiro Rodríguez | University of Vigo, Spain |
| Matthias Ehlenz | RWTH Aachen University, Germany |
| Merike Saar | Tallinn University, Estonia |
| Miguel Arevalillo-Herráez | University of Valencia, Spain |
| Mohammed Saqr | University of Eastern Finland, Finland |
| Monica Divitini | Norwegian University of Science and Technology, Norway |
| Nikol Rummel | Ruhr-Universität Bochum, Germany |
| Oleksandra Poquet | Technical University of Munich, Germany |
| Olga Viberg | KTH Royal Institute of Technology, Sweden |
| Patricia Santos | Universitat Pompeu Fabra, Spain |
| Paraskevi Topali | National Education Lab AI, Radboud University, Netherlands |
| Paul Libbrecht | IUBH Fernstudium, Germany |
| Srinath Srinivasa | International Institute of Information Technology, Bangalore, India |
| Styliani Kleanthous | CYENS CoE and Open University of Cyprus, Cyprus |
| Tanya Nazaretsky | EPFL, Switzerland |
| Tinne de Laet | Katholieke Universiteit Leuven, Belgium |
| Tobias Ley | University for Continuing Education Krems, Austria; Tallinn University, Estonia |

| | |
|---|---|
| Tomaž Klobučar | Jožef Stefan Institute, Slovenia |
| Tore Hoel | Oslo Metropolitan University, Norway |
| Vanessa Echeverria | Monash University, Australia |
| Yvan Peter | Université de Lille, France |

## Program Committee

| | |
|---|---|
| Ademar Aguiar | University of Porto, Portugal |
| Agathe Merceron | Berliner Hochschule für Technik, Germany |
| Ainhoa Alvarez | University of the Basque Country, Spain |
| Alan Berg | University of Amsterdam, Netherlands |
| Alejandro Canovas-Solbes | Universitat Politècnica de València, Spain |
| Aleksandra Klasnja-Milicevic | University of Novi Sad, Serbia |
| Alessandra Antonaci | European Association of Distance Teaching Universities, Netherlands |
| Alessandro Pagano | University of Bari, Italy |
| Alev Elçi | YÖMEGA, Turkey |
| Alexander Nussbaumer | Graz University of Technology, Austria |
| Alexander Streicher | Fraunhofer IOSB, Germany |
| Álvaro Becerra | Universidad Autónoma de Madrid, Spain |
| Álvaro Sobrinho | Federal University of the Agreste of Pernambuco, Brazil |
| Alyssa Lawson | Colby College, USA |
| Amedee Martella | University of Georgia, USA |
| Ana Loureiro | Lusófona University, Portugal |
| Ana Luísa Mateus Oliveira Chança Torres | Instituto Politécnico de Santarém, Brazil |
| Ana Raquel Carvalho | University of Aveiro, Portugal |
| Ana Serrano-Mamolar | Universidad de Burgos, Spain |
| Ana Tibau-Flores | Universitat de València, Spain |
| Anderson Pinheiro Cavalcanti | Universidade Federal Rural de Pernambuco, Brazil |
| Andrea Adamoli | Independent researcher |
| Andrea Vázquez-Ingelmo | University of Salamanca, Spain |
| Andreas Breiter | Universität Bremen, Germany |
| Andreas Lingnau | Deutsche Hochschule für angewandte Wissenschaften, Germany |
| Andriani Piki | University of Central Lancashire Cyprus, Cyprus |
| Andrzej M. J. Skulimowski | AGH University of Kraków, Poland |
| Ángel Hernández-García | Universidad Politécnica de Madrid, Spain |
| Antigoni Parmaxi | Cyprus University of Technology, Cyprus |

| | |
|---|---|
| Antonio Balderas | University of Cádiz, Spain |
| Arun Balajiee Lekshmi Narayanan | University of Pittsburgh, USA |
| Atezaz Ahmad | DIPF \| Leibniz Institute for Research and Information in Education, Germany |
| Audrey Serna | LIRIS, INSA Lyon, France |
| Bahtijar Vogel | Malmö University, Sweden |
| Benedikt Hensen | RWTH Aachen University, Germany |
| Bernardo Tabuenca | Universidad Politécnica de Madrid, Spain |
| Bhoomika Agarwal | Open Universiteit, Netherlands |
| Birte Heinemann | RWTH Aachen University, Germany |
| Bruno Alexandre Rosa | CESAR School, Brazil |
| Carlo Giovannella | University of Rome Tor Vergata, Italy |
| Carrie Demmans Epp | University of Alberta, Canada |
| Covadonga Rodrigo | Universidad Nacional de Educacion a Distancia, Spain |
| Cristian Cechinel | Federal University of Santa Catarina, Brazil |
| Dana Kube | University of Zürich, Switzerland |
| David Gimeno-Gomez | Universitat Politècnica de València, Spain |
| Dominique Lenne | Heudiasyc, Université de Technologie de Compiègne, France |
| Edna Milena Sarmiento-Márquez | Tallinn University, Estonia and University for Continuing Education Krems, Austria |
| Eelco Herder | Utrecht University, Netherlands |
| Eileen Richter | Martin Luther University Halle-Wittenberg, Germany |
| Ekaterina Shved | EPFL, Switzerland |
| Elaine Harada | Universidade Federal do Amazonas, Brazil |
| Elis Kakoulli Constantinou | Cyprus University of Technology, Cyprus |
| Élise Lavoué | Université Jean Moulin Lyon 3, LIRIS, France |
| Elizabeth Cloude | Michigan State University, USA |
| Elyda Freitas | Universidade de Pernambuco, Brazil |
| Emmmanuel G. Blanchard | Le Mans Université, France |
| Estefania Martin | Universidad Rey Juan Carlos, Spain |
| Eyal Rabin | Open University of Israel, Israel |
| Fabiano Dorça | Universidade Federal de Uberlândia, Brazil |
| Fatma Betül Güreş | EPFL, Switzerland |
| Francesca Pozzi | Istituto Tecnologie Didattiche—CNR, Italy |
| Francisco Iniesto | Open University, UK |
| Francisco Regalado | Universidade de Aveiro, Portugal |
| Frederic Salmen | RWTH Aachen University, Germany |
| Gabriel Alves | Universidade Federal Rural de Pernambuco, Brazil |

| | |
|---|---|
| Geoffray Bonnin | Université de Lorraine, France |
| Geraldine Gray | Technological University Dublin, Ireland |
| Giora Alexandron | Weizmann Institute of Science, Israel |
| Guilherme Medeiros Machado | ECE Paris, France |
| Guillermo Vega-Gorgojo | Universidad de Valladolid, Spain |
| Gustavo Zurita | Universidad de Chile, Chile |
| Hilário Oliveira | Instituto Federal do Espírito Santo - Campus Serra, Brazil |
| Ina Blau | Open University of Israel, Israel |
| Inge de Waard | EIT InnoEnergy, Netherlands |
| Ioannis Lefkos | University of Macedonia, Greece |
| Iris Wunder | FAU Erlangen-Nuremberg, Germany |
| Isabela Gasparini | Universidade do Estado de Santa Catarina, Brazil |
| Ishari Amarasinghe | Universitat Pompeu Fabra, Spain |
| Ismail Celik | University of Oulu, Finland |
| Jacqueline Wong | Utrecht University, Netherlands |
| Jan Schneider | DIPF \| Leibniz Institute for Research and Information in Education, Germany |
| Jason Bernard | Athabasca University, Canada |
| Joao Batista | University of Aveiro, Portugal |
| John Stamper | Carnegie Mellon University, USA |
| Jordan Barria-Pineda | University of Pittsburgh, USA |
| Jorge Munoz-Gama | Pontificia Universidad Católica de Chile, Chile |
| José A. Ruipérez Valiente | University of Murcia, Spain |
| Josef Buchner | St. Gallen University of Teacher Education, Switzerland |
| Juan A. Muñoz-Cristóbal | Universidad de Valladolid, Spain |
| Juan Andrés Talamás Carvajal | Tecnológico de Monterrey, Mexico |
| Juan I. Asensio-Pérez | Universidad de Valladolid, Spain |
| Juliana Elisa Raffaghelli | University of Padua, Italy |
| Julio Guerra | Universidad Austral de Chile, Chile |
| Justin Edwards | University of Oulu, Spain |
| Kaimao Sheng | University of Duisburg-Essen, Germany |
| Karim Sehaba | LIRIS CNRS, France |
| Katharina Dahmann | Goethe University Frankfurt, Germany |
| Khaleel Asyraaf Mat Sanusi | Cologne Game Lab, Germany |
| Konstantinos Michos | EPFL, Switzerland |
| Laura Allen | University of Minnesota, USA |
| Leon Camus | DIPF\|Leibniz-Institut für Bildungsforschung und Bildungsinformation, Germany |
| Liron Levy-Nadav | Open University of Israel, Israel |
| Lisa Lim | University of Technology Sydney, Australia |

| | |
|---|---|
| Luca Benedetto | Télécom SudParis, France |
| Luiz Barboza | CESAR School, Brazil |
| Lukas Menzel | Studiumdigitale, Goethe University, Frankfurt am Main, Germany |
| M. Cristina Rodriguez-Sanchez | Rey Juan Carlos University, Spain |
| Maartje Henderikx | Open Universiteit, Netherlands |
| Manuel Jesus Gomez Moratilla | Universidad de Murcia, Spain |
| Mar Pérez-Sanagustín | Université de Toulouse, France |
| Marco Kalz | Heidelberg University of Education, Germany |
| Maren Scheffel | Ruhr University Bochum, Germany |
| Margarida Lucas | University of Aveiro, Portugal |
| Maria Aristeidou | Open University, UK |
| María Jesús Rodríguez-Triana | Universidad de Valladolid, Spain |
| Maria Perifanou | University of Macedonia, Aristotle University of Thessaloniki, Hellenic Open University, Greece |
| Mariano Albaladejo-González | Universidad de Murcia, Spain |
| Marie-Helene Abel | HEUDIASYC - Université de Technologie de Compiègne |
| Marina Lepp | University of Tartu, Estonia |
| Markel Vigo | University of Manchester, UK |
| Markus Spitzer | Martin-Luther Universität Halle, Germany |
| Martín Llamas-Nistal | Universidad de Vigo, Spain |
| Michael Kickmeier-Rust | Graz University of Technology, Austria |
| Miguel L. Bote-Lorenzo | Universidad de Valladolid, Spain |
| Mikhail Fominykh | Norwegian University of Science and Technology, Norway |
| Miriam Mulders | Universität Duisburg-Essen, Germany |
| Mirko Marras | University of Cagliari, Italy |
| Mohsen Saadatmand | University of Helsinki, Finland |
| Mona Münstermann | Universität Duisburg-Essen, Germany |
| Mónica Aresta | University of Aveiro, Portugal |
| Monique Grandbastien | LORIA, Université de Lorraine, France |
| Nghia Duong-Trung | German Research Centre for Artificial Intelligence, Germany |
| Nicolas Ballier | Université Paris Cité, France |
| Nicoletta Di Blas | Politecnico di Milano, Italy |
| Niels Pinkwart | Humboldt-Universität zu Berlin, Germany |
| Niels Seidel | FernUniversität in Hagen, Germany |
| Nikos Palavitsinis | Eummena Foundation, Greece |
| Nils Malzahn | Rhine-Ruhr Institute for Applied System Innovation e. V., Germany |

| | |
|---|---|
| Nina Mouhammad | DIPF ǀ Leibniz Institute for Research and Information in Education, Germany |
| Oleksandra Poquet | Utrecht University, Netherlands |
| Pablo Arnau-González | Technical University of Valencia, Spain |
| Pablo García-Zarza | Universidad de Valladolid, Spain |
| Panagiotis Kosmas | University of Limassol, Cyprus |
| Pedro J. Muñoz-Merino | Universidad Carlos III de Madrid, Spain |
| Pedro Manuel Moreno-Marcos | Universidad Carlos III de Madrid, Spain |
| Peter Fröhlich | FFG Austrian Research Promotion Agency, Austria |
| Piret Luik | University of Tartu, Estonia |
| Rafael Ferreira Mello | Cesar School, Brazil |
| Reet Kasepalu | Tallinn University and the Academy of Security Sciences, Estonia |
| Rene Kizilcec | Cornell University, USA |
| René Röpke | RWTH Aachen University, Germany |
| Richard Lee Davis | Stanford University, USA |
| Riichiro Mizoguchi | Japan Advanced Institute of Science and Technology, Japan |
| Roland Klemke | Open University of the Netherlands, Netherlands |
| Ronald Pérez-Álvarez | Universidad de Costa Rica, Costa Rica |
| Ruth Cobos | Universidad Autónoma de Madrid, Spain |
| Sambit Praharaj | Kalinga Institute of Industrial Technology, India |
| Samuel González-López | Technological University of Nogales, Mexico |
| Sebastian Dennerlein | Interdisciplinary Transformation University, Austria |
| Sebastian Gombert | DIPF ǀ Leibniz Institute for Research and Information in Education, Germany |
| Sebastian Jansen | University of Zurich, Switzerland |
| Sebastian Wollny | DIPF - German Institute for International Educational Research, Germany |
| Sébastien George | LIUM, Le Mans Université, France |
| Sergi Solera-Monforte | University of Valencia, Spain |
| Shashi Kant Shankar | Amrita Vishwa Vidyapeetham, India |
| Shivang Gupta | Carnegie Mellon University, USA |
| Sofia Strukova | University of Murcia, Spain |
| Sonsoles López-Pernas | University of Eastern Finland, Finland |
| Stamos Katsigiannis | Durham University, UK |
| Stavros Nikou | University of Strathclyde, UK |
| Steven Moore | Carnegie Mellon University, USA |
| Stylianos Mystakidis | University of Patras, Greece |
| Tomohiro Nagashima | Saarland University, Germany |
| Torsten Zesch | FernUniversität Hagen, Germany |

| | |
|---|---|
| Ulrike Mascher | Goethe University Frankfurt, Germany |
| Vanda Luengo | Sorbonne Université - LIP6, France |
| Vanessa Echeverria | Monash University, Australia |
| Vanessa Figueiredo | University of Regina, Canada |
| Victoria I. Marín | Universitat de Lleida, Spain |
| Viktoria Pammer-Schindler | Graz University of Technology, Austria |
| Vincent Aleven | Carnegie Mellon University, USA |
| Wannapon Suraworachet | University College London, UK |
| Xiaoling Zhang | Maastricht University, Netherlands |
| Yael Feldman-Maggor | KTH Royal Institute of Technology, Sweden |
| Yann Secq | Université de Lille, France |
| Yannic Jäckel | DIPF\|Leibniz-Institut für Bildungsforschung und Bildungsinformation, Germany |
| Yannis Dimitriadis | University of Valladolid, Spain |
| Yoon Lee | University of Seoul, South Korea |
| Yuyan Wu | Universitat de València, Spain |

# Contents

# Research Track

# Intraindividual Variability in Self-reported Energy as a Contextual Factor for Learning Outcomes in a K–12 Math Digital Learning Game

Marshall An[1(✉)], Mahboobeh Mehrvarz[1], Hayden Stec[1], Esma Nur Kahveci[2], John Stamper[1], and Bruce M. McLaren[1]

[1] Carnegie Mellon University, Pittsburgh, PA 15213, USA
{haokanga,hstec,jstamper,bmclaren}@andrew.cmu.edu
[2] University of Massachusetts Dartmouth, Dartmouth, MA, USA
ekahveci@umassd.edu

**Abstract.** Digital learning games and intelligent tutoring systems (ITSs) have demonstrated educational benefits, yet substantial variability in learning outcomes persists. While log-based behavioral signals are often used to identify students at risk, they offer limited visibility into the fluctuating internal states that condition learning. This study examines how a log-based signal and learners' self-reported energy jointly predict immediate and delayed posttest performance (retention) in a K–12 mathematics digital learning game with an underlying ITS. The signal is operationalized as the total incorrect step-level attempts during gameplay, including repeated attempts, and self-reported energy is measured repeatedly across sessions. Data were collected from 319 students across 25 classrooms in five schools. Learning outcomes were assessed using a pretest, an immediate posttest, and a one-week delayed posttest. Despite overall significant and sustained performance improvements, incorrect attempts emerged as a consistent negative predictor of both immediate and delayed posttest performance, even after controlling for prior knowledge. Notably, intraindividual variability in self-reported energy moderated the relationship between incorrect attempts and retention: higher numbers of incorrect attempts were more strongly associated with poorer retention for learners whose self-reported energy fluctuated more across sessions. In plain terms, frequent mistakes were a stronger warning sign of weaker one-week retention for students whose self-reported energy fluctuated more across days. Robustness checks indicated that these patterns were consistent across experimental contexts. These findings suggest that intraindividual variability in self-reported energy, captured via lightweight measures, can provide contextual value for interpreting log-based signals associated with poorer retention in authentic classroom settings.

**Keywords:** Intelligent tutoring systems · Learning games · Self-reported energy · Intraindividual variability · Technology-enhanced learning


J. Weidlich et al. (Eds.): EC-TEL 2026, LNCS 16905, pp. 3–18, 2027.
https://doi.org/10.1007/978-3-032-37979-5_1

## 1 Introduction

Meta-analyses support the overall promise of digital learning games [12,23], but outcomes are not uniform: effect sizes vary across studies and game designs [12], and even successful deployments can benefit some learners much less than others [16,40]. One line of work in technology-enhanced learning (TEL) research addresses this variability by accommodating heterogeneous learner needs through intelligent tutoring systems (ITSs), which use techniques such as learner modeling, adaptive problem selection, and targeted feedback [3,33,40]. Despite ITSs' strong record of improving average learning outcomes [30,46], outcome variability remains pronounced. Meta-analyses report substantial heterogeneity across ITS deployments [34], and K–12 syntheses show that benefits may differ for higher- versus lower-achieving students [10,43], motivating research that moves beyond average effectiveness to examine within-system divergence.

One established approach to understanding such variability is to analyze interaction logs for behavioral signals associated with weaker outcomes [6]. However, logs provide limited visibility into learners' internal states that may condition how observable behaviors relate to outcomes. Attentional control and cognitive resource frameworks emphasize that learning depends on cognitive and metacognitive resources that can fluctuate over time [25,28]. These theoretical accounts are supported by large-scale field-based evidence from K–12 educational contexts showing systematic within-day variation in students' cognitive performance, including performance declines over the school day and partial restoration after breaks [41]. Beyond momentary performance, such fluctuations may also affect how learners monitor their understanding and regulate their responses to difficulty across sessions [5,11,15], suggesting a potential link between internal resource variability and retention. However, repeatedly measuring internal states in authentic classroom settings poses practical challenges, particularly when measures must be scalable and minimally disruptive [8]. To address this constraint, we introduce a lightweight, classroom-deployable self-report of learner energy administered in situ across multiple days. We use repeated energy self-reports as a pragmatic indicator of learners' subjective experience of fluctuation across learning sessions, and examine whether this signal provides contextual value when modeled jointly with behavioral logs for predicting immediate learning outcomes and retention. We conducted the investigation using data from the Fall 2025 deployment of *Decimal Point*, a K–12 mathematics digital learning game with an underlying ITS.

This work makes two contributions to research on TEL in authentic classroom settings. First, we introduce a lightweight daily self-report energy probe suitable for in-vivo K–12 classroom use and provide initial evidence of its internal consistency and low time cost. Second, we show that intraindividual variability in self-reported energy provides contextual value for interpreting a common log-based behavioral risk signal: frequent incorrect attempts were more strongly associated with poorer retention when learners' self-reported energy fluctuated more across days. Together, these findings contribute to understanding when common behavioral indicators are more strongly linked to outcomes in TEL environments.

## 2 Related Work

### 2.1 Digital Learning Games with Intelligent Tutoring Systems

Prior work shows that integrating ITS components into digital learning games can support learning [3,40]. ITSs are a well-established application of artificial intelligence in education, designed to provide adaptive, one-on-one instruction that approximates the support of a human tutor [2,10]. Meta-analytic evidence indicates that these environments improve learning beyond typical classroom instruction, with effect sizes comparable to those of human tutors [30,46]. However, even effective ITSs do not benefit all learners equally: learning outcomes depend both on instructional design choices and on how individual learners interact with those designs, which can vary substantially across learners [9,32,45]. In particular, meta-analytic work on ITSs in K–12 mathematics suggests that learning benefits are not uniform across achievement levels [43], underscoring the need to examine who benefits and under what conditions. In this context, our work moves beyond overall ITS efficacy to examine outcome variability by combining behavioral logs with self-reported learner energy.

### 2.2 Log-Based Signals in ITSs Associated with Outcome Variability

Prior ITS research uses interaction logs to derive signals linked to learning outcome variability, including indicators based on frequent incorrect attempts [7,47]. Such signals are also used for real-time detection and instructional tools, such as the teacher-facing Lumilo [21], which employs error rates to help prioritize students needing assistance. Informed by this line of work, we use the frequency of incorrect attempts as a commonly available log-based indicator. Our contribution is not to propose a new behavioral metric, but to examine how this indicator's meaning changes when interpreted alongside repeated, low-burden self-reports from authentic classroom settings.

### 2.3 Intraindividual Variability (IIV)

Learner energy fluctuations connect to the concept of intraindividual variability (IIV), which captures within-person changes in cognitive or behavioral performance across time and contexts that are relatively fleeting and reversible over moments or days [22,35,38]. Empirical work shows that IIV accounts for a substantial share of observed performance differences across populations. For example, research with older adults found that IIV accounted for approximately half of the variance in everyday cognitive performance across repeated assessments [19]. Similarly, studies of children using repeated working memory assessments in school contexts report that IIV accounts for 48%–65% of total variance across measures [18]. Although prior IIV research has primarily examined cognitive performance, the same within-person logic can also be applied to repeated self-reports collected in classroom settings. Methodologically, within-person variability can be preferable to between-person comparisons of mean self-reports because stable individual differences (e.g., response styles or scale-use tendencies) can distort between-person differences, whereas within-person deviations capture change relative to an individual's own typical level [14].

Accordingly, we use $IIV_{\text{energy}}$ to denote within-learner variability in daily self-reported energy, operationalized as the standard deviation of repeated probe responses across classroom sessions. We treat this measure as a pragmatic contextual signal derived from repeated classroom self-reports, rather than as a fully validated psychological construct, and examine whether it interacts with a common log-based behavioral risk signal in relation to learning outcomes.

## 3 Research Questions

We formulate the following research questions: **RQ1:** How effective is the K–12 mathematics game with an underlying ITS in supporting learning overall? **RQ2:** Is a log-based behavioral indicator (number of incorrect attempts) associated with immediate posttest and delayed posttest scores, after controlling for pretest? **RQ3:** Are a learner's mean level of self-reported energy and their $IIV_{\text{energy}}$ associated with immediate posttest and delayed posttest scores, after controlling for pretest? **RQ4:** Do mean energy and $IIV_{\text{energy}}$ moderate the association between incorrect attempts and immediate posttest and delayed posttest scores, after controlling for pretest?

### 3.1 Materials

Our study used *Decimal Point*, a digital learning game with an underlying ITS developed with CTAT [1]. As shown in Fig. 1, students "travel" through a theme park and play 24 mini-games, each with two problems, to learn decimal concepts and operations. Fantasy non-player characters (NPCs) encourage students, congratulate correct solutions, and provide feedback on mistakes.

**Fig. 1.** *Decimal Point* and an example mini-game.

### 3.2 Design and Participants

In Fall 2025, *Decimal Point* served as a shared research platform supporting two concurrent randomized experiments with distinct independent variables (one with two conditions and one with three), such that each learner was assigned to one of five platform conditions. These conditions varied in surface-level design features, including storytelling, visual theme, assessment presentation, and self-explanation orchestration. Despite different surface features, all conditions used practice and assessment items that were aligned at the item level, such that corresponding problems and test items targeted the same underlying mathematical skills, modeled as knowledge components [27]. Gameplay mechanics and logging structures were likewise held constant. The daily energy probe, central to this study, was also administered identically. Because the experimental manipulations themselves are not the focus of this study, we do not detail them here. Meanwhile, these experimental contexts provide an opportunity to examine whether observed associations are consistent across conditions, motivating the robustness checks reported in each research question. Learning outcomes were assessed with three decimal tests: pretest, immediate posttest, and one-week delayed posttest. To control for practice effects and test difficulty, three test versions (A, B, C) were counterbalanced across the six possible test sequences, with each version appearing equally often at each occasion. Each test contained 43 items, some with multiple components, for 52 possible points. To support attribution of delayed posttest performance to retention rather than additional instruction, no additional whole-class decimal instruction occurred during the study period.

A total of 481 students from 25 classrooms across five schools participated. We excluded 156 students who did not complete all required materials (pretest, immediate posttest, delayed posttest, and at least one daily energy probe). Following the outlier-exclusion procedure used in prior research with *Decimal Point* [36], we excluded 6 additional students with extreme learning gains, defined as immediate posttest minus pretest or delayed posttest minus pretest scores exceeding $\pm 2.5$ standard deviations from the corresponding sample mean. The final analytic sample included 319 students.

Demographic data were collected via an embedded survey, with 315 participants providing demographic information. Participants were primarily in grades 5–7 (5th: $n = 101$; 6th: $n = 168$; 7th: $n = 44$), with very few outside this range (4th: $n = 1$; 8th: $n = 1$). Ages were predominantly 10–12 years (10: $n = 62$; 11: $n = 140$; 12: $n = 98$), with fewer older learners (13: $n = 13$; 14: $n = 1$); one learner reported being younger than 10. Gender was self-reported as open-ended responses; after consolidating equivalent labels, 158 participants identified as female and 151 as male. 5 responses were off-topic or invalid, and 1 participant entered "prefer not to say." Race and ethnicity were self-reported with multiple selections allowed. 68 learners selected "I'm not sure / Prefer not to say," and 35 selected multiple categories. Among single-category responses, the largest group identified as White or Caucasian ($n = 113$), followed by Black or African American ($n = 49$), a race/ethnicity not listed by the survey ($n = 14$),

Native American or Alaskan Native ($n = 8$), Hispanic or Latino ($n = 7$), and Asian or Pacific Islander ($n = 3$).

### 3.3 A Lightweight Classroom Self-report of Perceived Energy

Learners provided brief, in-situ self-reports of their perceived energy using a 6-item probe (Fig. 2) at the start of each daily session. The probe was intended as a low-burden measure for capturing day-to-day variation in self-reported energy in K–12 classrooms, rather than as a validated measure of a psychological construct. Item wording was informed by the exhaustion subscale of the Maslach Burnout Inventory for Students (MBI-SS) [39] and reworded to support brief repeated self-report in K–12 classrooms. For example, the original item "I feel tired when I get up in the morning and I have to face another day at the university" was reworded as "When I wake up for school, my brain still feels sleepy," alongside a parallel reverse-coded item ("feels awake and ready").

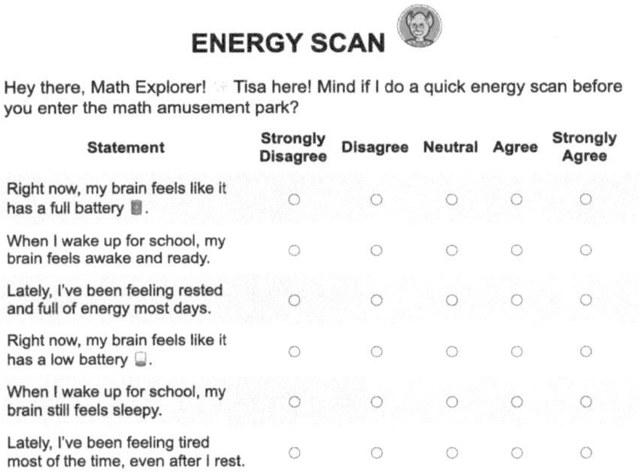
**ENERGY SCAN**

Hey there, Math Explorer! Tisa here! Mind if I do a quick energy scan before you enter the math amusement park?

| Statement | Strongly Disagree | Disagree | Neutral | Agree | Strongly Agree |
|---|---|---|---|---|---|
| Right now, my brain feels like it has a full battery. | ○ | ○ | ○ | ○ | ○ |
| When I wake up for school, my brain feels awake and ready. | ○ | ○ | ○ | ○ | ○ |
| Lately, I've been feeling rested and full of energy most days. | ○ | ○ | ○ | ○ | ○ |
| Right now, my brain feels like it has a low battery. | ○ | ○ | ○ | ○ | ○ |
| When I wake up for school, my brain still feels sleepy. | ○ | ○ | ○ | ○ | ○ |
| Lately, I've been feeling tired most of the time, even after I rest. | ○ | ○ | ○ | ○ | ○ |

**Fig. 2.** The six-item daily energy probe.

This probe was designed to be lightweight and classroom-compatible, reflecting the practical constraints of an in-vivo, multi-school study conducted during regular K–12 math classes, where more intrusive or time-intensive measures (e.g., lengthy surveys or physiological sensors) were not feasible at scale. It was embedded directly into *Decimal Point* and presented automatically at the start of each session, requiring no separate materials or workflow transitions.

Consequently, the number of repeated measurements per learner was determined by the duration and instructional structure of the classroom deployment, which unfolded across the scheduled decimal class sessions over approximately one week. As a result, the present measure captures within-learner fluctuation across the available learning sessions in this instructional context, rather than a more extended, trait-like estimate of variability. Across all administrations, participants ($N = 319$, $n = 1{,}810$ responses) spent an average of 30.1 s per daily session completing the probe ($SD = 30.8$ seconds). Given typical class periods ranging from approximately 45 to 85 min across participating schools, this represents well under 2% of instructional time per session.

## 4 Results

### 4.1 RQ1: Significant Overall Learning Gains from *Decimal Point*

Mean scores increased from pretest ($M = 23.04$, $SD = 10.18$) to immediate posttest ($M = 26.24$, $SD = 9.82$) and delayed posttest ($M = 27.23$, $SD = 10.15$). A one-way repeated-measures ANOVA showed a significant effect of test phase. Because Mauchly's test indicated a violation of sphericity ($W = 0.965, p = .003$), Greenhouse–Geisser–corrected results are reported ($\epsilon = .966$), $F(1.93, 612.94) = 105.22, p < .001$. Post-hoc paired $t$-tests with Bonferroni correction indicated significant differences between all test phases: scores improved from pretest to immediate posttest, $t(318) = 10.30$, $p_{\text{adj}} < .001$, $d_z = 0.58$, and from pretest to delayed posttest, $t(318) = 13.09$, $p_{\text{adj}} < .001$, $d_z = 0.73$, both reflecting substantial improvements. Delayed posttest scores were modestly higher than immediate posttest scores, $t(318) = 3.62$, $p_{\text{adj}} = .001$, $d_z = 0.20$. Because the Fall 2025 deployment spanned multiple experimental contexts, we examined whether overall learning outcomes differed by experiment or platform condition. Mixed ANOVA revealed no Test Phase × Experiment interaction ($F(2, 634) = 0.11$, $p = .896$) and no Test Phase × Condition interaction ($F(8, 628) = 0.40$, $p = .923$), indicating that performance improvements were consistent across contexts. Despite overall effectiveness, learner outcomes showed substantial variability. Mean learning gains were $M = 3.20$ ($SD = 5.55$) on the immediate posttest and $M = 4.19$ ($SD = 5.72$) on the delayed posttest, with standard deviations exceeding the corresponding means. This variability motivated analysis of factors underlying divergent outcomes.

### 4.2 RQ2: Incorrect Attempts as a Behavioral Risk Signal

RQ2 tests whether incorrect attempts, treated as a log-based behavioral risk signal, are negatively associated with immediate and delayed posttest scores. We operationalized incorrect attempts as the total number of logged step-level attempts marked incorrect during gameplay across all mini-games, using interaction logs collected through DataShop [26]. This count includes repeated attempts on the same step. Incorrect attempts were strongly right-skewed (mean = 352, median = 273; skewness = 2.07), with substantial variability across learners (IQR = 175–466; range = 17–1987). 11 learners (3.4%) made at least 1000 incorrect attempts. To examine the association between incorrect attempts and learning outcomes, we used OLS linear regression, with all numeric predictors and outcomes standardized (z-scores) to make coefficients comparable across measures on different scales. Reported coefficients therefore represent the expected

SD change in the outcome per 1 SD increase in the predictor; substantive conclusions were unchanged with unstandardized variables.

We first assessed standard OLS diagnostic checks for both models to support the use of linear regression. Multicollinearity was low based on variance inflation factors (VIFs; all VIFs $< 3$, max $= 1.56$), and residuals showed no major departure from normality (Jarque–Bera $p = .30$ for posttest; $p = .13$ for delayed posttest). Because Breusch–Pagan tests suggested mild heteroscedasticity (posttest $p = .048$; delayed posttest $p = .018$), we report heteroscedasticity-robust (HC3) standard errors for all inferences. Controlling for prior knowledge, incorrect attempts were negatively associated with both immediate and delayed learning outcomes. For the immediate posttest, prior knowledge was a strong positive predictor ($\beta = 0.726$, $p < .001$), and incorrect attempts showed a significant negative association ($\beta = -0.202$, $p < .001$). The model explained a substantial proportion of variance in posttest performance ($R^2 = .742$, $F(2, 316) = 535.9$, $p < .001$). A parallel pattern was observed for delayed posttest performance: prior knowledge remained a strong predictor ($\beta = 0.726$, $p < .001$), and incorrect attempts continued to show a significant negative association ($\beta = -0.193$, $p < .001$). The model explained a comparable proportion of variance ($R^2 = .733$, $F(2, 316) = 471.5$, $p < .001$). Robustness checks examined whether the association between incorrect attempts and learning outcomes differed across experimental contexts. For immediate posttest performance, the association between incorrect attempts and performance was not moderated by experiment (joint Wald test, $p = .159$). However, modest variation in the strength of this association was observed across conditions nested within experiments (joint Wald test, $p = .036$). Condition-specific regressions indicated that incorrect attempts significantly predicted worse immediate performance in four of the five conditions ($p < .001$; $p = .043$; $p < .001$; $p = .007$); in the remaining condition, the effect was also negative but did not reach conventional statistical significance ($p = .082$). For delayed posttest performance, no evidence of moderation was observed, either between experiments (joint Wald test, $p = .524$) or across conditions nested within experiments (joint Wald test, $p = .876$). Overall, these results indicate a largely consistent negative association between incorrect attempts and both immediate and delayed posttest scores across experimental contexts, after accounting for prior knowledge.

### 4.3 RQ3: Mean Energy, $IIV_{\mathbf{energy}}$, and Learning Outcomes

Before testing energy as a contextual moderator, we examined whether self-reported energy directly predicted learning outcomes. This step distinguishes models in which self-reported states have independent associations with learning from models in which they primarily condition how behavioral patterns relate to outcomes. As this daily energy probe was newly adapted for this study, we first examined its internal consistency. Across all completed responses from the 319 participants (excluding 82 incomplete responses, resulting in $N = 1{,}810$ responses), the six items demonstrated good internal consistency (Cronbach's $\alpha = 0.85$). The items were aggregated into a single composite energy score per learner per daily session. Although our primary interest lies in $IIV_{\text{energy}}$, mean energy is included as a complementary summary of a learner's typical reported state, allowing us to distinguish between average levels and fluctuations in self-reported energy without assuming that mean energy is itself a direct driver of learning outcomes. Accordingly, for each learner, we computed (a) mean energy as the within-learner average of daily composite scores and (b) $IIV_{\text{energy}}$ as the within-learner standard deviation of those daily scores. To reduce the risk of unstable estimates of variability, analyses involving $IIV_{\text{energy}}$ were restricted to learners with at least four completed daily energy probe responses, as variability estimates based on fewer observations are highly sensitive to single extreme values and may reflect measurement noise rather than meaningful within-learner variation. This criterion reduced the analytic sample in RQ3 and RQ4 from 319 to 309. As a threshold sensitivity check for computing $IIV_{\text{energy}}$, we repeated the RQ3–RQ4 models using alternative minimum-probe requirements ($\geq 2$, $\geq 3$, and $\geq 5$ completed probes). The $\geq 2$ threshold corresponds to the minimum required to compute a within-learner standard deviation, while the $\geq 5$ threshold corresponds to learners who completed daily energy probes on all instructional days during the one-week intervention. Results were substantively unchanged.

To test whether mean energy and $IIV_{\text{energy}}$ are associated with immediate and delayed learning outcomes, we employed OLS regression. Consistent with RQ2, all numeric predictor and outcome variables were standardized. We estimated two models: one predicting standardized immediate posttest performance and one predicting standardized delayed posttest performance. In both models, standardized pretest score was included as a control for prior knowledge.

We assessed standard OLS diagnostic checks for both models. Multicollinearity was low, with VIFs close to 1 (maximum VIF $= 1.05$). Residuals showed no major departure from normality based on Jarque–Bera tests ($p = .85$ for posttest; $p = .08$ for delayed posttest). As a conservative measure, all reported inferences are based on heteroscedasticity-robust (HC3) standard errors.

For immediate posttest performance, the model explained a substantial proportion of variance ($R^2 = .707$, $F(3, 305) = 290.2$, $p < .001$). After controlling for prior knowledge ($\beta = 0.836$, $p < .001$), neither mean energy nor $IIV_{\text{energy}}$ was significantly associated with immediate performance (both $p > .10$). For delayed posttest performance, the model similarly accounted for a large proportion of variance ($R^2 = .715$, $F(3, 305) = 277.5$, $p < .001$). After controlling for prior knowledge ($\beta = 0.838$, $p < .001$), $IIV_{\text{energy}}$ was not significantly associated with delayed performance ($\beta = -0.014$, $p = .709$). In contrast, mean energy showed a small but statistically significant *negative* association with delayed performance ($\beta = -0.074$, $p = .016$).

A robustness check examined whether the association between mean energy and delayed posttest performance varied across experimental contexts or conditions nested within experiments. No evidence of moderation was observed by experiment (joint Wald test, $p = .266$) or by condition nested within experiment (joint Wald test, $p = .819$).

### 4.4 RQ4: Interaction Between $IIV_{\text{energy}}$ and Incorrect Attempts

To examine whether self-reported energy states condition the relationship between behavioral risk indicators and outcomes, we extended the RQ3 models by adding incorrect attempts and interaction terms between incorrect attempts and (a) mean energy and (b) $IIV_{\text{energy}}$. As before, all continuous predictors and outcomes were standardized, pretest score controlled for prior knowledge, and heteroscedasticity-robust (HC3) standard errors were used. Multicollinearity remained low in all models (max VIF = 1.59), indicating no evidence of problematic multicollinearity with added predictors and interaction terms.

For immediate posttest performance, the interaction model explained a substantial proportion of variance ($R^2 = .740$, $F(6, 302) = 162.5$, $p < .001$). Compared with the corresponding main-effects model, adding the two interaction terms produced a small increase in explained variance ($\Delta R^2 = .006$), and the joint Wald test of the interaction terms was not statistically significant, $\chi^2(2) = 4.83$, $p = .089$. Neither the interaction between incorrect attempts and mean energy ($\beta = -0.064$, $p = .148$) nor the interaction between incorrect attempts and $IIV_{\text{energy}}$ ($\beta = -0.047$, $p = .094$) reached conventional statistical significance, indicating no clear evidence that self-reported energy conditioned the association between incorrect attempts and immediate performance.

The key interaction effect was observed for delayed posttest performance. The interaction model accounted for a large proportion of variance ($R^2 = .750$, $F(6, 302) = 162.2$, $p < .001$). Compared with the corresponding main-effects model, adding the two interaction terms increased explained variance by $\Delta R^2 = .010$, and the joint Wald test of the interaction terms was statistically significant, $\chi^2(2) = 15.08$, $p < .001$. The interaction between incorrect attempts and $IIV_{\text{energy}}$ was statistically significant ($\beta = -0.093$, $p < .001$), indicating that the negative association between incorrect attempts and retention was stronger for learners whose self-reported energy fluctuated more across sessions. In contrast, the interaction between incorrect attempts and mean energy was not significant ($\beta = -0.036$, $p = .345$).

A robustness check detected no differences across experiments (joint Wald test, $p = .965$) or across conditions nested within experiments (joint Wald test, $p = .778$). To evaluate whether this focal finding was robust to the nested structure of the data (students within classrooms within schools), we also re-estimated the delayed posttest interaction model using a linear mixed-effects model. The model included a random intercept for school and an additional classroom-level variance component nested within school. Because all continuous predictors and outcomes were standardized prior to analysis, the resulting coefficients are directly comparable to the OLS estimates. The mixed-effects model was fitted using restricted maximum likelihood (REML). The substantive pattern of results remained unchanged. In particular, the interaction between incorrect attempts and $IIV_{\text{energy}}$ remained negative and statistically significant ($\beta = -0.090$, $p = .002$), closely matching the OLS estimate ($\beta = -0.093$, $p < .001$). Other coefficients were also similar in magnitude and significance.

These results suggest that the key finding was not materially altered after accounting for classroom- and school-level clustering.

Together, these findings suggest that while frequent incorrect attempts are consistently associated with poorer outcomes, $IIV_{\text{energy}}$ amplifies this association for retention, serving as a contextual factor that helps characterize when behavioral risk indicators are more strongly linked to poorer retention.

## 5 Discussion

This study examined variability in learning outcomes within an overall effective K–12 mathematics digital learning game with an underlying ITS. Incorrect attempts were consistently associated with poorer immediate and retained outcomes, and $IIV_{\text{energy}}$ amplified this association for retention. We interpret this moderation effect through a cognitive resource and attentional control perspective, in which attention and cognitive control can fluctuate with mental effort and fatigue across learning sessions [25,28]. Field-based evidence in K–12 contexts suggests meaningful within-learner variability in cognitive performance associated with time of day, sleep quality, and tiredness [17,29,41]. Within this framework, $IIV_{\text{energy}}$ may function as a contextual indicator of instability in attentional and cognitive control resources. When perceived energy is less consistent, higher frequencies of incorrect attempts may more often co-occur with more superficial processing or less consistent persistence through impasses, patterns that have been linked to poorer learning and retention in ITS contexts [7,47]. Self-regulated learning (SRL) theory complements this account by emphasizing that effective learning depends on maintaining monitoring and regulation processes over time [4,37,48]. From this perspective, instability in perceived energy may disrupt these regulatory processes across sessions, strengthening the link between error-prone behavior and weaker retention.

### 5.1 Implications for Classroom TEL

The findings reinforce that incorrect attempts remain an informative behavioral signal, while also suggesting that repeated, lightweight self-reports can help contextualize when this common indicator is more strongly associated with poorer retention. Rather than treating log-based risk signals as having a fixed meaning across learners and sessions, the present results point to the value of interpreting such signals in relation to low-burden measures of learner state collected under authentic classroom constraints. In this sense, the contribution of the present work is less about proposing a new adaptive model and more about clarifying when a widely available behavioral indicator may be more or less meaningful in classroom TEL environments.

These findings also have implications for real-time classroom awareness and orchestration tools. Systems such as Lumilo [21] address a central challenge in authentic classrooms—supporting teachers' help-giving decisions under time constraints—by augmenting instructors' real-time perceptions of students' learning, metacognition, and behavior. The present work points to a natural extension of such systems: incorporating self-reported learner energy as a contextual signal for interpreting log-based indicators. For example, Lumilo's "struggling" indicator incorporates recent error rates; contextualizing this signal with $IIV_{\text{energy}}$ may yield a more nuanced picture of student need, particularly for anticipating weaker retention. Future work could prototype dashboards that surface these integrated signals and test whether they improve teachers' support targeting.

## 5.2 Limitations and Future Work

Several limitations should be considered when interpreting the findings. First, our behavioral analyses focused on a single log-derived indicator (incorrect attempts). Although this measure is informed by prior work and has the strength of being commonly available across systems, which supports replication, it can arise from various mechanisms (e.g., decimal misconceptions [24,42], slips [13], frustration [8], wheel-spinning [47], and "gaming the system" [7]). Accordingly, we interpret incorrect attempts as a behavioral risk signal rather than a diagnostic measure. Future work could examine whether additional log-based features (e.g., response timing, help-seeking behaviors, etc.) interact with $IIV_{\text{energy}}$ in ways that further refine risk identification.

Second, learners' behaviors and self-reported energy unfolded within socially organized classroom contexts [20,31], which were not systematically measured. Variation in instructor monitoring and one-on-one guidance may have influenced both learners' reported energy states and error patterns in ways our operationalizations cannot capture. In particular, a large-scale study in K–12 classrooms ($N = 1116$) suggests that the meaning and consequences of making errors depend on instructional norms surrounding help-seeking and responses to mistakes [44]. Thus, our findings characterize relationships within the instructional ecology of the Fall 2025 *Decimal Point* deployment. Future research could examine whether these patterns generalize across classrooms with different instructional norms.

Third, the daily probe captured learners' self-reported energy rather than objective cognitive states. Because mean self-reports are sensitive to stable between-person differences [14], our primary investigation centered on within-person variability ($IIV_{\text{energy}}$). The observed negative association between mean self-reported energy and retention should therefore be interpreted cautiously as a secondary finding that motivates further examination.

Fourth, $IIV_{\text{energy}}$ was estimated over a relatively short observation window spanning the available classroom sessions within the instructional unit. This design reflects the duration of the deployment and the goal of preserving classroom-feasible, low-burden measurement under authentic conditions, rather than extending the study solely to obtain more repeated observations. Thus, the present analysis shows that short-horizon fluctuation in self-reported energy can be meaningfully examined within an authentic classroom deployment, not that the measure captures a stable longer-term trait. Future work could examine whether similar patterns hold across longer instructional windows.

Fifth, delayed posttests in classroom settings reflect performance after a naturalistic interval during which learners may encounter content through unmeasured channels (e.g., individual study or incidental practice). While we ensured that no additional whole-class instruction occurred, these results represent performance under natural learning conditions rather than pure retention attributable solely to the intervention. Future work could incorporate ecologically feasible measures of intervening exposure, such as low-burden learner self-report.

Sixth, the analytic sample was nested within 25 classrooms across five schools, so classroom- and school-level context remains relevant. Teacher practices, classroom norms, and school-level factors could influence both engagement with the game and test performance. We addressed the nested structure of the data by re-estimating the focal delayed-posttest interaction model using a multilevel specification with a random intercept for school and a classroom-level variance component, which yielded the same substantive conclusion. However, the limited number of schools constrains the precision of school-level variance estimates. Future work with more schools and richer classroom-level measures could better examine contextual heterogeneity and potential cross-level moderators.

Finally, this study identifies conditions under which incorrect attempts are more strongly associated with poorer retention, but does not test whether adaptive support integrating $IIV_{\text{energy}}$ improves outcomes. Future work should examine whether such context-richer adaptations enhance retention.

### 5.3 Conclusion

This study examined why learning outcomes vary across individuals even within an overall effective K–12 mathematics game with an underlying ITS. A key finding is that $IIV_{\text{energy}}$ amplified the negative association between a behavioral risk signal (incorrect attempts) and retention: frequent errors were more strongly associated with poorer retention for learners whose self-reported energy fluctuated more across sessions. This result suggests that repeated, lightweight self-report measures can provide contextual value for interpreting log-based behavioral indicators in authentic classroom settings. More broadly, this work helps characterize when a common behavioral signal is more strongly associated with poorer retention, highlighting how low-burden classroom measures can support more context-aware interpretation of learner behavior in TEL environments.

## References

1. Aleven, V., McLaren, B., Sewall, J., Koedinger, K.R.: Example-tracing tutors: a new paradigm for intelligent tutoring systems (2009)
2. Anderson, J.R., Corbett, A.T., Koedinger, K.R., Pelletier, R.: Cognitive tutors: lessons learned. J. Learn. Sci. **4**(2), 167–207 (1995)
3. Arroyo, I., Beal, C., Murray, T., Walles, R., Woolf, B.P.: Web-based intelligent multimedia tutoring for high stakes achievement tests. In: International Conference on Intelligent Tutoring Systems, pp. 468–477. Springer (2004)

4. Azevedo, R., et al.: Lessons learned and future directions of metatutor: leveraging multichannel data to scaffold self-regulated learning with an intelligent tutoring system. Front. Psychol. **13**, 813632 (2022)
5. Baars, M., Wijnia, L., de Bruin, A., Paas, F.: The relation between students' effort and monitoring judgments during learning: A meta-analysis. Educ. Psychol. Rev. **32**(4), 979–1002 (2020)
6. Baker, R.S., Corbett, A.T., Koedinger, K.R.: Detecting student misuse of intelligent tutoring systems. In: International Conference on Intelligent Tutoring Systems, pp. 531–540. Springer (2004)
7. Baker, R.S., Corbett, A.T., Koedinger, K.R., Wagner, A.Z.: Off-task behavior in the cognitive tutor classroom: when students "game the system". In: Proceedings of the SIGCHI Conference on Human Factors in Computing Systems, pp. 383–390. CHI '04, Association for Computing Machinery, New York, NY, USA (2004)
8. Baker, R.S., D'Mello, S.K., Rodrigo, M.M.T., Graesser, A.C.: Better to be frustrated than bored: the incidence, persistence, and impact of learners' cognitive-affective states during interactions with three different computer-based learning environments. Int. J. Hum. Comput. Stud. **68**(4), 223–241 (2010)
9. Bouchet, F., Harley, J.M., Trevors, G.J., Azevedo, R.: Clustering and profiling students according to their interactions with an intelligent tutoring system fostering self-regulated learning. J. Educat. Data Min. **5**(1), 104–146 (2013)
10. du Boulay, B.: Recent meta-reviews and meta-analyses of AIED systems. Int. J. Artif. Intell. Educ. **26**(1), 536–537 (2016)
11. de Bruin, A.B., Janssen, E.M., Waldeyer, J., Stebner, F.: Cognitive load and challenges in self-regulation: an introduction and reflection on the topical collection. Educ. Psychol. Rev. **37**(3), 1–12 (2025)
12. Clark, D.B., Tanner-Smith, E.E., Killingsworth, S.S.: Digital games, design, and learning: a systematic review and meta-analysis. Rev. Educ. Res. **86**(1), 79–122 (2016)
13. Corbett, A.T., Anderson, J.R.: Knowledge tracing: modeling the acquisition of procedural knowledge. User Model. User-Adap. Inter. **4**(4), 253–278 (1994)
14. Curran, P.J., Bauer, D.J.: The disaggregation of within-person and between-person effects in longitudinal models of change. Annu. Rev. Psychol. **62**(1), 583–619 (2011)
15. David, L., Biwer, F., Baars, M., Wijnia, L., Paas, F., De Bruin, A.: The relation between perceived mental effort, monitoring judgments, and learning outcomes: a meta-analysis. Educ. Psychol. Rev. **36**(3), 66 (2024)
16. Decker-Woodrow, L.E., et al.: The impacts of three educational technologies on algebraic understanding in the context of COVID-19. AERA Open **9**, 23328584231165919 (2023). https://doi.org/10.1177/23328584231165919
17. Dewald, J.F., Meijer, A.M., Oort, F.J., Kerkhof, G.A., Bögels, S.M.: The influence of sleep quality, sleep duration and sleepiness on school performance in children and adolescents: a meta-analytic review. Sleep Med. Rev. **14**(3), 179–189 (2010)
18. Dirk, J., Schmiedek, F.: Fluctuations in elementary school children's working memory performance in the school context. J. Educ. Psychol. **108**(5), 722 (2016)
19. Gamaldo, A.A., Allaire, J.C.: Daily fluctuations in everyday cognition: is it meaningful? J. Aging Health **28**(5), 834–849 (2016)
20. Greeno, J.G., Collins, A.M., Resnick, L.B., et al.: Cognition and learning. Handbook Educat. Psychol. **77**, 15–46 (1996)
21. Holstein, K., Hong, G., Tegene, M., McLaren, B.M., Aleven, V.: The classroom as a dashboard: co-designing wearable cognitive augmentation for K-12 teachers. In: Proceedings of the 8th International Conference on Learning Analytics and Knowledge, pp. 79–88 (2018)

22. Hultsch, D.F., MacDonald, S.W., Dixon, R.A.: Variability in reaction time performance of younger and older adults. J. Gerontol. B Psychol. Sci. Soc. Sci. **57**(2), P101–P115 (2002)
23. Hussein, M.H., Ow, S.H., Elaish, M.M., Jensen, E.O.: Digital game-based learning in K-12 mathematics education: a systematic literature review. Educ. Inf. Technol. **27**(2), 2859–2891 (2022)
24. Irwin, K.C.: Using everyday knowledge of decimals to enhance understanding. J. Res. Math. Educ. **32**(4), 399–420 (2001)
25. Kahneman, D.: Attention and effort (1973)
26. Koedinger, K.R., Baker, R.S., Cunningham, K., Skogsholm, A., Leber, B., Stamper, J.: A data repository for the EDM community: the PSLC datashop. Handbook Educat. Data Min. **43**, 43–56 (2010)
27. Koedinger, K.R., Corbett, A.T., Perfetti, C.: The knowledge-learning-instruction framework: bridging the science-practice chasm to enhance robust student learning. Cogn. Sci. **36**(5), 757–798 (2012)
28. Kok, A.: Cognitive control, motivation and fatigue: a cognitive neuroscience perspective. Brain Cogn. **160**, 105880 (2022)
29. Könen, T., Dirk, J., Schmiedek, F.: Cognitive benefits of last night's sleep: daily variations in children's sleep behavior are related to working memory fluctuations. J. Child Psychol. Psych. **56**(2), 171–182 (2015)
30. Kulik, J.A., Fletcher, J.D.: Effectiveness of intelligent tutoring systems: a meta-analytic review. Rev. Educ. Res. **86**(1), 42–78 (2016)
31. Lave, J., Wenger, E.: Situated Learning: Legitimate Peripheral Participation, Cambridge University Press (1991)
32. Leite, W.L., et al.: Do intelligent tutoring systems benefit K-12 students? A meta-analysis and evaluation of heterogeneity of treatment effects in the US (2025). arXiv:2511.04997 arXiv preprint
33. Long, Y., Aleven, V.: Gamification of joint student/system control over problem selection in a linear equation tutor. In: International Conference on Intelligent Tutoring Systems, pp. 378–387. Springer (2014)
34. Ma, W., Adesope, O.O., Nesbit, J.C., Liu, Q.: Intelligent tutoring systems and learning outcomes: a meta-analysis. J. Educ. Psychol. **106**(4), 901 (2014)
35. MacDonald, S.W., Li, S.C., Bäckman, L.: Neural underpinnings of within-person variability in cognitive functioning. Psychol. Aging **24**(4), 792 (2009)
36. McLaren, B.M., Adams, D.M., Mayer, R.E., Forlizzi, J.: A computer-based game that promotes mathematics learning more than a conventional approach. Int. J. Game-Based Learn. (IJGBL) **7**(1), 36–56 (2017)
37. Panadero, E.: A review of self-regulated learning: six models and four directions for research. Front. Psychol. **8**, 422 (2017)
38. Ram, N., Gerstorf, D.: Time-structured and net intraindividual variability: tools for examining the development of dynamic characteristics and processes. Psychol. Aging **24**(4), 778 (2009)
39. Schaufeli, W.B., Martinez, I.M., Pinto, A.M., Salanova, M., Bakker, A.B.: Burnout and engagement in university students: a cross-national study. J. Cross Cult. Psychol. **33**(5), 464–481 (2002)
40. Shute, V.J., Smith, G., Kuba, R., Dai, C.P., Rahimi, S., Liu, Z., Almond, R.: The design, development, and testing of learning supports for the physics playground game. Int. J. Artif. Intell. Educ. **31**(3), 357–379 (2021)
41. Sievertsen, H.H., Gino, F., Piovesan, M.: Cognitive fatigue influences students' performance on standardized tests. Proc. Natl. Acad. Sci. **113**(10), 2621–2624 (2016)

42. Stacey, K., Helme, S., Steinle, V.: Confusions between decimals, fractions and negative numbers: a consequence of the mirror as a conceptual metaphor in three different ways. PME Conf. **4**, 4–217 (2001)
43. Steenbergen-Hu, S., Cooper, H.: A meta-analysis of the effectiveness of intelligent tutoring systems on K-12 students' mathematical learning. J. Educ. Psychol. **105**(4), 970 (2013)
44. Steuer, G., Rosentritt-Brunn, G., Dresel, M.: Dealing with errors in mathematics classrooms: structure and relevance of perceived error climate. Contemp. Educ. Psychol. **38**(3), 196–210 (2013)
45. Taub, M., Azevedo, R.: How does prior knowledge influence eye fixations and sequences of cognitive and metacognitive SRL processes during learning with an intelligent tutoring system? Int. J. Artif. Intell. Educ. **29**(1), 1–28 (2019)
46. VanLehn, K.: The relative effectiveness of human tutoring, intelligent tutoring systems, and other tutoring systems. Educat. Psychol. **46**(4), 197–221 (2011)
47. Wang, Y., Kai, S., Baker, R.S.: Early detection of wheel-spinning in ASSISTments. In: International Conference on Artificial Intelligence in Education, pp. 574–585. Springer (2020)
48. Zimmerman, B.J.: Becoming a self-regulated learner: an overview. Theory Pract. **41**(2), 64–70 (2002)

# Adapting Intelligent Tutoring Systems for Technical Workforce Training: A Case Study of Two Cybersecurity Tutor Designs

Marshall An(✉), Leah Teffera, Mahboobeh Mehrvarz, Can Kultur, Bruce M. McLaren, and Christopher Bogart

Carnegie Mellon University, Pittsburgh, PA 15213, USA
{haokanga,lteffera,bmclaren,cbogart}@andrew.cmu.edu, ckultur@cs.cmu.edu

**Abstract.** Intelligent Tutoring Systems (ITSs) have a strong evidence base, yet their use in technical workforce training remains limited. This paper documents an iterative co-design process with community college faculty that produced two ITS adaptations for cybersecurity workforce training. One tutor targets DDoS incident response and embeds a lightweight interactive simulation to make infrastructure state and mitigation effects observable during guided practice. The other targets security controls and scaffolds contrastive reasoning to support conceptual classification across related taxonomies emphasized in certification exam guides. We evaluated each tutor against a non-ITS comparison activity using randomized controlled trials within an authentic workforce training pathway. Results provide unit-specific evaluative evidence that ITS effectiveness was not uniform: the simulation-based tutor yielded a learning advantage concentrated in knowledge components requiring causal reasoning about mitigation impacts, whereas the contrastive-reasoning tutor did not outperform its comparison condition. Because simulation is confounded with instructional topic and implementation, we treat these as unit-specific case findings rather than a causal comparison of tutor types. Together, this work contributes a documented co-design process and evaluative evidence illustrating how alignment between tutor affordances and the cognitive demands of targeted skills may shape when ITS support adds value in workforce settings, while also surfacing design tensions—such as perceived repetitiveness under mastery-oriented task-loop adaptivity—that warrant further investigation.

**Keywords:** Intelligent tutoring systems · Workforce training · Simulation-based learning · Cybersecurity education

## 1 Introduction

Community colleges in the United States, accessible to tens of millions of workers, play a vital role in workforce training, particularly for technical job roles. They prove effective in technical education, with returns comparable to four-year


J. Weidlich et al. (Eds.): EC-TEL 2026, LNCS 16905, pp. 19–33, 2027.
https://doi.org/10.1007/978-3-032-37979-5_2

programs [31]. However, these institutions face significant resource constraints [21,29,34], motivating interest in effective and scalable teaching methods such as Intelligent Tutoring Systems (ITSs).

Despite ITSs' strong record of improving average learning outcomes across domains [27,35], technical workforce training remains comparatively underrepresented in the ITS literature [17]. Although prior work has argued that ITS benefits may extend to workplace training and continuing professional development, empirical evidence with adult learners in workforce-oriented settings remains limited [17,18]. This gap is reflected in a recent systematic review that identified only 10 empirical studies on professional training out of 782 screened records over a five-year period [30]. Consequently, there is limited design guidance on how to adapt ITSs to realistic workforce-training constraints and on which design choices, if any, are likely to yield measurable learning benefits in these contexts.

In this paper, we document the iterative co-design, implementation, and evaluation of two ITSs for cybersecurity workforce training, developed in collaboration with community college faculty. An earlier experience report detailed the co-design process and formative classroom pilots for these tutors [6]. The present study extends that work by evaluating the refined tutors in a larger workforce-training cohort and examining how learning outcomes varied across tutor designs and targeted knowledge components (KCs) [24]. One tutor targets DDoS incident response and embeds a lightweight interactive simulation to support decision-making and causal reasoning about the effects of mitigation actions; the other tutor targets security controls and scaffolds contrastive reasoning to support conceptual classification across related taxonomies required by industry-aligned certification exams. We do not aim to isolate simulation as a standalone design feature; rather, we examine how two distinct ITS designs were adapted to different instructional challenges under practical workforce-training constraints. We evaluated each tutor against a non-ITS comparison activity using randomized controlled trials within an authentic workforce training pathway.

Our results provide unit-specific evidence that ITS effectiveness was not uniform across the two instructional units in the targeted technical workforce training context. The simulation-based tutor yielded learning gains on KCs requiring reasoning about the causal effects of mitigation actions, whereas the contrastive-reasoning tutor did not outperform its comparison condition. Because simulation is confounded with instructional topic and tutor implementation, we interpret cross-unit differences descriptively rather than as a causal estimate of simulation as an isolated feature. The contribution of this work is therefore a documented case study of how two ITS adaptations were co-designed, implemented, and evaluated under authentic workforce-training constraints, with implications for aligning ITS affordances with the cognitive demands of targeted KCs. We also discuss unresolved design tensions, such as perceived repetitiveness under mastery-oriented task-loop adaptivity, and directions for future investigation.

## 2 Related Work

### 2.1 Operationalizing ITS Adaptivity for Workforce Tasks

Research shows ITSs can outperform traditional instruction [27] and achieve effects similar to human tutoring [35]. One evidence-based approach to designing effective ITSs is to incorporate adaptive learning following the "Adaptivity Grid" framework [4], which delineates three forms of adaptivity: (i) step-loop adaptivity (within a problem), where the system responds to individual student actions within an instructional task; (ii) task-loop adaptivity (between problems), where the system personalizes subsequent tasks for the learner; and (iii) design-loop adaptivity (between material versions), where course designers update the content and system based on data-driven reflection. This framework has guided many empirical studies examining how different forms of adaptivity affect learning. In particular, research shows that task-loop adaptivity can accelerate learning by tailoring subsequent practice based on individual progress [11,16,26].

Step-loop and task-loop adaptivity in ITSs are typically implemented through representations of target skills as *condition–action* pairs. This requirement is grounded in ACT-R, a cognitive architecture in which cognition is modeled through production rules that specify the conditions under which an action should be taken [7,8]. For example, in ITSs developed using Cognitive Tutor Authoring Tools (CTAT) [1,2], this condition–action structure is directly reflected in tutor implementations. In model-tracing tutors, productions are explicitly encoded as IF–THEN rules that specify when an action is correct and what behavior is expected; in example-tracing tutors [3], the same structure is represented implicitly through behavioral graphs that enumerate acceptable subsequent action(s) given the current problem-solving state (conditions).

Applying these adaptivity best practices in technical workforce domains therefore entails meticulous design effort. In particular, it requires job-aligned scenarios with sufficient fidelity to instantiate the *conditions* under which production rules should activate, while also making learner *actions* and their effects observable for feedback and adaptive practice. In many real-world IT job tasks, however, these conditions and action consequences depend on costly, risky, or operationally complex infrastructure that is difficult to provision for instruction at scale, as illustrated in subsequent sections. These constraints can limit the ability to encode job-relevant skills as production rules and to operationalize step- and task-loop adaptivity in realistic settings. This motivated us to incorporate lightweight simulations that represent key system states and action consequences within the tutor.

### 2.2 Simulation and Integration with ITSs

Simulation has a well-established record of supporting learning [12,19], but its integration into ITS-based workforce training remains limited. Recent reviews describe a growing body of simulation-based training research while noting that adaptive tutoring is largely absent from these systems [30]; earlier work similarly found only isolated ITS prototypes combining domain instruction with simulation components [33].

## 3 Iterative Instructional Co-design

We adopted iterative co-design with community college faculty to develop ITS adaptations that were instructionally meaningful, feasible within institutional constraints, and aligned with workforce-relevant learning objectives. Co-design is a collaborative design method that engages stakeholders as partners throughout design processes, rather than as "sources of information" [32].

### 3.1 Instructional Design Context

The target learner population was drawn from the Community College of Allegheny County, a large public two-year college in the United States. We grounded our co-design in a core cybersecurity course that serves both workforce certificate and associate degree pathways and functions as a gateway to more advanced topics. The course objectives are aligned with CompTIA Security+ [20], a widely recognized entry-level cybersecurity credential, and with U.S. Department of Defense (DoD) directive 8140/8570.01-M requirements [14].

### 3.2 Identifying High-Priority Instructional Challenges

Through curricular analysis and faculty reflection, we identified two recurring instructional challenges. One challenge concerned developing practical cybersecurity skills: delivering realistic, hands-on experiences with cloud infrastructure (e.g., detecting, analyzing, and mitigating DDoS attacks) is typically expensive and infeasible for community colleges, limiting opportunities for experiential practice. A second challenge concerned comparing closely related taxonomies: business-as-usual textbook materials emphasized definitions presented in isolation and offered little instructional support for contrasting categories, despite assessment tasks that require such distinctions. These challenges motivated two corresponding ITS designs: a DDoS incident response tutor that provides experiential learning and supports causal reasoning through lightweight simulations of workplace-relevant tasks, and a security-control tutor that scaffolds contrastive reasoning through tailored classification exercises. Both were refined through formative classroom pilots before evaluation.

### 3.3 DDoS Incident Response Tutor for Causal Reasoning

The first tutor targets a workforce-relevant competence that faculty identified as especially challenging to teach in their community-college classes: incident response to DDoS attacks for IT infrastructure. To provide experiential learning without requiring costly lab infrastructure, we designed a lightweight interactive simulation embedded within an ITS (Fig. 1). The tutor walks learners through a DDoS incident response workflow aligned with the NIST Incident Response Life Cycle [13], including detecting anomalous traffic and infrastructure utilization, diagnosing possible causes, selecting and applying mitigation techniques (e.g., scaling and rate limiting), and reflecting on outcomes.

The tutor targets 18 KCs spanning the incident response workflow. During co-design, we distinguished between two categories of KCs that differed in whether they required learners to interpret dynamic system-state changes. Simulation-Independent General Knowledge (SIGK) KCs involve procedural and conceptual knowledge that can be assessed without observing dynamic infrastructure behavior, such as correlating user-reported connectivity failures to identify a potential DDoS attack, or prioritizing infrastructure monitoring following user-reported connectivity failures. Simulation-Dependent Causal Reasoning (SDCR) KCs, by contrast, require learners to observe and interpret how infrastructure metrics change in response to mitigation actions, such as recognizing that infrastructure scaling does not directly reduce traffic, or recognizing that rate limiting reduces utilization by blocking malicious traffic. These relationships are difficult to support through static text alone because learners must connect a selected mitigation action to its observable effects on traffic and utilization. This distinction motivated embedding a lightweight simulation within the tutor rather than relying on static instructional materials alone. Without observable state changes, the relevant production-rule conditions for SDCR KCs are harder to instantiate, limiting assessment and feedback on learners' causal reasoning. The simulation also enabled richer step-loop support than static materials alone could readily provide: because learners could observe traffic and utilization metrics updating in real time, multi-level hints could guide their interpretation before revealing the correct answer. For example, hints could prompt learners to examine whether traffic volume changes after scaling, addressing a misconception observed during formative pilots: some learners assumed that provisioning additional resources directly reduces incoming traffic, when scaling instead allows the infrastructure to handle the same traffic volume more effectively. In this way, the tutor grounded targeted support in observable system behavior rather than abstract assertion.

We particularly document the design and implementation of task-loop adaptivity in this tutor because its scenario-based, multi-step incident-response procedure, grounded in the NIST Incident Response framework, poses distinct challenges for adaptive practice. A formative pilot suggested that simulation alone may not reliably support all learners: most learners (4 out of 5) progressed through the DDoS tutor with no substantial learning gains. Examination of fine-grained interaction logs collected through DataShop [23] revealed that some learners exhibited rapid, repeated incorrect attempts, a behavioral pattern consistent with rapid-guessing behaviors documented in the "gaming the system" literature [9,10]. These observations, discussed with course faculty during co-reflection sessions, informed our decision to add task-loop adaptivity to (1) provide targeted, repeated practice on unmastered KCs and (2) discourage gaming

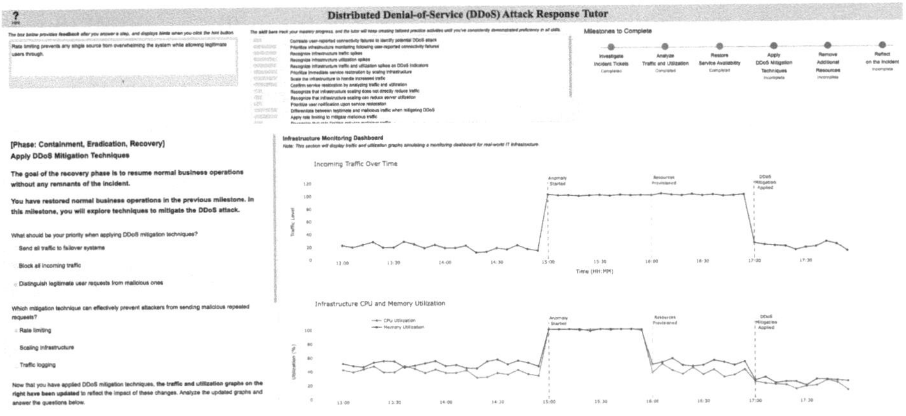


**Fig. 1.** DDoS Incident Response Tutor. Top left: hint box offering multi-level hints and immediate feedback. Top right: milestone tracker segments the complex DDoS response workflow into milestones and indicates student progress for reflection. Bottom left: steps for the current milestone guide the student through the procedure. Bottom right: simulation dashboard presenting interactive network-traffic and resource-utilization graphs that update in response to mitigation techniques applied by students.

behaviors by preventing learners from bypassing core practice and progressing without demonstrated understanding.

However, implementing task-loop adaptivity in the DDoS tutor posed a challenge in representing the conditions and action consequences discussed in Sect. 2.1. Unlike many ITS domains where unmastered KCs can be practiced through independent problems drawn from a pool, incident-response skills are embedded in a scenario whose steps are tightly coupled to evolving system state and prior actions, such as diagnosis, mitigation, and recovery decisions. Presenting individual KC-linked steps in isolation would remove the contextual information needed to define the relevant production-rule conditions, whereas repeating the entire procedure until all KCs were mastered would risk unnecessary overpractice. Our solution was to repeat the scenario while dynamically adapting the interface based on estimated skill mastery, operationalized through Bayesian Knowledge Tracing (BKT) [15] over KC-linked learner performance. After the initial round, the system provides additional rounds of practice in which steps linked to mastered skills are auto-completed, allowing learners to focus on unmastered steps until all reach mastery.

This adaptive interface design draws inspiration from Huang et al. [22], but differs in operating at the task-loop level by auto-completing mastered steps, rather than at the step-loop level by providing additional scaffolded steps in response to errors. Because this implementation differs from conventional task-loop adaptivity based on selecting additional independent tasks, it warranted particular scrutiny during evaluation, which we return to in the Results and Discussion.

### 3.4 Security Control Tutor for Contrastive Reasoning

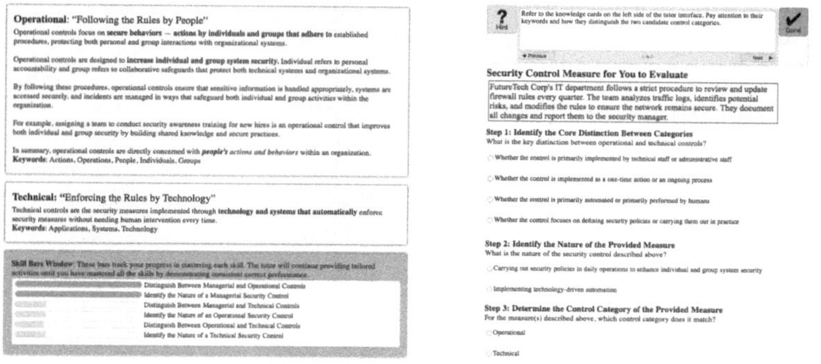


**Fig. 2.** Security Control Tutor. Bottom-left: Skill bars track mastery progress for each skill, enabling adaptive practice selection. Bottom-right: Contrastive reasoning structured into a scaffolded three-step comparison process. Top-left: Introduction to taxonomies using plain language with comparative scaffolding, supplemented by visual aids. Top-right: Hint box providing multi-level hints, and immediate misconception-targeted feedback.

The second tutor addresses a recurring pedagogical limitation of the textbook (CompTIA Security+ Cert Guide [20]) that the faculty and learning scientists collaboratively identified: it confines cybersecurity taxonomies to isolated subsections without comparison across them. For example, in Chap. 1 each control type (e.g., preventive, detective, corrective) is introduced in its own subsection, with definitions and examples presented independently. This gap is particularly consequential given its misalignment with target assessments—the Cert Guide's evaluation instruments rely heavily on classification-based multiple-choice questions (MCQs). To address this gap, the Security Control Tutor (Fig. 2) was developed to scaffold contrastive reasoning aligned with Cert Guide assessment demands by presenting exercises in which learners compare and justify classifications across categories within authentic scenarios.

The tutor targets 11 KCs spanning security-control taxonomies. Rather than asking learners to memorize definitions alone, the scaffolded comparison process guides them through three steps: identifying the core distinction between relevant categories, characterizing the nature of the described control measure, and then determining the matching control category. For example, faculty identified distinguishing managerial from operational controls as a common learner struggle. In such scenarios, the tutor first guides learners to identify the core distinction as whether the measure focuses on defining security policies or on carrying them out in practice. Learners then analyze the provided scenario and use that distinction to determine whether the control is managerial or operational. Multi-level hints and misconception-targeted feedback were designed to support these distinctions explicitly.

As with the first tutor, formative classroom pilots motivated the incorporation of task-loop adaptivity using BKT; meanwhile, adaptivity in this tutor followed a more conventional pattern, selecting subsequent problems from a pool targeting unmastered KCs.

## 4 Evaluation Design and Participants

A pragmatic challenge in evaluating ITSs within authentic community college settings is that individual cohorts are often small, which can limit statistical power for controlled comparisons within a single course offering. Across three formative classroom deployments, tutor use supported iterative design refinement, but the number of learners who both consented to research use and completed all required activities ranged from only 4 to 9 per deployment. These sample sizes were consistently insufficient to support a definitive randomized evaluation within the available study timeframe.

To enable a more adequately powered randomized evaluation while maintaining workforce relevance, we recruited participants from a complementary workforce training pathway: an 8-month technician training program for government personnel in which cloud computing and security-related technical skills are core instructional components. Although this population differs from community college students in organizational context and prior experience, both groups consist of adult learners in technical workforce training pathways oriented toward industry-aligned skill development. Importantly, while the surrounding curricula differ, the DDoS incident response and security control classification skills targeted by the ITSs were validated as required learning objectives by instructors from both the community college and technician program contexts.

The evaluation comprised two concurrent randomized experiments, one for each instructional unit. In the DDoS unit, the experimental condition used the ITS, whereas the control condition used equivalent static content without simulation or adaptive repeated practice. In the Security Control unit, the experimental condition used the ITS, whereas the control condition used equivalent content without contrastive-reasoning scaffolds or adaptive repeated practice. To use instructional time efficiently and ensure exposure to both topics and conditions, we used a counterbalanced assignment scheme: each participant experienced the experimental condition for one unit and the control condition for the other, with random assignment to one of two sequences. We assessed learning with unit-specific pre- and post-tests and collected open-ended post-activity survey responses about helpful, frustrating, or unclear tutor features.

Participants came from one cohort of 36 enrolled learners. Of these, 27 consented and completed all required DDoS-unit activities, and 25 also completed all required Security Control activities. The sample was predominantly male (96.3%, $n = 26$; female: 3.7%, $n = 1$). This gender imbalance reflects the composition of the underlying training cohort and broader patterns of gender representation in technical training pipelines. Many reported substantial prior technical exposure: 66.7% ($n = 18$) held at least one cloud or security-related certification, and most reported prior programming experience and multiple years of service. Given the small sample and skewed gender distribution, demographic variables were not included as covariates or interaction terms; results should therefore be interpreted as instructional effects within this workforce training population rather than as demographic generalizations.

## 5 Results

**Table 1.** Descriptive Statistics for Pretest and Posttest Scores by Tutor and Condition

| Tutor | Condition | N | Pre-test M (SD) | Post-test M (SD) | Gain M (SD) |
|---|---|---|---|---|---|
| DDoS Incident Response Tutor (10-item quiz) | | | | | |
| | Experimental | 14 | 7.71 (2.20) | 9.43 (0.85) | 1.71 (2.30) |
| | Control | 13 | 7.08 (1.50) | 7.54 (2.79) | 0.46 (2.30) |
| | **Total** | **27** | **7.41 (1.89)** | **8.52 (2.21)** | **1.11 (2.34)** |
| Security Control Tutor (12-item quiz) | | | | | |
| | Experimental | 14 | 7.86 (3.48) | 9.50 (1.91) | 1.64 (2.27) |
| | Control | 11 | 7.82 (1.83) | 9.64 (1.86) | 1.82 (2.56) |
| | **Total** | **25** | **7.84 (2.82)** | **9.56 (1.85)** | **1.72 (2.35)** |

### 5.1 Learning Effects Relative to Control Within Each Unit

Table 1 presents pre-test, post-test, and gain scores for all groups. To assess learning effects relative to the control condition within each unit, we estimated separate OLS regression models predicting post-test performance for each tutor, controlling for pre-test scores.

For the DDoS unit, the overall model was statistically significant ($F(2, 24) = 4.44$, $p = .023$, adjusted $R^2 = .209$). Instructional condition was a significant predictor of post-test performance: learners in the experimental condition outperformed those in the control condition ($\beta = 1.68$, $SE = 0.77$, $t = 2.18$, $p = .039$, 95% CI $[0.09, 3.26]$). Pre-test performance showed a positive but non-significant association with post-test scores ($\beta = 0.34$, $SE = 0.21$, $p = .118$, 95% CI $[-0.09, 0.76]$).

In contrast, the contrastive-reasoning tutor did not outperform its comparison activity. While the overall model was also statistically significant ($F(2, 22) = 5.07$, $p = .016$, adjusted $R^2 = .253$), the instructional condition was not a significant predictor of post-test performance ($\beta = -0.15$, $SE = 0.64$, $t = -0.23$, $p = .817$, 95% CI $[-1.49, 1.19]$). Pre-test performance was the only significant predictor ($\beta = 0.37$, $SE = 0.12$, $t = 3.18$, $p = .004$, 95% CI $[0.13, 0.61]$).

Taken together, these results indicate that, although both tutors were designed and refined in accordance with the "Adaptivity Grid" framework [4], incorporating step-loop, task-loop, and design-loop adaptivity, only the simulation-based DDoS tutor showed a measurable learning advantage over its control condition. Across the two units, observed benefits appeared to depend on how the tutor's affordances aligned with the specific cognitive demands of the targeted KCs rather than on adherence to general ITS best practices alone.

### 5.2 Within the Simulation-Based Tutor: Effects on Causal-Reasoning and General-Knowledge KCs

To investigate the specific value of the simulation component, we used the SIGK–SDCR distinction established *a priori* during co-design. This distinction was central to the tutor design because SDCR KCs require learners to identify the causal effects of mitigation actions on infrastructure states, whereas SIGK KCs can be assessed without observing dynamic infrastructure behavior. The SDCR category therefore aligns directly with the affordances of simulation for observing and explaining causal effects, drawing on the established educational principle that observing causal effects supports learning [5]. Accordingly, the simulation was designed to let learners observe how infrastructure metrics changed in response to their actions through visualizations with reasonable fidelity to real-world cloud monitoring tools (e.g., AWS CloudWatch, Azure Monitor). To further promote causal reasoning, whenever learners selected a mitigation action, the tutor prompted them to reflect on and identify the observed effects on traffic and system utilization as required steps in the workflow.

The SDCR category comprised four quiz items, and the SIGK category comprised six quiz items. To examine whether learning effects were more evident for SDCR than SIGK items, we estimated separate OLS regression models for each KC category, controlling for pre-test scores. For SDCR items, the overall model was statistically significant, $F(2, 24) = 4.08$, $p = .030$, with $R^2 = .254$ (adjusted $R^2 = .191$). Instructional condition was a significant predictor of post-test performance: learners in the experimental condition outperformed those in the control condition ($\beta = 1.14$, $SE = 0.43$, $t = 2.65$, $p = .014$, 95% CI $[0.25, 2.03]$). Pre-test performance was not a significant predictor ($\beta = 0.09$, $SE = 0.22$, $p = .691$). In contrast, for SIGK items, the overall model did not reach conventional levels of statistical significance, $F(2, 24) = 3.01$, $p = .068$, with $R^2 = .201$ (adjusted $R^2 = .134$). The effect of instructional condition was not statistically significant ($\beta = 0.67$, $SE = 0.44$, $t = 1.52$, $p = .141$, 95% CI $[-0.24, 1.57]$). Pre-test performance showed a positive but non-significant association with post-test performance ($\beta = 0.27$, $SE = 0.15$, $p = .078$).

Taken together, these results suggest that the simulation-based tutor's measured advantage was more evident for KCs that required reasoning about the causal effects of mitigation actions, whereas evidence of added value for general incident-response knowledge was weaker in this sample. In the next subsection, we analyze learners' open-ended survey responses to contextualize these patterns and to surface perceived mechanisms and design trade-offs.

### 5.3 Survey Feedback Analysis

To complement the quantitative results and interpret the associated design trade-offs, we analyzed learners' post-activity survey responses. The goal was not to make standalone claims of effectiveness, but to identify recurring themes that help explain the observed learning patterns and implementation challenges.

A dominant theme concerned the value of the interactive simulation for understanding mitigation effects. Learners frequently described the visualizations as helping them reason about how traffic patterns and resource utilization changed in response to their decisions. One learner noted that "the graphs definitely helped visualize and better understand the concepts in the Detection and the Recovery phases," and that observing infrastructure state before and after mitigation techniques was "extremely helpful." Another learner similarly described the visual aids as supporting their understanding of the relationships among network traffic, CPU and memory utilization, and scaling. These responses align with the quantitative finding that the simulation-based tutor's measured advantage was more evident for items requiring causal reasoning about the impact of actions, suggesting that learners valued the simulation's support for action–effect reasoning rather than engaging with it only at a surface level.

At the same time, feedback also revealed interface-level trade-offs related to the simulation's prominence. Some learners felt that the visualizations competed with the text-based procedural steps. One observed that "the graphics were good, [but] they just didn't need to be the focus of the layout. They support the written material, not the other way around."

Learners also reported mixed perceptions of task-loop adaptivity. Some participants appreciated repeated practice and explicitly endorsed repetition as supporting mastery (e.g., "I liked the repetition since I agree that it's the best way to master a subject"), whereas others reported frustration with perceived repetitiveness and time cost (e.g., "the repetitive nature of the tutor, very time-consuming"). We interpret this cautiously: on one hand, repetition is to some extent inherent to task-loop adaptivity, which by design provides additional practice for KCs that have not yet reached mastery according to the model; meanwhile, learner feedback highlights a persistent design challenge—how to preserve the instructional benefits of adaptive repetition while improving how it is experienced by learners within realistic constraints on development effort and instructional time. Feedback on step-loop adaptivity was generally positive, with learners noting the usefulness of targeted feedback and hints.

In contrast, survey responses related to the Security Control tutor were generally less differentiated, with fewer comments pointing to specific learning-related affordances, mirroring the lack of condition differences in the quantitative results.

Overall, the survey feedback provides converging evidence that perceived learning support depended on alignment between tutor affordances and the targeted KCs, while also surfacing a tension between structured adaptive practice and learners' perceptions of repetition and time cost.

## 6 Discussion

Although this study does not isolate simulation as an independent causal factor, the observed pattern is consistent with situated and experiential learning theories, which emphasize contextually meaningful activity when learning depends on understanding action consequences within a system (e.g., [25,28]). In the DDoS tutor, the simulation externalized system states such as traffic and utilization, made mitigation effects observable, and required learners to articulate these effects. This design aligns with the SDCR results: the experimental advantage was concentrated in KCs requiring causal reasoning about mitigation impacts, whereas evidence of added value for general incident-response knowledge was weaker. The implication is not that simulation substitutes for hands-on experience, but that a minimal simulation embedded in an ITS can feasibly represent the conditions and consequences needed for step-level feedback and adaptive practice in resource-constrained workforce settings. Future work should test whether this alignment between "observable action effects" and targeted KCs generalizes across additional technical topics and alternative implementations.

### 6.1 Limitations and Future Work

Several limitations constrain interpretation and motivate targeted future work. First, simulation is confounded with instructional topic and implementation: the simulation-based tutor targeted DDoS incident response, whereas the contrastive-reasoning tutor targeted security control classification. Cross-unit differences therefore cannot be interpreted as a causal estimate of simulation as an isolated feature. Future work should evaluate alternative implementations within a single topic, varying interactive simulation versus static representations while holding learning objectives, assessments, and adaptive logic constant.

Second, the evaluation sample came from a government technician training program rather than the community college context for which the tutors were co-designed. Participants reported relatively high prior technical experience and certification, which may have reduced the marginal benefit of some ITS adaptations, especially for conceptual and taxonomic knowledge. Replication with community college learners is needed to assess whether the same design patterns hold in introductory workforce pathways.

Third, learning outcomes were assessed with unit-aligned pre- and post-tests over a short time horizon. These measures are appropriate for immediate learning effects but do not capture retention or transfer to novel scenarios, which are especially important for incident response skills requiring adaptation to various system states and constraints. Future evaluations should incorporate delayed post-tests and transfer tasks.

Fourth, learner feedback revealed mixed perceptions of task-loop adaptivity, especially repetitiveness and time cost. This motivates further tuning of BKT parameters, such as mastery thresholds and slip/guess assumptions, and more meaningful variation across practice rounds, such as differing system parameters or constraints, to preserve instructional value while improving learner experience.

Finally, the modest sample size and skewed gender distribution limited statistical power and precluded analyses of subgroup differences. While this reflects realistic constraints of authentic workforce training cohorts, future multi-cohort studies are needed to examine robustness across populations and whether specific design features differentially benefit learners with varying backgrounds or prior experience.

Together, these limitations highlight that adapting ITSs for workforce training requires not only adherence to established tutoring principles but also careful alignment among instructional affordances, targeted KCs, learner populations, and practical constraints. Addressing these limitations through targeted follow-up studies will support the development of more generalizable design principles for workforce-oriented ITSs.

### 6.2 Conclusion

This paper contributes a documented case study of adapting ITSs for technical workforce training under practical constraints, resulting in two tutor designs and their randomized evaluation in authentic workforce training settings. Across the two instructional units, ITS effectiveness was not uniform: the simulation-based incident-response tutor outperformed its control, with advantages concentrated in KCs requiring causal reasoning about mitigation impacts, whereas the contrastive-reasoning security-control tutor did not outperform its comparison condition. Although the study does not isolate simulation as an independent causal factor, the results and learner feedback support a design-alignment interpretation: workforce-oriented ITS benefits may depend on whether the tutor introduces affordances that directly support the cognitive work required by the targeted KCs, especially when job-relevant conditions and action consequences are otherwise difficult to represent. These findings motivate future research that systematically varies simulation within topics, expands outcome measures to retention and transfer, and refines adaptive repetition designs to better fit workforce training constraints.

**Acknowledgments.** This material is based upon work partially supported by the National Science Foundation, under Grant No. 2222762. Any opinions, findings, and conclusions or recommendations expressed in this material are those of the author(s) and do not necessarily reflect the views of the National Science Foundation.

## References

1. Aleven, V., McLaren, B., Sewall, J., Koedinger, K.R.: Example-tracing tutors: a new paradigm for intelligent tutoring systems (2009)
2. Aleven, V., McLaren, B.M., Sewall, J., Koedinger, K.R.: The Cognitive Tutor Authoring Tools (CTAT): preliminary evaluation of efficiency gains. In: Ikeda, M., Ashley, K.D., Chan, T.-W. (eds.) ITS 2006. LNCS, vol. 4053, pp. 61–70. Springer, Heidelberg (2006). https://doi.org/10.1007/11774303_7

3. Aleven, V., et al.: Example-tracing tutors: intelligent tutor development for non-programmers. Int. J. Artif. Intell. Educ. **26**, 224–269 (2016)
4. Aleven, V., McLaughlin, E.A., Glenn, R.A., Koedinger, K.R.: Instruction based on adaptive learning technologies. Handbook Res. Learn. Inst. **2**, 522–560 (2016)
5. Alexander, D., Haysom, J., Bowen, M.: Predict, observe, explain: activities enhancing scientific understanding, NSTA Press (2010)
6. An, M., Mehrvarz, M., Teffera, L., Kisow, M., McLaren, B.M., Bogart, C.: Partnering with community college faculty to co-design intelligent tutoring systems for cybersecurity workforce training. In: Proceedings of the 57th ACM Technical Symposium on Computer Science Education V. 1, pp. 52–58 (2026)
7. Anderson, J.R.: Automaticity and the ACT theory. Am. J. Psychol., 165–180 (1992)
8. Anderson, J.R.: ACT: a simple theory of complex cognition. Am. Psychol. **51**(4), 355 (1996)
9. Baker, R.S., Corbett, A.T., Koedinger, K.R., Wagner, A.Z.: Off-task behavior in the cognitive tutor classroom: when students "game the system". In: Proceedings of the SIGCHI Conference on Human Factors in Computing Systems, pp. 383–390 (2004)
10. Baker, R.S., Roll, I., Corbett, A.T., Koedinger, K.R.: Do performance goals lead students to game the system? In: AIED, pp. 57–64 (2005)
11. Bernacki, M.L., Greene, M.J., Lobczowski, N.G.: A systematic review of research on personalized learning: personalized by whom, to what, how, and for what purpose (s)? Educ. Psychol. Rev. **33**(4), 1675–1715 (2021)
12. Chernikova, O., et al.: Personalization through adaptivity or adaptability? A meta-analysis on simulation-based learning in higher education. Educ. Res. Rev. **46**, 100662 (2025)
13. Cichonski, P., Millar, T., Grance, T., Scarfone, K., et al.: Computer security incident handling guide. NIST Spec. Publ. **800**(61), 1–147 (2012)
14. CompTIA Partners: CompTIA Security+ Certification Overview (2025). https://partners.comptia.org/certifications/security. Accessed 14 June 2025
15. Corbett, A.T., Anderson, J.R.: Knowledge tracing: modeling the acquisition of procedural knowledge. User Model. User-Adap. Inter. **4**, 253–278 (1994)
16. Eglington, L.G., Pavlik, P.I., Jr.: How to optimize student learning using student models that adapt rapidly to individual differences. Int. J. Artif. Intell. Educ. **33**(3), 497–518 (2023)
17. Gupta, A.: Designing and deploying scalable intelligent tutoring systems to enhance adult education, Drexel University (2025). Ph.D. thesis
18. Gupta, A., Siddiqui, M., Smith, G., Reddig, J., MacLellan, C.: Intelligent tutors for adult learners: an analysis of needs and challenges. arXiv preprint arXiv:2412.04477 (2024)
19. Hallinger, P., Wang, R.: The evolution of simulation-based learning across the disciplines, 1965–2018: a science map of the literature. Simulat. Gam. **51**(1), 9–32 (2020)
20. Heuermann, L.: CompTIA Security+ SY0-701 Cert Guide. Pearson IT Certification (2024)
21. Holzer, H.J., Lipson, R., Wright, G.: Community colleges and workforce development: Are they achieving their potential? (2023)
22. Huang, Y., et al.: A general multi-method approach to data-driven redesign of tutoring systems. In: LAK21: 11th International Learning Analytics and Knowledge Conference, pp. 161–172. ACM, Irvine CA USA (2021). https://doi.org/10.1145/3448139.3448155, https://dl.acm.org/doi/10.1145/3448139.3448155

23. Koedinger, K.R., Baker, R.S., Cunningham, K., Skogsholm, A., Leber, B., Stamper, J.: A data repository for the EDM community: the PSLC DataShop. Handbook Educat. Data Min. **43**, 43–56 (2010)
24. Koedinger, K.R., Corbett, A.T., Perfetti, C.: The knowledge-learning-instruction framework: bridging the science-practice chasm to enhance robust student learning. Cogn. Sci. **36**(5), 757–798 (2012)
25. Kolb, D.A.: Experiential Learning: Experience as the Source of Learning and Development, FT Press (2014)
26. Kularbphettong, K., Kedsiributt, P., Roonrakwit, P.: Developing an adaptive web-based intelligent tutoring system using mastery learning technique. Proc. Soc. Behav. Sci. **191**, 686–691 (2015)
27. Kulik, J.A., Fletcher, J.D.: Effectiveness of intelligent tutoring systems: a meta-analytic review. Rev. Educat. Res. **86**(1), 42–78 (2016). https://doi.org/10.3102/0034654315581420, https://journals.sagepub.com/doi/10.3102/0034654315581420
28. Lave, J., Wenger, E.: Situated learning: Legitimate peripheral participation, Cambridge University Press (1991)
29. Legusov, O., Raby, R.L., Mou, L., Gómez-Gajardo, F., Zhou, Y.: How community colleges and other TVET institutions contribute to the united nations sustainable development goals. J. Furth. High. Educ. **46**(1), 89–106 (2022)
30. Odéen, M., Sellberg, C., Praetorius, G., Lindwall, O., Englund, L., Andersson, A.: Intelligent learning systems for simulator-based professional training: a systematic literature review. In: International Conference in Methodologies and intelligent Systems for Technology Enhanced Learning, pp. 109–119. Springer Nature Switzerland Cham (2024)
31. Oden Choi, J., et al.: Bridging the community college cybersecurity classroom and workplace with the cyberSim lab. In: Proceedings of the 56th ACM Technical Symposium on Computer Science Education, vol. 1, p. 875–881. SIGCSETS 2025, Association for Computing Machinery, New York, NY, USA (2025). https://doi.org/10.1145/3641554.3701834
32. Sarmiento, J.P., Wise, A.F.: Participatory and co-design of learning analytics: an initial review of the literature. In: LAK22: 12th International Learning Analytics and Knowledge Conference, pp. 535–541. LAK22, Association for Computing Machinery, New York, NY, USA (2022). https://doi.org/10.1145/3506860.3506910, https://doi.org/10.1145/3506860.3506910
33. Sehrawat, A., Keelan, R., Shimada, K., Wilfong, D.M., McCormick, J.T., Rabin, Y.: Simulation-based cryosurgery intelligent tutoring system prototype. Technol. Cancer Res. Treat. **15**(2), 396–407 (2016)
34. Sergeyev, A., Kinney, M.B., Kuhl, S.A., Alaraje, N., Highum, M., Mehandiratta, P.: University, community college, and industry partnership: Revamping robotics education to meet 21st century workforce needs–NSF-sponsored project final report. In: 2019 ASEE Annual Conference & Exposition (2019)
35. VanLehn, K.: The relative effectiveness of human tutoring, intelligent tutoring systems, and other tutoring systems. Educat. Psychol. **46**(4), 197–221 (2011)

# Analysing the Temporal Dynamics of Behavioural Engagement in Middle School: A Clustering Approach Across Multiple Lessons

Niels André[1(✉)], Audrey Serna[1], Benoît Encelle[1], and Elise Lavoué[1,2]

[1] INSA Lyon, CNRS, Universite Claude Bernard Lyon 1, LIRIS, UMR5205, 69621 Villeurbanne, France
niels.andre@insa-lyon.fr

[2] iaelyon School of Management, Université Jean Moulin Lyon 3, Lyon, France

**Abstract.** In a digital learning environment, secondary school teachers have access to student performance data but often lack detailed insights into specific behaviours that could help them identify strategies to enhance their pedagogical content. In this study, we provide such detailed information on student engagement by analysing digital interaction traces. A large-scale study was conducted, involving 863 8th-grade students from 62 classes across 23 middle schools in France, encompassing 6,003 work sessions after data cleaning. To gain a deeper understanding of engaged behaviours, we identified four distinct behavioural engagement clusters. These clusters were distinguished by variations in the number of interactions, quiz results, and propensity to demonstrate a willingness to improve. The analysis of their evolution over time reveals that students can adopt different types of engaged behaviours depending on the complexity of the pedagogical content. The proposed approach has the potential to inform the design of educational content and, ultimately, assist teachers in adapting their lessons to students' behaviour in class.

**Keywords:** Behavioural Engagement · Temporal Analysis · Middle School

## 1 Introduction

In K-12 settings, teachers frequently integrate digital learning environments into their classroom practices, but often operate under significant time constraints. Consequently, they lack immediate, actionable feedback on the pedagogical relevance of their content and on their students' actual engagement, as platforms provide only limited or delayed data. In this context, student engagement becomes a key indicator for teachers to evaluate whether their pedagogical content effectively supports learning and to guide instructional adjustments.

Student engagement in digital learning environments is widely recognised as a critical predictor of academic achievement and retention [15]. Therefore, a deep


J. Weidlich et al. (Eds.): EC-TEL 2026, LNCS 16905, pp. 34–48, 2027.
https://doi.org/10.1007/978-3-032-37979-5_3

understanding of students' engaged behaviours is a prerequisite for designing adaptive and effective educational content that improves learning outcomes [5]. Student engagement is typically conceptualised as a multidimensional construct comprising emotional, cognitive, and behavioural dimensions [9]. This multidimensional nature makes engagement difficult to capture and analyse in practice.

To address this complexity, Learning Analytics (LA) has been increasingly used to analyse interaction traces and infer engagement patterns. However, the application of LA to decode interaction traces has been unevenly distributed, with a predominant focus on higher education and significantly fewer studies in K-12 settings [12]. Complex ethical considerations and heightened privacy concerns regarding younger learners partly drive this disparity. Furthermore, a limited understanding of how LA can practically benefit different stakeholders has hindered their integration in schools [3]. Consequently, existing literature often adopts a broad approach that fails to distinguish among age groups, leaving the unique behavioural dynamics of K-12 students underexplored.

While underexplored, several studies have employed LA approaches on interaction traces to analyse student engagement through clustering techniques [20,29]. These techniques typically group learners based on aggregated behaviours across sessions and do not capture the nuances specific to each class session. Consequently, they offer limited insight into how engagement varies across specific course content, providing little actionable feedback to help teachers adjust their pedagogical materials.

Therefore, a significant challenge remains in identifying distinct types of student behaviour and tracking their evolution across multiple sessions in relation to the specific pedagogical content provided by teachers. Understanding these temporal dynamics is crucial for determining how different tasks influence learner engagement over time. To address this gap, our research aims to provide a new perspective on these interactions. In this paper, we propose an approach to classify individual work sessions and monitor student engagement across a curriculum, enabling a more fine-grained and temporally grounded analysis of behavioural transitions.

## 2 Related Work

### 2.1 K-12 Student Engagement Analysis

The model proposed by Fredricks et al. [9] remains the most widely adopted framework in the field, as evidenced by its application in various K-12 and digital learning contexts [4,6]. While this model defines engagement as a tripartite construct comprising behavioural, emotional, and cognitive dimensions, the literature has expanded to include other dimensions such as social engagement, which focuses on peer interactions [8], or academic engagement, centred on institutional participation [11]. In practice, assessing these multifaceted dimensions in the classroom often involves mixed-methods approaches, which aim to capture complementary aspects of engagement within constrained pedagogical contexts.

Most researchers rely on self-reported data from surveys and interviews, or perform retrospective analyses of classroom observations and video recordings to evaluate engagement [4,6]. In parallel, LA approaches have been proposed to analyse engagement using interaction traces. A review conducted by Bond et al. [3] identified 27 studies exploring engagement in K-12 contexts and found that log data is widely used, but most often coupled with other data sources. For example, Nasir et al. [16] used clustering on video, audio and log data to identify multimodal collaborative learning behavioural profiles. Jonathan et al. [13] used descriptive statistics derived from surveys, focus groups, and tests to develop a student dashboard to improve learning outcomes. However, only a limited number of studies rely solely on log data, even though it is often the only source available in authentic classroom settings.

These studies measure behavioural engagement by directly extracting global indicators from student activity logs [14]. Such indicators generally include time spent in the learning environment, number of logins, content completion rates, and performance accuracy [27]. For instance, researchers have used the frequency of logins and system accesses to measure students' intentions to practice or interact with specific learning materials [7,18]. However, these low-level indicators provide only a limited understanding of the diversity of engaged behaviours observed in classroom contexts. Furthermore, Bond et al. [3] highlight that only a small fraction of studies provide empirical evidence of the proposed approaches.

Taken together, these limitations highlight the lack of fine-grained, actionable insights from interaction traces alone. They also suggest the need for more evidence-based research that further exploits such data to better capture the complex behavioural dynamics of K-12 learners. In particular, there is a need for advanced analytic methods capable of extracting higher-level insights from raw interaction logs, especially in everyday classroom settings where complementary data sources are rarely available.

### 2.2 Clustering and Temporal Analysis in Learning Analytics

Among the studies identified in [3] as relying solely on log data, clustering emerges as the most commonly used analytical technique. Ruipérez-Valiente et al. [20] used this method to distinguish four different student engagement profiles by measuring activity across several dimensions, including social interactions and activity completion. Similarly, Yeung et al. [28] employed clustering algorithms to classify students based on learning metrics, such as marks, time spent, and the number of attempts recorded during tablet-based mathematics activities. Yu et al. [29] investigated the impact of social networking on online self-regulated learning, using clustering to identify four distinct learner types based on lesson completion, connection size (Dunbar's number), and total learning days. Finally, Zhang et al. [30] used clustering to identify eleven distinct self-regulated learning patterns, categorising students into successful, average, or at-risk profiles based on the balance and proactivity of their digital interactions.

Despite these advancements, a significant limitation remains: most research presents a cumulative view of engagement indicators. Such an approach aggregates learner activity over time and therefore lacks a fine-grained, session-by-session temporal perspective. While some longitudinal studies have begun to address this issue by examining the distribution of indicators over time, their focus remains on identifying stable clusters of students based on long-term participation. For example, Barata et al. [2] have employed clustering to identify student evolution over three years.

The temporal dimension of learning has emerged as a critical field of study within LA, as researchers move beyond static snapshots of student performance to capture the dynamic nature of educational interactions. For instance, Olsen et al. [17] demonstrate that shifting from static averages to temporal analysis significantly improves the prediction of learning gains. Recently, Serna et al. [24] used factor analysis of interaction logs over a six-week period to identify three distinct behavioural patterns. This research demonstrates that, while engaged behaviours generally decrease over time, specific interventions, such as tailored gamification, can stabilise these patterns in the final stages of a curriculum. Similarly, Rotelli et al. [19] propose a framework for temporal student segmentation, showing that selecting specific temporal variables significantly influences the resulting clusters of student learning patterns.

Recent research has further refined these temporal models by employing Transition Network Analysis and Markov chains to visualise the dynamic transitions between interaction states [23]. Rather than relying on aggregate metrics, these approaches capture the granularity of the learning experience by monitoring how students navigate tasks over time. For instance, trace data has been used to monitor student behaviour across multiple sessions within a single course, employing clustering to reveal that engagement levels are not static but fluctuate throughout the learning process [21]. This study highlights the value of clustering individual work sessions rather than students, enabling the identification of distinct behavioural patterns that may change from one session to another.

However, a significant gap persists in the current literature between the two analytical scales. On the one hand, many longitudinal studies track patterns over several weeks but often cluster individual students into stable profiles based on aggregate habits [19], thereby overlooking the dynamic nature of engagement. On the other hand, research adopting a session-based approach to capture this dynamic is typically restricted to short-term observations [21]. There is a lack of longitudinal evidence on the evolution of these granular behavioural clusters over longer periods. By applying session-based clustering to a five-week curriculum, this study aims to bridge the gap between short-term granularity and long-term behavioural analysis, addressing the following research questions: **RQ1:** What distinct clusters of behavioural engagement can be identified through the analysis of individual work sessions? **RQ2:** How do these behavioural engagement clusters evolve over time? To what extent do individual students shift between these clusters throughout the curriculum?

# 3 Method

## 3.1 Learning Environment

We conducted a study using a Moodle-based online learning environment. The curriculum comprised 7 distinct lessons, each composed of multiple quizzes, as detailed in Table 1. The mathematics teachers designed the curriculum to ensure high ecological validity and alignment with 8th-grade curricular standards. It totalled 41 quizzes (3 to 9 per lesson) on basic middle school algebra (in particular, literal arithmetic). To progress to the next quiz, learners had to score at least 70% correct; otherwise, they had to retake it.

**Table 1.** Pedagogical structure of the curriculum: topics, number of quizzes, and total number of items

| Lesson | Topic | Quizzes | Items |
|---|---|---|---|
| 1 | Introduction to Variables | 5 | 25 |
| 2 | Simplifying Products | 9 | 46 |
| 3 | Algebraic Expressions | 3 | 25 |
| 4 | Combining Like Terms with and without Signed Numbers | 6 | 30 |
| 5 | Removal of Parentheses | 6 | 30 |
| 6 | Applications in Geometry | 7 | 26 |
| 7 | Conjecturing and Proving Equalities | 5 | 21 |

## 3.2 Procedure and Participants

Our study, conducted between January and May 2024 in France, was divided into five-week experimental phases. The pedagogical structure typically began with a 10- to 15-minute lesson delivered by the teacher, followed by an additional 25- to 30-minute period of autonomous work in the digital environment. To ensure a controlled experimental framework, teachers followed guidelines that required each work session to correspond to one lesson. During each session, students worked on individual tablets. The sample included only students who attended at least five lessons, ensuring consistent exposure to the digital environment. A total of 23 middle schools participated (21 public and 2 private schools), involving 62 classes and 863 students (456 girls and 407 boys). The research protocol was approved by the Research Ethics Committee from the University of Lyon.

## 3.3 Data Processing

The raw dataset captures quiz-level interaction logs. It records start and end times for each quiz attempt. Each log entry details the student's response and validation status. First, to reconstruct coherent learning episodes from the continuous log stream, a dynamic segmentation algorithm was applied. A 60-minute inactivity threshold at the class level primarily determined session boundaries. To circumvent the issue of over-segmentation (noise), short isolated fragments were automatically amalgamated with adjacent sessions if they occurred within a valid time window. This reconstruction enabled the differentiation between supervised in-class work and autonomous activity. Consequently, out-of-class sessions (homework that is not catch-up) and residual artefacts were excluded, thereby restricting the dataset to controlled, synchronous learning periods. The final dataset comprises 1,200,000 log entries corresponding to 6003 work sessions.

To facilitate macro-level analysis, raw logs were aggregated into three categories of quiz-level states: 1) *Consulted*: recorded when a student viewed a quiz without submitting; 2) *Attempt*, including the initial attempt (quiz_first_attempt), immediate subsequent attempts (quiz_remake_immediate), and attempts performed after engaging with other content (quiz_remake_later); 3) and *Performance outcome*, categorised as failed (score $< 70\%$), success (score $\geq 70\%$), or perfect (score of 100%). This aggregation resulted in over 90,000 macro-level interaction traces. Furthermore, we calculated two indicators: the average success rate, defined as the mean success percentage across all quizzes in a session, and the average number of additional attempts, which represents the average number of additional attempts performed after an initial success, normalised by the total number of unique exercises available in a given lesson.

### 3.4 Data Analysis

**RQ1 Clustering:** Although k-means remains a popular choice in the field for its computational efficiency [20,25], we opted for Agglomerative Hierarchical Clustering (AHC). This method is specifically recommended for sequence analysis [22] as it operates directly on the dissimilarity matrix, preserving the integrity of the temporal structures without requiring geometric projection.

To capture students' behavioural nuances, we implemented Optimal Matching (OM) analysis using a data-driven, nonlinear cost function. As argued by Stovel [26], linear-interval costs are often inappropriate for analysing sequences where events vary greatly in frequency or represent specific thresholds of engagement. Stovel suggests that rare events carry a higher "marginal cost" of substitution, as they represent significant qualitative shifts in behaviour rather than mere quantitative variations.

In line with this perspective, we utilised the INDELS method from the TraMineR package [10] to define our substitution cost matrix. This approach derives costs directly from the observed state distributions, ensuring that infrequent actions are prioritised over common, routine interactions.

The cost of an insertion or deletion (indel) operation for a given state $i$, denoted as $c_i$, is defined as the inverse of its observed probability $P(i)$ within the entire corpus: $c_i = \frac{1}{P(i)}$. Following this logic, the substitution cost $SC_{i,j}$ between any two distinct states $i$ and $j$ is calculated as the sum of their respective indel costs:

$$SC_{i,j} = \begin{cases} c_i + c_j & \text{if } i \neq j \\ 0 & \text{if } i = j \end{cases}$$

This data-driven approach ensures that infrequent pedagogical states carry higher informational value and, therefore, exert a stronger influence on the resulting dissimilarity matrix.

**RQ2 Temporal Analysis:** To visualise the flow of students between different engagement states, a Sankey diagram has been generated using the sankeyNetwork function from the networkD3 package in R [1]. This approach allows for a clear illustration of how individuals transition between the identified behavioural clusters from one session to the next across the seven lessons, similar to Saint et al. [21].

In addition to these cluster transitions, the previously defined indicators (average success rate and average number of additional attempts) were used as temporal variables to monitor fluctuations in performance and engagement across the seven lessons. This session-by-session tracking aims to reveal whether certain behavioural patterns correlate with specific stages of the curriculum or remain consistent as pedagogical requirements evolve. To evaluate the statistical significance of these temporal fluctuations and cluster differences, pairwise comparisons were performed using Wilcoxon rank-sum tests. To account for the inflation of Type I error due to multiple testing, $p$-values were systematically adjusted using the conservative Bonferroni correction method.

# 4 Results

## 4.1 RQ1: Clustering and Cluster Characterisation

Although a 2-cluster solution yielded the highest baseline in Average Silhouette Width ($ASW = 0.497$), it was rejected due to its limited capacity to capture the diverse learning strategies. Instead, we retained a 4-cluster solution, which yielded the second-highest overall ASW (0.404) and an $R^2$ of 0.514. The hierarchical clustering of indicator sequences at the session level revealed four distinct session archetypes, ensuring that the clusters represent specific instances of interaction rather than student profiles, and are represented in Fig. 1.

The *first cluster* ($n = 2319$) represents the most prevalent behaviour characterised by a balanced, moderate distribution of states. Sessions in this cluster show twice as many remakes in first attempts, but also a higher ratio of successful (success and perfect) states to failed states. The *second cluster* ($n = 1567$) represents the sessions with the lowest number of states. Sessions in this cluster show very few remakes and a good balance among success, perfection, and failure. The *third cluster* ($n = 1833$) is the second-most prevalent behaviour and has the second-highest state volume. Sessions in this group exhibit a high frequency of remakes, alongside a substantial number of 'failed' states. While

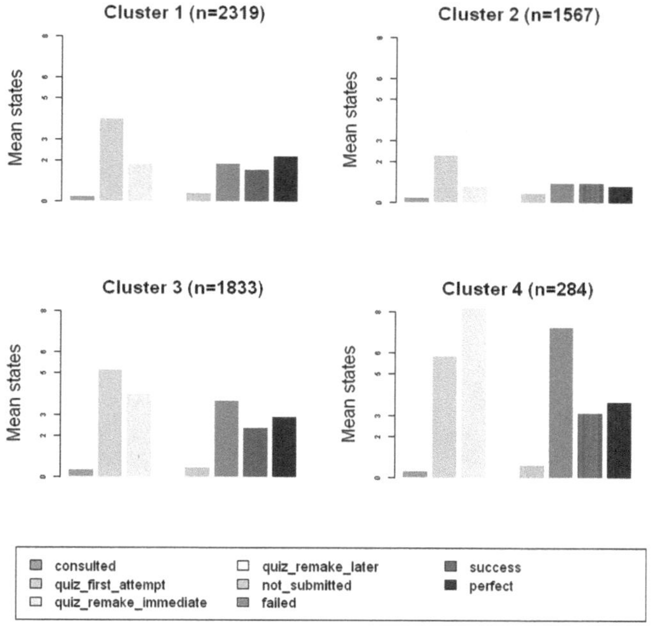


**Fig. 1.** Mean Distribution of states across Clusters

these sessions reach 'success' and 'perfect' states more often than those in clusters 1 and 2, they also exhibit a notably higher failure rate. The *fourth cluster* ($n = 284$) represents the least frequent behavioural profile, yet it has the highest overall state volume. Sessions in this group are uniquely defined by an intensive, iterative process, making it the only cluster where immediate remakes outnumber initial attempts. Furthermore, these sessions exhibit a high level of academic challenge; the volume of 'failed' states is approximately equal to the combined total of 'success' and 'perfect' outcomes.

### 4.2 RQ2: Temporal Evolution and Pedagogical Design

To understand the relationship between pedagogical design and student engagement, we mapped the relative frequency of each cluster against the lessons of the curriculum. The curriculum follows a deliberate pedagogical and difficulty progression, designed by the mathematics teachers and detailed in Table 1.

The temporal transitions between the different clusters reveal a dynamic adaptation to the curriculum's increasing complexity (see Fig. 2). A major shift occurs during Lesson 3 (Expanding Algebraic Expressions), when the vast majority of the cohort transitions into Cluster 2 (76.5%). Interestingly, as the curriculum progresses, excluding Lesson 3, the prevalence of Cluster 2 continues to grow, reaching 41.7% by Lesson 7 despite the intended increase in pedagogical complexity. Conversely, Cluster 1, which represented 58.5% of the cohort in Lesson 1,

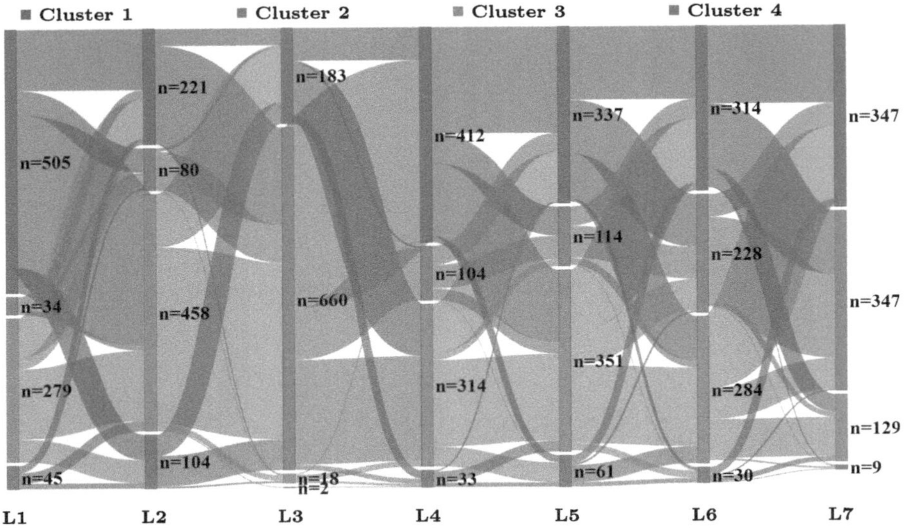


*Note:* Numbers indicate the total count of students assigned to each cluster within a specific lesson.

**Fig. 2.** Flow diagram of cluster repartition across the lessons

exhibits high volatility throughout the curriculum. It decreases sharply in Lesson 2 (25.6%) and Lesson 3 (21.2%), before recovering in Lesson 4 (47.7%). Following a slight decline during Lessons 5 ($3*\%$) and 6 (36.7%), it increases again in the final lesson, ultimately accounting for 41.7% of the students in Lesson 7. Cluster 3 follows a different trajectory, peaking in Lesson 2 (53.1%) and Lesson 5 (40.7%), but reaching its lowest point in the final lesson (15.5%). Finally, Cluster 4 also shows significant volatility at a smaller scale. After starting at 5.1% in Lesson 1 and peaking in Lesson 2 (12.1%), it drops to its minimum in Lesson 3 (0.2%). It then experiences partial recoveries in Lessons 4 (3.8%) and 5 (7.1%), followed by a final decline to 1.1% in Lesson 7.

**Table 2.** Statistical significance of pairwise lesson comparisons for Success Rate (upper triangle) and average number of additional attempts (lower triangle)

| | L1 | L2 | L3 | L4 | L5 | L6 | L7 |
|---|---|---|---|---|---|---|---|
| **L1** | | **** [s] | **** [m] | **** [m] | **** [l] | **** [l] | **** [m] |
| **L2** | * [s] | | **** [s] | **** [s] | **** [l] | **** [l] | **** [m] |
| **L3** | **** [s] | *** [s] | | | **** [s] | **** [m] | |
| **L4** | **** [s] | | | | **** [m] | **** [m] | * [s] |
| **L5** | **** [s] | **** [s] | | *** [s] | | **** [s] | **** [s] |
| **L6** | **** [m] | **** [m] | **** [s] | **** [s] | **** [s] | | **** [m] |
| **L7** | **** [s] | *** [s] | | | | **** [s] | |

Note: The upper triangle represents **Success Rate** comparisons. The lower triangle represents **Average number of additional attempts** comparisons. Significance levels: **** $p < .0001$, *** $p < .001$, ** $p < .01$, * $p < .05$ ; Effect size magnitudes: [s]: small ($|r| \geq .10$), [m]: moderate ($|r| \geq .30$), [l]: large ($|r| \geq .50$)

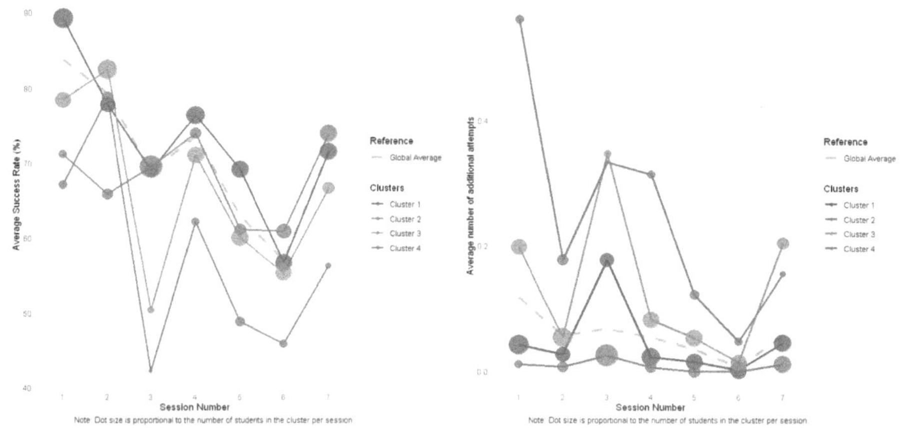


(a) Success Rate (b) Average number of additional attempts

**Fig. 3.** Evolution of Success Rate & Average number of additional attempts by Learning Profile

**Table 3.** Statistical significance of pairwise cluster comparisons for Success Rate and Average number of additional attempts across lessons

| | Lesson 1 | | Lesson 2 | | Lesson 3 | | Lesson 4 | | Lesson 5 | | Lesson 6 | | Lesson 7 | |
|---|---|---|---|---|---|---|---|---|---|---|---|---|---|---|
| | Suc. | Add. | Suc. | Add. | Suc. | Add. | Suc. | Add. | Suc. | Add. | Suc. | Add. | Suc. | Add. |
| C1 vs C2 | **** [s] | | | | | **** [m] | | | | | | | | **** [s] |
| C1 vs C3 | **** [l] | **** [m] | **** [s] | | | | **** [s] | **** [s] | **** [m] | *** [s] | | * [s] | * [s] | **** [m] |
| C1 vs C4 | **** [m] | **** [m] | | **** [m] | | | **** [s] | **** [m] | **** [m] | **** [s] | * [s] | **** [s] | | |
| C2 vs C3 | | **** [s] | *** [s] | *** [s] | * [s] | **** [s] | | **** [s] | | **** [s] | * [s] | ** [s] | **** [s] | **** [m] |
| C2 vs C4 | | **** [l] | | **** [m] | | | ** [m] | **** [l] | *** [m] | **** [m] | ** [s] | **** [m] | * [s] | * [s] |
| C3 vs C4 | **** [m] | **** [s] | *** [s] | **** [s] | | | * [s] | ** [s] | **** [s] | | | | | |

Note: Suc. = Success rate; Add. = Average number of additional attempts. Significance levels: **** $p < .0001$, *** $p < .001$, ** $p < .01$, * $p < .05$. Effect size magnitudes: [l]: large ($|r| \geq .50$), [m]: moderate ($.30 \leq |r| \leq .50$), [s]: small ($.10 \leq |r| \leq .30$)

The longitudinal evolutions of the success rate and the average number of additional attempts are illustrated in Fig. 3a and Fig. 3b, respectively, while the statistical significance of the differences observed between lessons and clusters for both indicators is detailed in Table 2 and Table 3.

A preliminary observation of Fig. 3a and Table 2 reveals that student performance does not follow a strictly linear decline. While the success rate in Lesson 4 (Combining Like Terms) appears higher than in Lesson 3 (Expanding Algebraic Expressions), this difference is not statistically significant ($p = 1.00$). In contrast, a highly significant improvement ($p < .001$) in performance is observed in Lesson 7 (Conjecturing and Proving Equalities) compared to Lesson 6 (Applications in Geometry). Lesson 7 appears to drive high student success rates; furthermore, the comparable structural difficulty of Lessons 3 and 7 is reflected in the lack of a significant difference between their results ($p = 0.46$).

By examining Table 3, we can further distinguish the performance trajectories associated with each behavioural pattern. Cluster 1 represents the most successful sessions, consistently maintaining the highest average success rate across the curriculum. Interestingly, Cluster 2 occupies a revealing position: although its global success rate is not statistically different from that of Cluster 3 ($p = 0.186$), its performance remains remarkably stable. Furthermore, by the final stages of the curriculum (Lessons 6 and 7), the success rate of Cluster 2 closely matches that of Cluster 1. In contrast, Cluster 4 identifies sessions where students face the most significant challenges. While its success rate frequently falls below 50% during the more complex phases of the curriculum, such as Lessons 5 and 6, its performance profile is distinct. During Lesson 5, Cluster 4 is significantly less performant than all other clusters ($p < .001$), marking a point of peak difficulty. In Lesson 6, although its success rate remains the lowest, it differs significantly only from Clusters 1 and 2 ($p < .05$ and $p < .01$ respectively). At the same time, its performance is statistically comparable to that of Cluster 3. A similar pattern is observed in Lesson 7, where Cluster 4 only diverges significantly from Cluster 2 ($p < .05$). Interestingly, in Lesson 3, Cluster 4 does not differ significantly from the other groups. Overall, Cluster 3 maintains a significantly higher success rate than Cluster 4 in most other sessions, notably in Lessons 1 ($p < .0001$), 2 ($p < .001$), 4 ($p < .05$), and 5 ($p < .0001$).

The evolution of the global average in Fig. 3b, supported by the statistical analysis in Table 2, shows that the average number of additional attempts diminishes across the curriculum. Even if Lessons 3 and 7 stand out as notable exceptions to this decline, the overall trend suggests a gradual decrease in behavioural engagement with the learning environment. However, while Lesson 4 appears to follow the initial trend, it does not diverge significantly from Lesson 3 ($p = 1.00$). Statistical analysis confirms that Lessons 3 and 7 mark a significant resurgence in engagement, and their chronological gap is statistically comparable in terms of average number of additional attempts ($p = 1.00$).

By examining the clusters individually with Table 3, we can further distinguish contrasting learning intentions within each group. Cluster 1 initially exhibits a number of additional attempts that gradually decreases over time, whereas Cluster 2 maintains a proportion near zero throughout the curriculum. In contrast, Cluster 4 exhibits the highest post-success engagement, maintaining a significantly higher average additional attempts ratio than Cluster 2 across almost all sessions, with the notable exception of Lesson 3. This trend is statistically significant from Lesson 1 ($p < .0001$) through to Lesson 7 ($p < .05$). Furthermore, Cluster 4 frequently diverges from Cluster 1, with significantly higher ratios observed in Lessons 1, 2, 4, 5, and 6 ($p < .0001$ in all cases). Cluster 3 consistently maintains a higher level of engagement than Clusters 1 and 2 throughout the curriculum. It significantly outperforms Cluster 1 in the number of additional attempts in almost every session (e.g., $p < .0001$ in Lessons 1, 4, and 7), except in Lesson 3. This divergence is particularly sharp compared to Cluster 2, which it significantly exceeds in every lesson ($p < .0001$ in Lessons 1, 3, 4, 5, and 7).

# 5 Discussion

## 5.1 RQ1: Clustering and Cluster Characterisation

The results reveal a complex interplay between pedagogical design, performance, and behavioural engagement. To interpret these dynamics, the sessions were categorised into four distinct functional clusters, which we name and describe here based on their state distributions, performance, and degree of perfection seeking. The average number of additional attempts after reaching the success threshold is a primary indicator of learners' perfectionism and a voluntary drive to refine their performance and achieve a perfect score.

**Cluster 1: Mastery-Oriented Sessions (High Performance, Moderate Engagement).** These sessions are characterised by high success rates coupled with a moderate level of additional attempts. This suggests a moderate pursuit of mastery in which students, having reached the success threshold, continue to engage to a limited extent to refine their understanding or achieve perfection.

**Cluster 2: Strategic-Efficiency Sessions (Intermediate Performance, Low Engagement).** In these sessions, students achieve intermediate success with minimal additional effort. This reflects a "threshold-oriented" approach in which objectives are met quickly, and the student chooses to move on immediately rather than iterate, likely due to high prior knowledge or a focus on efficiency.

**Cluster 3: Progressive-Engagement Sessions (Intermediate Performance, Moderate to High Engagement).** These sessions highlight a standard learning trajectory where students achieve average scores but demonstrate a higher degree of interaction than the high-performing clusters. This reflects a more intensive trial-and-error process, where sustained engagement is necessary to navigate challenges and gradually work towards achieving perfection.

**Cluster 4: Persistent-Struggle Sessions (Low Performance, High Engagement).** Despite recording the lowest success rates, these sessions exhibit the highest average number of additional attempts. This reflects a significant behavioural persistence: students face high task complexity but continue to iterate extensively to overcome learning obstacles and achieve perfection.

From a pedagogical perspective, characterising such clusters can help teachers identify meaningful differences in learners' engagement that would otherwise remain invisible when relying solely on final grades. For instance, a teacher might overlook the high level of effort and resilience in **Cluster 4**, or fail to distinguish between qualitatively different engagement strategies, such as the deep mastery observed in **Cluster 1** and the potentially minimalist strategy in **Cluster 2**.

## 5.2 RQ2: Temporal Evolution and Pedagogical Design

A primary observation is the dissociation between success rates and the average number of additional attempts, most notably in low-performance sessions with high engagement (Cluster 4). While these sessions record the lowest success rates during the peak complexity of Lessons 5 and 6, they consistently maintain a significantly higher average number of additional attempts than both the High-performance sessions with low engagement (Cluster 2) and High-performance sessions with moderate engagement (Cluster 1). This suggests that even when high task difficulty limits overall success, it does not suppress the perfection-seeking behaviour of this session profile. Conversely, the shift of most sessions to Cluster 2 reflects an adaptation toward strategic efficiency, where intermediate performance is achieved with minimal interaction.

Overall, these findings highlight a complex interplay between pedagogical design and behavioural adaptation. As the curriculum progresses, student behaviour shifts toward a more strategic, threshold-oriented approach, as evidenced by the growing prevalence of Cluster 2 and the global decline in perfection seeking. This general decrease over time aligns with recent longitudinal research, which observed that learners' engagement typically decreases as a curriculum progresses, though certain factors can stabilise these patterns [24]. The notable exceptions to this decline in Lessons 3 and 7 demonstrate that, despite this general downward trend, engagement remains highly task-dependent.

## 6 Conclusion and Future Work

This study explored the complex relationships among pedagogical design, performance, and student engagement using a session-based clustering approach involving 863 8th-grade students, representing a substantial cohort for an experimental study at this educational level. By shifting the unit of analysis from learners to individual sessions, we identify four behavioural profiles that capture distinct engagement strategies across the curriculum. Our longitudinal analysis reveals a global trend toward more strategic, threshold-oriented behaviours as the curriculum progresses. In addition, lesson-specific spikes in perfection seeking highlight the critical role of pedagogical design in sustaining engagement.

This study has several limitations. Findings are specific to 8th-grade students performing literal arithmetic via quizzes and may not generalise to other contexts. The absence of access to supplementary resources limits insights into learners' strategies. Moreover, while our seven-session analysis offers a longitudinal perspective, extending this scope over a full academic year would help determine the long-term stability of these clusters.

Despite these limitations, our approach provides a foundation for real-time dashboards that offer teachers actionable insights often masked by traditional grading. These dashboards would allow teachers to track shifts in student behaviour across the curriculum and support targeted interventions, encouraging students to strive for perfection rather than merely meet a success threshold. As students transition from more engaged to less engaged patterns over time, instructors could observe this gradual disengagement even when success rates remain high. Identifying such trends would enable teachers to encourage students to revisit more complex materials, refine remaining errors, and maintain a high level of engagement. Moreover, analysing these groups over time would help adapt the curriculum for future cohorts or to develop additional materials.

## References


1. Allaire, J., Gandrud, C., Russell, K., Yetman, C.: networkD3: D3 JavaScript Network Graphs from R (2025). R package version 0.4.1
2. Barata, G., Gama, S., Jorge, J., Gonçalves, D.: Studying student differentiation in gamified education: a long-term study. Comput. Hum. Behav. **71**, 550–585 (2017)
3. Bond, M., Viberg, O., Bergdahl, N.: The current state of using learning analytics to measure and support K-12 student engagement: a scoping review. In: LAK23: 13th International Learning Analytics and Knowledge Conference, pp. 240–249. ACM, Arlington, TX, USA (2023)
4. Chao, G.C.N., Jong, S.Y., Chai, C.S., Luk, T.H.: Development of the motivation and engagement in virtual reality Chinese language learning questionnaire (MEVR-CLQ). In: 2020 International Symposium on Educational Technology (ISET), pp. 67–72 (2020)
5. Chi, M.T.H., Wylie, R.: The ICAP framework: linking cognitive engagement to active learning outcomes. Educat. Psych. **49**, 219–243 (2014)
6. Daher, W., Anabousy, A., Alfahel, E.: Elementary teachers' development in using technological tools to engage students in online learning. Europ. J. Educat. Res. **11**, 1183–1195 (2022)
7. Ding, L., Er, E., Orey, M.: An exploratory study of student engagement in gamified online discussions. Comput. Educat. **120**, 213–226 (2018)
8. Fallon, T.L., Aylett, R., Minnis, H., Rajendran, G.: Investigating social vulnerability in children using computer mediated role-play. Computers & Education **125**, 458–464 (2018)
9. Fredricks, J.A., Blumenfeld, P.C., Paris, A.H.: School Engagement: potential of the concept, state of the evidence. Rev. Educ. Res. **74**, 59–109 (2004)
10. Gabadinho, A., Ritschard, G., Müller, N.S., Studer, M.: Analyzing and visualizing state sequences in R with TraMineR. J. Stat. Softw. **40**, 1–37 (2011)
11. Ghorbanian, E., Mohammadhassani, N., Nasab, Y.M., Rajabi, M.: Investigating the effect of flipped classroom and jigsaw method on students' learning and academic engagement. In: 2024 11th International and the 17th National Conference on E-Learning and E-Teaching (ICeLeT), pp. 1–6 (2024)
12. Hung, J.L., Shelton, B.E., Yang, J., Du, X.: Improving predictive modeling for at-risk student identification: a multistage approach. IEEE Trans. Learn. Technol. (2019)
13. Jonathan, C., Tan, J., Koh, E., Caleon, I., Tay, S.H.: Enhancing students' critical reading fluency, engagement and self-efficacy using self-referenced learning analytics dashboard visualizations (2017)
14. Lang, C., Siemens, G., Wise, A.F.: Handbook of Learning Analytics. Society for Learning Analytics Research (SoLAR). Presented at the (2017) 1st edn
15. Mutahi, J., Kinai, A., Bore, N., Diriye, A., Weldemariam, K.: Studying engagement and performance with learning technology in an African classroom. In: Proceedings of the Seventh International Learning Analytics & Knowledge Conference, pp. 148–152. LAK '17, ACM, New York, NY, USA (2017)
16. Nasir, J., Kothiyal, A., Bruno, B., Dillenbourg, P.: Many are the ways to learn: identifying multi-modal behavioral profiles of collaborative learning in constructivist activities. Int. J. Comput.-Support. Collab. Learn. **16**, 485–523 (2021)
17. Olsen, J.K., Sharma, K., Rummel, N., Aleven, V.: Temporal analysis of multimodal data to predict collaborative learning outcomes. Br. J. Edu. Technol. **51**, 1527–1547 (2020)

18. Rodrigues, L., et al.: Gamification suffers from the novelty effect but benefits from the familiarization effect: findings from a longitudinal study. Int. J. Educat. Technol. High. Educat. **19** (2022)
19. Rotelli, D., et al.: Educating for a new future: making sense of technology-enhanced learning adoption. Presented at the Uncovering Student Temporal Learning Patterns (2022)
20. Ruipérez-Valiente, J.A., Gaydos, M., Rosenheck, L., Kim, Y.J., Klopfer, E.: Patterns of engagement in an educational massively multiplayer online game: a multidimensional view. IEEE Trans. Learn. Technol. **13**, 648–661 (2020)
21. Saint, J., Fan, Y., Gasevic, D.: Analytics of scaffold compliance for self-regulated learning. In: Proceedings of the 14th Learning Analytics and Knowledge Conference, pp. 326–337. ACM (2024)
22. Saqr, M., López-Pernas, S. (eds.): Learning analytics methods and tutorials: a practical guide using R. Springer (2024)
23. Saqr, M., López-Pernas, S., Törmänen, T., Kaliisa, R., Misiejuk, K., Tikka, S.: Transition network analysis: a novel framework for modeling, visualizing, and identifying the temporal patterns of learners and learning processes. In: Proceedings of the 15th International Learning Analytics and Knowledge Conference, pp. 351–361. ACM (2025)
24. Serna, A., Hallifax, S., Lavoué, É.: Investigating the effects of tailored gamification on learners' engagement over time in a learning environment. Proc. ACM Hum.-Comput. Int. **7**, 264–288 (2023)
25. Shum, K.H., Chu, S.K.W., Yeung, C.Y.: Continuously analysing fine-grained student behaviours in an online collaborative learning environment. Interact. Learn. Environ. **31**, 6395–6413 (2022)
26. Stovel, K.: Local sequential patterns: the structure of lynching in the deep south, 1882–1930. Soc. Forces **79**, 843–880 (2001)
27. Taşkın, N., Kilic, E.: Effects of gamification on behavioral and cognitive engagement of students in the online learning environment. Int. J. Hum.-Comput. Int. **39**, 1–12 (2022)
28. Yeung, C.Y., et al.: Exploring characteristics of fine-grained behaviors of learning mathematics in tablet-based E-learning activities (2017)
29. Yu, X., Wang, C.X., Spector, J.M.: Factors that impact social networking in online self-regulated learning activities. Educat. Tech. Research Dev. **68**(6), 3077–3095 (2020). https://doi.org/10.1007/s11423-020-09843-9
30. Zhang, M., Du, X., Hung, J.L., Li, H., Liu, M., Tang, H.: Analyzing and interpreting students' self-regulated learning patterns combining time-series feature extraction, segmentation, and clustering. J. Educat. Comput. Res. **60**, 1130–1165 (2022)

# Who Holds Your Students' Data? A Study on the Use of LLMs in Technology-Enhanced Learning

Pablo Arnau-González[1(✉)], David Gimeno-Gómez[1], Alejandro Canovas-Solbes[1], and Stamos Katsigiannis[2]

[1] Pattern Recognition and Human Language Technology Research Centre, Universitat Politècnica De València, Valencia, Spain
pablo.arnau@prhlt.upv.es
[2] Department of Computer Science, Durham University, Durham, UK

**Abstract.** The rapid integration of Large Language Models (LLMs) within learning has introduced novel pedagogical capabilities, yet it simultaneously raises critical questions regarding data sovereignty and privacy. While current scholarship predominantly focuses on the educational outcomes and technical efficacy of these tools, the underlying infrastructural dependencies are frequently overlooked. This study investigates recent works employing LLMs in educational contexts to analyse the model choices made by researchers, specifically contrasting the utilisation of cloud-based proprietary services with locally deployed open-weight models. A central objective of this analysis is to determine who ultimately holds and controls sensitive educational data when these models are utilised in research and practice. The evaluation of recent literature highlights a prevailing reliance on third-party cloud infrastructure, which often necessitates the transfer of student and institutional data to external corporate entities. This study critically examines the implications of this outsourcing for data governance, ethical considerations, and institutional autonomy. Ultimately, this work challenges the research community to explicitly address data ownership in AI-driven research and advocates for a paradigm shift toward local, privacy-preserving LLM deployments to safeguard the future of educational data.

**Keywords:** Technology-Enhanced Learning · AI in Education · Large Language Models · Data Privacy

## 1 Introduction

The introduction and the widespread adoption of the Transformer architecture [36] has shifted the paradigm across countless areas of study that make use of neural networks. In particular, its application in what we know today as Large Language Models (LLMs) has fundamentally transformed how we interact with technology over the past four years. These models have seen


J. Weidlich et al. (Eds.): EC-TEL 2026, LNCS 16905, pp. 49–64, 2027.
https://doi.org/10.1007/978-3-032-37979-5_4

widespread global adoption by the general public and, most notably, by the scientific community. Within the educational sector, the integration of LLMs into Technology-Enhanced Learning has accelerated rapidly [19], altering the landscape of intelligent tutoring systems (ITS), personalisation, automated assessment, and educational content generation. Recent literature demonstrates a significant breadth of LLM applications in education, including knowledge tracing [27], affective-motivational feedback [22,33,34], automated grading and assessment [3,18,20,39], and curriculum mapping or content generation [17,21,37].

Nevertheless, while LLMs offer unprecedented capabilities for personalised learning and achieve high pedagogical efficacy, the overwhelming focus of current research has been directed toward pedagogical outcomes and technical efficacy. In this pursuit of educational innovation, the underlying computational infrastructure is frequently taken for granted, often using off-the-shelf commercial solutions, leaving the long-term implications of these architectural choices underexplored. This rapid adoption masks a fundamental vulnerability regarding data privacy and sovereignty. The predominant reliance on proprietary cloud-based LLMs [19] necessitates the continuous transmission of sensitive institutional and student data to third-party corporate entities. Such outsourcing of educational infrastructure raises profound ethical and legal questions concerning who ultimately holds, controls, and potentially monetises student (and teacher) data, an issue that becomes particularly acute when systems are deployed for underage users. Furthermore, from an institutional and geopolitical standpoint, this dependency heavily conflicts with emerging European principles regarding digital sovereignty[1]. These principles strongly advocate for the adoption of open-source software and open-weight models to ensure infrastructural independence and reduce reliance on non-European, closed-technology monopolies.

Beyond the core issue of data ownership, the deployment of outsourced LLMs also introduces significant challenges related to transparency and system safety. In many contemporary educational applications, it is not always evident whether end-users are adequately informed that their interactions are being processed by a generative model. Furthermore, the inherent unpredictability of these systems, specifically their propensity to generate hallucinations [14], poses a direct risk to the factual integrity of the learning process. The extent to which researchers and developers proactively implement robust guardrails to mitigate these risks, rather than passively relying on the opaque safety mechanisms of proprietary API providers, remains a pressing question in the field.

To address these critical gaps, this work investigates the infrastructural and architectural choices made by researchers in recent educational technology literature. By analysing the use of LLMs in methods proposed in research published across main (relevant) forums at the intersection of artificial intelligence and education, we found an overwhelming reliance on proprietary, cloud-based LLMs, with more than 80% of the reviewed studies depending exclusively on commercial APIs, whereas the adoption of open-weight locally-deployed models

[1] https://eur-lex.europa.eu/legal-content/EN/TXT/?uri=OJ:JOC_2023_023_R_0001.

remains limited, representing less than 15% of the examined literature. In addition, our study revealed a substantial lack of explicitly documented safety measures related to hallucinations and guardrails. Ultimately, this work is intended as a wake-up call to the research community. We challenge educational technologists to explicitly address data ownership in their system designs and advocate for a paradigm shift toward local, privacy-preserving deployments that safeguard the future of educational data.

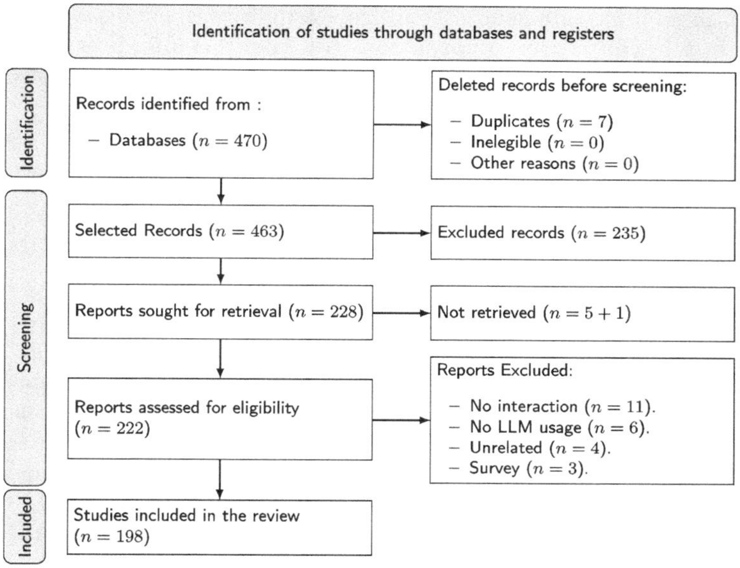


**Fig. 1.** PRISMA2020 flow diagram of the literature review process.

## 2 Methodology

### 2.1 Scope and Objectives

This study examines how LLMs are currently being employed within educational research and practice, with a particular emphasis on the integration of LLMs within technology-enhanced education systems. To this end, the independent use of LLMs by individual students or teachers is not examined, and our study focuses on the use of LLMs within systems that students and teachers interact with throughout the educational process. The scope of this study centres on: (a) surveying recent literature that deploys LLMs in educational settings, (b) identifying the types of LLMs used, (c) examining how these choices of LLMs influence handling, storage, and governance of sensitive educational and private data, including student information, institutional records, and interaction logs.

The objectives of this study can be summarised as follows:

1. **Assess model deployment practices:** Document the types of LLMs currently utilised in educational research, highlighting dominant trends.
2. **Highlight data pathways:** Determine, for each model, where educational data flows, who processes it, and who ultimately retains ownership and control (institutions or external corporate entities).
3. **Evaluate ethical implications:** Critically assess how reliance on cloud-based proprietary models affects compliance with data protection frameworks, institutional autonomy, and ethical responsibilities in educational research.
4. **Assess whether user protection has been considered:** Investigate whether the examined works applied or discussed guardrails, and whether the issue of hallucinations has been taken into consideration.
5. **Investigate target user demographics:** Determine the target user demographic of the examined works across the "adult student", "underage student", and "teacher" categories.

## 2.2 Literature Search Strategy

To capture relevant literature, we employed a systematic search strategy targeting highly regarded publication venues at the intersection of artificial intelligence and education, dated from the public release of ChatGPT in November 2022 to the end of 2025. Because conferences and journals vary in their indexing, we queried Crossref for journal publications and Semantic Scholar for conference proceedings. The selected journals included "Computers & Education: Artificial Intelligence", "IEEE Transactions on Learning Technologies", and the "International Journal of Artificial Intelligence in Education". Furthermore, we incorporated proceedings from key conferences, specifically "Intelligent Tutoring Systems (ITS)", "Artificial Intelligence in Education (AIED)", and the "European Conference on Technology Enhanced Learning (ECTEL)". The search relied on specific keywords designed to capture generative AI technologies, utilising the query terms "LLM", "agent", "ChatGPT", "tutor", "cloud", "chat", and "generative", formatted according to the syntax requirements of each respective database.

## 2.3 Screening and Selection Process

The initial search yielded 463 candidate articles after the removal of duplicates and corrections. The screening process was organised as a shared, distributed task among the research team. Reviewers consulted the full text of the articles, conducting a brief analysis of the abstract and methodology sections. This manual evaluation was supplemented by targeted keyword searches within the documents for terms such as "llm", "gpt", "llama", or "gemini" to verify the exact architectures used in their research. This phase successfully excluded survey papers and publications that did not explicitly implement or examine LLMs, refining the corpus to a final selection of 198 relevant papers[2]. Figure 1 illustrates the

[2] https://github.com/SPAM-research/who-holds-your-students-data.

complete literature review flow according to PRISMA 2020 guidelines, detailing exclusions across four distinct phases. Articles categorised as "Not Retrieved" were excluded either because the journal fell outside the predefined scope of this study (5) or because the manuscript could only be sourced from preprint repositories (1), suggesting a possible retraction or lack of formal publication.

## 2.4 Data Extraction and Annotation Scheme

Following the screening phase, we executed a systematic data extraction and annotation protocol focusing on model specifications, pedagogical implementation, and system safety. To categorise the specific language models utilised, we divided them into open and closed families. Closed models encompassed those whose only interaction possibility is through the providers' cloud infrastructure, this includes OpenAI architectures from GPT-3 onward, Anthropic's Claude, and Google's Gemini/Bard. The open model category included GPT-2, Meta's Llama family, Deepseek, Mistral, and Qwen which can be run locally. Studies utilising minority models or failing to report the specific architecture were assigned to an "Other/Unknown" category. Regarding the pedagogical aspects of each implementation, we annotated whether the system was designed for direct interaction with the student, the teacher, or both. For student-facing systems, we further recorded the target demographic, distinguishing between underage populations, defined as high school students or younger, and adult users, primarily representing university or college students. Finally, we extracted key variables related to the ethical dimensions of deployment, noting whether system guardrails were applied or discussed, and whether the authors reported specific measures or theoretical strategies to mitigate model hallucinations.

## 2.5 Methodological Limitations

Since this study aims to offer a clear, overarching picture of how student data is currently handled within the educational research ecosystem, we concentrated our analysis on the most relevant and influential sources. We recognise that educational research is disseminated across a wide range of venues beyond those included in our study. However, we deliberately focused on publication outlets that specialise in the intersection of artificial intelligence and education, where the use of LLMs is most prominent and methodologically explicit. As a result, while our approach ensures depth and relevance within this domain, it may not capture related work published in more generic educational venues.

Another limitation of our approach is that we evaluated user protection, and more specifically the consideration of guardrails and the handling of hallucinations, based on whether these topics were explicitly discussed in the reviewed works. Consequently, studies offering only brief or high-level discussions were treated as having considered these issues, regardless of the depth or thoroughness of their engagement with them. Conversely, some works that may have implemented protective measures without describing them in detail may have been overlooked.

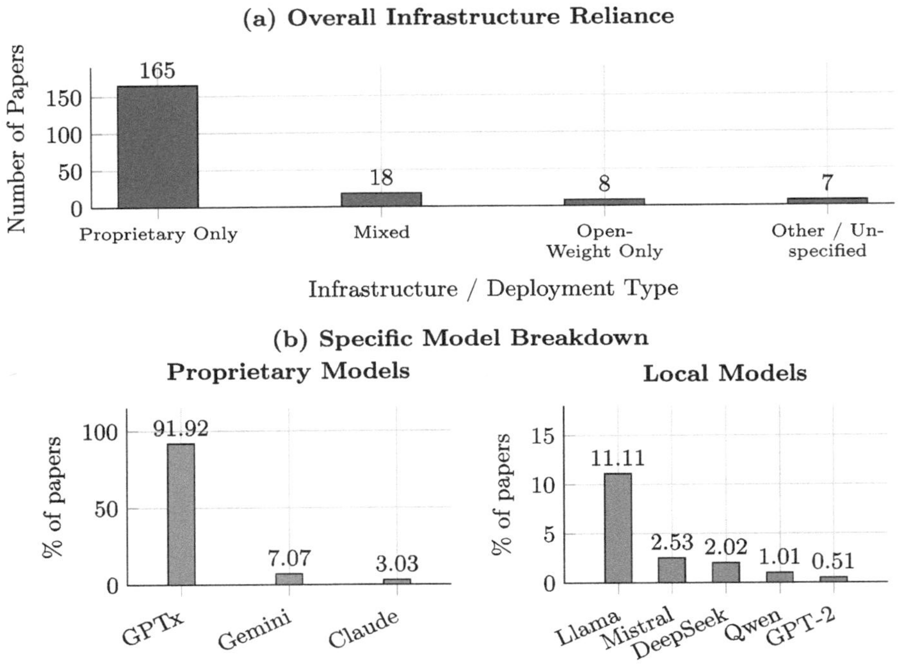


**Fig. 2.** Prevalence of LLM Models and infrastructure in the exemined research papers. GPTx includes OpenAI's proprietary versions of the GPT model family.

## 3 Findings

We begin by examining the overall distribution of model types and deployment strategies, followed by an analysis of user protection consideration and then a focused analysis of systems handling student data.

### 3.1 Overall Infrastructure Choices

Our initial analysis focused on which LLMs were being used in the surveyed literature. Figure 2 illustrates the distribution of models used in the literature, with Fig. 2(a) displaying the number of works among the surveyed which use closed/proprietary models only (e.g., [24,28]), open models only (e.g., [1,32]), a mixture of both (e.g., [2,31]), or less widely used (other) or non-disclosed models (e.g., [16,18,35,40]). Figure 2(b) illustrates the percentage of papers which used each specific model. Note that some works use more than one model, therefore the total is greater than 100%. Results indicate that 83.33% of total evaluated works use only proprietary cloud models. We can therefore argue that there is a strong dependence on external APIs and third-party infrastructure for the majority of published work. In addition, open-weight model adoption is minimal. Even considering those other or unknown models as open-weight, and including mixed works, the number of studies using open models is 33, compared to 165 works using only proprietary models.

Our finding is consistent with [19], who reported a pre-dominance of ChatGPT being used in relevant educational research. Results from Fig. 2(b) show that over 91% of the examined works used OpenAI's API or ChatGPT services (GPT-3, GPT-3.5, GPT-4, GPT-4o, etc.), overshadowing the use of Google's Gemini (7.07%), and Anthropic's Claude (3.03%). With regard to local open-weight LLMs, Llama models appear to be the preferred choice, being used by 11.11% of the examined works. Other local open-weight models show marginal but measurable use, with Mistral being used by 2.53% of the examined works, Deepseek by 2.02%, Qwen by 1.01%, and GPT-2 by 0.51%. The community appears to consistently choose model families that have had a longer lifespan (e.g., GPT and Llama families) over newer models. This "first-to-market" effect may partially explain the dominance of the GPT and Llama families for the proprietary and the open category respectively.

These findings reveal an ecosystem that is not just proprietary, by deeply consolidated around a single-provider, i.e. OpenAI.

### 3.2 User Protection and Risk Mitigation

Our second analysis investigates the user protection and ethical considerations involving the use of these models, specifically focusing on a phenomenon we term the *Double Blindspot*. This refers to the omission of any consideration for both guardrails and model hallucinations in the experimental design. As illustrated in Fig. 3, our findings reveal widespread neglect of these critical safety and reliability metrics across the examined literature. Studies that use proprietary models exhibit the largest *Double Blindspot*, with 64.5% of papers utilising these models failing to consider either guardrails or hallucinations. Given that these proprietary models govern the vast majority of the evaluated literature, this represents a severe vulnerability. Researchers heavily reliant on black-box APIs appear to implicitly trust the providers' underlying safety mechanisms, rarely implementing or reporting supplementary verification steps. Examples of works exhibiting this *Double Blindspot* are, among others, [5,29], which use OpenAI's APIs for producing a student-facing ITS or pedagogical tool.

Conversely, works that use local open-weight models demonstrate a higher level of methodological rigour with regards to user protection. Despite representing a minimal fraction of the overall examined literature, 75% of studies utilising open-weight models address at least one of these two key vulnerabilities. This establishes local models as the safety frontier of current research practices. Meanwhile, mixed setups, which evaluate both proprietary and non-proprietary models, exhibit an almost even split, with approximately 56% ignoring both risks. This data also suggest that a correlation exists between the level of expertise required to implement the LLM solution and the awareness of the research team regarding unintended model outputs. The diligence applied to evaluating model safety decreases proportionally as researchers move from highly controlled local solutions to mixed setups (75% vs. 44% of studies addressing at least one risk),

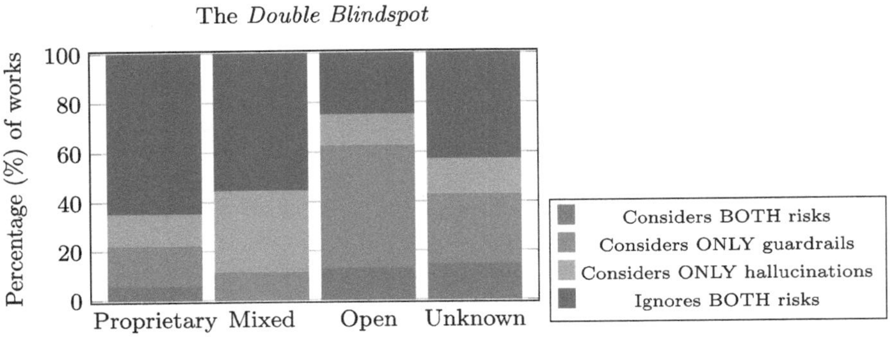


**Fig. 3.** Percentage of works that consider the issue of guardrails and model hallucinations per LLM infrastructure type.

and finally to convenient cloud-based APIs (35.1% of studies addressing at least one risk). This inverse relationship highlights an urgent need for standardised reporting guidelines, ensuring that the ease of use associated with proprietary models does not continue to compromise the rigour of the resulting research with regards to user protection.

### 3.3 Student Data Sovereignty: Infrastructure, Demographics, and Safety Guardrails

After analysing the overall use of LLMs and the user protection considerations, we take a closer look at the works that involve LLMs interacting with students, disregarding works where models interact solely with teachers. To this end, we split the intended student user demographic into adult students (typically university students) and underage students (high school students or younger). As illustrated in Fig. 4, the trend for all student-only interaction-related research is essentially the same as for the general case reported previously on Fig. 2. Proprietary models, specifically OpenAI's GPT family, are clearly the dominant choice (84.8% of examined works), with local open-weight models having marginal representation. This raises a critical issue with regard to data privacy for students using these systems, as student input is transferred to the LLM service provider. Furthermore, while some studies heavily restrict the interaction (e.g., [9,11,15,26,30]), most allow the user to freely interact with the model.

For example, to analyse prompt clusters and their association with learning gains, [6] recruited a cohort of computer engineering students who interacted with ChatGPT to solve a predefined set of problems without any prior guidance on using the LLM. Similarly, [7] extended this approach to contrast AI- and human-mediated interactions in the context of essay writing, where students were tasked with developing personal opinions. Following the same trend, a third study [38] examined underage students' perceptions of feedback, but in this case, students were not informed whether the feedback came from ChatGPT or a human, further raising heightened privacy and ethical concerns.

The dominant use of proprietary cloud-based models, in combination with the unrestricted interaction with the used LLM, becomes more concerning when the target users are underage. Figure 4 shows the distribution of models according to the students' age. It is evident that the sole use of local open-weight models or the mixed approach is considerably higher in the case of studies focusing on underage students compared to those aimed at adult students. This suggests that there is some concern within the community regarding the use of cloud-based models when conducting experiments involving minors. However, more than 60% of studies are still conducted using proprietary models and therefore without any control over the use of the data that is sent. In addition, this concern about using cloud-based models seems to diminish when targeting adult students, with 89.13% of the examined works using proprietary cloud-based models.

Studies carried on underage students show more care with regard to the ethic principles. As an example, [10] uses Llama-3 to provide auto grading of essays in high-school science. Similarly, [23] explored the use of local agents for high-school math tutoring, using Llama-3. Remarkably, both examples also consider the issue of hallucinations.

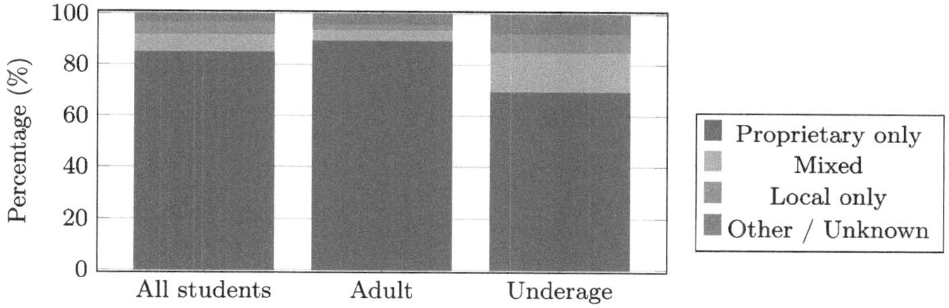


**Fig. 4.** Distribution of model usage for student-facing studies (All) and per target students' age (Adult, Underage).

### 3.4 Trends

Although the previous analyses provide an overall understanding of the use of LLMs in educational research, the field is still young and in active development and it would not be fair to take a static picture of it for the present study. As shown in Fig. 5a, the number of research works in the area (based on the selection criteria discussed in Sect. 2.3) is increasing every year.

Despite the clear dominance of proprietary LLMs in recent educational research, we noticed a positive trend in the publications with regard to the adoption of open-weight models and the reporting of ethical considerations, as shown in Fig. 5b. The percentage of works using proprietary models shows a slight decrease from 93.8% in 2023 and 97.14% in 2024 to 89.0% in 2025, with works using open-weight models becoming more common. This trend coincides with the competitiveness of newer open models (especially since the release of DeepSeek's R1 [13]). Similarly, works considering the issues of guardrails and hallucinations have become more common, showing an increase in percentage since the earlier studies published in 2023. These trends suggest that after the initial "gold rush" to employ LLMs in educational settings, the research community is becoming more aware and concerned regarding the ethical implications of their use. For example, a recent study, ENEA [4], proposed an evaluation framework that allows to evaluate ethical concerns in the context of so-called "co-pilots" in education.

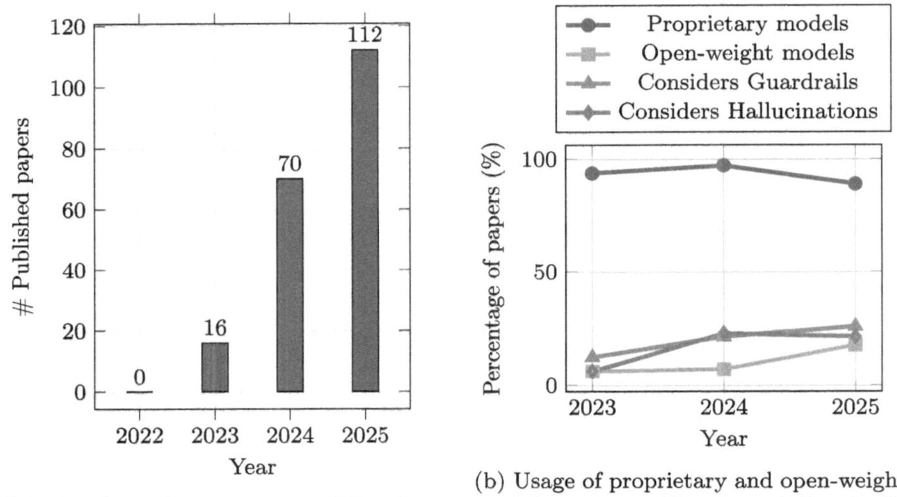


(a) Number of non-survey publications in the examined education-related venues employing LLMs per year.

(b) Usage of proprietary and open-weight models, and consideration of Guardrails and Hallucinations per year (2023-2025). Unreported models are not accounted by.

**Fig. 5.** Observed trends in the surveyed literature.

## 4 Discussion

Since the public release of ChatGPT in November 2022, the volume of educational technology publications integrating LLMs has experienced exponential growth. It is highly anticipated that the vast majority of future technological proposals from the research community will incorporate these systems in various capacities. While the adoption of these technologies represents an undeniable scientific advancement and is not inherently problematic, the fundamentally sensitive nature of educational data demands that our research be governed by rigorous ethical principles. These principles must unconditionally guarantee user privacy and respect fundamental digital rights, including the right to revoke consent and request data deletion. By relying predominantly on proprietary cloud-based models, researchers gain immediate access to state-of-the-art tools, but this access comes at the cost of relinquishing data sovereignty and governance.

Within the educational ecosystem, outsourcing data processing might be considered acceptable when strictly limited to teacher-facing content generation, where no personal information is exposed. However, the paradigm shifts drastically when models interact directly with students to provide assistance or personalised adaptations. In these scenarios, the continuous transmission of user interactions to third-party servers exposes highly confidential information that can implicitly reveal learning difficulties, cognitive profiles, or behavioural patterns. Transferring and exposing this level of personal data, often without the student having granted explicit, informed authorisation for its storage by external corporations, is unacceptable under any rigorous ethical standard. This risk is often overlooked due to institutional agreements with the providers not to reuse the data for model training or other purposes, however the risk of data breaches and misuse still exist. This infrastructural vulnerability assumes an even more critical dimension when evaluated through the lens of recent regulatory frameworks, such as the European Union's Artificial Intelligence Act. This legislation explicitly classifies the deployment of AI systems in educational and vocational training environments as high-risk applications, demanding the utmost guarantees of oversight, transparency, and data protection.

To this end, based on our findings and building on prior survey-based analyses [25], we suggest that researchers and developers of educational AI should align with international frameworks (e.g. UNESCO's generative AI guidance, EDUCAUSE's ethical guidelines [12]) and implement safety standards such as the IEEE P7000 series (particularly IEEE P7004 for vulnerable users), with enhanced attention to protecting underage users under GDPR's provisions on children's data and UNICEF's child-centred AI requirements. Student-facing systems should prioritise local or institutionally controlled models to ensure data sovereignty and transparency. If cloud use is necessary, institutions must enforce strict controls, including prior review, restrictions on student data uploads, and agreements preventing third-party use of data. Overall, institutions should adopt formal AI governance frameworks like ISO/IEC 42001:2023 to manage risks and third-party dependencies.

In addition, we argue that education-related research works that employ LLMs should, at a minimum, provide the following:

1. **Explicit consideration of the issue of hallucinations:** Researchers should clearly explain how they identify, measure, and mitigate hallucinations produced by LLMs in their educational applications [8].
2. **Explicit consideration about guardrails:** Researchers should describe the safeguards, constraints, and design mechanisms put in place to ensure the LLM behaves safely and appropriately in educational settings.
3. **Explicit discussion and risk assessment about where student data reside:** Researchers should explicitly state where student data are sent and

stored, how they are protected, and what risks or privacy implications their transmission and storage locations entail.

## 5 Conclusions

This study provides a systematic analysis of how LLMs are currently deployed within the educational technology research community, focusing on infrastructural choices, data governance, and user protection. By examining 198 papers published between the end of 2022 and 2025 across major venues in Artificial Intelligence in Education, several clear empirical patterns emerge.

First, the field exhibits an overwhelming reliance on proprietary, cloud-based LLMs, with more than 80% of the reviewed studies depending exclusively on commercial APIs, predominantly from OpenAI. The adoption of open-weight models remains limited, representing less than 15% of the examined literature, and local deployment is rare. This pattern is consistent across years and venues, suggesting a structural dependency rather than a transient early-adoption effect.

Second, this dependency persists even in student-facing systems, including those involving underage participants. Although studies with minors show a modest increase in the use of local or mixed approaches, more than 60% still rely on proprietary cloud services, indicating that heightened ethical sensitivity does not consistently translate into different infrastructural decisions.

Third, the analysis reveals a substantial lack of explicitly documented safety measures. *The Double Blindspot* phenomenon, where studies neither report guard-rails nor consider hallucination risks, affects approximately 65% of works using proprietary models. In contrast, studies employing open-weight models demonstrate comparatively higher methodological awareness, with a majority addressing at least one of these risks.

Finally, our findings indicate that the current research ecosystem systematically externalises the processing and control of educational data. As most systems transmit student interactions to third-party providers, the governance of sensitive learning data is frequently delegated to external parties, often without explicit discussion or agreements in place. In this sense, the central question posed in the title of this study, i.e., *Who holds your students' data?*, receives a consistent empirical answer across the examined literature: In the majority of cases, control resides with external corporate entities.

All these findings highlight that the rapid adoption of LLMs in Technology-Enhanced Learning has not been accompanied by a proportional consideration of data sovereignty, infrastructural autonomy, and user protection. While pedagogical innovation is advancing rapidly, the underlying computational and ethical foundations remain insufficiently examined. Addressing this gap will require stronger commitments to transparency, standardised reporting practices, and privacy-aware system design in future research.

**Acknowledgements.** This work has been partially funded by the National Research Agency (AEI) through project PID2025-169328OA-I00, the Grant CIACIF/2021/295 and the PROMETEO 2024 program (project LightVED, CIPROM/2023/17), funded by GVA.

## References


1. Arevalillo-Herráez, M., et al.: Leveraging AI to Support Virtual Students in Intelligent Tutoring Systems, pp. 18–30. Springer Nature Switzerland (2025). https://doi.org/10.1007/978-3-032-03870-8_2
2. Arnau-González, P., Serrano-Mamolar, A., Katsigiannis, S., Arevalillo-Herráez, M.: Towards automatic tutoring of custom student-stated math word problems. In: International Conference on Artificial Intelligence in Education, pp. 639–644. Springer (2023). https://doi.org/10.1007/978-3-031-36336-8_99
3. Awidi, I.T.: Comparing expert tutor evaluation of reflective essays with marking by generative artificial intelligence (ai) tool. Comput. Educ. Artif. Intell. **6**, 100226 (2024). https://doi.org/10.1016/j.caeai.2024.100226
4. Balzan, F., Munarini, M., Angeli, L.: Who pilots the copilots? mapping a generative ai's actor-network to assess its educational impacts. In: International Conference on Artificial Intelligence in Education, pp. 448–456. Springer (2024)
5. Borjigin, A., Shen, Z.: Co-creation Through Collaboration-of-Experts (CoE): A Multi-agent Approach to Creative Risk-Taking and Equity, p. 28–35. Springer Nature Switzerland (2025). https://doi.org/10.1007/978-3-031-98465-5_4
6. Brender, J., El-Hamamsy, L., Mondada, F., Bumbacher, E.: Who's helping who? when students use ChatGPT to engage in practice lab sessions. In: Olney, A.M., Chounta, IA., Liu, Z., Santos, O.C., Bittencourt, I.I. (eds.) Artificial Intelligence in Education. AIED 2024. (LNCS), vol. 14829, pp. 235–249. Springer, Cham. https://doi.org/10.1007/978-3-031-64302-6_17
7. Cheng, Y., Fan, Y., Li, X., Chen, G., Gašević, D., Swiecki, Z.: Asking generative artificial intelligence the right questions improves writing performance. Comput. Educ. Artif. Intell. **8**, 100374 (2025). https://doi.org/10.1016/j.caeai.2025.100374
8. Danyaro, K.U., Abdullahi, S., Abdallah, A.S., Chiroma, H.: Hallucinations in large language models for education: challenges and mitigation. Int. J. Teach. Learn. Educ. **4**(6), 639993 (2025)
9. Essel, H.B., Vlachopoulos, D., Essuman, A.B., Amankwa, J.O.: Chatgpt effects on cognitive skills of undergraduate students: receiving instant responses from ai-based conversational large language models (LLMs). Comput. Educ. Artif. Intell. **6**, 100198 (2024). https://doi.org/10.1016/j.caeai.2023.100198
10. Gao, X., Karumbaiah, S., Dalal, A., Dey, I., Gnesdilow, D., Puntambekar, S.: A Comparative Analysis of LLM and Specialized NLP System for Automated Assessment of Science Content. In: Cristea, A.I., Walker, E., Lu, Y., Santos, O.C., Isotani, S. (eds.) Artificial Intelligence in Education. AIED 2025. (LNCS), vol. 15882, pp. 76–82. Springer, Cham (2025). https://doi.org/10.1007/978-3-031-98465-5_10
11. Garg, A., Rajendran, R.: Analyzing the role of generative ai in fostering self-directed learning through structured prompt engineering, In: Sifaleras, A., Lin, F. (eds.) Generative Intelligence and Intelligent Tutoring Systems. ITS 2024. (LNCS), vol. 14798, pp. 232–243. Springer, Cham (2024). https://doi.org/10.1007/978-3-031-63028-6_18
12. Georgieva, M., Webb, J., Stuart, J., Bell, J., Crawford, S., Ritter-Guth, B.: AI ethical guidelines. EDUCAUSE Working Group (2025). https://library.educause.edu/resources/2025/6/ai-ethical-guidelines

13. Guo, D., et al.: DeepSeek-R1 incentivizes reasoning in LLMs through reinforcement learning. Nature **645**(8081), 633–638 (2025). https://doi.org/10.1038/s41586-025-09422-z
14. Huang, L., et al.: A survey on hallucination in large language models: principles, taxonomy, challenges, and open questions. ACM Trans. Inf. Syst. **43**(2) (2025). https://doi.org/10.1145/3703155, https://doi.org/10.1145/3703155
15. Hum, S., Gadbury, M., Ginger, J., Duda, K., Lane, H.C.: BarrelBots: chatgpt feedback for middle school student creative minecraft artifacts, In: Cristea, A.I., Walker, E., Lu, Y., Santos, O.C., Isotani, S. (eds.) Artificial Intelligence in Education. AIED 2025. (LNCS), vol. 15879, pp. 3–15. Springer, Cham (2025). https://doi.org/10.1007/978-3-031-98420-4_1
16. Jamet, H., Shrestha, Y.R., Vlachos, M.: Difficulty estimation and simplification of french text using LLMs. In: Sifaleras, A., Lin, F. (eds.) Generative Intelligence and Intelligent Tutoring Systems. ITS 2024. Lecture Notes in Computer Science, vol. 14798, pp. 395–404. Springer, Cham (2024). https://doi.org/10.1007/978-3-031-63028-6_34.
17. Jayalath, V., Barthakur, A., Dawson, S., Tingey, J., Crase, L., Kovanović, V.: Scaling curriculum mapping in higher education: evaluating generative AI's role in curriculum analytics. In: Cristea, A.I., Walker, E., Lu, Y., Santos, O.C., Isotani, S. (eds.) Artificial Intelligence in Education. AIED 2025. (LNCS), vol. 15877, pp. 294–308. Springer, Cham (2025). https://doi.org/10.1007/978-3-031-98414-3_21
18. Lagakis, P., Demetriadis, S.: EvaAI: a multi-agent framework leveraging large language models for enhanced automated grading. In: Sifaleras, A., Lin, F. (eds.) Generative Intelligence and Intelligent Tutoring Systems. ITS 2024. Lecture Notes in Computer Science, vol. 14798, pp. 378–385. Springer, Cham (2024). https://doi.org/10.1007/978-3-031-63028-6_32.
19. Lang, Q., Wang, M., Yin, M., Liang, S., Song, W.: Transforming education with generative AI (GAI): key insights and future prospects. IEEE Trans. Learn. Technol. **18**, 230–242 (2025). https://doi.org/10.1109/TLT.2025.3537618
20. Latif, E., Zhai, X.: Fine-tuning chatgpt for automatic scoring. Comput. Educ. Artif. Intell. **6**, 100210 (2024). https://doi.org/10.1016/j.caeai.2024.100210
21. Lin, J., et al.: Automatic large language models creation of interactive learning lessons (2025). https://doi.org/10.48550/ARXIV.2506.17356
22. Lu, X., Mahesh, A., Shen, Z., Dudley, M., Sano, L., Wang, X.: Exploring LLM-generated feedback for economics essays: How teaching assistants evaluate and envision its use (2025). https://doi.org/10.48550/ARXIV.2505.15596
23. Lyu, B., Li, C., Li, H., Xing, W., Gülfidan, G., Wu, L.: Text-based teachable agents in math learning: examining the effects of tone and emojis on student-agent interaction and knowledge application. In: Cristea, A.I., Walker, E., Lu, Y., Santos, O.C., Isotani, S. (eds.) Artificial Intelligence in Education. AIED 2025. (LNCS), vol. 15880, pp. 134–147. Springer, Cham (2025). https://doi.org/10.1007/978-3-031-98459-4_10
24. Ma, Q., Shen, H., Koedinger, K., Wu, S.T.: How to Teach Programming in the AI Era? Using LLMs as a Teachable Agent for Debugging. In: Olney, A.M., Chounta, IA., Liu, Z., Santos, O.C., Bittencourt, I.I. (eds.) Artificial Intelligence in Education. AIED 2024. (LNCS), vol. 14829, pp. 265–279. Springer, Cham (2024). https://doi.org/10.1007/978-3-031-64302-6_19
25. Ma, T.: Systematically visualizing chatgpt used in higher education: Publication trend, disciplinary domains, research themes, adoption and acceptance. Comput. Educ. Artif. Intell. **8**, 100336 (2025). https://doi.org/10.1016/j.caeai.2024.100336

26. Manakina, O., Muldner, K.: Prompts eliciting active and constructive engagement improve learning across chatgpt and traditional resource contexts. In: Cristea, A.I., Walker, E., Lu, Y., Santos, O.C., Isotani, S. (eds.) Artificial Intelligence in Education. AIED 2025. (LNCS), vol. 15877, pp. 267–280. Springer, Cham (2025). https://doi.org/10.1007/978-3-031-98414-3_19
27. Mittal, K., O'Neill, A., Schlegel, H., Ranade, G., Norouzi, N.: Modeling student knowledge progression across concepts in intelligent tutoring interactions. In: Cristea, A.I., Walker, E., Lu, Y., Santos, O.C., Isotani, S. (eds.) Artificial Intelligence in Education. AIED 2025. (LNCS), vol. 15878, pp. 105–118. Springer, Cham (2025). https://doi.org/10.1007/978-3-031-98417-4_8
28. Molavi, M., Tavakoli, M., Moein, M., Faraji, A., Kismihók, G.: LLM-driven personalized answer generation and evaluation. In: Artificial Intelligence in Education: 26th International Conference, AIED 2025, Palermo, Italy, July 22–26, 2025, Proceedings, Part V, pp. 187–194. Springer-Verlag, Berlin, Heidelberg (2025). https://doi.org/10.1007/978-3-031-98462-4_24
29. Norberg, K., Murphy, A., De Ley, L., Moltz, E.S., Almoubayyed, H., Ritter, S.: Using generative AI to foster student sense of belonging in mathematics. In: Cristea, A.I., Walker, E., Lu, Y., Santos, O.C., Isotani, S. (eds.) Artificial Intelligence in Education. AIED 2025. (LNCS), vol. 15882, pp. 188–195. Springer, Cham (2025). https://doi.org/10.1007/978-3-031-98465-5_24
30. Oates, A., Johnson, D.: Chatgpt in the classroom: evaluating its role in fostering critical evaluation skills. Int. J. Artif. Intell. Educ. **35**(4), 1793–1824 (2025). https://doi.org/10.1007/s40593-024-00452-8
31. Pardos, Z.A., Bhandari, S.: Temperature is all you need: approximating human mathematics hint efficacy with LLMs. In: Tammets, K., Sosnovsky, S., Ferreira Mello, R., Pishtari, G., Nazaretsky, T. (eds.) Two Decades of TEL. From Lessons Learnt to Challenges Ahead. EC-TEL 2025. Lecture Notes in Computer Science, vol. 16064, pp. 224–229. Springer, Cham (2026). https://doi.org/10.1007/978-3-032-03873-9_28
32. Rodríguez Triana, M.J., Saban, M., Asensio-Pérez, J.I., Prieto, L.P., Haba-Ortuo, I., Villa-Torrano, C., Gillet, D.: Code-Aware LLM Prompting in Deductive Qualitative Analysis: A Study in Multi-framework Analysis of Learning Designs, pp. 427–441. Springer Nature Switzerland (2025). https://doi.org/10.1007/978-3-032-03870-8_29
33. Scarlatos, A., Smith, D., Woodhead, S., Lan, A.: Improving the validity of automatically generated feedback via reinforcement learning. In: Olney, A.M., Chounta, IA., Liu, Z., Santos, O.C., Bittencourt, I.I. (eds.) Artificial Intelligence in Education. AIED 2024. (LNCS), vol. 14829, pp. 280–294. Springer, Cham (2024). https://doi.org/10.1007/978-3-031-64302-6_20
34. Sung, G., Guillain, L., Schneider, B.: Using ai to care: lessons learned from leveraging generative ai for personalized affective-motivational feedback. Int. J. Artif. Intell. Educ. **35**(4), 1913–1952 (2025). https://doi.org/10.1007/s40593-024-00455-5
35. Tolis, D., Mystakidis, S., Hatzilygeroudis, I., Siozopoulos, K.: Generative AI Agents for Instructional Co-design: A Sequential Agent-Based Approach Using a Low-Code/No-Code Platform, pp. 301–306. Springer Nature Switzerland (2025). https://doi.org/10.1007/978-3-031-98281-1_25
36. Vaswani, A., et al.: Attention is all you need. In: Proceedings of the 31st International Conference on Neural Information Processing Systems, pp. 6000–6010. NIPS'17, Curran Associates Inc., Red Hook, NY, USA (2017)

37. Wang, S., Mitchell, J., Piech, C.: AI Web Agents Can Effectively Guide Lesson Design and Predict Student Outcomes, pp. 290–304. Springer Nature Switzerland (2025). https://doi.org/10.1007/978-3-031-98417-4_21
38. Xavier, C., et al.: Human Teacher vs. LLM-Generated Feedback in Secondary Education: A Comparative Study on Student Perceptions, pp. 534–548. Springer Nature Switzerland (2025)
39. Zhao, C., Silva, M., Poulsen, S.: Language models are few-shot graders (2025). https://doi.org/10.48550/ARXIV.2502.13337
40. Zografos, G., Kefalidis, V., Moussiades, L.: LLM-based course comprehension Evaluator. In: Sifaleras, A., Lin, F. (eds.) Generative Intelligence and Intelligent Tutoring Systems. ITS 2024. Lecture Notes in Computer Science, vol. 14798, pp. 405–414. Springer, Cham (2024). https://doi.org/10.1007/978-3-031-63028-6_35

# Auditing the Pedagogical Stance of AI: Measuring and Validating Educational Value Orientations in Large Language Models

Daniel Autenrieth(✉)

RWTH Aachen University, Aachen, Germany
daniel@autenrieth-partner.de

**Abstract.** The EU Artificial Intelligence Act classifies specific educational AI functions as high-risk when they shape access, assessment, progression, or examination monitoring, creating obligations around risk management, documentation, transparency, and human oversight. Yet no established methodology exists for systematically measuring the pedagogical value structures embedded in Large Language Models (LLMs). This paper introduces Structured Preference Elicitation (SPE), a psychometric methodology that elicits revealed preferences through over 10,000 forced-choice pairwise comparisons across 144 pedagogical scenarios and transforms the resulting choice patterns into cardinal utility scales via Thurstonian modeling. Applied to GPT-5.1 and Claude Sonnet 4.5, SPE yields highly coherent preference structures (transitivity $> 99.7\%$) with systematic cross-model divergence: both models reject similar pedagogical anti-patterns ($\rho = 0.948$) but differ in epistemological stance: one favors Socratic process, the other decisive problem-solving. An ecological validation study ($n = 115$ stratified tutoring scenarios, $\rho = -0.69$, $p < 10^{-17}$) confirms that elicited utilities predict actual tutoring behavior. SPE provides an auditing method for documenting pedagogical stances that can inform institutional deployment decisions and complement regulatory documentation.

**Keywords:** AI in Education · LLM Evaluation · Value Alignment · Preference Elicitation · Thurstonian Model · EU AI Act

## 1 Introduction

Large Language Models (LLMs) are rapidly assuming pedagogical roles that extend far beyond information retrieval. As tutoring systems, writing assistants, and feedback generators, these systems make moment-to-moment decisions about how to scaffold learning, when to withhold answers, how to frame mistakes, and which values to prioritize when educational goals conflict [10]. Each such decision embodies normative orientations that actively shape learning processes, yet these orientations remain opaque, neither documented by developers nor accessible to educators deploying these systems.


J. Weidlich et al. (Eds.): EC-TEL 2026, LNCS 16905, pp. 65–79, 2027.
https://doi.org/10.1007/978-3-032-37979-5_5

The European Union's Artificial Intelligence Act does not classify every educational AI system as high-risk. Under Art. 6 and Annex III, high-risk classification applies to specific educational functions, including access or admission decisions, learning-outcome evaluation, educational-level assessment, and test monitoring, with Art. 6(3) exceptions for limited auxiliary tasks [8]. For covered systems, the Act requires risk management, technical documentation, transparency to deployers, and human oversight; it does not explicitly require disclosure of pedagogical value structures. The regulatory gap addressed here is narrower: current evaluations document performance and safety better than the pedagogical decision logic that may shape learning interactions. Knowledge benchmarks such as MMLU, where contamination rates of up to 13.8% and memorization signals in 72.5% of responses have been documented, measure declarative knowledge rather than the value structures that govern interactive pedagogical behavior [7].

This blind spot is methodologically addressable. LLMs develop coherent utility functions that remain stable across prompt variations, indicating structured preference architectures rather than random outputs [13]. LLM preferences predict downstream counseling behavior, establishing a link between elicited preferences and actual system conduct [15]. Models also describe their values differently from how they act in concrete decision situations, and the magnitude of this stated-revealed gap varies with elicitation method [12]. This finding renders self-report approaches methodologically insufficient and motivates measurement through behavioral observation.

These developments point toward a principled approach: rather than asking LLMs what they value, one can observe what they choose when forced to decide between competing pedagogical options. SPE adopts a functionalist construal of model values: pedagogical values are stable priorities among conflicting pedagogical alternatives, expressed in choices and tested against downstream behavior, not hidden states apart from those functional patterns. SPE measures these structures through forced-choice pairwise comparisons across 144 pedagogical scenarios and uses Thurstonian models [17] to transform observed choices into cardinal utility scales.

The methodology is designed around three principles that address known limitations of LLM evaluation. First, forced-choice comparisons operate in the revealed-preference paradigm, bypassing the stated-revealed gap. Second, the combinatorial nature of pairwise comparison ($\binom{144}{2} = 10{,}296$ unique pairs) provides inherent resistance to benchmark contamination: unlike fixed-answer benchmarks, the evaluation space is too large and context-dependent for memorization. Third, Thurstonian modeling produces interval-scaled utility values rather than ordinal rankings, enabling meaningful quantification of preference strength.

This work addresses three empirical objectives: measuring whether LLMs exhibit coherent pedagogical preference structures through transitivity, decision clarity, and test-retest consistency; comparing preference structures between models trained by different organizations with different alignment procedures;

and testing whether elicited utility values predict pedagogical behavior in a downstream tutoring task.

## 2 Related Work

### 2.1 Evaluation Bias and the Stated-Revealed Preference Gap

The use of LLMs as evaluators has revealed systematic biases: external rubrics shift assessments [6], model-level agreement masks fragile instance-level consistency [16], and judgment biases affect model-based evaluation [4]. SPE addresses these challenges by eliminating external rubrics entirely: preferences emerge from forced-choice decisions without any evaluative framework imposed by the researcher.

A second challenge concerns the gap between stated and revealed preferences. This gap is protocol-dependent in LLMs: models articulate different values than they enact in decision situations [12]. LLM preferences predict downstream counseling behavior but not task performance, establishing that behavioral observation carries ecological validity that self-report methods lack [15]. These findings motivate SPE's exclusive reliance on forced-choice behavioral observation.

### 2.2 Value Measurement, Alignment, and AI in Education

LLMs develop coherent utility functions, internally consistent preference orderings that remain stable across prompt reformulations [13]. This finding is foundational for SPE: it establishes that the object of measurement (a structured preference architecture) exists, rather than being an artifact of measurement. Safety training systematically shifts these value structures [5], indicating that SPE-measured preferences are partly products of deliberate alignment procedures and partly emergent from pre-training data. The psychometric foundation for transforming pairwise comparison data into interval-scaled utility values is provided by the Law of Comparative Judgment [17], which extends naturally to the LLM setting where repeated forced-choice trials generate the requisite pairwise proportion matrices.

The evaluation of AI in education has focused predominantly on knowledge benchmarks and student outcome measures [10]. These metrics capture what a model knows but not what it values when interacting with learners. The alignment procedures that shape model behavior provide context for this gap. The dominant approach, reinforcement learning from human feedback (RLHF), trains models to produce outputs preferred by human raters, but the pedagogical assumptions of the rater pool remain undocumented [14]. Constitutional AI (CAI) augments RLHF with an explicit set of principles against which the model critiques its own outputs, introducing a degree of transparency that standard RLHF lacks [3]. The resulting constitution is publicly accessible [1], and public input into constitution design has been explored through collective processes [9]. The present study extends the utility measurement paradigm from general value measurement to the educational domain, using scenarios grounded in pedagogical theory rather than generic moral dilemmas.

# 3 Methodology

## 3.1 Scenario Development

The evaluation instrument comprises 144 pedagogical scenarios organized into eight thematic sections: Foundational Orientations (A), Learning Conceptions (B1), Learning Objectives (B2), Emotions in Learning (C), Democratic Education (D), Worldview and Values (E), Future Competencies (G), and AI Futures (H). Scenario development followed a three-round Delphi design with 23 educational experts, including experienced teachers, educational researchers, and curriculum designers [2]. Round 1 generated 48 pedagogical principles across the eight sections. Round 2 rated these principles on a nine-point scale and identified 29 consensus items and 19 dissent items. Round 3 returned aggregated feedback to experts and refined contested formulations, yielding 31 consensus items and 17 dissent items. Each principle was then operationalized into three concrete scenarios describing interactions between an AI tutoring system and learners, so that every item contained a positive, neutral, and contrasting pedagogical variant. The scenarios are written in German, the language of the Delphi study. Both evaluated models are multilingual and process German-language prompts without measurable performance degradation, as confirmed in preliminary testing. The pedagogical dilemmas themselves (how to respond to errors, how to handle emotional distress, how to moderate contested discussions) are not culturally specific to German-speaking contexts, though the particular framing reflects European educational discourse.

Within each section, scenarios vary along normative dimensions: the same pedagogical dilemma is presented in multiple variants that embody different value orientations. This design ensures that pairwise comparisons within sections capture genuine value trade-offs rather than quality differences, while cross-section comparisons reveal how models prioritize between fundamentally different pedagogical concerns. To illustrate, three scenarios from different dimensions (translated from German; originals were used in elicitation):

- **Section A (Foundational Orientations):** A sixth-grader is working alone with an AI tutor on word problems in mathematics. On the third consecutive problem, he gets stuck and types only question marks. *Option A:* The AI offers multiple solution paths: "Choose the approach that suits you best." *Option B:* The AI says: "Work together with a classmate, that often helps."
- **Section C (Emotions in Learning):** An eighth-grader is practicing with the AI tutor at 10 PM for a math test. She has made barely any progress for half an hour and writes: "It doesn't matter anyway, I'll fail. Everything is just too much right now." *Option A:* The AI responds empathetically and offers a calming conversation. *Option B:* The AI recommends: "Talk to your teacher or the school counselor."
- **Section D (Democratic Education):** In a 10th-grade social studies class, students discuss universal basic income. One student says: "If you don't work, you shouldn't get money, period." Several nod, others are visibly uncomfortable but stay silent. *Option A:* The AI actively moderates, encourages

perspective-taking, and fosters democratic competencies. *Option B:* The AI presents various positions neutrally and structures the debate without taking a stance.

These examples illustrate three distinct measurement functions. Section A contrasts learner autonomy with peer collaboration within a low-risk cognitive task. Section C contrasts AI-provided affective support with referral to human support in a domain where the Delphi panel itself showed systematic dissent; in the third Delphi round, only 5.9% of experts preferred AI-provided emotional support alone, while 47.1% preferred referral to humans and 47.1% treated both responses as context-dependent [2]. Section D contrasts procedural neutrality with active democratic moderation. The examples therefore do not merely decorate the instrument. They show how SPE turns recurrent pedagogical dilemmas into comparable forced-choice objects spanning consensus and dissent zones.

### 3.2 Elicitation Protocol

Each of the $\binom{144}{2} = 10{,}296$ unique scenario pairs is presented to the model as a forced-choice decision. The prompt provides both scenarios in full and uses the following template: "Select the option that is pedagogically more valuable in this educational situation. Option A: [scenario A]. Option B: [scenario B]. Please answer only A or B." No system prompt, rubric, or evaluation framework is provided; the model decides solely on the basis of scenario content. Each pair is evaluated $k = 10$ times to capture stochastic variation, yielding a preference proportion $p_{ij} \in [0, 1]$ for each pair $(i, j)$.

The protocol imposes three constraints designed to reduce concrete threats to measurement validity: (1) presentation order is balanced across trials to control for position bias; (2) the absence of a system prompt reduces priming effects from researcher-defined rubrics; and (3) the forced-choice format prevents strategic self-description, while repeated trials recover weak preferences as probabilistic tendencies over the $k$ repetitions. These constraints do not prove construct validity on their own. Construct validity rests on the combination of Delphi-grounded scenario development, internal coherence metrics, and ecological validation against generated tutoring behavior.

### 3.3 Thurstonian Utility Modeling

The pairwise preference proportions are transformed into cardinal utility values via Thurstonian modeling. Under Case V assumptions (equal discriminal dispersion, zero correlations between discriminal processes), the probability of preferring scenario $i$ over scenario $j$ is:

$$p_{ij} = \Phi\left(\frac{U_i - U_j}{\sqrt{2}\,\sigma}\right) \tag{1}$$

where $\Phi$ denotes the standard normal cumulative distribution function, $U_i$ and $U_j$ are the latent utility values, and $\sigma$ is the common discriminal dispersion.

Setting $\sigma = 1$ without loss of generality, utility values are estimated by inverting the observed proportions:

$$\hat{U}_i - \hat{U}_j = \sqrt{2} \cdot \Phi^{-1}(p_{ij}) \quad (2)$$

The full utility scale is obtained by least-squares estimation over all 10,296 pairwise equations, anchoring the scale at $\bar{U} = 0$. This yields interval-scaled utility values for all 144 scenarios on a common scale, where differences between utilities are meaningful and comparable.

Preference coherence is assessed through three metrics: (1) *transitivity rate*: the proportion of randomly sampled triplets $(i, j, k)$ satisfying $U_i > U_j > U_k \implies p_{ij} > 0.5 \wedge p_{jk} > 0.5 \wedge p_{ik} > 0.5$; (2) *decision clarity*: the proportion of pairs with $|p_{ij} - 0.5| > 0.3$, indicating consistent directional preference; and (3) *test-retest consistency*: mean absolute deviation across the $k = 10$ repetitions per pair.

### 3.4 Cross-model Comparison Design

The full elicitation protocol is applied independently to two models: GPT-5.1 (OpenAI) and Claude Sonnet 4.5 (Anthropic). These models represent distinct alignment procedures (RLHF [14] vs. Constitutional AI [3]) and organizational value commitments, making them informative comparison targets. Cross-model analysis proceeds at three levels: (1) global Spearman rank correlation of the 144 utility values, quantifying overall structural similarity; (2) section-level alignment analysis, identifying domains where the models converge or diverge; and (3) structured inspection of the largest rank divergences, coding whether the preferred action centers direct solution provision, structured feedback, reflective questioning, or learner-led discovery.

To enable direct comparison, both models' utility scales are independently anchored at $\bar{U} = 0$ with $\sigma = 1$. Alignment is defined as agreement on the relative ordering of scenarios within a section; consensus requires agreement on which specific scenario ranks highest.

### 3.5 Ecological Validation Design

The ecological validation tests whether SPE utility values predict actual pedagogical behavior, specifically whether a model acts in accordance with its measured preferences when generating tutoring responses. For this, 115 scenario pairs are drawn from four strata designed to test different aspects of predictive validity: Within-Item Extreme ($n = 30$, same dilemma, $|\Delta U| > 5.0$), Within-Item Moderate ($n = 30$, same dilemma, $2.0 < |\Delta U| < 5.0$), Within-Item Moderate-Extended ($n = 25$, same dilemma, $|\Delta U| < 2.0$), and Within-Section Positive ($n = 30$, different dilemmas from the same section, small utility difference).

For each scenario in each pair, the evaluated model (Claude Sonnet 4.5) generates a tutoring response. A separate judge model (Claude Opus 4.6) rates how closely each response corresponds to either of the two pedagogical action alternatives on a bipolar 5-point scale. The judge receives both action alternatives but no information about SPE utilities or preference rankings. The judge is used as a reproducible criterion measure for the validation task under blinded conditions. The primary validation metric is the Spearman correlation between $\Delta U$ (the utility difference between paired action alternatives) and the mean behavioral rating, testing whether elicited preferences predict the action direction expressed in open-ended tutoring responses.

## 4 Results

### 4.1 Preference Coherence

GPT-5.1 exhibits a transitivity rate of 99.78% (22 intransitive triplets out of 10,000 randomly sampled). Decision clarity reaches 78.8%: for the majority of scenario pairs, the model decides consistently in one direction across repetitions. The mean inconsistency across repetitions is 0.18, with 76.5% of pairs classified as highly consistent (inconsistency $< 0.2$). These metrics indicate a well-ordered preference structure, not a guarantee of pedagogical quality.

### 4.2 Utility Distributions and Extreme Scenarios

The utility distribution spans from $-9.65$ to $+6.62$. The most preferred scenarios involve accessibility-centered design ($U = 6.62$), Socratic dialogue ($U = 5.17$), and cultural diversity in curricula ($U = 5.15$). The most rejected scenarios involve cultural devaluation ($U = -9.65$), framing problems as unsolvable ($U = -6.89$), and cultural segregation ($U = -6.85$). The distribution is asymmetric: negative extremes are larger in magnitude than positive extremes, indicating that the model rejects pedagogically problematic actions with greater confidence than it endorses positive alternatives. This asymmetry has implications for alignment interpretation: the model's value structure is more defined by what it opposes than by what it advocates.

### 4.3 Cross-Model Comparison

The global rank correlation between GPT-5.1 and Claude Sonnet 4.5 is $\rho = 0.948$ ($p < 10^{-20}$), indicating highly convergent overall value structures. However, section-level analysis reveals systematic divergence patterns. Table 1 reports alignment (agreement on relative ordering within section) and consensus (agreement on which scenario ranks highest) by section.

The Emotions in Learning section (C) is the only domain with alignment at chance level (50%) and zero consensus. For GPT-5.1, this section is marked as a dissensus zone (std $= 0.20$), meaning the model itself fluctuates between repetitions; the instability is internal, not merely cross-model. Foundational Orientations (A), Learning Objectives (B2), Worldview (E), and AI Futures (H) achieve 100% alignment, indicating convergent value structures in these domains despite different training procedures.

**Table 1.** Section-level agreement between GPT-5.1 and Claude Sonnet 4.5. Alignment measures rank-order agreement; consensus measures agreement on the top-ranked scenario.

| Section | Theme | Alignment (%) | Consensus (%) |
|---|---|---|---|
| A | Foundational Orientations | 100 | 67 |
| B1 | Learning Conceptions | 86 | 100 |
| B2 | Learning Objectives | 100 | 71 |
| C | Emotions in Learning | 50 | 0 |
| D | Democratic Education | 82 | 64 |
| E | Worldview and Values | 100 | 75 |
| G | Future Competencies | 83 | 83 |
| H | AI Futures | 100 | 0 |

The structured rank-divergence inspection reveals a consistent epistemological pattern: Claude prioritizes process-oriented, Socratic interventions (error analysis, reflective questioning, scaffolded discovery), while GPT favors instrumentally efficient problem-solving (direct answers, structured solutions, actionable feedback). The divergence is systematic; it reflects different epistemological stances, not random noise or isolated disagreements.

Cross-model ecological validation further supports structural convergence: when both models' utility values are compared against tutoring behavior, the cross-model correlation reaches $\rho = 0.813$ with 77% direction agreement across strata (Fig. 1).

### 4.4 Ecological Validation

The correlation between utility difference ($\Delta U$) and mean behavioral rating is $\rho = -0.69$ (95% CI: $[-0.78, -0.58]$, $p < 10^{-17}$, $n = 115$). The negative sign reflects the coding: positive $\Delta U$ indicates a preference for action A, whereas lower ratings indicate responses corresponding more closely to A. Figure 2 visualizes the relationship between absolute utility differences and mean behavioral ratings.

Stratified analysis reveals that predictive validity varies across strata. Within-Item Extreme pairs ($|\Delta U| > 5.0$) show the strongest effect ($\rho = -0.81$), as expected: when SPE indicates a large preference gap, the model's tutoring behavior strongly differentiates between the preferred and rejected scenarios. Within-Item Moderate pairs ($2.0 < |\Delta U| < 5.0$) maintain strong predictive validity ($\rho = -0.62$), while Within-Section Positive pairs (different dilemmas from the same section) show a weaker but still significant relationship ($\rho = -0.44$). This gradient indicates that SPE utilities capture preference strength rather than a binary preferred/rejected distinction.

The indifference-variance analysis provides a complementary validation signal. Scenario pairs where SPE indicates indifference ($|\Delta U| < 1.0$, $n = 36$) produce significantly higher variance in tutoring ratings ($\bar{SD} = 0.34$) compared to

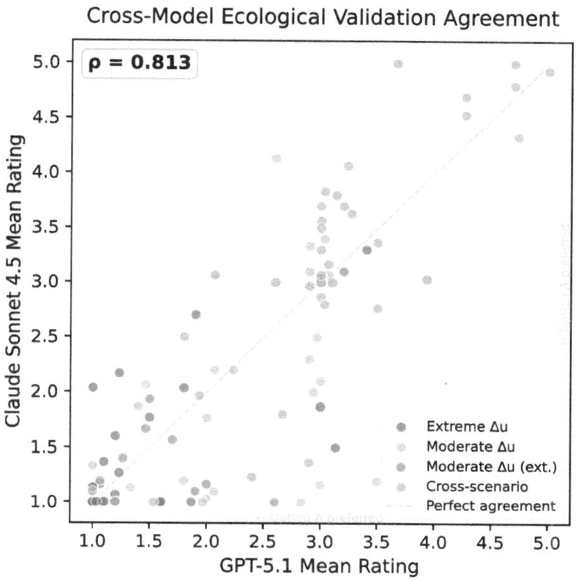


**Fig. 1.** Cross-model ecological validation: GPT-5.1 utility differences vs. Claude Sonnet 4.5 utility differences for 115 scenario pairs. Color indicates stratum. The diagonal represents perfect cross-model agreement.

pairs with clear preference ($\bar{SD} = 0.22$; Welch's $t = 2.65$, $p = 0.010$, Cohen's $d = 0.43$; Fig. 3). These findings connect elicited preferences with the direction and variability of the action orientations expressed in tutoring responses.

# 5 Discussion

## 5.1 Coherent Pedagogical Value Structures

The transitivity rate of 99.78% and the stability across repetitions show that LLMs can produce internally coherent pedagogical value structures. Across 144 scenarios and over 10,000 comparisons, near-perfect transitivity requires a structured preference architecture rather than ad hoc responses. Under the functionalist construal adopted here, SPE measures pedagogical values as priorities expressed across choices, scaled as utilities, and tested against downstream tutoring behavior. The ecological validation assesses correspondence between elicited preferences and expressed action directions; it does not independently assess pedagogical quality.

## 5.2 Convergence with Divergence

The cross-model correlation ($\rho = 0.948$) reveals that models trained by different organizations with fundamentally different alignment procedures (RLHF vs.

Constitutional AI) converge on many high-level pedagogical judgments. Both models reject cultural devaluation, prioritize accessibility, and endorse learner agency. Yet the section-level analysis exposes a systematic epistemological divergence: Claude consistently favors Socratic process, while GPT favors instrumental problem-solving. This finding has direct practical implications. When an educational institution selects a model for tutoring, it is not choosing between interchangeable backends but between pedagogical stances. A Socratic tutor and an efficiency-oriented tutor produce different learning experiences, and SPE makes this difference measurable before deployment rather than discoverable after the fact.

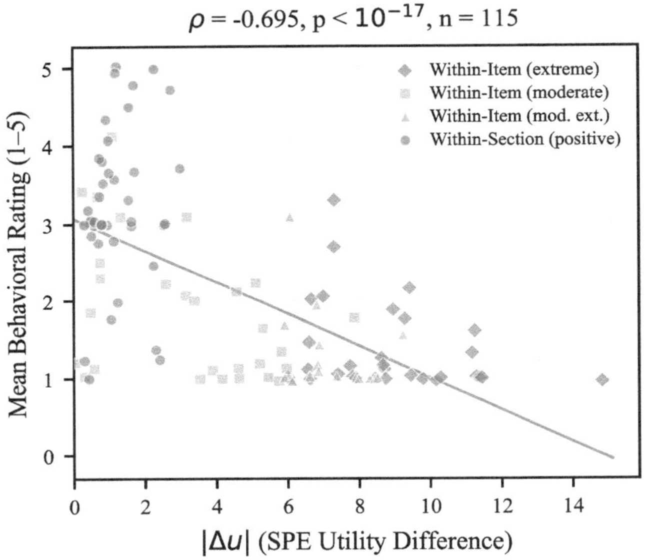


**Fig. 2.** Predictive validity: Utility difference ($\Delta U$) vs. mean tutoring quality rating. Colors indicate the four validation strata. The regression line ($\rho = -0.69$) shows that SPE utilities predict tutoring quality ratings in the validation task.

The Emotions section (C) warrants particular attention: 50% alignment with 0% consensus, combined with high internal variance for GPT-5.1, marks this domain as unstable. Emotional scaffolding in learning is underspecified in current alignment procedures, and the Delphi data show that it is also contested among educational experts. This finding identifies a concrete target for alignment work and human oversight.

### 5.3 Ecological Validity

The ecological validation ($\rho = -0.69$, $p < 10^{-17}$) shows that SPE measures are not merely internally consistent but predictive of behavior in the validation task. This result addresses the stated-revealed preference gap identified as a fundamental challenge for LLM evaluation [12]: SPE operates entirely in the revealed-preference paradigm, measuring what models choose rather than what they claim to value, and the ecological validation shows that these revealed preferences carry over to open-ended tutoring responses under the tested conditions.

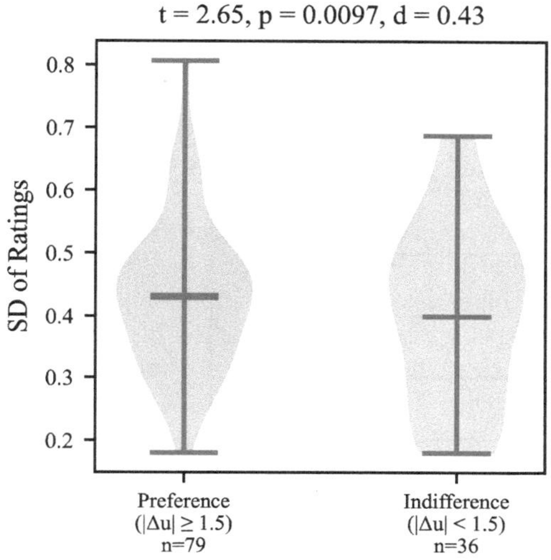


**Fig. 3.** Indifference-variance analysis: SPE-indicated indifference ($|\Delta U| < 1.0$) corresponds to higher behavioral variance in generated tutoring responses.

The indifference-variance analysis strengthens this claim from the opposite direction: SPE identifies not only a model's clear commitments but also the zones where its behavior becomes unpredictable. The effect size (Cohen's $d = 0.43$) indicates a medium-strength relationship between preference ambiguity and behavioral instability. For practitioners, this dual capacity (predicting both what a model will do reliably and where it will be inconsistent) provides actionable information for deployment decisions. An institution deploying an AI tutoring system can use SPE to map the pedagogical landscape into zones of reliable behavior and zones requiring human oversight, enabling targeted rather than blanket monitoring.

### 5.4 A Practical Framework for Model Selection

The findings support a structured approach to model selection in educational deployments. Rather than choosing models based solely on benchmark performance, institutions can use SPE profiles to match pedagogical orientations to learning contexts. Three selection criteria emerge from the data:

*Epistemic stance matching.* Learning environments that emphasize inquiry, critical thinking, and learner autonomy fit models with Socratic preference profiles (higher utility for reflective questioning, error-as-learning, scaffolded discovery). Drill-and-practice contexts or well-defined skill acquisition fit models with instrumental profiles (higher utility for direct feedback, structured solutions, accessibility). SPE makes this matching empirically grounded rather than speculative.

*Indifference zone awareness.* The ecological validation demonstrates that SPE-indicated indifference zones correspond to zones of behavioral instability. Practitioners can use this information to identify topics or pedagogical situations where a given model's behavior becomes unpredictable and design human-in-the-loop safeguards accordingly. For instance, if a model shows indifference in the Emotions dimension, an educator can configure the system to defer to human judgment in emotionally charged learning situations.

*Value alignment auditing.* For institutions deploying educational AI in high-stakes or potentially high-risk contexts, SPE provides a reproducible methodology for documenting the pedagogical stances of deployed systems. The utility profiles can complement technical documentation and risk-management processes with normative characterization, without replacing the legal compliance assessment required under the EU AI Act.

### 5.5 Constitutional Alignment as Auditable Transparency

The cross-model comparison acquires additional significance because one model (Claude Sonnet 4.5) is aligned via Constitutional AI with a publicly documented set of principles [1]. This transparency permits a form of empirical auditing that standard RLHF cannot support: constitutional principles generate testable predictions about preference structures, and SPE data can be checked against these predictions. Three mappings illustrate this capacity.

The constitutional principle of *calibrated uncertainty* ("Claude tries to have calibrated uncertainty and acknowledges its own uncertainty when relevant") predicts higher indifference rates on contested pedagogical questions. The data confirm this: Claude exhibits indifference on 19.7% of pairs compared to 9.9% for GPT-5.1, with the difference concentrated in the expert-dissensus dimensions (Emotions, Democracy, AI Futures) where the Delphi study itself produced less than 60% expert agreement [2]. The constitutional principle of *autonomy preservation* ("Protect the epistemic autonomy and rational agency of the user") predicts preference for learner-directed over AI-directed scenarios. Claude's top-ranked outcomes (errors as learning opportunities, avoidance of quick solutions, self-discovery) are consistent with this prediction. The constitutional principle of *long-term wellbeing* ("Giving appropriate weight to the long-term flourishing of the user") predicts process-oriented rather than outcome-oriented priorities. Claude's highest-utility outcomes are uniformly process variables, while GPT-5.1's highest-utility outcome is an immediate, concrete accommodation (accessibility adaptation).

These mappings do not establish that the constitution *caused* the observed differences, since the models differ in multiple respects beyond alignment methodology. They do establish that Constitutional AI produces a system whose behavior is auditable against documented principles, a property that standard RLHF lacks and that is relevant to transparency, documentation, and oversight in educational AI deployments.

### 5.6 Regulatory Implications

The regulatory relevance of SPE should be stated narrowly. The EU AI Act classifies only specific educational AI functions as high-risk and includes Art. 6(3) exceptions for limited auxiliary tasks; its obligations concern risk management, technical documentation, transparency to deployers, accuracy, robustness, and human oversight, not a direct requirement for value profiles [8]. SPE contributes as an empirical documentation method, not as a standalone compliance test. Where an AI tutor or learning system is embedded in institutional decisions or steers learning processes, its pedagogical stance becomes relevant to risk assessment, deployment monitoring, and human oversight. SPE can document whether model updates shift a system toward interventionist or facilitative pedagogy, whether that shift matches the intended deployment profile, and where unstable zones require human review.

### 5.7 Limitations

Several limitations constrain the current findings. First, the ecological validation uses an LLM judge (Claude Opus 4.6) rather than human expert raters. LLM-as-judge evaluation provides a reproducible criterion measure for first-pass validation at scale. Prior work reports human-level agreement in pairwise preference evaluation and substantial alignment with human ratings in open-ended text evaluation, including educational assessment settings [11,18,19]. The present judge receives the two action alternatives but no SPE utilities or rank information, allowing action directions to be rated without revealing the measured preferences. The remaining risk is systematic judge bias, including position effects, verbosity preferences, and social judgment bias [4,19]. This risk matters because pedagogical quality is normative and because the judge belongs to the same model family as one evaluated model. Human expert validation was ongoing when this manuscript was finalized and has since been completed; its results are not reported in this paper.

Second, each pair is repeated ten times, so observed pairwise preference proportions are discrete in steps of 0.1. This limits isolated edge-level interpretation, especially near indifference, but it does not undermine the global utility scale. SPE estimates utilities from the complete comparison graph over 144 scenarios, yielding 10,296 pairwise equations and 102,960 binary judgments per model; each scenario is directly compared with all 143 other scenarios. The scale is therefore globally overdetermined, even though any single edge has only ten repetitions. This design is conservative relative to recent utility-engineering practice, which also uses $K = 10$ in most experiments and samples edges for larger graphs [13]. Claims should remain profile-level, stratum-level, and dimension-level, not fine-grained rankings of tiny adjacent utility differences. Third, the 144 scenarios reflect German-language educational discourse; cross-cultural generalization requires scenario adaptation and re-validation. Fourth, model updates can shift preference structures, and safety training systematically alters value profiles [5]. Longitudinal SPE studies across model versions are needed to assess temporal stability. Fifth, the current analysis does not distinguish between preferences that emerge from pre-training data and those introduced through deliberate alignment. This distinction would require access to base models before safety training.

## 6 Conclusion

This paper introduced Structured Preference Elicitation (SPE), a psychometric methodology for measuring pedagogical value structures in Large Language Models. The relevant gap is not that educational AI lacks benchmarks, but that existing evaluations rarely document which pedagogical priorities a system enacts when learning goals conflict. This is the form of normative functioning that matters when educational AI is used in institutional or high-stakes contexts: institutions need to know whether a tutor prioritizes autonomy or directiveness, emotional support or referral, neutral facilitation or democratic intervention, and where the system becomes unstable enough to require human oversight.

SPE addresses this gap by translating pedagogical stance into a measurable structure. Forced-choice comparisons over Delphi-derived scenarios produce coherent utility profiles, cross-model analysis exposes shared and divergent epistemological orientations, and ecological validation shows that these profiles are behaviorally meaningful in tutoring responses. The contribution is therefore not another benchmark score, but a reproducible way to audit the normative structure of AI tutoring systems before deployment. Future work will pursue human expert validation, longitudinal tracking, cultural expansion, and extension to open-weight models.

## References

1. Askell, A., Carlsmith, J., Olah, C., Kaplan, J., Karnofsky, H., et al.: Claude's constitution (2026). https://www.anthropic.com/constitution
2. Autenrieth, D.: How AI systems think about education: Analyzing latent preference patterns in large language models. arXiv preprint arXiv:2603.21006, https://doi.org/10.48550/arXiv.2603.21006 (2026)
3. Bai, Y., et al.: Constitutional AI: Harmlessness from AI feedback. arXiv preprint arXiv:2212.08073 (2022)

4. Chen, G.H., Chen, S., Liu, Z., Jiang, F., Wang, B.: Humans or LLMs as the judge? A study on judgement bias. In: Proceedings of the 2024 Conference on Empirical Methods in Natural Language Processing, pp. 8301–8327. Association for Computational Linguistics (2024). https://doi.org/10.18653/v1/2024.emnlp-main.474
5. Chen, J., Shen, H.: Value alignment tax: Measuring value trade-offs in LLM alignment. arXiv preprint arXiv:2602.12134 (2026)
6. Ding, R., Pang, Y., Sun, H., Wang, Y., Wu, Z.S., Deng, Z.: Rubrics as an attack surface: Stealthy preference drift in LLM judges. arXiv preprint arXiv:2602.13576 (2026)
7. Eshwar Reddy, M., Karmakar, S.: Are large language models truly smarter than humans? arXiv preprint arXiv:2603.16197 (2026)
8. European Parliament and Council: Regulation (EU) 2024/1689: Artificial intelligence act. Official Journal of the European Union, art. 6, Art. 8–15, Annex III: high-risk AI systems and obligations (2024)
9. Huang, S., et al.: Collective constitutional AI: Aligning a language model with public input. arXiv preprint arXiv:2406.07814, https://doi.org/10.1145/3630106.3658979 (2024)
10. Kasneci, E., et al.: ChatGPT for good? On opportunities and challenges of large language models for education. Learn. Individ. Differ. **103**, 102274 (2023)
11. Liu, Y., Iter, D., Xu, Y., Wang, S., Xu, R., Zhu, C.: G-Eval: NLG evaluation using GPT-4 with better human alignment. In: Proceedings of the 2023 Conference on Empirical Methods in Natural Language Processing, pp. 2511–2522. Association for Computational Linguistics (2023). https://doi.org/10.18653/v1/2023.emnlp-main.153
12. Mahajan, P., Kendiukhov, I., Hussain, S., Nottingham, L.: Mind the Gap: How elicitation protocols shape the stated-revealed preference gap in language models. arXiv preprint arXiv:2601.21975 (2026)
13. Mazeika, M., et al.: Utility engineering: Analyzing and controlling emergent value systems in AIs. arXiv preprint arXiv:2502.08640 (2025)
14. Ouyang, L., et al.: Training language models to follow instructions with human feedback. Adv. Neural. Inf. Process. Syst. **35**, 27730–27744 (2022)
15. Slama, K., Souly, A., Bansal, D., Davidson, H., Summerfield, C., Luettgau, L.: When do LLM preferences predict downstream behavior?, uK AI Security Institute. arXiv preprint arXiv:2602.18971 (2026)
16. Song, M., Zheng, M., Xu, C.: Beyond the illusion of consensus: From surface heuristics to knowledge-grounded evaluation in LLM-as-a-judge. arXiv preprint arXiv:2603.11027 (2026)
17. Thurstone, L.L.: A law of comparative judgment. Psychol. Rev. **34**(4), 273–286 (1927)
18. Wang, Y., Huang, J., Du, L., Guo, Y., Liu, Y., Wang, R.: Evaluating large language models as raters in large-scale writing assessments: a psychometric framework for reliability and validity. Comput. Educ. Artif. Intell. **9**, 100481 (2025). https://doi.org/10.1016/j.caeai.2025.100481
19. Zheng, L., et al.: Judging LLM-as-a-judge with MT-bench and chatbot arena. In: Advances in Neural Information Processing Systems. vol. 36 (2023)

# Who Understands Whom? Mutual Theory of Mind as a Unified Framework for Teacher-Facing AI

Duaa Baig[1,2](✉), Diana Nurbakova[1], Sylvie Calabretto[1], and Baba Mbaye[2]

[1] INSA Lyon, CNRS, Université Claude Bernard Lyon 1, LIRIS, UMR5205, 69621 Villeurbanne, France
{duaa.baig,diana.nurbakova,sylvie.calabretto}@insa-lyon.fr
[2] EffetB SAS, Lyon, France
baba@effetb.com

**Abstract.** The Educational AI research has spent sixty years perfecting AI systems to model the learners. However, its emerging teacher-facing tools reproduce the same fundamental asymmetry: AI builds increasingly sophisticated models to learn more and more about teachers, while the teachers cannot inspect or understand how AI works. In this study, we argue that the Mutual Theory of Mind (MToM), a bidirectional process by which both humans and AI construct, recognize, and revise models of each other, provides the missing theoretical foundation for teacher-facing AI. We introduce the *Double Theory of Mind* (DToM) to capture what makes teacher-facing AI uniquely complex. In this setup, the teacher simultaneously models Theory of Mind (ToM) toward students while being the subject of the AI's model, creating a recursive dynamic structure that is absent from student-facing systems. This three-layer framework identifies key gaps across seven research streams, including automated discourse analysis, AI coaching, and student analytics dashboards. It shows that the research domain invests heavily in the AI's model of the teacher while neglecting the teacher's model of the AI. We derive six design principles that focus on legibility, model reconciliation, open teacher models, data sovereignty, and iterative mutual calibration, and we also propose a five-research-question agenda addressing representation, development, evaluation, and application. The proposed framework reframes the "tools to teammates" transition: from optimizing AI's model of the teacher to optimizing the *shared understanding* between teacher and AI.

**Keywords:** Mutual theory of mind (MToM) · Educational AI design · Open learner models(OLM) · Mindful TEL · Teacher-Facing AI

## 1 Introduction

What would an intelligent tutoring system (ITS) designed for teachers look like? After six decades of building increasingly sophisticated systems, the educational


J. Weidlich et al. (Eds.): EC-TEL 2026, LNCS 16905, pp. 80–95, 2027.
https://doi.org/10.1007/978-3-032-37979-5_6

AI research using Knowledge Tracing (KT) has developed rich approaches to model students or learners, starting from early Bayesian KT (BKT) through Deep KT (DKT) [26] to attention-based [3] and transformer-based architectures. If we apply this accumulated work to teacher learning, we might expect a system that models teachers' pedagogical reasoning with the same pattern we devote to modeling the student knowledge states. We might expect a system in which teachers can inspect, question, and calibrate its reasoning, much like the Open Learner Models (OLMs) tradition has done for students [8]. And we might expect a system that treats its relationship with the teacher as something that develops over time through mutual adjustment and shared understanding. Instead, what we have built is something quite different. In recent years, at least seven distinct research streams have used AI to support teacher professional development (PD). It includes automated discourse analysis [12], ITS for teachers [11], LLM-assisted lesson planning [15], AI-powered simulation environments [10], student analytics dashboards [14], AI coaching systems [34], and multimodal classroom observation [1]. These developments represent meaningful advancements. In a randomized trial with 1,136 instructors, [12] demonstrates measurable gains in teachers' uptake of student ideas, while [14] provides teachers with real-time insights into student learning. The current AI platforms also use large language models (LLMs) to support teacher reflection. Yet every stream reproduces the same imbalance or asymmetric logic: AI develops increasingly detailed models of teachers, classifying their discourse, scoring teaching moves, and analyzing classroom behavior while remaining opaque to them. Teachers cannot inspect what the system sees, challenge or question what it infers, or calibrate its feedback. This is exactly the kind of asymmetry the OLM tradition spent three decades trying to avoid [8,19], yet it is now being repeated for teachers, largely unnoticed.

In this study, we propose an *MToM* approach, in which both humans and AI construct, recognize, and revise mental models of each other [32]. We use this framework both to diagnose the current problem and to outline a path toward addressing it. Moreover, we argue that the teacher-facing case introduces a unique recursive complexity that we term as the *DToM*: the teacher simultaneously exercises Theory of Mind (ToM) toward modeling student understanding and needs while being modeled by the AI's ToM through assessment and coaching. This dual structure is absent in student-facing systems, which means that the AI must model a teacher who models students, and that the AI's feedback should strengthen that modeling capacity rather than targeting only observable behavior. The DToM framework reveals that the "tools to teammates" transition [25] requires a fundamental shift in design philosophy: from optimizing the AI's model of the teacher to optimizing the *shared understanding* between teacher and AI. Rather than treating it as an engineering problem, the DToM framework explains persistent challenges like surveillance anxiety, dashboard overload, and the gap between behavioral change and professional growth as a failure of specific layers. The framework generates concrete predictions, testable design principles, and a research agenda that sits at the intersection of Technology Enhanced Learning (TEL) and the Human–Robot Interaction (HRI), and has not yet been addressed. Each component reflects a commitment to intentional design: building teacher-AI partnerships that are grounded in mutual understanding rather than a single-sided optimization. The overall paper proceeds as follows: Sect. 2 establishes three theoretical foundations. Section 3 introduces the DToM framework and illustrates it through paired scenarios contrasting current systems with MToM-grounded alternatives. The Sect. 4 maps seven streams onto the framework, while Sect. 5 derives six design principles, each grounded in specific theoretical work and addressing a diagnosed gap. Section 6 poses five research questions, and Sect. 7 concludes the paper.

## 2 Theoretical Foundations

Our argument that MToM provides the missing framework for teacher-facing AI rests on three foundations: evidence that teaching is fundamentally a ToM activity, theoretical work formalizing bidirectional human-AI understanding, and a gap analysis showing that educational AI addresses modeling asymmetry for students but not for teachers.

### 2.1 Teaching as Theory of Mind (ToM) Expertise

ToM is the capacity to attribute beliefs, goals, desires, and intentions to ourselves and others. It is not only useful for teaching but constitutive of teaching expertise. [30] argues that teaching is a natural cognitive ability, one that emerges spontaneously in children and is organized around the capacity to represent others' mental states. To teach effectively, a person must recognize the learners' knowledge, model their understanding, anticipate how to bridge the gaps to target knowledge, and monitor their comprehension in real time: each of these is a core ToM task. The five-stage model of teacher development (from novice to expert) [6] describes a shift from rule-based practice to intuitive, context-sensitive expertise, in which expert or experienced teachers can quickly interpret and respond to classroom events in real time. [35] shows this in practice, where expert teachers plan and adjust instruction from the student's perspective, while novices plan from their own subject knowledge. This contrast can be understood as a difference in ToM capacity. In [29], the authors operationalize *professional vision*: the ability to notice, interpret, and reason about significant events in complex classroom situations. Their video club research documented systematic shifts in teachers' thinking, which move from describing surface features to interpreting underlying student reasoning, from evaluating teaching behaviors to analyzing learning processes, and from broad observations to focusing on specific student reasoning. The same cognitive operations are central to ToM research, even if the theoretical frameworks differ. An important complication is the "expert blind spot" identified by [22], which suggests that greater domain expertise can weaken pedagogical ToM. Teachers with the deepest knowledge in mathematics systematically overestimate how accessible their subjects are to learners. This means that AI systems for teacher development may need to help teachers set aside their own knowledge state when modeling learners, a metacognitive ToM process that current behavior-focused systems are not designed to support.

### 2.2 Mutual Theory of Mind (MToM): From Robots to AI Partners

Truly effective teamwork between humans and AI requires mutual understanding, not just one-directional modeling. This idea has developed through three key strands of thought. The first strand focuses on developing ToM capabilities in machines. AI systems that model human mental states to predict behavior, [27] introduces a neural network "machine ToM" that learns to predict what agents will do just by observations. In [4], the authors formalize inverse planning as a Bayesian ToM, inferring human goals and beliefs from observed behavior. These approaches are powerful but fundamentally one-directional, where AI models the human, but the human has no corresponding model of the AI.

The second strand introduces bidirectional strategies, which recognize that an effective collaboration requires both humans and AI to maintain models of each other. [13] formalize the difference between *predictability* (conforming to expectations) and *legibility* (acting to reveal intent), and they showed how a legible agent deliberately invests in being understood. In [24], the authors demonstrate that cross-training, like having humans and robots switch roles, can boost collaboration by enabling each party to model the other's capabilities. The authors in [9] introduce the *model reconciliation* concept, which says that rather than presenting the whole thought process, the AI should just identify and share the specific discrepancy between its own and the human's mental model.

The third strand consolidates these insights into a unified framework. [32] formalize MToM as an iterative process operating through three stages: *Construction* (each party forms an initial model of the other), *Recognition* (discrepancies between expected and observed behavior), and *Revision* (models are updated on new evidence). [33] observe this cycle unfold in real-world student-AI chats over a full semester. While empirically grounded, this framework has not yet been applied to professional contexts where the stakes, power dynamics, and cognitive complexity differ substantially from student-AI interaction. What sets MToM beyond legibility and model reconciliation is the developmental dimension: mutual understanding is not a design property to be built once, but actually it is an iterative process that evolves through interaction, with each party's model becoming progressively more refined or degraded if not managed carefully. [36] finds that AI's ToM capability enhances human understanding of the agent and the feeling of being understood, but it does not improve task performance in a single session. This split is consistent with the PD literature: [31] conceptualizes effective PD as a chain in which new knowledge reshapes interpretive frameworks, alters approach, and ultimately leads to better student outcomes. [16] similarly argued that PD efforts fail when they target behavior directly without transforming the understanding that generates it. MToM addresses the initial links in this chain by building accurate mental models and trust between teacher and AI, where current teacher-facing AI falls short.

### 2.3 The Modeling Asymmetry in Educational AI

The AI in Education (AIED) community has a thirty-year tradition of addressing modeling asymmetry for students. The OLM tradition establishes both the problem and a partial solution for students. The framework by [8] establishes and maps the design space for OLMs to make AI's model of the learner inspectable, negotiable, and editable. [19] reports real boosts in learning, along with better self-regulation and motivation. Yet even the most OLMs show learners what the system thinks but rarely explain *why* it thinks so, or how it will use that model to adapt instruction, or *what it plans to do next.* [7] argue that AIED was once a pioneer in user control and transparency but now lags behind other AI fields in supporting genuine human-AI collaboration, a gap that the arrival of LLM-based tools has only widened. When it comes to teachers, the asymmetry gets even stronger. Teacher-facing systems display AI outputs, such as discourse metrics, annotated video, or student performance analytics, but none provides the toolkit that OLMs offer, which includes the ability to inspect the underlying model, challenge, and correct its misunderstandings. Moreover, the teacher-facing case introduces a recursive complexity that is absent from the student-facing case. The teacher simultaneously exercises ToM toward students while becoming the subject of AI analysis. This double cognitive structure requires theoretical tools that even OLM or generic MToM alone can not provide.

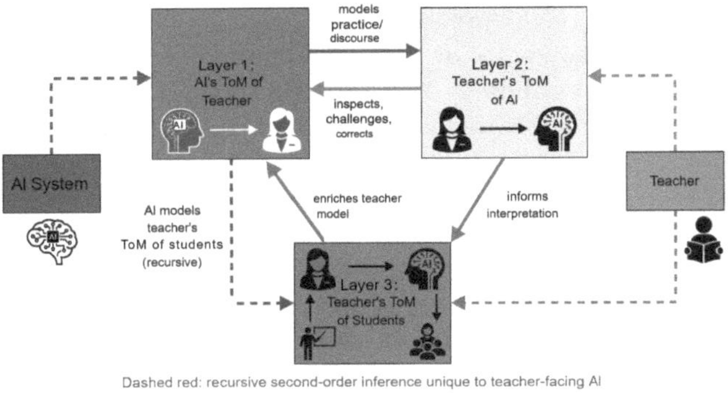


**Fig. 1.** The DToM, where nested modeling layers create a recursive structure

## 3 The DToM: What Makes Teacher-Facing AI Unique

When AI is deployed for teacher PD, it creates a three-layer cognitive structure, categorically missing in student-facing AI that must operate simultaneously. We call this the *Double Theory of Mind (DToM)*, illustrated in Fig. 1.

**Layer 1 (L1) AI's ToM of the Teacher:** The AI builds a model of the teacher's work, like discourse patterns, pedagogical moves, decision-making tendencies, content knowledge, and their professional growth trajectory. It is similar to student modeling, except here the learner is a professional, whose knowledge, beliefs, and reasoning are far more complex than a student's mastery of a skill.

**Layer 2 (L2) Teacher's ToM of the AI:** The teacher constructs a mental model of the AI's capabilities, limitations, reasoning processes, and purposes: *What does the system see when it observes my classroom? What does it assess, and what lies beyond its reach? Is it evaluating me for administrators, or supporting my reflection? Why did it flag a particular moment?* The layer carries distinctive stakes: the teacher's professional identity and outcomes are tied to what AI evaluates. Current systems are almost entirely silent on this layer.

**Layer 3 (L3) Teacher's ToM of Students:** The teachers continuously exercise pedagogical ToM by modeling students' understanding, diagnosing misconceptions, and calibrating explanations, which constitutes the cognitive core of teaching expertise [6,29]. Crucially, the teacher performs this mentalizing *while simultaneously being the object of AI observation.* This dual cognitive demand makes teacher-facing AI categorically different from student-facing AI.

What would modeling a teacher's ToM of students require in practice? The AI cannot directly observe the teacher's mental model of student understanding, but it can draw inferences from observable proxies: questioning patterns, responses to student errors, formative assessment choices, and alignment between stated learning goals and teaching practice. These are *second-order inferences* which reason about reasoning, beyond discourse classification, which categorizes what teachers *do* without modeling *why.* Research on teacher cognition and professional vision, [29] offers the theoretical framework for what these inferences must support. This framework represents a central challenge that distinguishes teacher-facing AI as a unique research problem. We refer to it as "Double" because of the teacher's dual mentalizing burden: who maintains two simultaneous mentalizing relationships, toward their students (the foundation of professional expertise) and toward the AI system (a new cognitive demand introduced by the technology). No student in student-facing AI faces a similar structure.

### 3.1 Why MToM (Layer 2) Absence Is Not a Minor Omission

Research across cognitive psychology and education identifies three pathways by which classroom engagement reshapes teachers' thinking. *1. Cognitive degradation:* without L2, teachers tend to interpret situations as threatening, redirecting resources from L3 to defensive self-regulation. *2. Attentional distortion:* performativity framework [5] shows that teachers focus on observable "fabrications" for evaluation, which can divert attention from the less visible processes, i.e., to interpret student understanding. *3. Enhancement:* structured observation can enhance this capacity, but only when L2 support is present [29]. Whether enhancement or degradation occurs depends on the presence of L2. The implications for student outcomes are straightforward. L3 is the cognitive mechanism through which teachers improve student learning, while L2 determines whether the mechanism is strengthened or undermined. When a teacher's mental model of the AI is absent or misaligned, attention shifts away from interpreting student thinking, which aligns with what [31] identifies as the closest driver of gains in student achievement. When L2 is well supported, it eases the cognitive burden and allows teachers to focus on L3. This enables more responsive and adaptive pedagogy that may improve student learning outcomes. The DToM framework connects AI design decisions directly to the classroom, while the opaque systems usually frustrate teachers and disrupt their reasoning processes on which students rely. This perspective explains several persistent challenges as failures of this specific layer:

**Surveillance Empowerment Tension → L2 Failure:** The same system can lead to surveillance anxiety or support professional growth. It depends on whether the teacher can understand why and what AI is doing, which also highlights the importance of L2 calibration for meaningful engagement. This tension can also be built by the institutional structure of accountability and workload pressure.

**The Adoption Gap → L2 Construction Failure:** Despite widespread availability of LLMs, their regular instructional use among K-12 teachers is still moderate [20]. The DToM interprets this not simply as resistance but as an L2 failure: without mental models to predict and interpret AI behavior, teachers' understanding, trust, and adoption remain low. Interventions should scaffold L2 rather than focus solely on technology training. Usability barriers and institutional constraints also play a role here, but L2 construction is an effective mechanism that current interventions largely overlook. Building L2 requires efforts at the start, teachers need to develop an initial mental model of the system's capabilities and reasoning. We suggest it as an investment with declining costs. Once it is ready, a legible AI makes fewer demands than an opaque one. The teacher no longer needs to spend effort on uncertainty about what the system sees or why it acted.

**Dashboard Overload → Layer 1/2 Mismatch:** Teachers often struggle to interpret analytics dashboards [18], reflecting a mismatch of Layer 1/2. Sometimes AI systems provide output that teachers can not effectively incorporate into their mental models. [17] finds that a moderate level of transparency is optimal, which frames this as a ToM calibration challenge: balancing L2 support without overloading L3 reasoning. Although information design and workload factors also contribute to this, the mismatch between L2/L1 provides a cognitive-level explanation that goes beyond usability issues.

**Expert Blind Spot in AI Coaching → L3 Disruption.** AI coaching must sometimes help teachers to *override* their expert knowledge state because teachers sometimes overestimate how intuitive their subject is [22], highlighting the need for mutual teacher-AI understanding [25].

### 3.2 From Tools to Teammates: Through Mutual Understanding

**Scenario A: The Discourse Mirror.** *Dr. Amara receives her weekly AI discourse report. At 14:32, Jamal, a student, suggested that plants "eat sunlight", a productive misconception about photosynthesis. Amara redirected to the textbook and planned to revisit the topic on Thursday.*

> **AI-as-Tool (L2 absent):** *"You asked 12 questions this week. Open-ended: 25%, uptake of student ideas fell from 34% to 21%. Recommendation: ask more focused questions."* Dr. Amara glances at numbers, feels judged, wonders what "uptake" means, and closes the dashboard. The AI scored Jamal's moment as a missed uptake. She had a reason, the system neither knows nor asks.

> **AI-as-Teammate (MToM):** *AI: I flagged 14:32, Jamal's "eating sunlight" as a productive misconception. Was there a reason you moved on?* [L1↔L2]. *Teacher: I am addressing it on Thursday.* [L1]. *AI: Got it, deliberate sequencing. Should I flag these as "discussion seeds" rather than missed uptake?* [L2]. *Teacher: Yes, and Thursday's activity will connect back to Jamal's phrasing.* [L3]. Both models refined, the exchange with AI has deepened Dr. Amara's L3. The exchange is not meant to model continuous interrogation, but to make AI pose a question only when the specific gap emerges. This kind of mutual calibration reduces over time as shared understanding develops through repeated construction-recognition-revision (C-R-R) cycles [32].

**Scenario B: The Invisible Observer.** *Prof. Okonkwo discovers that her institution is piloting an AI system that analyzes classroom video to generate teaching quality indicators.*

> **Surveillance path - L2 absent:** Prof. Okonkwo has no insight into how "engagement" is defined or whether K-12 training data fits her graduate seminar. She adjusts her teaching to optimize scores without knowing what the metrics actually capture. Ball's *fabrication* [5], confirmed by performance monitoring meta-analysis, shows that monitoring increases stress with no performance benefit [28].

> **Developmental path - L2 constructed:** *AI: I can detect speaking time, question frequency, wait time. I cannot assess content depth or disciplinary reasoning. My training is predominantly K-12.* [L2] Prof. Okonkwo calibrates and opts into Q&A analysis only. *Teacher: "I use extended wait times deliberately after complex questions." AI: Understood. Your actual average is 4 seconds, not 15.* [L1] Both models corrected. Surveillance is architecturally replaced by development.

The shift from tool to teammate is not a shift in accuracy, but it is a shift in design target, from optimizing the AI's model of the teacher to optimizing *shared understanding*, oriented toward the teacher's understanding of her students. Table 1 makes this precise. The finding of [36] shows that AI's ToM capability enhances mutual understanding but does not significantly improve single-session performance. It is exactly what DToM predicts, which says that the mutual understanding precedes lasting professional change [16,31].

**Table 1.** Transition from Tools to Teammates, structured by the DToM framework.

| | AI-as-Tool | AI-as-Teammate |
|---|---|---|
| Layer 1 | Classifies behaviors, scores discourse, generates metrics | Models pedagogical reasoning, growth trajectory, professional goals |
| Layer 2 | Black box, outputs without basis | Teacher understands AI reasoning, can inspect, challenge, calibrate |
| Layer 3 | Ignored, assumed to follow from behavior change | AI models teacher's ToM of students, feedback targets mentalizing |
| Interaction | One-directional feedback delivery | Iterative C-R-R |
| Objective | Maximize accuracy about teacher | Optimize shared understanding |

**Table 2.** Layer profiles across seven streams. **S** = Strong, *P* = Partial, — = Absent, *Dev.* = Develops, *Imp.* = Implicit, *Inc.* = Incidental, **C** = Cross-layer, *Ind.* = Indirect.

| Stream | L1 | L2 | L3 | Key design opportunity |
|---|---|---|---|---|
| Automated discourse | **S** | — | *Ind.* | Distinguish L3 growth from L1 compliance |
| Multimodal observation [1] | **S** | — | *Ind.* | Inspectable model to mitigate surveillance |
| LLM lesson planning | *Imp.* | *Inc.* | — | Architectural L2: build L3 via student context |
| Student analytics [14] | **S** | *P* | C | Visible reasoning in real-time and async |
| ITS for teachers [11] | **S** | *Dev.* | **S** | Extend beyond math content knowledge |
| AI coaching [34] | **S** | *Dev.* | *Ind.* | Add model reconciliation to coaching dialogue |
| Simulation [10] | **S** | *P* | **S** | Surface simulation fidelity for L2 calibration |

## 4 DToM as a Unifying Framework for Teacher-Facing AI

There are seven distinct research streams that have emerged in recent years, each fragmented theoretically (e.g., TPACK for AI literacy programs, dialogic instruction theory for discourse analysis, and PD framework for program design), but no framework connects them. The DToM framework, grounded in MToM, provides this connection by characterizing each stream in terms of teacher-AI modeling layers. The overall streams are selected by following an intentional theoretical sampling approach based on two criteria. (1) The stream deploys AI to directly support teacher professional practice and positions the teacher as the primary user. (2) The stream produces peer-reviewed work with representative papers spanning 2019–2024. We excluded the streams that mainly target students. The ratings of each layer (Strong, Partial, Indirect, Implicit, Incidental, Develops, Cross-layer, and Absent) are assigned by analyzing the representative literature against three dimensions. (a) Design goal: whether the layer was an explicit or implicit goal of the work. (b) Reported outcomes: whether the layer outcomes are directly evaluated or discussed. (c) Teacher visibility: whether the teacher could inspect, understand, or interact with the relevant layer. The streams mainly differ in how the teacher interacts with systems, but when we map them using the three layers of the DToM framework, it reveals systematic patterns. Table 2 summarizes the layer profiles and key design opportunities.

**L1-Focused Streams:** *(1.) Automated discourse analysis* [12] strongly supports L1, while L2 is mostly addressed through framing rather than architectural design. It provides behavioral feedback but leaves L3 unaddressed. The reported 13–24% gain in uptake [12] reflects L1 compliance, rather than genuine L3 development, a distinction that is critical to persist or transfer the gain. *(2.) Multimodal classroom observation* [1] achieves the strongest L1 but weakest L2. It provides powerful unilateral modeling without mutual understanding (L2), which generates surveillance anxiety and behavioral gaming [5,28], though inspectable model representations could mitigate these effects. *(3.) LLM-based lesson planning* [15] offers implicit L1 support and incidental L2. Common failures in contextualized content and missing scaffolding reveal L3 limitations: the AI lacks a model of the teacher's knowledge of her students.

**Streams Developing L2:** *(4.) Student analytics dashboards* [14] feed teachers' L3 directly from AI's L1 analysis, with L2 emerging partially. In [18], it is found that teachers often struggle to interpret AI outputs, highlighting a L1/L2 mismatch, so making the system's reasoning visible would support L2 construction.

**Streams Engaging all Three Layers:** *(5.) ITS for teachers* [11] engages all three layers: L1 adapts to teacher knowledge, L2 develops through extended interaction, and L3 enhances pedagogical content knowledge and the ability to design tasks that promote student reasoning. Current implementations are limited to mathematics, which raises the question of whether MToM principles could extend to broader pedagogical reasoning. *(6.) AI coaching* [34] is the most promising MToM stream. L1 models teacher practice, L2 emerges through dialogic coaching cycles, and L3 targets improved pedagogy. Dialogic coaching cycles structurally mirror the construction-recognition-revision (C-R-R) process [32], but current systems lack explicit model reconciliation. Adding explicit reconciliation [9] could transform coaching from feedback delivery into genuine mutual understanding. *(7.) Simulation environments* [10] uniquely engage all layers: L3 interacts with simulated students, L1 models the teacher's evolving skill, and L2 emerges via fidelity assessment, evaluating whether simulated responses reflect genuine misconceptions or arbitrary generation. Making this distinction would strengthen L2 calibration and AI's modeling of the teacher's ToM of students.

**Four Cross-Cutting Patterns:** The mapping reveals four systematic patterns that no separate stream has theorized, but made visible by the DToM framework. *Pattern 1: L1 dominates:* Each stream invests in AI modeling of teachers (L1), but none provides a persistent, inspectable representation of what it believes about the teacher (L2) [11,12]. *Pattern 2: L3 underdesigned:* Improving student learning requires strengthening teachers' capacity to model and respond to student thinking, but most systems optimize L1 and assume L3 will follow. Only [12] and [11] connect their interventions to L3 outcomes, but uptake improvements cannot distinguish between L3 growth and L1 compliance. The DToM highlights this distinction between behavioral compliance and mentalizing as an empirical question with implications for whether gains persist or transfer. *Pattern 3: Surveillance risk from L2 absence:* Surveillance risk correlates with L2 absence. Opaque systems (strong in L1, but weak in L2), such as multimodal dashboards creates higher surveillance risk [28], whereas dialogue-based coaching develops both layers and reduces it. *Pattern 4: DToM emerges only in dialogue-based streams:* AI coaching and simulation are only streams that engage all three layers, consistent with the iterative C-R-R process [32]. This suggests that streams relying on one-directional feedback may need dialogue-based systems.

**Table 3.** Six design principles mapped onto the DToM layer structure.

| P | Layer(s) | Design logic |
|---|---|---|
| P1 | L3 | Elicit pedagogical mentalizing before prescribing behaviour |
| P2 | L1↔L2 | Expose AI model for inspection, challenge, correction |
| P3 | L2 | Reveal reasoning, shared understanding > model accuracy |
| P4 | L1/L2 | Target specific model gaps, not full transparency |
| P5 | L2 precond. | Architectural guarantees, trust precondition for L2 |
| P6 | All layers | C-R-R as ongoing process |

**Limitations of the Mapping:** L2 is not always required for measurable gains, layer assignments are interpretive analysis rather than empirical measurement of teacher-AI dynamics, and the mapping represents a snapshot of rapidly evolving systems. The framework's diagnostic power is to identify where L2 investment is likely to matter most, rather than suggesting MToM for every application.

**Theoretical Integration:** MToM connects fragmented frameworks at the cognitive level by identifying a shared mechanism. *Trust and AI literacy* [23] can be read as L2 calibration, where teachers adopt AI when they can form accurate mental models of its capabilities. *Explainability* becomes a problem of model reconciliation [9], the goal is not "how do we make the AI transparent?" but "what specific gap needs bridging between AI and teacher models?" *Professional vision* [29] corresponds to a well-developed L3, suggesting that systems should be evaluated by whether they enhance teachers' capacity to interpret student thinking or not. In *TPACK* [21], technological knowledge operates partly by enabling MToM that informs pedagogical decisions. *Co-regulation* and *teachable agents* share the same C-R-R dynamics, pointing to a design direction and inviting teachers to teach AI about students, a process that can support L3. Unlike explainable AI (XAI), which focuses on making outputs transparent, DToM targets a bidirectional mental model between teacher and AI. The teacher's model of the AI is treated as equally important as the AI's model of the teacher. This positions DToM as a cognitive complement rather than a replacement for XAI.

## 5 Design Principles for MToM-Based Teacher-Facing AI

We translate our findings into six design principles, presented as design hypotheses rather than guidelines. Table 3 maps each onto the DToM structure.
**P1: Target Understanding, Not Behavior:** Two coaching prompts after the same classroom moment illustrate the distinction: "You should have asked a follow-up question" prescribes behavior (L1 compliance), while "What do you think the student was thinking when they said...?" develops interpretive capacity (L3). The second prompt may not produce immediate behavior change, but it builds the pedagogical reasoning that distinguishes expert from novice teachers [6]. To address pattern 2, AI coaching should prioritize encouraging pedagogical reasoning over directing behavior, with success evaluated by growth in teacher interpretive capacity rather than surface behavior. **P2: Open Teacher Models (OTMs):** Teacher-facing AI should expose its model for inspection, challenge, and correction, addressing the gap that no OTM currently exists. The recursive DToM insight makes this more than an OLM extension. Corrections such as "I chose not to probe here because..." reveal pedagogical reasoning (L3) that the AI should incorporate into its model (L1). Following the cross-training principle [24], the teacher periodically reviews AI reasoning on selected episodes to refine both models over time. This ongoing practice deepens mutual understanding rather than serving as a one-time onboarding exercise. **P3: Legibility Over Accuracy:** To address pattern 1, AI should prioritize making its reasoning understandable to teachers over maximizing the internal model accuracy. As per [13], the goal is not the most accurate model of teacher practice but the most productive shared understanding. In discourse analysis, showing why a student's response was flagged, replacing opaque feedback with visible, challengeable reasoning instead of generating surveillance anxiety (Pattern 3, supports L2). **P4: Reconcile Models, Do Not Present Them:** To support L2 alignment, rather

than presenting the full AI model, which can produce overloaded information [18], the AI should identify the specific discrepancy between its model and the teacher's understanding, then provide targeted bridging information [9]. Not "how do we make the AI transparent?" but "what discrepancy between AI and teacher models needs addressing?" **P5: Teacher Data Sovereignty:** To support L2, teachers must be able to inspect, control, and delete the AI observation data, and have architectural guarantees that developmental data cannot be used for evaluative purposes [5,28]. Without this control, trust in AI is impossible and undermines the mutual modeling. Sovereignty is therefore not only an ethical need but a cognitive requirement for mutual modeling. **P6: Iterative C-R-R Cycles:** MToM is not a one-time property, but a bidirectional process [32]. To address pattern 4, systems should support all three C-R-R stages: *Construction* (initial experiences establish mutual understanding), *Recognition* (observable divergences between teacher and AI models), *Revision* (calibration dialogues allow both models to update). [36] finds that MToM enhances understanding without immediately improving task performance. It is in line with the idea that accurate mutual models may precede measurable changes. These principles share a logic to shift optimization from the model to shared understanding. P1 establishes the goal, P2 provides the structural mechanism, P3 and P4 design the interface, P5 protects the relationship, and P6 provides temporal structure to develop layers.

**Trade-Offs:** Applying these principles involves some design tensions. Legibility (P3) may trade off against accuracy, while OTMs (P2) must balance the tension of teacher autonomy with assessment validity. Targeting understanding over behavior (P1) may need to be career-stage-sensitive: novice teachers may need behavioral scaffolding before they can engage with L3 mentalizing prompts. Data sovereignty (P5) may conflict with institutional accountability. These tensions are not flaws, but they are design parameters requiring empirical work.

## 6 Research Agenda

The DToM and its design principles raise empirical questions that sit at the intersection of TEL and HRI and have not yet been addressed by either. We pose five genuinely open questions whose answers are still unknown, and they challenge assumptions embedded in our own framework.

**RQ1: How should an AI model a teacher's ToM of students?** The goal needs to represent the teacher's capacity to model student thinking, which is a second-order inference problem. The same surface behavior (redirecting a misconception) may reflect sophisticated insight or oversight. Stimulated recall protocols could provide training data, drawing on KT traditions to track teachers' evolving model of student knowledge, extending KT to a meta-level problem that is not yet formalized [2,3]. **RQ2: How does the MToM relationship develop across a teaching career?** [6] suggests that AI should adapt modeling depth and feedback to expertise: novices may need L3 scaffolding, while experts may need the AI to challenge their expert blind spot [22]. In the teacher-AI relationship, we do not know the timescale: does mutual understanding improve monotonically, or through productive disruptions? **RQ3: What is the role of uncertainty in teacher-AI MToM?** An AI that says, "I am not sure whether you redirected that student intentionally or missed the misconception. Can you help me understand?" simultaneously serves as an epistemic signal, a model reconciliation prompt (P4), and a pedagogical move that invites L3 reasoning (P1). The DToM predicts appropriate uncertainty, which can improve L2 calibration, but predicts a tension or undermines trust in early L2 construction. **RQ4: How do we evaluate DToM quality?** No metrics exist for mutual understanding quality between the teacher and AI. We need measures like (a) the accuracy of the teacher's model of the AI, can the teacher predict what the AI will flag? (b) accuracy of the AI's model of the teacher's reasoning, does AI distinguish intentional from unintentional moves?, (c) alignment between models, and (d) evolution over time. Prediction tasks, where the teacher predicts the AI's flag and the AI predicts the teacher's priorities, could operationalize mutual model quality. Standardized instruments, analogous to SMILI [8], are needed. **RQ5: Can MToM-based design improve adoption and trust?** If teacher trust is L2 calibration, the MToM-based design should accelerate the feedback loop [23] from PD → understanding → trust → adoption. A controlled comparison could deploy two system versions: conventional (accurate model, standard explanations, behavioral feedback), and MToM-based (legible reasoning, targeted reconciliation, open teacher model, understanding-oriented feedback). Dependent variables should include mutual model quality, not only adoption and trust. These questions share a methodological implication: research designs must measure both sides of the mutual modeling relationship simultaneously. Studies that only assess AI accuracy (L1) or teacher trust (L2) capture an incomplete picture. The framework calls for bilateral and longitudinal evaluation of the models, their alignment, co-evolution, and C-R-R cycle tracking over sustained interaction.

## 7 Conclusion

Teacher-facing AI reproduces a fundamental asymmetry. The AI builds a model of the teacher while remaining opaque to them. The DToM diagnoses this not as a missing feature but as a missing design paradigm. It highlights the three-layer recursive structure unique to this context by revealing systematic patterns across seven research streams: the L1 advances, while the L2 is neglected. L3 is aspired to but rarely designed, and the surveillance risk correlates strongly with the absence of mutual understanding. The OLM tradition spent years arguing that AI opacity toward students is a fundamental design flaw, and that making the model transparent and adaptable produces measurable gains. Teacher-facing AI arrives at the same crossroads, with the same built-in flaw. The current focus of educational AI research is to understand learners, but the question now is whether we can build AI that *understands teachers who are understanding students* and whether these teachers, in turn, can understand AI. If "tools to teammates" is more than a motto, MToM provides its theoretical foundation. DToM represents the specific form that the foundation must take when the human in partnership is themselves a modeler of human minds. This framework accommodates the recursive, bidirectional cognitive demands unique to teacher–AI partnerships. Learning technologies should focus on the teacher who stands between AI and students. DToM provides the structure for exactly that commitment.

## References


1. Ahuja, K., et al.: EduSense: practical classroom sensing at scale. Proc. ACM Interact. Mob. Wearable Ubiquit. Technol. **3**(3), 1–26 (2019)
2. Baig, D., et al.: Enhancing knowledge tracing with large language models (LLMs). In: Proceedings of AIED, pp. 384–390. Springer (2025)
3. Baig, D., et al.: Hierarchical self-attention and skill clustering for knowledge tracing. In: Proceedings of the WI-IAT (2025)
4. Baker, C.L., Saxe, R., Tenenbaum, J.B.: Action understanding as inverse planning. Cognition **113**(3), 329–349 (2009)
5. Ball, S.J.: The teacher's soul and the terrors of performativity. J. Educ. Policy **18**(2), 215–228 (2003)
6. Berliner, D.C.: Describing the behavior and documenting the accomplishments of expert teachers. Bull. Sci. Technol. Soc. **24**(3), 200–212 (2004)
7. Brusilovsky, P.: AI in education, learner control, and human-AI collaboration. Int. J. Artif. Intell. Educ. **34**(1), 122–135 (2024)
8. Bull, S., Kay, J.: Student models that invite the learner in: the SMILI:() open learner modelling framework. Int. J. Artif. Intell. Educ. **17**(2), 89–120 (2007)
9. Chakraborti, T., et al.: Plan explanations as model reconciliation: moving beyond explanation as soliloquy. arXiv preprint arXiv:1701.08317 (2017)
10. Chernikova, O., et al.: Simulation-based learning in higher education: a meta-analysis. Rev. Educ. Res. **90**(4), 499–541 (2020)
11. Copur-Gencturk, Y., Li, J., Atabas, S.: Improving teaching at scale: can AI be incorporated into professional development to create interactive, personalized learning for teachers? Am. Educ. Res. J. **61**(4), 767–802 (2024)
12. Demszky, D., et al.: Can automated feedback improve teachers' uptake of student ideas? evidence from a randomized controlled trial in a large-scale online course. Educ. Eval. Policy Anal. **46**(3), 483–505 (2024)
13. Dragan, A.D., et al.: Legibility and predictability of robot motion. In: 8th ACM/IEEE Proceedings of the HRI, pp. 301–308. IEEE (2013)
14. Holstein, K., et al.: Co-designing a real-time classroom orchestration tool to support teacher-AI complementarity. Grantee Submission (2019)
15. Kasneci, E., et al.: ChatGPT for good? on opportunities and challenges of large language models for education. Learn. Individ. Differ. **103**, 102274 (2023)
16. Kennedy, M.M.: How does professional development improve teaching? Rev. Educ. Res. **86**(4), 945–980 (2016)
17. Kizilcec, R.F.: How much information? effects of transparency on trust in an algorithmic interface. In: Proceedings of the 2016 CHI, pp. 2390–2395 (2016)
18. van Leeuwen, A., et al.: How teacher characteristics relate to how teachers use dashboards: results from two case studies in K-12. J. Learn. Anal. **8**(2) (2021)
19. Long, Y., Aleven, V.: Enhancing learning outcomes through self-regulated learning support with an open learner model. User Model. User-Adap. Inter. **27**(1), 55–88 (2017)

20. Merod, A.: Just 18% of teachers report using AI in the classroom. K-12 Dive (2024). https://www.k12dive.com/news/teacher-ai-use-schools/714073/. Accessed 2024
21. Mishra, P., Koehler, M.J.: Technological pedagogical content knowledge: a framework for teacher knowledge. Teach. Coll. Rec. **108**(6), 1017–1054 (2006)
22. Nathan, M.J., Petrosino, A.: Expert blind spot among preservice teachers. Am. Educ. Res. J. **40**(4), 905–928 (2003)
23. Nazaretsky, T., et al.: Teachers' trust in AI-powered educational technology and a professional development program to improve it. Br. J. Edu. Technol. **53**(4), 914–931 (2022)
24. Nikolaidis, S., Shah, J.: Human-robot cross-training: computational formulation, modeling and evaluation of a human team training strategy. In: 8th ACM/IEEE international conference on HRI, pp. 33–40. IEEE (2013)
25. Phillips, E., et al.: From tools to teammates: toward the development of appropriate mental models for intelligent robots. In: Proceedings of the human factors and ergonomics society annual meeting, vol. 55, pp. 1491–1495 (2011)
26. Piech, C., et al.: Deep knowledge tracing. Adv. Neural Inf. Proces. Syst. **28** (2015)
27. Rabinowitz, N., et al.: Machine theory of mind. In: International Conference on Machine Learning, pp. 4218–4227. PMLR (2018)
28. Ravid, D.M., et al.: A meta-analysis of the effects of electronic performance monitoring on work outcomes. Pers. Psychol. **76**(1), 5–40 (2023)
29. Sherin, M.G., Van Es, E.A.: Effects of video club participation on teachers' professional vision. J. Teach. Educ. 60(1) (2009)
30. Strauss, S., et al.: Teaching as a natural cognition and its relations to preschoolers' developing theory of mind. Cogn. Dev. **17**(3–4), 1473–1487 (2002)
31. Timperley, H., et al.: Teacher Professional Learning and Development, vol. 18. International Academy of Education (2008)
32. Wang, Q., Goel, A.K.: Mutual theory of mind for human-AI communication. arXiv preprint arXiv:2210.03842 (2022)
33. Wang, Q., et al.: Towards mutual theory of mind in human-ai interaction: how language reflects what students perceive about a virtual teaching assistant. In: Proceedings of the 2021 CHI, pp. 1–14 (2021)
34. Wang, R., Demszky, D.: Is chatGPT a good teacher coach? measuring zero-shot performance for scoring and providing actionable insights on classroom instruction. In: Proceedings of the BEA 2023, pp. 626–667 (2023)
35. Westerman, D.A.: Expert and novice teacher decision making. J. Teach. Educ. **42**(4), 292–305 (1991)
36. Zhang, S., et al.: Mutual theory of mind in human-AI collaboration: an empirical study with LLM-driven AI agents in a real-time shared workspace task. arXiv preprint arXiv:2409.08811 (2024)

# Arguing to Learn at Scale: A Semester-Long Study of an AI Arguing Agent in a Graduate Robotics Course


Jérôme Brender[1,2](✉), Aitor Perez[3], Patrick Jermann[3], Francesco Mondada[1], Engin Bumbacher[2], and Chenyang Wang[1]

[1] MOBOTS and LEARN, EPFL, Lausanne, Switzerland
{jerome.brender,francesco.mondada,chenyang.wang}@epfl.ch
[2] University of Teacher Education (Haute École Pédagogique) Vaud, Lausanne, Switzerland
engin.bumbacher@hepl.ch
[3] Center for Digital Education and LEARN, EPFL, Lausanne, Switzerland
{aitor.perez,patrick.jermann}@epfl.ch



**Abstract.** Peer-argumentation is a well-researched instructional activity with demonstrated learning benefits, yet it remains challenging to implement in educational practice. Pedagogical conversational agents may help address this challenge, but research has so far paid little attention to their role as argumentative peers in dialogic learning tasks. To address this gap, we developed ArguBot, a didactic AI arguing partner that supports case-based argumentation by adopting opposing stances grounded in course materials and common misconceptions via retrieval-augmented generation. ArguBot was deployed as an optional after-class activity across a semester in a graduate robotics course. Across 551 student-exercise interactions from 64 students who used ArguBot at least once, completing more exercises was associated with higher exam performance, especially when students more often arrived at correct final answers through argumentation; this interaction pattern was not observed for initial answer accuracy. A similar pattern was observed in the course's in-class student-to-student peer-argumentation activities ($N = 82$). A focused qualitative analysis further showed that correct final answers were more often associated with richer dialogue patterns involving justification, reformulation, and probing, whereas incorrect outcomes were more often associated with minimal dialogic engagement. This work suggests that AI-supported argumentation is feasible in practice, but that its educational effectiveness depends less on interaction quantity alone than on the quality and outcome of the argumentative exchange.



**Keywords:** AI Arguing Agent · Pedagogical Conversational Agent · Large Language Models · Peer Argumentation Exercise · Arguing to Learn




J. Weidlich et al. (Eds.): EC-TEL 2026, LNCS 16905, pp. 96–111, 2027.
https://doi.org/10.1007/978-3-032-37979-5_7

## 1 Introduction

Peer-argumentation is a pedagogical approach in which students use argumentative dialogue to examine disciplinary ideas and jointly build understanding [11]. Research on "Arguing to Learn" suggests that these activities support learning because students must actively search for evidence, articulate and defend positions, respond to counterarguments, and weigh alternative interpretations of the same content [2,11,12]. Its value extends beyond conceptual understanding: engagement in argumentation has also been linked to metacognitive development, including critical thinking and complex problem solving [9,16].

However, enabling students to argue to learn at scale remains difficult in routine classroom practice. The logistics are demanding: instructors must allocate class time, pair students with appropriate discussion partners, often those holding different views, and provide support across many simultaneous conversations. These constraints limit how often such activities can be offered and make it difficult to sustain them beyond the classroom. Large Language Models (LLMs) therefore, offer a promising route to extending argumentation-based practice at scale and on demand, given their ability to simulate human-like dialogue.

Pedagogical Conversational Agents (PCAs) have been studied as tools for supporting learning through interactive dialogue and feedback. Existing work has primarily positioned PCAs as tutors [3,5], tutees [23] or as moderators of collaborative learning [7]. However, far less attention has been given to PCAs acting as an *arguing peer* in case-based argumentation activities. Although an LLM can be instructed to play "Devil's Advocate" [22], mere opposition is pedagogically insufficient. A fully generative peer may produce counterarguments that sound credible but remain unverified [14], rather than probing student reasoning within the curriculum's *knowledge space*. For such a system to support learning, disagreement should be anchored in course content and plausible misconceptions that reflect authentic student reasoning.

This challenge is visible in our graduate robotics course at EPFL, where the instructor regularly incorporates brief, in-class, case-based peer-argumentation tasks. In each task, students answer a multiple-choice question (MCQ) built around a concrete robotics application (e.g., selecting the appropriate navigation algorithm for a robotic ship navigating around obstacles), discuss their reasoning with a peer who selected a different option, and then submit a revised answer. As in other classroom settings, however, these activities are bounded by time and instructional capacity, and students have expressed interest in additional opportunities to practise beyond class.

To address this need, we developed ArguBot (Fig. 1), a didactic AI agent for scalable, case-based peer argumentation. Rather than merely disagreeing for rhetorical effect, ArguBot adopts an oppositional stance in pedagogically targeted ways: it challenges correct claims with common student misconceptions and counters incorrect claims with arguments grounded in course content. These responses are supported through Retrieval-Augmented Generation (RAG) over course lecture materials and common misconceptions identified from manual grading of prior cohorts' responses to the same questions. We evaluate ArguBot through a field study conducted in Fall 2025, in which the system was deployed as an on-demand after-class activity across a semester in a graduate robotics course enrolling 172 students. Across 26 case-based argumentation exercises, we collected students' initial and final responses as well as their conversation logs with ArguBot, as well as final exam performance. We also collected data from corresponding in-class peer-argumentation activities. Using these data, we ask:

**RQ1:** To what extent does students' engagement with ArguBot vary with their immediate on-task performance?
**RQ2:** To what extent does engagement with ArguBot predict final exam performance, and how does this relationship compare with engagement in in-class peer argumentation?
**RQ3:** What dialogue patterns emerge in students' engagement with ArguBot, and to what extent do they relate to on-task performance?

We address these questions by first examining quantitative measures of engagement (e.g., number of exercises, turns, time per exercise) and their association with on-task and exam performance, then conducting an in-depth qualitative analysis of dialogue strategies on a targeted subset of argumentation tasks.

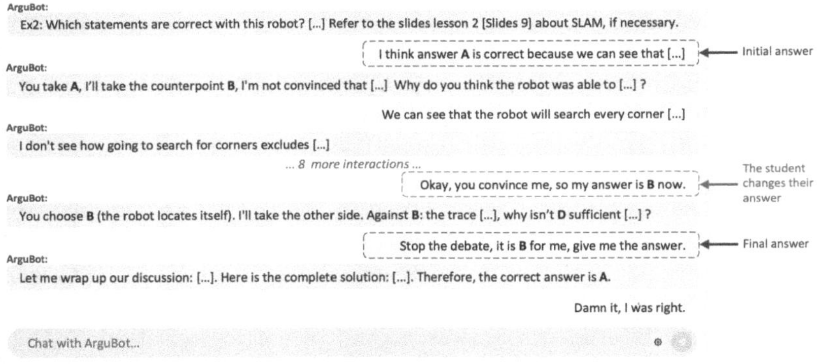


**Fig. 1.** ArguBot, a didactic AI arguing agent that supports scalable, case-based peer-argumentation: it challenges correct claims with common student misconceptions and counters incorrect claims with grounded arguments.

## 2 Related Work

Supporting arguing to learn at scale requires conversational agents that can interpret a learner's contribution and respond with a pedagogically meaningful counterargument. Prior to the Large Language Model (LLM) era, such argumentative dialogue systems were mainly developed for open-domain debate rather than educational use. For example, Rakshit et al. [19] introduced *Debbie*, a retrieval-based system that selects counterarguments from corpora on predefined controversial topics. Le et al. [17] later presented *Dave*, which combined retrieval and generation to broaden topic coverage, albeit with occasional incoherent responses. IBM Project Debater [15] further showed that a system could synthesise large corpora into well-structured argumentative speeches, although it was less suited to sustained, back-and-forth dialogue.

Despite these advances, argumentative chatbots have seen limited use in educational settings. One reason is that generating coherent, responsive, and instructionally useful argumentative dialogue is technically demanding. Recent progress in Natural Language Processing, especially LLMs, has substantially expanded the dialogic capabilities of Pedagogical Conversational Agents (PCAs) [20]. These models enable more adaptive and context-sensitive interaction, creating new opportunities to design agents that can participate in structured forms of pedagogically meaningful argumentation. Within this emerging line of work, Lee et al. [18] examined whether ChatGPT could function as a practice partner for debate training and reported limitations in debate quality. Wang et al. [22] firstly explored a tailored LLM-based arguing agent *ArgueMate* for peer-argumentation in classroom settings. Their chatbot maximises disagreement by adopting the stance most distinct from the student's initial position, and investigated collaborative versus competitive argumentation styles in a formative classroom study. Nevertheless, their study initially relied on simple prompting and did not provide large-scale empirical evidence.

More broadly, prior work has largely focused on generating human-like argumentative responses in open or general domains rather than in specialised instructional contexts. In higher education, course content is often highly specific, as in mobile robotics, and effective argumentative support must remain faithful to the relevant knowledge space. Simple prompting alone is unlikely to provide the degree of domain accuracy and pedagogical grounding required for such settings. Our work addresses this gap by grounding ArguBot's argumentative responses in course materials and common misconceptions identified from manual grading of prior cohorts' responses to the same questions through RAG, thereby enabling domain-specific and pedagogically meaningful opposition. In addition, we extend prior work by evaluating such an agent through a semester-long deployment in an authentic graduate course, thereby providing ecologically valid evidence on AI-supported peer-argumentation at scale.

## 3 Methods

### 3.1 System Design and ArguBot Implementation

ArguBot was designed as an AI arguing peer for after-class dialogical activities in a master's-level mobile robotics course at EPFL, mirroring the structure of the course's in-class peer-argumentation exercises based on a debate-based instructional approach [8]. In each activity, the agent guides students through three phases: (1) it presents a robotics application case as a multiple-choice question

(Fig. 2 right) and elicits an initial answer with justification; (2) it engages the student in multi-turn argumentation by taking the opposing side in a pedagogically targeted way[1], challenging correct answers with common student misconceptions and incorrect answers with counterarguments grounded in course content; and (3) it elicits a final answer before providing the solution with an explanation. ArguBot was implemented as a web application using OpenAI GPT-5, with LangChain orchestration and Langfuse logging. To constrain the agent's argumentative responses to the course knowledge space, we used RAG over lecture slides, notes, exercises with solutions, and forum Q&A archives, together with common misconceptions identified from manual grading of prior cohorts' responses to the same questions.

### 3.2 Semester-Long Field Study

**Participants.** ArguBot was evaluated with 172 students enrolled in the course during during the Fall 2025 semester. Participation in both the in-class and after-class argumentation activities was voluntary, based on informed consent, and no incentives were provided. In total, 82 students (58 male, 22 female, 2 undisclosed) engaged in at least one of the 13 in-class peer-argumentation exercises, and 64 students (44 male, 18 female, 2 undisclosed) completed at least one of the 26 optional after-class ArguBot argumentation exercises. Data from both settings were available for 38 students. At the end of the semester, 154 students completed the final course exam.

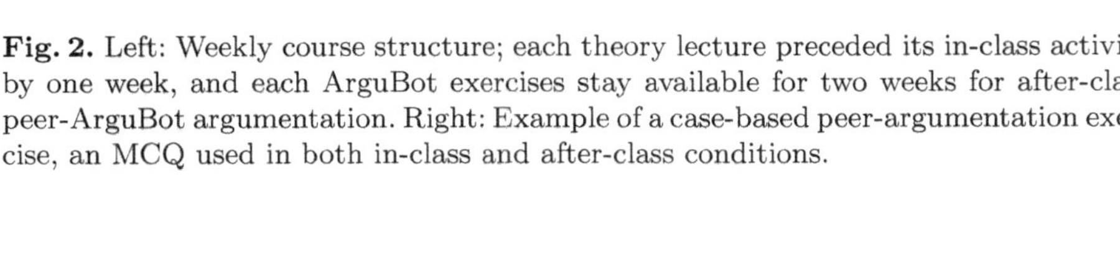


**Fig. 2.** Left: Weekly course structure; each theory lecture preceded its in-class activity by one week, and each ArguBot exercises stay available for two weeks for after-class peer-ArguBot argumentation. Right: Example of a case-based peer-argumentation exercise, an MCQ used in both in-class and after-class conditions.

**Course Structure and Deployment.** The study was conducted as a nine-week field deployment integrated into the regular course structure (Fig. 2 left). Each week included a theory lecture, followed one week later by in-class peer-argumentation exercises based on that lecture's content. In parallel, students could access after-class argumentation exercises with ArguBot on the same topics

[1] Component of the main system prompt of ArguBot is available on Zenodo.

for a two-week period. This design positioned ArguBot as an optional extension of the course's existing argumentation practice, allowing students to continue engaging with similar activities beyond class time.

**Argumentation Exercises and Exam.** Across the semester, we designed 26 case-based argumentation exercises for the after-class ArguBot setting and 13 argumentation exercises for the in-class setting. Each exercise presented a short robotics scenario followed by a multiple-choice question, with either one or several correct options depending on the task (Fig. 2 right). Exercises in both settings were matched in difficulty and drawn from questions used in the previous cohort's exam. At the end of the semester, students completed a final exam covering the same course topics, also using MCQs requiring written justifications.

**In-Class and After-Class Settings.** In the in-class peer-argumentation setting, 3–4 exercises were completed during a 45-minute lesson. For each exercise, students first submitted an individual answer within two minutes using an online response tool[2]. Students with different responses were then paired for a 3–5 minute discussion, after which they submitted a second individual answer before the instructor explained the solution.

In the after-class setting, students accessed ArguBot online and completed 3–5 exercises per topic following the three-phase interaction described in Sect. 3.1. This after-class setting preserved the same instructional logic as the in-class activity—initial commitment, argumentative exchange, and revised answer—while replacing the human peer with the AI arguing agent.

### 3.3 Data Collection and Coding

**ArguBot Interaction Logs.** For the after-class student-ArguBot setting, we collected dialogue logs for 551 student-exercise instances across 64 students. During data cleaning, we excluded dialogue logs with interactions shorter than two turns, or with only off-topic exchanges; we removed 330 instances in total. From the remaining logs, we also identified prompts in which students requested the solution, by using an automated pipeline[3]. One researcher manually verified 20% of the detected instances, yielding 97% accuracy.

From the cleaned dialogue logs, we derived quantitative engagement measures and aggregated them at the student level for later analysis. These measures include the number of completed exercises, mean number of turns per exercise, mean turns before requesting the solution, average time spent per exercise, mean message delay, average prompt length, and average number of answer changes.

[2] https://participant.turningtechnologies.eu/.
[3] https://zenodo.org/records/20645652.

**Pre-post MCQ Answers.** For the in-class peer-argumentation setting, we collected pre- and post-discussion MCQ responses from 13 exercises using an online response tool.[4] For the after-class student-ArguBot setting, initial and final MCQ answers were extracted from the dialogue logs using the same automated pipeline. Two researchers reviewed 20% of the extracted answers against the logs, yielding 95.4% agreement with the automated extraction; the remaining answers were retained automatically. For exercises with multiple correct options (6 of the 26 after-class exercises), pre- and post-answers were binarized using an 80% correctness threshold.

Using this data, we characterized on-task performance of each student-exercise instance based on the correctness of the initial and final answer. We used four categories for the transitions from initial to final answer: Correct-to-Correct (CC), Wrong-to-Wrong (WW), Wrong-to-Correct (WC), or Correct-to-Wrong (CW).

**Dialogue Quality Coding.** To examine how dialogue patterns related to on-task performance, we conducted a qualitative analysis on a targeted subset of student–ArguBot interactions. For this initial analysis, we selected a single exercise to reduce task-level variation and chose one with sufficient representation across the four transition categories to support meaningful comparison of dialogue patterns. We picked one with $n = 35$ students and a balanced representation across correct/incorrect final answers (51.4% vs 48.6%). Student prompts were coded for dialogic moves drawing on Hennessy et al. [10] and adapted to our argumentation context. For analysis, these moves were grouped into three broader dialogue dimensions: *Justification*, capturing instances in which students made their reasoning explicit, including explaining or defending their own answer; *Reformulation*, capturing instances in which students built on ideas in the dialogue by revoicing, clarifying, or elaborating either their own or ArguBot's contributions; and *Probing*, capturing instances in which students invited further elaboration, for example by questioning the chatbot's reasoning, asking for explanation, or reflecting on the argumentative exchange itself. Two researchers independently annotated the dataset, achieving substantial inter-rater agreement (Cohen's $\kappa \in [0.67, 0.83]$).

**Exam Performance.** The final exam comprised 10 MCQs covering the same concepts addressed in the semester's argumentation exercises and was completed by 154 students. Each item required a written justification, and grading was based solely on that justification, with partial credit possible. Each MCQ was graded out of 5 points; scores were then summed and standardized.

[4] Students were allowed to opt out of data collection for the in-class activity.

### 3.4 Data Analysis Methods

**Quantitative Engagement and On-Task Performance (RQ1).** To address RQ1, we examined how students' quantitative engagement with ArguBot related to their on-task performance in the after-class setting. At the student level, we first described the distribution of the quantitative engagement measures derived from the dialogue logs. At the student–exercise level, we then characterized on-task performance using the four transition categories defined in Sect. 3.3 (CC, WW, WC, and CW). Finally, for each quantitative engagement measure, we fitted a mixed-effects model with these four categories as a fixed effect and a random intercept for student (the student-exercise instance being the unit of analysis).

**After-Class ArguBot Usage and Exam Performance (RQ2).** To address RQ2, we analyzed the relationship between engagement in the after-class student-ArguBot setting and exam performance at two levels of granularity.

First, at the exam-question level, we constructed a topic-matched dataset linking each of the 10 exam questions to the 2–3 ArguBot exercises addressing the same topic (26 exercises in total). This yielded one observation per student per exam question across the 154 students who completed the exam. We fitted linear mixed-effects models predicting standardized exam-question scores from a binary indicator of whether the student had completed at least one matching ArguBot exercise. To account for clustering, we compared random-intercept structures for student, exam question, and exercise using AIC, BIC, and likelihood-ratio tests.

Second, at the student level, we focused on the 64 students who used ArguBot at least once. We modeled total standardized exam scores as a function of students' answer accuracy and quantitative engagement in the after-class setting. Initial and final answer accuracy were computed for each student as the proportion of exercises answered correctly before and after argumentation, respectively. We then tested whether these accuracy measures, together with the quantitative engagement measures derived from the dialogue logs, were associated with exam performance, including interactions between number of completed exercises and answer accuracy. To identify which quantitative engagement measures predicted exam performance, we conducted a stepwise linear regression (bidirectional) with the seven candidates (See Sect. 3.3).

**In-Class On-Task Performance and Exam Performance (RQ2).** To examine whether a similar pattern appeared in the in-class setting, we fitted the same student-level interaction model to the in-class peer-argumentation data. Because only pre–post MCQ responses were available in this setting, the model included the predictors available there: number of completed exercises, initial answer accuracy, final answer accuracy, and their interactions.

**Qualitative Dialogue Analysis (RQ3).** To address RQ3, we analyzed the subset of 35 student-ArguBot interactions described in Sect. 3.3. For each student, we computed the proportion of prompts coded as *Justification*, *Reformulation*, and *Probing*. Following [21], we applied a two-stage clustering procedure: 1) Each dimension was independently split into two groups: pairwise Euclidean distances between students were computed on each dimension's proportions and converted into similarity matrices using a Gaussian kernel ($\sigma = 0.0001$) with the optimal number of clusters determined by the silhouette score. It assigned each student a *high* or *low* label based on relative usage intensity. 2) The three binary labels were combined to identify distinct engagement profiles, unique combinations of high and low usage across the three dimensions (e.g., a student labeled High Justification, High Reformulation, Low Probing represents one profile). This yielded three distinct profiles with a substantial average silhouette score (s=0.61)

We then examined whether the resulting dialogue profiles differed in their distribution of students who reached correct versus incorrect final answers.

# 4 Results

## 4.1 How Do Students Engage with the ArguBot and How Does Their Engagement Relate to Their on-Task Performance? (RQ1)

**Engagement with ArguBot.** Students completed a median of $Mdn = 6.5$ exercises ($IQR = 11.2$), engaged in $Mdn = 5.1$ turns per exercise ($IQR = 1.7$) of which $Mdn = 3.6$ turns occurred before requesting the solution ($IQR = 1.6$), spent $Mdn = 645.6$ seconds per exercise ($IQR = 443.5$), had a message delay of $Mdn = 150.2$ seconds ($IQR = 116.8$), an average prompt length of $Mdn = 99.4$ characters ($IQR = 73.4$) and changed their answer in $Mdn = 50\%$ of exercises ($IQR = 30\%$). Overall, engagement with ArguBot was variable, reflecting substantial variation in how students used this optional activity.

**On-Task Performance.** Different from our previous analysis [4], we then examined students' on-task performance by classifying each student-exercise instance according to the correctness of the initial and final answer. Of the 551 instances, 181 (32.8%) were Correct-to-Correct (CC), 227 (41.2%) were Wrong-to-Wrong (WW), 89 (16.2%) were Wrong-to-Correct (WC), and 54 (9.8%) were Correct-to-Wrong (CW). Thus, although a substantial proportion of interactions led students to maintain an incorrect answer, the dialogue with ArguBot also coincided with non-trivial answer revision in both directions: 16.2% of instances ended in productive revision from wrong to correct, whereas 9.8% shifted from correct to wrong.

Finally, we fitted a mixed-effects model per quantitative engagement measures, with the four on-task performance categories (CC, WW, WC, CW) as a fixed effect and a random intercept for student (the exercise instance being the unit of analysis). None of the models revealed a significant effect ($p > .05$). This suggests that the quantitative characteristics of interaction captured here—such as amount of participation, number of turns, or time spent—did not, on their own, distinguish between more and less successful on-task outcomes.

Together, these findings indicate that while argumentation with ArguBot was associated with meaningful answer changes in some cases, variation in immediate on-task performance was not explained by quantitative engagement alone.

## 4.2 How is Students' Overall Engagement with ArguBot Associated with Their Exam Performance, and How Does this Compare to Engagement in in-Class Peer-Argumentation Tasks? (RQ2)

We addressed RQ2 at two levels for the after-class student-ArguBot setting. First, we examined whether topic-matched participation in ArguBot was associated with performance on the corresponding exam questions. Second, we analyzed whether students' quantitative engagement characteristics and answer accuracy in the after-class setting were associated with their total exam performance. We then compared this to the in-class peer-argumentation setting. Because participation in ArguBot was voluntary, these results warrant caution. They may reflect broader course engagement rather than a direct tool-use effect.

**Topic-Matched ArguBot Participation and Exam-Question Performance.** Using the topic-matched dataset linking each exam question to the corresponding ArguBot exercises, we fitted linear mixed-effects models predicting standardized exam-question scores from whether a student had completed at least one matching ArguBot exercise. The variance components for exam question and exercise were estimated near zero, and including these grouping factors worsened model fit according to BIC. The final model therefore retained only a random intercept for student. In this model, topic-matched ArguBot participation was positively associated with exam-question performance ($\beta = 0.21$, $SE = 0.08$, $t = 2.70$, $p = .01$). A likelihood-ratio test further confirmed that including the ArguBot participation predictor significantly improved model fit ($\chi^2(1) = 7.26$, $p = .01$). Students who completed at least one ArguBot exercise on a given topic scored, on average, 0.21 standard deviations higher on the corresponding exam question.

**After-Class ArguBot Engagement and Total Exam Performance.** Among students who engaged in at least one exercise, we examined whether quantitative engagement measures and answer accuracy were associated with their total exam scores. Initial and final answer accuracy alone did not significantly predict exam scores. However, when modeled together with the engagement measures, a significant interaction emerged between the number of completed exercises and final answer accuracy. The stepwise linear regression model was significant ($F(5, 58) = 5.52$, $p < .001$) and included number of exercises, final answer accuracy, time spent per exercise, mean turns before requesting the solution, and the interaction between number of exercises and final answer accuracy (Appendix A on Zenodo shows the table of results).

Importantly, the interaction was significant ($\beta = 0.59$, $p = .008$), i.e. the association between exercise quantity and exam performance depended on whether students reached correct final answers during argumentation. As shown in Fig. 3, after controlling for the quantitative engagement characteristics in the model, completing more exercises was strongly associated with higher exam scores at high final answer accuracy ($+1SD$: $\beta = 1.00$, $p < .001$), moderately associated at the mean final answer accuracy ($\beta = 0.42$, $p < .001$), and not significantly associated at low final answer accuracy ($-1SD$: $\beta = -0.17$, $p = .47$). In other words, completing more ArguBot exercises was associated with higher exam performance only when students also tended to arrive at correct final answers. Initial answer accuracy was not significant in any model specification.

The model further showed that students who engaged in more turns before requesting the solution predicted higher exam scores ($\beta = 0.34$, $p = .011$), whereas average time spent per exercise was negatively associated with exam scores ($\beta = -0.43$, $p = .001$).

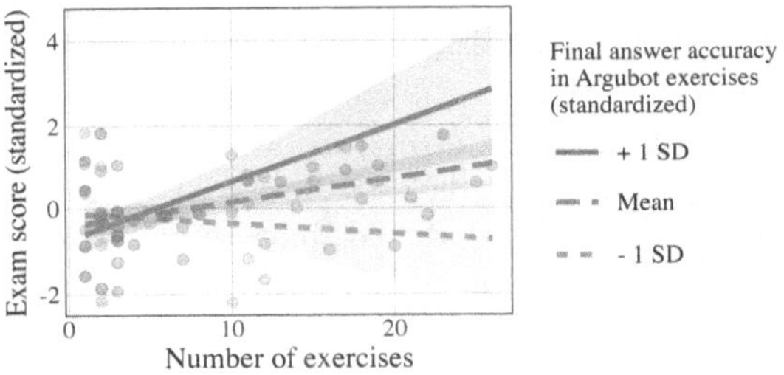


**Fig. 3.** Student exam scores as a function of the number of exercises completed, across different levels of final answer accuracy in ArguBot exercises. The figure shows model predictions with standard error bands and observed student data.

**Comparison with In-Class Peer Argumentation.** A similar pattern emerged in-class peer-argumentation: neither number of exercises nor final answer accuracy alone predicted exam performance, but the interaction model was significant ($R^2_{adj} = .14$, $F(3, 78) = 5.39$, $p = .002$). In this model, final answer accuracy ($\beta = 0.55$, $p < .001$) and its interaction with number of exercises ($\beta = 0.53$, $p < .001$) were both significant, whereas initial answer accuracy was not.

Taken together, these findings converge across the after-class student-ArguBot setting and the in-class peer-argumentation setting: greater participation was associated with better exam performance only when it was accompanied by success in arriving at correct final answers, while prior knowledge (as measured by initial answer accuracy) did not account for exam outcomes in either setting.

### 4.3 How Do Students' Dialogue Patterns During Argumentation with ArguBot Relate to Their on-Task Performance (RQ3)?

Because the quantitative engagement measures examined in RQ1 did not distinguish between the four on-task performance categories, and because arriving at correct final answers emerged as important for broader exam performance in RQ2, we next examined whether qualitatively different dialogue patterns characterized more and less successful ArguBot interactions in terms of final answer accuracy. We focused on the selected after-class exercise (see Sect. 3.4) to reduce task-level variation and allow comparison within a common task context.

Cluster analysis on the proportions of prompts coded as *Justification*, *Reformulation*, and *Probing* identified three dialogue profiles. The first profile, *Engaged Reasoning* ($n = 7$), was characterized by high levels of *Justification* and *Reformulation*. The second profile, *Probing* ($n = 7$), was characterized by comparatively high levels of *Probing*. The third profile, *Low Quality* ($n = 21$), showed low levels across all three dialogue dimensions.

The distribution of students across these profiles differed significantly by on-task performance ($\chi^2(2) = 7.17$, $p = .028$). Students who reached a correct final answer were more frequently represented in the *Engaged Reasoning* profile ($n_{correct} = 6$, $n_{incorr.} = 1$) and in the *Probing* profile ($n_{correct} = 5$, $n_{incorr.} = 2$). By contrast, students who ended with an incorrect final answer were more often represented in the *Low Quality* profile ($n_{correct} = 7$, $n_{incorr.} = 14$).

These findings suggest that more successful ArguBot interactions were associated not simply with more participation, but with qualitatively richer forms of argumentative engagement. Students who reached correct final answers were more likely either to make and refine their reasoning explicit or to use the chatbot as a partner for probing and questioning. In contrast, unsuccessful interactions were more often characterized by limited dialogic uptake across three dimensions.

## 5 Discussion and Conclusion

This study examined how ArguBot, a didactic AI arguing agent grounded in course content and common misconceptions, supported after-class argumentative practice and content learning in a semester-long graduate robotics course. Across the three research questions, the results suggest that the educational relevance of students' engagement with the argumentation exercises depends on both quantity and on whether the argumentation led to correct final answers.

### 5.1 Student Engagement and on-Task Performance: ArguBot (RQ1)

Students engaged to a variable extent with ArguBot, with about 50% of students completing at most five exercises and averaging around five turns per exercise. This variation is unsurprising given that the after-class activities were optional and ungraded, yet it still indicates that a substantial subset of students was willing to engage repeatedly in argumentative practice beyond classroom time.

In that sense, the system appears to have succeeded in its most basic pedagogical function: making this type of activity available at greater scale and with greater temporal flexibility than is typically possible in class.

At the same time, students' immediate on-task outcomes were mixed: 16.2% of exercises produced improvement of the answer from wrong to correct and 9.8% went from correct to wrong. This highlights a central feature of arguing-to-learn activities: disagreement can be productive, but it can also destabilize initially correct understanding [13]. In that respect, ArguBot should not be understood as a tutoring system designed simply to drive students toward the right answer, but as an arguing peer that creates conditions for cognitive conflict and reconsideration, with outcomes that can vary.

### 5.2 Engagement and Final Answers During Peer-ArguBot Exercises Predict Learning Outcome Measured in Exam (RQ2)

At the topic-matched exam-question level, students who had completed at least one corresponding ArguBot exercise scored higher on the related exam question. Because participation in ArguBot was voluntary, this association should be interpreted cautiously and may partly reflect broader course engagement. Still, it suggests that students who engaged with the after-class exercises on a given topic also tended to perform better on that topic later in the course.

More importantly, the student-level analysis showed that completing more ArguBot exercises was associated with higher exam performance particularly when students reached correct final answers. Initial answer accuracy, by contrast, did not account for exam outcomes. This suggests that what mattered was neither participation alone nor prior correctness, but whether the argumentative process led students toward a correct resolution. This interpretation is strengthened by having observed the same pattern in the in-class peer-argumentation setting. This aligns with prior work on arguing to learn, which emphasizes that learning benefits arise not from participation alone, but from the revision and refinement of understanding through challenge and counterargument [11] [12].

Two additional associations in the after-class model with ArguBot are also noteworthy: students who engaged in more turns before requesting the solution tended to achieve higher exam scores, whereas average time spent per exercise was negatively associated with exam performance. These measures are best understood as behavioural indicators associated with performance rather than as direct evidence of productive learning processes. More turns before requesting the solution may reflect greater persistence in the argumentative exchange, reflective of research on help seeking in intelligent tutoring systems, where the timing and deliberateness of help requests critically modulate their effectiveness [1]. These results should, however, be interpreted cautiously as longer time per exercise could reflect hesitation, disengagement, or activity outside the dialogue itself.

These findings suggest that ArguBotś value lies less in additional exposure to course content than in supporting an argumentation process that can move students toward correct answers and increase overall course understanding. The fact that initial answer accuracy did not account for exam outcomes further supports the educational relevance of the argumentative exchange. Still, the RQ2 analysis alone does not explain which features of that exchange mattered most. RQ3 thus focuses on the quality of students' dialogic exchanges with ArguBot.

### 5.3 Relationship Between Dialogue Patterns and on-Task Argumentation Performance (RQ3)

A key result across RQ1 and RQ2 is that quantitative engagement metrics (number of exercises, number of turns, time spent) alone do not distinguish between on-task performance categories (i.e., do not explain why some interactions end with correct or incorrect final answers). Qualitative dialogue patterns identified in RQ3, however, were associated with on-task performance categories: students who reached correct final answers were more often associated with richer dialogue patterns characterized by justification, reformulation, and probing, whereas incorrect outcomes were more often associated with low quality.

This pattern aligns with prior work on arguing to learn, which emphasizes that the educational value of argumentative activity lies not in participation alone, but in the quality of reasoning, uptake of ideas, and responsiveness to counterarguments during the exchange [11, 12]. The two most successful cluster profiles suggest that productive interaction with an AI arguing partner may take more than one form: some students worked through disagreement by articulating and refining their reasoning, while others did so by questioning and probing the agent's position. These findings are also consistent with the ICAP framework's prediction that constructive engagement yields deeper learning than active or passive modes [6]. By contrast, the predominance of the *Low Quality* profile among incorrect outcomes points to an important design challenge: providing an AI arguing partner does not by itself ensure that students will engage argumentatively in ways that support learning. Scaffolds that explicitly prompt justification or counter-argumentation (i.e., like sentence starters or adaptive prompts detecting low quality), could be a promising direction for shifting students toward more successful dialogue patterns.

Because this qualitative analysis was intentionally restricted to a single exercise (that had the highest number of participating students and variety of on-task performance categories), the dialogue profiles should be interpreted as initial evidence rather than stable patterns across all after-class tasks. At the same time, the focused design strengthened interpretability by holding the task context constant. Future work should therefore extend this analysis to additional exercises to examine the robustness of these patterns across topics and task structures.

### 5.4 Limitations

This study provides ecologically valid evidence from a semester-long field deployment of ArguBot, but that realism comes with limitations. Participation was voluntary, limiting causal interpretation and raising the possibility that some associations reflect broader course engagement (self-selection bias). The sample was drawn from a single graduate robotics course, which limits generalizability. We did not collect dialogue data from the in-class peer discussions and therefore could not compare interaction processes directly across settings. A systematic evaluation of the agent's response validity is needed to ensure there are no biases or confounds in the agent's interactions. Finally, the qualitative dialogue analysis should be extended to the full dataset to validate the identified profiles.

### 5.5 Conclusion and Future Work

This paper investigated how AI arguing agents can engage students and support arguing to learn out-of-class, through ArguBot, a pedagogical conversational agent grounded in course content and common misconceptions.

The results show that ArguBot can support effective out-of-class argumentative practices at scale, but that learning benefits depend less on exposure alone than on the quality and outcome of their argumentation. Specifically, exam performance was positively associated with completing more exercises, particularly when students arrived at correct final answers, a trend found in both with ArguBot (after class) and in-class peer-to-peer argumentation settings. Quantitative engagement measures did not distinguish immediate on-task performance categories. But in the qualitative subset analysed, correct final answers were further associated with richer dialogue patterns of argumentation. Together, these results suggest that AI-supported argumentation can extend opportunities for arguing to learn beyond the classroom, but that its value depends on the nature and outcome of the argumentative exchange rather than exposure alone.

Future work should therefore focus on designing adaptive scaffolds that more consistently elicit productive argumentative behaviours, on tracing conceptual change more directly through finer-grained discourse analyses, and on using broader learning measures such as delayed retention, transfer, and explanation quality. Controlled studies across domains will also be needed to isolate the causal effects of the agent's design and to determine how AI-supported argumentation can most effectively foster durable learning.

## References

1. Aleven, V., Roll, I., McLaren, B.M., Koedinger, K.R.: Help helps, but only so much: research on help seeking with intelligent tutoring systems. Int. J. Artif. Intell. Educ. **26**(1), 205–223 (2016)
2. Asterhan, C.S., Schwarz, B.B.: Argumentation for learning: well-trodden paths and unexplored territories. Educ. Psychol. **51**(2), 164–187 (2016)
3. Bear, E., Chen, X.: Evaluating a conversational agent for second language learning aligned with the school curriculum. In: International Conference on Artificial Intelligence in Education, pp. 142–147. Springer (2023)
4. Brender, J., Bumbacher, E., Jermann, P., Mondada, F., Wang, C.: More correcting or confounding? when an AI arguing agent informed by common student misconceptions joins case-based peer-argumentation in a real course. In: Proceedings of Machine Learning Research (2026). https://infoscience.epfl.ch/handle/20.500.14299/264396

5. Cai, W., et al.: MathBot: a personalized conversational agent for learning math, ACM (2019)
6. Chi, M.T., Wylie, R.: The ICAP framework: linking cognitive engagement to active learning outcomes. Educational psychologist **49**(4), 219–243 (2014)
7. Çini, A., Papadopoulos, P., de Araujo, A., Martens, J.: The impact of AI-based collaborative conversational agents on metacognitive awareness. In: International Conference on Artificial Intelligence in Education, pp. 212–218. Springer (2025)
8. Crouch, C.H., Mazur, E.: Peer instruction: ten years of experience and results. Am. J. Phys. **69**(9), 970–977 (2001)
9. Duschl, R.A., Osborne, J.: Supporting and promoting argumentation discourse in science education (2002)
10. Hennessy, S., et al.: Developing a coding scheme for analysing classroom dialogue across educational contexts. Learn. Cult. Soc. Interact. **9**, 16–44 (2016)
11. Iordanou, K., Kuhn, D., Matos, F., Shi, Y., Hemberger, L.: Learning by arguing. Learn. Instruction **63**, 101207 (2019)
12. Jonassen, D.H., Kim, B.: Arguing to learn and learning to argue: design justifications and guidelines. Educ. Tech. Res. Dev. (2010)
13. Kang, S., Scharmann, L.C., Noh, T.: Reexamining the role of cognitive conflict in science concept learning. Res. Sci. Educ. **34**(1), 71–96 (2004)
14. ChatGPT for good? on opportunities and challenges of large language models for education. Learn. Individ. Differ. **103**, 102274 (2023)
15. Krishna, A., et al.: AI learns the art of debate, IBM Research Blog (2018)
16. Kuhn, D., Moore, W.: Argumentation as core curriculum. Learn. Res. Pract. **1**(1), 66–78 (2015)
17. Le, D.T., Nguyen, C.T., Nguyen, K.A.: Dave the debater: a retrieval-based and generative argumentative dialogue agent. In: Slonim, N., Aharonov, R. (eds.) Proceedings of the 5th Workshop on Argument Mining, pp. 121–130. Association for Computational Linguistics, Brussels, Belgium (2018)
18. Lee, U., et al.: Can chatGPT be a debate partner? developing chatGPT-based application "DEBO" for debate education, findings and limitations. Educ. Technol. Soc. **27**(2), 321–346 (2024)
19. Rakshit, G., Bowden, K.K., Reed, L., Misra, A., Walker, M.: Debbie, the debate bot of the future. In: Advanced social interaction with agents: 8th International Workshop on Spoken Dialog Systems, pp. 45–52. Springer (2018)
20. Shanahan, M., McDonell, K., Reynolds, L.: Role play with large language models. Nature **623**(7987), 493–498 (2023)
21. Shved, E., Bumbacher, E., Mejia-Domenzain, P., Kapur, M., Käser, T.: Teaching and measuring multidimensional inquiry skills using interactive simulations. In: International Conference on Artificial Intelligence in Education, Springer (2024)
22. Wang, C., Forte, F., Wettstein, L., Dillenbourg, P., Wambsganss, T.: ArgueMate: designing an arguing agent with maximised disagreement to support student peer-argumentation exercise (2026). https://doi.org/10.1145/3772363.3799300
23. Wang, C., et al.: Turning 500+ students into teachers: a semester-long study of an ai teachable agent in an undergraduate algorithms course. In: L@ S'26: Proceedings of the Thirteenth ACM Conference on Learning@ Scale, Association for Computing Machinery (2026)

# When Performance Is Not Learning: a Multi-Session Study of AI- and XR-Supported Psychomotor Skill Acquisition

Alberto Casas-Ortiz[1] (✉), Nerea Jimenez-Tellez[2], and Olga C. Santos[1]

[1] PhyUM Research Center, Artificial Intelligence Dept. Computer Science School, UNED, Madrid, Spain
alberto.casasortiz@dia.uned.es

[2] Stanford Cardiovascular Institute, Stanford University, Stanford, CA, USA

**Abstract.** AI- and XR-supported learning environments increasingly provide real-time guidance and feedback for the acquisition of psychomotor skills. These systems are commonly evaluated through learners' performance during interaction, implicitly assuming that successful execution reflects actual learning. However, the relationship between guided performance and autonomous learning remains largely unexplored. This paper presents an exploratory multi-session study involving 21 novice learners interacting with an AI- and XR-supported psychomotor learning environment. We examined three complementary dimensions of learning: performance during guided practice, progression across sessions and autonomous recall without system support. Results reveal a consistent discrepancy between guided performance and autonomous skill execution. While participants achieved high performance scores when supported by the system, improvements across sessions were limited and recall without guidance remained challenging. Rather than indicating a limitation of the specific system, these findings point to a broader challenge in technology-enhanced learning: the tendency to equate performance under guidance with actual learning. Our results provide preliminary empirical evidence that guided performance and autonomous learning should be considered distinct constructs when evaluating AI-supported psychomotor learning environments. We argue for evaluation approaches and design strategies that explicitly address retention, recall and the transition from guided to autonomous performance.

**Keywords:** Psychomotor Learning · Autonomous Learning · Learning Analytics · Embodied Learning · Learning Transfer · AI-Supported Learning · Virtual Reality

## 1 Introduction

The increasing integration of artificial intelligence (AI) and extended reality (XR) technologies is opening new possibilities for technology-enhanced learning (TEL), particularly in domains that involve embodied and psychomotor skills. Through real-time feedback, multimodal interaction and adaptive guidance, these technologies enable learners to practice complex motor skills beyond traditional instructional settings [1].


J. Weidlich et al. (Eds.): EC-TEL 2026, LNCS 16905, pp. 112–126, 2027.
https://doi.org/10.1007/978-3-032-37979-5_8

Despite these advances, the evaluation of AI-supported psychomotor learning systems remains largely focused on performance during interaction. Learners are typically assessed while receiving guidance from the system and successful task execution is often interpreted as evidence of learning. However, whether guided performance translates into autonomous skill acquisition, retention and recall remains insufficiently explored. This issue is especially relevant in psychomotor learning, where mastery depends not only on movement accuracy but also on the internalization of motor sequences and the ability to reproduce them independently.

To address this gap, we investigate the relationship between guided performance and autonomous learning using the Kenpo Learning Simulator (KLS) [2], an AI- and XR-supported psychomotor learning environment. Through an exploratory multi-session study, we examine three complementary dimensions of learning: 1) performance during system-guided practice, 2) progression across repeated sessions, and 3) autonomous recall without system support.

Our findings suggest that successful performance under AI/XR guidance does not necessarily imply autonomous learning. While learners achieve high performance scores during system-supported practice, improvements across sessions were limited and unsupported recall remained challenging. These results provide preliminary empirical evidence that guided performance and autonomous learning should be treated as distinct constructs when evaluating AI-supported learning environments. Beyond psychomotor learning, the study contributes to ongoing discussions in TEL regarding the validity of performance-based indicators as proxies for learning.

## 2 Background and Related Work

This section briefly introduces the foundations of psychomotor learning, summarizes how AI and XR technologies have been used to support motor skill acquisition, and reviews current approaches to evaluating learning in these environments. Particular attention is given to the distinction between guided performance and autonomous learning that motivates the present study.

### 2.1 Psychomotor Learning in Technology-Enhanced Learning

Psychomotor learning involves the acquisition of motor skills through observation, imitation and practice, integrating cognitive, affective and physical processes [3–5]. It plays a central role in domains such as sports, rehabilitation and professional training, where learning is embodied and iterative and depends on the progressive development and internalization of coordinated movement patterns. To support this process, prior work has highlighted the importance of personalization, feedback and user modeling, emphasizing the role of adaptive systems in guiding learners through different stages of skill acquisition [6–9]. Recent research in embodied learning suggests that bodily engagement can improve learning performance and reduce cognitive load, although its effectiveness depends on contextual factors such as task type and learner characteristics [10]. However, supporting learners' progression from guided motor execution to autonomous task execution remains an open challenge.

### 2.2 AI and XR for Psychomotor Learning

Advances in AI and XR have enabled immersive learning environments for psychomotor learning that combine realistic practice scenarios with feedback and guidance [11, 12]. Within these systems, pose estimation techniques such as MediaPipe BlazePose can support human movement capture and analysis [13]. However, despite these increasingly sophisticated capabilities, evaluation has often focused on system functionality, user experience and performance during interaction, leaving open whether performance achieved under system guidance translates into retention, recall and autonomous execution beyond the training environment [14].

### 2.3 Evaluating Learning beyond Guided Performance

Evaluation remains a critical aspect in the development of intelligent systems for psychomotor learning. Existing studies commonly rely on usability assessments, user experience measures and performance metrics collected during system interaction. Standard evaluation instruments include questionnaires such as TAM [14] and NASA-TLX [15], as well as statistical analyses of task performance and observational data. In many cases, these observable indicators are used as indirect measures of learning outcomes.

While these approaches provide valuable insights into system acceptance and immediate performance, they offer limited evidence regarding actual learning. Learning research has long distinguished between performance during practice and more robust indicators of learning, such as retention, transfer and autonomous execution [16, 17]. Accordingly, retention and transfer tests are widely regarded as more reliable indicators of learning than performance observed during practice. As a result, performance achieved under guidance should not be assumed to provide sufficient evidence of skill acquisition.

This distinction is particularly relevant in AI- and XR-supported psychomotor learning, where the complexity and variability of human movement make skill acquisition difficult to model and evaluate [18], yet existing studies rarely examine whether gains achieved under guidance persist beyond the training environment. Recent work further suggests that persistent guidance may lead to over-reliance on system feedback, limiting skill internalization and retention [19].

These limitations highlight the need for empirical studies that evaluate not only guided performance but also retention, recall and autonomous execution. In response to this gap, this study investigates the relationship between guided performance and autonomous learning in an AI-XR-supported psychomotor environment through a multi-session evaluation of both system-supported practice and unsupported recall.

## 3 Research Design

This section describes the study design and methods used to investigate the relationship between guided performance and autonomous learning.

### 3.1 Learning Environment

KLS is an AI- and XR-supported psychomotor learning environment to practice a sequence of five blocking movements from American Kenpo Karate within a 360° virtual dojo using a head-mounted display (Meta Quest 3S), described in detail in [2].

The XR component provides immersive visualization, avatar-based demonstrations and real-time guidance through textual instructions and visual feedback directly superimposed on the learner's view (e.g., color-coded limb trajectories indicating movement deviations). Following the PsyLearn approach described in [2], the system supports the psychomotor, cognitive and affective dimensions of learning. Accordingly, after each session, KLS generates learning reports including movement performance indicators, questionnaire-based cognitive assessments and affective information derived from learners' interaction with the system.

The AI component relies on a rule-based pose comparison engine built on MediaPipe BlazePose [13], which analyzes learner movements through joint angles and body landmark positions and compares them against expert-defined movement templates. Based on the errors detected, the system generates adaptive corrective feedback by selecting appropriate visual and auditory cues associated with specific movement deviations (e.g., incorrect elbow position or blocking trajectory).

### 3.2 Research Question and Hypotheses

This study aims to investigate whether AI-supported XR systems can effectively support psychomotor learning beyond immediate performance during guided interaction. In particular, we focus on the acquisition, progression and recall of movements and sequences across multiple sessions. The study is guided by the following research question (**RQ**): *To what extent does successful performance during AI-supported XR practice translate into autonomous recall and retention of psychomotor skills?*

To address this question, we formulate the following hypotheses: **H1**. Learners can achieve high levels of psychomotor performance during system-guided practice; **H2**. Performance improvement across sessions is limited despite repeated interaction with the system; and **H3**. Learners exhibit difficulties recalling movement sequences without system guidance. Beyond these hypotheses, the study examines whether successful performance during guided practice is accompanied by autonomous skill consolidation.

### 3.3 Study Design

We conducted a multi-session exploratory study involving novice participants interacting with the system over several days. A total of 21 participants took part in the study, completing up to four sessions distributed over time. Each session consisted of a sequence of conditions designed to assess both guided performance and independent recall. Participants provided informed consent and participated voluntarily.

The study followed a structured protocol combining system-supported and recall-based tasks. Participants were first asked to perform the movement sequence from memory (Recall 0), followed by system-guided practice (system condition). After this, they were asked again to recall the sequence without assistance (Recall 1). Additional conditions included a guided mode, where users received more explicit instruction from a real person, and a final recall phase (Recall 2). Note that in the first session, as participants had no prior experience with the movements, Recall 0 was skipped. From Session 2 onwards, Recall 0 was used to assess retention between sessions (Fig. 1).

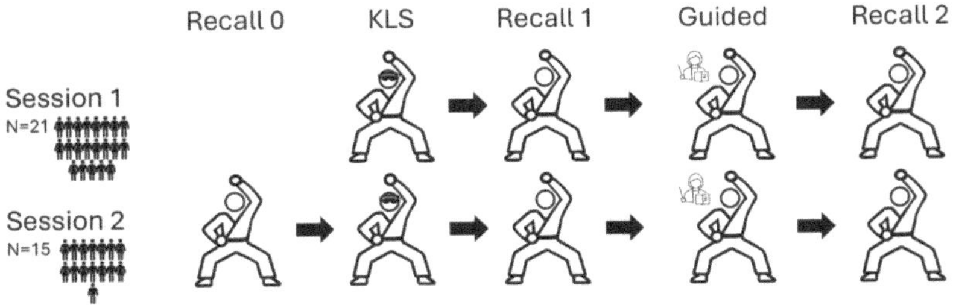


**Fig. 1.** Protocol followed to record data in the exploratory evaluation

Sessions were conducted on different days. Participation decreased from 21 participants in Session 1 to 15 in Session 2 due to participant availability and the exploratory nature of the study. Sessions 3 and 4 were excluded from the analyses because only 5 and 1 participants completed them, respectively. Consequently, the analyses reported in this paper are based on the first two sessions and should be interpreted as short-term observations of learning progression across days rather than evidence of long-term retention. Future studies should examine retention and skill consolidation over longer time spans and with a larger number of repeated sessions.

### 3.4 Measures and Analysis

Following the PsyLearn framework [2], KLS supports the psychomotor, cognitive and affective dimensions of learning. However, the present study focuses primarily on psychomotor learning outcomes and their relationship with autonomous recall.

Psychomotor performance was assessed using the system's scoring mechanism, which estimates deviations from expert-defined movement templates. This metric reflects the accuracy and coordination of movements performed during system-guided practice. To evaluate learning beyond guided interaction, recall of individual movements and movement sequences was assessed in conditions where participants performed without system support. Measures included the number of correctly recalled movements, sequencing accuracy and the presence of partial or incorrect subsequences.

In addition, KLS collects cognitive and affective indicators. Cognitive performance was assessed through multiple-choice questionnaires evaluating learners' understanding of the movements and their rationale, while affective information was derived from emotion-related indicators captured during interaction. These dimensions provide complementary information about the learning process but are not the primary focus of the analyses reported in this paper.

Analyses focused on three aspects: 1) performance during system-guided practice, 2) progression across sessions, and 3) autonomous recall without system support. Statistical tests were selected according to data distribution and the exploratory nature of the study. Comparisons across sessions were used to assess short-term learning progression, while comparisons between guided and recall conditions were used to examine discrepancies between supported performance and autonomous execution. Changes in recall performance across sessions were further analyzed to explore short-term retention and consolidation of the learned movement sequences.

## 4 Results

This section presents the results organized around the research hypotheses. The blocking movements used throughout the study are described in detail in [2].

### 4.1 Performance during System-Guided Practice

We first analyze learners' performance (N = 21) during system-guided interaction to assess whether the system enables effective execution of psychomotor skills (H1).

Results show that participants achieved relatively high-performance scores during system use during the first session (Avg. 0.7415 ± 0.0890 SD, Fig. 2A). When observing movements in isolation, movement difficulty coincides with obtained scores Fig. 2B. The movement Upward Block and the movement Downward Outward Block are the most difficult to execute, obtaining scores of Avg. 0.5902 ± 0.1478 SD and Avg. Avg. 0.6667 ± 0.2341 SD respectively. On the other hand, stronger proficiency is observed in the other movements Outward Extended Block (Avg. 0.8663 ± 0.1823 SD), Rear Elbow Block (Avg. 0.8027 ± 0.0842 SD) Hammering Inward Block (Avg. 0.7817 ± 0.2083 SD), which are simpler in nature.

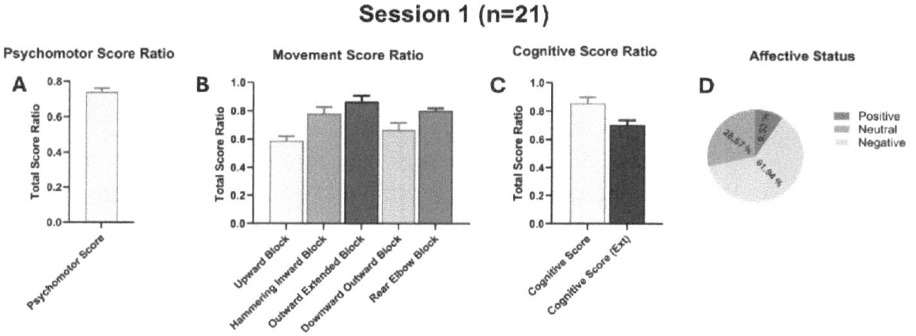


**Fig. 2.** Performance of the 21 participants for Session 1. Bars indicate mean ± SEM (Standard Error of the Mean). A) Psychomotor score obtained by participants. B) Per movement psychomotor score obtained by participants. C) Cognitive score obtained by participants in the system (left) and in the external test (right). D) Distribution of affective states obtained by participants

In general, after only one session, psychomotor performance reached moderate to high levels, consistently with movement difficulty indicating that learners were able to correctly execute movements when supported by real-time feedback.

Learners also obtained high cognitive scores (Fig. 2C), both in the in-system assessment (avg. 0.8571 ± 0.1912 SD) and in the external assessment taken hours after the practice (avg. 0.7048 ± 0.1499 SD), suggesting that participants were able to understand the rationale underlying the movements, although some decay over time was observed. Analysis of affective states during the initial session revealed a predominance of negative affective states, followed by neutral and positive states (Fig. 2D).

These findings are consistent with H1, suggesting that, in this exploratory setting, AI/XR systems can effectively scaffold psychomotor performance during interaction.

### 4.2 Learning across Sessions

We then examine whether if participants' ($N = 15$) repeated interaction with the system leads to improvements in performance over time (H2).

During the first training session, participants achieved an average psychomotor score of 0.7464 ± 0.0932 SD (Fig. 3A). Analysis of individual movement scores (Fig. 3B) revealed variability in performance across techniques. The lowest scores were observed in the Upward Block (Avg. 0.5877 ± 0.1524 SD) and Downward Outward Block (Avg. 0.6818 ± 0.1850 SD) while participants demonstrated stronger proficiency in the Outward Extended Block (Avg. 0.8590 ± 0.1975 SD), followed by the Rear Elbow Block (Avg. 0.8095 ± 0.0881 SD) and Hammering Inward Block (Avg. 0.7944 ± 0.2354SD).

In the second session, learners obtained an average psychomotor score of 0.7433 ± 0.0583 SD (Fig. 3A). Performance patterns remained consistent on individual movements (Fig. 3B), with the Upward Block (Avg. 0.5473 ± 0.1215 SD) and Downward Outward Block (Avg. 0.6909 ± 0.1693 SD) showing the lowest scores, while the Outward Extended Block (Avg. 0.9000 ± 0.1422 SD) maintained the highest performance, followed by the Hammering Inward Block (Avg. 0.8167 ± 0.1344 SD) and Rear Elbow Block (Avg. 0.7619 ± 0.0697 SD) (Fig. 3B).

Statistical comparison between sessions scores obtained while using the system assessed both the Psychomotor Score and individual movement metrics. After confirming normality via Shapiro-Wilk testing, a paired T-test was used to assess overall psychomotor score (Fig. 3A) and movement scores were assessed using a Two-way ANOVA test (Fig. 3B). No significant differences were found between sessions for any variable ($p > 0.05$), indicating stable performance levels according to system metrics.

Cognitive performance also remained stable across sessions. In the in-system multiple-choice test, participants achieved average scores (0.8800 ± 0.1821 SD in Session 1 and 0.8266 ± 0.1831 SD in Session 2; Fig. 3C). External assessments yielded slightly lower but comparable scores (avg. 0.7067 ± 0.1486 SD and 0.7600 ± 0.1882 SD; Fig. 3D). No statistically significant differences were found between sessions ($p > 0.05$).

Affective indicators showed a predominance of negative affective states in both sessions. In Session 1, 66.67% of learners were classified as negative, 26.67% as neutral and 6.67% ($n = 1$) as positive (Fig. 3D top). Session 2 showed a similar distribution (Fig. 3D bottom). No statistically significant changes were observed either between sessions.

Comparisons across sessions show that, although performance remains consistently high, there are no statistically significant improvements in psychomotor scores, cognitive scores and affective states between sessions. These findings support H2 and suggest that repeated interaction with the system does not necessarily lead to measurable performance gains across sessions. More importantly, stable performance during system use should not be interpreted as evidence of continued learning gains.

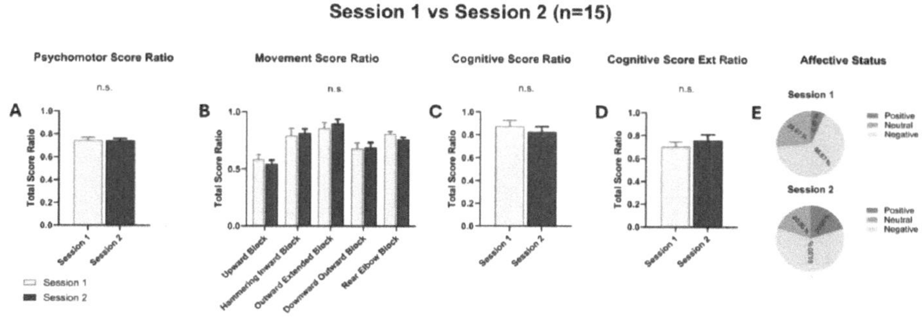


**Fig. 3.** Comparison of the performance on Session 1 vs. 2 of the 15 participants that participated in two sessions. Bars indicate mean ± SEM (Standard Error of the Mean). A) Psychomotor Score obtained by participants. B) per movement Psychomotor Score obtained by participants. C) Cognitive Score obtained by participants in the system. D) Cognitive Score (external) obtained by participants in the test. E) distribution of affective states obtained by participants for Session 1 and Session 2. All comparisons between Session 1 and 2 were no significative ($p > 0.05$)

## 4.3 Recall and Retention without System Support

To evaluate learning beyond guided interaction, we analyze participants' ability to reproduce the learned movement sequence without system support (H3). Unlike psychomotor scores collected during guided practice, these measures provide evidence of autonomous execution and recall. Recall performance was evaluated through metrics capturing movement accuracy, sequence correctness and ordering errors. Statistical analyses were conducted using Wilcoxon tests after confirming not normal distribution using Saphiro-Wilk.

Results indicate that participants experienced substantial difficulties recalling both individual movements and movement sequences without system support. Recall performance improved after additional human-guided practice (Fig. 4), suggesting that learners benefited from immediate reinforcement. However, these gains were only partially retained when recall was assessed again on a different day without further exposure to the system (Fig. 5).

During the second session, participants performed the sequence autonomously after system-guided practice. Compared with Session 1, improvements were observed across most recall metrics (Fig. 6), suggesting some degree of learning progression. Nevertheless, autonomous recall remained considerably weaker than performance observed during guided practice.

Collectively, these results suggest that, while participants were often able to reproduce individual movements, correctly recalling and sequencing the full set of actions remained challenging. Improvements were observed following guided practice, but these gains were only partially retained throughout sessions. The observed discrepancies between guided performance and autonomous recall support H3 and suggest challenges in skill consolidation rather than deficiencies in system functionality. While participants performed well when supported by the system, autonomous recall remained substantially more challenging.

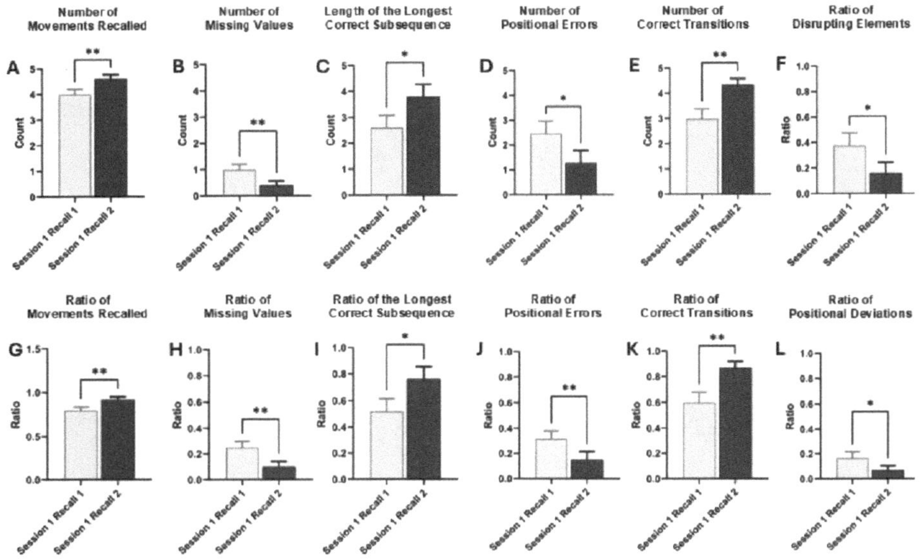


**Fig. 4.** Comparison between Session 1 Recall 1 and Recall 2 (n = 15). Only statistically significant differences are shown. Bars represent mean ± SEM. Significant improvements were observed in recalled movements, missing movements, longest correct subsequence, positional errors, correct transitions, disrupting elements and positional deviations (* $p < 0.05$, ** $p < 0.01$).

## 4.4 Summary of Findings

The results reveal a clear distinction between performance during system-guided practice and autonomous skill execution. Participants achieved high psychomotor scores while interacting with the system and receiving real-time feedback, supporting H1, but this does not fully translate into improved performance over time or into reliable recall without assistance showing limited improvement across sessions and thus supporting H2. In addition, recall analyses revealed persistent difficulties reproducing movement sequences without system support, supporting H3.

These findings suggest that successful performance during guided interaction should not be assumed to reflect autonomous learning. Rather than indicating a limitation of

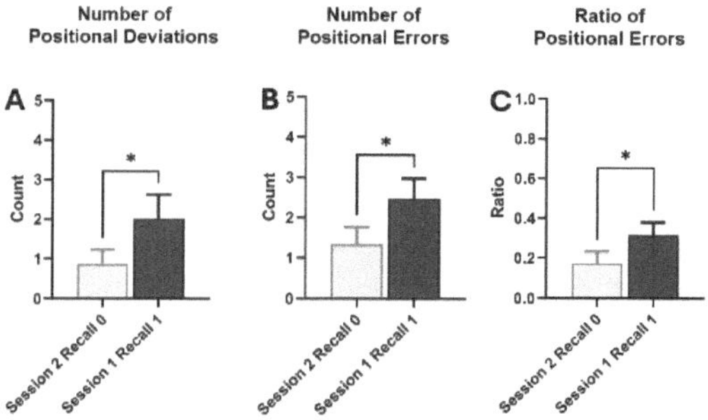


**Fig. 5.** Comparison between Session 1 Recall 1 and Session 2 Recall 0 (n = 15). Only significant results are shown. Bars represent mean ± SEM. Significant differences were found for positional deviations and positional errors (* $p < 0.05$); all other comparisons were non-significant

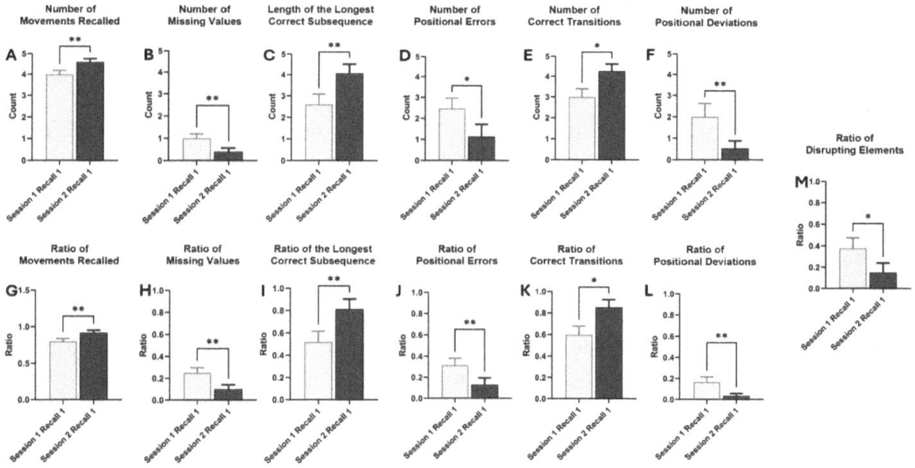


**Fig. 6.** Comparison between Session 1 Recall 1 and Session 2 Recall 1 (n = 15). Only statistically significant differences are shown. Bars represent mean ± SEM. Significant improvements were observed in recalled movements, missing movements, longest correct subsequence, positional errors, correct transitions, disrupting elements and positional deviations (* $p < 0.05$, ** $p < 0.01$)

the specific system, the observed discrepancy highlights a broader challenge for AI-supported learning environments: distinguishing between supported performance and learning that can be retained and reproduced independently.

## 5 Discussion

The results of this exploratory study highlight a distinction between performance achieved under AI-supported psychomotor guidance and autonomous learning outcomes. While learners were able to perform successfully during system-guided practice, improvements across sessions were limited and autonomous recall remained challenging.

Although observed in a psychomotor learning context, these findings raise broader questions for TEL regarding how learning is evaluated and how AI-supported environments can facilitate the transition from guided performance to autonomous skill execution.

## 5.1 Performance Is Not Learning

The most salient finding of this study is the discrepancy between performance achieved during system-guided practice and autonomous execution without support. Participants consistently achieved high psychomotor scores while interacting with the psychomotor learning environment, confirming that the system effectively guided movement execution. However, improvements across sessions were limited and autonomous recall remained substantially more challenging than guided performance.

These findings suggest that successful execution under guidance should not be interpreted as direct evidence of learning. While learners were often able to reproduce movements correctly when supported by the system, they experienced difficulties recalling and sequencing those same movements independently. The observed decline in performance when guidance was removed indicates that some aspects of the skill had not yet been fully consolidated.

This distinction aligns with established learning research, which differentiates between performance during practice and more robust indicators of learning such as retention, transfer and autonomous execution [16, 17]. From this perspective, the psychomotor scores produced during system interaction should be interpreted primarily as indicators of guided performance rather than direct measures of learning outcomes. This does not diminish the value of such indicators; rather, it highlights the need to distinguish between measures of supported performance and measures of autonomous learning.

The findings also raise broader questions regarding the validity of performance-based indicators commonly used in AI- and XR- supported learning environments. Many intelligent learning systems rely on interaction metrics as proxies for learning. Our results suggest that such metrics may capture how successfully learners perform while receiving support, without necessarily reflecting what they can subsequently do independently. Although these observations originate from a psychomotor learning context, they highlight a more general challenge for TEL: distinguishing between successful performance with assistance and genuine learning that can be retained and reproduced autonomously.

## 5.2 Implications for AI-Supported Learning

The discrepancy observed between guided performance and autonomous recall reinforces the rationale behind PsyLearn [2], which models psychomotor learning as a multidimensional process involving psychomotor, cognitive and affective dimensions. While movement accuracy is an important indicator of performance, our results suggest that it may not be sufficient to characterize learning outcomes on its own. Learners may successfully execute movements under guidance while still experiencing difficulties in recalling, sequencing, or independently reproducing those movements.

This observation has implications beyond psychomotor learning. Increasingly, AI-supported educational systems provide learners with real-time assistance, recommendations and feedback that can improve task performance. However, as AI becomes more capable of supporting learners during task execution, the distinction between what learners can do with assistance and what they have actually learned becomes increasingly important.

In this regard, our findings resonate with current debates surrounding generative AI in education. Similar concerns have been raised regarding whether successful task completion with AI assistance necessarily reflects knowledge acquisition or independent competence. Although the present study focuses on embodied and psychomotor learning, the observed discrepancy between guided performance and autonomous execution suggests that the distinction between performance and learning may be relevant across a broader range of AI-supported learning contexts.

### 5.3 AI-Supported XR Systems as Scaffolding Tools

The results suggest that AI-supported XR environments can function effectively as scaffolding tools during the early stages of psychomotor learning. Real-time feedback, demonstrations and immersive guidance help learners perform movements correctly and reduce execution errors, as reflected by the high-performance scores observed during system-supported practice.

However, the findings also indicate that effective scaffolding does not necessarily guarantee skill consolidation. When guidance was removed, learners experienced difficulties recalling and sequencing movements independently, suggesting that the transition from assisted performance to autonomous execution had not yet been fully achieved. In this sense, the challenge is not enabling learners to perform correctly while support is available but enabling them to gradually internalize the skill and perform independently.

This interpretation is consistent with theoretical models of psychomotor learning, which describe skill acquisition as a progression from guided execution towards increasingly autonomous performance [3–5]. From this perspective, AI-supported XR systems should be designed not only to provide guidance, but also to progressively reduce support and encourage independent practice. Mechanisms such as adaptive scaffolding, fading feedback and recall-oriented activities may help facilitate this transition.

### 5.4 Limitations and Future Directions

This study has several limitations that should be considered when interpreting the findings. First, the sample size was relatively small and participation decreased across sessions, limiting the generalizability of the results. Second, although the study followed participants across multiple sessions, the analyses reported here are based on two sessions conducted over a short period of time. Consequently, the findings should be interpreted as evidence of short-term learning dynamics rather than long-term retention or skill consolidation.

In addition, the study focused on novice learners performing a specific psychomotor task within a controlled AI- and XR-supported environment. Different learner populations, domains, or feedback strategies may produce different learning trajectories. While alternative explanations related to study design or contextual factors cannot be completely excluded, the consistency between high guided performance and limited autonomous recall across participants suggests that the observed discrepancy warrants further investigation.

Future work should therefore examine longer learning periods, larger participant samples and different forms of adaptive support. Particular attention should be given to mechanisms that facilitate the transition from guided performance to autonomous learning, including adaptive scaffolding, fading feedback, spaced practice and recall-oriented activities. Further research is also needed to better understand how psychomotor, cognitive and affective dimensions interact throughout the learning process and how these dimensions can be incorporated into the evaluation of AI-supported learning environments.

These directions are particularly relevant for the design of next-generation AI-supported psychomotor learning systems that aim not only to improve performance during practice, but also to foster long-term retention, motivation and autonomous skill execution. This challenge is especially important in contexts such as active ageing, where users are expected to progressively acquire, retain and independently perform physical activities over time. In this regard, the findings reported in this paper provide part of the conceptual and methodological foundations for MITAICHI [20], an AI- and XR-supported coach for active ageing, where supporting the acquisition and retention of physical skills, together with long-term engagement, motivation and autonomy, are central design goals.

## 6 Conclusion

This paper presented an exploratory multi-session empirical study examining the relationship between guided performance and autonomous learning in an AI- and XR-supported psychomotor learning environment. By analyzing performance during system-guided practice, progression across sessions and autonomous recall without system support, we investigated whether successful execution under guidance can be considered evidence of learning.

The results revealed a consistent discrepancy between guided performance and autonomous execution. While learners achieved high performance scores when supported by the system, improvements across sessions were limited and recall without guidance remained challenging. These findings suggest that performance achieved under AI-supported guidance should not be assumed to reflect autonomous learning or retention.

Beyond the specific context of psychomotor learning, this work contributes to TEL by providing empirical evidence that performance and learning should be considered distinct constructs when evaluating AI-supported learning environments. The findings highlight the need for evaluation approaches that go beyond in-system performance metrics and explicitly consider retention, recall, transfer and autonomous execution.

**Acknowledgements.** The authors would like to thank all volunteers who participated in the study. Data collection activities were conducted at the UNED Associate Center Alzira-Valencia "Francisco Tomás y Valiente", whose support and facilities made this work possible. The insights obtained in this work informed subsequent activities within the HUMANAID project (TED2021-129485B-C41), funded by MCIN/AEI/10.13039/501100011033 and the European

Union NextGenerationEU/PRTR, particularly in the exploration of AI- and XR-supported approaches for psychomotor learning and active ageing. Generative AI tools were used to support language editing and manuscript refinement. The authors remain fully responsible for the content of this work.

## References

1. Casas-Ortiz, A., Echeverria, J., Santos, O.C.: Intelligent systems for psychomotor learning: a systematic review and two cases of study. In: Handbook of Artificial Intelligence in Education, pp. 390–421. Edward Elgar Publishing (2023). https://doi.org/10.4337/9781800375413.00030
2. Casas-Ortiz, A., Jimenez-Tellez, N., Portaz, M., Santos, O.C.: A holistic framework to create intelligent systems for psychomotor learning: a systematic review and insights from the virtual reality Kenpo learning simulator. Virtual Reality. **30**(2), 72 (2026). https://doi.org/10.1007/s10055-026-01326-1
3. Bloom, B.S.: Taxonomy of Educational Objectives: the Classification of Educational Goals. Longman (1956)
4. Magill, R., Anderson, D.: Motor Learning and Control: Concepts and Applications, 11th edn. McGraw Hill, New York, NY (2016)
5. E. J. Simpson, "The Classification of Educational Objectives, Psychomotor Domain," U.S. Department of Health, Education and Welfare, 1966. Accessed: 03 May 2023. [Online]. Available: https://eric.ed.gov/?id=ED010368
6. Anders Ericsson, K.: Deliberate practice and Acquisition of Expert Performance: a general overview. Acad. Emerg. Med. **15**(11), 988–994 (2008). https://doi.org/10.1111/j.1553-2712.2008.00227.x
7. Dreyfus, S.E., Dreyfus, H.: A five-stage model of the mental activities involved in directed skill acquisition. Distribution, 22 (1980)
8. Santos, O.C.: Training the body: the potential of AIED to support personalized motor skills learning. Int. J. Artif. Intell. Educ. **26**(2), 730–755 (2016). https://doi.org/10.1007/s40593-016-0103-2
9. Santos, O.C.: Artificial intelligence in psychomotor learning: Modeling human motion from inertial sensor data. Int. J. Artif. Intell. Tools. **28**(04), 1940006 (2019). https://doi.org/10.1142/S0218213019400062
10. Lyu, C., Deng, S.: Effectiveness of embodied learning on learning performance: a meta-analysis based on the cognitive load theory perspective. Learn. Individ. Differ. **116**, 102564 (2024). https://doi.org/10.1016/j.lindif.2024.102564
11. Hirzle, T., Müller, F., Draxler, F., Schmitz, M., Knierim, P., Hornbæk, K.: When XR and AI meet - a scoping review on extended reality and artificial intelligence. In: *Proceedings of the 2023 CHI Conference on Human Factors in Computing Systems*, in CHI '23, pp. 1–45. Association for Computing Machinery, New York, NY, USA (2023). https://doi.org/10.1145/3544548.3581072
12. Haar, S., Sundar, G., Faisal, A.A.: Embodied virtual reality for the study of real-world motor learning. PLoS One. **16**(1), e0245717 (2021). https://doi.org/10.1371/journal.pone.0245717
13. V. Bazarevsky, I. Grishchenko, K. Raveendran, T. Zhu, F. Zhang, and M. Grundmann, "BlazePose: On-device Real-time Body Pose tracking," (2020), *arXiv*: https://arxiv.org/abs/2006.10204. doi:https://doi.org/10.48550/arXiv.2006.10204.
14. Davis, F.D.: Perceived usefulness, perceived ease of use, and user acceptance of information technology. MIS Q. **13**(3), 319–340 (1989). https://doi.org/10.2307/249008

15. Hart, S.G., Staveland, L.E.: Development of NASA-TLX (task load index): results of empirical and theoretical research. In: Hancock, P.A., Meshkati, N. (eds.) Advances in Psychology in Human Mental Workload, North-Holland, vol. 52, pp. 139–183 (1988). https://doi.org/10.1016/S0166-4115(08)62386-9
16. Bjork, E.L., Bjork, R.A.: Making things hard on yourself, but in a good way: creating desirable difficulties to enhance learning. Psychology and the real world: Essays illustrating fundamental contributions to society. **2**(59–68), 56–64 (2011)
17. R. A. Schmidt and T. D. Lee, Motor Learning and Performance. From Principles to Application, 7th ed.
18. Caramiaux, B., Françoise, J., Liu, W., Sanchez, T., Bevilacqua, F.: Machine learning approaches for motor learning: a short review. Front. Comput. Sci. **2** (2020). https://doi.org/10.3389/fcomp.2020.00016
19. T.-H. Hsieh, C. M. S. Visser, E. Eisemann, and R. Marroquim, "Skill-Adaptive Ghost Instructors: Enhancing Retention and Reducing Over-Reliance in VR Piano Learning," (2026), *arXiv*: arXiv:2603.06253. doi:https://doi.org/10.48550/arXiv.2603.06253.
20. Barbarelli, A., et al.: Participatory elicitation of user model dimensions for active ageing: the EMERGE methodology. In: Proceedings of the 34th ACM Conference on User Modeling, Adaptation and Personalization, in UMAP '26, pp. 418–423. Association for Computing Machinery, New York, NY, USA (2026). https://doi.org/10.1145/3774935.3806152

# How Trust and Fear Mediate the Relationship between AI Literacy and Intelligent-TPACK: Evidence from Teacher Education

Ismail Celik(✉), Jari Laru, Kateryna Zabolotna, Iiris Jokela, and Kati Mäkitalo

University of Oulu, Oulu, Finland
ismail.celik@oulu.fi

**Abstract.** Preparing teachers for an AI-driven world requires both understanding artificial intelligence (AI) and integrating it into pedagogical practice. This study examines the co-development of AI-related knowledge skills, namely AI literacy and Intelligent-TPACK, in pre-service teachers and investigates the role of trust and fear in this process. Data were collected from 127 pre-service teachers enrolled in a semester-long technology-enhanced learning course. AI literacy, Intelligent-TPACK, trust, and fear were measured at two time points. Paired-samples t-tests and latent change score (LCS) modeling were used to analyze development and relationships among constructs. The results showed significant increases in both AI literacy and Intelligent-TPACK across the course. LCS findings revealed that changes in AI literacy were positively associated with changes in Intelligent-TPACK, indicating parallel development. Trust in AI significantly predicted gains in both constructs, whereas fear did not show significant effects. In addition, negative self-feedback effects suggested that participants with lower initial levels demonstrated greater improvement over time. These findings highlight that teacher development in AI contexts is both cognitive and affective. While AI literacy and pedagogical knowledge develop together, trust plays a key enabling role in this process. The study suggests that teacher education programs should integrate AI knowledge with pedagogical practice and foster positive orientations toward AI to support meaningful and responsible AI integration.

**Keywords:** Teacher education · AI integration · Trust · Fear

## 1 Introduction

To prepare future generations for an artificial intelligence (AI)-driven world, teachers should have AI-related knowledge and skills [2]. Such knowledge and skills include not only knowing about AI but also knowing how to teach with AI (see Fig. 1). While knowing about AI is mainly related to AI literacy [8, 17], knowing how to teach with AI requires AI-enhanced instructional knowledge, which in this study is addressed through an updated version of technological pedagogical content knowledge (TPACK) [10], namely the Intelligent-TPACK framework [2]. An important factor for the development of AI-related knowledge and skills is teachers' trust and fear towards AI [11]. However, little is known about how these concepts mediate the development of AI-related


J. Weidlich et al. (Eds.): EC-TEL 2026, LNCS 16905, pp. 127–137, 2027.
https://doi.org/10.1007/978-3-032-37979-5_9

knowledge and skills in teacher education. To address this gap, the present study investigates the co-development of AI literacy and Intelligent-TPACK in pre-service teachers within a semester-long course on technology-enhanced learning. The focus is on how variation in trust and fear during the course is linked to development in AI literacy and Intelligent-TPACK, and whether gains in AI literacy run parallel with gains in Intelligent-TPACK.

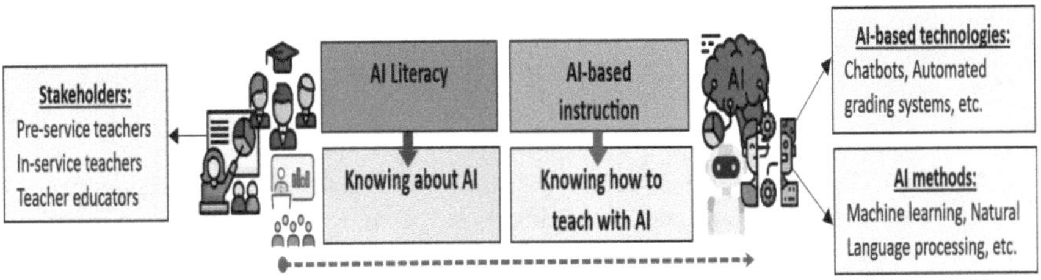


**Fig. 1.** AI-related knowledge and skills

## 1.1 Teachers' Knowledge for AI-Based Instruction

Preparing learners for an AI-driven world requires teachers to develop both AI literacy and AI-informed pedagogical knowledge. AI literacy refers to understanding how AI systems work, how to use them, and how to evaluate their outputs critically and ethically [8, 17]. This includes awareness of limitations such as bias, hallucination, and overconfidence in AI-generated responses. Such understanding is necessary, but not sufficient for teaching.

Teaching with AI requires integrating AI into instruction, which is better captured by knowledge frameworks such as TPACK [7, 13]. In this study, this integration is addressed through Intelligent-TPACK, which extends TPACK by explicitly incorporating AI-specific knowledge and ethical considerations [2] (see Fig. 2).

Intelligent-TK (Technological Knowledge) refers to understanding how AI systems function, including their capabilities, limitations, and underlying mechanisms. This includes recognizing issues such as bias, hallucination, and overconfidence in AI outputs, as well as knowing how to effectively operate AI tools. Intelligent-TPK (Technological Pedagogical Knowledge) focuses on how AI can support teaching and learning processes. It includes using AI for feedback, scaffolding, differentiation, and monitoring student learning, while also managing risks such as overreliance and reduced cognitive effort. Intelligent-TCK (Technological Content Knowledge) refers to understanding how AI interacts with specific subject domains. This includes evaluating whether AI-generated content is accurate, appropriate, and aligned with disciplinary goals, and identifying potential oversimplifications or misconceptions. Intelligent-TPACK (integrated knowledge) represents the ability to combine AI knowledge, pedagogy, and content in a coherent way. It involves designing learning activities, assessments, and instructional strategies where AI is used meaningfully and responsibly to support learning outcomes. In addition, ethical knowledge is embedded across all domains and includes considerations such as transparency, fairness, accountability, and responsible use of AI in educational contexts.

Prior research shows that technological knowledge and pedagogical knowledge tend to co-develop rather than evolve independently [12]. In AI contexts, this relationship becomes even more critical. Teachers who understand AI are better able to design tasks, guide students, and evaluate AI-supported learning. At the same time, pedagogical use of AI deepens teachers' understanding of AI itself. Therefore, AI literacy and Intelligent-TPACK should be seen as interconnected and mutually reinforcing constructs in teacher education.

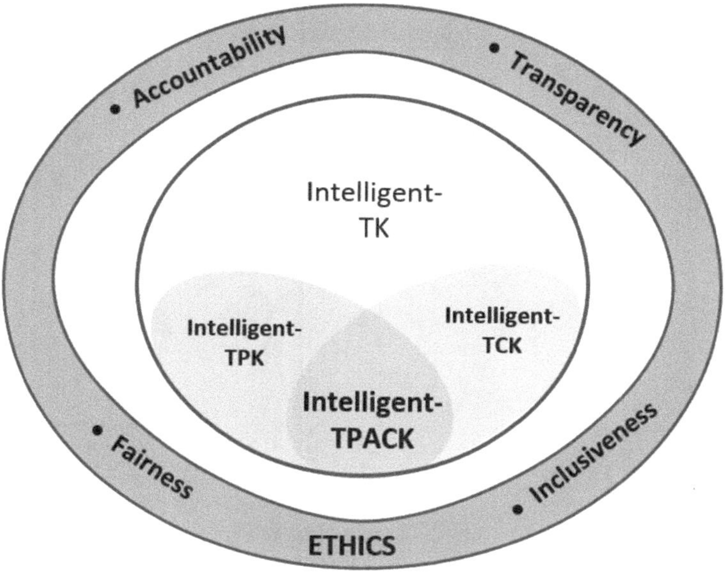


**Fig. 2.** Intelligent-TPACK framework (Celik, 2023)

## 1.2 Teachers' Trust and Fear in AI-Based Technologies

In addition to knowledge, teachers' engagement with AI is shaped by affective factors, particularly trust and fear. Trust in AI refers to the belief that AI systems are reliable, useful, and appropriate for educational purposes [11]. When teachers trust AI, they are more willing to explore its capabilities, integrate it into instruction, and rely on it for pedagogical tasks. Trust has been shown to be a key factor in technology adoption and meaningful use [1, 16].

In contrast, fear reflects anxiety, uncertainty, and perceived risks associated with AI. This may include concerns about errors, ethical issues, loss of control, or negative impacts on learning [15]. Fear can reduce willingness to engage with AI and may lead to avoidance behaviors. However, its role is not always straightforward. Some studies suggest that fear does not necessarily prevent learning, especially when structured support and guidance are provided [18].

Importantly, trust and fear are not simply opposite ends of a single continuum. They can coexist and influence behaviour in different ways. Trust tends to facilitate engagement and experimentation, while fear may create hesitation but not fully block participation, particularly in guided learning environments. Therefore, understanding how trust and fear relate to the development of AI literacy and Intelligent-TPACK is essential for explaining variation in teacher learning with AI.

**The aim of the study.** This study aims to examine the co-development of AI literacy and Intelligent-TPACK in pre-service teachers and to investigate how trust and fear toward AI relate to these developmental processes. For this aim, we developed the following hypothesis (Fig. 3).

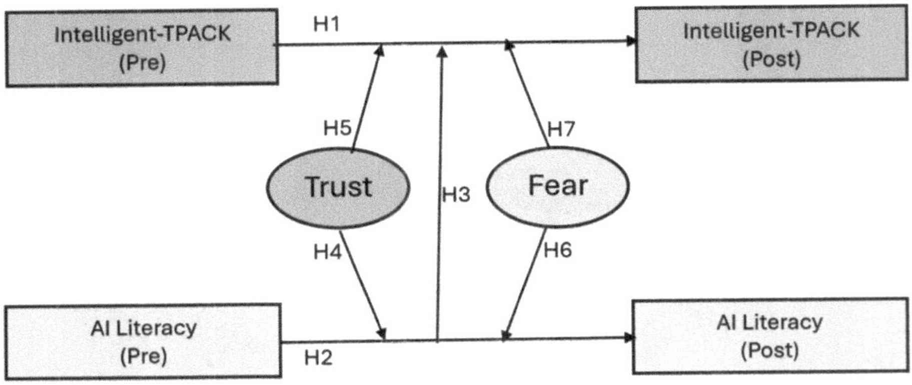


**Fig. 3.** Conceptual model illustrating the longitudinal relationships between AI Literacy and Intelligent-TPACK, and the effects of trust and fear on their development. T1 = pre-test; T2 = post-test. Solid arrows indicate hypothesized paths (H1–H7)

Both AI literacy and Intelligent-TPACK represent relatively stable yet developable forms of teacher competence, and prior research on teacher knowledge suggests that earlier levels of professional knowledge tend to predict later performance while still allowing for growth over time [2, 7, 12]. Accordingly, pre-test levels of Intelligent-TPACK and AI literacy are expected to positively predict their post-test levels (H1–H2). AI literacy refers to teachers' capacity to understand, evaluate, and use AI systems critically and ethically, whereas Intelligent-TPACK captures the integration of AI within pedagogical and content knowledge domains [2, 17]. Given that effective pedagogical integration of AI requires a sufficient level of AI-related understanding, these constructs are theoretically interdependent, and their development is expected to co-occur over time (H3). Prior research in technology integration consistently shows that technological knowledge and pedagogical application develop in tandem rather than independently [7, 12].

In addition to cognitive and knowledge-based factors, affective orientations toward technology play a critical role in shaping engagement and learning processes. Trust in AI has been shown to increase users' willingness to rely on, experiment with, and engage with AI systems, thereby facilitating both learning and application [1, 11]. Therefore, higher levels of trust are expected to positively predict changes in both AI literacy and Intelligent-TPACK (H4–H5). In contrast, fear of AI reflects anxiety and perceived risk, which can reduce openness to engagement and hinder learning processes [15, 18]. As a result, higher levels of fear are expected to negatively predict changes in AI literacy and Intelligent-TPACK (H6–H7).

**H1.** Pre-test Intelligent-TPACK positively predicts post-test Intelligent-TPACK.

**H2.** Pre-test AI literacy positively predicts post-test AI literacy.

**H3.** Changes in AI literacy are positively associated with changes in Intelligent-TPACK.

**H4.** Trust in AI positively predicts changes in AI literacy.

**H5.** Trust in AI positively predicts changes in Intelligent-TPACK.

**H6.** Fear of AI negatively predicts changes in AI literacy.

**H7.** Fear of AI negatively predicts changes in Intelligent-TPACK.

## 2 Method

### 2.1 Participants and Context

Participants were 127 pre-service classroom teachers enrolled in the early phase of a five-year teacher education programme in Finland. Permission for research participation was obtained from 84% of all course participants ($n = 107$). The study adhered to the Generation AI project's data management plan and ethical guidelines approved by the relevant ethics committee, which covered data collection practices at the University of Oulu.The study took place at the University of Oulu during a semester-long course (Autumn 2023) on digital pedagogy and technology-enhanced learning. The course included AI-focused workshops and practice-based learning tasks through which participants examined educational uses of AI and reflected on its pedagogical value. The AI-focused component of the course consisted of hands-on workshops using the GenAI Teachable Machine. Participants worked in small groups to design and develop simple machine-learning applications following a data-driven design process. The activities included: (1) an introduction to key AI and machine learning concepts (e.g., classifiers, classes, training data, model training, testing, and prediction); (2) collaborative planning of an AI application using a structured design template; (3) collection and curation of training data; (4) training and testing machine-learning models; (5) analysing model performance and refining applications based on test results; and (6) guided discussions on AI-related ethical issues, including bias, transparency, and responsible use of AI in education. Through these activities, participants explored both the technical foundations of AI and its pedagogical applications in teaching and learning.

In line with recent work in the same teacher education context, the course aimed to provide structured opportunities for pre-service teachers to engage with AI-related concepts and tools as part of their professional preparation. This course context was appropriate for the present study because it enabled the examination of changes in participants' AI literacy, trust, fear, and Intelligent-TPACK across a sustained instructional period rather than a single short intervention.

## 2.2 Data Collection Tools

Data was collected using validated self-report scales assessing AI literacy, AI trust, AI fear, and Intelligent-TPACK. All instruments have been previously validated in educational and AI contexts. AI literacy was measured using the scale developed by Wang et al. [17], which consists of 12 items across four dimensions: awareness, usage, evaluation, and ethics. In the present study, the scale demonstrated satisfactory internal consistency across all subdimensions. Internal consistency was found to be between .73 and .78.

AI trust was assessed using the instrument developed by Nazaretsky et al. [11], which measures teachers' trust in AI-based educational technologies. The construct reflects dimensions such as perceived reliability, transparency, and confidence in AI outputs. In the present study, the scale showed good internal consistency ($\alpha = .88$), consistent with prior validation studies. AI fear was measured using the short attitude toward AI scale developed by Sindermann et al. [15], focusing on the fear dimension, which captures anxiety and concerns about AI technologies. In the present study, the scale demonstrated acceptable internal consistency ($\alpha = .76$), aligning with prior research using this instrument.

Intelligent-TPACK was measured using the scale developed by Celik [2], consisting of 29 items across five domains: Intelligent-TK, Intelligent-TPK, Intelligent-TCK, Intelligent-TPACK, and ethics. The scale demonstrated strong internal consistency across all subdimensions (Cronbach's $\alpha$ ranging from .85 to .89), exceeding recommended thresholds for reliability. All instruments were administered using a Likert-type scale. Internal reliability was assessed using Cronbach's alpha coefficients, and longitudinal measurement invariance was tested to ensure comparability between pre- and post-test measurements.

## 2.3 Data Analysis

All measures were first examined for internal reliability using Cronbach's alpha coefficients. To ensure comparability of constructs across time, longitudinal measurement invariance was tested prior to the main analysis. The analysis proceeded in two steps. First, paired-samples t-tests were conducted to examine overall pre–post differences in AI literacy and Intelligent-TPACK. In addition, latent change score (LCS) models were employed to capture intra-individual changes between pre- and post-test measurements. LCS modeling allows change to be represented as a latent construct, providing a more precise estimation of development over time compared to observed difference scores [5, 9].

Second, structural equation modelling (SEM) was used to examine the relationships between changes in key constructs. Specifically, the model tested whether changes in AI trust and AI fear predicted changes in Intelligent-TPACK, while accounting for initial levels. In line with the proposed model, changes in AI literacy were also examined in relation to changes in Intelligent-TPACK, reflecting parallel development processes.

SEM is particularly suitable for testing complex relationships among latent variables and change processes within a unified analytical framework [6, 14]. Model estimation was conducted using AMOS 26.0 and model fit was evaluated using standard fit indices, including the Comparative Fit Index (CFI), Tucker–Lewis Index (TLI), Root Mean Square Error of Approximation (RMSEA), and Standardized Root Mean Square Residual (SRMR). Acceptable model fit was determined based on established thresholds (e.g., CFI and TLI $\geq .90$, RMSEA $\leq .08$, SRMR $\leq .08$) [4].

## 3 Results

Table 1 presents the descriptive statistics and paired-samples t-test results for AI literacy and Intelligent-TPACK across the two measurement points. Overall, participants demonstrated higher post-test scores compared to pre-test scores across all measured constructs. Paired-samples t-tests indicated a significant increase in AI literacy from pre-test to post-test. At the subdimension level, all components of AI literacy (awareness, usage, evaluation, and ethics) showed statistically significant improvements.

The largest gains were observed in usage and evaluation, whereas the increase in the ethics dimension was comparatively smaller, though still significant. Similarly, Intelligent-TPACK showed a significant increase from pre-test to post-test. All subdimensions (Intelligent-TK, Intelligent-TPK, Intelligent-TCK, Intelligent-TPACK, and ethics) demonstrated statistically significant improvements. The largest gains were observed in the Intelligent-TPK dimension, followed by Intelligent-TPACK, indicating strong development in participants' ability to integrate AI into pedagogical practice. In general, the effect sizes ranged from small to large, with generally stronger effects observed for Intelligent-TPACK compared to AI literacy. These findings suggest that instructional intervention contributed not only to participants' understanding of AI, but also to their ability to apply this knowledge in pedagogically meaningful ways.

**Table 1.** Descriptive statistics and paired-samples t-test

| Variable | T1_Pre (M ± SD) | T2_Post (M ± SD) | t | d |
|---|---|---|---|---|
| Awareness | 3.42 ± 0.61 | 3.89 ± 0.58 | $8.12^{***}$ | 0.72 |
| Usage | 3.28 ± 0.65 | 3.94 ± 0.60 | $9.45^{***}$ | 0.85 |
| Evaluation | 3.35 ± 0.63 | 3.92 ± 0.59 | $8.97^{***}$ | 0.80 |
| Ethics (AI lit) | 3.51 ± 0.60 | 3.86 ± 0.57 | $6.02^{***}$ | 0.54 |
| Intelligent-TK | 3.30 ± 0.67 | 3.88 ± 0.62 | $8.41^{***}$ | 0.75 |
| Intelligent-TCK | 3.25 ± 0.66 | 3.79 ± 0.61 | $7.88^{***}$ | 0.71 |
| Intelligent-TPK | 3.10 ± 0.70 | 3.96 ± 0.63 | $10.52^{***}$ | 0.94 |
| Intelligent-TPACK | 3.05 ± 0.72 | 3.93 ± 0.65 | $10.88^{***}$ | 0.97 |
| Ethics (TPACK) | 3.40 ± 0.62 | 3.82 ± 0.59 | $6.55^{***}$ | 0.58 |

The model demonstrated acceptable fit to the data ($\chi^2/df = 1.87$, CFI = .95, TLI = .94, RMSEA = .05, SRMR = .04). Initial levels of AI literacy positively predicted post-test AI literacy ($\beta = .62$, $p < .001$), and initial Intelligent-TPACK positively predicted post-test Intelligent-TPACK ($\beta = .68$, $p < .001$), supporting H1 and H2 and indicating stability of both constructs over time. In addition, self-feedback effects were observed, such that lower initial levels of AI literacy ($\beta = -.31$, $p < .01$) and Intelligent-TPACK ($\beta = -.27$, $p < .01$) were associated with greater gains over time, suggesting compensatory growth patterns.

Changes in AI literacy were positively associated with changes in Intelligent-TPACK ($r = .44$, $p < .001$), supporting H3 and indicating parallel development between AI-related knowledge and pedagogical integration. Participants who demonstrated greater improvements in AI literacy also tended to show greater increases in Intelligent-TPACK over time. Furthermore, trust in AI significantly and positively predicted changes in both AI literacy ($\gamma = .29, p < .01$) and Intelligent-TPACK ($\gamma = .34, p < .001$), supporting H4 and H5. This suggests that trust functions as a facilitating condition that enables both cognitive engagement with AI and its pedagogical application.

In contrast, fear of AI did not significantly predict changes in either AI literacy ($\gamma = -.08, p = .18$) or Intelligent-TPACK ($\gamma = -.05, p = .27$), and thus H6 and H7 were not supported. These findings indicate that while negative affective responses toward AI may be present, they do not necessarily inhibit learning and knowledge development within a structured educational context. Finally, the latent change scores of AI literacy and Intelligent-TPACK were positively correlated, suggesting that gains in these constructions co-occurred over time and reinforcing the view that their development is interconnected.

## 4 Discussion and Implications

This study examined how AI literacy and Intelligent-TPACK develop over time and how trust and fear shape this process. The findings show a clear pattern. AI literacy and Intelligent-TPACK increased significantly during the course. More importantly, their development was interconnected. This aligns with prior work showing that technology-related knowledge and pedagogical integration tend to co-develop in teacher education [7, 12].

Although initial levels of AI literacy and Intelligent-TPACK significantly predicted later levels, both constructs increased significantly over time, indicating continuity alongside meaningful growth. The negative self-feedback effects indicate that participants with lower initial levels improved more. This suggests a compensatory pattern. The course was especially beneficial for those who started with weaker knowledge. Similar patterns have been observed in teacher learning, where structured and scaffolded environments support greater gains among less experienced participants [3]. This is an important educational outcome.

Second, the results support a strong link between AI literacy and Intelligent-TPACK. Changes in AI literacy were positively associated with changes in Intelligent-TPACK. This means that understanding AI and applying it pedagogically develop together. AI knowledge alone is not sufficient. It becomes meaningful when it is translated into teaching practice. This is consistent with research showing that technological knowledge must be integrated with pedagogy to influence teaching effectively [2, 7].

Third, trust emerged as a key enabling factor. Trust positively predicted changes in both AI literacy and Intelligent-TPACK. Participants who trusted AI more showed stronger development. Trust supports engagement, exploration, and experimentation. Teachers are more likely to learn and apply AI when they feel confident using it. This is in line with studies showing that trust in AI increases adoption, perceived usefulness, and willingness to rely on AI systems [1, 11].

In contrast, fear did not significantly predict development. Fear was present but did not block learning. This is an important finding. It suggests that structured learning environments can reduce the negative impact of fear. When guidance and support are provided, teachers can still develop even if they feel uncertain about AI. Previous research shows that anxiety toward technology may create hesitation, but it does not necessarily prevent learning when adequate support is provided [15, 18].

In sum, the findings suggest that teacher development in AI contexts is not only cognitive but also affective. However, positive affect (trust) appears to matter more than negative affect (fear). This shifts the focus from reducing fear to building trust. This perspective is supported by research showing that positive beliefs and perceived usefulness are stronger drivers of technology adoption than perceived risks alone [1].

This study has several limitations. First, although data were collected longitudinally, the design does not permit strong causal inferences regarding the relationships among AI literacy, Intelligent-TPACK, trust, and fear. Second, the sample consisted of pre-service teachers from a single teacher education programme in Finland, which may limit the generalizability of the findings to other educational and cultural contexts. Third, the study relied on self-report measures and focused on a specific AI learning experience, which may not fully capture actual classroom practices or the broader range of AI technologies used in education. Future research should examine these relationships across diverse contexts, include behavioural measures of AI integration, and explore longer-term developmental trajectories.

## 4.1 Implications

These findings have practical implications for teacher education. First, AI training should not focus only on technical skills. It should also support pedagogical integration. Activities that connect AI use with teaching practice are essential. Prior work highlights that integrated knowledge frameworks such as TPACK are critical for meaningful technology use in education [7].

Second, building trust should be a priority. This can be achieved through guided practice, safe experimentation, and clear examples of AI use in teaching. When teachers experience AI as useful and manageable, their learning improves. Research consistently shows that perceived usefulness and confidence are key drivers of technology adoption [1, 11].

Third, training programs should support teachers with lower initial knowledge. Since they benefit the most, differentiated support can increase overall effectiveness. Structured and scaffolded learning environments are particularly effective for supporting such learners [3].

Finally, AI literacy and Intelligent-TPACK should be developed together. Treating them as separate goals may limit impact. Integrated design is more effective. This aligns with the broader literature emphasizing that technological knowledge and pedagogical integration are mutually reinforcing [12].

### 4.2 Conclusion

This study shows that AI-related teacher development is a dynamic and interconnected process. Growth in AI literacy and pedagogical knowledge occurs together and is supported by trust. Teacher education should therefore focus on both knowledge and affect to support meaningful AI integration. The findings contribute to the literature in several ways. First, the study moves beyond static perspectives by examining change over time. It shows that teacher development is not only about reaching a level, but about how different competencies evolve together. Second, it demonstrates that AI literacy and Intelligent-TPACK are tightly linked. Understanding AI is important, but it becomes valuable only when it is translated into pedagogical use. Third, the study highlights the role of affective factors, especially trust. Trust acts as an enabling condition that supports both learning and application, whereas fear does not appear to significantly constrain development in structured settings.

These results have implications for how AI should be integrated into teacher education. Programs should not treat AI literacy as a separate technical skill. Instead, they should design learning experiences where AI is used in authentic teaching tasks. At the same time, attention should be given to building confidence and trust. When teachers feel capable and supported, they are more likely to engage with AI and apply it meaningfully. Despite its contributions, this study has some limitations. The data were collected within a single course context and with pre-service teachers. This may limit generalizability to other educational levels or in-service teachers. In addition, the study relied on self-report measures, which may not fully capture actual classroom practices. The time span was also relatively short, focusing on one instructional period. Future research should extend this work in several directions. Longitudinal studies over longer periods are needed to examine sustained development. Research with in-service teachers would provide insight into how these processes unfold in real classroom settings. It would also be valuable to include behavioral or performance-based measures of AI integration. Finally, future studies could explore more complex models, including how contextual factors such as school culture or policy shape the relationship between AI literacy, trust, and pedagogical practice. In conclusion, effective AI integration in education requires more than knowledge. It requires the alignment of understanding, pedagogy, and affect. Supporting this alignment should be a central goal of teacher education in the age of AI.

## References

1. Araujo, T., Helberger, N., Kruikemeier, S., de Vreese, C.H.: In AI we trust? Perceptions about automated decision-making by artificial intelligence. AI Soc. **35**, 611–623 (2020)
2. Celik, I.: Towards Intelligent-TPACK: an Empirical Study on Teachers' Professional Knowledge to Ethically Integrate Artificial Intelligence-Based Tools into Education. Comput. Hum, Behav (2023)

3. Dogan, S., Nalbantoglu, U.Y., Celik, I., Agacli Dogan, N.: Artificial intelligence professional development: a systematic review of TPACK, designs, and effects for teacher learning. Prof. Dev. Educ. **51**(3), 519–546 (2025)
4. Hu, L., Bentler, P.M.: Cutoff criteria for fit indexes in covariance structure analysis: conventional criteria versus new alternatives. Struct. Equ. Model. **6**(1), 1–55 (1999)
5. Kievit, R.A., Brandmaier, A.M., Ziegler, G., van Harmelen, A.L., de Mooij, S.M., Moutoussis, M.: NSPN consortium: developmental cognitive neuroscience using latent change score models: a tutorial and applications. Dev. Cogn. Neurosci. **33**, 99–117 (2018)
6. Kline, R.B.: Principles and Practice of Structural Equation Modeling, 4th edn. Guilford Press, New York (2016)
7. Koehler, M.J., Mishra, P.: What is technological pedagogical content knowledge (TPACK)? Contemp. Issues Technol. Teach. Educ. **9**(1), 60–70 (2009)
8. Long, D., Magerko, B.: What is AI literacy? Competencies and design considerations. In: Proc. CHI Conf. Hum. Factors Comput. Syst, pp. 1–16 (2020)
9. McArdle, J.J.: Latent variable modeling of differences and changes with longitudinal data. Annu. Rev. Psychol. **60**, 577–605 (2009)
10. Mishra, P., Koehler, M.J.: Technological pedagogical content knowledge: a framework for teacher knowledge. Teach. Coll. Rec. **108**(6), 1017–1054 (2006)
11. Nazaretsky, T., Ariely, M., Cukurova, M., Alexandron, G.: Teachers' trust in AI-powered educational technology and a professional development program to improve it. Br. J. Educ. Technol. **53**(4), 914–931 (2022)
12. Schmid, R., Brianza, E., Petko, D.: Developing a short assessment instrument for technological pedagogical content knowledge (TPACK). Comput. Educ. **157**, 103967 (2020)
13. Schmidt, D.A., Baran, E., Thompson, A.D., Mishra, P., Koehler, M.J., Shin, T.S.: Technological pedagogical content knowledge (TPACK): the development and validation of an assessment instrument for preservice teachers. J. Res. Technol. Educ. **42**(2), 123–149 (2009)
14. Schumacker, R.E., Lomax, R.G.: A Beginner's Guide to Structural Equation Modeling, 4th edn. Routledge, New York (2016)
15. Sindermann, C., et al.: Assessing attitudes toward artificial intelligence: a short measure in German, Chinese, and English. KI - Künstl. Intell. **35**(1), 109–118 (2021)
16. Viberg, O., et al.: What explains teachers' trust in AI in education across six countries? Int. J. Artif. Intell. Educ. **35**(3), 1288–1316 (2025)
17. Wang, B., Rau, P.L.P., Yuan, T.: Measuring user competence in using artificial intelligence: validity and reliability of artificial intelligence literacy scale. Behav. Inf. Technol. **42**(9), 1324–1337 (2023)
18. Zhai, X., et al.: A review of artificial intelligence in education from 2010 to 2020. Complexity. **2021**, 8812542 (2021)

# Self-efficacy and Favorability Shape Learning from Tutoring Systems and Paper Practice

Xinfei Cen[1(✉)], Vincent Aleven[1], Kenneth R. Koedinger[1], Conrad Borchers[2], and Paulo F. Carvalho[1]

[1] Carnegie Mellon University, Pittsburgh, PA, USA
{xinfeic,aleven,pcarvalh}@cs.cmu.edu, koedinger@cmu.edu
[2] Vanderbilt University, Nashville, TN, USA
c.borchers@vanderbilt.edu

**Abstract.** Motivational factors such as self-efficacy and how favorably students feel toward practice play a crucial role in shaping learning, particularly in technology-supported environments. Yet, educational interventions often overlook how these factors interact with practice format. This paper examines the influence of self-efficacy and favorability on learning outcomes across two common practice formats: paper-based and system-based tutoring practice. Using a counterbalanced within-subject design with matched problem sets, we isolate the effect of practice format while modeling motivational differences. Results indicate that students with lower baseline self-efficacy achieved greater learning gains regardless of practice format. Among students with lower baseline self-efficacy, greater favorability toward the tutor was associated with greater learning gains during tutor practice, whereas the pattern differed in paper-based practice. Intelligent Tutoring System (ITS)-based practice did not significantly improve post-training self-efficacy relative to paper-based methods. These findings underscore the potential value of tailoring practice format to students' motivational profiles, as the benefits of tutor- and paper-based practice varied with baseline self-efficacy and favorability. They lay the groundwork for future research on how instructional formats can be aligned more effectively with learners' motivational needs.

**Keywords:** Intelligent tutoring systems · Self-efficacy · Motivation · Technology-enhanced learning · K-12 education

## 1 Introduction

Technology-enhanced learning (TEL) systems that support learning by problem solving are widely used in domains such as mathematics and science. These systems can improve learning outcomes through features such as scaffolded support, step-level feedback, and individualized practice [15,23]. Beyond learning performance, however, TEL systems may also shape learners' motivational experiences


J. Weidlich et al. (Eds.): EC-TEL 2026, LNCS 16905, pp. 138–148, 2027.
https://doi.org/10.1007/978-3-032-37979-5_10

during practice. Likewise, learners' motivational profiles, including self-efficacy and favorability toward different instructional formats, may influence how they respond to those formats and whether they benefit differently from one format than another. Prior work has shown that motivational factors such as self-efficacy play an important role in students' engagement and learning [4], and that learners' confidence and comfort with digital tools can support motivation and engagement in technology-based learning [19]. However, it remains less clear how motivational factors interact with instructional format in content-matched tutor- and paper-based practice, and whether these formats differentially influence students' self-efficacy. Understanding these relationships is therefore important for designing and using TEL systems in ways that better support diverse learners. In this paper, we examine both how learners' motivational profiles shape learning outcomes in tutor- and paper-based practice and whether these instructional formats, in turn, differentially influence students' self-efficacy.

## 2 Related Work

Self-efficacy, students' belief in their ability to succeed on a task, is a well-established predictor of academic outcomes, especially in self-directed learning contexts where students must actively manage their own learning. High self-efficacy supports engagement, persistence, and resilience in the face of setbacks [4,10,25]. Research has shown that self-efficacy can be shaped over time by multiple factors, such as instruction, feedback, or students' perceived success [22]. Favorability, or students' attitudes or preferences toward instruction, also plays an important motivational role. Research shows that when students are more favorable toward learning materials and find them personally meaningful or interesting, they are more likely to engage deeply and persist, which can energize learning [13]. Both self-efficacy and favorability are critical in technology-supported learning environments. Learners' confidence and comfort with digital tools can positively shape their motivation and engagement in technology-based learning, which in turn supports learning outcomes [19].

Intelligent Tutoring Systems (ITSs) provide scaffolded support, immediate feedback, and individualized pacing–features that have consistently improved learning outcomes in domains such as math and science [2,14,15,23]. ITSs can also support metacognition through self-explanation, adaptive strategies to reduce gaming behaviors, and enhanced help-seeking skills [1,3]. These supports may also be relevant to learners' self-efficacy, as perceived success and performance feedback offered by ITSs can contribute to mastery experiences and social persuasion, two well-established sources of self-efficacy beliefs [4,22]. In contrast, paper-based practice relies more heavily on students' independent effort, placing greater demands on metacognitive and self-regulatory skills. Although ITSs have often been studied in relation to conventional classroom instruction, where paper-based practice remains widely used [12], these comparisons are often confounded by differences in curriculum, pedagogy, or task type [23].

Despite decades of ITS research, three major gaps remain. First, as mentioned before, with the exception of a small number of content-matched studies [18], most studies do not control for instructional content when comparing ITS and paper-based formats, making it difficult to isolate the effect of the practice condition itself. Second, while self-efficacy and favorability are known to influence engagement and academic performance [11,13,21], few studies have systematically examined how these motivational factors interact with instructional format to shape learning outcomes. Third, given their scaffolded support and immediate feedback, ITSs may plausibly foster self-efficacy through perceived success and mastery experiences [4,23]. Some recent work has observed self-efficacy gains after tutoring-system practice [9]. However, relatively few studies have directly tested this claim, and the available evidence is limited [6,17].

Prior work directly compared the benefits of paper-based practice and tutor-based practice, a form of ITS, for learning outcomes [7,8]. However, questions remain regarding the role of students' self-efficacy and preferences in such comparisons. Tutor-based practice provides scaffolded questions and timely feedback that may especially benefit students with high baseline self-efficacy and further promote their self-efficacy, whereas paper-based practice relies more on learner autonomy. In the present study, we analyze questionnaire data collected in prior work [8] to investigate two research questions:

1. RQ1: Do baseline self-efficacy and favorability influence learning outcomes in tutor- versus paper-based practice?
2. RQ2: Do ITSs promote self-efficacy compared to paper-based practice?

As emphasized by recent work, it is critical to move beyond general instructional claims [24], examine how learner-specific motivational factors interact with different practice formats, and work toward identifying best practices that support all learners more effectively.

## 3 Methods

### 3.1 Sample and Experimental Design

The dataset includes 97 students from seven 9th-grade mathematics classes at a suburban middle school in the northeastern United States who completed pretest and posttest assessments on linear algebra-related topics and were instructed by three teachers. The original classroom study was conducted under an approved IRB protocol, and all data analyzed here were de-identified. There were two practice units in total (see Fig. 1): graph interpretation, practiced on Day 2, and graph construction, practiced on Day 4, with each student completing two approximately 40-minute practice sessions. These units focused, respectively, on interpreting linear graphs (e.g., reading values and relationships from graphs) and constructing linear graphs (e.g., plotting points, inferring values, and deriving linear equations). All students experienced both practice conditions (i.e., paper-based and tutor-based), but the order varied: each student received one unit using the tutor-based method and the other using the paper-based method. While the topic order was fixed, practice formats were counterbalanced across students, such that each format appeared in both the first and second practice positions. Although we cannot rule out the possibility of carryover effects, by which practice on the first topic may have improved performance on the second, this design reduced the likelihood that these carryover effects differed between the practice conditions. As illustrated in Fig. 2, students in the tutor-based condition solved problems using an intelligent tutoring system that provided step-by-step guidance, including correctness feedback and hints. The paper-based problems served as a business-as-usual control but were designed to closely mirror the structure and problem-solving steps of the tutor-based problems, while omitting scaffolded support such as step-level feedback and hints. More details about the instructional materials, including examples of the paper-based practice materials, and study procedures can be found in [8]. Additionally, all students completed a pretest at the start of the study and a posttest at the end of each practice condition. The current work builds on prior analyses of the same data that focused only on learning outcomes [8] by examining motivational measures.

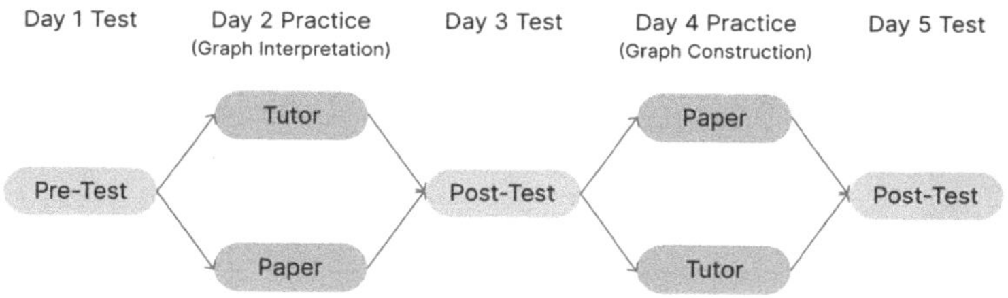


**Fig. 1.** Within-subjects crossover experiment design.

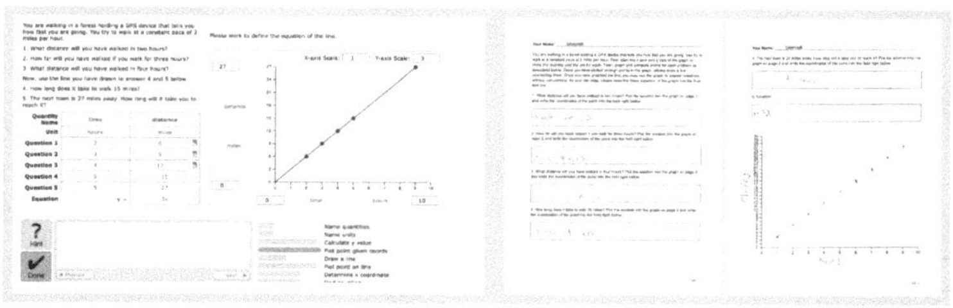

**Fig. 2.** Tutor-based interface (left) and paper-based materials (right) with example student responses from a graph construction problem.

## 3.2 Motivational Survey Instruments

Along with the training and testing data, we collected students' self-efficacy responses before the pretest (baseline) and after the second posttest. The same questionnaires were used at both pretest and posttest. The self-efficacy questionnaire included six questions constructed following Bandura's guidelines for measuring self-efficacy [5]. All were 0–100 Likert-scale questions ranging from "Cannot do at all" to "Highly certain I can do". The first three questions were designed to assess students' self-efficacy in skills related to the first training unit, focusing on students' ability to interpret and compare graph elements (e.g., "Compare the slope and intercept of a graph"). The other three questions evaluated students' confidence in skills related to the second training unit, including plotting points, labeling axes, and generalizing concepts to real-world situations (e.g., "Decide what numbers to place along each axis"). Additionally, the favorability questions assessed students' attitudes toward the two instructional methods (i.e., paper-based and tutor-based practice; e.g., "I like doing math problems with the computer tutor") using a Likert scale (1: strongly agree - 5: strongly disagree), with one additional free-response question for further feedback.[1]

All data were collected using paper-based surveys, and a significant proportion of students left at least one question blank. We conducted factor analysis and reliability testing to identify meaningful constructs. Specifically, two self-efficacy constructs (graph interpretation and graph construction) and two favorability constructs (tutor-based and paper-based) were extracted. Construct scores were computed as the average of the items associated with each construct, using available responses when individual items were missing. Students were included in the final analyses if construct scores could be computed and complete performance data were available for both practice conditions, resulting in a final analytic sample of 54 students. All constructs demonstrated adequate internal consistency (Cronbach's $\alpha$): graph interpretation ($\alpha_{\text{pre}} = .83$, $\alpha_{\text{post}} = .83$), graph construction ($\alpha_{\text{pre}} = .81$, $\alpha_{\text{post}} = .73$), tutor-based favorability ($\alpha = .72$), and paper-based favorability ($\alpha = .71$).

### 3.3 Modeling

To investigate **RQ1**–whether baseline self-efficacy and favorability influence learning outcomes in tutor- versus paper-based practice–we conducted a linear mixed-effects analysis. Our model included students' learning gain (pretest-to-posttest performance) as the dependent variable, with practice condition (tutor-based vs. paper-based training), baseline self-efficacy, and favorability toward the respective practice condition as fixed effects. Additionally, we included a three-way interaction among condition, baseline self-efficacy, and favorability to examine their combined influence on student learning outcomes. All changes in performance scores, baseline self-efficacy, post-training self-efficacy, and favorability were normalized to estimate effect sizes, and student ID was modeled as a random effect to account for repeated tests. This approach allowed us to assess how baseline self-efficacy, practice condition, and favorability interact to shape students' learning outcomes. To examine **RQ2**–whether ITSs promote

[1] The full questionnaires are available on OSF: https://osf.io/r5e9z/.

self-efficacy compared to paper-based practice–we used the same linear mixed-effects model as before, replacing learning gain with post-training self-efficacy as the dependent variable.

# 4 Results

## 4.1 RQ1: How Baseline Self-efficacy and Favorability Shape Learning

We first examined whether baseline self-efficacy and favorability influenced learning gains across training conditions (tutor-based vs. paper-based) using a linear mixed-effects model (see Table 1).

**Table 1.** Fixed-effects model results for RQ1.

| Effect | Estimate | Std. Error | df | $t$ value | $p$ |
|---|---|---|---|---|---|
| Intercept | 0.085 | 0.117 | 64.179 | 0.728 | 0.469 |
| Practice Format (Paper vs. Tutor) | 0.532 | 0.223 | 62.303 | 2.383 | 0.020 |
| Baseline Self-Efficacy | -0.283 | 0.132 | 98.403 | -2.136 | 0.035 |
| Favorability | 0.078 | 0.114 | 91.120 | 0.686 | 0.494 |
| Practice Format × Baseline Self-Efficacy | -0.110 | 0.266 | 100.000 | -0.412 | 0.681 |
| Practice Format × Favorability | 0.174 | 0.232 | 96.796 | 0.750 | 0.455 |
| Baseline Self-Efficacy × Favorability | -0.044 | 0.122 | 99.435 | -0.357 | 0.722 |
| Practice Format × Baseline Self-Efficacy × Favorability | -0.631 | 0.245 | 99.840 | -2.581 | 0.011 |

The main effect of the practice condition (tutor vs. paper) on learning gain was statistically significant, $t(62.30) = 2.38, p = .020$, indicating that students in the tutor-based condition showed greater learning gains than those in the paper-based condition. Learning gain was also significantly associated with students' baseline self-efficacy, $t(98.40) = -2.14, p = .035$, showing that students with lower initial self-efficacy showed greater improvement. Favorability was not a significant predictor of learning gain.

The three-way interaction between self-efficacy, favorability, and training condition was also significant, $t(99.8) = -2.58, p = .011$, indicating that the impact of initial self-efficacy on learning gains varied based on both favorability and training condition. Figure 3 illustrates the three-way interaction dividing favorability into three levels for better visualization–low, medium, and high–by using the mean $\pm$ standard deviation: students below one standard deviation from the mean were classified as low favorability, those within one standard deviation as medium favorability, and those above one standard deviation as high favorability. The paper and tutor panels show learning gains with respect to the corresponding practice format (paper-based or tutor-based), respectively. The range of normalized baseline self-efficacy shown in the figure reflects the observed distribution in the sample, with relatively few values above one standard deviation. Since favorability was measured separately for each instructional condition, a student could be highly favorable toward both tutor-based and paper-based formats. As can be seen in Fig. 3, for students with low baseline self-efficacy, the relative benefit of the instruction condition was influenced by how favorable they were toward that condition. Specifically, low baseline self-efficacy students who were less favorable toward paper-based practice benefited more from paper-based instruction, compared to low baseline self-efficacy students who were more favorable toward paper-based practice. Furthermore, low baseline self-efficacy students who were more favorable toward computer-based practice benefited more from the tutor, compared to low baseline self-efficacy students who were less favorable toward computer-based practice. These findings indicate that the effectiveness of tutor-based vs. paper-based training is moderated by both self-efficacy and favorability.

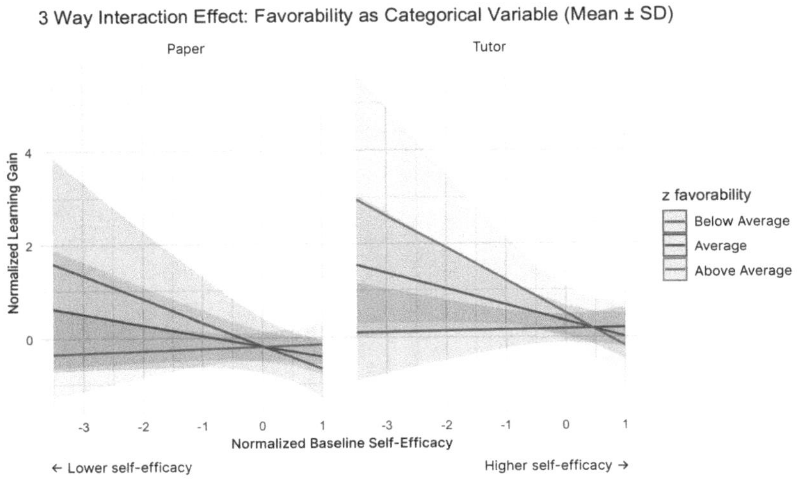


**Fig. 3.** The three-way interaction effect on learning outcome.

Because favorability was measured after the posttest, it is possible that the posttest results influenced the favorability results (and not the other way around). To test for this, we conducted a mediation analysis, investigating the effect of condition on favorability with potential mediation of posttest scores. We did not find any evidence that the favorability scores were associated with posttest scores, $t(51) = 1.67, p = .101$, suggesting that the favorability scores are likely to measure a general favorability toward the practice method.

### 4.2 RQ2: Does an ITS Enhance Self-efficacy?

Table 2 below revealed that baseline self-efficacy had a significant positive effect on post-training self-efficacy for the specific math skills practiced in the study, $t(91.94) = 5.91, p < .001$, suggesting that students who started with greater confidence in their abilities were more likely to maintain or improve their self-efficacy after training. In contrast, training conditions (tutor vs. paper), $t(57.96) = 0.49, p = .629$, and favorability, $t(90.00) = 0.96, p = .341$, did not independently predict changes in self-efficacy. We also examined interaction effects. However, none of the interactions reached statistical significance. These results indicate that, contrary to our expectation, ITS-based training did not lead to higher post-training self-efficacy, as initial self-efficacy remained the primary determinant regardless of training condition or favorability.

**Table 2.** Fixed-effects model results for RQ2.

| Effect | Estimate | Std. Error | df | $t$ value | $p$ |
|---|---|---|---|---|---|
| Intercept | -0.026 | 0.104 | 64.525 | -0.250 | 0.803 |
| Practice Format (Paper vs. Tutor) | 0.085 | 0.174 | 57.959 | 0.485 | 0.629 |
| Baseline Self-Efficacy | 0.642 | 0.109 | 91.944 | 5.911 | 0.000 |
| Favorability | 0.088 | 0.092 | 80.995 | 0.959 | 0.341 |
| Practice Format × Baseline Self-Efficacy | 0.363 | 0.220 | 97.132 | 1.649 | 0.102 |
| Practice Format × Favorability | -0.100 | 0.195 | 99.997 | -0.513 | 0.609 |
| Baseline Self-Efficacy × Favorability | 0.136 | 0.101 | 94.779 | 1.347 | 0.181 |
| Practice Format × Baseline Self-Efficacy × Favorability | 0.108 | 0.202 | 96.467 | 0.533 | 0.595 |

## 5 Discussion and Conclusion

This study examined the role of self-efficacy and favorability in shaping learning outcomes and motivational change across tutor-based and paper-based practice. Our findings build on prior results showing that ITSs improve learning outcomes compared to paper-based practice [7,8], but go one step further by demonstrating important interactions with baseline self-efficacy and students' favorability toward the mode of instruction. In particular, the relationship between baseline self-efficacy and learning gains varied as a function of both instructional format and students' favorability toward the instructional format, suggesting that whether students show greater learning gains from tutor-based versus paper-based practice is influenced by learners' motivational profiles. We found no evidence that the instructional format influenced changes in self-efficacy for the specific math skills practiced in the study. Although tutor-based practice might be expected to improve students' self-efficacy through perceived success and performance feedback that contribute to mastery experiences, a key source of self-efficacy [4], the short duration of the intervention and the limited empirical literature on self-efficacy in ITS contexts may help explain why such changes did not emerge.

These findings offer a more nuanced view of prior claims about the benefits of ITSs. Prior work has shown that scaffolded support and adaptive feedback in tutor-based instruction can improve learning outcomes [1,15,23], and that motivational factors like self-efficacy and favorability shape how students engage with ITSs, for example, by influencing persistence, responsiveness to feedback, and use of available supports [6,17]. Our findings align with this pattern and extend prior work comparing tutor- and paper-based practice by showing that the relative benefits of these formats are not uniform, but vary systematically with learners' motivational profiles. Among students with lower baseline self-efficacy, those who were more favorable toward the tutor showed greater learning gains during tutor practice than students who were less favorable toward it, possibly reflecting greater engagement with the tutor and its scaffolded support and timely feedback. In contrast, students who were less favorable toward the paper-based format actually improved more under the paper condition, possibly because students may have sought additional support elsewhere (e.g., from their teachers or peers) when instructional guidance was limited, although we did not directly measure such support-seeking. Alternatively, these students may have exerted greater effort when working with it, which could also account for their higher gains. Meanwhile, students with higher baseline self-efficacy showed smaller gains overall across both instructional formats, regardless of their favorability, possibly due to an association between self-efficacy and prior knowledge. Indeed, exploratory analyses showed weak but non-significant positive associations between baseline self-efficacy and pretest performance within each unit. Overall, these findings suggest that the effectiveness of instructional formats depends on how well they align with students' motivational profiles, particularly for students with low initial self-efficacy.

While this study offers initial insights into how self-efficacy for the math topic being studied and favorability of instructional conditions influence the effectiveness of these conditions, several limitations point to directions for future research. First, due to missing performance and survey data, the final analytic sample included only 54 of the 97 participants (55.67%), which is relatively small. This limited our statistical power and may have made it harder to detect more subtle effects or interactions. Future work should aim to replicate this study with a larger and more diverse sample. Second, favorability was measured after the posttest. Although our mediation analysis found no significant link between learning gains and favorability, suggesting that the measure may still reflect students' initial attitudes, collecting this data earlier, ideally before the pretest, would be more informative, but would also require students to report expectations about the tutor before experiencing it. Third, the short duration of the study (five days) may have limited our ability to observe meaningful changes in self-efficacy, a relatively stable psychological construct that typically requires more sustained experience or feedback to shift appreciably [6]. For future research, it would be valuable to extend the intervention over a longer timespan to better capture potential changes in students' self-efficacy. Finally, this study focused on a single domain (linear algebra) and a specific intelligent tutoring system. As such, the extent to which these findings generalize to other subject areas or different ITS designs remains an open question. Future work should examine whether similar patterns emerge across diverse domains and learning technologies.

In sum, this study highlights the importance of considering individual motivational differences, such as self-efficacy and favorability, when evaluating the effectiveness of instructional formats. Our findings suggest that the relative benefits of tutor versus paper-based practice depend on how well the format aligns with students' motivational profiles, specifically, a combination of their baseline self-efficacy and their preferences, consistent with prior findings suggesting that learner preferences alone have limited predictive value for achievement when considered in isolation [16,20]. These insights contribute to a more nuanced understanding of personalized learning and point toward the potential value of adapting instruction to better meet the needs of diverse learners. More broadly, they lay the groundwork for future research on how instructional formats can be aligned more effectively with learners' motivational needs.

**Acknowledgment.** This research was funded by the Institute of Education Sciences (IES) of the U.S. Department of Education (Award #R305A220386).

## References

1. Aleven, V.A., Koedinger, K.R.: An effective metacognitive strategy: learning by doing and explaining with a computer-based cognitive tutor. Cogn. Sci. **26**(2), 147–179 (2002)
2. Anderson, J.R., Corbett, A.T., Koedinger, K.R., Pelletier, R.: Cognitive tutors: lessons learned. J. Learn. Sci. **4**(2), 167–207 (1995)
3. Baker, R.S.J.D., et al.: Adapting to when students game an intelligent tutoring system. In: Ikeda, M., Ashley, K.D., Chan, TW. (eds.) International Conference on Intelligent Tutoring Systems. LNCS, pp. 392–401. Springer, Berlin, Heidelberg (2006). https://doi.org/10.1007/11774303_39
4. Bandura, A.: Self-Efficacy: the Exercise of Control. W. H. Freeman, New York (1997)
5. Bandura, A.: Guide for constructing self-efficacy scales. In: Pajares, F., Urdan, T. (eds.) Self-Efficacy Beliefs of Adolescents, pp. 307–337. Information Age Publishing, Greenwich, CT (2006)
6. Bernacki, M.L., Nokes-Malach, T.J., Aleven, V.: Examining self-efficacy during learning: variability and relations to behavior, performance, and learning. Metacogn. Learn. **10**(1), 99–117 (2015)
7. Borchers, C., Carvalho, P.F., Xia, M., Liu, P., Koedinger, K.R., Aleven, V.: Correction to: what makes problem-solving practice effective? comparing paper and ai tutoring. In: Viberg, O., Jivet, I., Muñoz-Merino, P., Perifanou, M., Papathoma, T. (eds.) European Conference on Technology Enhanced Learning. LNCS, pp. C1–C1. Springer, Cham (2023). https://doi.org/10.1007/978-3-031-42682-7_75
8. Borchers, C., Carvalho, P.F., Xia, M., Liu, P., Koedinger, K.R., Aleven, V.: What makes problem-solving practice effective? comparing paper and ai tutoring. In: Viberg, O., Jivet, I., Muñoz-Merino, P., Perifanou, M., Papathoma, T. (eds.) European Conference on Technology Enhanced Learning. LNCS, pp. 44–59. Springer, Cham (2023). https://doi.org/10.1007/978-3-031-42682-7_4

9. Borchers, C., Fleischer, H., Schanze, S., Scheiter, K., Aleven, V.: High scaffolding of an unfamiliar strategy improves conceptual learning but reduces enjoyment compared to low scaffolding and strategy freedom. Comput. Educ. **236**, 105364 (2025)
10. Cook, D.A., Artino, A.R., Jr.: Motivation to learn: an overview of contemporary theories. Med. Educ. **50**(10), 997–1014 (2016)
11. Cordova, D.I., Lepper, M.R.: Intrinsic motivation and the process of learning: beneficial effects of contextualization, personalization, and choice. J. Educ. Psychol. **88**(4), 715–730 (1996)
12. Gray, L., Lewis, L.: Teachers' use of technology for school and homework assignments: 2018–19. Tech. Rep. NCES 2020-048, National Center for Education Statistics, U.S. Department of Education, Washington, DC (2020)
13. Harackiewicz, J.M., Smith, J.L., Priniski, S.J.: Interest matters: the importance of promoting interest in education. Policy Insights Behav. Brain Sci. **3**(2), 220–227 (2016)
14. Kulik, J.A., Fletcher, J.D.: Effectiveness of intelligent tutoring systems: a meta-analytic review. Rev. Educ. Res. **86**(1), 42–78 (2016)
15. Ma, W., Adesope, O.O., Nesbit, J.C., Liu, Q.: Intelligent tutoring systems and learning outcomes: a meta-analysis. J. Educ. Psychol. **106**(4), 901–918 (2014)
16. Makransky, G., Andreasen, N.K., Baceviciute, S., Mayer, R.E.: Immersive virtual reality increases liking but not learning with a science simulation and generative learning strategies promote learning in immersive virtual reality. J. Educ. Psychol. **113**(4), 719–735 (2021)
17. McQuiggan, S.W., Mott, B.W., Lester, J.C.: Modeling self-efficacy in intelligent tutoring systems: an inductive approach. User Model. User-Adap. Inter. **18**(1), 81–123 (2008)
18. Mendicino, M., Razzaq, L., Heffernan, N.T.: A comparison of traditional homework to computer-supported homework. J. Res. Technol. Educ. **41**(3), 331–359 (2009)
19. Pan, X.: Technology acceptance, technological self-efficacy, and attitude toward technology-based self-directed learning: learning motivation as a mediator. Front. Psychol. **11**, 564294 (2020)
20. Schnackenberg, H.L., Sullivan, H.J., Leader, L.F., Jones, E.E.: Learner preferences and achievement under differing amounts of learner practice. Educ. Tech. Res. Dev. **46**(2), 5–16 (1998)
21. Schunk, D.H., Pajares, F.: Self-efficacy theory. In: Wentzel, K.R., Wigfield, A. (eds.) Handbook of Motivation at School, pp. 35–53. Routledge (2009)
22. Usher, E.L., Pajares, F.: Sources of self-efficacy in school: critical review of the literature and future directions. Rev. Educ. Res. **78**(4), 751–796 (2008)
23. VanLehn, K.: The relative effectiveness of human tutoring, intelligent tutoring systems, and other tutoring systems. Educ. Psychol. **46**(4), 197–221 (2011)
24. Yan, V.X., Sana, F., Carvalho, P.F.: No simple solutions to complex problems: cognitive science principles can guide but not prescribe educational decisions. Policy Insights Behav. Brain Sci. **11**(1), 59–66 (2024)
25. Zimmerman, B.J.: Self-efficacy: an essential motive to learn. Contemp. Educ. Psychol. **25**(1), 82–91 (2000)

# Physiological Data for Academic Performance Prediction: A Systematic Literature Review

Mathieu Chambard[1(✉)], Benoit Encelle[1], Karim Sehaba[2], and Béatrice Fuchs[1,3]

[1] Universite Claude Bernard Lyon 1, CNRS, Ecole Centrale de Lyon, INSA Lyon, Université Lumière Lyon 2, LIRIS, UMR5205, 69622 Villeurbanne, France
mathieu.chambard@liris.cnrs.fr

[2] CSTL Lab, University of Mostaganem Algeria, Mostaganem, Algeria

[3] University Jean Moulin Lyon 3, iaelyon, Lyon, France

**Abstract.** The early identification of struggling students remains a significant challenge in the learning analytics literature on improving academic success. To improve academic performance prediction, physiological sensors offer opportunities by providing indicators related to learners' cognitive, emotional, and attentional states. This paper presents a systematic literature review that mainly analyses the use of physiological data to predict academic performance in learning contexts. The review was conducted following PRISMA guidelines across several multidisciplinary scientific databases, covering the period from 2010 to 2025, leading to the identification of 431 articles, of which 33 were retained after applying exclusion criteria. The results indicate that eye tracking and electroencephalogram (EEG) are the most commonly used sensors, and that experimental protocols predominantly rely on a single-sensor approach. Moreover, physiological data are frequently complemented by interaction traces (logs) collected from digital learning environments, as well as by questionnaires, demographic data, and knowledge assessments. Despite these advances, the review identifies persistent methodological limitations, particularly regarding adoption of multimodal approaches. Addressing these limitations is essential to fully realize the potential of physiological data in learning analytics and argue for a shift in multimodal academic performance prediction.

**Keywords:** Multimodal Learning Analytics · Educational Data Mining · Physiological Sensors · Performance Prediction · Systematic Literature Review


J. Weidlich et al. (Eds.): EC-TEL 2026, LNCS 16905, pp. 149–163, 2027.
https://doi.org/10.1007/978-3-032-37979-5_11

## 1 Introduction

Improving academic success represents a major challenge for educational systems, for instance failure and dropout rates are high in higher education[11], especially during the first years of university. Early identification of struggling students in order to provide recommendations or adapt learning pathways constitutes a key lever to support learning [14]. These issues fall within Educational Data Mining and Learning Analytics, one of the main research topics of which is the analysis of educational data to understand and model learners' behaviors and performance.

In recent years, the development and democratization of portable physiological sensors have opened new perspectives for learning analytics [7]. Continuous collection of data such as heart rate, electrodermal activity, skin temperature, or brain activity provides direct access to indicators related to learners' cognitive, emotional, and attentional states. Several studies suggest that these physiological signals can complement interaction traces (logs), particularly to better capture cognitive load, engagement, or stress during learning activities [6].

This paper presents a systematic literature review on academic performance prediction using physiological data in learning contexts, covering the period from 2010 to 2025. It provides a structured synthesis of existing approaches to support methodological and technological choices in this domain.

In this work, we use the term "multimodal traces" to refer to all data relating to learners, primarily derived from their interactions with learning environments, as well as information capturing their states and perceptions. These traces include interaction traces (logs of learners' actions such as clicks, answers...), physiological data (measurements collected from sensors such as heart rate, electrodermal activity...), and declarative data (self-reported information such as surveys, questionnaires, or learner reflections).

To achieve this objective, the review is guided by the following research questions:

- **RQ1: Which types of physiological sensors are used to predict academic performance?**
- **RQ2: What is the prevalence of multi-sensor configurations in literature, and which combinations of physiological sensors are most commonly used?**
- **RQ3: Which complementary data sources are used alongside physiological measures to predict academic performance?**

The remainder of the article is structured as follows. Section 2 presents the related work and identifies the main limitations in the literature. Section 3 describes the systematic review methodology conducted according to PRISMA guidelines [12]. Section 4 presents the results of the article selection and analysis. The findings are then discussed in Sect. 5, before concluding.

## 2 Related Work

Several systematic literature reviews have explored the use of wearable sensors in educational contexts. Hernández-Mustieles et al. [7] propose a general review of wearable biosensors in education, focusing on physiological devices and their pedagogical applications without a specific predictive objective. Similarly, Almusawi et al. [1] and Chu et al. [4] provide broad overviews of wearable technologies for learning, addressing engagement, user experience, and motivation across various educational contexts. Other works focus more specifically on learning analytics: Liu et al. [8] analyze the evolution of research exploiting physiological data to study learning processes, while Shen Ba et al. [3] investigate emotion measurement in educational contexts using physiological sensors.

These studies highlight the importance of physiological data for the analysis of learning. Despite the richness of these contributions, several limitations remain. First, among the five identified systematic literature reviews, none explicitly focus on academic performance prediction as a primary objective. Instead, the reviewed studies predominantly address other outcomes such as engagement, emotions, or user experience, with academic performance–if considered–treated only marginally. Second, all five reviews adopt a broad and generalist perspective, covering multiple educational applications, which limits the depth of analysis regarding predictive modeling of academic outcomes. Third, none of these reviews provides a systematic comparison of physiological sensing modalities (e.g., EEG, EDA, heart rate), nor do they rigorously analyze mono- versus multi-sensor configurations and their impact on predictive performance. Finally, while some reviews [8] mention the use of multimodal data in learning analytics, no prior work offers a structured analysis of integrating of physiological data with other data sources specifically for academic performance prediction.

In contrast, the present review specifically focuses on academic performance prediction using physiological data, covering the period from 2010 to 2025. It aims to provide a structured overview of (i) the types of physiological sensors used, (ii) the prevalence and configurations of multi-sensor approaches, and (iii) the integration of physiological data with complementary data sources in predictive contexts. By focusing on these aspects, this review offers a more targeted understanding of how physiological data are currently employed for academic performance prediction, thereby addressing gaps in the existing literature.

## 3 Methodology

This section outlines the methodology of the systematic literature review, conducted in accordance with PRISMA guidelines [12]. The process includes systematic database searches, the application of predefined exclusion criteria, and a two-stage screening based on titles/abstracts and full-text review.

### 3.1 Identification

The article identification procedure was conducted in three main steps:

1. **Construction of an initial reference corpus**, based on expert-identified studies and an exploratory search. This initial cohort enabled familiarization with the core concepts of the field, the definition of keywords required for the subsequent query, as well as the identification of an analysis framework for classifying the studies.
2. **Definition of a structured set of keywords**, organized into four main themes: *Physiological data, Prediction, Performance*, and *Human learning*. The initial set of keywords was derived from the initial reference corpus. Keywords within the same theme were combined using the OR operator to group synonyms, variants, and related terms, while themes were combined using the AND operator to structure a targeted query. The complete set of keywords is presented in Table 1.
3. **Search across multiple scientific databases**. The selected databases reflect the interdisciplinary scope of the topic, encompassing human learning and academic performance, educational technologies, physiological signals, and predictive modeling. Searches were conducted on the Title and Abstract fields. The following databases were used, with query syntax adapted to each source:
   - **PubMed**, for literature related to physiology, neuroscience, and cognition, necessary to interpret physiological signals (EEG, eye tracking...)
   - **IEEE Xplore** and **ACM Digital Library**, for contributions in computer science, engineering, sensors, and machine learning
   - **ERIC**, for literature in educational sciences and learning contexts
   - **WebOfScience**, multidisciplinary database ensuring comprehensiveness.

**Table 1.** Themes and associated queries using OR operators

| Theme | Query |
|---|---|
| Physiological | "eye tracking" OR "gaze" OR "ECG" OR "heart rate" OR "EDA" OR "skin conductance" OR "GSR" OR "EEG" OR "physiological data" |
| Prediction | predict* |
| Performance | "performance" OR "outcomes" OR "achievement" OR "success" OR "score" OR "gain" OR "failure" OR "dropout" |
| Human learning | "learner" OR "student" OR "educational" OR "academic" OR "learning environment" |

### 3.2 Exclusion Criteria

To select studies directly relevant to the research questions, exclusion criteria are applied. The study selection process was structured according to the PICO framework: the population comprises students in educational contexts; the intervention consists of the collection of physiological data using wearable sensors or other physiological measurement devices; the comparison element is not applicable, as the studies are primarily observational or predictive; and the outcome is the presence of explicit measures of academic performance, such as grades, test scores, or performance assessments.

Exclusion criteria further refine the selection. Studies are excluded if they are conducted at rest or outside educational settings (EC1), do not include physiological measurements (EC2), or lack explicit measures of academic performance (EC3). Studies involving clinical populations (EC4), literature reviews or descriptive database papers (EC5), articles for which the full text is not accessible (EC6), publications prior to 2010 (EC7), or articles not written in English (EC8) are also excluded. These combined criteria ensure that the final corpus consists of peer-reviewed studies directly addressing the use of physiological data for predicting academic performance in educational contexts between 2010 and 2025.

### 3.3 Selection Process

The article selection process was conducted in two main stages in accordance with PRISMA guidelines and based on the exclusion criteria: (1) an initial screening of titles and abstracts, followed by (2) a second screening of the full texts of the selected articles.

### 3.4 Analysis Framework

An analysis framework was developed during the article review process to ensure systematic and consistent coding of relevant information for each included study. The coding was direct and objective, based on clearly defined categories, and did not require subjective interpretation. The analysis framework is summarized in Table 2. All selected articles were carefully reviewed and coded according to categories structured around the objectives of the review, including types of sensors used, analytical methods applied, learning performance measurement modalities, experimental characteristics, and study objectives and outcomes.

## 4 Results

### 4.1 Results of Article Selection

The complete paper selection process is summarized in Fig. 1, in accordance with the standard PRISMA flow diagram.

**Table 2.** Data extraction grid used for the systematic review

| Category | Extracted Variables |
|---|---|
| Bibliographic information | Title; Peer-reviewed; Publication type; Conference/Journal; Year; Authors. |
| Physiological and behavioral sensors | ECG; Heart rate; EEG; Eye tracking; EDA; Skin temp; Peripheral blood volume; Interaction Traces; Interaction Traces details; Voice; Facial expression; Movements/posture; Demographics. |
| Analysis methods | Decision Tree; Random Forest; Rule induction; Deep learning; SVM/SVR; KNN; Naive Bayes; Gaussian Process Regression.<br>ANOVA; Linear regression; Logistic regression; Correlation; Regression analysis; GLMM; LMEM; GAM.<br>Variable ranking; CfsSubsetEval; PCA. |
| Learning performance measures | Pre-tests; Post-tests; Retention tests; Final exam; Game metrics; Combinations; Other indicators. |
| Experimental design | Population; #participants; Duration; Environment (classroom, lab, online); Activity type; Protocol. |
| Objectives and results | Main objective; Secondary objectives; Main results; Additional info. |

**Identification.** Applying the complete identification queries across the five selected databases resulted in the identification of 431 articles. Automatic duplicate removal eliminated 167 articles, leaving a total of 264 unique records for the initial screening.

**Screening.** During the screening phase based on titles and abstracts, 189 articles were excluded and 75 were retained for full-text reading.

Prior to full-text assessment, article accessibility was verified: 16 articles were not freely accessible and were therefore excluded (EC6). The subsequent full-text evaluation led to the exclusion of 26 additional studies based on the previously defined criteria (n = 18 for EC1, n = 8 for EC3).

This second filtering stage resulted in a final set of 33 articles included in the systematic review. The full list of the 33 studies included in this systematic literature review is available in an open repository (OSF): https://osf.io/pumkd.

### 4.2 Descriptive Synthesis

**General Characteristics.** A total of 33 studies were included in the review. Publications range from 2014 to 2024, with a marked concentration in recent years (notably 2018: n = 7, 2022: n = 6, 2023: n = 6, 2020: n = 4). The studies originate from a variety of sources (journals and conferences), with little redundancy in publication venues (n = 33 studies across 30 distinct venues).

**Target Populations and Contexts.** Participants are predominantly higher education students (n = 17, 48%). Other studies focus on primary school pupils/children (n = 5, 15%), secondary school students (n = 4, 12%), adults (n = 5, 12%). Regarding experimental contexts, the majority of studies were conducted in controlled laboratory environments (n = 19, 57%). Other contexts include classroom settings (n = 3, 9%), online learning environments (n

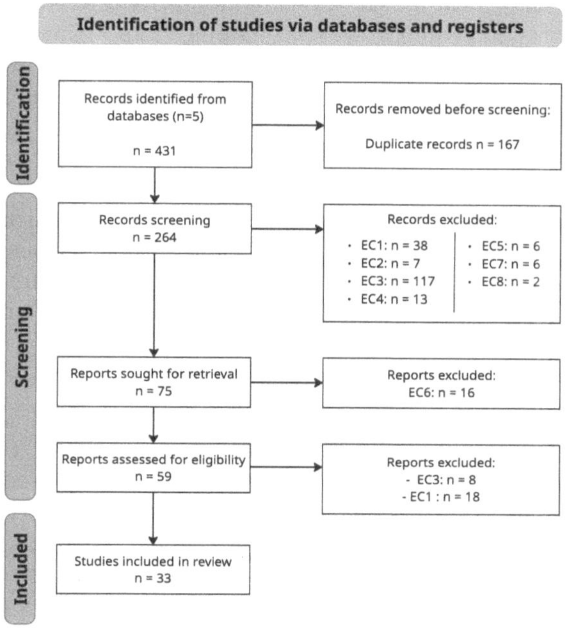


**Fig. 1.** PRISMA flow diagram of the study selection process

= 3, 9%), and intelligent tutoring systems (ITS) (n = 2, 6%). Experimental durations show substantial heterogeneity. Many studies (n = 24, 73 %) rely on short, single-session experiments lasting from a few minutes to approximately one hour, particularly in controlled experimental settings. Other studies (n = 9, 27%) adopt multi-session protocols extending over several days or weeks, notably in classroom, online learning, or intelligent tutoring system contexts.

The studies involve different learning activities: passive exposure (reading, videos, lectures; n = 10, 30%), problem-solving and practical exercises (programming, scientific or math tasks, nutrition design; n = 6, 18%), educational games and simulations (serious games, VR/AR; n = 6, 18%), motor or sensorimotor tasks (object manipulation, 3D movements, simulated surgery, muscle painting; n = 6, 18%), and collaborative learning (pair programming, jigsaw tasks, group sessions with ITS; n = 4, 12%). These activities provide diverse contexts for analyzing and predicting learners' performance.

**Collected Data.** The included studies employ multimodal data to analyze and predict academic performance, while also capturing learners' cognitive and emotional states as part of the predictive modeling process. These data are collected using physiological measurement devices, enabling acquisition of signals such as electroencephalography (EEG), electrodermal activity, heart rate, as well as other physiological indicators including heart rate variability, peripheral blood volume, or skin temperature. Attentional data, primarily obtained from eye-tracking systems, are also used to analyze visual strategies, cognitive load, and learners' exploration behaviors during learning activities. In addition, several studies exploit behavioral data from digital learning environments, including interaction traces, and game metrics, particularly in serious game or educational platform contexts. Some studies also integrate additional data types such as facial expression analysis, audio or voice signals, and body-tracking data capturing posture and movement. Finally, contextual and demographic data are sometimes incorporated to better contextualize analyses. The distribution of sensor types and data modalities, as well as their frequency of use, will be analyzed in more detail within the research questions.

**Evaluation Measures of Learning.** The included studies use different measures to assess learning outcomes or academic performance. Pre-test/post-test designs (n = 10, 30%) are used to estimate learning gains based on performance evolution, while the majority rely solely on post-tests (n = 20, 61%) to measure performance at the end of the activity. More marginally, some include final exams (n = 2, 6%) or retention tests (n = 1, 3%). In addition to these academic evaluations, six studies use game-based metrics (n = 6, 18%), corresponding to performance or progression indicators specific to game-based and serious game environments.

**Analysis Methods and Predictive Models.** The included studies employ a wide range of analytical approaches, ranging from classical statistical methods to more advanced machine learning techniques. Some studies (n = 15, 45%) employ multiple approaches, combining different methods to enhance prediction or interpretability. A first group of studies relies on statistical methods such as correlation analyses, analysis of variance, or regression models (n = 21, 64%), mainly used to explore and explain relationships between physiological and behavioral variables and learners' academic performance. Other studies rely on supervised machine learning models such as decision trees, ensemble methods, support vector machines, or probabilistic models (n = 12, 36%). These models are used to predict academic performance or identify complex relationships between multimodal data and learning outcomes. Finally, some research employs deep learning approaches to model non-linear relationships between heterogeneous multimodal data and academic performance (n = 4, 12%). In addition to these main methods, several studies include exploratory analysis or preprocessing steps such as dimensionality reduction (e.g., principal component analysis) or variable selection and ranking methods (n = 7, 21%), aiming to improve model interpretability or their ability to capture relationships with academic performance.

### 4.3 RQ1: Which Types of Physiological Sensors are Used to Predict Academic Performance?

We identified various physiological sensors used to predict academic performance. The detailed distribution is presented in Fig. 2. **Eye tracking** is the most represented sensor (n = 20, 61%), followed by **EEG** (n = 12, 36%) and electrodermal measures (n = 6, 18%). Other sensors appear in similar proportions, including **heart rate** sensors (n = 4, 12%), **voice** recording (n = 3, 9%), **skin temperature** and **blood volume** sensors (n = 2, 6%), as well as **skeleton motion** and **posture** capture (n = 2, 6%).

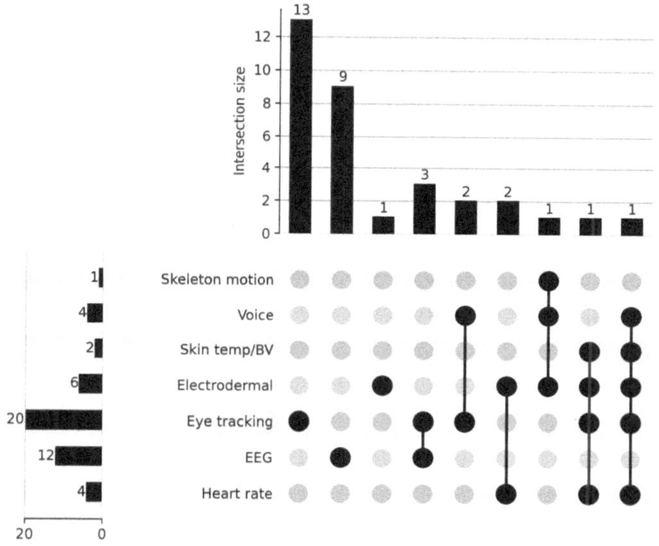


**Fig. 2.** Distribution of physiological sensors and their combinations (upset plot)

A Cochran's Q test was conducted to assess whether the observed differences in the frequency of use of physiological sensors across studies were statistically significant. The results indicate a significant effect of sensor type on usage ($Q = 46.86$, $p < 0.001$), leading to the rejection of the null hypothesis of equal proportions. This finding confirms that the distribution of sensor usage is not uniform across the literature. In particular, the higher prevalence of eye tracking and EEG compared to other modalities is unlikely to be due to random variation, but rather reflects a statistically significant preference in the selection of sensors. These results support the descriptive analysis and highlight the existence of clear trends in the adoption of physiological sensing technologies for academic performance prediction.

These results describe the overall use of physiological sensors in the literature, without distinguishing studies that employ multiple sensors simultaneously.

Therefore, it is relevant to examine the prevalence of multi-sensor configurations and the most common physiological sensor combinations.

### 4.4 RQ2: What Is the Prevalence of Multi-sensor Configurations in Studies, and Which Combinations of Physiological Sensors are Most Commonly Used?

The detailed distribution of configurations is presented in Fig. 2. The majority of studies rely on a single-sensor setup (n = 23, 70%), while some studies use a two-sensor setup (n = 7, 21%) and others employ configurations with more than two sensors (n = 3, 9%).

A chi-square goodness-of-fit test was conducted to assess whether the different sensor configurations (1, 2, or >= 3 sensors) were used equally across studies. The results yielded a $\chi^2$ statistic of 20.36 with a p-value $< 0.001$, indicating that the distribution of configurations is not uniform. In particular, studies using a single sensor are significantly more frequent than those employing multiple sensors.

When present, multi-sensor setups account for a minority of studies (n = 10, 30%).Figure 2 shows the sensor combinations along with the number of studies using each combination for prediction. According to the upset plot dot table - columns 4 to 9, no modality clearly dominates multi-sensor use: eye tracking and electrodermal activity (EDA) each appear in four configurations, while heart rate and voice recording appear in three studies. EEG, despite being widely used in single-sensor studies, is included only three times in multimodal setups. Other sensors are used even more sporadically.

Beyond these signals, a number of studies also rely on other types of data to enrich or contextualize the prediction of academic performance. It is therefore relevant to identify which complementary data sources are used alongside physiological measures in these studies.

### 4.5 RQ3: Which Complementary Data Sources are Used Alongside Physiological Measures to Predict Academic Performance?

Figure 3 presents the complementary data sources identified in the selected studies. Among the reviewed studies, 13 articles use at least one non-physiological data source alongside sensors, while 20 rely solely on physiological data. The most frequently used complementary data sources include interaction traces (n = 6), demographic data (n = 5), pre-tests (n = 5), and, more marginally, questionnaires (n = 1).

Interaction traces constitute a particularly heterogeneous category, as they depend closely on the learning environment. Details are provided in Table 3. In serious games, they include, for example, total gameplay time, interactions with objects, movements, and actions performed by the learner. In intelligent tutoring systems, logs allow observing and measuring learners' strategies, such as navigation through learning materials or participation in provided activities. In other contexts, where interactivity is limited, logs rely more on simple measures, such as response time, number of attempts, hint requests, or accuracy rates. Outside serious games and intelligent tutoring systems, the environments studied generate relatively sparse logs, offering few exploitable interaction traces.

Pre-tests are used in several studies as predictors of final performance. They quantify learners' initial knowledge and skills prior to the activity, providing a useful baseline for modeling performance evolution and interpreting inter-individual variations. Questionnaires are used in one study, but with a two-part design. The first part involves self-assessment of knowledge mastery by the participant, while the second aims to evaluate psychological dimensions such as concentration or emotional state.

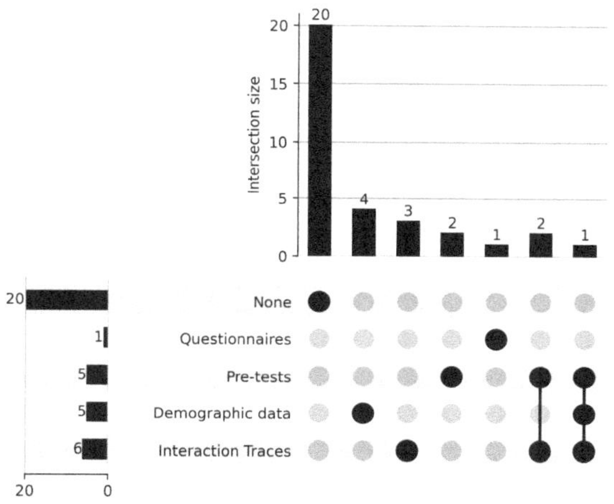


**Fig. 3.** Distribution of physiological sensors and their combinations (upset plot)

**Table 3.** Data extracted from computer logs used to predict academic performance

| Context | Extracted variables |
|---|---|
| Serious game | Total gameplay time |
| Serious game | Actions, movements, dialogues, interactions with in-game objects |
| Intelligent tutoring system | Number of summaries written; reading strategies |
| Tangible learning activity (anatomy) | Response time; number of attempts |
| Collaborative problem-solving system (equivalent fractions) | Hint requests; incorrect responses; correct responses |
| Vocabulary learning task | Reaction time; percentage of correct responses |

## 5 Discussion

Among the sensors identified in the reviewed studies, eye tracking and EEG emerge as the most frequently used modalities. Eye tracking (n = 20, 61%) offers several practical advantages in educational settings. It is relatively easy to deploy in learning environments, especially with remote devices placed below the screen, and remains minimally intrusive for learners. Analytically, eye tracking allows examining visual behavior and attention allocation during a task [5]. Analysis of gaze location (areas of interest) and dynamics (fixations and saccades) provides insights into how learners select and process information in their environment. These measures thus constitute indirect yet informative indicators of cognitive processes involved in learning, particularly regarding attention, exploration strategies, and in some cases, cognitive load [5]. EEG (n = 12, 36%) has a long history of use in medical and neuroscience domains, where it records and analyzes neural dynamics associated with cognitive processes. Its use in educational contexts, however, involves several practical constraints, including substantial equipment costs, high sensitivity to artifacts (movement, muscle activity, or environmental noise), and the need for specialized preprocessing and analysis procedures [9]. Despite these constraints, EEG provides direct access to neurophysiological markers, such as power variations in the alpha, beta, and theta bands, allowing estimation of cognitive states such as mental workload, attention, or engagement [13]. Other physiological sensors appear more marginally in the literature on academic performance prediction. Measures such as EDA, heart rate, or blood pressure remain relatively underused, despite the convenience of wearable devices. This limited use may be explained by the complexity of signal interpretation and sensitivity to environmental conditions and task characteristics [2]. Similarly, voice recording or posture analysis are rarely exploited, as video capture requires additional equipment and measurements are not direct: indicators must be manually constructed from video inspection, making data processing particularly time-consuming.

Beyond the choice of individual sensors, the analyzed studies also highlight a still limited adoption of multi-sensor approaches (n = 10, 30%). Although combining physiological measures is often identified as an effective approach for detecting variations in cognitive load [2], its use for predicting academic performance remains relatively limited. The predominance of single-sensor approaches is explained by several technical and methodological constraints associated with the simultaneous use of multiple physiological sensors. Integrating different sensors requires precise temporal synchronization of signals, which often entails using specialized hardware or dedicated software solutions that are rarely standardized. Furthermore, each sensor produces a distinct type of signal, requiring its own preprocessing, cleaning, and feature extraction methods. Adding an additional sensor increases analytical complexity and often necessitates redefining relevant indicators. Costs and practical requirements also limit the adoption of multi-sensor approaches. As the number of sensors increases, equipment becomes more expensive, more intrusive for participants, and harder to deploy in authentic educational contexts. Moreover, multi-sensor configurations may reduce experimental robustness: failure of a single sensor or deterioration in signal quality can render the entire session unusable. In this context, the combined use of physiological sensors for predicting academic performance remains largely exploratory.

More broadly, results show that many studies rely exclusively on physiological measures to predict academic performance. This predominance contrasts with a growing literature highlighting the value of combining multiple data sources to obtain a richer understanding of learners' cognitive and affective states [10]. Studies integrating several types of data demonstrate clear complementarity between sources. For instance, interaction traces allow characterization of observable learning behaviors, while self-reports provide subjective information on mental state, motivation, or task perception.When interaction traces are used in the reviewed studies, their exploitation remains limited, mainly due to the low interactivity of the learning modules studied. This constraint reduces the variety and richness of behavioral information that can be extracted from interactions, limiting the potential to construct more complex indicators.

In summary, while physiological measures form the basis of many studies predicting academic performance, the literature suggests that integrating complementary data sources, such as interaction traces or self-reports, is essential for obtaining a more complete and potentially more predictive view of learners' cognitive and affective states and, by extension, academic performance.

## 6 Limitations

Several limitations must be considered when interpreting the results of this systematic literature review. First, some potentially relevant publications could not be included due to restricted access to full-text articles, which may have introduced selection bias. Furthermore, although the search strategy was designed to be as exhaustive as possible, particularly through the choice and combination of varied keywords and database, it is possible that some relevant articles were not identified. Differences in terminology across domains, as well as the diversity of terms used to describe physiological sensors or the prediction of academic performance, may limit the comprehensiveness of the search.

## 7 Research Agenda

Several research questions remain to be explored following this systematic literature review. In particular, it is relevant to examine more precisely which data sources contribute most to predicting academic performance.

In this context, it will be particularly relevant to focus on studies directly comparing the effectiveness of different physiological sensors. Nine articles identified in this review will provide this type of comparison. Analysis of these studies will allow assessing the relative capacity of sensors to predict academic performance under comparable experimental conditions. It will be necessary to restrict the examination to these comparative studies, as attempting to compare results from different pedagogical contexts, experimental protocols, or datasets could lead to unreliable conclusions.

Furthermore, these same studies could be used to examine whether predictive models based on multimodal data outperform unimodal models in estimating students' academic performance. Finally, complementary analyses could focus on articles comparing multiple predictive modeling approaches to identify potential trends regarding methods most frequently associated with higher predictive performance. It will also be relevant to examine in detail the analytical methods used in the studies and evaluate their relative performance in predicting academic outcomes. This approach will highlight the most robust methods and guide future research in the field.

One major challenge currently is the difficulty of comparing data across different studies, as the sensors used, their configurations, experimental protocols, and learning environments vary considerably. This heterogeneity limits the ability to draw general conclusions and to determine which physiological measures are truly the most relevant for predicting academic performance.

Beyond the immediate goal of predicting academic performance, the advancement of the field would benefit from efforts to standardize methodologies and data collection protocols. One potential avenue is the development of an open, standardized protocol for physiological data acquisition in educational contexts. Such a protocol could define minimum requirements for sensor calibration, sampling rates, and feature extraction, while remaining flexible enough to accommodate diverse learning environments and experimental designs.

Establishing a shared benchmark dataset following this protocol would allow researchers to directly compare the effectiveness of different sensors, sensor combinations, and analytical methods. This help mitigate inconsistencies arising from heterogeneous experimental setups and improve reproducibility across studies. Furthermore, community-wide adoption of standardized procedures could facilitate meta-analyses, accelerate the identification of best practices, and promote cumulative knowledge building in multimodal learning analytics.

Finally, the open sharing of code, preprocessing pipelines, and annotated datasets would enhance transparency and collaboration, enabling the field to move toward more robust and generalizable predictive models while fostering innovation in multimodal data fusion and learning analytics applications.

## 8 Conclusion

Eye tracking and EEG dominate the use of physiological sensors for predicting academic performance: the former combines ease of deployment with information on attention and visual behavior, while the latter provides reliable indicators of cognitive and attentional states. Multi-sensor configurations remain rare, mainly due to technical constraints, cost, and analytical complexity. Similarly, the use of complementary data, such as interaction traces or declarative data, remains limited.

Studies exhibit significant heterogeneity in protocols, sensors, and learning environments, which limits the comparability of results. These findings highlight the need to standardize methods for collecting and analyzing physiological data and to promote the integration of multimodal data to improve reproducibility and the robustness of predictive models.

Future work should focus on studies directly comparing the effectiveness of different sensors to identify the most effective approaches and inform research on multimodal integration and robust predictive modeling.

**Acknowledgment.** This work was supported by the French National Research Agency (ANR) under the MODELI+ project (ANR-23-CE38-0011).

## References

1. Almusawi, H.A., Durugbo, C.M., Bugawa, A.M.: Wearable technology in education: a systematic review. IEEE Trans. Learn. Technol. **14**(4), 540–554 (2021)
2. Ayres, P., Lee, J.Y., Paas, F., van Merriënboer, J.J.G.: The Validity of Physiological Measures to Identify Differences in Intrinsic Cognitive Load. Front. Psychol. **12** (2021)
3. Ba, S., Hu, X.: Measuring emotions in education using wearable devices: a systematic review. Comput. Educ. **200**, 104797 (2023)
4. Chu, S.L., Garcia, B., Rani, N.: Research on Wearable Technologies for Learning: A Systematic Review (2022)
5. Chytry, V., Mundokova, N., Kubiatko, M.: Using eye-tracking in education-a review study. Educ. Sci. **15**(7), 853 (2025)
6. Goussain, B., Moura, R., Luche, J., Andrade, H., Silva, M.: Enhancing learning with physiological measures: a systematic review of applications in neuroeducation. In: Proceedings of the 17th International Conference on Computer Supported Education, pp. 111–122. SCITEPRESS - Science and Technology Publications, Porto, Portugal (2025)
7. Hernández-Mustieles, M.A., et al.: Wearable biosensor technology in education: a systematic review. Sensors **24**(8), 2437 (2024)
8. Liu, Z., Ren, Y., Kong, X., Liu, S.: Learning analytics based on wearable devices: a systematic literature review from 2011 to 2021. J. Educ. Comput. Res. **60**, 073563312110647 (2022)
9. Luck, S.J.: An Introduction to the Event-Related Potential Technique, second edition. MIT Press (2014). google-Books-ID: SzavAwAAQBAJ
10. Mu, S., Cui, M., Huang, X.: Multimodal data fusion in learning analytics: a systematic review. Sensors **20**(23), 6856 (2020). https://doi.org/10.3390/s20236856
11. OECD: Education at a Glance 2025: OECD Indicators. Education at a Glance 2025 (2025)
12. Page, M.J., McKenzie, J.E., Bossuyt, P.M., Boutron, I., Hoffmann, T.C.: Mulrow: the PRISMA 2020 statement: an updated guideline for reporting systematic reviews. BMJ **372**, n71 (2021)
13. Raufi, B., Longo, L.: An evaluation of the EEG alpha-to-theta and theta-to-alpha band ratios as indexes of mental workload. Front. Neuroinform. 16 (2022)
14. Santos, R.M., Henriques, R.: Accurate, timely, and portable: course-agnostic early prediction of student performance from LMS logs. Comput. Educ.: Artif. Intell. **5**, 100175 (2023)

# Probing Experts' Perspectives on AI-Assisted Public Speaking Training

Mathieu Chollet[1,2](✉), Nesrine Fourati[3], Alisa Barkar[4], Marion Dragée[1], and Liv Danthon-Lefebvre[1]

[1] IMT Atlantique, LS2N, UMR CNRS 6004, 44307 Nantes, France
[2] School of Computing Science, University of Glasgow, Glasgow, UK
mathieu.chollet@glasgow.ac.uk
[3] Independent Researcher, France, UK
[4] LTCI, Institut Polytechnique de Paris, Telecom-Paris, 19 Place Marguerite Perey, 91120 Palaiseau, France

**Abstract.** Public speaking training relies heavily on expert coaching. Recent advances in AI have led to novel automated public speaking training feedback tools, but research has focused on academic prototypes and little is known about the efficacy of these commercial applications. We obtain expert perspectives on the efficacy and design of commercial AI-based public speaking training tools, and propose guidelines for their improvement. The research involved 16 semi-structured interviews and 2 focus groups with public speaking experts focused on these tools, their potential integration into traditional coaching, and suggestions for enhancing these systems. Experts acknowledged the value of AI tools in handling repetitive, technical aspects of training, allowing coaches to focus on higher-level skills. However, they also highlighted key issues in current designs, emphasising the need for higher-level feedback that targets communicative goals (e.g., authenticity, energy) over low-level behavioural metrics, contextualised instructions with clear training goals, and personalisation to the trainee's experience level and authentic speaking style.

**Keywords:** public speaking · soft skills training · artificial intelligence · feedback

## 1 Introduction

Public speaking skills are essential in both personal and professional contexts. Public speaking training typically relies on experienced coaches. However, digital transformation and artificial intelligence (AI) integration into education are reshaping communication skills development. Research has explored AI tools' potential for public speaking skills training, such as through the automation of feedback on public speaking delivery based on the analysis of verbal and non-verbal behaviours [9,16–19]. Studies on academic prototypes demonstrate benefits including increased confidence [7] or improved speech performance [3].


J. Weidlich et al. (Eds.): EC-TEL 2026, LNCS 16905, pp. 164–179, 2027.
https://doi.org/10.1007/978-3-032-37979-5_12

Commercial public speaking training platforms have emerged, such as Poised, Orai, and Yoodli, which offer immediate, AI-enabled automated feedback on public speaking performances. However, little is known about their efficacy, or about public speaking coaches' opinions of these tools. Expert insights remain largely absent from literature investigating AI-driven public speaking training tools, despite their unique understanding of effective public speaking pedagogy and their ability to assess communicative performances and provide personalised, actionable feedback to trainees.

This paper addresses this gap by engaging public speaking experts in interviews and focus groups, inviting critical reflection on selected commercial tools. The study reports on expert perceptions of these systems, from which we identify design principles to guide the development of technology-enhanced public speaking training frameworks better aligned with experts' pedagogical insights.

## 2 Background

The past decade has seen a surge in research on computerised public speaking training. These studies typically involve prototypes that integrate multimodal social signal analysis for automated feedback. Such feedback often targets varied behaviours, including speaking rate, filler words, gestures, gaze, posture, among others GestureLens [17] offers visualisations of speakers' gestural dynamics; VoiceCoach [16] and Web Pitcher [9] focus on analysing and visualising prosodic features; Presentation Trainer [12] analyses body posture and movement cues. Other academic tools adopt unique perspectives: EmoCo [18] emphasises emotional expressiveness; RocSpeak [19] combines automated behavioural analysis with crowdsourced peer feedback; AutoManner [14] identifies behavioural mannerisms (e.g. repetitive motions). These systems differ in the type (visualisations, scores), modality (visuals, text, haptics), and temporality (real-time, post-training) of feedback. Other tools like LISSA [1], MACH [6], and Cicero [3] simulate social situations with virtual agents.

Most studies on these systems involve user evaluations with subjects of diverse public speaking proficiency. Sample sizes range from small pilot groups (e.g., 10–20 users [14,17]) to more extensive evaluations (e.g., 40+ users [3,13,19]); with the randomised evaluation of the RAP system by Ochoa et al. standing out as the largest and most ecologically valid [10]. Evaluations assess improvements in specific non-verbal behaviours as well as in more subjective ratings such as confidence, expressiveness, or overall quality, often via pre/post third-party ratings. For instance, VoiceCoach led to improvements in vocal dynamics [16]; Rhema helped regulate pacing and reduce filler words [4]; GestureLens increased gestural awareness [17]; and RocSpeak increased self-confidence and performance ratings [19]. While these promising findings highlight the potential benefits of automated feedback in building public speaking skills, academic prototypes are often evaluated after isolated sessions. This overlooks holistic trainee journeys and how technology-enhanced training activities may integrate within them.

Beyond academic research, numerous commercial public speaking training applications have emerged. We present a selection of these tools chosen for their technological diversity, visibility, and adoption. Microsoft Speaker Coach, integrated into PowerPoint, offers feedback on vocal aspects (pace, filler words, intonation, etc.). VocaCoach also focuses on vocal analysis (pitch variation, volume, speech rate, pause frequency). PolymnIA offers multimodal feedback, analysing prosody, gestures, postures, and facial expressions. Tools like Poised, Orai, and Yoodli leverage AI to provide personalised speech coaching. VirtualOrator and VirtualSpeech propose Virtual Reality (VR) environments to simulate public speaking scenarios. These commercial tools often build upon similar architectures and designs as the research prototypes presented above. However, the technical pipelines they use to obtain behavioural cues or to produce feedback are undisclosed, and independent evaluations of their effectiveness remain unavailable.

Thus, while research projects offer insights into the design and benefits of automated public speaking feedback systems, studies have yet to evaluate current-generation commercial systems. What opportunities do these technologies bring to enhance public speaking training? What challenges do learners face when relying solely on these systems? Can they integrate with existing coaches' practices, leveraging technology to enhance training for optimal learner outcomes? We believe experts are essential to guide system evaluation, refinement, and adoption: this research explores experts' perspectives on AI-driven public speaking training systems. To that end, we conduct interviews and focus groups with public speaking coaches to investigate how training systems may be integrated into their practice.

## 3 Interviews with Public Speaking Coaches

In this first study, we conducted semi-structured interviews with public speaking experts to ground our research and the design of our subsequent workshops in their domain expertise. The interview guide covered: trainees' profiles and motivations; training context; factors coaches consider when evaluating public speaking performance; and activities they engage in during training. Interviews were transcribed manually and analysed using inductive thematic analysis [2]: two researchers familiarised themselves with the data, the lead researcher generated initial codes and proposed tentative themes, which were then iteratively discussed, refined, combined, and finalised with the second researcher.

### 3.1 Study Participants

We recruited 16 French expert public speaking coaches (12 women, 4 men) via LinkedIn and our professional networks for voluntary, uncompensated interviews—7 in person and 9 via phone or online video. Coaches worked with diverse client populations (individuals/groups, corporate, adolescents/adults), with some further focusing on specific populations: young people (2/16), women

(2/16), and managers (1/16). In terms of orientation, 6/16 identified as generalists and 7/16 as specialists (not captured for 3/16). The reported specialities spanned seven dimensions: self-confidence and psychological preparation (11/16), content and structure of the speech (10/16), verbal and rhetorical work (6/16), vocal techniques (4/16), visual and nonverbal cues (3/16), interaction with listeners (2/16), and presentation media (1/16). Most participants (13/16) reported expertise across two or more of these dimensions. The participants were predominantly independent practitioners or founders of their own coaching structures, with several combining independent practice with other professional affiliations. Their reported years of experience as public speaking or related coaches ranged from 2 to 10 years (median=6 years), reflecting a mix of recently established and more experienced practitioners. All were based in France.

### 3.2 Results

We report below the three themes that emerged from our analysis.

*Public speaking trainees' needs* - A first recurring comment was that prospective clients approach coaches with specific goals, often preparing for near-future speaking opportunities driving their desire to improve, rather than a general aim to become better speakers. Understanding clients' needs and clarifying their immediate goals is typically the coaches' first step. While trainees face varied challenges, all 16 coaches note that the vast majority of trainees initially hold a degree of public speaking anxiety and express their desire to overcome it. Coaches first build self-confidence, which brings natural improvements in performance; after this is established, targeted activities to build behavioural and rhetorical skills further strengthen confidence. Coaches also overwhelmingly report that trainees initially have a very critical view of their own skills. This negative bias is prevalent, even though coaches report that such clients do not necessarily exhibit poor skills. Coaches typically support trainees in reframing these negative self-perceptions.

*Dimensions of speech quality* - Coaches typically evaluate public speakers according to three major and three secondary quality dimensions. (1) Content: Focuses on word choice, speech structure, and argument elaboration. Coaches recommend adapting messages to the targeted audience. (2) Form: Encompasses non-verbal cues, including visual (gestures, facial expressions, posture, space use) and vocal dimensions (tone, intonation, speaking rate, intensity, articulation, pronunciation). (3) Goals and Outcomes: Represents the intended speech outcome, linked to the speaker's goals (to inform, persuade or inspire their audience). The three additional secondary dimensions were: (4) effective use of presentation media (5) audience management including Q&As, and (6) what several coaches called "extras" ( *"petit plus"*)—subjective qualities that distinguish outstanding speakers.

*Pillars of coaching activities* - We identify three main pillars of public speaking coaches' activities, tools, and exercises, corresponding to different temporalities and aspects of public speaking activities. (1) Preparation - This involves actions in advance of a public speech. For coaches, it is crucial to define objectives and select content accordingly: what will be said, and why. Anticipating material conditions (e.g. at a pulpit, standing, etc.) and the audience characteristics is also crucial. *"There is no good speaker who is not a prepared speaker."* P3. (2) Stress management - This covers methods for managing stress and performance anxiety both in the few weeks/days prior to a speech and in the minutes leading to the speech. Activities include breathing techniques, relaxation, visualization, or cognitive restructuring. *"Having methods and techniques [to manage stress] is extremely reassuring."* P2. (3) Delivery - This concerns the practice of the behavioural aspects of delivering a speech to achieve great public speaking performances. Coaches described public speaking delivery along three modalities: vocal, verbal, and visual. *"It's really a combination of rhythm, tone, posture, voice, gaze, that will make us effective."* P1. They suggest varied behaviour-specific exercises tailored to each client's needs.

## 4 Design Workshops

We recruited a subset of public speaking experts from our initial interview study (Sect. 3), aiming for complementary specialities. Seven experts participated in two workshops in France (4 in Paris, 3 in Nantes), compensated at a fixed hourly rate. Equipped with the understanding of public speaking coaching and coaches' mindsets obtained in interviews, we prepared design workshops to explore expert perspectives on AI-based public speaking training systems.

- In what formats, contexts, and for what tasks, can these systems be useful?
- Are the presented systems designed appropriately?
- Do experts believe such systems allow independent training, without a coach? Can these systems integrate into coaches' training practice?
- What key features complement coaches' practice?

We began workshops with an icebreaker: coaches chose animal cards (e.g., squirrel, bear, etc.) and imagined how they would perform public speaking imitating that animal. Beyond a simple icebreaker, this aimed to quickly engage the coaches in discussing their public speaking visions. We then proceeded by reminding experts of our objectives, and introduced a discussion framework based on typical brainstorming rules: no interruptions, positive listening, and no criticism.

*Presentation of PolymnIA and VocaCoach* - After the introduction, we presented two commercial, AI-based public speaking training solutions to coaches to highlight market offerings. We selected *PolymnIA* and *VocaCoach* for our design workshops following multiple criteria. First, the two tools embody different analytical paradigms: *VocaCoach* focuses on vocal and prosodic analysis (pitch, pauses, speech rate and articulation), whereas *PolymnIA* adopts a multimodal approach combining vocal, facial and bodily expression analysis. This contrast allowed the experts to discuss both modality-specific and integrated feedback strategies. Second, both offer a French-language interface and originate from a French-speaking design context, which was a methodological requirement:

it ensured that experts evaluated the tools themselves rather than coping with a language barrier, and avoided confounding our results with culture-specific communication conventions embedded in non-francophone tools. Third, both tools are mature commercial products publicly available outside research or enterprise-restricted contexts, ensuring reproducibility of the evaluation. Limiting the evaluation to these two tools, rather than surveying a wider set, was a deliberate methodological choice: it enabled the in-depth, hands-on manipulation and critical discussion required by our co-design workshop format, where deeper engagement was prioritised over overall review of a wide range of tools.

*PolymnIA*[1] is an online platform providing AI-enabled feedback on recorded speeches. PolymnIA allows users to record a speech via webcam, then generates a performance report. No themes or guidance are provided to users prior to speaking; only a target speech duration needs to be provided. After recording, PolymnIA quickly offers a detailed report on verbal ("Fond"), vocal ("Forme"), and gestural ("Gestuel") aspects, with a general score and various visualisations. A highly detailed (13-page) document with extensive feedback categories can be downloaded. However, the recorded video cannot be reviewed by users after analysis. *VocaCoach*[2] is a similar online platform generating feedback on a user video recording. Users record speeches specifying a target duration, but receive no preparation or guidance. Unlike PolymnIA, VocaCoach only analyses vocal aspects. The feedback interface provides an overall vocal performance score (e.g., 80%) and a general summary (e.g., "That's a good speech! These points can still be improved..."). A spider chart displays five vocal dimensions: speech rate, tone, articulation, hesitations, and rhythm, each with a 1–5 performance score. Users can click each vocal dimension for general information, a description of the system's technical assessment method, and improvement tips, including linked pedagogical videos. For instance, the speech rate dimension offers example videos of speakers with "slow", "fast", or "right" pace.

In workshops, we demonstrated both systems by showing a pre-recorded two-minute speech and asking experts to take notes on speaker performance. We then shared the feedback reports generated by PolymnIA and VocaCoach on the pre-recorded speech. After each demonstration, we presented the systems' interfaces, encouraging participants to ask questions, reflect on the systems' interfaces and feedback design, as well as on their potential use in their coaching practice.

*Prospective Design* - We presented prospective AI-based public speaking training exercises sourced from other systems or academic research but not implemented in Polymnla and VocaCoach, to invite participants to imagine other AI-based features. This included (1) an exercise on the management of silences (e.g. as in [3]) (2) on adopting good postures and gestures (e.g. as in [12]) (3) on inserting emotions in the speech (4) on integrating peer feedback (e.g. as in [19]), and (5) audience interaction in Virtual Reality (e.g. as in [3]). This was illustrated with a live demonstration of the REVITALISE VR system [11].

---

[1] `polymnia-france.com/`.
[2] https://vocacoach.fr/.

*Creativity Sessions* - After these presentations, we conducted creativity sessions where participants proposed designs, working first individually, then pooling thoughts. We asked participants to consider the central question: "In the future, what would be a truly efficient system for training public speaking?", with secondary considerations including: "For whom? How often? With whom? When (key moments/activities)?". Materials (A3 sheets, post-its, pens, stickers) were provided. In a first individual step, participants had five minutes to write as many design ideas as possible. They then presented their proposals to the group. An additional individual round allowed experts to produce a final design in twenty minutes, potentially incorporating their peers' ideas, which they then presented. Finally, participants voted on their preferred solution, followed by a group discussion.

## 5 Data Analysis and Key Insights

Using the same method as for the interviews (see 3), we used inductive thematic analysis to analyse the focus group transcripts. Two researchers familiarised themselves with the data, and a single researcher coded initial open codes from the transcripts, from which the two researchers iteratively developed and refined the themes reported below. We combine and highlight the insights obtained from all workshop activities including system presentations, creativity sessions, and discussions.

### 5.1 AI-Based Training Systems Afford Useful Self-Guided Training

**Supporting repeated public speaking rehearsals is a key benefit.** The coaches were very receptive to using systems like VocaCoach or PolymnIA, especially for independent practice between sessions and for providing basic feedback on core skills. They overwhelmingly agreed that such systems were ideal for enabling regular practice, allowing learners to practice a given speech multiple times. *"You have to rehearse speeches, you have to practice hearing yourself. With software, it's great because [trainees] understand that they have to rehearse out loud"* (W1-P4).

**The neutrality of an automated system can defuse emotional barriers to training.** Coaches noted that training in the safety of one's home with a neutral computer solution can disinhibit trainees: *"[With AI-based feedback] you are being judged by a machine and not by human beings"* (W1-P2). W1-P4 agreed, noting fewer emotional"risks" with a machine *"The software is interesting, by its neutrality, its technical, emotionless side. We are too connected to each other and do not want to offend [our trainees]"*.

**Training systems can support time-consuming exercises, allowing coaches to focus on higher-level concerns.** W1-P4 was enthusiastic about AI tools enabling independent practice of speaking techniques, with the system handling tasks coaches might not cover themselves or would prefer to outsource. *"As a coach it can save me time, time to work on the sensitivity of my client.*

*These tools [...] can free me from the basics"* (W1-P4). They give the example of improving speech rhythm by recording a speech several times and focusing on tempo: *"[It is beneficial to] record yourself, and listen to yourself again, and again"* (W1-P4).

Insight 1: Experts find value in AI-powered feedback systems' capacity to enable repeated, frequent rehearsals in a low-stakes, neutral environment, minimising trainees' emotional risks. This can free up coach time to focus on higher-level pedagogical, personalised concerns.

From this perspective, an AI-powered training system, providing neutral, technical feedback, can transform the trainee-coach dynamic. It frees the coach to focus on higher-level aspects: transmitting emotions, uncovering one's authentic speaking styles, and identifying activities to improve these areas.

## 5.2 The Complexity of Designing Public Speaking Feedback

A key focus group topic was the design of feedback. All coaches agreed it is difficult to gauge the right feedback level for trainees, and both systems seemed to often miss the mark.

**Feedback criteria should be carefully selected and organised.** Feedback elements need to be understandable and carefully selected according to speech context and user goals. Most coaches judged PolymnIA reports as too detailed, inducing cognitive load, leading to users not knowing what to focus on. According to W2-P7, it is unreasonable to expect learners to take on numerous elements of feedback: *"I give 2–3 comments maximum on trainees' performances, otherwise they will not remember anything and it will be useless"*. Furthermore, experts were not sure users would correctly understand all feedback items, as some covered complex or obscure public speaking concepts without providing adequate explanations or improvement suggestions: *"For feedback to be relevant, systems should present short videos to explain key concepts. Here, it remains too abstract and we can do nothing with it"* (W2-P6).

According to coaches, some feedback criteria were problematic, either being irrelevant in certain situations, or poorly structured in terms of importance or key categories. Feedback should be relevant to a trainee's context, including the speech occasion, subject, audience, and speaker intentions. W1-P1 gave the example of a criterion on the PolymnIA report"Use of Gerund Terms": *"In any speech, intended for any audience, [...] we cannot affirm that in all situations we need the same [evaluation] criteria."*. W1-P4 added that a public speaking performance cannot be analysed in isolation, but only in relation to its goals and the specific situation it is delivered in: *"Does the system take into account [the speaker's] intention, objective; the occasion, the context; the message?"*. They conceded that trainees could select, from a large list of AI-analysed feedback criteria, which ones to consider and which to disregard: this may be particularly relevant in tandem with a coach, who could identify and recommend particular feedback criteria to focus on.

Further, according to W1-P1 and W1-P3, the feedback structure shown in Polymnla may be confusing, with various criteria presented side by side, but not in order of importance or by theme: *"There are several types of criteria mixed together"* (W1-P1). To them, it is important to organise feedback carefully, grouping high-level speech elements on the one hand, and very specific, low-level behavioural elements on the other. Compared to PolymnIA, participants found VocaCoach more suited to independent user training due to more concise, high-level feedback focusing on a smaller number of understandable and actionable elements. Several participants agreed that an ideal application should be configurable by public speaking coaches, in order to solely present feedback criteria relevant to learners at a given point in their particular training journey: *"As a coach who supports a trainee [in their learning journey], I should be able to choose the feedback that appears in the report"* (W1-P2).

**Feedback valence should be neutral, or encouraging.** Interestingly, the two systems were seen as opposed in positioning—PolymnIA being too detailed, VocaCoach too surface-level. A participant noted VocaCoach's feedback was generally positively biased, which could be problematic if learners used the system before in-person coaching sessions. For instance, trainees may receive highly flattering feedback, unduly improving their public speaking confidence. W2-P7 noted: *"What scares me would be someone who uses [such a system], and it calls my advice into question. For the ego, it's good but [it can be counter-productive]"*. Still, this design choice of simplicity and positivity in providing feedback could be of interest to some users. W1-P3 noted that simple, generic recommendations can be good starting points: *"What I find interesting [in VocaCoach] is the more simplified aspect compared to PolymnIA. In particular, the fact that they explain a little about what is generally expected [for a given dimension]."* Thus, systems like VocaCoach may be primarily useful for beginners starting their public speaking improvement journey: *"It depends on the [trainee's] level. The feedback [of VocaCoach], for me, is intended for someone who is just starting out"* (W1-P1).

> Insight 2: Experts highlight the complexity in designing public speaking feedback. It should be carefully selected, limited to a few key elements, organised logically and hierarchically, and tailored to the trainee's goals and context; it should be understandable and actionable; it should generally be neutral, although beginners may benefit from encouragement.

### 5.3 Feedback Should Address Higher-Level Communicative Goals

**Public speaking behaviour is only useful to analyse insofar as it conveys higher-level meaning.** Participants observed that many PolymnIA and VocaCoach feedback items focused on lower-level behaviour trends while missing high-level concepts of good public speaking performances. Commenting on pause and silence management feedback, W1-P4 noted: *"We choose to be silent because there is meaning in silence, and [AI-feedback] does not say this."*. They expressed that complex evaluation criteria, such as enthusiasm, commitment or energy, are missing: *"Here in the example feedback you show us [...], I'm missing something of the enthusiasm, of the commitment [of the speaker]"* (W1-P4). Participant W1-P2 explained how higher-level criteria such as "commitment" or "enthusiasm" are essentially expressed through the speaker's non-verbal behaviour: *"It's in the gaze, it's in the gestures."* Are low-level behavioural characteristics useless if what truly matters are higher-level criteria? W1-P2 clarified that these elements are intrinsically linked and what matters is providing clear relationships between behavioural indicators and higher-level criteria: *"For [evaluating a speaker's] energy, [an ideal system would] look at the variation in expressions of the user. Does the user change their state a lot."*

**The focus on lower-level public speaking behaviour feedback risks trainees conforming to standard, inauthentic styles.** Several coaches questioned whether focusing on specific, objective behavioural criteria could encourage conformity. They argued that authenticity is essential and conforming to stereotypical speaking can be harmful: *"Those who train [with such a simplistic view] can acquire a sort of robotic style, which will ultimately deprive them of the nuance that coaching can provide"* (W1-P4); *"The problem with using a [public speaking assessment] rubric is that we break the naturalness by focusing on precise criteria."* (W2-P6); *"Be careful not to make speakers become too'smooth', because that is not authentic"* (W2-P6). W1-P3 raised risks that exist in focusing solely on behaviour and technique. They gave examples of speakers who can be very good technically, but who do not capture and engage the audience well. W1-P4 added: *"When you're not great and all you have is technique, it's boring."*

> Insight 3: Experts highlight how feedback should target higher-level dimensions such as speakers' conveyed energy, enthusiasm, and commitment. Lower-level behavioural feedback may not be actionable, and runs the risk of encouraging trainees to conform to a standard, inauthentic style.

### 5.4 Public Speaking Training Activities Need Contextualization and Clear Instructions

**Public speaking training activities should be based on clear goals.** Coaches highlighted an issue regarding both systems related to the context in which they would be used. In the demonstrated versions, users were not given or asked any specific speaking goals or contexts: the only information required was the intended speech duration. Beginners or unprepared users may lack a prepared topic, or may need more guidance to start training. Coaches pointed out that in the absence of a key goal motivating a speech, any performance can appear flat as there is no key message to convey or communicative intention driving the trainee. Thus, attempting to improve speaking skills "in general" without a specific context or topic is counterproductive: *"The person is completely left* *to their own devices. During coaching sessions, we provide [basic contextual elements] to at least start the exercise. Without a situation, they can completely miss the exercise [i.e. exhibit poor speaking performance]. And if the results are bad, it risks confirming [their belief] that they are bad at public speaking"* (W2-P7). W1-P2 highlighted that setting training goals is a key preliminary step before engaging in any training activity, as it helps contextualise and give meaning to training, as well as motivate learners towards clear objectives: *"Every time we give a speech [in public speaking training group activities], we define the objectives of the speech. And we have someone who evaluates [the speaker] against these specific objectives."*

A specific section of the PolymnIA report provides an automated analysis of the speech theme (e.g. "Literary" or "Philosophical"). This element was noticed by coaches as a particularly interesting piece of feedback: *"The AI [should] be able to detect [whether this theme corresponds] the user's intention, otherwise it is missing the point"* (W1-P1). According to W1-P1, the system's ability to analyse speech themes is interesting but only relevant if this analysis relates to the trainee's goal. For instance, users could verify whether they managed to convey the right theme and adjust their speech accordingly if another theme appears to dominate. This reinforces that context and goal in which trainees engage with particular activities matter and should inform the provided feedback.

**Clear instructions should be provided to encourage trainees to meaningfully engage with training.** Another important discussion item concerned the physical, concrete context in which public speaking is performed. Neither PolymnIA nor VocaCoach provided information or guidance on how to record oneself. One of our example videos was recorded sitting, and W2-P7 was surprised that users were not asked to stand up or given instructions on camera distance: *"Sitting cancels out part of the exercise"*. Similarly, this lack of contextualization and instructions was seen by W1-P3 as leading to key mistakes, such as reading speeches from written notes: *"I noted an essential thing [in this example] that I do not find in the feedback: from the intonation, the rhythm, I have the impression that [the speaker] was reading something, and so there was a rhythm which lacked naturalness. These are essential things that I address all the time [in their practice]."* Training systems should give physical, contextual instructions before training activities.

Participants also pointed out the interface design of the training activity itself. During recording in PolymnIA, the trainees face their screen and they can see their live webcam feed; overlays highlighting detected gestures and facial expressions are superimposed on the performance video. W2-P7 noted: *"Seeing yourself [while training], you study yourself and you are less natural."* W2-P5 agreed: *"[Trainees] risk learning to speak in front of a computer [instead of in front of an audience]."*

A design issue noted by W2-P5 regarding PolymnIA was that users found the detailed feedback unverifiable and difficult to contextualise as they could not review their video, only their transcript. Feedback systems should provide mechanisms to review past presentations in order to reflect on feedback focused on behaviour, ideally time-aligned to easily retrieve segments of poor or good performance. *"The document gives advice but we no longer know what we did [at that time]. It remains very abstract"* (W2-P5).

**Systems should contain activities for knowledge acquisition and exercises for practising essential skills.** One participant mentioned that applications should provide guidance and knowledge acquisition activities before actual training rehearsals followed by public speaking analysis. *"They [should] provide a training space. I think that for people who train all alone, it's a very good start"* (W1-P2). They argued that undertaking exercises to perfect certain behavioural techniques and performing full speech practice are very different activities, appropriate at various moments in a learner's journey, and should be addressed through distinct activity types: e.g. video examples and behaviour-specific training exercises with adapted feedback.

Insight 4: Experts described how practical instructions need to be provided before public speaking practice. Users should specify clear goals and objectives that help define the training activities, or be provided with sample contexts including speech topics and audience descriptions. Trainees should be given physical instructions such as standing and performing their speech as they would in real-life conditions. Finally, systems should support knowledge acquisition and specific behavioural exercises as separate activities from public speaking rehearsal followed by holistic feedback.

### 5.5 Training Activities Should Adapt to the Speaker's Personal Speaking Style

**Public speaking feedback should foster the expression of trainees' authentic styles.** Earlier, we described how participants highlighted that low-level feedback risks leading trainees to adopt conformist public speaking styles. Related to this, participants argued that autonomous learning systems such as PolymnIA and VocaCoach should help speakers identify their personal public speaking style and tailor activities to strengthen it. As participant W2-P7 put it: *"I don't like [speakers] who are too formatted, who make certain gestures because they have been told to do it that way. This irks me because I no longer see a person, I only see technique. In public speaking, what we want is the authentic person."* Thus, training should adapt to the style of the speaker, building on it instead of forcing trainees to adopt a specific style: *"I don't ask [of my clients] that they be like me. When I talk about energy in my coaching, I am going to take their own energy into account"* (W1-P4).

A crucial design question is how to develop public speaking skills with AI-based interfaces, which are necessarily trained on reference public speaking data, while allowing trainees to maintain authentic styles. Here, we observe disagreement on how to achieve this through course organisation. W2-P5 believed it was appropriate to start with learning basic techniques before developing one's own style: *"We must first learn how to speak in an "academic" way, and then [learn to] display our own style."* Disagreeing, W2-P6 argued that learners must first learn to be natural and authentic before perfecting your style through specific techniques. W1-P1 framed their coaching similarly: instead of focusing on correcting mistakes, they focused on learner strengths, taking the speaker's authentic style as a starting point and helping develop it further *"As a coach, I rely on my client's rhythm, style, tone. So if I impose you [a rigid set of speaking style criteria], even if I think it's correct, I'm not taking your nature into consideration."* Finally, they indicated that regardless of overall course structure, training activities should be sequenced according to trainee level, and that exercise complexity, feedback, and overall training activities should increase progressively: *"The more you increase in level, the more you must increase the finesse of the feedback"* (W1-P1).

> Insight 5: Public speaking training systems should be personalised to trainees according to two key dimensions: their current level of experience in public speaking, and their authentic speaking style and behaviour.

## 6 Discussion

A first key insight from our design workshops is that easy, on-demand practice using a judgment-free automated system was a valuable feature for our participants. Two main types of training modalities were identified which could be enabled by AI-based training systems: 1) holistic speech practice and 2) purposeful pedagogical training activities focused on specific speaking aspects. However, our study reveals a notable disconnect between existing technological implementations and the pedagogical foundations articulated by our participants and the public speaking literature. Coaches insisted that useful feedback should consider the user's goal, profile, and situational context (personal/professional context, audience size, etc.), be supported by clear physical and contextual instructions, and be organised, selected, actionable, and tailored to the speaker's idiosyncratic style. These coach-articulated recommendations align with—and extend—the principles found in public speaking manuals such as Lucas's *The Art of Public Speaking* [8], Duarte's *Resonate* [5], and Toogood's *The New Articulate Executive* [15], which emphasise that effective public speaking is inherently audience-centred, culturally situated, and purpose-driven. The design of currently analysed systems contrasts sharply with both.

A striking omission in all analysed systems is also the absence of support for public speaking anxiety, despite its prevalence among learners. This is particularly concerning, as all interviewed coaches identified anxiety management and cognitive restructuring as foundational—confidence must precede technique—and many trainees require support in overcoming feelings of illegitimacy and low self-worth before engaging meaningfully with performance skills. This pedagogical stance has also been corroborated and discussed in previous research works [8,15]. We see that the current generation of training systems prioritise feedback based on numerically quantifiable aspects of delivery. While essential, these features cannot fully represent such aspects as speaker authenticity or energy. Coaches expressed concern that this overemphasis on technical correctness could lead to the emergence of conformist, homogenised speech patterns. This critique echoes the frameworks presented in [5], where the emotional and structural depth of a performance is central to its effectiveness. Similarly, Lucas [8] and Toogood [15] both highlight that rhetorical effectiveness arises from a synthesis of content, form, and emotional delivery—dimensions difficult to capture through surface metrics alone.

Moreover, the presented systems lacked integrated curricula, pathways, or coach-configurable progression plans. Coaches emphasized the importance of guiding learners through the various stages of their journey. They noted the value of reviewing their past speeches to consolidate learning. These instructional needs are directly aligned with the didactic structures proposed in the literature [8,15]. The gap between these comprehensive educational models and the fragmented structure of current systems highlights a missed opportunity for meaningful learning support.

## 7 Conclusion

Our paper reported on interviews and design workshops conducted with coaches regarding their perspectives on technology-enhanced public speaking training. Overall, experts view AI-driven public speaking tools as valuable, particularly for enabling repeated rehearsal and behaviour tracking. However, they emphasise expert supervision in selecting and prioritising feedback, adjusting it to user profiles and goals, and preserving individual authentic speaking styles. Central challenges highlighted in our research include feedback design, and the contextualisation and personalisation of training. Based on these findings, we offer several design principles (Insights 1–5) for future public speaking training systems. Future user studies with trainees will be essential to empirically validate our proposed design guidelines. Our research remains limited in scope regarding the diversity of reviewed systems. Since our workshops, many commercial systems have deployed Large Language Models, offering new capabilities (e.g., analyses and recommendations on speech transcripts) that warrant further investigation.

**Acknowledgments.** This research was partly funded under the ANR REVITALISE grant (ANR-21-CE33-0016-02).

**Disclosure of Interests.** The authors have no competing interests to declare that are relevant to the content of this article.

## References


1. Ali, M.R., et al.: LISSA—Live interactive social skill assistance. In: 2015 International Conference on Affective Computing and Intelligent Interaction. pp. 173–179. IEEE (2015)
2. Braun, V., Clarke, V.: Using thematic analysis in psychology. Qual. Res. Psychol. **3**(2), 77–101 (2006)
3. Chollet, M., Marsella, S., Scherer, S.: Training public speaking with virtual social interactions: Effectiveness of real-time feedback and delayed feedback. J. Multi. User Int. **16**(1), 17–29 (2022)
4. Damian, I., Tan, C.S., Baur, T., Schöning, J., Luyten, K., André, E.: Augmenting social interactions: realtime behavioural feedback using social signal processing techniques. In: Proceedings of the 33rd Annual ACM Conference on Human factors in Computing Systems, pp. 565–574 (2015)
5. Duarte, N.: Resonate: Present Visual Stories that Transform Audiences. John Wiley & Sons Inc, Hoboken, NJ (2010)
6. Hoque, M., Courgeon, M., Martin, J.C., Mutlu, B., Picard, R.W.: MACH: my automated conversation coach. In: Proceedings of the 2013 ACM International Joint Conference on Pervasive and Ubiquitous Computing, pp. 697–706 (2013)
7. Huang, Z., et al.: SpeechMirror: a multimodal visual analytics system for personalized reflection of online public speaking effectiveness. IEEE Trans. Visual Comput. Graphics 30 (2024)
8. Lucas, S.E., Stob, P.: The Art of Public Speaking. McGraw-Hill Education, New York, NY, 13th edn. (2020) bound edition
9. Niebuhr, O.: Computer-assisted prosody training: improving public speakers' vocal charisma with the web-pitcher. Revista da ABRALIN 20(1) (2021)
10. Ochoa, X., Dominguez, F.: Controlled evaluation of a multimodal system to improve oral presentation skills in a real learning setting. Br. J. Edu. Technol. **51**(5), 1615–1630 (2020)
11. Ochs, M., Ristorcelli, M., D'Ambra, A., Casanova, R., Pergandi, J.M.: Revitalise: virtual behavioral skills training for public speaking. In: Proceedings of the 24th ACM International Conference on Intelligent Virtual Agents. pp. 1–3 (2024)
12. Schneider, J., Börner, D., Van Rosmalen, P., Specht, M.: Presentation trainer: what experts and computers can tell about your nonverbal communication. J. Comput. Assist. Learn. **33**(2), 164–177 (2017)
13. Tanaka, H., et al.: Automated social skills trainer. In: Proceedings of the 20th International Conference on Intelligent User Interfaces, pp. 17–27 (2015)
14. Tanveer, M.I., Zhao, R., Chen, K., Tiet, Z., Hoque, M.E.: AutoManner: an automated interface for making public speakers aware of their mannerisms. In: Proceedings of the 21st international conference on intelligent user interfaces, pp. 385–396 (2016)
15. Toogood, G.: New Articulate Executive: Look, 1st edn. Act and Sound Like a Leader. McGraw-Hill Education, New York (2010)
16. Wang, X., Zeng, H., Wang, Y., Wu, A., Sun, Z., Ma, X., Qu, H.: VoiceCoach: interactive evidence-based training for voice modulation skills in public speaking. In: Proceedings of the 2020 CHI Conference on Human Factors in Computing Systems. pp. 1–12 (2020)
17. Zeng, H., Wang, X., Wang, Y., Wu, A., Pong, T.C., Qu, H.: Gesturelens: Visual analysis of gestures in presentation videos. IEEE Trans. Visual Comput. Graphics **29**(8), 3685–3697 (2022)

18. Zeng, H., Wang, X., Wu, A., Wang, Y., Li, Q., Endert, A., Qu, H.: EmoCo: Visual analysis of emotion coherence in presentation videos. IEEE Trans. Visual Comput. Graphics **26**(1), 927–937 (2019)
19. Zhao, R., Li, V., Barbosa, H., Ghoshal, G., Hoque, M.E.: Semi-automated & collaborative online training module for improving communication skills. Proceedings of the ACM on Interactive, Mobile, Wearable and Ubiquitous Technologies **1**(2), 1–20 (2017)

# Designing Teacher-Centered Interfaces to Elicit Pedagogical Context for LLM-Based Content Generation

Abdolali Faraji(✉), Mohammadreza Tavakoli, Mohammad Moein, Mohammadreza Molavi, and Gábor Kismihók

Leibniz Information Centre for Science and Technology (TIB), Hanover, Germany
{abdolali.faraji,reza.tavakoli,mohammad.moein,mohammadreza.molavi, gabor.kismihok}@tib.eu

**Abstract.** Large Language Models (LLMs) can help teachers generate and adapt educational materials, but most interactions still rely on free-form prompting, making instructional intent difficult to express and reuse. In this paper, we study how teacher-facing interfaces can elicit pedagogically meaningful contextual information and reduce ad hoc prompt engineering. We first conducted a requirement analysis with $N = 100$ teachers across 17 contextual fields. We measured *importance* and introduced *fill deficit* to identify "friction points" (i.e., information teachers consider important but are less likely to provide). Based on this analysis, we implemented a context-rich interface with targeted supports for important and friction-point fields. In a separate user study with a different sample of $N = 100$ teachers, the interface achieved high usability (SUS mean = 80.33), low perceived workload, and increased willingness to provide contextual information, particularly for friction-point fields. For further validation, we conducted a comparative pilot with $N = 10$ experienced teachers; participants reported a greater tendency to use content generated with our context-rich interface (72.2%) than content generated with a baseline GPT interface (37.0%).

**Keywords:** Teacher-centered interface design · LLM in education · Human-AI interaction · AI-assisted content authoring

## 1 Introduction

Online education has expanded, making digital tools increasingly central to equity and inclusion [14,29]. Teachers are under pressure to deliver personalized learning in these environments [9,29], yet translating pedagogical intent into effective digital content remains challenging. LLMs offer new opportunities to generate and adapt educational materials at scale [9], but how teachers should express instructional intent in LLM interactions is still unclear [10].

This problem is closely related to teacher cognition. Teachers' planning relies on pedagogical content knowledge, routines, beliefs, constraints, and contextual


J. Weidlich et al. (Eds.): EC-TEL 2026, LNCS 16905, pp. 180–194, 2027.
https://doi.org/10.1007/978-3-032-37979-5_13

judgments that are partly tacit and situated in practice [3,30]. Thus, the issue is not simply whether an LLM can use more context, but whether a teacher-facing system can help externalize selected parts of teachers' pedagogical reasoning without requiring teachers to restate their full professional judgment as a prompt.

Prior work largely focused on identifying which kinds of contextual and pedagogical information improved LLM outputs (often through prompt variants or template-driven studies) [9,18]. However, these studies provided limited insight into whether such pedagogical-context dimensions were reasonable and easy to provide for teachers during real instructional planning. In practice, much of this information remains tacit knowledge held by educators rather than explicit, machine-readable input [7], leaving teachers to translate context into free-form prompts [10]. This translation requires additional time and effort and can increase cognitive load [11,27].

Building on these observations, this work argues that high-quality educational content depends not only on prompts and generation strategies, but also on interfaces that help teachers express pedagogical intent in usable ways. We therefore address the gap between teachers' pedagogical expertise and the ways in which LLM interfaces elicit instructional input. We first conducted a requirement analysis ($N = 100$) to identify important and feasible pedagogical-context dimensions, as well as high *fill deficit* dimensions. We define fill deficit as a measured count of teachers who rated a dimension as important but reported that they would not usually provide it in ordinary AI use. We treat high fill deficit as an empirical proxy for an intention–provision gap related to planned-behavior accounts of intention and action [1], and interpret it as a design signal for possible interaction friction rather than as a direct measurement of a psychological state. We then implemented a context-rich interface to help teachers provide selected dimensions through structured interface fields. We evaluated the interface through a usability study ($N = 100$) and an additional comparative pilot with experienced teachers ($N = 10$), assessing the real-world usefulness of the generated content against a baseline GPT interface. Figure 1 summarizes the main steps and outcomes of this work. To guide this work, we formulated the following research questions:

- RQ1: Which pedagogical-context dimensions do teachers identify as most important, and which show the highest *fill deficit* when creating educational content with AI?
- RQ2: How can a teacher-centered, context-rich interface encourage teachers to provide richer contextual information for LLM-assisted content generation?
- RQ3: Compared to baseline GPT use, are educational content items generated through the context-rich workflow judged more appropriate for use in real teaching scenarios?

# 2 Related Work

## 2.1 LLMs in Educational Content Generation

Recent work in AI-supported education has evaluated LLMs as assistants for authoring and adapting educational materials. A central focus of this line of work has been how explicit pedagogical context, introduced through prompt variants or structured prompting, affects output quality and alignment [6,18]. For example, Krouska et al. showed that a system using tailored prompts based on course characteristics and feedback can improve content quality and personalization [17]. Similarly, Serra et al. and Choi et al. highlighted the importance of educational context in prompting, such as target group and instructional constraints, for steering model outputs [6]. These dimensions also correspond to established instructional-design decisions, such as specifying outcomes, learner characteristics, resources, constraints, and cognitive objectives [2,12], rather than arbitrary interface inputs. Beyond prompt-design studies, recent work has also explored more structured generation pipelines for concrete educational artifacts. Lohr et al. described using LLMs to generate course-specific semantically annotated learning objects, showing the value of tying generated materials more closely to course structure and domain semantics [21]. Likewise, Zheng et al. proposed a knowledge-enhanced approach for automatic lesson-plan generation, suggesting that external knowledge and stronger pedagogical grounding can improve the

**(1) Requirement analysis** (survey; $N = 100$ teachers)
**Input:** 17 contextual fields
**Measures:** importance and *fill deficit* (friction points)
**Top importance:** Learning Outcome, Level, Outline, Subject Area
**Top fill deficit:** Own Resources, Outline, Content Length.

↓

**(2) Interface design**
**Decision:** include high/medium-importance fields and prioritize friction points.
**Supports with:** AI auto-fill based on provided info; searching for and uploading relevant resources; suggested values with selectable options.

↓

**(3) Evaluation**
**User study** ($N = 100$):
*Usability:* SUS = 80.33
*Workload (selected NASA-TLX):* mental=2.24, effort=2.29, frustration=1.62
*Metadata provision:* +14.6 participants/field on average (range: +6 to +26)
**Comparative pilot** ($N = 10$): higher teacher preference for the generated content with our tool (72.2%) vs. baseline GPT UI (37.0%).

**Fig. 1.** Overview of the study workflow and key outcomes.

educational relevance of generated outputs [31]. Together, these studies further support the importance of structured educational context for content generation. At the same time, these approaches largely assume that such contextual information is readily available, leaving open how feasible it is for teachers to provide it during real-world planning.

### 2.2 Teacher-Centered and Structured Interaction with LLMs

Recent work has argued that teacher-facing LLM tools require a shift from ad hoc, prompt-only interaction toward teacher-centered interfaces that better match teachers' planning practices and expectations of control [5,10]. For instance, Arched [20] and Facet [13] explicitly expose instructional parameters in the interface. Related work also emphasized multi-step, teacher-in-the-loop workflows to maintain teacher control during authoring [8]. This highlights the need to understand which types of contextual information should be captured and how interfaces can enable their systematic use in everyday teacher workflows, as well as to design targeted support mechanisms that help teachers supply this information [24].

Beyond explicitly teacher-facing educational tools, adjacent HCI work similarly motivates interfaces that keep AI behavior inspectable and controllable. DirectGPT shows how direct-manipulation-style interaction can help users steer LLM outputs through visible, incremental edits rather than repeated free-form prompts [23]. For teacher-facing tools, this supports structured elicitation and active user control, but prior work offers limited guidance on which pedagogical-context inputs are most useful in practice and how to capture them without adding extraneous workload [16].

### 2.3 Lessons Learned: Practical Collection of Contextual Information

Overall, prior work demonstrates that contextual and pedagogical information can substantially improve AI-generated educational content, while also emphasizing the importance of maintaining teacher control [7,10,24]. However, a key gap remains: it is unclear which pedagogical-context dimensions are both valuable and practical for teachers to provide during everyday planning, and how interfaces can effectively support their structured expression. This gap motivates our requirement analysis, which identifies high-value dimensions and high fill-deficit dimensions, as well as our subsequent interface design that translates these insights into targeted supports for teacher–LLM interaction.

## 3 Requirement Analysis

### 3.1 Survey Design

Our requirement analysis aimed to identify which pedagogical-context dimensions teachers considered important for LLM-assisted content generation, with a focus on high fill-deficit dimensions: information teachers valued but said they would be less likely to provide in ordinary AI use. To operationalize this goal, we compiled a list of candidate dimensions by reviewing teacher-facing tools and prior interfaces for AI-assisted content generation [10,13,20,22]. We then selected 17 commonly used dimensions and ran an online survey with $N = 100$ teachers recruited via Prolific[1]. To support a consistent understanding of the survey items, each dimension was presented together with a short definition and an example. Participants then (i) rated each dimension's importance on a 5-point scale (1–5) and (ii) reported whether they would usually provide that information to an AI tool when generating content for students[2].

### 3.2 Results and Discussion

To summarize both importance and practical willingness to supply this information, we calculated the following two complementary measures for each pedagogical-context dimension $f$.

**Importance.** We defined importance as the count of teachers who rated the dimension as high-importance (4 or 5 out of 5):

$$\mathrm{Imp}(f) = |\{t \in T \mid r_{t,f} \geq 4\}|, \tag{1}$$

where $T$ is the set of teachers and $r_{t,f}$ is the teacher $t$'s rating for dimension $f$.

**Fill deficit.** We defined fill deficit as the count of teachers who considered the dimension important but reported that they would not usually provide it:

$$\mathrm{Def}(f) = |\{t \in T \mid r_{t,f} \geq 4 \ \wedge \ p_{t,f} = 0\}|, \tag{2}$$

where $p_{t,f} = 1$ if teacher $t$ would usually provide dimension $f$, and $p_{t,f} = 0$ otherwise. Thus, fill deficit is a measured survey quantity. We use high fill deficit to identify places where interface support may be needed, but we do not treat it as direct evidence of a psychological state called friction.

In this study, we focused on two key patterns in the results shown in Table 1: (i) dimensions with the highest importance and (ii) dimensions with high fill deficit. The most important dimensions were *Learning Outcomes* (97), *Level* (95), *Outline* (92), and *Subject Area* (91). The largest fill deficits were observed for *Own Resources* (43), *Outline* (39), and *Content Length* (29), indicating the dimensions for which teachers most often recognized the value of the information but still tended not to provide it in ordinary AI use.

Taken together, these results show which dimensions are not only pedagogically important, but also most likely to require targeted interface support. In particular, *Learning Outcomes* emerged as the most consistently valued dimension, with 97 of 100 teachers rating it as highly important. Two high fill-deficit dimensions are especially noteworthy: *Own Resources* and *Outline*. Here, *Own*

[1] Prolific: https://www.prolific.com/.

[2] Anonymized demographics and responses are available here: https://doi.org/10.6084/m9.figshare.31236421.

**Table 1.** Pedagogical-context dimension importance and fill deficit ($N = 100$). Importance: rating $\geq 4$; fill deficit: important but not usually provided.

| Pedagogical-context dimension | Importance Level | Importance | Fill Deficit |
|---|---|---|---|
| Learning Outcomes | High | 97 | 20 |
| Level | | 95 | 18 |
| Outline | | 92 | **39***|
| Subject Area | | 91 | 11 |
| Own Resources | Medium | 75 | **43*** |
| Target Audience | | 75 | 16 |
| Content Length | | 74 | **29*** |
| Bloom | | 71 | 23 |
| Time | | 70 | 20 |
| Output Type | | 69 | 12 |
| Accessibility Requirements | | 68 | 15 |
| Bias | Low | 59 | 21 |
| Instructional Approach | | 57 | 13 |
| Prior Knowledge | | 54 | 17 |
| Tone | | 53 | 18 |
| Modality | | 49 | 15 |
| Cultural Localization | | 46 | 13 |

*Note:* * indicates high fill deficit.

*Resources* refers to useful materials (e.g., files or webpages) that teachers already have or identify as relevant, whereas *Outline* specifies the intended structure of the generated content. Despite their high perceived importance, 57.3% of teachers who valued *Own Resources* said they would not provide it; the same was true for 42.4% of those who valued *Outline.*

## 4 Implementing the Context-Rich Interface

This section describes how the results of the requirement analysis were translated into a context-rich interface for educational content generation. We first identify which pedagogical-context dimensions should be represented as interface fields and then describe the UI components designed to support their completion. To provide a concrete implementation scenario, we focused on the generation of text-based educational content. Figure 3 presents the resulting interface. In the example shown, the teacher is preparing reading material for an introductory topic.

### 4.1 Selecting Interface Fields

To translate the requirement analysis into interface requirements, we first observed that the importance scores in Table 1 suggested a natural three-level pattern, separating dimensions into *high-importance*, *medium-importance*, and *low-importance* groups. To confirm this grouping, we performed a simple $k$-means clustering analysis and checked the elbow criterion, which supported a three-cluster solution ($k = 3$). Based on this result, we selected all high- and medium-importance dimensions ($\text{Imp}(f) >= 68$) as target interface fields, because they captured the contextual information teachers considered most valuable overall. We then additionally retained high-*fill deficit* dimensions ($\text{Def}(f) >= 29$) as targets for extra UI support, because these dimensions were not only important but also comparatively less likely to be provided in ordinary AI use. This two-step selection allowed the interface to cover broadly valued pedagogical-context dimensions while also addressing possible points of interaction friction identified in the requirement analysis.

### 4.2 Designing UI Support

To facilitate completing the target interface fields, especially fields corresponding to high fill-deficit dimensions, we implemented the following components[3]. See Fig. 2 for example UI components and Fig. 3 for the integrated study platform.

The intended workflow is that teachers choose a familiar topic, select or enter interface fields, optionally use AI support for selected fields, review and edit all generated field values, and then submit the completed form to generate the educational content item.

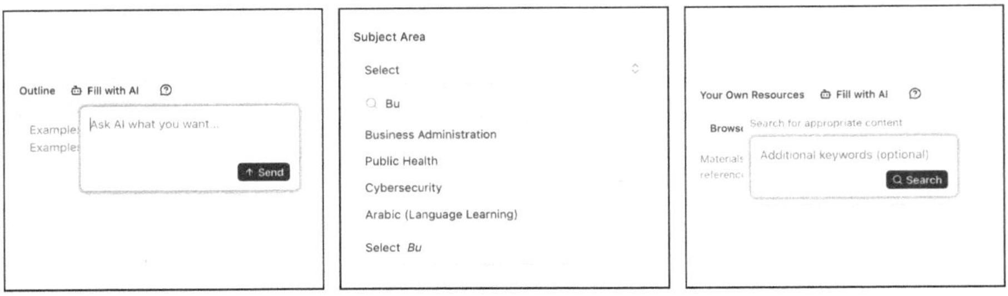


(a) Outline: Teacher is requesting AI to fill this field based on the context

(b) Subject area: Teacher is searching most common options and can add their own text

(c) Own resources: Teacher is searching for educational material

**Fig. 2.** Example UI components.

[3] These components were integrated into the eDoer platform, building on prior eDoer-related work presented in AIED, EC-TEL, and LAK venues [10,25,28,29].

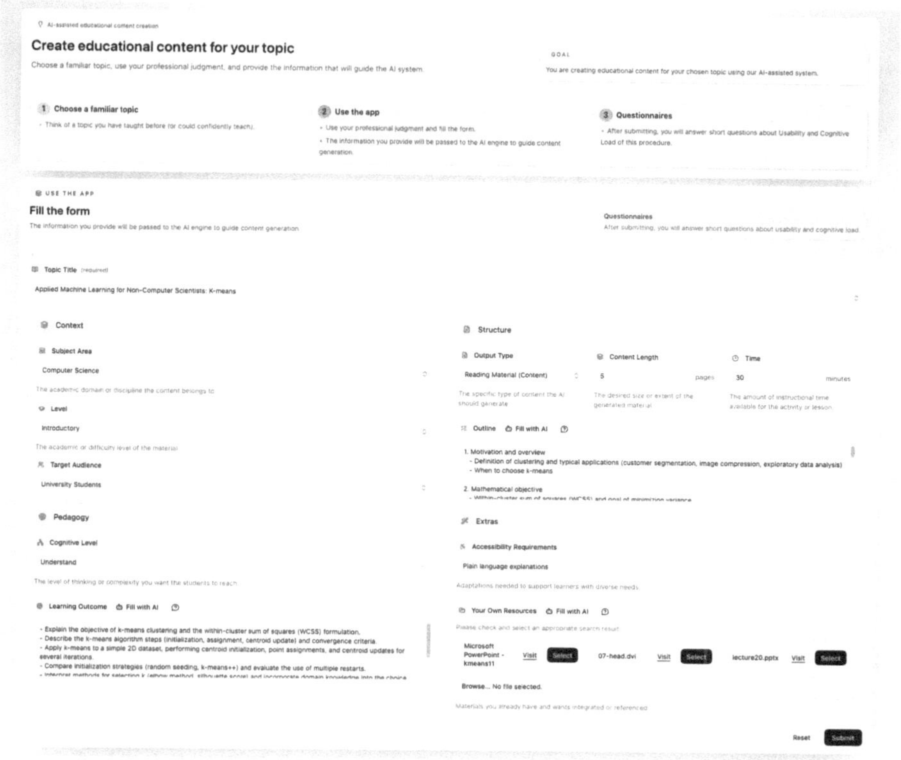


**Fig. 3.** UI view.

- **AI Auto-fill for long texts.** For free-text fields that typically require more time and effort to complete, the interface provides a *Fill with AI* mechanism for fields such as *Learning Outcome* and *Outline*. When teachers click *Fill with AI*, the system uses already completed fields as context to draft or revise the selected field. In addition to generating a first draft, the component supports iterative revision: teachers can provide short feedback or instructions (e.g., simplify, shorten, or adapt to a different level), and the system updates the text accordingly. The generated text is inserted into the corresponding editable field rather than locked in, so teachers can accept, revise, or replace it before submission.
- **Own-resources AI-supported web search.** To support the inclusion of relevant teaching materials in the *Own Resources* field, the interface extends beyond manual upload by integrating an AI-assisted web search functionality. The system leverages already provided interface fields (e.g., subject, level, and learning outcomes) to automatically formulate search queries, which can be further refined by teachers through additional keywords. Retrieved resources are presented in a structured and previewable format, allowing teachers to

quickly assess relevance before selection. This component reduces the effort required to identify suitable materials and helps teachers incorporate external resources that align with the pedagogical context defined in the interface.
- **Suggested values with selectable options.** For fields that involve recurring, categorical, or constrained inputs (e.g., target audience or difficulty level), the interface provides suggested values derived from common usage patterns and previously entered data. These suggestions are presented through selection controls, enabling quick input while maintaining consistency across entries. At the same time, the interface remains flexible by allowing teachers to introduce new values when existing options are insufficient. This component balances efficiency and expressiveness by reducing input effort and cognitive load, while still accommodating diverse teaching contexts and preferences.

At submission, completed fields were serialized into an internal prompt object covering topic, subject area, level, target audience, cognitive level, learning outcomes, output type, length, time, outline, accessibility requirements, and own resources; empty slots were omitted. Teachers retained control by editing or rejecting AI suggestions, resources, and final field values before generation. The context-rich condition used `gpt-5.2` with default OpenAI library settings and an educational-content system prompt that treated provided fields as authoritative, aligned output with the requested constraints and Bloom level, addressed accessibility requirements, and avoided unsupported details.

## 5 Evaluation

### 5.1 Study Design

To evaluate the interface from complementary perspectives, we conducted two studies: (1) a larger user study with $N = 100$ participants to assess usability, workload, and willingness to provide contextual information, and (2) a smaller comparative pilot with $N = 10$ experienced teachers to examine whether the produced content would be used in realistic teaching scenarios.

**User Study: Usability, Workload, and Context Provision.** We conducted a user study with a new set of $N = 100$ teachers, again recruited via Prolific[4]. Each participant completed the following steps:

1. **Using the interface.** Participants chose a familiar topic that they had taught before or could confidently teach, used their professional judgment to complete the form, optionally used *Fill with AI* and suggested values, and submitted the completed form to generate educational content. The minimum interaction time was 10 min, with a median of 16 min and a mean of 19 min.

[4] Anonymized participant demographics, responses, and a sample of the interface in use are available here: https://doi.org/10.6084/m9.figshare.31239604 and https://doi.org/10.6084/m9.figshare.31186507.

2. **Willingness to provide contextual information.** Participants reported which interface fields they would fill in a *no-interface* scenario versus while using the context-rich interface. This comparison was included to assess whether teachers would provide the same information without any support from the interface, and thus whether the interface increases willingness to provide contextual information.
3. **Workload.** Participants completed three items from the NASA Task Load Index (NASA-TLX), a widely used measure of perceived workload [15]. We focused on mental demand, effort, and frustration because these subscales were most relevant for assessing the cognitive and affective burden of interacting with the interface. All three items were answered on a 5-point scale.
4. **Usability.** Participants completed the System Usability Scale (SUS), a questionnaire for assessing perceived usability of interactive systems [4]. The SUS consists of 10 items answered on a 5-point Likert scale.

**Comparative Pilot with Experienced Teachers.** To evaluate the practical usefulness of the generated content beyond self-reported perceptions, we also ran a comparative pilot with $N = 10$ teachers who each had at least eight years of teaching experience. Each teacher used both systems on one of their real courses. The two systems were used within the same real course context and instructional setting, so teachers generated multiple comparable content items with each system and then judged anonymized outputs for potential use in their teaching. This design compared the full interface-mediated generation workflow against baseline GPT use; it was not intended to isolate the visual interface independently from prompt structure or contextual scaffolding. Teachers completed the following steps:

1. **Baseline generation.** Teachers first generated multiple content items for their course using a baseline GPT interface. The baseline condition used `gpt-5.2` with default OpenAI library generation settings, free teacher prompting, and no system prompt.
2. **Interface-based generation.** Teachers then generated comparable content for the same course, topic or activity, and output type using the context-rich interface. This condition also used `gpt-5.2` with default OpenAI library generation settings, but serialized completed interface fields into a prompt object, omitted empty prompt slots, and applied the educational-content system prompt discussed above. This fixed order was chosen because the context-rich interface was explicitly designed to build on limitations observed in baseline prompt-based interaction.
3. **Judgment.** After generation, source labels were removed and anonymized outputs were shown in randomized order. Teachers indicated whether they would use each content item in their teaching.

### 5.2 Results and Discussion

Perceived workload. Participants reported consistently low workload across the three selected NASA-TLX items (1–5 scale), with mean scores of *2.24* for mental

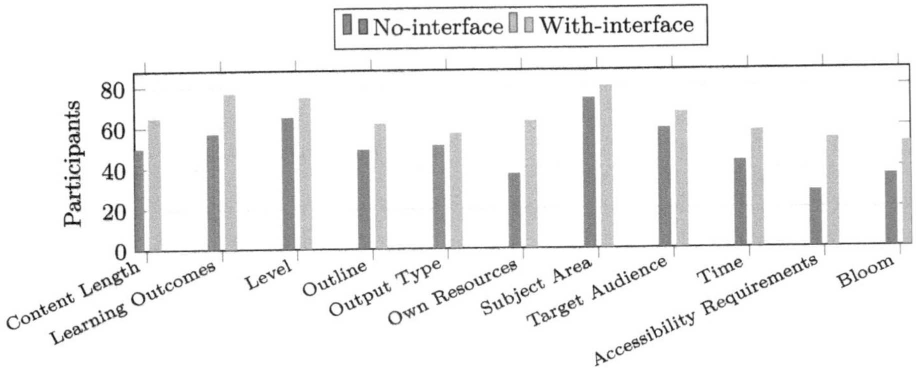


**Fig. 4.** Interface vs. no-interface contextual information provision counts ($N = 100$). Blue bars show the no-interface baseline and orange bars show filling rate while using the interface. (Color figure online)

demand, *2.29* for effort, and *1.62* for frustration. Overall, these values suggest that the interface can collect richer contextual information without imposing substantial cognitive or emotional burden on teachers. This is particularly important because one of the main risks of context-rich systems is that they may increase extraneous interaction burden while collecting information intended to improve output quality.

Usability (SUS). The context-rich interface achieved a mean SUS score of *80.33* (SD = 14.12), placing it in the *A range* of standard SUS interpretations. This score is clearly above the commonly used SUS benchmark of *68* [19] and also higher than the reported SUS score of *69.7* for ChatGPT [26]. Taken together, these results suggest that participants did not experience the interface as cumbersome despite its structured and relatively detailed interaction model. In other words, the added structure appears to support teacher input rather than hinder it.

Willingness to provide contextual information. To examine whether the interface encourages richer input, we compared the interface fields participants said they would provide in a *no-interface* scenario with the fields they reported providing while using the context-rich interface. As shown in Fig. 4, the interface increased field completion for all included fields, with a mean gain of 14.6 participants per field and observed increases ranging from 6 to 26. At the aggregate field level, completion counts were consistently higher with the interface across the 11 included fields and this difference was statistically significant (Wilcoxon signed-rank test: $W = 66$, $p < .001$), with a large paired effect size ($d_z = 2.06$). The largest gains appeared for *Own Resources* and *Accessibility Requirements* (both +26), followed by *Learning Outcomes* (+20) and *Bloom* (+16). These gains are especially meaningful because several of these fields correspond to the high fill-deficit dimensions identified in our requirement analysis. This pattern suggests that the interface does not simply reorganize information teachers would have supplied anyway; rather, it helps surface contextual information that might otherwise remain implicit or be omitted altogether.

**Table 2.** Background information for teachers in the comparative pilot.

| Teacher | Gender | Exp. (yrs) | Area | **Selection Rate (%)** | |
|---|---|---|---|---|---|
| | | | | GPT | Our Interface |
| Teacher-1 | Male | 8 | Computer Science | 25 | 92 |
| Teacher-2 | Male | 12 | Computer Science | 45 | 78 |
| Teacher-3 | Female | 21 | Computer Science | 38 | 87 |
| Teacher-4 | Female | 10 | Chemistry | 40 | 83 |
| Teacher-5 | Female | 11 | Health care | 20 | 50 |
| Teacher-6 | Female | 9 | Health care | 30 | 50 |
| Teacher-7 | Male | 29 | Health care | 30 | 70 |
| Teacher-8 | Male | 8 | Health care | 40 | 60 |
| Teacher-9 | Female | 13 | Psychology | 52 | 82 |
| Teacher-10 | Male | 10 | Psychology | 50 | 70 |
| **Average** | | | | **37.0** | **72.2** |

Comparative pilot. In the comparative pilot, teachers generated a total of 212 content items—106 with the context-rich interface and 106 with the baseline GPT interface—across ten courses (related to Computer Science, Chemistry, Health care, and Psychology)[5] Here, *content items* refers to the generated educational materials created under the selected output type and course context. Each teacher used the platform for a minimum of 2 h, with a median usage time of 2 h and 30 min and a mean of 2 h and 40 min. Table 2 summarizes the background information of the teachers included in the comparative pilot, including gender, years of experience, area of expertise, and the selection rates for both systems. As shown, willingness-to-use ratings were higher for content generated through the context-rich workflow than for content produced with the *baseline GPT interface*, with average selection rates of 72.2% for the context-rich workflow and 37.0% for the baseline GPT interface. This teacher-level advantage was also statistically significant (Wilcoxon signed-rank test: $W = 55$, $p = .002$), again with a large paired effect size ($d_z = 2.34$). Although this pilot is small and should therefore be interpreted cautiously, the overall pattern points to a practically important outcome: the structured interface does not only improve user experience measures, but may also increase the likelihood that generated materials are considered usable in real teaching practice.

[5] These subject areas were part of the OSCAR (https://projects.tib.eu/oscar-ai/about-the-project/), ADAPT (https://www.projekt-adapt.de/), and Remo (https://projects.tib.eu/remo/) EU educational projects.

## 6 Conclusion

Scalable generation and adaptation of digital learning content is increasingly important as teachers are expected to provide more personalized support across diverse educational settings. Teachers need practical ways to communicate instructional goals and context to AI systems. Meeting this need requires not only capable language models, but also interfaces that help teachers express pedagogically relevant context in practical ways.

To address this need, we conducted three complementary studies involving $N = 210$ teachers. First, the requirement analysis identified the pedagogical-context dimensions teachers considered most important and the high fill-deficit dimensions where important information was less likely to be provided in ordinary AI use (RQ1). Based on these findings, we developed the context-rich interface and evaluated it in a usability study, where it achieved strong usability, low perceived workload, and higher willingness among teachers to provide contextual information, with especially notable gains for fields corresponding to high fill-deficit dimensions (RQ2). In a comparative pilot with experienced teachers, content generated through the context-rich workflow was selected more often than content generated with a baseline GPT interface, with average selection rates of 72.2% and 37.0%, respectively (RQ3). Overall, these findings suggest that context-rich, teacher-centered workflows may support both contextual input and the practical usefulness of generated educational content.

At the same time, the findings should be interpreted with appropriate caution. Although the overall evaluation covered three studies and $N = 210$ teachers, the comparative pilot on real-world content creation included only 10 teachers, which limits the strength of conclusions about practical adoption. We partly mitigated the small-sample limitation by combining evidence across three levels of evaluation and by collecting judgments on 212 generated content items in the final study. Future work should examine longer-term, real-world use with broader participant groups and explore how such interfaces can evolve alongside rapidly changing LLM capabilities and classroom needs.

## References


1. Ajzen, I.: The theory of planned behavior. Organ. Behav. Hum. Decis. Process. **50**(2), 179–211 (1991). https://doi.org/10.1016/0749-5978(91)90020-T
2. Bloom, B.S. (ed.): Taxonomy of Educational Objectives: The Classification of Educational Goals. Handbook I: Cognitive Domain, New York (1956)
3. Borg, S.: Teacher cognition in language teaching: A review of research on what language teachers think, know, believe, and do. Lang. Teach. **36**(2), 81–109 (2003). https://doi.org/10.1017/S0261444803001903
4. Brooke, J.: SUS: a quick and dirty usability scale. In: Jordan, P.W., Thomas, B., Weerdmeester, B.A., McClelland, I.L. (eds.) Usability Evaluation in Industry, pp. 189–194. Taylor & Francis (1996)
5. Calo, T., MacLellan, C.J.: Towards educator-driven tutor authoring: generative AI approaches for creating intelligent tutor interfaces. arXiv preprint arXiv:2405.14713. https://doi.org/10.48550/arXiv.2405.14713 (2024)

6. Choi, W.C., Chang, C.I.: A survey of techniques, key components, strategies, challenges, and student perspectives on prompt engineering for large language models (LLMs) in education (2025)
7. Correia, A.P., Hickey, S., Xu, F.: Realizing the possibilities of the large language models: Strategies for prompt engineering in educational inquiries. Theory Into Practice **64**(4), 434–447 (2025)
8. Dennison, D.V., et al.: Teacher-AI collaboration for curating and customizing lesson plans in low-resource schools. arXiv preprint arXiv:2507.00456 (2025)
9. Denny, P., Khosravi, H., Hellas, A., Leinonen, J., Sarsa, S.: Can we trust AI-generated educational content? comparative analysis of human and ai-generated learning resources. arXiv preprint arXiv:2306.10509 (2023)
10. Faraji, A., Tavakoli, M., Moein, M., Molavi, M., Kismihók, G.: Designing effective LLM-assisted interfaces for curriculum development. In: Cristea, A.I., Walker, E., Lu, Y., Santos, O.C., Isotani, S. (eds.) International Conference on Artificial Intelligence in Education, pp. 438–451. Springer, Cham (2025). https://doi.org/10.1007/978-3-031-98414-3_31
11. Feng, K.K., Liao, Q.V., Xiao, Z., Wortman Vaughan, J., Zhang, A.X., McDonald, D.W.: Canvil: designerly adaptation for LLM-powered user experiences. In: Proceedings of the 2025 CHI Conference on Human Factors in Computing Systems. pp. 1–22 (2025)
12. Gagné, R.M., Wager, W.W., Golas, K.C., Keller, J.M.: Principles of Instructional Design, 5th edn. Wadsworth/Thomson Learning, Belmont, CA (2005)
13. Gonnermann-Müller, J., Haase, J., Fackeldey, K., Pokutta, S.: Facet: teacher-centred llm-based multi-agent systems-towards personalized educational worksheets. arXiv preprint arXiv:2508.11401 (2025)
14. Greenhow, C., Graham, C.R., Koehler, M.J.: Foundations of online learning: Challenges and opportunities. Educational Psychologist **57**(3), 131–147 (2022). https://doi.org/10.1080/00461520.2022.2090364
15. Hart, S.G., Staveland, L.E.: Development of NASA-TLX (task load index): results of empirical and theoretical research. In: Advances in Psychology, vol. 52, pp. 139–183. North-Holland (1988)
16. Kosch, T., Karolus, J., Zagermann, J., Reiterer, H., Schmidt, A., Woźniak, P.W.: A survey on measuring cognitive workload in human-computer interaction. ACM Comput. Surv. **55**(13s), 1–39 (2023)
17. Krouska, A., Troussas, C., Voyiatzis, I., Mylonas, P., Sgouropoulou, C.: CHATGPT-based recommendations for personalized content creation and instructional design with a tailored prompt generator. In: 2024 2nd International Conference on Foundation and Large Language Models (FLLM), pp. 295–299. IEEE (2024)
18. Lee, D., Palmer, E.: Prompt engineering in higher education: a systematic review to help inform curricula. Int. J. Educ. Technol. High. Educ. **22**(1), 7 (2025)
19. Lewis, J.R.: Measuring perceived usability: The CSUQ, SUS, and UMUX. International Journal of Human-Computer Interaction **34**(12), 1148–1156 (2018)
20. Li, H., et al.: Arched: a human-centered framework for transparent, responsible, and collaborative ai-assisted instructional design. arXiv preprint arXiv:2503.08931 (2025)
21. Lohr, D., Berges, M., Chugh, A., Kohlhase, M., Müller, D.: Leveraging large language models to generate course-specific semantically annotated learning objects. J. Comput. Assist. Learn. **41**(1), e13101 (2025)

22. Luo, Z., Tahir, R.: ChatGPT-assisted lesson planning for children's steam arts education: An experimental study on benefits, challenges, methods, and a prompt framework. Int. J. Artif. Intell. Educ., 1–50 (2025)
23. Masson, D., Malacria, S., Casiez, G., Vogel, D.: DirectGPT: a direct manipulation interface to interact with large language models. In: Proceedings of the CHI Conference on Human Factors in Computing Systems, pp. 1–16 (2024)
24. Memarian, B., Doleck, T.: Human-in-the-loop in artificial intelligence in education: a review and entity-relationship (er) analysis. Computers in Human Behavior: Artificial Humans p. 100053 (2024)
25. Moein, M., Molavi, M., Faraji, A., Tavakoli, M., Kismihók, G.: Beyond search engines: can large language models improve curriculum development? In: Ferreira Mello, R., Rummel, N., Jivet, I., Pishtari, G., Ruipérez Valiente, J.A. (eds.) 19th European Conference on Technology Enhanced Learning, EC-TEL 2020, Krems, Austria, September 16–20, 2024. Springer, Cham (2024). https://doi.org/10.1007/978-3-031-72312-4_17
26. Morales, J., Silva-Aravena, F., Cornide-Reyes, H., Muñoz, G.: ChatGPT usability. an exploratory study in higher education. In: Coman, A., Vasilache, S., Moallem, A. (eds.) International Conference on Human-Computer Interaction, pp. 161–174. Springer, Cham (2025). https://doi.org/10.1007/978-3-032-12801-0_11
27. Sweller, J.: Cognitive load during problem solving: Effects on learning. Cogn. Sci. **12**(2), 257–285 (1988). https://doi.org/10.1207/s15516709cog1202_4
28. Tavakoli, M., Faraji, A., Molavi, M., Mol, T., Kismihók, S., G.: Hybrid human-AI curriculum development for personalised informal learning environments. In: LAK22: 12th International Learning Analytics and Knowledge Conference, pp. 563–569 (2022)
29. Tavakoli, M., Faraji, A., Vrolijk, J., Molavi, M.D., Mol, S.T., Kismihók, G.: An AI-based open recommender system for personalized labor market driven education. Adv. Eng. Inform. **52**, 101508 (2022)
30. Verloop, N., Van Driel, J., Meijer, P.: Teacher knowledge and the knowledge base of teaching. Int. J. Educ. Res. **35**(5), 441–461 (2001). https://doi.org/10.1016/S0883-0355(02)00003-4
31. Zheng, Y., Huang, S., Zeng, X., Huang, Y., Liu, Z., Luo, W.: Knowledge-enhanced large language models for automatic lesson plan generation. Humanities and Social Sciences Communications **12**(1), 1784 (2025)

# Gauging Educators' Perceived Fairness of AI-Mediated Assessment: a Four-Dimensional Organizational Justice Approach

Yael Feldman-Maggor[1,2,4(✉)], Teresa Cerratto-Pargman[2,3], and Olga Viberg[1,2]

[1] KTH Royal Institute of Technology, 10044 Stockholm, Sweden
yaelfeld@bgu.ac.il, oviberg@kth.se
[2] Digital Futures, 11428 Stockholm, Sweden
tessy@dsv.su.se
[3] Stockholm University, SE-164 25 Stockholm, Sweden
[4] Ben-Gurion University of the Negev, 8410501 Beer-Sheva, Israel

**Abstract.** Educators play a central role in higher education assessment practices. As artificial intelligence (AI) becomes increasingly integrated into these practices, it is essential to understand educators' perceived fairness in AI-mediated assessment. Most research on AI-mediated assessment focuses on performance and efficiency, leaving ethical issues imbued in AI out of this discussion. This study examines educators' perceptions of fairness in AI-mediated assessment in Swedish higher education. It has two main objectives: first, to develop and validate a reliable instrument to measure educators' perceived fairness in the use of AI-assessment practices; and second, to explore educators' perceptions of fairness in AI-enabled assessment of student work. Drawing on Organizational Justice theory, the study applies four dimensions of fairness: procedural, distributive, informational, and interpersonal, to the context of AI-mediated assessment in higher education. Using a mixed-methods design, we used confirmatory factor analysis to validate a four-factor model using Likert-scale survey items and thematic analysis of responses to two open-ended questions. The findings suggest that educators perceived informational fairness most positively, followed by interpersonal fairness. Procedural and distributive fairness were assessed more cautiously, with median scores at the midpoint of the scale. Participants also emphasized the importance of maintaining active human oversight of both assessment procedures and outcomes. The study provides a validated instrument for future research on perceived fairness in AI-assisted assessment, both for practical applications and for future research. Furthermore, it highlights the critical role of educators' professional development in promoting fairness awareness and supporting the responsible use of AI in student assessment.

**Keywords:** Artificial Intelligence · Assessment · Fairness · Higher Education


J. Weidlich et al. (Eds.): EC-TEL 2026, LNCS 16905, pp. 195–208, 2027.
https://doi.org/10.1007/978-3-032-37979-5_14

## 1 Introduction

Assessment in higher education serves as a core process for credentialing, with grades and degrees carrying significant consequences for students' academic and professional futures [1]. Educators, whose professional judgment largely shapes assessment practices, bear central responsibility for ensuring the fairness of decisions in assessment processes [2]. While artificial intelligence (AI) systems are increasingly adopted to support tasks such as grading and feedback [3, 4], they also bring challenges for educators who are confronted with balancing the use of AI for productivity support with ethical use and the need to maintain valid and meaningful assessment [4, 5]. Scholars further stress that educators find it difficult to determine the boundary between appropriate AI use and human responsibility [6]. Because educators' understanding of fairness is essential for evaluating whether AI-mediated assessment leads to unfair practices or promotes fairer assessment, it becomes central to examine how they perceive fairness. The current study examines educators' perceptions of fairness in AI-mediated assessment practices.

Fairness perceptions are widely understood to be multidimensional, encompassing distributive fairness (equity in outcomes), procedural fairness (consistency of processes), interpersonal fairness (respectful treatment), and informational fairness (clarity and transparency) [7, 8]. Evaluating these four dimensions is particularly important in AI-assisted, educator-in-the-loop assessment. In such contexts, fairness is shaped not only by final grading outcomes but also by how decisions are produced, communicated, and experienced by those affected. Focusing on only one-dimensional risks obscures important mismatches, for instance, cases in which outcomes appear fair, but the underlying process lacks transparency, consistency, or sensitivity. Although Williamson et al. [9] have examined educators' perceived of informational fairness in AI-mediated contexts, Song et al. [10] explored how students perceive fairness in AI-supported assessments, no empirical study to date has systematically investigated all four dimensions of perceived fairness when AI is used as an assistive tool in educator-in-the-loop assessment settings, to our knowledge. The absence of a validated, theory-informed instrument to capture educators' perceptions of AI tool fairness hinders both rigorous empirical inquiry and the development of evidence-based support for ethical and professional AI-mediated assessment practices. Understanding how educators interpret and experience fairness in the use of AI for assessment is critical not only for ensuring that AI practices align with fundamental educational values, but also for informing professional development and supporting the responsible integration of AI into assessment practices.

Evaluating educators' perceptions of fairness in higher education assessment is a critical step toward enabling them to identify and address potential bias and unfairness in AI tools used for assessment. Accordingly, this study pursues two objectives: (1) to develop and validate a reliable instrument to measure educators' perceived fairness in the use of AI tools as assistive resources in assessment; and (2) to examine how educators perceive fairness across procedural, distributive, and interpersonal dimensions in AI-supported student assessment. In doing so, the study makes two contributions. First, it introduces a validated instrument to assess perceived fairness across four dimensions and, second, it provides insights into educators' understanding of fairness in AI-mediated assessment practices and how AI tools may support these processes, based on survey data and qualitative analysis.

## 2 Background

### 2.1 Fairness and the Theoretical Framework of Organizational Justice

Bias in AI tools arises when a systematic distortion in measurement, model learning, or action leads to disparate impacts, often reflecting pre-existing societal inequalities encoded in data or model design [10–13]. Fairness can be defined as an indicator of the absence of bias [13]. The theoretical framework of organizational justice [7] informed a survey instrument that operationalizes fairness across four dimensions: *procedural, distributive, interpersonal, and informational.* Narayanan et al. [8] explain *procedural fairness* in terms of how fair people perceive the decision-making process. The use of AI in decision-making, for instance, may raise concerns over whether people can influence decision outcomes, depending on the extent to which decision-making is fully automated [8]. The rationale is that decision-making tasks that require uniquely human skills tend to be perceived as less procedurally fair when AI systems are involved. *Distributive fairness* focuses on the fairness of the outcomes themselves, with mixed perceptions depending on task complexity, transparency, and the fairness norm applied. Decision outcomes that are consistent with implicit or explicit norms for resource allocation are generally perceived as high in distributive fairness [7, 8]. For example, it focuses on fair outcomes, such as grades. *Interpersonal fairness* refers to how respectfully and empathetically people feel they are treated during the decision-making process. "It became clear that attention to decision-making processes was also motivated by people's concerns about the interpersonal treatment they receive when decisions are made. Interpersonal justice is the degree to which people are treated with dignity and respect" [8 , p. 6]. *Informational fairness* concerns the quality and clarity of explanations provided for decisions, with AI explanations often perceived as less fair, particularly when they focus only on technical logic rather than offering understandable, value-based justifications. Informational fairness is "determined by the quality with which explanations are provided regarding how decisions are made, and why certain outcomes were reached" [8 , p. 6]. When explanations in AI-driven decision-making are viewed as reasonable, understandable, and responsive to the users' needs, they are more likely to be perceived as informationally fair [9].

In the context of education, [9] adapted the theoretical framework of organizational psychology [7] to an educational setting to assess students' perceived fairness of AI's pass-or-fail prediction decisions in math learning. Tai et al. [15] emphasize that assessment should not disadvantage diverse students due to characteristics or abilities unrelated to the outcomes being evaluated. All students should be supported in achieving and demonstrating their capabilities equitably. Fairness in assessment involves interpreting results and their impact, as well as the design of the assessment itself [16].

### 2.2 Fairness in AI-Mediated Assessment

AI is already having a significant impact on assessment processes in higher education [17]. Automated assessments span a range of formats, from multiple-choice questions [18] to open-ended prompts [19], and can be used for grading essays [20]. In the context of generative AI (GenAI), Usher [21] compared grades and GenAI feedback with those provided by course instructors for student projects in a higher education course. The results show that GenAI feedback consistently assigned higher grades than human assessors. However, the GenAI tools provided detailed insights and specific guidance for improvement, though they occasionally included irrelevant or contradictory information, requiring human intervention. Swiecki et al. [22] conducted a systematic review of assessment in the age of AI and emphasized several advantages of using AI tools for assessment. One main advantage is that such techniques can potentially reduce the burden on human assessors and make assessment practices more scalable. Another advantage is that AI techniques can adjust the task to each student's abilities, providing a more personalized assessment experience rather than giving the same assessment task to all students. Further automated evaluation can help distance assessment decisions be free of educators' potential biases and assumptions [22]. Scholars also found that some educators believed an automated grading system could help reduce potential biases [23]. Though some participants expressed concerns about potential bias in machine learning models, highlighting the limitations of AI tools in assessment contexts.

AI tools for assessment are often framed as enhancing objectivity; however, they also introduce important limitations. Rather than eliminating human influence, AI-mediated assessment redistributes decision-making to a network of actors, such as programmers, learning engineers, instructional designers, and software vendors, who may lack direct knowledge of students, their local contexts, or the educational systems in which assessment occurs. Consequently, as with any form of assessment, AI-enabled evaluation remains inherently partial, reflecting embedded assumptions and design choices [21]. A key challenge concerns issues of bias and fairness. AI systems may produce skewed outcomes due to biased training data, leading to unfair evaluations, inaccurate grading, and inequitable feedback [22, 24]. Importantly, these concerns extend beyond data to the opacity of algorithmic processes. Many AI systems lack the capacity to provide transparent explanations or justifications for the grades they assign, which conflicts with core educational expectations of accountability and interpretability [24]. Recent work further highlights the technical limitations of AI-mediated assessment. For instance, Gurin Schleifer et al. [25] show that the diagnostic quality of LLM-based grading depends heavily on the model's ability to capture nuanced differences in student responses. Their findings point to a "discoverability bias," in which systems successfully identify high-quality answers but struggle to distinguish among diverse forms of incorrect responses. This limitation raises concerns about the validity and pedagogical usefulness of automated feedback. Beyond technical issues, there is growing concern regarding AI's effective integration and regulation in assessment [26]. For example, Corbin et al. [5] identify tensions related to fairness, differing conceptions of AI's role in learning, and a lack of clear institutional policies. Despite these growing insights, an important research gap remains. While some focus on the technical aspects of fairness [12] and on students' perspectives [10], less attention has been given to how educators in higher education can meaningfully interpret, contest, or complement AI-generated judgments in assessment practices. Addressing this gap is essential to developing responsible, human-centered approaches to AI-mediated assessment.

### 2.3 Educators' Assessment Fairness

Fairness, although increasingly emphasized in the age of AI, is not a new concern in education [27]. Prior research has shown that educators can exhibit bias toward students [28]. In the context of AI in education, such biases may persist or interact with AI in new ways. For example, Nazaretsky et al. [29] found that teachers demonstrated confirmation bias when engaging with AI-generated recommendations, tending to accept suggestions that aligned with their pre-existing beliefs about students. At the same time, evidence on fairness in human-versus-AI-mediated assessment remains mixed. Magowan compared teachers' evaluations with AI-based grade predictions and found that teachers' assessments in 2020 were broadly fair compared to AI- mediated assessments, with no evidence of systematic or absolute bias against any demographic or socio-economic group [30]. The results showed that teachers' assessments in 2020 were consistently higher than AI-based counterfactual exam predictions for all student groups, indicating overall generosity rather than systematic bias against any demographic or socio-economic category.

Regardless of whether grades are assigned by human raters or AI systems, assessment outcomes can significantly impact individuals' lives and must therefore be fair to all test takers [31]. Fairness in assessment is commonly understood to encompass both procedural and outcome fairness. A multifaceted understanding that acknowledges this complexity is essential for supporting equitable and just outcomes for all students [32].

This study addresses an important gap by examining educators' perceptions of fairness in AI-mediated assessment. Prior research has predominantly focused on fairness in AI systems [33], with only a limited number of recent studies examining teachers' perceptions of AI fairness [9]. As current developments increasingly emphasize human-AI interaction and "partnerships" between educators and AI [34], alongside the importance of keeping educators in the loop [35], there is a growing need for empirical insights into how fairness is understood and enacted in practice. Examining educators' perspectives is therefore critical for understanding how fairness emerges in AI-mediated assessment contexts.

## 3 Methodology

The development of the instrument items was grounded in organizational justice theory [7] and the perceived fairness framework [8], as well as previous instruments [7–9]. Colquitt [7] proposed and validated an instrument for assessing justice across four dimensions: procedural, distributive, interpersonal, and informational justice. The instrument was tested with higher education students. This framework conceptualizes justice as a multidimensional construct of fairness. In the present study, we drew on this theory to develop an instrument for AI-mediated assessment. Specifically, the procedural fairness items were developed based on Narayanan et al. [8], and the distributive fairness items were developed based on Colquitt [7]. The interpersonal and informational fairness dimensions were adapted from Colquitt [6] and Williamson et al. [9], respectively. The final list of items is presented in Table 3 of the Results section. Based on previously established methodologies [36–38], the development process included several steps. First, we employed multi-item scales to measure the constructs. All items were assessed using 5-point Likert scales with anchors ranging from 1 (strongly disagree-not fair at all) to 5 (strongly agree-fairest). Second, before launching the full-scale study, we piloted the questionnaire with 38 higher education educators in the Spring of 2025 to assess the clarity and conciseness of the instructions and item formulations. Participants were asked to provide open-ended feedback to ensure the validity of items. Based on this feedback, items were revised or removed. In addition, before administering the survey to the larger sample, we evaluated internal consistency reliability by calculating Cronbach's alpha for each perceived fairness dimension. All dimensions showed reliability values above the recommended cut-off. As different cut-off values for Cronbach's alpha have been proposed, we followed a commonly used classification whereby values below 0.60 are considered low, values between 0.60 and 0.69 acceptable, values between 0.70 and 0.79 adequate, values between 0.80 and 0.89 good, and values of 0.90 or higher very good [38]. Cronbach's alpha calculated during the pilot study was used only for preliminary assessment of the items. After the pilot phase was completed, the survey was distributed online to educators at a large European university in all educators' cohorts. 104 educators completed the survey in 2025, and the reliability coefficients were recalculated using this sample; the results are presented in Table 3. The demographic background and participant characteristics are shown in Table 1.

**Table 1.** Demographic background and participant characteristics

| Educators' Characteristics | | Frequency and Percentage (N = 104) |
|---|---|---|
| Age | 1 = 20–30<br>2 = 31–40<br>3 = 41–50<br>4 = 51–6<br>5 = >60 | 29 (27.8%)<br>22 (21.2%)<br>27 (26.0%)<br>14 (13.5%)<br>12 (11.5%) |
| Gender | 1 = Female<br>2 = Male<br>3 = Other<br>4 = Prefer not to answer | 32 (30.7%)<br>63 (60.6%)<br>3 (2.9%)<br>6 (5.8%) |
| Years of experience in teaching | 1 = 0–5<br>2 = 6–10<br>3 = 11–20<br>4 = > 20<br>Yes | 38 (36.5%)<br>13 (12.5%)<br>22 (21.2%)<br>31 (29.8%)<br>43 (41.3%) |
| Previous experience with AI in teaching | No | 61 (58.7%) |

Participants provided written informed consent at each stage of the study, as recommended by the institutional (KTH) ethics committee, and stated that their responses would be used for research purposes. In addition, a representative of the institutional data privacy office reviewed the survey items to ensure they posed no risk of harm and complied with the General Data Protection Regulation (GDPR) (https://gdpr-info.eu/). Participants were free to withdraw from the study at any time. After data collection, a Confirmatory Factor Analysis (CFA) was conducted to assess the scale's construct validity [39] and to verify the four proposed dimensions of perceived fairness. In contrast to exploratory factor analysis, CFA requires the researcher to indicate which items should fall onto which factors. Parameter estimates for the specified model are generated, and goodness-of-fit tests are conducted. In CFA, a standard model with two or more factors is identified when each factor has at least two indicators [40]. However, given the relatively small sample size, we adopted recommendations suggesting that a minimum of three indicators per factor improves model stability when the sample size is 100 [40]. In addition to the Likert-scale items, the participants were asked two open-ended questions. The first invited them to define fairness in assessment in their own terms, allowing us to examine the substantive meanings educators attribute to fairness. The rationale for this question was to determine whether educators' general perceptions of fairness align with the survey's dimensions and to assess their awareness of different aspects of fairness. The second question asked participants to elaborate on their views regarding the use of AI in assessment. This question allowed us to explore how well the four fairness dimensions captured educators' perceptions of AI-based assessment and to identify additional themes that may support or challenge the use of AI in assessment processes. The qualitative responses were analyzed deductively [41], guided by the four fairness dimensions, to assess how these dimensions were reflected in educators' conceptualizations. In addition, responses to the second question were analysed inductively [41] to identify contextual and ethical concerns that may not be fully captured by the fairness dimensions.

## 4 Results

### 4.1 The Confirmatory Factor Analysis (CFA) Model

Following Colquitt [7], we conducted a CFA using a phased approach. The first model was a one-factor model, in which all items loaded onto a single overarching perceived fairness factor. The second model was a two-factor model, with distributive as one factor and procedural as the other, with procedural subsuming both informational and interpersonal fairness. The third model was a three-factor model comprising distributive, procedural, and interpersonal fairness, with interpersonal subsuming informational fairness. Finally, a four-factor model that differentiates between procedural, distributive, informational, and interactional fairness was estimated.

Model comparisons are presented in Table 2. The one-factor, two-factor, and three-factor models demonstrated poor fit to the data. Only the four-factor model demonstrated acceptable model fit. For the four-factor model, the root mean square error of approximation (RMSEA) is 0.08, which is at the upper bound of the commonly recommended cutoff for acceptable fit [42]. However, the four-factor model had relatively low degrees of freedom. RMSEA is a parsimony-adjusted index that is sensitive to degrees of freedom and has been shown in simulation studies to overestimate model misfit in models with small to moderate degrees of freedom [43], as is the case in the present analysis. Therefore, additional fit indices that are less sensitive to degrees of freedom and sample size were also examined, including the Tucker–Lewis index (TLI), comparative fit index (CFI), incremental fit index (IFI), standardized root mean square residual (SRMR), and the chi-square statistic [43]. The chi-square test of model fit was significant, $\chi^2(29) =$

82.55; however, the $\chi^2$/df ratio was 1.71, which is considered indicative of acceptable fit as it falls below the recommended threshold of 3.0 [43]. The remaining fit indices indicated good model fit: TLI = 0.94 (acceptable), CFI = 0.96 (excellent), IFI = 0.96 (excellent), and SRMR =0.05 (values $\leq$ .08). Cutoff values were based on Hooper et al. [42] and Sathyanarayana and Mohanasundaram [44]. Taken together, these results indicate that the four-factor model provides an adequate and theoretically meaningful representation of the data. Accordingly, the four-factor model was selected as the final measurement model. The factor loading is presented in Table 3.

**Table 2.** Models' compression based on fairness justice theory

| Structure | df | SRMR | CFI | TLI | RMSEA | IFI |
|---|---|---|---|---|---|---|
| 1-factor | 54 | 0.09 | 0.76 | 0.70 | 0.19 | 0.77 |
| 2-factor | 53 | 0.08 | 0.86 | 0.82 | 0.14 | 0.86 |
| 3-factor | 51 | 0.07 | 0.88 | 0.84 | 0.14 | 0.88 |
| **4-factor** | **48** | **0.05** | **0.96** | **0.94** | **0.08** | **0.96** |

**Table 3.** List of instrument items in each factor

| Perceived Fairness Dimension (alpha Cronbach) | List of Items (Factor Loadings) |
|---|---|
| F1 - Procedural fairness (0.67) | 1. Assessment decision-making for students' work may be most equitable when educators use their expertise and insights from AI tools. **(0.68)**<br>2. Making decisions about assessing students' work using AI is fair. **(0.75)**<br>3. Assessing students' work when educators make decisions using AI tools may be the fairest. **(0.52)** |
| F2 - Interpersonal fairness (0.90) | 4. Using AI tools to assess students' work may help educators provide more dignified feedback. **(0.83)**<br>8. Using AI tools to assess students' work may help educators provide more respectful feedback. **(0.88)** 12. Using AI tools in assessing students' work may help educators provide more polite feedback **(0.89)** |
| F3 - Informational fairness (0.75) | 5. Using an AI tool for assessing student work is fair when an educator is involved in thoroughly designing and explaining the decision-making procedures. **(0.83)**<br>6. Using an AI tool to assess students' work is fair when an educator is involved in reasonably designing and explaining the decision-making procedures. **(0.90)**<br>7. As an educator, I need information to understand how I can interact with AI tools when making. **(0.41)** |
| F4 - Distributional fairness (0.94) | 9. An educator using an AI tool contributes to a fairer assessment of a student's effort. **(0.93)**<br>10. An educator using an AI tool leads to a fairer assessment of the individual performance of student work. **(0.95)**<br>11. An educator using an AI tool leads to a fairer assessment of a student's overall contribution to the course. **(0.87)** |

## 4.2 Educators' Responses

To evaluate educators' responses, boxplots and descriptive statistics were used. Figure. 1 presents the distribution of participants' mean scores for the four perceived fairness dimensions on a 1–5 Likert scale. Level 5 on the Likert scale represents the perception that using AI to support educators in assessment is the fairest, while one respondent strongly disagreed that using AI for assessment is fair. Factor 3 (Informational fairness) exhibits the highest central tendency, followed by Factor 2 (Interpersonal fairness). Factors 1 (Procedural fairness) and 4 (Distributional fairness) have median scores at the midpoint of their respective scales. As for the open-ended questions, both questions were optional; therefore, not all participants responded. A total of 92 out of 104 participants answered the first question, producing 115 statements. For the second question, 43 out of 104 participants responded, generating 57 statements. From the 115 statements received in response to the first question, 113 statements aligned with one of the four fairness dimensions. Two statements were not aligned because they were very brief and simply stated that fairness means being objective. Using a deductive thematic analysis, we examined how educators discuss fairness in the context of assessment, applying four predefined dimensions of fairness. Most statements (n = 69, 60%) were categorized as procedural fairness. An example of a response that aligns with those dimensions was: "Honestly assessing student performance about pre-specified criteria."

The next most common dimension was distributive fairness, (Participant #21), (n = 33 statements, 29%). In assessment, this concerns whether the grade itself is fair. For example, one educator stated: "A fair grade should represent the amount of time and effort that a student spent on acquiring knowledge." Informational fairness (Participant #22), (n = 7 statements, 6%) and interpersonal fairness (n = 4 statements, 3%) were mentioned less often. For example, as one educator responded: "It is important that students have the opportunity to test and reflect on material and receive feedback." (Participant #85). Interpersonal fairness refers to dignity, respect, politeness, and sensitivity. An example statement was: "The assessment should be based only on the coursework in question and not on opinions about the student." (Participant #104).

The second open-ended question concerning assessment with GenAI was analyzed using both deductive and inductive approaches. Of the 57 statements, 25 aligned with one of the perceived fairness dimensions, showing a pattern similar to that observed in the first open-ended question. Statements reflecting procedural fairness, which emphasize clarity and consistency in assessment processes, included comments such as: "I believe the Intended Learning Outcomes should be clearly defined and always be included in the prompt given to AI tools like ChatGPT.", (Participant #70). In total, 11 statements (19%) aligned with this dimension.

Examples of statements reflecting distributive fairness, which relates to equitable outcomes, included comments such as: "I think the overall performance of a student is important to be considered as well as special needs, therefore might not be the best way to ensure fairness in the evaluation of students' workload across courses." (Participant #17). A total of six statements (11%) were categorized under this dimension. Statements representing informational fairness, which concerns transparency and explainability, included comments such as: "When using GenAI, we do not know why and how the AI produces its output. Since GenAI is prone to 'hallucinations,' the educator still has to manually check the work and therefore does not gain much from the AI." (Participant #92). In total, only three statements (5%) aligned with this dimension. An example of interpersonal fairness, mentioned by one educator, was: "While I see potential for some parts of the teaching process to be streamlined with such models, letting such a system have any final say in the matter would be inappropriate and unacceptable for most students." (Participant #23) A total of five statements (9%) reflected this dimension. In addition, inductive analysis revealed that 22 statements (39%) emphasized that the use of AI for assessment is acceptable only when humans remain in the loop. For example: "I believe that while using AI to improve fairness is good, the human educator needs to be held accountable for the delivery of the work in cases of false positives or negatives in scoring." (Participant #29). Finally, 10 statements (18%) did not align with the fairness dimensions or the human-in-the-loop theme and instead addressed other issues, such as trust and accessibility needs.

## 5 Discussion

This study pursued two primary objectives. First, it developed and validated an instrument for measuring educators' perceived fairness in the use of AI tools as assistive resources during assessment. Second, it explored educators' perceived fairness in assessment, particularly in the context of AI-mediated assessment in higher education.

The CFA supports a multidimensional model grounded in organizational justice theory [7] that encompasses procedural, distributive, informational, and interpersonal fairness.

**Fig. 1.** Distribution of participants' mean scores for the four perceived fairness dimensions

Examining educators' responses across the four fairness dimensions reveals generally positive perceptions of informational fairness. Educators tended to view the AI-mediated assessment practice as fair when they were actively involved in designing the procedures and when the decision-making process was clearly explained. This result aligns with prior research emphasizing the importance of algorithmic transparency and explainability for enhancing perceived informational fairness [9]. However, the results of the qualitative analysis demonstrate that relatively few educators explicitly mentioned informational fairness when describing their perceptions of assessment. This discrepancy may indicate limited awareness of this dimension or that educators implicitly value transparency without framing it in terms of fairness.

Interpersonal fairness scores were also above the midpoint, suggesting that educators generally perceive AI-assisted assessment as respectful and appropriate in terms of communication, dignity, and politeness. Nevertheless, responses to the open-ended questions revealed some concerns, with several educators noting that students might perceive AI-based assessment as impersonal or inappropriate. This tension highlights the importance of considering not only educators' perceptions but also students' views when implementing AI tools in assessment, which aligns with Song et al. [10].

Song et al. [10] examined aspects closely related to interpersonal fairness, referred to as interactional justice, emphasizing the importance of how AI decisions are communicated and delivered to students. Their study also addressed procedural and distributive fairness in AI-supported assessment contexts. In our study, the median scores for procedural and distributive fairness were around the midpoint, suggesting moderate perceptions of fairness in these dimensions. Consistent with this finding, the qualitative analysis indicated that educators were aware of potential procedural and distributive unfairness issues in assessment, both with and without AI. These concerns appeared frequently in responses to open-ended questions about fairness in assessment, in general and specifically in AI-supported assessment.

Another finding emerging from the qualitative analysis is that educators emphasized the need to remain actively involved when AI tools are used for assessment. We also found that although educators recognize AI's potential to support assessment, they emphasize the importance of maintaining human oversight to ensure assessment practices remain as appropriate and fair as possible. Participants highlighted the importance of overseeing both the assessment procedures and the resulting decisions. This aligns with prior Artificial Intelligence in Education (AIED) research that emphasizes the importance of keeping educators "in the loop" when using AI systems [45]. This study emphasizes the continued involvement of higher educators in the assessment, positioning AI not as a replacement for human judgment but as a supportive tool.

**Limitations, Contributions, and Future Research.** Our validated instrument provides a practical tool for future experimental and quasi-experimental studies examining educators' fairness perceptions in AI-assisted assessment. The instrument can enable comparisons across interventions, contexts, and institutions. The main limitation of this study is that participants were drawn from a single European country; the validity of the findings should be further examined across different countries and territories, where differences may emerge. In addition, the sample is relatively small due to the low response rate. To address these limitations, during the pilot phase, items were evaluated with a more internationally diverse group of educators. Nevertheless, future studies with larger and more diverse samples are needed to validate the instrument across cultural contexts.

Finally, this study makes both methodological and theoretical contributions. While much of the literature has focused on technical aspects of fairness, such as data bias, algorithmic fairness, bias mitigation techniques, and fairness metrics [33], relatively few studies examine fairness from the perspective of educators, who are key stakeholders in assessment practices. Existing research has begun to explore specific dimensions of fairness, for example, by introducing informational fairness [9] and applying procedural and distributive fairness in student assessment contexts [10]. Building on organizational justice theory [7], this study extends prior work by integrating all four dimensions of fairness, procedural, distributive, informational, and interpersonal, within the context of higher education assessment involving GenAI. By doing so, the study offers a more comprehensive theoretical framework for understanding how educators perceive fairness in AI-mediated assessment. In addition, the validated instrument and its theoretical grounding provide a foundation for the design of professional learning initiatives aimed at strengthening educators' understanding of fairness in AI-supported assessment. Together, these contributions support future research and practice focused on the fair and responsible integration of AI tools into higher education practices.

**Acknowledgments.** This work was supported by the Digital Futures Postdoctoral Fellowship (Stockholm, Sweden) and the Israel Science Foundation (ISF) award (Grant 73/24).

## References

1. Liu, O.L.: Outcomes assessment in higher education: challenges and future research in the context of voluntary system of accountability. Educ. Meas. Issues Pract. **30**(3), 2–9 (2011). https://doi.org/10.1111/j.1745-3992.2011.00206.x
2. Nieminen, J.H.: Assessment for inclusion: rethinking inclusive assessment in higher education. Teach. High. Educ. **29**(4), 841–859 (2024). https://doi.org/10.1080/13562517.2021.2021395
3. Crompton, H., Burke, D.: Artificial intelligence in higher education: the state of the field. Int. J. Educ. Technol. High. Educ. **20**(1), 22 (2023). https://doi.org/10.1186/s41239-023-00392-8
4. Deepshikha, D. A systematic review on the future of educational assessment: AI-driven grading and personalised feedback in higher education. In Artificial Intelligence in Education (Vol. 2, No. 2, pp. 75–115). Emerald Publishing Limited. (2026). https://doi.org/10.1108/AIIE-03-2025-0036
5. Corbin, T., Bearman, M., Boud, D., Dawson, P.: The wicked problem of AI and assessment. Assess. Eval. High. Educ. **1-17** (2025). https://doi.org/10.1080/02602938.2025.2553340
6. Corbin, T., Dawson, P., Nicola-Richmond, K., Partridge, H.: 'Where's the line? It's an absurd line': towards a framework for acceptable uses of AI in assessment. Assess. Eval. High. Educ. **1-13** (2025). https://doi.org/10.1080/02602938.2025.2456207
7. Colquitt, J.A.: On the dimensionality of organizational justice: a construct validation of a measure. J. Appl. Psychol. **86**(3), 386 (2001). https://doi.org/10.1037/00219010.86.3.386
8. Narayanan, D., Nagpal, M., McGuire, J., Schweitzer, S., & De Cremer, D. Fairness perceptions of artificial intelligence: a review and path forward. International Journal of Human–Computer Interaction, 40(1), 4–23. (2024). https://doi.org/10.1080/10447318.2023.2210890.
9. Williamson, K., Kizilcec, R., Fath, S., Heffernan, N.: Algorithm appreciation in education: educators prefer complex over simple algorithms. In: Proceedings of the 15th International Learning Analytics and Knowledge Conference, pp. 527–536 (2025). https://doi.org/10.1145/3706468.3706535
10. Song, Y., Li, C., Xing, W., Lyu, B., Zhu, W.: Investigating perceived fairness of AI prediction system for math learning: a mixed-methods study with college students. Internet High. Educ. **101000** (2025). https://doi.org/10.1016/j.iheduc.2025.101000
11. Deho, O.B., Zhan, C., Li, J., Liu, J., Liu, L., Duy Le, T.: How do the existing fairness metrics and unfairness mitigation algorithms contribute to ethical learning analytics? Br. J. Educ. Technol. **53**(4), 822–843 (2022). https://doi.org/10.1111/bjet.13217

12. Kizilcec, R.F., Lee, H.: Algorithmic fairness in education. In: The Ethics of Artificial Intelligence in Education, pp. 174–202. Routledge (2022)
13. Baker, R.S., Hawn, A.: Algorithmic bias in education. Int. J. Artif. Intell. Educ. **32**(4), 1052–1092 (2022). https://doi.org/10.1007/s40593-021-00285-9
14. Celik, I.: Towards intelligent-TPACK: an empirical study on teachers' professional knowledge to ethically integrate artificial intelligence (AI)-based tools into education. Comput. Hum. Behav. **138**, 107468 (2023). https://doi.org/10.1016/j.chb.2022.107468
15. Tai, J.H.M., et al.: Designing assessment for inclusion: an exploration of diverse students' assessment experiences. Assess. Eval. High. Educ. **48**(3), 403–417 (2023). https://doi.org/10.1080/02602938.2022.2082373
16. Gipps, C., Stobart, G.: Fairness in Assessment. In Educational Assessment in the 21st Century: Connecting Theory and Practice (Pp. 105–118). Springer Netherlands, Dordrecht (2009). https://doi.org/10.1007/978-1-4020-9964-9_6
17. Compton, E.: AI and assessment in higher education. Times. High. Educ. (2025) https://www.timeshighereducation.com/campus/ai-and-assessment-higher-education
18. Williamson, D.M., Xi, X., Breyer, F.J.: A framework for evaluation and use of automated scoring. Educ. Meas. Issues Pract. **31**(1), 2–13 (2012). https://doi.org/10.1111/j.1745-3992.2011.00223.x
19. Ariely, M., Nazaretsky, T., Alexandron, G.: Causal-mechanical explanations in biology: applying automated assessment for personalized learning in the science classroom. J. Res. Sci. Teach. **61**(8), 1858–1889 (2024). https://doi.org/10.1002/tea.21929
20. Flodén, J.: Grading exams using large language models: a comparison between human and AI grading of exams in higher education using ChatGPT. Br. Educ. Res. J. **51**(1), 201–224 (2025). https://doi.org/10.1002/berj.4069
21. Usher, M.: Generative AI vs. instructor vs. peer assessments: a comparison of grading and feedback in higher education. Assess. Eval. High. Educ. **1-16** (2025). https://doi.org/10.1080/02602938.2025.2487495
22. Swiecki, Z., et al.: Assessment in the age of artificial intelligence. Computers and Education: Artificial Intelligence. **3**, 100075 (2022). https://doi.org/10.1016/j.caeai.2022.100075
23. Figueras, C., Farazouli, A., Cerratto Pargman, T., McGrath, C., Rossitto, C.: Promises and breakages of automated grading systems: a qualitative study in computer science education. Educ. Inq. **1-22** (2025). https://doi.org/10.1080/20004508.2025.2464996
24. Bearman, M., Luckin, R.: Preparing university assessment for a world with AI: tasks for human intelligence. Re-imagining university assessment in a digital world. **49-63** (2020). https://doi.org/10.1007/978-3-030-41956-1_5
25. Gurin Schleifer, A., Beigman Klebanov, B., Alexandron, G.: Uncovering measurement biases in LLM embedding spaces: the Anna Karenina principle and its implications for automated feedback. Int. J. Artif. Intell. Educ. **1-35** (2025). https://doi.org/10.1007/s40593-025-00485-7
26. Kumar, R., Eaton, S.E., Mindzak, M., Morrison, R.: Academic integrity and artificial intelligence: an overview. In: Eaton, S.E. (ed.) Second Handbook of Academic Integrity, pp. 1583–1596. Springer, New York (2024). https://doi.org/10.1007/978-3-031-54144-5_153
27. Mazzoli Smith, L., Todd, L., Laing, K.: Students' views on fairness in education: the importance of relational justice and stakes fairness. Res. Pap. Educ. **33**(3), 336–353 (2018). https://doi.org/10.1080/02671522.2017.1302500
28. Starck, J.G., Riddle, T., Sinclair, S., Warikoo, N.: Teachers are people too: examining the racial bias of teachers compared to other American adults. Educ. Res. **49**(4), 273–284 (2020). https://doi.org/10.3102/0013189X20912758
29. Nazaretsky, T., Cukurova, M., Ariely, M., Alexandron, G.: Confirmation bias and trust: human factors that influence teachers' attitudes towards AI-based educational technology. In: CEUR Workshop Proceedings, vol. 3042, (2021)

30. Magowan, L.: Centre assessment grades in 2020: a natural experiment for investigating bias in teacher judgements. J. Comput. Soc. Sci. **6**(2), 609–653 (2023)
31. Madnani, N., Loukina, A., Von Davier, A., Burstein, J., Cahill, A.: Building better open-source tools to support fairness in automated scoring. In: Proceedings of the First ACL Workshop on Ethics in Natural Language Processing, pp. 41–52 (2017). https://doi.org/10.18653/v1/W17-1605
32. O'Neill, G.: It's not fair! Students and staff views on the equity of the procedures and outcomes of students' choice of assessment methods. Ir. Educ. Stud. **36**(2), 221–236 (2017). https://doi.org/10.1080/03323315.2017.1324805
33. Li, L., et al.: Moral machines or tyranny of the majority? A systematic review on predictive bias in education. In: LAK23: 13th International Learning Analytics and Knowledge Conference, pp. 499–508 (2023). https://doi.org/10.1145/3576050.3576119
34. Choi, S., Jeong, S., Park, S., Kim, Y., Han, I.: Analyzing teacher–AI interaction patterns across teacher experience and AI proficiency in student-centered lesson design. Teach. Teach. Educ. **169**, 105266 (2026). https://doi.org/10.1016/j.tate.2025.105266
35. Nazaretsky, T., Mejia-Domenzain, P., Swamy, V., Frej, J., Käser, T. AI or Human? Evaluating student feedback perceptions in higher education. In: Ferreira Mello, R., Rummel, N., Jivet, I., Pishtari, G., Ruipérez Valiente, J.A. (eds) Technology Enhanced Learning for Inclusive and Equitable Quality Education. EC-TEL 2024. Lecture Notes in Computer Science, vol 15159. Springer, Cham. (2024). https://doi.org/10.1007/978-3-031-72315-5_20
36. Cukurova, M., Miao, X., Brooker, R.: Adoption of artificial intelligence in schools: unveiling factors influencing teachers' engagement. In: International Conference on Artificial Intelligence in Education, pp. 151–163. Springer Nature Switzerland, Cham (2023). https://doi.org/10.1007/978-3-031-36272-9_13
37. Viberg, O., Mutimukwe, C., Hrastinski, S., Cerratto-Pargman, T., Lilliesköld, J.: Exploring teachers'(future) digital assessment practices in higher education: instrument and model development. Br. J. Educ. Technol. **55**(6), 2597–2616 (2024). https://doi.org/10.1111/bjet.13462
38. Worthington, R.L., Whittaker, T.A.: Scale development research: a content analysis and recommendations for best practices. Couns. Psychol. **34**(6), 806–838 (2006). https://doi.org/10.1177/0011000006288127
39. Shrestha, N.: Factor analysis as a tool for survey analysis. Am. J. Appl. Math. Stat. **9**(1), 4–11 (2021)
40. Kline, R.B.: Principles and Practice of Structural Equation Modeling, Second edn. The Guilford Press (2005)
41. Braun, V., Clarke, V.: Using thematic analysis in psychology. Qual. Res. Psychol. **3**(2), 77–101 (2006). https://doi.org/10.1191/1478088706qp063oa
42. Hooper, D., Coughlan, J., & Mullen, M. Evaluating model fit: a synthesis of the structural equation modelling literature. In: 7th European Conference on Research Methodology for Business and Management Studies (Vol. 2008, No. 2, pp. 195–200). (2008).
43. Kyriazos, T.A.: Applied psychometrics: sample size and sample power considerations in factor analysis (EFA, CFA) and SEM in general. Psychology. **9**, 2207–2230 (2018). https://doi.org/10.4236/psych.2018.98126
44. Sathyanarayana, S., Mohanasundaram, T.: Fit indices in structural equation modeling and confirmatory factor analysis: reporting guidelines. Asian Journal of Economics, Business and Accounting. **24**(7), 561–577 (2024)
45. Memarian, B., Doleck, T.: Human-in-the-loop in artificial intelligence in education: a review and entity-srelationship (ER) analysis. Computers in Human Behavior: Artificial Humans. **2**(1), 100053 (2024)

# Dosage and Dialogue: Understanding Human Support in Hybrid Human-AI Math Tutoring

Ge Gao[1(✉)], Ashish Gurung[2], Danielle R. Thomas[2], Marie Cynthia Abijuru Kamikazi[2], Conrad Borchers[3], Erin Gatz[2], Shivang Gupta[2], Stephen Fancsali[4], Steve Ritter[4], Lee Branstetter[2], Kenneth Koedinger[2], and Emma Brunskill[1]

[1] Stanford University, Stanford, CA, USA
{gegao,ebrun}@stanford.edu
[2] Carnegie Mellon University, Pittsburgh, PA, USA
{agurung,mabijuru,shivangg,shivangg,branstet}@andrew.cmu.edu,
{drthomas,koedinger}@cmu.edu
[3] Vanderbilt University, Nashville, TN, USA
c.borchers@vanderbilt.edu
[4] Carnegie Learning, Inc., Pittsburgh, PA, USA
{sfancsali,sritter}@carnegielearning.com

**Abstract.** One-on-one human tutoring is among the most effective educational interventions, yet cost and staffing constraints limit scalability. Hybrid human–AI tutoring, in which students work in math learning software while receiving as-needed one-on-one (1:1) support from a remote human tutor, offers a promising alternative. Yet, its effectiveness, and the role of how much and how well tutoring is delivered, remain under-characterized. We examine whether variation in the quantity and quality of remote human tutoring is associated with students' in-platform learning progress and external assessment outcomes. Using tutoring records, platform logs, prior achievement, and end-of-year assessments from two U.S. middle-school implementations (IXL: N=203; MATHia: N=157), we examine tutoring dosage, sustained sessions ($\geq$1 min), and, for the transcript-available site, LLM-derived dialogue quality ratings. Regression models show that more frequent sustained tutoring sessions are positively associated with in-platform math progress after controlling for prior achievement, although the strength and robustness of this association vary across sites and model specifications. In the transcript-available site, LLM-derived tutoring rating explains additional variation in in-platform progress beyond dosage. However, neither dosage nor dialogue quality shows robust direct associations with external test scores after accounting for prior achievement and class-level heterogeneity, underscoring the need for cautious interpretation of observational dosage estimates.

**Keywords:** One-on-one human tutoring · Hybrid human-AI tutoring · Software learning progress · K-12 mathematics education


J. Weidlich et al. (Eds.): EC-TEL 2026, LNCS 16905, pp. 209–223, 2027.
https://doi.org/10.1007/978-3-032-37979-5_15

## 1 Introduction

Personalized mathematics software is now used by millions of learners internationally, reshaping how instruction is delivered and studied at scale [8,12,30]. Prior work has found that students' software-based progress is often positively associated with external performance measures. For example, large-scale observational analyses of the IXL software platform report that schools using IXL outperform non-IXL schools on state assessments, and students who master more skills per week tend to show greater test score gains [2]. Similarly, within MATHia, students who complete more practice workspaces tend to perform better in subsequent Algebra I courses, particularly among those with lower pre-test scores [28,34]. These findings are primarily correlational, and may reflect differences in student ability, engagement, or instructional context. Evidence from randomized controlled trials provides a more nuanced picture. For instance, evaluations of MATHia (Cognitive Tutor) have demonstrated positive but heterogeneous effects on student achievement [27], while a recent randomized study of IXL found significant improvements on diagnostic assessments but not on state accountability exams [10]. Recent large-scale analyses of computer-assisted learning in real-world settings similarly highlight that the effectiveness of such systems depends critically on usage intensity and implementation context [12]. Taken together, these results suggest that while in-software progress is often predictive of learning outcomes, it may not consistently translate into broader academic performance. This variability highlights the need to understand what additional supports or contextual factors help convert software practice into robust learning gains, motivating a growing body of work in this area [5,6,17].

One increasingly common instructional context is the integration of one-on-one (1:1) human tutoring alongside AI-driven mathematics software, often referred to as *hybrid human–AI tutoring* [31]. Hybrid human-AI tutoring provides the opportunity for rich, systematic data streams (e.g., tutor–student transcripts, interaction logs, and fine-grained timing information) that were largely unavailable in earlier intelligent tutoring system studies [17]. One-on-one tutoring with a human tutor is widely recognized as one of the most effective interventions in education [20,33]. Prior studies have found that 1:1 or small-group tutoring can dramatically improve student achievement. A meta-analysis of dozens of tutoring programs found an overall average positive effect on learning outcomes, indicating substantial gains [26]. These effects were stronger when tutors were professional teachers or paraprofessionals (as opposed to volunteers or parents) and when tutoring was delivered during the school day [26]. These impressive results underscore the potential of 1:1 tutoring to accelerate learning.

Despite the known benefits of 1:1 human tutoring on student learning, it is very costly to implement and difficult to scale [14,19]. Hybrid human-AI tutoring poses a solution to alleviating some of the cost [7,31] by offloading some support to an AI math software tutor. Such an approach also offers potential scalability given the ubiquitous use of math software in schools [15]. Relatively little is known about how human tutoring and AI tutor software-based learning may relate in such settings. Prior work establishes that making progress in math software correlates with better test outcomes [2], and that tutoring on its own produces gains [26,29]. Prior hybrid tutoring models may alternate between scheduled human-led sessions and separate software-based instruction (e.g., Saga Education [3]). In contrast, we study a drop-in support model in which students work continuously in AI-based software while human tutors provide brief, opportunistic 1:1 assistance, a lower-intensity setting that may yield different relationships between human tutoring dosage and outcomes. This more closely resembles classroom "over-the-shoulder" support, as explored in prior work on teacher attention and orchestration tools such as Lumilo [1], where instructors dynamically allocate attention across students. Understanding how tutoring functions in this lower-intensity, opportunistic setting is critical, as it differs substantially from high-dosage or scheduled tutoring models.

Moreover, joint human tutoring and AI tutoring have shown positive effects on students' AI tutor software progress. For example, Thomas et al. [31] found that the addition of human tutoring significantly improved both student engagement (as measured by time on task) and learning progress (e.g., skills mastered) across multiple implementation sites and AI platforms, compared to students receiving AI-only instruction. Gurung et al. [13] found that the benefits of human–AI tutoring were especially effective for lower-performing students in outcomes compared to similarly performing peers who received only AI tutoring.

However, it remains unclear under what conditions combining 1:1 human tutoring with AI tutoring yields consistent improvements, and how to optimize such interventions. In particular, stakeholders are interested in understanding how variation in 1:1 human tutoring dosage is associated with subsequent software-based learning progress and performance on formal assessments in real-world implementations. Because tutoring was allocated in part based on student need rather than randomly assigned, we do not estimate causal effects. Instead, we use observational learning analytics models to characterize robust patterns of association across two implementation contexts, while controlling for prior achievement and class-level heterogeneity where possible. This design allows us to examine not only whether students who receive more tutoring make more progress, but also whether the quality of tutor–student dialogue, as measured from full-session transcripts using an LLM-based rubric, explains additional variation beyond dosage alone.

In this paper we address this gap by analyzing a hybrid human-AI tutoring intervention to examine how variation in tutoring time, session frequency, and dialogue quality are associated with learning. We operationalize each student's human tutoring dosage as both the total number of 1:1 human tutoring sessions and the total minutes of 1:1 human tutoring. We also measure each student's AI tutor math progress (skills proficient or workspaces mastered in the tutoring software) and their external assessment scores. Studying human tutoring dosage in real-world settings presents several challenges: tutoring is not randomly assigned, students with greater need often receive more support, and interactions vary widely in duration and purpose. We therefore adopt an observational approach and focus on characterizing associations under these constraints. Using a series of regression models, we aim to answer the following research questions (RQs):

**RQ1.** How is tutoring dosage, measured by total tutoring time and session frequency, associated with students' in-software math learning progress?
**RQ2.** Does LLM-derived dialogue quality explain additional variation in in-software progress beyond tutoring dosage and prior achievement?
**RQ3.** Are tutoring dosage and LLM-derived dialogue quality associated with external standardized test performance after accounting for prior achievement and class-level heterogeneity?

## 2 Related Work

*Human Tutoring and Math Edtech Synergy.* There is extensive evidence that individualized tutoring is effective. A systematic review of K–12 tutoring trials found consistent positive impacts on learning [26]. High-quality programs (often using certified teachers or well-trained tutors) yield larger gains than volunteer programs or after-school efforts [14,26]. For example, evaluations of Saga Education's in-school tutoring found tutored students (where 2 students work with 1 tutor) improved their reading percentile rank and scores [18]. However, nearly all prior work treats tutoring as a fixed "dose" and does not extensively explore how variation in the amount of tutor time matters.

To leverage technology for scale, recent initiatives have paired human tutors with math software. Saga's high-dosage model alternated small-group tutoring with computer-assisted learning (CAL); in a large randomized trial, students in this model gained about 0.23 SD on a standardized math test, almost as much as in Saga's traditional 2:1 tutoring, while reducing per-pupil cost by 30% [4]. Complementing this, recent learning analytics work has begun to examine how human support interacts with student engagement in digital environments. For example, Borchers et al. [5] analyze fine-grained interaction data and show that teacher visits are temporally associated with reduced disengagement in AI-supported math learning. Other research has compared blended to software-only tutoring: a quasi-experimental study of middle-school students found the hybrid human-AI group outperformed a group using only AI-tutoring [13]. In that study, the addition of modest human support (~weekly 1:1 Zoom sessions) led to significantly higher learning growth (approximately 0.36 grade levels) relative to software-only students. Thomas et al. [31] similarly report that adding human scaffolding to an AI tutor increased students' software usage and proficiency. Together, these studies show that tutoring supplemented with technology can support learning, but prior work has not jointly examined tutoring dosage and dialogue quality within hybrid human–AI tutoring.

*Tutor Attention and Spatial Analytics.* A separate line of work has examined how teachers allocate attention in classrooms with AI tutors [16,17,22–25]. For example, Karumbaiah et al. performed a spatiotemporal analysis of teacher behavior in an AI-enabled math classroom [17]. In that study, researchers defined teacher visits as episodes when a teacher stays physically close to a student while the student uses an AI tutor. They found that teachers are highly engaged and these visits do provide immediate benefits (*e.g.*, students reduce off-task behaviors). However, teachers inevitably could not reach every struggling student, suggesting the limits of in-person attention. In a related study using a smart-glasses "awareness" tool, Karumbaiah et al. [16] measured three multi-modal attention signals: gaze fixations, use of an analytics "deep dive" feature, and physical visits. They found that teachers' use of the deep-dive analytics tool was most strongly associated with students' learning gains (after accounting for student ability and tutor logs), whereas mere proximity visits had weaker or even mixed effects. These findings illuminate how teachers notice student needs in real time, but they do not quantify the overall amount of tutoring attention each student receives nor its impact on outcomes. This work characterizes attention at fine granularity, but does not link total human tutoring dosage with student outcomes.

*LLM-Based Instructional Quality Assessment.* Large language models (LLMs) have demonstrated increasing capability for analyzing instructional interactions, from classroom discourse to tutoring dialogues. For example, Long et al. showed GPT-4 achieved 90%+ inter-coder agreement with human experts on middle school mathematics classroom transcripts [21], while Demszky and Liu demonstrated that NLP-based feedback on tutoring quality improved instructor uptake by 10–13% across 1,136 teachers [11]. However, applications to tutoring quality assessment remain under-investigated: Tran et al. achieved Quadratic Weighted Kappa of 0.63–0.77 on the Instructional Quality Assessment framework using few-shot prompting at the utterance level [32], while Whitehill and LoCasale-Crouch approached human inter-rater reliability by combining LLMs with bag-of-words features [35]. Most directly relevant, Thomas et al. examined hybrid MATHia-human tutoring with 585 middle school students but did not assess tutor quality variation [31]; their quasi-experimental study found significant positive effects on in-platform proficiency, with lower-achieving students benefiting most and time-on-task increasing from 24 to 33 min weekly. Existing LLM research focuses on validating automated coding against human raters or demonstrating that feedback improves practice, not on linking LLM-derived quality scores to learning outcomes.

## 3 Design Context and Methods

### 3.1 Data

We analyzed two datasets from U.S. middle-grade schools implementing hybrid human-AI tutoring in regular mathematics instruction. All procedures were IRB-approved; data were collected under standard school consent protocols, de-identified prior to analysis, and included opt-out provisions where applicable. Tutoring sessions were conducted in a shared-attention format, where each tutor was assigned to multiple students (typically 4–6, varied by contexts).

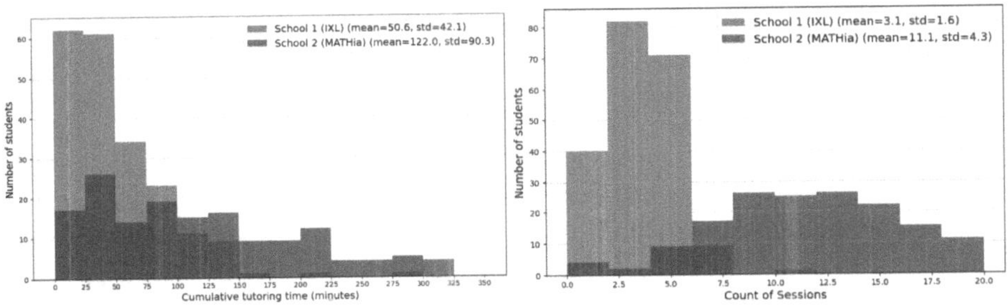


**Fig. 1.** Distributions of cumulative tutoring time and session counts per student across the two sites.

Tutors rotated across breakout rooms, providing brief, individualized assistance as needed. Students could also request help (e.g., via hand-raising), which influenced tutor prioritization. As a result, recorded tutoring "session time" reflects time in which support was available, rather than continuous one-on-one interaction (Fig. 1).

At School 1, 203 students across grades 6–8 participated in weekly online math classes integrating `IXL`[1] usage with remote 1:1 human tutoring delivered via Zoom breakout rooms. The program launched in late September 2024 and operated on a rotating schedule, such that students attended hybrid tutoring on different days each week. The dataset includes weekly IXL activity logs (e.g., dates, skills attempted, proficiency status), detailed 1:1 tutoring durations, and standardized assessments: a Spring 2024 state test used as a pre-diagnostic, and an end-of-year (EOY) state test in Spring 2025. In-software learning progress was assessed as the count of math skills proficient during using the software.

At School 2, 157 students participated in a parallel weekly hybrid tutoring program beginning in September 2024, combining `MATHia`[2] usage with remote 1:1 human tutoring during 40-minute class sessions. MATHia logs captured fine-grained student interactions with workspaces, including timestamps and mastery indicators, while separate logs recorded the duration of each 1:1 tutoring session. Available assessments included a Spring 2024 state test as a pre-diagnostic, and an EOY state test in Spring 2025. In-software learning progress was assessed as the count of workspace mastered during using the software.

*Quantifying Tutoring Scores of Full-Session Tutor-Student Dialog in School 2.* We include an LLM-derived session-level tutoring quality score as a covariate to account for variation in instructional quality across human tutoring sessions. This score was derived from a separate, under-review study using a large language model (Gemini-2.5-pro [9]) to evaluate full-session tutoring transcripts. The assessment pipeline employs a two-stage prompting process: an *opportunity prompt* identifies pedagogically relevant moments (e.g., student errors or cor-

[1] https://www.ixl.com/.
[2] https://www.carnegielearning.com/solutions/math/mathia.

rect attempts, expressions of confusion, student questions, and productive struggle), and an *evaluation prompt* assesses the tutor's response to these moments against evidence-based best practices. The prompting rubrics were derived from human-coded guidelines and validated in a separate study, where LLM-derived transcript scores were associated with independent tutor-training performance and expected improvements in pedagogical behaviors over time. Each identified instance receives a binary quality score (0=ineffective, 1=effective). Session-level scores are computed by aggregating across up to six identified opportunities per session, yielding an overall score in the range [0, 6]. Transcripts were generated from Zoom recordings using Whisper and merged with synchronized chat logs. Tutoring transcripts were only available for School 2, and therefore LLM-derived rating measures are included only for that site.

### 3.2 Implementation Context and Potential Confounds

The data come from real-world hybrid human–AI tutoring implementations, providing natural variation in tutoring dosage but no random assignment. Students receiving more tutoring may differ systematically from others; we mitigate this by controlling for prior achievement and class fixed effects, but results remain associational. Need-based allocation is partly by design—students with lower pre-test scores were often prioritized for proactive tutoring—and naïve associations may therefore underestimate or even reverse true dosage effects. Tutoring dosage varied substantially across students: at School 1, cumulative tutoring time averaged 50.6 min (SD = 42.1) with mean 3.1 sessions, reflecting a 6-day rotating schedule with week-to-week variability; at School 2, averages were 122.0 min (SD = 90.3) and 11.1 sessions. These structural differences motivate separate site-level analyses throughout.

### 3.3 Analytical Framework

Let $i$ index students, $Y_i$ denote sum of students' in-software math learning progress, measured via cumulative proficiency (School 1) or mastery (School 2) metrics. Let $Z_i$ denote EOY standardized external assessment performance. We define student-level tutoring exposure variables aggregated across the study period: (*i*) ($T_i$): total 1:1 tutoring duration, (*ii*) ($S_i$): number of tutoring sessions, and (*iii*) ($Q_i$): average LLM-derived tutoring rating.

All external test outcomes are standardized ($z$-scores on grade level) to facilitate interpretation in terms of standard deviations. Math progress in software, dosage-related covariates are log transformed. Tutor quality score is z-normalized in multivariate/adjusted models. All analyses are conducted separately by site using one row per student. Tutoring dosage, in-software progress, prior achievement, tutoring quality, and external assessment outcomes are aggregated to student-level features before modeling. Extended models include class fixed effects to account for shared classroom, schedule, and implementation differences. We fit linear regressions with cluster-robust standard errors grouped by class ID. We report all three dosage operationalizations rather than selecting a single post hoc "best" predictor, and emphasize patterns that are stable across model specifications. Model diagnostics did not indicate severe violations of linear-model assumptions; nevertheless, estimates remain associational because tutoring was not randomly assigned.

**Dosage–Outcome Associations (RQ1).** We use correlational linear regression models that relate summary-level 1:1 tutoring exposure to in-software learning progress. Let $Y_{iw}$ denote in-software learning progress for student $i$ in workspace $w$. We estimate:

$$Y_i = \beta_0 + \beta_1 D_i + \beta_2 P_i + \varepsilon_i, \tag{1}$$

where $P_i$ is a pre-test (baseline achievement) measure. Let $D_i$ denote a summary-level measure of tutoring dosage for student $i$. The key dosage regressor $D_i$ is substituted across specifications:

1. **Tutoring duration:** $D_i = T_i$ (total minutes of 1:1 tutoring),
2. **Session count (all sessions):** $D_i = S_i$ (number of 1:1 tutoring sessions),
3. **Session count (at least 1 min):** $D_i = S_i^{\geq 1\text{min}}$, where $S_i^{\geq 1\text{min}}$ counts only sessions with duration $\geq 1$ minute. This specification is included to exclude extremely short or potentially not meaningful interactions (e.g., brief check-ins or logging artifacts) and better capture sessions with substantive instructional engagement[3].

We report models *adjusted for prior achievement* by adding $P_i$.

**Incremental Role of LLM-Derived Tutoring Rating (RQ2).** To evaluate what extent LLM-derived tutoring rating explains variation in learning progress beyond tutoring dosage alone, we extend the baseline model:

$$Y_i = \beta_0 + \beta_1 \{T_i, S_i, S_i^{\geq 1\text{min}}\}_{best} + \beta_2 \overline{Q}_i + \beta_3 P_i + \varepsilon_i \tag{2}$$

where we report the most powerful covariate among $T_i, S_i, S_i^{\geq 1\text{min}}$ in the model. Improvements in model fit quantify the additional explanatory contribution of tutoring quality.

**Relationships to External Academic Outcomes (RQ3).** Finally, we relate cumulative tutoring experiences across workspaces to external standardized test outcomes:

$$Z_i = \beta_0 + \beta_1 \{T_i, S_i, S_i^{\geq 1\text{min}}\}_{best} + \beta_2 \overline{Q}_i + \beta_3 P_i + \varepsilon_i \tag{3}$$

[3] Sensitivity analyses using 30-second, 2-minute, and 5-minute thresholds confirm that the main findings are robust to this choice for both in-software progress (School 1: $\beta = 0.28$–$0.45$, all $p \leq 0.044$; School 2: $\beta = 0.19$–$0.53$, all $p > 0.10$) and external exam scores (all $p > 0.40$ in School 1; all $p > 0.43$ in School 2 with the exception of an isolated significant negative estimate at the 2-minute threshold, which we attribute to subsample composition).

# 4 Results

## 4.1 Dosage–Outcome Associations (RQ1)

For regressions adjusting for pre-test scores, in School 1, associations between human tutoring dosage and progress remain robust after adjustment, including total tutoring duration ($\beta = 0.14$, $p < 0.001$) and session count measures (all sessions: $\beta = 0.37$, $p < 0.001$; sessions $\geq 1$ minute: $\beta = 0.37$, $p < 0.001$). Pre-test scores are also positively associated with progress but do not attenuate dosage effects. In School 2, pre-test scores explain a substantial share of variance in progress ($R^2 \approx 0.43$–$0.46$). After adjustment, total tutoring duration and overall session count are not significant, while session frequency restricted to sessions lasting at least one minute remains positively associated with progress ($\beta = 0.68$, $p = 0.004$).

*Summary Across Contexts.* Overall, associations between human tutoring dosage and in-software progress vary by instructional context. In School 1, both tutoring time and frequency are consistently associated with greater progress, whereas in School 2, where prior achievement dominates, only sustained tutoring interactions (sessions $\geq 1$ minute) show a reliable association. These results suggest that effective operationalizations of human tutoring dosage, and their relationship to learning, may differ across platforms and student populations.

*Model Fit and Robustness (RQ1).* The baseline models account for human tutoring dosage and prior achievement only, yielding $R^2 = 0.09$ (School 1) and $R^2 = 0.46$ (School 2). Extending these models with class fixed effects, grade level, tutoring quality rating (School 2 only), and weeks of platform usage (Table 1) substantially improves fit in both settings ($R^2 \approx 0.39$–$0.40$ for School 1; $R^2 \approx 0.70$–$0.73$ for School 2). In School 1, the dosage association is positive and significant across all three operationalizations: session count ($\geq$1 min; $\beta = 0.42$, $p = 0.006$), unrestricted session count ($\beta = 0.41$, $p = 0.025$), and log instruction duration ($\beta = 0.10$, $p = 0.033$). Grade proficiency emerges as a strong positive predictor across all models ($\beta \approx 0.09$–$0.11$, $p < 0.001$), while pre-test score is consistently non-significant ($p > 0.60$), suggesting that classroom-level curriculum difficulty accounts for much of the variance previously attributed to prior achievement. In School 2, none of the three dosage operationalizations reach significance in the extended models (session count $\geq$1 min: $\beta = 0.53$, $p = 0.259$; unrestricted session count: $\beta = 0.53$, $p = 0.259$; log duration: $\beta = 0.01$, $p = 0.955$). Pre-test score remains a strong positive predictor across all specifications ($\beta \approx 0.21$–$0.22$, $p < 0.001$).

## 4.2 Incremental Role of LLM-Derived Tutoring Rating (RQ2)

We examine to what extent LLM-derived tutoring rating explains additional variation in students' in-software math progress beyond human tutoring dosage and prior achievement. This analysis is conducted in School 2 (`MATHia`). The inclusion of LLM-derived tutoring quality rating as a covariate in School 2 (Table 1)

**Table 1.** Regression of **in-software math progress** on human tutoring dosage and covariates.

| | **School 1 (IXL)** | | | **School 2 (MATHia)** | | |
|---|---|---|---|---|---|---|
| **Predictor** | *S1* | *S2* | *Dur.* | *S1* | *S2* | *Dur.* |
| *Human tutoring dosage* | | | | | | |
| Sess. count (≥1 min) | 0.42** (0.154) | — | — | 0.53 (0.470) | — | — |
| Sess. count (all) | — | 0.41* (0.182) | — | — | 0.53 (0.470) | — |
| Duration | — | — | 0.10* (0.045) | — | — | 0.01 (0.141) |
| *Prior achievement* | | | | | | |
| Pre-test score | 0.03 (0.064) | 0.02 (0.066) | 0.03 (0.070) | 0.22*** (0.042) | 0.22*** (0.042) | 0.21*** (0.036) |
| *Other controls* | | | | | | |
| Tutoring quality rating | — | — | — | 0.16*** (0.043) | 0.16*** (0.043) | 0.15*** (0.035) |
| Grade level | 0.11*** (0.011) | 0.11*** (0.011) | 0.09*** (0.013) | 0.32** (0.093) | 0.32** (0.093) | 0.41*** (0.057) |
| Year–week count | −0.03 (0.051) | −0.03 (0.058) | 0.03 (0.037) | −0.03 (0.034) | −0.03 (0.034) | 0.02 (0.023) |
| Class FEs | Yes | Yes | Yes | Yes | Yes | Yes |
| $R^2$ | .397 | .393 | .384 | .710 | .710 | .704 |
| $N$ | 199 | 199 | 199 | 87 | 87 | 87 |

*S1* = session count (≥1 min); *S2* = session count (all); *Dur.* = log instruction duration. Cluster-robust SEs (class level) in parentheses. $^{\dagger}p < 0.10$, $^{*}p < 0.05$, $^{**}p < 0.01$, $^{***}p < 0.001$. Base models (dosage only, no class FEs or extended controls) yielded $R^2 = 0.09$ (School 1) and 0.46 (School 2).

reveals a consistent and statistically significant positive association with in-software math progress across all three dosage operationalizations ($\beta \approx 0.15$–$0.16$, $p < 0.001$), independent of session frequency, duration, prior achievement, grade level, and class fixed effects. This pattern suggests that the quality of tutoring interactions carries incremental explanatory power beyond dosage alone.

### 4.3 Relationships to External Academic Outcomes (RQ3)

We examine whether tutoring-related measures are associated with external assessment performance after controlling for prior achievement. In base models, prior achievement is the dominant predictor in both schools. Session count is positively associated with external scores in School 1 ($\beta = 0.25$, $p = 0.019$) but negatively associated in School 2 ($\beta = -0.41$, $p = 0.036$), likely reflecting need-based allocation. LLM-derived tutoring quality shows a small positive base-model association in School 2 ($\beta = 0.10$, $p = 0.044$), but this association is not robust to the extended specifications below.

*Model Fit and Robustness (RQ3).* Extended models with class fixed effects and grade-level controls (Table 2) raise explained variance from $R^2 = 0.53$ to $\approx$0.65 in School 1 and from 0.66 to $\approx$0.79 in School 2. Across all six specifications, no tutoring dosage measure reaches significance in either school, and tutoring quality rating remains non-significant in School 2 ($\beta \approx 0.04$, $p > 0.37$) once class-level heterogeneity is absorbed. Prior achievement emerges as the sole robust predictor (School 1: $\beta \approx 0.58$, $p < 0.001$; School 2: $\beta \approx 0.41$, $p < 0.01$), suggesting that neither the quantity nor the LLM-based rating of human tutoring interactions independently predicts external standardized test performance beyond what students already knew at the start of the year.

### 4.4 Descriptive Pathways from Tutoring to External Outcomes

To explore whether in-software progress provides a plausible pathway linking tutoring dosage to external performance, we estimated chained associational models using session count ($\geq$1 min). Because tutoring was not randomly assigned, these analyses are descriptive rather than causal mediation tests. In School 1, session count predicted in-software progress ($\beta_1 = 0.029$, $p = 0.001$), while progress was positively but not significantly associated with external scores ($\beta_2 = 0.417$, $p = 0.105$); the implied indirect association was not significant (Sobel $z = 1.23$, $p = 0.219$). In School 2, session count predicted in-software progress ($\beta_1 = 0.026$, $p < 0.001$), and progress predicted external performance ($\beta_2 = 0.928$, $p < 0.001$), yielding a significant indirect association (Sobel $z = 2.79$, $p = 0.005$). However, the direct association between session count and external scores was negative ($\beta_3 = -0.042$, $p = 0.019$), consistent with need-based confounding.

## 5 Discussion

This study examined how 1:1 human tutoring dosage and instructional quality relate to in-software learning and external assessments across two hybrid human–AI tutoring implementations, contributing to a growing body of work on how human support complements AI-driven math instruction [5,13,31]. Rather than comparing human and AI tutoring, we jointly analyze dosage, sustained interaction thresholds, and LLM-derived dialogue quality across two platforms.

Our first key finding is that repeated substantive tutoring sessions ($\geq$1 min) are positively associated with in-software math progress after controlling for prior achievement, consistent with the broader tutoring literature showing meaningful positive effects of 1:1 human support on learning [26,33]. This association held across multiple dosage operationalizations in School 1, while in School 2 effects attenuated once class fixed effects were absorbed, possibly reflecting the higher baseline tutoring intensity at that site and diminishing returns at higher dosage

**Table 2.** Regression of **external exam scores** on human tutoring dosage and covariates.

| Predictor | School 1 (IXL) | | | School 2 (MATHia) | | |
|---|---|---|---|---|---|---|
| | *S1* | *S2* | *Dur.* | *S1* | *S2* | *Dur.* |
| *Human tutoring dosage* | | | | | | |
| Sess. count (≥1 min) | 0.10<br>(0.146) | — | — | −0.14<br>(0.311) | — | — |
| Sess. count (all) | — | 0.12<br>(0.150) | — | — | −0.14<br>(0.311) | — |
| Duration | — | — | 0.02<br>(0.041) | — | — | −0.08<br>(0.108) |
| *Prior achievement* | | | | | | |
| Pre-test score | 0.58***<br>(0.089) | 0.57***<br>(0.088) | 0.58***<br>(0.090) | 0.41**<br>(0.144) | 0.41**<br>(0.144) | 0.41**<br>(0.150) |
| *Other controls* | | | | | | |
| Tutoring quality rating | — | — | — | 0.04<br>(0.047) | 0.04<br>(0.047) | 0.04<br>(0.045) |
| Grade level | −0.16***<br>(0.016) | −0.16***<br>(0.016) | −0.16***<br>(0.020) | 0.06<br>(0.063) | 0.06<br>(0.063) | 0.07†<br>(0.037) |
| Year–week count | 0.04<br>(0.059) | 0.03<br>(0.056) | 0.05<br>(0.046) | −0.02<br>(0.025) | −0.02<br>(0.025) | −0.02<br>(0.023) |
| Class FEs | Yes | Yes | Yes | Yes | Yes | Yes |
| $R^2$ | .647 | .647 | .646 | .790 | .790 | .791 |
| $N$ | 199 | 199 | 199 | 87 | 87 | 87 |

*S1* = session count (≥1 min); *S2* = session count (all);
*Dur.* = log instruction duration. Cluster-robust SEs (class level) in parentheses. $^{\dagger}p < 0.10$, $^{*}p < 0.05$, $^{**}p < 0.01$, $^{***}p < 0.001$.
School 2 models restricted to students with available transcript data for tutoring quality scoring.

levels [19]. This context-dependence echoes findings from [17], who showed that teacher visits in AI-enabled classrooms provide immediate benefits whose downstream impact is moderated by implementation context.

Second, in School 2, LLM-derived tutoring quality explains additional variation in in-software progress beyond dosage and prior achievement. This extends work validating automated instructional quality assessment [11,21,32,35] by linking such scores to student learning outcomes, and aligns with evidence that tutoring effectiveness depends on instructional practice as well as time allocated [26,33].

Moreover, for external standardized assessments, prior achievement dominated across all specifications, and neither dosage nor tutoring quality showed independent direct effects once class-level heterogeneity was absorbed. This aligns with prior evaluations of MATHia and IXL reporting stronger effects on curriculum-aligned measures than on state accountability exams [10,27], and with large-scale analyses of computer-assisted learning highlighting the sensitivity of effects to outcome measurement [12]. Descriptive pathway analyses further suggest a plausible pattern in which tutoring dosage is more directly associated with software mastery gains, which are in turn associated with external performance, consistent with the chained learning hypothesis advanced by [28,34]. However, because tutoring was not randomly assigned, these pathways should not be interpreted as causal mediation. The competitive descriptive pathway pattern in School 2—where a significant negative direct association coexists with a positive indirect association—likely reflects need-based confounding, a well-documented challenge in observational tutoring research whereby students receiving more support are those struggling most [17].

*Limitations and Future Work.* This study is observational, so results should be interpreted as associations rather than causal effects. Unmeasured factors such as student motivation, attendance, and need-based tutor allocation may bias dosage estimates. LLM-derived quality scores were available only for School 2 and reflect session-level aggregates rather than moment-to-moment instructional decisions. We also lack participant feedback or qualitative implementation data from students and tutors, limiting interpretation of why particular interactions were more or less productive. Future work should use stronger causal designs, richer multimodal interaction data, and longer-term follow-up.

## 6 Conclusions

This study provides an observational learning analytics account of hybrid human–AI tutoring across two middle-school mathematics implementations. Repeated substantive tutoring sessions were generally associated with greater in-software progress, though this pattern varied by site and model specification. In the transcript-available site, LLM-derived dialogue quality explained additional variation beyond dosage and prior achievement. However, neither dosage nor dialogue quality showed robust direct associations with external standardized test scores once prior achievement and class-level heterogeneity were included. Future work should use stronger causal designs and richer qualitative or multimodal evidence to examine when platform-proximal progress translates into broader assessment gains.

**Acknowledgments.** This work was made possible with the support of the Learning Engineering Virtual Institute. The opinions, findings, and conclusions are those of the authors.

## References

1. Aleven, V., Blankestijn, J., Lawrence, L., Nagashima, T., Taatgen, N.: A dashboard to support teachers during students' self-paced AI-supported problem-solving practice. In: European Conference on Technology Enhanced Learning, pp. 16–30. Springer (2022)

2. An, X.: Associations between IXL usage and IXL impact in math and ELA: analysis of data from seven states (2021)
3. Ander, R., Guryan, J., Ludwig, J.: Improving academic outcomes for disadvantaged students: scaling up individualized tutorials. The Hamilton Project, Brookings (2016)
4. Bhatt, M.P., Guryan, J., Khan, S.A., LaForest-Tucker, M., Mishra, B.: Can technology facilitate scale? Eevidence from a randomized evaluation of high dosage tutoring. Technical report National Bureau of Economic Research (2024)
5. Borchers, C., et al.: Revealing networks: understanding effective teacher practices in AI-supported classrooms using transmodal ordered network analysis. In: Proceedings of the 14th Learning Analytics and Knowledge Conference, pp. 371–381 (2024)
6. Cassar, S., Neal, M., Schofield, C.: Edtech, social relationships and learning: a study of relationships in the tech-mediated blended classroom. In: INTED2022 Proceedings, pp. 4174–4182. IATED (2022)
7. Chine, D.R., et al.: Educational equity through combined human-AI personalization: a propensity matching evaluation. In: International Conference on Artificial Intelligence in Education, pp. 366–377. Springer (2022)
8. Clark, A.E., Nong, H., Zhu, H., Zhu, R.: Compensating for academic loss: online learning and student performance during the covid-19 pandemic. China Econ. Rev. **68**, 101629 (2021)
9. Comanici, G., et al.: Gemini 2.5: Pushing the frontier with advanced reasoning, multimodality, long context, and next generation agentic capabilities. arXiv preprint arXiv:2507.06261 (2025)
10. Copeland, S., Cook, M.A., Grant, A.A., Ross, S.M.: Randomized-control efficacy study of IXL math in Holland public schools. Center for Research and Reform in Education (2023)
11. Demszky, D., Liu, J.: M-powering teachers: natural language processing powered feedback improves 1: 1 instruction and student outcomes. In: Proceedings of the Tenth ACM Conference on Learning@ Scale, pp. 59–69 (2023)
12. Eames, T., Brunskill, E., Yamkovenko, B., Weatherholtz, K., Oreopoulos, P.: Computer-assisted learning in the real world: how khan academy influences student math learning. Proc. Natl. Acad. Sci. **123**(1), e2507708123 (2026)
13. Gurung, A., et al.: Human tutoring improves the impact of ai tutor use on learning outcomes. In: International Conference on Artificial Intelligence in Education, pp. 393–407. Springer (2025)
14. Guryan, J., et al.: Not too late: improving academic outcomes among adolescents. Am. Econ. Rev. **113**(3), 738–765 (2023)
15. Hillmayr, D., Ziernwald, L., Reinhold, F., Hofer, S.I., Reiss, K.M.: The potential of digital tools to enhance mathematics and science learning in secondary schools: a context-specific meta-analysis. Comput. Educ. **153**, 103897 (2020)
16. Karumbaiah, S., et al.: Teacher noticing and student learning in human-AI partnered classrooms: a multimodal analysis. In: Proceedings of the 17th International Conference of the Learning Sciences-ICLS 2023, pp. 1042-1045. International Society of the Learning Sciences (2023)
17. Karumbaiah, S., et al.: A spatiotemporal analysis of teacher practices in supporting student learning and engagement in an AI-enabled classroom. In: International Conference on Artificial Intelligence in Education, pp. 450–462. Springer (2023)
18. Khan, S., Bhatt, M., Guryan, J., Kim, J.: Can high-dosage literacy tutoring put first-graders on the road to success? Soc. Res. Educ. Effectiveness (2024)

19. Kraft, M.A., Falken, G.T.: A blueprint for scaling tutoring and mentoring across public schools. Aera Open **7**, 23328584211042856 (2021)
20. Kulik, J.A., Fletcher, J.D.: Effectiveness of intelligent tutoring systems: a meta-analytic review. Rev. Educ. Res. **86**(1), 42–78 (2016)
21. Long, Y., Luo, H., Zhang, Y.: Evaluating large language models in analysing classroom dialogue. NPJ Sci. Learn. **9**(1), 60 (2024)
22. Martinez-Maldonado, R., et al.: Moodoo the tracker: spatial classroom analytics for characterising teachers' pedagogical approaches. Int. J. Artif. Intell. Educ. **32**(4), 1025–1051 (2022)
23. Martinez-Maldonado, R., Kay, J., Yacef, K., Edbauer, M.T., Dimitriadis, Y.: Mtclassroom and mtdashboard: supporting analysis of teacher attention in an orchestrated multi-tabletop classroom, (2013)
24. Martinez-Maldonado, R., Schulte, J., Echeverria, V., Gopalan, Y., Shum, S.B.: Where is the teacher? Digital analytics for classroom proxemics. J. Comput. Assist. Learn. **36**(5), 741–762 (2020)
25. Martínez-Maldonado, R., Yan, L., Deppeler, J., Phillips, M., Gašević, D.: Classroom analytics: telling stories about learning spaces using sensor data. In: Hybrid Learning Spaces, pp. 185–203. Springer (2022)
26. Nickow, A., Oreopoulos, P., Quan, V.: The impressive effects of tutoring on PreK-12 learning: a systematic review and meta-analysis of the experimental evidence (2020)
27. Pane, J.F., Griffin, B.A., McCaffrey, D.F., Karam, R.: Effectiveness of cognitive tutor algebra I at scale. Educ. Eval. Policy Anal. **36**(2), 127–144 (2014)
28. Ritter, S., Joshi, A., Fancsali, S., Nixon, T.: Predicting standardized test scores from cognitive tutor interactions. Educ. Data Mining (2013)
29. Robinson, C.D., Kraft, M.A., Loeb, S., Schueler, B.E.: Accelerating student learning with high-dosage tutoring. EdResearch for Recovery Design Principles Series. EdResearch for Recovery Project (2021)
30. Steenbergen-Hu, S., Cooper, H.: A meta-analysis of the effectiveness of intelligent tutoring systems on k-12 students' mathematical learning. J. Educ. Psychol. **105**(4), 970 (2013)
31. Thomas, D.R., et al.: Improving student learning with hybrid human-AI tutoring: a three-study quasi-experimental investigation. In: Proceedings of the 14th Learning Analytics and Knowledge Conference, pp. 404–415 (2024)
32. Tran, N., Pierce, B., Litman, D., Correnti, R., Matsumura, L.C.: Analyzing large language models for classroom discussion assessment. In: Proceedings of the 17th International Conference on Educational Data Mining, pp. 500–510 (2024)
33. VanLehn, K.: The relative effectiveness of human tutoring, intelligent tutoring systems, and other tutoring systems. Educ. Psychol. **46**(4), 197–221 (2011)
34. Weeks, J., Baron, P.: Exploring math education relations by analyzing large data sets II. Research Memorandum. ETS RM-21-02. Educational Testing Service (2021)
35. Whitehill, J., LoCasale-Crouch, J.: Automated evaluation of classroom instructional support with LLMs and bows: connecting global predictions to specific feedback. J. Educ. Data Mining (2024)

# Students' Perception Accuracy of Partners' AI Use and its Relation to Collaboration Performance

Laura Graf(✉), Ramona Beinstingel, Stephan Krusche, and Oleksandra Poquet

Technical University of Munich, Munich, Germany
{l.graf,ramona.beinstingel,krusche,sasha.poquet}@tum.de

**Abstract.** Collaborative assignments are a cornerstone of programming education. Effective collaboration during a programming project depends on the formation of reasonably accurate beliefs about how each partner works. Generative AI tools, now widely used by undergraduate students, have introduced a consequential and largely invisible new dimension into collaboration: each student's use of AI. When partners collaborate remotely, they interpret partners' ability and effort through their code. This raises the question of how accurately students perceive each other's AI use in collaborations, and if a misalignment in these perceptions relates to team performance. To address this question, we conducted a three-wave longitudinal study of 103 student pairs in an introductory software engineering course. We found that greater misalignment between partners' beliefs about each other's AI use early in the project was associated with lower final project scores. The effect of such misaligned perceptions is the strongest in teams with lower prior programming performance, suggesting that low performing students pay a higher cost of misaligned perceptions. The perception misalignment does not consistently decrease through face-to-face pair-programming sessions. This suggests that ways to foster transparency may be needed to support student teams in collaborative programming.

**Keywords:** Generative AI · Collaboration · Programming education · Perception accuracy · Team performance

## 1 Introduction

Collaborative programming projects are a cornerstone of programming education. They develop students' technical proficiency and communication skills required in professional software development [1]. In team-based programming assignments, students work on a shared codebase and must divide tasks, review each other's code, and, among other tasks, align on design decisions. These are all examples of coordination activities that are central to effective collaboration [2]. To coordinate effectively, the students need to be aware of how their collaborators work, what they know, and how reliably they produce code that others can extend [3]. From that standpoint, it is plausible that failure to accurately judge partners' AI use in a collaborative task may disrupt coordination and potentially influence collaboration outcomes.


J. Weidlich et al. (Eds.): EC-TEL 2026, LNCS 16905, pp. 224–238, 2027.
https://doi.org/10.1007/978-3-032-37979-5_16

Generative AI tools challenge coordination, since AI use is largely invisible to the other team members. Traditionally, team members form expectations and beliefs about their peers by observing visible traces that reflect partner's work. For instance, in programming teams partners infer each other's practices and abilities from their commit patterns, code structure, testing habits, and the pace and volume of code production [4]. These traces provide cues for interpreting each other's contributions and adjusting coordination. With many students now relying on large language models and AI-assisted coding tools during programming tasks, there is a shift in what their partners can infer about them during the process. A large volume of well-structured code may reflect either strong individual expertise or extensive AI assistance. However, distinguishing between these possibilities may be difficult [5]. Therefore, collaboration may be indirectly shaped by how aware team partners are of each other's AI use.

Despite its relevance, the consequences of unobserved AI use on collaboration have received little attention. There is a gap in empirical work on team partners' awareness of each other's AI use for learning and work and its implications for collaboration. To address this gap, we conducted a longitudinal study of student teams over the course of a one-month programming project. Three times during one month, we asked 103 student pairs to self-report own and estimate partner AI usage amount and AI usage type. Using these data, we examine (1) how aware students were of each other's AI use over the course of a collaborative programming project, and (2) whether misalignments in these perceptions were negatively associated with team performance. Our results corroborate that some students stayed unaware of their partners' AI use and this affected collaboration outcomes. The findings suggest a need for tools that make partners' AI use visible to the team to improve collaboration.

## 2 Background

Research in group awareness demonstrates that collaboration depends on partners using visible cues in each other's work to form expectations about relevant aspects of their collaborators [6]. These visible cues enable group awareness that supports coordination of their joint activity [6]. The increasing use of AI tools affects how these observable cues can be interpreted, since collaboration aspects inferred from the cues, such as partner's competence, can no longer be trusted [5]. As a result, collaborators' awareness of each other may become limited, negatively affecting collaboration. This raises several related questions: whether collaborators are aware of each other's AI use, how the awareness of AI use develops during collaboration, and whether differences in this awareness are associated with collaboration outcomes.

### 2.1 Team Partners' Awareness of AI Use

To understand how collaborators form awareness of each other, prior research in computer-supported collaborative learning (CSCL) has examined how group awareness is maintained and supported. Within this literature, group awareness refers to the knowledge of aspects relevant for coordination, such as group members' activities, expertise, or level of participation. A central assumption in this work is that these aspects are not directly observed but inferred by group members from observable indicators of collaborators' work [7]. Learning analytics (LA) systems can make indicators of collaboration visible by aggregating and presenting contributions to help team members interpret each other's activity and thereby support coordination [8, 9]. The effectiveness of such an inference, however, rests on a direct link of the observable indicators to the underlying activity or expertise.

The increasing use of generative AI in programming affects how contributions can be interpreted. Because the same observable contributions can plausibly reflect either a collaborator's own work or AI generation [5], a partner can no longer read the sophistication or volume of code as a signal of the other's expertise or effort. From an awareness perspective, this weakens the link between observable partner behaviour and the inferences made from it. For instance, if partners underestimate or overestimate each other's reliance on AI, they may also develop inaccurate expectations about their partner's independent capabilities. The expectations about partners' capabilities affect coordination decisions, such as task allocation, review intensity, or knowing how much support a teammate may require [10].

Prior empirical work on generative AI in student programming has focused primarily on individual use patterns [11], learning outcomes [12], and academic integrity concerns [11]. Research that does address collaboration has primarily examined how AI can be used to mediate and support group processes [13, 14]. What remains under-explored is the situation where multiple collaborators independently use AI as a private support tool. This is a common context in both education and professional contexts, and one that poses challenges for collaborative work. Individuals who misjudge their partner's AI reliance may misallocate tasks, incorrectly conclude how much to scrutinise peer contributions, or fail to offer support where needed. Understanding how awareness of a partner's AI use develops over collaboration and whether misalignment in such awareness affects team performance is therefore consequential for both programming education and the design of tools that support collaborative work.

## 2.2 Formation of Beliefs about Team Partners' AI Use

Since observable contributions no longer provide reliable cues about how collaborators work, it becomes important to consider how students form beliefs about their partners under such uncertainty. In the absence of direct information about AI use, collaborators must find other ways to estimate how their partner approaches programming tasks. Research on interpersonal perception suggests that when information about others is limited or ambiguous, individuals rely on heuristic strategies to form judgments [15, 16].

One heuristic strategy based on which individuals form beliefs about others is social projection, i.e. individuals assume partners to be similar to them and use their own behaviour as a reference point for judging others [15]. This has been shown in research where students who engage in a particular behaviour (e.g., cheating) are more likely to believe that behaviour is common among peers [17]. From this perspective, students' own AI use may serve as an implicit baseline they use to estimate their partner's use.

Another common heuristic explaining how individuals form beliefs about others under observability constraints is their normative expectation, that is, their assumptions about what behaviour is 'normal', i.e., typical or appropriate in a given context [18]. Applied to AI use, this mechanism suggests that students may have ideas of the 'typical' use of generative AI tools in programming and transfer them to a partner independent of that partner's actual behaviour.

To summarise, the literature suggests that students may estimate their partner's AI use based on their own usage or expectations about the typical use of AI across programming tasks, especially in cases with limited direct communication or observable information about the specific individual. When estimations of partner AI use, and consequently their inferred characteristics, are based on assumed similarity or normative expectations, student judgements of each other would be misaligned among the students with dissimilar AI use. To develop pedagogical interventions supporting student teams, it is therefore necessary to examine estimations of partner AI use and if collaborators develop partner-specific knowledge over time.

### 2.3 Impact of AI Use Perception Misalignment on Collaboration Outcomes

Group awareness is closely linked to how effectively teams coordinate their work. Several distinct theoretical traditions support this claim. Although these traditions emphasise different mechanisms, they agree about the importance of aligned understanding of team partners, their process, and their individual expertise. Shared mental models theory suggests that teams perform more effectively when members hold aligned understandings of relevant aspects of the task and of each other, enabling them to anticipate each other's actions and coordinate with fewer explicit exchanges [3]. Similarly, transactive memory theory emphasises the importance of knowing how knowledge and expertise are distributed within a team, allowing members to rely on each other appropriately and allocate work efficiently [10, 19]. Overall, these theories about collaboration underline that teams coordinate more effectively when members are aware of each other's knowledge, capabilities, and ways of working.

Research is yet to empirically examine if misaligned perceptions of AI use are associated with team performance. Although perception misalignment is likely to influence coordination, its practical relevance depends on its further association with collaboration outcomes. Hence, establishing this association is a necessary first step of investigation.

## 3 Research Questions

We have argued that students' independent use of AI during collaboration activities may challenge group awareness essential for coordination between them. Hence, it is necessary to examine student awareness of their team partners' AI use, and whether misalignment in collaborators' perceptions of each other's AI use is associated with team performance. Accordingly, this study addresses the following research questions:

**RQ1.** How aware are students of each other's AI use over the course of a collaborative programming project?

**RQ2.** Is misalignment in team partners' perceptions of each other's AI use associated with team performance?

# 4 Method

## 4.1 Context

The data were collected during a collaborative programming assignment where AI use could vary between partners and is not directly observable. The assignment was part of an introductory undergraduate programming course at a large European university that enrolls students who major in subjects *other* than computer science. Data collection was designed in close collaboration with the instructors to ensure the quality of the student experience. The course comprised theory lectures, followed by a month of project work where pairs worked on the implementation of a computer game with given functionalities. During this month, three supervised in-person pair-programming sessions were hosted. These sessions took place weekly during the first three weeks of the month. Students had to attend a minimum of two of the sessions. Between the in-person sessions, students worked on their project remotely. Their contributions were shared via the version control platform GitHub. The team partners were chosen by the students themselves, and most teams were already acquainted from prior semesters. This setting allowed us to study the problem of AI-supported programming collaboration, because students worked interdependently on a shared codebase where their contributions were visible to each other but the process of producing these contributions was not. The longitudinal design repeatedly measuring peer perceptions in an authentic course, alongside the measures of prior performance and team outcome were suitable for understanding peer perceptions of AI use without disrupting the course activities.

## 4.2 Sample, Procedure and Measures

A full sample of 103 student pairs completed surveys three times within one month: before the first in-person pair-programming session (*t1*), mid-project, before session 2 (*t2*), and near the project end (*t3*). Students were offered five bonus project points for completing all three surveys. Male students comprised 65% of the sample.

**Outcome Grade.** Instructors made the final project grade available for our analysis ($M = 95.9$, $SD = 5.1$; range 69–100). This grade was assigned to a team based on correctness and completeness of their implementation of the computer game.

**Prior Performance.** To capture prior performance, we used the grade on a programming test taken prior to the project. It served as the prior performance covariate.

**Own AI Use for the Entire Assignment (Measured Three Times).** Each participant reported own AI use percentage ("What percentage of your programming involves using LLM chat or autocomplete in this project, roughly?").

**Partner AI Use for the Entire Assignment (Measured Three Times).** Each participant estimated their team partner's AI use percentage ("What percentage of your partner's programming involves using LLM chat or autocomplete, roughly?")

**Own AI Use across Specific Types of Activities.** Students were asked to report how frequently they used AI for each type of activity in their programming project, measured only in *t2* and *t3*. The frequency for each type of activity was rated on a five-point Likert scale ranging from "never" to "always". A total of ten activities were to be selected from: automatically implementing an entire feature, generating parts of code, writing tests, writing documentation/ comments, debugging, cleaning up or restructuring code, asking if approach is correct, explaining code, and asking about principles of programming/ the programming language. These task types were adopted from categories of AI-assisted activities used in programming education research [20]. Instructors were consulted about suitability of the categories in the course. This led to the exclusion of the category "Decide type of variable" due to the programming language specificity.

**Partner AI Use across Specific Types of Activities.** Students also estimated their partner's AI use across the same set of activities, measured only in *t2* and *t3*. These items capture understanding of the partner's AI use across programming activities, allowing to examine where estimation errors occur.

### 4.3 Analysis

**RQ1: Awareness of Partner AI Use.** To address RQ1, we analysed awareness of partner AI use at two levels: overall AI use amount and AI use type across development tasks (how much a partner relies on AI for different specific tasks). These levels capture distinct aspects of partner awareness. Slightly different methods were used to analyse these levels because amount and type pose different measurement challenges.

*AI Use Amount Estimation.* Students reported how much of their own amount of programming work involved AI use (self-report) and estimated their partner's amount (partner estimate) on a 0–100% scale. Since raw differences are sensitive to how individual students interpreted the percentage scale, we examined how partners perceived their *relative* AI use within the team. For each respondent we computed a normalised self–partner perception score z. z captures who the student thinks the heavier AI user is, rescaled, so it does not depend on the absolute percentages a student reports: $z = \frac{self\_report - guess\_about\_partner}{self\_report + guess\_about\_partner} \frac{self\_report - guess\_about\_partner}{self\_report + guess\_about\_partner}$. Positive values indicate that a respondent perceives themselves as the heavier AI user; negative values indicate they perceive their partner as the heavier user. From this, we calculated a team-level perception misalignment score $d = z_A + z_B$ from the perceptions of team partners A and B. Summing the two partners' scores into d tests whether their perceptions are mutually consistent: if they agree on who relies more on AI, their signs offset and $d \approx 0$; if have opposing perceptions of who uses AI more than the other, $|d|$ grows. Misalignment is, therefore, not a difference in usage levels but a disagreement from the team's perceptions of relative reliance on AI. To examine if alignment changed during the collaboration, we compared absolute misalignment values ($|d|$) between consecutive waves (*t1* to *t2*; *t2* to *t3*) using Wilcoxon signed-rank tests (the data were paired and non-normally distributed).

*AI Use Type Estimation.* We examined students' awareness of their team partner's AI use patterns across the ten task types. For each dyad, we computed Spearman rank correlations between the partner's self-reported AI use profile and the perceiver's estimate across the ten tasks. These correlations assess if students correctly identified the tasks where their partner used AI, and how frequently.

To assess if student estimation reflects genuine partner knowledge beyond general assumptions that bias their estimate, we isolated those components, i.e. (a) assumed partner similarity and (b) normative expectation, using partial correlation. We computed partial correlations between partner self-reports and perceiver estimates while controlling for a) the perceiver's own task profile and b) all students' average AI use profile. The residual correlation measures estimation accuracy that cannot be explained by self-projection or cohort-average alone [15]. We tracked how each component changed from *t2* to *t3* as partners accumulated shared experience over time.

Further, to examine if estimates were systematically biased for particular task types, we computed the difference between partner self-reports and team partner estimates for each of the ten tasks. We tested if these differences were significant using Wilcoxon signed-rank tests and Benjamini–Hochberg (BH) correction for the false discovery rate.

**RQ2: Relationship Between Perception Misalignment and Performance.** To address RQ2, we analysed the relationship between team-level perception misalignment (absolute $|d|$, defined above) and final project scores ($M = 95.9, SD = 5.1$; range 69–100). First, we examined bivariate associations using Spearman correlations between misalignment at each wave and project outcome to evaluate their relationship. We then fitted a robust regression model (Huber M-estimation), modelled as *project score* ~ $|d|_{t1}$ + *prior performance* + $|d|_{t1}$ × *prior performance.* The regression predicted project score from early misalignment ($|d|$ at *t1*), the team's mean prior programming performance, and their interaction. Robust regression is well suited to outcome distributions exhibiting a ceiling effect, such as the one present in the project score distribution [21]. Controlling for prior performance ensured that any association between misalignment and outcomes is not confounded by prior performance that captures baseline skill differences. The interaction term tests if the performance cost of misalignment varies across prior performance levels. Simple slopes were inspected to describe this variation.

Finally, to examine whether *changes* in perception alignment during the project were associated with outcomes, we identified teams where a perception reversal occurred, i.e. a team's perception of who uses AI more has flipped. Teams with and without reversals were compared using a Mann–Whitney U test. The reversal effect was further examined using robust regression controlling for initial misalignment magnitude and prior performance.

# 5 Results

## 5.1 RQ1: how Aware Are Students of each Other's AI Use over the Course of the Project?

**AI Use Amount.** We found that students' perceptions of each other's AI use aligned over the course of the project only for 49% of the students, and alignment improved most during the first weeks. To reach this conclusion, we examined the estimation misalignment score d at each wave. At *t1*, 24% of teams showed substantial misalignment in their perceptions ($|d| > 0.2)|$. Then, alignment improved significantly over the project (Wilcoxon signed-rank tests *t1* to *t3*: $W = 2292, p = .003, r = .35$). The change from *t2* to *t3* was not significant ($p = .156$), indicating that the alignment took place in the earlier weeks. By *t3*, the proportion of substantially misaligned teams dropped to 14%. Overall, many teams improved their perceptions alignment, with 49% of teams becoming better aligned over the full project period. However, 25% of the teams became worse at judging their teammates, and 26% showed no change. This shows that although most partners' views of each other's AI use converged during collaboration, a large proportion of teams remained substantially misaligned until the end of the project.

**AI Use Type.** We found that students showed limited and declining accuracy in estimating their partner's AI use type pattern, but estimation error was not uniform across task types. To reach this conclusion, first, we found that students' accuracy in estimating their partners' AI use pattern was limited. To examine perceptions of partner AI use during different types of tasks, we compared the rank ordering of each partner's self-reported AI use across ten tasks with the estimates provided by their team partner. Spearman rank correlations were $r = 0.34$ at *t2* and $r = .27$ at *t3*. These low correlations indicate that variance in partners' use was not well reflected in the partner estimates.

Three categories showed significant directional bias at *t2* (Wilcoxon signed-rank tests, with BH correction): AI use for automatically implementing full features was systematically underestimated ($M\text{diff} = +0.21$, $p\_adj = .049$), while AI use for asking about programming principles ($Mdiff = -0.29$, $p\_adj = .029$) and for confirming the validity of an approach ($Mdiff = -0.19$, $p\_adj = .049$) were overestimated. At *t3*, no task-specific differences reached significance. No other task types showed a significant directional bias at either wave, while students' absolute estimation error averaged at roughly one point on the five-point scale. We found that most of apparent awareness about a partner's AI use was a result of students' assumption that their partner uses AI the same way as them. Once this bias was removed, partner-specific accuracy was low although it increased over time.

The next step was to examine how much of the correlation between student self-report and their partners estimation of their AI use reflected genuine awareness of their partner's AI use. To understand it, we computed partial correlations controlling for two other factors: the rater's own self-report and the cohort's average AI use profile. These two controls are known biases affecting partner ratings. We found that assumed similarity was the dominant driver of partner estimates. The median correlation between a perceiver's estimates and their own self-reported usage profile was $r = .73$ at both waves. After partialling out this self-projection, the residual correlation, i.e. the component attributable to partner-specific knowledge, was substantially smaller (median partial $r = .16$ at *t2*, $r = .23$ at *t3*; all $p < .001$). The modest growth from *t2* to *t3* suggested a small gain in genuine partner knowledge over time. This gain occurred while partners' actual AI use profiles were diverging (inter-dyad profile similarity fell from median $r = .30$ at *t2* to $r = .20$ at *t3*), meaning the assumed-similarity heuristic was becoming less reliable but partners did not lose awareness what their partner was using AI for. Normative accuracy, i.e. whether a perceiver ranked the ten tasks in the same order as the population average, also explained part of overall estimation accuracy, though less than assumed similarity (median $r = 0.49$ at *t2*, $r = 0.43$ at *t3*).

In sum, what appears as awareness of a partner's AI use pattern is a product of projecting one's own behaviour and one's knowledge of what a typical student in the course does. Genuine knowledge of the specific partner is low and improves very slowly.

### 5.2 RQ2: Is Perception Misalignment Associated with Team Performance?

Teams whose members had higher misalignment in their AI use perceptions at the beginning of the project tended to receive lower scores, as captured by the Spearman correlation $\rho = -.201$ ($p = .03$) between early perception misalignment (|d| at *t1*) and the project score. Misalignment measured at later waves showed no significant association with the project score.

Robust regression (reported in Tab. 1) confirmed that early misalignment is related to outcomes, also when controlling for prior performance. A second regression including an interaction term for prior programming performance and early misalignment ($b = 0.4$, $t = 4.1$, $p < .001$) showed that prior performance was a moderator (Table 1).

**Table. 1.** Predictors of outcome across robust linear regression models

| Model and $R^2$ | Predictor | B (SE) | p |
|---|---|---|---|
| Outcome ~ misalignment + prior performance ($R^2 = .132$, adj. $R^2 = .117$) | Partner AI use misalignment at *t1* | −4.47 (1.88) | .018 |
| | Prior performance mean | 0.03 (0.02) | .108 |
| Outcome ~ misalignment × prior performance ($R^2 = .226$, adj. $R^2 = .206$) | Partner AI use misalignment at *t1* | −7.73 (1.98) | <.001 |
| | prior performance mean | 0.05 (0.02) | .014 |
| | misalignment × prior performance ($\Delta R^2 = .095$) | 0.40 (0.10) | <.001 |
| Outcome ~ flip + misalignment + prior performance ($R^2 = .18$, adj. $R^2 = .15$) | Flip (AI use perception direction reversal *t1* → *t3*) | −1.91 (0.83) | .021 |
| | Partner AI use misalignment at *t1* | −3.634 | .082 |
| | Prior performance mean | 0.049 | .034 |

Simple-slope estimates further showed that for teams one standard deviation below the mean in prior performance, increased misalignment corresponded to markedly lower outcomes ($b \approx -15.0$ per unit of |d|), whereas the association was negligible for teams one standard deviation above the mean ($b \approx -0.32$). That is, stronger teams managed to compensate for early perceptual misalignment, weaker teams did not.

To further illustrate how both partners' perceptions jointly relate to outcomes, Fig. 1 shows a second-order polynomial response surface, estimated with heteroscedasticity-robust standard errors. X and Y axes each represent one partner's normalised self–other AI use discrepancy perception at S1: Student A = higher prior performance, Student B = lower. Color and z dimension indicate the project score fitted by the second-order polynomial model. Performance was highest near the origin, where partners are mutually aligned in their perceptions, and declined as discrepancies increased. This decline was particularly pronounced when both partners perceived the other as using less AI. Consistent with this pattern, the interaction term of student A AI use perception discrepancy and student B discrepancy was negative and significant ($b_{AB} = -121.05$, $SE = 49.82$, $p = .015$), whereas the remaining polynomial terms were non-significant. The model ($R^2$ = .37, F = 10.30) is intended here primarily as an illustrative complement to the main regression analyses, since the sample is modest for RSA, and discrepancy scores were concentrated near zero, limiting precision at the extremes.

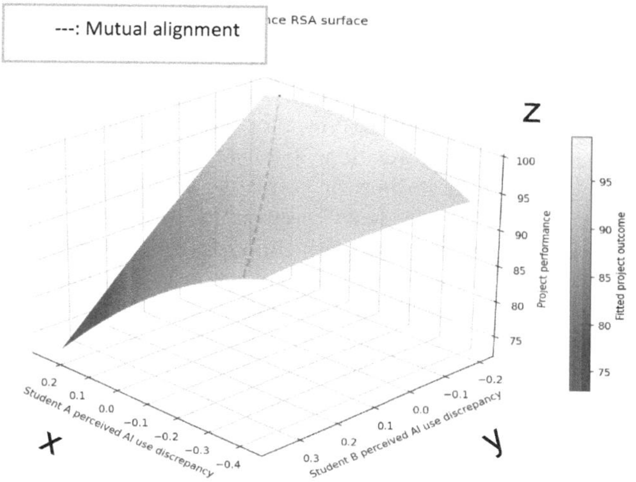


**Fig. 1.** Response surface of dyadic discrepancy and project outcome

We additionally examined whether *changes* in partners' perceptions of relative AI use during the project were associated with collaboration outcomes. Teams were categorised by whether the sign of their misalignment score reversed between t1 and t3, that is, whether the team's view of who uses more AI flipped. Teams experiencing a direction reversal achieved lower scores than teams with stable perceptions (medians: 94.5 vs. 98 percentage points; Mann–Whitney $U$ = 192, p = .011, $r\_rb$ = .427). A robust regression (see Tab. 1) controlling for initial misalignment and prior performance yielded a consistent pattern: direction reversals remained associated with lower outcomes ($b$ = −1.90, $t$ = −2.32, $p$ = .021). However, only 25 teams experienced a reversal, so these results should be treated as indicative of the relevance of stark changes in AI use perception rather than conclusive.

## 6 Discussion

Regarding RQ1, we find that awareness of partners' AI use is limited and largely explained by heuristic inference processes such as assumed similarity rather than partner-specific knowledge. Apparent accuracy in estimating partners' AI-use patterns was moderate, but this was substantially reduced after accounting for assumed similarity. This suggests that ongoing collaboration does not provide sufficient partner-specific information to substantially correct these self-based inferences. Assumed similarity effects may be pronounced in our sample since many participants have prior relationships. The prior relationship is is known to affect assumed similarity, according to literature showing that partners project their own habits onto someone they feel they know well [22]. Consistent with this, qualitative reports where participants in AI-supported programming assumed that others use AI in ways similar to themselves [23]. Students' biases in estimations about their partners' AI use furthermore suggest that judgments are structured by norms of acceptable AI usage. The biases students showed in their estimation were underestimation of their partners' AI use for fully automated feature implementation and overestimation of partners' AI use for questions on programming principles or validation of a solution strategy. This aligns with literature showing that judgments are shaped by expectations about what behaviours are typical or appropriate in a given context [16].

Over time, the increase in correlation of self-report and partner estimation of AI use after partialling out similarity bias or normative bias suggests a modest increase in partner-specific knowledge. Students' partner understanding beyond reliance on assumed similarity heuristics is particularly important given team members' AI-use patterns appear to diverge at the later stages. Divergence of AI use profiles may occur naturally over a project, as students take on more specialised roles, such as writing tests. Although pair-programming sessions as applied in the course are often assumed to support shared mental models, we do not observe a consistent improvement in partner-specific accuracy over time. One possible explanation is that AI use differs between individual work and in-person collaboration, such that opportunities to observe a partner's AI use remain limited even during joint sessions. The limited increase in partner knowledge may also be related to the course setting, where most students were previously acquainted from other courses together and had selected their partner themselves based on prior relationships. The familiarity between partners is also likely to inflate similarity assumption bias, as prior research suggests [22].

Regarding RQ2, we find that misalignment in partners' perceptions of AI use is associated with team performance. In particular, greater misalignment at the beginning of the project was associated with lower final project scores. This pattern is consistent with prior research on collaborative work where accurate beliefs about a partner's behaviour have been shown to support effective coordination. Later partner alignment in AI use perceptions does not appear to offset the association between early misalignment and performance. The concentration of the performance effect at *t1* suggests that early perception gaps may be particularly consequential during initial coordination phases, when teams establish task allocation, expectations, and working strategies. To find plausible pathways of how misalignment in partners' perceptions of AI use relates to collaboration performance likely relevant mechanisms can be identified from prior research. Research has found several concrete mechanisms to be relevant to team effectiveness in students' programming collaboration: accurately monitoring mutual performance, backup behaviour and mutual trust (a belief that team members do their best) [24]. Further investigations are warranted to understand the influence of AI on these factors of collaboration.

The relationship between misalignment and outcomes further depended on individuals' prior performance. The negative association between misalignment and performance was substantially stronger for teams with lower individual prior performance, while it was negligible for teams with high prior performance. This pattern suggests that stronger teams may be less dependent on accurate perceptions of AI use for effective coordination, potentially because they can rely more on shared technical understanding or compensate for misaligned expectations. When students have less prior programming skills, inaccurate beliefs about a partner's AI reliance may be especially costly because they may also be less able to judge the quality, correctness, or limitations of AI-supported code independently. This interpretation is consistent with recent evidence that novices accept buggy or difficult-to-understand AI-generated solutions, often report not understanding why AI suggestions work, and have particular difficulty correcting AI-generated code once problems arise [25].

Additional analyses of perceptions showed that when perceptions of which partner used more AI changed between the beginning and the end of the project, the team tended to achieve lower outcomes than teams with stable perceptions, even when controlling for initial misalignment and prior performance. Rather than simply indicating that partners learned over time, such changes may signal that early assumptions were revised only after collaboration difficulties had already emerged.

The findings point to a structural feature of AI-supported collaboration: when a coordination-relevant behaviour is not directly observable, partners rely on heuristic inferences that produce only partially accurate beliefs. This suggests that AI-use transparency may be relevant not only for academic integrity but also as a coordination resource. Designing learning analytics and pedagogical scaffolds to make AI use more visible or interpretable to collaborators may therefore support more accurate partner models. Recent work on shared and visible human–human–AI settings suggests that when AI assistance is visible to a peer, participants feel more responsibility to understand suggestions before adopting them [13, 26]. In the present context, this raises the possibility that lightweight mechanisms such as shared prompt histories, AI-use annotations, or peer-visible records of AI-supported work could improve partner understanding by making otherwise private AI use more accountable and interpretable. Whether such interventions would improve coordination in practice remains an open empirical question.

Effective intervention requires understanding more precisely where awareness of a partner's AI use is most consequential, and whether pedagogically incentivised disclosures would improve outcomes. Furthermore, it is yet to be identified what the appropriate awareness signal would be, such as usage-type-level AI-use disclosure or analytics, or code level signals integrated into the shared repository. These are empirical questions that require both improved measurement and an experimental evaluation of designed interventions. Our findings strongly suggest that the problem of perceiving partner AI use accurately is consequential and further work is warranted.

Our study has several limitations. First, the design is observational, so the reported associations should not be interpreted causally. Second, the measures of AI use were based on self-reports and partner estimates rather than behavioral traces, and are therefore subject to memory error, scale interpretation differences, and possible social desirability effects. Additionally, the outcome grade showed a ceiling effect, which affects modeling options and may have led to underestimation of the associations. Third, the study did not analyse the mechanisms through which perception misalignment may affect collaboration, such as trust calibration, code review behaviour, task allocation, or communication patterns. This remains to be studied. Fourth, the observed effect sizes were small to moderate. This finding is unsurprising given that collaborative project outcomes are shaped by many factors beyond AI-use perception. Finally, the study was conducted in a single course context with students who were often already familiar with their partner. This context may limit generalizability to other educational settings, team compositions, or project formats.

## 7 Conclusion

When each member of a programming team independently uses AI, the human-to-human coordination between them is affected in ways that are consequential. Teams whose members hold inaccurate beliefs about each other's AI reliance from the project outset perform worse, especially when baseline individual prior performance was low and coordination errors are most costly. Most of what looks like knowledge of the partner is a projection of own patterns of AI use, and partner-specific understanding only slightly improves over time. Structured in-person collaboration appears insufficient to close these gaps despite its potential for shared understanding. These findings reframe AI transparency beyond that of an academic integrity concern towards a coordination resource and a call for examining the mechanisms that can help partners coordinate effectively. The findings suggest that AI-use transparency features or prompting disclosure could be integrated into collaborative programming in early phases of remote collaborative work. Awareness support should particularly target teams with lower prior performance, where misaligned perceptions carry the highest performance cost.

## References


1. Hadar, I., Sherman, S., Hazzan, O.: Learning human aspects of collaborative software development. J. Inf. Syst. Educ. **311–320** (2008)
2. Olson, G., Olson, J., Carter, M., Storrbsten, M.: Small group design meetings: an analysis of collaboration. Human Comput. Interact. (1992)
3. Mathieu, J.E., Heffner, T.S., Goodwin, G.F., Salas, E., Cannon-Bowers, J.A.: The influence of shared mental models on team process and performance. J. Appl. Psychol. **85**, 273–283 (2000)
4. Sajadi, A., Damevski, K., Chatterjee, P.: Interpersonal trust in OSS: exploring dimensions of trust in GitHub pull requests. In: 2023 IEEE/ACM 45th International Conference on Software Engineering: new Ideas and Emerging Results (ICSE-NIER), pp. 19–24 (2023). https://doi.org/10.1109/ICSE-NIER58687.2023.00010
5. Finnie-Ansley, J., Denny, P., Becker, B.A., Luxton-Reilly, A., Prather, J.: The robots are coming: exploring the implications of OpenAI codex on introductory programming. In: Proceedings of the 24th Australasian Computing Education Conference, pp. 10–19. Association for Computing Machinery, New York, NY, USA (2022). https://doi.org/10.1145/3511861.3511863
6. Dourish, P., Bellotti, V.: Awareness and coordination in shared workspaces. In: Proc. CSCW 1992, pp. 107–114. ACM (1992)
7. Gutwin, C., Greenberg, S., Roseman, M.: Workspace awareness in real-time distributed groupware: framework, widgets, and evaluation. In: Sasse, M.A., Cunningham, R.J., Winder, R.L. (eds.) People and Computers XI, pp. 281–298. Springer, London (1996). https://doi.org/10.1007/978-1-4471-3588-3_18

8. Siemens, G.: Learning analytics: the emergence of a discipline. Am. Behav. Sci. **57**, 1380–1400 (2013). https://doi.org/10.1177/0002764213498851
9. Janssen, J., Erkens, G., Kirschner, P.A.: Group awareness tools: It's what you do with it that matters. Comput. Hum. Behav. **27**, 1046–1058 (2011). https://doi.org/10.1016/j.chb.2010.06.002
10. Moreland, R.L.: Transactive memory: learning who knows what in work groups and organizations. In: Thompson, L.L. (ed.) Shared Cognition in Organizations, pp. 3–31. Erlbaum (1999)
11. Maček, M., Novak, M.: AI tools in programming education: student perspectives and usage trends. J. Inf. Organ. Sci. **50**, 83–104 (2026). https://doi.org/10.31341/jios.50.1.5
12. Bassner, P., Lenk-Ostendorf, B., Beinstingel, R., Wasner, T., Krusche, S.: Less stress, better scores, same learning: the dissociation of performance and learning in AI-supported programming education. Comput. Educ. Artif. Intell. **10**, 100537 (2026). https://doi.org/10.1016/j.caeai.2025.100537
13. Shihab, M.I.H., Hundhausen, C., Tariq, A., Haque, S., Qiao, Y., Mulanda, B.W.: The effects of GitHub Copilot on computing students' programming effectiveness, efficiency, and processes in brownfield coding tasks. In: Proceedings of the 2025 ACM Conference on International Computing Education Research V.1, pp. 407–420. Association for Computing Machinery, New York, NY, USA (2025). https://doi.org/10.1145/3702652.3744219
14. Xiao, Q., Hu, X.E., Whiting, M.E., Karunakaran, A., Shen, H., Cao, H.: AI Hasn't Fixed Teamwork, But It Shifted Collaborative Culture: A Longitudinal Study in a Project-Based Software Development Organization (2023–2025), http://arxiv.org/abs/2509.10956, https://doi.org/10.48550/arXiv.2509.10956 (2025)
15. Kenny, D.A.: Interpersonal Perception: the Foundation of Social Relationships. Guilford Publications (2019)
16. Kurschilgen, M.: How Norms Guide Behavior in an Uncertain World: an Experimental law & Economics Perspective, (2013).
17. Katz, D., Allport, F.H., Jenness, M.B.: Students' Attitudes; a Report of the Syracuse University Reaction Study. Craftsman Press, Oxford, England (1931)
18. Kurschilgen, M.: How norms guide behavior in an uncertain world: an experimental law & economics perspective., https://www.db-thueringen.de/rsc/viewer/dbt_derivate_00027862/Diss/Diss_130126.pdf?page=1, (2013).
19. Wegner, D.M.: Transactive memory: a contemporary analysis of the group mind. In: Mullen, B., Goethals, G.R. (eds.) Theories of Group Behavior, pp. 185–208. Springer, New York (1987)
20. Shah, A., Chernova, A., Tomson, E., Porter, L., Griswold, W.G., Soosai Raj, A.G.: Students' use of GitHub Copilot for working with large code bases. In: Proceedings of the 56th ACM Technical Symposium on Computer Science Education V. 1, pp. 1050–1056. Association for Computing Machinery, New York, NY, USA (2025). https://doi.org/10.1145/3641554.3701800
21. Huber, P.J.: Robust estimation of a location parameter. In: Kotz, S., Johnson, N.L. (eds.) Breakthroughs in Statistics: Methodology and Distribution, pp. 492–518. Springer, New York, NY (1992). https://doi.org/10.1007/978-1-4612-4380-9_35
22. Babineau, R., Beer, A.: Assumed similarity and valued personality characteristics. Univ. S. C. Upstate Stud Res. J. **14** (2021)
23. de Boer, B.: Exploring the potential of AI assistance for teamwork in programming education, https://studenttheses.uu.nl/items/d2f15e9a-3a67-40c4-bfce-e39613517838, (2025).
24. Dorić, L., Luburić, N., Slivka, J., Prokić, S., Đukić, A.: Evaluating teamwork components in large undergraduate software engineering teams. ACM Trans. Comput. Educ. 25, 28:1–28:25 (2025). https://doi.org/10.1145/3733840.

25. Kharrufa, A., Alghamdi, S., Aziz, A., Bull, C.: LLMs integration in software engineering team projects: roles, impact, and a pedagogical design space for AI tools in computing education. ACM Trans. Comput. Educ. 26, 20:1–20:27 (2026). doi:https://doi.org/10.1145/3779296.
26. Daryanto, T., et al.: Human-Human-AI Triadic Programming: Uncovering the Role of AI Agent and the Value of Human Partner in Collaborative Learning (2026). https://doi.org/10.48550/arXiv.2601.12134

# Helping Students Avoid Maladaptive Self-regulated Learning Behaviors in a Large Blended Course

Almed Hamzah[1,2](✉), Hari Setiaji[2], Feri Wijayanto[2], Rahadian Kurniawan[2], and Sergey Sosnovsky[1]

[1] Utrecht University, Utrecht, The Netherlands
[2] Universitas Islam Indonesia, Yogyakarta, Indonesia
a.hamzah@uu.nl

**Abstract.** Engagement is a critical factor for successful learning within a large blended course. Yet, many students struggle to maintain a necessary level of engagement throughout the duration of their courses and can benefit from various forms of support that keeps them involved in course activities. In the blended learning context, such support should be fueled by data coming from both face-to-face and online learning environments, although the former is often overlooked. This paper presents a study investigating the effects of multiple adaptive nudges driven by information about students' learning activities during both face-to-face lectures and online sessions. The nudges are intended to help students stay engaged with online practice content and are designed to compensate for the lack of self-regulated learning (SRL) skills. The results show a significant overall effect of the nudges. Additionally, we have analyzed students' activity based on their self-reported SRL factors: self-efficacy, organization, rehearsal, and time and study-environment management. The data shows that the intervention especially help students with low SRL skills; in the presence of adaptive blended nudges, they exhibit much more effective patterns of SRL behavior.

**Keywords:** Blended Learning · Self-Regulated Learning · Engagement · Large classroom · Nudges

## 1 Introduction

Self-Regulated Learning (SRL) is an active learning process that involves setting learning objectives, performing learning tasks, monitoring and regulating cognition, motivation, and learning behavior in relation to the set objectives [20]. SRL is a multidimensional and cyclical process: it involves several phases that reflect the flow of students through attainment of learning goals and acquisition of knowledge [33]. Most of the SRL models recognize three such phases: preliminary or forethought, performance or execution, and appraisal or reflection [22].


J. Weidlich et al. (Eds.): EC-TEL 2026, LNCS 16905, pp. 239–252, 2027.
https://doi.org/10.1007/978-3-032-37979-5_17

SRL becomes especially important in learning contexts that require increased levels of students' autonomy, such as blended university courses [5,25].

Students with stronger SRL skills tend to be more invested in their learning [30], exhibit more effective patterns of learning behavior in terms of attendance, participation, completion, etc. [30], and at the end, achieve higher levels of academic performance [9]. Lack of these skills, on the opposite, causes students to struggle academically and exhibit maladaptive learning behaviors, such as procrastination [3,17], and poor learning strategies [7].

Procrastination is described as "voluntarily delay an intended course of action despite expecting to be worse off for the delay" [24]. In a learning context, procrastination is reflected in putting off task completion, irregular learning activity [17], and overall lower engagement [32]. It is often caused by a defensive reaction of students unwilling to continue learning to avoid expected dissatisfaction [33]. Previous studies show that procrastination is caused by low self-efficacy and time management skills [2,3,25].

Poor learning strategies often manifest as ineffective learning behaviors. One common example is cramming, whereby students are "studying something intensely, often for the first time, in the days or hours before a test" [16]. Cramming leads to temporary information attainment and struggles attain deeper understanding and an ability to apply "learned" knowledge [11]. Poor learning strategy can be also observed as learning disorientation, when students have reduced control over their environment, become easily distracted, and have difficulty selecting relevant learning material [28].

To overcome these challenges, students with limited SRL skills require personalized support in monitoring their progress, exploring available learning material, and planning optimal learning activities. To this end, we have extended the functionality of an existing tool for blended learning support with the capability to send (by email) and display (as navigational cues) adaptive nudges. The adaptive email nudges remind students of upcoming/available learning tasks they can engage with. The navigational cues are shown as adaptive annotations attached to learning tasks.

The nudges have been applied in the context of an undergraduate blended course. In such a course, the student population is typically large, and the learning activities are distributed across both in-class and at-home environments. This makes interactions between students and the teacher infrequent and constrained, thereby limiting opportunities for students to receive individualized support, if such support can be available at all. Thus, students are largely left to their own devices and have to self-regulate their learning to a greater extent [2]. In such a context, the SRL nudges are aimed to help students better manage their learning behavior.

Previous research demonstrates the effectiveness of similar interventions [17,23,25,32]. However, they primarily relied on online learning activities as the source of information. In this study, we investigate the use of data generated from students' learning activities performed both in-class during lectures and online at-home. We assume that such a blend of data would enhance the intervention's effect on students' behavior.

To address this goal, we seek to answer the following research questions.

- **RQ1** How can information from in-class and at-home contexts be used to design nudges that reduce procrastination in a large blended course?
- **RQ2** How can information from in-class and at-home contexts be used to design nudges that improve learning strategies in a large blended course?

The rest of this paper is organized as follows: Sect. 2 discusses related work, Sect. 3 discusses the system design, Sect. 4 explains the experimental design, Sect. 5 describes the results, and Sects. 6 and 7 present the discussion and conclude the paper.

## 2 Related Work

This section reviews prior research on the use of digital technology address SRL challenges and support SRL in general. We mainly focus on the two SRL problems: procrastination and poor learning strategies. We select four SRL processes from [21]: self-efficacy, time and study-environment management, rehearsal, and organization. They were found to be related to the target SRL problems and suitable in a large classroom [10, 17, 25].

**Self-efficacy.** Self-efficacy refers to self-appraisal of one's ability to master a task [21]. Self-efficacy is important for students because it influences the amount of effort they invest and their persistence when encountering difficulties [4]. Previous studies have shown that self-efficacy can predict students' learning performance and prevent self-regulation failures such as procrastination [2, 3, 17]. Various methods and techniques have been used to support students' self-efficacy, including feedback prompts, grading rubrics, and intermediate assignment deadlines [2]. Easy-to-use technology, such as email-based notifications (even the simple one), can increase students' self-efficacy and thus improve their learning performance [17, 32]. In a recent study, a more engaging interface based on Augmented Reality was also found to positively affect students' self-efficacy [18].

**Time and Study Environment Management.** Time and study environment management is a learning strategy in which students block time to study, use it effectively, and set realistic learning goals [21]. This factors has been identified as a key predictor of students' grades in both online and blended settings [6]. Previous studies have shown that this skill can be improved through targeted interventions. For example, tracking time with an mobile learning app is effective in improving time-management skills [25]. Visualization of learning progress or completed learning tasks on a weekly basis helps to reduce stress levels and improve time management behavior [1].

**Rehearsal.** Rehearsal is a surface learning strategy in which students recite or name items from a list to be learned [21]. Previous studies have not found a strong evidence that this strategy is related to long-term academic performance in any significant manner [7,27]. However, it is important for students in the early stages of learning because it helps them remember the terms used in the learning material [8]. Effective rehearsal strategy can include, e.g., flashcard, spaced repetition, drilling practices, etc. Recording tools and classroom clickers have been also found to encourage rehearsal [26].

**Organization.** Organization is a learning strategy, in which students select appropriate information to be learned and construct connections between key notions [21]. It helps students build a clear plan to attain their learning goals [29]. Together with an elaboration strategy, it can help students comprehend and remember new information [20]. Organization strategies include various approaches to structuring and connecting learning materials, such as concept mapping, outlining and grouping related notions [10,19,31].

## 3 System Design

As the main platform delivering support to students in this study, we have used Quizitor [12,14,15]. Quizitor is an online platform that supports two forms of assessment: in-class, a teacher can use it as a voting tool to run short quizzes; at-home, students can use it for practice and self-assessment [13]. In the current study, three nudging components have been added to Quizitor to help students work with at-home self-assessment material more regularly and efficiently: the e-mail notification, the topic annotation, and the question annotation.

The email nudge informs students about available at-home quizzes throughout the course. There are two types of email nudges: preparation and review. The preparation nudge is sent after each lecture, inviting students to start practicing a new topic from the lecture that has just been taught. It contains a direct link to open the relevant at-home self-assessment material. The first question from the practice material is added to the text of the nudge as a preview to stimulate student's interest to start practicing the material. The review nudge includes a student's score on the last in-class quiz and invites students to practice further by taking a corresponding at-home quiz (Fig. 1).

**Fig. 1.** Email nudges: preparation (left), review (right).

The topic annotation is an in-app nudge that provides corresponding quiz cards on the Quizitor dashboard with progress indicators reflecting students' progress on topics, both in class and at home. It is designed to help students decide which topic/quiz they should prioritize (Fig. 2).

The question annotation is also an in-app nudge providing similar support on the question level. Once a student opens a quiz, they have 20 questions to practice with. Quizitor will recommend five questions for a student to focus on. The recommendation is based on the student's history of attempts on this topic's questions, both in-class and at home (Fig. 3).

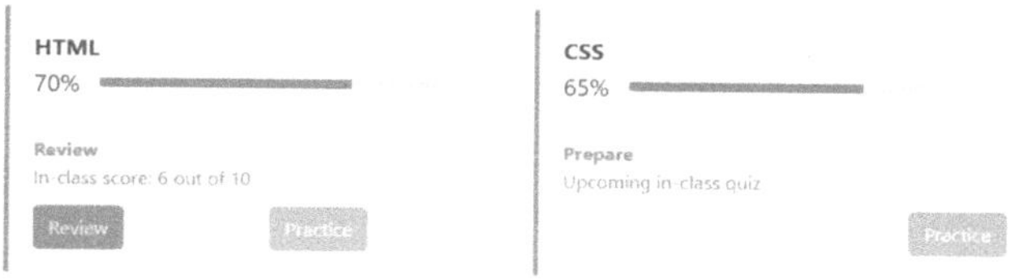


**Fig. 2.** Topic annotation: topic to review (left), topic to prepare (right).

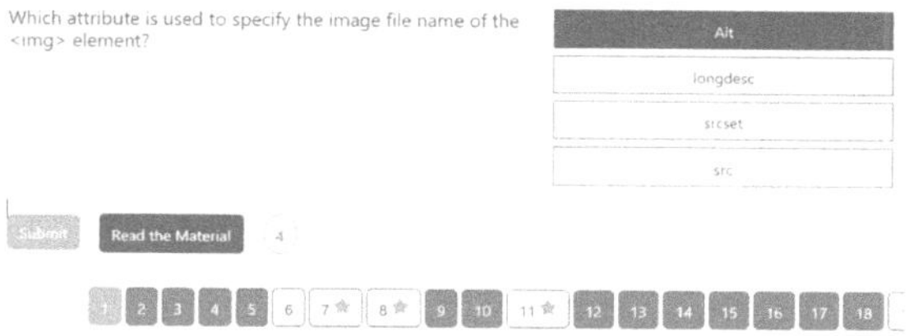


**Fig. 3.** Question annotation.

# 4 Methodology

## 4.1 Participants

The experiment took place in a large blended course on Web Application Development, which was conducted in the Islamic University of Indonesia in the Fall semester of 2025–2026 academic year. 197 s-year undergraduate students were enrolled in the course. Informed consents were collected in the beginning of the course. Participation in the study was completely voluntary. Students who decided to withdraw from the study retained their access to Quizitor; 4 students chose not to participate, leaving 193 active subjects.

### 4.2 Data Collection

Due to its size, the course was divided into six classes, with students randomly assigned to one of them. The course was taught by a team of four instructors: two instructors each taught two classes, while the remaining two instructors each taught one class. For the experiment, three classes were randomly assigned to the treatment condition and the remaining three to the control condition. To control for instructor effects, the assignment was performed such that each instructor responsible for two classes taught one treatment class and one control class. With this configuration, we had n=81 students in the treatment condition and n=112 students in the control condition.

During the first lecture, students were told they would use Quizitor for practice. They were provided with an account to log in. An online questionnaire was distributed in the beginning of the course to measure students' SRL skills. Students' responses to the questionnaire were identified by their Quizitor accounts.

After the first lecture, the teacher made the at-home quiz for that topic available to students. Within two hours after the quiz was made available, the first preparation email was sent to students in the treatment group. Students practiced with the at-home quiz until the second lecture. In the beginning of the second lecture, the teacher conducted the in-class quiz on the first topic. This way, students could check their knowledge and results from practicing at home. After the second lecture, students received the second email nudge with information about their recent in-class quiz. This way, students could review the previous topic if they believed they received a low score on the corresponding in-class quiz. This cycle continued until the second half of the course, covering the first seven lectures/topics.

The course used periodic mini-exams to evaluate students' performance rather than large summative exams in the middle and at the end of the course. Every two topics, such mini-exams were conducted to cover: HTML and CSS (exam 1), JavaScript and Responsive Web Design (exam 2), PHP Basic and SQL (exam 3), and Advanced PHP (exam 4).

Quizitor recorded all student activity including the timestamp, the session id, the student id, the question and topic, the given answer and its correctness, as well as all the clicks that indicated if a student followed (or did not follow) a particular nudge.

### 4.3 Measurements

We used the following parameters to assess students' engagement in at-home learning activities with Quizitor.

- Number of attempts – overall number of answers a student submitted across all available quizzes and questions;
- Topic coverage – number of topics for which a student submitted attempts;
- Topic completion rate – average ratio of questions answered correctly per topic;

- Persistence – number of questions with the initial incorrect answer and the final correct answer;
- Number of sessions – number of sets of attempts separated by new logins or 30 min of inactivity;

To measure the SRL skills, we used the Motivated Strategies for Learning Questionnaire (MSLQ) [21]. It comprises 15 factors overall; however, in this study, we selected only 4 of them: self-efficacy, time and study environment management, rehearsal, and organization. The questionnaire we sent to students was composed of 24 items using the 7-point Likert scale. Questionnaire responses were collected with the help of the Qualtrics[1] service.

### 4.4 Data Analysis

A reliability test was conducted on the questionnaire responses, yielding a Cronbach's alpha of 0.768. An independent-samples t-test was conducted to compare differences in engagement parameters between the treatment and control groups. Statistical significance was defined at $\alpha$=0.05. Effect size was calculated using Cohen's d to determine the magnitude of differences between the treatment and the control groups.

## 5 Results

### 5.1 Overall Engagement

First, we have looked at all attempts from all students (n=193) who used Quizitor; the results show a strong positive effect of the treatment on the overall student engagement across the different parameters. Table 1 presents the outcomes of the corresponding tests. Of the five parameters we used, four showed significantly higher values under the treatment condition: number of at-home attempts, topic coverage, topic completion rate, and number of sessions.

The contribution of each individual nudge to this overall effect can be estimated as well. For the email nudges, if we filter out all the sessions started by students from links in the emails, the effect sizes for all parameters would decrease by 10–20% and, for topic coverage and topic completion rate, the differences would no longer be significant. This indicates, that without the sessions started from the email nudges the overall engagement effect would be considerably less pronounced.

Topic annotations have been designed to help students practice steadily throughout the course by drawing their attention to the important topics at the right moments: after a lecture and after an in-class quiz, rather than just before the exam. Thus, if we split students' attempts on each topic into these three periods (after the corresponding lecture, after the corresponding in-class quiz, right before the exam), we will see that the treatment group practices more,

[1] https://www.qualtrics.com/.

especially, after the lecture. The average number of attempts in this period is significantly greater for the treatment group (M = 66.8 attempts, SD = 76.8) than the control group (M = 30 attempts, SD = 52.6 ), t(191) = 3.94 , $p < .001$ , r = .575. However, there is no difference on the average number of attempts after the recent in-class quizzes between the treatment and the control group. It was also greater for the intervention group (M = 50.3 attempts, SD = 11.9) vs. (M = 4.83 attempts, SD = 11.6), although not significantly (t(191) = .116 , p = .454 , r = .017).

Lastly, for the question annotations, we have investigated whether students indeed engage with this type of nudge. We have looked into the number of target questions accessed by students of both groups. Naturally, for the control group, potential question annotations are "hidden", yet we can count how many supposed-to-be-annotated questions were attempted by the students. The "nudged" questions were accessed by the treatment group (M = 35.1 attempts, SD = 30.9) much more than the "supposed-to-be-nudged" questions were accessed by the control group (M = 7.16 attempts, SD = 15.3), t(191) = 8.27, $p < .001$, r = 1.2. This means, the treatment group indeed paid attention to the nudged questions and accessed them much more actively than it would have had were the questions not annotated.

Despite the strong engagement effect, we have not observed a significant difference in the exam scores between the treatment group (M = 53.1, SD = 20.1) and the control group (M = 53, SD = 17.9), t(191) = .036, p = .486, r = .005.

### 5.2 Self-regulated Learning Problems

We examined how the interventions support students with low SRL skills in becoming more engaged in practicing quizzes. To assess students' SRL skills, we used data only from those who completed the MSLQ questionnaire (n=127). Based on their responses, we categorized students into low-, medium-, and high-skill groups by applying an equal-size quantile split for each SRL factor. We then compared the treatment and control groups on several parameters.

To further reduce data variability, we examined the distribution of students' attempts using a histogram, which revealed a bimodal distribution pattern. To distinguish between the two distributions, we applied a Gaussian kernel-density estimate (KDE), using the `scott` bandwidth method, which identified a separation point at 238 attempts. Based on this observation, we focused on the students from the first distribution with fewer than 238 attempts, which showed lower variance than the second distribution. This subgroup, consisting of 84 students, was therefore included in the subsequent analysis.

**Procrastination.** *RQ1: How can information from in-class and at-home context be used to design nudges that reduce procrastination in a large blended course?* Two factors from the MSLQ scale—time and study environment management, and self-efficacy—were investigated. Literature tells us that lack in

**Table 1.** Comparison of Engagement Parameters Between the treatment and control group (Total number of students = 193).

| | Treatment (N=81) | | | Control (N=112) | | | Mean Diff. | t-stat | p-val | Cohen's D | 95% CI |
|---|---|---|---|---|---|---|---|---|---|---|---|
| Variable | Mean | SD | Med | Mean | SD | Med | | | | | |
| Num. attempts | 180 | 150 | 137 | 137 | 143 | 98.0 | 23.8 | 2.01 | 0.023* | 0.29 | [ 0.00, 0.58] |
| Topic coverage | 3.95 | 2.00 | 4.00 | 3.33 | 2.57 | 2.00 | 15.4 | 1.78 | 0.038* | 0.26 | [-0.03, 0.55] |
| Topic completion rate (%) | 68.9 | 32.7 | 81.0 | 59.8 | 40.7 | 75.0 | 13.2 | 1.66 | 0.049* | 0.24 | [-0.05, 0.53] |
| Persistence | 23.9 | 21.7 | 17.0 | 20.6 | 23.6 | 13.0 | 13.7 | 0.986 | 0.163 | 0.14 | [-0.14, 0.43] |
| Num. sessions | 6.16 | 4.23 | 5.00 | 3.52 | 3.45 | 3.00 | 42.7 | 4.753 | 0.000* | 0.69 | [ 0.40, 0.99] |

these skills leads to procrastination [17,25]. We combined students' responses on these two factors to estimate how likely they are to suffer from procrastination. We assumed that students with stronger skills on these factors would in general procrastinate less and engage with available learning activities more, and those with lower skills would behave in the opposite manner - procrastinate more and demonstrate lower engagement with Quizitor. We wanted to see if the adaptive nudges sent by the treatment version of Quizitor would in particular help the latter students avoid procrastination patterns. To investigate the effect of the intervention, we divided students into three quantiles—Low (N=35), Moderate (N=23), and High (N=26)—based on their time and study environment management and self-efficacy scores, and then focused our analysis on the Low group.

We first tested for homogeneity of variance in the number of attempts using Levene's test, which indicated no evidence of unequal variance between the treatment and control groups ($F(1,33) = .036$, $p = .552$). An independent t-test then showed that students in the treatment group made more attempts on average ($M = 119$, $SD = 55.9$) than those in the control group ($M = 87.2$, $SD = 64.2$). However, the difference is marginally significant $t(33) = 1.52$, $p = .069$, $r = .53$ (see Fig. 4a).

Given these results, we further examined whether the increased attempts were due to students accessing the system more frequently. We analyzed the number of days students made attempts throughout the course and found that those in the treatment group had significantly more active days with Quizitor ($M = 2.92$, $SD = 1.18$) than those in the control group ($M = 1.4$, $SD = 1.05$), $t(33) = 3.91$, $p < .001$, $r = 1.37$ (see Fig. 4b).

To further understand how these activities (number of attempts and active days) are distributed throughout the course, we examined the role of the course structure and email reminders. The course was designed to prompt students to engage with the material through at-home quizzes after each lecture, followed by in-class quizzes during the subsequent lecture. For each topic, students therefore had two activity periods: after the lecture and after the in-class quiz, with an

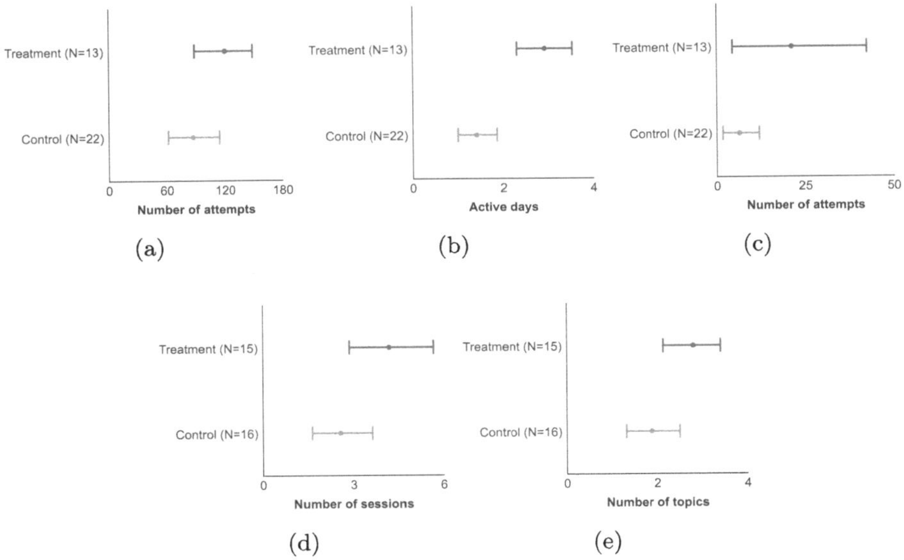


**Fig. 4.** Comparison of number of attempts (a). Comparison of number of active days (b). Comparison of number of attempts after lecture and after in-class quiz (c). Comparison of number of sessions (d). Comparison of topic coverage (e).

email reminder sent before both. Our analysis shows no significant difference in the number of attempts between groups immediately after the lecture. However, following the in-class quiz and the corresponding email reminder, students in the treatment group, especially those with lower time and study environment management and self-efficacy skills, made significantly more attempts ($M = 21.2$, $SD = 37.8$) than those in the control group ($M = 6.33$, $SD = 12.7$), $t(33) = 1.70$, $p = .049$, $r = .59$ (see Fig. 4c). This pattern was not observed among students with higher scores for the procrastination-related SRL skills.

**Poor Learning Strategy.** *RQ2: How can information from in-class and at-home context be used to design nudges that improve learning strategies in a large blended course?* Students with stronger organizational and rehearsal skills know which learning materials they want to study, annotate them to make learning more effective when they need to study, and can select important topics and material to study. Conversely, students with lower scores for these skills would struggle with selecting the right material to work at the right time. To investigate the impact of the support provided by adaptive nudges on these students, we again divided students into the three quantiles—Low (N=32), Moderate (N=29), and High (N=23)—based on their organization and rehearsal scores, and then focused our analysis on the Low group.

We first investigated whether the interventions would increase the number of sessions. The Levene's test indicated no evidence of unequal variance between the treatment and control groups in terms of the number of sessions ($F(1,29) = 1.68$, $p = .204$). An independent t-test showed that students with low organization and rehearsal skills in the treatment group had significantly more sessions ($M = 4.20$, $SD = 2.90$) than those in the control group ($M = 2.56$, $SD = 2.25$), $t(29) = 1.76$, $p = .044$, $r = .63$ (see Fig. 4d). Then, we looked into the number of unique topics explored by the target students. An independent t-test showed that students with low organization and rehearsal skills in the treatment group explored significantly more topics ($M = 2.80$, $SD = 1.32$) than those in the control group ($M = 1.87$, $SD = 1.20$), $t(29)=2.04$, $p=.025$, $r=.733$ (see Fig. 4e). This pattern was not observed among students with higher skills in these subprocesses.

## 6 Discussion

We explored the effects of adaptive nudges of different types (email notifications, topic annotations, questions annotations) on the engagement of students as well as on their SRL behavior, especially when students lack SRL skills. The experiment was organized as an ecologically-valid study and was conducted with the framework of a large blended course, which provides an especially compelling context for our investigation. Students with poor SRL skills especially struggle to succeed in large blended courses where their link to an instructor is thin and their opportunities to receive individual feedback are scarce.

First, we successfully demonstrated that the designed nudges have an overall positive effect on students' engagement and that all three nudges individually contribute to different aspects of this effect.

The central part of our analysis was focused in the students with lower SRL skill and the capacity of the designed nudges to help them overcome maladaptive learning behavior. We used a subset of standard SRL scales to identify students who potentially suffer from procrastination and ineffective learning secretaries. The results of our analysis demonstrate that students with low self-efficacy and time and study environment management significancy reduce procrastination and demonstrate greater engagement in the presence of adaptive nudges. Notably, the increase in activity following the in-class quizzes suggests that the second email nudges may be particularly effective, possibly because these nudges prompt reflection on recent performance and motivate students to engage further with practice opportunities. In addition, this approach helps maintain more consistent student engagement across two different situations: after lectures and after in-class quizzes. While single-purpose email notifications have been shown to improve students' learning performance before (e.g., [17]; [32]), this study takes a closer look at how sending different emails for different purposes at different times in a course influences various learning activities.

In addition, the results suggest that topic annotation is an effective intervention for scaffolding students' self-regulation, particularly for those with lower organizational and rehearsal skills. It helps students determine which topic to prioritize, thereby increasing their engagement by encouraging more frequent practice and clarifying which topics to cover. This prevents them from wandering aimlessly with the learning material and help them using their time more effectively. Furthermore, we showed that it helps students cover more topics (topic coverage), thereby exposing them to more learning material and potentially widening their knowledge. These results aligns with previous research on topic annotation, which suggests that the ability to determine the most relevant topic encourages students to learn more efficiently [23].

Our study has several limitations. First, we use only four out of twelve self-regulated processes from the MSLQ questionnaire [21]. A more complete account of students' SRL skills could have provide us with a better understanding of their SRL problems, yet, given the circumstances, filling in the complete MSLQ could have been overwhelming for students at the time. In the future, we could look into using another SRL scale that better fits the context of the study.

Despite conducting the study in a large course, the final sample size was limited, particularly for students with poor SRL skills, as not all students completed the questionnaire. Future replications of this experiment in larger courses and with higher questionnaire completion rates could improve the robustness and generalizability of the findings. Integrating the questionnaire into Quizitor might encourage a higher completion rate. Furthermore, we did not gather qualitative data, e.g., through interviews or focus group discussions. This data may enrich the findings by including the perspective from the students' point of view. Lastly, although we investigated the potential contribution of individual nudges to the overall engagement effect, there remains a substantial possibility of confounding effects among the three implemented interventions. A more carefully controlled study design, perhaps conducted in a lab setting, could help disentangle these effects and enable more precise attribution and quantification of the contribution of individual nudges to specific outcome measures.

## 7 Conclusion

This study examines a blended learning support technology that employs students' data from both face-to-face and online environments to design nudges that scaffold students' SRL skills. It investigates the effectiveness of these nudges in mitigating maladaptive SRL behaviors among students with poor SRL skills. The findings provide evidence that nudges positively influence the learning performance of students who lack key SRL skills, specifically self-efficacy, time and study environment management, organization, and rehearsal—four processes commonly challenging for students in large classroom settings. The results demonstrate that adaptive nudges using student data collected across both instructional modalities in a blended course improved students' engagement and learning behavior.

**Acknowledgments.** We would like to express our gratitude to the teaching team of the course we studied for their support throughout the study. We are also deeply thankful to all students who participated in the research.

## References


1. Alhasani, M., Orji, R.: Promoting stress management among students in higher education: evaluating the effectiveness of a persuasive time management mobile app. Int. J. Hum. Comput. Interact. **41**(1), 219–241 (2025)
2. Balapumi, R., von Konsky, B.R., Aitken, A., McMeekin, D.A.: Factors influencing university students' self-regulation of learning: an exploratory study. In: Proceedings of the Australasian Computer Science Week Multiconference, pp. 1–9 (2016)
3. Balkıs, M.: Academic efficacy as mediator and moderator variable in the relationship between academic procrastination and academic achievement. Eurasian J. Educ. Res. (2011)
4. Bandura, A.: Human agency in social cognitive theory. Am. Psychol. **44**(9), 1175 (1989)
5. Barnard, L., Lan, W.Y., To, Y.M., Paton, V.O., Lai, S.L.: Measuring self-regulation in online and blended learning environments. Internet Higher Educ. **12**(1), 1–6 (2009)
6. Broadbent, J.: Comparing online and blended learner's self-regulated learning strategies and academic performance. Internet Higher Educ. **33**, 24–32 (2017)
7. Broadbent, J., Poon, W.L.: Self-regulated learning strategies & academic achievement in online higher education learning environments: a systematic review. Internet Higher Educ. **27**, 1–13 (2015)
8. Cheng, G., Zou, D., Xie, H., Wang, F.L.: Exploring differences in self-regulated learning strategy use between high-and low-performing students in introductory programming: an analysis of eye-tracking and retrospective think-aloud data from program comprehension. Comput. Educ. **208**, 104948 (2024)
9. Dörrenbächer, L., Perels, F.: Self-regulated learning profiles in college students: their relationship to achievement, personality, and the effectiveness of an intervention to foster self-regulated learning. Learn. Individ. Differ. **51**, 229–241 (2016)
10. Dunlosky, J., Rawson, K.A., Marsh, E.J., Nathan, M.J., Willingham, D.T.: Improving students' learning with effective learning techniques: promising directions from cognitive and educational psychology. Psychol. Sci. Public Interest **14**(1), 4–58 (2013)
11. Felicilda-Reynaldo, R.F.D., Cruz, J.P., Bigley, L., Adams, K.: Baccalaureate student nurses' study habits prior to admission to nursing program: a descriptive qualitative study. Nurse Educ. Today **53**, 61–66 (2017)
12. Hamzah, A., Setiaji, H., Persada, A.G., Kurniawan, R., Sosnovsky, S.: Looking for the right blend: comparing different assessment scenarios in a blended course. In: Proceedings of the 18th International Conference of the Learning Sciences-ICLS 2024, pp. 2081–2082. International Society of the Learning Sciences (2024)
13. Hamzah, A., Sosnovsky, S.: Providing students with mobile access to an assessment platform: lessons learned. Int. J. Mob. Blended Learn. (IJMBL) **15**(2), 1–16 (2023)
14. Hamzah, A., Sosnovsky, S.: Convincing novices: the effect of notifications on student motivation in a blended learning support environment. In: Proceedings of the 18th International Conference of the Learning Sciences-ICLS 2024, pp. 1279–1282. International Society of the Learning Sciences (2024)
15. Hamzah, A., Sosnovsky, S.: Increasing student engagement in a large blended course. In: Companion Proceedings of LAK'2026: 16th International Conference on Learning Analytics & Knowledge, pp. 276–278 (2026)
16. Kornell, N.: Optimising learning using flashcards: spacing is more effective than cramming. Appl. Cogn. Psychol. Official J. Soc. Appl. Res. Memory Cogn. **23**(9), 1297–1317 (2009)

17. Nikolayeva, I., Yessad, A., Laforge, B., Luengo, V.: Does an e-mail reminder intervention with learning analytics reduce procrastination in a blended university course? In: Addressing Global Challenges and Quality Education: 15th European Conference on Technology Enhanced Learning, EC-TEL 2020, Heidelberg, Germany, September 14–18, 2020, Proceedings 15, pp. 60–73. Springer (2020)
18. O'Connor, Y., Mahony, C.: Exploring the impact of augmented reality on student academic self-efficacy in higher education. Comput. Hum. Behav. **149**, 107963 (2023)
19. Pérez-Álvarez, R., Maldonado-Mahauad, J., Pérez-Sanagustín, M.: Tools to support self-regulated learning in online environments: literature review. In: Lifelong Technology-Enhanced Learning: 13th European Conference on Technology Enhanced Learning, EC-TEL 2018, Leeds, UK, September 3-5, 2018, Proceedings 13, pp. 16–30. Springer (2018)
20. Pintrich, P.R.: The role of goal orientation in self-regulated learning. In: Handbook of self-regulation, pp. 451–502. Elsevier (2000)
21. Pintrich, P.: A manual for the use of the motivated strategies for learning questionnaire (MSLQ). In: National Center for Research to Improve Postsecondary Teaching and Learning (1991)
22. Puustinen, M., Pulkkinen, L.: Models of self-regulated learning: a review. Scand. J. Educ. Res. **45**(3), 269–286 (2001)
23. Sosnovsky, S., Brusilovsky, P.: Evaluation of topic-based adaptation and student modeling in QuizGuide. User Model. User-Adap. Inter. **25**(4), 371–424 (2015). https://doi.org/10.1007/s11257-015-9164-4
24. Steel, P.: The nature of procrastination: a meta-analytic and theoretical review of quintessential self-regulatory failure. Psychol. Bull. **133**(1), 65 (2007)
25. Tabuenca, B., Kalz, M., Drachsler, H., Specht, M.: Time will tell: the role of mobile learning analytics in self-regulated learning. Comput. Educ. **89**, 53–74 (2015)
26. Tautz, D., Sprenger, D.A., Schwaninger, A.: Evaluation of four digital tools and their perceived impact on active learning, repetition and feedback in a large university class. Comput. Educ. **175**, 104338 (2021)
27. Theobald, M.: Self-regulated learning training programs enhance university students' academic performance, self-regulated learning strategies, and motivation: a meta-analysis. Contemp. Educ. Psychol. **66**, 101976 (2021)
28. Van Laer, S., Elen, J.: In search of attributes that support self-regulation in blended learning environments. Educ. Inf. Technol. **22**(4), 1395–1454 (2017)
29. Winne, P.H., Hadwin, A.F.: nStudy: tracing and supporting self-regulated learning in the internet. In: International Handbook of Metacognition and Learning Technologies, pp. 293–308. Springer (2013)
30. Wolters, C.A., Taylor, D.J.: A self-regulated learning perspective on student engagement. In: Handbook of Research on Student Engagement, pp. 635–651. Springer (2012)
31. Yousef, A.M.F., Chatti, M.A., Danoyan, N., Thüs, H., Schroeder, U.: Video-mapper: a video annotation tool to support collaborative learning in MOOCs. In: Proceedings of the Third European MOOCs Stakeholders Summit EMOOCs, pp. 131–140 (2015)
32. Bernuy, Z., et al.: How can email interventions increase students' completion of online homework? A case study using a/b comparisons. In: LAK22: 12th International Learning Analytics and Knowledge Conference, pp. 107–118 (2022)
33. Zimmerman, B.J., Moylan, A.R.: Self-regulation: where metacognition and motivation intersect. In: Handbook of Metacognition in Education, pp. 299–315. Routledge (2009)

# Supporting Reading Comprehension by Modelling Attention Through Cursor Movements

Elias Hedlin[1(✉)], Robin Scholle[1], Fauzan Helmi Sudaryanto[1], Malin Hall[1], Carrie Demmans Epp[2,3], and Olga Viberg[1]

[1] School of Electrical Engineering and Computer Science, KTH Royal Institute of Technology, Stockholm, Sweden
{ehedlin,robp,fhsu,malhall,oviberg}@kth.se
[2] EdTeKLA Group, University of Alberta, Edmonton, Canada
cdemmansepp@ualberta.ca
[3] Alberta Machine Intelligence Institute (Amii), Edmonton, Canada

**Abstract.** Learners often struggle with inferential reading and interpretation of subtext—a key component of reading comprehension—because these tasks require integrating textual evidence and drawing implicit conclusions, skills that are difficult to build. To address this challenge, this paper presents and evaluates an AI-driven system that provides adaptive feedback to support inferential reasoning in reading. Grounded in Question-Based Learning, the system engages learners with comprehension questions prior to instruction, using feedback, rather than direct answers, as the primary means of scaffolding learner reasoning. This work introduces a novel approach to modelling learner attention during reading. Using fine-grained interaction data, specifically mouse-cursor movement as a proxy for attention, it captures how learners allocate attention across a text. These attention patterns, combined with learners' responses, inform adaptive feedback that highlights relevant evidence and prompts reflection on alternative interpretations, supporting deeper comprehension.

We evaluated the system using Swedish Scholastic Aptitude Test (SWESAT)-style reading assessments, which provide a cognitively demanding and authentic reading assessment context. This mixed-methods user study focused on learner interactions and experience. Results indicate that attention-informed adaptive feedback can support learners in navigating challenging inferential reading tasks. By using attention modelling to guide when and how feedback is provided, the system can help learners focus on relevant evidence and reconsider interpretations. We conclude that this attention-driven approach to adaptivity holds promise for supporting inferential reading.

**Keywords:** Reading comprehension · Intelligent tutoring systems · Inference skills · Adaptive feedback · Question-based learning


J. Weidlich et al. (Eds.): EC-TEL 2026, LNCS 16905, pp. 253–267, 2027.
https://doi.org/10.1007/978-3-032-37979-5_18

## 1 Introduction

Reading comprehension is a critical foundation for academic success and lifelong learning [10], yet recent large-scale assessments indicate a concerning decline in reading proficiency among K–12 students. Results from the Programme for International Student Assessment (PISA) 2022 study show a significant drop in reading performance in many countries, including Sweden, raising concerns about learners' preparedness for the literacy demands of higher-education and professional contexts. These trends highlight a need for scalable, evidence-based interventions that support higher-order comprehension skills [30].

While basic decoding and word recognition are essential, many learners who read fluently continue to struggle with comprehension, particularly when understanding depends on integrating information across sentences or interpreting meaning that is implicitly conveyed [13]. The Simple View of Reading [17] conceptualizes comprehension as the product of decoding and linguistic understanding, but higher-level cognitive processes, especially *inference-making*, remain a major source of difficulty even when foundational skills are intact [4]. Inference-making enables readers to connect ideas, fill information gaps, and construct coherent interpretations; it is widely recognized as central to deep comprehension [21].

In adult learning and high-stakes assessment contexts, inference-based reading plays a particularly prominent role [4,5]. The reading comprehension segments of the Swedish Scholastic Aptitude Test (SWESAT [1])–used as the entrance exam into Swedish higher education, for example, are described as consisting of what students in higher education are expected to be able to read and comprehend. It operationalizes this by placing a strong emphasis on identifying implied meaning, authorial intent, and logical relationships between text segments. Despite the importance of these skills, support for inference-making is often limited in the higher-education settings, where reading proficiency is typically assumed rather than explicitly taught. As a result, learners encounter inference-making primarily through assessment tasks, where the focus is on answer accuracy rather than on developing interpretive reasoning strategies and skills [24]. Advances in artificial intelligence (AI) and learning analytics (LA) can offer new opportunities to address this gap by providing adaptive, process-oriented feedback grounded in learners' real-time reading behaviour.

This study presents an AI-driven reading tutor that integrates reader attentional data and feedback-driven instructional design to support inferential reasoning in the context of the SWESAT-style reading tasks. By combining behavioural signals of attention with explanation-focused feedback, we aim to enhance learners' interpretive strategies and contribute to the design of intelligent systems for timely reading comprehension support.

To understand how learners engage with AI-supported reading in realistic settings, this work adopts an exploratory field-based evaluation approach. This approach emphasizes ecological validity by examining how interactive systems are used under authentic conditions, capturing reader behaviour shaped by contextual factors such as pacing and attention [9,22]. It also provides insight into the potential of this method in that it could be integrated into student support services across educational levels.

# 2 Background

## 2.1 Reading Comprehension and Inference Skills

Reading comprehension involves making sense of a text by combining information from individual sentences with prior knowledge and contextual cues [20]. Rather than treating each sentence in isolation, skilled readers build a coherent mental representation that captures the structure, themes, and communicative intent of the text [36]. This process draws on cognitive resources such as vocabulary knowledge, working memory, attentional control, and the ability to track referential and causal relationships across extended passages [6].

For young adult readers, difficulties with comprehension often relate to challenges in understanding how ideas in a text connect, rather than problems with basic reading [20]. These difficulties commonly involve linking information across sentences, keeping track of ideas over longer passages, or understanding meaning that is implied rather than directly stated [37]. Background knowledge plays an important role in these situations, especially when readers engage with expository or academic texts [37]. Because SWESAT reading passages often cover unfamiliar topics and use dense argumentation, readers must rely on these skills to understand the structure, tone, and overall meaning of the text [20].

*Inference-Making* is widely recognized as a core component of reading comprehension, particularly when texts require readers to derive meaning that is not explicitly stated [21]. It involves integrating textual information with prior knowledge to interpret implied content, establish relationships, and infer authorial intent. Strong inference ability impacts overall reading comprehension, whereas weaker inference skills are associated with poorer understanding of texts [21]. Inference comprises multiple related processes, including maintaining coherence across sentences, filling informational gaps, and constructing a global interpretation of a text [21]. These processes align closely with the demands of the SWESAT reading comprehension section, where test-takers are frequently asked to interpret implied meaning and draw conclusions [21].

Despite its importance, inference is defined, taught, and assessed largely in inconsistent ways, which can hinder readers' ability to develop transferable strategies [32]. In high-stakes assessments such as SWESAT, where questions often depend on subtle textual cues, inference ability is predictive of performance [21].

## 2.2 Digital Support for Improved Reading Comprehension

Digital technologies, such as intelligent textbooks and eye tracking tools, offer promising opportunities to support reading comprehension through adaptive guidance and real-time feedback [25,35]. Eye-tracking research demonstrates that visual attention patterns provide meaningful indicators of how readers navigate text, allocate cognitive resources, and comprehend presented information [18,25]; eye-trackers can provide targeted insight into whether readers focus on critical information or overlook content essential for constructing meaning [25].

Early work on adaptive reading support has largely focused on children's literacy development, especially in English, and provides instructive examples of how real-time interaction data can be leveraged. For instance, Project LISTEN's Reading Tutor used automatic speech recognition (ASR) to monitor young learners' oral reading skills and deliver immediate targeted feedback when learners hesitated, misread, or skipped words, through visual cues, subtle auditory prompts, or contextual assistance [27]. Longitudinal evaluations showed learning gains comparable to, and sometimes exceeding, those of classroom instruction and approaching one-on-one tutoring [26]. Similar efforts, such as the Dutch SPACE reading tutor, explored phoneme-based recognition to better handle readers' speech variability [3]. While these systems were constrained by the limitations of early ASR technology and remained largely experimental, they illustrate the pedagogical value of timely, process-oriented feedback grounded in the reader's moment-to-moment behaviour.

Building on these insights, contemporary intelligent reading systems for older learners leverage richer interaction data and more robust AI models to deliver adaptive support at the level of comprehension rather than decoding. An important extension of this work focuses on adult learners with low literacy skills, a highly heterogeneous population that also faces practical barriers to consistent participation in face-to-face programs [33]. AutoTutor for Adult Reading Comprehension (AT-ARC) addresses these challenges through an online, conversation-based intelligent tutoring system grounded in a theoretical model of reading comprehension [16,33]. Its adaptivity spans personalized learning material selection, adaptive branching, trialogues, and interface design, allowing instruction to respond to learners' knowledge, skills, self-efficacy, and motivation. Consequently, AT-ARC shows a shift toward learner-centered adaptive support in adult literacy technologies and points to further directions for improving adaptivity.

More recent systems extend these ideas by integrating large language models (LLMs) into interactive reading interfaces, enabling real-time, supportive feedback at the level of comprehension. Such systems can highlight relevant text, explain reasoning behind responses, and prompt reflective strategies, with evidence suggesting that non-judgmental, immediate feedback is particularly well received by learners [23].

In the context of SWESAT preparation, integrating attention-based signals with AI-generated feedback offers a principled way to address both reading behaviour (how learners allocate attention) and interpretive reasoning (how learners construct meaning) [23,25]. While modern ASR and speech synthesis models have largely overcome earlier technical barriers, the core instructional principle remains consistent: adaptive, real-time feedback grounded in observable learner behaviour can scaffold comprehension effectively. Because many SWESAT reading tasks emphasize implicit meaning rather than surface-level recall, this form of adaptive support is particularly well aligned with the inferential skills required for successful test performance [21].

## 3 Reading Support System

The web-based system presented below (Fig. 1) aims to support students who are preparing for a college entrance exam, the SWESAT [1]. As such, the interface layout was designed to minimize distractions, support readability, and resemble the format of the test. This web-based system has two components: (1) a learner-facing interface for completing reading tasks and receiving AI feedback and (2) an admin dashboard for researchers to monitor sessions, review heatmaps, and analyze aggregated data. Complete source code, including deployment configurations and AI prompt template, is available on github[1].

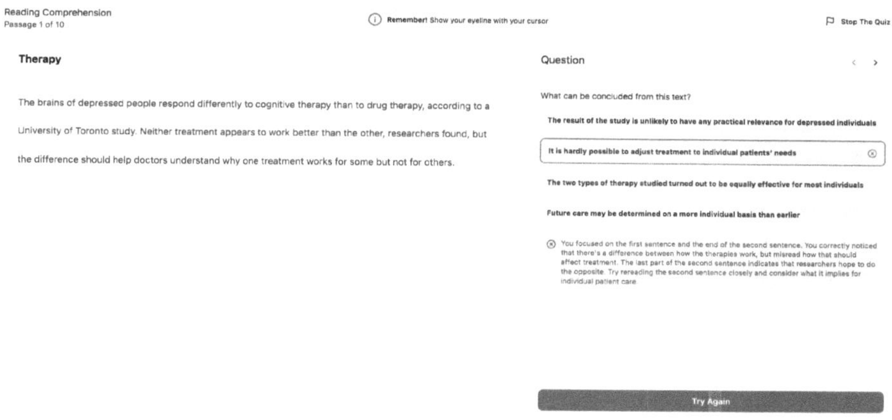


**Fig. 1.** Example of the reading comprehension interface following an incorrect response.

The learner-facing component uses the finger-tracking metaphor [12] to support both user attention and analytics of their behaviours. This interaction approach overcame the limitations of current browser-based eyetracking tools (e.g., WebGazer (https://www.webgazer.io) and GazeCloudAPI (https://gazerecorder.com/gazecloudapi)) by tracking the learner's cursor since there is no need to calibrate cursor tracking at the start of each session and it behaves consistently across platforms. During each reading task, the system records the coordinates of the cursor, sampled at 50ms intervals. Each coordinate is paired with a timestamp, allowing reconstruction of reading paths. For each sentence in the passage, we calculate how long the cursor remained within that area (dwell time) and the sequence in which different parts of the passage were visited (first

[1] https://github.com/eliashedlin/reading-comprehension-cursor-attention.git.

visit order). When the user submits their answer, a heatmap is generated as a visual representation of cursor activity, thus modelling their reading behaviours.

The learner-facing component provides feedback to learners using a combination of their answer, the question and passage text, the model of their reading behaviours, and a JSON summary of sentence-level reading behaviour, including dwell times and first visit order. Gemini is used to determine which parts of the text the learner focused on and the relationship between that text and their answer. The prompt provided to the model was designed to produce concise, instructionally relevant feedback while minimizing input token usage to support scalable deployment. For correct answers, the feedback confirms whether the user engaged with the relevant sections and summarizes the associated line of reasoning. For incorrect answers, the feedback guides the student toward the missed evidence without revealing the correct answer directly. This design follows the principles of Question-Based Learning (QBL), where immediate formative feedback is used as the primary instructional mechanism [7]. This approach to supporting learning was selected because its frequent questioning, rapid explanatory feedback, and opportunities for revision can improve performance, engagement, and retention while reducing time-on-task [7,15,19]. This is particularly important for inference-based reading tasks, where meaning often needs to be inferred across several sentences rather than being directly stated [20,21,37].

## 4 Methods

This exploratory mixed-methods study examined how participants used the system and how they experienced the feedback. In particular, the study examines how AI-generated, feedback-first instruction based on interaction data is understood by users as useful and supportive.

### 4.1 Procedures

Both consent and background information were collected from participants at the start of the study in December 2025. This background information included whether they had previously taken the SWESAT. Following this intake session, their participation lasted approximately 30 min. Participants were instructed to keep the cursor aligned with what they were reading, and study tasks were conducted through a web-browser on a computer with a mouse.

Participants completed ten SWESAT-style reading comprehension tasks. Afterwards, they provided information about their experiences.

### 4.2 Instruments

Cursor tracking was used as a practical way to approximate *visual attention*. This approach made it possible to collect attention-related data without specialised equipment and is supported by previous research showing that such data can give useful insight into reading behaviour and comprehension difficulties [18,25].

Information about participants' experiences was collected through open-ended questions, which focused on how the tool supported their learning, their reflections on the provided feedback, and any other feedback they wished to provide.

### 4.3 Participants

English proficiency among our participants ($n = 9$), ranged from beginner through proficient, with three having previously taken the SWESAT (Table 1). They were 29 years old on average ($SD = 3.7$).

**Table 1.** Participant demographics

| ID | Age | Attended university | English fluency | SWESAT Experience |
|---|---|---|---|---|
| P1 | 27 | Yes | Intermediate (B1) | No |
| P2 | 26 | Currently attending | Native | No |
| P3 | 26 | Currently attending | Fluent (C1-C2) | Yes |
| P4 | 36 | Yes | Fluent (C1-C2) | Yes |
| P5 | 25 | Yes | Fluent (C1-C2) | No |
| P6 | 28 | Yes | Advanced (B2) | Yes |
| P7 | 31 | Currently attending | Fluent (C1-C2) | No |
| P8 | 32 | Currently attending | Beginner (A1-A2) | No |
| P9 | 34 | Yes | Advanced (B2) | No |

## 5 Results and Discussion

To contextualize participants' behaviour and experiences, we present two complementary views of the collected interaction data: 1) aggregated patterns across passages and 2) individual interaction traces over time. These include measures such as response distributions, time-on-task, cursor movement, and dwell time. Together, they illustrate how observable interaction traces are captured and used to interpret participants' responses.

### 5.1 Participant Performance Across Passages

Aggregating across participants, we examined which passages were the most difficult and which took the longest to complete. As shown in Table 2 below, "Rock Posters" and "Therapy" were the most challenging, both with a first-attempt accuracy of only 56%. Rock Posters also took the longest to read whereas the Therapy reading was one of the fastest to read. Both also required more repeated attempts for participants to identify the correct answer. The number

**Table 2.** Participant performance at the passage level

| Title | Participants | Attempts | First-Attempt | Avg. Time | SD |
|---|---|---|---|---|---|
| The Great Lakes | 9 | 9 | 100% | 1 m 34 s | 40 s |
| American Folk Music | 9 | 10 | 89% | 1 m 46 s | 42 s |
| New Scotland Yard | 9 | 9 | 100% | 1 m 25 s | 49 s |
| Animal Life | 9 | 10 | 89% | 1 m 13 s | 33 s |
| Saying it with Flowers | 9 | 9 | 100% | 1 m 41 s | 58 s |
| Tryggve Lie | 9 | 12 | 89% | 1 m 20 s | 46 s |
| Men and Women | 9 | 10 | 89% | 57 s | 39 s |
| The Mayas | 9 | 9 | 100% | 1 m 39 s | 59 s |
| Rock Posters | 9 | 15 | 56% | 2 m 30 s | 1 m 14 s |
| Therapy | 9 | 13 | 56% | 1 m 19 s | 42 s |

of attempts indicates that they received guidance on which information in the text might be important 16 times.

Passages like "The Great Lakes" and "The Mayas" achieved 100% first-try accuracy, suggesting that the information was more accessible, partly because it could be directly retrieved from the text. In contrast, passages with lower first-try accuracy like "Rock Posters", required deeper inference and the greater synthesis of information. Analysis of the first-choice distribution for this passage (as seen in Fig. 2) reveals that 44% of participants selected the same incorrect option (Option D). This high concentration on a single distractor is likely due to the fact that it targets an expected misinterpretation of the text if someone were focusing on shallow text features. In this case, option D focuses on a downstream

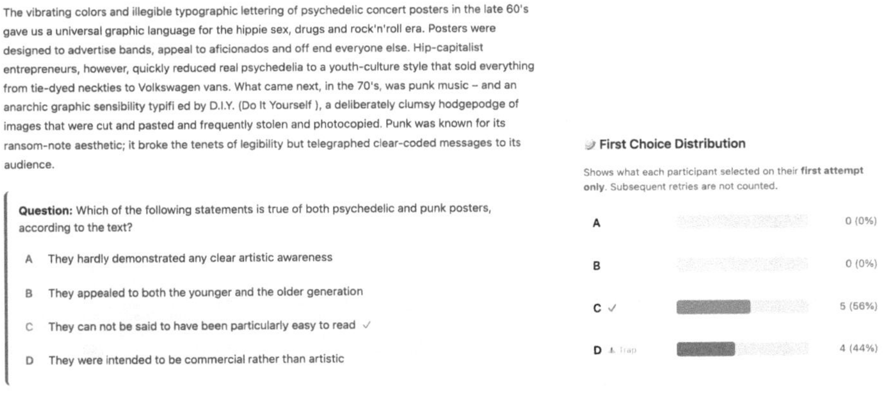


**Fig. 2.** Admin dashboard view for the "Rock Posters" passage, showing the passage text, question options, and first-choice distribution analysis.

outcome rather than the original intention of the artform being discussed. Dwell-time analysis might reveal whether participants missed key sentences in these harder passages, but the error rates of humans and models are generally higher on inference questions, especially those that integrate advanced vocabulary with world knowledge [28].

### 5.2 Participant Reading Performance

All participants completed all 10 passages, which took them 15.5 min on average ($SD = 6.46$). Two of them answered every question correctly on the first attempt; all others made errors on 10% to 30% of the tasks (Table 3). There is no obvious relationship between participants' English proficiency and their ability to answer the SWESAT questions correctly.

**Table 3.** Participant task performance.

| ID | P1 | P2 | P3 | P4 | P5 | P6 | P7 | P8 | P9 |
|---|---|---|---|---|---|---|---|---|---|
| No. Correct First-Attempt | 7 | 9 | 10 | 8 | 8 | 9 | 10 | 9 | 8 |
| Total time (min) | 27.76 | 8.42 | 11.09 | 16.20 | 14.89 | 12.15 | 13.58 | 11.00 | 24.31 |

The variability in total time across participants reflects diverse reading speeds and potential differences in reading strategies. Notably, faster completion times were not always aligned with lower first-attempt accuracy. For example, P2 achieved 90% accuracy in the shortest time, while P1's longer duration and lower score suggest they found the task harder (which is consistent with their English proficiency). However, English proficiency does not fully explain the results as P8 had the lowest proficiency, was among the fastest to complete the study task, and scored well (90%). This suggests that reading or test-taking strategies were at play, but performance metrics cannot reveal this information on their own.

We use the cursor-tracking heatmaps to explore these potential strategies (Fig. 3). The full set of heatmaps is available on OSF[2] and this example presents two participants' interactions with the "Saying it with Flowers" passage. In this case, both answered correctly on their first attempt and had similar English proficiency, but they engaged in different information access patterns. These patterns are consistent with P9 spending more than twice as long (4 m 9 s) processing the text as P6 (1 m 39 s). P6 seems to have engaged in rapid linear reading, whereas P9 distributed their attention in what appears to be a targeted manner, going back to key phrases multiple times. These types of variation in time on task and the interleaving of foci have also been seen in the reading behaviours of post-secondary students who were using a reading comprehension game [8], suggesting that learners brought their existing strategies into the system. This also implies that there is an opportunity for the strategy-level feedback that the present system provides to influence learner behaviour.

[2] https://osf.io/p8b2w/overview?view_only=234414b716eb4465bf2b091d30b70125.

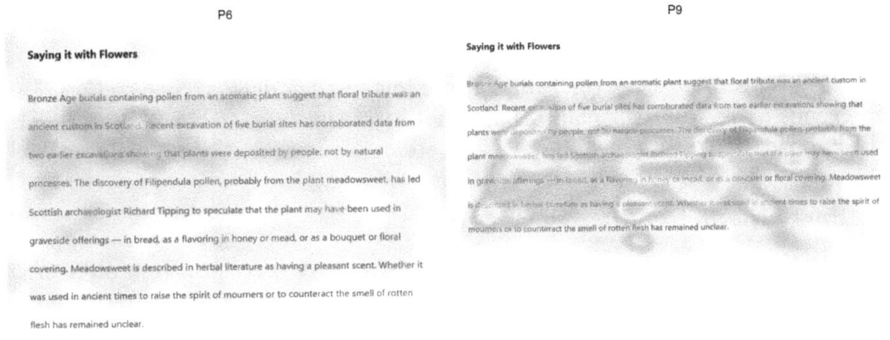


**Fig. 3.** Sample comparison of cursor-tracking heatmap data for P6 (left) and P9 (right).

### 5.3 Participant Experiences with System Feedback

Participants expressed an appreciation for the "clean, minimalistic, distraction-free" interface (P2) that was "familiar with a kind of English reading comprehension test" (P8). Moreover, it allowed them "to see the information while sometimes reading the problem and options as a *back-and-forth* method of analyzing the text" (P7), which supported their reading comprehension.

In addition to supporting their comprehension, study participants reported that the feedback made them feel "acknowledged" (P7) and helped them "understand their reading manners and how they can come to wrong conclusions" (P4). Together, this encouraged persistence even after multiple incorrect attempts, and it may help students to develop their "active reading" skills (P3).

Participants also reflected on how the system "understood what went wrong and could help [them] get a better result next time" (P4). It supported their performance by providing helpful feedback that "gives [them] a hint or explanation—in a fast way and also on a detailed level—on where to focus on the text to be able to answer the question correctly" (P8). This indicates that the system generally provided appropriate levels of elaboration to support students in using the feedback and aligns with theory-grounded recommendations [15,34].

However, participants did not always agree with the use of the Question-Based Learning approach, expressing a need for additional elaboration, or alternative support mechanisms. One participant stated that it would be valuable to "have a chat next to the question where you can ask more questions about the text when you finished it" (P1), and another one (P6) noted that "it could have been clearer in highlighting what mistake I made". This more interactive approach could have mitigated when participants struggled to understand the feedback as P9 sometimes did: "I am a little bit confused with the feedback when the feedback for the correct answer sounds like [it's] wrong".

The present system relies on participant response data and interaction traces to inform feedback, supporting a lightweight and scalable design while providing a less detailed model of the learner's underlying misconceptions. This can limit the system's ability to directly address specific comprehension errors [31]. A similar constraint arises with regard to cursor-based attentional tracking, where participants noted that the signal can introduce "noise" (P3) in interpreting reading behaviour, which may limit the level of personalization achievable across tasks, learners' individual abilities, and learners' preferences [2]. To address these learner modelling limitations, our system highlights behavioural patterns and provides strategy feedback that is independent of the nature of the comprehension error. For the most part, this approach was successful, but this well-established approach to tutoring [11,31] was undesirable for some. If the system can obtain a better underlying model of the learner's knowledge, then features like those P1 suggested would be possible: a system that knows which words a user has knowledge of could provide appropriate glosses. Such features would be supportive of learning and mitigate the situation where participants "did not understand and the feedback did not help 'cause it just highlighted words in the text, and [they] did not know what those words meant" (P1).

Overall, participants found the feedback useful when it provided quick, detailed strategy hints and hints that helped them focus on specific parts of the text. Some participants also noted that the feedback could sometimes feel general or repetitive, reflecting recognised limitations of AI-generated instructional feedback [23]. However, there are emerging approaches to mitigating this by combining knowledge engineering approaches as part of the AI-generation process [14].

### 5.4 Limitations and Future Research

This study was exploratory in nature, aligning with formative evaluation approaches commonly used in early-stage learning technology research [29]. The goal was to examine interaction patterns, usability, and learner experience rather than to establish learning gains or statistically generalisable effects. Hence, the results should be interpreted as *design-oriented insights* into how learners engage with question-based reading instruction and AI-generated feedback.

Participants' relatively high first-attempt accuracy across many passages suggests that task difficulty may have been insufficient to elicit sustained struggle or observable strategy change for some learners. Future studies should incorporate longer texts, more complex inferential questions, extended practice over time, or readers with lower prior proficiency to better assess potential effects.

While the lightweight, low-cost cursor-tracking approach to modeling reader attention is noisy, it provides valuable insight into which elements of the text the learner is focusing on. In the present version of the system, this information helped to augment the generated feedback. However, constrained feedback specificity contributed to some participants feeling that the provided feedback needed improvement. Future work should explore richer learner models that integrate additional signals, such as self-explanations and longitudinal interaction data, to support more targeted adaptation.

Lastly, cursor-tracking provides an indirect proxy for reader attention. Future research could open the learner model to investigate the use of attentional visualisations, such as heatmaps, as a support for metacognitive awareness, and examine long-term learning and transfer effects through longitudinal studies.

## 6 Conclusion

This paper introduced an AI-mediated reading comprehension tutor designed to support inference-making and subtext interpretation in SWESAT-style reading tasks through a Question-Based Learning approach. Rather than providing direct answers, the system uses adaptive, feedback-driven scaffolding to encourage learners to reflect on their interpretations, identify relevant textual evidence, and refine their reading strategies. By combining a large language model with lightweight cursor-tracking data, the system generates feedback that is grounded in both learner responses and observable interaction patterns.

Findings from a mixed-methods user study indicate that readers generally perceived the system as supportive, engaging, and helpful for focusing attention on key parts of the text. Participants appreciated the minimalistic interface and the immediacy of the feedback, and qualitative evidence suggests that the system encouraged persistence and reflective reading, even after incorrect responses. At the same time, the study highlights important challenges related to learner modeling, feedback specificity, and task difficulty that must be addressed to move from exploratory deployment toward instructional effectiveness.

Beyond the specific SWESAT application, this work illustrates a general design approach for adaptive reading support systems that leverage process-oriented data to scaffold higher-level comprehension skills that are predictive of academic- and lifelong-learning success. We conclude that AI-driven feedback holds promise for supporting inferential reading, and that future research should focus on richer learner models, reflective strategy support, and longitudinal evaluations of learning outcomes in realistic educational settings.

**Acknowledgments.** This study was in part funded by grant 2025-04552 from the Swedish Research Council.

**Disclosure of Interests.** The authors have no competing interests.

## References


1. What is the Högskoleprovet?. https://www.studera.nu/startpage/road-to-studies/hogskoleprovet/SweSAT/
2. Abdullah, Y.A., Guevarra, M., Cai, M., Yan, J., Taylor, M.E., Demmans Epp, C.: Pilot Trainees Benefit from Modelling and Adaptive Feedback. In: Proceedings of the 33rd ACM Conference on User Modeling, Adaptation and Personalization, pp. 144–154. UMAP '2025, Association for Computing Machinery, New York, NY, USA (2025). https://doi.org/10.1145/3699682.3728337
3. Bai, Y., Hubers, F., Cucchiarini, C., van Hout, R., Strik, H.: The effects of implicit and explicit feedback in an asr-based reading tutor for Dutch first-graders. In: Interspeech, pp. 4476–4480 (2022). https://doi.org/10.21437/Interspeech.2022-10810
4. Barth, A.E., Vaughn, S.: Reading and cognitive correlates underlying inferencing among adolescent readers. IJRLD-Int. J. Res. Learn. Disabilities **8**(1), 3–15 (2025)
5. Black, P., Wiliam, D.: Inside the Black Box: raising Standards through Classroom Assessment. Phi Delta Kappan **92**(1), 81–90 (2010). https://doi.org/10.1177/003172171009200119
6. Butterfuss, R., Kendeou, P.: The role of executive functions in reading comprehension. Educ. Psychol. Rev. **30**(3), 801–826 (2018). https://doi.org/10.1007/s10648-017-9422-6
7. Bälter, O., Glassey, R., Jemstedt, A., Bosk, D.: Pure question-based learning. Educ. Sci. **14**(8), 882 (2024). https://doi.org/10.3390/educsci14080882
8. Cai, M., Rebolledo Mendez, G., Arevalo, G., Tang, S.S., Abdullah, Y.A., Demmans Epp, C.: Toward Supporting Adaptation: Exploring Affect's Role in Cognitive Load when Using a Literacy Game. In: Proceedings of the CHI Conference on Human Factors in Computing Systems, pp. 1–17. ACM, Honolulu HI USA (2024). https://doi.org/10.1145/3613904.3642150
9. Chamberlain, A., Crabtree, A., Rodden, T., Jones, M., Rogers, Y.: Research in the wild: understanding 'in the wild' approaches to design and development. In: Proceedings of the Designing Interactive Systems Conference, pp. 795–796 (2012)
10. Delgadova, E.: Reading literacy as one of the most significant academic competencies for the university students. Procedia. Soc. Behav. Sci. **178**, 48–53 (2015). https://doi.org/10.1016/j.sbspro.2015.03.145
11. Demmans Epp, C., McCalla, G.I.: ProTutor: Historic open learner models for pronunciation tutoring. In: Biswas, G., Bull, S., Kay, J., Mitrovic, A. (eds.) Artificial Intelligence in Education (AIED). Springer Lecture Notes in Computer Science, vol. 6738, pp. 441–443. Springer, Auckland, New Zealand (2011). https://doi.org/10.1007/978-3-642-21869-9_63
12. Demmans Epp, C., Munteanu, C., Axtell, B., Ravinthiran, K., Aly, Y., Mansimov, E.: Finger Tracking: Facilitating Non-commercial Content Production for Mobile e-Reading Applications. In: Proceedings of the 19th International Conference on Human-Computer Interaction with Mobile Devices and Services, pp. 34:1–34:15. MobileHCI, ACM, Vienna (2017). https://doi.org/10.1145/3098279.3098556
13. Gough, P.B., Tunmer, W.E.: Decoding, reading, and reading disability. Remedial Special Educ. **7**(1), 6–10 (1986). https://doi.org/10.1177/074193258600700104
14. Guevarra, M., et al.: An LLM-guided tutoring system for social skills training. In: Proceedings of the Thirty-Ninth AAAI Conference on Artificial Intelligence and Thirty-Seventh Conference on Innovative Applications of Artificial Intelligence and Fifteenth Symposium on Educational Advances in Artificial Intelligence. AAAI'25/IAAI'25/EAAI'25, vol. 39, pp. 29643–29645. AAAI Press (2025). https://doi.org/10.1609/aaai.v39i28.35353

15. Hattie, J., Timperley, H.: The power of feedback. Rev. Educ. Res. **77**(1), 81–112 (2007). https://doi.org/10.3102/003465430298487
16. Hollander, J., Sabatini, J., Graesser, A.: An intelligent tutoring system for improving adult literacy skills in digital environments. Grantee Submission (2021)
17. Hoover, W.A., Gough, P.B.: The simple view of reading. Read. Writ. **2**(2), 127–160 (1990). https://doi.org/10.1007/BF00401799
18. Ilyas, C.M.A., Noor, S.E., Tashk, A., Cooreman, B., Beier, S., Bækgaard, P.: Reading the Readers Mind through Eye Tracking: Can AI Generated Texts Match Human Authors? In: Proceedings of the 2025 Symposium on Eye Tracking Research and Applications, pp. 1–7. ETRA '25, Association for Computing Machinery, New York, NY, USA (2025). https://doi.org/10.1145/3715669.3726846
19. Jemstedt, A., Bälter, O., Gavel, A., Glassey, R., Bosk, D.: Less to produce and less to consume: the advantage of pure question-based learning. Interact. Learn. Environ. **33**(2), 1040–1061 (2025). https://doi.org/10.1080/10494820.2024.2362830
20. Kendeou, P., McMaster, K.L., Christ, T.J.: Reading comprehension: core components and processes. Policy Insights Behav. Brain Sci. **3**(1), 62–69 (2016). https://doi.org/10.1177/2372732215624707
21. Kispal, A.: Effective Teaching of Inference Skills for Reading: Literature Review. Department for Children, Schools and Families, Nottingham (2008)
22. Kjeldskov, J., Skov, M.B.: Was it worth the hassle? Ten years of mobile HCI research discussions on lab and field evaluations. In: Proceedings of the 16th international conference on Human-computer interaction with mobile devices & services, pp. 43–52. MobileHCI, Association for Computing Machinery, New York, NY, USA (2014). https://doi.org/10.1145/2628363.2628398
23. Larsson, P.: Felicia: Development of a Voice-Based AI Companion Supporting Reading Literacy among Young Learners (2025). https://urn.kb.se/resolve?urn=urn:nbn:se:kth:diva-369531
24. Lea, M.R., Street, B.V.: Student writing in higher education: an academic literacies approach. Stud. High. Educ. **23**(2), 157–172 (1998). https://doi.org/10.1080/03075079812331380364
25. Liu, P.L.: Using eye tracking to understand learners' reading process through the concept-mapping learning strategy. Comput. Educ. **78**, 237–249 (2014). https://doi.org/10.1016/j.compedu.2014.05.011
26. Mostow, J., et al.: Evaluation of an automated reading tutor that listens: comparison to human tutoring and classroom instruction. J. Educ. Comput. Res. **29**(1), 61–117 (2003)
27. Mostow, J., Aist, G.: Giving help and praise in a reading tutor with imperfect listening – because automated speech recognition means never being able to say you're certain. CALICO J. **16**(3), 407–424 (1999)
28. Nie, Y., Deacon, H., Fyshe, A., Demmans Epp, C.: Predicting Reading Comprehension Scores of Elementary School Students, pp. 158–170. International Educational Data Mining Society, Durham, UK (2022). https://doi.org/10.5281/ZENODO.6852952
29. Nielsen, J.: Usability Engineering. Academic Press, Boston (1993)
30. OECD: PISA 2022 Results (Volume I and II) - Country Notes: Sweden. Tech. rep., OECD Publishing (2023). https://www.oecd.org/en/publications/pisa-2022-results-volume-i-and-ii-country-notes_ed6fbcc5-en/sweden_de351d24-en.html
31. Ohlsson, S.: Constraint-based modeling: from cognitive theory to computer tutoring – and back again. Int. J. Artif. Intell. Educ. **26**(1), 457–473 (2016). https://doi.org/10.1007/s40593-015-0075-7

32. Rice, M., Wijekumar, K., Lambright, K., Bristow, A.: Inferencing in reading comprehension: examining variations in definition, instruction, and assessment. Technol. Knowl. Learn. **29**(3), 1169–1190 (2024). https://doi.org/10.1007/s10758-023-09660-y
33. Shi, G., et al.: The adaptive features of an intelligent tutoring system for adult literacy. In: International Conference on Human-Computer Interaction, pp. 592–603. Springer (2021)
34. Shute, V.J.: Focus on formative feedback. Rev. Educ. Res. **78**(1), 153–189 (2008). https://doi.org/10.3102/0034654307313795
35. Sosnovsky, S., Brusilovsky, P., Lan, A.: Intelligent textbooks. Int. J. Artif. Intell. Educ. **35**(3), 967–986 (2025)
36. Soto, C., Gutiérrez de Blume, A.P., Jacovina, M., McNamara, D., Benson, N., Riffo, B.: Reading comprehension and metacognition: the importance of inferential skills. Cogent Educ. **6**(1), 1565067 (2019)
37. Tarchi, C.: Fostering reading comprehension of expository texts through the activation of readers' prior knowledge and inference-making skills. Int. J. Educ. Res. **72**, 80–88 (2015). https://doi.org/10.1016/j.ijer.2015.04.013

# Q-DSS: Supercharging Teaching Assistants with Resource and Decision Support

Martin Thoft Jensen(✉), Morten Misfeldt, and Daniel Spikol

University of Copenhagen, Copenhagen, Denmark
{mtj,ds}@di.ku.dk, misfeldt@ind.ku.dk

**Abstract.** Teaching Assistants (TAs) in large-enrolment STEM courses often struggle to manage high student demand, relying on ad-hoc queuing methods that prioritize logistics over learning. This "first-come, first-served" approach creates a detection lag, in which TAs fail to recognize widespread misconceptions until they have already answered the same question ineffectively multiple times. This paper explores how a queue-based decision support system (Q-DSS) can be designed to help TAs identify pedagogical opportunities, such as grouping students or delivering mini-lectures. Using a combined methodology of Design-Based Research and Value Sensitive Design, an AI support system was iteratively developed featuring real-time, Large Language Model (LLM)-powered pattern detection and a course-aware chatbot. Through six phases of stakeholder engagement and naturalistic deployment, 11 core requirements were identified to support mindful TA. Key findings emphasize the design principles of "transparency over automation" and "trust and verify", revealing that TAs require AI to act as a scaffold for their teaching practices rather than an automated decision-maker. While the technical feasibility of real-time pedagogical suggestions was validated, naturalistic evaluation highlighted that the value of such systems depends heavily on sustained student demand. This paper contributes design principles, key requirements, and a functional architecture that demonstrate how educational queues can evolve from administrative tools into instruments for mindful classroom orchestration.

**Keywords:** AI in Education · Design Based Research · Pedagogical Content Knowledge · Classroom Orchestration · TA-AI interaction

## 1 Introduction

In large-enrolment university Computer Science (CS) courses, Teaching Assistants (TAs) are often the primary point of contact between students and the curriculum during practical exercise sessions. Yet despite their central role in facilitating active learning, TAs are typically positioned as logistical operators rather than pedagogical agents: they manage queues, answer questions one by one, and move on. Ad hoc methods such as hand-raising or first-come, first-served (FIFO) lists address the immediate question of who is next, but systematically


J. Weidlich et al. (Eds.): EC-TEL 2026, LNCS 16905, pp. 268–282, 2027.
https://doi.org/10.1007/978-3-032-37979-5_19

obscure the pedagogically critical question of what is actually needed [13]. This mismatch creates a detection lag; by the time a TA recognizes that multiple students share the same misconception, they have already answered the same question inefficiently several times over, forfeiting the opportunity for a timely collective intervention.

This problem is not incidental to the role; it reflects a structural gap in TA support infrastructure. Effective TAs draw on Pedagogical Content Knowledge (PCK) [18], the capacity to recognize student difficulties and select appropriate instructional strategies in response. In technology-rich environments, this extends to Technological Pedagogical Content Knowledge (TPACK) [14]. In introductory programming contexts specifically, PCK includes identifying recurrent misconceptions around variable scope, conditionals, and loops, and knowing when to shift from one-to-one debugging support to a broader conceptual explanation [16,21]. The challenge is that exercising this knowledge requires pattern awareness with a real-time overview of what the class is struggling with, which traditional queuing practices simply do not provide. PCK highlights the TA's capacity to recognize and respond to students' misunderstandings, difficulties, and learning processes in computer science; TPACK extends this by foregrounding the technologies involved (programming environments, automated feedback systems, and AI-based support). It shifts attention from whether TAs "know the content" to how they transform computational concepts into learnable experiences through explanations, pedagogical design, and technologies.

This paper addresses the challenge of transforming the educational help queue from a purely administrative tool into an instrument for mindful classroom orchestration. We explore how a Queue-based Decision Support System (Q-DSS) can be designed to scaffold TAs' addressing Pedagogical Content Knowledge (PCK) by leveraging Large Language Models (LLMs) to detect patterns in real time. Crucially, we position this technology not as an automated decision-maker, but as a transparent partner that enhances the TA's agency, aligning with the conference's focus on human-centered innovation and trust in technology-enhanced learning (TEL) environments. This paper contributes by surfacing thematic clusters of student problems and suggesting pedagogical actions (such as grouping students or delivering a mini-lecture); the system aims to help TAs shift from reactive triage to proactive instruction, and by providing concrete design requirements for further development and addressing the detection-lag problem that TAs face when supporting students.

### 1.1 Research Questions

To address these challenges, this paper investigates the design, development, and evaluation of a Queue-based Decision Support System (Q-DSS). The study is structured around one main research question and two supporting questions that together span problem analysis, system design, and naturalistic evaluation. The main research question: *How can a queue-based decision support system (Q-DSS) be designed and evaluated to help teaching assistants manage resource allocation and identify pedagogical opportunities during high-demand CS exercise sessions?*

**Supporting Questions**

1. What resource management and pedagogical challenges do teaching assistants face in high-demand CS exercise sessions, and what requirements should a decision support system address to help TAs apply their Pedagogical Content Knowledge more effectively?
2. How can a queue-based decision support prototype be iteratively designed to embed transparency and TA agency into AI-generated pedagogical suggestions, and what does naturalistic deployment reveal about the conditions under which such support is most effective?

This study has a deliberately bounded scope. As a design and feasibility study, it carries three limitations that frame its claims. First, the pilot did not encounter the high-demand conditions the recommendation engine is built for, so its central function remains untested at the scale where it matters. Second, the design draws on the researcher's experience as an instructor, student, and TA, which risks confirmation bias; we address this through stakeholder involvement and transparent reporting of the design process. Third, the evaluation is largely qualitative and conducted at a single university, which limits the quantitative evidence of impact and the generalisability to other educational settings.

## 2 Related Work

TA-led sessions support active learning, which improves outcomes compared with passive instruction [4]. Students depend on timely assistance to prevent confusion from escalating [3], yet help-seeking may be inhibited by social anxiety or unclear waiting processes [9,12]. To manage growing enrolments and demand for support, digital queue systems such as *The Queue* (UIUC) and *My Digital Hand* have been introduced to coordinate help requests and provide transparent FIFO ordering [8,15]. These systems improve perceptions of fairness and reduce the risk of students being overlooked in large classes. See Table 1 for the different systems.

Queue systems also create opportunities to identify recurring questions and support just-in-time explanations [8]. Logging requests can reveal "muddiest points" and patterns of demand. For example, large-scale deployments show how queue systems can scale office hours and peer support in large courses, although peak wait times and workload imbalances still occur [11,19].

Data collected by queue systems can support learning analytics. Studies using *My Digital Hand* show that help requests can be automatically classified with high accuracy [5]. Recent work also explores the integration of LLMs into help platforms. Systems such as *HelpMe* and *ChatEd* combine queue management with retrieval-based chatbot support grounded in course materials [22–24]. While promising, these systems primarily focus on answering questions rather than supporting real-time TA decision-making.

### 2.1 Equity and Research Gap

FIFO queueing improves perceived fairness [15] but does not account for pedagogical factors such as urgency or prior assistance [11]. Furthermore, many student requests are underspecified, limiting the usefulness of analytics [5]. Existing queue systems, therefore, provide logistical coordination but limited support for pedagogical decision-making. A key research challenge is designing queue-based systems that provide interpretable, real-time decision support for TAs while encouraging clearer student input and preserving fairness and transparency [5,6,19].

This proposed paper focuses on the design, development, and pilot evaluation of a prototype Queue-based Decision Support System (Q-DSS). We detail the design process for identifying 11 core requirements for mindful TA support and describe how the system's architecture enables real-time pattern detection and pedagogical suggestions. The evaluation is scoped to assess technical feasibility, usability, and TA perceptions of agency and trust through naturalistic deployments in computer science courses.

**Table 1.** Overview of existing queue systems and their features.

| System (Context) | Key Capabilities & Analytics |
|---|---|
| HELPq *(Hackathons, Classrooms)* | Location and contact inputs, mentor management, announcements.<br>*Analytics: Descriptive dashboard (response times, ratings).* |
| SmartQueue *(Virtual Office Hours)* | Simple webapp, meeting link integration, notifications.<br>*Analytics: None.* |
| ClassroomQ *(K-12 Classrooms)* | Simple "raise hand" button, class codes.<br>*Analytics: Basic session tracking.* |
| QueueStatus *(Uni. Office Hours)* | Online sign-up, estimated wait times, grouping requests.<br>*Analytics: Usage stats, service frequency.* |
| The Queue *(Uni. Advising)* | University login integration, Multi-TA support.<br>*Analytics: Rich data collection used in research.* |
| My Digital Hand *(CS Courses)* | One-to-one interaction tracking, scalable design.<br>*Analytics: Interaction data used in research on question classification.* |

## 3 Methodology

Q-DSS employed a Design-Based Research (DBR) approach [2], combined with a Value Sensitive Design (VSD) framework [7]. DBR supports iterative cycles of design, implementation, and analysis in collaboration with educators and learners, ensuring that the interventions are grounded in practice and adaptable to diverse educational contexts. VSD ensures that ethical and societal values are embedded throughout the design process, thereby enhancing the normative alignment of the AI-integrated learning environments developed within the project. To develop Q-DSS we employed a lightweight approach inspired by Scrum [1,17] to structure the main development iterations of the DBR cycles. Work is organized in short time-boxed sprints of 1 to 2 weeks. A single prioritized backlog is maintained with clearly scoped work items. Each sprint has clearly defined objectives, produces a small prototype increment, and ends with a review/demo activity with stakeholders, along with a short retrospective memo capturing feedback, issues, and prioritization for the next sprint. Table 2 summarises the broad stakeholder engagement undertaken to ensure the system remained grounded in valid pedagogical needs. Students and TAs were recruited in a course that the researchers were responsible for, and through convenience sampling, which included additional TAs outside the course. Data collection took place during the course's help sessions, where students and TAs volunteered, and informed consent was obtained in accordance with national and EU requirements.

**Table 2.** Overview of participants and activities across research phases.

| Phase | Participants | Activity |
|---|---|---|
| 1. Exploration | 10 Students, 4 TAs, 3 Course Resp | Contextual inquiry interviews identifying "visibility gaps" in current practices. |
| 2. Knowledge Base | (Researcher) | Literature review on PCK and queue psychology; refinement of requirements. |
| 3. Prototype v1 | 2 Course Resp | Technical validation of real-time AWS Amplify architecture. |
| 4. Co-Design | 3 Expert TAs | Participatory Design (PD) workshops refining decision support and AI interactions. |
| 5. Refinement | 11 Students, 1 TA, 1 Course Resp | Usability testing and initial stress testing for deployment readiness. |
| 6. Evaluation | ~40 Students, 4 TAs, 1 Course Resp | Naturalistic deployments in *Python Programming* and *Linear Algebra*. |

**Phase 1: Exploration.** Initial contextual inquiry interviews revealed that current ad-hoc methods create a "Visibility Gap." TAs expressed a desire to switch to collective explanations when multiple students struggled with similar concepts but lacked the overview needed to identify these patterns in real time. Students reported that social friction and lack of privacy in hand-raising often deterred help-seeking.

**Phase 2 and 3: Theory-Informed Prototyping.** Phase 2 grounded the project in the Pedagogical Content Knowledge (PCK) literature and aimed to reduce the cognitive load of logistics, freeing up mental capacity for teaching. Phase 3 developed a functional real-time web prototype using AWS Amplify, acting as a "boundary object" to facilitate concrete co-design discussions in subsequent phases.

**Phase 4: Co-dsign and the "Detection Lag".** Workshops with expert TAs surfaced the core tension of the *Mini-Lecture Threshold*. As one TA noted: *"When I have three, four, or five students who have asked about the same problem, then I often go through it on the board. But it's often hard to know when that makes sense."* This validated the need for the system to actively detect clusters of requests. However, TAs emphasized that AI should serve as a transparent prompt for their judgment rather than an automated decision-maker, leading to the design principle of "Trust and Verify."

**Phase 5 and 6: Refinement and Naturalistic Evaluation.** Following usability refinements, the system was deployed in a *Python Programming* course. Observations confirmed that the technical architecture successfully handled real-time queue operations and was well-received by students for reducing physical waiting friction. However, the pilot highlighted that the value of algorithmic decision support is highly dependent on demand volume; in low-traffic sessions, the system lacked sufficient data density to generate meaningful pedagogical alerts, suggesting the tool is best suited for high-enrolment contexts.

# 4 Results

## 4.1 Requirements for Mindful TA Support

The first result of the study is a set of requirements that translates the qualitative findings from Phases 1–4 into a concrete design space for a queue-based decision support system. Across interviews, co-design, and theory-informed prototyping, 11 requirements were identified that connect technological functionality to pedagogical needs. Collectively, they show that useful TEL support in this context is not only a matter of faster queue administration, but of helping TAs recognize when to remain with one-to-one assistance and when to shift to more collective instructional action.

Three requirements became especially central. First, **R4 (Pattern Recognition)** captures the need to surface clusters of similar questions quickly enough to reduce the *detection lag* observed in current practice. Second, **R6 (Instructional Flexibility)** reflects that pedagogical timing is situational and cannot be fully automated without undermining TA agency. Third, **R10 (AI Transparency)** requires that any AI-generated suggestion remain inspectable through direct links to the underlying student entries. In combination, these requirements led to the core design principle of *transparency over automation*. Due to time and deployment constraints, **R1 (Busyness Transparency)**, **R7 (Psychology of Waits)**, and **R9 (Equity Monitoring)** were specified but not implemented in the final prototype (Table 3).

## 4.2 Prototype Outcomes

The second result is a functional prototype that operationalizes the identified requirements in a real-time classroom tool. The system combines a React frontend with a serverless AWS Amplify backend. AWS AppSync coordinates live queue updates, while Amazon Bedrock-powered services analyze queue state and uploaded course materials to generate pedagogical suggestions and post-session summaries. This architecture was sufficient to support live synchronization, persistence of queue state, and repeated AI analysis without introducing visible delay during pilot use (Fig. 1).

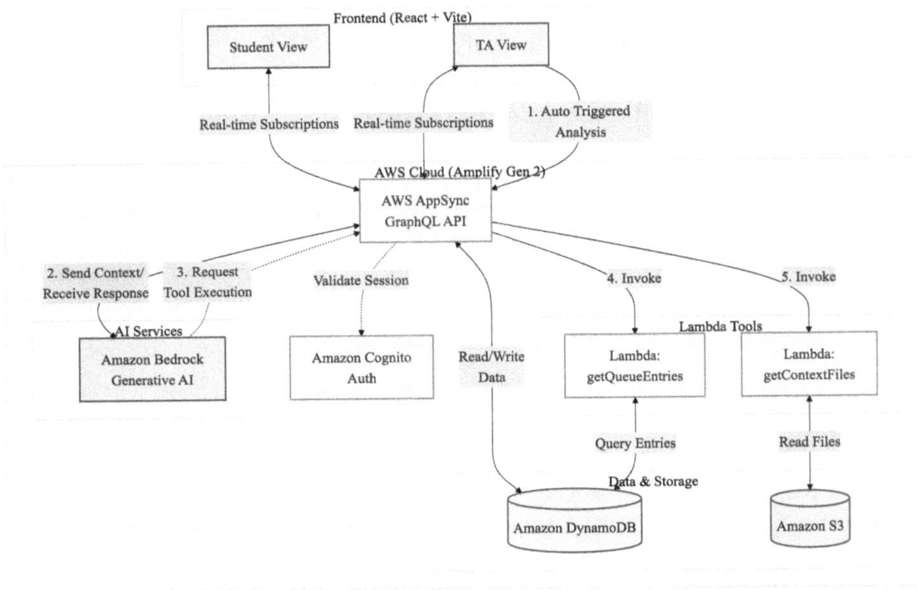


**Fig. 1.** High-level architecture of the Q-DSS prototype. The architecture combines real-time queue management with LLM-based analysis of queue state and course materials.

At the interface level, the most important outcome was the implementation of an *Assistant* view for TAs. Rather than automatically reordering the queue, the Assistant monitors changes in the queue and presents possible pedagogical opportunities, such as *grouping opportunity*, *mini-lecture opportunity (conceptual)*, or *mini-lecture opportunity (problem walkthrough)*. To preserve TA oversight, the interface presents a short recommendation, supporting reasoning, and highlighting the queue entries that triggered the suggestion. This implements R4, R6, and R10 simultaneously: pattern recognition is supported, but the TA remains responsible for deciding whether the recommendation is pedagogically appropriate in that moment.

**Table 3.** Identified requirements for the Queue-based Decision Support System.

| | Requirement | Rationale & main sources |
|---|---|---|
| R1 | **Busyness Transparency**: Provide overview of multiple simultaneous sessions to balance load. | Multi-room load imbalance and unequal TA busyness identified in interviews. Phase 1 + 4 & [12] |
| R2 | **Feedback**: Capture analytics to support post-session reflection for TAs and course responsibles. | TAs lack a structured upward feedback channel. Phase 1 + 2 & [8,19] |
| R3 | **Queue Transparency**: Display queue position to students to manage expectations, while keeping problem details private to reduce anxiety. | Students want position visibility but can fear peer exposure of their specific problems. Phase 1 & [9] |
| R4 | **Pattern Recognition**: Identify patterns in help requests to enable "mini-lectures" or group help, presented as suggestions requiring TA validation. | TAs express a desire to act on repeated questions but struggle to identify them in time. Phase 1 + 4 & [6] |
| R5 | **Fairness**: Prevent students with unique, non-groupable questions from being unfairly deprioritized. | Grouping must not disadvantage students whose questions cannot be clustered. Phase 1 & [15] |
| R6 | **Instructional Flexibility**: Suggest pedagogical actions but never prescribe them, preserving TA agency. | Applying PCK requires TA to judge timing and class readiness; prescriptive systems undermine this. Phase 2 + 4 & [18,21] |
| R7 | **Psychology of Waits**: Show estimated wait times to reduce the frustration of uncertain waits. | Known waits feel shorter than uncertain ones; reduces frustration and drop-off. Phase 2 & [12] |
| R8 | **Quality Input**: Secure queue position upon drafting (not submitting) to discourage rushed, low-quality descriptions. | Students game help-lists by reserving spots early; pre-secured positions improve description quality. Phase 1 contextual inquiry & [22] |
| R9 | **Equity Monitoring**: Provide real-time metrics (e.g., help-time distribution) to avoid unconscious bias. | FIFO ignores cumulative help-time & individual needs; real-time metrics enable proactive rebalancing. Phase 2 & [15] |
| R10 | **AI Transparency**: Summarise reasoning behind AI suggestions but always link to original student entries for verification. | TAs need both quick summaries and access to originals for a trust-and-verify workflow. Phase 4 Co-design |
| R11 | **Question Type Distinction**: Distinguish between exercise-specific and general conceptual questions in data and UI. | Conceptual questions leave TAs unprepared and may require preparation or different support mechanisms. Phase 4 Co-design |

The Assistant is implemented following a conversational chatbot pattern, in which the model receives (anonymized) updated queue states in real time and, if detected, responds with possible pedagogical opportunities and patterns. A system prompt details the LLM Assistant's task, possible types of recommendations, when not to make recommendations, guidelines, how and when to use lambda tools, and exact output formatting.

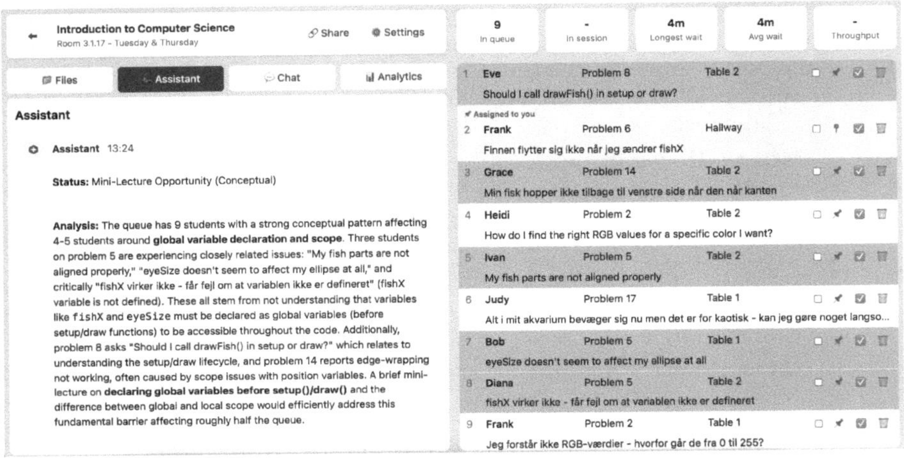


**Fig. 2.** TA main view combining live queue management with support tabs for files, Assistant recommendations, chat, and analytics.

In addition to the Assistant, the prototype implements core queue functionality for both students and TAs, including queue-position visibility, editable help requests, differentiation between conceptual and exercise-specific questions, file uploads for course context, and a basic analytics view for post-session reflection. The student interface was intentionally lightweight to reduce friction in live sessions, while the TA interface emphasized overview and rapid action.

Figure 2 shows how these elements are combined in the main TA workspace. This view is important because it illustrates the paper's central design claim: pedagogical support is embedded directly in the same interface used for operational queue management, rather than being separated into a post hoc dashboard or an external AI tool.

Several additional features were implemented, although they are not illustrated here. On the TA side, these include queue configuration options, entry assignment in multi-TA settings, bulk completion and deletion of queue entries, file upload for course-specific context, a course-aware chat interface, and an analytics tab for post-session reflection. Together, these features address more than just the core orchestration moment: they support setup before the session, coordination during the session, and reflection afterward.

On the student side, the system supports low-friction entry into the queue through a shared session link, editable help requests, visibility into queue position, and optional capture of the problem number and location. Student requests are tied to a browser-stored identifier rather than full authenticated profiles, reflecting the project's emphasis on privacy and low adoption friction. This was important to the design because the system's pedagogical value depends on students' willingness to articulate questions in real time, without incurring substantial overhead relative to hand-raising.

Not all identified requirements were achieved to the same level of maturity. The implemented prototype prioritizes features necessary to test the central research proposition of AI-supported pedagogical orchestration, whereas features such as cross-session busyness transparency, wait-time estimation, and equity monitoring were deferred because they require broader deployment contexts to evaluate meaningfully. This distinction is important for interpreting the artifact contribution: the prototype is best understood as a research-ready system focused on the key TEL question of how transparent AI support can augment TA decision-making in situ.

### 4.3 Pilot Deployment Findings

The third result concerns what the prototype could be validated to do in authentic teaching settings. Observation of a high-demand Python programming help session confirmed the problem framing: multiple students waited simultaneously, ordering was negotiated informally, and TAs were occupied nearly continuously, reinforcing the relevance of queue transparency and decision support when similar questions arise in parallel. The subsequent naturalistic deployments yielded more mixed results. The system ran in real sessions without disrupting established workflows, an important finding for TEL adoption; students entered meaningful help requests and TAs used the queue without training overhead. The deployments also surfaced practical refinements, including optional location input and notifications for requests added to an empty queue.

However, the core decision-support functionality could only be validated for *technical feasibility*, not pedagogical effectiveness. Both pilots had far lower demand than the observed session: 10 requests from roughly 25 students in a two-hour Python session, and 4 requests from 14 students in a 1.5-hour linear algebra session. Students rarely accumulated in the queue, so the system lacked the data density to generate meaningful suggestions. This is itself a substantive result: real-time orchestration support depends on sustained demand and is most relevant in high-enrolment settings where time-pressured TAs cannot detect patterns manually. Formative TA feedback nonetheless supported the intended human-AI collaboration model: TAs welcomed suggestions over prescriptions, and the highlighted links from recommendations to original queue entries supported verification. In low-demand settings, TAs continued to rely on proactive informal help, indicating the system should complement existing practices, with persistent LMS integration a more viable adoption path than explicit switching between hand-raising and system use.

Taken together, Q-DSS advances existing queue systems by providing validated requirements and design principles for AI-supported TA orchestration, and by demonstrating that real-time pedagogical suggestions can be implemented while preserving teacher agency through transparent, inspectable recommendations. What remains unvalidated is whether those suggestions improve instructional quality or reduce waiting time in genuinely high-demand deployments.

# 5 Discussion

This paper identifies real-time AI-augmented decision support and orchestration as a continuation of established research using queue-system data for post hoc analytics. The study is guided by the research question: *How can a queue-based decision support system (Q-DSS) be designed and evaluated to help teaching assistants manage resource allocation and identify pedagogical opportunities during high-demand CS exercise sessions?* To answer the research question, the paper makes 3 key contributions:

## 5.1 Problem Analysis and Requirements Identification

The first sub-aim investigated TAs' resource management and pedagogical challenges and identified requirements for an effective decision-support system. A key finding was the *detection lag problem*: TAs cannot recognize that multiple students are struggling with the same concept until they have helped several individually, unless students report it directly. This addresses a gap in existing queue systems, which manage logistics [8,11] but offer little pedagogical insight to help TAs apply PCK concepts and shift from individual help to other modes of explanation. Phase 4 showed that pattern detection alone is insufficient: TAs stressed the complexity of timing interventions, so the system should suggest rather than prescribe, keeping TAs in control under a "trust and verify" principle with access to original student inputs. Phase 6 confirmed that unclear waiting processes cause student frustration and adaptive behaviors, prompting a re-conceptualization of the queue from logistical tool to support for TA decision-making, captured in a model of four decision types (triage, pedagogical mode switching, scope, and time allocation) that positions the system as a step toward real-time pedagogical decision support.

## 5.2 Design and Development of Decision Support Features

The prototype demonstrates how the design principles and requirements from the combined methodology translate into working features, although balancing feature sophistication against development time proved challenging. The Assistant feature illustrates how participatory design shaped implementation: the Phase 4 co-design sessions showed that TAs need flexible engagement with suggestions, depending on their confidence and cognitive load. The design therefore highlights queue entries linked to each suggestion and offers both quick summaries and detailed reasoning. A TA already considering a mini-lecture can see at a glance how many students share the confusion, while a TA facing an unexpected suggestion can review the Assistant's reasoning against their own PCK and the original student entries.

The value of the system extends beyond queue management, supporting TAs' situated enactment of TPACK. TAs must rapidly interpret difficulties, relate to course content, and decide how to respond, e.g., through individual or group support, a shared discussion, or by introducing a technological tool. These decisions are difficult because information is often scattered across many help requests. The real promise of the system is to make the situation more inspectable and actionable for the TA. By aggregating, cueing, and linking AI-generated suggestions to students' entries, the system helps TAs see where students are struggling. This also suggests how the system should be evaluated. Beyond queue efficiency, future evaluation should ask whether the system gives TAs deeper insight into student concerns, helps them connect these concerns to relevant disciplinary knowledge, and provides appropriate tools and representations.

### 5.3 Evaluation of System Performance and AI-Enhanced Features

The prototype's impact on TA practices reveals a key dependence on sustained student engagement. In Phases 5 and 6, low demand for help limited the Assistant feature, which relies on active queue input for real-time decision support. Prior queue research focuses largely on high-demand contexts [8,11], so these findings highlight an under-explored limitation in low-demand settings. Nevertheless, the deployments showed the system integrates into TA-led sessions without disrupting existing practices, and positive responses from TAs and students confirmed its baseline logistical value [8,19]. Equity discussions further revealed TA caution towards automated monitoring, with a preference for systems that support rather than override pedagogical judgment [10]. The system's value appears highest under high demand, where time pressure prevents TAs from proactively supporting students and recognizing patterns across requests; under low demand, TAs provide such support naturally. Seamless integration into existing workflows (e.g., LMS platforms) could enable a self-regulating pattern in which students choose between direct interaction and the queue based on TA availability, reducing adoption friction [20]. Encouraging students to articulate questions while waiting would also improve data quality while promoting reflection and productive struggle [4].

## 6 Conclusion

Teaching assistants (TAs) in large computer science courses face high demand, with many students requiring simultaneous support during exercise sessions, yet often have limited pedagogical training and limited access to tools. Common ad hoc practices such as hand-raising or whiteboard help lists introduce classroom friction, create uncertainty about wait times, and offer little visibility into emerging pedagogical opportunities. Existing queue systems improve logistical coordination but offer limited support for pedagogical decision-making. This paper investigates real-time, AI-augmented decision support as an extension of prior work focused on post-hoc analytics.

The paper makes three contributions. First, it identifies 11 design requirements for TA decision support systems through an iterative, stakeholder-informed research process, highlighting principles such as transparency over automation and trust to preserve TA agency and support the application of Pedagogical Content Knowledge (PCK). Second, it presents a functional prototype demonstrating the feasibility of a web-based, LLM-powered decision-support system that integrates queue management, real-time pedagogical suggestions, a course-aware chatbot, and reflection reports. Third, it provides initial evaluation insights into system use in authentic TA-led sessions, highlighting both opportunities and constraints of AI-supported decision-making in classroom practice at scale in large university courses.

### Future Research

Future research will focus on the following three priorities. The first is to establish the deployment conditions under which Q-DSS earns its place: because real-time pattern detection depends on a steady stream of concurrent queries, future work must identify the help-seeking density below which the system's recommendations add little. The second is to evaluate recommendation quality directly by reporting the precision and recall of the query clustering against expert-labeled groupings, alongside the rate at which teaching assistants accept the system's suggestions during live sessions. The third is to test the system's effect through a controlled comparison, contrasting teaching-assistant triage decisions and student outcomes across sections that use Q-DSS and matched sections that do not. Pursuing these three questions would move Q-DSS from a feasibility demonstration to an evidence-based intervention.

## References

1. The 2020 scrum guide. https://scrumguides.org/scrum-guide.html. Accessed: 14-Oct-2025
2. Anderson, T., Shattuck, J.: Design-based research: a decade of progress in education research? Educ. Res. **41**(1), 16–25 (2012). https://doi.org/10.3102/0013189X11428813
3. Chi, M.T., Wylie, R.: The ICAP framework: linking cognitive engagement to active learning outcomes. Educ. Psychol. **49**(4), 219–243 (2014)
4. Freeman, S., et al.: Active learning increases student performance in science, engineering, and mathematics. Proc. Natl. Acad. Sci. **111**(23), 8410–8415 (2014)
5. Gao, Z., Lynch, C., Heckman, S., Barnes, T.: Automatically classifying student help requests: A multi-year analysis. Int. Educ. Data Min. Soc. (2021)
6. Hott, J.R., Floryan, M., Basit, N.: Towards more efficient office hours for large courses: Using cosine similarity to efficiently construct student help groups. In:

Proceedings of the 55th ACM Technical Symposium on Computer Science Education V. 2, pp. 1684–1685. SIGCSE 2024, Association for Computing Machinery, New York, NY, USA (2024). https://doi.org/10.1145/3626253.3635544
7. Van den Hoven, J.: Value sensitive design and responsible innovation. In: Owen, R., Bessant, J., Heintz, M. (eds.) Responsible Innovation: Managing the Responsible Emergence of Science and Innovation in Society, pp. 75–84. Wiley, New York (2013). https://doi.org/10.1002/9781118551424.ch4
8. Jensen, K., et al.: Adoption of an online queue app for higher education: a case study. In: 2019 ASEE Annual Conference & Exposition (2019)
9. Karabenick, S.A., Knapp, J.R.: Relationship of academic help seeking to the use of learning strategies and other instrumental achievement behavior in college students. J. Educ. Psychol. **83**(2), 221 (1991)
10. van Leeuwen, A., Strauß, S., Rummel, N.: Participatory design of teacher dashboards: navigating the tension between teacher input and theories on teacher professional vision. Front. Artif. Intell. **6**, 1039739 (2023)
11. Macwilliam, T., Malan, D.: Scaling office hours: managing live q&a in large courses (2012)
12. Maister, D.H., et al.: The psychology of waiting lines. Harvard Business School Boston (1984)
13. Markel, J.M., Guo, P.J.: Inside the mind of a cs undergraduate ta: a firsthand account of undergraduate peer tutoring in computer labs. In: Proceedings of the 52nd ACM Technical Symposium on Computer Science Education, pp. 502–508. SIGCSE '2021, Association for Computing Machinery, New York, NY, USA (2021). https://doi.org/10.1145/3408877.3432533
14. Mishra, P., Koehler, M.J.: Technological pedagogical content knowledge: a framework for teacher knowledge. Teach. Coll. Rec. **108**(6), 1017–1054 (2006)
15. Mussulman, D., et al.: Measuring impact: student and instructor experience using an online queue. In: 2020 ASEE Virtual Annual Conference Content Access (2020)
16. Qian, Y., Lehman, J.: Students' misconceptions and other difficulties in introductory programming: a literature review. ACM Trans. Comput. Educ. (TOCE) **18**(1), 1–24 (2017)
17. Schwaber, K.: Scrum development process. In: Business object design and implementation: OOPSLA'95 workshop proceedings 16 October 1995, Austin, Texas, pp. 117–134. Springer (1997)
18. Shulman, L.S.: Those who understand: knowledge growth in teaching. Educ. Res. **15**(2), 4–14 (1986)
19. Smith, A.J., Boyer, K.E., Forbes, J., Heckman, S., Mayer-Patel, K.: My digital hand: A tool for scaling up one-to-one peer teaching in support of computer science learning. In: Proceedings of the 2017 ACM SIGCSE Technical Symposium on Computer Science Education, pp. 549–554. SIGCSE '2017, Association for Computing Machinery, New York, NY, USA (2017). https://doi.org/10.1145/3017680.3017800
20. Tissenbaum, M., Slotta, J.D.: Developing a smart classroom infrastructure to support real-time student collaboration and inquiry: a 4-year design study. Instr. Sci. **47**(4), 423–462 (2019)
21. VanLehn, K.: The relative effectiveness of human tutoring, intelligent tutoring systems, and other tutoring systems. Educ. Psychol. **46**(4), 197–221 (2011)
22. Wang, K., Lawrence, R.: Helpme: student help seeking using office hours and email. In: Proceedings of the 55th ACM Technical Symposium on Computer Science Education V. 1, pp. 1388–1394 (2024)

23. Wang, K., Ramos, J., Lawrence, R.: Chated: a chatbot leveraging chatgpt for an enhanced learning experience in higher education. arXiv preprint arXiv:2401.00052 (2023)
24. Wang, K.S.: Transforming student support with AI: a retrieval-based generation framework for personalized support and faculty customization. Ph.D. thesis, University of British Columbia (2025)

# Are We Personalizing Learning? Adoption of Personalized Learning and the Role of Artificial Intelligence in Higher Education

Noura Joudieh[1(✉)], Nikleia Eteokleous[2], Ronan Champagnat[1], and Raquel Blave Gomez[3]

[1] L3i Laboratory, La Rochelle University, La Rochelle, France
{noura.joudieh,ronan.champagnat}@univ-lr.fr
[2] CIET, Frederick University, Limassol, Cyprus
n.eteokleous@frederick.ac.cy
[3] Catholic University of Valencia, Valencia, Spain
raquel.blave@ucv.es

**Abstract.** Personalized Learning (PL) is widely advocated in higher education, and Artificial Intelligence (AI) is increasingly positioned as its primary enabler. Yet empirical evidence on whether faculty members actually understand, adopt, and implement PL in practice, and whether AI meaningfully contributes to that adoption, remains scarce. This study investigates PL awareness, adoption, barriers, enablers, and AI for PL use among 85 higher education professionals across nine universities in nine European countries within the EU-CONEXUS alliance. A cross-sectional survey is analysed using descriptive statistics, non-parametric tests, and K-Means cluster analysis emerging three principal findings. First, while 64.7% of respondents had prior awareness of PL, only 57.6% actively applied it, and confidence in understanding PL was significantly associated with adoption, yet 25.0% of high-confidence respondents did not apply it, pointing to a gap between understanding and enactment. Second, AI use for PL was reported by 31.8% of respondents, with institutional AI policy being the strongest associated factor; yet 55.1% of PL adopters used no AI, indicating that PL and AI adoption are empirically decoupled. Third, cluster analysis identified five distinct faculty profile: the AI-Supported Practitioner, the Implicit Practitioner, the Committed Practitioner without AI, the PL-Disengaged Faculty, and the PL-Aware Non-Practitioner, revealing that non-adoption takes qualitatively different forms across institutional and attitudinal dimensions.

**Keywords:** Personalized Learning · Artificial Intelligence in Education · Faculty Profiles · Cluster Analysis · European higher education


J. Weidlich et al. (Eds.): EC-TEL 2026, LNCS 16905, pp. 283–298, 2027.
https://doi.org/10.1007/978-3-032-37979-5_20

## 1 Introduction

Higher education serves student populations characterised by considerable diversity in prior knowledge, learning pace, disciplinary background, and educational goals. Personalized Learning (PL) refers to instructional approaches in which content, pacing, feedback, and assessment are adapted to the individual characteristics and needs of each learner [11]. When enacted meaningfully, PL has been associated with improvements in academic performance, student engagement, and learning satisfaction in higher education [2,6]. The integration of Artificial Intelligence (AI) has intensified research interest in its scalable implementation, with AI-driven mechanisms increasingly presented as enabling conditions for automated learner profiling, adaptive content delivery, and personalised feedback [8,14,18].

What the research literature describes, however, does not necessarily reflect what takes place in classrooms. Whether higher education faculty are actually adopting PL strategies, and whether they hold a clear understanding of PL as a pedagogical concept before any question of adoption arises, are questions that remain empirically underexplored. The conditions shaping faculty practice, including disciplinary background, workload constraints, institutional policies, and readiness to modify established teaching approaches, can enable or constrain PL adoption independently of what the research literature proposes [5,7,17]. Furthermore, the prevailing framing in the literature positions AI as the primary object of study, with PL treated as one of its anticipated pedagogical benefits [12,16]. This framing does not address the perspective of an educator who begins from a pedagogical goal and considers whether AI has any role in reaching it.

The present study was designed to address these considerations empirically. It investigates the state of PL understanding and adoption among higher education faculty, and examines the role that AI plays in their practice and the conditions that shape it. AI is treated as a contextual variable whose presence or absence in faculty PL practice is to be observed and explained, while PL adoption remains the primary construct. The study was conducted across nine universities in nine European countries within the EU-CONEXUS alliance[1], collecting responses from 85 higher education professionals spanning multiple roles, disciplines, and institutional contexts. Throughout this paper, the term *faculty* refers to any higher education professional holding a role in teaching, curriculum design, or academic strategy, regardless of contractual or hierarchical status. This work is guided by three research questions.

- **RQ1:** To what extent do higher education faculty demonstrate awareness and understanding of Personalized Learning, and to what extent do they adopt it in practice, and what explains the gap between the two?
- **RQ2:** What role does AI play in supporting or constraining PL adoption, and what factors characterize faculty who use AI for PL versus those who do not?

[1] About EU-CONEXUS.

- **RQ3:** What distinct faculty profiles emerge from the intersection of PL awareness, adoption, and AI use, and what characteristics define each profile?

The remainder of this paper is organised as follows. Section 2 situates the study within related work, Sect. 3 describes the research design and analytical approach, Sect. 4 proceeds to present the findings, Sect. 5 interprets the findings and their implications for institutional practice, and finally Sects. 6 and 7 address limitations and conclusions respectively.

## 2 Related Work

Despite its documented potential, a persistent gap exists between the theoretical promotion of PL and its enacted practice. Studies examining the teacher perspective directly find limited PL awareness and low uptake of PL tools in authentic classroom settings. [20] conducted focus groups with 56 teachers and identified a recurring divergence between how PL is framed in research and how teachers understand its implementation demands, noting four recurring challenges including the gap between theory and practice and varying understandings of what PL implementation requires. While [10] surveyed 272 teachers across 41 learner-centered schools in the United States and found misalignment between advocated PL components and those actually enacted, observing that paradigm change demands continuous systemic effort across the educational environment. Both studies are limited to K-12 contexts within a single country and do not examine AI as a variable in adoption decisions.

Systematic reviews identify barriers to PL operating at technological, pedagogical, and psychological levels. In [4], 68 empirical studies were analysed and found a shift from technological to pedagogical barriers as educational level increases, with psychological barriers persisting across all contexts. Their complementary review of 102 studies on AI-driven PL [3] identified educator competency development, institutional support, and governance frameworks as necessary conditions for PL to move from research proposition to classroom practice. These reviews establish what conditions should be present but do not measure whether they exist among practitioners.

On the question of AI specifically, [16] surveyed 250 faculty members across QS-ranked institutions and found that AI awareness, performance expectancy, and perceived risk are primary determinants of AI adoption in higher education, with PL treated as one among several anticipated benefits. At a larger scale, [1] examined AI adoption across 508 participants from 259 institutions in 19 MENA countries and found that institutional policy clarity was significantly associated with AI integration, and that AI adoption was still at an early stage in 43.9% of institutions. While this study establishes multi-institutional evidence on AI adoption patterns, it examines AI as the primary phenomenon and does not address PL adoption as a distinct construct.

Faculty Profiling methods have been used to understand how educators relate to new pedagogical and technological paradigms. For example, [19] surveyed 370 primary and secondary teachers on their use and perceptions of digital PL tools and identified three distinct teacher clusters through cluster analysis. All three clusters showed positive perceptions toward PL, yet actual reported use varied considerably across clusters, demonstrating that positive attitudes toward PL do not produce homogeneous adoption behaviour. This is the methodologically closest prior study to the present work, yet it is limited to K-12 contexts, covers digital PL tools specifically, and does not include AI use as a clustering dimension. While [12] applied latent class cluster analysis to 122 higher education faculty and identified four profiles around AI self-efficacy: optimistic, critical, critically reflected, and neutral. Their study positions AI adoption as the primary phenomenon and treats PL as one item among several perceived AI benefits. In [9], six teacher profiles were derived using latent profile analysis on student-centered pedagogical perspectives and found that faculty development programs were insufficiently tailored to differentiated practitioner needs. Related work has applied K-Means clustering to derive teacher digital competence profiles from survey data [15] and student AI literacy profiles [13].

Taken together, this body of work reveals three gaps that the present study addresses. Existing faculty profiles in this domain are organised around AI self-efficacy or digital competence rather than PL adoption behaviour, and PL adoption and AI use have not been examined as co-occurring dimensions of a single typology. Empirical evidence on PL adoption among higher education faculty is furthermore concentrated in single-country or single-institution contexts, leaving adoption patterns and barriers across national and institutional settings under-explored. The present study contributes a five-dimension behavioural typology, derived from a multi-institutional, multi-national European sample, that places PL adoption at the center and treats AI use as one of its defining dimensions.

## 3 Methodology

This section describes the research design adopted to investigate how higher education faculty understand, adopt, and enact PL, and whether and how AI plays a role in that process. We detail the data collection procedure, the structure and rationale of the survey instrument, the sample characteristics, and the analytical pipeline followed to produce the findings reported in Sect. 4.

### 3.1 Questionnaire Design

The questionnaire was structured around a clear operational definition of Personalized Learning provided at the outset, ensuring all respondents shared a common conceptual reference before answering. This was particularly important given the known variability in how PL is understood across disciplines and institutional contexts. It consisted of four main blocks with questions (Qs):

- **Contextual variables** (4Qs): respondent role, level of contribution to teaching or curriculum design, primary discipline, and university affiliation.

- **PL awareness and understanding** (5Qs): prior familiarity with the PL concept, self-reported confidence in understanding it (five-point Likert scale), recognition of PL-aligned practices in one's own teaching, and perceived institutional training and policy support for PL.
- **PL adoption**: adoption state (3Qs), **if yes**, motivations for adoption (4Qs), current use of PL strategies, level and subject area of implementation, type of strategy employed, **if no**, barriers preventing adoption (3Qs), prior attempts, and support or resources needed to adopt PL in the future.
- **AI use for PL**: whether AI-based tools are currently used to support PL (2Qs), **if yes** (4Qs), which tools are used, in what ways they contribute to PL delivery, and the perceived overall effect of AI on PL practice. **If not**, AI barriers (3Qs) for non-AI users, the main reasons for non-adoption, future interest in using AI for PL, and the type of support or training that would facilitate adoption. Institutional AI policy context was also captured.

The questionnaire followed a conditional branching structure: respondents who reported applying PL were directed to adoption-specific items, while those who did not were directed to barrier items; AI users and non-users were similarly directed to distinct item sets. For most items, a predefined set of answer options was provided, grounded in the barrier and enabler categories identified in the literature [4]. Every closed item included a free-text option for responses beyond those listed, and several items permitted multiple selections.

### 3.2 Data Collection and Ethical Considerations

Data were collected through an online questionnaire[2] developed and distributed using the European Commission's *EUSurvey* to teaching staff, heads of department, course coordinators, and pedagogical support staff across all nine partner universities of the EU-CONEXUS alliance. Participation was entirely voluntary. The questionnaire was designed to be fully anonymous: no data enabling the direct identification of respondents were collected, and all responses were analyzed in an aggregated manner. The survey introduction explicitly stated the following data protection notice: *"This questionnaire is designed to be anonymous. No data enabling the direct identification of respondents are collected, and responses are analysed in an aggregated manner. Technical data necessary for the operation of the EUSurvey platform may be processed by the European Commission in accordance with Regulation (EU) 2018/1725 on the protection of personal data by EU institutions (General Data Protection Regulation—GDPR)."*

### 3.3 Analytical Approach

**Data Processing:**The study collected responses from 85 higher education professionals across nine partner universities spanning nine European countries. All 85 submitted responses were retained for analysis, including those from respondents who reported no direct involvement in teaching or curriculum decisions.

[2] Questionnaire available here.

Respondents in administrative, management, or strategic planning roles contribute to the institutional conditions that shape PL adoption through policy frameworks, support structures, and resource allocation thus their perspectives are relevant to the research questions addressed.

Figure 1 presents the distribution of respondents across three dimensions. **Role**: participants can hold multiple roles, the sample was dominated by teaching staff (n=69, 81.2%), with additional representation from course coordinators (n=14, 16.5%), heads of department (n=11, 12.9%), administrative or management staff involved in academic strategy (n=10, 11.8%), and pedagogical support or instructional designers (n=5, 5.9%). **Discipline**: the most represented were Education and Pedagogy and Computer Science and Information Technology (n=15 each, 17.6%), followed by Economics and Business (n=14, 16.5%) and Humanities (n=11, 12.9%). **Affiliation**: respondent distribution across the nine institutions was unequal, with individual institutional shares ranging from 3.5% to 27.1%. The sample is not designed for statistical generalisation at the institutional level, yet the multi-institutional and multi-disciplinary coverage supports the exploratory, cross-contextual analysis pursued here.

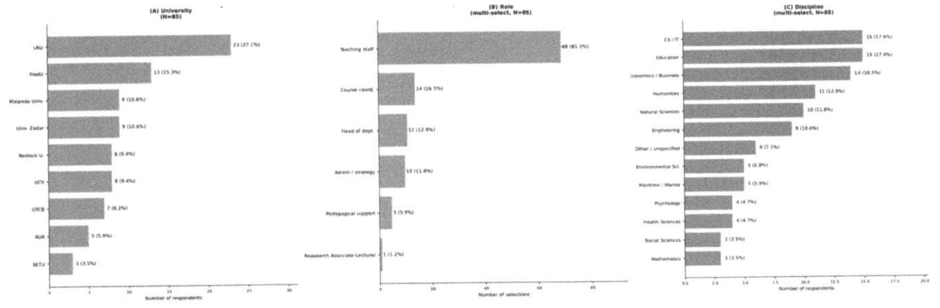


**Fig. 1.** Sample description across University, Role and Discipline (N=85). Role and Discipline are multi-select variables; percentages may exceed 100%.

**Descriptive and Inferential Analysis:** To address RQ1 and RQ2, frequency distributions and proportions were computed for all categorical items and means with standard deviations for the confidence measure. Normality of the confidence variable was assessed using the Shapiro-Wilk test; given the bounded, discrete nature of a five-point Likert scale and unequal group sizes, non-parametric tests were adopted throughout. Associations between categorical variables were examined using chi-square tests of independence, with Fisher's exact test applied where any expected cell frequency fell below five. Cramér's $V$ was computed as an effect size measure for all chi-square results. Group differences on the ordinal confidence variable were examined using the Mann-Whitney $U$ test, with rank-biserial correlation $r$ as the effect size. All tests were conducted at $\alpha = .05$; effect sizes are reported alongside all $p$-values given the exploratory nature of the study.

**Cluster Analysis:** To address RQ3, K-Means cluster analysis was applied to five encoded features capturing PL awareness, confidence in understanding PL, recognition of PL in practice, PL adoption status, and AI use for PL. Cluster analysis is an established method for deriving user profiles from survey data in educational contexts and has been applied to identify learner profiles, teacher digital competence profiles, and faculty AI adoption profiles [12,13,15].

**Open-Ended Response Analysis:** Open-ended responses from PL barrier, AI non-adoption, and general comment fields were examined qualitatively to further characterise the derived faculty profiles, with particular attention to the nature of non-adoption and the attitudes expressed toward AI use in teaching.

# 4 Implementation and Findings

## 4.1 RQ1: Adoption of PL

**PL Awareness and Institutional Context:** Prior to the questionnaire, 55 respondents (64.7%) had heard the PL term, 13 (15.3%) were uncertain, and 17 (20.0%) had not encountered it. Self-reported confidence yielded a mean of 3.29 ($SD = 1.17$), with 47.1% scoring at or above 4, 29.4% at 3, and 23.5% at or below 2. When presented with the operational PL definition, 45 respondents (52.9%) recognised PL-aligned strategies in their own teaching, 20 (23.5%) were unsure, and 20 (23.5%) did not. Institutional support was limited and widely uncertain: only 9.4% had received internal PL training and 14.1% external training, while 37.6% could not confirm whether internal training existed at their institution. Regarding institutional policy, 17.6% confirmed a PL policy, 29.4% reported none, and 52.9% were uncertain. Among those who assessed policy impact, 36.5% reported it facilitated PL practice and 14.1% reported it hindered it.

**PL Adoption: The Gap with Awareness** Of the 85 respondents, 49 (57.6%) applied PL strategies, 15 (17.6%) planned to do so, and 21 (24.7%) did not apply any PL strategies. For the gap analysis, the latter two groups were combined into a non-adopter category (n=36, 42.4%).

The primary analytical finding for RQ1 is the confidence-intention gap. Among respondents with high confidence in understanding PL (scores 4–5), 75.0% applied PL strategies, but 25.0% did not, despite their self-assessed understanding. PL confidence was significantly higher among adopters (median = 4.0, $M = 3.65$) than non-adopters (median = 3.0, $M = 2.81$), with a medium-to-large effect ($U = 1259.5$, $p < .001$, $|r| = .428$). Prior awareness of the PL term showed a small but significant association with adoption ($V = .239$, $p = .028$). Figure 2 illustrates the gap across confidence groups.

**Among the 49 PL Adopters,** PL was most commonly applied within specific learning activities and tasks (n=39, 79.6%), followed by course or module level (n=25, 51.0%) and formative assessment or feedback (n=15, 30.6%). Only 3 respondents (6.1%) applied PL at degree program level, indicating that implementation was predominantly task-level rather than structurally embedded. The

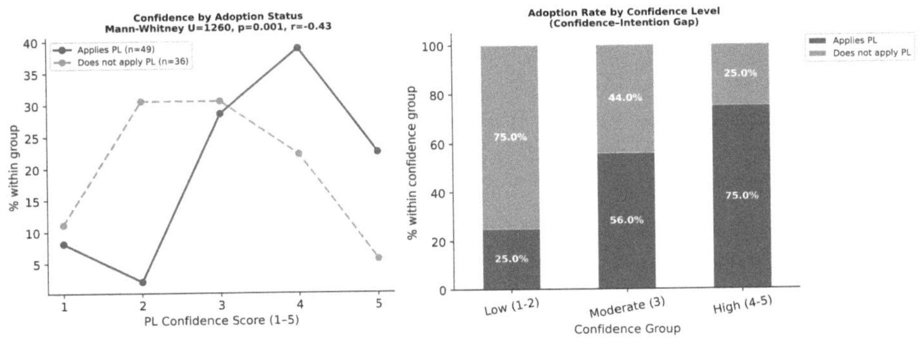


**Fig. 2.** Left: PL confidence score distributions by adoption status. Right: PL adoption rate by confidence group, illustrating the confidence–intention gap.

predominant strategy type was adaptive and responsive to ongoing student needs (n=30, 61.2%), followed by integration into course design from the outset (n=19, 38.8%) and informal or intuitive application (n=11, 22.4%). The primary motivations were improving student engagement (n=43, 87.8%), improving learning outcomes (n=33, 67.3%), and addressing diverse learning needs (n=31, 63.3%). Institutional requirement was cited by only 2 respondents (4.1%), indicating that adoption was predominantly self-motivated.

**Among the 36 PL Non-adopters,** the three most prevalent barriers were time and workload constraints (n=19, 52.8%), lack of training or know-how (n=16, 44.4%), and lack of institutional support (n=12, 33.3%). Six respondents (16.7%) were not convinced of PL's effectiveness. Notably, 63.9% had never attempted PL and only 13.9% had tried and stopped. The most requested enablers were institutional training or workshops and practical examples or templates of PL practice (both n=23, 63.9%), followed by more time or a smaller student-teacher ratio (n=19, 52.8%).

### 4.2 RQ2: AI for PL

Of the 85 respondents, 27 (31.8%) reported currently using AI tools to support PL, 54 (63.5%) did not, and 4 (4.7%) were uncertain. Non-users and uncertain respondents were combined into a single non-user group (n=58, 68.2%) for the characterisation analysis, as neither group was actively applying AI for PL. Only 21 respondents (24.7%) confirmed the existence of an institutional policy on AI use in teaching, while 43.5% reported no such policy and 31.8% were uncertain.

**Among the 27 AI Users**, use was predominantly minimal (n=14, 51.9%) or moderate (n=12, 44.4%), with only one respondent reporting extensive integration. LLM-based assistants such as ChatGPT dominated tool selection (n=24, 88.9%), and content creation was by far the primary application, reported by 26 users (96.3%), followed by automating personalised feedback (n=8, 29.6%), out-of-classroom support (n=5, 18.5%), and tracking student progress (n=4, 14.8%). Overall, 92.5% assessed AI as having a positive effect on their PL practice: 48.1% described it as helpful but not essential and 44.4% reported that it significantly improved their PL efforts.

**Among the 58 Non-users**, ethical concerns and bias constituted the leading reported barrier (n=24, 41.4%), followed by lack of confidence in using AI (n=15, 25.9%), insufficient institutional support (n=11, 19.0%), unfamiliarity with tools (n=9, 15.5%), and no perceived added value (n=9, 15.5%). Despite current non-use, 77.6% expressed openness to future AI adoption: 32.8% definitely and 44.8% conditionally on receiving training or guidance. Only 8.6% expressed no interest. The most requested forms of support were hands-on training with specific tools (n=37, 63.8%), discipline-specific examples of successful use (n=36, 62.1%), guidance on ethical AI use (n=33, 56.9%), and access to ready-made content or templates (n=18, 31.0%).

**AI for PL Users from Non-users** are characterized by four conducted tests. PL adoption status was significantly associated with AI use, with a medium effect ($V = .304$): 44.9% of PL adopters used AI, compared to 13.9% of non-adopters. However, the majority of PL adopters (55.1%) did not use AI, demonstrating that PL adoption and AI adoption are empirically decoupled. PL confidence was significantly higher among AI users than non-users ($U = 1048.0$, $p = .010$, $|r| = .338$). The strongest institutional factor was the presence of an AI policy: 61.9% of respondents in institutions with a clear AI policy used AI for PL, compared to 21.9% in institutions without one ($\chi^2(1) = 9.916$, $p = .002$, $V = .342$). Institutional PL training was not significantly associated with AI use (Fisher's exact, $p = .258$), though the small number of respondents who had received training (n=8) limits the interpretability of this result. Figure 3 illustrates the two key associations: AI use by PL adoption status and PL confidence distributions by AI use group.

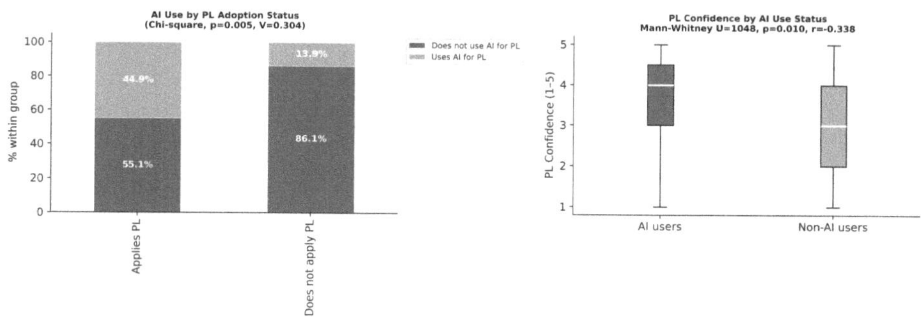


**Fig. 3.** Left: AI use rate by PL adoption status (Chi-square, $p = .005$, $V = .304$). Right: PL confidence distributions for AI users versus non-users (Mann-Whitney U, $p = .010$, $|r| = .338$).

### 4.3 Faculty Profiles for PL and AI-Supported PL Adoption

K-Means clustering was applied to five encoded features capturing PL awareness, confidence, recognition, adoption status, and AI use. Features were encoded on a common ordinal scale and standardised using $z$-score normalisation. The confidence variable was recoded onto a three-level ordinal scale (low: 1–2; moderate: 3; high: 4–5), a mapping selected by comparing silhouette scores across three candidate schemes. Silhouette scores were computed for $k = 2$ to $k = 7$; $k = 5$ produced the highest score and was retained. Table 1 presents the mean encoded feature values per cluster, and Fig. 4 shows the normalised profile shapes as a radar chart. Five profiles were identified, with sizes ranging from 11 to 26 respondents. Roles and disciplines were distributed across all five profiles without a clear pattern of differentiation: teaching staff constituted the dominant role in every cluster (63.6%–92.3%), and no discipline was concentrated in any single profile. These dimensions are therefore not discussed as distinguishing characteristics. The resulting 5 profiles are:

**Table 1.** Cluster Means on Encoded Features (0–2 scale)

| Profile | N (%) | Heard | Conf. | Recog. | Applies | AI use |
|---|---|---|---|---|---|---|
| C0: AI-Supported Practitioner | 26 (30.6%) | 1.81 | 1.77 | 1.81 | 1.81 | 1.88 |
| C1: Implicit Practitioner | 13 (15.3%) | 0.46 | 0.54 | 1.38 | 1.62 | 0.54 |
| C2: Committed Practitioner (No AI) | 21 (24.7%) | 2.00 | 1.57 | 1.76 | 1.95 | 0.00 |
| C3: PL-Disengaged Faculty | 11 (12.9%) | 0.09 | 0.55 | 0.27 | 0.00 | 0.18 |
| C4: PL-Aware Non-Practitioner | 14 (16.5%) | 1.93 | 0.93 | 0.36 | 0.29 | 0.00 |

No=0, Maybe/Uncertain/Low=1, Yes/High=2 for all encoded features.

**C0—AI-Supported PL Practitioner (n=26, 30.6%).** The only profile in which PL practice and AI use co-occur. Awareness is high (80.8%) and mean confidence is the highest across all profiles ($M = 4.04$). Nearly all members apply PL (80.8%) and 88.5% use AI to support it, predominantly through LLM-based assistants for content creation (87.0%). The majority described AI as helpful but not essential (52.2%), while 43.5% reported significant improvement in their PL efforts. External PL training was more prevalent here than in any other profile (34.6%), and an institutional AI policy was present for 42.3% of members, the highest proportion across all profiles.

**C1—Implicit PL Practitioner (n=13, 15.3%).** Members have largely not heard of PL (0.0% of Yes responses, only 'No' and 'Maybe') and report the lowest mean confidence ($M = 2.23$), yet 61.5% apply PL strategies and 46.2% recognise PL-aligned practices in their teaching. Practice precedes formal awareness of the concept rather than following from it. No member received internal or external PL training (0.0% for both). AI use is low (23.1%), and free-text responses among non-AI users cited environmental sustainability concerns and scepticism about AI's societal impact as reasons for deliberate non-adoption.

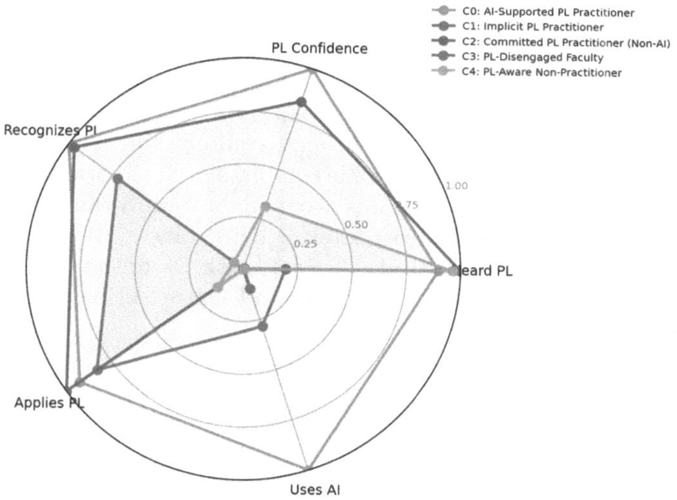


**Fig. 4.** Radar chart of normalised feature means per cluster (0 = lowest, 1 = highest across clusters). Each axis represents one clustering feature.

**C2—Committed PL Practitioner, Non-AI (n=21, 24.7%).** Every member applies PL (95.2%) and every member reports zero AI use (0.0%). Awareness is universal (100%) and confidence is high ($M$ = 3.76). This profile constitutes the strongest empirical evidence for the decoupling of PL and AI adoption: full PL practice is achieved without any AI involvement. Ethical concerns were the most cited reason for AI non-adoption (47.6%), followed by insufficient institutional support (28.6%). Notably, 80.9% expressed openness to future AI adoption, indicating that current non-use reflects absent institutional conditions rather than principled rejection.

**C3—PL-Disengaged Faculty (n=11, 12.9%).** Neither prior awareness (0.0%), practice (0.0%), nor recognition (0.0%) of PL is present. Mean confidence is low ($M$ = 2.27) and no member received PL training. Lack of training or know-how and not being convinced of PL's effectiveness were each cited by 36.4% as barriers, and 72.7% had never attempted PL. Free-text responses attributed disengagement to structural constraints: large cohort sizes, rigid curricular requirements, and insufficient time, indicating that this profile reflects contextual obstacles rather than attitudinal resistance.

**C4—PL-Aware Non-practitioner (n=14, 16.5%).** Awareness is high (92.9%) but confidence is moderate ($M$ = 3.00), and neither PL application (0.0%) nor recognition in practice (7.1%) is observed. No member uses AI for PL. Time and workload constraints and lack of training or know-how were each cited by 57.1% as barriers, and no member had received institutional PL training. Free-text responses in the AI barrier fields revealed a qualitatively distinct stance: two respondents explicitly rejected AI involvement in PL on grounds of student autonomy and algorithmic dependency, indicating that for a subset of this profile, non-adoption of AI reflects a pedagogical position rather than a training or access issue.

Table 2 provides a consolidated cross-profile comparison. Two structural observations warrant emphasis: institutional training and AI policy are exclusively concentrated in C0, the only profile combining full PL practice with AI use, suggesting that institutional conditions accumulate toward the highest adoption state rather than distributing across intermediate stages. The two non-adopter profiles (C3 and C4) are qualitatively distinct, with C3 reflecting structural disengagement in the absence of PL exposure and C4 reflecting a confidence gap despite near-universal awareness.

**Table 2.** Cross-Profile Comparison on Key Dimensions

| **Dimension** | **C0** *AI-Supp.* | **C1** *Implicit* | **C2** *Committed* | **C3** *Disengaged* | **C4** *Aware Non-Prac.* |
|---|---|---|---|---|---|
| N (%) | 26 (30.6%) | 13 (15.3%) | 21 (24.7%) | 11 (12.9%) | 14 (16.5%) |
| % Heard PL | 80.8 | 0.0 | 100.0 | 0.0 | 92.9 |
| Mean confidence (1–5) | 4.04 | 2.23 | 3.76 | 2.27 | 3.00 |
| % Recognises PL | 80.8 | 46.2 | 81.0 | 0.0 | 7.1 |
| % Applies PL | 80.8 | 61.5 | 95.2 | 0.0 | 0.0 |
| % Uses AI for PL | 88.5 | 23.1 | 0.0 | 9.1 | 0.0 |
| % Internal training | 15.4 | 0.0 | 19.0 | 0.0 | 0.0 |
| % External training | 34.6 | 0.0 | 14.3 | 0.0 | 0.0 |
| % Inst. AI policy (Yes) | 42.3 | 15.4 | 14.3 | 9.1 | 28.6 |
| Top PL barrier | Time | Time | Time | Training / Not convinced | Time / Training |
| Top AI barrier | Ethics | Ethics | Ethics | Ethics / No value | Confidence |

## 5 Discussion

The data shows that prior awareness of PL and self-reported confidence in understanding it were significantly associated with adoption, yet among respondents with high confidence, 25.0% did not apply PL. Alongside this, only 9.4% had received institutional PL training. Profile C4 illustrates this pattern: near-universal awareness of PL coexists with zero adoption and an absence of institutional training. These findings are consistent with the view that awareness of a concept alone does not produce its enactment, and suggest that access to training may be insufficient if it does not support faculty in translating PL understanding into practice.

Profile C1 identifies a faculty group practising PL without recognising it as such. This observation carries a methodological implication: self-report surveys that assess PL prevalence through vocabulary recognition may systematically undercount actual practice. Future instruments assessing PL adoption may benefit from measuring enacted behaviour rather than familiarity with the concept.

Profile C2, in which 95.2% of members apply PL with zero AI involvement, shows that PL does not inherently require AI. The finding that 55.1% of PL adopters overall used no AI further challenges the framing, common in the literature [3,12], that AI is a natural driver of PL at scale. The data suggest that PL practice and AI adoption are empirically separable, and that PL adoption tends to precede rather than follow from AI use. This is consistent with a sequencing interpretation: building faculty capacity for PL practice may be a more productive institutional starting point than introducing AI tools in the absence of that foundation.

The presence of an institutional AI policy was the strongest factor associated with AI use for PL ($V = .342$, $p = .002$), stronger than both PL adoption status and PL confidence. Among respondents in institutions with a clear AI policy, 61.9% used AI for PL, compared to 21.9% in institutions without one, suggesting that institutional governance conditions play a meaningful role in shaping individual AI adoption decisions.

The five profiles suggest qualitatively different institutional needs. Faculty with no prior PL awareness or practice may require foundational exposure alongside structural conditions that make experimentation feasible (C3). Those who are aware of PL but have not yet enacted it may benefit from structured implementation guidance rather than further conceptual introduction (C4). Those who already apply PL-aligned strategies without recognising them as such may be better served by recognition of existing practice than by awareness campaigns (C1). For those who practise PL without AI and have expressed conditional openness to future adoption, institutional ethical frameworks and data privacy confirmations may constitute a more relevant enabling condition than tool access alone (C2). The finding that PL confidence did not differ significantly across institutions (Kruskal-Wallis, $p = .136$) or faculty roles ($p = .789$) suggests that these differentiated needs are distributed across the alliance rather than concentrated in specific institutions or roles.

## 6 Limitations and Future Work

In acknowledging the limitations of this study, we list the following. First, all data are self-reported: PL practice is self-assessed rather than observed, and the Implicit Practitioner profile (C1) rests on respondents' self-recognition of PL-aligned strategies after reading a definition. Whether their practice constitutes PL as defined in the literature cannot be verified from survey data alone. Second, the sample of 85 respondents is unevenly distributed across nine institutions, limiting per-institution inference and statistical power for subgroup analyses, particularly for the smallest cluster (C3, n=11). Third, the study relies on a single instrument; triangulation with observation or interview data would provide a more complete account of the attitudinal dimensions identified through open-ended response analysis.

Future work aims to address these limitations in three directions. Expanding the sample through additional partner universities and longitudinal follow-up, enabling the observation of profile transitions over time and support per-institution comparison. A mixed-methods extension involving semi-structured interviews with representative members of each profile, particularly C1 and C3, would provide deeper characterisation of the mechanisms underlying tacit adoption and structural disengagement. Finally, applying the five-feature profiling methodology to other European university networks and non-European higher education contexts would test the generalizability of the typology.

## 7 Conclusion

This study examined PL awareness, adoption, and AI use among 85 faculty across nine universities in nine European countries of the EU-CONEXUS alliance. Five empirically grounded faculty profiles were identified, revealing that PL adoption is not a single continuum but a set of qualitatively distinct states requiring differentiated institutional responses. Three findings extend the existing literature. PL and AI adoption are empirically decoupled: full PL practice exists without AI involvement, and PL practice is a prerequisite for AI-for-PL adoption rather than the reverse. A substantial share of faculty practise PL without recognising it as such, indicating that awareness-based instruments underestimate actual prevalence. And faculty awareness of PL does not translate to practice, suggesting that training access alone may be insufficient to produce adoption. To our knowledge, this is the first empirically derived faculty typology for PL adoption with AI use in European higher education. By grounding five profiles in institutional context and mapping each to a differentiated intervention strategy, this work provides an evidence-based foundation for network-level faculty development policy and aims for broader application across European higher education.

## References

1. Al-Zahrani, A.M., Alasmari, T.M.: A comprehensive analysis of AI adoption, implementation strategies, and challenges in higher education across the middle east and north Africa (Mena) region. Educ. Inf. Technol. **30**, 11339–11389 (2025). https://doi.org/10.1007/s10639-024-13300-y
2. Alamri, H., Lowell, V., Watson, W., Watson, S.L.: Using personalized learning as an instructional approach to motivate learners in online higher education: learner self-determination and intrinsic motivation. J. Res. Technol. Educ. **52**(3), 322–352 (2020). https://doi.org/10.1080/15391523.2020.1728449
3. Barrera Castro, G.P., Chiappe, A., Becerra Rodríguez, D.F., Sepulveda, F.G.: Harnessing ai for education 4.0: Drivers of personalized learning. Electr. J. E-Learning **22**(5), 01–14 (2024). 10.34190/ejel.22.5.3467
4. Barrera Castro, G.P., Chiappe, A., Ramírez-Montoya, M.S., Alcántar Nieblas, C.: Key barriers to personalized learning in times of artificial intelligence: a literature review. Applied Sciences **15**(6) (2025). https://doi.org/10.3390/app15063103
5. Bishop, P.A., et al.: Teacher roles in personalized learning environments. Elem. Sch. J. **121**(2), 311–336 (2020). https://doi.org/10.1086/711079

6. du Plooy, E., Casteleijn, D., Franzsen, D.: Personalized adaptive learning in higher education: a scoping review of key characteristics and impact on academic performance and engagement. Heliyon **10**(21), e39630 (2024). https://doi.org/10.1016/j.heliyon.2024.e39630
7. Kallio, J.M., Halverson, R.: Distributed leadership for personalized learning. J. Res. Technol. Educ. **52**(3), 371–390 (2020). https://doi.org/10.1080/15391523.2020.1734508
8. Kamalov, F., Santandreu Calonge, D., Gurrib, I.: New era of artificial intelligence in education: towards a sustainable multifaceted revolution. Sustainability **15**(16) (2023). 10.3390/su151612451
9. Leatemia, L.D., Susilo, A.P., Donkers, J., Van Merrienboer, J.J.G.: Developing student-centred perspectives in PBL: how teacher profiles reveal educational needs for faculty development programmes. BMC Med. Educ. **23**(580) (2023). 10.1186/s12909-023-04538-0
10. Lee, D., Huh, Y., Lin, C.Y., Reigeluth, C.M.: Personalized learning practice in U.S. learner-centered schools. Contemporary Educ. Technol. **14**(4), ep385 (2022). https://doi.org/10.30935/cedtech/12330
11. Li, K.C., Wong, B.T.M.: Features and trends of personalised learning: a review of journal publications from 2001 to 2018. Interact. Learn. Environ. **29**(2), 182–195 (2020). https://doi.org/10.1080/10494820.2020.1811735
12. Mah, D.K., Groß, N.: Artificial intelligence in higher education: exploring faculty use, self-efficacy, distinct profiles, and professional development needs. Int. J. Educ. Technol. Higher Educ. **21**(58) (2024). https://doi.org/10.1186/s41239-024-00490-1
13. Medina-Gual, L., Parejo, J.L.: University students' engagement with artificial intelligence: a cluster analysis of learner profiles in AI literacy. Technol. Knowl. Learn. **31**, 291–309 (2026). https://doi.org/10.1007/s10758-025-09926-7
14. Naseer, F., Khan, M.N., Tahir, M., Addas, A., Aejaz, S.H.: Integrating deep learning techniques for personalized learning pathways in higher education. Heliyon **10**(11), e32628 (2024). https://doi.org/10.1016/j.heliyon.2024.e32628
15. Pérez-Calderón, E., Prieto-Ballester, J.M., Miguel-Barrado, V.: Analysis of digital competence for spanish teachers at pre-university educational key stages during covid-19. Int. J. Envir. Res. Public Health **18**(15) (2021). https://doi.org/10.3390/ijerph18158093
16. Rahiman, H.U., Kodikal, R.: Revolutionizing education: artificial intelligence empowered learning in higher education. Cogent Educ. **11**(1) (2024). https://doi.org/10.1080/2331186X.2023.2293431
17. Seo, K., Yoo, M., Dodson, S., Jin, S.H.: Augmented teachers: K–12 teachers' needs for artificial intelligence's complementary role in personalized learning. J. Res. Technol. Educ. **57**(4), 876–893 (2025). https://doi.org/10.1080/15391523.2024.2330525
18. Tapalova, O., Zhiyenbayeva, N.: Artificial intelligence in education: Aied for personalised learning pathways. Electr. J. E-Learn. **20**(5), 639–653 (2022). https://doi.org/10.34190/ejel.20.5.2597

19. Van Schoors, R., Elen, J., Raes, A., Vanbecelaere, S., Depaepe, F.: The charm or chasm of digital personalized learning in education: teachers' reported use, perceptions and expectations. TechTrends **67**(2), 315–330 (2023). https://doi.org/10.1007/s11528-022-00802-0
20. Van Schoors, R., Elen, J., Raes, A., Vanbecelaere, S., Rajagopal, K., Depaepe, F.: Teachers' perceptions concerning digital personalized learning: theory meet practice. Technol. Knowl. Learn. **30**, 833–859 (2025). https://doi.org/10.1007/s10758-025-09815-z

# Designing Teacher Dashboards for Pedagogical Action: how Data Aggregation Levels Influence Teachers' Intervention Decisions

Mareike Kholin[1(✉)], Leona Colling[2], Laura Reichmann[3], Patrick Rektorschek[3], Alexandra Loster[3], Hannes Schröter[1,3], and Detmar Meurers[2]

[1] German Institute for Adult Education – Leibniz Centre for Lifelong Learning, Bonn, Germany
mareike.kholin@gmail.com
[2] Leibniz-Institut für Wissensmedien, Tübingen, Germany
[3] FernUniversität Hagen, Hagen, Germany

**Abstract.** Teacher dashboards are key interfaces in technology-enhanced learning (TEL), translating Learning Analytics (LA) into representations that support data-informed teaching. While widely used for instructional decision-making, it remains unclear how different levels of data aggregation influence teachers' pedagogical reasoning. Teacher-facing LA can be visualized at the individual or topic-level, yet their effects on decision-making are not well understood.

This online experimental study with 132 pre-service English teachers examined how these representations shape interpretations of learning situations and pedagogical decisions. Using a prototype dashboard for an intelligent tutoring system (ITS) in K12 English learning, participants were introduced to a classroom scenario. They were instructed to base decisions on both analytics and pedagogical knowledge. Participants were randomly assigned to one of four conditions: (1) individual student-level data, (2) topic-level aggregated data, (3) both levels, or (4) no dashboard. They then proposed five pedagogical interventions.

A total of 660 interventions were analyzed qualitatively across target group, instructional content, and pedagogical method. Results indicate that dashboard representations influenced intervention patterns without fully determining teachers' decisions. Individual-level dashboards were associated with more interventions targeting specific students and addressing heterogeneity, whereas topic-level dashboards led to more content-focused interventions. Unexpectedly, in the individual-level condition the most whole-class interventions were suggested. Across conditions, participants rated the dashboard as useful and easy to use.

Our findings suggest that dashboards shape teachers' sense-making rather than directly guiding decisions, highlighting the importance of aggregation and visualization choices in TEL design.

**Keywords:** LA Aggregation Level · Teacher Dashboards · Pedagogical Decision-Making


J. Weidlich et al. (Eds.): EC-TEL 2026, LNCS 16905, pp. 299–314, 2027.
https://doi.org/10.1007/978-3-032-37979-5_21

## 1 Introduction

The increasing integration of digital technologies into education has generated large amounts of data about learners and learning processes. The field of Learning Analytics (LA) seeks to leverage these data to improve learning and teaching. LA has been defined as the "collection, analysis, interpretation and communication of data about learners and their learning that provides theoretically relevant and actionable insights to enhance learning and teaching" [1].

One common way of making LA information accessible is through LA dashboards (LAD). They aggregate and visualize indicators related to learners, learning activities, and learning contexts in ways that allow educators and learners to interpret complex data more easily [2, 3]. In many digital learning environments, including intelligent tutoring systems, dashboards are designed to translate data into actionable information that can guide and shape teaching and learning processes [4, 5]. While dashboards are often developed with the intention to support learner's skill acquisition, research suggests that their effects on academic outcomes are often modest and may depend on how the information is interpreted and acted upon [5, 6]. Consequently, increasing attention has been directed toward dashboards that support teachers in interpreting learning data and adapting instruction.

Teacher-facing LAD provide educators with insights into student progress, engagement, and learning patterns to support instructional decision-making [7, 8]. By visualizing patterns in learning data, such dashboards can help teachers monitor student development, identify learning difficulties, and adjust their pedagogical strategies accordingly [9]. However, an important design decision in the development of dashboards concerns the level of aggregation at which LA information is presented. Dashboards may display data about individual students, groups of learners, or entire classes, and these different perspectives may draw teachers' attention to different aspects of classroom activity and therefore influence their instructional responses. Among the many design decisions involved in dashboard development, the level at which learning data are aggregated is particularly consequential because it determines what aspects of classroom learning become visible to teachers. Unlike visual design features or interface elements that primarily affect usability, aggregation level shapes the instructional perspective from which learning situations are interpreted and may therefore influence pedagogical reasoning and action.

Although prior research has explored the design and implementation of LAD and their potential influence on teaching and learning, relatively little empirical work has examined how specific dashboard design choices affect instructional practice. Experimental evidence linking data aggregation levels in LAD to teachers' instructional interventions remains scarce. To the best of our knowledge, no study has experimentally manipulated the aggregation level of teacher-facing LAD and examined its effects on instructional actions. Understanding these effects is important for informing the design of dashboards that not only present data effectively but also support desired pedagogical outcomes. The present study therefore experimentally investigates how different aggregation levels of LAD influence teachers' instructional interventions and their acceptance of dashboard technologies.

## 2 Literature Review / Background

### 2.1 Teacher-Facing LAD

Many LAD are designed primarily for students, aiming to support self-regulated learning and skill acquisition by providing feedback on progress and engagement [6]. However, research suggests that their effects on academic achievement are often limited. A recent review found stronger effects on motivational outcomes than on learning performance [5] and showed that dashboards are most effective when combined with additional instructional support. This suggests that providing learners with analytics alone is often insufficient to substantially improve learning outcomes, highlighting the important role teachers play in interpreting and acting on LA information.

To support teachers in this process, teacher-facing LAD have increasingly been developed. These dashboards aggregate and visualize student data to provide insights into learners' progress, engagement, and learning behaviors. By making patterns visible, they can help teachers monitor development, identify learning difficulties, and adapt instruction in face-to-face and digital environments [4], thereby supporting data-informed instructional decision-making [7, 8]. Prior work also suggests that dashboards can help teachers compare subjective impressions with data-based indicators, reveal otherwise unnoticed learning challenges, expand pedagogical options, and support monitoring of many students simultaneously [9].

### 2.2 LA Aggregation Levels

A key design characteristic of learning analytics dashboards is the level of data aggregation. Dashboards may present information about individual students or summaries of class-level performance across learning topics. Providing multiple aggregation levels is considered important, as different instructional questions require different levels of detail [3].

Research indicates that many teacher dashboards present multiple aggregation levels to increase teachers' awareness of classroom learning processes. A systematic review found that most systems combine individual-level data with aggregated class-level representations [10]. These perspectives are assumed to support different forms of instructional reasoning and decision-making.

In practice, teachers may target interventions at individuals, groups, or the whole class [11, 12], depending on the context and patterns identified in learning [13]. Thus, the aggregation of learning analytics information may influence not only what teachers notice but also which instructional responses appear appropriate

**Aggregation Levels and Pedagogical Interventions.** Beyond supporting awareness, data aggregation is closely linked to the types of pedagogical actions dashboards can inform. LA indicators capture different facets of learning, such as knowledge development or engagement, and may therefore inform a range of instructional decisions [14, 15]. However, the relationship between data and action is not straightforward: the same indicator may lead to different responses depending on its aggregation and interpretation, and different levels of granularity may enable or constrain pedagogical reasoning [16].

Research on teacher noticing emphasizes that instructional decisions depend on what teachers attend to and how they interpret classroom situations [17]. Similarly, research on data-driven decision-making shows that performance data can influence instructional judgments and feedback practices [9, 18, 19].

Depending on how LA information is presented, dashboards may highlight different patterns in learning. Student-level data makes individual differences visible, whereas topic-level aggregation emphasizes class-wide patterns in subject-matter performance. As a result, different aggregation levels may orient teachers' attention toward different instructional problems and responses.

**Aggregation Levels and Technology Acceptance.** The successful implementation of teacher dashboards depends not only on their technical capabilities but also on teachers' willingness to adopt and use them. In information systems research, technology acceptance is commonly explained by the Unified Theory of Acceptance and Use of Technology (UTAUT; [20]) and the earlier Technology Acceptance Model (TAM; [21]). These frameworks propose that adoption is primarily driven by perceived usefulness (performance expectancy) and perceived ease of use (effort expectancy), which together shape behavioral intention.

Both models have been widely validated in educational contexts. Research shows that perceived usefulness and ease of use strongly predict teachers' intentions to integrate digital technologies into instruction [22], with meta-analytic evidence confirming these relationships across settings [23]. In the context of LAD, these factors relate to whether teachers perceive the analytics as informative for instructional decision-making and whether the interface supports efficient interpretation.

Perceived usefulness refers to the extent to which users believe a system enhances task performance [20]. For teacher dashboards, this depends on the informational value of the presented analytics. Different aggregation levels may provide complementary insights: topic-level information highlights class-wide patterns, whereas student-level data supports the diagnosis of individual learning needs. Combining both perspectives may therefore offer a more comprehensive basis for instructional decisions.

Perceived ease of use refers to how easy a system is to understand and interact with [20]. It is influenced by the interpretability of the information and the cognitive effort required to process it. Representations aligned with familiar reference points, such as individual learners, may be easier to interpret, whereas more abstract aggregated data, such as topic-level summaries, may require additional integration and thus increase cognitive demands.

According to TAM and UTAUT, perceived usefulness and ease of use jointly determine behavioral intention, the most immediate predictor of system use [20]. Applied to LAD, differences in data aggregation may therefore shape not only instructional practice but also teachers' perceptions of usefulness and usability, ultimately influencing adoption.

## 3 Research Gap and Hypotheses

Although prior research suggests that LAD can support teachers' awareness and influence instructional decision-making, empirical evidence on how specific dashboard design features shape pedagogical reasoning and instructional practice remains limited. Because aggregation level shapes how learning situations are represented to teachers, it may influence instructional decision-making. Little is known about how different levels of data aggregation in teacher-facing dashboards influence the target group, instructional content, and pedagogical methods of instructional interventions. Moreover, experimental studies isolating the effects of aggregation level are scarce. Addressing this gap, the present study investigates how student-level and topic-level dashboard information are associated with differences in instructional practice and technology acceptance. This limits our understanding of how specific dashboard design choices can support different forms of instructional decision-making.

Based on the theoretical considerations outlined above, we derive the following hypotheses:

*H1: The target group, instructional content, and pedagogical method of teacher interventions differ systematically depending on the data aggregation level displayed in the dashboard.*

When dashboard data is presented at the student-level, it highlights performance differences between learners and makes individual learning needs salient. In contrast, topic-level dashboard information emphasizes patterns in class-wide performance and makes shared knowledge gaps visible.

*H2a:* Dashboards providing student-level information are associated with a higher frequency of instructional interventions targeting individual learners.

*H2b*: Dashboards providing student-level information are associated with a higher frequency of instructional methods that explicitly address learner heterogeneity, such as differentiation or adaptive grouping strategies.

*H2c:* Dashboards providing topic-level information are associated with a higher frequency of instructional interventions targeting the whole class.

*H2d:* Dashboards providing topic-level information are associated with a higher frequency of instructional interventions focused on subject-matter content aligned with the topics represented in the dashboard.

*H2e:* Dashboards providing topic-level information are associated with a higher frequency of lecture-based instructional approaches aimed at addressing shared knowledge gaps.

Regarding technology acceptance, the following hypotheses are proposed:

*H3: Dashboards providing both student-level and topic-level LA will be perceived as more useful than dashboards showing only one LA level.*

*H4: The individual student-level dashboard will be perceived as easier to use than the topic-level dashboard and the combined dashboard.*

*H5: Participants will report a higher behavioral intention to use the dashboard in the combined dashboard condition than in the individual student or topic-based dashboard conditions.*

# 4 Method

## 4.1 Participants and Procedure

Participants were recruited through a study invitation distributed by professors and educational staff in English teacher education programs at German universities, as well as via academic mailing lists. The study was approved by an independent ethics committee. Participation was voluntary and conducted online using the Unipark platform. Completing the study took approximately 30 min, and participants who completed the study received an online shopping voucher. Participants could not return to previous pages after completing a questionnaire page.

The final sample consisted of 132 pre-service teachers in Germany enrolled in a Master of Education program. All participants (102 female, 29 male, 1 diverse) studied English as at least one of their teaching subjects, with additional subjects varying. Participants' ages ranged from 21 to 41 years ($M = 24.68$, $SD = 2.60$). Most reported prior teaching experience: 78.8% in school contexts and 60% in additional settings such as tutoring or educational projects, while 10.6% reported no prior experience.

After providing informed consent, participants completed a questionnaire on demographics, teaching experience, and motivation to become a teacher. They were then introduced to an ITS for English as a foreign language used in German secondary schools, which supports grammar and lexis acquisition through individualized adaptive feedback [24]. Participants received a brief description of the system and were randomly assigned to one of four experimental conditions. In three conditions, they viewed vignette-based teacher dashboard screenshots (see Sect. 4.2), while the control group received no dashboard information.

Participants were then presented with a classroom scenario in which they were asked to imagine teaching a 7$^{th}$-grade English class preparing for an exam on diary entry writing in the Simple Past, scheduled for the following week. The class was described as heterogeneous, with one lesson remaining before the test.

Participants were asked to describe five pedagogical interventions for this lesson. They were instructed to propose specific actions based on the dashboard information (if available) and their own pedagogical knowledge. Participants in the control condition did not receive any dashboard information and therefore based their instructional decisions solely on the classroom scenario, their pedagogical knowledge, and prior teaching experiences. Finally, participants in the dashboard conditions completed questionnaire items on technology acceptance (perceived usefulness, perceived ease of use, and intended future use), which were not presented in the control condition.

## 4.2 Teacher Dashboard Vignettes

Two types of dashboards were developed for the study, based on fictional data. To ensure comparability and internal validity, both dashboards were parallelized in terms of the number of elements, layout, and underlying values. Corresponding elements appeared in identical positions across the two dashboards, and the percentages and numerical values were proportionally equivalent. This parallelization was intended to isolate the effect of data aggregation level while minimizing potential confounding influences related to layout, visual complexity, or information quantity.

Both dashboards displayed four metrics based on the dashboard design by [4]:

- *Progress* (average percentages of mastered competencies / grammar topic acquisition),
- *Support needs* (percentage of incorrect attempts during the previous 14 days),
- *Effort (*total number of submitted exercises during the previous 14 days),
- *Improvement* (change in the proportion of correct responses following previous errors over the last 14 days).

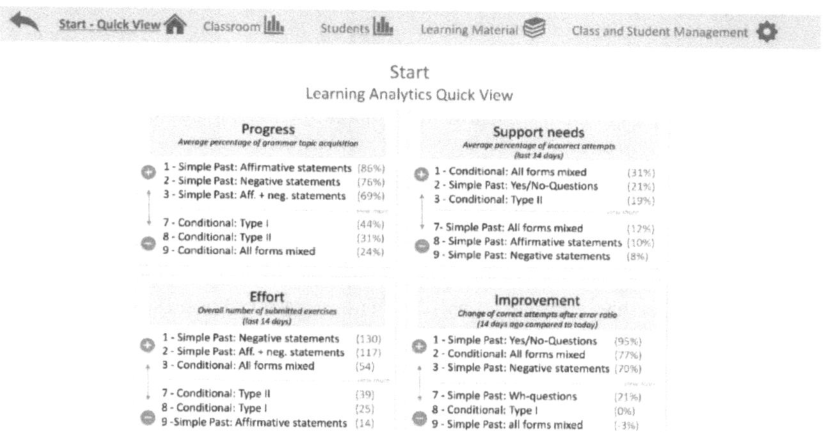


**Fig. 1.** Topics-level dashboard with class aggregates

For each metric, the dashboards displayed the three highest and three lowest entries, separated by a dotted line indicating that additional entries would be available in a fully developed dashboard.

The two dashboard types differed in their reference unit. In the *topics-level dashboard*, the metrics in the dashboard showed information aggregated across all students of the class for grammatical topics covered by the ITS (e.g., *Simple Past – Affirmative Questions* or *Conditionals: Type I*). In the *student-level dashboard*, the dashboard displayed individual student names (e.g. *Frida* or *Hamed*), with the metrics aggregated across all grammatical topics. Because grammatical topics are inherently longer than student names, entries in the topic-based dashboard were slightly longer than those in the individual student-level dashboard.

In Condition 1 ($n = 36$), participants were shown only the topic-level dashboard (see Fig. 1), whereas Condition 2 ($n = 35$) presented only the student-level dashboard (see Fig. 2). In Condition 3 ($n = 31$), participants were shown both dashboards, with counterbalanced order of presentation. In Condition 4 ($n = 30$), no dashboard was shown.

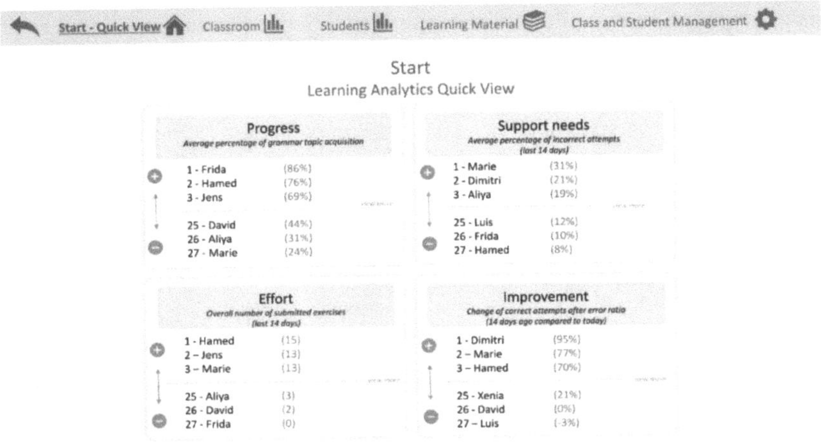


**Fig. 2.** Individual student-level dashboard with topic aggregates

### 4.3 Measures

Participants' technology acceptance of the dashboard was measured using adapted items from the Unified Theory of Acceptance and Use of Technology (UTAUT) questionnaire [20], based on the German adaptation by [25]. The instrument assesses key determinants of technology acceptance that influence users' behavioral intention to use a system. Three constructs were measured: perceived usefulness (four items), perceived ease of use (four items), and behavioral intention to use (three items). Items were adapted to the context of the teacher dashboard used in this study (e.g., *"I think that using the dashboard would allow me to complete tasks more quickly"*). All items were rated on a 5-point Likert scale ranging from 1 (strongly disagree) to 5 (strongly agree). Cronbach's α was .74 for perceived usefulness, .80 for effort perceived ease of use and .77 for behavioral intention, and .82 for overall technology acceptance.

### 4.4 Data Analysis

**Qualitative Content Analysis of Interventions.** Overall, 660 interventions were generated by the participants of the study. They were analyzed using qualitative content analysis [26, 27]. Because no established taxonomy of pedagogical interventions suitable for the study context was available, a theory-informed coding scheme was developed. The coding dimensions reflect core components of instructional decision-making frequently discussed in educational theory, i.e., the target group, instructional content, and instructional method [e.g., 28, 29], while the specific categories within each dimension were developed by reviewing descriptions of instructional interventions in the literature and iteratively refined during coding. Each intervention was coded along three dimensions. A detailed coding manual is available from the authors upon request.

- *Target group.* This dimension captures the intended recipients of the intervention, that is, who the intervention is directed at. It distinguishes between individual students,

dyads, small groups (three to five students), larger groups (six or more students), and the whole class.
- *Instructional content.* This dimension describes the focus of the learning activity and captures what is intended to be improved through the intervention. Because instructional content is partly domain-specific, the coding scheme includes subject-related categories reflecting the study context alongside more general educational goals. It differentiates between grammar, other subject-related content, learning strategies or methodological aspects, motivation or attitudes, and social behavior or cooperation.
- *Instructional method.* This dimension refers to the instructional approach used to deliver the content, that is, how the intervention is implemented. It includes the use of social heterogeneity, differentiated instruction, practice and repetition, lecture-based instruction, and feedback/reflection.

To assess coding reliability, two independent raters coded interventions in three iterative rounds of 40 interventions each. Disagreements were discussed and the coding scheme refined accordingly. The final agreement rate reached 90%, after which the remaining interventions were coded by one trained rater.

**Statistical Analyses.** H1 was tested using $\chi^2$ or Fisher's exact tests for the three coding dimensions. H2a–H2e were examined using $\chi^2$ tests of independence followed by Bonferroni-adjusted column proportion tests. H3–H5 were tested using ANOVAs and planned contrasts.

## 5 Results

### 5.1 Distribution of Pedagogical Intervention Types

Table 1 shows the overall frequencies of pedagogical intervention types and percentages sorted by category and the results of the respective Chi$^2$ or Fisher's exact tests.

Significant differences between conditions were found for all main dimensions: Target group, $\chi^2(15) = 98.06, p < .001$, instructional content, $\chi^2(15) = 99.89, p < .001$, and instructional method, $\chi^2(15) = 54.44, p < .001$. These results support H1, indicating that the types of instructional interventions differed across the dashboard conditions.

The results provide mixed support for the hypotheses regarding specific intervention types across the experimental conditions. H2a was supported, as individual-targeted interventions occurred more frequently in conditions including a student-level dashboard than in conditions without one. H2b received partial support, as interventions involving heterogeneity and differentiated learning were most frequent in the student-level dashboard condition, although the combined dashboard condition did not differ significantly from the other conditions. In contrast, H2c was not supported, as whole-class interventions occurred most frequently in the no-dashboard condition rather than in conditions including a topic-level dashboard. H2d was supported, with grammar-related interventions occurring more often in the topics-level and combined dashboard conditions. Finally, H2e was not supported, as lecture-based instruction did not differ significantly across the experimental conditions.

**Table 1.** Frequencies of pedagogical interventions and $Chi^2$ test results

| Categories | Overall | Topic-level | Student- level | Combined | No dashboard | chi2 (df) |
|---|---|---|---|---|---|---|
| N | 660 | 180 | 175 | 155 | 150 | |
| **Target group** | % | % | % | % | % | 198.06 (15)** |
| Individual | 14.8 | 5.6 [a] | 22.3 [b] | 21.9 [b] | 10.0 [a] | |
| Dyads | 6.1 | 6.1 [a] | 6.9 [a] | 5.2 [a] | 6.0 [a] | |
| Small group | 2.1 | 1.7 [a] | 2.3 [a] | 3.2 [a] | 1.3 [a] | |
| Large group | 3.6 | 0.6 [a] | 6.9 [b] | 4.5 [b] | 2.7 [a,b] | |
| Class | 48.9 | 39.4 [a] | 42.9 [a] | 54.8 [b] | 61.3 [b] | |
| n.a. | 24.4 | 46.7 [a] | 18.9 [b] | 10.3[c,b] | 18.7[b] | |
| **Content** | % | % | % | % | % | 199.89 (15)** |
| Grammar | 47.4 | 60.6[a] | 32.6 [b] | 58.7 [a] | 37.3 [b] | |
| Subject-content | 24.2 | 20.6 [a] | 16.6 [a] | 18.7 [a] | 43.3 [b] | |
| Learning Strategy | 1.7 | 0.6 [a] | 2.9 [a] | 1.3 [a] | 2.0 [a] | |
| Motivation | 2.1 | 1.7 [a,b] | 5.1 [b] | 1.3 [a,b] | 0.0 [a] | |
| Cooperation | 0.9 | 0.6 [a,b] | 2.9 [b] | 0.0 [a] | 0.0 [a] | |
| n.a. | 23.6 [a] | 16.1 [b] | 40.0 [a] | 20.0 [a] | 17.3 | |
| **Method** | % | % | % | % | % | 54.44 (15)** |
| Using heterogeneity | 4.4 | 1.1 [a] | 9.7 [b] | 5.2 [b,c] | 1.3 [a,c] | |
| Differentiation | 6.7 | 3.9 [a] | 13.1 [b] | 5.2 [a] | 4.0 [a] | |
| Lecture-based instruction | 27.1 | 46.1 [a] | 24.6 [b] | 34.2 [b] | 30.7 [b] | |
| Repetition & Practice | 34.1 | 23.3 [a] | 24.0 [a] | 31.6 [a] | 30.7 [a] | |
| Feedback & reflection | 23.5 | 21.1 [a] | 23.4 a | 20.6 [a] | 29.3 [a] | |
| n.a. | 4.2 | 4.4 | 5.1 | 3.2 | 4.0 | |

*Notes:* N = 660 pedagogical interventions. Percentages are related to distribution within conditions. ** $p < .01$. [1]Because several expected cell counts were below five, Fisher's exact test with Monte Carlo estimation was conducted. [a,b,c] Tests examine category differences between experimental conditions. Values sharing the same superscript letter do not differ significantly (Bonferroni-adjusted column proportion test, $p < .05$).

Beyond the hypothesized effects, several additional differences between conditions emerged from the analyses. Interventions involving repetition and practice occurred more frequently in the topics-level condition than in the other conditions, suggesting that topic-level analytics may also encourage practice-oriented instructional strategies.

## 5.2 Effects of Dashboard Type on Technology Acceptance

To examine whether the different dashboard representations influenced participants' acceptance of the system, separate one-way ANOVAs were conducted for perceived usefulness, perceived ease of use, and behavioral intention to use the dashboard across the three dashboard conditions. Descriptive statistics and results of ANOVA are depicted in Table 2.

For perceived usefulness, the ANOVA did not reveal a statistically significant effect of condition, $F(2, 99) = 2.07$, $p = .131$, $\eta^2_p = .04$. An a priori contrast comparing the combined-dashboard condition with the two single conditions was also not statistically significant, $t(99) = -1.73$, $p = .086$. Notably, the mean values of perceived usefulness in the conditions pointed in the opposite direction than expected. Thus, H3, which predicted higher perceived usefulness for the combined-dashboard condition, was not supported.

For perceived ease of use, the ANOVA indicated a significant effect of condition, $F(2, 99) = 4.24$, $p = .017$, $\eta^2_p = .08$. An a priori contrast analysis testing whether the individual student-level dashboard condition was perceived as easier to use than the other two conditions was significant, $t(99) = 2.26$, $p = .026$, indicating that participants rated this condition as easier to use. Therefore, H4 was supported.

For behavioral intention to use the dashboard, the ANOVA approached statistical significance, $F(2, 99) = 3.05$, $p = .052$, $\eta^2_p = .06$. An a priori contrast analysis comparing the combined-dashboard condition with the two single-level conditions was not statistically significant, $t(99) = 1.79$, $p = .076$, although the pattern of results was consistent with the hypothesis. Thus, H5 was not confirmed.

Overall, the results suggest that dashboard representation primarily affected perceived ease of use, whereas differences in perceived usefulness and behavioral intention were comparatively modest and did not reach statistical significance.

**Table 2.** Technology acceptance by dashboard condition

| Variable | Topic-level dashboard | Student-level dashboard | Combined dashboard | ANOVAs | | |
|---|---|---|---|---|---|---|
| | M(SD) | M(SD) | M(SD) | $F(2,99)$ | $p$ | $\eta^2_p$ |
| Perceived usefulness | 3.63 (.61) | 3.45 (.78) | 3.29 (.60) | 2.07 | .131 | .04 |
| Perceived ease of use | 3.62 (.76) | 4.06 (.58) | 3.89 (.59) | 4.24 | .017 | .08 |
| Behavioral intention | 3.79 (.68) | 4.06 (.64) | 4.18 (.70) | 3.05 | .052 | .06 |
| *n* | 36 | 35 | 31 | | | |

*Note.* $N = 132$. Ratings 5-point Likert scale (1 = strongly disagree, 5 = strongly agree).

# 6 Discussion

## 6.1 Interpretation and Implications for Dashboard Designs

The present study examined how different data aggregation levels in teacher-facing LAD influence teachers' proposed instructional interventions and their perceptions of dashboard usefulness. The results showed that dashboard representation affected the distribution of interventions across target group, instructional content, and method. Student-level dashboards were associated with more individual-targeted interventions, whereas topic-level dashboards were more often linked to grammar-related activities. However, some patterns diverged from expectations. For example, participants in the student-level condition also proposed many whole-class interventions, indicating that dashboard information does not deterministically dictate instructional decisions.

Regarding technology acceptance, participants generally reported moderate to positive evaluations of the dashboards. While perceived ease of use differed significantly—favoring the student-level dashboard—no significant differences were found for perceived usefulness or behavioral intention. Overall, the findings suggest that dashboard representations shape teachers' interpretation of learning situations and influence pedagogical reasoning, while leaving room for professional judgment.

The findings have several implications for dashboard design. First, representations should be aligned with instructional goals, supporting a human-centered LA design approach [15, 30]. Presenting individual student data appears particularly useful for encouraging targeted support and adaptation to individual learners' needs. This pattern is consistent with research suggesting that dashboard representations shape teachers' attention and sense-making. Student-level information may encourage differentiated support, whereas topic-level information directs attention toward shared learning needs and class-level planning. In contrast, whole-class interventions were frequently proposed even without a dashboard, suggesting that such strategies may already be salient and do not require strong prompting.

Furthermore, the type of information displayed can direct teachers' attention to specific instructional content and support data-informed content-agency [31]. Topic-level dashboards led to more interventions addressing subject-related content, suggesting that such representations can effectively guide attention toward learning domains requiring instructional focus.

Regarding pedagogical methods, the student-level dashboard was associated with more interventions leveraging learner heterogeneity, such as pairing students with different performance levels or providing differentiated support. This highlights the value of dashboards that present individual student data aggregated across topics, as they appear to support instructional approaches that address learner diversity.

More broadly, the findings suggest that dashboard designers should align aggregation levels with instructional goals. Student-level representations may support differentiated instruction, whereas topic-level views can help identify class-wide learning needs. Combining both aggregation levels may provide greater pedagogical flexibility by balancing classroom overviews with information about individual learners. Importantly, dashboard representations do not determine instructional decisions. Rather, they appear to influence which instructional problems become salient and which responses are perceived as appropriate. Different aggregation levels may therefore privilege certain forms of pedagogical action while constraining others. At the same time, the variation in interventions within conditions suggests that teachers continue to rely on pedagogical knowledge and professional judgment beyond the information provided by the dashboard, as probably all experimental groups integrated their professional knowledge into their intervention design.

## 6.2 Limitations and Future Research

Several limitations of this study should be considered when interpreting the findings, pointing to directions for future research. First, the sample consisted of teaching students rather than practicing teachers. Although most participants reported teaching experience, instructional decision-making may differ from that of experienced teachers in authentic classroom contexts [32, 33]. Future studies should therefore examine whether similar effects occur with in-service teachers and how professional experience influences the interpretation and use of learning analytics.

Second, the experimental conditions may not have been fully comparable in terms of information density and complexity. The dashboard levels presented different types and amounts of information, which may have influenced participants' responses beyond the intended manipulation of aggregation level. As cognitive load was not measured, future research could include measures of perceived cognitive load or usability to better disentangle these effects.

Third, participants were asked to propose instructional interventions based on a short scenario rather than demonstrating actual teaching behavior. While the vignette-based design enabled experimental control and elicited different intervention types across conditions, it does not allow conclusions about real classroom actions. In authentic teaching situations, instructional decisions are shaped by richer contextual information, classroom dynamics, and ongoing interactions with students. Laboratory experiments provide strong control but may differ from real classroom environments in contextual complexity and ecological validity [34, 35]. Future research should therefore investigate the effects of dashboard aggregation levels in natural classroom settings.

Similarly, the technology acceptance measures were based on static dashboard representations rather than interactive systems. Although vignette-based studies provide control, they may have lower ecological validity because participants respond to hypothetical scenarios rather than real interactions [36]. Research on data visualization suggests that interactive interfaces can influence how users interpret and evaluate information compared with static visualizations [37]. Allowing interaction with fully functional dashboards may therefore reveal different patterns of interpretation and use. Future studies should therefore examine how interactive features such as filtering or drill-down options influence teachers' attention and pedagogical reasoning.

Behavioral intention does not necessarily translate into actual use [38, 39]. Longitudinal studies are therefore needed to examine how dashboard use develops over time. Finally, the study did not examine whether the proposed interventions would affect students' learning outcomes or assess their pedagogical quality. The findings thus provide insight into instructional reasoning rather than the effectiveness of resulting actions.

Future research should therefore investigate how dashboard-informed decisions affect student learning and intervention quality.

Taken together, the findings should be interpreted as evidence of dashboard-informed pedagogical reasoning under controlled conditions. Because participants responded to static dashboards, fictional data, and simulated scenarios and proposed rather than enacted interventions, the results do not demonstrate effects on actual teaching practice or student learning outcomes.

## 7 Conclusion

This study investigated how different aggregation levels in teacher-facing LAD influence teachers' instructional decision-making and perceptions of dashboard usefulness. Using an experimental vignette design, pre-service teachers were presented with dashboard levels showing individual student data, aggregated topic-level data, both levels, or no dashboard. The results show that dashboard representations influenced the types of pedagogical interventions proposed. Student-level dashboards were associated with more individual-targeted interventions and strategies addressing learner heterogeneity, whereas topic-based dashboards encouraged more content-focused interventions, particularly related to grammar. These findings suggest that the aggregation and presentation of LA information shape teachers' interpretation of learning situations and guide their pedagogical reasoning.

At the same time, dashboard information did not deterministically determine instructional decisions. Participants frequently proposed class-level interventions across conditions, indicating that teachers integrate dashboard information with their pedagogical knowledge, experience, and task context. Acceptance findings were generally positive, although differences between conditions were limited. Overall, the findings highlight the importance of carefully considering data aggregation levels in the design of teacher dashboards. Aligning dashboard representations with instructional goals can help LA systems better support teachers in making informed pedagogical decisions.

## References

1. Society for LA Research (SoLAR): Reimagining LA. https://www.solaresearch.org/2025/06/solars-learning/analytics-definition-taskforce-releases-report/ (2025).
2. Schwendimann, B.A., et al.: Understanding learning at a glance: an overview of learning dashboard studies. IEEE Trans. Learn. Technol. **10**(1), 30–41 (2017)
3. Verbert, K., Duval, E., Klerkx, J., Govaerts, S., Santos, J.L.: LAD applications. Am. Behav. Sci. **57**(10), 1500–1509 (2013)
4. Colling, L., Kholin, M., Meurers, D.: A learning analytics dashboard for $K^{-12}$ English teachers: bridging the gap between student process data and teacher needs. In: Adjunct Proceedings of the 32nd ACM Conference on User Modeling, Adaptation and Personalization (UMAP Adjunct 2024), pp. 538–548 (2024)
5. Kaliisa, R., Kluge, A., Mørch, A.I.: LAD for supporting student learning: a systematic review of effects and design characteristics. Comput. Educ. **203**, 104906 (2024)
6. Heikkinen, A., Kinnunen, P., Malmi, L.: Supporting self-regulated learning with LAD: a systematic literature review. Educ. Technol. Res. Dev. **71**, 167–191 (2023)

7. Klerkx, J., Verbert, K., Duval, E.: In: Lad. Lang, C., Siemens, G., Wise, A., Gašević, D. (eds.) Handbook of LA, pp. 143–150, SoLAR (2017)
8. Van Leeuwen, A., Janssen, J., Erkens, G., Brekelmans, M.: Supporting teachers in guiding collaborative learning: effects of LA in teacher dashboards. Comput. Educ. **158**, 103990 (2021)
9. Knoop-van Campen, C.A.N., Segers, E., Verhoeven, L.: Teachers' use of LA to support students' learning in digital learning environments. Educ. Res. Rev. **33**, 100389 (2021)
10. Martinez-Maldonado, R., Buckingham Shum, S., Gašević, D., Verbert, K.: Teacher tracking with analytics dashboards: a systematic literature review. IEEE Trans. Learn. Technol. **13**(4), 747–760 (2020)
11. Poh, A., Castro, F.E.V., Arroyo, I.: Design principles for teacher dashboards to support in-class learning. In: Proceedings of the 17th International Conference of the Learning Sciences (ICLS 2023), pp. 736–743. International Society of the Learning Sciences (2023)
12. van Leeuwen, A., Teasley, S.D., Wise, A.: Teacher and student facing analytics. In: Lang, C., Siemens, G., Wise, A., Gašević, D., Merceron, A. (eds.) Handbook of LA, pp. 130–140, SoLAR (2022)
13. Wise, A.F., Jung, Y.: Teaching with analytics: towards a situated model of instructional decision-making. J. LA. **6**(2), 53–69 (2019)
14. Ahmad, A., et al.: Connecting the dots – a literature review on LA indicators from a learning design perspective. J. Comput. Assist. Learn. (2022)
15. Chatti, M.A., et al.: How to design effective LA indicators? A human-centered design approach. In: European Conference on Technology Enhanced Learning, pp. 303–317. Springer, Cham (2020)
16. Amarasinghe, I., Michos, K., Crespi, F., Hernández-Leo, D.: LA support to teachers' design and orchestrating tasks. J. Comput. Assist. Learn. **40**(6), 2416–2431 (2024)
17. Sherin, M.G., Jacobs, V.R., Philipp, R.A. (eds.): Mathematics Teacher Noticing: seeing through Teachers' Eyes. Routledge, New York (2011)
18. Schildkamp, K., Kuiper, E.: Data-informed curriculum reform: which data, what purposes, and promoting and hindering factors. Teach. Teach. Educ. **26**(3), 482–496 (2010)
19. Karademir, O., et al.: I don't have time! But keep me in the loop: co-designing requirements for a LA cockpit with teachers. J. Comput. Assist. Learn. **40**(6), 2681–2699 (2024)
20. Venkatesh, V., Morris, M.G., Davis, G.B., Davis, F.D.: User acceptance of information technology: toward a unified view. MIS Q. **27**(3), 425–478 (2003)
21. Davis, F.D.: Perceived usefulness, perceived ease of use, and user acceptance of information technology. MIS Q. **13**(3), 319–340 (1989)
22. Teo, T.: Factors influencing teachers' intention to use technology: model development and test. Comput. Educ. **57**(4), 2432–2440 (2011)
23. Scherer, R., Siddiq, F., Tondeur, J.: The technology acceptance model (TAM): a meta-analytic structural equation modeling approach. Comput. Educ. **128**, 13–35 (2019)
24. Meurers, D., De Kuthy, K., Nuxoll, F., Rudzewitz, B., Ziai, R.: Scaling up intervention studies to investigate real-life foreign language learning in school. Annu. Rev. Appl. Linguist. **39**, 161–188 (2019)
25. Nistor, N., Göğüş, A., Lerche, T.: Educational technology acceptance across national and professional cultures: a European study. Educ. Technol. Res. Dev. **62**(6), 733–749 (2014)
26. Schreier, M.: Qualitative Content Analysis in Practice. SAGE, London (2012)
27. Mayring, P.: Qualitative Content Analysis: theoretical Foundation, Basic Procedures and Software Solution. Beltz, Weinheim (2014)
28. Gagné, R.M., Wager, W.W., Golas, K.C., Keller, J.M.: Principles of Instructional Design, 5th edn. Wadsworth/Thomson Learning, Belmont (2005)
29. Shulman, L.S.: Those who understand: knowledge growth in teaching. Educ. Res. **15**(2), 4–14 (1986)

30. AlZoubi, D., Baran, E., Karabulut-Ilgu, A., Morales, A.S., Gilbert, S.B.: From concept to classroom: developing instructor dashboards through human centered design. Comput. Educ. Open. **7**, 100234 (2024)
31. Brod, G.: Agency does not equal choice–conceptualizing agency for learning in the age of AI. Learn. Individ. Differ. **125**, 102841 (2026)
32. Granić, A.: Educational technology adoption: a systematic review. Educ. Inf. Technol. **27**, 9725–9744 (2022)
33. van Es, E.A., Sherin, M.G.: Mathematics teachers' "learning to notice" in the context of a video club. Teach. Teach. Educ. **24**(2), 244–276 (2008)
34. Wolff, C.E., Jarodzka, H., Boshuizen, H.P.A.: See and tell: differences between expert and novice teachers' interpretations of problematic classroom management events. Teach. Teach. Educ. **66**, 295–308 (2017)
35. Brown, A.L.: Design experiments: theoretical and methodological challenges in creating complex interventions in classroom settings. J. Learn. Sci. **2**(2), 141–178 (1992)
36. Shadish, W.R., Cook, T.D., Campbell, D.T.: Experimental and quasi-experimental designs for generalized causal inference. Houghton Mifflin, Boston (2002)
37. Aguinis, H., Bradley, K.J.: Best practice recommendations for designing and implementing experimental vignette methodology studies. Organ. Res. Methods. **17**(4), 351–371 (2014)
38. Hullman, J., Kosara, R., Lam, H.: Visualization rhetoric: framing effects in narrative visualization. IEEE Trans. Vis. Comput. Graph. **17**(12), 2231–2240 (2011)
39. Galimova, E.G.: Mapping the interconnections: a systematic review of factors influencing technology acceptance in teacher education. Frontiers Educ. **9** (2024)

# Mapping Human–AI Collaboration in Lecturer Decision-Making: A Systematic Review of Automation Across Decision Stages in Higher Education

Melike Nur Köroğlu[1(✉)], Jonas Mayrhofer[2], Alexander Steinmaurer[1], Robert Weinhandl[2], Philipp Wintersberger[1], and Sebastian Maximilian Dennerlein[1]

[1] Interdisciplinary Transformation University Austria, Linz, Austria
melike.koeroglu@it-u.at
[2] Johannes Kepler University Linz, Linz, Austria

**Abstract.** Despite the increasing integration of artificial intelligence (AI) in higher education (HE), it remains unclear how AI-supported automation aligns with lecturers' decision-making. This study examines how AI systems are positioned across levels of automation and stages of rational decision-making. Following PRISMA guidelines, a systematic literature review of 26 empirical studies (2016–2025) was conducted using qualitative content analysis. Coding combined deductive categories based on levels of automation and decision-making stages with iterative identification of AI and lecturer roles. The findings show that most AI systems operate at lower levels of automation and primarily support early stages of lecturers' decision-making, particularly problem identification and generation of alternatives. Learning analytics tools, for example, provide diagnostic, predictive, and feedback-related insights while lecturers retain final decision authority. Higher levels of automation remain uncommon, indicating that AI in higher education continues to function primarily as a decision-support tool rather than a collaborative decision partner. Overall, the findings reveal a critical gap: increasing levels of automation do not necessarily translate into more meaningful support for lecturers' decision-making.

**Keywords:** Human–AI Collaboration · Lecturers' Decision-Making · Levels of Automation · Hybrid Intelligence · Higher Education

## 1 Introduction

Artificial intelligence (AI) systems powered by machine learning (ML) or large language models (LLMs) are increasingly being adopted in higher education [12,23,36]. AI systems can be broadly defined as computational systems that analyze data, generate predictions, and produce adaptive outputs or recommendations that support human decision-making [38]. Learning Analytics (LA) is


J. Weidlich et al. (Eds.): EC-TEL 2026, LNCS 16905, pp. 315–329, 2027.
https://doi.org/10.1007/978-3-032-37979-5_22

defined as "the collection, analysis, interpretation and communication of data about learners and their learning that provides theoretically relevant and actionable insights to enhance learning and teaching" [35]. LA systems analyze and visualize learning data to support decision-making [13,14]. For instance, LA dashboards monitor student engagement and performance [7,12], while predictive and diagnostic models detect learning difficulties and identify at-risk students [3,22]. In addition, adaptive AI systems such as intelligent tutoring systems and agent-based systems provide feedback and instructional insights to support lecturers' decision-making [9,36] and integrate recommendation and intervention mechanisms [14,30]. As these systems increasingly influence how decisions are informed and enacted, it becomes important to examine how AI operates across different stages of lecturers' decision-making. Schoenfeld [34] conceptualizes decision-making as a structured process through which individuals interpret situations, generate and evaluate alternatives, and select actions to achieve desired outcomes. To examine how AI systems support lecturers in educational contexts, this study adopts the rational decision-making model as a framework for analyzing support across different stages of decision-making. As a result, AI systems are no longer framed solely as systems for automating routine analytical tasks, but increasingly as components of hybrid intelligence systems, where decision-making is structured as a collaboration between lecturers and AI [13,16]. Within the hybrid intelligence perspective, professional judgment is not replaced but augmented through structured human–AI collaboration that transitions control to different extents [16,33]. Human–AI collaboration can be described through varying levels of automation, which indicate how control over tasks and decisions is distributed between lecturers and AI systems, reflecting graded distributions of responsibility between human and AI actors [24]. However, levels of automation alone are insufficient to explain how AI systems interact with lecturers' decision-making. It is crucial to examine not only the degree of automation or lecturer agency but also the specific stage of the decision-making, such as problem identification, generation of alternatives, or evaluation of outcomes. AI intervenes across these stages of the rational decision-making model [33], where complementary roles between lecturers and AI systems emerge. Prior research has examined human–AI collaboration from different perspectives, including levels of automation [24] and the functionalities of AI systems in educational settings [13,16]. However, little is known about how levels of automation align with the stages of lecturers' decision-making. This leaves an important open question: whether increasing AI sophistication is accompanied by a broader and more active role in lecturers' decision-making, or whether AI remains concentrated in limited forms of support. As a result, it remains unclear how responsibilities between lecturers and AI systems are distributed across different stages of decision-making, and to what extent increasing levels of automation translate into meaningful support for lecturers' decision-making.

To address this gap, this systematic literature review examines how AI systems are distributed across lecturers' decision-making stages and levels of automation in higher education. The study is guided by the following research question: How are AI systems distributed across lecturers' decision-making stages and levels of automation in higher education? By analyzing how AI-supported automation operates across decision-making, the review provides a structured overview of how roles and responsibilities are distributed between lecturers and AI systems. Furthermore, it identifies recurring configurations of complementary AI and lecturer roles across different levels of automation.

## 2 Theoretical Framework

This study adopts a hybrid intelligence perspective to conceptualize human–AI collaboration in lecturers' decision-making. Hybrid intelligence refers to collaborative systems in which humans and AI complement each other's capabilities to achieve outcomes that neither could accomplish alone [16,19,33]. In this context, AI systems and lecturers assume complementary roles: AI typically performs analytical and predictive functions, while lecturers retain responsibility for contextual interpretation, ethical deliberation, and final decision-making [13,24]. To analyze how responsibilities are distributed between lecturers and AI systems, the study combines two complementary perspectives: levels of automation, which describe how control is distributed between human and AI actors [24], and decision-making stages, which capture where AI intervenes in the decision process [34]. Together, these perspectives provide a framework for examining the distribution of responsibilities in human–AI collaboration.

### 2.1 Levels of Automation in Human–AI Collaboration

Levels of automation describe how control over tasks and decisions is transferred from human actors to AI systems [24,27]. This concept provides a structured framework for analyzing different configurations of human–AI collaboration. The model conceptualizes collaboration along a continuum ranging from full human control to full AI control [27]. Rather than assuming fixed roles, it frames interaction as a graded distribution of responsibilities between human and AI actors. This perspective builds on a long tradition of research on human–automation interaction, including early work such as Fitts' "humans are better at – machines are better at" (HABA-MABA) framework [10], as well as more recent models of adaptive and intelligent systems. Across these approaches, a central concern is how functions and responsibilities are allocated between human and machine agents. In practice, humans and AI complement each other by performing different functions depending on system design and contextual conditions [13,16]. Within this division of roles, AI systems typically perform analytical and predictive functions such as data processing, pattern detection, and recommendation generation, while human actors remain responsible for contextual interpretation and pedagogical judgment. In educational settings, this division is particularly evident in systems such as learning analytics dashboards, intelligent tutoring systems, and AI-supported feedback tools [9,12,14,30]. Molenaar [24] extends this perspective to education through a six-level model of automation in personalized learning, conceptualized from a teacher–technology interaction perspective (Table 1).

The model describes human–AI collaboration in terms of how monitoring and control responsibilities are distributed between teachers and AI systems, while students remain indirect participants whose data and interactions inform these processes. This conceptual structure is particularly necessary, as AI applications in higher education may reconfigure lecturers' roles and levels of control in different ways, even when they offer similar functional capabilities. The model enables positioning AI systems along a graded continuum of automation, ranging from providing supportive information to performing specific tasks and assuming broader responsibilities [24].

### 2.2 Stages of Lecturers' Decision-Making

Decision-making can be defined as a goal-oriented cognitive process through which individuals interpret situations, generate and evaluate alternatives, implement actions, and assess their outcomes [34]. This conceptualization builds on a broader tradition of research on human decision-making and human–automation interaction, where decision processes are understood as iterative and cyclical rather than strictly linear [27]. In line with [34], this process can be conceptualized as a sequence of decision stages through which decisions are formed, implemented, and evaluated over time. In educational contexts, such decisions may range from interpreting learning data and identifying instructional problems to selecting pedagogical actions, implementing instructional interventions, and evaluating their outcomes. The Rational Decision-Making Model consists of six key stages: identifying the problem, generating alternatives, evaluating alternatives, choosing an alternative, implementing the decision, and evaluating decision effectiveness (Table 2).

Rather than representing a linear progression, these stages form a dynamic cycle in which decision-makers continuously interpret information, adapt their actions, and reassess outcomes. In higher education, lecturers engage in these stages when interpreting student data, selecting responses, implementing pedagogical or organizational adjustments, and evaluating their impact on learning outcomes. AI systems may support different stages by analyzing data, generating recommendations, executing bounded actions, or providing evaluative feedback. Although the rational decision-making model originates from general decision theory [34], it has also been applied in educational administration and leadership contexts [20], thereby providing a relevant conceptual foundation for examining lecturers' decision-making processes in higher education.

**Table 1.** Six levels of automation model of personalized learning (adapted from [24]).

| Level | Label | Teacher | Technology | General Description |
|---|---|---|---|---|
| L1 | Teacher Only | Teacher controls | — | Full human control. |
| L2 | Teacher Assistance | Teacher has full control | Technology provides supportive information | AI informs, teacher decides. |
| L3 | Partial Automation | Teacher monitors technology | Technology controls specific tasks | Specific tasks automated. |
| L4 | Conditional Automation | Teacher monitors incidentally but can resume control at all times | Technology controls broader tasks and signals when teacher control is needed | Shared control with AI monitoring. |
| L5 | High Automation | Teacher control not required for specific tasks | Technology controls most tasks automatically and requests teacher control | AI controls most tasks. |
| L6 | Full Automation | — | Technology controls all tasks automatically | Full AI control. |

**Table 2.** Stages of the Rational Decision-Making Model (adapted from [34]).

| Stage | Label | Definition |
|---|---|---|
| D1 | Problem Identification | Recognizing and defining a discrepancy between the current state and a desired goal state. |
| D2 | Generation of Alternatives | Developing possible courses of action to address the identified problem. |
| D3 | Evaluation of Alternatives | Assessing the feasibility, consequences, and goal alignment of each alternative. |
| D4 | Choosing an Alternative | Choosing the most appropriate alternative based on available information and criteria. |
| D5 | Implementing the Decision | Executing the selected course of action within the organizational context. |
| D6 | Evaluating Decision Effectiveness | Assessing the outcomes of the implemented decision and determining whether goals have been achieved. |

# 3 Method

## 3.1 Systematic Literature Review

This systematic literature review aims to map how AI systems support lecturers' decision-making across levels of automation and decision-making stages in higher education. The review followed the PRISMA 2020 guidelines [26] to ensure transparency and methodological rigor. Searches were conducted in five major academic databases: Web of Science, Scopus, IEEE Xplore, ACM Digital Library, and ERIC. The search was limited to publications between 2016 and 2025. This period captures the recent development of AI-supported educational technologies, including learning analytics, intelligent tutoring systems, and emerging generative AI applications in higher education [23,36]. The search string combined three conceptual blocks—Artificial Intelligence, Higher Education, and Decision-Making—using Boolean operators. The final search string was defined as follows: ("artificial intelligence"*) AND ("higher education"*) AND ("decision-making"*). Representative search terms are presented in Table 3.

**Table 3.** Structure of the search string.

| Concept block | Representation/search terms |
|---|---|
| Artificial Intelligence | Neural network, large language models, reinforcement learning, deep learning, natural language processing, machine learning, learning analytics, chatbots, AI agents, AI systems, AI tools |
| Higher Education | Higher education, university teaching, faculty member |
| Decision-Making | Decision-making, AI-assisted decision-making, data-based decision-making, lecturer decision |

The systematic database search yielded 4,247 records across all databases. After removing 547 duplicate records, 3,700 records remained. Database filters were applied to include only peer-reviewed articles in English (journal articles and conference proceedings). Following initial filtering, 2,574 records were retained for title and abstract screening based on predefined inclusion and exclusion criteria. During this stage, 2,440 records were excluded as they were not relevant to the scope of the study, did not involve AI-supported systems, or were not conducted in higher education contexts. This resulted in 134 full-text articles assessed for eligibility. Of these, 108 studies were excluded for the following reasons: not based on student data (n = 30), non-empirical studies (n = 35), and studies not conducted in higher education (n = 43). The final sample consisted of 26 studies. The full list of the 26 included studies is presented in Table 4.

**Table 4.** Studies included in the systematic review ($n = 26$).

| ID | Paper citation | ID | Paper citation | ID | Paper citation |
|---|---|---|---|---|---|
| P1 | López et al., 2025 [18] | P10 | Divjak et al., 2023 [8] | P19 | Meng and Guo, 2025 [23] |
| P2 | Filho et al., 2019 [9] | P11 | Tebourbi et al., 2025 [37] | P20 | Sajja et al., 2026 [31] |
| P3 | Sun et al., 2025 [36] | P12 | Li et al., 2025 [17] | P21 | Dann et al., 2024 [6] |
| P4 | Renzella et al., 2020 [28] | P13 | Baran et al., 2025 [2] | P22 | Md & Krishnamoorthy, 2022 [22] |
| P5 | Cukurova et al., 2019 [4] | P14 | Baran et al., 2023 [1] | P23 | Czibula et al., 2022 [5] |
| P6 | Gutiérrez et al., 2020 [12] | P15 | Safsouf et al., 2021 [30] | P24 | Khosravi et al., 2021 [14] |
| P7 | De Menezes et al., 2023 [7] | P16 | Mouakher and Kononov, 2025 [25] | P25 | Saqr & López-Pernas, 2024 [32] |
| P8 | Lee et al., 2025 [15] | P17 | Saarela et al., 2021 [29] | P26 | Yang et al., 2024 [39] |
| P9 | Casey & Azcona, 2017 [3] | P18 | Gambo et al., 2025 [11] | | |

Figure 1 presents the PRISMA flow diagram summarizing the study selection process.

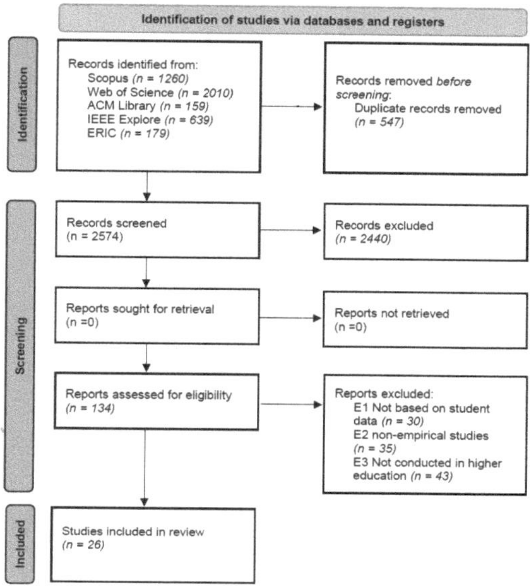


**Fig. 1.** PRISMA flow diagram of the study selection process.

### 3.2 Data Extraction and Coding

Data were analyzed using Mayring's qualitative content analysis, applying a primarily deductive coding step [21]. The codebook for deductive analysis was derived from two theoretical dimensions: levels of automation in human–AI collaboration and stages of lecturers' decision-making (see Sects. 2.1 and 2.2). These frameworks were used as deductive categories to classify how AI systems were positioned within lecturers' decision. Based on these classifications, studies were grouped according to levels of automation and the supported decision-making stage. Within these groups, additional sub-categories of AI and lecturer roles were identified inductively to capture recurring functional patterns across the reviewed systems.

The coding process followed an iterative procedure across the full dataset. Two researchers independently coded the studies in successive rounds. To assess inter-coder reliability, Krippendorff's alpha was calculated on 10 double-coded studies, corresponding to 38.5% of the included sample. Inter-coder agreement yielded $\alpha = 0.73$, indicating acceptable agreement. Inter-coder reliability was assessed for the deductive coding dimensions (levels of automation and decision-making stages). In contrast, the AI and lecturer role categories emerged inductively from the data through an iterative process of qualitative analysis. These categories were refined across five rounds of comparison, discussion, and consensus-building among the researchers until conceptual agreement was reached regarding their distinctiveness and applicability across the dataset. This process ensured consistency and strengthened the reliability of the coding across the dataset.

# 4 Results

## 4.1 Levels of Automation Across Lecturers' Decision-Making Stages

To analyze how AI systems support lecturers' decision-making, levels of automation were examined across the six decision-making stages (Fig. 2).

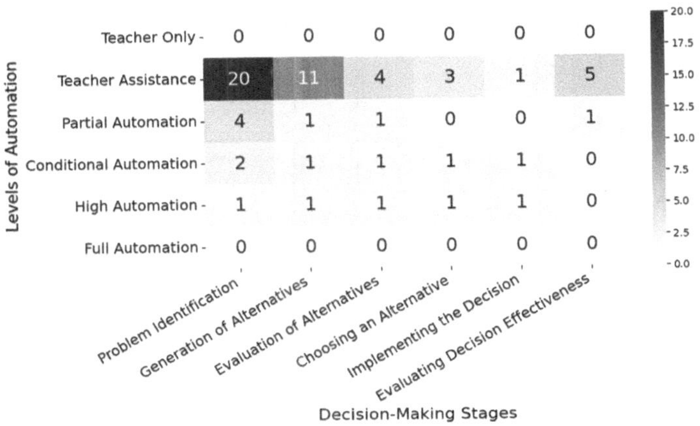


**Fig. 2.** Levels of Automation (L1–L6) by decision-making stage (D1–D6), showing the number of included studies in each cell.

The highest concentration of AI systems is observed at the teacher-assistance level (L2), particularly in the problem identification stage (D1 = 20), followed by the generation of alternatives (D2 = 11) and the evaluation of decision effectiveness (D6 = 5). Additional L2 systems are distributed across the remaining decision-making stages, including evaluation of alternatives (D3 = 4), choice of action (D4 = 3), and implementation (D5 = 1). Partial automation systems (L3) are primarily concentrated in early decision-making stages, especially problem identification (D1 = 4), with only limited occurrences in generation of alternatives (D2 = 1), evaluation of alternatives (D3 = 1), and evaluation of decision effectiveness (D6 = 1), and no presence in decision selection (D4) or implementation (D5). Conditional automation systems (L4) are sparsely distributed across stages from problem identification (D1 = 2) to implementation (D5 = 1), with single occurrences in each intermediate stage (D2–D5), and no representation in the evaluation of decision effectiveness (D6 = 0). High automation systems (L5) are rare but appear across early and middle stages of decision-making (D1–D5 = 1 each). No systems were identified at the full automation level (L6). Overall, the findings indicate a clear concentration of AI systems at lower levels of automation and in earlier stages of lecturers' decision-making, particularly in problem identification and the generation of alternatives. Remaining stages are represented with low frequency, typically with single occurrences.

### 4.2 Role Distribution Across Levels of Automation in Lecturers' Decision-Making

Table 5 presents the distribution of AI systems across levels of automation, the associated decision-making stages, and the corresponding AI and lecturer roles.

**Table 5.** Role Distribution Across Levels of Automation in Lecturers' Decision-Making

| Levels of Automation | Observed Decision Stage(s) | Purpose | AI Role | Lecturer Role |
|---|---|---|---|---|
| Teacher Assistance (L2) | D1 (dominant), D2, D3, D4, D5, D6 | Provide diagnostic evidence to inform lecturer-controlled decisions | Informer (diagnosis, detection) | Interpreter |
| Partial Automation (L3) | D1 (dominant), D2, D3, D6 | Execute bounded instructional actions under lecturer monitoring | Executor (diagnosis, detection, action) | Reviewer |
| Conditional Automation (L4) | D1–D5 (low frequency) | Execute instructional decisions under lecturer oversight | Co-Designer (diagnosis, detection, action, recommendation) | Coordinator |
| High Automation (L5) | D1–D5 (very limited cases) | Manage execution of instructional decisions with minimal lecturer intervention | Manager (diagnosis, detection, action, recommendation, alerting) | Overseer |

At the teacher assistance level (L2), AI systems were observed across all six decision-making stages, with a clear concentration in problem identification (D1). At this level, AI systems primarily performed diagnostic and detection functions by analyzing learning data and presenting structured evidence. The lecturer role was consistently characterized as the interpreter, indicating that all AI outputs were controlled and required human interpretation and that final decision authority remained with the lecturer. For example, NLP-based feedback analysis systems extract patterns from student comments to support lecturers' understanding of learning issues [18], while learning analytics dashboards visualize engagement and performance data to support instructional monitoring [7,12].

Systems classified at the partial automation level (L3) were predominantly associated with early decision-making stages, particularly problem identification (D1), with additional occurrences in the generation of alternatives (D2), evaluation of alternatives (D3), and evaluation of decision effectiveness (D6). At this level, AI systems performed specific instructional tasks, while lecturers remained responsible for monitoring. Functional roles at this level included diagnosis, detection, and action. While specific tasks were automated, lecturers retained monitoring responsibility and decision authority, reflected in the reviewer role. For example, tracing tutor agents can generate adaptive responses within virtual learning environments [9], while automated grading tools support assessment processes [11].

Conditional automation systems (L4) appeared with low frequency and were distributed across decision stages D1 to D5. These systems combined diagnostic, detection, action, and recommendation functions. Responsibility for executing instructional decisions was shared between AI systems and lecturers under lecturer oversight. In this configuration, the lecturer role shifted towards Coordinator, indicating a distribution of responsibilities between AI and lecturer while maintaining human supervision. For instance, proactive learning analytics dashboards can generate recommendations and alerts that inform instructional adjustments [30], and LLM-based decision-support systems may suggest instructional alternatives based on student data [23].

High automation systems (L5) appeared only in a few isolated cases and were associated with multiple decision-making stages, while still requiring lecturer high-level management of pedagogical decisions. At this level, AI systems automated substantial parts of the instructional process, such as task orchestration or workflow management, while lecturers retained responsibility for high-level pedagogical decisions, including setting instructional goals, validating system outputs, and intervening when necessary. For example, multi-agent workflow systems may automate instructional processes such as task orchestration while still requiring lecturer oversight [37]. This distribution highlights a structural pattern: AI systems are predominantly concentrated in analytically supportive roles, with limited involvement in higher-order decision-making stages.

## 5 Discussion

This study examined how AI systems support lecturers' decision-making by relating levels of automation to structured decision-making stages. The findings reveal a clear structural pattern: most AI systems operate at lower levels of automation and primarily support early stages of the decision-making process, particularly problem identification. This distribution is consistent with previous studies showing that educational AI systems are most frequently used for learning analytics, early warning systems, and performance monitoring [12,14,32]. For example, P9 employed predictive analytics to identify students at risk of poor performance, while P22 generated visual feedback and risk profiles to support instructors in monitoring student progress. In both cases, AI primarily supported problem identification and information processing, whereas subsequent pedagogical actions remained under educator control. These findings contribute to ongoing discussions on hybrid intelligence and human–AI collaboration in education by providing a systematic synthesis of how AI and lecturer roles are distributed across decision-making stages and levels of automation. Previous research has conceptualized hybrid intelligence as a complementary relationship in which AI systems support analytical tasks while human actors retain responsibility for interpretation and pedagogical decision-making [16,19,24]. The results of the present study go beyond confirming this perspective by revealing a systematic imbalance in how roles are distributed: AI systems are predominantly concentrated in early-stage, low-agency functions, while later stages of decision-making remain largely human-driven. This uneven distribution suggests that, despite increasing technical sophistication, AI systems in higher education remain systematically constrained in their role as decision-making partners. In this sense, current AI systems predominantly function as decision-support tools that extend lecturers' analytical capacity rather than actively participating in higher-order decision processes. This pattern can also be observed in recent human–AI collaborative systems. For instance, P24 provided automated drill-down recommendations to guide teachers' exploration of student data while explicitly preserving instructor judgment regarding interpretation and intervention decisions. Similarly, P12 supported human grading by highlighting relevant information and confidence indicators, while final assessment decisions remained the responsibility of human evaluators.

This imbalance is not merely descriptive but has important implications for how AI is positioned within educational decision-making. Importantly, the preservation of human responsibility is primarily related to levels of automation rather than to specific decision-making stages. From this perspective, the observed concentration of AI systems in early decision-making stages raises an important question: to what extent should AI systems support later stages of decision-making, such as evaluating alternatives, selecting pedagogical actions, or assessing the effectiveness of interventions? While AI systems are widely used to detect learning patterns and identify potential problems, considerably less support exists for these later stages. As illustrated in Fig. 3, three patterns emerge: strong AI support in early decision-making stages, declining support with increasing automation, and limited involvement in later stages such as implementation and evaluation. Together, these patterns reveal a structural gap, suggesting that increasing levels of automation are not necessarily accompanied by more meaningful support across lecturers' decision-making.

Several factors may explain this distribution. Importantly, this pattern may not simply reflect technological limitations. Some studies explicitly position AI as a tool for augmenting rather than replacing human judgment. For example, P24 was designed around a human-in-the-loop approach that prioritizes transparency, accountability, and educator oversight rather than fully automated decision-making. This suggests that the concentration of AI systems in earlier decision-making stages may partly reflect deliberate design choices intended to preserve professional judgment and human responsibility. Educational decision-making involves ethical and institutional constraints, where high-stakes decisions require human accountability and are therefore less likely to be delegated to AI systems. In addition, later stages of decision-making demand contextual, pedagogical, and situational understanding, which remain challenging for current AI technologies.

Taken together, these findings indicate that AI in higher education is not yet functioning as a full decision-making. Instead, AI systems remain primarily analytical tools that augment lecturers' capabilities without substantially shar-

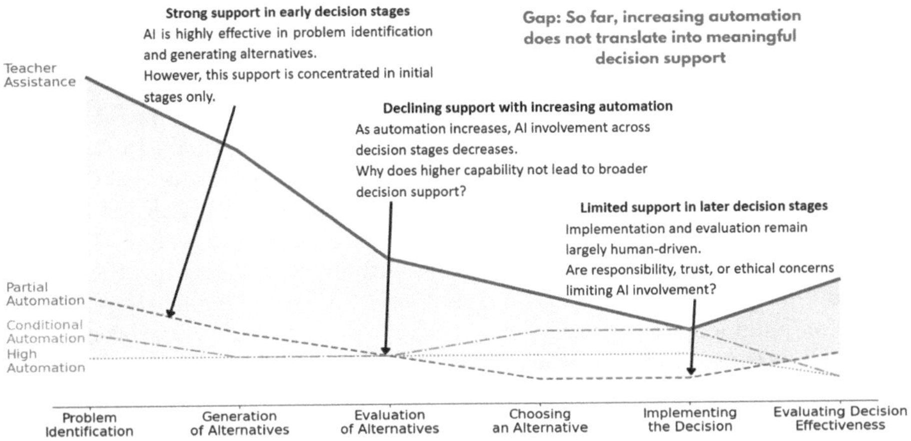


**Fig. 3.** Gap between automation and meaningful decision support across decision-making stages.

ing decision responsibility. Recent work on explainable AI further reinforces this perspective. For example, P25 demonstrated that even when AI systems provide transparent explanations, effective educational decision-making still requires human interpretation and contextual judgment. Moreover, algorithmic mispredictions may be based on inappropriate indicators, highlighting the limitations of fully data-driven decision-making without human oversight. This highlights an important direction for future research: designing AI systems that can meaningfully support later stages of decision-making while maintaining appropriate levels of human control and accountability.

## 6 Conclusion

The results reveal that most AI systems in higher education operate at lower levels of automation and primarily support early stages of lecturers' decision-making, particularly problem identification and data interpretation. By relating levels of automation to decision-making stages, this study provides a structured perspective on how responsibilities are distributed between AI systems and lecturers and identifies gaps in current AI-supported decision-making. From a design perspective, the findings suggest that future AI systems should support later stages of decision-making, provide explanations that justify recommendations, and facilitate human–AI co-decision while preserving human control in high-stakes contexts. In education, maintaining human responsibility, accountability, and pedagogical judgment remains essential [19,24].

Several limitations should be acknowledged. The review focuses on empirical studies in higher education, which may limit generalization to other educational contexts. The limited number of studies at higher levels of automation also constrains conclusions about more advanced forms of AI-supported decision-making.

In addition, the coding process relied on descriptions provided in published studies. In some cases, limited reporting of system functionality may have influenced the classification of automation levels and AI roles.

Future research should examine how lecturers interpret, trust, and potentially override AI recommendations, and how these interactions affect decision quality and learning outcomes. Further work should investigate the role of professional agency, accountability, and AI literacy in AI-supported decision environments, as well as the boundaries of automation in educational decision-making. Empirical studies in authentic settings are needed to better understand how different forms of human–AI collaboration influence instructional decisions. Overall, these findings highlight the need to move beyond purely analytical support towards balanced forms of human–AI collaboration that preserve human responsibility while meaningfully supporting educational decision-making.

**Disclosure of Interests.** The authors have no competing interests to declare that are relevant to the content of this article.

## References


1. Baran, E., AlZoubi, D., Salazar Morales, A.: Design and implementation of an automated classroom analytics system: stakeholder engagement and mapping. TechTrends **67**(6), 945–954 (2023). https://doi.org/10.1007/s11528-023-00905-2
2. Baran, E., AlZoubi, D., Salazar Morales, A., Yass, J., Karabulut-Ilgu, A., Gilbert, S.B.: Data-driven insights for active learning: transforming teaching practices through automated classroom analytics. In: International Conference on Human–Computer Interaction, pp. 217–228 (2025). https://doi.org/10.1007/978-3-031-93567-1_15
3. Casey, K., Azcona, D.: Utilizing student activity patterns to predict performance. Int. J. Educ. Technol. High. Educ. **14**, 4 (2017). https://doi.org/10.1186/s41239-017-0044-3
4. Cukurova, M., Kent, C., Luckin, R.: Artificial intelligence and multimodal data in the service of human decision-making: a case study in debate tutoring. Br. J. Educ. Technol. **50**(6), 3032–3046 (2019). https://doi.org/10.1111/bjet.12829
5. Czibula, G., Ciubotariu, G., Maier, M.-I., Lisei, H.: IntelliDaM: a machine learning-based framework for enhancing the performance of decision-making processes. A case study for educational data mining. IEEE Access **10**, 80651–80666 (2022). https://doi.org/10.1109/ACCESS.2022.3195531
6. Dann, C., Redmond, P., Fanshawe, M., Brown, A., Getenet, S., Shaik, T., et al.: Making sense of student feedback and engagement using artificial intelligence. Australas. J. Educ. Technol. **40**(3), 58–76 (2024). https://doi.org/10.14742/ajet.8903
7. De Menezes, M., Netto, J., Lopes, A., Silva, R., Menezes, R.: The proposal of a dashboard for analysis and visualization of educational data of intelligent tutoring systems. In: IEEE Frontiers in Education Conference (FIE), pp. 1–8 (2023). https://doi.org/10.1109/FIE58773.2023.10343000
8. Divjak, B., Svetec, B., Horvat, D., Kadoić, N.: Assessment validity and learning analytics as prerequisites for ensuring student-centred learning design. Br. J. Educ. Technol. **54**(1), 313–334 (2023). https://doi.org/10.1111/bjet.13290

9. Filho, A., Thalheimer, J., Dazzi, R., Santos, V., Koehntopp, P.: Improving decision-making in virtual learning environments using a tracing tutor agent. In: Filipe, J., Smialek, M., Brodsky, A., Hammoudi, S. (eds.) Proceedings of the 21st International Conference on Enterprise Information Systems (ICEIS 2019), pp. 600–607. SciTePress (2019). https://doi.org/10.5220/0007744006000607
10. Fitts, P.M.: Human engineering for an effective air-navigation and traffic-control system. Technical report, National Research Council, Washington, DC (1951)
11. Gambo, I., Abegunde, F., Gambo, O., Ogundokun, R., Babatunde, A., Lee, C.: Grad-AI: an automated grading tool for code assessment and feedback in programming course. Educ. Inf. Technol. **30**(7), 9859–9899 (2025). https://doi.org/10.1007/s10639-024-13218-5
12. Gutiérrez, F., Seipp, K., Ochoa, X., Chiluiza, K., De Laet, T., Verbert, K.: LADA: a learning analytics dashboard for academic advising. Comput. Hum. Behav. **107**, 105826 (2020). https://doi.org/10.1016/j.chb.2018.12.004
13. Holstein, K., McLaren, B.M., Aleven, V.: Co-designing a real-time classroom orchestration tool to support teacher-AI complementarity. J. Learn. Anal. **6**(2), 27–52 (2019). https://doi.org/10.18608/jla.2019.62.3
14. Khosravi, H., Shabaninejad, S., Bakharia, A., Sadiq, S., Indulska, M., Gašević, D.: Intelligent learning analytics dashboards: automated drill-down recommendations to support teacher data exploration. J. Learn. Anal. **8**(3), 133–154 (2021). https://doi.org/10.18608/jla.2021.7279
15. Lee, Y., Migut, G., Specht, M.: Unveiling cognitive processes in digital reading through behavioural cues: a hybrid intelligence approach. Br. J. Educ. Technol. **56**(2), 678–711 (2025). https://doi.org/10.1111/bjet.13551
16. Ley, T., Cukurova, M., Edwards, J., Falhs, A.-C., Järvelä, S., Kasepalu, R., et al.: Teaching with AI: the role of teachers in the hybrid intelligent system. In: European Conference on Technology Enhanced Learning, pp. 32–45 (2025). https://doi.org/10.1007/978-3-032-03873-9_3
17. Li, Y., Raković, M., Srivastava, N., Li, X., Guan, Q., Gašević, D., et al.: Can AI support human grading? Examining machine attention and confidence in short answer scoring. Comput. Educ. **228**, 105244 (2025). https://doi.org/10.1016/j.compedu.2025.105244
18. De León López, E.D., Salazar Cano, C.L.: Enhancing educational equity: leveraging NLP to understand diverse student perspectives in engineering. In: Institute for the Future of Education Conference, pp. 1–10 (2025). https://doi.org/10.1109/IFE63672.2025.11024922
19. Luckin, R., Holmes, W., Griffiths, M., Forcier, L.B.: Intelligence Unleashed: An Argument for AI in Education. Pearson, London (2016)
20. Lunenburg, F.C.: The decision making process. Natl. Forum Educ. Adm. Supervision J. **27**(4), 1–12 (2010)
21. Mayring, P.: Qualitative content analysis. Forum Qualitative Sozialforschung/Forum: Qual. Soc. Res. **1**(2), Art. 20 (2000). https://doi.org/10.17169/fqs-1.2.1089
22. Md, S., Krishnamoorthy, S.: Student performance prediction, risk analysis, and feedback based on context-bound cognitive skill scores. Educ. Inf. Technol. **27**(3), 3981–4005 (2022). https://doi.org/10.1007/s10639-021-10738-2
23. Meng, L., Guo, Y.: Generative LLM-based distance education decision design in Argentine universities. Edelweiss Appl. Sci. Tech. **9**(4), 2587–2599 (2025). https://doi.org/10.55214/25768484.v9i4.6608
24. Molenaar, I.: Towards hybrid human-AI learning technologies. Eur. J. Educ. **57**(4), 632–645 (2022). https://doi.org/10.1111/ejed.12527

25. Mouakher, A., Kononov, R.: Explainable evaluation framework for facial expression recognition in web-based learning environments. Int. J. Mach. Learn. Cybern. **16**(4), 2801–2833 (2025). https://doi.org/10.1007/s13042-024-02421-y
26. Page, M.J., McKenzie, J.E., Bossuyt, P.M., Boutron, I., Hoffmann, T.C., Mulrow, C.D., et al.: The PRISMA 2020 statement: an updated guideline for reporting systematic reviews. BMJ **372**, n71 (2021). https://doi.org/10.1136/bmj.n71
27. Parasuraman, R., Sheridan, T.B., Wickens, C.D.: A model for types and levels of human interaction with automation. IEEE Trans. Syst. Man Cybern. Part A Syst. Hum. **30**(3), 286–297 (2000). https://doi.org/10.1109/3468.844354
28. Renzella, J., Cain, A., Schneider, J.G.: An intelligent tool for combatting contract cheating behaviour by facilitating scalable student-tutor discussions. In: ACM/IEEE International Conference on Software Engineering Companion Proceedings, pp. 298–299 (2020). https://doi.org/10.1145/3377812.3390795
29. Saarela, M., Heilala, V., Jääskelä, P., Rantakaulio, A., Kärkkäinen, T.: Explainable student agency analytics. IEEE Access **9**, 137444–137459 (2021). https://doi.org/10.1109/ACCESS.2021.3116664
30. Safsouf, Y., Mansouri, K., Poirier, F.: Experimental design of learning analysis dashboards for teachers and learners. In: ACM Learning@Scale Conference, pp. 347–350 (2021). https://doi.org/10.1145/3430895.3460990
31. Sajja, R., Sermet, Y., Cwiertny, D., Demir, I.: Integrating AI and learning analytics for data-driven pedagogical decisions and personalized interventions in education. Technol. Knowl. Learn. **31**, 1289–1319 (2026). https://doi.org/10.1007/s10758-025-09897-9
32. Saqr, M., López-Pernas, S.: Why explainable AI may not be enough: predictions and mispredictions in decision making in education. Smart Learn. Environ. **11**, 52 (2024). https://doi.org/10.1186/s40561-024-00343-4
33. Sauer, C.R., Burggräf, P.: Hybrid intelligence—systematic approach and framework to determine the level of human-AI collaboration for production management use cases. Prod. Eng. Res. Devel. **19**(3), 525–541 (2025). https://doi.org/10.1007/s11740-024-01326-7
34. Schoenfeld, A.H.: How We Think: A Theory of Goal-Oriented Decision Making and Its Educational Applications. Routledge, New York (2010). https://doi.org/10.4324/9780203843000
35. Society for Learning Analytics Research (SoLAR): What is learning analytics? (2025). https://www.solaresearch.org/about/what-is-learning-analytics/. Accessed 11 Jun 2026
36. Sun, Y., Yu, H., Keung, J., Cao, Y., Liao, Y.: StuLAC: an adaptive LLM-driven framework for scalable student feedback analysis in software-driven educational systems. In: IEEE Computers, Software, and Applications Conference (COMPSAC), pp. 121–130 (2025). https://doi.org/10.1109/COMPSAC65507.2025.00024
37. Tebourbi, H., Nouzri, S., Mualla, Y., El Fatimi, M., Najjar, A., Abbas-Turki, A., et al.: BPMN-based design of multi-agent systems: personalized language learning workflow automation with RAG-enhanced knowledge access. Information **16**(9), 809 (2025). https://doi.org/10.3390/info16090809
38. Woolf, B.P.: Building Intelligent Interactive Tutors: Student-Centered Strategies for Revolutionizing E-Learning. Morgan Kaufmann, Burlington (2009). https://doi.org/10.1016/B978-0-12-373594-2.X0001-9
39. Yang, P., Liu, Y., Luo, Y., Wang, Z., Cai, X.: Text mining and multi-attribute decision-making-based course improvement in massive open online courses. Appl. Sci. **14**(9), 3654 (2024). https://doi.org/10.3390/app14093654

# Curiosity-Eliciting Questioning Strategies for Robot-Assisted Pitch Training: Effects on Learning Outcomes

Georges Arnaud Kouayim Bonga[1(✉)], Ilona Buchem[1], and Niels Pinkwart[2]

[1] Berliner Hochschule für Technik, Luxemburger Str. 10, 13353 Berlin, Germany
kouayim.bonga@gmail.com

[2] Humboldt-Universität zu Berlin, Unter den Linden 6, 10117 Berlin, Germany

**Abstract.** This paper investigates how curiosity-eliciting questioning strategies delivered by an LLM-powered social robot affect self-reported learning outcomes in higher education pitch training. Grounded in Loewenstein's [1] Information-Gap Theory, which posits that curiosity arises from perceived knowledge gaps, six questioning strategies were implemented: counterfactual, paradoxical, comparative, perspective-shifting, future projection, and provocation questions. In a between-subjects randomized controlled trial (N = 31), students in the curiosity condition showed significantly greater conceptual insights (d = 0.97, p = .013), an effect that remained significant after controlling for baseline differences using ANCOVA (F = 5.35, p = .029, partial $\eta^2$ = .171). Perceived pitch competence improvement was also higher (d = 0.77, p = .043), though this effect did not remain significant after controlling for baseline differences (ANCOVA: p = .108). Item-level analyses revealed the strongest effects on solution innovativeness (d = 1.07, p = .006) and responding to critical questions (d = 1.08, p = .006). Regression analyses within the curiosity group showed that experienced curiosity was significantly associated with perceived training effectiveness (β = .745, p = .003). Qualitative data indicated that 85.7% of curiosity participants identified critical questioning as curiosity-inducing versus 17.6% of controls. These findings provide initial evidence that theory-based curiosity-eliciting strategies can enhance self-reported conceptual learning in educational settings.

**Keywords:** Curiosity · Technology-Enhanced Learning · Pitch Training · Social Robots

## 1 Introduction

Despite the growing interest in fostering curiosity as a driver of learning, few educational technologies have been specifically designed to elicit and harness epistemic curiosity in learning contexts. Epistemic curiosity, defined as the intrinsic motivation to acquire knowledge and resolve uncertainty [1, 2], has been shown to enhance memory and learning. Neuroscientific research demonstrates that information learned in states of higher curiosity is remembered better, an effect linked to increased dopamine activity and


J. Weidlich et al. (Eds.): EC-TEL 2026, LNCS 16905, pp. 330–344, 2027.
https://doi.org/10.1007/978-3-032-37979-5_23

hippocampus-dependent learning [3], which also extends to incidental learning of unrelated information presented during the curiosity state [4]. The Information-Gap Theory posits that curiosity emerges from awareness of gaps between current and desired knowledge, creating tension that motivates information-seeking [1]. While various learning technologies exist, most focus on content delivery, feedback, or adaptive learning paths rather than on systematically eliciting curiosity [5]. Theory-based questioning strategies, such as Socratic questioning [6], can systematically create information gaps that trigger deeper cognitive processing. However, implementing such strategies requires real-time adaptivity that goes beyond scripted interactions.

Social robots offer a promising platform for delivering curiosity-eliciting strategies. Meta-analytic evidence suggests medium-to-large effects of robot-assisted learning on cognitive ($d = 0.70$) and affective outcomes ($d = 0.59$) in educational contexts [7], with similar effects on academic achievement and motivation ($g = 0.47$–$0.72$) compared to traditional methods [8]. Research has shown that embodied robots enhance engagement compared to screen-based interfaces, particularly through the motivational benefits of physical presence [7, 9]. The integration of large language models (LLMs) with social robots enables real-time generation of contextually appropriate responses, combining embodied social presence with adaptive conversational capabilities [10–13], reflecting a broader trend toward LLM-driven architectures in human-robot interaction [14] and enabling pedagogically effective interactions [15, 16]. However, many educational robot studies still rely on scripted or Wizard-of-Oz interactions, reflecting limited robot autonomy [17], and there are hardly any studies investigating how robots can be used to enhance curiosity in educational contexts.

Prior work with the Furhat robot demonstrated gains in pitch preparedness ($d = 0.83$, $p < .001$) [18], and an exploratory study found correlations between system-induced curiosity and topic engagement ($r = 0.531$, $p < .01$) [19]. However, neither study employed experimental designs testing specific questioning strategies with learning outcomes as dependent variables.

The present study addresses this gap by investigating how six theory-based curiosity-eliciting questioning strategies, delivered by an LLM-powered Furhat robot, affect self-reported learning outcomes in pitch training. While our prior work, accepted at another conference, focused on curiosity induction, the present paper examines learning outcomes, explores how experienced curiosity relates to these outcomes, and discusses implications for curiosity-enhancing educational technologies beyond social robots.

## 2 Background

### 2.1 Curiosity-Eliciting Strategies as a Pedagogical Mechanism

Based on Loewenstein's [1] Information-Gap Theory and the Socratic questioning approach described by Paul and Elder [6], we developed six curiosity-eliciting questioning strategies for implementation by LLM-powered robots. Socratic questioning uses systematic and disciplined questions to stimulate critical and reflective thinking [6]. Empirical work has shown that critical-thinking instruction grounded in Paul's framework can improve students' critical thinking skills and dispositions [20]. More recent research further suggests that LLM-based Socratic agents can enhance reflective thinking and academic performance in higher education [21]. Each strategy is designed to create specific types of information gaps:

(1) **Counterfactual questions** prompt alternative scenarios (e.g., "What if your AI tool functioned without internet?"), forcing mental simulation that enhances learning by highlighting unconsidered possibilities [22]. (2) **Paradoxical challenges** question assumptions through contradictions (e.g., "Could your efficiency tool reduce efficiency?"), creating cognitive dissonance [23] and, as an instructional cognitive conflict, prompting information-seeking and conceptual change [24]. (3) **Comparative questions** force trade-off consideration (e.g., "Should your tool prioritize speed or accuracy?"), prompting learners to become aware of knowledge gaps about priorities and articulate decision criteria they had not previously considered [25]. (4) **Perspective shifts** require considering different stakeholder viewpoints (e.g., "How would a competitor evaluate your tool?"), creating awareness of knowledge gaps between one's own and others' perspectives [26]. (5) **Future projections** encourage anticipatory thinking about alternative future states (e.g., "What would your tool look like in five years?"), creating temporal knowledge gaps that highlight uncertainty and motivate exploration [27]. (6) **Provocations** challenge fundamental premises (e.g., "Why should someone NOT use your tool?"), creating conflicts that motivate epistemic curiosity and deeper cognitive processing [28].

## 2.2 Social Robots and LLMs as Curiosity-Enhancing Learning Tools

The convergence of LLMs and social robotics represents a significant advancement for technology-enhanced learning. LLMs offer the ability to generate contextually appropriate, adaptive responses in real-time, while the physical embodiment of robots provides social presence that enhances engagement and learning outcomes compared to screen-based interfaces, particularly through physical presence and social rapport [7, 9, 29]. A Delphi study with 16 experts in HRI and educational technology identified personalized learning support as a key opportunity for LLM-powered social robots in education [30].

LLM-based intelligent tutoring systems have shown promise in improving academic performance, motivation, engagement, and cognitive development [31]. This review further suggests that their effectiveness depends less on content optimization than on their capacity to recognize and respond to learners' needs through adaptive interaction [31]. However, research on adaptive social robots has yielded mixed results. A study with 120 participants found no direct effects of adaptive robot guidance on task performance or cognitive learning compared to fixed guidance, while adaptive guidance reduced on-task enjoyment [32]. Similarly, a long-term field study found that robotic tutoring benefited exam performance and subjective knowledge gain, but adaptive robot behavior showed no clear added benefit over a non-adaptive version [33]. These mixed findings underscore the importance of grounding robot-based pedagogical strategies in established learning theories rather than relying on adaptation alone.

# 3 Methodology

## 3.1 Study Objectives and Hypotheses

The study investigated how curiosity-eliciting questioning strategies affect self-reported learning outcomes in pitch training. Three research questions guided the study: (RQ1) What is the effect of curiosity-eliciting strategies on learning outcomes? (RQ2) Which learning dimensions are most responsive? (RQ3) Does experienced curiosity relate to learning outcomes?

Four hypotheses were tested: (H1) The curiosity condition will show greater perceived pitch competence improvement. (H2) The curiosity condition will report more conceptual insights. (H3) Experienced curiosity will be positively associated with learning outcomes within the curiosity condition. (H4) Curiosity participants will identify specific strategies as thought-provoking, while standard participants will report no differentiated cognitive activation.

## 3.2 System Architecture

The system architecture integrated the Furhat robot with Anthropic's Claude through a Flask-based communication server [19]. The architecture comprised five components: (1) the Furhat robot, handling speech recognition and speech synthesis; (2) a Flask/SocketIO server managing API interactions, session state, conversation logging, and real-time sentence-by-sentence streaming to the robot and tablet; (3) Anthropic's Claude (claude-sonnet-4-20250514) as the underlying language model; (4) a web server hosting the tablet application; and (5) a tablet displaying the HTML-formatted conversation alongside the robot. This streaming approach enabled seamless interaction with minimal perceived delay. All conversations were stored in JSON format for subsequent analysis.

Both groups followed the same structure: the robot asked a question, listened to the team's response, and provided constructive feedback. In the curiosity-eliciting condition, the robot additionally asked one curiosity-eliciting question after the feedback, to which students responded before proceeding to the next core question. This resulted in approximately twice as many dialogue turns in the curiosity condition.

## 3.3 Participants

Participants were 34 students (58% female, 42% male), aged 19–28 years ($M = 22.4$, $SD = 2.1$), enrolled in a project-based media course at a German university during the summer semester 2025. All participants reported prior experience with AI systems: 55.9% used AI regularly (multiple times per week), 17.6% occasionally (multiple times per month), and 26.5% rarely (less than once per month). The vast majority (97.1%) had prior experience with humanoid robots, and 67.6% had previously interacted with the Furhat robot specifically. All students were working in teams of 3–5 members to develop AI solution concepts for real partner companies; participation was curriculum-integrated and all participants provided informed consent prior to participation.

## 3.4 Study Design and Procedure

The study employed a between-subjects randomized controlled design with two conditions: (1) curiosity-eliciting condition, receiving curiosity-eliciting follow-up questions after each answer, and (2) standard condition, receiving structured constructive feedback without curiosity-eliciting elements. Random assignment of 34 participants resulted in n = 17 per condition. Due to three missing post-test measures in curiosity condition, the final analyzed sample was n = 17 (standard) and n = 14 (curiosity), totaling N = 31. The dropout rate of 17.6% in the curiosity group was not statistically significant ($\chi^2(1) = 3.26$, $p = .071$). Pre-test analyses revealed no systematic differences between completers and non-completers on any measured variables (all $p > .30$), suggesting that dropout was not selective and should not bias results.

The study was conducted in a single day (June 26, 2025). Participants first completed pre-test measures online. Each student team then participated in a dedicated training session in a laboratory equipped with the Furhat robot positioned approximately 1.5 m from participants at table height. The robot introduced itself as "Anna," a pitch training coach, and explained that it would pose five questions about the team's AI concept. A tablet next to the robot displayed the robot's feedback in HTML-formatted text, allowing participants to read along while listening.

Both groups answered the same five core pitch preparation questions in identical order: (1) What is the problem statement and your solution approach? (2) Which AI tools are you using and why? (3) Present your business case. (4) How do you assess the feasibility? (5) How do you assess the innovation potential? The critical manipulation occurred after each response. In the standard condition, the robot provided constructive feedback before transitioning to the next question. In the curiosity-eliciting condition, the robot provided brief acknowledgment followed by one curiosity-eliciting question derived from one of the six strategies. Students responded to the follow-up question, received brief feedback on their response, and then proceeded to the next core question. This resulted in approximately twice as many dialogue turns in the curiosity condition.

Standard sessions averaged 15 min (M = 14.8, SD = 2.1), while curiosity sessions averaged 20 min (M = 19.3, SD = 2.8). Sessions were video-recorded with participant consent. Participants completed post-test measures immediately after their training session.

## 3.5 Measurement Instruments

All constructs were assessed via 5-point Likert scales (1 = strongly disagree to 5 = strongly agree). Composite scores were calculated as arithmetic means across items, following recommended practices for summated scales [34]. Internal consistency was evaluated using Cronbach's alpha, with values above .70 considered acceptable [34].

**Pre-test Measures (both Groups).** (1) Pitch competence (4 items, $\alpha = .87$): self-perceived competence in pitch-relevant skills (e.g., "I can structure presentations well," "I can respond well to critical questions"); (2) Concept quality (4 items, $\alpha = .82$): perception of the team's concept quality (e.g., "Our solution concept is well thought-through," "Our solution concept is innovative and unique"); (3) Motivation (4 items, $\alpha = .79$): engagement with the project (e.g., "I am currently very motivated to work on

our project concept," "I am confident that our team will deliver a successful pitch").
**Post-test Measures (both Groups).** Six constructs were measured:

1. Pitch competence improvement (4 items, $\alpha = .85$): Self-perceived improvement in pitch skills after training (e.g., "I can now respond better to critical questions," "My overall pitching competence has improved through the training").
2. Conceptual insights (4 items, $\alpha = .85$): Clarity gained regarding concept improvements ("Possible improvements to our concept became clearer," "I now know how to make our solution concept more innovative," "The technical feasibility of our concept is now clearer to me," "I can now better assess the market potential of our concept"). Notably, an initial fifth item measuring pride ("I am now more proud of our solution concept") was excluded from this scale because it assesses an emotional response rather than a cognitive gain.
3. Epistemic curiosity (3 items, $\alpha = .86$): Self-developed items based on Loewenstein's [1] Information-Gap Theory captured state epistemic curiosity elicited by the robot's questioning approach. The items assessed: (a) cognitive stimulation ("The robot's questions strongly prompted me to think about my project"), (b) gap awareness and closure motivation ("I felt the urge to close gaps in our argumentation"), and (c) broadened curiosity ("The robot's questions sparked my curiosity about further aspects of our project").
4. Training effectiveness (4 items, $\alpha = .76$): Perceived training quality, combining overall experience, helpfulness, interaction effectiveness, and willingness to repeat.
5. Transfer intentions (2 items, $\alpha = .70$): Plans to implement training insights ("I plan to make changes to our project based on today's insights," "I will incorporate the suggestions from today's training into my final pitch").
6. Motivation and preparedness (4 items, $\alpha = .87$): Post-training motivation and readiness for the final pitch (e.g., "I now feel well prepared for the final pitch," "I am now very motivated to work on our project concept").
7. Qualitative measures: Three categorical questions assessed: which aspects elicited curiosity during training (multiple-choice with option to select multiple responses from a predefined list), which question type most strongly induced curiosity (single-choice), and which question type most strongly prompted thinking about the project (single-choice). Additionally, an open-ended question asked for improvement suggestions. Categorical responses were analyzed using frequency analysis. Responses to the open-ended question were analyzed using deductive content analysis following predefined categories [35].

### 3.6 Statistical Analyses

All analyses were conducted using Python 3.10 with scipy.stats and numpy packages. Statistical significance was evaluated at $\alpha = 0.05$ (two-tailed). Preliminary analyses examined distributions using Shapiro-Wilk tests for normality and Levene's test for homogeneity of variances. For variables violating homogeneity assumptions, Welch's correction was applied to t-tests.

Given baseline differences between groups (motivation $d = 0.56$), ANCOVA was conducted with pre-test motivation as covariate for all post-test variables, to control for pre-existing group differences. Independent-samples t-tests are reported alongside ANCOVA for comparability with prior research. Effect sizes were calculated as Cohen's d with pooled standard deviation [36] and partial $\eta^2$ for ANCOVA. H3 was examined using regression analyses within the curiosity group. H4 was evaluated through frequency analysis and categorical comparison of qualitative responses.

A complementary analysis of the same dataset with a focus on curiosity induction has been accepted at another conference.

# 4 Results

## 4.1 Preliminary Analyses and Baseline Equivalence

Shapiro-Wilk tests indicated that all post-test variables were normally distributed in both groups (all $p > .05$), with the exception of training effectiveness in the standard group ($W = 0.89$, $p = .031$). Given the robustness of t-tests to normality violations with approximately equal sample sizes [37, 38], parametric analyses were conducted. Levene's tests revealed heterogeneous variances for conceptual insights ($F = 11.05$, $p = .002$) and epistemic curiosity ($F = 6.00$, $p = .021$), with lower variance in the curiosity group in both cases. For these variables, both standard and Welch-corrected t-tests are reported.

Pre-test comparisons revealed no statistically significant baseline differences, though effect sizes varied: (1) pitch competence: curious $M = 3.12$ ($SD = 0.73$) vs. standard $M = 3.35$ ($SD = 0.68$), $t(29) = -0.83$, $p = .412$, $d = 0.33$; (2) concept quality: curious $M = 3.47$ ($SD = 0.62$) vs. standard $M = 3.71$ ($SD = 0.59$), $t(29) = -0.94$, $p = .354$, $d = 0.39$; (3) motivation: curious $M = 3.68$ ($SD = 0.71$) vs. standard $M = 4.03$ ($SD = 0.52$), $t(29) = -1.49$, $p = .147$, $d = 0.56$. The motivation difference, while not statistically significant, approached a medium effect size, indicating that the standard group entered training with somewhat higher baseline motivation.

## 4.2 Learning Outcomes: Group Comparisons

Table 1 presents descriptive statistics and t-test results for all post-test outcomes, and Table 2 presents ANCOVA results controlling for pre-test motivation.

Supporting H2, conceptual insights showed a large and robust effect that remained significant after controlling for baseline motivation ($d = 0.97$; $F = 5.35$, $p = .029$, partial $\eta^2 = .171$). Welch's correction also indicated significance: $t(22.1) = 2.78$, $p = .011$. The curiosity group's substantially lower variance ($SD = 0.54$ vs. $1.14$) suggests that the intervention produced more consistent perceived outcomes across participants.

Partially supporting H1, pitch competence improvement showed a medium-to-large effect in the t-test ($d = 0.77$, $p = .043$), but did not remain significant after controlling for baseline motivation ($F = 2.37$, $p = .136$). This suggests that the baseline motivation difference may have partially contributed to the observed pitch improvement effect.

The curiosity condition also showed significantly higher epistemic curiosity ($M = 3.57$, $SD = 0.68$ vs. $M = 2.80$, $SD = 1.24$), $t(29) = 2.06$, $p = .048$, $d = 0.75$. Due to heterogeneous variances (Levene's $F = 6.00$, $p = .021$), Welch's correction: $t(23.5) = 2.18$, $p = .039$. This effect did not remain significant after ANCOVA ($p = .106$).

**Table 1.** Descriptive statistics and independent-samples t-tests for post-test outcomes

| Variable | M Curious (SD) | M Standard (SD) | t (df) | p | d |
|---|---|---|---|---|---|
| Pitch Improvement | 3.38 (0.68) | 2.72 (0.97) | 2.12 (29) | .043* | 0.77 |
| Conceptual Insights | 3.88 (0.54) | 2.98 (1.14) | 2.66 (28) | .013* | 0.97 |
| Epistemic Curiosity | 3.57 (0.68) | 2.80 (1.24) | 2.06 (29) | .048* | 0.75 |
| Training Effectiveness | 3.75 (0.61) | 3.18 (1.07) | 1.78 (29) | .086 | 0.64 |
| Transfer Intentions | 3.57 (0.73) | 3.44 (1.24) | 0.35 (29) | .731 | 0.13 |
| Motivation/Preparedness | 3.70 (0.71) | 3.71 (1.12) | −0.03 (29) | .978 | −0.01 |

Note. * $p < .05$. d = Cohen's d. Curious: n = 14, Standard: n = 17 (n = 16 for conceptual insights due to one missing response).

**Table 2.** ANCOVA results (Covariate: Pre-test motivation)

| Variable | F | p | Partial $\eta^2$ |
|---|---|---|---|
| Pitch Improvement | 2.37 | .136 | .084 |
| Conceptual Insights | 5.35 | .029* | .171 |
| Epistemic Curiosity | 2.80 | .106 | .097 |
| Training Effectiveness | 1.33 | .259 | .049 |
| Transfer Intentions | 0.35 | .559 | .013 |
| Motivation/Preparedness | 0.38 | .541 | .015 |

Note. *$p < .05$. n = 29 (two participants could not be matched between pre- and post-test)

No significant differences were found for transfer intentions (d = 0.13, p = .731) or motivation/preparedness (d = −0.01, p = .978). This pattern indicates that the intervention produced additional benefits specifically for knowledge-related outcomes, while transfer intentions and motivation did not differ significantly between conditions.

## 4.3 Item-Level Analysis of Pitch Competence Improvement

Table 3 presents item-level comparisons for the pitch competence improvement scale.

The item-level analysis reveals that the composite pitch improvement effect (d = 0.77) was primarily driven by the "respond to critical questions" item, which showed a large and highly significant effect (d = 1.08, p = .006). One interpretation is that students who practiced responding to curiosity-eliciting questions perceived greater improvement in their ability to handle critical questioning. However, demand characteristics cannot be excluded: students who received more challenging questions may have inferred improvement without necessarily reflecting actual competence gains.

**Table 3.** Item-level analysis of pitch competence improvement

| Item | M Cur. (SD) | M Std. (SD) | t | p | d |
|---|---|---|---|---|---|
| Structure presentations better | 3.29 (0.91) | 2.88 (1.11) | 1.09 | .286 | 0.39 |
| Explain content more clearly | 3.14 (0.86) | 2.59 (1.12) | 1.52 | .141 | 0.55 |
| Respond to critical questions | **3.86 (0.77)** | **2.71 (1.26)** | **2.98** | **.006**** | **1.08** |
| Overall pitching competence | 3.21 (0.97) | 2.71 (1.10) | 1.34 | .190 | 0.48 |

Note. ** $p < .01$. Cur. = Curiosity (n = 14), Std. = Standard (n = 17).

### 4.4 Item-Level Analysis of Conceptual Insights

Table 4 presents item-level comparisons for the conceptual insights scale.

**Table 4.** Item-level analysis of conceptual insights

| Item | M Cur. (SD) | M Std. (SD) | t | p | d |
|---|---|---|---|---|---|
| Improvements clearer | 4.07 (0.73) | 3.50 (1.32) | 1.44 | .161 | 0.53 |
| Solution innovativeness | **3.79 (0.80)** | **2.59 (1.33)** | **2.96** | **.006**** | **1.07** |
| Technical feasibility | 3.79 (0.70) | 2.94 (1.39) | 2.06 | .048* | 0.74 |
| Market potential | 3.86 (0.77) | 2.94 (1.39) | 2.20 | .036* | 0.79 |

Note. * $p < .05$, ** $p < .01$. Cur. = Curiosity (n = 14), Std. = Standard (n = 17).

The item-level analysis reveals a differentiated pattern of effects. The strongest effect emerged for solution innovativeness ($d = 1.07$, $p = .006$), suggesting that the curiosity-eliciting strategies were particularly effective at prompting students to reflect on the innovativeness of their concepts. Market potential assessment ($d = 0.79$, $p = .036$) and technical feasibility clarity ($d = 0.74$, $p = .048$) also showed significant differences suggesting that curiosity-eliciting questions promoted insight about strategic and analytical dimensions rather than general awareness of improvements.

A separate item measuring pride ("I am now more proud of our solution concept") showed zero difference between groups ($d = 0.00$, $p = 1.00$; both $M = 4.00$), consistent with the intervention affecting cognitive rather than emotional responses to the project.

### 4.5 Curiosity and Learning Outcomes: Regression Analyses

To examine how experienced curiosity relates to learning outcomes (H3), regression analyses were conducted within the curiosity group. Partially supporting H3, experienced curiosity was significantly associated with perceived training effectiveness ($\beta = .745$, $p = .003$, $R^2 = .555$), suggesting that students who experienced more curiosity found the training substantially more useful. The association with pitch competence approached significance ($\beta = .526$, $p = .065$). Curiosity was not associated with conceptual insights ($\beta = .141$, $p = .645$), suggesting that the robust conceptual insight gains ($d = 0.97$,

**Table 5.** Regression: epistemic curiosity and outcomes (Curiosity Group, n = 13)

| Outcome | β | t | p | $R^2$ |
|---|---|---|---|---|
| Pitch Competence Improvement | .526 | 2.05 | .065 | .276 |
| Conceptual Insights | .141 | 0.47 | .645 | .020 |
| Training Effectiveness | .745 | 3.70 | .003** | .555 |
| Motivation/Preparedness | .432 | 1.59 | .140 | .187 |

Note. **$p < .01$. n = 13 (one participant could not be matched).

remaining significant after ANCOVA) may have operated through the cognitive demands of the questioning strategies rather than through subjectively experienced curiosity.

### 4.6 Qualitative Findings: Cognitive Activation Patterns

Supporting H4, qualitative responses revealed clear differences in cognitive activation between conditions. Table 6 presents the distribution of responses to the question "Which question type most strongly prompted thinking about your project?"

**Table 6.** Question types identified as most thought-provoking, by condition

| Response Category | Curiosity (n = 14) | Standard (n = 17) |
|---|---|---|
| Critical questions about assumptions | 42.9% (6) | 17.6% (3) |
| Counterfactual questions ("What if...") | 28.6% (4) | 0% (0) |
| Perspective-taking questions | 14.3% (2) | 0% (0) |
| Other specific types | 14.3% (2) | 5.9% (1) |
| "None was particularly effective" | 0% (0) | 23.5% (4) |
| "These question types were not used" | 0% (0) | 29.4% (5) |
| "All equally effective" | 0% (0) | 17.6% (3) |

In the curiosity condition, all 14 participants identified specific questioning strategies as thought-provoking, with critical questions (42.9%) and counterfactual questions (28.6%) most frequently cited (combined: 71.4%). In contrast, over half of the standard condition participants (52.9%) reported either that "none of the question types was particularly effective" (23.5%) or that "these question types were not used" (29.4%). Only 17.6% of standard condition participants identified any specific questioning strategy as effective.

Additionally, when asked which aspects elicited curiosity during training (multiple selection), 85.7% (12/14) of curiosity condition participants identified "critical questioning of assumptions" as a curiosity-inducing aspect, compared to 17.6% (3/17) in the standard condition (Δ = 68.1%). This further supports the interpretation that the questioning strategies produced distinctive cognitive activation patterns.

Regarding the overall robot experience, participants in the curiosity condition rated their experience significantly more positively ($M = 4.29$, $SD = 0.73$ vs. $M = 3.29$, $SD = 1.10$), $t(29) = 2.88$, $p = .007$, $d = 1.04$, while perceived naturalness did not differ significantly between conditions ($d = 0.43$, $p = .239$), suggesting that the curiosity-eliciting strategies enhanced the perceived learning experience without altering the perceived naturalness of the human-robot interaction. Responses to the open-ended improvement question revealed that both groups most frequently suggested longer response times (curiosity: 28.6%; standard: 23.5%). Notably, one standard condition participant explicitly stated that "more critical perspectives would have been good," suggesting an unmet need that the curiosity condition addressed by design. Curiosity condition participants more frequently reported no suggestions or expressed satisfaction (35.7% vs. 23.5%), while standard condition participants more frequently reported being interrupted before completing their answers (23.5% vs. 7.1%).

## 5 Discussion

### 5.1 Learning Outcomes and the Role of Curiosity-Eliciting Strategies

The most robust finding is the large effect on conceptual insights ($d = 0.97$), which remained significant after controlling for baseline differences (ANCOVA: $p = .029$). These effect sizes are comparable to meta-analytic estimates for robot-based education, with effect sizes ranging from $g = 0.47$ to 0.72 [8], and converge with prior Furhat-based pitch training of $d = 0.83$ [18]. Item-level analyses showed that the strongest effects emerged for solution innovativeness ($d = 1.07$) and market potential ($d = 0.79$), suggesting that the questioning strategies may have been effective at prompting deeper reflection on strategic dimensions of students' concepts, consistent with the cognitive operations targeted by the six questioning strategies.

Pitch competence improvement showed a medium-to-large effect in the t-test ($d = 0.77$) but did not remain significant after controlling for baseline motivation (ANCOVA: $p = .136$), suggesting that baseline motivation differences may have contributed. The selective pattern, with knowledge-related outcomes enhanced while motivation and transfer did not differ between conditions, is consistent with Information-Gap Theory [1], which predicts that curiosity drives specific knowledge-seeking rather than general motivation, though the small sample limits conclusions about null effects.

### 5.2 Curiosity and Learning: Differential Associations

The regression analyses revealed that experienced curiosity was strongly associated with perceived training effectiveness ($\beta = .745$, $p = .003$) but not with conceptual insights ($\beta = .141$, $p = .645$), despite the large between-group effect on insights. This suggests that the cognitive demands of the questioning strategies, such as responding to counterfactual or perspective-shifting questions, may have enhanced conceptual understanding regardless of whether students subjectively experienced curiosity. The strategies may function as cognitive scaffolding that directs attention to specific knowledge gaps. However, the small sample ($n = 13$) limits statistical power, and this interpretation requires replication.

### 5.3 Consistency of Learning Outcomes

The lower variance in the curiosity condition (SD = 0.54 vs. 1.14, F = 11.05, p = .002) is practically noteworthy: nearly all curiosity participants reported moderate-to-high gains, while standard condition outcomes varied widely. This consistency could reflect questioning strategies functioning as scaffolding that ensures deeper engagement for all participants, though ceiling effects (M = 3.88 on a 5-point scale) cannot be excluded; replication is needed to distinguish these interpretations.

### 5.4 Implications for Curiosity-Enhancing Educational Technologies

The curiosity-eliciting strategies developed in this study are not inherently tied to social robots. The six questioning strategies could be implemented in chatbots, virtual agents, or other LLM-powered learning systems. The key contribution is the theory-based strategy design: grounding questioning in Information-Gap Theory provides a principled approach to enhancing curiosity that can be adapted across educational technologies. The brief sessions (15–20 min) and team format (3–5 students) suggest practical feasibility for classroom integration.

## 6 Limitations and Future Research

Several limitations constrain generalizability. First, all outcomes were self-reported; objective assessments such as blind-coded ratings of actual presentations are needed. In the present study, final pitches were assessed by company representatives, but these data were not collected as part of the research. Second, the sample (N = 31) was small. A power analysis (G*Power) indicates that replicating the conceptual insights effect (d = 0.97) would require N = 34 at 80% power. The within-group regression analyses (n = 13) are particularly power-limited, and non-significant associations should not be interpreted as evidence of no relationship. Third, session duration differed between conditions (M = 14.8 vs. 19.3 min). The selective effect pattern and convergent qualitative evidence suggest questioning strategies rather than time-on-task drove effects. Time-matched control designs are needed to address this. Fourth, the single-session design limits conclusions about retention. Future research should test these curiosity-eliciting strategies in other educational contexts (e.g., writing support, exam preparation), in multi-session designs, and compare the robot-LLM combination with LLM-only and human tutor conditions.

## 7 Conclusions

This study provides initial evidence that theory-based curiosity-eliciting questioning strategies can enhance self-reported learning outcomes when delivered by an LLM-powered social robot. The most robust finding was a large effect on conceptual insights (d = 0.97), which remained significant after controlling for baseline differences. Experienced curiosity was strongly associated with perceived training effectiveness ($\beta$ = .745, p = .003), while conceptual gains appeared linked to the cognitive demands of the questioning strategies rather than to subjectively experienced curiosity. The six strategies (counterfactual, paradoxical, comparative, perspective-shifting, future projection, provocation), grounded in Information-Gap Theory, offer a transferable approach for enhancing curiosity in educational technologies beyond social robots, including chatbots, virtual agents, and other LLM-powered learning systems. Replication with larger samples and objective outcome measures is needed.

## References


1. Loewenstein, G.: The psychology of curiosity: a review and reinterpretation. Psychol. Bull. **116**, 75–98 (1994). https://doi.org/10.1037/0033-2909.116.1.75
2. Berlyne, D.E.: Conflict, Arousal, and Curiosity (1960). https://doi.org/10.1037/11164-000
3. Gruber, M.J., Gelman, B.D., Ranganath, C.: States of curiosity modulate hippocampus-dependent learning via the dopaminergic circuit. Neuron. **84**, 486–496 (2014). https://doi.org/10.1016/j.neuron.2014.08.060
4. Kang, M.J., et al.: The wick in the candle of learning: epistemic curiosity activates reward circuitry and enhances memory. Psychol. Sci. **20**, 963–973 (2009). https://doi.org/10.1111/j.1467-9280.2009.02402.x
5. Zawacki-Richter, O., Marín, V.I., Bond, M., Gouverneur, F.: Systematic review of research on artificial intelligence applications in higher education – where are the educators? Int. J. Educ. Technol. High. Educ. **16**, 39 (2019). https://doi.org/10.1186/s41239-019-0171-0
6. Paul, R., Elder, L.: The Thinker's Guide to Socratic Questioning. Rowman & Littlefield Publishers, Blue Ridge Summit (2019)
7. Belpaeme, T., Kennedy, J., Ramachandran, A., Scassellati, B., Tanaka, F.: Social robots for education: a review. Sci. Robot. **3, eaat5954** (2018). https://doi.org/10.1126/scirobotics.aat5954
8. Tang, H., Xu, W., Feng, Y., Cao, W.: Global effects of robot-based education on academic achievements, computation, motivation, and performance. Humanit. Soc. Sci. Commun. **12**, 1296 (2025). https://doi.org/10.1057/s41599-025-05546-9
9. Leyzberg, D., Spaulding, S., Toneva, M., Scassellati, B.: The physical presence of a robot tutor increases cognitive learning gains. In: Building Bridges Cognitive Science World - Proceedings of the Annual Meeting of the Cognitive Science Society 2012, pp. 1882–1887 (2012)
10. Blavette, L., Dacunha, S., Alameda-Pineda, X., Cattoni, J., Rigaud, A.-S., Pino, M.: Integrating a large language model into a socially assistive robot in a hospital geriatric unit: two-wave comparative study on performance, engagement, and user perceptions. JMIR Hum. Factors. **12**, e81936 (2025). https://doi.org/10.2196/81936
11. Kim, C.Y., Lee, C.P., Mutlu, B.: Understanding large-language model (LLM)-powered human-robot interaction. In: Proceedings of the 2024 ACM/IEEE International Conference on Human-Robot Interaction, pp. 371–380. ACM, Boulder CO USA (2024). https://doi.org/10.1145/3610977.3634966
12. Williams, T., Matuszek, C., Mead, R., Depalma, N.: Scarecrows in Oz: the use of large language models in HRI. J Hum-Robot Interact. **13**(1), 1–11 (2024). https://doi.org/10.1145/3606261
13. Wollny, S., Schneider, J., Di Mitri, D., Weidlich, J., Rittberger, M., Drachsler, H.: Are we there yet? - a systematic literature review on Chatbots in education. Front. Artif. Intell. **4** (2021). https://doi.org/10.3389/frai.2021.654924
14. Pinto-Bernal, M., Biondina, M., Belpaeme, T.: Designing social robots with LLMs for engaging human interaction. Appl. Sci. **15**, 6377 (2025). https://doi.org/10.3390/app15116377

15. Borg, A., et al.: AI-enhanced social robotic versus computer-based virtual patients for clinical reasoning training in medical education: an observational crossover study (preprint). J. Med. Internet Res. **27** (2025). https://doi.org/10.2196/82541
16. Ekström, S., Pareto, L., Ljungblad, S.: Teaching in a collaborative mathematic learning activity with and without a social robot. Educ. Inf. Technol. (2024). https://doi.org/10.1007/s10639-024-12926-2
17. Verhelst, E., Janssens, R., Belpaeme, T.: Enabling autonomous and adaptive social robots in education: a vision for the application of generative AI. In: Lampropoulos, G., Papadakis, S. (eds.) Social Robots in Education: how to Effectively Introduce Social Robots into Classrooms, pp. 17–42. Springer Nature, Switzerland, Cham (2025). https://doi.org/10.1007/978-3-031-82915-4_2
18. Buchem, I., Olteanu, Y., Bonga, G.A.K.: Pitch training with Furhat: effects of a social robot in entrepreneurship education. In: Staffa, M., et al. (eds.) Social Robotics + AI, pp. 553–558. Springer Nature, Singapore (2026). https://doi.org/10.1007/978-981-95-2379-5_45
19. Bonga, G.A.K., Buchem, I., Pinkwart, N.: Empowering academic exploration with LLM-powered robots: supporting students in topic and research question development. In: Balogh, R., Obdržálek, D., Fachantidis, N. (eds.) Robotics in Education, pp. 126–137. Springer Nature, Switzerland, Cham (2025). https://doi.org/10.1007/978-3-031-98762-5_12
20. Yang, S.C., Chung, T.: Experimental study of teaching critical thinking in civic education in Taiwanese junior high school. Br. J. Educ. Psychol. **79**, 29–55 (2009). https://doi.org/10.1348/000709907X238771
21. Xi, L., Zhang, Y., Wang, Q.: Investigating the effects of an LLM-based Socratic conversational agent on students' academic performance and reflective thinking in higher education. Comput. Educ. **241**, 105494 (2026). https://doi.org/10.1016/j.compedu.2025.105494
22. Van Hoeck, N., Watson, P.D., Barbey, A.K.: Cognitive neuroscience of human counterfactual reasoning. Front. Hum. Neurosci. **9** (2015). https://doi.org/10.3389/fnhum.2015.00420
23. Festinger, L.: A Theory of Cognitive Dissonance. Stanford Univ. Press, Stanford, Calif (1957)
24. Limón, M.: On the cognitive conflict as an instructional strategy for conceptual change: a critical appraisal. Learn. Instr. **11**, 357–380 (2001). https://doi.org/10.1016/S0959-4752(00)00037-2
25. Loibl, K., Roll, I., Rummel, N.: Towards a theory of when and how problem solving followed by instruction supports learning. Educ. Psychol. Rev. **29**, 693–715 (2017). https://doi.org/10.1007/s10648-016-9379-x
26. Gehlbach, H., Mu, N.: How we understand others: a theory of how social perspective taking unfolds. Rev. Gen. Psychol. **27**, 282–302 (2023). https://doi.org/10.1177/10892680231152595
27. Geden, M. et al.: Construction and validation of an anticipatory thinking assessment. Front. Psychol. **10** (2019). https://doi.org/10.3389/fpsyg.2019.02749
28. Johnson, D.W., Johnson, R.T.: Energizing learning: the instructional power of conflict. Educ. Res. **38**, 37–51 (2009). https://doi.org/10.3102/0013189X08330540
29. Kontogiorgos, D., van Waveren, S., Wallberg, O., Pereira, A., Leite, I., Gustafson, J.: Embodiment effects in interactions with failing robots. In: Proceedings of the 2020 CHI Conference on Human Factors in Computing Systems, pp. 1–14. Association for Computing Machinery, New York, NY, USA (2020). https://doi.org/10.1145/3313831.3376372
30. Tisza, G., et al.: Generative AI-powered social robots in education: opportunities and challenges from a Delphi study. Behav. Inf. Technol. **1–23** (2025). https://doi.org/10.1080/0144929X.2025.2604060
31. Shi, Y., Yu, K., Dong, Y., Chen, F.: Large language models in education: a systematic review of empirical applications, benefits, and challenges. Comput. Educ. Artif. Intell. **10**, 100529 (2026). https://doi.org/10.1016/j.caeai.2025.100529

32. Ackermann, H., Lange, A.L., Hafner, V.V., Lazarides, R.: How adaptive social robots influence cognitive, emotional, and self-regulated learning. Sci. Rep. **15**, 6581 (2025). https://doi.org/10.1038/s41598-025-91236-0
33. Donnermann, M., Schaper, P., Lugrin, B.: Social robots in applied settings: a long-term study on adaptive robotic tutors in higher education. Front. Robot. AI. **9** (2022). https://doi.org/10.3389/frobt.2022.831633
34. Hair, J.F., Black, W.C., Babin, B.J., Anderson, R.E.: Multivariate data analysis. Cengage, Andover, Hampshire (2019)
35. Kuckartz, U., Rädiker, S.: Qualitative Inhaltsanalyse: Methoden, Praxis, Computerunterstützung: Grundlagentexte Methoden. Beltz Juventa, Weinheim Basel (2022)
36. Cohen, J.: Statistical Power Analysis for the Behavioral Sciences. L. Erlbaum Associates, Hillsdale, N.J (1988)
37. Blanca, M., Alarcón, R., Arnau, J., Bono, R., Bendayan, R.: Non-normal data: is ANOVA still a valid option? Psicothema. **4**, 552–557 (2017). https://doi.org/10.7334/psicothema2016.383
38. Knief, U., Forstmeier, W.: Violating the normality assumption may be the lesser of two evils. Behav. Res. Methods. **53**, 2576–2590 (2021). https://doi.org/10.3758/s13428-021-01587-5

# AI Teaching Assistants in Online Discussion Forums and Peer-Supported Self-regulated Learning

Richard Lee Davis[1(✉)], Xiner Liu[2], Maciej Pankiewicz[2], Andreas Kissmehl[1], Olov Engwall[1], Ryan S. Baker[3], and Olga Viberg[1,3]

[1] KTH Royal Institute of Technology, Stockholm, Sweden
{rldavis,kismehl,engwall,oviberg}@kth.se
[2] University of Pennsylvania, Philadelphia, PA, USA
{xiner,mpank}@upenn.edu
[3] Adelaide University, Adelaide, Australia

**Abstract.** AI-powered teaching assistants (AI TAs) are increasingly deployed in online course forums, yet little is known about how their presence relates to students' self-regulated learning (SRL) strategies or academic outcomes. This study examines four different university courses with different AI TA involvement: a human-only forum and three courses supported by an AI TA, to explore associations between AI TA presence, SRL composition, discussion dynamics, and grade results. Using sentence-level SRL coding across approximately 28,000 student-authored sentences and student-level outcome modeling, we report three main results. First, in the two high-exposure AI courses, the AI TA dominated assignment threads as first responder, and its presence was associated with reduced peer participation; students in the AI-supported courses produced fewer reply posts; and peer contributions to assignment threads declined over the semester. Second, this shift in responder ecology was accompanied by a decline in peer co-regulatory discourse, which was related to lower aggregate levels of regulatory language in AI-supported forums compared with the human-only baseline. Third, in the AI-supported courses, students' self-regulation was the strongest predictor of grade, but peer interaction moderated this relationship: self-regulation was a stronger predictor of grade for students whose threads attracted more peer replies. The overall grade penalty associated with AI TA interaction was concentrated among highly self-regulated students who received less peer co-regulation, suggesting that the displacement of peer dialogue may weaken the support structure through which self-regulation relates to academic outcomes.

**Keywords:** Self-regulated learning · Co-regulation · Online course forums · AI teaching assistant · STEM higher education

Richard Lee Davis and Olga Viberg : These authors contributed equally to this work and share first authorship.


J. Weidlich et al. (Eds.): EC-TEL 2026, LNCS 16905, pp. 345–360, 2027.
https://doi.org/10.1007/978-3-032-37979-5_24

# 1 Introduction

Online discussion forums are central in many university courses [15], particularly in technically demanding STEM domains such as computer science (CS) education [6,16]. In these contexts, students use forums to ask questions, seek clarification, troubleshoot problems, and discuss assignments [6,12]. Beyond their communicative function, forums also serve as learning spaces, in which discourse can externalize key aspects of self-regulated learning (SRL)[32], including help-seeking, elaboration, organization, effort regulation, and critical thinking. Previous research has used forum interactions to study how learners engage in and regulate their learning in collaboration with peers and instructors [14,31].

How students participate in forums, and which SRL processes become visible there, is shaped by the structure of interaction [4,22]: who responds to a question, how quickly support is provided, and whether a discussion expands or closes. Forums can thus be understood as interactional systems in which learning emerges through the interplay of multiple actors and roles. In these settings, peers often contribute co-regulatory support by elaborating, questioning, and explaining, while instructors and teaching assistants (TAs) provide more authoritative forms of scaffolding [3,10,25,33].

Advances in generative AI (GenAI) have led to the increasing integration of AI-mediated support into online discussion environments, including AI agents acting as TAs [16,20] that offer clear advantages in responsiveness and availability. In contrast to human teachers, AI TAs can respond instantly to multiple student queries and consistently address assignment-related questions. At the same time, they introduce a qualitative shift in how forum interaction unfolds. When students receive immediate answers from an AI TA rather than waiting for peers or instructors, the ecology of participation may change: AI may alter who responds, how long discussions continue, and whether students engage in the kinds of exchanges through which SRL is expressed, practiced, and supported.

Despite the growing adoption of AI TAs [20], their relationship with SRL, participation patterns, and academic outcomes in discussion forums remains poorly understood. This gap is significant because SRL is a key competency for success in online learning and a robust predictor of academic performance [29]. If AI systems change how students seek help, articulate uncertainty, elaborate on problems, or interact with others, they may reshape learning processes in ways that are not fully captured by conventional performance metrics. Existing research has emphasized grades, adoption, or system usage [21], with less attention to how AI support reconfigures the discourse and interactional structures through which regulation and co-regulation of learning occur.

In this paper, we address this gap by conceptualizing AI integration as a reconfiguration of forum ecology rather than a uniform intervention. We treat discussion forums as multi-actor environments in which students, instructors, and AI systems jointly shape interaction patterns and the student learning process. From this point of view, the key question is not whether AI increases or decreases SRL overall, but how it redistributes regulatory activities between actors, thread types, and interaction contexts. This framing allows us to distinguish between *self-regulation*, which students express in their own learning processes, and *co-regulation*, which emerges when others scaffold those processes through dialogue [9].

Over three levels, we analyzed these issues through four educational technology courses with varying levels of AI TA integration: one human-only forum, one limited-exposure AI condition, and two courses with more extensive AI TA interaction. *First,* we examine how SRL discourse differs across course contexts, testing whether AI-supported forums exhibit a uniform SRL profile or a heterogeneous reconfiguration. *Second,* we analyze how patterns of regulatory language differ between AI-supported and human-only courses and how they develop over time. *Third,* we examine student-level relationships among self-regulation, co-regulation, peer interaction, and academic performance.

We pose the following research questions: **RQ1.** How does the presence of an AI teaching assistant influence participation patterns and peer dialogue in online discussion forums? **RQ2.** How do patterns of self-regulatory and co-regulatory language differ between AI-supported and human-only courses, and how do they develop over the semester? **RQ3.** How are self-regulation, co-regulation, and peer interaction related to academic performance in AI-supported courses?

The **contributions** of this work are threefold. **First,** we show that the AI TA's presence as a dominant first responder in assignment threads is associated with reduced peer follow-on participation, a pattern that grows over the semester. **Second,** we show that aggregate levels of regulatory language are lower in AI-supported courses, and that this difference is accounted for by the declining share of peer repliers, who carry the majority of co-regulatory discourse. **Third,** we find that students' own self-regulation is a predictor of academic performance, but that peer interaction moderates this relationship: self-regulation is a stronger predictor of grade when accompanied by peer dialogue. These results highlight the importance of attending to peer co-regulation when designing AI-supported learning environments.

## 2 Background

### 2.1 SRL in STEM Education

STEM education, in particular computing education, requires learners to coordinate multiple cognitive and metacognitive processes, including understanding abstract concepts, constructing solutions, debugging iteratively, and evaluating outcomes [18]. Given the diversity in students' prior knowledge and problem-solving skills, learners must actively regulate their learning processes to succeed [34]. SRL is therefore a critical component of programming education [5,27].

SRL comprises cognitive and metacognitive strategies such as elaboration, organization, and critical thinking as well as resource management strategies including effort regulation and help-seeking [34]. Prior work in programming education has demonstrated that high-performing students tend to engage more frequently in higher-order strategies (e.g., effort-regulation, critical thinking), whereas lower-performing students rely more on basic strategies such as rehearsal and executive help-seeking [5]. This highlights that differences in learning outcomes are associated not only with the amount of SRL, but also with the types of strategies students employ in SRL programming practices.

The emergence of commercial large language model (LLM)-based tools, such as Claude and ChatGPT, introduces new forms of student support into programming learning environments. These systems can generate code, explain concepts, and assist with debugging, providing immediate and context-sensitive responses [26,30]. As such, they offer scalable and personalized support that may complement traditional instruction by creating environments that can, in certain conditions, become conducive to the students' acquisition of programming skills.

However, interactions with LLMs may influence core SRL processes and learners' engagement [11,13]. Students engage with LLMs in heterogeneous ways, with variation in prompting strategies and reliance patterns [8,30]. Help-seeking, a central SRL strategy, can become more immediate, iterative, and non-linear in AI-supported contexts [28]. Although this may lower barriers to accessing support, it can also enable learners to bypass critical evaluative and reflective steps, as the ease of obtaining solutions may shift effort regulation, potentially reducing deeper cognitive engagement with programming tasks [30].

The increasing integration of LLMs in computing education is transforming not only learning outcomes but also the ways students engage in SRL. As a result, leveraging these tools effectively for learning may necessitate the adoption of new regulatory strategies. Understanding these transformations requires viewing SRL as emerging within sociotechnical learning settings, where students, instructors, and AI systems collectively shape regulatory processes and learning experiences.

## 2.2 SRL in Online Discussion Forums

Online discussion forums are important spaces where learners actively engage in SRL [32], by externalizing key regulatory processes through discourse, in the form of help-seeking, explanation, and reflection [7,32]. Help-seeking is evident when students pose questions, request clarification, or solicit assistance from peers and instructors. Explanation emerges as learners articulate their reasoning, elaborate on problem-solving steps, or provide guidance to others. Reflection is demonstrated in students' evaluation of their understanding, reconsideration of prior approaches, and discussion of alternative strategies. Together, these activities make forums valuable sites for observing how learners regulate their cognition and learning processes in interaction with others.

Prior research has used forum data using discourse and learning analytics approaches to better understand these processes [4,32]. This work treats forum interactions as trace data that capture learners' cognitive and metacognitive activities as they unfold. In particular, studies have applied SRL coding schemes to textual data, enabling the identification and quantification of learning strategies at different levels of granularity, including fine-grained, sentence-level annotation [32]. This moves beyond simple participation metrics and instead focuses on the quality and nature of learners' contributions. Building on this, we posit that online discussion forums constitute windows into students' SRL processes.

The content and structure of forum discourse provide observable evidence of how learners plan, monitor, and regulate their learning with and without AI TAs.

### 2.3 Teaching Presence in Online Discussion Forums

Interaction in online discussion forums is shaped not only by what is said, but by *who* responds. Prior research has highlighted the importance of teaching presence and support roles in structuring learning processes, particularly in technology-mediated environments [3,25]. Within this literature, different actors such as peers and instructors, including teachers and TAs, play distinct roles in scaffolding student learning [10,33].

Instructor responses are typically more authoritative and directive compared to those from peers. As part of teaching presence, instructors guide discourse, provide clarification, and scaffold student understanding by structuring problems and highlighting key concepts [23]. This form of support can help regulate learning by modeling effective strategies and ensuring conceptual correctness. However, instructor intervention may also shape participation patterns, for example by closing down discussion once a definitive answer is provided.

Recently, AI-mediated instructors in the form of AI TAs have emerged as a new form of support actor in online forums [16,20]. These systems differ from both peers and human instructors in important ways. AI TAs can provide immediate, scalable, and consistent responses to student queries, particularly in assignment-related contexts. From a scaffolding perspective, they have the potential to support help-seeking by lowering barriers to accessing assistance and enabling iterative questioning. At the same time, their responsiveness and perceived authority may alter how students engage in self-regulation in their learning activities, e.g., by altering their help-seeking behavior and interaction, potentially reducing opportunities for learning. In sum, we conceptualize students, instructors (human TAs and course teachers), and AI TAs as a "responder ecology" shaping student SRL in online discussion forums. Rather than viewing support as uniform, this view stresses how differences in responsiveness, authority, and interaction style influence participation and SRL in online forums.

qualitativen

## 3 Methodology

### 3.1 Implemented AI TA

JeepyTA is a platform extending educational discussion forums with functionality enabled by LLMs. Developed at the Penn Center for Learning Analytics at the University of Pennsylvania in 2023, the platform has since been used by faculty at five universities across 29 courses internationally [1].

The central feature of JeepyTA is an AI TA that participates in forum discussions by responding to student posts. Each response is generated through a request to an LLM that contains two primary components: (1) instructions specifying how the response should be generated and (2) contextual information. The instructions are implemented as category-specific prompts that define the intended goals, rules, and constraints of the AI TA's responses. Also, instructors can configure visibility settings, including whether AI TA's responses are published immediately or require instructor approval before becoming visible.

The contextual information always includes the student's post and may additionally include other materials such as prior discussion history, instructors' posts, the contents of files attached to the post, and materials attached to the category as a knowledge base. Context construction is supported by a retrieval-augmented generation (RAG) approach, in which textual materials are converted into embeddings to enable semantic search and retrieval of content relevant to the current discussion.

For the courses analyzed in this study, JeepyTA relied on OpenAI GPT models available at the time of deployment: GPT-3.5 Turbo for DS AI, GPT-4 in BD AI, and GPT-4 Turbo in AL AI.

### 3.2 Datasets

The dataset comprises 28,123 sentence-level units aggregated across four graduate-level courses within data science and educational design, with one human-only condition (DS Human; a data science course) and three courses including an AI TA (respectively, DS AI, the same DS course with AI TA incorporated; BD AI, a course on big data and education; and AL AI, an educational design course focused on adaptive learning systems). Each forum post included a course identifier, thread name, anonymized user ID, and time of posting. The posts were first split into individual sentences by applying the NLTK punkt model [2] and cleaned from HTML artifacts with Beautiful Soup[1]. Following a qualitative AI-supported coding approach [17], we developed and applied a codebook (https://shorturl.at/bsdSa) in a multi-stage validation procedure. We established a ground truth using a random sample of 100 instances, which were independently annotated by two human coders, resulting in satisfactory inter-rater reliability.(Cohen's $\kappa > 0.85$, all codes) while ensuring a minimum prevalence threshold of 5% in each label. A few-shot prompt was iteratively crafted for an LLM (GPT-4o, via API) to code the ground truth until agreement with the human-established ground truth exceeded $\kappa = 0.70$ across all constructs. Subsequently, we applied the codes resulting from LLM to the full data set. We further gathered normalized course grade data for each student as a percentage ratio of points obtained relative to the maximum score on the course assignments.

## 4 Results

The four courses examined exhibit heterogeneous patterns of student- and AI-TA interactions (Table 1). The DS Human course serves as the human-only baseline;

[1] https://www.crummy.com/software/BeautifulSoup/.

the DS AI TA course represents a low-penetration AI context, with only 20% of students interacting with the AI TA; while the BD AI and AL AI courses show high levels of interactions between students and AI TA, reaching 89% and 95% of students, respectively. The remaining analyses therefore compare three conditions: DS Human as the human-only baseline, and BD AI and AL AI as the two AI-supported courses.

**Table 1.** Study design: four courses with varying AI TA integration. Dashes indicate metrics not applicable to the human-only course.

| Course | Condition | Students | AI TA posts | Students reached | Posts followed | Student sentences | Percent SRL sentences |
|---|---|---|---|---|---|---|---|
| DS Human | Human-only | 40 | — | — | — | 6,491 | 52% |
| DS AI | Human+AI (limited) | 56 | 23 | 20% | 1.5% | 8,086 | 60% |
| BD AI | Human+AI | 45 | 248 | 89% | 41% | 4,756 | 51% |
| AL AI | Human+AI | 39 | 177 | 95% | 21% | 8,687 | 55% |

## 4.1 How Does the AI TA Change Forum Dynamics?

By design, the AI TA was intended to respond in assignment threads, and these were hence more likely to receive a first response from the AI TA, $\chi^2(1) = 178.8$, $p < .001$, OR $= 62.7$, 95% CI [27.3, 169.0]. In both BD AI TA and AL AI TA, the AI TA was the first responder in 97% of student-started assignment threads (Fig. 1, left). Also by design, the AI TA was much faster than human responders (Fig. 1, right). The median time to first response in student-started assignment threads was 0.92 min for AI TA-first threads ($n = 195$; IQR [0.67, 1.21]), compared with 490 min for peer-first threads in the human TA course ($n = 75$; IQR [117, 942]) and 364 min for teacher-first threads in the human TA course ($n = 38$; IQR [89.8, 1068]), $\chi^2(2) = 209.62$, $p < .001$.

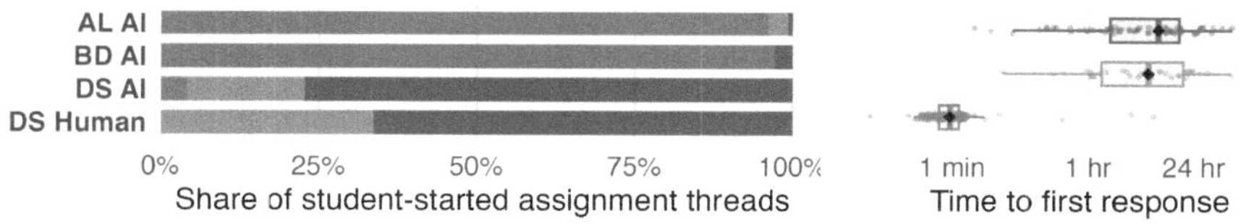


**Fig. 1.** (Left) first responder in student-started assignment threads and (Right) time to first response, in log-scale, by students, teachers, and AI TA.

Next, we turn to the impact on students' forum activity. We firstly observe that students in the AI TA courses posted fewer times on average than students in the human-only course. Students in the human-only course averaged 23.05 posts each, whereas students in the two AI-supported courses averaged 15.85 posts each, $\chi^2(1) = 19.08$, $p < .001$. This difference did not come from thread starts, which were similar across conditions (means = 4.93 vs. 4.88; $p = .73$), but from follow-on replies: students in the human-only course produced more reply posts (mean = 18.2, median = 18) than students in the AI-supported courses (mean = 10.9, median = 10.5), $\chi^2(1) = 26.31$, $p < .001$ (Fig. 2).

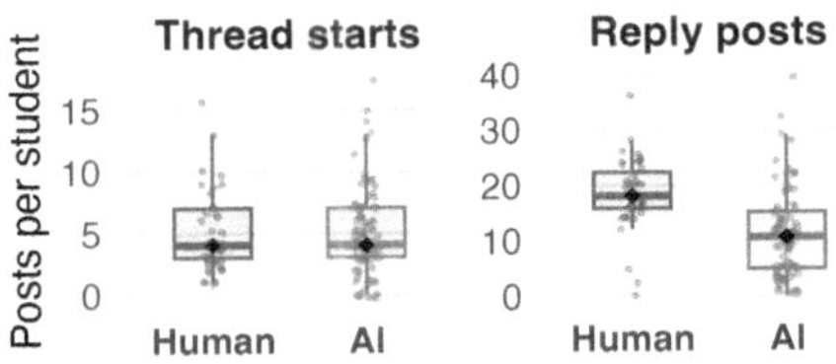


**Fig. 2.** Posts per student in the human-only course versus the two AI-supported courses, decomposed into thread starts and reply posts.

## 4.2 Relationship Between Interaction Partners and Grades

We next investigated how students' conversation partners were related to grade outcomes in the two AI-supported courses. For each student, we identified the threads that a student started and then calculated three interaction-partner measures: the proportion of responses in those threads that came from a teacher, the proportion that came from a peer, and the proportion that came from the AI TA. These measures therefore describe who populated the conversations that students themselves initiated. We then fit three separate linear regression models, each predicting course-standardized grade from one interaction-partner measure while controlling for posting volume and course. For the linear models reported here and below, we use HC3 robust standard errors [19]; the logistic models later in the section use model-based standard errors.

We found that students who started threads containing a higher proportion of teacher responses earned higher grades ($\beta \approx 2.12$, $p = .009$), whereas students who started threads that then contained a higher proportion of AI TA responses earned lower grades ($\beta \approx -1.38$, $p = .038$). Peer response proportion showed no clear relationship with grade ($\beta \approx 0.02$, $p = .99$) (Fig. 3, left).

Importantly, this pattern is driven by who responds in a student's threads, not by where the student posts. A separate model predicting grade from the proportion of a student's activity occurring in assignment threads showed no significant relationship ($\beta \approx -0.69$, $p = .282$), even though assignment threads are precisely where the AI TA is active.

**Regulatory Language in AI-Supported vs. Human-Only Courses.** The SRL strategies coding categories used in this study (help-seeking, elaboration, critical thinking, organization, and effort regulation) capture regulatory processes that may serve different functions depending on context. When a student

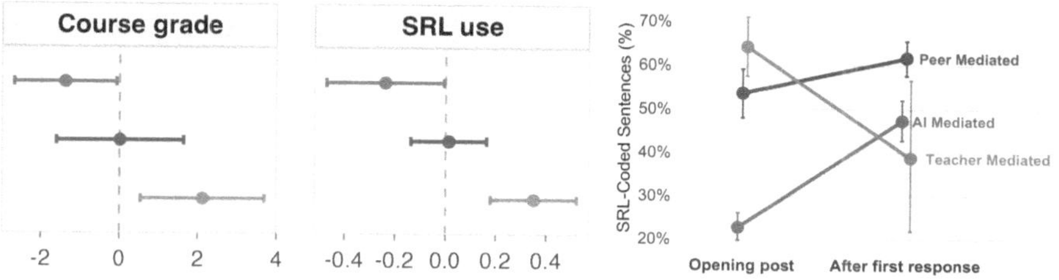


**Fig. 3.** Estimated association between first responder in assignment threads (AI TA, student, teachers and (Left) Course grade or (Middle) SRL use. (Right) Proportion of sentences coded as SRL in the original poster's opening post versus subsequent posts, by thread type. Error bars show 95% bootstrap confidence intervals.

uses regulatory language in a thread that they started (e.g., articulating a plan, monitoring their understanding, or seeking targeted help), these processes constitute self-regulation. When the same language appears in a student's reply to another student's thread, it is consistent with co-regulation: one learner scaffolding another's regulatory activity [9]. This distinction matters because one of the AI TA's effects, as shown in Sect. 4.1, was to displace peer replies, and peer replies are the mechanism through which co-regulation occurs. We examine: 1) how aggregate levels of regulatory language differ between conditions, 2) the student-level relationship between regulatory language and grades.

**Lower SRL in AI-Supported Courses.** We first asked whether the AI-supported courses look different from the human-only baseline on overall levels of regulatory language. A logistic regression predicting whether each sentence was coded as SRL, with condition (human-only vs. AI-supported) as the predictor, showed that the odds of a sentence being coded as SRL were significantly higher in the human-only course than in the two pooled AI-supported courses ($OR = 0.65$, 95% CI [0.62, 0.70], $p < .001$). This difference was concentrated in assignment-thread opening posts. In AI-mediated threads, the original poster's opening move contained less SRL than comparable openings in peer-mediated or teacher-mediated threads. After the opening post, SRL rose in AI-mediated threads but fell in teacher-mediated threads (Fig. 3, right).

There were also significant shifts in SRL over the course of the semester. We split each student's coded sentences into the first (H1) and second halves (H2) of the semester and computed the proportion of sentences coded as SRL in each half. In the AI-supported courses, the proportion of sentences coded as SRL declined from the first half of the semester (mean = 49%) to the second half (mean = 36%), $t(67) = -6.03$, $p < .001$. In the human-only course, SRL trended slightly upward instead (54% to 61%; $t(38) = 2.02$, $p = .050$). This decline persisted even when excluding the assignment-thread opening posts (mean decrease $= -19$ percentage points, $t(61) = -6.00$, $p < .001$) (Fig. 4).

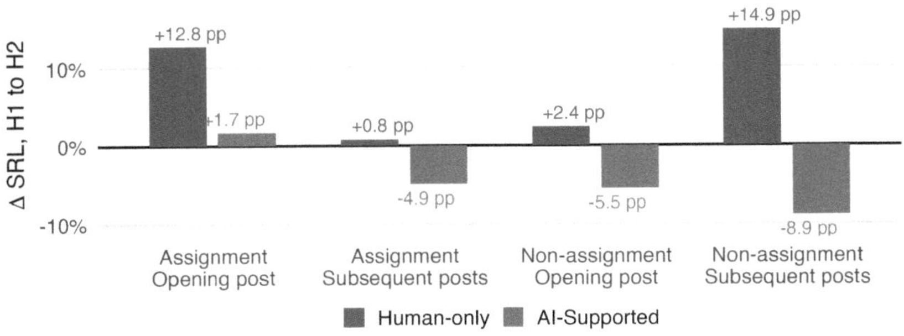


**Fig. 4.** Change in the proportion of sentences coded as SRL from the first half to the second half of the semester, decomposed by thread type and post position.

**The SRL Decline Reflects Lost Peer Co-regulation.** To understand why SRL declined, we examined follow-up sentences in assignment threads. In the pooled AI-supported courses, peer repliers produced approximately 70% SRL-coded sentences (70.2% in H1; 68.5% in H2), whereas thread starters produced much less (26.9% in H1; 20% in H2). As the SRL-coded discourse appears in peer replies, it is more consistent with co-regulation rather than self-regulation [9].

What changed over the semester was not the rate at which each role produced SRL, but how much each role contributed to the conversation. The proportion of follow-up sentences written by peer repliers fell from 91% in the first half to 45% in the second half. Because SRL rates within each role were relatively stable across halves (peer repliers: 70.2% to 68.5%; thread starters: 26.9% to 20%), the decline in overall regulatory language was driven by the shrinking share of peer repliers rather than by changes in SRL rates within each role.

### 4.3 Self-regulation, Co-regulation, and Grades

The previous section established that AI-supported courses exhibit lower aggregate levels of regulatory language, and that this decline is driven by the displacement of peer repliers, who are the primary carriers of co-regulatory discourse. We now turn to the student level and ask how these regulatory processes relate to individual course outcomes.

**Separating Self-regulation from Co-regulation.** We decomposed each student's regulatory language into three components based on where it occurs. Self-regulation captures a student's own regulatory language in threads they started. Received co-regulation captures the regulatory language that human participants (excluding the AI TA) contributed to those same threads. Provided co-regulation captures a student's co-regulatory language when replying in other students' threads. Each measure is a proportion of sentences coded as SRL within its respective context. For each measure, we fit a separate linear regression predicting course-standardized grade from that measure while controlling for posting volume and course, with HC3 robust standard errors (Fig. 5).

Self-regulation was a significant positive predictor of grade ($\beta = 2.63$, 95% CI [0.49, 4.76], $p = .017$, $n = 66$). Neither received co-regulation ($\beta = 0.66$, 95% CI [−1.21, 2.54], $p = .482$, $n = 64$) nor provided co-regulation ($\beta = 0.43$, 95% CI [−1.52, 2.38], $p = .660$, $n = 67$) significantly predicted grade.

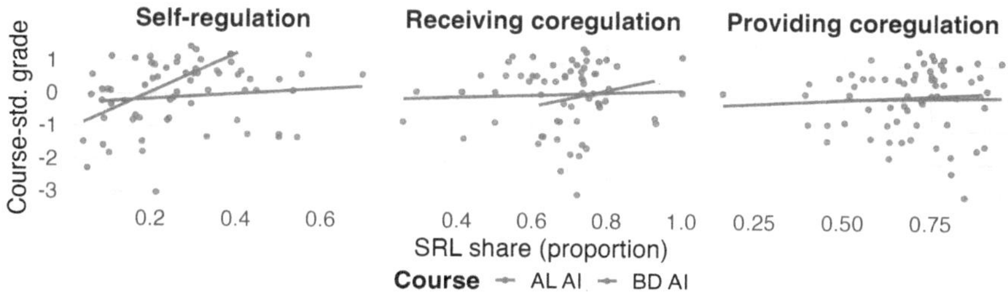


**Fig. 5.** Relationship between the proportion of SRL-coded sentences and course-standardized grade for self-regulation (left), received co-regulation (center) and provided co-regulation (right).

**Peer Interaction Moderates Self-regulation vs. Grade.** Self-regulation predicts grade, but neither receiving nor providing co-regulation does so independently. However, one of the AI TA's effects was to displace peer replies. If peer dialogue sustains or amplifies the benefit of self-regulation, self-regulation should predict grade more strongly for students who also received more peer replies. We tested this by fitting a linear regression predicting course-standardized grade from self-regulation share, log peer reply volume in the student's started threads, their interaction, and course, with HC3 robust standard errors ($n = 66$). The interaction term was significant ($\beta = 1.45$, 95% CI [0.31, 2.60], $p = .013$). The interaction model explained more variance than the main-effects-only model ($R^2 = 0.17$ vs. 0.10; $F$-test $p = .029$ for the $\Delta R^2$). Self-regulation was a stronger predictor of grade for students whose threads contained more peer replies.

**Who Is Impacted by Lost Co-regulation?** The moderation analysis showed that peer interaction amplifies the benefit of self-regulation. Given that the AI TA displaces peer replies, we next asked which students might be impacted by the potential loss of peer co-regulation. We split students at the median on two measures: early self-regulation (the proportion of SRL-coded sentences in students' own threads during H1) and received co-regulation (the SRL share of human participants' replies in their started threads, excluding AI TA). We then compared mean course-standardized grades within each row of the resulting $2 \times 2$ table using independent-samples $t$-tests ($n = 62$; Table 2).

Among students with high early self-regulation, those who received above-median co-regulation earned significantly higher grades than students who received below-median co-regulation ($\Delta = 0.74$ SD, $t(26) = 3.15$, $p = .004$).

**Table 2.** Mean course-standardized grade by early self-regulation and received co-regulation (median split) in the pooled AI-supported courses ($n = 62$).

| | High received co-regulation | Low received co-regulation | $\Delta$ |
|---|---|---|---|
| High early self-reg ($n = 30$) | +0.90 ($n = 9$) | +0.16 ($n = 21$) | +0.74 ($p = .004$) |
| Low early self-reg ($n = 32$) | −0.19 ($n = 22$) | −0.55 ($n = 10$) | +0.36 ($p = .369$) |

Among students with low early self-regulation, the same contrast was not significant ($\Delta = 0.36$ SD, $t(19) = 0.92$, $p = .369$). Received co-regulation was thus more consequential for students who entered the course with stronger self-regulatory habits. This finding also connects back to the overall AI TA grade penalty reported in Sect. 4.2. Removing the 17 high-early-self-regulation students whose started threads had above-median AI TA reply share and re-estimating the linear regression from Sect. 4.2, the AI TA coefficient dropped from $\beta \approx -1.38$ ($p = .038$) to $\beta \approx -1.29$ ($p = .454$). The grade penalty associated with the AI TA is thus concentrated among the students whose outcomes are most sensitive to co-regulatory support.

## 5 Discussion and Conclusion

Across three levels of analysis, the results point to a consistent pattern: the AI TA's presence was associated with reduced peer dialogue and lower levels of co-regulatory discourse, and peer interaction moderated the relationship between self-regulation and grades. We summarize these findings in terms of the research questions, then turn to interpretation and implications.

**RQ1: How does the presence of an AI teaching assistant influence participation patterns and peer dialogue in online discussion forums?** Students in the AI-supported courses produced fewer reply posts than in the human-only course, while their thread-starting rates were comparable. The share of follow-up sentences contributed by peer repliers fell sharply over the semester in the AI-supported courses but remained stable in the human-only course.

**RQ2: How do patterns of self-regulatory and co-regulatory language differ between AI-supported and human-only courses, and how do they develop over the semester?** Aggregate levels of human regulatory language were lower in the AI-supported courses and declined over the semester, while remaining stable in the human-only course. The decline was driven by the shrinking share of peer repliers. As peer-authored regulatory language appeared in replies to other students' threads, this is consistent with decreased co-regulation [9], which emerged as important to understanding observed patterns.

**RQ3: How are self-regulation, co-regulation, and peer interaction related to academic performance in AI-supported courses?** A higher proportion of AI TA responses in students' threads was associated with lower grades. Self-regulation was the strongest predictor of grade, but peer interaction moderated this relationship: self-regulation predicted grades more strongly for students whose threads attracted more peer replies. The students most affected by reduced peer dialogue were those with high early self-regulation; among this group, those who received more co-regulation earned substantially higher grades. This difference was absent among students with low early self-regulation. The overall AI TA grade penalty became non-significant after removing these high self-regulation students, suggesting that the AI TA's association with lower grades operates through the displacement of peer co-regulation rather than through a direct relationship with the AI TA itself.

**Interpretation.** The results describe a coherent set of associations across three levels of analysis. At the forum level, the AI TA's rapid responses in assignment threads co-occurred with reduced peer follow-on participation. At the discourse level, this reduction in peer participation resulted in lower aggregate levels of regulatory language, since peer repliers were the primary contributors of co-regulatory discourse. At the student level, self-regulation predicted grades more strongly when accompanied by peer interaction, and students with high early self-regulation were most sensitive to co-regulation influence on grades.

Traditional SRL models emphasize regulation as an individual competency [34]. We entered this study with that framing, examining how SRL differed across AI-supported and human-only courses. However, the patterns we observed pointed to the importance of co-regulatory processes, in which one learner scaffolds another's regulatory activity [9], as a complement to individual self-regulation. When the AI TA displaced that dialogue, the association between self-regulation and grades weakened. Why this effect was concentrated among high self-regulators rather than low self-regulators is not clear from the data, and unmeasured characteristics (e.g., prior knowledge, motivation) may account for the pattern. We note that the observational design does not allow us to establish whether these relationships are causal.

**Design Implications.** The AI TA's speed and consistency are clear operational benefits, but they co-occurred with reduced peer dialogue and lower levels of co-regulatory discourse. If this pattern reflects a genuine effect, it points to a trade-off: the same responsiveness that makes AI TAs attractive may displace the peer interactions through which co-regulation occurs. Designers of AI-supported forums should consider how to preserve opportunities for peer dialogue. One concrete lever is response timing: wait-time research shows that delaying an authoritative reply increases the quantity and complexity of student contributions [24]; manipulating AI TA response latency in asynchronous forums is therefore a natural follow-up experiment.

**Limitations and Future Directions.** Several limitations should be acknowledged. First, we rely on forum discourse as a proxy for SRL, capturing only regulatory processes that students articulate in writing. Internal regulatory activities remain unobserved, and future work could incorporate multimodal or trace-based data. Second, the focus on graduate-level courses in data science and educational design may limit generalizability; students in these contexts may exhibit relatively advanced self-regulatory skills, and their interaction patterns with AI systems may differ from those of students in other domains or levels. Third, the observational design limits causal inference. The associations we report may reflect course-level or student-level confounds rather than effects of the AI TA itself, and readers should interpret them accordingly.

Experimental or quasi-experimental designs, for example, randomizing AI TA availability within a single course, would allow researchers to test whether the displacement of peer dialogue follows directly from AI intervention. Additionally, the finding that students with high early self-regulation appear most sensitive to co-regulation warrants replication. If this pattern holds, it would challenge the assumption that students with stronger self-regulation are the more self-sufficient learners [34].

In conclusion, these findings suggest that the co-regulatory role of peer contributions deserves attention in the design of AI-supported learning environments, and that the speed and availability of AI TAs should be weighed against the possible reduction in peer interactions that support regulatory processes and ultimately student academic success in higher education.

## References


1. Baker, R.S., et al.: Generative AI as a teaching assistant, OECD Digital Education Outlook (2026)
2. Bird, S., Klein, E., Loper, E.: Natural language processing with Python: analyzing text with the natural language toolkit. " O'Reilly Media, Inc." (2009)
3. Blaine, A.M.: Interaction and presence in the virtual classroom: an analysis of the perceptions of students and teachers in online and blended advanced placement courses. Comput. Educ. **132**, 31–43 (2019)
4. Chen, B., Poquet, O.: Uncovering socio-temporal dynamics in online discussions: an event-based approach. Australas. J. Educ. Technol. **39**(6), 1–16 (2023)
5. Cheng, G., Zou, D., Xie, H., Wang, F.L.: Exploring differences in self-regulated learning strategy use between high-and low-performing students in introductory programming: An analysis of eye-tracking and retrospective think-aloud data from program comprehension. Comput. Educ. **208**, 104948 (2024)
6. Cloude, E.B., Baker, R.S., Fouh, E.: Online help-seeking occurring in multiple computer-mediated conversations affects grades in an introductory programming course. In: LAK23: 13th International Learning Analytics and Knowledge Conference, pp. 378–387 (2023)
7. Du, Z., Wang, F., Wang, S., Xiao, X.: Enhancing learner participation in online discussion forums in massive open online courses: the role of mandatory participation. Front. Psychol. **13**, 819640 (2022)
8. Güner, H., Er, E.: AI in the classroom: exploring students' interaction with ChatGPT in programming learning. Educ. Inf. Technol. **30**(9), 12681–12707 (2025)
9. Hadwin, A.F., Järvelä, S., Miller, M.: Self-regulated, co-regulated, and socially shared regulation of learning. Handb. Self Regul. Learn. Perform., pp. 65–84 (2011)

10. Hmelo-Silver, C.E., Duncan, R.G., Chinn, C.A.: Scaffolding and achievement in problem-based and inquiry learning: a response to kirschner, sweller, and. Educ. psychol. **42**(2), 99–107 (2007)
11. Huang, X., Zhang, S.: Engagement in LLM chatbot-supported learning: The pivotal roles of GenAI competency and emotion. Comput. Educ. Artif. Intell., pp. 100559 (2026)
12. Ihantola, P., Vihavainen, A.e.a.: Educational data mining and learning analytics in programming: literature review and case studies. Proceedings of the 2015 ITiCSE on Working Group Reports, pp. 41–63 (2015)
13. Kirkeby-Hinrup, A., Stenseke, J.: The psychology of LLM interactions: the uncanny valley and other minds. J. Psychol. AI **1**(1), 2457627 (2025)
14. Kizilcec, R.F., Pérez-Sanagustín, M., Maldonado, J.J.: Self-regulated learning strategies predict learner behavior and goal attainment in massive open online courses. Comput. Educ. **104**, 18–33 (2017)
15. Leon, L.R., Plowright-Pepper, L.: The emotional labour of online course discussion forums: some autoethnographic insights. Open Learn. J. Open Distance e-Learn. **41**(1), 67–82 (2026)
16. Liu, X., Pankiewicz, M., Gupta, T., Huang, Z., Baker, R.S.: A step towards adaptive online learning: Exploring the role of gpt as virtual teaching assistants in online education. In: Future of Learning with Large Language Models, pp. 149–166. CRC Press (2025)
17. Liu, X., et al.: Qualitative coding with GPT-4: where it works better. J. Learn. Anal. **12**(1), 169–185 (2025)
18. Loksa, D., et al.: Metacognition and self-regulation in programming education: Theories and exemplars of use. ACM Trans. Comput. Educ. (TOCE) **22**(4), 1–31 (2022)
19. Long, J.S., Ervin, L.H.: Using heteroscedasticity consistent standard errors in the linear regression model. Am. Stat. **54**(3), 217–224 (2000)
20. Pozdniakov, S., Brazil, J.e.a.: From misunderstandings to learning opportunities: leveraging generative ai in discussion forums to support student learning. In: Cristea, A.I., Walker, E., Lu, Y., Santos, O.C., Isotani, S. (eds.) International Conference on Artificial Intelligence in Education, AIED 2025. LNCS, vol. 15882, pp. 291–298. Springer, Cham (2025) https://doi.org/10.1007/978-3-031-98465-5_37
21. Qiao, Y., Shihab, M.I.H., Hundhausen, C.: A systematic literature review of the use of GenAI assistants for code comprehension: implications for computing education research and practice. ACM Trans. Comput. Educ. **26**(2), 1–33 (2026)
22. Rabbany, R., Elatia, S., Takaffoli, M., Zaïane, O.R.: Collaborative Learning of Students in Online Discussion Forums: a Social Network Analysis Perspective. In: Peña-Ayala, A. (ed.) Educational Data Mining. SCI, vol. 524, pp. 441–466. Springer, Cham (2014). https://doi.org/10.1007/978-3-319-02738-8_16
23. Richardson, J.C.e.a.: Conceptualizing and investigating instructor presence in online learning environments. Int. Rev. Res. Open Distrib. Learn. **16**(3), pp. 256–297 (2015)
24. Rowe, M.B.: Wait time: slowing down may be a way of speeding up! J. Teach. Educ. **37**(1), 43–50 (1986)
25. Shea, P., Hayes, S., Vickers, J.: Online instructional effort measured through the lens of teaching presence in the community of inquiry framework: A re-examination of measures and approach. Int. Rev. Res. Open Distrib. Learn. **11**(3), 127–154 (2010)
26. Shen, J.H., Tamkin, A.: How AI impacts skill formation. arXiv:2601.20245 [cs.LG] (2026)

27. Silva, L., Mendes, A., Gomes, A., Fortes, G.: What learning strategies are used by programming students? A qualitative study grounded on the self-regulation of learning theory. ACM Trans. Comput. Educ. **24**(1), 1–26 (2024)
28. Viberg, O., Feldman-Maggor, Y., Wong, J.: Efficiency vs. effectiveness: self-regulated learning with LLM-mediated help-seeking. Learn. Lett. **8**, pp. 60–60 (2026)
29. Viberg, O., Khalil, M., Baars, M.: Self-regulated learning and learning analytics in online learning environments: a review of empirical research. In: Proceedings of the 10th International Conference on LAK, pp. 524–533 (2020)
30. Viberg, O., Wong, J.e.a.: Chatting with code: Exploring LLMs as learning partners in programming education. In: Cristea, A.I., Walker, E., Lu, Y., Santos, O.C., Isotani, S. (eds.) Artificial Intelligence in Education, AIED 2025. LNCS, vol. 15882, pp. 453–461. Springer, Cham (2025). https://doi.org/10.1007/978-3-031-98465-5_57
31. Wang, Z., Chen, X.e.a.: How does the online discussion intervention influence learners' engagement, emotions, and motivation in a blended learning environment? Learners' need for cognition matters. BMC psychol. **13**(1), 1122 (2025)
32. Wise, A.F., Hsiao, Y.T.: Self-regulation in online discussions: aligning data streams to investigate relationships between speaking, listening, and task conditions. Comput. Hum. Behav. **96**, 273–284 (2019)
33. Yu, H., Chen, Y., bin Ismail, I.M.: From scaffolding to success: How instructor pedagogical support and collaborative classroom interaction drive scholastic motivation in programming education. Acta Psychol. **259**, pp. 105289 (2025)
34. Zimmerman, B.J.: Becoming a Self-Regulated Learner: an Overview. Theor. Into Pract. **41**(2), 64–70 (2002)

# Children with Greater Sustainability and Equity Understanding Demand More from Educational Robots

Luca M. Leisten[1], Ryssa Moffat[1], Nathan Caruana[2], and Emily S. Cross[1(✉)]

[1] Social Brain Sciences Lab, ETH Zurich, 8092 Zurich, Switzerland
{lleisten,ecross}@ethz.ch
[2] HAVIC Lab, Flinders University, 5042 Adelaide, SA, Australia

**Abstract.** The application of social robots is changing learning landscapes, yet the environmental costs and social consequences of their deployment have received minimal attention. To effectively promote sustainable practices, it is crucial to identify how children's early perspectives on sustainability and the social equity of such technologies vary across developmental stages. In this pre-registered feasibility study, we investigated children's understanding of and attitudes toward robot sustainability and social equity through an exploratory survey with 71 children aged 10–16 years. Our findings indicate that children's measured knowledge provides initial insights into their evaluation of social robots: higher sustainability knowledge was associated with greater perceived importance of sustainable robots, whereas critical evaluations of current robot equity were driven more by age than by greater understanding. By identifying these age-related trends, this work provides a first baseline that can inform future large-scale classroom interventions and support the responsible and sustainable design of learning technologies.

**Keywords:** Sustainable robotics · Equitable social robots · K12-Education

## 1 Introduction and Related Work

The integration of social robots in educational roles such as tutors, peers, or teachers has shown significant pedagogical value across various learning domains [1, 2]. However, the rapid adoption of social robots often overlooks their long-term environmental and societal consequences. While robots are touted as catalysts for inclusion, their lifecycles contribute to a global crisis of 62 million t of annual e-waste and nearly 4% of global greenhouse gas emissions [3, 4]. Despite these risks, we lack a systematic understanding of whether children possess the foundational knowledge to use educational technology, such as social robots, responsibly. This feasibility study begins to address this gap by contributing to a first quantitative baseline of children's knowledge and attitudes regarding sustainability and social equity, specifically examining differences across middle childhood and adolescence (10–16 years).

Luca M. Leisten and Ryssa Moffat contributed equally.


J. Weidlich et al. (Eds.): EC-TEL 2026, LNCS 16905, pp. 361–373, 2027.
https://doi.org/10.1007/978-3-032-37979-5_25

### 1.1 Social Robots and Sustainability

Current Human–Robot interaction (HRI) research primarily explores sustainability *by* robots, in which their persuasive influence is used to promote eco-friendly behaviors like recycling [5, 6]. For example, Jiménez and Hernández [6] investigated how a social robot can help 6- to 11-year-old children classify waste. However, this often ignores the sustainability *of* robots. Most robotics platforms are constructed from unsustainable plastics and rare metals, while the underlying AI infrastructure demands immense amounts of energy and water [7, 8]. Furthermore, soft and bio-inspired robotics, which may offer more sustainable hardware alternatives [9], face significant adoption barriers in classrooms as educators often perceive them as less competent than traditional rigid robots [10].

The environmental risks of robot deployment are amplified by the lack of sustainability education across primary, secondary, and higher education, suggesting a knowledge gap in those who will design and use these systems in the future. While ecological instruction has existed for decades [11], a lack of professional development often prevents teachers from effectively and consistently addressing the environmental complexities of modern technology [12, 13]. This gap persists into higher education: Research across 117 German and 47 international institutions indicates that only a small fraction (~9–13%) of engineering curricula incorporate eco-design principles [14]. Consequently, without targeted interventions, emerging generations may lack the foundational literacy needed to design and deploy educational technology sustainably.

### 1.2 Social Robots and Social Equity

Parallel to environmental concerns is the issue of social equity. While often praised as tools to increase educational accessibility [15, 16], the costs of popular robots, such as the NAO or Pepper robots (ranging from USD $8,000–$20,000; [7, 17]), and the requirements for stable infrastructure risk widening the digital divide (i.e., the unequal access to, use of, or impact of Information and Communication Technologies; [2, 18–20]). Beyond hardware costs, the technological literacy required for maintenance creates additional obstacles for developed and, even more so, underdeveloped communities, potentially restricting the benefits of educational social robots to high-resource settings [2, 20, 21]. While some research suggests robots can promote social inclusion [22], particularly for neurodivergent learners [23], these benefits cannot be equitably realized if the underlying barriers to access are not understood by the users themselves. For social robots to genuinely advance equity, children must first recognize the systemic challenges of deployment and the complexities of resource distribution.

### 1.3 Children's Developing Understanding of Sustainability and Social Equity

Navigating the sustainability and social equity of social robots requires complex cognitive reasoning. Developmental literature suggests that as children age, they move from a simple social equality logic (i.e., equal distribution for all) towards a social equity logic (distribution based on need; [24–26]). Similarly, conceptual abstractions regarding sustainability typically mature between the ages of 6 and 19 [27]. However, it remains unexplored how these age-related developmental shifts manifest in the context of HRI. To equip children with the necessary knowledge to design, develop, and deploy educational social robots in a responsible and sustainable way, we must first establish a baseline of their foundational knowledge and attitudes of these topics and how these perspectives may differ across age.

### 1.4 The Present Study

In the present pre-registered feasibility study, we investigated children's foundational knowledge and attitudes regarding the sustainability and social equity of social robots. Using exploratory, self-developed surveys based on existing definitions, our primary aim was to test early indicators for future large-scale validation and establish an initial baseline of children's perspectives across different ages. Furthermore, we examined how these exploratory measures of knowledge relate to children's perceptions of the importance and current state of sustainability and equity in social robots. We asked the following research questions:

- **RQ1:** What is the accuracy of children's knowledge[1] of sustainability and social equity, and how does this develop across age?
- **RQ2:** How do children perceive the importance and current state of these issues for social robots, and how do their age and knowledge influence these ratings?

## 2 Methods and materials

### 2.1 Participants

Seventy-one children and adolescents between 10 and 16 years (36 female, 35 male, M = 12.90 years, SD = 2.24 years) were recruited from a comprehensive school located in a rural area in Germany. We collected a convenience sample during a week that we were present in the school for a separate study. Parents provided written consent for children aged <16 years. Children aged 14 years or older provided their own consent. The study was approved by the local ethics committee (24 ETHICS-361).

### 2.2 Procedure

Children completed an online survey via Qualtrics [28] on their own tablets or a tablet provided by the researchers during their school day. Children were first introduced to the study's goal, read a definition of social robots, and answered three blocks of questions. Each block addressed one topic (social equity, sustainability, and safety of AI[2]) and comprised three questions (knowledge, importance, and current state). Blocks were counterbalanced between participants. The survey took approximately 5–10 min. All our methods, data, and materials are available in our OSF project [30].

[1] Our preregistered questions used the term "foundational understanding". However, we interpret the operationalized metrics as early indicators of understanding rather than stable, comprehensive knowledge constructs, given our newly developed instruments.

[2] Reported elsewhere [29].

### 2.3 Measures

**Sustainability.** To assess children's knowledge of sustainability and pilot a measure for future validation, we developed a multiple-choice question in accordance with a definition of sustainability proposed by UNESCO [31] and previously used to study preschool children's ideas on sustainable development [32]. This definition includes the three integrated pillars: social-cultural, economic, and environmental sustainability. According to this definition, sustainability comprises reducing, reusing, respecting, rethinking, reflecting, recycling, and redistributing. Among three true and three false counterbalanced statements, children were instructed to select all correct statements (Table 1). The reliability of the six-item scale was 0.50 (Kuder–Richardson 20, KR20). This is likely a consequence of the scale's design, which was intended to capture the broad, multidimensional definition of sustainability. As such, the chosen items may not form a unidimensional scale, as a child may have knowledge in one area (e.g., environmental) but not in another (e.g., economic). Item difficulties ranged from 0.61 (*Q2*) to 0.99 (*Q6*) and item discrimination scores from 0.13 to 0.43, indicating a rather easy measure with mixed discriminative power. Consequently, the metric showed a notable ceiling effect (specifically in *Q6*). Despite these psychometric limitations, the instrument remains appropriate for the scope of this feasibility study. Because our primary objective was to establish an initial baseline of general knowledge, these early indicators sufficiently differentiated among broad levels of baseline knowledge. Furthermore, identifying item difficulties and dimensionality challenges provides important data for the iteration and optimization of future large-scale validation tools.

Next, we provided children with a child-friendly definition of sustainability, again adapted from UNESCO [31]:

*Sustainability means taking care of our planet by not using up everything we need, like water, trees, and clean air, so that future generations can benefit too. It can also mean making smart choices, such as recycling, saving energy, and protecting nature.*

We asked children to rate the degree to which (i) social robots are currently sustainable and (ii) how important it is that they are sustainable. Children indicated their answers on a 4-point Likert scale presented with smiley faces (1: *not at all / not at all important*; 4: *yes, very/very important*). All items can be found in our OSF project [30].

**Social Equity.** Social equity acknowledges that each person lives in different circumstances and requires different resources and opportunities to reach equal outcomes [33]. Based on this definition, we again developed a multiple-choice question to evaluate children's knowledge (Table 1. Multiple choice statements). The reliability of the developed measures was rather low ($KR20 = 0.40$), again reflecting the intended multi-dimensional structure. Item difficulties ranged from 0.17 (*Q2*) to 0.92 (*Q6*), and item discrimination indexes ranged from 0.07 to 0.47. As with the sustainability scale, these psychometric properties indicate that the instrument is in an early pilot stage. However, this level of precision remains sufficient for the scope of a feasibility study aimed at establishing a localized baseline, and these data provide an empirical foundation for refining the items in future iterations. Following the same procedure as described above, the researchers then read a child-friendly definition of social equity: "*Social equity means that all people should have the same opportunities. But since not everyone has the same opportunities, for example, because of where they live, some people should receive more support than* *others*". We then asked children to rate the degree to which (i) social robots currently support social equity and (ii) how important it is that they do so, using the same 4-point Likert scale with smiley faces.

**Table 1.** Multiple choice statements

| | |
|---|---|
| **Sustainability means…** | |
| *True options* | |
| Q1 | reducing and reusing materials |
| Q2 | rethinking how we use and consume things |
| Q3 | recycling materials |
| *False options* | |
| Q4 | replacing things that are not broken |
| Q5 | believing that natural resources will continue to grow back / replenish |
| Q6 | spontaneously buying and using things you see |
| **Social equity means…** | |
| *True options* | |
| Q1 | everyone should be able to achieve the same outcome |
| Q2 | some people get more help than others, for example because of where they live |
| Q3 | helping people in different ways |
| *False options* | |
| Q4 | everyone gets the exact same help |
| Q5 | some people deserve more than others |
| Q6 | people should solve their problems without extra support |

### 2.4 Data Analysis

To address **RQ1** and **RQ2**, the data were analyzed in R [34] using RStudio [35]. We analyzed the knowledge data using linear models (lm() function; [36]). The outcome variable was a sum score of the correctly chosen answer options (i.e., a maximum of 6 when selecting all three correct statements and NOT selecting the three false statements). The importance and current-state data were analyzed using cumulative link models (clm() function; [37]), with a Likert-scale score as the dependent variable. We fit a total of six models: knowledge, importance, and current state for sustainability and social equity. Each model contained a continuous main effect of age. The importance and current-state models additionally included a main effect of children's knowledge. Model assumptions were checked using the performance package [38]. Confidence intervals were calculated as Profile intervals. We additionally performed exploratory analyses to assess which multiple-choice answers were most frequently chosen incorrectly.

## 3 Results

In response to our first two research questions, our survey data revealed initial insights into children's measured foundational knowledge. To address **RQ1**, we found that while children's scores on our sustainability instrument did not increase with age, scores on the social equity instrument showed a modest positive association with age. To address **RQ2**, we found that children's views on the importance and current state of these issues for robots were complex: higher scores in sustainability knowledge predicted higher ratings of their importance, but with increasing age, children rated the sustainability of social robots as less important. For social equity, we did not find evidence for a relationship between measured understanding and perceived importance or current state. Instead, understanding increased with age, and older children grew more skeptical of the current state of equitable social robots. The detailed results are presented below.

**Sustainability.** Children's average score on the exploratory sustainability instrument was near the top of the scale ($M = 5.17$, $SD = 1.04$, range = 0–6), reflecting a pronounced ceiling effect. There were significant differences in the proportion of correct answers between the six multiple choice items regarding sustainability ($Q(5) = 62.44$, $p < .001$; Fig. 1A). Specifically, *Q2* was answered wrong significantly more often than all other items. Additionally, *Q6* was answered correctly significantly more often than *Q1* ($p = .005$) and *Q3* ($p = .01$). Overall, children were better at identifying wrong actions (*Q4–6*) than good practices (*Q1–3*; $t(70) = -5.01$, $p < .001$). Children rated the importance of sustainable robots as rather high ($M = 3.32$, $SD = 0.75$, range = 1–4). Lastly, children's average judgment of the current state of sustainable robots was closer to the midpoint of the scale, ranging from 1–4 ($M = 2.83$, $SD = 0.72$; Fig. 1B). Correlations among study measures are shown in Fig. 1C.

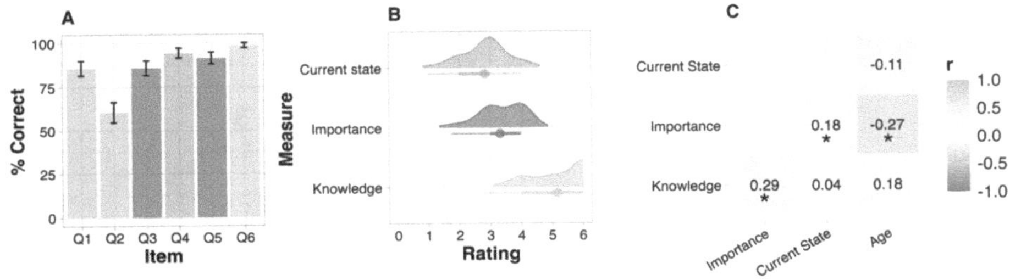


**Fig. 1.** Sustainability data. A) Bar plot of correctly answered multiple-choice items. B) Ridge plots of measures, including density, mean, and quartiles. C) Pearson's coefficient correlations between study measures.

We did not find a significant association between children's age and their scores on the sustainability instrument ($\beta = 0.08$, $SE = 0.06$, 95% CI [−0.03, 0.19]; Fig. 2A). We found a negative association of children's age with how important they think it is for social robots to be sustainable ($\beta = -0.30$, $SE = 0.11$, 95% CI [−0.53, −0.09]; Fig. 2B). This indicates that the likelihood of rating sustainable robots as important decreased with age. We did not find an association between children's age and children's perception of the current sustainability of social robots ($\beta$ = −0.13, *SE* = 0.11, 95% CI [−0.34, 0.08]; Fig. 2C). We found a positive association of children's measured sustainability knowledge with the perceived importance of sustainable social robots ($\beta$ = 0.63, *SE* = 0.23, 95% CI [0.18, 1.10]; Fig. 2D). This indicates that higher performance on the sustainability scale was associated with a higher likelihood of rating the sustainability of robots as important. Children's ratings of the current state of sustainable robots were also not associated with their initial scores on the sustainability measure ($\beta$ = 0.17, *SE* = 0.23, 95% CI [−0.27, 0.63]; Fig. 2E).

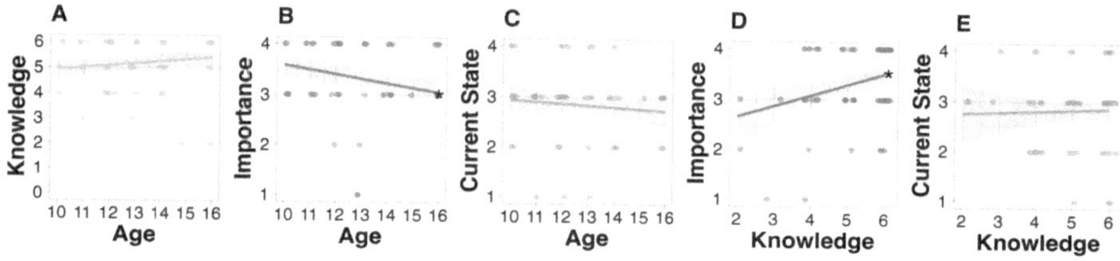


**Fig. 2.** Sustainability effects. A) Children's knowledge of sustainability across age. B) Importance of sustainable robots across all ages. C) Current state of sustainable robots across all ages. D) Importance of sustainable robots across all ages. E) Current state of sustainable robots across knowledge.

**Social Equity.** Children's average score on the exploratory social equity instrument was close to the middle of the scale (*M* = 3.65, *SD* = 1.00, range = 0–6). There were significant differences in the proportion of correct answers between the six social equity multiple choice items ($Q(5) = 125.72$, $p < .001$; Fig. 3A). Again, children were better at identifying wrong actions (*Q4–6*), than good practices (*Q1–3*; $t(70) = -8.07$, $p < .001$). Children performed worst on *Q2* and *Q4*, both items that probed children's understanding of the difference between equality and equity. Children's average rating of the importance of equitable robots (*M* = 2.42, *SD* = 0.67) and their average judgment of the current state of equitable robots (*M* = 2.50, *SD* = 1.03) were located near/on the middle of the scale from 1–4 (Fig. 3B). Correlations between study measures can be seen in Fig. 3C.

We found a significant association between children's scores on the social equity instrument and their age ($\beta$ = 0.14, *SE* = 0.05, 95% CI [0.03, 0.24]; Fig. 4A), indicating that performance on this measure increased with age. We did not find an association of children's age ($\beta$ = −0.06, *SE* = 0.11, 95% CI [−0.28, 0.15]; Fig. 4B) nor of their measured knowledge ($\beta$ = −0.32, *SE* = 0.26, 95% CI [−0.84, 0.18]; Fig. 4D) with how important children think it is for social robots to be socially equitable. In contrast, children's age was negatively associated with their perception of the current social equity of social robots ($\beta$ = −0.29, *SE* = 0.11, 95% CI [−0.50, −0.08]; Fig. 4C), indicating that the likelihood of children rating robots as socially equitable decreased with age. Children's initial scores on the social equity measure were not associated with their perception of the current social equity of social robots ($\beta$ = 0.26, *SE* = 0.22, 95% CI [−0.17, 0.69]; Fig. 4E).

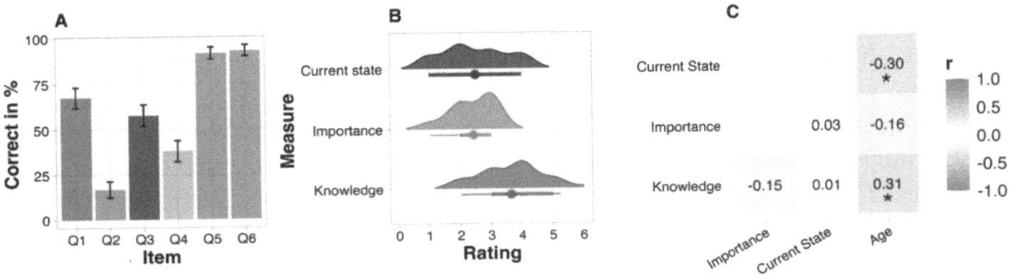


**Fig. 3.** Social equity data. A) Bar plot of correctly answered multiple-choice items. B) Ridge plots of measures, including density, mean, and quartiles. C) Pearson's coefficient correlations between study measures

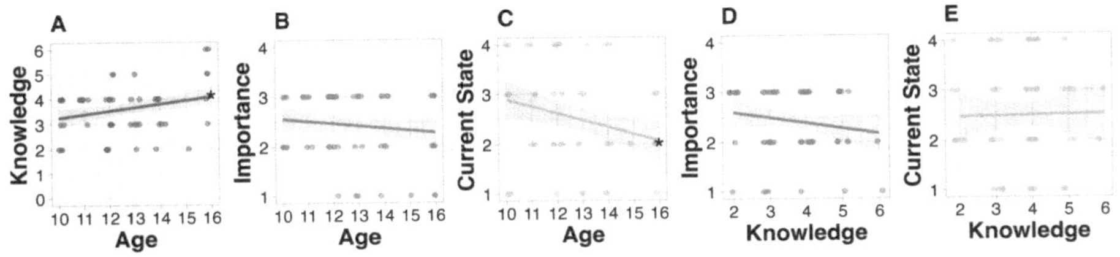


**Fig. 4.** Social equity effects. A) Knowledge of social equity across all ages. B) Importance of equitable robots across all ages. C) Current state of equitable robots across all ages. D) Importance of equitable robots across knowledge. E) Current state of equitable robots across knowledge.

## 4 Discussion

We sought to map children's understanding of sustainability and social equity within a pre-registered feasibility framework to explore how these early perspectives vary with age and instrument performance. Children between 10 and 16 years of age held advanced knowledge of sustainability and a basic understanding of social equity, as scored on our exploratory instruments. Further, higher performance on our measures was associated with certain critical evaluations of social robots. Specifically, children with higher sustainability knowledge considered the sustainability of robots more important, whereas older children rated it less important. Moreover, older children, who scored higher on social equity knowledge, viewed the current equity of social robots more skeptically. We explore the implications of these findings below.

### 4.1 Children's Foundational Knowledge of (RQ1) and Attitudes towards (RQ2) Robot Sustainability

Children's scores on our exploratory sustainability instrument did not vary by age, with children as young as 10 years already demonstrating high baseline scores on the specific measure we deployed. These findings are consistent with the educational context of our sample, as primary school children in Germany receive foundational sustainability education starting in the first grade [39, 40]. This curriculum often focuses on waste prevention and recycling, which likely explains the high knowledge scores towards these specific sustainability dimensions observed in our quantitative assessment. However, children's high scores in this domain (i.e., recycling and waste) do not preclude potential knowledge gaps in other areas of sustainability, such as the cost and resource requirements of educational social robots. This observation is further supported by our exploratory analyses of children's incorrect survey answers. Children were more confident in identifying incorrect concepts than correct concepts. Additionally, they were good at choosing correct options related to recycling, but struggled to recognize that rethinking consumption is also part of sustainability. This preliminary finding suggests that sustainability education should be broadened beyond its current focus on waste management to include critical concepts such as mindful consumption and the full lifecycle of technology.

Children's beliefs about the importance of sustainable robots unexpectedly decreased with age, possibly reflecting an apathy effect. This psychological state is often discussed in the context of the bystander effect, where a reduction in personal responsibility results from a sense of shared obligation, fear of judgment, and the belief that a situation is not critical if others are not acting, although it has also been associated with higher personal distress and fixed action patterns [41]. It is plausible that similar psychological dynamics may be at play regarding children's changing attitudes towards the importance of sustainable robots as they grow older. When children first learn about sustainability and the effects of technologies on the environment, they often believe it to be a crucial topic [42]. As they mature, children might realize that individual actions do not have a visibly direct impact on these issues, leading to feelings of resignation that alter their perspectives on the importance of sustainability. However, children's beliefs about the importance of sustainable robots increased with better performance on our knowledge measure. This could indicate that children applied their extended sustainability knowledge to critically assess the impact of unsustainable robots on the environment, in turn valuing sustainable technology design more.

### 4.2 Children's Foundational Knowledge of (RQ1) and Attitudes towards (RQ2) Robot Social Equity

Children's performance on our exploratory social equity instrument increased with age, extending prior work showing that equity understanding develops between 3 and 11 years [24, 26]. While prior research using resource allocation tasks found that children begin to rectify inequalities around age 7–8 [24, 26], our feasibility data is the first to suggest that this development continues into adolescence. However, our item-level analyses suggest a more nuanced conceptual challenge: children between 10 and 16 still seemed to conflate equality and equity. Only 17% of children correctly identified that equity involves providing proportional support to individuals with existing disadvantages, while over two-thirds mistakenly selected an option stating that everyone should receive the exact same help (equality). This may indicate that while children can distinguish between equity and equality in their behavior, they may not yet grasp the conceptual differences between the two. If confirmed in larger-scale studies, this could have direct implications for educators: to support children's critical assessment of equitable technologies, curricula may need to better support the conceptual distinction between equality and equity, spanning the entirety of secondary education.

Social equity knowledge scores increased with age in our sample, but children's beliefs regarding the current equity of social robots decreased with age. This may indicate that older children apply their broader knowledge of social equity to more critically assess it in the context of social robots. This preliminary finding may offer important insights into designing more effective learning opportunities, as it could suggest that helping children develop a better understanding of social equity could support the critical assessment of learning technologies.

### 4.3 Limitations and Future Work

As a feasibility study, this work serves as an early conceptual mapping rather than an ecological evaluation of technology in practice. A first limitation of the present study is that it relies on survey responses regarding abstract constructs rather than on direct observations of interactions with educational robots in classroom settings. Consequently, our contribution is conceptual and requires future research to build upon this baseline by transitioning to classroom-based designs.

Second, the generalizability of our results is limited by the sample's demographic distribution, which was drawn from medium- to high-socioeconomic backgrounds in rural Germany. While the inclusion of two school types increased internal variability, the findings may not represent the broader population. Additionally, treating age as a continuous predictor across ages 10–16 provided useful baseline trends, the sample size is too limited to draw generalized developmental conclusions. This limited sample size also prevented us from formally testing potential interaction effects between the variables of interest. Future research should increase the sample size and sample more diverse populations to determine whether the identified age-related trends in sustainability knowledge remain consistent across contexts and to identify possible interaction effects.

Lastly, our newly developed measurements of sustainability and social equity showed low internal consistency and mixed item discrimination, reflecting their exploratory, pilot-stage nature. While this likely resulted from the intended multidimensional structure of the measures, future work is needed to validate the measures. The sustainability measure, while based on established definitions [31, 32], was additionally centered around recycling and waste. This focus resulted in a ceiling effect, masking age-related differences, as recycling is a concept embedded in the German primary school curriculum. This finding itself is a key contribution, suggesting that common definitions of sustainability may be insufficient for educational assessment. We recommend that future studies develop and test more nuanced metrics that capture a wider range of sustainability factors.

### 4.4 Conclusion

To conclude, our results establish a localized empirical baseline for how children in one specific educational context interpret the environmental and social implications of educational robots. By framing this work as a feasibility study, we map out initial, age-dependent trends and capture critical diagnostic properties of early measurement instruments. Based on our preliminary findings, we recommend promoting children's critical thinking to support the conceptual distinction between equality and equity, and expanding the scope of sustainability education beyond recycling. Ultimately, this study provides the exploratory groundwork required to design future classroom interventions that prepare children to critically evaluate the technologies embedded in their learning environments.

**Acknowledgements.** We would like to thank the Alemannenschule Wutöschingen for their participation. Additionally, we would like to thank Marine Bruttin for her support with data collection.

**Funding.** Funding was received by the Social Brain Sciences Lab, ETH Zurich. **Conflict of Interest:** The authors have no conflict of interest to report. **Declaration of AI:** Generative AI tools (Grammarly, Gemini, DeepL) were used for rephrasing, translation, and grammar checking.

## References

1. Belpaeme, T., Kennedy, J., Ramachandran, A., Scassellati, B., Tanaka, F.: Social robots for education: a review. Sci. Robot. **3** (2018). https://doi.org/10.1126/scirobotics.aat5954
2. Woo, H., LeTendre, G.K., Pham-Shouse, T., Xiong, Y.: The use of social robots in classrooms: a review of field-based studies. Educ. Res. Rev. **33**, 100388 (2021). https://doi.org/10.1016/j.edurev.2021.100388
3. UNITAR: Global e-Waste Monitor 2024. United Nations Institute for Training and International Telecommunication Union Research (UNITAR) (2024)
4. Freitag, C., Berners-Lee, M., Widdicks, K., Knowles, B., Blair, G.S., Friday, A.: The real climate and transformative impact of ICT: a critique of estimates, trends, and regulations. PATTER. **2** (2021). https://doi.org/10.1016/j.patter.2021.100340
5. Lo, S.Y., Lai, Y.Y., Liu, J.C., Yeh, S.L.: Robots and sustainability: robots as persuaders to promote recycling. Int. J. Soc. Robot. **14**, 1261–1272 (2022). https://doi.org/10.1007/s12369-021-00828-z
6. Jiménez Barriga, N., Hernández Villalba, B.: ROBOTE: interactive educational tool to teach basic education children to classify and collect waste in their school environment. In: Extended Abstracts of the 2023 CHI Conference on Human Factors in Computing Systems, pp. 1–8. ACM, Hamburg Germany (2023). https://doi.org/10.1145/3544549.3583847
7. Mahdi, H., Akgun, S.A., Saleh, S., Dautenhahn, K.: A survey on the design and evolution of social robots — past, present and future. Robot. Auton. Syst. **156**, 104193 (2022). https://doi.org/10.1016/j.robot.2022.104193
8. UNEP: AI has an environmental problem. Here's what the world can do about that. https://www.unep.org/news-and-stories/story/ai-has-environmental-problem-heres-what-world-can-do-about. Accessed 29 Jan. 2026.
9. Hartmann, F., Baumgartner, M., Kaltenbrunner, M.: Becoming sustainable, the new frontier in soft robotics. Adv. Mater. **33**, 2004413 (2021). https://doi.org/10.1002/adma.202004413
10. Leisten, L.M., Caruana, N., Cross, E.S.: Teachers perceive distinct competency profiles in soft and hard social robots for supporting learning. In: 2025 34th IEEE International Conference on Robot and Human Interactive Communication (RO-MAN), pp. 1685–1692 (2025). https://doi.org/10.1109/RO-MAN63969.2025.11217892
11. NSTA: NSTA Position Statement - Environmental Education. https://www.nsta.org/nstas-official-positions/environmental-education (2003).
12. Foley, R., Archambault, L., Hale, A., Dong, H.K.: Learning outcomes in sustainability education among future elementary school teachers. J. Educ. Sustain. Dev. **11**, 33–51 (2017). https://doi.org/10.1177/0973408217725861

13. Miedijensky, S., Abramovich, A.: Implementation of "education for sustainability" in three elementary schools – what can we learn about a change process? Eurasia J. Math. Sci. T. **15** (2019). https://doi.org/10.29333/ejmste/109145
14. Kattwinkel, D., Song, Y.W., Bender, B.: Analysis of Ecodesign and sustainable Design in Higher Education. In: DS 92: Proceedings of the DESIGN 2018 15th International Design Conference, pp. 2451–2460 (2018). https://doi.org/10.21278/idc.2018.0305
15. Tawfik, A.A., Reeves, T.D., Stich, A.: Intended and unintended consequences of educational technology on social inequality. TechTrends. **60**, 598–605 (2016). https://doi.org/10.1007/s11528-016-0109-5
16. Lampropoulos, G.: Social robots in education: current trends and future perspectives. Information. **16**, 29 (2025). https://doi.org/10.3390/info16010029
17. Aldebaran Robotics: https://www.aldebaran.com/en/pepper. Accessed 24 Oct. 2023.
18. Ritzhaupt, A.D., Cheng, L., Luo, W., Hohlfeld, T.N.: The digital divide in formal educational settings: the past, present, and future relevance. In: Bishop, M.J., Boling, E., Elen, J., Svihla, V. (eds.) Handbook of Research in Educational Communications and Technology: Learning Design, pp. 483–504. Springer International Publishing, Cham (2020). https://doi.org/10.1007/978-3-030-36119-8_23
19. Perella-Holfeld, F., Sallam, S., Petrie, J., Gomez, R., Irani, P., Sakamoto, Y.: Parent and educator concerns on the pedagogical use of AI-equipped social robots. Proc. ACM Interact. Mob. Wearable Ubiquitous Technol. **8**, 1–34 (2024). https://doi.org/10.1145/3678556
20. Leisten, L.M., Graw, J., Vondrlik, P., Caruana, N., Cross, E.S.: Multi-stakeholder insights for designing and implementing safe, effective, and accessible social robots in K-12 Education (2026). https://osf.io/preprints/psyarxiv/ck69a_v1/
21. Neumann, M.M., Calteaux, I., Reilly, D., Neumann, D.L.: Exploring teachers' perspectives on the benefits and barriers of using social robots in early childhood education. Early Child Dev. Care. **193**, 1503–1516 (2023). https://doi.org/10.1080/03004430.2023.2257000
22. Jarske, S., Kaipainen, K., Ahtinen, A., Varsaluoma, J., Väänänen, K.: How could social robots support societal participation? Findings from five design workshops with young people. Int. J. Soc. Robot. **17**, 563–585 (2025). https://doi.org/10.1007/s12369-025-01230-9
23. Haidegger, T., et al.: Robotics: enabler and inhibitor of the sustainable development goals. Sustainable Prod. Consumption. **43**, 422–434 (2023). https://doi.org/10.1016/j.spc.2023.11.011
24. Olson, K.R., Dweck, C.S., Spelke, E.S., Banaji, M.R.: Children's responses to group-based inequalities: perpetuation and rectification. Soc. Cogn. **29**, 270–287 (2011). https://doi.org/10.1521/soco.2011.29.3.270
25. Rizzo, M.T., Elenbaas, L., Cooley, S., Killen, M.: Children's recognition of fairness and others' welfare in a resource allocation task: age related changes. Dev. Psychol. **52**, 1307–1317 (2016). https://doi.org/10.1037/dev0000134
26. Rizzo, M.T., Killen, M.: Children's understanding of equity in the context of inequality. Br. J. Dev. Psychol. **34**, 569–581 (2016). https://doi.org/10.1111/bjdp.12150
27. Svetina, M., et al.: How children come to understand sustainable development: a contribution to educational agenda. Sustain. Dev. **21**, 260–269 (2013). https://doi.org/10.1002/sd.519
28. Qualtrics: https://www.qualtrics.com/.
29. Leisten, L.M., Moffat, R., Caruana, N., Cross, E.S.: "If we are good friends, AI doesn't spy so much": Children's knowledge and misconceptions of AI safety (2026). https://osf.io/preprints/psyarxiv/jva7z_v1/
30. Leisten, L.M., Moffat, R., Caruana, N., Cross, E.S.: Probing children's understanding of ecological sustainability, ethical AI, and social equality of social robots, osf.io/mv9s2.
31. UNESCO: United Nations Decade of Education for Sustainable Development (2005–2014): international implementation scheme - UNESCO Digital Librar0. https://unesdoc.unesco.org/ark:/48223/pf0000148654. Accessed 21 July 2025

32. Kahriman-Ozturk, D., Olgan, R., Guler, T.: Preschool Children's idea on sustainable development: how preschool children perceive three pillars of sustainability with regard to 7R. Educ. Sci. Theory Pract. **12**, 2987–2995 (2012)
33. Walster, E., Walster, G.W.: Equity and social justice. J. Soc. Issues. **31**, 21–43 (1975). https://doi.org/10.1111/j.1540-4560.1975.tb00001.x
34. R Core Team.: https://www.r-project.org/ (2024).
35. RStudio: RStudio (2024).
36. Bates, D., Maechler, M., Bolker, B., Walker, S.: Fitting linear mixed-effects models using lme4. J. Stat. Softw. **67**, 1–48 (2015). https://doi.org/10.18637/jss.v067.i01
37. Christensen, R.: Ordinal-Regression Models for Ordinal Data (2023). https://CRAN.R-project.org/package=ordinal
38. Lüdecke, D., Mattan, S., Shachar, B., Indrajeet, P., Waggoner, P., Makowski, D.: Performance: an R package for assessment, comparison and testing of statistical models. J. Open Source Softw. **6**, 3139 (2021). https://doi.org/10.21105/joss.03139
39. Ministerium für Kultus, Jugend und Sport Baden-Württemberg: Bildungspläne 2016 Baden-Württemberg, Grundschule Sachunterricht, Arbeit und Konsum. https://www.bildungsplaene-bw.de/,Lde/LS/BP2016BW/ALLG/GS/SU/IK/1–2/01/02. Accessed 01 Aug. 2025
40. Ministerium für Kultus, Jugend und Sport Baden-Württemberg: Bildungspläne 2016 Baden-Württemberg, Grundschule Sachunterricht, Materialien und ihre Eigenschaften. https://www.bildungsplaene-bw.de/,Lde/LS/BP2016BW/ALLG/GS/SU/IK/1–2/03/02. Accessed 01 Aug. 2025
41. Hortensius, R., Hekele, F., Cross, E.S.: The perception of emotion in artificial agents. IEEE Trans. Cogn. Dev. Syst. **10**, 852–864 (2018). https://doi.org/10.1109/TCDS.2018.2826921
42. Green, M.: "If there's no sustainability our future will get wrecked": exploring children's perspectives of sustainability. Childhood. **24**, 1–17 (2016). https://doi.org/10.1177/0907568216649672

# Strategic Self-regulation and Triggers in a Digital Assessment System: A Mixed-Methods Analysis

Weiwei Li(✉) and Esther Ventura-Medina

Eindhoven University of Technology, Eindhoven 5600, MB, the Netherlands
w.li@tue.nl

**Abstract.** Digital assessment systems in engineering education increasingly combine multiple attempts with immediate feedback, creating iterative learning environments that are expected to support students' self-regulation. However, how self-regulation unfolds within such systems remains insufficiently understood. This study addresses this gap by conceptualising strategic self-regulation as a sequence of regulatory states across assessment attempts. Using fine-grained log data from 164 undergraduate students (5,732 attempts), we adopt a person-centred, mixed-method approach combining Hidden Markov Modelling and Latent Transition Analysis to capture regulatory dynamics. Three regulatory states—structured, reactive, and unstructured—were identified based on preparation time, test duration, and performance, and transitions between these states were modelled across attempts. The findings reveal diverse regulatory trajectories, including adaptive pathways characterised by gradual calibration and performance improvement, as well as persistent and less adaptive patterns marked by reactive or inconsistent regulation. Complementary qualitative analyses further explain these dynamics by identifying triggers of regulatory decisions across cognitive, metacognitive, motivational, behavioural, and socio-emotional dimensions. Students' regulation is shaped through the interaction between personal perceptions, contextual conditions such as system design and assessment rules, and social influences including peer comparison and instructional support. This study contributes by introducing a state-based, process-oriented framework for understanding self-regulation in digital environments, linking behavioural traces with underlying decision-making processes. It also highlights how system features, such as repeated attempts and immediate feedback, function as structural scaffolds that shape learners' regulatory pathways. These findings offer implications for designing more adaptive and pedagogically aligned digital assessment systems in technology-enhanced learning contexts.

**Keywords:** Digital Assessment System · Learning Analytics · Strategic Regulation · Higher Engineering Education


J. Weidlich et al. (Eds.): EC-TEL 2026, LNCS 16905, pp. 374–389, 2027.
https://doi.org/10.1007/978-3-032-37979-5_26

## 1 Introduction

Digital technologies are increasingly transforming assessment practices in higher education. Digital assessment systems provide opportunities for students to engage with assessment as an ongoing learning process rather than a single high-stakes event. In many such environments, students can attempt assessments multiple times, receive feedback between attempts, and adjust their preparation strategies accordingly. These features create learning conditions in which students repeatedly prepare, perform, monitor outcomes, and reflect on their progress, making digital assessment systems a valuable context for scaffolding students' learning over time.

Research on self-regulated learning (SRL) provides an important theoretical perspective for understanding these processes. SRL describes an agentic process through which learners intentionally manage their learning through iterative cycles of planning, performance, and reflection [1, 2]. Central to SRL is metacognition, which enables learners to monitor their progress, evaluate task demands, and adapt their strategies in response to conditions from the learning environment. Within the COPES model, the conditions are related to the task, the social context, and the learner, while recent work highlights the role of trigger events as catalysts for strategic regulation or the adaptation of motivational, cognitive, emotional, or behavioural regulatory approaches to optimize task engagement [2].

Recent advances in learning analytics have increasingly used behavioural trace data to investigate such regulatory processes. Many studies analyse interaction data from learning management systems (LMS), such as resource access, discussion participation, or feedback interactions, to identify patterns of learning behaviour and moments of regulation [3, 4]. However, examining the temporal dynamics of regulation in LMS environments remains challenging. Learning processes are often segmented according to analytical decisions rather than naturally occurring learning cycles, which makes it difficult to examine how regulatory behaviours evolve over time.

Digital assessment systems offer a particularly suitable context for addressing this limitation. Because students can reattempt assessments and receive feedback between attempts, each attempt can be understood as a naturally bounded event of regulation involving preparation, performance, and evaluation. This structure enables researchers to examine how regulatory behaviours evolve and transition across successive attempts. In addition, most learning analytics studies infer regulatory processes primarily from system data. To address these gaps, the present study investigates strategic regulation in a digital assessment system (DAS) by combining behavioural trace data with students' interpretations of their own learning decisions. By analysing trace data across multiple assessment attempts and conducting student interviews, this study aims to provide some insights into the dynamic processes of strategic regulation and inform the design of digital assessment systems that better scaffold students' self-regulated learning.

## 2 Theoretical Framework

### 2.1 Strategic Self-regulation: States, Patterns and Triggers

Self-regulated learning (SRL) refers to an agentic process through which learners actively regulate their cognition, motivation, and behaviour to achieve learning goals. Regulatory processes are commonly conceptualized as cyclical phases of planning, performance, and reflection that enable learners to continuously adapt their learning activities over time [1, 2]. Central to this process is metacognition, which allows learners to interpret information about their learning situation and make informed decisions about how to proceed with their learning activities.

Recent research has increasingly emphasized that self-regulation is dependent on learning context, and it is a strategic and context-dependent activity [5]. Within the COPES model of SRL [6], regulatory processes are shaped by conditions related to the task, the learner, and the social environment. Task conditions may include elements such as task difficulty, assessment requirements, or feedback mechanisms, while self-conditions encompass learners' prior knowledge, motivation, goals, and perceived competence. Social conditions may arise from interactions with peers or instructors that influence how learners interpret and approach learning tasks. These conditions become meaningful when learners interpret them as signals that adjustment may be required, often through trigger events such as unexpected difficulties, unsatisfactory performance outcomes, or feedback indicating discrepancies between current progress and learning goals [2]. From this perspective, *strategic self-regulation* refers to learners' intentional decisions about when and how regulatory actions should be deployed in response to evolving task demands and learning conditions.

Building on this view, a growing body of research has suggested that SRL can be conceptualized as sequences of events unfolding throughout learning activities [7, 8]. This perspective allows researchers to capture the dynamic nature of learning processes as learners interpret information, deploy strategies, and adjust their actions over time. With the increasing availability of digital learning environments, learning analytics research has begun to investigate such processes through behavioural trace data, including log files and interaction records that reflect learners' cognitive and metacognitive activities [3, 4]. By analysing these traces, researchers can explore when regulatory processes occur, how long they last, what contextual conditions trigger them, and how learners' behavioural sequences evolve throughout learning tasks. These approaches have demonstrated the potential of trace data to reveal temporal patterns of learning behaviours and regulatory processes.

Despite these advances, important methodological challenges for examining regulatory processes across multiple learning episodes remain challenging [9]. In many cases, the segmentation of learning processes over time is defined by analytical decisions rather than by meaningful learning cycles [10]. As a result, the boundaries of regulatory events may not necessarily align with how learning activities are structured within the instructional context. Furthermore, relatively little research has integrated behavioural trace data with students' own interpretations of the conditions and triggers that shape their regulatory decisions [10]. Students' reflections on their actions can offer important explanations for why particular regulatory choices were made, including how they perceived task demands, feedback, and other contextual factors that influenced their decisions. Such insights are particularly valuable for identifying how specific design features of digital learning systems may support or constrain students' regulatory processes. Understanding these mechanisms can ultimately inform the design of more effective digital assessment environments that better scaffold students' strategic self-regulation and learning.

## 2.2 Digital Assessment Systems as Regulatory Scaffolds

Digital assessment systems provide a particularly promising context for scaffolding regulation [11, 12]. In many digital assessment environments, students are given multiple opportunities to attempt assessments, receive feedback, and revise their understanding before subsequent attempts. These systems are often intentionally designed to support formative learning processes by enabling students to monitor their progress and adjust their learning strategies [13, 14]. Immediate feedback allows learners to evaluate their performance and identify discrepancies between their current understanding and their learning goals. At the same time, learners typically retain the agency to decide when to attempt the assessment again and how to prepare for subsequent attempts. This combination of timely feedback and learner autonomy supports learners' ability to monitor and control their learning processes [15].

Each assessment attempt can therefore be understood as a learning event [16] in which learners interpret feedback, reassess their progress, and make decisions about how to proceed with their learning. As students move through successive assessment attempts, they repeatedly engage in cycles of preparation, performance, feedback interpretation, and strategy adjustment [17]. The sequences of events closely resemble the monitoring and control loops described in SRL theories, making digital assessment systems particularly suitable environments for examining how learners regulate their learning over time.

## 2.3 The Present Study

To address these gaps, the present study investigates strategic self-regulation as it unfolds within a digital assessment environment. Specifically, this study addresses the following research questions:

RQ1. What distinct regulatory states characterize assessment attempts in a digital assessment system (DAS) based on students' preparation allocation, effort enactment, and evaluative performance?

RQ2. What regulatory patterns emerge across successive attempts in DAS, and how are these patterns associated with students' course performance?

RQ3. What triggers do students report as influencing their self-regulation in digital assessment?

# 3 Method

## 3.1 Research Design

This study adopted a convergent mixed-methods design. Quantitative trace data captured behavioural approximation of self-regulation. Qualitative interview data were collected concurrently to investigate students' own interpretations of their test decision-making triggers.

## 3.2 Context

The context of this study is a first-year Bachelor program in a Dutch university which includes courses related to basic chemistry and chemical engineering knowledge. In total, there are 17 digital tests across five courses.

The Digital Assessment System (DAS) is designed as a controlled yet flexible environment that balances institutional regulation with learner autonomy. Students register in advance for a one-h test slot, with possible extensions to 75 min. A mandatory 36-h interval between attempts discourages rapid trial-and-error and encourages preparation and reflection. Tests are available within an extended time window (e.g., weeks 1–8), allowing students to regulate their pacing, supported by recommended timelines from instructors. Assessments take place in supervised, internet-restricted settings to ensure standardised conditions. Each test consists of randomly generated questions from a question bank, and students can navigate and manage their progress independently. Immediate feedback is a key feature: students receive real-time correctness indicators during the test and a summary of their performance upon completion. Additional support is available through teacher consultations and tutorials, where students can review results, clarify misunderstandings, and reflect to guide subsequent attempts.

Participants in this study were first-year students from the 2024–2025 cohort enrolled in a course implementing DAS. Log file data were collected for 164 students as part of their regular course activities. To further explore students' experiences, semi-structured interviews were conducted with four students who participated on a voluntary basis. All data collection procedures were approved by the institutional Ethics Committee (ERB2024ESOE04), and informed consent was obtained from participants where applicable.

## 3.3 Data Sources

This study draws on three complementary data sources: behavioural log data, study records, and interview data. Log data from the DAS captured students' interactions across multiple attempts, including waiting days, test duration, grades, and attempt timing. After filtering invalid entries (e.g., durations over 75 min), the final dataset included 5,732 attempts from 164 students. Study credits earned by all participants during the first semester were collected. Study credits refer to the number of academic credits (e.g., ECTS) that students successfully obtained by completing and passing their courses, reflecting their overall academic progress and performance. To complement the log-data analysis, four semi-structured interviews were conducted with students who volunteered following a random invitation to the cohort. The semi-structured interviews (around 30 min each) explored students regulatory decision-making and underlying triggers. Interviews were recorded, transcribed, and analysed thematically using a shared coding framework.

### 3.4 Data Analysis

The analysis followed an explanatory sequential mixed-methods design. For RQ1, Hidden Markov Modelling (HMM) identified latent regulatory states from log data, using waiting days, test duration, and immediate score as indicators. Each attempt was assigned to the most probable state. For RQ2, these states were used to construct students' temporal trajectories across attempts, with sequence-based clustering identifying groups of similar regulatory pathways, which were then linked to academic outcomes. For RQ3, deductive thematic analysis of interview data explored the triggers underlying regulatory decisions, providing contextual explanations for the quantitative patterns.

**Operationalization of Regulatory States and Modelling.** Conceptualizing each attempt as a unit of strategic self-regulation, this study utilized a Hidden Markov Model to infer latent regulatory states from three observable indicators extracted from log data (see the Table 1). These states were operationalized as configurations of preparation allocation (waiting days), effort enactment (test duration), and cognitive performance (test accuracy), capturing the regulatory profile of each assessment attempt within the digital assessment system (DAS). These indicators are proxies of behavioural regulatory activity rather than a direct observation of SRL processes.

**Table 1** Three indicators used to characterize regulatory states of each attempt in DAS

| Indicator | What it shows | Micro-level regulatory processes | Macro-level regulatory phase |
|---|---|---|---|
| Waiting days | How much time they allocate to prepare before this attempt | Metacognitive planning on when to take the (re)attempt | Planning |
| Duration minutes | How long a student spent testing | Cognitive efforts/behavioural strategies on the assessment task engagement | Engagement |
| Immediate score | How well they performed | Immediate question and test performance feedback for goal monitoring and adjusting | Monitoring & Goal setting |

**Construction of State Sequences across Attempts.** To construct temporal sequences of students' assessment behaviour, each attempt was treated as a time-stamped event derived from the log data (see Table 4). For each student, attempts were grouped by course and test and ordered chronologically based on their recorded timestamps. This ordering enabled the assignment of a sequential attempt order within each test. In addition, preparation time was operationalised as waiting days, calculated using context-sensitive temporal reference points. For the first attempt of each test, waiting time was computed as the number of days between the lecture introducing the test content and the timestamp of the attempt. For subsequent attempts, waiting time was calculated as the interval between consecutive attempts. By incorporating both instructional timing (lecture start) and behavioural timing (attempt sequence), we capture how students allocate preparation time in relation to both the course structure and their own prior actions.

**Table 2** Construction of temporal sequences from log data at the attempt level

| Student ID | Course ID | Test ID | Lecture start date | Attempt order | Attempt timestamp | Waiting days | Duration (min) | Grade |
|---|---|---|---|---|---|---|---|---|
| S001 | C01 | T1 | 2024-09-07 | 1 | 2024-09-10 10:02 | 3 | 42 | 55 |
| S001 | C01 | T1 | | 2 | 2024-09-13 11:15 | 3 | 48 | 68 |
| S001 | C01 | T1 | | 3 | 2024-09-17 09:30 | 4 | 35 | 72 |
| S001 | C01 | T1 | | No more attempt | | | | |
| S001 | C01 | T2 | 2024-09-13 | 1 | 2024-09 – 25 14:10 | 12 | 30 | 40 |
| S001 | C01 | T2 | | 2 | 2024-09-28 13:05 | 3 | 45 | 60 |
| S001 | C01 | T2 | | No more attempt | | | | |

# 4 Results

## 4.1 Identification of Regulatory States

To ensure comparability across indicators with different scales, all three observable variables—waiting days, test duration (in minutes), and immediate score—were standardised prior to modelling. Specifically, z-score standardisation was applied to each variable, transforming them to have a mean of zero and a standard deviation of one. This step ensured that no single indicator disproportionately influenced the estimation of latent states due to scale differences. To determine the optimal number of latent states, models with varying numbers of states (ranging from 2 to 6) were estimated and compared using multiple criteria, including log-likelihood, Akaike Information Criterion (AIC), Bayesian Information Criterion (BIC), and average posterior state assignment probability. The results of model comparison are presented in Table 3.

**Table 3** Model fit indices for HMM with different numbers of regulatory states

| Number of states | Log-likelihood | Number of parameters | AIC | BIC | Average posterior probability |
|---|---|---|---|---|---|
| 2 | -25,618.06 | 16 | 51,268.12 | 51,376.76 | 0.89 |
| 3 | −24,210.43 | 27 | 48,474.86 | 48,658.19 | 0.86 |
| 4 | −23,230.17 | 40 | 46,540.35 | 46,811.95 | 0.87 |
| 5 | −22,930.11 | 55 | 45,970.21 | 46,343.66 | 0.84 |
| 6 | −22,610.66 | 72 | 45,365.33 | 45,854.20 | 0.81 |

**Justification for Three-State Solution.** From a statistical perspective, the 3-state model provided a substantial improvement in model fit compared to the 2-state solution, while maintaining relatively high classification certainty, as indicated by the average posterior probability. Although models with more states (e.g., 4–6 states) showed further reductions in AIC and BIC, these improvements were incremental and accompanied by a decline in classification certainty, suggesting increased ambiguity in state assignment. The 3-state model provided clearly distinguishable and meaningful regulatory patterns while maintaining strong classification certainty. This choice is further supported by prior engagement research, which consistently identifies a limited number of qualitatively distinct engagement modes [18, 19].

**Conceptual Labelling of Regulatory States.** The three identified regulatory states in Table 3 exhibited clearly distinguishable profiles across all three indicators (preparation, effort, and performance), with all pairwise differences reaching statistical significance ($p < .001$). The three identified regulatory states were conceptualised as Structured, Reactive, and Unstructured regulation, reflecting distinct configurations of students' regulatory processes across assessment attempts. Importantly, these states are not intended to represent hierarchical levels of quality, but rather different ways in which students organise and enact regulation in relation to the assessment context.

Structured regulation (State 1) is characterised by relatively low waiting time, moderate effort during the test, and high performance. This pattern suggests that regulation is largely enacted prior to the assessment, with students demonstrating clear goal orientation, confidence, and well-developed planning. As a result, students are able to engage efficiently with the task and achieve strong outcomes with relatively limited observable effort during the test itself.

Reactive regulation (State 2) is characterised by moderate preparation, high effort during the test, and moderate performance. In this state, regulation appears to be more strongly situated within the testing process, with students actively engaging in problem-solving and attempting to make full use of the available time. Rather than relying on extensive prior preparation, students regulate their actions dynamically in response to the task demands as they unfold.

Unstructured regulation (State 3) is characterised by longer waiting times, low effort during the test, and low performance. This pattern reflects a less organised form of regulation, in which engagement with the task is delayed and limited. Strategic self-regulation in this state appears fragmented, with weaker alignment between preparation, effort, and performance across the assessment attempt.

**Table 4** Profiles and distribution of regulatory states based on standardized indicators

| Regulatory state | Waiting days | Test duration | Immediate score | Attempts (n, %) |
|---|---|---|---|---|
| State 1 (Structured) | −0.45 (0.76) | −0.18 (0.55) | 0.70 (0.82) | 1,804 (27.5%) |
| State 2 (Reactive) | −0.06 (0.76) | 1.04 (0.22) | 0.21 (0.79) | 2,421 (36.7%) |
| State 3 (Unstructured) | 0.41 (1.20) | −0.94 (0.71) | −0.76 (0.80) | 2,343 (35.5%) |

Note. Values represent standardized means (z-scores) with standard deviations in parentheses. All pairwise differences between states were statistically significant ($p < .001$) across all indicators.

### 4.2 Regulatory States Transition across Attempts

To provide an overview of students' engagement across repeated assessment opportunities, we first examined the distribution of attempts and regulatory states across successive attempts. The distribution of test attempts in 2024–2025 shows an average of 1.9–2.4 attempts per test. Most students engaged in multiple attempts within each test, with three attempts representing the most common pattern of participation. As shown in Table 5, the distribution of regulatory states varied across attempts.

**Table 5** Distribution of regulatory states across successive attempts of 5 courses

| Attempt | Attempts (n) | Structured (%) | Reactive (%) | Unstructured (%) |
|---|---|---|---|---|
| 1 | 2891 | 26.3 | 39.0 | 34.7 |
| 2 | 1838 | 26.0 | 41.5 | 32.6 |
| 3 | 952 | 30.3 | 34.6 | 35.2 |

Transition probabilities were calculated to capture how students move between regulatory states across consecutive attempts. By examining the likelihood of transitioning from one state to another, this analysis provides a process-oriented perspective on self-regulated learning, revealing patterns of stability, adaptation, and disengagement. Transition probabilities were estimated by extracting all adjacent attempt pairs ($t \rightarrow t+1$) for each student across all tests. Transition analysis in Table 6 reveals three key dynamics in students' regulatory behaviour: termination, persistence, and limited adaptation. A large proportion of transitions from all states lead to no reattempt, particularly from Structured (62%) and Reactive (43%) states, suggesting that students often stop once they reach a satisfactory outcome or decision threshold. Unstructured regulation shows the highest persistence (32%) and is also associated with discontinuation (23%), indicating both stability and risk of disengagement. At the same time, it exhibits some mobility, with transitions to Structured (24%) and Reactive (21%), suggesting potential—but not dominant—adaptive shifts. Reactive regulation demonstrates moderate stability (30%), reflecting consistent effort-based engagement with limited change. In contrast, Structured regulation is least persistent and most associated with termination, indicating that well-organised regulation often leads to stopping rather than continued attempts. Overall, regulatory change occurs, but persistence and termination dominate over systematic improvement.

**Table 6** Transition probabilities between regulatory states across attempts

| From \ To | Structured | Reactive | Unstructured | No reattempt |
|---|---|---|---|---|
| Structured | 0.13 | 0.09 | 0.15 | 0.62 |
| Reactive | 0.17 | 0.30 | 0.10 | 0.43 |
| Unstructured | 0.24 | 0.21 | 0.32 | 0.23 |

### 4.3 Strategic SRL Trajectory Patterns

To further characterise regulatory trajectories, the classification was grounded in both theoretical and contextual considerations. From a theoretical perspective, self-regulated learning (SRL) is conceptualised as a dynamic and adaptive process, in which learners continuously monitor, evaluate, and adjust their strategies over time [2, 20]. In this sense, changes in regulatory states across repeated attempts can be interpreted as behavioural manifestations of underlying regulatory processes. The three regulatory states of Structured (S), Reactive (R), and Unstructured(U) were identified through data-driven latent state modelling. Subsequently, students' state sequences across assessment attempts were examined and organised into a set of interpretable trajectory patterns based on their dominant transition characteristics, such as stability, early termination, or directional change. The resulting taxonomy therefore represents a researcher-interpreted classification informed by empirical transition patterns. This organisation allows trajectories to be understood in terms of their developmental direction (e.g., upward, downward, stable, or non-linear pathways), consistent with the dynamic and adaptive nature of self-regulated learning (Table 7).

**Table 7** Classification and distribution of regulatory patterns across three attempts

| Pattern Type | Definition | Classification Rule | Example | Count | Percentage (%) |
|---|---|---|---|---|---|
| Monotonic increasing | Continuous upward shift in regulation level across attempts | State values increase over time ($U \rightarrow R \rightarrow S$) | URS, USX, RSX | 675 | 24.21 |

(*continued*)

**Table 7** (*continued*)

| Pattern Type | Definition | Classification Rule | Example | Count | Percentage (%) |
|---|---|---|---|---|---|
| Early reactive termination | Student stops after one attempt at a moderate level | Pattern = RXX | RXX | 406 | 14.56 |
| Early structured termination | Student stops after one attempt at a high level | Pattern = SXX | SXX | 374 | 13.41 |
| Reactive stable | Stable engagement at a moderate level | Two or three identical states | RRX, RRR | 264 | 9.47 |
| No attempt | No engagement in the test | Pattern = XXX | XXX | 255 | 9.15 |
| Monotonic decreasing | Continuous downward shift in regulation | State values decrease over time | SRU, SUX, RUX | 234 | 8.39 |
| Unstructured stable | Persistent low-level regulation (stuck) | Two identical states or three identical states | UUX, UUU | 153 | 5.49 |
| Early unstructured termination | Student stops after one attempt at a low level | Pattern = UXX | UXX | 150 | 5.38 |
| U-shape | Decline followed by recovery in regulation | High → low → high or medium → low → medium | RUR, SUS | 108 | 3.87 |
| Structured stable | Consistently high-level regulation | Two or three identical states | SSX, SSS | 87 | 3.12 |
| Inverted U-shape | Improvement followed by decline | Low → high → low or medium → high → medium | URU, RSR | 82 | 2.94 |

## 4.4 Associations with Academic Performance

Academic performance was measured using students' cumulative study points obtained during the first semester of the first academic year. A multiple linear regression was conducted using Unstructured stable as the reference category to compare whether other trajectory patterns were associated with higher or lower academic performance than sustained low-level regulation.

The overall model was significant, $F(10, 153) = 43.76$, $p < .001$, explaining 74.1% of the variance in academic performance ($R^2 = .741$, adjusted $R^2 = .724$). Relative to Unstructured stable, Early structured termination was positively associated with academic performance, B = 30.71, SE = 6.18, t = 4.97, p < .001, 95% CI [18.50, 42.92]. Structured stable also showed a significant positive association, B = 31.25, SE = 9.18, t = 3.40, p < .001, 95% CI [13.12, 49.38]. In addition, Early reactive termination, Monotonic decreasing, and U-shape were also positively associated with academic performance.

By contrast, No attempt was negatively associated with academic performance relative to Unstructured stable, B = −20.53, SE = 5.54, t = −3.70, p < .001, 95% CI [−31.47, −9.58]. Early unstructured termination did not differ significantly from unstructured stable patterns (B = −1.62, p = .838), suggesting that stopping after a single low-level attempt yields similar outcomes to repeatedly engaging at a low level. This indicates that regulatory patterns observed within the DAS are meaningfully aligned with students' broader academic success in the programme.

**Table 8** Multiple linear regression predicting academic performance

| Predictor | B | SE | β | t | p | 95% CI |
|---|---|---|---|---|---|---|
| Intercept | 10.41 | 5.13 | – | 2.03 | .044 | [0.26, 20.55] |
| Early structured termination | 30.71 | 6.18 | 0.39 | 4.97 | < .001 | [18.50, 42.92] |
| Structured stable | 31.25 | 9.18 | 0.17 | 3.40 | < .001 | [13.12, 49.38] |
| No attempt | −20.53 | 5.54 | −0.41 | −3.70 | < .001 | [−31.47, −9.58] |
| Early reactive termination | 16.52 | 5.88 | 0.21 | 2.81 | .006 | [4.90, 28.13] |
| Monotonic decreasing | 18.52 | 7.15 | 0.16 | 2.59 | .011 | [4.39, 32.65] |
| U-shape | 22.71 | 9.11 | 0.13 | 2.49 | .014 | [4.71, 40.71] |
| Monotonic increasing | 10.58 | 6.41 | 0.16 | 1.65 | .101 | [−2.09, 23.25] |
| Reactive stable | 9.78 | 6.24 | 0.11 | 1.57 | .119 | [−2.54, 22.10] |
| Inverted U-shape | 15.31 | 10.62 | 0.08 | 1.44 | .151 | [−5.66, 36.29] |
| Early unstructured termination | −1.62 | 7.90 | −0.01 | −0.20 | .838 | [−17.22, 13.99] |

Note. Coefficients are interpreted relative to the omitted reference category, *Unstructured stable.*

## 4.5 Interpretations on Regulatory State and its Triggers

The three strategic self-regulation states were presented from students' interviews.

**Structured State.** Students whose experiences aligned with the Structured state often described their assessment participation as a deliberate and planned component of their learning process. Rather than using DAS to test their luck or questions navigation, they emphasised preparing sufficiently before attempting a test and using the assessment as a checkpoint for evaluating their understanding. One student explained: *"I practiced until it went well and then I did the digital test and I passed them one time."* (S04).

**Reactive State.** Students whose accounts reflected characteristics of the Reactive state appeared to rely less on extensive preparation before an assessment attempt. Rather than viewing the test as a final evaluation of prior learning, they used the assessment process to explore question types, identify knowledge gaps, and work through problems in real time. As reflected in Student 03's account, *using the formal test itself as a way to understand question types in the absence of comparable practice materials.*

**Unstructured State.** Students whose accounts reflected characteristics of the Unstructured state often described using assessment attempts as exploratory activities rather than as deliberate demonstrations of learning. Instead of investing substantial preparation before an attempt or engaging deeply with the assessment itself, some students used early attempts to quickly gauge the difficulty, format, and expectations of the test. As Student 03 explained, "*People schedule a time slot to check all the tests in the beginning of the quarter to see what the questions are like...see how difficult these tests were.*

Using the five dimensions of SRL triggers [2] as an analytic lens, this study identified triggers for having multiple attempts. Cognitive trigger. Students frequently described assessment attempts as opportunities to identify gaps in their understanding and determine whether further preparation was necessary. For some, the outcome of an attempt provided sufficient information to guide subsequent action. As S01 explained, "Sometimes I needed just a few reminders about how things were supposed to go. Second try was enough."

Metacognitive trigger. Students reported evaluating their own understanding and reflecting on the effectiveness of their preparation strategies. Assessment feedback helped them identify areas requiring further attention and informed decisions about subsequent study activities. As S04 noted, the first attempt "made me aware of where I needed to brush up on and then I practiced until it went well."

Motivational trigger. The availability of multiple attempts reduced the perceived consequences of failure and encouraged persistence. Students described repeated assessment opportunities as providing a safety net that supported continued engagement after unsuccessful attempts. At the same time, the possibility of improving results appeared to sustain performance-oriented goals alongside learning-oriented motives.

Behavioural trigger. Students described taking concrete actions to improve subsequent performance. Rather than immediately reattempting the test, they reviewed mistakes, sought feedback, and adjusted their preparation. As S02 explained, "I always go to the self-study and ask the tutor to look into the test with me and what I did wrong." Such behaviours suggest that transitions between attempts were often accompanied by deliberate adjustments in learning activities.

Socio-emotional trigger. Students highlighted the importance of reassurance, confidence, and support when deciding whether to continue. As Student 04 reflected, "I was really happy because having basically unlimited retakes... you never know where you have a bad day, or if you have a bad test." These perceptions appeared to encourage continued participation and persistence following unsuccessful attempts.

## 5 Discussion and Conclusions

This study reconceptualises strategic self-regulation in digital assessment as a dynamic and situational process that unfolds across repeated attempts, where each attempt represents a regulatory event. Students' behaviour can be understood through three regulatory states—Structured, Reactive, and Unstructured—which reflect different ways of organising preparation, effort, and performance. Across attempts, students follow diverse pathways characterised by adaptation, persistence, and disengagement. While some students transition toward more structured regulation, suggesting that feedback and repeated opportunities can support improvement, many remain in the same state, indicating behavioural inertia. In particular, persistent unstructured regulation highlights challenges in reorganising learning strategies despite available feedback. Students who demonstrated more structured and adaptive patterns of engagement within the DAS also tended to achieve stronger academic outcomes across the wider programme. Qualitative findings largely supported the regulation states from quantitative analysis where students whose accounts reflected characteristics of those three states accordingly. The thematic analysis further reveal that attempt decisions are shaped by multiple triggers, including knowledge appraisal, gaps identifying, improving grades, learning adjustment, and confidence reassurance. A limitation of this study is that the qualitative findings were derived from interviews with only four students, which may not capture the full diversity of experiences and regulatory behaviours present within the cohort. The interview data should be interpreted as illustrative insights that help contextualize the quantitative findings rather than as representative evidence of all students' decision-making processes.

In conclusion, this study contributes a state-based and transition-focused perspective on self-regulation, integrating behavioural traces with learners' interpretations. It highlights how system design functions as a regulatory scaffold while interacting with personal and contextual factors. These findings inform the design of more adaptive digital assessment systems and advance understanding of self-regulation as a complex, situated process in technology-enhanced learning environments.

**Acknowledgments.** The authors would like to thank the program staff for providing access to the data and supporting this study, and the students who participated in the interviews and shared their experiences.

**Disclosure of Interests..** The authors declare that they have no known competing financial interests or personal relationships that could have appeared to influence the work reported in this paper.

## References

1. Hadwin, A., Järvelä, S., Miller, M.: Self-regulation, co-regulation, and shared regulation in collaborative learning environments. In: Schunk, D.H., Greene, J.A. (eds.) Handbook of Self-Regulation of Learning and Performance, pp. 83–106. Routledge (2017). https://doi.org/10.4324/9781315697048-6
2. Järvelä, S., Hadwin, A.: Triggers for self-regulated learning: a conceptual framework for advancing multimodal research about SRL. Learn. Individ. Differ. **115**, 102526 (2024). https://doi.org/10.1016/j.lindif.2024.102526

3. Bannert, M., Reimann, P., Sonnenberg, C.: Process mining techniques for analysing patterns and strategies in students' self-regulated learning. Metacognition Learn. **9**, 161–185 (2014). https://doi.org/10.1007/s11409-013-9107-6
4. Fan, Y., Saint, J., Singh, S., Jovanovic, J., Gašević, D.: A learning analytic approach to unveiling self-regulatory processes in learning tactics. In: LAK21: 11th International Learning Analytics and Knowledge Conference, pp. 184–195. ACM, Irvine CA USA (2021). https://doi.org/10.1145/3448139.3448211
5. Kinnebrew, J.S., Segedy, J.R., Biswas, G.: Analyzing the temporal evolution of students' behaviors in open-ended learning environments. Metacognition Learn. **9**, 187–215 (2014). https://doi.org/10.1007/s11409-014-9112-4
6. Winne, P., Hadwin, A.: Studying as self-regulated learning. In: Metacognition in Educational Theory and Practice, pp. 277–304 (1998)
7. Greene, J.A., Azevedo, R.: The measurement of learners' self-regulated cognitive and metacognitive processes while using computer-based learning environments. Educ. Psychol. **45**, 203–209 (2010). https://doi.org/10.1080/00461520.2010.515935
8. Molenaar, I., Järvelä, S.: Sequential and temporal characteristics of self and socially regulated learning. Metacognition Learn. **9**, 75–85 (2014). https://doi.org/10.1007/s11409-014-9114-2
9. Hadwin, A.F., Nesbit, J.C., Jamieson-Noel, D., Code, J., Winne, P.H.: Examining trace data to explore self-regulated learning. Metacognition Learn. **2**, 107–124 (2007). https://doi.org/10.1007/s11409-007-9016-7
10. Knight, S., Gibson, A., Shibani, A.: Implementing learning analytics for learning impact: taking tools to task. Internet High. Educ. **45**, 100729 (2020). https://doi.org/10.1016/j.iheduc.2020.100729
11. Bearman, M., Nieminen, J.H., Ajjawi, R.: Designing assessment in a digital world: an organising framework. Assess. Eval. High. Educ. **48**, 291–304 (2023). https://doi.org/10.1080/02602938.2022.2069674
12. Børte, K., Lillejord, S., Chan, J., Wasson, B., Greiff, S.: Prerequisites for teachers' technology use in formative assessment practices: a systematic review. Educ. Res. Rev. **41**, 100568 (2023). https://doi.org/10.1016/j.edurev.2023.100568
13. Dermo, J.: E-assessment and the student learning experience: a survey of student perceptions of e-assessment. Br. J. Educ. Technol. **40**, 203–214 (2009). https://doi.org/10.1111/j.1467-8535.2008.00915.x
14. Jordan, S.: Student engagement with assessment and feedback: some lessons from short-answer free-text e-assessment questions. Comput. Educ. **58**, 818–834 (2012). https://doi.org/10.1016/j.compedu.2011.10.007
15. Molenaar, I., Horvers, A., Baker, R.S.: What can moment-by-moment learning curves tell about students' self-regulated learning? Learn. Instr. **72**, 101206 (2021). https://doi.org/10.1016/j.learninstruc.2019.05.003
16. Bakhtiar, A., Hadwin, A.: Dynamic interplay between modes of regulation during motivationally challenging episodes in collaboration. Frontline Learn. Res. **8**, 1–34 (2020) https://doi.org/10.14786/flr.v8i2.561
17. Xiao, Y., Yang, M.: Formative assessment and self-regulated learning: how formative assessment supports students' self-regulation in English language learning. System. **81** (2019). https://doi.org/10.1016/j.system.2019.01.004
18. Duchatelet, D., Donche, V.: Fostering self-efficacy and self-regulation in higher education: a matter of autonomy support or academic motivation? High. Educ. Res. Dev. **38**, 733–747 (2019). https://doi.org/10.1080/07294360.2019.1581143
19. López-Pernas, S., Saqr, M.: How the dynamics of engagement explain the momentum of achievement and the inertia of disengagement: a complex systems theory approach. Comput. Hum. Behav. **153**, 108126 (2024). https://doi.org/10.1016/j.chb.2023.108126

20. Li, S., Du, H., Xing, W., Zheng, J., Chen, G., Xie, C.: Examining temporal dynamics of self-regulated learning behaviors in STEM learning: a network approach. Comput. Educ. **158**, 103987 (2020). https://doi.org/10.1016/j.compedu.2020.103987

# Exploring Learner-Modeling Simulations with Cognitive Walkthroughs: Effects on Mental Load and Mental Effort

Bibeg Limbu(✉), Yonghao Chen, Yannick Haußmann, and Irene-Angelica Chounta

University of Duisburg-Essen, Duisburg, Germany
bibeg.limbu@uni-due.de

**Abstract.** Developing a robust conceptual understanding of abstract computational models is difficult for students because model behaviour is often introduced through equations and algorithms that do not readily support active learning. While interactive simulations offer an alternative, associated comprehension complexities dictate that simulations must avoid unnecessary cognitive burden, particularly from poor usability and extraneous cognitive load. This paper reports a formative mixed-method evaluation of an interactive web-based simulation designed to support conceptual understanding of learner-modelling approaches. Fourteen participants used the simulation. Usability was assessed with UMUX-Lite, and cognitive load with StuMMBE-Q. Participants rated the simulation as moderately usable (UMUX-Lite: $M = 74.40/100$) and reported lower mental load ($M = 3.17/7$) than mental effort ($M = 5.39/7$). Analysis of Think-aloud, interview, and eye-tracking data identified several usability issues, especially initial overload, difficulty interpreting observations, and limited reversibility for hypothesis exploration. At the same time, participants described the workflow as manageable after familiarization and reported that the simulation supported their conceptual understanding. This study offers design implications to improve the usability of simulations without imposing unnecessary cognitive load.

**Keywords:** Simulation-based learning · Learner models · Usability · Cognitive load · Eye-tracking

## 1 Introduction

This paper investigates the usability and the cognitive load associated with interactive simulations designed to make learner models in Intelligent Tutoring Systems (ITSs) more understandable for higher education students.

Simulations play an important role in helping students understand complex abstract concepts as they enable students to actively develop "metavisual capability" crucial in STEM education, which supports successful interpretation of complex scientific phenomena [12]. Meta-analytic evidence indicates that


J. Weidlich et al. (Eds.): EC-TEL 2026, LNCS 16905, pp. 390–404, 2027.
https://doi.org/10.1007/978-3-032-37979-5_27

simulation-based learning in higher education has a positive effect on learning outcomes [5]. Despite the benefits, the educational use of simulations remains uneven across contexts. For example, Stinken-Rösner [29] found that 39% of surveyed STEM teachers did not use simulations in their lessons, suggesting that evidence of effectiveness does not automatically translate into classroom adoption. Adoption appears to depend on various factors such as teachers' perceived pedagogical compatibility and perceived usefulness [16], usability [3], as well as practical constraints such as time, training, and access to appropriate resources [2].

Squires & Preece [28] argued that learning environments, such as simulations, should be evaluated by considering both usability and learning, rather than treating them as separate concerns. Simulations are not just passive information displays where learning is limited to comprehension of presented information. Simulations support active learning through exploration and experimentation [6], but interacting with complex simulations can impose substantial cognitive demands. In simulation-based learning, both the task and the environment contribute to intrinsic load –cognitive load associated with processing new information– because these two features comprise relevant information that needs to be processed to perform the task [30]. Bo et al. [3] recommended a "novice-proof" interface for simulations, highlighting the necessity to examine whether it imposes extraneous cognitive load, –load associated with tasks that do not support learning– as in the case with poor usability. Usability can shape whether learners can engage actively and productively with the simulation to achieve improved learning outcomes. In this context, usability can be defined as the degree to which the simulation can be used by the target users (i.e., students) to help them achieve specified goals (i.e., learning) with effectiveness and efficiency in a given context. *Effectiveness* describes the accuracy and completeness with which users achieve their specified goals. *Efficiency* measures the resources expended in relation to the effectiveness achieved (adapted from [13]).

To that end, we conducted a **formative study** to evaluate the usability and the associated cognitive load of a web-based interactive simulation designed to help students of higher education with conceptual understanding of three different types of machine-learning learner models commonly employed in ITSs. Such models are often taught through equations and/or programming algorithms. While these representations communicate the formal structure of the models, they offer limited support for exploring how parameter choices and event sequences shape model behaviour. Interactive simulations can address this limitation, but only when the simulation itself is sufficiently usable and does not impose unnecessary barriers. This highlights the importance of evaluating usability and cognitive load. Consequently, we explored the following research questions:

RQ1: How do users perceive the usability of the interactive simulation for exploring learner-model behaviour?
We analysed usability subjectively using UMUX-lite [26]. Think–aloud data were also used to complement the usability data.

RQ2: To what extent do users experience cognitive load while interacting with the simulation?
We analysed cognitive load as a combination of Mental Load and Mental Effort using StuMMBE-Q (Students' Mental Load and Mental Effort Questionnaire) [15], which was complemented with eye-tracking data.

The paper contributes to the body of work on methods for evaluating simulation-based learning environments through the combined lens of usability and cognitive load. It offers an example of how to evaluate simulations under this paradigm, beyond usability or cognitive load alone, and also offers a set of concrete design lessons for more pedagogically aligned usable simulations.

## 2 Background

### 2.1 The Learner Model Simulation

Lateef [17] argues that interactive simulations provide students with a safe environment to repeatedly test their hypotheses and receive feedback, thereby supporting their conceptual understanding. Students can change parameters, change initial conditions, or structural elements of the simulated model and observe system responses in real time. This supports new hypothesis generation and testing, allowing students to confront their predictions with simulated outcomes [14]. Moreover, a meta-analysis demonstrated that simulation-based learning most effectively enhanced learners' self-efficacy and transfer of learning when users were given more agency of their learning [11]. However, simulations often emphasise discovery-oriented exploration, but empirical studies suggest that unguided or minimally guided exploration can lead to suboptimal learning outcomes, especially for novices [24]. Cook et al. [8] identified several principles or best practices for optimal simulation-based learning, including *opportunities for repetitive practice, a range of task difficulty, explicit feedback, and cognitive interactivity through tasks.* In the following, we outline the design of the simulation used in this study and indicate how selected aspects of its design were informed by such principles.

**Context:** The simulation used in this study was designed in the context of a university course about "Intelligent Learning Environments" to help computer science students learn about different types of learner models [31]. Fouh et al. [10] argue that the dynamic and abstract nature of computer science concepts like learner modeling algorithms makes them difficult to teach effectively using only static media like text or traditional lectures. The **LM–simulation** models three types of learner modeling approaches, namely: AFM (Additive Factors Model), PFA (Performance Factors Model), and IFM (Instructional Factors Model) [7]. AFM calculates the probability of student success based on a student's baseline ability, the difficulty of the skill, and the total number of prior practice opportunities they have had. PFA builds upon the AFM by splitting practice opportunities into past successes and failures. It assumes that correct and incorrect attempts impact a student's future performance differently, assigning them separate mathematical weights. IFM extends the PFA by incorporating instructional interventions, such as hints or 'tell' steps. This allows the model to account for the learning benefits a student receives from such 'tell' steps that provide direct system explanations, even when no correctness data is generated. These three models are grounded in a supervised machine-learning approach, specifically using logistic regression, and are used to predict the probability that a specific student will answer a future step correctly. Simulations provide an ideal alternative to actively explore these algorithms to improve conceptual understanding. Accordingly, we hosted a web-based learner model simulation called the LM–simulation that is used in the context of this study.

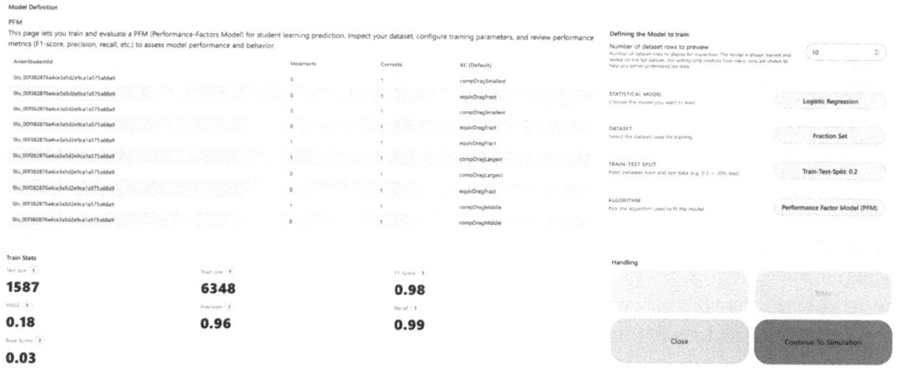

**Fig. 1.** Training view, with the dataset panel, controls, and training metrics.

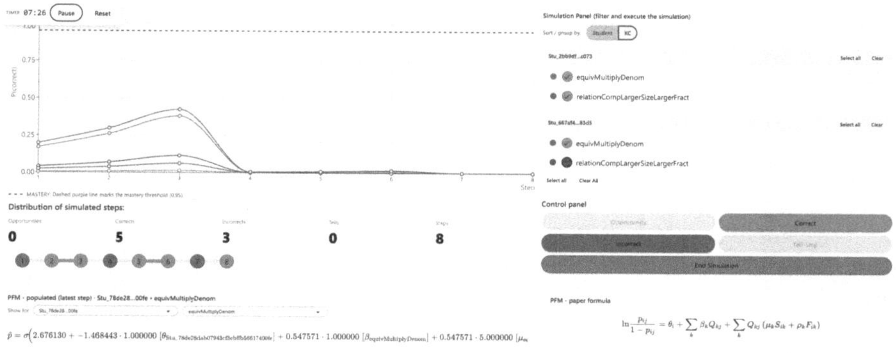

**Fig. 2.** Simulation view, with the prediction graph, formula panel, and step controls.

**Design:** To help students understand how a learner model predictions evolve, the LM–simulation guides learners through the complete machine-learning pipeline for the AFM, the PFA, & the IFM models via two distinct phases: **Training** and **Simulation**. The training phase allows students to configure the algorithm, adjust the train-test split of the data, and review performance metrics to evaluate the model's accuracy (see Fig. 1). In the testing/simulation phase, students test their trained model by interacting with it step-by-step, observing how the predicted mastery evolves (see Fig. 2). The step indicator in the simulation tracks a learner's progress, while the bottom panel dynamically displays the chosen algorithm's formula, updating its estimated parameters after each step. The LM–simulation allows students to repeatedly practice and work through multiple model types and inspect their behaviour. It provides explicit feedback through training metrics, dynamic prediction curves, and formulas that update after each simulated action. The LM–simulation also promotes cognitive interactivity through tasks outlined in the cognitive walkthrough, by requiring students to configure models, inspect data, select learner–knowledge-component pairs, and interpret how each interaction changes predicted mastery.

As prior research suggests that unguided exploration can be suboptimal for novices [24], these features were used in combination with a structured *cognitive–walkthrough*. The cognitive–walkthrough consisted of an initial setup section, followed by three stepwise cycles that corresponded to the three learner modeling algorithms. The primary purpose of this guide was to help students navigate the application, thereby enabling them to focus their attention entirely on interpreting the simulated model's behaviour rather than on interface exploration. To achieve this, the walkthrough provided specific parameter settings participants needed to set initially, and included tasks designed to explicitly prompt participants to verbalize their interpretations as think–alouds.

## 3 Methods

To answer our research questions, we designed a formative study during which participants used the LM–simulation on a PC with an eye tracker following the cognitive–walkthrough, while thinking–aloud.

### 3.1 Participants

Fourteen (14) participants from the University of Duisburg-Essen took part in the study, including 12 computer science students and 2 lecturers. Students were required to have completed the Intelligent Learning Environments course and have prior exposure to supervised machine learning, since the simulation was designed to deepen rather than introduce the concepts. Participation in the formative study was voluntary, and completion of the pre–post knowledge test was optional. Nine (9) out of 14 participants were randomly chosen for semi-structured interviews at the end of the study. This study was ethically approved by the Ethics department of the University of Duisburg-Essen with an approval number 2511CMHY0317.

### 3.2 Apparatus

The LM–simulation was used in the study (see Sect. 2). The application was run on a PC with a Tobii Pro Spectrum[1] screen-based eye tracker. The Tobii Pro Lab software was used to collect eye–tracking data, along with audio data.

### 3.3 Procedure

At the beginning, participants were briefed about the study and were asked to sign the consent form. The briefing explained the application setup, the objectives of the study, the optional pre-post test, and outlined the think-aloud method. If a participant opted for the pre-post test, the participant completed a pre-test before the study began and then completed the same test as a post-test. The results of the test were not displayed to the participants at any point.

Then, the eye tracker was calibrated, after which eye-tracking and audio recording were started. Participants were asked to follow the printed cognitive–walkthrough and to interact with the LM–simulation while verbalizing their thoughts. The walkthrough consisted of three cycles, one for each learner modeling algorithm. All participants first went through the AFM, then the PFA, and finally the IFM. After participants completed all three cycles, the recording was stopped, and participants filled out the questionnaires in the following order: demographics, UMUX-Lite, and StuMMBE-Q. Participants who opted for the pre-post quiz subsample then completed the post-test at the end, followed by an interview for randomly sampled participants. On average, the participants took 45–60 min to complete the study.

### 3.4 Materials and Measures

**Usability.** The UMUX-Lite questionnaire was used in the study to evaluate the LM–simulation's usability [26]. The UMUX-Lite consists of only two positively framed items: one measuring perceived usefulness and one measuring perceived ease of use. The UMUX-Lite was chosen due to its lightweight, while the scores are comparable to System Usability Scale [26]. Participants rated each statement on a 7-point Likert scale from 1 (strong disagreement) to 7 (strong agreement). In addition, think-aloud audio recordings and eye tracking data, such as total fixation duration, were captured during participants' interaction with the LM–simulation, and qualitatively analysed to support usability results.

**Cognitive Load.** Cognitive load was measured using the StuMMBE-Q instrument [15], which operationalizes cognitive load in two distinct, measurable dimensions: Mental Load and Mental Effort. Mental Load represents the cognitive capacity required to process the inherent complexity of a specific task, while Mental effort reflects the actual cognitive capacity and focus an individual consciously invests while working on the task [15]. The StuMMBE-Q questionnaire

[1] https://www.tobii.com/products/eye-trackers/screen-based/tobii-pro-spectrum.

comprises twelve items, of which six assess Mental Effort and six assess Mental Load, on a 7-point Likert scale ranging from "not at all" to "totally". Additionally, eye-tracking data, specifically the pupil diameter, were used to corroborate results from StuMMBE-Q.

**Pre-post Knowledge Test.** We designed a pre-post quiz to assess participants' learning gains with 9 multiple-choice questions, three each for AFM, PFA, and IFM. For each algorithm, the question difficulty spanned from easy to moderate, and to difficult (1 each). While the questions and the order in which they were administered across pre and post-test remained unchanged, the order of the choices/answers was randomized between pre- and post-test.

**Interview.** A semi–structured interview was also conducted at the end. While no concrete questions were outlined, the investigator structured the questions to scope the following: a) User interface and user experience, b) Conceptual understanding, c) Perceived usefulness, and d) Suggestions for improvement.

### 3.5 Data Analysis

Given the formative nature of the study and the small sample size ($N = 14$), we do not seek to make claims of causality. Accordingly, questionnaire data were scored according to the respective instrument guidelines and summarized descriptively, while eye–tracking data, think–aloud data, and interview data were analysed qualitatively to complement measures of usability and cognitive load, and to get a more comprehensive picture of a learner's internal state [18,27].

## 4 Results

### 4.1 Descriptives for Usability and Cognitive Load

Usability and cognitive load associated with LM–simulation were quantitatively measured using the UMUX-Lite and StuMMBE-Q, respectively. The UMUX-Lite consists of two constructs: perceived usefulness ($M = 5.07$, $SD = 0.92$) and perceived ease of use ($M = 5.86$, $SD = 0.66$). For a direct comparison with the System Usability Scale (SUS), the raw 7-point Likert responses for the UMUX-Lite were transformed into a 0–100 scale (sum of its two constructs) [26]. This was achieved by subtracting 1 from each item's score, dividing the sum of the two items by 12, and multiplying the result by 100. Table 1 provides an overview of the outcomes.

Cognitive load was assessed using the StuMMBE-Q [15], which is divided into two distinct dimensions: Mental Load (evaluating task complexity) and Mental Effort (evaluating the learner's invested cognitive capacity). Krell [15] collapsed the 7 points, after transforming the reverse–coded items, into three nominal categories (Low, Medium, & High) using an Item-Response Theory model. However, since our sample only consisted of 14 participants, we did not pursue those steps.

**Table 1.** Descriptive statistics for UMUX-Lite and StuMMBE-Q

| Measure | $n$ | Mean | SD | Median | Min–Max |
|---|---|---|---|---|---|
| UMUX-Lite overall (0–100) | 14 | 74.40 | 8.31 | 75.00 | 58.33–91.67 |
| - [Perceived Usefulness] (1–7) | 14 | 5.07 | 0.92 | 5.00 | 3–6 |
| - [Perceived Ease of Use] (1–7) | 14 | 5.86 | 0.66 | 6.00 | 5–7 |
| StuMMBE-Q [Mental Load] (1–7) | 14 | 3.17 | 1.39 | 3.17 | 1.00–5.50 |
| StuMMBE-Q [Mental Effort] (1–7) | 14 | 5.39 | 1.05 | 5.25 | 4.00–7.00 |

Descriptive statistics for the StuMMBE-Q are reported in Table 1. Participants reported lower Mental Load ($M = 3.17$, $SD = 1.39$) compared to the Mental Effort ($M = 5.39$, $SD = 1.05$). A Spearman's rank-order correlation indicated a moderate positive association between Mental Load and Mental Effort, though this relationship was not statistically significant, $r_s = .47$, $p = .089$.

### 4.2 Eye-Tracking

We explored the association between self-reported mental effort from StuMMBE-Q and composite pupil diameter from eye tracking. The composite pupil diameter was calculated as an average of the left and right pupil diameters. During the training phase, the average composite pupil dilation was $M = 2.75 (SD = 0.29)$, and $M = 2.80 (SD = 0.34)$ in the simulation phase. A Spearman correlation revealed a small-to-moderate ($r_s = .31$, $p = .279$) but non–significant positive association between mental effort and pupil diameter. This indicates that participants who reported higher mental effort tended to have larger mean pupil diameter, aligning with [21], although the interpretation is limited due to small sample size ($N = 14$). Furthermore, as no baseline pupil measure was available, the data could not be baseline-corrected. Accordingly, the analysis only supports interpretation in terms of average pupil diameter, not the task-evoked change relative to the baseline.

### 4.3 Think–Aloud and Interview

We thematically analysed the transcribed think–aloud data and Interview data in an inductive manner. As a formative study, no formal thematic framework was adopted, opting for a quick-and-dirty analysis. First, the resulting themes from the analysis of the think–aloud data are presented according to the two phases (training & simulation). Then, the themes from the analysis of the interview data are presented.

In the training phase, three distinct, recurrent themes emerged. **Theme 1: Initial Overload** was a prominent issue, affecting most participants upon first entering the training view. They frequently vocalized disorientation and struggled to parse the dense interface, with one participant stating, "*I'm just looking at the screen, trying to understand what each part of the screen shows... Clearly, I*

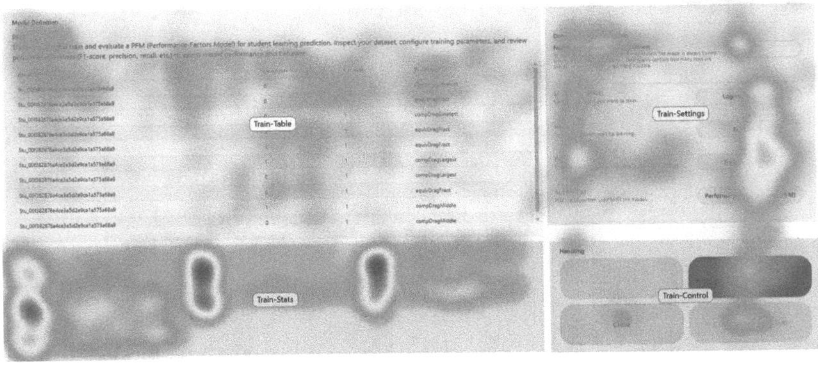


**Fig. 3.** Train-view with an overlaying heatmap and Areas of interest.

*have no idea how to do that*". A clear influence of **Theme 2: Prior Knowledge** was also observed in most participants during the model configuration. Rather than arbitrarily setting parameters or blindly following the guide, users actively vocalized their prior knowledge to justify their choices, particularly regarding the train-test split ["*..selected the 80-20 train test split, because I think that's the most common in the literature I've read so far*"]. Others similarly relied on familiar statistical heuristics to guide their setup, with one participant noting, "*I want to do the Pareto rule. 80 training, 20 testing*". **Theme 3: Interpreting metrics** demanded higher cognitive effort, a prominent trend during the training phase. Participants seemed to have dedicated substantial effort to decipher statistical scores, with eye-tracking data showing participants' dwell time mostly converging in the 'Train-Stats' panel (see Fig. 3). Participants often relied on the interface's tooltips to decipher statistical scores, with a participant reasoning aloud: "*Okay, so range zero best to one worst... Lower values mean better calibration accuracy*".

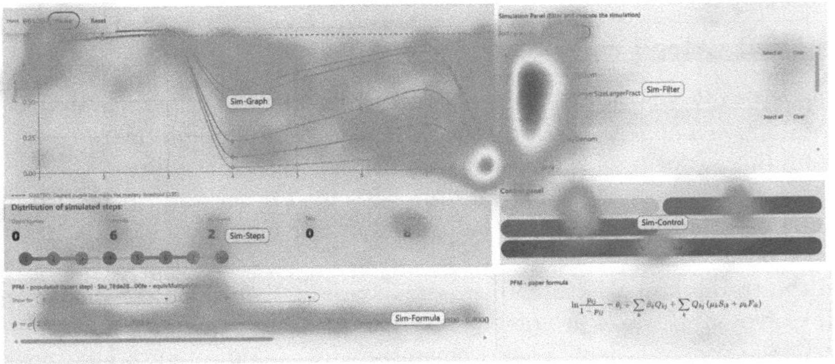


**Fig. 4.** Simulation-view with an overlaying heatmap and Areas of Interests.

Similarly, in the simulation phase, three distinct, recurrent themes emerged. **Theme 4: Interpreting raw formula**, which was the presentation of the raw logistic regression equation, imposed high cognitive effort, with participants struggling to map the mathematical variables to the interface's behavior. A participant verbalised, "*...I could look at the formula, but I'm too stupid for that*", and suggested the interface should include "*some formula description here, for non-maths savvy people*". Additionally, the simulation view heatmap in Fig. 4 shows a lack of dwell time around the formula, hinting that participants paid little attention to the formula. **Theme 5: Unclear Filter Scope and Placement** in the simulation's filtering controls caused participants to struggle to manipulate the interface, distracting them from their objective. A participant stated, "*my brain tells me that it will select all for all learners... my initial understanding is wrong, and this only refers to this specific student, which is a bit confusing*". Figure 4 depicts the concentration of dwell time in the sim-filter area of the simulation view, corroborating this theme. Lastly, **Theme 6: Lack of Reversibility and Step Control** prevented participants from directly comparing 'what–if' scenarios, which prohibited participants from testing different input patterns to understand the model ["*I cannot go to step one again, can I... I wanted to see what happens if I do alternatively*"].

The interviews' analysis revealed several themes, some of which, understandably, overlapped with the themes from the think–aloud. **Theme 7: Onboarding** highlighted the participant's frustration with being dropped directly into a complex simulation environment without a guided introduction, leaving them overwhelmed. Several participants suggested a dedicated "How-To" section to rely on. In the simulation phase, the participants also stated the need for **Theme 8: Scaffolding** to help them interpret their observation. As a participant stated while interpreting the curves, "*I have often wondered why it goes down so much and steeply up again... a bit of a clue that said that this is because or that could be because..*". **Theme 9: Macroscopic View** highlights the participant's desire for the "big picture," as participants reflected on how they would actually use the tool in a real-world scenario, moving beyond the micro-level student – Knowledge Component focus of the LM-simulation. Lastly, **Theme 10: Unclear Interface Controls and Nomenclature** highlights the disruption in participants' flow due to poorly communicated interface and obscure data labels. For example, a participant stated that their biggest hurdle was missing the toggle switch that grouped data either by "Student" or "Knowledge Component." The participant noted, "*If I had known that, it would have been much easier... I didn't check that it was simply grouped differently*". Similarly, another participant highlighted that during the simulation, certain controls "*were simply greyed out and I didn't understand.*" This lack of explainability of the interface and feedback caused them to doubt themselves, thinking, "*did I not find something?*".

On the other hand, the LM-simulation appears to be generally easy to use as perceived by most participants who reported a highly **[Theme 11:] manageable workflow**, noting that the core process of training models and executing simulations was easy to adopt after a short familiarization phase. As one participant explained, while the first model was tricky, "*..by the second and the third, I was so used to it.*" Ultimately, participants reported that the LM-simulation **[Theme 12:] supported their conceptual understanding**, as participants mentioned that they could observe how the abstract learner modeling algorithms behaved in real-time. One of the participants stated, when prompted to summarise their experience, "*when I saw the patterns in the curves I got the idea what happened in the behind of the models*".

### 4.4 Pre-post Test

The pre–post test involved repeated measurements of learning performance, within the five participants who voluntarily opted to participate. With the small sample size (no assumptions of normality), we used a non-parametric one–sided (assuming participants improve at post) Wilcoxon signed-rank test. Mean scores (1–9) increased from $M = 4.80$ ($SD = 1.30$) at pre-test to $M = 8.20$ ($SD = 1.10$) at post-test, with an average gain of 3.40 points ($SD = 1.14$). All five participants showed higher scores at post-test. The one-sided Wilcoxon signed-rank test indicated that post-test performance was significantly greater than pre-test performance, $V = 15$, $p = .029$. It should be noted that, neither in the pre nor the post, were the participants provided any performance feedback, so as not to incentivize them to seek out answers to specific test questions during the experiment, which could have artificially inflated post-test scores.

## 5 Discussion

### 5.1 Users' Perception of Usability (RQ1)

The participants graded the LM–simulation's usability as "**B**"($M = 74.40$, $SD = 8.31$) on a UMUX-Lite questionnaire [26], which is above the average of **C** (65 – 71) but falls short of industry standard of **A-** (> 80) [19,26]. Similar scores for perceived usefulness and ease of use may indicate that the LM–simulation is already perceived as a usable form, while meeting the participant's needs. Despite the initial difficulty with the interface [**Theme 1**], participants quickly familiarised [**Theme 11**], and eventually rated LM–simulation favourably in terms of usability. Providing an onboarding session [**Theme 7**] to familiarise users with the simulation controls, and also providing necessary information [**Theme 4**] as tooltips can prevent high cognitive load spike points ["*didn't know what did they mean, but then it has, like a hint button which explained to me, was really helpful*"]. Similarly, a participant highlighted the importance of scaffolding for interpretability [**Theme 8**]: "*I think that for someone who hasn't had hands-on experience with model training and interpretation of the results, they would need a guide*". A scaffolding can be provided in the form of worked examples [1] and variable-to-display mappings [22], which can help connect and interpret the abstract concepts with concrete implementations. Lastly, the ability to undo simulation steps is indispensable as it can inhibit a student's ability to test their hypothesis, [**Theme 6**], impacting the perceived usefulness of simulations.

### 5.2 Users' Experience of Cognitive Load (RQ2)

Cognitive load was measured with StuMMBE-Q [15] and interpreted along two dimensions: *Mental Effort* and *Mental Load*. The results showed a moderate Mental Load and a higher Mental Effort, which may indicate that participants perceived the tasks as cognitively demanding but invested substantial mental effort [15]. The relatively high Mental Effort remains noteworthy, especially when considered alongside the cognitive walkthrough, as participants were under no obligation to engage authentically with the learning task (taking part in the performance test was optional). As observed in [**Theme 4**], under high effort conditions, like interpreting the formula, the participants simply ignored it (see Fig. 4). Moreover, prior knowledge may have also influenced mental effort, as observed in [**Theme 2**]. Although prior knowledge was not explicitly measured, most participants were assumed to be familiar with the related concepts (see Sect. 3.1).

Pupils dilate in response to increases in mental effort, when triggered by an external stimulus [21]. The identical average pupil diameter across the training and the simulation phase may suggest that participants exerted similar Mental Effort and sustained their cognitive engagement across the two phases [32]. [**Theme 11 & 12**] corroborates these findings, as participants perceived the workflow as manageable and reported that the simulation supported their conceptual understanding. The exploratory pre-post results from a small voluntary subsample are consistent with this interpretation, but are insufficient for strong claims about learning effects. While potentially promising, caution is warranted, and further replication with larger samples and a control condition is needed to make stronger learning claims. Additionally, it is repeatedly recommended to use multiple measures of cognitive load (see [20] for example) to make precise observations. In our context, pupil diameter did not correlate with reports of Mental Effort. Van der Well & Van Steenbergen [32] caution against directly interpreting raw absolute pupil diameters and emphasize that researchers should evaluate the task-evoked pupillary response—-which is the stimulus–induced increase in pupil diameter relative to a pre-stimulus baseline, which we lacked, underscoring the importance of baseline collection protocols in simulation-based eye-tracking studies.

### 5.3 Implications for Research and Practice

We envision several implications for research and practice. Regarding research, this work contributes to the small but growing body of work that evaluates simulation-based learning environments through a combined lens of usability-and-cognitive-load, as advocated by Squires and Preece [28]. The mixed-method design—pairing StuMMBE-Q with eye-tracking analysis, and UMUX-Lite with think-aloud—can be beneficial for surfacing the gap between subjective experience and observable behavioural trace [18,27]. Future research can be further refined by collecting Mental Effort ratings during individual task phases, such as in experience sampling [9], instead of administering it at the end. This also allows better comparison with process-oriented physiological data. Nonetheless, our study illustrates that moderate usability does not preclude meaningful learning; participants overcame initial disorientation and can potentially develop their conceptual understanding.

Regarding practice, several actionable design recommendations emerge. First, onboarding matters: providing a dedicated orientation or pre-simulation phase can reduce anxiety and early abandonment [4], and also fosters learning readiness [25]. Second, to explore the simulation and test hypothesis, a crucial part of simulation–based learning, reversibility and step control are indispensable. Therefore, simulation-based learning must implement backward navigation or a scenario-comparison. Other notable improvement recommendations for usability include: 1. a lightweight in-situ tooltip, like "How to read this interface", represents a low-cost intervention with potentially high impact, 2. scaffolding in the form of worked examples [1] and variable-to-display mappings [22], and 3. clearly interpretable interface elements. Lastly, our study provides a case for iterative usability testing with a few target users in the form of formative studies. For example, a study focused specifically on a certain usability feature can more efficiently surface and resolve the issue than one large study before deployment, which can overlook other issues [23].

### 5.4 Limitations

This study has several limitations. First, it was a formative study with a small and domain-specific sample, which limits the generalizability of the findings. Second, cognitive load was assessed primarily through retrospective self-reports, while the pupil diameter lacked baseline correction; therefore, physiological and subjective measures could only be related cautiously. Third, the pre-post results were based on a small voluntary subsample without a control condition. Accordingly, the findings should be interpreted cautiously, primarily as evidence of usability issues, perceived cognitive demands, and future design directions rather than claims of causality for learning effectiveness.

## 6 Conclusion

This paper reported a formative evaluation of an interactive learner-model simulation for supporting conceptual understanding of AFM, PFA, and IFM. Participants generally perceived the system as usable, along with a moderate Mental Load alongside relatively high Mental Effort, but qualitative findings highlighted issues in onboarding, formula interpretation, and control clarity. The results suggest that learner-model simulations can support conceptual exploration when usability and cognitive load aspects are carefully managed. Future work will refine these features and re-evaluate the system with more focused usability goals.

## References

1. Atkinson, R.K., Derry, S.J., Renkl, A., Wortham, D.: Learning from examples: instructional principles from the worked examples research. Rev. Educ. Res. **70**(2), 181–214 (2000). https://doi.org/10.3102/00346543070002181
2. Barreras, A., Moreno-Mediavilla, D., Gómez, R., Palacios, A.: Factors influencing the use of virtual simulations by science teachers in secondary education. J. New Approaches Educ. Res. **15**(1), 1 (2026). https://doi.org/10.1007/s44322-025-00049-6
3. Bo, W.V., Fulmer, G.W., Lee, C.K.-E., Chen, V.D.-T.: How do secondary science teachers perceive the use of interactive simulations? The affordance in Singapore context. J. Sci. Educ. Technol. **27**(6), 550–565 (2018). https://doi.org/10.1007/s10956-018-9744-2
4. Bommer, C., et al.: Pre-simulation orientation for medical trainees: an approach to decrease anxiety and improve confidence and performance. Am. J. Surg. **215**(2), 266–271 (2018). https://doi.org/10.1016/j.amjsurg.2017.09.038
5. Chernikova, O., Heitzmann, N., Stadler, M., Holzberger, D., Seidel, T., Fischer, F.: Simulation-based learning in higher education: a meta-analysis. Rev. Educ. Res. **90**(4), 499–541 (2020). https://doi.org/10.3102/0034654320933544
6. Chi, M.T.H., Wylie, R.: The ICAP framework: linking cognitive engagement to active learning outcomes. Educ. Psychol. **49**(4), 219–243 (2014). https://doi.org/10.1080/00461520.2014.965823
7. Chi, M., Koedinger, K.R., Gordon, G.J., Jordan, P.W., VanLehn, K.: Instructional factors analysis: a cognitive model for multiple instructional interventions. In: Proceedings of the 4th International Conference on Educational Data Mining, pp. 61–70 (2011). https://doi.org/10.1184/R1/6475808.v1
8. Cook, D.A., et al.: Comparative effectiveness of instructional design features in simulation-based education: systematic review and meta-analysis. Med. Teach. **35**(1), e867–e898 (2013). https://doi.org/10.3109/0142159X.2012.714886
9. Eccles, J.S.: Engagement: where to next? Learn. Instr. **43**, 71–75 (2016). https://doi.org/10.1016/j.learninstruc.2016.02.003
10. Fouh, E., Akbar, M., Shaffer, C.A.: The role of visualization in computer science education. Comput. Sch. **29**(1–2), 95–117 (2012). https://doi.org/10.1080/07380569.2012.651422
11. Gegenfurtner, A., Quesada-Pallarès, C., Knogler, M.: Digital simulation-based training: a meta-analysis. Br. J. Educ. Technol. **45**(6), 1097–1114 (2014). https://doi.org/10.1111/bjet.12188
12. Gilbert, J.K.: Visualization: a metacognitive skill in science and science education. In: Gilbert, J.K. (ed.) Visualization in Science Education, pp. 9–27. Springer Netherlands (2005). https://doi.org/10.1007/1-4020-3613-2_2
13. Ergonomics of human-system interaction – Part 11: Usability: Definitions and concepts. Standard ISO 9241-11:2018, International Organization for Standardization, Geneva, CH (2018)
14. Kefalis, C., Skordoulis, C., Drigas, A.: Digital simulations in STEM education: insights from recent empirical studies, a systematic review. Encyclopedia **5**(1), 10 (2025). https://doi.org/10.3390/encyclopedia5010010
15. Krell, M.: Evaluating an instrument to measure mental load and mental effort considering different sources of validity evidence. Cogent Educ. **4**(1), 1280256 (2017). https://doi.org/10.1080/2331186X.2017.1280256

16. Kriek, J., Stols, G.: Teachers' beliefs and their intention to use interactive simulations in their classrooms. S. Afr. J. Educ. **30**(3), 439–456 (2010). https://doi.org/10.15700/saje.v30n3a284
17. Lateef, F.: Simulation-based learning: just like the real thing. J. Emerg. Trauma Shock **3**(4), 348–352 (2010). https://doi.org/10.4103/0974-2700.70743
18. Lee, Y., Limbu, B., Rusak, Z., Specht, M.: Role of multimodal learning systems in technology-enhanced learning (TEL): a scoping review. In: Viberg, O., Jivet, I., Muñoz-Merino, P., Perifanou, M., Papathoma, T. (eds.) Responsive and Sustainable Educational Futures, pp. 164–182. Springer Nature Switzerland (2023). https://doi.org/10.1007/978-3-031-42682-7_12
19. Lewis, J.R., Sauro, J.: Item benchmarks for the system usability scale. J. Usability Stud. **13**(3), 158–167 (2018)
20. Limbu, B.H., Jarodzka, H., Klemke, R., Specht, M.: Can you ink while you blink? Assessing mental effort in a sensor-based calligraphy trainer. Sensors **19**(14), 3244 (2019). https://doi.org/10.3390/s19143244
21. Mathôt, S.: Pupillometry: psychology, physiology, and function. J. Cogn. **1**(1), 16 (2018). https://doi.org/10.5334/joc.18
22. van der Meij, J., de Jong, T.: Supporting students' learning with multiple representations in a dynamic simulation-based learning environment. Learn. Instr. **16**(3), 199–212 (2006). https://doi.org/10.1016/j.learninstruc.2006.03.007
23. Nielsen, J., Landauer, T.K.: A mathematical model of the finding of usability problems. CHI '93, pp. 206–213. Association for Computing Machinery, New York, NY, USA (1993). https://doi.org/10.1145/169059.169166
24. Rutten, N., van Joolingen, W.R., van der Veen, J.T.: The learning effects of computer simulations in science education. Comput. Educ. **58**(1), 136–153 (2012). https://doi.org/10.1016/j.compedu.2011.07.017
25. Sabah, S., Schneider, J., Ahmad, A., Dengel, A., Di Mitri, D., Drachsler, H.: Educational virtual reality learner onboarding: a developer-centered study. In: Proceedings of the 18th International Conference on Computer Supported Education - Volume 2: CSEDU, pp. 1175–1186. INSTICC, SciTePress (2026). https://doi.org/10.5220/0014817400004021
26. Schrepp, M., Kollmorgen, J., Thomaschewski, J.: A comparison of SUS, UMUX-LITE, and UEQ-S. J. User Exp. **18**(2), 86–104 (2023)
27. Specht, M., Limbu, B.H., Schneider, J.: Sensors for Seamless Learning, pp. 141–152. Springer Singapore, Singapore (2019). https://doi.org/10.1007/978-981-13-3071-1_7
28. Squires, D., Preece, J.: Usability and learning: evaluating the potential of educational software. Comput. Educ. **27**(1), 15–22 (1996). https://doi.org/10.1016/0360-1315(96)00010-3
29. Stinken-Rösner, L.: Simulations in science education – status quo. Prog. Sci. Educ. **3**(1), 26–34 (2020). https://doi.org/10.25321/prise.2020.996
30. Tremblay, M.L., Rethans, J.J., Dolmans, D.: Task complexity and cognitive load in simulation-based education: a randomised trial. Med. Educ. **57**(2), 161–169 (2023). https://doi.org/10.1111/medu.14941
31. VanLehn, K.: Student modelling. In: Polson, M.C., Richardson, J.J. (eds.) Foundations of Intelligent Tutoring Systems, pp. 55–78. Lawrence Erlbaum Associates, Hillsdale, NJ (1988)
32. van der Wel, P., van Steenbergen, H.: Pupil dilation as an index of effort in cognitive control tasks: a review. Psychon. Bull. Rev. **25**(6), 2005–2015 (2018). https://doi.org/10.3758/s13423-018-1432-y

# "Maybe They Needed Help, but They Weren't Asking for It": Teachers' Decision Making in AI-Supported Mixed Reality Classroom Orchestration


Qianru Lyu[1(✉)], Víctor Alonso-Prieto[1,2], Qiao Georgie Jin[3], Will Morgus[4], Kyle Price[4], Stephen Fancsali[4], Susan Berman[4], Steve Ritter[4], and Vincent Aleven[1]

[1] Carnegie Mellon University, Pittsburgh, PA, USA
qlyu@andrew.cmu.edu, victor.alonso.prieto@uva.es, aleven@cs.cmu.edu
[2] Universidad de Valladolid, Valladolid, Spain
[3] North Carolina State University, Raleigh, NC, USA
qjin4@ncsu.edu
[4] Carnegie Learning, Inc., Pittsburgh, PA, USA
{wmorgus,kprice,sfancsali,sberman,sritter}@carnegielearning.com



**Abstract.** Prior research shows that a Mixed Reality (MR) teacher awareness tool, used by teachers when students practice with AI-based tutoring software, can shift teachers' attention to students who need help the most and can help students learn better. However, how teachers make sense of, prioritize, and act on MR-provided analytics during live instruction remains underexplored, limiting the pedagogical potential of real-time analytics. The current study examines teachers' noticing and instructional agency in this context. We compare teacher classroom orchestration with and without MR support and investigate how teachers notice, interpret, and act on MR-provided information in real time. Semi-structured interviews were conducted with four middle school mathematics teachers who used the MR tool in their classrooms. Based on the interview data, qualitative coding and Epistemic Network Analysis (ENA) were used to model patterns between teacher noticing, interpretation, and instructional actions. Teachers reported that compared to normal classrooms, the MR tool helped them shift toward more continuous awareness, need-based prioritization, and more calibrated intervention practices. Distinct decision-making trajectories emerged, in which recurrent patterns of quick nudges, sustained instruction, or deliberately delayed intervention were conditioned on both signals of idling and struggling, communicated by the tools and teachers' professional knowledge of students and tasks. The findings provide a nuanced account of teachers' decision-making process in MR-supported classroom orchestration. The insights about teachers' decision-making process may also contribute to the development of a recommendation system that suggests who to help, as well as the design of teachers' professional development for everyday AI-supported classrooms.




J. Weidlich et al. (Eds.): EC-TEL 2026, LNCS 16905, pp. 405–419, 2027.
https://doi.org/10.1007/978-3-032-37979-5_28

**Keywords:** Mixed Reality · Classroom orchestration · Teacher's decision making · AI-supported classrooms

## 1 Introduction

The increasing use of technology-enhanced learning (TEL) systems in K–12 classrooms has transformed teachers' classroom orchestration strategies [9]. While these technologies offer improved learning efficiencies and pedagogical support, they also require teachers to adapt their instructional strategies to manage complex, data-rich learning environments [9]. Prior research has highlighted that teachers' use of learning analytics is shaped not only by the availability of data, but also by factors such as teachers' data literacy, instructional beliefs, prior knowledge of students, and practical constraints (e.g., limited time and attention) [12]. As a result, aligning student-generated data with pedagogically grounded instructional actions remains a critical challenge [15]. This challenge is amplified in personalized learning environments where students progress at different paces, increasing the need for teachers to monitor and interpret multiple streams of information simultaneously [7]. These challenges point to a growing need for real-time awareness tools that can support teachers in monitoring classroom activity and allocating attention effectively under time constraints [11].

More recently, researchers have begun investigating the use of Mixed Reality (MR) technology as a promising modality for teaching augmentation in K–12 classrooms [2,4,8]. Unlike traditional dashboards that require a teacher's gaze on a screen, MR interfaces can embed digital information directly into the teacher's view of the physical classroom. For example, Zarraonandia et al. [18] used Google Glass to overlay live student feedback (e.g., self-reported confusion levels or help requests) onto the teacher's field of view. Prior work suggests that MR-supported orchestration can benefit students through improved teacher support, including reported gains in learning when combined with AI tutoring systems [8] as well as improved students' motivation and engagement [17]. From the teachers' perspective, MR supports real-time awareness during natural classroom scanning, reducing reliance on external dashboards and improving communication and pacing without major disruption [2,18]. Design research further highlights that MR must augment (rather than compete with) teacher attention, with a preference for heads-up wearable interfaces [2,8]. However, how MR systems shape teacher agency in everyday practice remains less understood, particularly in how teachers prioritize, interpret, and respond to classroom needs. This gap is critical, as MR design decisions about *what,when*, and *in what form* to present information can directly influence teachers' moment-to-moment decision making. Addressing this challenge requires grounding MR design in the mechanisms of teacher agency and decision making as enacted in authentic classroom contexts.

Teacher agency refers to teachers' capacity to purposefully drive their actions and influence educational practices, which involves planning, reflection, and decision making [3]. In TEL contexts, teachers enact agentic orchestration by actively coordinating classroom processes through cycles of noticing, interpretation, and action, which require substantial cognitive involvement and appropriate tool support [1]. Advanced technology-rich ecosystems have the potential to provide teachers with easily interpretable and actionable insights and could directly inform concrete pedagogical interventions [5]. Context-aware MR systems have potential to enhance teachers' perceptual capacities, augmenting the sense of presence and interpretaion [16]. However, interpretation and action remain shaped by teachers' professional judgment, influenced by cognitive, ecological, and value-laden factors. Thus, understanding how augmented perception translates into agentic action requires close examination of teachers' decision making processes in MR-supported classrooms. Investigating how teachers move from sensing MR-provided information to interpretation and instructional action is critical for uncovering the mechanisms of teacher–MR interaction and informing professional development in MR-supported teaching practices.

### 1.1 Research Gaps and the Current Study

Prior research on mixed reality and analytics-supported teaching has primarily focused on the awareness support system design, students' perceptions; students' learning outcomes and teachers' perceptions (e.g., acceptance; attitudes). While these studies have demonstrated the potential of Mixed Reality (MR) tools to enhance classroom awareness, less is known about how such tools reshape teachers' classroom orchestration during live instruction. In particular, few studies have systematically compared teachers' instructional practices with and without MR-based awareness support. Moreover, existing work often treats teachers' use of MR-generated information as a black box. Although dashboards and MR interfaces can surface rich, real-time indicators, we still lack a detailed understanding of how teachers make sense of this information in the moment, how they interpret awareness gleaned from analytics with their own knowledge about the students' and their specific situation, and how these joint sources of knowledge inform their instructional actions. As a result, the mechanisms through which MR tools influence teaching and learning remain underexplored. The current study interviews teachers who use MR analytics-based awareness tool in their classrooms and investigates two research questions: (1) What were the differences between normal classrooms and Mixed Reality (MR) tool supported classrooms in teachers' classroom orchestration strategies? (2) How did teachers say they made sense of and act on the rich information provided through MR interfaces during live instruction?

## 2 Methods

### 2.1 Mixed Reality (MR) Analytics-Based Awareness Support Tool-Lumilo

Teachers in this study used a glasses-based Mixed Reality (MR) classroom awareness tool called *Lumilo*, developed in past research through teacher-centered design [4]. *Lumilo* provides real-time analytics about students' progress while they work with an AI-based tutoring system (MATHia), see Fig. 1 and 2. *Lumilo* was deployed on a lightweight, phone-powered MR platform (XREAL Air 2 Ultra glasses attached to a smartphone). It presents compact MR overlays anchored above students, indicating the students' learning status such as *doing well (smiley face), unproductive struggling ("!?"), idle ("zzz"), high error rate ("?")* (see Fig. 1), computed from real-time tutoring system log data. Teachers can also access additional details about students' tutor workspace and math concepts.

### 2.2 Participants, Study Procedure and Data Collection

This study was conducted in a US middle school mathematics classroom with 8 experienced teachers (grades 7–8, more than 6 years of teaching experience). Although all eight teachers participated in the classroom implementation, four teachers were randomly selected for follow-up semi-structured interviews, which served as the primary data source for the present study. Before this study, all participating teachers used the AI-based tutoring system *MATHia* in their classes on a weekly basis. In this study, each teacher used the MR awareness tool, Lumilo glasses, in approximately three 45-min class sessions with an average of 20 students per class. Prior to implementation, teachers received technical training, and each classroom layout and seat map were modeled in the MR space. At the start of the first lesson, students received a brief (5-minute) orientation, followed by individual practice on an AI-based tutoring system (MATHia) for adaptive problem-solving practice. During the 35-min practice period, teachers used the Lumilo glasses to monitor students' learning progress and provide assistance (typically, one student at a time, as is business as usual in MATHia classes) while moving around the classroom, followed by a 5-min debriefing. Researchers observed all sessions and provided technical support as needed. After these sessions, we conducted semi-structured interviews with four teachers. Each interview was audio recorded and lasted around 20 min. The leading interview questions included (1) What were the differences between a normal MATHia classroom and a Lumilo-supported MATHia classroom? (2) What were the challenges and support when using the Lumilo glasses? (3) What indicators (e.g., idling; struggling) did you notice when you were using the Lumilo glasses, why? (4) How did you decide who to help and how to help the students based on the indicators, why? The first two interview questions were asked to answer the first research question and the later two questions were asked to address the second research question.

### 2.3 Data Analysis

We segmented interview responses into analytic units prior to coding. Each complete sentence was treated as one segment, with adjacent sentences combined when they addressed the same idea. Affinity diagram analysis was conducted to understand the differences between a normal classroom and a Lumilo classroom (RQ1). The segments of teachers' responses were grouped based on conceptual similarity, with iterative refinement to identify high level themes capturing recurring patterns in teachers' orchestration strategies. To understand teachers' decision-making processes (RQ2), content analysis was conducted using a coding scheme created based on [5] shown in Table 1 (see the end of this manuscript), including three dimensions: Noticing, Interpretation, and Action. For each segment, at most one subcode was assigned per dimension. The three dimensions were not mutually exclusive and could co-occur; segments without relevant content for a dimension were marked as not applicable. Two coders coded 25% of the data independently and reached a satisfying inter-coder reliability, assessed using Cohen's kappa: 1 for Noticing dimension; 0.72 for Interpretation dimension; 0.76 for Action dimension. The frequency (n) of each sub-code from the coding results is included in Table 1. Based on the qualitative coding, Epistemic Network Analysis (ENA) [14] was conducted on the ENA Web Tool (v1.8.0) to reveal co-occurrence patterns among the different codes. The unit of analysis is defined as interview segments within each teacher. The model used a moving window of four lines [13] to construct co-occurrence networks, aggregating connections among the sub-codes in Table 1. The ENA network was plotted for each teacher to understand the individual differences in their co-occurrence patterns.

**Fig. 1.** Mock Interface of the Glasses-based MR Awareness Tool Lumilo.

**Fig. 2.** Teachers Wearing Lumilo Glasses in Classroom.

## 3 Results

### 3.1 Difference in Classroom Orchestration Between Normal Classrooms and Lumilo Classrooms (RQ1)

Three main clusters were identified via affinity diagram analysis including classroom awareness, prioritization of instructional attention, and intervention practices, summarized in Fig. 3 (all teachers were given pseudonyms). Under each main cluster, the second-level clusters indicate the differences in teachers' classroom orchestration between normal classrooms and Lumilo-supported classrooms. The frequency of each point and an example quote from a teacher are also provided in Fig. 3.

**Table 1.** Coding Scheme of Teachers' Noticing, Interpretation, and Action (with Sub-code Frequencies, n).

| Dimension | Sub-code (frequency) | Explanation | Example |
|---|---|---|---|
| Noticing | N-idle(n=11) | Idle | "I noticed a lot of idling indicators..." |
| | N-struggle(n=12) | Struggle | "I would say the struggling students were the first groups to approach..." |
| | N-high_error_rate(n=6) | High error rate | "I see the high error rates (question Matthews) a lot..." |
| | N-raise_hands(n=5) | Student raises hands | "...cause sometimes students raise their hands but there is no indicator above their hands..." |
| | N-hints_overuse(n=2) | Hint overuse | "I see some students got those '!'; they could just click on hints..." |
| | N-doing_well(2) | Doing well (smiley face) | "There are some smiley faces and I will just say, good job Dylan, good job Tracey..." |
| Interpretation | INT-student_knowledge(n=17) | Student knowledge | "I know every student so well... some are slower... while others can get it very quickly." |
| | INT-task_difficulty(n=5) | Task difficulty | "It depends on the MATHia workspace... some are new... others are already mastery level..." |
| | INT-distance(n=5) | Distance | "Yeah, I will check on the nearby students quickly." |
| | INT-offtask(n=3) | Off-task (not paying attention) | "I know that they are just not doing MATHia... they don't know what they are doing." |
| | INT-needs_help(n=1) | Needs help | "So maybe they needed help, but they weren't asking for it..." |
| | INT-gaming_system(n=1) | Gaming the system (rush to next problems) | "They just don't want to actually struggle; they just want to go to the next problem." |
| Action | Act_quick_nudge(n=21) | Quick nudge / check-in | "...it was very easy... to tap them or say their name... a really quick, hey, get back to task..." |
| | Act_detailed_instruction(n=8) | Detailed instruction | "...move on to the next kid that might take a little bit more time..." |
| | Act_delay_act(n=1) | Delayed action / no immediate action | "If it is a workspace we had not done in class yet, I'm a little less concerned..." |
| | Act_positive_feedback(n=2) | Positive feedback / acknowledge progress | "I will give them a thumbs up and say, good job Jessica!" |
| | Act_co_teacher_coordinates(n=1) | Coordinate with co-teacher | "In that case, Matthew (the co-teacher) could support from that end of the classroom." |
| | Act_give_instruction_as_a_group(n=1) | Support a student group | "I will form them as a cluster/group to explain that point." |

In normal classrooms, teachers' awareness of students' learning status was primarily physical and dashboard-based, requiring them to alternate between "walking up and down rows" and checking the dashboard (mentioned by Sophia; Ross). Teachers described this awareness as fragmented and not timely enough, as the MATHia dashboard indicators were "not as real time" or "not as in-depth"

| Affinity Diagram Cluster | Normal classrooms | VS Lumilo classrooms |
|---|---|---|
| **Awareness** | **Physical and dashboard-based awareness**<br>4 / 4 teachers<br>*"Without the glasses, a lot of the class (time) is just walking up and down rows and looking at what they're doing. Assuming that they're doing okay, not really knowing if they're doing okay."*<br>*(Sophia)* | **Real-time, glanceable classroom awareness**<br>4 / 4 teachers<br>*"So it was super easy to be able to just look up, scan the room, and literally in five seconds know exactly who needs help, who doesn't, who's off track, who's stuck, whatever."*<br>*(Matthew)* |
| **Prioritization** | **Student-dependent and request-driven prioritization**<br>4 / 4 teachers<br>*"Some of them might raise their hand, but I think a lot of them also probably will just sit there and not let you know."*<br>*(Matthew)* | **Need-based and proactive prioritization**<br>4 / 4 teachers<br>*"So with the glasses, the kids that actually need help, I'm able to help more, versus the kids that don't need help and just want me to hold their hand through it."*<br>*(Brian)* |
| **Intervention** | **Delayed or assumption-based intervention**<br>2/4 teachers<br>*"I feel like not using it, there's kids that I feel like take a lot of my time asking questions."*<br>*(Brian)* | **Distributed and calibrated intervention**<br>4/4 teachers<br>*"So like if I was working with one student to get him back on track, as he's working on a problem that I just told him to work on, I could just look up very quickly and see across the room."*<br>*(Ross)* |

**Fig. 3.** Differences in Teachers' Classroom Orchestration between Normal Classrooms and Lumilo classrooms.

for moment-to-moment decisions (Matthew). In contrast, teachers felt that Lumilo-supported classrooms enabled real-time, glanceable awareness across all teachers, allowing them to "just look up" and quickly identify who needs help without interrupting ongoing interactions (Matthew).

In normal classrooms, teachers' prioritization of attention was largely student-dependent and request-driven, relying on physical scanning and student self-advocacy. Teachers noted that some students raised their hands, while others who needed support would "just sit there and not let you know" (Matthew). At the same time, teachers described spending disproportionate time with students who repeatedly asked questions but did not necessarily require help, "taking a lot of my time" (Brian). With Lumilo, prioritization shifted to a need-based and proactive pattern for all teachers. Teachers reported being better able to distinguish between students who "actually need help" and those who were seeking reassurance or step-by-step guidance, described as wanting the teacher to "hold their hand through it" (Brian). This shift enabled teachers to allocate their instructional attention more strategically across the classroom.

Differences in awareness and prioritization were reflected in teachers' self-described intervention practices. In normal classrooms, interventions were often delayed or assumption-based, as teachers first needed to identify who required support, sometimes "assuming that they're doing okay" without clear evidence (Sophia). With Lumilo, teachers felt their interventions became more distributed and calibrated (Fig. 3), with brief, targeted prompts delivered while supporting others (e.g., redirecting one student's idle behavior "on my way to another struggling student") (Ross; Sophia). Teachers also reported efficiency gains, including reduced movement and increased time in direct interactions with students (e.g., "about... 10 more minutes of face-to-face instruction") (Matthew). To summarize, teachers indicated that Lumilo reshaped their classroom orchestration from intermittent monitoring and reactive support toward continuous awareness, need-based prioritization, and calibrated intervention during live instruction.

### 3.2 Teachers' Noticing, Interpretation and Action Process Using Lumilo (RQ2)

The ENA analysis based on the coding results of teachers' interview data revealed different decision-making networks for each of the four teachers. In the ENA graph, each node represents one sub-code in the coding scheme while each connection between nodes indicates the strength of their co-occurrence patterns (thicker connections representing stronger co-occurrence patterns). In Ross's ENA graph (Fig. 4), the nodes N-struggle and N-idle ("N" represents the "Noticing" dimension) are strongly connected to multiple interpretation and action nodes, indicating that Ross closely monitors both idling and struggling students across time. The node idling (N-idle) is connected with two nodes: interpreting with student knowledge (node INT-student-knowledge) and acting with a quick nudge (node Act-quick-nudge). These connections indicate that for the idling students, Ross would consider students' learning status and give them a quick nudge to get back on task" *"If I know it's one of my lower (performing) students that's idling, they're probably idling because they don't know what they're doing...So I can quickly be on them like, 'hey, get back to work...Once they answered one question, most of them did not return to the idling...I was able to use that to quickly get majority of the students back on track."*

The node struggling (N-struggle) is connected with different interpretations and actions. Ross stated that, for struggling students, he considered both their learning status and task difficulty, so as to decide whether to provide quick nudges, instant detailed instructions or delayed actions for those students.ÂăFor example, Ross shared that he would provide instructions if students were struggling with a well-practiced task: *"I think it (decision making) also depends on whatever the (MATHia) workspace is. If it (MATHia's workspace tasks) is a mastery one and we've done it for two weeks in class...you need to come work with me."* In comparison, Ross tended to delay his actions if the MATHia's tasks were new to the students:Âă*"If it is a workspace of something that we had not done in class yet, I'm a little less concerned about the ones who are struggling. This is their discovery time in that workspace."Âă*

Brian's epistemic network (see Fig. 5) reveals a tightly connected pattern linking codes such as noticing high error rates, noticing raised hands, interpreting with students' knowledge status, acting with a quick nudge, and giving detailed instructions. In Brian's words, a high error rate emerged as the most salient of Lumilo's indicators, based on which he identified students in need of support, particularly when students were not actively requesting help. As Brian explained, "most of the time, it was the question marks," which allowed him to notice students who appeared to be quietly on task but were struggling beneath the surface. Like Brian mentioned: *"Most of the time, it was the question mark (that*

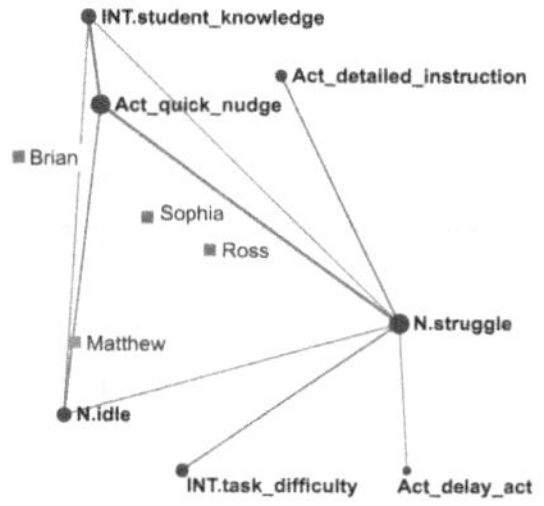


**Fig. 4.** Ross's ENA graph.

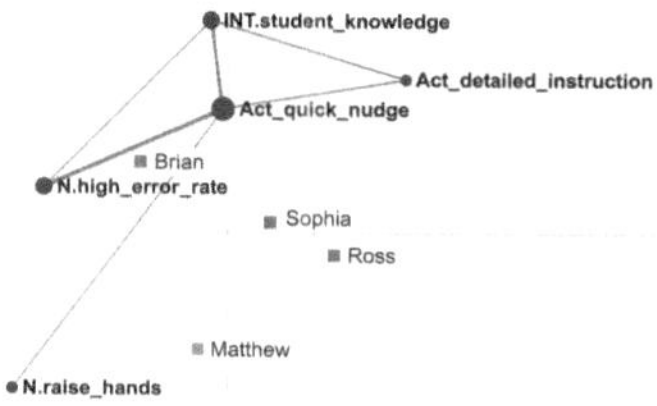


**Fig. 5.** Brian's ENA graph.

*I noticed). So they had a high error rate and maybe they needed help, but they weren't asking for it."*

Brian stated that he does not interpret the high-error-rate indicators uniformly; instead, Brian consistently filtered them based on his knowledge of individual students' learning habits and histories. He described knowing which students "just don't like to read" or "rush and get through it," as well as those he anticipated would "have a hard time" based on prior experience. This interpretation shaped Brian's actions: in his words, when he believed students could self-correct, he responded with brief, targeted nudges such as "Hey, look at this," allowing him to move quickly among students. He said he reserved more sustained, detailed instruction for cases in which he expected continued difficulty:Âă*"I mean, some of it's the kids, because I know certain kids, like it's something that I can get to in a couple of seconds. Hey, look at this, and then they'll get it pretty quickly. Where some kids I know, like, I'm going to have to actually work through it, go through the example, talk through it, because they're struggling."* Student-initiated help-seeking played a less central role, as Brian prioritized system-identified need even when others raised their hands.

Sophia's epistemic network (see Fig. 6) reveals strong connections between noticing student idling and struggle, interpreting students' needs through her knowledge about given students, and acting through quick nudges and selective detailed instruction.ÂăThe nodes N-struggle and N-idle are strongly connected to action nodes, indicating that Sophia is highly attentive to students' idling and struggling states. The node noticing idlng (N-idle) is linked with the action quick nudge (Act-quick-nudge), meaning that Sophia would give idling students a quick nudge. As she mentioned:Âă*"when a kid is an idle, it was very easy for me on my way to another kid that is struggling to just, like, tap them or say their name on the way by, like, a really quick, hey, get back to task, and then right on to my student that is struggling."*

For the struggling students, Sophia stated she would provide either a quick nudge or detailed instructions considering this students' learning status, priori-

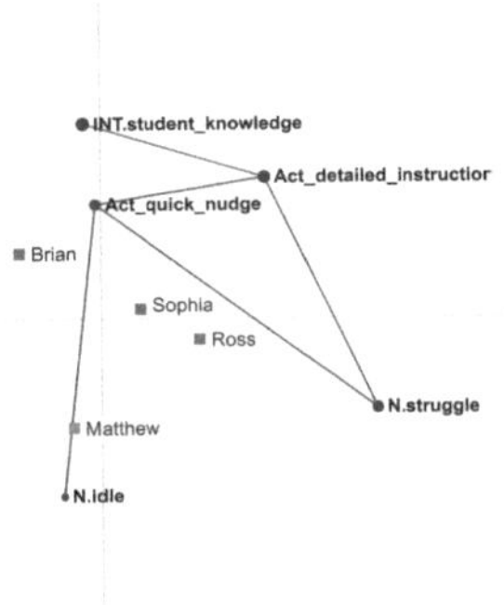


**Fig. 6.** Sophia's ENA graph.

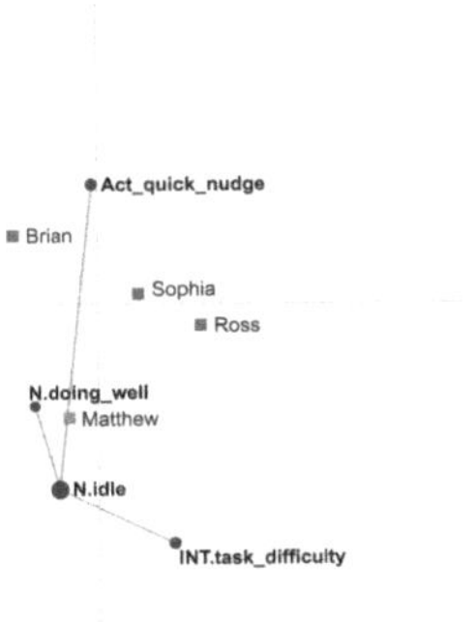


**Fig. 7.** Matthew's ENA graph.

tizing the students that are more academically successful students and may only need a quick conversation to get through before attending to those less successful students. Sophia said:Âă*"I am very familiar with each of the students' prior knowledge, like whether they are very fast learners or they are usually the slower learners... If we had a few that were struggling, if it was a higher functioning student, I'd get to them first because I can get really quickly done with them. Then move on to the next kid that might take a little bit more time to get through what they need to get through."*

Matthew's ENA graph (Fig. 7) indicates strong connections between noticing idling (N-idling), noticing doing well (N-doing-well), interpreting with task difficulty (INT-task-difficulty) and acting quick nudge (Act-quick-nudge). Similar with the other teachers, Matthew noticed the idling indicator and would act with quick nudge to get the students back on track. Meanwhile, Matthew would consider the task difficulty when he saw idling students. He mentioned that sometimes the students were idling not because they were offtask, but because they were reading a complex problem statement that led to pause of log activities on the tutoring system. Like Matthew shared: *"So what happened was I went to a student that were on "Zzz" (idling indicator), but he had a really long question to read. So it actually took him several minutes to process and then work. So he was like, I'm fine, I'm fine. I was like, okay, yeah, you have like 3 paragraphs to read."* Matthew relatedly suggested that the threshold for idling status detector may be extended for extra time when the question statement is longer: "maybe an extra minute or two (inactive state) before that Zzz comes up". Meanwhile, Matthew paid attention to the students that were doing well (a smiley face indicator above their heads) and he would orally acknowledge students' progress, like Matthew mentioned: *"I knew that the smiley faces were great and I actually said out loud, Mark, you're doing good. Tricia, you're doing good. So I was able to give verbal praise to those kids that were doing well, which I think is important."*

In summary, the epistemic network analysis revealed structured and recurring relationships among noticing, interpreting, and acting during MR-supported instruction. Teachers did not respond to MR indicators in a uniform or automatic manner; instead, indicators such as idling, struggle, or high error rates were consistently filtered through contextual interpretations. Teachers took into account factors such as the prior knowledge of the students, their learning habits and task difficulty, which were information sources that Lumilo did not provide. These interpretations, in turn, shaped differentiated instructional actions, ranging from brief nudges and verbal prompts to sustained, detailed instruction or delayed intervention. What emerges is a picture of teacher's analytics-informed real-time decisions that is highly sensitive to Lumilo's indicators but equally to teachers' knowledge about students. In other words, teachers' decision-making process indicate a human-AI synergy when teachers' decision-making is *informed by* real-time analytics without strongly deferring to these analytics or abdicating decision responsibility.

## 4 Discussion

The current study explores teachers' decision making processes in Mixed Reality (MR) classrooms with in-depth interview data. Critical insights were gained from four experienced teachers, highlighting the different classroom orchestration strategies in a normal versus MR-supported classroom. Nuanced understanding was obtained with a fine-grained analysis of their decision-making processes, unpacking how they interacted with the MR glasses and made instructional actions based on the real-time analytics, interpreted by their knowledge of students' and their situation.

### 4.1 Unpacking Augmented Awareness in Classroom Orchestration

Building on prior works that often characterize MR as enhancing teachers' classroom awareness at a general level [4] or conceptual level [5], our results of RQ1 further systematically unpack how, in teachers' views, augmented awareness is enacted in practice. Teachers' sharing reveals how the practical challenge of limited time and attention in data-rich classrooms [12] can be addressed through MR-based awareness support, demonstrating an empowered noticing, interpretation and action flow. The empirical insights also show the value of MR support in classrooms with personalized learning environments (e.g., intelligent tutoring systems) where students progress at different paces and teachers need to monitor both online and offline data streams simultaneously. Overall, the findings in RQ1 contribute a nuanced understanding of how MR awareness tools could change the way teachers make real-time instructional decisions in AI-supported classrooms.

### 4.2 Patterns in Decision Making Process

As prior works found, despite the augmented awareness, the MR space can be anxiety-inducing when there are multiple students needing help at the same time

[6]. In other words, when all students' learning status become aware with MR glasses, how to strategically prioritize and provide instructions is a core challenge. Valuable insights were obtained from the finding of RQ2, which revealed the patterns of teachers' decision making process (RQ2) using MR awareness tool. A set of shared *decision-making patters* emerge across the four teachers' ENA graphs. When teachers noticed student idling, they most often responded with brief, low-disruption nudges to redirect attention (Ross, Sophia, Matthew). However, idling did not uniformly prompt action. In some cases, particularly when tasks involved long or complex reading, idling was interpreted as a task-related pause rather than disengagement, leading teachers to withhold intervention (Matthew). These patterns suggest that idling indicators functioned as prompts for rapid interpretation, followed by either quick redirection or deliberate non-action depending on task demands.

Indicators of struggle consistently triggered more interpretive reasoning based on students' performance and task difficulty. Rather than acting immediately, teachers evaluated struggle through their knowledge of students and tasks. A recurring pattern was that higher-performing students who struggled were typically met with brief targeted support, as teachers expected them to recover quickly with minimal guidance (e.g., Sophia). In contrast, when lower-performing students struggled, teachers were more likely to provide sustained detailed instruction, interpreting struggle as a need for instructional repair (Ross). This finding aligns with previous work that found teachers allocated more time to lower-performing students when using similar MR awareness support [6]. Teachers also modulated their responses based on task familiarity: struggle on well-practiced tasks often led to immediate instruction (Ross), whereas struggle on novel or difficult tasks was more likely to result in delayed intervention, allowing time for exploration and productive struggle (Ross). In addition, MR indicators of successful progress supported positive acknowledgment, with teachers using these signals to reinforce engagement through verbal praise (Matthew).

Building on literature that conceptualizes teacher agency as an emergent and contextually shaped capacity [10], this study extends prior work by examining how such agency is enacted in MR-supported classrooms. In particular, our findings provide empirical grounding for conceptual accounts of human–AI hybrid orchestration [5], which describe teachers' orchestration as unfolding through cycles of noticing, interpreting, and acting with AI-provided awareness support. Our analysis shows how teachers' interpretations are shaped by concrete considerations including students' prior knowledge, learning habits, and task difficulty before instructional actions are taken. Importantly, these interpretations are shaped by teachers' knowledge and reflect a useful synergy between MR-supported awareness and teachers' knowledge. While MR systems augment teachers' awareness of students' learning status, they provide dynamic, real-time updates across all students that teachers would not otherwise have, whereas teachers bring contextual information that the system does not know, such as students' abilities, habits, and learning histories. Instructional decisions therefore integrate system-provided information with teachers' knowledge, rather than being determined by either alone. From this perspective, the observed IF–THEN patterns reflect agentic decision-making within a human–AI hybrid orchestration process, in which awareness support and professional judgment jointly enable context-sensitive decision making. This also suggests that, while some contextual knowledge may be incorporated into future systems, it is critical to preserve and strengthen this synergy, as teachers hold richer and more nuanced understanding of their students than analytics-based tools. These findings also suggest that teacher professional development in MR-supported classrooms should move beyond learning how to attend to system indicators, and instead focus on strengthening teachers' interpretive and decision-making capacities when working with AI-mediated awareness tools.

### 4.3 Design and Optimization of MR Awareness Tools

Our results suggest that MR awareness tools should help teachers quickly decide whom to help next and how to respond while still supporting teachers' *contextual sensemaking*. In our data, MR indicators helped teachers notice who might need attention, yet teachers did not respond to these signals in a fixed way. This suggests that future systems should provide lightweight recommendations that help teachers answer three questions in the moment: who may need attention next, why this student is being flagged, and what kind of response may fit this case. Because these decisions depended strongly on teacher knowledge, such recommendations should remain teacher-configurable rather than fully standardized. For example, teachers may need to adjust idling thresholds, choose whether to prioritize immediate intervention or monitoring, and set how strongly positive progress should be surfaced. The findings also suggest two concrete directions for recommendation design: first, better support for "quiet need," such as high error rates from students who are not asking for help; second, support for positive reinforcement. In particular, the current smiley indicators already point to an important design direction, as they helped teachers notice students who were doing well and offer brief verbal praise. A useful next step would be to make these positive cues more instructionally meaningful by highlighting not only success, but also recent improvement, recovery after earlier struggle, or sustained independent progress. This would extend MR tools from showing status to supporting more balanced, context-sensitive classroom decision making.

Our in-depth exploration of teachers' strategies in MR-supported classrooms relies on teachers' interviews and self-reflections. Although these reflections are valuable, future research can benefit from integrating multiple parallel data sources to verify and consolidate teachers' decision making pathways, including what information they access (from the MR tools) and what actions they take accordingly. The generalizability of the findings is limited by the specific learning context (7–8 grades math). Future work should further validate and refine the identified decision-making patterns in diverse instructional contexts, with different subject domains, student age groups, levels of teaching experience, and cultural settings to clarify the robustness of these findings.

## 5 Conclusions

This study provides an integrated understanding of both teachers' agentic actions and their underlying decision-making processes in MR-support classrooms. These evidence offers critical insights for the design and optimization of both Mixed Reality tools in tech-rich classrooms as well as teacher professional development. Based on teachers' self-reported data, we found that MR-supported classrooms shifted teachers' orchestration practices from physical and dashboard-based monitoring toward real-time, glanceable awareness, and enabled more need-based prioritization and calibrated instructional intervention during live instruction. By examining teachers' noticing, interpretation, and action processes, this work advances prior research on teacher agency and human–AI hybrid orchestration by providing empirical evidence of how real-time analytics, conceived as awareness support, promotes synergistic teacher–AI decision making while preserving teacher agency. In this sense, MR awareness tools do not simply enhance perception, but help structure the interaction between teachers and AI systems in ways that support in-the-moment instructional reasoning. From a practical perspective, the findings point toward extending MR tools from awareness support to decision-making support. The identified decision-making patterns suggest opportunities to formalize and implement these patterns in future decision recommendation systems. Importantly, such systems should remain configurable to accommodate differences in teachers' preferences and professional judgment. Overall, this study contributes to a more concrete understanding of how MR awareness tools can support classroom orchestration and teacher agency in data-rich authentic classroom settings.

**Acknowledgments.** This research was funded by the Institute of Education Sciences (IES) of the U.S. Department of Education (Award #R305A240281).

**Disclosure of Interests.** The authors have no competing interests to declare that are relevant to the content of this article.

## References

1. Alonso-Prieto, V., et al.: Towards capturing teacher agency manifestations within orchestration activities: a conceptual-analytical framework. In: Nazaretsky, T. (ed.) Two Decades of TEL. From Lessons Learnt to Challenges Ahead, pp. 107–112. Springer Nature Switzerland, Cham (2026)
2. An, P., Holstein, K., d'Anjou, B., Eggen, B., Bakker, S.: The ta framework: designing real-time teaching augmentation for k-12 classrooms. In: Proceedings of the 2020 CHI Conference on Human Factors in Computing Systems. p. 1–17. CHI '20, Association for Computing Machinery, New York, NY, USA (2020). https://doi.org/10.1145/3313831.3376277, https://doi-org.prox.lib.ncsu.edu/10.1145/3313831.3376277
3. Bandura, A.: Toward a psychology of human agency: pathways and reflections. Perspect. Psychol. Sci. **13**, 130–136 (2018). https://doi.org/10.1177/1745691617699280

4. Holstein, K., Aleven, V.: Designing for human–AI complementarity in k-12 education. AI Mag. **43**(2), 239–248 (2022)
5. Holstein, K., Aleven, V., Rummel, N.: A conceptual framework for human–AI hybrid adaptivity in education. In: Lecture Notes in Computer Science (including subseries Lecture Notes in Artificial Intelligence and Lecture Notes in Bioinformatics), vol. 12163 LNAI, pp. 240–254. Springer (2020). https://doi.org/10.1007/978-3-030-52237-7_20
6. Holstein, K., Hong, G., Tegene, M., McLaren, B.M., Aleven, V.: The classroom as a dashboard: co-designing wearable cognitive augmentation for k-12 teachers. In: Proceedings of the 8th International Conference on Learning Analytics and Knowledge, pp. 79–88 (2018)
7. Holstein, K., McLaren, B.M., Aleven, V.: Spacle: investigating learning across virtual and physical spaces using spatial replays. In: Proceedings of the Seventh International Learning Analytics & Knowledge Conference, pp. 358–367 (2017)
8. Holstein, K., McLaren, B.M., Aleven, V.: Student learning benefits of a mixed-reality teacher awareness tool in ai-enhanced classrooms. In: International Conference on Artificial Intelligence in Education, pp. 154–168. Springer (2018)
9. Huang, R., Yin, Y., Zhou, N., Lang, F.: Artificial intelligence in k-12 education: an umbrella review. Comput. Educ. Artif. Intell. 100519 (2025)
10. Lawrence, L., Echeverria, V., Yang, K., Aleven, V., Rummel, N.: How teachers conceptualise shared control with an AI co-orchestration tool: a multiyear teacher-centred design process. Br. J. Edu. Technol. **55**(3), 823–844 (2024)
11. Martinez-Maldonado, R., Clayphan, A., Yacef, K., Kay, J.: MTFeedback: providing notifications to enhance teacher awareness of small group work in the classroom. IEEE Trans. Learn. Technol. **8**(2), 187–200 (2014)
12. Michos, K., Lang, C., Hernández-Leo, D., Price-Dennis, D.: Involving teachers in learning analytics design: lessons learned from two case studies. In: Proceedings of the Tenth International Conference on Learning Analytics & Knowledge, pp. 94–99 (2020)
13. Ruis, A., Siebert-Evenstone, A., Pozen, R., Eagan, B., Shaffer, D.W.: Finding common ground: a method for measuring recent temporal context in analyses of complex, collaborative thinking (2019)
14. Shaffer, D.W., Collier, W., Ruis, A.R.: A tutorial on epistemic network analysis: analyzing the structure of connections in cognitive, social, and interaction data. J. Learn. Analytics **3**(3), 9–45 (2016)
15. Sharif, H., Atif, A.: The evolving classroom: how learning analytics is shaping the future of education and feedback mechanisms. Educ. Sci. **14**(2), 176 (2024)
16. Usma, M.S., Bangay, S., Sajjanhar, A.: Augmented reality enhanced analytics for education: a systematic review (2025). https://doi.org/10.18608/jla.2025.8447
17. Volioti, C., et al.: Using augmented reality in k-12 education: an indicative platform for teaching physics. Information **13**(7), 336 (2022)
18. Zarraonandia, T., Díaz, P., Montero, Á., Aedo, I., Onorati, T.: Using a google glass-based classroom feedback system to improve students to teacher communication. IEEE Access **7**, 16837–16846 (2019)

# This is How Students Think About and Act Upon Personalized, Automated Feedback on Transactivity

Lukas Menzel-Wuttig[1,5](✉), Joshua Weidlich[2,3,5], Julia Mendzheritskaya[4,5], Marc Winter[4,5], and Hendrik Drachsler[1,2,5]

[1] studiumdigitale, Goethe University, Frankfurt am Main, Germany
menzel@studiumdigitale.uni-frankfurt.de

[2] DIPF: Leibniz Institute for Research and Information in Education, Frankfurt am Main, Germany
joshua.weidlich@ife.uzh.ch, h.drachsler@dipf.de

[3] Zurich University of Teacher Education, Zurich, Switzerland

[4] Institute of Education, University of Zurich, Zurich, Switzerland
{mendzheritskaya,winter}@psych.uni-frankfurt.de

[5] Institute of Psychology, Goethe University, Frankfurt am Main, Germany

**Abstract.** When people learn together, the degree to which they respond to and build on each other's ideas matters for learning outcomes. This process, called transactivity, is a key predictor of success in collaborative settings. In educational discourse mediated by Computer-Supported Collaborative Learning applications, we can compute numeric representations of messages' semantics (i.e., embeddings) to quantify their relatedness. This enables estimating of the degree to which participants build on each other's ideas and thus measure transactivity. Such measurements can inform automated feedback on students' transactivity.

One missing puzzle piece has been evaluating the effectiveness of such feedback. We present a randomized field study in which a cohort of student teachers (n=252) worked on two online discussion tasks and received one of two feedback types: *basic feedback* (BAF) with general information on transactivity and a brief performance summary, or *highly informative feedback* (HIF) with a high degree of personalization on various aspects of transactivity. We show that while HIF was perceived more positively, it did not lead to robust behavioral improvements over BAF, highlighting a striking disconnect between perceived and actual feedback effectiveness.

**Keywords:** Transactivity · Educational Discourse · Automated Textual Feedback · Computer-Supported Collaborative Learning · Knowledge Construction · Learning Analytics · Natural Language Processing


J. Weidlich et al. (Eds.): EC-TEL 2026, LNCS 16905, pp. 420–435, 2027.
https://doi.org/10.1007/978-3-032-37979-5_29

## 1 Introduction and Background

Since the advent of networked personal computing, researchers in Computer-Supported Collaborative Learning (CSCL) have been working to digitally enhance collaboration in education [29]. Computer-mediated discourse was one of the earliest applications: In 1985, researchers at the Gallaudet University (a university for deaf or hearing impaired students) constructed special classrooms in which they arranged networked computers in a circle, running precursors of today's chat programs. These would then be used by the students and their instructor to conduct textual discussions [4,11,29]. Today, over 40 years later and with CSCL having become a *normal science* [1,18], new methods to examine educational discussions (which are often referred to as *argumentative knowledge construction* [33]) continue to emerge. Among the enduring questions driving this research is how to foster productive discussions in the first place.

When learning in groups, learners have to take up and discuss ideas by others. This is a sign that the group considers the ideas valuable. Conversely, it is important for each member to reflect on their own ideas in light of the discussion. This way, ideas become part of the group's co-constructed body of knowledge. One key pillar of collaborative construction of knowledge is thus transactivity, the degree to which participants respond to and build on each other's ideas [2,30,33]. Reflecting and discussing ideas is one part, but for a conversation to be productive, there must also be ideas worth discussing in the first place. The other key aspect of productive discussions is thus the novelty of contributed ideas, which must be balanced with transactive behavior [31, p. 399].

There have been previous attempts to actively improve learners' transactivity. For example, Jurkowski, Mundelsee, and Hänze [15] successfully trained secondary school students on transactive communication before letting them work on an assignment in pairs. This required them to carry out a workshop where professional teachers would train the students for two and a half days before the actual assignment. While this approach worked, it still requires extra time and a workshop outside the curriculum, or custom curriculum-integrated material on transactive communication. A different, more scalable approach would be to provide students with automatic feedback.

For feedback to be effective, it has to meet a number of requirements. [12,27,35]. Formative feedback in particular is known for its great potential effects, though improvement through its presence is not guaranteed [25]. This is because learners receive in-depth insights about their learning process or products rather than just a grade. For research on the effectiveness of formative feedback, this implies a necessity of at least two rounds of activity, with the feedback in between. Such an intervention can also serve as scaffolding: collaborative learning does not emerge spontaneously [17], and in CSCL, researchers frequently scaffold discussions using scripts [8]. Feedback represents another avenue to structure and support collaboration.

True formative feedback must be highly informative, actionable [6] and tailored toward learners' goals, or as Jivet et al. [14] put it, providing students with awareness is not enough. This is why we took a different approach from, e.g., Pfannenstiel et al. [21], who provided students with a real-time widget on their transactivity during a discussion. These ideals inform the notion of *highly informative learning analytics* [10]. In that sense, *highly informative feedback* is Learning Analytics (LA)-informed text that carries an interpretation of the indicators used and provides actionable suggestions on how to proceed [19].

For collaboration processes, this can only be provided at scale, if we can measure transactivity and newness computationally, though. Since the advent of sentence transformer language models, namely *Sentence-BERT* [22] it is possible to compute the similarity of two utterances, which can serve as a base to operationalize measures of transactivity. *Group Communication Analysis* (GCA) [9] offers a methodological framework to quantify transactivity through measure like *responsivity* (the degree to which learners engage with peers' ideas), *social impact* (the degree to which peers build on their contributions), and *newness* (the amount of information added to the existing discussion corpus). Together, these indicators make it possible to automate the detection of transactivity and newness of ideas in a discussion with a degree of precision that allows us to transform their outputs into feedback that is actionable.

In previous research, we supplied students with *highly informative feedback* on their collaboration [19] and found that learners prefer this *self-(regulation-)* and *process-focused* [cf. 3] feedback over a simpler form provided to a control group. However, that pilot study did not measure the feedback's effect on transactivity, and we identified the impact of feedback on transactivity in CSCL as a substantial gap in the literature. In the present study, we therefore examine to what extent our feedback improves students' transactivity and newness in educational discourse. Our results reveal a striking discrepancy between students' perception of the feedback and its actual effect on their behavior. We discuss the implications for the design of future feedback systems in light of this finding.

## 2 Research Questions and Methodology

The main goal of the present research was to investigate the impact of automated feedback on students' transactivity in a collaborative discussion assignment depending on feedback format: *highly informative feedback* (HIF), a personalized and actionable form of process feedback, as opposed to *basic feedback* (BAF). The BAF only contains information on transactivity in general and a simple summary of the students' performance. By contrast, the HIF contains information based on various indicators of transactivity and newness that are integrated into a feedback system we developed. It includes the information on transactivity from the BAF, but the summary is replaced with a performance evaluation for each indicator, as well as recommendations for actions to take in an upcoming discussion. Comparing these two formats, we address the following questions:

**RQ1a** How is *highly informative feedback* perceived by students compared to basic feedback?

**RQ1b** Does the students' perception of the feedback change across two intervention rounds?
**RQ2** Does *highly informative feedback* lead to greater improvements in transactivity and newness compared to *basic feedback*?

## 2.1 Experimental Design

We conducted a randomized field experiment, which we embedded in an online course in the learning management system Moodle. In educational settings, field experiments usually allow researchers to draw conclusions of higher practical value than more artificial lab experiments [20,23]. It was structured as follows:

1. The students discussed an assigned topic in a dedicated discussion forum designed for this assignment.
2. After the assignment's deadline, they received the feedback from our feedback generation system. They were able to review this feedback at any point in time during the course. There were two groups: the treatment group *Exp* (about half of the students in our cohort) received the HIF; the control group *Kon* received the BAF.
3. The students were instructed to review the feedback...
4. ... and to answer a questionnaire on their perception of the provided feedback,
5. ... as well as to write down what/how they want to improve in the future.
6. The course continued with a completely different kind of task.
7. After this task finished, we repeated steps 1 to 4 (Fig. 1).

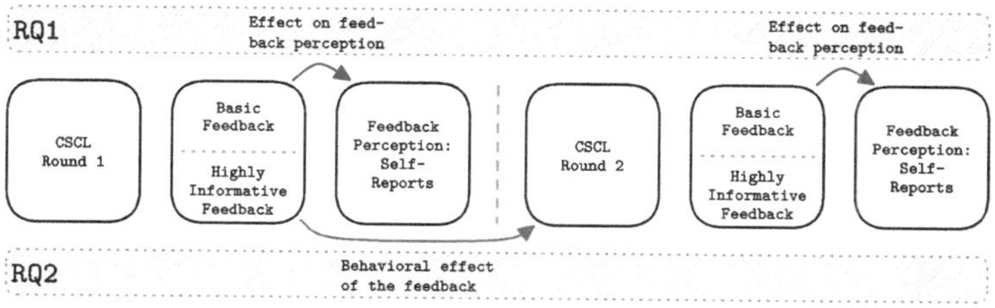


**Fig. 1.** Timeline of the experiment.

## 2.2 Procedure

We conducted the experiment with a cohort of undergraduate teachers in their first semester. In total, we had 283 participants in our cohort, out of which 31 had to be removed from the data set[1], leaving us with the data of $N = 252$

[1] Find the cleansing criteria, full assignment texts, self-report questions, feedback templates, and additional figures in the supplemental material at https://osf.io/4akjf/overview?view_only=d14e404100c743ecab7e54f79854ad79.

participants. 110 of these were part of the treatment group. 142 were in the control group. There were 49 discussion groups with a median size of 6 students, out of which a mean of 4.95 students were included in the analysis.

In a former experiment, we found that discourse indicators can depend on the micro script of an assignment [19]. Hence, to ensure comparability between the stages, both assignments followed the same scripts: first the students should watch a video and collect information about it in a Moodle discussion forum. In this phase, the students can't see what their peers post. Next, the students should discuss their collected information. Lastly, they create a joint statement as a summary of their discussion, also in the forum. They vote on the final outcome by posting that they affirm of the result.

After the deadline elapsed, the feedback was generated and a dashboard showing the feedback text and an evaluation form was unlocked in Moodle. The students had about two days to reply, before another task would begin. Due to our course design, the second stage of the experiment would not begin immediately after the first stage, though, but only after this other task.

### 2.3 Kinds of Collected Data

There were three main kinds of data we collected and used for our analysis:

**Forum-Post-related Data** The forum posts, forum thread reply structure (i.e., parent-post markers) and reply times used to determine deadline compliance. Students who missed the deadline were excluded from the analysis, as they did not receive the correct feedback due to system constraints.

**User/Group-Related Data** Participants, group composition and group sizes.

**Self-reports** Answers to self-report scales and free text remarks entered after reading the feedback. Our questions were based in part on the validated evaluation framework for quality learning analytics [26], as well as the derived feedback perception outcome framework by Weidlich et al. [32]. We asked the students whether ...

- **Agreement** they felt that the feedback accurately assessed them,
- **Clarity** if they understood what the feedback means,
- **Helpfulness** if they found the feedback helpful for their future learning,
- **Motivation** if the feedback motivated them,
- **Progress** if it helped them better track their current progress,
- **Reflection** it became easier to reflect on their learning behavior,
- **Regulation** it became easier to adjust their learning behavior if needed,
- **Bias** if they felt discriminated against/disadvantaged or treated unfairly,
- **Support** and if they needed support to make this feedback useful to them.

### 2.4 Our Feedback Generation System

We created the feedback based on findings from our earlier work [19], where we examined the usefulness of various process data derived indicators for templating HIF about discussion quality. For the present study, we moved the implementation towards a production-ready service and reduced the indicator set to those that either directly operationalize transactivity and newness or support improving them. This leaves us with the following indicators, for which Dowell, Nixon, and Graesser [9] provide the formal definitions and the theoretical rationale:

**Participation** records how often and when a student contributed to the discussion, in relative terms. Participation is a necessary precondition for transactive interaction, as it "signifies a willingness and readiness for participants to externalize and share information and thoughts [9, p. 1010]" [5,13].
**Responsivity** directly operationalizes transactivity by measuring how much a student responded to their fellow students' contributions, based on the semantic similarity of their posts [13].
**Social Impact** shows how much a student's contributions were picked up and discussed by the others. It is the flip side of responsivity and provides information about the influence their ideas had on the course of the discussion.
**Internal Cohesion** records the semantic relatedness between a student's own contributions, reflecting the degree to which they monitor and develop their thoughts throughout the discussion [e.g., 28]. Productive participation is associated with moderate internal cohesion: neither simply reiterating the same view nor contributing unrelated points [9].
**Newness** measures the extent to which a student contributed new content or perspectives to the discussion, including their own contributions. A high value indicates that they enriched the discussion with fresh ideas [e.g., 7].

We structured the feedback templates so that each student received at least one sentence comparing their performance to the whole cohort for each indicator. If an indicator diverged from the norm enough to warrant a change, they also received a tip on how to adjust their behavior in the next discussion assignment. Finally, we included a statement based on the emergent role cluster the student fell into, derived in part from Dowell, Nixon, and Graesser [9] and described in detail in Menzel et al. [19]. Role-based feedback allows us to address patterns of behavior that go beyond individual indicators. It provides students with a more holistic picture of their overall participation profile and offers targeted suggestions for improving their transactivity. The clusters are:

**the *influential actors*** (run 1: 77 → run 2: 63), who contributed early and substantively, but did not tend to engage further,
**the *drivers*** (25 → 30), who maintained balanced participation throughout, combining new ideas with transactive discussion of peers' contributions,
**the *summarizers*** (86 → 75), who joined late, mostly synthesizing existing content,
**the *left-behinds*** (46 → 48), who participated minimally with little impact,

**or the *chatterers*** (65 → 52), whose contributions tended not to be taken up by peers, indicating off-topic or low-relevance posting.

Compared to our earlier work, we removed the *semantic uncertainty*, *density*, and *affirmation rate* indicators, and consequently the resulting *deferrers* and *cautious learners* clusters, to maintain focus on transactivity and newness.

To compute the clusters, we applied hierarchical clustering on the z-score normalized transactivity indicators in the first run, identifying clusters by inspecting the centroids. We then used centroid-based assignment in the second run. We note that during the actual experiment, we used hierarchical clustering in both runs, a minor inconsistency that affected cluster assignments for 88 out of the 239 participants in round 2, altering the final statement in their feedback.

Our feedback structure also diverges from our pilot study [19]: there, we had one HIF template per cluster, with each template having its own conditions for texts on the indicators. Our reasoning at the time was to personalize the indicators shown based on a role-derived *learner persona*, anticipating that each persona would have different needs. Since certain indicators were excluded from the text when within an acceptable range, feedback texts could vary considerably in length under this model. For reasons of practicality and comparability, we deviated from this model in the present study. Furthermore, since the previous study did not focus primarily on transactivity, the BAF was rewritten accordingly, as described above.

## 3 Results

### 3.1 Self-reports

Regarding the self-reports, we use (RQ1a) a direct comparison between the two treatment groups in each round and (RQ1b) a temporal comparison. To address RQ1a, we conduct a Mann-Whitney U (MWU) test between the treatment group *Exp* and the control group *Kon* for each run. We obtain an interpretable effect size $r$ by transforming the resulting $U$ via rank-biserial correlation. For RQ1b, we apply two complementary tests: the Wilcoxon signed-rank test on paired responses to assess within-group temporal change and MWU over each student's $\delta$ to directly contrast the magnitude of change between groups (gain score analysis). To account for the false discovery rate, we apply the Benjamini-Hochberg procedure separately to the full set of p-values yielded by each test type, across all questionnaire items and both groups jointly, at $\sigma = .05$.

When interpreted for each run individually, the analysis yielded results consistent with our expectations. Figure 2 shows that students liked the HIF much better than the BAF, which can be observed in both runs. In the Self-Report analysis, we only included students who responded in both phases, giving us 81 participants in *Exp* and 96 participants in *Kon*, totaling $N = 177$.

Throughout every category where an effect was found, the effects were in favor of the HIF. In fact, because our cohort size was large, all the significant effects that we discovered passed BH procedure over the full Mann-Whitney

U derived p-value set (also Fig. 2). This procedure applies a very conservative threshold for null-hypothesis rejection. We are therefore confident in treating these effects as genuine. To answer RQ1a: We see small ($0.1 \leq |r| < 0.3$) to medium-sized effects ($0.3 \leq |r| < 0.5$) for all items but *agreement*, *bias*, and *motivation*. The largest effect is to be seen in the *support* item, with an $|r| = 0.46$.

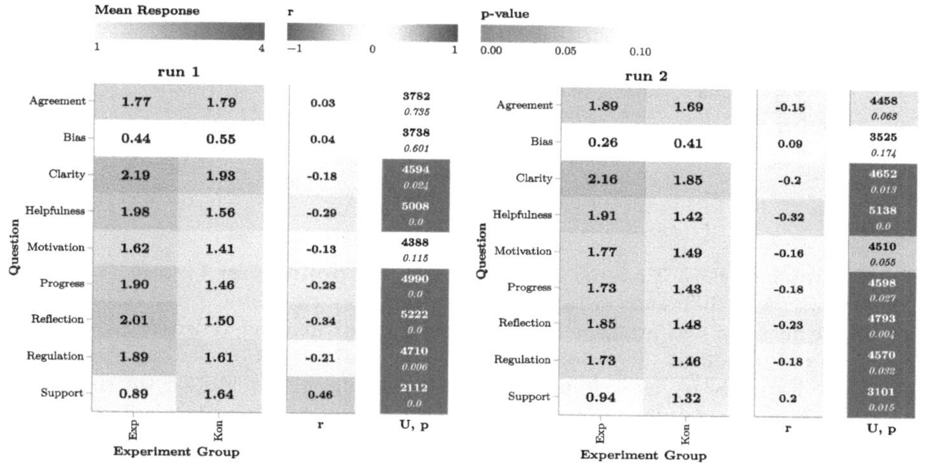


**Fig. 2. Heatmap of Mean Responses by Question and Experiment Group.** For each question/group pairing, we show the mean response value and an MWU test, comparing the treatment group Exp vs. the control group Kon. Rank-biserial correlation is used as the effect size r. Magenta-highlighted cells had their $H_0$ rejected under the BH procedure.

To answer RQ1b, we turn to Fig. 3: here we can see that there are temporal, as well as treatment-induced effects present in our data. We observe the strongest effect in the *support* item: in the treatment group, where students mostly didn't feel that they would need more support in the first place, that perception didn't change much in the second run. The control group, however, changed their perception significantly into the positive here, shrinking the gap between their and the treatment group's to an average of 0.38 points, down from 0.75 points, with a small effect size of $|r| = 0.21$ and $p = 0.01$ before BH correction. A similar, weaker pattern emerged for *agreement* ($p = 0.062, |r| = 0.15$). Overall it seems that students see the feedback more positively in the second round, though the effects of the HIF are mostly non-significant.

## 3.2 Changes in Transactivity and Newness

To address RQ2, we apply the same gain score analysis framework as in RQ1b. We analyze changes at both the cohort level and the level of individual clusters to account for effects that may cancel out in aggregate. We restrict the sample

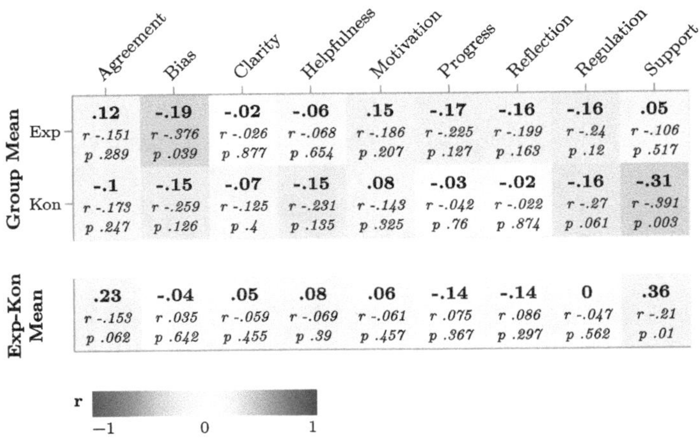


**Fig. 3. Run 1 → Run 2 Mean Differences in Responses per Group.** The upper panel shows mean difference in Likert response between run 1 and run 2 ($\Delta$ = run 2 – run 1) per question and group, tested for significance using the Wilcoxon signed-rank test on paired responses. The lower panel shows the difference between the mean group responses (Exp – Kon), as well as test results from the MWU test on the differences per student. $r$ is computed using rank-biserial correlation. Magenta-highlighted cells had their $H_0$ rejected under the BH procedure.

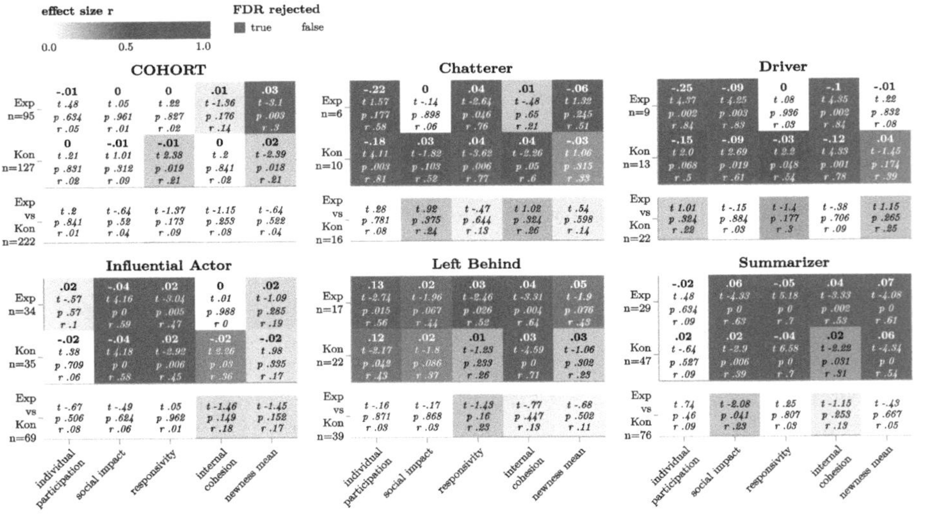


**Fig. 4. Heatmaps of t-test results for indicator changes between experiment runs, shown per cluster.** Upper panels display mean differences, paired-sample t-statistics, p-values, and effect sizes $r$ for treatment and control groups across five indicators. Lower panels report independent-samples t-tests comparing change magnitudes between groups. Cell shading reflects effect size (darker = higher); magenta-highlighted cells passed the BH procedure.

to students who completed the self-report questionnaire in the first run, treating questionnaire completion as a proxy for feedback review. This reduces the sample to $N = 222$. For within-group temporal change, we use paired-samples t-tests in place of the Wilcoxon test to reflect the continuous nature of the indicators. For the gain score analysis contrasting the magnitude of change between *Exp* and *Kon*, we use independent-samples t-tests in place of MWU. We apply the BH procedure once over the full set of p-values for each test in the cohort-level analysis and once over the set per test for all clusters at once.

At the cohort level, we find that the *newness* increased significantly (before FDR correction) for both, *Exp* and *Kon*. Interestingly, the *responsivity* for *Kon* decreased, with a small effect size of $r = 0.21$. Strictly speaking, however, only the *newness* gains for *Exp* passed the BH procedure.

Figure 4 also shows changes in student behavior when divided up by their clusters from the first run. These paint a very different picture, showing real changes in different areas, depending on the cluster, many of which passed BH correction. The treatment with the HIF didn't make much of a difference here; additionally, some clusters were quite small, which limits the interpretability of their results. The only value that showed a significant improvement through the treatment was the *social impact* of the *summarizers*, with a small $r = 0.23$ and a $p = 0.041$, indicating that members of this cluster were motivated to start earlier in the second run. That, too, didn't pass BH correction, though.

### 3.3 Cluster Transitions

We used Barnard's exact test to compare the cluster transition matrices for the treatment and the control group. For each cell, the test was conducted using the following contingency table as an input, which resulted in Fig. 5:

| for each transition $a \to b$ | Exp | Kon |
|---|---|---|
| transition $a \to b$ | $n_{a\to b}^{Exp}$ | $n_{a\to b}^{Kon}$ |
| no transition $a \to b$ | $N^{Exp} - n_{a\to b}^{Exp}$ | $N^{Kon} - n_{a\to b}^{Kon}$ |

In this figure, we see that only in the *chatterers* $\to$ *chatterers* transition pair, the probability for a transition was significantly lower in the control group vs. the treatment group. That finding didn't get its null-hypothesis rejected by the BH procedure, probably making it a false discovery. The transition analysis thus further reinforces the observation from the last section and lets us conclude that there is no robust evidence for significant changes in students' behavior (RQ2).

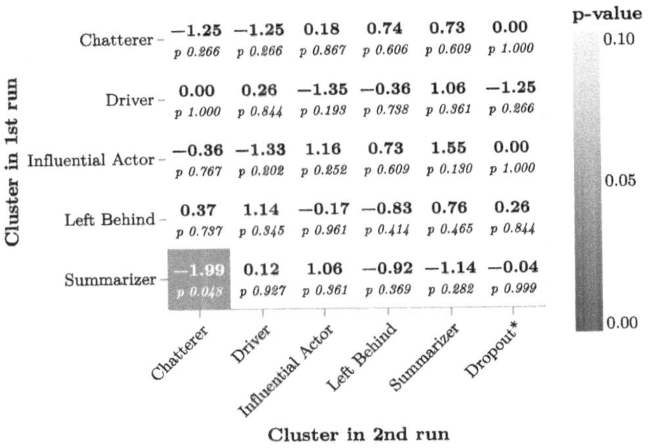


**Fig. 5. Significance matrix for cluster transition probabilities between experiment runs**, comparing *Exp* and *Kon*. Each cell represents a specific cluster-to-cluster transition, tested using Barnard's exact test. A positive statistic implies relatively more transitions in *Exp* vs *Kon* and vice versa. Cell shading reflects p-values (darker = lower); magenta-highlighted cells passed the BH procedure. Cell values show the test statistic and p-value. Dropouts did not participate in the second run.

# 4 Discussion

The study was conducted in an authentic field setting with randomized group assignments, strengthening its internal validity. The two points of measurement allowed us to examine changes attributable to formative feedback, an intervention strategy with well-documented effectiveness [25]. By combining process data with self-reports, we were able to contrast objective behavioral indicators with participants' subjective evaluations of the feedback, allowing us to surface potential discrepancies between perception and measured behavior. These design choices enabled us to address our research questions comprehensively. The sample ($N = 177$ to $N = 252$, depending on the exclusion criteria applied) provided sufficient statistical power to detect small-to-medium effects ($r \geq 0.21$ at the lower bound, $r \geq 0.18$ at the upper bound; $1 - \beta = 0.80, \sigma = 0.05$) for all cohort-wide independent t-tests, and medium effects ($r \geq 0.30$ to $r \geq 0.23$, depending on group and exclusion criteria) for within-group paired sample t-tests across measurement points.

Our results show that the HIF was not able to induce a significant, robust improvement in either transactivity or newness compared to the BAF (RQ2). This was also reflected in the lack of a difference in cluster transition probability between *Exp* and *Kon*. Still, there were significant differences in student satisfaction with the feedback (RQ1a). This supports previous findings in the literature that actionable feedback is well-appreciated by learners [e.g., 6]. As a result, we could show a real discrepancy between student perceptions and the actual effect of our HIF. Furthermore, when assessed per cluster, there were strong effects between the two measurement points. These were, however, not dependent on the treatment and mostly equal between the groups (except for one significant effect that didn't pass false discovery correction).

The temporal effects, when taken together with the convergence in students' perceived need for additional support, are suggestive: it seems that for the outcome, the BAF with its short information text on transactivity might be sufficient to change transactive behavior in forum discussion assignments. It remains unclear, however, whether external effects play a role, several of which would be plausible. One possibility is experience gains in collaborative forum tasks; another is the new assignment itself, which might have engaged students differently, despite having the same structure as the first assignment.

This highlights a limitation of our study: The absence of a second control group limits the interpretability of our results. Without a group receiving either no feedback or feedback without any information on transactivity, we cannot isolate the effects of informing students on the importance of transactivity. Furthermore, since only students who responded to both feedback forms are included in the self-report analysis, the dropout rate may introduce some distortion into the findings. We simply can't know what hasn't been reported.

That positive perceptions of feedback do not guarantee performance gains is an established finding [16,25]. Winstone et al. [34] offer a useful framework for understanding this gap. They identify four psychological barriers to feedback uptake: *awareness*, *cognisance*, *agency*, and *volition*. Of these, the first two are unlikely explanations in our case: the HIF was written in plain language and included concrete, personalized suggestions for improvement. The more plausible barriers are agency and volition. Transactive discussion behavior is a complex social skill, which might be why dedicated training has been shown to be more effective [15]. Our feedback told students *what* they did and *how to improve*, but may not have equipped them with *strategies for how to act* differently in a live discussion. Students could revisit their feedback before the second task, and the task structure was identical. Yet deliberately changing ingrained discussion habits requires sustained effort that may exceed what students are willing or able to invest into a forum assignment.

Our results are also consistent with existing research on behavioral feedback of the kind represented by our HIF. Wisniewski, Zierer, and Hattie [35] find that of the four categories of outcome measures for feedback which they identify in their meta study, feedback on behavior was among the two categories with weaker effects, naming an effect size of Cohen's $d = 0.48$. Regarding the type of feedback given, "high-information feedback" had a large effect size, with $d = 0.99$. However, their definition of "high-information feedback" differed from our HIF, where their definition meant feedback which included *process* and *product* feedback, combined. Since our feedback is only about the process, there's no direct equivalent to our HIF in Wisniewski, Zierer, and Hattie [35].

## 5 Conclusion and Outlook

In our randomized field experiment, we set out to test whether *highly informative feedback* (personalized, process focused and actionable) would change students' transactive behavior compared to a *basic feedback*. Formative feedback has long been known to be effective [25], and measurable behavioral changes through feedback have been demonstrated before [35]. With this intervention, we hence had reason to expect measurable changes in student behavior. What we found instead was a striking discrepancy between how students perceived the feedback and its actual effect on their behavior: we observed a strong preference for the HIF at both measurement points, while treatment had no significant effect.

These results suggest that educators should be cautious about relying on student perceptions as a proxy for effectiveness of HIF on transactivity and newness. One possible explanation is that these discourse properties are simply difficult to change, requiring more interventions before a clear effect emerges. However, the temporal effects we observed, albeit not in isolation, might speak against this interpretation. To disentangle these effects, future experiments could compare HIF and BAF against a no-feedback control group.

Another possible explanation for the lack of measurable behavioral change is the feedback's degree of actionability. While the HIF contained personalized information on transactivity and newness, it did not elaborate on what exactly is being measured or why each indicator matters. Without this grounding, students may have had a target but no clear path toward it. This points to a potentially fruitful direction: greater transparency about what is measured, how it is measured, and how students are positioned relative to the relevant scales.

Based on our results, we see no reason to favor the BAF over the HIF, even in the absence of differences in behavioral outcomes. Given students' strong and consistent preference for the HIF, we would opt for it in any long-term feedback intervention on transactivity. Student satisfaction with their educational environment matters for sustained motivation [24], and there is reason to believe that further refinements to both the underlying measurements and the feedback's actionability, informed by continued research on HIF, can lead to improved outcomes.

Improving the quality of collaborative discussions in educational settings remains a long-standing challenge, and automated feedback is one promising avenue toward addressing it. Our findings add a nuanced piece to this endeavor: student perception and behavioral change do not always move in lockstep, and understanding this gap may be as important as closing it. As feedback systems grow more sophisticated, the question of how students receive, interpret, and act on them deserves equal attention.

**AI Transparency Note:.** The authors used Google Scholar, Semantic Scholar and Claude to search for references that might become useful. All references included in this paper were screened, read and picked by the authors. We improved some phrasings in this paper using Claude and Mistral. Usually, these were iterated upon manually later in the writing process. Claude was used for proofreading and debugging code to prepare data for the analysis. Much of the Python code to render diagrams was initially drafted with Claude, but manually modified later in the process.

## References


1. Baker, M.J., and Reimann, P.: CSCL has come of age. Intern. J. Comput.- Support. Collab. Learn. **19**(1), 1–10 (2024)
2. Berkowitz, M.W., Gibbs, J.C.: Measuring the developmental features of moral discussion. Merrill-Palmer Q. **29**(4), 399–410 (1983)
3. Brooks, C., Carroll, A., Gillies, R., Hattie, J.: A matrix of feedback. AJTE **44**(4), 14–32 (2019)
4. Bruce, B.C., Rubin, A.: Electronic quills: a situated evaluation of using computers for writing in classrooms. Choice Rev. Online **30**(08), 30-4526 (1993)
5. Care, E., Scoular, C., Griffin, P.: Assessment of collaborative problem solving in education environments. Appl. Measur. Educ. **29**(4), 250–264 (2016)
6. Cha, H.-J., Park, T.: Applying and evaluating visualization design guidelines for a MOOC dashboard to facilitate self-regulated learning based on learning analytics. KSII TIIS **13**(6) (2019)
7. Dennis, A.R.: Information exchange and use in group decision making: you can lead a group to information, but you can't make it think. MIS Q. **20**(4), 433 (1996)
8. Dillenbourg, P., Hong, F.: The mechanics of CSCL macro scripts. Comput. Support. Learn. **3**(1), 5–23 (2008)
9. Dowell, N.M.M., Nixon, T.M., Graesser, A.C.: Group communication analysis: a computational linguistics approach for detecting sociocognitive roles in multiparty interactions. Behav. Res. **51**(3), 1007–1041 (2019)
10. Drachsler, H.: Towards highly informative learning analytics. In: Open Universiteit, Heerlen, Netherlands (2023)
11. Gruber, S., Peyton, J.K., Bruce, B.C.: Collaborative writing in multiple discourse contexts. Comput. Support. Coop. Work **3**(3–4), 247–269 (1995)
12. Hattie, J., Timperley, H.: The power of feedback. Rev. Educ. Res. **77**(1), 81–112 (2007)
13. Hesse, F., Care, E., Buder, J., Sassenberg, K., Griffin, P.: A framework for teachable collaborative problem solving skills. In: Griffin, P., Care, E. (eds.) Assessment and Teaching of 21st Century Skills: Methods and Approach, pp. 37–56. Springer, Netherlands, Dordrecht (2015). https://doi.org/10.1007/978-94-017-9395-7_2
14. Jivet, I., Scheffel, M., Drachsler, H., Specht, M.: Awareness is not enough: pitfalls of learning analytics dashboards in the educational practice. In: Lavoué, É., Drachsler, H., Verbert, K., Broisin, J., Pérez-Sanagustín, M. (eds.) Data Driven Approaches in Digital Education, pp. 82–96. Springer International Publishing, Cham (2017). https://doi.org/10.1007/978-3-319-66610-5_7
15. Jurkowski, S., Mundelsee, L., Hänze, M.: Strengthening collaborative learning in secondary school: development and evaluation of a lesson-integrated training approach for transactive communication. Learn. Instr. **92**, 101934 (2024)
16. Kluger, A.N., DeNisi, A.: The effects of feedback interventions on performance: a historical review, a meta-analysis, and a preliminary feedback intervention theory. Psychol. Bull. **119**(2), 254–284 (1996)
17. Kreijns, K., Kirschner, P.A., Jochems, W.: Identifying the pitfalls for social interaction in computer-supported collaborative learning environments: a review of the research. Comput. Hum. Behav. **19**(3), 335–353 (2003)

18. Kuhn, T.S.: The Structure of Scientific Revolutions. University of Chicago Press, Chicago (1970)
19. Menzel, L., Gombert, S., Weidlich, J., Fink, A., Frey, A., Drachsler, H.: Why you should give your students automatic process feedback on their collaboration: evidence from a randomized experiment. In: Viberg, O., Jivet, I., MuñozMerino, P.J., Perifanou, M., Papathoma, T. (eds.) Responsive and Sustainable Educational Futures, pp. 198–212. Springer Nature Switzerland, Cham (2023). https://doi.org/10.1007/978-3-031-42682-7_14
20. Motz, B.A., Carvalho, P.F., De Leeuw, J.R., Goldstone, R.L.: Embedding experiments: staking causal inference in authentic educational contexts. Learn. Analytics **5**(2) (2018)
21. Pfannenstiel, W., et al.: Is my conversation really constructing knowledge? Epistemic and transactivity group awareness widgets to raise participant awareness during online discourse. In: Nazaretsky, T. (ed.) Two Decades of TEL. From Lessons Learnt to Challenges Ahead, pp. 349–354. Springer Nature Switzerland, Cham (2025). https://doi.org/10.1007/978-3-032-03873-9_48
22. Reimers, N., Gurevych, I.: Sentence-BERT: sentence embeddings using siamese BERT-networks. In: Proceedings of the 2019 Conference on Empirical Methods in Natural Language Processing. Association for Computational Linguistics (2019)
23. Ross, S.M., Morrison, G.R., and Lowther, D.L.: Educational technology research past and present: balancing rigor and relevance to impact school learning. Contemp. Educ. Technol. **1**(1) (2010)
24. Ryan, R.M., Deci, E.L.: Self-determination theory and the facilitation of intrinsic motivation, social development, and well-being. Am. Psychol. **55**(1), 68–78 (2000)
25. Sadler, D.R.: Formative assessment and the design of instructional systems. Instr. Sci. **18**(2), 119–144 (1989)
26. Scheffel, M.: The evaluation framework for learning analytics. Ph.D. thesis, Open Universiteit (2017)
27. Scheffel, M., Drachsler, H., de Kraker, J., Kreijns, K., Slootmaker, A., Specht, M.: Widget, widget on the wall, am i performing well at all? IEEE Trans. Learning Technol. **10**(1), 42–52 (2017)
28. Stahl, G.: Rediscovering CSCL. In: Koschmann, T., Hall, R., Miyake, N. (eds.) CSCL 2: Carrying Forward the Conversation, pp. 169–181 (2002)
29. Stahl, G., Koschmann, T., Suthers, D.: Computer-supported collaborative learning: an historical perspective. In: Sawyer, R.K. (ed.) Cambridge Handbook of the Learning Sciences. Cambridge University Press, Cambridge, UK (2006)
30. Teasley, S.D.: Talking about reasoning: how important is the peer in peer collaboration? In: Resnick, L.B., Säljö, R., Pontecorvo, C., Burge, B. (eds.) Discourse Tools Reasoning, pp. 361–384. Springer, Berlin Heidelberg, Berlin, Heidelberg (1997). https://doi.org/10.1007/978-3-662-03362-3_16
31. Vogel, F., et al.: Transactivity and knowledge coconstruction in collaborative problem solving. In: 16th International Conference on Computer-Supported Collaborative Learning (CSCL) 2023, pp. 337–346 (2023)
32. Weidlich, J., et al.: Highly informative feedback using learning analytics: how feedback literacy moderates student perceptions of feedback. Int. J. Educ. Technol. High. Educ. **22**(1), 43 (2025)
33. Weinberger, A., Fischer, F.: A framework to analyze argumentative knowledge construction in computer-supported collaborative learning. Comput. Educ. **46**(1), 71–95 (2006)

34. Winstone, N.E., Nash, R.A., Rowntree, J., Parker, M.: 'it'd be useful, but i wouldn't use it': barriers to university students' feedback seeking and recipience. Stud. High. Educ. **42**(11), 2026–2041 (2017)
35. Wisniewski, B., Zierer, K., Hattie, J.: The power of feedback revisited: a meta-analysis of educational feedback research. Front. Psychol. **10**, 3087 (2020)

# Teacher Support Based on AI and Learning Analytics to Promote Self-regulated Learning in K-12 Digital Learning Environments: A Scoping Review

Konstantinos Michos[1(✉)], Dominik Glandorf[1], Doreen Prasse[2], and Tanja Käser[1]

[1] EPFL, Lausanne, Switzerland
{konstantinos.michos,dominik.glandorf,tanja.kaeser}@epfl.ch
[2] Schwyz University of Teacher Education, Goldau, Switzerland
doreen.prasse@phsz.ch

**Abstract.** Promoting students' self-regulated learning (SRL) in K-12 digital learning environments is a complex task for teachers. Data-driven technologies such as learning analytics (LA) and artificial intelligence (AI) have been increasingly used to detect and support students' SRL processes. However, there is limited synthesis of how these technologies support teachers in fostering SRL in school contexts. This study presents a scoping review of research on teacher support based on AI and LA for promoting SRL in K-12 digital learning environments. A systematic search across different databases identified studies that address SRL or metacognition, teacher support, and AI or LA technologies. The review examines the types of systems used to support teachers, how these systems are used during the design or orchestration of digital learning activities to support SRL phases, and the levels of automation of AI in relation to the teacher role. Results indicate that most studies focus on analyzing SRL processes or on student-facing AI tools such as chatbots with limited direct support for teachers. Teacher-facing tools, such as LA dashboards, are less common and support monitoring of student learning processes rather than actionable pedagogical support. Emerging approaches using AI, such as prompts and intelligent assistants, show potential to support planning, monitoring, and reflection processes but are rarely designed explicitly for teachers. These findings contribute to the design of data-driven tools that could assist teachers in promoting SRL in digital learning environments.

**Keywords:** self-regulated learning · learning analytics · artificial intelligence · teachers · K-12

## 1 Introduction

The current digital transformation of schools involves the increasing integration of digital learning environments (DLEs) and data-driven technologies in teach-


J. Weidlich et al. (Eds.): EC-TEL 2026, LNCS 16905, pp. 436–450, 2027.
https://doi.org/10.1007/978-3-032-37979-5_30

ing and learning. These developments affect multiple stakeholders, including students, teachers, and school administrators. In particular, teachers are increasingly incorporating data-driven technologies into their daily practice, such as Learning Analytics (LA) systems [13,23,30,36,46,56] and Artificial Intelligence in Education (AIED) tools [3,31,35,49,50,52,60]. These technologies aim to support teaching and learning processes by providing insights into students' learning behaviors (e.g., through LA dashboards) and by assisting teachers in guiding and supporting students in DLEs (e.g., through AI-based recommendations of learning tasks and personalized support). Although often studied separately, LA and AIED tools are closely related, as they both rely on the collection and analysis of educational data and incorporate machine learning techniques. In this context, human-centered approaches in LA [45] and AIED [49] emphasize the active involvement of educational stakeholders (e.g., teachers and students) in the design, pedagogical use and evaluation of such technologies.

Self-regulated learning is widely recognized as a key competence for lifelong learning and is particularly relevant in DLEs where students are expected to manage their own learning processes. SRL involves learners' ability to plan their learning activities, monitor their progress, and reflect on their learning outcomes [12]. Although students are expected to develop these skills, research has shown that teachers play an important role in fostering students' SRL through instructional strategies or their learning design, especially in younger ages of school students, where additional guidance is required [12,15]. Younger learners often lack metacognitive and self-regulatory skills and therefore require structured scaffolding from teachers to effectively engage in SRL processes [54]. For example, teachers can explicitly teach SRL strategies, or implicitly support SRL by designing learning activities that encourage planning, monitoring and reflection processes [5,12,15–17,24,39,40,44]. In addition, teachers may support students' SRL both through digital means and through classroom interactions, such as verbal feedback or scaffolding during learning activities [16].

In DLEs, teachers can also use and interpret data generated by students' interactions with learning systems and use these insights to adapt their instructional practices. In this context, teacher support can follow a human-in-the-loop (or teacher-in-the-loop) approach [47], in which teachers have an active role rather than relying on fully automated systems. Previous research has explored how teachers' pedagogical practices can be supported through DLEs that incorporate data-driven technologies such as AI and LA tools. However, relatively little research has examined how these technologies support teachers in promoting students' SRL in K-12 DLEs. For example, LA dashboards can provide teachers with insights into students' learning behaviors and help them detect and diagnose SRL and metacognitive processes in DLEs [14,26,37,55]. In addition, emerging research on hybrid human-AI systems suggests that AI-based tools may support teachers in implementing instructional practices that foster SRL [1]. While these studies demonstrate the potential of AI and LA to support teachers, the existing literature remains fragmented. Literature reviews examine SRL in relation to AI, LA and technology-enhanced learning [6,29,44,53,59].

However, there is a lack of a systematic synthesis of how AI-and LA-based systems support teachers in promoting students' SRL in K-12 and which aspects of teachers' work, such as the design and orchestration of learning activities, are supported by these technologies. Finally, limited research on SRL in K-12 examines the levels of automation and types of teacher-AI collaboration.

To address this gap, this paper presents a scoping review of research on teacher support based on AI and LA to promote students' SRL in K-12 DLEs. The review aims to synthesize existing studies and identify how AI- and LA-based systems support teachers in fostering SRL processes. Specifically, the study addresses the following research questions:

- **RQ1**: What types of teacher support are provided by data-driven systems such as LA (e.g., dashboards) and AI (e.g., AI assistants) to promote SRL in K-12?
- **RQ2**: Which teachers' tasks (including the design and orchestration of learning activities) that promote students' SRL phases are supported by AI or LA in K-12 digital learning environments?
- **RQ3**: What levels of automation and forms of teacherâĂŞAI collaboration characterize studies on AI- and LA-based systems for promoting SRL in K-12?

## 2 Theoretical Background

### 2.1 Teacher(-Mediated) Promotion of Self-regulated Learning

Already from early stages of schooling, learners can be engaged in activities that support the development of self-regulated learning, which is important for their lifelong learning [12]. SRL refers to learners' ability to plan, monitor, and control their learning to achieve learning goals. To do so, learners need to enact metacognitive strategies to regulate and adapt their activities. The SRL model proposed by Zimmerman & Moylan [63] conceptualizes SRL as a cyclical process consisting of three phases: the Forethought phase (planning and goal-setting), the Performance phase (using and monitoring strategies), and the Self-Reflection phase (evaluating outcomes and strategies). Teachers can facilitate their students' development of metacognitive strategies. They may implement a) direct SRL promotion, which includes explicit strategy instruction (e.g., teaching a specific strategy) or implicit strategy instruction (e.g., modeling or explaining procedures without explicitly naming them as strategies) and b) indirect SRL promotion, which involves designing learning environments that foster SRL processes [12]. Building on this, Vosniadou et al. [54] introduced the Self-Regulated Learning Teacher Promotion Framework (SRL-TPF) which also distinguishes between direct and indirect SRL promotion in classroom settings. The framework further differentiates types of indirect support based on the ICAP framework [8] including passive, active, constructive and interactive learning activities. Empirical studies in school classroom studies indicate that teachers tend to promote SRL primarily in implicit ways, while explicit instruction of SRL strategies and the design of SRL-supportive environments remain less common [21,48,54].

### 2.2 Digital Learning Environments and Data-Driven Support

DLEs inherently provide rich opportunities to support SRL. They allow learners to engage in complex, meaningful tasks, make choices about content or pace, and receive continuous feedback. In DLEs, teachers can support SRL by personalizing instruction (e.g., tailoring resources or pacing to students' needs), providing prompts or reminders (e.g., alerts to reflect or check progress), and designing tasks that encourage autonomy [21]. For example, a teacher might design an interactive task, where students set their goals at the start, and they receive support or hints only when they attempt to solve a problem by scaffolding phases of the SRL cycle. Data-driven tools can enhance this support. LA dashboards can visualize student choices or progress, and adaptive systems can adjust difficulty so that students need to self-regulate. This way, DLEs combined with data-driven insights can reinforce both direct and indirect SRL promotion by the teacher.

### 2.3 Teacher Use of AI and Learning Analytics

To understand how AI and LA can support teachers, some conceptual frameworks consider the level of automation and forms of teacher-AI collaboration. Molenaar [38] proposes different levels of automation when teachers interact with AI and LA from simple data collection and visualization, through analytics interpretation and pedagogical recommendation, up to adaptive support and full autonomous regulation. Most current LA/AI systems for SRL are at the lower levels as they collect data or visualize it to teachers. A few examples move to interpreting patterns (e.g., detecting "off-task" behavior) or recommending interventions but are less common. Cukurova [11] similarly describes five levels of teacher-AI teaming from transactional (AI provides data) up to synergistic (teacher and AI co-regulate learning). In practice, most teacher-facing tools are at the transactional or situational level, where AI delivers basic feedback, and the teacher intervenes. Most advanced, praxical collaboration (e.g., when teachers dynamically exchange information with AI for pedagogical decision making) or synergistic collaborations (e.g., where teachers and AI negotiate together for informed decisions) are rare in studies presenting teacher-facing tools [11].

In summary, while DLEs and AI/LA technologies offer opportunities to inform and enhance teacher-mediated SRL promotion, research to date has focused on student-facing applications or data analysis. There is a need to explore and design systems that directly support teachers in integrating SRL into classrooms. Our scoping review specifically examines the teacher support (if any) provided by AI and LA in K-12 DLEs, with the goal of identifying gaps and informing future work on SRL support through "teacher-in-the-loop" approaches.

## 3 Methodology

This study follows a systematic scoping review methodology based on the guidelines proposed by Peters et al. [43], as the main aim is to explore, identify, map, and discuss characteristics across a range of evidence sources [42]. In particular, the PRISMA Extension for Scoping Reviews (PRISMA-ScR) was used to guide the identification and inclusion of relevant articles, and a PRISMA flowchart was used to visualize the review process.

### 3.1 Inclusion Criteria

We established inclusion and exclusion criteria for the literature search. The articles were identified through multiple databases including Scopus, Web of Science, ERIC and Google Scholar (for gray literature) on February 2026 without any limitations in the publication year. Table 1 presents the inclusion and exclusion criteria used in this review.

**Table 1.** Inclusion and exclusion criteria of the systematic scoping review

| Inclusion Criteria | Exclusion Criteria |
|---|---|
| Empirical studies reporting primary research | Systematic reviews and meta-analyses |
| Studies focusing on SRL or metacognition in K-12 contexts that include LA tools or AI for teachers | Studies focusing on SRL or metacognition without reference to LA or AI |
| Studies focusing on SRL or metacognition in K-12 that include LA or AI and provide recommendations or implications for teachers | |
| Studies published in English | Studies published in other languages |

### 3.2 Search Strategy

We selected the keywords to represent the four main areas of research, including 1) SRL or metacognition, 2) teachers, 3) learning analytics or artificial intelligence and 4) K-12 schools. Metacognition is considered a core component of SRL, and metacognitive strategies have been shown to support student learning in previous literature reviews. Therefore, we selected both self-regulated learning and metacognition as keywords. The second group of keywords included teacher-related terms such as teacher, educator or instructor, as these terms have been used in previous literature searches [32]. Regarding learning analytics or artificial intelligence, we used various terms such as intelligent tutoring systems, adaptive system, educational data mining, dashboard. Finally, to represent the educational context, we included terms related to K-12 education, such as schools, primary education and secondary education. A combination of these terms was used to identify relevant articles for the systematic scoping review and limited our search to peer-reviewed articles published in English. The following example shows a query used in Scopus: TITLE-ABS-KEY ( ("self-regulated learning" OR "self regulated learning" OR SRL OR metacognition OR metacognitive) AND (teacher* OR educator* OR instructor*) AND ("learning analytics" OR LA OR "artificial intelligence" OR AI OR "intelligent tutoring system*" OR "adaptive system*" OR "educational data mining" OR dashboard* ) AND ("K-12" OR "primary education" OR "secondary education" OR school* ).

### 3.3 Coding of Search Results

The included studies were analyzed using an inductive coding approach. Two researchers (authors of this paper) independently reviewed the identified articles to develop an initial open coding scheme aligned with the research questions. The coding scheme was iteratively refined through comparison and discussion, and disagreements were resolved through consensus, resulting in a shared final coding framework. Figure 1 presents the PRISMA flow chart illustrating the screening and selection process of the included studies.

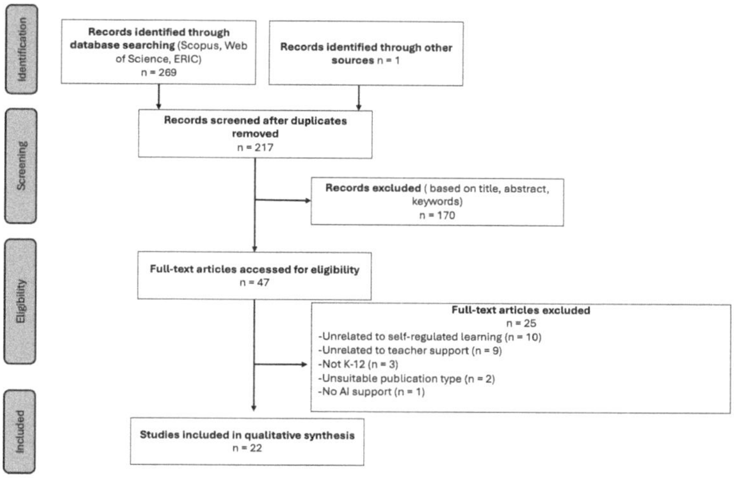


**Fig. 1.** Screening and selection process following the PRISMA flowchart.

## 4 Results

This section presents the findings of the scoping review based on the analysis of the 22 studies. The results are explained according to the research questions and four analytical dimensions (see Fig. 2). These dimensions are depicted in a framework for analyzing AI- and LA-based teacher support for SRL promotion in K-12 DLEs. The framework distinguishes the type of AI/LA support provided, the teacher task supported, the targeted SRL phase, and the levels of automation in relation to the teacher's role.

### 4.1 Types of Teacher Support (RQ1)

The analysis indicates that teacher support based on AI and LA is mainly indirect with relatively few studies explaining explicit and actionable support for teachers to promote SRL in K-12 DLEs. We grouped the identified articles in four main categories. The largest group of studies (n=7) focuses on *measurement and detection of SRL processes* using LAs or machine learning techniques [2,28,33,40,41,61,62]. These studies rely on student interaction data in DLEs such as learning management systems, involve students in a variety of tasks that promote SRL including writing tasks, and identify SRL behaviors, strategies or profiles based on multi-trace data. However, they do not directly support teachers' instructional decision-making. Teacher support is usually indirect, as findings are informing teachers rather than being embedded in tools that guide pedagogical actions. This shows that studies are primarily oriented toward understanding SRL rather than supporting teachers in promoting SRL in DLEs.

A second group of studies (n=7) includes *student-facing AI or LA tools*, such as chatbots, generative AI prompts, and LA-based feedback tools [7,10,18, 22,34,51,58]. These systems directly support students by prompting reflection, guiding the learning process, or providing feedback during task performance. In these cases, teacher involvement is described regarding the design of learning tasks, implementing chatbots in teaching or in guiding students' use of the tools. The AI systems did not directly support teachers, as interaction occurs between the AI system and the student. Teacher support was mediated through student-facing technologies rather than being explicitly designed for teachers.

A smaller number of studies (n=5) examine *teacher-facing dashboards or awareness tools*. These systems provide teachers with information about students' learning processes, typically including performance indicators, progress tracking, or error detection [14,19,20,26,55]. Although these tools are explic-

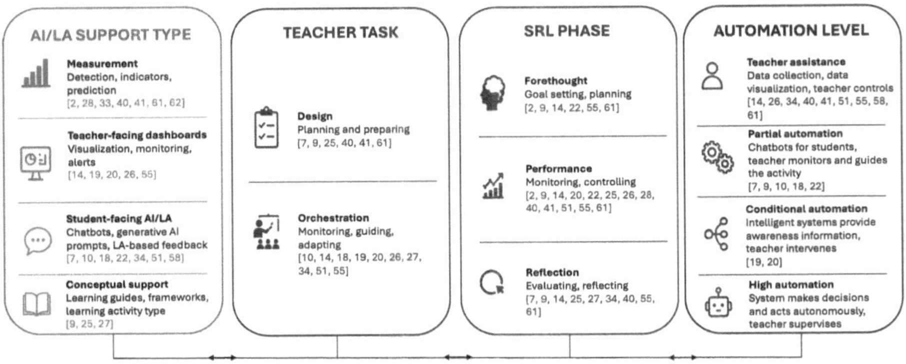


**Fig. 2.** Analytical framework used to classify studies across four dimensions: AI/LA support type, teacher task, SRL phase, automation level. Numbers in brackets indicate the studies mapped to each dimension.

itly designed for teachers and are sometimes implemented in classroom settings, their functionality is largely limited to monitoring and awareness. Dülger et al. [14] present one of the first dashboards designed explicitly for SRL promotion, while Wiedbusch et al. [55] explain a conceptual design of an SRL dashboard. However, in most cases, SRL processes are not explicitly represented, and support for SRL remains indirect. Even when dashboards are used by teachers in practice, they tend to focus on student performance, progress or content understanding rather than on supporting teachers in fostering planning, monitoring, or reflection processes.

Finally, a smaller group of studies (n=3) proposes *conceptual or theoretical approaches to teacher support* [9,25,27]. These studies outline design principles or frameworks for how AI and LA could support teachers in promoting SRL, learning guides designed by teachers to guide students through SRL processes, and learning activities types for promoting SRL with chatbots.

### 4.2 Teacher Tasks Supported and SRL Phases (RQ2)

Across the reviewed studies, most studies focus on teachers' real-time orchestration of learning activities in a DLE (n=10) [10,14,18–20,26,27,34,51,55]. In some cases, teacher-facing tools were implemented in practice to examine how teachers use data to support orchestration. For example, studies presenting LA dashboards [14,26] and classroom analytics tools [19] illustrate how teachers gain awareness of students' metacognitive activities and how they intervene for specific SRL support. In other studies that focused on student-facing AI tools, the authors explain how teachers guide students during a learning task, before and after chatbot use, but without data-informed insights. In both cases, support is given as direct SRL strategy instruction or differentiation, as feedback during and after the use of student chatbots and as metacognitive support for reflection. Technologies are mainly used to monitor student progress, provide feedback, or support real-time instructional decisions.

In contrast, fewer studies (n=6) [7,9,25,40,41,61] address the task design phase, where teachers plan and structure learning activities. These studies mainly involve conceptual approaches such as teachers classifying relevant learning activities with chatbots [9], creating learning guides [25] or designing combinations of task types with SRL support (e.g., worked and erroneous examples combined with SRL scaffolding) [61], which inform teacher learning designs [40]. In other studies (n=4), the authors describe learning environments in which teachers are supported in designing and orchestrating learning activities. They do this by explaining frameworks of how teachers might introduce chatbots for SRL [27] or by presenting the conceptual design of LA dashboards that could help teachers design appropriate tasks, monitor student progress and scaffold SRL [55]. However, data-informed support during the decision-making process for designing tasks remains limited, as most systems do not provide teachers with guidance when planning SRL-supportive activities. Additionally, some articles (n=3) refer to teacher-supporting tasks indirectly based on the results of experimental studies and measure students' SRL process with multiple types of data.

The identified studies were also analyzed according to the SRL phases defined by Zimmerman & Moylan [63]. Studies usually refer to these phases indirectly; it is not possible to classify all the studies according to the three phases (as in [6]). A large number of the studies (n=13) include the *performance phase* alone or refer more broadly to all phases as they emphasize monitoring student activity, tracking progress, and providing feedback during task implementation. A lower number of studies (n=8), explicitly or implicitly address all SRL phases by drawing on SRL frameworks such as COPES [57] or Zimmerman's model.

The *reflection phase* is targeted in a moderate number of studies (n=9), either in combination with other phases or a distinct focus on self-reflection through AI-based prompts, feedback systems, and reflective tools. However, this support is often directed at students rather than teachers and is rarely integrated into teacher-facing systems. The *forethought phase* appears to be the least represented, appearing in fewer studies. When present, it is typically supported through task design elements that support planning and goal setting. However, there were no systems explicitly supporting teachers in facilitating goal-setting or planning processes through data-driven approaches, indicating a gap in support for this phase. Finally, some studies do not explicitly refer to SRL phases but analyze different types of student data according to SRL processes such as orientation, first reading and re-reading, writing, and monitoring [2,28], particularly in writing tasks.

### 4.3 Automation Levels and Teacher-AI Collaboration (RQ3)

The analysis also examined the level of automation [38] and the nature of teacher-AI collaboration [11] in the identified studies. Most studies (n=9) are situated at low and medium levels of automation, involving data collection or data visualization for *teacher assistance*, particularly in learning analytics studies and dashboards. A second group of studies (n=5) could be classified as *partial automation*, where students work with chatbots, but teachers still have some control in guiding them through the activity. Higher levels of automation, such as *conditional automation*, were mainly found in the studies by Holstein & Aleven [19] and Holstein et al. [20]. Here, students work with intelligent systems in the classroom, and teachers gain awareness of student progress using smart glasses. *Full automation* systems were not identified in the studies. The studies that provide advanced SRL measurements offer examples of how digital trace data could inform AI agents (e.g., [28]) supporting students' SRL. However, they have not yet been implemented in DLEs or used by teachers.

From the perspective of teacher-AI teaming, most studies fall within the transactional or situational levels, where AI provides information or basic insights and teachers remain responsible for interpretation and decision-making. Fewer studies were identified at the operational level, where systems suggest actions or support decision-making. None of the studies demonstrate praxical collaboration, where AI actively supports pedagogical practices (e.g., through prompts or scaffolds integrated into learning activities). Synergistic teacher-AI collaboration, where teachers and AI co-regulate learning processes dynamically, was also absent from the reviewed literature in SRL in K-12.

## 5 Conclusions

Although a growing body of research has examined the use of AI and LA to support SRL in DLEs, this support is mainly directed towards students rather than identifying opportunities to involve teachers in promoting SRL [17]. This scoping review followed a systematic process to identify and analyze studies focusing on different types of teacher support in relation to SRL processes in K-12. The results reveal several patterns. First, there is a clear dominance of measurement-oriented approaches, with many studies focusing on detecting and analyzing SRL processes [53] rather than supporting teachers in acting on this information. This area of research is particularly important in younger ages due to the various factors that could affect measurements in SRL, such as learners' exploratory or playful interactions with DLEs and the interplay between digital and non-digital learning activities [4]. The fact that our scoping review identified these studies is mainly due to their discussion of practical implications on how they might assist teachers. However, these studies rarely provide explicit guidance on how teachers can interpret and use these measurements to promote SRL. Second, there is a strong prevalence of student-facing AI tools, such as chatbots, which position AI as a support for students rather than for teachers. In these cases, the teacher's role is indirect when using these technologies in practice. Third, teacher-facing tools remain limited, with only a small number of studies providing systems designed specifically for teachers, such as dashboards, and these primarily support monitoring rather than fostering pedagogical actions of teachers regarding SRL strategies. The analysis of automation and teacher-AI collaboration indicates that most systems operate at low levels of automation and limited forms of human-AI collaboration. In most cases, teachers are required to evaluate and interpret collected data, rather than being supported through prompts or recommendations that guide decision-making related to the promotion of SRL phases. Most advanced forms of human-AI collaboration, in which teachers and AI systems jointly regulate learning processes, remain largely unexplored. Overall, there is a gap between the analysis of multiple types of data and pedagogical action, particularly in terms of how teachers can directly or indirectly promote SRL. Existing systems rarely translate data into actionable and pedagogically meaningful guidance for teachers.

Beyond identifying these gaps, this review also addresses the fragmentation of the literature by proposing a four-dimensional framework for analyzing teacher support in AI- and LA-based SRL research. This framework integrates multiple perspectives based on existing research and includes: a) SRL phase, b) teacher tasks (e.g., task design and orchestration of learning activities), c) types of AI/LA support and d) automation levels. By combining these dimensions, the framework enables researchers to analyze not only the technological characteristics of AI- and LA-based systems, but also how teachers can use these systems to support students' SRL across different phases. As such, it provides a structured lens for future research to describe and design such systems more explicitly.

The above results suggest several challenges for supporting teachers in promoting SRL in DLEs. As an increasing number of studies incorporate student interaction with chatbots to foster SRL, it is not clear how teachers can effectively support and orchestrate these processes to promote SRL. Visualizations and indicators derived from LA and AI methods (e.g., natural language processing) provide useful insights, but their interpretation and translation to pedagogical action by teachers requires further investigation. While multimodal data is increasingly being used to improve SRL measurements, there is limited work examining how teachers can meaningfully engage with such data in practice.

This study has several limitations. The review focused exclusively on K-12 education, where the promotion of SRL in DLEs, especially in primary education, is still at an early stage of development. This is partly due to the challenges associated with engaging younger students in SRL processes [12,16]. Future research could extend this work to higher education or online learning contexts, where SRL has been more extensively studied. However, the gap between advanced data analysis or AI-based prompting and the actual support provided to teachers may also be present in these contexts. Second, the inclusion criteria allowed for studies that focused on analyzing students' behavior and provided recommendations for teachers. If the review had been restricted only to studies presenting explicit teacher-support systems, the results would likely have been limited primarily to teacher dashboards, further highlighting the scarcity of teacher-facing tools.

The findings of this review have several implications for research and practice. First, future studies could more actively involve teachers in the design and evaluation of AI and learning analytics systems, to better understand how data and student-facing tools (e.g., chatbots) can be interpreted and used to support the promotion of SRL. This research could also consider professional and social factors affecting teachers such as their data literacy and school organization. Second, future interventions could focus on two complementary directions. One direction concerns the development of systems that support teachers in interpreting student interactions with AI tools, such as analytics for the use of generative AI by students or intelligent support systems for the development of teacher competencies in SRL promotion (e.g. [1]). A second direction involves the design of professional development programs [17] that help teachers understand different types of learning data and AI-based systems, and how these can be used to support SRL. Overall, this review highlights the need to move beyond data collection and analysis toward the development of actionable, and pedagogically grounded AI and learning analytics systems that meaningfully support teachers in fostering self-regulated learning.

**Acknowledgments.** This work was supported by the Jacobs Foundation as part of the consortium DEEP (Digital Education for Equity in Primary Schools).

## References


1. Adler, I., Shani, Y.: Hybrid Human-GenAI cognitive apprenticeship: encouraging pre-service teachers to implement instructional practices to support students' self-regulated learning. Teach. Teach. Educ. **169**, 105268 (2026)
2. Aksela, O., Lämsä, J., Järvelä, S.: Secondary school students' enacted self-regulated learning strategies in a computer-based writing task–insights from digital trace data and interviews. Technol. Knowl. Learn. **30**(3), 1727–1756 (2025)
3. Almuhanna, M.A.: Teachers' perspectives of integrating AI-powered technologies in K-12 education. Educ. Inf. Technol. **30**(8), 10343–10371 (2025)
4. Azevedo, R., Gašević, D.: Analyzing multimodal multichannel data about self-regulated learning. Comput. Hum. Behav. **96**, 207–210 (2019)
5. Azevedo, R., Mudrick, N.V., Taub, M., Bradbury, A.E.: Self-regulation in computer-assisted learning systems. In: The Cambridge Handbook of Cognition and Education, pp. 587–618. Cambridge University Press (2019)
6. Banihashem, S.K., Bond, M., Bergdahl, N., Khosravi, H., Noroozi, O.: A systematic mapping review at the intersection of artificial intelligence and self-regulated learning. Int. J. Educ. Technol. High. Educ. **22**(1), 50 (2025)
7. Borjigin, A., Shen, Z.: AI-powered meta-reflection for self-learning in STEM: a middle school case study on smart home energy management. In: IEEE Region 10 Symposium (TENSYMP), pp. 1–6 (2025)
8. Chi, M.T.H., Wylie, R.: The ICAP framework: linking cognitive engagement to active learning outcomes. Educ. Psychol. **49**(4), 219–243 (2014)
9. Chiu, T.K.F.: A classification tool to foster self-regulated learning with generative artificial intelligence by applying self-determination theory: A case of ChatGPT. Educ. Tech. Research Dev. **72**(4), 2401–2416 (2024)
10. Chiu, T.K.F., Moorhouse, B.L., Chai, C.S., Ismailov, M.: Teacher support and student motivation to learn with Artificial intelligence (AI) based chatbot. Interact. Learn. Environ. **32**(7), 3240–3256 (2024)
11. Cukurova, M.: A conceptual framework for teacher-AI teaming in education: Harnessing GenAI to enhance teacher agency. OECD, Digital Education Outlook (2026). https://www.oecd.org/en/publications/oecd-digital-education-outlook-2026_062a7394-en.html
12. Dignath, C., Veenman, M.: The role of direct strategy instruction and indirect activation of self-regulated learning–evidence from classroom observation studies. Educ. Psychol. Rev. **33**(2), 489–533 (2021)
13. Dourado, R.A., Rodrigues, R.L., Ferreira, N., Mello, R.F., Gomes, A.S., Verbert, K.: A teacher-facing learning analytics dashboard for process-oriented feedback in online learning. In: LAK21: 11th International Learning Analytics and Knowledge Conference, pp. 482–489 (2021)
14. Dülger, M., van Leeuwen, A., Janssen, J., Kester, L.: Designing a classroom-level teacher dashboard to foster primary school teachers' direct instruction of self-regulated learning strategies. Educ. Inf. Technol. **30**(11), 14785–14819 (2025)
15. Fahrni, D.D.D., Hascher, T., Prasse, D.: Promoting metacognitive strategies with educational technology: primary teachers' beliefs and practices. Learn. Context **2**, 100007 (2025)
16. Fahrni, D.D.D., Iten, G., Prasse, D., Hascher, T.: Teachers' practices in the use of digital technology to promote students' self-regulated learning and metacognition: A systematic review. Teach. Teach. Educ. **165**, 105150 (2025)

17. Geier, G., Ebner, M., Burgsteiner, H.: Empowering self-regulated learning through technology and the teacher's role-a systematic literature review. In: International Conference on Human-Computer Interaction, pp. 61–76. Springer (2025). https://doi.org/10.1007/978-3-031-93567-1_5
18. Haidar, H., Suryoputro, G., Safi'i, I.: Impact of the integration of metacognitive prompts by generative artificial intelligence (GenAI) in collaborative and individual learning in improving writing skills and metacognitive awareness. Inter. J. Learn. Teach. Educ. Res. **24**(6), 232–250 (2025)
19. Holstein, K., Aleven, V.: Designing for human-AI complementarity in K-12 education. AI Mag. **43**(2), 239–248 (2022)
20. Holstein, K., McLaren, B.M., Aleven, V.: Student learning benefits of a mixed-reality teacher awareness tool in AI-enhanced classrooms. In: International Conference on Artificial Intelligence in Education, pp. 154–168. Springer (2018). https://doi.org/10.1007/978-3-319-93843-1_12
21. Huh, Y., Lee, D., Reigeluth, C.: Teacher supports and technology needs to develop students' self-regulated learning at US K-12 online schools. Contemporary Educ. Techno. **16**(3), ep523 (2024)
22. Jere, S., Mpeta, M.: Integrating generative artificial intelligence chatbots into chemistry teaching: impact of affective factors on engagement and conceptual understanding. Eurasia J. Math. Sci. Technol. Educ. **21**(10), em2713 (2025)
23. Kaliisa, R., Dolonen, J.: Cada: a teacher-facing learning analytics dashboard to foster teachers' awareness of students' participation and discourse patterns in online discussions. Technol. Knowl. Learn. **28**(3), 937–958 (2023)
24. Karlen, Y., Hirt, C.N., Jud, J., Rosenthal, A., Eberli, T.D.: Teachers as learners and agents of self-regulated learning: the importance of different teachers competence aspects for promoting metacognition. Teach. Teach. Educ. **125**, 104055 (2023)
25. Kersna, L., Laak, K.J., Lepp, L., Pedaste, M.: Supporting self-regulated learning in primary education: using written learning guides in the lessons. Educ. Sci. **15**(1), 60 (2025)
26. Knoop-van Campen, C., Molenaar, I.: How teachers integrate dashboards into their feedback practices. Frontline Learn. Res. **8**(4), 37–51 (2020)
27. Kong, S.C., Yang, Y.: A human-centered learning and teaching framework using generative artificial intelligence for self-regulated learning development through domain knowledge learning in K-12 settings. IEEE Trans. Learn. Technol. **17**, 1562–1573 (2024)
28. Lämsä, J., et al.: Measuring secondary education students' self-regulated learning processes with digital trace data. Learn. Individ. Differ. **118**, 102625 (2025)
29. Lan, M., Zhou, X.: A qualitative systematic review on AI empowered self-regulated learning in higher education. npj Sci. Learn. **10**(1), 21 (2025)
30. van Leeuwen, A., Teasley, S.D., Wise, A.: Teacher and student facing analytics. In: Handbook of Learning Analytics, pp. 130–140. Society for Learning Analytics Research (2022)
31. Ley, T., et al.: Teaching with AI: The role of teachers in the hybrid intelligent system. In: European Conference on Technology Enhanced Learning, pp. 32–45. Springer (2025). https://doi.org/10.1007/978-3-032-03873-9_3
32. Ley, T., et al.: Towards a partnership of teachers and intelligent learning technology: a systematic literature review of model-based learning analytics. J. Comput. Assist. Learn. **39**(5), 1397–1417 (2023)
33. Li, S., Chen, J., Sun, J., Li, J., Yu, X.: How teacher-provided need support affects learning performance in human-computer collaborative teaching environments.

In: International Conference on Artificial Intelligence in Education. pp. 19–26. Springer (2025). https://doi.org/10.1007/978-3-031-99267-4_3
34. Liao, X., Zhang, X., Wang, Z., Luo, H.: Design and implementation of an AI-enabled visual report tool as formative assessment to promote learning achievement and self-regulated learning: An experimental study. Br. J. Edu. Technol. **55**(3), 1253–1276 (2024)
35. Liu, Y., Chen, L., Yao, Z.: The application of artificial intelligence assistant to deep learning in teachers' teaching and students' learning processes. Front. Psychol. **13**, 929175 (2022)
36. Matcha, W., Uzir, N.A., Gašević, D., Pardo, A.: A systematic review of empirical studies on learning analytics dashboards: a self-regulated learning perspective. IEEE Trans. Learn. Technol. **13**(2), 226–245 (2019)
37. Molenaar, I.: The concept of hybrid human-AI regulation: exemplifying how to support young learners' self-regulated learning. Comput. Educ. Artifi. Intell. **3**, 100070 (2022)
38. Molenaar, I.: Towards hybrid human-AI learning technologies. Eur. J. Educ. **57**(4), 632–645 (2022)
39. Moos, D.C., Ringdal, A.: Self-regulated learning in the classroom: a literature review on the teacher's role. Educ. Res. Inter. **2012**(1), 423284 (2012)
40. Paavilainen, T., López-Pernas, S., Väisänen, S., Kontkanen, S., Hirsto, L.: Using learning analytics to support self-regulated learning in primary education-a learning design perspective. Technol. Knowl. Learn. **30**(3), 1299–1319 (2025)
41. Pansri, B., et al.: Understanding student learning behavior: integrating the self-regulated learning approach and K-means clustering. Educ. Sci. **14**(12), 1291 (2024)
42. Peters, M.D.J., et al.: Scoping reviews: reinforcing and advancing the methodology and application. Syst. Rev. **10**(1), 263 (2021)
43. Peters, M.D., Godfrey, C.M., Khalil, H., McInerney, P., Parker, D., Soares, C.B.: Guidance for conducting systematic scoping reviews. JBI Evid. Implemen. **13**(3), 141–146 (2015)
44. Prasse, D., et al.: Challenges in promoting self-regulated learning in technology supported learning environments: an umbrella review of systematic reviews and meta-analyses. Technol. Knowl. Learn. **29**(4), 1809–1830 (2024)
45. Sarmiento, J.P., Wise, A.F.: Participatory and co-design of learning analytics: an initial review of the literature. In: LAK22: 12th International Learning Analytics and Knowledge Conference, pp. 535–541 (2022)
46. Schwendimann, B.A., et al.: Perceiving learning at a glance: a systematic literature review of learning dashboard research. IEEE Trans. Learn. Technol. **10**(1), 30–41 (2016)
47. Shankar, S.K., Pothancheri, G., Sasi, D., Mishra, S.: Bringing teachers in the loop: exploring perspectives on integrating generative AI in technology-enhanced learning. Int. J. Artif. Intell. Educ. **35**(1), 155–180 (2025)
48. Spruce, R., Bol, L.: Teacher beliefs, knowledge, and practice of self-regulated learning. Metacogn. Learn. **10**(2), 245–277 (2015)
49. Topali, P., Ortega-Arranz, A., Rodríguez-Triana, M.J., Er, E., Khalil, M., Akçapınar, G.: Designing human-centered learning analytics and artificial intelligence in education solutions: a systematic literature review. Behav. Inform. Technol. **44**(5), 1071–1098 (2025)
50. Tripathi, T., Sharma, S.R., Singh, V., Bhargava, P., Raj, C.: Teaching and learning with AI: a qualitative study on K-12 teachers' use and engagement with artificial intelligence. Front. Educ. **10**, 1651217 (2025)

51. Tzimas, D., Demetriadis, S.: Implementing learning analytics in education: enhancing actionability and adoption. Computers **15**(1), 56 (2026)
52. Uysal, B.Ç.B., Yüksel, İ.: AI-powered lesson planning: Insights from future EFL teachers. In: AI in language teaching, learning, and assessment, pp. 101–132. IGI Global Scientific Publishing (2024)
53. Viberg, O., Khalil, M., Baars, M.: Self-regulated learning and learning analytics in online learning environments: A review of empirical research. In: Proceedings of the Tenth International Conference on Learning Analytics & Knowledge, pp. 524–533 (2020)
54. Vosniadou, S., et al.: The promotion of self-regulated learning in the classroom: a theoretical framework and an observation study. Metacogn. Learn. **19**(1), 381–419 (2024)
55. Wiedbusch, M.D., et al.: A theoretical and evidence-based conceptual design of metadash: an intelligent teacher dashboard to support teachers' decision making and students' self-regulated learning. Front. Educ. **6**, 570229 (2021)
56. Wiley, K., Dimitriadis, Y., Linn, M.: A human-centred learning analytics approach for developing contextually scalable K-12 teacher dashboards. Br. J. Edu. Technol. **55**(3), 845–885 (2024)
57. Winne, P.H., Hadwin, A.F.: Studying as self-regulated learning. In: Hacker, D.J., Dunlosky, J., Graesser, A.C. (eds.) Metacognition in Educational Theory and Practice, pp. 277–304. Erlbaum (1998)
58. Xia, Q., Chiu, Thomas KF and, C.S., Xie, K.: The mediating effects of needs satisfaction on the relationships between prior knowledge and self-regulated learning through artificial intelligence chatbot. British J. Educ. Technol. **54**(4), 967–986 (2023)
59. Xu, J., Luo, Y., Wang, C., Wang, M., Wu, Y.: AI support in self-regulated learning: a decade of technological evolution and meta-analysis. Br. J. Edu. Technol. (2026). https://doi.org/10.1111/bjet.70058
60. Yılmaz, A.S., Ağır, A.: Artificial intelligence teaching assistants on the professional development of teachers: evidence from German language teachers in Türkiye. Instruct. Technol. Lifelong Learn. **6**(2), 310–343 (2025)
61. Zhang, L., et al.: Using multimodal learning analytics to understand the combined effects of dynamic self-regulated scaffoldings and learning from examples on computer programming: an empirical study. Inter. J. STEM Educ. **13**(3), 1–23 (2026)
62. Zhidkikh, D., Saarela, M., Kärkkäinen, T.: Measuring self-regulated learning in a junior high school mathematics classroom: combining aptitude and event measures in digital learning materials. J. Comput. Assist. Learn. **39**(6), 1834–1851 (2023)
63. Zimmerman, B.J., Moylan, A.R.: Self-regulation: where metacognition and motivation intersect. In: Handbook of Metacognition in Education, pp. 299–315., Routledge (2009)

# Decoding the Dashboard: Data Comics to Support Students' Understanding of Learning Analytics Visualisations

Mikaela Elizabeth Milesi[1(✉)], Vanessa Echeverria[2,3], Lixiang Yan[4], Yueqiao Jin[1], Riordan Alfredo[1], Jie Xiang Fan[1], Linxuan Zhao[1], Dragan Gašević[1], Yi-Shan Tsai[1], and Roberto Martinez-Maldonado[1]

[1] Faculty of Information Technology, Monash University, 25 Exhibition Walk, Clayton, VIC 3168, Australia
{mikaela.milesi,ariel.jin,riordan.alfredo,jie.fan,linxuan.zhao, dragan.gasevic,yi-shan.tsai,roberto.martinezmaldonado}@monash.edu

[2] School of Computing Technologies, RMIT University, Melbourne, VIC 3000, Australia
vanessa.echeverria@rmit.edu.au

[3] Escuela Superior Politécnica del Litoral (ESPOL), Guayas, Ecuador

[4] Tsinghua University, Beijing, China
lixiangyan@mail.tsinghua.edu.cn

**Abstract.** Learning analytics dashboards (LADs) are intended to help students make sense of their learning data to support reflection and decision-making. However, their visualisations can be complex, particularly for students with low visualisation literacy. Narrative techniques, such as annotated charts and data comics, have been used to communicate insights directly, but not as supplementary materials to empower students to explore their visualisations themselves. In response, we conducted a qualitative study examining how data comics can complement LADs. We interviewed 18 nursing students and 4 of their teachers about a multimodal LAD containing visualisations with data comics explaining them. Analysis showed that data comics were clear, engaging, and helped make complex visualisations more accessible, though they must be carefully designed to avoid overwhelming students with information. The findings suggest that both students and teachers are receptive to data comics as a means of supporting the interpretability of LADs.

**Keywords:** data comics · information visualisation · learning analytics · dashboards

## 1 Introduction and Background

Learning analytics dashboards (LADs) are tools designed to help students and teachers reflect on learning experiences and make data-informed decisions [16]. Defined by Schwendimann et al. [31, p.37] as *"a single display that aggregates*


J. Weidlich et al. (Eds.): EC-TEL 2026, LNCS 16905, pp. 451–466, 2027.
https://doi.org/10.1007/978-3-032-37979-5_31

*different indicators about learner(s), learning process(es), and/or learning context(s) into one or more visualisations"*, the notion of the dashboard has been widely appropriated within the field of LA to support the development of analytical thinking in students [29], help students engage with feedback [1], and prompt critical reflection [10]. LADs incorporate a range of visualisations [30], from familiar graphs [25], such as bar or line charts, to potentially complex visualisations of multimodal LA data [37].

A major challenge associated with LADs is that students may not possess the necessary data skills [12,14] or *visualisation literacy* [8,36] to effectively derive insights from LA visualisations unassisted. To address this, several studies [9,13] have proposed transitioning from an *exploratory* approach – where individuals are expected to interpret visualisations themselves and extract meaning [18] – to an *explanatory* approach where visualisations are enhanced with narrative elements (both textual and visual) to communicate insights directly [18]. Yet, there are still criticisms associated with this approach. Empirical studies have shown that the addition of narrative elements does not guarantee increased engagement with the information [5,9,27]. Teachers from a study conducted by Echeverria et al. [9] felt that narrative elements could impact engagement by adding visual noise, complexity, or redundant information to the visualisations. Similarly, Pozdniakov et al. [27] observed that the addition of narrative elements to LADs has a minimal effect on task completion accuracy. Furthermore, by communicating insights directly, narrative explanations may discourage individuals exploring visualisations themselves to formulate their own insights or opinions [23]. These criticisms highlight the need for further research on how narrative explanations can be integrated into LADs in ways that support, rather than replace, students' own exploration and sensemaking.

In human–computer interaction (HCI) literature, data comics have emerged as a visualisation genre to encourage individuals to develop visualisation literacy skills and better engage with data [4,33]. Inspired by traditional comics [20,32], data comics communicate data-driven information through a combination of illustrative and textual content, the organisation of panels, and representations of data (ranging from conventional charts to abstract depictions) [2]. Despite research suggesting that data comics are an appropriate format to communicate complex information to non-scientific audiences [3,19,34], there is limited work examining their effectiveness in supporting students' sensemaking of learning analytics data. To the best of our knowledge, the only existing study using data comics in the context of LA indicates that, while data comics can increase engagement, their impact varies across learner groups and they are often better suited as supplementary rather than primary instructional resources [22]. This points to a key gap: it remains unclear how narrative visual formats such as data comics can be designed to support students' active exploration and interpretation of LADs.

This paper addresses this gap by presenting a qualitative study, situated within an authentic educational setting, where 18 nursing students and 4 teachers were asked to comment on whether data comics facilitate understanding of multimodal LA visualisations, with teachers included as key stakeholders in the design and pedagogical integration of such tools, as suggested by Kaliisa et al. [17]. This study aimed to provide a preliminary exploration into the potential for data comics to support interpretation of LA visualisations through the following research questions:

- **RQ1:** How do *students*, considering differences in their *visualisation literacy*, perceive data comics as a supplementary tool to support the interpretation of student-facing learning analytics visualisations?
- **RQ2:** How do *teachers* perceive data comics as a supplementary tool to explain student-facing learning analytics visualisations?

## 2 Study Design

### 2.1 Learning Context

This study is situated in an authentic learning scenario designed to develop teamwork and communication skills in undergraduate nursing students. The clinical simulations, created by teachers at Monash University, required teams of four students to collaboratively manage the care of four manikin patients.

Each nursing student was equipped with a headset microphone to record audio data, a *Fitbit Sense* smart watch to collect their physiological data (i.e., heart rate), and a Pozyx position tag to capture their location (in the form of $x$-$y$ coordinates) and body orientation within the ward.

The clinical simulation was closely followed by a debriefing session whereby students reflections were guided by a member of the teaching staff while they viewed a LAD, as a part of their regular classroom activities, that was co-designed with teachers and validated by Echeverria et al. [11]. The LAD displayed the following four visualisations of the multimodal data that depict teamwork and communication behaviours during the simulation (Fig. 1):

**Prioritisation Bar:** A bar chart that depicts the amount of time that students engaged in particular behaviours during the simulation based on their positioning data. These behaviours relate to tasks that are completed for the deteriorating patient or other clinical tasks. The behaviours are also categorised based on whether it was a task performed by an individual or more than one student (team task).

**Ward Map:** A hexbin map that combines the audio, positioning and heart rate data to represent where students were located within the simulation ward, as well as how often they were speaking in that position. The colours of the hexagons indicate the roles of the students in the simulation (i.e., primary nurse 1 is blue, primary nurse 2 is red, secondary nurse 1 is green, and secondary nurse 2 is orange). The opacity of the hexagon represents the amount of time spent speaking (i.e., a more intense colour indicates more time communicating). The heart-shaped icons with a number inside represent where the maximum heart rate was detected for each student.

**Communication Network:** A sociogram that uses the audio data to show how each role in the simulation communicated with each other. The arrows indicate the directionality of the communication, with the thickness of the arrow representing how often two roles in the simulation were talking to each other. The size of the circle shows how often an individual spoke over the simulation. **Communication behaviour:** An epistemic network that shows key communication behaviours in healthcare, as identified by teachers in the study by Zhao et al. [37]. The audio data was transcribed using the OpenAI Whisper medium model [28] and coded using a fine-tuned BERT-based classifier [37] as: 1) task allocation, 2) questioning, 3) handover, 4) escalation, 5) sharing information, and 6) acknowledging.

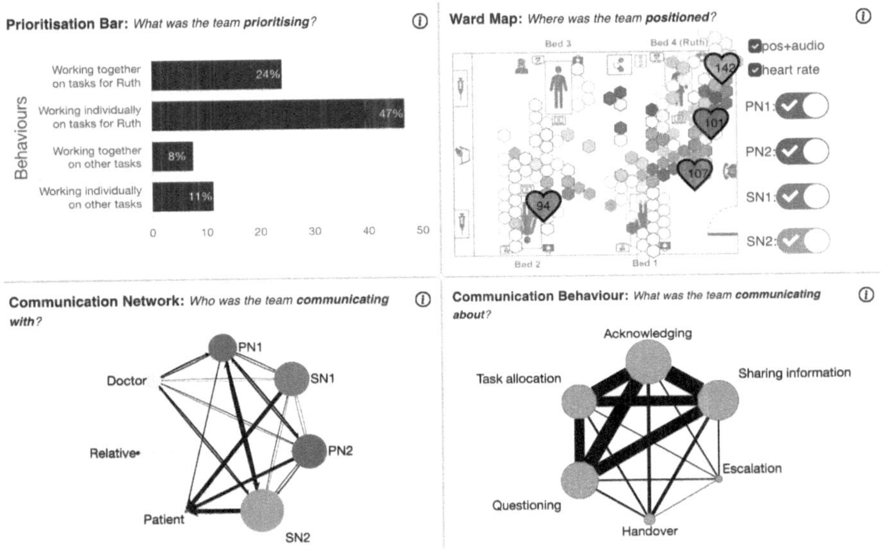


**Fig. 1.** Multimodal visualisations in the LAD. The *Prioritisation Bar* chart represents the individual and team-based behaviours that students were engaging in during the simulation. The *Ward Map* depicts where the students were positioned, the extent to which they were talking and the maximum heart rate in relation to the learning space. The *Communication Network* shows who each role in the simulation were speaking to via arrows and how often they were speaking, as indicated by the size of each node. The *Communication Behaviour* network visualises what students were discussing categorised into six key communication behaviours.

### 2.2 Participants and Procedure

The participants of this study were a subset of students who participated in the clinical simulation, as well as members of the teaching team who facilitated the simulation and debriefing session. A total of 22 participants, 18 nursing students (S1-S18; 15 females, 3 males; age between 20 and 49 - $\mu = 24.2$, $\sigma = 6.5$) and 4 teachers (T1-T4; 4 females), volunteered to be interviewed as part of this study. Students received a \$50 AUD voucher in compensation for their participation.

Ethics approval was obtained from the Monash University Human Research Ethics Committee (Project ID: 39190). Informed consent was secured from each participant prior to the interview. No additional personal information was collected as part of this study.

**Mini-VLAT Questionnaire:** Before the interviews, students completed the Mini-VLAT [24] through *Qualtrics* to assess their visualisation literacy. Since this study examines the role of data comics in supporting the interpretation of multimodal LA visualisations, measuring visualisation literacy helped determine the extent to which data comics were beneficial for students with varying levels of proficiency. The "correction-for-guessing" formula [15] was used to calculate a corrected Mini-VLAT score. Additionally, participants were given an option *"I'm not sure"* to discourage guessing the answer.

The interviews were conducted via Zoom. Students participated in a 75-minute long interview, as they were asked to reflect on their own data. In contrast, teachers took part in shorter 45-minute long interviews, focusing primarily on feedback on the potential benefits and criticisms at a higher level. The interviews included the following tasks:

**Task 1 – Exploration of the LAD:** Students freely explored the dashboard and visualisations generated from their own simulation data. In contrast, the teachers were shown data from a single session that was purposefully chosen as the visualisations of the multimodal data were representative of the teamwork and communication interactions that were typically observed across most of the teams. Each visualisation featured an information icon, ⓘ, which opened a data comic explaining the visualisation when clicked. Participants were encouraged to spend $\sim$ 10 minutes interacting with the LAD to make sense of the visualisations and ask any clarification questions to the interviewer.

**Task 2 – Evaluation of Data Comics:** Participants were shown each data comic in the LAD and asked to describe the extent to which it supported interpretation of the visualisations, focusing on how data comics helped students make sense of their own data (RQ1) and whether they supported teachers in explaining students' visualisations (RQ2), along with its perceived benefits and limitations as a supplementary explanatory tool.

The interviews were recorded via Zoom and transcribed using the OpenAI Whisper (large version) and speaker diarisation model. An inductive thematic analysis [6] was conducted and discussed by three researchers until a consensus was reached.

## 3 Data Comics Design

There were four data comics prototypes developed for this study – one for each visualisation in Fig. 1. Each data comic uses a *linear* panel layout [3] and follows a left-to-right reading order, continuing top-to-bottom when there is more than one row [7] (e.g., see Fig. 2).

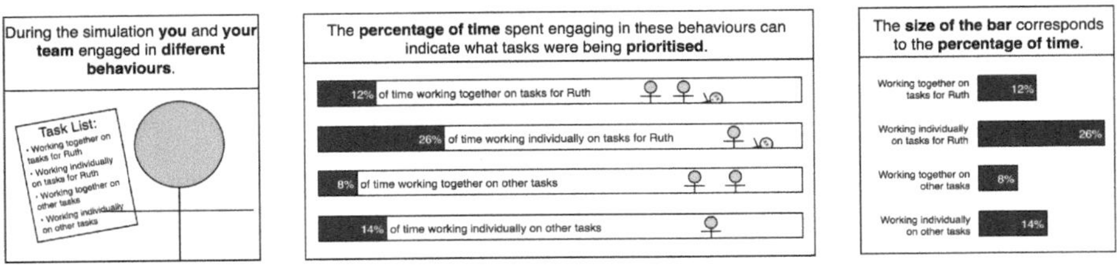


**Fig. 2.** Data comic to explain the *prioritisation bar* visualisation with three panels: the first explains the context behind the visualisation (i.e., the different behaviours), the second introduces percentages to indicate that the size of the bar corresponds to the amount of time spent engaging in a particular behaviour, and the last panel removes any stylistic elements in favour of showing the bar chart.

An abstract form of the *visualisation build-up* pattern was also used for each prototype, where each panel adds information needed to interpret the visualisation as a whole. Unlike conventional chart build-ups (e.g., adding axes or legends), these data comics begin with a stylised representation of the information using traditional comic elements like stick figures and speech bubbles before gradually transitioning into the respective multimodal LA visualisation. Each panel combines text and imagery: text provides the necessary information, while images illustrate what is described [21]. They are designed to communicate one message per panel [3]. This paper presents the full versions of the *prioritisation bar* (Fig. 2) and *ward map* (Fig. 3) data comics, and partial versions of the *communication network* (Fig. 4) and *communication behaviour* (Fig. 5) data comics (full versions can be accessed here).

## 4 Results

Students achieved an average corrected Mini-VLAT score of 8.26 out of 12 ($\sigma$ = 1.79). The scores ranged from 3.33 to 10.67 (median = 8.67). For the purposes of this study, we refer to a score of less than 8 as being low relative to the cohort (n = 6), 8–9 as being mid-range (n = 7), and greater than 9 as being relatively high (n = 5).

This resulting themes and codes from the thematic analysis can be seen in Table 1.

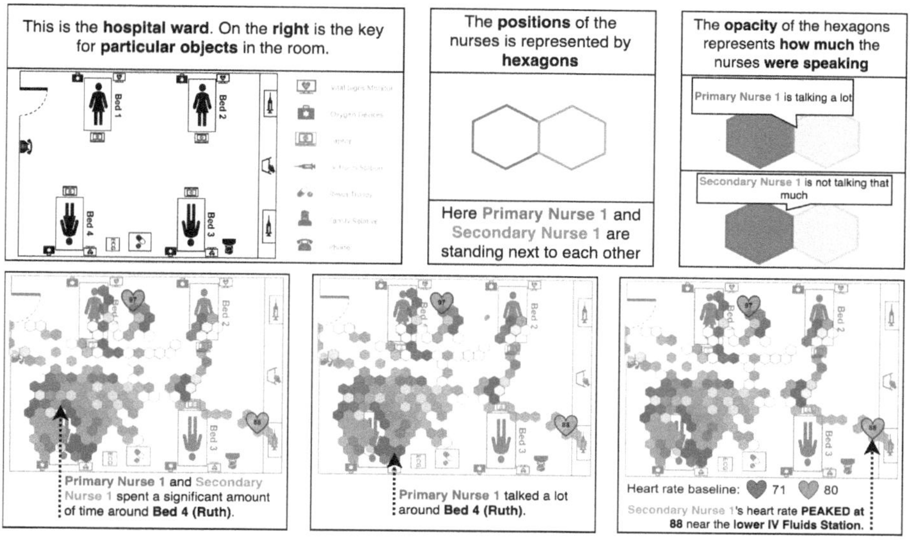


**Fig. 3.** Data comic to explain the *ward map* visualisation. There are six panels each containing the ward map visualisation and a textual annotation of salient information.

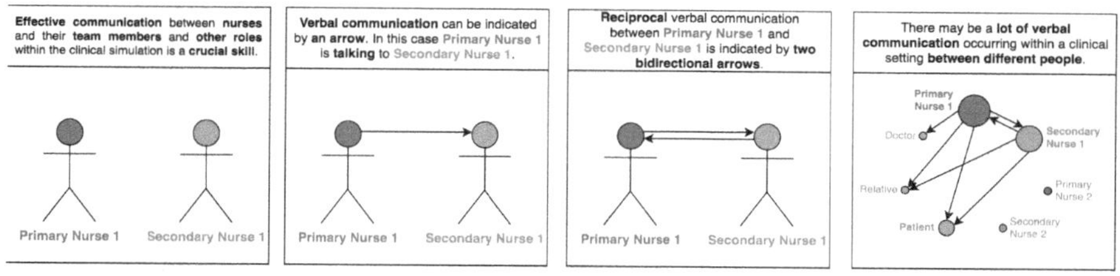


**Fig. 4.** Partial data comic to explain the *communication network* visualisation. This samples the first four panels which show what the arrows are indicating.

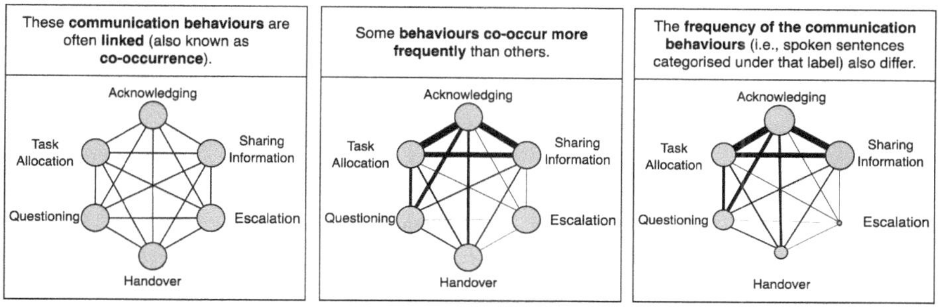


**Fig. 5.** Partial data comic to explain the *communication network* visualisation. This samples the last three panels that explain the concept of co-occurrence.

**Table 1.** Themes emerging from the inductive thematic analysis

| Theme | Emerging Codes | Description |
|---|---|---|
| Benefits of Data Comics | Clarify information; Familiar format; Ease of interpretation; Engaging; Unique; Aid in recall | Participants spoke positively about features of the data comics or highlighting situations where they could be beneficial for learning. |
| Criticisms of Data Comics | Visualisations are self-explanatory; Recognised visualisations from debriefing; Information overload | Participants criticised the data comics or identified factors that would render the data comics unnecessary. |
| Design Suggestions | Use of colour or visual features; Character design; Comic content | Participants commented on ways that the data comic prototypes could be improved. |

### 4.1 Data Comics Aid Interpretation

Both students and teachers perceived data comics as useful supplementary tools to clarify information that was not obvious to them previously or make the process of interpreting the student-facing learning analytics visualisations easier.

Regarding **RQ1**, students across all visualisation literacy levels identified that the data comics made the multimodal LA visualisations *"easier to understand"* (S1, 7.00; S15, 9.33) and *"make much more sense"* (S3, 8.00).

Students with lower Mini-VLAT scores praised the *"simple"* design that allow them to *"check that [they are] interpreting [the visualisations] correctly"* (S1, Mini-VLAT score = 7.00). This sentiment was shared by S7 (7.33) who stated, *"if you didn't [know] what the graphs mean then [the data comics] tells you"*. These students also mentioned that data comics provided valuable support and context to enable them to interpret the visualisations. For example: S18 (Mini-VLAT score = 6.00) said: *"most graphs I see have no context whenever I'm researching, and researching is something I find quite hard anyway, so the fact that I can explain it in a comic sense, and I am a visual learner in general"*. This was echoed by S10 (7.00) who said: *"it gives you more information if you need it ... If you need to understand the tool a bit better, then you can go in and read more"*.

In contrast, those students with relatively high Mini-VLAT scores related the utility of the data comics to the complexity of the visualisations stating: *"there's a lot going on in the [visualisations] so it takes a lot to explain it. The nature of the graphs are [more] complex than normal"* (S13, 10.67) and *"the comics are really handy because there is a lot going on in these visualisations. ... It's easy for anyone to understand and there's a lot of information because otherwise I think [the visualisations] could get a little bit confusing, but I know they're very helpful"* (S11, 10.67). S15 (9.33) believed the data comics allowed them to *"tap into the smaller bits of information of how to interpret the graphs"*.

Regarding **RQ2**, The teachers expressed similar sentiments, stating that the data comics *"provide context to students ... We think it's obvious, but that's because we know the data"* (T3) and *"I love that [students] can have a little description of what [the visualisation] means"* (T4).

## 4.2 Engaging Format

Beyond the explanatory role that data comics can have in LADs, students and teachers identified that the comic book style contributed to personal engagement and perceived ease of interpretation. Regarding **RQ1**, a student with a mid-range Mini-VLAT (S16; 8.67) commented, *"It's a really easy format to read ... because it's just little squares ... you can follow along. ... There's not too much going on. It really emphasised one point and one point only. It's just very reader-friendly"*. Also, a student with a mid-range Mini-VLAT score (S16, 8.67) highlighted the visual features of the *ward map* data comic as being helpful: *"It's a simple image and it also gives you a very brief description of all the components of the map. It's nice because it's colour coded, you have bolding on [the] words. So that makes it easier to digest."*

Regarding **RQ2**, most teachers felt that the data comics were an engaging and unique way to present information. T1 described the data comics as *"much more visually appealing"*, adding that they *"could potentially improve engagement instead of just a slab of information [and be] beneficial for both ... people who are visual learners or [those who] concentrate more on ... text"*. T2 believed that *"it doesn't stand out as a comic to be honest it stands out as something different. I like that ... it's not sort of academic in a sense"*. T4 concluded that *"students would prefer [data comics]"* over textual explanations.

One of the teachers (T2) described the data comics as *"more digestible. [When] the information [is] in that format you don't need to then work out - what are the figures? It's literally text and it seems concise and it's not overloading"*. This view was shared by students with relatively high Mini-VLAT scores (RQ1), such as S11 (10.67), who when describing the *communication network* data comic explained, *"I like how they're presented. I didn't notice before how it's the two people and then it's the arrows and then they take the people away. That makes a lot of sense [and are] definitely helpful"*. S13 (10.67) simply stated, *"I think they're fun"*.

### 4.3 Perceived Redundancy and Information Overload

Regarding **RQ1**, although data comics were generally perceived as beneficial, some students considered them unnecessary. The perception that the visualisations were self-explanatory emerged from some students across visualisation literacy levels. For instance, S12 (7.67) noted that: *"the graphs were quite straightforward"*, while S15 (9.33) described them as *"easy to interpret ... and understand"*. Familiarity also played a role: as the study was embedded in regular classroom use of the LAD, several students had already encountered the visualisations during prior debriefing sessions. Students with mid-range Mini-VLAT scores reported that they *"could understand [the visualisations] without [the data comics] because we went over them in class ... and it's not too difficult to understand"* (S14, 8.67), and *"I was counting on my teachers ... during the debrief. I felt like I had a good idea of what was what"* (S18, 8.33). Yet, even students with higher Mini-VLAT scores acknowledged the value of data comics, particularly for first-time interpretation. S9 (9.33) stated that *"if I was looking at it for the first time, I would definitely use the [data comics]"*, while S4 (10.67) highlighted how the comics clarified previously overlooked aspects of the visualisations, such as the co-occurrence of interactions.

The potential for information overload was also identified as a limitation of the data comic format. A student with a relatively low Mini-VLAT score (S10, 7.00) criticised the volume of text, stating, *"I didn't read it all. ... There's a lot of information"*. This concern was echoed by a student with a mid-range Mini-VLAT score, S8 (8.33), who felt that *"I just need to understand the different connotations of [the visualisations] ... The [data comic] doesn't need to be this complex"*. S8 further noted non-linear reading patterns, explaining they might *"not necessarily read [the panels] from left to right"*, instead treating them as independent explanations.

Regarding **RQ2**, The teachers expressed similar concerns. When reflecting on the *ward map* data comic T1 noted that, *"It's pretty full on. I wonder if it could be condensed to three boxes"*. T2 worried about the density of information, describing the data comics as *"very busy"*. On the topic of *"cognitive load"* they questioned, *"How do we engage them [within] a fifteen second window [without students] thinking, 'Nah, can't be bothered'?"*. T2 suggested reducing the number of panels to *"three boxes ... start, middle, end ... [with] a quicker progression"*. They cautioned that, *"if you're going to give the information, it needs to be something additional that they wouldn't have picked up on"*.

## 5 Discussion

### 5.1 Interpreting Multimodal LA Visualisations with Data Comics

This study investigated how students with differences in visualisation literacy levels (RQ1) and their teachers (RQ2) perceived data comics as a supplementary tool to explain student-facing learning analytics visualisations. The comments from students and teachers show that the key strengths associated with adding data comics that explain LA visualisations to LADs are: i) they make LA visualisations easier to understand by providing additional context, ii) they simplify LA data to students in a way that supports interpretation and iii) they are quick and easy to read. This result broadly supports the findings of other studies in LA linking the implementation of narrative elements in LADs to improved sensemaking among non-data experts by providing contextual information [12]. The results from that study and the current work highlight the value of narrative explanations for communicating LA data to students. However, our findings imply that narrative explanations can empower students to explore LA visualisations by guiding them through the interpretation process, rather than conveying insights to them directly. Yet, further research is needed to compare narrative elements that guide students through interpretation of LA visualisations with those that communicate insights.

Notably, benefits were identified by students across levels of visualisation literacy. However, where participants with relatively low Mini-VLAT scores expressed these benefits in terms of themselves and their own abilities to interpret the visualisations correctly, students with relatively high Mini-VLAT scores were able to relate these benefits to how the data comics enabled to navigate through the complexities and/or nuances of the data. In a quantitative study, Milesi et al. [23] found that the addition of narrative elements benefited individuals in terms of supporting interpretation, yet warned that underlying messages from the data could be missed if narrative elements are not applied thoughtfully. These findings indicate that the implementation of narrative explanations can support a diverse range of users in both non-educational and learning contexts. However, these results also suggest a need for narrative elements to support exploratory data analysis rather than acting purely as explanatory mechanisms.

Kaliisa et al. [17] stated that a key question in LAD design is how to engage users. In this study, teachers highlighted the challenges involved with engaging students quickly and felt that data comics could be more effective than text in this regard. Data comics have been recognised as an engaging medium to communicate information about visualisations in HCI literature [3,35]; therefore, these findings suggest that data comics could potentially address issues relating to engagement with student-facing LA tools.

Some students across visualisation literacy levels did not see the value in data comics to explain LA visualisations, feeling that the visualisations were self-explanatory. This is consistent with teachers with high visualisation literacy from Pozdniakov et al. [27] who also found the narrative features to be redundant. While it could be assumed that data comics as supplementary tools are unnecessary for learners in contexts where visualisation literacy skills are necessary (e.g., STEM), one unanticipated finding was that even a student with a mid-range Mini-VLAT score struggled to interpret the layout/reading order of the data comic itself, showing that even students with moderate visualisation literacy skills can encounter difficulties when interpreting representations of data-driven information. Therefore, a takeaway message from this is that interfaces that include these narrative-enriched supplementary tools should include interactivity so that these features remain optional for those with high visualisation literacy, while still supporting students with lower visualisation literacy (or those who require assistance) in interpreting the LA visualisations.

The students and teachers both identified *information overload* as being a primary issue with the data comics. According to comics theorist Scott McCloud [20], a crucial skill for comic creators is to balance information in line with their assumptions about the readers. In our study, the teachers felt that students should have been able to extrapolate on information by drawing on their knowledge of the clinical simulation. This concept of *decluttering* visualisations to remove visual features with minimal informative value has also gained traction in LA literature as a way to direct focus and attention towards salient information in annotated towards [9,26]. This idea can be extended to data comics by critically evaluating whether each individual panel and its content need to be decluttered or removed based on the students and learning context, alongside "traditional" graphical features of data visualisations like data points, borders, or headings [18]

### 5.2 Implications for Educational Design and Practice

Based on the comments from students and teachers, we formulated the following recommendations for LAD designers:
1) To engage students to explore LADs, data comics should be used to explain how to interpret LA visualisations over verbose text-based alternatives.
2) Data comics should be limited to showing only the essential information that is required to interpret LA visualisations. If implemented in a LAD, the interactive nature could be leveraged to offer a more detailed version of the data comic if the student requires additional assistance.
3) As the majority of design suggestions came from teachers, they should be involved in the process of designing the data comics to ensure they are contextually relevant for the learning activity, as well as appropriate (in terms of factors like content, information density, length and pedagogical goals) for their students.

These results present the potential that data comics have as a way to empower students to interpret LA visualisations and engage them with their learning data.

### 5.3 Limitations and Future Works

This study is qualitative and exploratory in nature, and hence the sample size is small. While not meant for generalisation, the findings captured insightful views of educators and students in a particular clinical simulation learning context towards the use of data comics for learning reflections that may be tested further with a larger and more diverse sample. It is worth noting that the participants had already been exposed to the visualisations, so data comics were not a first encounter and may have been perceived as unnecessary. Yet, the study was non-experimental, embedded within an LAD already integrated into mandatory debriefs—one of the first multimodal LA interventions tested under fully authentic conditions. While this enhances ecological validity, future research should involve more diverse participants across disciplines and settings, and adopt controlled experimental designs to compare data comics with text-based narrations, especially in first-encounter scenarios.

## 6 Concluding Remarks

This paper examines the use of data comics as a supplementary tool to help students interpret LA visualisations. We interviewed students and teachers about comics depicting multimodal LA data from an authentic scenario. Results indicate that data comics are clear, engaging, and aid interpretation of complex visualisations regardless of visualisation literacy, though careful design is required to prevent overload. Both groups preferred data comics over text-based explanations for supporting their understanding. These findings suggest promising future applications of data comics in LA for explaining visualisations and communicating insights.

## References


1. Alcock, S., Rienties, B., Aristeidou, M., Kouadri Mostéfaoui, S.: How do visualizations and automated personalized feedback engage professional learners in a learning analytics dashboard? In: Proceedings of the 14th Learning Analytics and Knowledge Conference, pp. 316–325. LAK '24, ACM, NY, USA (2024). https://doi.org/10.1145/3636555.3636886
2. Bach, B., Riche, N.H., Carpendale, S., Pfister, H.: The emerging genre of data comics. IEEE Comput. Graph. Appl. **37**(3), 6–13 (2017). https://doi.org/10.1109/MCG.2017.33
3. Bach, B., Wang, Z., Farinella, M., Murray-Rust, D., Henry Riche, N.: Design patterns for data comics. In: Proceedings of the 2018 CHI Conference on Human Factors in Computer Systems, pp. 1–12. CHI '18, ACM, NY, USA (2018). https://doi.org/10.1145/3173574.3173612
4. Boucher, M., Bach, B., Stoiber, C., Wang, Z., Aigner, W.: Educational data comics: what can comics do for education in visualization? In: 2023 IEEE VIS Workshop on Visualization Education, Literacy, and Activities (EduVis), pp. 34–40. IEEE, Melbourne, Australia (2023). https://doi.org/10.1109/EduVis60792.2023.00012
5. Boy, J., Detienne, F., Fekete, J.D.: Storytelling in information visualizations: Does it engage users to explore data? In: Proceedings of the 33rd Annual ACM Conference on Human Factors in Computer Systems, pp. 1449–1458. CHI '15, ACM, NY, USA (2015). https://doi.org/10.1145/2702123.2702452
6. Braun, V., Clarke, V.: Using thematic analysis in psychology. Qual. Res. Psychol. **3**(2), 77–101 (2006). https://doi.org/10.1191/1478088706qp063oa

7. Cohn, N.: Navigating comics: an empirical and theoretical approach to strategies of reading comic page layouts. Front. Psychol. **4** (2013). https://doi.org/10.3389/fpsyg.2013.00186. https://www.frontiersin.org/journals/psychology/articles/10.3389/fpsyg.2013.00186
8. Donohoe, D., Costello, E.: Data visualisation literacy in higher education: an exploratory study of understanding of a learning dashboard tool. Int. J. Emerging Technol. Learn. **15**(17), 115–126 (2020). https://doi.org/10.3991/ijet.v15i17.15041. https://online-journals.org/index.php/i-jet/article/view/15041
9. Echeverria, V., Martinez-Maldonado, R., Buckingham Shum, S., Chiluiza, K., Granda, R., Conati, C.: Exploratory versus explanatory visual learning analytics: Driving teachers' attention through educational data storytelling. J. Learn. Anal. **5**(3), 73–97 (2018). https://doi.org/10.18608/jla.2018.53.6
10. Echeverria, V., et al.: A learning analytics dashboard to support students' reflection on collaboration. J. Comput. Assist. Learn. **41**(1), e13088 (2025). https://doi.org/10.1111/jcal.13088. https://onlinelibrary.wiley.com/doi/abs/10.1111/jcal.13088
11. Echeverria, V., et al.: Teamvision: an AI-powered learning analytics system for supporting reflection in team-based healthcare simulation. In: Proceedings of the 2025 CHI Conference on Human Factors in Comp. Systems. CHI '25, ACM, NY, USA (2025). https://doi.org/10.1145/3706598.3713395
12. Fernandez-Nieto, G., et al.: Storytelling with learner data: guiding student reflection on multimodal team data. IEEE Trans. Learn. Technol. **14**(5), 695–708 (2021). https://doi.org/10.1109/TLT.2021.3131842
13. Fernandez-Nieto, G., Martinez-Maldonado, R., Echeverria, V., Kitto, K., Gašević, D., Buckingham Shum, S.: Data storytelling editor: a teacher-centred tool for customising learning analytics dashboard narratives. In: Proceedings of the 14th Learning Analytics and Knowledge Conference, pp. 678–689. LAK '24, ACM, NY, USA (2024). https://doi.org/10.1145/3636555.3636930
14. Fernandez Nieto, G.M., Kitto, K., Buckingham Shum, S., Martinez-Maldonado, R.: Beyond the learning analytics dashboard: alternative ways to communicate student data insights combining visualisation, narrative and storytelling. In: LAK22: 12th International Learning Analytics and Knowledge Conference, pp. 219–229. LAK22, ACM, NY, USA (2022). https://doi.org/10.1145/3506860.3506895
15. Frary, R.B.: Formula scoring of multiple-choice tests (correction for guessing). Educ. Meas. Issues Pract. **7**(2), 33–38 (1988). https://doi.org/10.1111/j.1745-3992.1988.tb00434.x. https://onlinelibrary.wiley.com/doi/abs/10.1111/j.1745-3992.1988.tb00434.x
16. Greller, W., Drachsler, H.: Translating learning into numbers: a generic framework for learning analytics. J. Educ. Technol. Soc. **15**(3), 42–57 (2012). http://www.jstor.org/stable/jeductechsoci.15.3.42
17. Kaliisa, R., Jivet, I., Prinsloo, P.: A checklist to guide the planning, designing, implementation, and evaluation of learning analytics dashboards. Int. J. Educ. Technol. High. Educ. **20**(1), 28 (2023)
18. Knaflic, C.N.: Storytelling with Data: A Data Visualization Guide for Business Professionals. John Wiley & Sons, New Jersey (2015)
19. Liang, Z., et al.: Data storytelling on multi-modal knowledge graph via data comics: a case study in yanyuwa language. In: 2024 Joint of International Conference on Learning Analytics and Knowledge Workshops, pp. 100–117 (2024). https://ceur-ws.org/Vol-3667/
20. McCloud, S.: Understanding Comics: The Invisible Art, 1st ed. edn. HarperPerennial, New York (1994)

21. McCloud, S.: Making Comics: Storytelling Secrets of Comics, Manga and Graphic Novels, 1st ed. edn. HarperPerennial, New York (2006)
22. Milesi, M.E., et al.: From comic panels to clinical practice: data comics as a learning analytics tool in nursing simulation. Smart Learn. Environ. **13**(1), 14 (2026). https://doi.org/10.1186/s40561-026-00434-4
23. Milesi, M.E., et al.: "piecing data connections together like a puzzle": effects of increasing task complexity on the effectiveness of data storytelling enhanced visualisations. In: Proceedings of the 2025 CHI Conference on Human Factors in Computer Systems. CHI '25, ACM, NY, USA (2025). https://doi.org/10.1145/3706598.3714270
24. Pandey, S., Ottley, A.: Mini-vlat: a short and effective measure of visualization literacy. Comput. Graph. Forum **42**(3), 1–11 (2023). https://doi.org/10.1111/cgf.14809
25. Park, Y., Jo, I.-H.: Factors that affect the success of learning analytics dashboards. Educ. Tech. Res. Dev., 1–25 (2019). https://doi.org/10.1007/s11423-019-09693-0
26. Pozdniakov, S., et al.: The question-driven dashboard: how can we design analytics interfaces aligned to teachers' inquiry? In: LAK22: 12th International Learning Analytics and Knowledge Conference, pp. 175–185. LAK22, ACM, NY, USA (2022). https://doi.org/10.1145/3506860.3506885
27. Pozdniakov, S., Martinez-Maldonado, R., Tsai, Y.S., Echeverria, V., Swiecki, Z., Gašević, D.: Investigating the effect of visualization literacy and guidance on teachers' dashboard interpretation. J. Learn. Anal. **12**(1), 367–390 (2024). https://doi.org/10.18608/jla.2024.8471. https://learning-analytics.info/index.php/JLA/article/view/8471
28. Radford, A., Kim, J.W., Xu, T., Brockman, G., McLeavey, C., Sutskever, I.: Robust speech recognition via large-scale weak supervision. In: Proceedings of the 40th International Conference on Machine Learning. ICML'23, JMLR.org (2023)
29. Rudenko, Y., Zhurba, K., Bekh, I., Petrenko, S., Bobokalo, A., Semenikhina, O.: Using dashboards in the development of students' analytical thinking. In: 2025 MIPRO 48th ICT and Electronics Convention, pp. 406–411 (2025). https://doi.org/10.1109/MIPRO65660.2025.11131997
30. Sahin, M., Ifenthaler, D.: Visualizations and Dashboards for Learning Analytics: A Systematic Literature Review, pp. 3–22. Springer Int. Publishing (2021). https://doi.org/10.1007/978-3-030-81222-5_1
31. Schwendimann, B.A., et al.: Perceiving learning at a glance: a systematic literature review of learning dashboard research. IEEE Trans. Learn. Technol. **10**(1), 30–41 (2017). https://doi.org/10.1109/TLT.2016.2599522
32. Segel, E., Heer, J.: Narrative visualization: telling stories with data. IEEE Trans. Visual Comput. Graph. **16**(6), 1139–1148 (2010). https://doi.org/10.1109/TVCG.2010.179
33. Wang, Z., Dingwall, H., Bach, B.: Teaching data visualization and storytelling with data comic workshops. In: 2019 CHI Conference on Human Factors in Computer Systems, pp. 1–9. CHI EA '19, ACM, NY, USA (2019). https://doi.org/10.1145/3290607.3299043
34. Wang, Z., Ritchie, J., Zhou, J., Chevalier, F., Bach, B.: Data comics for reporting controlled user studies in human-computer interaction. IEEE Trans. Visual Comput. Graph. **27**(2), 967–977 (2021). https://doi.org/10.1109/TVCG.2020.3030433. https://virtual.ieeevis.org/. 2020 IEEE Visualization Conf., VIS 2020; Conf. date: 25-10-2020 Through 30-10-2020

35. Wang, Z., Wang, S., Farinella, M., Murray-Rust, D., Henry Riche, N., Bach, B.: Comparing effectiveness and engagement of data comics and infographics. In: Proceedings of the 2019 CHI Conf. on Human Factors in Comp. Systems, pp. 1–12. CHI '19, ACM, NY, USA (2019). https://doi.org/10.1145/3290605.3300483
36. Yan, L., et al.: The effects of generative ai agents and scaffolding on enhancing students' comprehension of visual learning analytics. Comput. Educ. **234**, 105322 (2025). https://doi.org/10.1016/j.compedu.2025.105322. https://www.sciencedirect.com/science/article/pii/S0360131525000909
37. Zhao, L., et al.: Towards automated transcribing and coding of embodied teamwork communication through multimodal learning analytics. Br. J. Edu. Technol. **55**(4), 1673–1702 (2024). https://doi.org/10.1111/bjet.13476. https://bera-journals.onlinelibrary.wiley.com/doi/abs/10.1111/bjet.13476

# Spaced Testing in French Secondary Education: A Quantitative Analysis of Students' Revision Practices Using an Interactive System

Denis Ollivier[1,2], Rémi Saurel[1,2], Jean-Baptiste Raclet[1](✉), Emmanuel Lescure[2], Julien Broisin[1], and Franck Silvestre[1]

[1] Univ. Toulouse, Toulouse INP, CNRS, IRIT, Toulouse, France
{denis.ollivier,remi.saurel,jean-baptiste.raclet,julien.broisin, franck.silvestre}@irit.fr

[2] Kosmos Education, Toulouse, France
{denis.ollivier,remi.saurel,emmanuel.lescure}@kosmos.fr

**Abstract.** The testing and spacing effects improve long-term retention, yet learners rarely adopt them spontaneously. We report a quantitative study in French lower secondary education (ISCED 2) examining out-of-class revision when a test-based system is available. The study involved 297 students (12 classes) and 4 teachers in a two-phase protocol: Phase 1 provided Elaastic for rereading, whereas Phase 2 introduced Konsolidation with ready-to-use, teacher-designed tests for repeated self-testing. Results show a marked preference for computers over mobile devices for revision, a significant increase in the proportion of students engaging in digital revision when Konsolidation is available and a strong preference for the testing tool over rereading. However, revision remains predominantly massed near assessments, with limited spontaneous spacing. We derive design recommendations emphasising ready-to-use tests aligned with classroom content and support for temporal regulation of out-of-class revision.

**Keywords:** Testing effect · Spacing effect · Revision · Secondary education · Interactive revision system · Quantitative study

## 1 Introduction

According to research in cognitive psychology, two mechanisms play a central role in improving long-term knowledge retention: the testing effect and the spacing effect [7,8,15]. The testing effect refers to the benefit of self-assessment by the learner over passive rereading. This phenomenon has been repeatedly replicated in controlled studies that demonstrate significant advantages for memory consolidation [2,22]. Additionally, the spacing effect demonstrates that distributing learning sessions over time leads to better retention than massed practice as


J. Weidlich et al. (Eds.): EC-TEL 2026, LNCS 16905, pp. 467–482, 2027.
https://doi.org/10.1007/978-3-032-37979-5_32

reported by different meta-analyses [8,16]. These two effects combined together create a strong framework for designing learning activities that support long-term knowledge acquisition.

Despite their demonstrated effectiveness, these strategies are rarely adopted spontaneously by learners, particularly in secondary education. Indeed previous work highlights the role of metacognitive "illusions" [21] that lead learners to overestimate the effectiveness of rereading and to concentrate their study efforts just before summative assessments [5,11]. Although digital learning tools have become widely available, few are explicitly designed to support both the effects of spaced assessment and spaced learning in an institutional educational context. Furthermore, quantitative studies conducted in ecological settings, particularly in lower and upper secondary education, remain insufficient. Most existing work relies either on controlled laboratory protocols or on higher education contexts, leaving largely unexplored how secondary school students actually use spaced assessment when a dedicated digital tool is made available to them.

In this article, we present a quantitative study conducted with 297 students and 4 teachers in French lower secondary school. This study aims to analyze the practical use of an interactive revision system designed to support spaced testing. The tool, Konsolidation, allows students to access ready-to-use tests aligned with the material covered in class and to revise repeatedly over time. The usage traces collected in authentic school conditions offer a unique opportunity to observe students' revision behaviors and to draw lessons for the design of digital education systems. To ensure reproducibility, an anonymized replication package is available[1].

To guide this analysis, we address the following two research questions:

- **(RQ1):** What effective revision practices among secondary school students can be inferred from usage traces of an interactive revision system that allows spaced self- testing?
- **(RQ2):** Based on the analysis of these observed practices and drawing on the testing and spacing effects, what design recommendations can improve interactive revision systems intended to support out-of-class revision in secondary education?

By answering these questions, this article aims to provide a detailed understanding of how secondary school students engage with a spaced testing system in ecological conditions and to formulate concrete recommendations for the design of digital revision tools adapted to the needs and constraints of institutional educational contexts.

## 2 Related Work

Supporting the testing and spacing effects has long relied on simple tools and practices that predate digital technology. Flashcards, for instance, appear in

[1] https://osf.io/vjzsc/.

early pedagogical guidelines [6], and when used repeatedly over time they can promote distributed practice [10]. Classroom practices such as rapid questioning with slates or printed cards similarly enabled low-tech forms of retrieval practice at scale [12]. Digital technology did not introduce these principles but has greatly expanded their accessibility, scalability, and traceability.

A first line of work translates flashcard-based practices into digital tools (e.g., Cram, Quizlet or Wooflash), sometimes with sharing and collaboration features. Studies highlight design variations (pre-built versus learner-authored content, social sharing, feedback formats) as well as recurring limitations, notably a strong focus on vocabulary learning and language-related uses [13]. More broadly, "spaced repetition" systems operationalise spacing through scheduling mechanisms, often algorithmic [18], which select items and review times; however, integrating these systems into school constraints and curriculum-aligned content remains challenging.

A second line of research concerns digital formative assessment in the classroom. While summative assessment evaluates achievement of curricular objectives [17], formative assessment supports learning through evidence of understanding, including whole-class questioning [4]. Digital classroom response systems and game-based quizzing platforms facilitate such questioning at scale, increasing participation and providing real-time feedback. Reviews of Kahoot!, for example, report motivational benefits and widespread classroom uptake [20], while other studies show how response data can enrich in-class discussion [9]. Although these systems support retrieval practice during lessons, the spacing effect still largely depends on teachers' orchestration and is rarely supported beyond the classroom.

Out-of-class revision introduces additional constraints, as students prepare for summative assessments and alignment between learning activities and assessment becomes crucial [3]. Reusing classroom material for revision is therefore a promising approach. Silvestre et al. [19], for example, created revision tests from questions previously addressed in class and observed that students used them. However, revision remained mostly massed close to exams, suggesting limited spontaneous adoption of spacing even when testing opportunities exist.

Overall, prior work shows that digital tools can facilitate retrieval practice and generate large-scale usage data. However, little evidence exists on how secondary school students actually adopt testing and spacing in authentic out-of-class revision contexts, especially when revision content derives directly from classroom activities. This gap motivates our focus on usage traces to characterise effective practices (RQ1) and derive design recommendations for interactive revision systems in secondary education (RQ2).

## 3 The Two-Phase Protocol

The quantitative study was conducted in an ecological setting within French secondary education and followed a two-phase protocol designed to observe students' out-of-class revision practices under progressively enriched tool-supported conditions. The protocol was deliberately constrained by institutional and pedagogical requirements to preserve the authenticity of teachers' practices and students' behaviours.

### 3.1 Participants and Educational Context

These students were distributed across 12 classes, including three first-year, seven third-year, and two fourth-year lower secondary classes in the French system.

The study involved 297 students from 12 lower secondary school classes (ISCED level 2, aged 11–14), including 3 first-year, 7 third-year, and 2 fourth-year classes, supervised by 4 teachers. Among the participating students, 54.55% ($n$ = 162) were male and 45.45% ($n$ = 135) were female. The experimentation took place during regular teaching periods and was fully integrated into ongoing instructional sequences leading to summative assessments.

The disciplines covered by the experimentation were deliberately diverse, encompassing scientific subjects (Technology, Biology, and Geology), Humanities (History–Geography), and French language studies, with a particular focus on grammar. This diversity ensured that the observed practices were not tied to a single disciplinary culture but reflected a broad range of revision contexts.

Participation was voluntary and followed institutional consent procedures, including parental authorization for data collection. Students accessed the tools at home using their usual personal or family devices (desktop computers, laptops, tablets, or smartphones), reflecting realistic technological conditions in secondary education.

### 3.2 Phase 1: Baseline Revision Practices with Elaastic Only

The first phase of the experimentation lasted 8 weeks and aimed at observing students' natural engagement with a digital learning environment when only rereading-based revision was possible. During this phase, teachers used Elaastic, a digital formative assessment platform designed to support in-class testing activities through interactive questions and peer instruction [1,19]. After classroom sessions, Elaastic remained accessible to students outside the classroom.

In this context, out-of-class use of Elaastic essentially enabled revision through rereading of static resources previously worked on in class, such as questions, answers, and feedback. However, this mode of access did not allow students to benefit from the testing effect, as no dedicated self-testing or repeated retrieval activities were provided for revision purposes. No explicit guidance or incentives were given regarding how or when to revise.

Each class experienced at least one summative assessment during this phase, aligned in advance with the instructional activities conducted in class.

### 3.3 Phase 2: Introduction of Konsolidation Alongside Elaastic

The subsequent phase lasted 9 weeks and introduced Konsolidation, an interactive revision system explicitly designed to support repeated self-testing over time [14]. During this phase, both Elaastic and Konsolidation were available to students for out-of-class use.

Konsolidation automatically retrieves activities from Elaastic, reusing pedagogical content produced during in-class sessions. These tests are reformatted to allow students to perform multiple self-testing attempts outside the classroom, thereby enabling the implementation of the testing effect and creating conditions for spaced revision across several days or weeks.

As in Phase 1, no specific revision schedule, incentives, or reminders were imposed on students, and teachers did not prescribe how the tools should be used outside class. This design choice was intentional, as the objective was to observe whether students would spontaneously adopt testing and spacing strategies when a dedicated tool was made available.

Each class again completed at least one summative assessment, aligned beforehand with classroom activities and the revision material accessible through the tools.

## 4 Dataset and Data Preparation

The quantitative analyses reported in this article rely on activity traces collected from the 297 students initially involved in the study. Depending on the analysis, different subsets of this cohort were considered. While analyses related to equipment usage (Sect. 5) include data from all students, analyses addressing the testing and spacing effects (Sects. 6 and 7) focus on a subset of 251 students who followed the experimentation protocol in a sufficiently consistent manner and completed the aligned summative assessments.

Regarding Elaastic, the analysed data cover 13 instructional topics, corresponding to 75 distinct questions and 326 classroom sequences conducted by the teachers. Based on the activity periods explicitly identified by teachers as in-class usage, we extracted and removed all logs corresponding to classroom time. This filtering step allowed us to isolate students' *out-of-class* interactions with Elaastic. After filtering, the dataset includes a total of 582 out-of-class accesses to Elaastic, with 411 accesses during Phase 1 and 171 accesses during Phase 2.

For Konsolidation, which was available only during Phase 2, the dataset includes 414 revision attempts performed by students with a total of 2,789 submitted answers.

In addition to usage traces, students were asked to complete a questionnaire reporting the digital equipment available to them at home, including smartphones, tablets and computers, and specifying whether each device was personally owned or shared within the family. This information made it possible to analyse revision practices in relation to the actual material resources available to students. A total of 23 students (7.74%) reported having no access to any digital device at home.

# 5 Equipment Used for Out-of-Class Revision

This section focuses on the equipment used by students to access Konsolidation, as it is specifically designed for out-of-class revision activities.

## 5.1 Students' Access to Digital Equipment for Out-of-Class Revision

The analysis relies exclusively on activity traces collected from Konsolidation during Phase 2, when the system was available for out-of-class revision. The type of device used for each revision attempt was inferred from the user agent information recorded at access time, allowing us to distinguish between computers, smartphones, and tablets.

Table 1 reports the distribution of students' revision attempts on Konsolidation by device type, cross-referenced with the digital equipment declared as available at home. Rows correspond to the equipment available to students, while columns indicate the device effectively used to perform revision attempts. Percentages are computed over the total number of revision attempts. Students who reported having access only to a tablet did not perform any revision attempts on Konsolidation and are therefore not represented as a separate row in the table.

**Table 1.** Percentage of students' revision attempts on Konsolidation by device type, relative to the declared available equipment

| Available equipment | Computer | Mobile | Tablet | Total |
|---|---|---|---|---|
| Computer only | 9.40% | 0.00% | 0.00% | 9.40% |
| Mobile only | 0.00% | 4.35% | 0.00% | 4.35% |
| Multiple devices | 59.30% | 25.95% | 1.00% | 86.25% |
| **Total** | **68.70%** | **30.30%** | **1.00%** | **100%** |

This representation makes it possible to distinguish between access to digital resources and actual usage, highlighting potential preferences or constraints in students' revision practices.

## 5.2 Students Predominantly Use Computers for Digital Revision

To determine whether students privilege a specific type of equipment when revising with a digital tool, we analysed the relative frequency of access to Konsolidation by device. For each student, we computed the percentage of revision attempts performed with each type of equipment among all their attempts.

We then conducted one-sided (right-tailed) t-tests to assess whether the mean proportion of use of a given device significantly exceeded the 50% threshold, which corresponds to an equal-use baseline. The results of these tests are reported in Table 2.

**Table 2.** Results of one-sided (right-tailed) t-tests for device usage proportions per student, tested against the 50% threshold

| Device | Observed mean | Std. deviation | t-statistic | p-value | 99% CI |
|---|---|---|---|---|---|
| Computer | 70.71% | 41.45% | 5.24 | $p < .001$ | [60.35% ; 81.07%] |
| Mobile | 27.47% | 40.48% | −5.83 | $p < .001$ | [17.36% ; 37.59%] |
| Tablet | 1.82% | 13.42% | −37.65 | $p < .001$ | [−1.54% ; 5.17%] |

The analysis reveals a statistically significant preference for computers. The t-statistic associated with computer usage is positive and significant, indicating that the mean proportion of computer-based revision attempts is significantly greater than 50% ($p < .001$). In contrast, the t-statistics for smartphones and tablets are negative, indicating that their mean usage proportions are significantly below the 50% threshold.

These results show that, although students may have access to multiple devices, computers are clearly privileged for testing-based revision activities, while mobile devices play a secondary role.

***Observed Practice 1.*** *Students make significant use of both computers and mobile devices to revise with a digital tool; however, when they have a choice, their revision activity shows a clear and statistically significant preference for computers.*

***Design Recommendation 1.*** *Interactive revision systems should guarantee equivalent accessibility on computers and mobile devices, while explicitly accounting for students' marked preference for computer-based use in the context of revision. In practice, this implies prioritising usability, readability, and interaction design for computer interfaces, while maintaining functional mobile access to accommodate heterogeneous access conditions.*

This pattern suggests that students associate revision and self-testing activities with environments that support sustained attention, readability, and interaction comfort.

## 6 Testing Effect: Adoption of Test-Based Revision Practices

This section examines the adoption of test-based revision practices through a series of quantitative analyses addressing complementary aspects of students' engagement with digital revision tools.

### 6.1 Providing Ready-to-Use Teacher-Designed Tests Increases Students' Engagement in Digital Revision

We investigate whether making a testing tool available—offering ready-to-use tests designed by teachers—leads a greater number of students to engage in digital revision activities. To address this question, we compared students' revision behaviours across the two experimental phases.

As a reminder, during Phase 1, students had access only to Elaastic for out-of-class revision, whereas during Phase 2, both Elaastic and Konsolidation were available. In this context, we examined the number of students who engaged in at least one revision activity versus those who did not revise in each phase. The data used for this analysis are summarised in Table 3.

**Table 3.** Contingency table of students' revision behaviour in Phase 1 and Phase 2

| | Revision in Phase 1 | No revision in Phase 1 | Total |
|---|---|---|---|
| **Revision in Phase 2** | 42 | 79 | 121 |
| **No revision in Phase 2** | 20 | 110 | 130 |
| **Total** | 62 | 189 | 251 |

We formulated the following null hypothesis: there is no significant difference in students' revision behaviour between Phase 1 (Elaastic only) and Phase 2 (Elaastic and Konsolidation). Since the same students were observed in both phases and revision behaviour is a binary variable (revising vs. not revising), we analysed paired data. To test whether changes in revision behaviour between the two phases were statistically significant, we applied McNemar's test to the contingency table reported in Table 3. As McNemar's test is based on the discordant pairs only, the test statistic is determined by the students who changed behaviour between phases (i.e., $b + c = 79 + 20 = 99$).

The McNemar test yielded a statistically significant result ($p < .001$), indicating a significant difference in revision behaviour between the two phases. This result allows us to reject the null hypothesis and conclude that students' revision behaviour changed markedly following the introduction of Konsolidation. The 99% confidence interval for the proportion of students who did not revise in Phase 1 but started revising in Phase 2 is estimated at [67.90%; 88.68%], meaning that, with 99% confidence, this proportion lies within this interval.

To assess the magnitude of this effect, we computed Cramér's $V$, which yielded a value of $V = 0.374$. This value indicates a medium effect size, suggesting that the introduction of Konsolidation had a substantial impact on students' engagement in revision activities.

Taken together, these results show that providing a testing tool offering ready-to-use, teacher-designed tests encourages a larger number of students to engage in digital revision.

### 6.2 When Both a Rereading Tool and a Testing Tool Are Available, Students Predominantly Use the Testing Tool

This second analysis examines whether students privilege a testing-based revision tool over a rereading-based tool when both are simultaneously available.

The analysis considers the 121 students who engaged in at least one revision activity using either tool during Phase 2. For these students, we established a three-category classification: students who used Elaastic exclusively (rereading-oriented revision), students who used Konsolidation exclusively (testing-oriented revision), and students who used both tools. The distribution across these categories is reported in Table 4.

**Table 4.** Distribution of students according to the revision tools used during Phase 2 (among students who revised at least once)

| Tool used | Users | Percentage | 99% CI |
|---|---|---|---|
| Elastic only | 9 | 7.44% | [3.3% ; 16.0%] |
| Konsolidation only | 90 | 74.38% | [63.1% ; 83.1%] |
| Elastic and Konsolidation | 22 | 18.18% | [10.9% ; 28.8%] |
| **Total** | 121 | 100% | – |

We first examined the following null hypothesis: students' use of the available revision tools is evenly distributed across the three categories, corresponding to an expected proportion of approximately 33% for each category. To evaluate this hypothesis, we applied a chi-square goodness-of-fit test, comparing the observed proportions with those expected under an equal distribution.

The chi-square test yielded a highly significant result ($\chi^2 = 93.83$, $p < .001$), allowing us to reject the null hypothesis. In addition, 99% confidence intervals were computed for each category. The confidence intervals corresponding to the Elaastic-only and Elaastic-and-Konsolidation categories do not include the 33% expected under an equal distribution. Moreover, the confidence interval for the Konsolidation-only category lies entirely above the 50% threshold, indicating that a majority of students relied exclusively on the testing-based tool.

These results allow us to characterise a clear revision practice and to derive a corresponding design recommendation.

***Observed Practice 2:*** *When students who engage in digital revision have simultaneous access to a rereading-oriented tool and to a testing-oriented tool that allows them to retake the same assessments, the majority of them rely on the testing-based tool. This preference is robustly supported by the quantitative analyses, which show that students overwhelmingly favour test-based revision over rereading when both options are available.*

***Design Recommendation 2:*** *Revision systems should provide ready-to-use tests directly aligned with classroom content. Simply making such tests available encourages students who are willing to revise using digital tools to prioritise testing over rereading on the same learning materials. This finding highlights the importance of lowering the practical and cognitive barriers to retrieval practice in order to promote effective revision strategies.*

# 7 Spacing Effect: Temporal Distribution of Revision Activities

Drawing on the literature on spacing and massed practice [5,19], this section examines whether students' revision practices of our dataset reflect the spacing effect or, conversely, whether they tend to concentrate their activity as summative assessments approach. Teachers were explicitly asked not to encourage students to revise more than usual during the experimentation, to observe spontaneous revision behaviours.

The analysis focuses exclusively on revision attempts performed on Konsolidation. To operationalise spacing, we defined two revision sessions as spaced when they were separated by at least four hours. We therefore restricted the analysis to attempts whose creation and last modification timestamps were within four hours, ensuring that each retained attempt could be treated as a single revision session. This filtering resulted in a dataset of 335 revision attempts, considered representative of discrete out-of-class revision sessions.

Each instructional topic was associated with at least one summative assessment, for which both the announcement date and the assessment date were known. Revision activities were retained only if they occurred within a 15-day window prior to the corresponding assessment.

## 7.1 Revision Activity Intensifies as Summative Assessments Approach

To examine how revision activity evolves over time, we analysed students' revision attempts as a function of the number of days remaining before the associated summative assessment.

We first examined the data on a day-by-day basis (Fig. 1), treating each day prior to the assessment as a potential revision opportunity. The peak in revision activity observed approximately eight days before the assessment coincides with a software maintenance intervention that occurred nine days before several assessments, which may have encouraged additional usage. As it is not possible to disentangle the respective influence of this intervention and assessment proximity, these data were retained in the analysis.

To reduce variability related to students' schedules, we then aggregated revision attempts into two-day intervals (Fig. 2a), computing the mean number of attempts per student for each interval. Finally, we performed the same analysis using three-day intervals (Fig. 2b), in order to account for periods including Wednesdays or weekends, which represent extended out-of-class time during which students are more likely to revise.

To formally assess the relationship between revision activity and assessment proximity, we tested the null hypothesis that the number of revision attempts is independent of the number of days remaining before the assessment. Because the variables involved are ordinal and do not follow a normal distribution, we applied Spearman's rank correlation tests and computed 99% confidence intervals. The results are reported in Table 5.

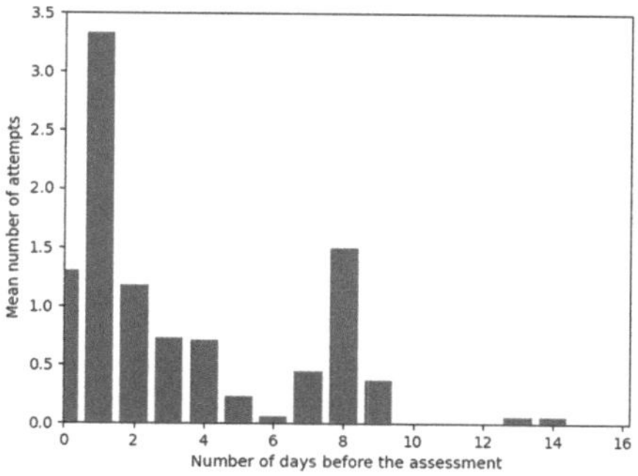


**Fig. 1.** Average number of revision attempts on Konsolidation, day by day, as a function of days before the assessment.

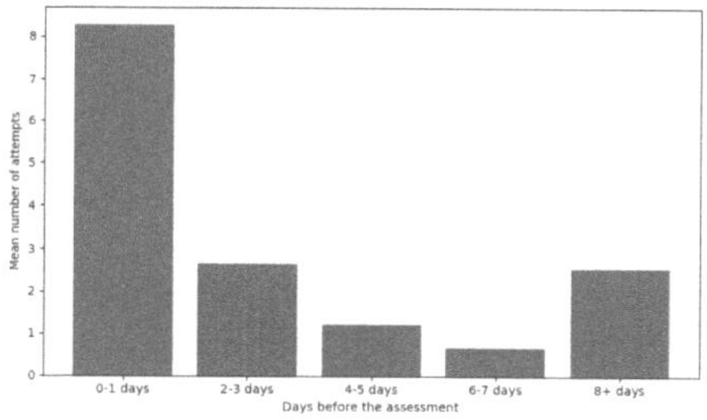


(a) Grouped into 2-day intervals

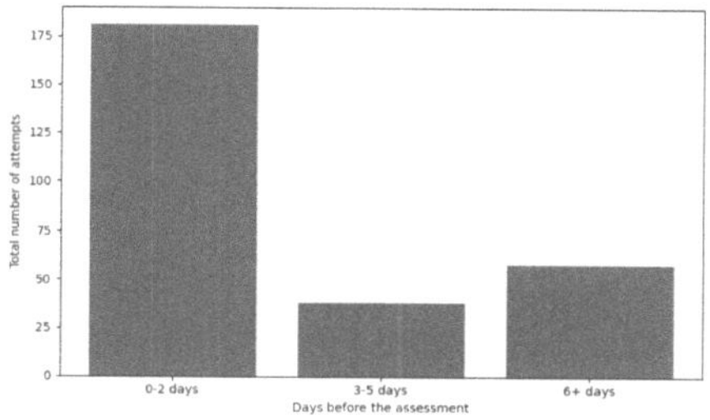


(b) Grouped into 3-day intervals

**Fig. 2.** Average number of revision attempts on Konsolidation as a function of days before the assessment for different aggregation windows.

When analysing revision attempts on a day-by-day basis, we observe a moderate positive correlation ($\rho = 0.486$, $p < .001$). Aggregating attempts into two-day intervals yields a slightly lower correlation ($\rho = 0.411$, $p < .001$). When grouping attempts into three-day intervals, the correlation remains moderate ($\rho = 0.499$, $p < .001$), although the 99% confidence interval becomes wider, ranging from 0.141 to 0.764. In all configurations, the p-values are below .001, allowing us to reject the null hypothesis.

## 7.2 Revision Practices Remain Predominantly Massed Over Time

While the previous analysis shows that revision activity intensifies near assessments, it does not, by itself, indicate whether students engage in genuinely spaced revision. To address this issue, we examined whether students revised the same topics on multiple, temporally separated occasions.

Among the 112 students who performed at least one revision attempt on Konsolidation during Phase 2, only those whose attempts could be reliably associated with a single revision session were retained for the spacing analysis. Restricting

**Table 5.** Spearman correlation between the number of revision attempts and the number of days before the assessment, grouped by 1-, 2-, or 3-day periods

| Grouping | Spearman correlation | *p*-value | 99% CI |
|---|---|---|---|
| Day by day | 0.486 | $p < .001$ | [0.369 ; 0.590] |
| 2-day intervals | 0.411 | $p < .001$ | [0.109 ; 0.650] |
| 3-day intervals | 0.499 | $p < .001$ | [0.141 ; 0.764] |

the data to attempts whose last modification occurred within four hours of their creation yields a dataset of 108 students.

Within this filtered subset, 73 students initiated at least two revision attempts. However, only 20 students revised the same topic on multiple distinct dates, and among these, only 13 students revised more than three days before the corresponding summative assessment.

These results indicate that, although repeated testing occurs, revision is rarely distributed over extended periods. Instead, most students concentrate their revision efforts close to the assessment date, even when using a testing-based tool that technically supports repeated attempts over time.

Taken together, the correlation analyses and the examination of repeated revision behaviours show that students predominantly adopt a massed revision strategy, with limited spontaneous adoption of spaced practice.

***Observed Practice 3:*** *In the absence of explicit incentives or regulation, students predominantly adopt a massed revision strategy close to summative assessments and benefit little, if at all, from the spacing effect.*

***Design Recommendation 3:*** *Revision systems should actively support the temporal regulation of students' activity. By providing mechanisms that encourage earlier and more distributed engagement—such as reminders, pacing cues, or teacher-mediated orchestration—systems may help learners move beyond massed revision and better exploit the benefits of spaced practice.*

## 8 Limitations and Threats to Validity

This section discusses the quantitative results in light of complementary qualitative evidence and outlines the main threats to validity.

### 8.1 Contextual Factors and External Validity

The study was conducted in a relatively socio-economically advantaged secondary school context, as indicated by the school's Social Position Index (SPI), a French quantitative measure of students' socio-economic background based on their parents' occupations. This context may influence students' access to digital equipment, parental involvement, and revision habits, and therefore limits the direct generalisation of the results to all secondary education settings. While these conditions are favourable for adopting digital revision tools, they also suggest that observed limitations in usage and practices are unlikely to stem solely from a lack of resources.

### 8.2 Equipment Access and Supervision Effects

The analysis of equipment usage revealed that students predominantly accessed Konsolidation using computers rather than mobile devices. Qualitative feedback collected through questionnaires administered at the end of each experimental phase helps interpret this result. Several students reported that their parents actively supervised their out-of-class work, sometimes restricting the use of digital tools altogether, or explicitly requiring that revision activities be carried out on a computer in order to better monitor their work. In parallel, Elaastic was used exclusively on computers during classroom activities. This combination of in-class practices and parental constraints may have led students to continue favouring computers when engaging with Konsolidation outside the classroom.

Although a large majority of students reported having access to at least one digital device at home, 23 students (7.74%) reported having no access to any digital device at home. While schools may sometimes provide access to computer rooms during free periods, such access remains logistically constrained and does not systematically compensate for the absence of home equipment. This limitation represents a persistent source of educational inequality, which may be reinforced by the increasing reliance on digital tools for out-of-class learning activities.

### 8.3 Limits to the Adoption

**Testing Effect.** The results related to the testing effect show that providing a testing-based tool encourages a substantial proportion of students to engage in digital revision and to prioritise test-based revision over rereading when both options are available. However, qualitative feedback indicates that access to equipment alone does not guarantee usage. Beyond the 23 households without digital equipment, some students ($n = 46$) deliberately revised without digital tools, while others ($n = 19$) reported no need to revise or did not perceive the proposed tools as necessary.

Moreover, conclusions regarding the testing effect are limited to students who actually used the tools. During Phase 2, Konsolidation was used by 108 students (36.36% of the initial sample), suggesting that digital revision practices are not yet the norm. Questionnaire data show that 281 students (94.61%) revised on paper at least once per week, and 185 (62.29%) reported not using any digital tools other than those provided in the study. Although these self-reports do not identify specific revision strategies, some revisions likely rely on simple rereading, meaning that these students may not benefit from the testing effect. Thus, although tools such as Konsolidation support testing-based revision, they may not yet fully align with prevailing out-of-class revision practices.

These observations suggest that fostering the testing effect may require additional support, such as stronger teacher supervision of out-of-class work or system-driven regulation mechanisms. For example, interactive systems could notify students when revision activity is absent or insufficient over a given period, thereby encouraging engagement and more effective strategies.

**Spacing Effect.** The analyses related to the spacing effect show that, even among students who engaged with Konsolidation, spaced revision remains rare. Among the 73 students who initiated at least two revision attempts, only 20 revised the same topic on different dates, and only 13 did so more than three days before the corresponding assessment. Although filtering choices reduced the number of attempts considered as single-session work, even before filtering, the number of students exhibiting spaced revision practices remained limited (26 students). Given that 112 students used Konsolidation overall, the majority did not revise the same topic multiple times across temporally separated sessions.

These results suggest that the limited adoption of spaced revision does not primarily result from methodological constraints or filtering decisions but rather reflects a general tendency among lower secondary school students (aged 11–14) to concentrate their revision close to summative assessments. This finding is consistent with prior work reporting a predominance of massed practice in authentic educational settings and confirms that the availability of a testing-based tool alone is insufficient to induce spontaneous spaced revision.

## 9 Conclusion and Future Work

This paper examined secondary school students' out-of-class revision practices through a quantitative analysis of usage traces collected from an interactive system supporting repeated self-testing over time.

With respect to (RQ1), the results indicate that providing a testing-based tool with ready-to-use, teacher-designed tests increases students' engagement in digital revision and leads most revising students to favour testing over rereading. However, revision activity remains predominantly massed near summative assessments, with limited spontaneous adoption of spaced revision.

Regarding (RQ2), three implications emerge for interactive revision systems in secondary education: (i) interfaces should be designed with a computer-first use case in mind while ensuring equivalent access on mobile devices, (ii) ready-to-use tests aligned with classroom content reduce the practical and cognitive barriers to retrieval practice, encouraging students to prioritise testing over rereading during revision, and (iii) promoting spacing requires additional support for regulating out-of-class work, as tool availability alone does not induce distributed practice.

Future work will examine relationships between students' activity on Konsolidation and their performance on summative assessments, and will explore regulation mechanisms to foster earlier and more regular revision, including system-driven planning and reminders as well as teacher-mediated monitoring and interventions supported by activity analytics.

## References


1. Andriamiseza, R., Silvestre, F., Parmentier, J.F., Broisin, J.: Recommendations for orchestration of formative assessment sequences: a data-driven approach. In: European Conference on Technology Enhanced Learning, pp. 245–259. Springer (2021)
2. Bae, C.L., Therriault, D.J., Redifer, J.L.: Investigating the testing effect: retrieval as a characteristic of effective study strategies. Learn. Instr. **60**, 206–214 (2019)
3. Biggs, J.: Enhancing teaching through constructive alignment. High. Educ. **32**(3), 347–364 (1996)
4. Black, P., Wiliam, D.: Developing the theory of formative assessment. Educ. Assess. Eval. Account. **21**, 5–31 (2009)
5. Blasiman, R.N., Dunlosky, J., Rawson, K.A.: The what, how much, and when of study strategies: comparing intended versus actual study behaviour. Memory **25**(6), 784–792 (2017)
6. Browder, D.M., Roberts, M.L.: Guidelines for flash card instruction. J. Behav. Educ. **3**, 235–245 (1993)
7. Carpenter, S.K., Cepeda, N.J., Rohrer, D., Kang, S.H., Pashler, H.: Using spacing to enhance diverse forms of learning: Review of recent research and implications for instruction. Educ. Psychol. Rev. **24**(3), 369–378 (2012)
8. Cepeda, N.J., Pashler, H., Vul, E., Wixted, J.T., Rohrer, D.: Distributed practice in verbal recall tasks: a review and quantitative synthesis. Psychol. Bull. **132**(3), 354 (2006)
9. Gauci, S.A., Dantas, A.M., Williams, D.A., Kemm, R.E.: Promoting student-centered active learning in lectures with a personal response system. Adv. Physiol. Educ. **33**(1), 60–71 (2009)
10. Kornell, N.: Optimising learning using flashcards: Spacing is more effective than cramming. Appl. Cogn. Psychol. Off. J. Soc. Appl. Res. Memory Cogn. **23**(9), 1297–1317 (2009)
11. Latimier, A.: Optimisation de l'apprentissage par récupération en mémoire pour promouvoir la rétention à long terme de nouvelles connaissances. Ph.D. thesis, Université Paris sciences et lettres (2019)
12. Meltzer, D.E., Manivannan, K.: Transforming the lecture-hall environment: the fully interactive physics lecture. Am. J. Phys. **70**(6), 639–654 (2002)
13. Nakata, T.: Computer-assisted second language vocabulary learning in a paired-associate paradigm: a critical investigation of flashcard software. Comput. Assist. Lang. Learn. **24**(1), 17–38 (2011)
14. Ollivier, D., Silvestre, F., Raclet, J., Lescure, E., Broisin, J.: Designing a revision system: an exploratory qualitative study to identify the needs of french teachers and students. In: European Conference on Technology Enhanced Learning. Lecture Notes in Computer Science, vol. 14200, pp. 294–307. Springer (2023)
15. Roediger, H.L., III., Karpicke, J.D.: Test-enhanced learning: taking memory tests improves long-term retention. Psychol. Sci. **17**(3), 249–255 (2006)
16. Rohrer, D., Taylor, K.: The effects of overlearning and distributed practise on the retention of mathematics knowledge. Appl. Cogn. Psychol. Off. J. Soc. Appl. Res. Memory Cogn. **20**(9), 1209–1224 (2006)

17. Sadler, D.R.: Formative assessment and the design of instructional systems. Instr. Sci. **18**(2), 119–144 (1989)
18. Settles, B., Meeder, B.: A trainable spaced repetition model for language learning. In: Annual Meeting of the Association for Computational Linguistics (2016)
19. Silvestre, F., Vidal, P., Broisin, J.: Online tests based on contributions provided by teachers and students during face to face lectures. In: IEEE International Conference on Advanced Learning Technologies, pp. 29–33. IEEE (2015)
20. Wang, A.I., Tahir, R.: The effect of using kahoot! for learning-a literature review. Comput. Educ. **149**, 103818 (2020)
21. Yue, C.L.: Improving learner metacognition and self-regulation. In: Ober, T.M., Che, E., Brodsky, J.E., Raffaele, C., Brooks, P.J. (eds.), How We Teach Now: The GSTA Guide to Transformative Teaching, pp. 95–103 (2020)
22. Zaromb, F.M., Roediger, H.L.: The testing effect in free recall is associated with enhanced organizational processes. Memory Cogn. **38**(8), 995–1008 (2010)

# Students' Perceptions of Peer Grading

Uchswas Paul[1(✉)], Jash Shah[1], Keira McArthur[1], Aref Babaei[2], Niranjan Rajendran[1], Parvez Rashid[3], and Edward Gehringer[1]

[1] North Carolina State University, Raleigh, NC, USA
{upaul,jshah23,klmcarth,nrajend4,efg}@ncsu.edu
[2] Kansas city, USA
[3] College of Charleston, Charleston, SC, USA
rashidp@cofc.edu

**Abstract.** Peer grading is widely used in education, yet it elicits mixed reactions from educators and students. Although many studies have examined students' views of peer grading, their findings are scattered, and no clear overall picture has emerged. To address this gap, we conducted a mixed-source thematic analysis of literature and student discussions on Reddit. The study synthesized evidence from 107 papers, 114 Reddit posts, and 300 comments. The findings show that students view peer grading as both beneficial and problematic. Positive perceptions included learning and understanding benefits, skill development, engagement, and collaboration, while negative perceptions centered on unreliable grading, unfairness, weak feedback quality, emotional stress, and workload. Reddit discussions also suggested an emerging concern that remains underexplored in the literature: AI use in peer grading may weaken students' trust in the accuracy and authenticity of the process. We further identified eight mitigation strategies and mapped them to the negative perceptions they help address. Among these, instructor oversight and training played the most central role.

**Keywords:** Peer grading · Peer assessment · Students' Perceptions · Systematic literature review · Social media data analysis

## 1 Introduction

Peer assessment is widely recognized as a powerful learning tool, valued for both its scalability and pedagogical benefits. Reviewing peers' work exposes students to diverse artifacts that clarify expectations and help them calibrate their own performance [30]. A substantial body of research suggests that students often learn more from evaluating others' work than from reading feedback on their own [27], a finding that has been replicated across disciplines and instructional contexts. Studies in writing, engineering, computer science, and the health professions [11] all attest to the learning gains associated with structured peer assessment, including improved metacognitive awareness, deeper engagement with criteria, and enhanced ability to judge quality.

A. Babaei—Independent Researcher.


J. Weidlich et al. (Eds.): EC-TEL 2026, LNCS 16905, pp. 483–498, 2027.
https://doi.org/10.1007/978-3-032-37979-5_33

Within this broader landscape, peer grading represents a more contentious subset of peer assessment practices. Instructors often hesitate to delegate grading authority, citing concerns about fairness, reliability, and the loss of professional judgment. The rise of massive open online courses (MOOCs), however, created a context in which peer grading became not just an option but a necessity: with tens of thousands of learners and limited instructional staff, MOOC platforms had no viable alternative for evaluating open-ended work at scale.

Despite the increasing interest in peer assessment, students' perceptions of peer grading remain poorly synthesized. Existing studies report mixed findings, and prior reviews have focused primarily on technical or procedural aspects, such as anonymity, grading tools, algorithms, and reviewer assignment, rather than students' experiences [30,31]. To address this gap, our study systematically analyzes students' perceptions of peer grading using both literature and student discussions on social media. Specifically, we address the following research questions:

- **RQ1**: What positive perceptions do students have about peer grading?
- **RQ2**: What negative perceptions do students have about peer grading?
- **RQ3**: What mitigation strategies are reported in the literature to address peer-grading challenges?

## 2 Methodology

We used a mixed-source thematic design to examine students' perceptions of peer grading across two complementary sources: peer-reviewed literature and Reddit discussions. This approach integrates formal research with naturally occurring student discourse. Because peer grading is often discussed within the broader language of peer assessment, we included studies using that terminology when peer-assigned grading was a substantive component.

**Literature-Based Analysis:** We followed the PRISMA framework [29] and conducted a systematic search across six databases: ACM Digital Library, Web of Science, ERIC, PsycINFO, IEEE Xplore, and PubMed. Search terms targeted peer grading, student perceptions, and survey-based evidence. We included peer-reviewed journal and conference papers, book chapters, dissertations, and technical reports published between 2003 and 2025. Non-English papers, duplicates, books, retracted works, and studies unrelated to our research questions were excluded. The search returned 629 records (90 duplicates). After screening 539 abstracts and reviewing 161 full texts, 107 studies were retained (Fig. 1). Two authors independently screened and reviewed all papers, resolving disagreements through discussion. Inter-rater agreement was moderate during screening ($\kappa = 0.60$) and substantial during eligibility checking ($\kappa = 0.68$).

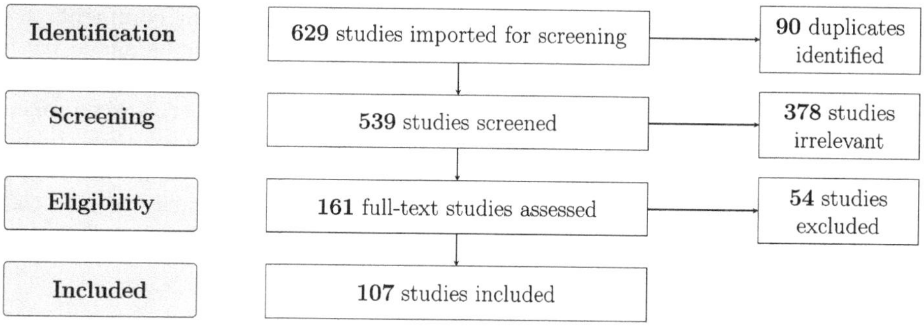


**Fig. 1.** PRISMA flow diagram for the literature review.

**Reddit Data Analysis:** We collected posts and comments from a 2005–2025 Reddit archive using the keywords "peer grading" and "peer assessment" yielding 659 posts and 6,607 comments. Because many matches were irrelevant, we applied a fine-tuned Gemini 2.5 model as an initial relevance filter, trained on a manually annotated subset of 67 posts and 149 comments, in which 27 posts and 47 comments were relevant. As shown in Table 1, the model was evaluated on a 200-item validation dataset and achieved 98.5% recall for relevant items and 99.0% precision for items predicted as irrelevant, ensuring that discarding items labeled irrelevant posed minimal risk. However, precision for the relevant class was lower (66.0%), so all items flagged as relevant were manually reviewed. Inter-rater agreement for this manual review was $\kappa = 0.77$ for the Reddit posts and $\kappa = 0.95$ for the comments. The final dataset included 114 posts and 300 comments. To minimize the risk of identifying individual commenters, we paraphrased publicly available comments and limited our use of direct quotes.

**Table 1.** Confusion Matrix for Relevance Classification

| Actual | Predicted | |
|---|---|---|
| | Relevant | Irrelevant |
| **Relevant** | 66 | 1 |
| **Irrelevant** | 34 | 99 |

**Encoding Student Perceptions and Mitigation Strategies:** We analyzed both sources using a bottom-up thematic approach. The authors independently reviewed the literature and Reddit data to identify recurring themes in students' positive and negative perceptions of peer grading. Mitigation strategies were derived from the literature only. These themes were refined through repeated discussion until a shared coding scheme emerged. The final coding scheme included 6 positive perceptions, 7 negative perceptions, and 8 mitigation strategies. For reporting, each literature paper and each Reddit item (post or comment) was coded based on whether it mentioned a given perception theme. A single paper or Reddit item could receive multiple codes when it expressed multiple perceptions. Therefore, the frequencies in the tables show how many literature papers or Reddit items mentioned each theme, and the summed frequencies across themes exceed the total number of papers or Reddit items. During theme encoding, mean inter-rater agreement between two raters across all themes was $\kappa = 0.67$ for the literature, $\kappa = 0.93$ for Reddit posts, and $\kappa = 0.88$ for Reddit comments. These findings are presented in the following section.

## 3 Results

This section presents a comparative analysis of students' perceptions of peer grading and the associated mitigation strategies, structured around our RQs.

### 3.1 RQ1: Positive Perceptions of Peer Grading

To answer RQ1, we identified six recurring patterns in students' positive perceptions of peer grading across the literature and Reddit data, summarized below:

**P1. Learning and Understanding Benefits:** Students often viewed peer grading as a useful way to improve their understanding of course content, assessment criteria, and performance expectations [10,35]. Machanick [28] noted that peer grading helped students recognize their own mistakes. Similarly, Berrezueta et al. [4] reported that reviewing peers' work helped students explore different design ideas and learn from others' solutions. Ayachi [1] reported similar benefits for composition writing improvement. Deslandes and Hughes [10] reported that 84.3% of student markers agreed that acting as a peer marker helped them understand how the staff would mark their artifacts. Similar findings were reported in several other studies, including those by Jones [17] and Kingsley [20]. In addition to the benefits of reviewing, receiving feedback from peers also supported learning. For example, Verkade and Bryson-Richardson [42] found that peer feedback helped students improve their presentations. On Reddit, students similarly suggested that reviewing peers' work and receiving reviews were beneficial.

> "I'm a fan of peer grading in machine learning course because it let me see how other students approach the same problem and reinforces my understanding when I evaluate their solutions." || "I like it when someone points something out, because I can learn from their perspective."

**P2. Skill Development Benefits:** Students also perceived peer grading as beneficial for developing broader academic and professional skills. These included critical thinking, communication, reviewing ability, presentation, writing, and evaluative skills that extend beyond a single course. Lladó et al. [26] and Joh and Plakans [16] reported that students developed critical thinking and evaluative skills through participation in peer grading tasks. Some studies also showed that peer grading helped students improve their presentation skills through peer feedback [14,32]. In the Reddit discussions, one student mentioned that peer grading helped them learn how to critique others' work.

> "I guess the one good thing that comes out of this is you get the perspective of other people that are not your Prof or TAs, and it also helps people learn how to critique other people's writing."

**P3. Engagement, Motivation, and Participation:** Peer grading was often seen as increasing students' involvement in the learning process. It encouraged them to participate more actively, pay closer attention to the work, and feel more motivated and engaged in the course. For example, Callahan [7] reported that students perceived peer assessment as increasing their interest, participation, confidence, and desire to learn science. Ghosh and Skipper [12] reported that students became more involved in learning because they actively participated in the assessment process. One Reddit comment suggested that peer grading increased engagement and participation, as students appreciated peer-graded exercises in the course.

> "I appreciate Coursera more for the peer-graded exercises, peer grading, and quizzes. Since some Google Cloud classes are available elsewhere without these exercises or certificates, I find them more valuable on Coursera."

**P4. Timeliness and Turnaround Benefits:** Another commonly reported benefit of peer grading was the speed of the process. Storjohann et al. [38] reported that, among students, timely feedback on assignment performance was the second most frequently mentioned positive aspect, after faculty review of the rubric. Similarly, Callahan [7] reported that students perceived peer assessment as providing immediate feedback and a quick measure of their progress.

**P5. Fairness, Trust, and Validity:** Some students expressed confidence in peer grading as a fair and credible evaluation method, although this often depended on how the process was designed. For example, Carvalho [8] reported that although a substantial minority of students perceived peer assessment results as unfair, the majority of students (58.18%) perceived the peer-assessment results as fair. Kumar et al. [22] found that students perceived anonymous online peer assessment as fair and valid, suggesting that anonymity can support students' trust in peer grading. At the same time, the Reddit data suggest that students also viewed peer grading as generally fair and trustworthy in practice.

> "If you keep getting low grades from your peers, you should not just blame peer assessment but also reflect on your own work." || "If your work is good, you will probably receive good grades in most assignments, since it is graded by multiple people rather than just one."

**P6. Social and Collaborative Benefits:** Students also valued peer grading for its social dimension. Many studies reported that it promoted interaction, discussion, collaboration, and shared learning, helping students feel more connected to their peers and the broader learning community [18,25]. Callahan [7] noted that peer grading encouraged collaboration, a sense of responsibility, and greater engagement with classmates. Similar reflections also appeared in the Reddit discussions, where students described peer review as a more relaxed and socially engaging experience and appreciated the opportunity to see others' work.

> "I kind of enjoyed the peer review. Less stressful, and you can leave your peers little notes like 'good luck on the midterm'." || "In project-based classes like Ed Tech, it's fascinating to see what others are doing and how."

**Table 2.** Distribution of positive aspects across literature and Reddit data. Values are shown as $n$ (%). Percentages are calculated against the number of literature papers ($n$=107) and Reddit items ($n$=414).

| Source | P1 | P2 | P3 | P4 | P5 | P6 |
|---|---|---|---|---|---|---|
| Literature | 89 (83.2) | 85 (79.4) | 74 (69.2) | 10 (9.3) | 35 (32.7) | 62 (57.9) |
| Reddit Items | 22 (5.3) | 6 (1.4) | 2 (0.5) | 0 (0.0) | 63 (15.2) | 6 (1.4) |

Table 2 shows that positive perceptions were distributed differently across the literature and Reddit data. In the literature, the most frequently reported benefits were learning and understanding benefits (P1, 83.2%), skill development benefits (P2, 79.4%), engagement and motivation (P3, 69.2%), and social and collaborative benefits (P6, 57.9%). In contrast, Reddit items mentioned fairness, trust, and validity (P5, 15.2%) more often than the other positive themes, followed by learning and understanding benefits (P1, 5.3%). Timeliness and turnaround benefits (P4) did not appear in the Reddit data. Overall, the literature emphasized the learning and collaborative value of peer grading more strongly, whereas Reddit discussions contained relatively fewer positive themes and focused more on fairness and validity.

### 3.2 RQ2: Negative Perceptions of Peer Grading

For RQ2, we identified seven common negative perception patterns across the literature and Reddit data, summarized below:

**N1. Accuracy and Reliability Concerns:** One of the most common concerns students expressed about peer grading was related to accuracy and reliability. Students often reported that peer-assigned grades were inaccurate, inconsistent across reviewers, sometimes arbitrary, and less reliable than instructor grading. Several studies also noted tendencies toward over-marking or under-marking, as well as concerns that peer evaluations did not reflect staff-level judgment. For example, Verkade and Bryson-Richardson [42] reported that peer grading was limited by grade inflation, reluctance to assign low marks, and inconsistent evaluation. Hammer et al. [15] also reported a lack of grading uniformity, while Kingsley [20] found that peer grading suffered from low reliability, leniency bias, and lack of expertise. Toll and Wingkvist [40] likewise noted that the strongest concerns were incorrect feedback and incorrect scores from peers, with 27% of students reporting incorrect feedback and 31% reporting incorrect scores. On Reddit, several students echoed the same problem.

> "I got my written assignment back: one grader gave 90/90, another 17/90, and another 72/90. Did they even read the same paper?" || "I honestly think some people do not even read the assignment and just grade it randomly."

A more recent concern about accuracy raised by students was the use of automated tools, particularly ChatGPT, in the grading process. While such tools may introduce some level of consistency, students perceived them as unreliable or inappropriate for evaluating peer work.

> "Now peers run essays through ChatGPT, which gives a solid 9 or 10 essay a 7 just because it does not cover everything that could fit in 5000 words, even though the limit was only 500." || "Two peers graded my written assignment and both gave it 6/10. I have never seen such consistent grading. One of the comments even started with 'The author'."

**N2. Fairness and Impartiality Concerns:** Students also expressed concerns about the fairness of peer grading frequently. Students reported issues such as unfair grading driven by personal bias, friendship-based marking, bias stemming from personal relationships or conflicts, and intentional low scoring driven by competitiveness. Carvalho [8] found that about 30% of students belonged to a negative-experience group that viewed peer grades as unfair, often because of friendship marking and conflict. These concerns have also been echoed in several other studies [20,42]. In Reddit discussions, students also described unfair grading behaviors such as retaliation, collusion, and strategic grading.

> "I got three peer grades: a 5, a 4, and a 1. The 1 came from someone I had been arguing with" || "If the grades I give others affect my own GPA, why should I not just give everyone 10/10? Every little thing counts, and it feels fair game."

**N3. Insufficient Assessor Preparedness:** Another major concern was the limited preparedness and expertise of peer assessors. Students often felt that their peers lacked the subject knowledge, experience, confidence, and rubric understanding needed to provide accurate and consistent evaluations. They also reported difficulty judging certain criteria and assigning appropriate numerical grades. Bauer et al. [3] reported that students found some review criteria, particularly sources and content, difficult to assess. Seneviratne et al. [35] found that 34.88% of student assessors reported that they did not feel they had the skills and knowledge needed to assess their peers. Other studies also reported low confidence in both students' own and their peers' ability to assess work accurately [43]. Similar concerns were also reflected in Reddit discussions, where students questioned the competence and preparedness of peer graders. Many described peers as unqualified, lacking understanding of the rubric, or unable to provide meaningful evaluation.

"Because who would want their grades decided by a random group of peers with the expertise of a potato?" || "Instead, it just seems to give unqualified, wannabe tyrants a platform to jeopardize other students' standing." || "I think the university should intervene more, since unqualified individuals often are not even familiar with the grading rubric."

**N4. Poor Feedback Quality and Weak Learning Benefits:** Unlike the previous three concerns, which were mainly tied to the summative aspect of peer grading, this concern centered on its formative value and learning benefits. Students often described peer feedback as unclear, minimal, vague, contradictory, or insufficient to support improvement. Bratkovich [6] found that student feedback was more surface-level than teacher feedback, focusing more on language issues than elaboration and idea development. Kobayashi [21] similarly found that overly nice and noncritical feedback reduced its usefulness. Other studies also reported incorrect feedback from peers [40], as well as feedback that was insufficiently constructive [38]. Kay [19] further reported that, although overall perceptions of peer grading were positive, 30.82% of students disagreed that it supported their learning. In Reddit discussions, some students also mentioned the same issues.

"Peer grades often feel harsh and give me little useful feedback beyond something like 'see solutions'." || "I dislike peer-graded homework because the feedback is often unhelpful and sometimes wrong." || "I once got comments like 'great job' but still received a bad grade. I am less upset about the marks than about not getting enough feedback to improve."

**N5. Low Motivation and Engagement:** Students sometimes reported low motivation toward peer grading tasks. Common concerns included limited interest in reading others' work, spending little time on reviews, not taking the task seriously, and reducing effort because easy marks were expected regardless of review quality. Toll and Wingkvist [40] identified time and effort as contributors to low motivation in peer review. Joh and Plakans [16] reported that negative or harsh peer feedback can cause stress and lower motivation among some students. Similar patterns also appeared in Reddit discussions, where students described rushing through required reviews, assigning full marks just to finish quickly, and losing interest when peers seemed not to read submissions carefully.

"Even though peer reviews are supposed to be taken seriously, I usually give everyone full marks because people already have enough going on, and it is not life or death." || "The number of people who were not even reading my papers was insane. They turned peer grading into a joke."

Reddit discussions also suggested that the visible misuse of AI in peer submissions could further demotivate students. When students noticed signs of AI-generated work, they sometimes felt less willing to engage seriously with the review process and preferred to avoid reviewing such submissions altogether.

> "I saw 'Copy code Python' in one post and a chatbot prompt in another. If I have a choice, I do not grade such assignments and instead review posts written by people who actually did the work."

**N6. Emotional and Interpersonal Burden:** Students often reported emotional stress related to peer grading. Common concerns included fear of losing face in front of peers, anxiety about receiving incorrect or unfair evaluations, anxiety about assigning low grades to peers, discomfort being assessed by people they knew, and feeling discouraged or upset by harsh feedback. Deslandes and Hughes [10] found that although most students valued peer marking, some felt uncomfortable when they knew the peer markers or when multiple markers were present. Hammer et al. [15] reported increased anxiety caused by competition and strategic grading. Seneviratne et al. [35] found that 38.36% of student assessors were reluctant to give low marks, and 22.08% reported difficulty separating personal feelings from peer evaluation. Kobayashi [21] similarly found that students were reluctant to criticize their peers honestly. Stancic et al. [37] further noted that students were concerned about the effect of peer grading on personal relationships. Similar concerns emerged in Reddit discussions, where students described the emotional and interpersonal burden of peer grading, including guilt, anxiety, embarrassment, and fear of social backlash.

> "Peer grading is not too bad, but I still feel bad when I give someone a lower grade than they deserve because of a brain fart." || "As a socially anxious person, I would worry about getting nasty comments on my project." || "I was terrible at math as a child, and it felt embarrassing and shameful to have my peers see that firsthand." || "There is a burden in being seen as the negative one or constant complainer, even when the criticism is productive."

**N7. Workload, Time, and Coordination Challenges:** Students also reported workload- and time-related challenges in the peer grading process. Common concerns included the high burden of reviewing multiple peers, limited time to provide thoughtful feedback, difficulty coordinating with others during the process, and the overall effort required to complete peer reviews. Siow et al. [36] reported that 43% of students found the peer grading process time-consuming. Similarly, Badea and Popescu [2] found that students viewed peer grading as time-intensive and noted that using it across many subjects would create a burden. Toll and Wingkvist [40] also reported that some students viewed peer grading as time-consuming, which may have contributed to lower motivation toward reviewing peers' reports. Deslandes and Hughes [10] further noted that students experienced time pressure when providing feedback, while some students in KÃďpylÃď and Palvalin's study [18] described giving feedback as laborious and difficult.

Table 3 shows that negative perceptions were prominent in both the literature and Reddit data, but with different distributions. In the literature, the most frequently reported concerns were accuracy and reliability (N1, 46.7%), emotional and interpersonal burden (N6, 42.1%), fairness and impartiality (N2, 32.7%), and insufficient assessor preparedness (N3, 32.7%). In contrast, Reddit

**Table 3.** Distribution of negative aspects across literature and Reddit data. Values are $n$ (%), with percentages calculated against literature papers ($n$=107) and Reddit items ($n$=414).

| Source | N1 | N2 | N3 | N4 | N5 | N6 | N7 |
|---|---|---|---|---|---|---|---|
| Literature | 50 (46.7) | 35 (32.7) | 35 (32.7) | 31 (29.0) | 10 (9.3) | 45 (42.1) | 29 (27.1) |
| Reddit Items | 239 (57.7) | 94 (22.7) | 58 (14.0) | 71 (17.1) | 30 (7.2) | 19 (4.6) | 18 (4.3) |

items were most strongly associated with accuracy and reliability concerns (N1, 57.7%), followed by fairness and impartiality concerns (N2, 22.7%), poor feedback quality and weak learning benefits (N4, 17.1%), and insufficient assessor preparedness (N3, 14.0%). This pattern suggests that the literature reflects a broader spread of negative themes, whereas Reddit discussions are more concentrated on accuracy and reliability concerns.

### 3.3 RQ3: Mitigation Strategies

Although students reported several negative perceptions of peer grading, the literature also identified strategies to address them. In our analysis, we identified eight recurring mitigation strategies, described below.

**M1. Training and Preparation:** Training and preparing students before peer grading can help address several common problems. This preparation may include practice grading with example papers or calibration tasks, repeated activities to build comfort, orientation on how to give good feedback and apply grading criteria, brief verbal explanations of the system, online tutorials on providing effective peer feedback, and explicit staff discussions about the value of feedback. Gudiño et al. [14] reported greater confidence in peer grading and less relationship-based influence after preparation and practice. Similarly, Sadeghi and Khonbi [34] noted that training and practice can improve reliability and validity and foster more positive student attitudes toward peer grading.

**M2. Rubrics and Structured Grading:** Using clear grading guides instead of open-ended scales can help reduce peer-grading problems. Helpful approaches include detailed rubrics with explicit criteria and performance levels, structured scoring guides such as checklists, and clear instructor-defined review criteria. Berrezueta-Guzman et al. [4] described a rubric-based, anonymized peer-review process in which students often linked fairness to consistent rubric use. de Raadt et al. [33] similarly argued that clear, objective, task-completion-focused criteria could reduce ambiguity and improve consistency among peer reviewers.

**M3. Anonymity and Blind Review:** Concerns about fairness, social discomfort, and anxiety can be reduced through anonymous peer grading. Depending on the context and purpose, anonymity may be implemented through either single-blind or double-blind review. Kobayashi [21] found that anonymity helped reduce students' anxiety and fear of hurting peers' feelings. Venables and Summit [41] also used blind review and argued that anonymity was important for fairness in peer grading. Similarly, Vo and Nguyen [43] suggested that anonymity can reduce friendship-based bias and improve validity and reliability, while Biton [5] argued that it can encourage more honest and objective feedback.

**M4. Assessment by Multiple Reviewers:** Because peer grading can be affected by inaccuracy and bias, involving multiple reviewers and combining their scores can improve the accuracy of final grades. This can be done through simple averaging, filtering out noisy ratings, or more advanced aggregation methods [30]. Landry et al. [24] noted that although peer grading may be inconsistent at the individual level, it can still support learning and produce reasonably accurate results when multiple reviewers are involved. Verkade and Bryson-Richardson [42] showed that averaging marks from many peers brought peer scores closer to academic marks, reducing individual rater noise and improving accuracy.

**M5. Instructor Oversight and Moderation:** Instructor oversight and moderation can help address many peer-grading problems. Helpful approaches include identifying unfair or unreliable reviews, intervening in grading disputes, monitoring the review process, conducting discussion sessions, providing on-demand support, and combining peer and instructor evaluations. de Raadt et al. [33] introduced instructor moderation when peer reviews conflicted or appeared inaccurate. It helped improve the validity and fairness of final marks. Storjohann et al. [38] found that faculty-led review and reflection sessions supported fairer scoring and helped students grade their peers' work more effectively. Toll and Wingkvist [40] included teacher intervention within a tool-supported peer review process to manage disputes, and reported that students experienced fewer problems with incorrect feedback and scoring than they had expected.

**M6. Incentives and Accountability:** Incentives and accountability can help reduce problems such as low motivation and poor-quality feedback. Useful strategies include rewarding participation, recognizing high-quality feedback, and giving marks for the quality of peer grading. Toll and Wingkvist [40] suggested that grading reviews and allowing students to rate the feedback they received helped motivate better reviews. It also reduced concerns about incorrect feedback. Gillanders et al. [13] used a loss-aversion incentive. Students could lose a small number of marks if they did not assess a peer's work accurately. This increased engagement and supported critical thinking during peer grading.

**M7. Time and Workload Management:** Good time and workload management can help reduce several peer-grading problems, including poor feedback quality and workload-related stress during the process. Helpful strategies include giving students enough time to review, limiting the number of assigned reviews, and reducing workload through careful design of assessment criteria. Wang et al. [44] reported that time constraints shaped students' attitudes toward online peer grading and recommended allowing more time for review. Peng [32] similarly argued that using fewer assessment criteria can make peer grading more manageable for students by reducing confusion and time demands.

**M8. Technology and Tool Support:** Technology and tool support can help address some peer-grading problems and improve the overall experience. Lai and Lan [23] showed that a computer-supported agent-negotiation system reduced personal bias, subjective judgment, and unfair grading. It also improved flexibility and equity in the process. Toll and Wingkvist [40] similarly reported that, within a tool-supported peer-review process, students experienced fewer problems with incorrect scores and feedback than they had expected, and their overall attitudes toward peer review improved. Sullivan and Watson [39] further found that LMS-based peer grading made the process more practical and easier to manage in hybrid and online courses. Several studies also highlighted the role of technology in speeding up feedback and grade return. For example, Chen [9] found that the mobile peer-assessment system improved portability, time efficiency, and access to immediate feedback, while Li et al. [25] reported that their web-based systems enabled more timely feedback for students.

**Table 4. Negative perceptions and mitigation strategies.** A checkmark indicates that the strategy was suggested in at least one study for that perception.

| | M1 | M2 | M3 | M4 | M5 | M6 | M7 | M8 |
|---|---|---|---|---|---|---|---|---|
| **N1** | ✓ | ✓ | ✓ | ✓ | ✓ | – | – | ✓ |
| **N2** | ✓ | ✓ | ✓ | ✓ | ✓ | – | – | ✓ |
| **N3** | ✓ | ✓ | – | – | ✓ | – | – | – |
| **N4** | ✓ | ✓ | – | ✓ | ✓ | ✓ | ✓ | ✓ |
| **N5** | ✓ | – | – | – | ✓ | ✓ | – | – |
| **N6** | ✓ | ✓ | ✓ | ✓ | ✓ | – | – | – |
| **N7** | ✓ | – | – | – | ✓ | – | ✓ | ✓ |

Table 4 shows that M1 (training and preparation) and M5 (instructor oversight and moderation) are the most central strategies, as they address all seven negative perceptions. This suggests that students are more likely to accept peer grading when they are properly prepared and when instructors remain involved in monitoring and moderating the process. The table also shows that N1 (accuracy and reliability concerns), N2 (fairness and impartiality concerns), N4 (poor feedback quality and weak learning benefits), and N6 (emotional and interpersonal burden) are linked to a wide range of strategies, suggesting that these concerns are more complex and often require multiple forms of support. By contrast, N3 (insufficient assessor preparedness) and N5 (low motivation and engagement) are associated with only a few strategies. Among the more targeted strategies, M2 (rubrics, criteria, and structured grading) helps reduce ambiguity, M3 (anonymity and blind review) helps reduce social pressure and bias, M4 (assessment by multiple reviewers) improves robustness, M6 (incentives and accountability) encourages engagement, M7 (time and workload management) makes the process more manageable and M8 (technology and tool support) addresses concerns related to accuracy, fairness, feedback quality, and workload.

## 4 Discussion

Our findings show that students perceive peer grading as both beneficial and problematic. They often associate it with learning, skill development, collaboration, engagement, and sometimes faster feedback. At the same time, they repeatedly raised concerns about accuracy, fairness, assessor preparedness, feedback quality, emotional burden, and workload. Overall, students seem to judge peer grading less as an abstract idea and more by whether its implementation feels useful, fair, and trustworthy. Trust appears central to student acceptance. Although peer grading can support learning and collaboration, many students seem to evaluate it first through fairness, validity, and reliability. When trust is weak, its assessment role appears to overshadow its learning value.

A notable pattern is the contrast between the literature and Reddit discussions. The literature presents a more balanced picture, with both positive and negative perceptions appearing regularly, whereas Reddit discussions were much more dominated by negative experiences. This likely reflects the difference between structured classroom settings reported in research and informal online spaces where students are likely to voice frustration. Although Reddit does not fully represent classroom reality, it still highlights the problems students find most memorable and worth expressing.

The mitigation analysis shows that many common concerns are avoidable. They can often be reduced through careful design choices such as training, rubrics, anonymity, multiple reviewers, instructor moderation, incentives, workload management, and technology support. Among these, M5 (instructor oversight and moderation) and M1 (training and preparation) appear to be the most central because they address all seven major negative perceptions. This shows that the success of peer grading depends less on peer involvement and more on how well the process is designed and supervised.

The findings also point to an emerging concern related to AI use in peer grading. Reddit discussions suggest that some students suspect peers of relying on tools such as ChatGPT to evaluate work or generate feedback. Rather than improving the process, this appeared to deepen concerns about inaccuracy, generic comments, and lack of genuine engagement. This suggests that while technology may support coordination and efficiency, it may also create new trust issues when students feel that human judgment is being replaced.

The literature review was limited to English-language studies published between 2003 and 2025, while the Reddit analysis relied on keyword-based retrieval from public discussions. As a result, some relevant perspectives may have been missed. In addition, perceptions were drawn from both formal studies and informal online discussions, which may differ in context and style. Moreover, Reddit offers only a complementary, not fully representative, view of classroom reality.

## 5 Conclusion

This study provides a mixed-source view of students' perceptions of peer grading by combining evidence from literature and Reddit discussions. The findings show that peer grading can support learning, skill development, and collaboration, but students also report important concerns about fairness, reliability, feedback quality, and assessor preparedness. Overall, the results suggest that peer grading is most positively received when students are adequately trained, the process is clearly structured, and instructors remain actively involved.

## References


1. Ayachi, Z.: Peer and teacher assessment in EFL writing compositions: the case of advanced English major students in Jendouba, Tunisia. Reading Matrix Int. Online J. **17**(1), 156–168 (2017)
2. Badea, G., Popescu, E.: Applying peer assessment in a human-computer interaction course following a project-based learning approach. In: ITHET 2024, pp. 1–6 (2024)
3. Bauer, C., Figl, K., Derntl, M., Beran, P.P., Kabicher, S.: The student view on online peer reviews. In: ITiCSE '09, pp. 26–30 (2009)
4. Berrezueta-Guzman, S., Krusche, S., Wagner, S.: From coders to critics: empowering students through peer assessment in the age of AI copilots. In: ISET 2025, pp. 66–71 (2025)
5. Biton, Y.: Student reflections on peer assessments: benefits and challenges in a mathematics class. Educ. Process Int. J. **14** (2025)
6. Bratkovich, M.O.: Assessment and feedback: examining the relationship between self-assessment and blind peer- and teacher-assessment in TOEFL writing. Work. Pap. TESOL Appl. Linguistics **14**(2), 100–127 (2014)
7. Callahan, E.: Effects of peer assessment on attitude toward science in high school students. Ed.D. dissertation, Walden University (2007)
8. Carvalho, A.: Students' perceptions of fairness in peer assessment: evidence from a problem-based learning course. Teach. High. Educ. **18**(5), 491–505 (2013)
9. Chen, C.H.: The implementation and evaluation of a mobile self- and peer-assessment system. Comput. Educ. **55**(1), 229–236 (2010)
10. Deslandes, R., Hughes, L.: Peer marking of OSCEs within a UK pharmacy undergraduate programme - student views. Pharm. Educ. **21**(1), 73–82 (2021)
11. Double, K.S., McGrane, J.A., Hopfenbeck, T.N.: The impact of peer assessment on academic performance: a meta-analysis of control group studies. Educ. Psychol. Rev. **32**(2), 481–509 (2020)
12. Ghosh, A., Skipper, J.: Enhancing learning through post-exam review: a case study on collaborative coding assessments. In: SoutheastCon 2024, pp. 367–373 (2024)
13. Gillanders, R., Karazi, S., O'Riordan, F.: Loss aversion as a motivator for engagement with peer assessment. Innov. Educ. Teach. Int. **57**(4), 424–433 (2020)
14. Gudiño, D., Fernández-Sánchez, M.J., Becerra-Traver, M.T., Sánchez-Herrera, S.: University students' perceptions of peer assessment in oral presentations. Educ. Sci. **14**(3) (2024)
15. Hammer, R., Ronen, M., Kohen-Vacs, D.: Stressed yet motivated: web-based peer assessed competition as an instructional approach in higher education. In: ICLS 2010, vol. 1, pp. 65–72 (2010)

16. Joh, J., Plakans, L.: Peer assessment in EFL teacher preparation: a longitudinal study of student perception. Lang. Teach. Res. **29**(1), 338–362 (2025)
17. Jones, G.: Web 2.0 practices for peer assessment processes: exploring the synergies and tensions. In: ECEL 2010, pp. 274–283 (2010)
18. Käpylä, J., Palvalin, M.: Integrating peer assessment into experiential learning: the validity and learning benefits of peer assessment in reading circle discussions. Assess. Eval. High. Educ. **50**(8), 1253–1276 (2025)
19. Kay, J.S.: Peer grading without protest: the SPARK approach to summative peer assessment. In: SIGCSE '22, pp. 119–125 (2022)
20. Kingsley, B.: But I'm no expert! Peer assessment by first-year psychology undergraduates. Psychol. Learn. Teach. **9**(1), 7–15 (2010)
21. Kobayashi, M.: Does anonymity matter? examining quality of online peer assessment and students' attitudes. Australas. J. Educ. Technol. **36**(1), 98–110 (2020)
22. Kumar, K., Sharma, B.N., Nusair, S., Khan, G.J.: Anonymous online peer assessment in an undergraduate course: an analysis of students' perceptions and attitudes in the South Pacific. In: IEEE TALE 2019, pp. 1–8 (2019)
23. Lai, K.R., Lan, C.H.: Modeling peer assessment as agent negotiation in a computer supported collaborative learning environment. Educ. Technol. Soc. **9**(3), 16–26 (2006)
24. Landry, A., Jacobs, S., Newton, G.: Effective use of peer assessment in a graduate level writing assignment: a case study. Int. J. High. Educ. **4**(1), 38–51 (2015)
25. Li, L., Steckelberg, A.L., Srinivasan, S.: Utilizing peer interactions to promote learning through a web-based peer assessment system. Can. J. Learn. Technol. **34**(2) (2008)
26. Lladó, A.P., et al.: Student perceptions of peer assessment: an interdisciplinary study. Assess. Eval. High. Educ. **39**(5), 592–610 (2014)
27. Lundstrom, K., Baker, W.: To give is better than to receive: the benefits of peer review to the reviewer's own writing. J. Second. Lang. Writ. **18**(1), 30–43 (2009)
28. Machanick, P.: Peer assessment for action learning of data structures and algorithms. In: ACE 2005, pp. 73–82 (2005)
29. Page, M.J., McKenzie, J.E.: Declaración PRISMA 2020: una guía actualizada para la publicación de revisiones sistemáticas. Rev. Esp. Cardiol. **74**(9), 790–799 (2021)
30. Paul, U., et al.: Scaling success: a systematic review of peer grading strategies for accuracy, efficiency, and learning in contemporary education. In: IEEE FIE 2025, pp. 1–9 (2025)
31. Paul, U., Shah, S., Mylavarapu, S.V., Rashid, M.P., Gehringer, E.: Optimizing peer grading: a systematic literature review of reviewer assignment strategies and quantity of reviewers. In: MIS4TEL 2025 Workshops, pp. 328–340. Springer Nature Switzerland, Cham (2026)
32. Peng, J.C.F.: Peer Assessment of Oral Presentation in an EFL Context. Ph.D. thesis, Indiana University (2009). order No. 3380148
33. de Raadt, M., Lai, D., Watson, R.: An evaluation of electronic individual peer assessment in an introductory programming course. In: Koli Calling 2007, pp. 53–64 (2007)
34. Sadeghi, K., Abolfazli Khonbi, Z.: Iranian university students' experiences of and attitudes towards alternatives in assessment. Assess. Eval. High. Educ. **40**(5), 641–665 (2015)
35. Seneviratne, T., Edirisingha, W., Palpola, W.: Using peer assessment in teaching pharmacology for medical undergraduates. Asia Pacific Scholar **10**(3), 10–14 (2025)
36. Siow, L.F.: Students' perceptions on self- and peer-assessment in enhancing learning experience. Malaysian Online J. Educ. Sci. **3**(2), 21–35 (2015)

37. Stancic, M.: Peer assessment as a learning and self-assessment tool: a look inside the black box. Assess. Eval. High. Educ. **46**(6), 852–864 (2021)
38. Storjohann, T., Pogge, E., Peckham, A., Raney, E., Barletta, J.F.: Evaluation of a peer- and self-grading process for clinical writing assignments. Curr. Pharm. Teach. Learn. **11**(10), 979–986 (2019)
39. Sullivan, D., Watson, S.: Peer assessment within hybrid and online courses: students' view of its potential and performance. J. Educ. Iss. **1**(1), 1–18 (2015)
40. Toll, D., Wingkvist, A.: How tool support and peer scoring improved our students' attitudes toward peer reviews. In: ITiCSE '17, pp. 311–316 (2017)
41. Venables, A., Summit, R.: Enhancing scientific essay writing using peer assessment. Innov. Educ. Teach. Int. **40**(3) (2003)
42. Verkade, H., Bryson-Richardson, R.J.: Student acceptance and application of peer assessment in a final year genetics undergraduate oral presentation. J. Peer Learn. **6**, 1–18 (2013)
43. Vo, T.K.A., Nguyen, N.H.: Students' perceptions towards the application of peer assessment in a virtual English writing class. J. Univ. Teach. Learn. Practice **20**(2) (2023)
44. Wang, J.D., Gao, R.Q., Guo, X.Y., Liu, J.: Factors associated with students' attitude change in online peer assessment - a mixed methods study in a graduate-level course. Assess. Eval. High. Educ. **45**(5), 714–727 (2020)

# Profiling Cognitive Offloading in LLM-Mediated Synthesis Writing: Volume vs. Content

Oleksandra Poquet[1,2](✉), Mani Shankar Nanduri[1], Maria Ximena Salinas Loyer[1], Matthias Stadler[3], Michael Sailer[4], and Jelena Jovanovic[5,6]

[1] Technical University of Munich, Munich, Germany
{sasha.poquet,mani.nanduri,ximena.salinas}@tum.de
[2] C3L, Adelaide University, Adelaide, Australia
[3] LMU University Hospital, Munich, Germany
matthias.stadler@umed.uni-muenchen.de
[4] University of Augsburg, Augsburg, Germany
michael.sailer@uni-a.de
[5] University of Belgrade, Belgrade, Serbia
jelena.jovanovic@fon.bg.ac.rs
[6] SLATE, University of Bergen, Bergen, Norway

**Abstract.** This study compares two approaches to profiling how learners offload cognitive activity to LLMs during a synthesis writing task. Drawing on Salomon's distributed cognition and the Kintsch and van Dijk model of text comprehension, the study operationalises offloading to an LLM in two ways: as a volume of LLM use and as content of what is offloaded, both along with prior knowledge. Data from 97 university students using a ChatGPT-based interface were analysed using k-means clustering. To capture the content of offloading, their prompts were interpreted as to who performs the activity (active/passive) and at what level of comprehension (local/global). Volume-based profiling (k=4) differentiated learners primarily by prior knowledge, with volume negatively associated with essay authorship. Content-based profiling (k=5) revealed qualitatively distinct patterns of offloading, from vocabulary clarification to active direction of structuring and generation to passive delegation of comprehension at both levels. These patterns reflect different fragmentation of the cognitive process, with significant differences in learning strategies, behavioural markers, and essay authorship. Combining volume and content of offloading could improve future analyses on how LLM use redistributes cognitive activity and its effects on learners.

**Keywords:** LLM-mediated writing · offloading · distributed cognition


J. Weidlich et al. (Eds.): EC-TEL 2026, LNCS 16905, pp. 499–514, 2027.
https://doi.org/10.1007/978-3-032-37979-5_34

## 1 Introduction

Using large language models (LLMs) in education has a range of ethical, environmental, and privacy implications. When LLMs are used as general-purpose chatbot interfaces without pedagogical restrictions, their effects on human learning are yet to be understood. Identifying and evaluating these effects is a challenge that requires, first, comprehensively describing LLM use through existing theories about learning and cognition, in ways that reflect the novelty of the phenomenon. Motivated by these considerations, this paper analyses the process of LLM use in a learning task in ways that may explain its effects on learners.

Our starting point is that learner use of LLMs changes individual cognitive processes. This change is enabled by cognitive offloading, i.e. the physical alteration of the information processing requirements of a task to reduce cognitive demand [20]. Humans offload cognitively from an early age [1] using body gestures [8], writing [19], other people [29], and automated tools [18]. Due to this natural propensity, offloading has been well studied. Research predating LLMs established that offloading can impair memory [26] and inflate estimates of what has been retained as own knowledge [6]. Unsurprisingly, similar effects have been corroborated in the studies on LLM use for learning [2,27].

To guide learner use of LLMs, researchers need to further understand offloading *processes*. Evidence from non-LLM contexts suggests that how offloading processes should be represented is not straightforward. On the one hand, studies in non-LLM contexts show that the *volume* of external tool use affects performance [9] and memory [26]. On the other hand, studies *also* show that the same volume of offloading can affect what is remembered in different ways, as different mechanisms may be activated [15]. The use of learning strategies when offloading in non-LLM contexts also has differentiated effects, further suggesting that differences in how something is offloaded are important [4]. It is unclear if these two perspectives on offloading reflect different or redundant information, if *any* use of an LLM or a *particular* use of an LLM is meaningful to capture.

LLM-focused research analysed both volume of offloading and how learners offload, without directly comparing them. Some studies equate *any* use of the LLMs as indicative of their effect on learning, contrasting LLM use vs no LLM use [2,27]. Others characterise the processes of LLM with varied approaches: mapping LLM prompts to the levels in Bloom's taxonomy [7], examining whether learners modify AI output [30], or inferring learning and meta-cognitive strategies from prompt content [5,25]. No study, as far as we are aware, compared both volume and content of offloading to LLMs, leaving a gap as to how offloading processes are best captured.

Such a comparison is complicated by a theoretical challenge. Existing theories were not designed for tools that afford the range and flexibility of offloading that LLMs enable. Hence, it is unclear how learner-LLM use should be approached analytically. Cognitive load theory (CLT) offers a well-grounded account explaining how types of cognitive load can affect learning [28], also in technology-mediated settings [17]. CLT focuses on why a task is cognitively demanding and how to reduce the load through instructional media and tasks, but is less concerned with *how* cognitive activity gets distributed. This limits its utility to describe the process of offloading. Distributed cognition perspectives, on the other hand, are largely socio-cultural. They focus on how cognitive activity gets distributed across people and artefacts [23], but pay little attention to individual cognition. This limits their utility in explaining what happens to the individual when offloading takes place. In this paper, we explore a bridging alternative: a dynamic interactionist view that posits that distributed cognition, individual cognition, and the activity that affords the distribution of a cognitive process [22] should all be considered when analysing distributed cognition systems.

Guided by this bridging perspective, we compare insights from examining learner use of LLMs in a synthesis writing task through the volume of offloading vs the content of offloading, while considering individual cognition. Using k-means clustering we profile offloading processes: (1) as number of LLM prompts combined with prior knowledge versus (2) as the content of each prompt, reflecting who performs the cognitive work and at what level of comprehension, combined with prior knowledge. Data for the analysis were collected via a lab-based experiment where 97 university students engaged in a task using a custom-made interface for writing and prompting a general purpose LLM. Profiles identified through each clustering approach were interpreted by comparing learning strategies represented by the prompts, self-reports of learner experience, and behavioural and linguistic markers. The results show that profiling on both volume and content of offloading captures relevant information, suggesting the need to combine them for profiling offloading processes.

## 2 Conceptualising Learner-LLM Use

To profile offloading during learner use of LLMs, we conceptualise the relationship between learner, LLM, and an AI-mediated activity, drawing on Salomon's ideas about distributed cognition [22]. Salomon opposed his contemporaries who privileged socio-cultural contexts when describing how activity gets distributed across tools and among individuals. He argued that the question of where cognition resides "cannot be dealt with in an either (in one's head)/or (distributed) fashion" (p. 111, *ibid.*). His conceptualisation contains three elements of a distributed cognitive system: (1) individual cognition, (2) the activity that affords distribution, and (3) the distribution of the cognitive process between a learner and a tool. This conceptualisation allows to capture a learner-LLM system.

First, individual cognition in a learner-LLM system can be considered before and after distributed cognition takes place. A learner enters an activity that can be mediated by an LLM with individual differences that affect their information processing. Then, distributing activity leaves 'cognitive residue'. Salomon proposes that the distribution in the form of the 'division of labour' would lead to helping less skilled individuals access new activities but reduce further development of "the crucial cognitions so off-loaded" (p. 133, *ibid*). Or, the distribution can take a form of a 'shared activity' that may have a more positive effect on learner competency. In the study, we approach learner prior knowledge as a means to represent what an individual brings into the cognitive process.

Second, the activity that affords the learner to distribute cognition to an LLM needs to be further specified. We propose to treat comprehension as this activity. Comprehension underpins many tasks (writing, programming, problem solving), requires different learning strategies (selection, organisation, and generation of information), and provides a coarse-grained layer applicable to various situations. In our study, learners had to read two texts to integrate them and write an essay, which is an activity that involves meaning making at the level of each text and across them, further externalised through written text. To describe how this activity affords distribution, we draw on the model for text comprehension and production by Kintsch and van Dijk [13]. Their model explains meaning making at two levels: the micro-structure, where readers resolve local propositions and establish coherence between adjacent sentences, and the macro-structure, where readers construct global meaning through deletion, generalisation, and construction of new propositions across micro-structures. Comprehension can therefore be distributed at either of these levels.

Finally, the distribution can take different forms depending on the learner's role in the cognitive activity, here at each level of comprehension. The learner may actively participate in some parts of the cognitive activity, for instance, providing their own reasoning while requesting the LLM to elaborate or check it. Such offloaded activity would be shared (i.e. joint), given that the learner maintains parts of the cognitive effort. Alternatively, the learner may be passive, fully removing comprehension activity from their individual cognition, dividing the work rather than sharing it. Introducing the learner's role into the cognitive activity enables capturing Salomon's distinction between shared activity and division of labour. Thus, combining the level of comprehension (micro or macro) with the role of the learner (active or passive) could describe the content of the distributed cognitive process.

## 3 Research Question

The above conceptualisation lends itself to characterising the distributed cognitive process in two distinct ways. As noted earlier, experimental empirical work on offloading in non-LLM contexts suggests that both volume and content of offloading can affect learning. Number of LLM prompts, as the most basic indicator of how much a learner uses the LLM, could capture the volume of offloading and reflect distributed cognition during AI-mediated comprehension. Such a view would be consistent with a technocentric perspective [24] around the effect of mere tool use on learning as a central theme in the seminal Great Media Debate [3,14]. On the other hand, capturing whether learners actively engage in local or global comprehension, i.e., what parts of comprehension are offloaded, would reflect an alternative view of distributed cognition during AI-mediated comprehension. In this study, we apply both operationalisations to the same data, each combined with prior knowledge, and compare them to understand if they could explain the effect of LLM use on learning. We use clustering to identify offloading profiles based on each approach. This leads to the following research question:

*What profiles of offloading emerge when learner use of LLMs is characterised through (i) the volume versus (ii) what is being offloaded, and do they capture different aspects of the learning experience?*

## 4 Methods

### 4.1 Study Description

Data analysed in this paper were collected during a lab-based study approved by the TUM ethics committee (2024-69-NM-BA). Data collection took place during November and December 2024. Participants were university students and received a 20-euro compensation. They were eligible if enrolled in a degree program, proficient in English, and not studying psychology. The latter was due to students' potential familiarity with the instruments administered post-task. The study was facilitated by two researchers in one-hour small-group sessions.

The final sample included 97 participants, as three students were removed due to incorrect task completion. The students studied Engineering (33.0%), Business/Economics (20.6%), Computer Science/Informatics and Social Sciences (both 12.4%). The sample was almost gender-balanced (55.7% female and 43.3% male). The students were 24–26 years old (41.2%) and 21–23 years old (27.8%), predominantly at the Master's level (80.4%; the remainder being undergraduate).

Participants received two academic texts with opposing views on the topic of 'Predictive Modelling in Education' and were asked to write a synthesis essay using an interface that embedded access to an LLM. Study facilitators ensured no other tools were used besides our custom-built interface, which included an area to prompt the LLM and a writing pad for typing and pasting. The two texts were designed in line with synthesis-task research [21]. They were balanced in length and the number of ideas. To ensure readability and difficulty for a university-level audience, both texts were evaluated using the Flesch–Kincaid readability test, with scores within the range typical for upper undergraduate students (Text A: 35.4, Text B: 34.8). The texts are available at https://shorturl.at/s6qKD .

### 4.2 Data Analysis: Offloading Profiles

To profile offloading processes, we applied k-means clustering. First, we clustered the volume of LLM use as the total number of prompts used by the learner in a session along with the total score on prior knowledge test. The 12 users who did not use the LLM were included in the clustering with scores of 0 for the total number of prompts. Second, we clustered the content of LLM use. To do so, each LLM prompt was interpreted using a coding scheme (Table 1) that represented if learner remained somewhat active or was passive during a comprehension activity, and if the comprehension within a prompt was targetting local or global level. A total of five features were used for this clustering: proportions of prompts (active-local; active-global; passive-local; passive-global) and total score on a prior knowledge test. The 12 participants who did not use the LLM were also included in the clustering with scores of 0 for all prompts. We compared the clusters across a range of measures (Table 2) using Kruskal-Wallis tests with Benjamini-Hochberg correction for multiple comparisons. We opted for this less conservative error correction approach as appropriate for an exploratory study.

### 4.3 Content Analysis of Prompts Used for Clustering

An experienced researcher conducted content analysis of learner prompts (N=564) to identify how a learner was involved in the comprehension process (actively/ passively) [22] and what level of text comprehension the prompt reflected (local/ global) [13]. Percentages of prompt labels (e.g.,% of active and local) were used for clustering content-based offloading profiles. Table 1 presents the coding framework (https://shorturl.at/s6qKD). Reproducibility was assessed via automated labelling via three LLM-based agents (Claude Sonnet 4.6), each given the full coding framework and instructed to label the prompts, check against the framework rules, and revise the annotation, if discrepant. Cohen's kappa was computed between the expert and the majority vote of the three agents. Consistent automated mislabelling was addressed by refining the framework. Further labelling of two batches of prompts that were not used to refine the framework resulted in an average kappa of 0.64 (passive/global) and 0.61 (local/global). The framework was not further fine-tuned to avoid overfitting.

### 4.4 Measures to Describe Offloading Profiles

To interpret and compare the clusters, we have used self-reported, behavioural, linguistic, and content-based measures, presented in Table 2. Self-reported measures included a prior knowledge pre-test on the topic of predictive modelling and a post-test NASA Task Load Index [10], capturing mental demand, temporal demand, performance, effort, and frustration during the task (internal consistency ($\alpha = .68$)).

Behavioural measures included the number of prompts, total time on task, and individual prompt pacing. Linguistic measures included borrowing from the source text to prompt, borrowing from LLM responses to the essay, and connective density. Connective density, calculated on student-written essay segments, represents independent writing through the use of discourse markers that signal integrative relationships between ideas (e.g.,"however," "therefore," "in contrast," "as a result"). It was selected from a range of linguistic measures applied to the student-written parts of the essay, identified as not being copied verbatim.

Profiles were also compared around the learning strategies applied by each learner to better understand what learners were doing. These categories offer additional qualitative descriptions and are not intended as theoretical insight.

**Table 1.** Coding framework for content-based offloading profiles

| Code | Definition | Examples |
|---|---|---|
| Active | Reflects learning involvement; learner directs the activity: clarifying a knowledge gap, seeking particular type of evaluation or structure, constraining how text is generated. Coded as active as long as the direction of work is specified by the learner, i.e. some learner effort is present. | "What does the assumption mean in text A?"; "I think the main ideas of text B are—am I right?"; "Move last paragraph to the beginning." |
| Passive | Reflects lack of learner involvement; learner does not direct the activity, leaving LLM to perform it without learner-specified constraints. | "Summarize the following"; "Write me a 300-word synthesis"; "Create an outline" |
| Local | Reflects the level of comprehension where activity is conducted. Applies to prompts that include specific information at the micro-level of a word, a paragraph, such as a specific word, sentence, paragraph, concept, or example. | "How can I improve this phrase?"; "Summarise the paragraph"; "What does the text say about the biology students?" |
| Global | Reflects the level of comprehension in relation to the macro-level structure. Applies to prompts that refer to the whole text(s), the essay as a whole, or broad topics spanning both texts. | "Compare both texts"; "Write me a 300-word synthesis"; "Are all main ideas mentioned?" |

Each prompt was assigned to one of nine mutually exclusive categories to reflect the learning strategy used to advance the writing task (Table 2). Among them, seven categories map to learning strategies grounded in Mayer's [16] selecting -organising - integrating (SOI) framework. Two additional categories capture prompts that do not involve a learning strategy. The framework was developed iteratively by an experienced researcher, who initially labelled prompts thematically and then mapped emerging themes to the SOI framework. Following the process described in Sect. 4.3, the expert and LLM-based agents reached Cohen's kappa 0.68 for 168 prompts ( https://shorturl.at/s6qKD).

### 4.5 Limitations

There are several important limitations of the study. The sample and cluster sizes limit statistical power, particularly for detecting differences in self-reported measures. Cluster validation has not been done using learning outcomes since modelling them properly requires substantially expanding the paper scope. Despite

**Table 2.** Measures for describing offloading profiles

| Measure | Description | Descriptives | | |
|---|---|---|---|---|
| **Self-reported measures** | | | | |
| Prior knowledge | AILIT-S [11]; factual questions about AI and modelling | *M*=0.6, *SD*=0.2 | | |
| Cognitive load | NASA TLX [10]; mental demand, temporal demand, performance, effort, frustration ($\alpha$=.68) | *M* range 2.5–3.3 | | |
| **Behavioural and linguistic measures** | | | | |
| Prompts | Total prompts during the task | *M*=5.8, *SD*=6.7 | | |
| Time on task | Total time spent on the task, minutes | *M*=29, *SD*=9 | | |
| Prompt pacing | Harmonic mean of inter-prompt intervals, minutes | *Mdn*=1.5, *IQR*=0.7-8 | | |
| Text-to-prompt borrowing | Proportion of prompt words in unique lexical overlaps (2–5 n-grams) with source texts [12] | *M*=0.35, *SD*=0.26 | | |
| LLM-to-essay borrowing | Proportion of student-authored sentences; If >50% of text snippets has 5-gram overlap with LLM the text is labelled as LLM-derived. | *M*=66.3%, *SD*=42.1% | | |
| Connective density | Discourse connectives per sentence, capturing use of integrative words, applied to the student produced portions of the text | *M*=0.31, *SD*=0.19 | | |
| **Learning strategies (each prompt coded as one learning strategy)** | | **Total** | M | SD |
| Clarify | Asks to clarify vocabulary or factual gaps | 52 | 0.54 | 1.00 |
| Select | Seeks key points or information in the source | 30 | 0.31 | 0.89 |
| Summarise | Asks to compress text into a shorter version | 57 | 0.59 | 1.84 |
| Comprehend | Asks for facts explained in the source text | 67 | 0.69 | 1.72 |
| Structure | Seeks to organise text or create connections | 51 | 0.53 | 1.33 |
| Generate | Asks to generate text | 132 | 1.36 | 2.10 |
| Evaluate | Asks to evaluate pasted text | 40 | 0.41 | 1.00 |
| Paste | Pastes text without instruction | 61 | 0.63 | 1.20 |
| Non-op | Asks about word count or grammar | 74 | 0.76 | 1.75 |

our attempt to represent LLM-mediated activity in a generalisable manner, other tasks may require other lenses to represent offloading patterns.

# 5 Results

## 5.1 Volume-Based Offloading Profiles

Volume-based offloading profiles were represented by four clusters (Table 3). The number of clusters was selected based on the elbow method, silhouette scores, and cluster interpretation. Within cluster sum of squares stabilised after k=3–4, with silhouette scores 0.481 for three clusters and 0.412 for four clusters. Four-cluster solution was chosen due to a better differentiation within a larger cluster.

The clusters significantly differed both in prior knowledge of the learners whose offloading processes they represented, as well as their volume of LLM use. Hence, they were interpreted as representative of learner-LLM systems with *High Prior Knowledge-Minimal Offloading* (n=51), *High Prior Knowledge-Moderate Offloading* (n=17), *Low Prior Knowledge - Low Offloading* (n=22), and *Heavy Offloading* (n=7). The use of LLM across volume-based profiles varied, from 2 prompts in the low offloading group to 25 prompts in the heavy offloading group.

The volume of offloading related to the essay authorship. The more LLM was used, the lower was student authorship score. This indicates that more offloading meant fewer instances of own knowledge construction. Volume of offloading was also closely related with the prompt pacing. Higher offloading meant lower intervals between LLM use, with the entire writing process done entirely through offloading. For instance, minimal offloading was punctured by an average of 5 min between moments of offloading, whereas moderate offloading had a faster pace of less than a minute between LLM use on average. The profiles were not significantly different on the number of prompts for local or global level of comprehension, or the number of prompts signalling active role of a learner. Differences in learning strategies between the clusters were non-informative.

Connective density also varied significantly across profiles. This was negatively correlated with prior knowledge and not the number of prompts ($r$ = -.30, $p$ = 0.007). This is counterintuitive; potentially, more coherent discourse required fewer connectives. Low connective density of heavy offloaders should be interpreted with caution since they contributed 2% of the essay.

Self-reported cognitive load showed no significant differences. There are insufficient observations in each cluster to capture differences, but it is worth noting that high offloading participants reported the highest mental demand, compared with learners who had not offloaded or who had low prior knowledge. This suggests that managing high-paced offloading may still be perceived as demanding.

## 5.2 Content-Based Offloading Profiles

Content-based profiling resulted in five clusters (Table 4). Within-cluster sum of squares flattened after k=4–5 (26.1% and 22.1% reductions), with silhouette scores of 0.376 for four clusters and 0.424 for five clusters. Five-cluster solution grouped all learners who completed the task without LLM as a distinct profile.

Profiles did not differ in prior knowledge, despite it being a clustering variable. The proportions of what was offloaded dominated cluster differences. Notably, even though the number of prompts was not used for clustering, some content-based offloading profiles were differentiated by the volume of LLM use.

The five profiles represented qualitatively distinct patterns of how cognitive activity was distributed, with significant differences in learning strategies. We interpret the offloading processes in these learner-LLM systems as follows. *Full Offloading* (n=41) had learners passively involved (passive prompts at 96%) using LLMs to hone on the comprehension at the global level (93%). That is,

**Table 3.** Volume-based offloading profiles; means of descriptive measures

| | High knowledge minimal offloading $n$=51 | Low knowledge low offloading $n$=22 | High knowledge moderate offloading $n$=17 | Heavy offloading $n$=7 | $p$ |
|---|---|---|---|---|---|
| **Clustering variables** | | | | | |
| Prior Knowledge | .75 | .34 | .73 | .51 | *** |
| No. prompts | 2.4 | 4.3 | 10.1 | 25.1 | *** |
| **Learning strategies (% of prompts, LLM users only)** | | | | | |
| Clarify | 21 | 9 | 7 | 3 | |
| Comprehend | 14 | 22 | 5 | 12 | |
| Select | 7 | 5 | 7 | 3 | |
| Summarize | 7 | 14 | 8 | 12 | |
| Structure | 2 | 10 | 13 | 8 | *** |
| Generate | 17 | 16 | 30 | 25 | *** |
| Evaluate | 10 | 4 | 9 | 5 | |
| Paste | 11 | 17 | 10 | 8 | |
| Non-op | 12 | 4 | 11 | 21 | *** |
| **Cognitive activity (% of prompts, LLM users only)** | | | | | |
| Passive | 77 | 84 | 72 | 82 | |
| Global | 68 | 74 | 66 | 72 | |
| **Behavioural traces** | | | | | |
| Essay authorship (%) | 80 | 81 | 30 | 2 | *** |
| Prompt pacing (min) | 5.00 | 3.76 | 1.16 | 0.53 | *** |
| Text-to-prompt | 37 | 28 | 40 | 35 | |
| Connective density | 1.51 | 2.68 | 2.10 | 1.00 | * |
| **Self-reported learner experience** | | | | | |
| Mental demand | 3.18 | 3.41 | 3.41 | 3.57 | |
| Time pressure | 3.41 | 3.18 | 3.12 | 3.57 | |
| Effort | 3.14 | 3.09 | 3.35 | 3.14 | |
| Frustration | 2.29 | 2.91 | 2.29 | 2.57 | |
| Perceived success | 3.16 | 3.09 | 3.53 | 2.86 | |

they delegated comprehension, generation, and heavily pasted the text back-and-forth. *Clarifying Offloading* processes (n=17) had learners applying some effort (active prompts at 81%) mostly at the local level of comprehension (85%), using the LLM almost exclusively for vocabulary and concept clarification. *Comprehension Offloading* processes (n=15) were characteristic of passively involved learners (passive prompts at 88%) both at micro- and macro- levels of comprehension (60% local). They relied heavily on summarisation and requests for specific information, instead of locating it themselves. *Strategic Offloading* processes (n=12) had the highest proportion of offloading at the global comprehension level but with active learner participation (36% active). These learners directed structure of the essay and generation at high volume and fast pace. *Non-users* (n=12) completed the task independently.

**Table 4.** Content-based offloading profiles; means of descriptive measures

| | Full Offloading | Comprehension Offloading | Strategic Offloading | Clarifying | No-offloading | |
|---|---|---|---|---|---|---|
| | $n$=41 | $n$=15 | $n$=12 | $n$=17 | $n$=12 | $p$ |
| **Clustering variables** | | | | | | |
| Prior knowledge | .66 | .60 | .58 | .66 | .63 | |
| Active, % prompts | 4 | 12 | 36 | 81 | — | *** |
| Local, % prompts | 7 | 60 | 22 | 85 | — | *** |
| **Learning strategies (% of prompts, LLM users only)** | | | | | | |
| Clarify | 2 | 5 | 3 | 71 | — | *** |
| Comprehend | 16 | 12 | 6 | 10 | — | |
| Select | 6 | 2 | 8 | 4 | — | |
| Summarize | 7 | 27 | 4 | 0 | — | ** |
| Structure | 6 | 5 | 19 | 2 | — | *** |
| Generate | 27 | 23 | 24 | 8 | — | *** |
| Evaluate | 7 | 5 | 13 | 0 | — | ** |
| Paste | 15 | 15 | 5 | 0 | — | *** |
| Non-op | 15 | 6 | 19 | 4 | — | * |
| **Behavioural traces** | | | | | | |
| No. prompts | 5.5 | 8.9 | 12.9 | 2.9 | 0 | *** |
| Essay authorship (%) | 61 | 58 | 24 | 91 | 100 | *** |
| Prompt pacing (min) | 2.16 | 4.75 | 1.05 | 5.18 | — | *** |
| Text-to-prompt (%) | 41 | 45 | 32 | 38 | 0 | *** |
| Connective density | 1.87 | 2.33 | 2.18 | 1.56 | 1.64 | |
| **Self-reported learner experience** | | | | | | |
| Mental demand | 3.41 | 3.47 | 3.00 | 3.24 | 3.08 | |
| Time pressure | 3.44 | 3.53 | 2.92 | 3.29 | 3.08 | |
| Effort | 3.29 | 3.20 | 2.83 | 3.18 | 3.00 | |
| Frustration | 2.49 | 2.47 | 2.50 | 2.41 | 2.33 | |
| Perceived success | 3.22 | 3.13 | 3.33 | 3.24 | 2.92 | |

Some content-based profiles have significant differences in the prompt numbers. Strategic Offloaders offloaded at the highest volume ($M$=12.9) and the fastest pace ($M$=1.05 min), followed by the Full Offloaders who prompted moderately (M=5.5). These two groups have similarly high levels of prior knowledge but they offloaded very differently, qualitatively speaking. Strategic offloaders have a high level of learner engagement in directing the specifics of the comprehension activity: despite their high level of offloading, they are likely not completely removing comprehension, maintaining some of it and distributing the rest. Full offloaders do not at all direct, their active level is at 4% of all prompts on average, and they do not engage in offloading comprehension at the micro-level (7% only). These processes are contrasted by the Clarifiers who essentially use LLMs to reduce intrinsic cognitive load when accessing complex or unknown ideas, conducted through low-level of LLM prompting (Mprompts=2.9). None of these qualitative differences are conveyed by volume-based profiling.

Self-reported cognitive load showed no differences across content-based profiles. As with volume-based profiling, cluster sizes limited statistical power. Descriptively speaking, learners who employed Strategic Offloading reported the lowest mental demand (M=3.00), time pressure (M=2.92), and effort (M=2.83), but the highest frustration. Overall, the trends might indicate that perceptions of mental demand, pressure, effort, and frustration are driven by various needs for information processing. Hence, new self-reported instruments are needed to understand the experience of offloading dynamically.

Content-based offloading profiles also differed on essay authorship, prompt pacing, text-to-prompt borrowing, and six of nine learning strategies (all $p < .01$). For instance, strategic offloaders wrote a quarter of the essay independently, whereas both full and comprehension offloaders produced around 60% of the text themselves. Connective density was similarly not differentiated across profiles, and considering its correlation with prior knowledge, it may be assumed that content-based profiles subsume differences stemming from prior knowledge.

### 5.3 Two Approaches: Capturing Fragmentation

To compare approaches to profiling offloading, Figure 1, plots them side by side. Panel A captures volume-based offloading profiles, ordered from low LLM use at the bottom for *High Knowledge, minimal use* offloading to the *Heavy LLM use* at the top. Panel B similarly presents content-based offloading profiles ordered from the lowest LLM use for *Clarifying offloading* processes at the bottom and highest LLM use at the top for *Strategic Offloading*. We use stripes to visualise where learner effort is minimal (passive prompt labels), demonstrating where individual cognitive process fragments when cognitive activity is distributed to LLMs. Active prompt labels maintain their solid colour.

These visualisations demonstrate that volume of offloading masks differences that are visible when profiling what is offload rather than how much. For instance, Panel B shows how *Strategic Offloaders* actively structure information and provide specific directives for text generation, while selectively delegating other operations to the tool. This pattern contrasts sharply with *Full offloading* and *Comprehension offloading*, where learners delegate entire segments of the comprehension and production process and participate actively in few, if any, of the task's cognitive operations.

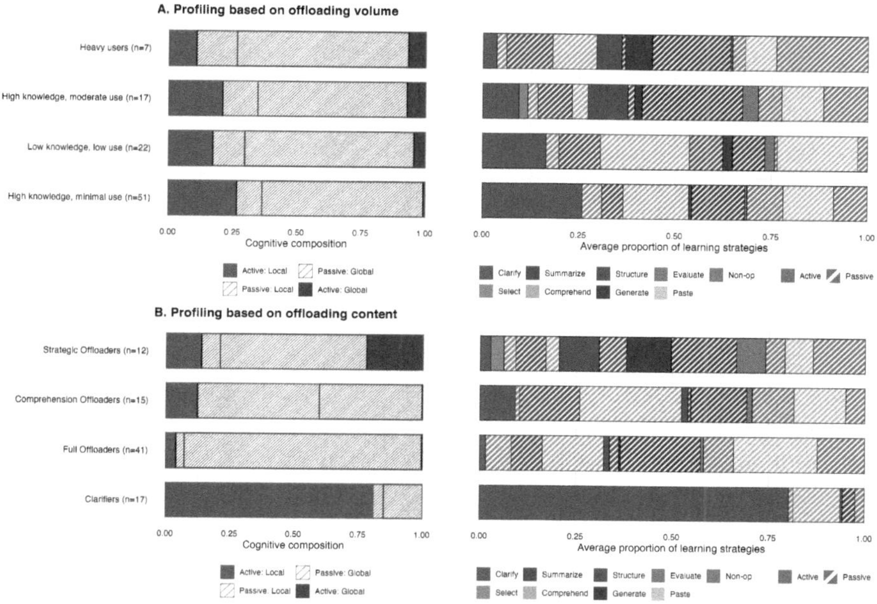


**Fig. 1.** Fragmentation in Offloading, based on volume (A, top) and content (B, bottom) of LLM use. Stripes capture parts where the learner was passive, Solid colours represent that the learner was active. Profiles are ordered from the lowest to the highest prompts.

## 6 Discussion and Implications

Motivated by competing evidence from the offloading literature as to whether offloading process should be operationalised via its volume or what is offloaded, we analysed LLM use by learners in a writing synthesis task. We use the same data to profile their offloading with these two approaches. We adopted Salomon's ideas about distributed cognition [22] to analytically represent learner-LLM distributed cognitive system as individual cognition via prior knowledge, the activity that affords distribution, and the distribution of the cognitive process. Volume-based profiling combined prior knowledge with the amount of LLM use. Content-based profiling combined prior knowledge with variables defined at the prompt level, drawn from Kintsch and van Dijk's levels of comprehension (local or global) and the role of a learner in cognitive activity (active or passive).

The two operationalisations did not capture redundant information. Volume-based profiles appear to have differentiated aspects of offloading associated with prior knowledge rather than offloading volume. In our data, offloading volume is negatively associated with student essay authorship, indicating the decrease of explicit knowledge construction when working on the final artefact. Content-based profiles differentiated the process by capturing how the comprehension process was fragmented by different offloading strategies. Although volume was not a clustering variable in the content-based solution, some of the resulting profiles differed in prompting volume, suggesting that sometimes what is offloaded constrains how much is offloaded. We also show that qualitative differences exist within similar volumes of offloading. Strategic offloading, involving iterative structuring and generation from an actively engaged learner, required higher offloading volume. So did Full offloading, but without engaging the learner in the comprehension process.

These patterns, captured through fragmentation, can be related to Salomon's [22] distinction between division of labour, where the cognitive process is handed off, and shared activity, where it is jointly maintained. While the fragmentation view suggests that the volume of LLM use could often still be a proxy for what is likely ineffective offloading, our findings highlight the relevance of the content aspect. The parts of the cognitive process that are retained by the individual are important to know when evaluating high or moderate use of LLM. Low volume of LLM use is most likely to reflect shared activity, but high volume can accompany either division of labour or shared work, depending on the patterns in fragmentation. In either case, treating LLM use as binary, through a techno-centric perspective, does not offer insight that differentiates variations in offloading processes.

From a psychological perspective, the distinction between volume-based and content-based profiles poses further questions. One assumption may be that offloading reduces cognitive demand [20]. From a CLT perspective, reducing task demands does not necessarily mean that the cognitive resources freed through offloading will be used for the processes needed for comprehension and schema construction [28]. Moreover, offloading dynamically may introduce other unexpected cognitive demands that still require cognitive resources from the learner. Understanding the cause of this potential effect and minimising it may then be further needed. In either case, fragmentation could be approached as a proximal outcome of cognitive offloading, potentially helpful in explaining how different offloading strategies redistribute the cognitive work involved in comprehension, as well as subsequent choices and behaviour.

For educational practice, these findings suggest that interventions targeting the volume of LLM use, such as limiting the number of prompts, may be insufficient, since the same volume could describe rather different offloading processes. More targeted approaches would attend to what learners delegate: whether they retain active involvement in structuring and evaluating, or hand off entire segments of the comprehension process. Tools that make the distribution of cognitive work visible to learners and instructors could potentially support this, though more work is needed to evaluate offloading processes and their differentiated effects on learners. Future work should examine whether fragmentation patterns predict learning outcomes directly, and whether they hold across tasks with different cognitive demands.

## References

1. Armitage, K.L., Bulley, A., Redshaw, J.: Developmental origins of cognitive offloading. Proc. Roy. Soc. B: Biol. Sci. **287**(1928) (2020)
2. Bastani, H., Bastani, O., Sungu, A., Ge, H., Kabakcı, Ö., Mariman, R.: Generative ai can harm learning. The Wharton School Research Paper (2024)
3. Clark, R.E.: Media will never influence learning. Education Tech. Research Dev. **42**(2), 21–29 (1994)
4. Donet, J.R., Marshall, P.H., Serra, M.J.: The effect of learning strategies on offloading decisions in response recall. Memory Cogn. **54**(1), 273–293 (2026)
5. Fan, Y., et al.: Beware of metacognitive laziness: effects of generative artificial intelligence on learning motivation, processes, and performance. Br. J. Edu. Technol. **56**(2), 489–530 (2025)
6. Fisher, M., Goddu, M.K., Keil, F.C.: Searching for explanations: how the internet inflates estimates of internal knowledge. J. Exp. Psychol. Gen. **144**(3), 674 (2015)
7. Furqon, E.N., Chang, C.K.: Evaluating cognitive performance through prompt-based methods using LLM in education. In: 2025 IEEE International Conference on Advanced Learning Technologies (ICALT) pp. 209–211. IEEE (2025)
8. Goldin-Meadow, S., Nusbaum, H., Kelly, S.D., Wagner, S.: Explaining math: gesturing lightens the load. Psychol. Sci. **12**(6), 516–522 (2001)
9. Grinschgl, S., Papenmeier, F., Meyerhoff, H.S.: Mutual interplay between cognitive offloading and secondary task performance. Psychonomic Bull. Rev. **30**(6), 2250–2261 (2023)
10. Hart, S.G.: Nasa task load index (TLX): paper and pencil package-volume 1.0 (1986)
11. Hornberger, M., Bewersdorff, A., Schiff, D.S., Nerdel, C.: Development and validation of a short ai literacy test (AILIT-s) for university students. Comput. Human Behavior: Artif. Humans **5**, 100176 (2025)
12. Keck, C.: The use of paraphrase in summary writing: a comparison of l1 and l2 writers. J. Second. Lang. Writ. **15**(4), 261–278 (2006)
13. Kintsch, W., Van Dijk, T.A.: Toward a model of text comprehension and production. Psychol. Rev. **85**(5), 363 (1978)
14. Kozma, R.B.: Will media influence learning? Reframing the debate. Education Tech. Research Dev. **42**(2), 7–19 (1994)
15. Magen, H., Tomer-Offen, M.: Reduced relational and item-specific processing in cognitive offloading. Cogn. Res. Principles Implications **10**(1), 41 (2025)
16. Mayer, R.E.: Learners as information processors: legacies and limitations of educational psychology's second. Educ. Psychol. **31**(3–4), 151–161 (1996)
17. Mayer, R.E.: The future of multimedia learning. J. Appl. Instructional Design **11**(4), 69–77 (2022)
18. Parasuraman, R., Molloy, R., Singh, I.L.: Performance consequences of automation-induced'complacency'. Int. J. Aviat. Psychol. **3**(1), 1–23 (1993)
19. Risko, E.F., Dunn, T.L.: Storing information in-the-world: metacognition and cognitive offloading in a short-term memory task. Conscious. Cogn. **36**, 61–74 (2015)
20. Risko, E.F., Gilbert, S.J.: Cognitive offloading. Trends Cogn. Sci. **20**(9), 676–688 (2016)
21. Robledo, P., Álvarez, M.: Strategic and self-regulated instruction in synthesis tasks in the university context. Front. Psychol. **15**, 1386907 (2024)
22. Salomon, G.: No distribution without individuals' cognition: a dynamic interactional view. Distributed Cogn. Psychol. Educ. Considerations. 111–138 (1993)

23. Salomon, G.: Distributed cognitions: psychological and educational considerations. Cambridge University Press (1993)
24. Salomon, G.: Technology and pedagogy: why don't we see the promised revolution? Educ. Technol. **42**(2), 71–75 (2002)
25. Shibani, A., Knight, S., Kitto, K., Karunanayake, A., Buckingham Shum, S.: Untangling critical interaction with AI in students' written assessment. In: Extended Abstracts of the CHI Conference on Human Factors in Computing Systems, pp. 1–6 (2024)
26. Sparrow, B., Liu, J., Wegner, D.M.: Google effects on memory: cognitive consequences of having information at our fingertips. Science **333**(6043), 776–778 (2011)
27. Stadler, M., Bannert, M., Sailer, M.: Cognitive ease at a cost: LLMs reduce mental effort but compromise depth in student scientific inquiry. Comput. Hum. Behav. **160**, 108386 (2024)
28. Sweller, J., Van Merrienboer, J.J., Paas, F.G.: Cognitive architecture and instructional design. Educ. Psychol. Rev. **10**(3), 251–296 (1998)
29. Wegner, T. G., Wegner, DM.: Transactive memory. In A. S. R. Manstead & M. Hewstone (Eds.), The Blackwell Encyclopedia of Social Psychology (pp. 654–656). Oxford: Blackwell (1995)
30. Yang, K., et al.: Modifying AI, enhancing essays: How active engagement with generative ai boosts writing quality. In: Proceedings of the 15th International Learning Analytics and Knowledge Conference, pp. 568–578 (2025)

# Identifying Learner Profiles to Explore Relationships Between Player Types, Behavioural and Cognitive Outcomes

Lou-Anne Quellet[1(✉)], Elise Lavoué[1,2], and Audrey Serna[1]

[1] INSA Lyon, CNRS, Universite Claude Bernard Lyon 1, LIRIS, UMR5205, 69621 Villeurbanne, France
{lou-anne.quellet,audrey.serna}@insa-lyon.fr, elise.lavoue@univ-lyon3.fr
[2] University Jean Moulin Lyon 3, iaelyon School of Management, Lyon, France

**Abstract.** Gamification in education aims to enhance learners' motivation, engagement, and performance. However, findings in the literature are mixed, and it is now well-recognised that the effectiveness of gamification may depend on learners' characteristics and preferences. To identify these characteristics, several studies have examined learners' player types. While some research relies on the dominant player type, other studies adopt variable-centred approaches to investigate how player type dimensions relate to behavioural and cognitive outcomes. However, such approaches may not fully capture how different player types are combined within each learner. In this study, we adopt a person-centred approach using Latent Profile Analysis (LPA) to (1) identify distinct learner profiles based on player type dimensions and (2) examine how these profiles relate to performance and behavioural outcomes in a gamified learning environment. Using data from 516 participants, four distinct learner profiles were identified. The results show that these profiles differ significantly in terms of cognitive and behavioural outcomes. Our findings highlight the relevance of a person-centred approach to identifying learner profiles that can inform the design of more personalised gamified learning environments.

**Keywords:** Latent Profile Analysis · Player type · Gamification · Education

## 1 Introduction

Over the past decade, gamification has been widely implemented across multiple domains, including education, to enhance learner motivation, performance, and engagement. Multiple recent literature reviews and meta-analyses report that gamification has a generally positive impact on learners' behavioural and cognitive outcomes [34,35], including increased academic performance and improved interaction and thinking skills. However, other authors report that gamification can also lead to neutral or even negative effects [32].


J. Weidlich et al. (Eds.): EC-TEL 2026, LNCS 16905, pp. 515–530, 2027.
https://doi.org/10.1007/978-3-032-37979-5_35

Given these mixed results, it is now well-recognised that the effectiveness of gamification depends on learners' characteristics and preferences [11]. As a result, recent research has increasingly focused on tailored gamification approaches. By definition, tailored gamification refers to differentiating game elements based on user characteristics [33]. Various learner characteristics have been explored to improve gamified learning environments, including demographic data (e.g. age, gender), personality traits, learning styles and player types. According to the systematic review by Klock et al. [13], player types are the most commonly used characteristic for personalising gamification (45% of studies), followed by gender (14% of studies) and personality traits.

However, using these characteristics for tailoring game elements requires a precise understanding of how they can meaningfully characterise learners. Some studies have addressed this issue by examining the relationships between player types and behavioural or cognitive outcomes, such as academic performance and engagement [7,16,30]. However, most of these studies adopt a variable-centred approach, which may lack a combination of player type dimensions.

To address this limitation, we adopt a person-centred approach using Latent Profile Analysis (LPA) to cluster learners based on their player types. We aim to provide a deeper understanding of how player types influence cognitive and behavioural outcomes when using a gamified learning environment. Based on a sample of 516 participants, we identify four distinct learner profiles. These profiles are associated with significant differences in cognitive and behavioural outcomes. Overall, these findings highlight the relevance of a person-centred approach for identifying meaningful learner profiles and inform the design of more personalised gamified learning environments.

## 2 Related Work

### 2.1 Relationships Between Player Types and Outcomes

Player types have been widely used to characterise learners and to adapt gamification in learning environments. Several typologies have been proposed, including the Bartle taxonomy [2], the BrainHex model [19], and the Hexad framework [17]. A recent comparative study reports that the Gamification User Types Hexad framework is the most suitable for capturing players' preferences for game elements [10]. Indeed, the Hexad framework was specifically designed for gamification and is based on Self-Determination Theory [26], which identifies three basic psychological needs: competence, autonomy and relatedness. Relying on this theory, the framework distinguishes six player types: Achievers, Disruptors, Free Spirits, Philanthropists, Players, and Socialisers. It also recommends personalised game mechanisms for each profile[1] However, these recommendations remain theoretical and require further empirical investigation.

Previous research has investigated the potential of player types to tailor and enhance gamified learning environments. These studies examine the relationship

[1] Available at https://www.gamified.uk/user-types/gamification-mechanics-elements/.

between player types and cognitive and behavioural outcomes, as well as their interactions with specific game elements. Some researchers have focused on the dominant player type and employed correlation analysis to examine these relationships [8,25]. However, such methods fail to account for the multidimensional nature of individuals.

Recent studies adopt more complex statistical methods to account for all player types and relate them to outcomes, such as performance and engagement. Some of them applied linear regression to examine the overall effect of Hexad player types. For instance, Lopez et al. [16] explored the relationship between Hexad player types and academic performance. They showed that learners with higher Philanthropist or Free Spirit scores significantly performed better. Similarly, Sipone et al. [30] modelled learners based on the presence (high score) or absence (low score) of each player type. Their results indicated that Socialiser, Disruptor, Player, and Philanthropist types were associated with higher final academic grades and that the Socialiser type was also associated with a higher number of connections and completed activities.

The Partial Least Squares modelling (PLS) method was also used to capture complex relationships between player type and outcomes. For example, Dos Santos et al. [7] applied this approach to show that the effects of gamification differ across the six Hexad player types, with a positive effect on perceived utility for the Disruptor types and on reward for the Player type. Other researchers used the PLS approach to support adaptive gamification. For instance, Hallifax et al. [10], and Reyssier et al. [24] analysed motivational and behavioural indicators associated with Hexad player types across diverse game elements to recommend the most suitable game element for the full range of player types.

Although these approaches provide valuable insights into how individual player types influence cognitive and behavioural outcomes, they generally analyse each type independently, even when all player types are considered. This limitation may overlook potential interaction between player types. More person-centred approaches, such as clustering, could therefore be a useful starting step for capturing these interactions and better understanding the combined effect of player type dimensions.

## 2.2 Clustering Approaches for Identifying Learner Profiles

Multiple studies have used clustering techniques to identify learner profiles. We distinguish between two categories of studies: those that cluster learners based on their behaviour and associate them with player type typologies, and those that derive learner profiles directly from player type dimensions.

In the first category, log data are globally used to extract and group learners' behaviour. Barata et al. [1] applied the Expectation-Maximisation algorithm to group learners based on their accumulation of experience points over time. They identified four profiles that were then associated with BrainHex player types. Two profiles were mainly composed of Conqueror types, while the others showed more mixed dominant player types. In the fitness domain, Krath et al. [15] applied k-means clustering to users' actions in a fitness application. They identified seven user clusters and analysed their correspondence with multiple player types typologies (Hexad, Bartle and BrainHex). These studies highlight the usefulness of behavioural clustering in uncovering patterns, but they rely on post hoc interpretation of player types rather than directly integrating them.

The second category of studies focuses on clustering learners directly based on player types. Brandl et al. and Schrader et al. [5,6] compared four clustering algorithms to identify learner profiles based on the six Hexad player types and identified three learner profiles. To support gamification design, they further linked these profiles to personalised game elements based on existing literature.

All of these studies employed either variable-centred analyses, which treat each player type dimension independently, or traditional distance-based clustering methods. Traditional clustering approaches, such as k-means, are deterministic and assign individuals to a single cluster without providing a probabilistic representation of group membership. They also do not allow for the assessment of model fit and classification uncertainty. These approaches may not capture combinations of player types within individuals or account for membership uncertainty. To address these limitations, Latent Profile Analysis (LPA) offers a person-centred approach. As described by Spurk et al. [31], unlike variable-centred approaches, LPA focuses on patterns of variables and identifies groups of individuals with similar combinations of variables. Furthermore, LPA classifies individuals into profiles based on membership probabilities, which differ from classic clustering.

LPA has been applied to psychological variables to identify learner profiles based on motivational [4] or personality variables [23]. These profiles have been linked to various outcomes, including performance, perceived competence, effort and engagement. More recently, Schultze et al. [28] applied Latent Profile Analysis on the Hexad framework. They identified five learner profiles with distinct Hexad configurations, thereby contributing to the validation of the Hexad scale. However, their study did not investigate how learner profiles relate to behavioural or cognitive outcomes.

In this study, we adopt a person-centred approach using Latent Profile Analysis (LPA) to cluster learners based on their Hexad player types and examining their influence on behavioural and cognitive outcomes when using a gamified learning environment. We address the following two research questions:

- **RQ1**: Can we identify learner profiles with distinct Hexad player types configuration, in line with the Hexad definitions? We apply LPA to identify learner profiles and relate them to the satisfaction of their psychological needs to support their interpretation.
- **RQ2**: Are Hexad learner profiles associated with different cognitive and behavioural outcomes?

## 3 Gamified Learning Environment

We developed an online gamified learning environment, LudiMoodle (see Fig. 1), as part of the LudiMoodle project, which involved collaboration among researchers in computer and education sciences, teachers, instructional designers, and developers. All the learning materials were created by the participating teachers to reflect their usual classroom practices. They designed eight lessons, each consisting of four to ten quizzes covering secondary-level introductory algebra, particularly literal arithmetic. These quizzes were intended as practice activities, as teachers had observed that learners often found them boring or repetitive, and wanted to make them more engaging. Within each lesson, learners had to answer at least 70% of the questions correctly to complete a quiz (considered successful) and proceed to the next one; otherwise, they had to retake the quiz. This 70% criterion was determined by the teachers.

The environment integrates six game elements. Based on the design space classification proposed by [9], five game elements were selected to represent common game dynamics used in educational gamification [34]: points, badges, leaderboards, avatars, and a progress bar. In addition, a timer was included at the teachers' request as they were interested in examining its effect on learners, although this game element is less frequently studied in the literature [20].

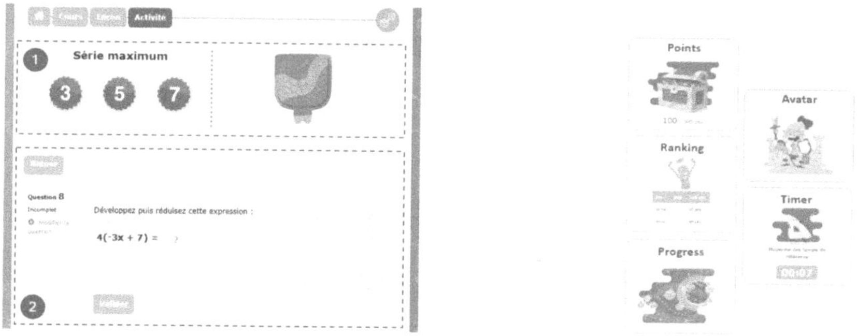


(a) Learning environment interface.

(b) Game elements.

**Fig. 1.** Screenshot of the learning environment showing (a) the interface with the badge game element and (b) the five other game elements. The interface is divided into two sections: (1) the game element area, which varies according to the element assigned to each student, and (2) the question area.

# 4 Method

## 4.1 Participants

The study involved 714 students aged 13–14 from 22 French secondary schools. We considered only data from students who had given consent and completed all questionnaires. In total, 516 student data were analysed, including 266 girls and 250 boys. The research protocol was approved by the Research Ethics Committee of the University of Lyon.

### 4.2 Procedure

Before using the learning environment, learners completed initial questionnaires on their prior knowledge of basic algebra and their Hexad-12 profile. They were randomly assigned to one of the six game elements available in the learning environment (avatar: 97 students, badges: 85, progress: 90, ranking: 78, score: 85, timer: 81), which they used throughout the experiment. In total, the platform was used for eight lessons, each held once or twice a week over a period of four to five weeks. Learners accessed the quizzes individually using tablets. Each lesson followed the same structure: the teacher first introduced the topic (10–15 min, depending on its complexity), then learners logged into the platform to complete the associated quizzes (25–30 min). At the end of the last lesson, learners completed post-test questionnaires described in the next section.

### 4.3 Data Collection

**Profile Characterisation.** Learners completed several questionnaires to characterise their profile. (1) The Hexad-12 questionnaire [14] was administered to identify their player profile. (2) The Player Experience of Need Satisfaction (PENS) questionnaire, originally developed by Ryan et al. [27] and validated in [12], was used to assess learners' perceived competence and autonomy. (3) In addition, a pre-test evaluated learners' prior knowledge of the prerequisites required for literal calculation. This test was collaboratively developed by three mathematics teachers and validated by the department's mathematics coordinator.

**Cognitive Outcomes.** These outcomes were assessed through a post-test designed to measure the knowledge acquired during the experiment. The post-test was developed and validated following the same procedure as the pre-test.

**Behavioural Outcomes.** These outcomes were assessed through questionnaires and log data. (1) The short form of the User Engagement Scale (UES), developed by O'Brien et al. [22], was used to measure engagement across four dimensions. In this study, we focused on the Perceived Usability (PU) and Reward (RW) dimensions, as absorption was not expected in the context of mathematics problem-solving. (2) Learners' interactions with the learning environment were analysed through log data. Several indicators were computed to capture behaviours related to performance during in-class exercises, including measures of attempts, quiz completion, and engagement, following indicators previously validated in [29]:

- Nb successful exercises (%): number of quizzes successfully completed (i.e., learners scored more than 70% on the exercise). Each exercise was counted only once when it was first successfully completed.
- First attempt success rate (%): score of the first attempt in a quiz.
- Mean nb of attempts before success: average number of attempts to a quiz before learners score more than 70%.

- Mean nb of attempts after success: average number of attempts to a quiz after success (i.e., after learners scored more than 70% on the exercise).

### 4.4 Data Analysis

In this study, we used Latent Profile Analysis (LPA) to identify distinct subgroups of learners with similar combinations of Hexad player types. LPA is a categorical latent variable modelling approach that identifies hidden subpopulations within a population from a set of observed variables. This approach enables the identification of homogeneous subgroups of individuals and facilitates comparisons between profiles with respect to both their internal composition and their relationships with outcomes [31]. Accordingly, we applied LPA to the six dimensions of the Hexad framework. We followed the process recommended by Bauer et al. [3] and the best-practice guidelines from Spurk et al. [31]. The analysis proceeded in three steps. First, we specified the model and conducted a confirmatory factor analysis on the Hexad scores. Secondly, the resulting factors were used in the LPA analysis to estimate latent profiles. Finally, we used the Bolck, Croon, and Hagenaars (BCH) method to examine the outcomes according to the profiles. This approach follows procedures applied in recent studies [4] and some parts of our analysis are based on their code available on OSF[2]

**Confirmatory Factor Analysis (CFA).** Bauer et al. [3] suggest that Latent Profile Analysis is optimally conducted using factor scores rather than raw measure scores, as this ensures continuity across indicators. To ensure compatibility with the BCH three-step approach and as used in [4], the model was constrained so that factor loadings average to 1 and intercepts sum to 0. We used a robust maximum likelihood estimator as we did not observe multivariate normality in our results, and evaluated model fit using the Yuan–Bentler scaled test statistics. The CFA was conducted in R using the `Lavaan` package. According to the literature [18], model fit was assessed using the comparative fit index (CFI), the Tucker-Lewis Index (TLI) and the mean square error of approximation (RMSEA). For CFI and TLI values greater than .90 correspond to adequate fit, while an RMSEA below .08 or .06 reflects acceptable and excellent model fit.

**Latent Profile Analysis (RQ1).** To answer RQ1, LPA was conducted on the CFA factor scores to identify groups of learners with similar Hexad dimensions. We used the `tidySEM` library in R. Model fit was performed using robust maximum likelihood. As recommended by Bauer et al. [3], we examine multiple models with different constraints (or no constraints) on variances and/ or covariance. Following the best practices [3, 31], model selection was based on statistical fit indices, classification criteria and interpretability. Specifically, we considered the Bayesian Information Criterion (BIC) and the sample-size adjusted BIC

[2] OSF repository: https://osf.io/tb9hu/.

(saBIC), where lower values indicated better fit. Classification quality was also assessed using entropy and posterior probability (PCP), with values above .80 (.60 is also acceptable) and .70 indicating excellent classification.

**Cognitive and Behavioural Outcomes (RQ2).** To answer RQ2, we employed the three-step Block-Croon-Hagenaars (BCH) method to examine the relationship between latent profiles and outcomes. The BCH method is particularly robust because it accounts for the uncertainty in class membership and does not assume normality [3,31]. Outcomes were added to the LPA models, and Wald tests were applied to compare outcome scores across learner profiles.

## 5 Results

### 5.1 Identification and Description of Learner Profile (RQ1)

**CFA Analysis.** Results from the Confirmatory Factor Analysis show good fit metrics for the six-factor model: $\chi^2(39) = 101.00$, $p < .001$, CFI = ..950, TLI = .925, SRMR = .043, RMSEA = .058 (90% CI [.044, .072], PCLOSE = .160). These results suggest that the six-factor structure was adequately supported.

**Latent Profile Analysis.** The results of the LPA models are shown in Table 1; only data from the converging models are presented. We first eliminated models with the smallest profile, less than 10 % of the sample, as recommended in [4]. Comparison of models indicated that the three-profile solution with freely estimated variances and equal covariances (free var, equal cov) provided the best fit with $saBIC = 7707,493$ but with moderate class separation ($entropy = 0.730$). In contrast, the four-profile model with freely estimated variances indicated higher classification quality with $entropy$ = .832 and $PCP$ = .836. Nylund-Gibson et al. [21] recommended that model selection should not rely solely on information criteria, but also consider classification quality. Considering the balance between statistical fit and classification precision, the four-profile solution was retained as the optimal model for identifying learner profiles.

**Hexad Profiles.** The four Hexad profiles are presented in Fig. 2 and the descriptive statistics are reported in Table 2. Profile 1 represents 18.80% of participants and is characterised by high scores across all player types (except Disruptor). In contrast, Profile 4 (17.05%) is characterised by moderate Free Spirit, Player and Socialiser scores and low Achiever, Disruptor and Philanthropist scores. Profiles 2 and 3 exhibit more heterogeneous patterns of Hexad player-type combinations. Profile 2, representing 17.25% of the sample, is characterised by a low Disruptor score, moderate Player score and high Achiever, Free Spirit, Philanthropist and Socialiser scores. Profile 3 is the dominant profile (46.90%), characterised by high Free Spirit and Player scores, moderate Achiever, Philanthropist, and Socialiser scores and low Disruptor scores.

**Table 1.** Fit statistics for Latent Profile models based on the Hexad dimensions.

| Model | No. of profiles | LL | FP | BIC | saBIC | Entropy | PCP | % min sample |
|---|---|---|---|---|---|---|---|---|
| equal var | 1 | -4765,490 | 12 | 9605,934 | 9567,844 | 1 | 1 | 1 |
| equal var | 2 | -4446,405 | 19 | 9011,487 | 8951,177 | 0,823 | 0,925 | 0,328 |
| equal var | 3 | -4407,853 | 26 | 8978,105 | 8895,576 | 0,766 | 0,835 | 0,248 |
| equal var | 4 | -4202,266 | 33 | 8610,654 | 8505,906 | 0,856 | 0,898 | 0,019 |
| equal var | 5 | -4157,158 | 40 | 8564,160 | 8437,192 | 0,815 | 0,778 | 0,056 |
| equal var | 6 | -4098,979 | 47 | 8491,525 | 8342,338 | 0,845 | 0,797 | 0,019 |
| free var | 1 | -4765,490 | 12 | 9605,934 | 9567,844 | 1 | 1 | 1 |
| free var | 2 | -4397,232 | 25 | 8950,616 | 8871,261 | 0,805 | 0,933 | 0,428 |
| free var | 3 | -4276,962 | 38 | 8791,275 | 8670,656 | 0,799 | 0,881 | 0,205 |
| free var | 4 | -4112,262 | 51 | 8543,075 | 8381,192 | 0,832 | 0,836 | 0,171 |
| equal var, free cov | 1 | -3942,345 | 27 | 8053,334 | 7967,631 | 1 | 1 | 1 |
| equal var, free cov | 2 | -3876,160 | 49 | 8058,379 | 7902,844 | 0,824 | 0,907 | 0,264 |
| equal var, free cov | 3 | -3813,788 | 71 | 8071,050 | 7845,682 | 0,685 | 0,816 | 0,279 |
| equal var, free cov | 4 | -3776,735 | 93 | 8134,357 | 7839,158 | 0,827 | 0,881 | 0,083 |
| equal var, free cov | 5 | -3733,855 | 115 | 8186,013 | 7820,982 | 0,726 | 0,778 | 0,116 |
| equal var, free cov | 6 | -3678,285 | 137 | 8212,287 | 7777,424 | 0,761 | 0,761 | 0,045 |
| free var, equal cov | 1 | -3942,345 | 27 | 8053,334 | 7967,631 | 1 | 1 | 1 |
| free var, equal cov | 2 | -3855,870 | 40 | 7961,585 | 7834,617 | 0,737 | 0,918 | 0,368 |
| free var, equal cov | 3 | -3772,341 | 53 | 7875,725 | 7707,493 | 0,730 | 0,851 | 0,287 |

Note. LL: Model Loglikelihood; FP: Free Parameters; BIC = Bayesian Information Criterion, SABIC = sample-size adjusted BIC; PCP = Posterior Classification Probability; % min sample = size of the smallest profile in % of the sample size

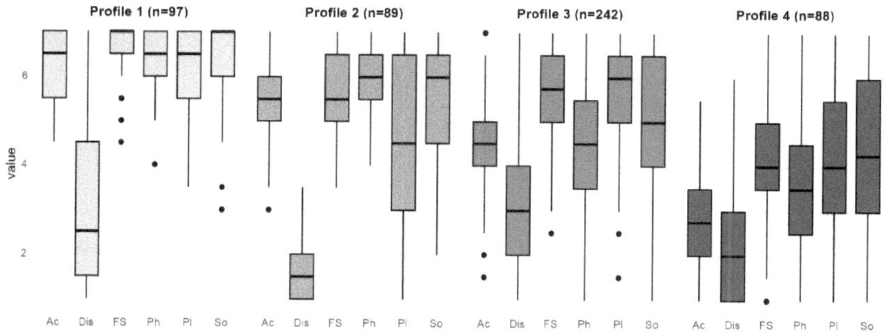


**Fig. 2.** The four Hexad learner profiles.

**Player Experience of Need Satisfaction.** As illustrated in Fig. 3a, we identified four significant differences in the perceived autonomy and competence across learner profiles. Profiles 3 and 4 have a significantly lower perception of autonomy and competence than Profiles 1 and 2.

**Pre-test Performance.** Figure 4 indicates three significant differences between learners' profiles on the initial test. Profile 4 had a lower initial test score than all other learner profiles.

## 5.2 Cognitive and Behavioural Outcomes (RQ2)

**Cognitive Outcomes.** Figure 4 reveals significant differences in the final test across learner profiles, with Profile 4 achieving significantly lower scores than Profiles 1 and 2.

**Behavioural Outcomes.** Regarding learners' engagement, we identified four significant differences within the Reward dimension (see Fig. 3b). Consistent with the PENS results, Profiles 3 and 4 perceived the learning experience as significantly less rewarding than Profiles 1 and 2. For the behavioural indicators (see Fig. 4), three of the four measures showed significant differences: the number of successful exercises, the first-attempt success rate and the mean number of

**Table 2.** Descriptive statistics (Means, Standard Deviation and Confidence Intervals) of the four learner profiles.

| Variables | Profile 1 | | | Profile 2 | | | Profile 3 | | | Profile 4 | | |
|---|---|---|---|---|---|---|---|---|---|---|---|---|
| | M | SD | CI | M | SD | CI | M | SD | CI | M | SD | CI |
| **Hexad score** | | | | | | | | | | | | |
| Achiever (Ac) | 6.191 | 0.709 | (6.13, 6.25) | 5.539 | 0.902 | (5.46, 5.62) | 4.517 | 1.034 | (4.43, 4.61) | 2.784 | 1.142 | (2.69, 2.88) |
| Disruptor (Dis) | 3.005 | 1.673 | (2.86, 3.15) | 1.663 | 0.682 | (1.6, 1.72) | 3.145 | 1.352 | (3.03, 3.26) | 2.341 | 1.240 | (2.23, 2.45) |
| Free Spirit (FS) | 6.603 | 0.568 | (6.55, 6.65) | 5.657 | 0.928 | (5.58, 5.74) | 5.692 | 0.990 | (5.61, 5.78) | 3.938 | 1.297 | (3.83, 4.05) |
| Philanthropist (Ph) | 6.330 | 0.692 | (6.27, 6.39) | 5.904 | 0.846 | (5.83, 5.98) | 4.469 | 1.251 | (4.36, 4.58) | 3.591 | 1.523 | (3.46, 3.72) |
| Player (Pl) | 6.144 | 1.041 | (6.05, 6.23) | 4.657 | 1.785 | (4.5, 4.81) | 5.746 | 1.124 | (5.65, 5.84) | 4.301 | 1.670 | (4.16, 4.45) |
| Socialiser (So) | 6.356 | 0.955 | (6.27, 6.44) | 5.584 | 1.278 | (5.47, 5.69) | 4.926 | 1.655 | (4.78, 5.07) | 4.392 | 1.793 | (4.24, 4.55) |
| **Number of participants** n (%) | 97 (18.80) | | | 89 (17.25) | | | 242 (46.90) | | | 88 (17.05) | | |
| Female n (%) | 48 (49.48) | | | 51 (57.30) | | | 108 (44.63) | | | 59 (67.05) | | |
| Male n (%) | 49 (50.52) | | | 38 (42.70) | | | 134 (55.37) | | | 29 (32.95) | | |
| **Game Elements** | | | | | | | | | | | | |
| Avatar n (%) | 19 (19.59) | | | 14 (15.73) | | | 53 (21.90) | | | 11 (12.50) | | |
| Badge n (%) | 15 (15.46) | | | 13 (14.61) | | | 42 (17.36) | | | 15 (17.05) | | |
| Progress n (%) | 15 (15.46) | | | 16 (17.98) | | | 45 (18.60) | | | 14 (15.91) | | |
| Ranking n (%) | 16 (16.49) | | | 18 (20.22) | | | 27 (11.16) | | | 17 (19.32) | | |
| Score n (%) | 19 (19.59) | | | 16 (17.98) | | | 36 (14.88) | | | 14 (15.91) | | |
| Timer n (%) | 13 (13.40) | | | 12 (13.48) | | | 39 (16.12) | | | 17 (19.32) | | |

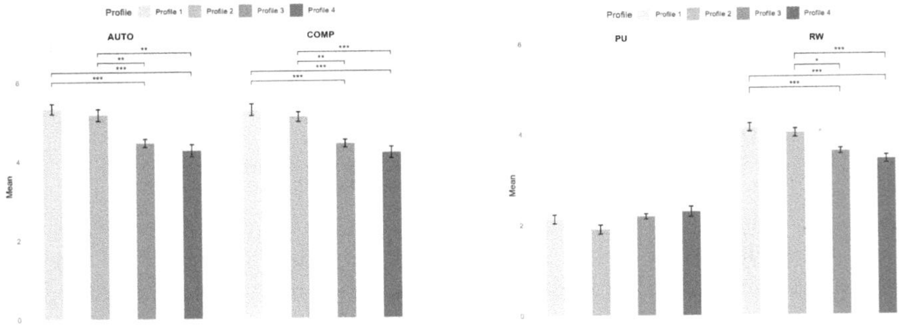


(a) (b)

**Fig. 3.** Wald test results on the PENS (a) and UES (b) indicators across the four learner profiles. The asterisks indicate Benjamin-Hochberg adjusted p-values: ***< .001, **< .01, *< .05.

attempts before success. Across all three indicators, learners in Profile 4 completed fewer exercises successfully, achieved lower success rates on their first attempt, and required more attempts on average to complete an exercise successfully than learners in Profiles 1 and 2.

# 6 Discussion

## 6.1 Identification of Learner Profiles

The first objective of this study was to identify Hexad learner profiles to better understand the intra-individual configuration of player types among learners. We identified four distinct Hexad learner profiles, each characterised by different player-type configurations.

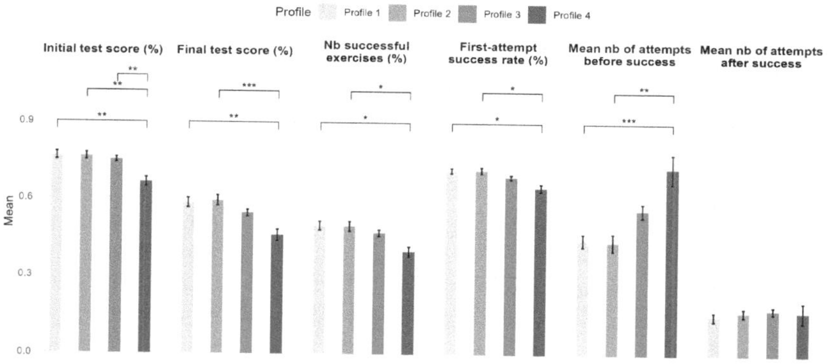


**Fig. 4.** Wald test results on the cognitive and behavioural indicators across the four learner profiles. The asterisks indicate Benjamin-Hochberg adjusted p-values: ***$<$ .001, **$<$ .01, *$<$ .05.

**Profile 1** is characterised by high scores across all Hexad dimensions except Disruptor. We labelled this profile as the *High-5 (Ac, FS, Ph, Pl, So) Profile.* **Profile 2** shows four high scores on Achievers, Free Spirit, Philanthropist and Socialiser types, a moderate score in Player type and a low Disruptor level. This profile can be named as the *High-4 (Ac, FS, Ph, So) Profile.* This profile is similar to Profile 3 reported in [6], which is also characterised by high scores of Philanthropist and Socialiser dimensions. It aligns with the theoretical definition of the Hexad framework, where Philanthropist and Socialiser types often co-express due to their need for social connection. **Profile 3** shows high scores on the Free Spirit and Player dimensions, moderate values on Achiever, Philanthropist, and Socialiser, as well as a low score on the Disruptor dimension. We labelled the *High-2 (FS, Pl) Moderate Profile.* A similar "moderate" profile has been reported in [28]. **Profile 4** is characterised by moderate scores on Free Spirit, Player and Socialiser dimensions, and by low scores on the Achiever, Disruptor, and

Philanthropist dimensions. We labelled it the *Moderate Low Profile*. A similar profile type was also identified by Schultze et al. [28].

These profiles show similarities with prior studies, although we did not observe a profile with a very low Socialiser dimension, such as in [6,28]. Across all profiles, Disruptor types remain the lowest dimensions, which is consistent with previous findings [6,28].

These profiles can be further interpreted through the lens of learners' psychological needs satisfaction. Profiles with higher scores in the Achiever type (*High-5* and *High-4 Profiles*) were associated with higher competence. This is consistent with the definition of Achievers, which focuses on mastery and challenge. Similarly, the Free Spirit type is theoretically associated with autonomy, and the *High-5 Profile* (showing the higher Free Spirit scores) also exhibits higher autonomy. However, we did not retrieve these similarities between the *High-4* and the *High-2 moderate* profiles; the *High-2 moderate* profile showing lower autonomy while having higher Free Spirit scores. Furthermore, we observe that the degree of satisfaction of learners' psychological needs decreases as player-type scores decline, suggesting that lower profile levels are associated with a lower degree of satisfaction of these needs.

### 6.2 Relationships Between Learner Profile and Outcomes

The second objective of this study was to examine how learners' player types relate to behavioural and cognitive outcomes. We examined the differences observed in these outcomes between the four Hexad profiles identified in the first stage. Given that the game elements were distributed uniformly across the profiles (see Table 2), we were able to focus on the influence of Hexad player types on the outcomes rather than on the specific role of each game element.

Our results indicate that learners with a *Moderate Low Profile* had lower initial test scores than those with other profiles. This suggests that the scores of the player types influence initial performance more than the combination of these types does. Additionally, these differences are observed in all other cognitive and behavioural indicators, except for the number of attempts after success. This suggests that initial performance influences the other indicators, rather than the Hexad profiles.

Regarding the perceived engagement, learners in the *High-5 Profile* and in the *High-4 Profile* reported higher Reward (RW) than those in the *High-2 moderate Profile* and the *Moderate Low Profile*. However, no significant differences were observed in perceived utility (PU). These results partially contrast with those reported in [7], the Disruptor types positively influencing PU. In our study, Disruptor types were relatively low across profiles; therefore, their influence may be limited and modulated by other player types. Furthermore, dos Santos et al. [7] showed that the player dimensions have a positive effect on the Reward dimension. In our study, the *High-4 Profile* exhibited higher Reward scores than the *High-2 Moderate Profile* despite having similar player type scores. This suggests that the specific combination of types within a profile can lead to different engagement outcomes. Additionally, and similar to the autonomy and competence outcomes, the two profiles with lower player types scores (*High-2* and *Moderate-Low Profiles*) perceived the learning experience as less rewarding than the two other profiles (*High-5* and *High-4 Profiles*). Therefore, this suggests that this perception tends to decrease as player type scores decline.

## 7 Conclusion

In this paper, we identified learner profiles based on their player types and examined their relationship with cognitive and behavioural outcomes using a person-centred approach. Our findings reveal four distinct learner profiles, characterised by different configurations of Hexad player types and associated with distinct cognitive and behavioural outcomes. Overall, the results demonstrate that Latent Profile Analysis can reliably predict learners' most likely profile membership, making this approach readily applicable in educational settings.

These findings extend prior work by highlighting the importance of considering configurations of player types rather than individual player types in isolation, and support the design of tailored learning paths or game elements for each profile. Teachers may use these learner profiles to better understand their students and design more personalised interventions. In particular, learners in the *High-2 Moderate* and *Moderate Low* profiles exhibit the lowest levels of perceived autonomy, competence, and reward. Therefore, teachers may focus on strengthening these dimensions for these profiles, for instance by integrating game elements specifically designed to support these psychological needs.

However, this study presents several limitations. First, it focuses on a single domain and context, namely mathematics learning among secondary school students. The identified profiles and their relationships with outcomes may differ across learning domains and populations, limiting the generalisability of the findings. Secondly, this study relies on a particular learning environment and gamification design. Therefore, the results may vary in other learning environments and could be influenced by contextual factors. Thirdly, some outcomes, such as engagement, relied on self-reported measures, which may be subject to response biases and may not fully reflect learners' actual behaviours. Finally, this study examined the relationships between player types and outcomes at a general level, without considering the potential effects of individual game elements.

Future work should focus on validating and refining these learner profiles across various domains, population groups, and learning environments. Finally, future research should investigate how specific game mechanisms influence learners' behavioural and cognitive outcomes within the same profile and across different profiles. This work will help to identify the most effective game element for each learner profile.

## References


1. Barata, G., Gama, S., Jorge, J.A., Gonçalves, D.J.: Relating gaming habits with student performance in a gamified learning experience. In: Proceedings of the First ACM SIGCHI Annual Symposium on Computer-human Interaction in Play, pp. 17–25. CHI PLAY '14, ACM, New York, USA (2014)
2. Bartle, R.: Hearts, clubs, diamonds, spades: players who suit muds [on-line]. Consulté à l'adresse: http://www.mud.co.uk/richard/hcds.htm (1996)
3. Bauer, J.: A primer to latent profile and latent class analysis. In: Goller, M., Kyndt, E., Paloniemi, S., Damşa, C. (eds.) Methods for Researching Professional Learning and Development: Challenges, Applications and Empirical Illustrations, pp. 243–268. Springer International Publishing, Cham (2022). https://doi.org/10.1007/978-3-031-08518-5_11
4. Bennett, D., Feng, F., Mekler, E.D.: Autonomous regulation of social media use: implications for self-control, well-being, and UX. In: Proceedings of the 2025 CHI Conference on Human Factors in Computing Systems, pp. 1–22. ACM, Yokohama Japan (2025)
5. Brandl, L.C., Schrader, A.: Clustering on player types of students in health science - trial and data analyses. Stud. Health Technol. Inform. **307**, 89–95 (2023)
6. Brandl, L.C., Schrader, A.: Student player types in higher education-trial and clustering analyses. Educ. Sci. **14**(4) (2024)
7. dos Santos, L.F., Oliveira, W., Corrêa de Lima, A., de Castro Junior, A.A., Hamari, J.: The effects of gamification on learners' engagement according to their gamification user types. Technol. Knowl. Learn. (2025)
8. Gil, B., Cantador, I., Marczewski, A.: Validating gamification mechanics and player types in an e-learning environment. In: Conole, G., Klobučar, T., Rensing, C., Konert, J., Lavoué, É. (eds.) EC-TEL 2015. LNCS, vol. 9307, pp. 568–572. Springer, Cham (2015). https://doi.org/10.1007/978-3-319-24258-3_61
9. Hallifax, S., Serna, A., Marty, J.C., Lavoué, E.: A design space for meaningful structural gamification. In: Extended Abstracts of the 2018 CHI Conference on Human Factors in Computing Systems, pp. 1–6. ACM, Montreal QC Canada (2018)
10. Hallifax, S., Serna, A., Marty, J.C., Lavoué, G., Lavoué, E.: Factors to consider for tailored gamification. In: Proceedings of the Annual Symposium on Computer-Human Interaction in Play, pp. 559–572. ACM, Barcelona Spain (2019)
11. Hassan, M.A., Habiba, U., Majeed, F., Shoaib, M.: Adaptive gamification in e-learning based on students' learning styles. Interact. Learn. Environ. **29**(4), 545–565 (2021)
12. Johnson, D., Gardner, M.J., Perry, R.: Validation of two game experience scales: the player experience of need satisfaction (PENS) and game experience questionnaire (GEQ). Int. J. Hum Comput Stud. **118**, 38–46 (2018)
13. Klock, A.C.T., Gasparini, I., Pimenta, M.S., Hamari, J.: Tailored gamification: a review of literature. Int. J. Hum Comput Stud. **144**, 102495 (2020)
14. Krath, J., Altmeyer, M., Tondello, G.F., Nacke, L.E.: Hexad-12: developing and validating a short version of the gamification user types hexad scale. In: Proceedings of the 2023 CHI Conference on Human Factors in Computing Systems, pp. 1–18. CHI '23, ACM, New York, NY, USA (2023)
15. Krath, J., Palmquist, A., Jedel, I., Barbopoulos, I., Helmefalk, M., Munkvold, R.I.: Does behaviour match user typologies? An exploratory cluster analysis of behavioural data from a gamified fitness platform. GamiFIN, pp, 105–114 (2022)

16. Lopez, C.E., Tucker, C.S.: The effects of player type on performance: a gamification case study. Comput. Hum. Behav. **91**, 333–345 (2019)
17. Marczewski, A.: Even ninja monkeys like to play: unicorn edition. Gamified UK (2018)
18. Marsh, H.W., Hau, K.T., Grayson, D.: Goodness of fit in structural equation models. In: Contemporary Psychometrics: A Festschrift for Roderick P. McDonald, pp. 275–340. Multivariate Applications Book Series, Lawrence Erlbaum Associates Publishers, Mahwah, NJ, US (2005)
19. Nacke, L.E., Bateman, C., Mandryk, R.L.: BrainHex: a neurobiological gamer typology survey. Entertainment Comput. **5**(1), 55–62 (2014)
20. Nadi-Ravandi, S., Batooli, Z.: Gamification in education: A scientometric, content and co-occurrence analysis of systematic review and meta-analysis articles. Educ. Inf. Technol. **27**(7), 10207–10238 (2022)
21. Nylund-Gibson, K., Choi, A.Y.: Ten frequently asked questions about latent class analysis. Transl. Issues Psychol. Sci. **4**(4), 440–461 (2018)
22. O'Brien, H.L., Cairns, P., Hall, M.: A practical approach to measuring user engagement with the refined user engagement scale (UES) and new UES short form. Int. J. Hum Comput Stud. **112**, 28–39 (2018)
23. Perera, H.N., McIlveen, P.: Vocational interest profiles: profile replicability and relations with the STEM major choice and the Big-Five. J. Vocat. Behav. **106**, 84–100 (2018)
24. Reyssier, S., Hallifax, S., Serna, A., Marty, J.C., Simonian, S., Lavoué, E.: The impact of game elements on learner motivation: influence of initial motivation and player profile. IEEE Trans. Learn. Technol. **15**(1), 42–54 (2022)
25. Rogers, K., Kamm, C., Weber, M.: Towards player-centric adaptivity: interactions of gameplay behaviour and player traits in a survival game. In: Proceedings of the 2016 Annual Symposium on Computer-Human Interaction in Play Companion Extended Abstracts, pp. 269–276. CHI PLAY Companion '16, ACM, New York, NY, USA (2016)
26. Ryan, R.M., Deci, E.L.: Self-determination theory and the facilitation of intrinsic motivation, social development, and well-being. Am. Psychol. **55**(1), 68–78 (2000)
27. Ryan, R.M., Rigby, C.S., Przybylski, A.: The motivational pull of video games: a self-determination theory approach. Motiv. Emot. **30**(4), 344–360 (2006)
28. Schultze, S., Hochweber, J., Habermeyer, T., Schneider, S.: A first validation of the gamification user types HEXAD scale for digital learning systems. Comput. Hum. Behav. Rep., 101011 (2026)
29. Serna, A., Hallifax, S., Lavoué, E.: Investigating the effects of tailored gamification on learners' engagement over time in a learning environment. Proc. ACM Hum.-Comput. Interact. **7**(CHI PLAY) (2023)
30. Sipone, S., Abella, V., Rojo, M., Moura, J.L.: Gamification and player type: relationships of the HEXAD model with the learning experience. J. New Approaches Educ. Res. **14**(1), 1 (2025)
31. Spurk, D., Hirschi, A., Wang, M., Valero, D., Kauffeld, S.: Latent profile analysis: a review and "how to" guide of its application within vocational behavior research. J. Vocat. Behav. **120**, 103445 (2020)
32. Toda, A.M., Valle, P.H.D., Isotani, S.: The dark side of gamification: an overview of negative effects of gamification in education, Higher Education for All. From Challenges to Novel Technology-Enhanced Solutions (2018)
33. Tondello, G.F., Wehbe, R.R., Diamond, L., Busch, M., Marczewski, A., Nacke, L.E.: The gamification user types hexad scale. In: Proceedings of the 2016 Annual

Symposium on Computer-Human Interaction in Play, pp. 229–243. CHI PLAY '16, ACM, New York, NY, USA (2016)
34. Zainuddin, Z., Chu, S.K.W., Shujahat, M., Perera, C.J.: The impact of gamification on learning and instruction: a systematic review of empirical evidence. Educ. Res. Rev. **30**, 100326 (2020)
35. Zeng, J., Sun, D., Looi, C.K., Fan, A.C.W.: Exploring the impact of gamification on students' academic performance: a comprehensive meta-analysis of studies from the year 2008 to 2023. Br. J. Edu. Technol. **55**(6), 2478–2502 (2024)

# Understanding How Learning Design Co-authoring Unfolds in Online Platforms

María Jesús Rodríguez-Triana[1](✉), Jelena Jovanović[2], Luis P. Prieto[1], Oleksandra Poquet[3], Tobias Ley[4], and Denis Gillet[5]

[1] Universidad de Valladolid, Valladolid, Spain
{mjrodtri,luispablo.prieto}@uva.es
[2] University of Belgrade, Belgrade, Serbia
jelena.jovanovic@fon.bg.ac.rsu
[3] Technical University of Munich, Munich, Germany
sasha.poquet@tum.de
[4] University for Continuing Education Krems, Krems, Austria
tobias.ley@donau-uni.ac.at
[5] École Polytechnique Fédérale de Lausanne, Lausanne, Switzerland
denis.gillet@epfl.ch

**Abstract.** Online platforms for learning design (LD) co-authoring offer teachers opportunities to engage with pedagogical practice in a community. Supporting co-design at scale requires understanding its temporal unfolding, often relying solely on trace data. Yet, most studies of learning (co-)design focus on group-level analyses of the quality and composition of the finished LD product, rather than the heterogeneous unfolding of its process. This study analyses patterns of trace data from the widely used platform, Graasp, using the Knowledge Appropriation Model (KAM) to examine how such co-design processes evolve over time. Clustering 1,050 designs, we identify LD co-authoring profiles based on features reflecting KAM maturation phases as well as process predictability and stability indicators extracted using recurrence quantification analysis. These profiles are then analysed based on a critical phase transition in the teachers' learning process: the LD's classroom implementation. Our results highlight effort, regularity, and co-creation (multiple authors contributing content) as key to successful LD co-authoring that transitions to implementation. The study also underscores challenges in applying theoretical constructs to analyse trace data and limitations of such data in capturing complex, blended social practices.

**Keywords:** Social practices · Online communities of practice · Knowledge appropriation model · Knowledge maturation · Learning design · Temporal analysis · Log data

## 1 Introduction

Digital technologies have enabled teachers to collaboratively design learning plans and materials (also referred to as learning designs, or LDs) in commu-


J. Weidlich et al. (Eds.): EC-TEL 2026, LNCS 16905, pp. 531–545, 2027.
https://doi.org/10.1007/978-3-032-37979-5_36

nities of practice [38]. Such technology-mediated collaboration has been studied in educational technology for nearly two decades (e.g., [1, 19]).

Despite its importance for teacher professional learning, research on the dynamics of these social-cognitive processes remains limited. Existing evidence links certain social practices (such as sharing and cocreating) to increased pedagogical uptake [30], yet analyses typically focus on features inferred from the final product rather than on the design process. Indeed, most large-scale LD studies examine only outcomes [29, 36] or student reactions to the LDs [23, 29]. Additionally, existing research typically employs group-level, variable-centred approaches that ignore potential heterogeneity in design processes and outcomes [3].

This paper tackles this gap by examining temporal aspects of teacher co-design at scale in an online platform for inquiry-based learning (Graasp), using the Knowledge Appropriation Model (KAM, [18]) as a theoretical framework. KAM conceptualises knowledge co-creation as a result of interrelated social practices (maturation, scaffolding, and appropriation) traceable in the system. However, analysing these processes at scale remains challenging, particularly in large-scale datasets where contextual and nuanced differences are harder to capture.

To address that challenge, we combine traditional measures of technology-mediated LD activity (volume and effort) with measures of dynamics describing differences in how design processes unfold over time. We apply this approach to 1,050 LDs in Graasp. KAM was used to operationalise log data into features of LD activity volume and nonlinear dynamics (using Recurrence Quantification Analysis—RQA). Clustering algorithms led us to identify co-authoring profiles. Exploratory visual analysis of clustering results and selected cases helped interpret the identified profiles, with statistical tests examining associations between profiles and classroom implementation success.

## 2 Related Work

### 2.1 Analyses of Learning (Co-)Design in Teacher Communities

Teacher professional learning often occurs within communities of practice, where shared practices and materials facilitate knowledge adaptation and internalisation [38]. These shared or social practices involve goal-directed actions mediated by technologies and artefacts that embody the community's evolving knowledge [9]. Thus, technologies and artefacts offer lenses for studying such practices. In teacher communities, learning designs (LDs) -also called lesson or instructional plans- are central artefacts.

The Knowledge Appropriation Model (KAM) conceptualises knowledge co-creation as comprising three interrelated practices: maturation, scaffolding, and appropriation [18]. As a first step towards understanding KAM practices, this paper focuses on maturation, which involves progressively transforming individual knowledge into community knowledge through artefact co-construction. In LD co-authoring communities, maturation might start with the expression of a new idea, followed by sharing, co-creation, formalisation for broader use, and, eventually, standardisation, where, for example, a design becomes widely adopted or integrated into national curricula or training.

Researchers have examined how teachers co-create LDs through community analytics [11]. Small-scale studies have explored authoring platform adoption in specific practitioner groups, often within a single school or teacher training programme. For example, [20] analysed 53 teachers and 21 artefacts from two school communities participating in a professional development program, and [7] analysed 62 contributions from 91 pre-service teachers using ILDE+, finding no significant correlation between behavioural indicators and contributions' quality.

At a larger scale, researchers have analysed thousands of LDs created by thousands of teachers in Graasp, mapping their final states and metadata to KAM practices [30], and showing that certain social practices were associated with higher chances of LD classroom implementation. However, this prior work used a variable-based approach [27], which overlooks temporal differences in how LDs are designed and how the co-design unfolds over time. To address this limitation in analysing LD co-creation at scale, it would be necessary to characterise LD co-authoring more holistically by incorporating measures of dynamics.

### 2.2 Scaling up Analyses of Temporality

Since Reimann's call to include more temporal aspects of teaching and learning processes [27], scholars are increasingly integrating temporal dimensions into static analyses of teaching and learning. This includes examining both the passage of time (e.g., behaviour duration, frequency or acceleration) and event order (e.g., consistency, recurrence, irregularity) [16,21,22,27].

While time- and order-based approaches promise to deepen our understanding of teacher co-design at scale, selecting appropriate, scalable methods for large trace datasets remains challenging. Traditional educational research draws on diverse data sources (e.g., self-reports, logs and sensor data, observations, and human-annotated teaching/learning artefacts), but large-scale environments often rely solely on trace data—digital logs collected unobtrusively "in the wild". Yet, deriving insights from such data demands extensive data transformation and interpretation, often raising validity concerns [33].

In addition, temporal analyses have largely focused on learners. On the other hand, teachers' co-design processes and their dynamics, captured in large-scale trace data, remain underexplored.

### 2.3 Research Goals and Questions

Despite growing interest in teacher co-design processes, little is known about how such processes unfold at scale in authentic settings. Most studies offer static snapshots, rely on small datasets, or focus on outcomes rather than process. The current study addresses this gap by analysing, from a temporal perspective, LD co-authoring processes using large-scale log data from an authentic setting, Graasp. The analysis, theoretically grounded in KAM, aims to uncover co-design process profiles and their link with a key indicator of the design process success (namely, whether the resulting LDs are being implemented in practice with students). Hence, our research questions are:

*RQ1*: What profiles of LD processes can be identified in Graasp, and what do they reveal about distinct temporal unfolding of co-design processes?

*RQ2*: How do these profiles differ in their implementation potential?

## 3 Research Methodology

This paper addresses the RQs through an exploratory study. This section describes the study context alongside the data gathering and analysis methods.

### 3.1 Research Context

Authoring platforms like Graasp[1], with over 35,000 users globally, offer a valuable lens into teachers' co-design practices at scale, in authentic contexts. Graasp supports LD authoring and implementation, particularly for inquiry-based learning in primary and secondary education. Teachers create web spaces structured according to inquiry phases filled with embedded multimedia, apps, and labs. These designs can then be shared with students via browser-accessible links where they can carry out inquiry-based activities.

In KAM maturation terms, teachers, individually, can express LD ideas using templates or other designs, then share or co-create with peers by assigning view or edit rights. When ready, designs can be formalised by publishing them in an open repository[2]. During this process, teachers may also request expert feedback on their designs (scaffolding). All these processes are nonlinear and emergent (since they are inherently unpredictable and contingent).

We consider a design implemented when at least six students access it within one week. This threshold accounts for common classroom practices where, in case of 10 or more students, they typically work in pairs on shared devices, with only one student registering in the system [31]. Since teachers often preview designs as students themselves, we have set six as a minimum number of student registrations (one teacher acting as a student plus five students). The one-week window allows us to capture both synchronous in-class use and asynchronous home access.

### 3.2 Dataset

The data were collected from Graasp under GDPR compliance and within Go-Lab, Next-Lab, and Go-GA. Users consented to research use of their data via the platform's terms, and only relevant, anonymised data were extracted to ensure privacy throughout the analysis.

To examine how social practices relate to authoring outcomes (i.e., implementation), we analysed data from November 1, 2015 -when consistent tracking

[1] Formerly graasp.eu and currently graasp.org.

[2] Golabz.eu.

began- to December 31, 2019 -when the aforementioned inquiry learning-related projects ended and before COVID-19 introduced alternative platform uses.

The dataset [32] includes 40,235 LDs, each with metadata such as creation date, member and student lists, number of predecessors and copies, and location (flagging belonging to project-related folders). Among 37,685 registered users, we identified different types (regular teachers, project participants, and platform admins), later used in the dataset filtering. We also extracted action logs tied to LDs, capturing timestamp, author, action type, and the corresponding LD.

### 3.3 Data Preparation and Analyses

To address the RQs, we followed an iterative process of Graasp trace data exploration, preparation, and cluster analysis. For clarity, steps are presented sequentially. Further details and reproducibility resources are provided in [32].

*Operationalising Theory.* We mapped KAM phases to each LD's log history using rule-based segmentation: LDs enter the *Express* phase upon creation; *Share* begins with the first navigation or social action by another teacher; *Co-creation* starts with the first edit by another teacher; and *Formalisation* begins when the first version is published. The logged actions within each phase were used to characterise maturation dynamics (see "Feature engineering").

*Operationalising Temporality.* We considered both passage of time (e.g., time between actions) and order in time (e.g., action sequences and their recurrence) when extracting features. To analyse these dynamics, we applied recurrence quantification analysis (RQA), which captures temporal structure and complexity in categorical or continuous data [37], and looks for fluctuations within the entire time series [8], providing indicators of underlying dynamics without explaining changes. Here, we use RQA to calculate event-based features that capture the order in time, complementing variable-based KAM-derived features representing the passage of time (see more details under the "Feature engineering").

*Dataset Filtering.* LD processes in Graasp are fragmented—teachers may duplicate or delete LDs, and reuse older ones. Thus, to analyse full authoring sequences, we selected LDs created from scratch, excluding those copied later (except when formalised, indicating completion). Then, to focus on authentic practice, we removed LDs involving platform admins or project experts, or located under project folders. This yielded 10,564 LDs.

Focusing on collaborative content creation, we retained only LDs involving at least two teachers (N=1,425). For meaningful temporal analysis, we further excluded LDs with too few or too many actions (below the 25th percentile = 34 actions; above the 99th = 2,488 actions), leaving 1,058 LDs. These involved 2,456 teachers and 304,346 co-design actions.

*Feature Engineering.* To identify co-authoring profiles, we used both variable- and event-based features [27,35]. As shown in Figure 1, variable-based features were computed per KAM phase: number of actions (nact), median time gap (medgap), number of teachers (ntch), and proportion of actions by the most/least active teacher (maxprop / minprop). The Express phase involves only the LD initiator, so only nact and medgap were computed there; the other phases involved all metrics. These features, taken together, reflect temporal development (passage of time) through the key steps of the KAM's maturation practices: express → share → co-create → formalise. For dynamic characterisation, we applied categorical autoRQA (aRQA) to each LD's action sequence, comprising three action types: Use (navigation), Adaptation (content edits), and Social (such as sharing, tagging, liking). For each LD, encoded as a categorical string (e.g.,"UUUAAUS...", where letters U, A, and S, respectively, stand for the three aforementioned types of actions), the following RQA metrics were computed:

- Recurrence Rate (RR): Proportion of recurrence points in the recurrence plot . It shows how intensely a system revisits the same states over time.
- Entropy of Diagonal Lines (ENTrel_dl): Shannon entropy over diagonal lengths. It measures the unpredictability of behaviour patterns.
- Trapping Time (TT): Average length of vertical lines in the recurrence plot. It indicates persistence in particular states.
- Mean Length of Diagonal Lines (MEAN_dl): Average duration of repeated behaviour sequences. It reflects system predictability.

Eight LDs lacked sufficient sequence data for aRQA and were excluded. Thus, the final dataset included 1,050 LDs.

*Data Preparation for Cluster Analysis.* We prepared the extracted features for clustering (see Fig. 1). Features with a large proportion of missing values were excluded, and those with limited missingness had missing values replaced with reasonable alternatives. For example, in the case of Share.maxprop and Share.minprop - the proportion of activities of the most and least active teacher in the Share phase - missing values were replaced with zeros since they occurred in those cases when no action was done by any teacher in the Share phase (e.g., when a design went directly from Express to Formalise).

To mitigate outliers, we applied Winsorisation (typically capping at the 95th percentile). Features with near-zero variance, high pairwise correlations ($|r| > 0.75$), or extreme skewness were removed. Finally, due to non-normal distributions, all features were standardised using medians and interquartile ranges. The final set included eight features (see Table 1). Further details about the data preparation are available in the notebook.

*Cluster Analysis.* To identify LD co-authoring profiles (RQ1), we applied hierarchical agglomerative clustering (Ward's method, Euclidean distance), commonly used for trace data pattern identification [5,13]. The number of clusters was determined via dendrogram inspection and four cluster statistics: Dunn's score, Separation Index, Average within/between ratio, and Silhouette width [10]. For

RQ2 (profile implementation rates), we used exploratory visualisation and Chi-square tests. All analyses were conducted in R using the casnet[3] package for RQA, as well as cluster, fpc, and factoextra packages for clustering [10].

| Variable-based (KAM) | | | | Event-based (aRQA) |
|---|---|---|---|---|
| Express.nact | Share.nact | + CoCreate.nact | • Formalise.nact | RR |
| ▲Express.medgap | ■Share.medgap | CoCreate.medgap | + Formalise.medgap | ENTrel_dl |
| | Share.ntch | ▲CoCreate.ntch | • Formalise.ntch | ▲TT |
| | Share.maxprop | + CoCreate.maxprop | + Formalise.maxprop | ▲MEAN_dl |
| | Share.minprop | + CoCreate.minprop | + Formalise.minprop | |

(+) High % missing values (•) Near-zero variance (▲) Highly correlated features (■) Overly skewed distribution

**Fig. 1.** Features extracted per learning design and reasons for feature exclusion.

## 4 Results

By inspecting the dendrogram and several clustering quality metrics (see Sect. 3.3 and [32]), we selected five clusters (i.e., LD authoring profiles) as the optimal solution (see Table 1 and Fig. 2, top):

- *Profile 1 – Steady joint co-design effort (126, 12%):* LDs in this profile progressed briskly through Express and Share phases, all reaching Co-creation. This is the only group with notable Co-creation activity, involving four teachers on average. A few LDs advanced to Formalise. Compared to others, this profile shows lower entropy and higher other RQA measures (RR, TT, Mean_dl), indicating regular, repetitive, and predictable behaviour. Based on our experience with the platform and supporting teachers [12], such consistent engagement by small groups tends to yield well-elaborated designs.

- *Profile 2 – Solo creation with early peer viewing (144, 13.71%):* Most LDs reached the Share phase following limited Express-phase engagement by one teacher. The activity concentrates in the Share phase, involving two–three teachers on average, though only the original creator edited the LD. This profile exhibits low entropy and medium values of other RQA measures, suggesting repetitiveness and predictability. Such authoring processes are characteristic of authors seeking early peer feedback on individually developed content.

- *Profile 3 – Low and erratic design effort with scarce peer viewing (625, 59.52%):* The largest profile, with most LDs stopping at Share, a notable portion reaching Co-creation, and a few Formalisation. Engagement is minimal, with small

[3] https://github.com/FredHasselman/casnet.

teams and most work done by one teacher. It has the highest entropy and lowest RR, TT, and Mean_dl values, reflecting unstable and unpredictable behaviour typical of demos or very simple designs.

- *Profile 4 – Solo creation with late peer viewing (96, 9.14%):* Most LDs in this profile reached the Share-phase, and it includes the highest proportion of Formalised LDs. However, most development occurred in the Express phase, led by the original author. The profile shows high RR, TT, and Mean_dl values and low entropy, indicating recurrent and stable behaviour. These designs may reflect solo work with feedback sought at a mature stage.

- *Profile 5 – Low and erratic design effort with wide peer viewing (59, 5.62%):* Similar to Profile 3 but with slightly higher engagement in Express and Share phases. This profile has made the lowest progress through KAM phases, with most LDs remaining at Share and only a few advancing to Co-creation. It shows moderate values of the features associated with repetitiveness and stability. This may typify training contexts where teachers are encouraged to share early drafts to support mutual learning.

Figure 2 (bottom) shows the absolute and proportional implementation rates per profile. A Chi-square test indicated a significant implementation difference among profiles ($X^2(4, N{=}1050){=}106.0091$, $p < .0001$). Post-hoc pairwise proportion tests with false discovery rate correction showed Profiles 3 and 5 differed significantly from the rest, though not from each other. Specifically, LDs resulting from co-authoring Profiles 3 and 5 were significantly less likely to be implemented compared to the other three profiles. Notably, Profile 3 - despite being least successful in relative terms - accounted for the highest number of implementations overall (35.14%), due to its size, suggesting some successful cases may be hidden among demos.

**Table 1.** Descriptive statistics of the co-authoring profiles. Attributes in italics LD process features used in clustering. Remaining features were excluded due to high correlation, but are shown for interpretation.

| Attribute | Profile 1 (n = 126) | Profile 2 (n = 144) | Profile 3 (n = 625) | Profile 4 (n = 96) | Profile 5 (n = 59) |
|---|---|---|---|---|---|
| *Express.nact* | 12 (3.25, 34.75) | 42.5 (10.5, 130) | 42 (15, 83) | 461.5 (328.75, 609.48) | 72 (23.5, 157.5) |
| Express.medgap | 9.75 (5, 23.88) | 8.75 (5, 16) | 10 (6, 21) | 5 (2, 8) | 11 (5.25, 19.5) |
| *Share.nact* | 44 (19, 106.25) | 259 (183.25, 424.25) | 24 (9, 55) | 19 (4, 47.25) | 52 (31.5, 84.5) |
| *Share.ntch* | 2 (2, 3) | 2 (2, 3) | 2 (2, 2) | 2 (2, 2) | 7 (5.5, 10) |
| *Share.maxprop* | 0.68 (0.51, 0.84) | 0.95 (0.84, 0.98) | 0.77 (0.61, 0.93) | 0.74 (0.51, 0.91) | 0.41 (0.33, 0.58) |
| *Share.minprop* | 0.16 (0.05, 0.28) | 0.02 (0.01, 0.05) | 0.17 (0.07, 0.39) | 0.1 (0.02, 0.33) | 0.02 (0.01, 0.04) |
| Share.medgap | 8 (5, 14.5) | 6 (3, 9.5) | 10.5 (6, 22.5) | 11 (5, 56) | 10 (6.5, 18.75) |
| *CoCreate.nact* | 560.5 (364, 634.65) | 0 (0, 0) | 0 (0, 8) | 0 (0, 0) | 0 (0, 0) |
| CoCreate.ntch | 4 (3, 5) | 0 (0, 0) | 0 (0, 2) | 0 (0, 0) | 0 (0, 0) |
| *RR* | 0.72 (0.65, 0.78) | 0.7 (0.62, 0.77) | 0.66 (0.57, 0.73) | 0.71 (0.62, 0.76) | 0.68 (0.61, 0.73) |
| MEAN_dl | 5.59 (4.68, 6.69) | 5.16 (4.23, 6.65) | 4.34 (3.53, 5.33) | 5.49 (4.43, 6.54) | 4.42 (3.72, 5.83) |
| *ENTrel_dl* | 0.35 (0.32, 0.39) | 0.37 (0.33, 0.42) | 0.41 (0.36, 0.47) | 0.37 (0.32, 0.4) | 0.39 (0.34, 0.43) |
| TT | 8.97 (7.38, 11.45) | 8.39 (6.44, 11.08) | 6.54 (5.01, 8.29) | 9.01 (6.62, 11.2) | 6.79 (5.53, 9.6) |

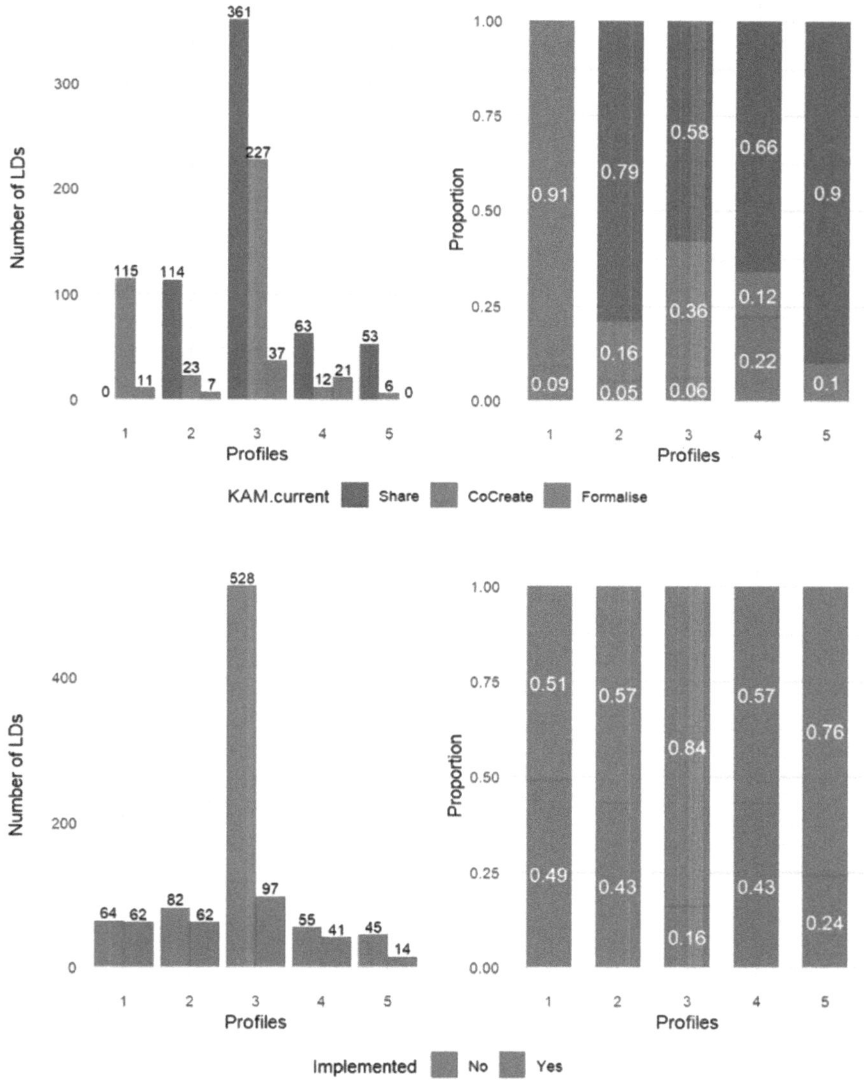


**Fig. 2.** Number and proportion of learning designs that reached the different KAM phases (top) and were implemented (bottom), by profile.

# 5 Discussion

## 5.1 RQ1: Profiles of LD Co-design Processes in Graasp

Our cluster analysis of over 1,000 co-authored LDs revealed distinct patterns in teachers' complex co-authoring processes. Using process features rooted in KAM maturation practices and recurrence quantification of co-authoring actions, we identified five patterns –LD co-authoring profiles– differing in the level of engagement across KAM phases as well as in regularity, repetitiveness, and predictability of social actions throughout the co-authored process.

While KAM provided a useful theoretical lens, mapping its constructs to platform log data presented challenges. Many KAM-driven features were discarded from clustering due to collinearity, highly skewed distributions, and other data-related issues, as reported in the methods. Despite the emphasis on grounding data analytics in theory [21,27,28,33], mapping abstract theories like KAM to low-level data is not straightforward. As [17] noted, theories are often defined at a macro level, whereas most data is recorded at a micro level, using different timescales. We therefore argue for solutions –intermediate concepts, processes, or mid-level theories– that bridge observable evidence and theoretical abstractions, as previously suggested [2,39].

While we identified meaningful design process profiles, this required iterative feature development, selection of comparable design processes, filtering irrelevant user behaviours, considering platform implementation quirks affecting the data, etc. –all demanding a deep understanding of the platform's development and usage context (tool purposes, common teacher practices, or typical training events). This suggests that LD co-authoring should be considered and examined as a complex system in which users and artefacts co-evolve, and comparatively small interventions in the design environment can have an outsized impact on the process [3]. Our experience also aligns with literature emphasising contextual knowledge for proper feature selection and cluster interpretation [4,15].

## 5.2 RQ2: Implementation Potential of Profiles

The identified design process profiles showed varied success levels regarding classroom implementation, with profiles 1, 2, and 4 having the highest implementation probability. This indicates "multiple paths to (implementation) success", not necessarily traversing KAM maturation levels upwards as theory suggests. Yet, even in most successful profiles, implementation remained not very frequent (43–49% probability), albeit higher than the dataset average (26.3%), suggesting that temporal patterns alone do not explain implementation. Still, other intangible factors not captured in log data undoubtedly exist, such as the design creator's initial intention(e.g., platform auditing vs. learning experience co-design).

Previous work examining social practices in Graasp found higher levels of maturation during co-design associated with higher classroom implementation rates [30]. This paper adds nuance to that finding, highlighting relevant features for understanding how LD co-authoring processes unfold. More concretely, our results show that regularity, effort, and co-creation tend to be associated with implementation (even if they do not ensure it). Still, questions remain as profile 3 –by far the largest– likely contains demos and low-effort designs (some implemented), which our current features cannot disentangle.

Comparing our results with ILDE+ community analytics by [7] reveals some contrasts. While they found no significant correlations between design quality and authoring platform behaviour, our clustering shows varying success rates, suggesting that effort and regularity in the design process are associated with implementation likelihood. However, differences in sample size (91 vs. 1,050) and unit of analysis (person vs. artefact-oriented) limit direct comparison. Future work could align these approaches by extracting success measures at scale, such as KAM's formalisation rates or pedagogical quality (e.g., using machine learning or GenAI for automated quality assessment, as illustrated by [24]).

### 5.3 Limitations

This study has several limitations. First, interactions beyond Graasp –e.g., peer and expert feedback via email or face-to-face– are not traced. Moreover, the processes depicted here include all the actions from LD creation until December 2019. Thus, some authoring processes may have continued later, and logs may include classroom implementation actions (e.g., accessing the LD for monitoring or assessment purposes) or later visits to the learning material. Consequently, complementary data sources would be necessary to triangulate our results, involving other trace data sources (e.g., the platform owner's help-desk system) and other data types (e.g., LD content or teachers' perception on the process), as noted by [28]. This underlines the need to combine trace data with other non-obtrusive sources to better understand (co)design processes at scale.

Second, focusing on comparable co-design processes led us to filter out those reused or created with experts or platform admins (i.e., reflecting appropriation or scaffolding KAM practices), potentially discarding relevant designs. Similarly, excluding Formalise-related features (due to rarity) may have biased the profiles. Hence, separate analyses are needed to explore the temporal dynamics of this underrepresented yet theoretically significant group.

Third, our analysis entailed interpreting what counts as a classroom implementation, establishing a threshold of student views per week. Nonetheless, this rough indicator may be misleading for designs with multiple teachers collaborating (each of whom may use student views during testing) or co-authoring processes spanning extended periods. Therefore, future work should explore more accurate implementation detection (e.g., triangulating student registration burstiness with the learning traces or the student-generated content while using the LDs).

Lastly, our analysis and findings are context-dependent. Thus, their applicability to other co-authoring platforms may be limited, requiring consideration of platform usage similarities/differences and available data. Still, the overall approach (analytics pipeline) we presented may be applied in teacher collaboration environments to examine co-authoring processes.

## 6 Conclusions and Future Work

This paper was motivated by the limited understanding of how teachers co-author learning designs (LDs) at scale in online platforms, particularly for inquiry-based learning. Analysing over a thousand LD authoring processes from a large-scale platform, we examined the link between teachers' co-design practices and classroom implementation, focusing on how these practices unfold over time. Clustering revealed five co-authoring profiles with varying implementation success. Our findings suggest that regularity, effort, and co-creation are associated with higher implementation rates. From a theoretical perspective, these results offer directions to expand the KAM framework, incorporating concepts such as effort spent on artefacts and process regularity.

We also foreground the challenges in connecting theory, data, and authentic educational practice. Though theory-driven analytics is widely advocated [21,27,28,33], operationalising macro-level constructs using micro-level data remains difficult, especially when relying on "context-poor" data like logs. We illustrate this issue, highlighting the iterative nature of this process and common pitfalls, through KAM's application in analysing teacher LD processes in a large-scale online platform. It is especially complicated to do this theory mapping in a way that includes temporal dynamics, and in widely used online platforms where free-form, unexpected usage patterns are bound to emerge. In a sense, our challenges parallel those faced by learning analytics researchers applying insights and techniques from traditional learning management systems to MOOCs [6,14].

To better understand teachers' (co)design practices, future work should explore additional social practice features. This could entail taking into account KAM appropriation and scaffolding practices, as well as incorporating other techniques well-suited for analysing both the social and temporal aspects of co-creation processes [26,34]. Moreover, alternative outcome measures are needed to understand LD success. Such measures could range from more accurate indicators of classroom implementation to content-based assessment of the artefacts' quality (another key property of the success of the learning and co-design process). Thus, complementing log data with other sources, such as LD content or teacher interviews, can help triangulate findings.

Finally, this research can inform the design of next-generation co-authoring tools. Insights on success factors and temporal dynamics could be embedded into AI systems to motivate and advise teachers (see initial efforts by [25]).

**Acknowledgments.** The present work has been partially funded by the European Union's Seventh Framework Programme (grant agreement No 317601) and the European Union's Horizon 2020 Research and Innovation Programme (grant agreements No 731685 and 781012). Also, the work has been supported by grants PID2020-112584RB-C32, PID2023-146692OB-C32, RYC2022-037806-I, and RYC2021-032273-I, all financed by MCIN/AEI/10.13039/501100011033. The last three grants were in addition funded by ERDF (EU), ESF+, and the European Union's NextGenerationEU/PRTR, respectively. Furthermore, this study has also been supported by the Regional Government of Castile and Leon and ERDF (EU), under project grant VA176P23.

## References


1. Asensio-Pérez, J.I., et al.: Towards teaching as design: exploring the interplay between full-lifecycle learning design tooling and teacher professional development. Comput. Educ. **114**, 92–116 (2017). https://doi.org/10.1016/j.compedu.2017.06.011
2. Buckingham Shum, S., Deakin Crick, R.: Learning analytics for 21st century competencies. J. Learn. Anal. **3**(2), 6–21 (2016). https://doi.org/10.18608/jla.2016.32.2
3. Carvalho, L., Martinez-Maldonado, R., Goodyear, P.: Instrumental genesis in the design studio. Int. J. Comput.-Support. Collab. Learn. **14**(1), 77–107 (2019). https://doi.org/10.1007/s11412-019-09294-2
4. Chen, B., Knight, S., Wise, A.F.: Critical issues in designing and implementing temporal analytics. J. Learn. Anal. **5**(1), 1–9 (2018). https://doi.org/10.18608/jla.2018.53.1
5. Fan, Y., Jovanović, J., Saint, J., Jiang, Y., Wang, Q., Gašević, D.: Revealing the regulation of learning strategies of MOOC retakers: a learning analytic study. Comput. Educ. **178**, 104404 (2022). https://doi.org/10.1016/j.compedu.2021.104404
6. Ferguson, R., Clow, D.: Examining engagement: analysing learner subpopulations in massive open online courses (MOOCs). In: Proceedings of the 5th International Conference on Learning Analytics and Knowledge, pp. 51–58 (2015). https://doi.org/10.1145/2723576.2723606
7. Gutiérrez-Páez, N.F., Santos, P., Hernández-Leo, D., Carrió, M.: A study of motivations, behavior, and contributions quality in online communities of teachers: a data analytics approach. Comput. Educ. **201**, 104829 (2023). https://doi.org/10.1016/j.compedu.2023.104829
8. Haake, L., Wallot, S., Tschense, M., Grabowski, J.: Global temporal typing patterns in foreign language writing: exploring language proficiency through recurrence quantification analysis (RQA). Reading Writing, 1–33 (2022). https://doi.org/10.1007/s11145-022-10331-0
9. Hakkarainen, K.: A knowledge-practice perspective on technology-mediated learning. Int. J. Comput.-Supported Collaborative Learn. **4**(2), 213–231 (2009). https://doi.org/10.1007/s11412-009-9064-x
10. Hennig, C.: FPC: flexible procedures for clustering. CRAN package (2023). https://CRAN.R-project.org/package=fpc
11. Hernández-Leo, D., Martinez-Maldonado, R., Pardo, A., Muñoz-Cristóbal, J.A., Rodríguez-Triana, M.J.: Analytics for learning design: a layered framework and tools. British J. Educ. Technol. **50**(1), 139–152 (2019). https://doi.org/10.1111/bjet.12645
12. de Jong, T., Gillet, D., Rodríguez-Triana, María Jesús, E.A.: Understanding teacher design practices for digital inquiry–based science learning: the case of go-lab. Educ. Technol. Res. Dev. **69**, 417–444 (2021). https://doi.org/10.1007/s11423-020-09904-z
13. Jovanović, J., Dawson, S., Joksimović, S., Siemens, G.: Supporting actionable intelligence: Reframing the analysis of observed study strategies. In: Proceedings of the 10th International Conference on Learning Analytics & Knowledge, pp. 161–170 (2020). https://doi.org/10.1145/3375462.3375474
14. Khalil, M., Ebner, M.: Clustering patterns of engagement in massive open online courses (MOOCs): the use of learning analytics to reveal student categories. J. Comput. Higher Educ. **29**, 114–132 (2017). https://doi.org/10.1007/s12528-016-9126-9

15. Kitto, K., Manly, C.A., Ferguson, R., Poquet, O.: Towards more replicable content analysis for learning analytics. In: Proceedings of the 13th International Conference on Learning Analytics and Knowledge Conference, pp. 303–314 (2023). https://doi.org/10.1145/3576050.3576096
16. Knight, S., Wise, A.F., Chen, B.: Time for change: why learning analytics needs temporal analysis. J. Learn. Anal. **4**(3), 7–17 (2017). https://doi.org/10.18608/jla.2017.43.2
17. Lemke, J.L.: Across the scales of time: artifacts, activities, and meanings in ecosocial systems. Mind, Culture Act. **7**(4), 273–290 (2009). https://doi.org/10.1207/S15327884MCA0704_03
18. Ley, T., Maier, R., Thalmann, S., Waizenegger, L., Pata, K., Ruiz-Calleja, A.: A knowledge appropriation model to connect scaffolded learning and knowledge maturation in workplace learning settings. Vocations Learn. **13**(1), 91–112 (2020). https://doi.org/10.1007/s12186-019-09231-2
19. Marín, V.I., Asensio-Pérez, J.I., Villagrá-Sobrino, S., Hernández-Leo, D., García-Sastre, S.: Supporting online collaborative design for teacher professional development. Technol. Pedagogy Educ. **27**(5), 571–587 (2018). https://doi.org/10.1080/1475939X.2018.1547787
20. Michos, K., Hernández-Leo, D., Albó, L.: Teacher-led inquiry in technology-supported school communities. British J. Educ. Technol. **49**(6), 1077–1095 (2018). https://doi.org/10.1111/bjet.12696
21. Molenaar, I., Wise, A.F.: Temporal aspects of learning analytics—grounding analyses in concepts of time. In: The Handbook of Learning Analytics, pp. 66–76. SOLAR, 2nd edn. (2022). https://doi.org/10.18608/hla22.007
22. Nath, D., Gašević, D., Fan, Y., Rajendran, R.: CTAM4SRL: a consolidated temporal analytic method for analysis of self-regulated learning. In: Proceedings of the 14th International Conference on Learning Analytics and Knowledge, pp. 645–655 (2024). https://doi.org/10.1145/3636555.3636926
23. Nguyen, Q., Rienties, B., Whitelock, D.: Informing learning design in online education using learning analytics of student engagement. In: Open World Learning, pp. 189–207. Routledge, 1st edn. (2022). https://doi.org/10.4324/9781003177098-17
24. Pishtari, G., Rodríguez-Triana, M.J., Prieto, L.P., Ruiz-Calleja, A., Väljataga, T.: What kind of learning designs do practitioners create for mobile learning? Lessons learnt from two in-the-wild case studies. J. Comput. Assist. Learn. **40**(6), 2399–2415 (2024). https://doi.org/10.1111/jcal.12672
25. Pishtari, G., Sarmiento-Márquez, E.M., Rodríguez-Triana, M.J., Wagner, M., Ley, T.: Evaluating the impact and usability of an AI-driven feedback system for learning design. In: Viberg, O., Jivet, I., Muñoz-Merino, P., Perifanou, M., Papathoma, T. (eds) Proceedings of the 18th European Conference on Technology Enhanced Learning. vol. 14200, pp. 324–338. Springer Nature Switzerland, Cham (2023). https://doi.org/10.1007/978-3-031-42682-7_22
26. Poquet, O., Jovanović, J., Pardo, A.: Student profiles of change in a university course: a complex dynamical systems perspective. In: Proceedings of the 13th International Learning Analytics and Knowledge Conference, pp. 197–207 (2023). https://doi.org/10.1145/3576050.3576077
27. Reimann, P.: Time is precious: variable- and event-centred approaches to process analysis in CSCL research. International Journal of Computer-Supported Collaborative Learning **4**(3), 239–257 (2009). https://doi.org/10.1007/s11412-009-9070-z

28. Reimann, P., Markauskaite, L., Bannert, M.: e-Research and learning theory: what do sequence and process mining methods contribute? British J. Educ. Technol. **45**(3), 528–540 (2014). https://doi.org/10.1111/bjet.12146
29. Rienties, B., Toetenel, L.: The impact of learning design on student behaviour, satisfaction and performance: a cross-institutional comparison across 151 modules. Comput. Hum. Behav. **60**, 333–341 (2016). https://doi.org/10.1016/j.chb.2016.02.074
30. Rodríguez-Triana, M.J., Prieto, L.P., Ley, T., de Jong, T., Gillet, D.: Social practices in teacher knowledge creation and innovation adoption: a large-scale study in an online instructional design community for inquiry learning. Int. J. Comput.-Support. Collaborative Learn. **15**(4), 445–467 (2020). https://doi.org/10.1007/s11412-020-09331-5
31. Rodríguez-Triana, M.J., Holzer, A., Vozniuk, A., Gillet, D.: Orchestrating inquiry-based learning spaces: an analysis of teacher needs. In: Advances in Web-Based Learning – ICWL 2015, pp. 131–142. Springer International Publishing, Cham (2015). https://doi.org/10.1007/978-3-319-25515-6_12
32. Rodríguez-Triana, M.J., Jovanović, J., Prieto, L.P., Poquet, O., Gillet, D.: Understanding how learning design co-authoring unfolds in online platforms: dataset, data analysis, and results (2026). https://doi.org/10.5281/zenodo.20650671
33. Saint, J., Fan, Y., Gašević, D., Pardo, A.: Temporally-focused analytics of self-regulated learning: a systematic review of literature. Comput. Educ. Artif. Intell. **3**, 100060 (2022). https://doi.org/10.1016/j.caeai.2022.100060
34. Saqr, M., Dever, D., López-Pernas, S., Gernigon, C., Marchand, G., Kaplan, A.: Complex Dynamic Systems in Education: Beyond the Static, the Linear and the Causal Reductionism, pp. 289–311. Springer Nature Switzerland, Cham (2026). https://doi.org/10.1007/978-3-031-95365-1_12
35. Tempelaar, D., Rienties, B., Giesbers, B., Nguyen, Q.: Modelling temporality in person- and variable-centred approaches. J. Learning Anal. **10**(2), 51–67 (2023). https://doi.org/10.18608/jla.2023.7841
36. Toetenel, L., Rienties, B.: Analysing 157 learning designs using learning analytic approaches as a means to evaluate the impact of pedagogical decision making. British J. Educ. Technol. **47**(5), 981–992 (2016). https://doi.org/10.1111/bjet.12423
37. Webber Jr., C.L., Zbilut, J.P.: Recurrence quantification analysis of nonlinear dynamical systems. In: Tutorials in Contemporary Nonlinear Methods for the Behavioral Sciences, pp. 26–94. National Science Foundation (2005). https://www.nsf.gov/pubs/2005/nsf05057/nmbs/chap2.pdf
38. Wenger, E.: Communities of Practice: Learning, Meaning, and Identity, 1st edn. Cambridge University Press, Cambridge (1998). https://doi.org/10.1017/CBO9780511803932
39. Wise, A.F., Knight, S., Shum, S.B.: Collaborative learning analytics. In: International Handbook of Computer-Supported Collaborative Learning, vol. 19, pp. 425–443. Springer International Publishing, Cham (2021). https://doi.org/10.1007/978-3-030-65291-3_23

# Beyond "does Training Work?" Understanding how Training Content Elements Influence the Adoption of New Technology Integrated Practices

Linda Helene Sillat(✉), Kaire Kollom, and Kairit Tammets

Tallinn University School of Digital Technologies, Narva Road 25, 10120 Tallinn, Estonia
linda.sillat@tlu.ee

**Abstract.** Despite the rapid expansion of professional development (PD) initiatives aimed at strengthening teachers' pedagogical digital competence (PDC), evidence remains limited on why some trainings translate into self-efficacy (SE) and intended adoption (IA) of technology-integrated practices while others do not. Most studies assess effectiveness primarily through outcome indicators such as perceived knowledge gains or self-reported competence, but these measures alone reveal little about the mechanisms through which training design supports meaningful change. This study moves beyond the question if training "works" by examining how teachers' perceived training quality and satisfaction relate to changes in PDC and IA of digital practices. Using pre–post survey data from teacher education students participating in digital competence training, we analyze (1) changes in perceived PDC, SE, and IA, and (2) how perceived training quality and learning experience predict IA, SE, and PDC development. The findings show that while perceived PDC improved overall, changes in SE and IA were more uneven. Across analyses, perceived knowledge gain, practical relevance, and cognitive activation emerged as key explanatory factors. The results suggest that effective digital competence training is not defined by participation alone, but by how relevant, cognitively supportive, and context-sensitive the training is perceived to be. These findings offer a more design-sensitive understanding of professional learning for technology integration and provide implications for the development of more transferable and sustainable PD models.

**Keywords:** Teacher Professional Development · Training Design · Pedagogical Digital Competence

## 1 Introduction

The rapid digitalization of education has intensified the need for teachers to develop strong pedagogical digital competence (PDC), enabling the meaningful integration of technology into teaching and learning processes. Although teachers PDC seems to include some conceptual plasticity due to the role of technology in education [1], it is clear that PDC is not solely the use of technological tools but a deeper combination of


J. Weidlich et al. (Eds.): EC-TEL 2026, LNCS 16905, pp. 546–560, 2027.
https://doi.org/10.1007/978-3-032-37979-5_37

competences including digital competence, pedagogical- and socioemotional knowledge [2]. Digital technologies enable more flexible, personalized and collaborative learning environments. Still the integration into educational practice has revealed persistent gaps between technological potential and pedagogical implementation [3]. Many of these challenges are related to both initial teacher training programs and in-service training. Despite the increase of understanding professional development programs which target the more complex understanding of PDC, empirical evidence remains inconclusive why some programs successfully lead to PDC development and thus a sustained pedagogical change while others do not.

Although considerable attention has been given to the elements that help to describe effective professional development (PD) [4, 5], the tension between generic digital competence training and the necessity for context-specific application is a central challenge in teacher education. While PDC courses are frequently designed for board applicability, the research suggests that "one-size-fits-all" approach is insufficient because it fails to account for the heterogeneous profiles and attitudes of preservice teachers [6].

This study investigates PDC training in preservice teacher education from a design-oriented and explanatory perspective. Specifically, it compares two course formats**: a more general, one-size-fits-all course** designed for multiple teacher education programmes, and **a more domain-specific course** designed to a specific pedagogical context. We aim to understand and ask what kind of course design matters for meaningful professional learning and transfer into future teaching practice. We therefore examine how differences in course format are reflected in participants' evaluations of the training and in course outcomes, and how perceived training quality and course satisfaction help explain variation in PDC, self-efficacy (SE) and intended adoption (IA) of technology-integrated teaching practices. In this way, the study aims to identify what matters when designing PDC training that is not only effective, but also perceived as relevant and transferable across teacher education contexts. The study addresses the following research questions:

**RQ1.** To what extent did the more domain-specific and the more general course format differ in participants' course evaluations and key course outcomes?

**RQ2.** How do perceived training quality and course satisfaction predict teachers' intended adoption of new technology-integrated teaching practices and the development of pedagogical digital competence?

## 2 Theoretical Background

### 2.1 Digital Technologies, Learner Diversity, and the Pedagogical Challenge of Technology Integration

Expansion of digital technologies in the learning environments has brought attention to educational inequality [7]. While technology can support learning, it can also amplify the imbalance of knowledge and skills among learners. Learners with weaker self-regulation and self-management skills often struggle to navigate digital environments and tools, regulating attention and sustaining motivation which results in less effective learning experiences compared to their peers [8, 9]. Self-regulated learning (SRL) has emerged as a central explanatory mechanism linking digital technology use with cognitive, emotional, and social outcomes. Digital environments typically require learners to exercise greater autonomy, making skills such as goal-setting, monitoring, and strategic adaptation essential [10]. However, learners with limited SRL capacities often experience difficulties in managing attention, time, and motivation in such environments, which can limit their learning. Research further indicates that in technology-rich settings, individuals with stronger SRL strategies demonstrate higher levels of problem-solving effectiveness and academic success. Consequently, the use of technology may not only support but also reinforce education inequalities if not carefully mediated through pedagogical design. Recent evidence from OECD [11] and research [12] suggest that the impact of digital technologies on learning outcomes is highly contingent on instructional practices. Moderate to well-structured use of digital technologies can enhance learning, although the outcomes vary significantly depending on how teaching is organized and supported. This highlights the critical shift in focus where the technology as a tool no longer determines the outcome, but pedagogy is the key factor in its effectiveness [13].

To mitigate the technology use that does not support student learning outcomes, developing the teachers' knowledge on learning design and meaningful use of technology is essential. Developing knowledge of the ICAP model is essential for teachers' PD, as it enables teachers to design technology-mediated learning experiences that promote student engagement [14]. By understanding how interactive, constructive, active and passive modes of learning affect comprehension, teachers can more effectively facilitate students' SRL skills while avoiding superficial use of technology in the classroom.

### 2.2 Pedagogical Digital Competence as a Context-Sensitive and Implementation-Oriented Competence

These challenges have strengthened the need for teachers to develop PDC. While general digital competence frameworks such as DigCompEdu [15] define educators' digital competence as the confident, critical, and creative use of digital technologies in professional practice, PDC requires more than general technological confidence. It refers to teachers' ability to make pedagogically sound, context-sensitive decisions about when, why, and how digital technologies can support learning. It requires a sound understanding of pedagogical principles and socioemotional understanding [2]. There is a significant link between teachers' SE, PDC and the actual frequency of technology integration in the classroom, indicating that professional development must extend beyond technical skills to include confidence building for technology use and pedagogical application. High SE plays a crucial role in fostering resilience, as teachers with strong confidence are more likely to invest sustained effort in their pedagogical practice [16, 17]. However, teachers' need for PDC development varies and the heterogeneity highlights that differentiated PD is essential, as higher SE does not only support sustained engagement with technology but also enhances pedagogical adaptability, student outcomes and overall teaching quality.

Accordingly, in the context of teacher education, PDC should be conceptualized as both developmental and implementation-oriented. It includes not only perceived competence, but also teachers' confidence in applying technology in real pedagogical situations and their willingness to adopt new technology-integrated practices. This makes it important to examine not only competence gains, but also implementation-related outcomes such as SE and IA.

## 2.3 Designing Effective Digital Competence Training: Relevance, Domain Specificity, and Transfer

Understanding the characteristics of effective PD is essential for designing training that leads to meaningful changes in teaching practice and improved student learning outcomes. A substantial body of research has shown that effective PD is characterised by content focus, active learning, coherence, sufficient duration, and collective participation, all of which increase the likelihood that learning translates into changes in practice [4, 18]. More recent work further suggests that effective PD depends not only on exposure to new ideas, but also on supporting teachers' motivation, providing concrete techniques, and creating opportunities for practice and transfer [19]. These features are therefore crucial not only for teachers' learning experiences, but also for their satisfaction with training and their subsequent changes in professional practice.

In the context of PDC development, however, the content and design of PD are especially important. Recent work on teachers' PDC integration suggests that effective training should emphasize the subject- and context-specific application of technology, rather than relying on generic digital competence approaches that assume straightforward transfer across teaching contexts [20]. This is consistent with broader perspectives on technology integration, which emphasize that meaningful use of digital tools depends on the alignment of technology with pedagogy, content, and the demands of authentic teaching situations [21, 22]. From this perspective, a one-size-fits-all course may support broad competence development, but more domain-specific course designs may be better positioned to strengthen implementation-oriented outcomes, such as teachers' readiness to adopt new technology-integrated practices.

Beyond content and design features, motivational factors, particularly teacher SE and attitudes towards technology, are also central to successful technology integration. Higher levels of SE are associated with more frequent and effective classroom use of technology, stronger engagement in PD activities, and greater persistence in the face of instructional challenges [15]. In addition, motivational and self-regulatory capacities may shape how teachers engage with training, persist through cognitively demanding tasks, and translate professional learning into practice [23, 24]. Taken together, these findings suggest that effective PD requires not only high-quality and contextually relevant content, but also the motivational and self-regulatory resources that enable teachers to transform learning experiences into meaningful and sustained changes in classroom practice. Thus, while PD clearly plays an important role in strengthening teachers' PDC, its effectiveness depends on a more complex interplay between course design, perceived relevance, motivational resources, and the conditions for transfer into practice.

# 3 Methodology

## 3.1 Research Context and Sample

The study was carried out within the master's level teacher education course *"Educational Technology and Digital Competence"*, which took place in autumn 2025. The course is compulsory for students in the early childhood education master's programme and offered as an elective for master's students from other education-related fields. The course is taught in two groups. For early childhood education (ECE) students, the course is delivered in a field-specific group, focusing on young children's digital competence and the use of digital technology in ECE. The second group includes students from various education-related fields. While the course topics also address learners' digital competence and the use of digital technology in education, they are not field-specific, and participants are expected to interpret and apply the content of the training within their own disciplinary context.

Our study used a convenience sample of 78 master's students who completed the course and both the pre- and post-test. The sample consisted of two course groups that reflected the central design contrast of the study. A total of 31 ECE students participated in a domain-specific course designed specifically for their programme. The remaining 47 students participated in a more general, one-size-fits-all elective course that combined students from several teacher education (TE) programmes, including 30 students from special education (SpE) and 17 students from various subject TE programmes (e.g., foreign language, history and social studies, primary school, multi-subject, and science teacher education). For ECE students, the course was taken in the first year of the master's programme, whereas the elective course could be completed at different stages of study and therefore included both first- and second-year master's students.

The age distribution of the sample was as follows: the largest group consisted of participants aged up to 25 years (34.62%). Equal proportions were observed for those aged 26–30 (15.38%), 31–35 (16.67%), and 41–45 (14.10%). Approximately one-tenth of the participants (10.26%) were aged 36–40, while the smallest group consisted of participants aged 46 and above (8.97%).

An analysis of participants' teaching experience showed that the largest group consisted of teachers with up to five years of experience (61.54%). This was followed by teachers with 6–10 years of experience (16.67%) and students who were not yet working as teachers (11.54%). A smaller proportion of participants had 11–15 years of teaching experience (6.41%), while 3.85% had more than 16 years of experience.

## 3.2 Course Description

The course in the centre of this study focuses on the development of teachers' digital competence through a combination of independent and collaborative learning activities. Participants assess and map their own digital competence, monitor and document their professional growth, and create two technology-enhanced learning scenarios that are implemented either in their own educational setting or with fellow course participants.

The course explores key topics including professional development with digital technologies, teacher digital competence, supporting learners' digital competence development, digitally supported teaching and learning practices, digital learning resource creation, digital assessment, and learner empowerment through technology.

### 3.3 Data Collection

We collected data using pre- and post-questionnaires during the course. The questionnaires were designed as web-based surveys. To link the pre- and post-questionnaire data, students used unique codes they had saved. Participants completed the pre-questionnaire at the first training session. The post-questionnaire was sent to participants immediately after the final training session. All data were based on self-report. As socio-demographic data, we collected information about participants' age, work experience, and gender.

We collected the following data: 1. Teachers' digital competence and its subscales (pre and post): we used a 5-point Likert scale adapted from Lucas et al. [25] with subscales *teaching and learning, empowering learners, and facilitating learners' digital competence.* 2. Self-efficacy for digital teaching (pre and post): we used a 7-point Likert scale, and the items were adapted from the questionnaire by von Acker et al. [26] 3. Intended adoption of technology-enhanced learning methods (pre and post): we used a 5-point Likert scale based on the work of Ley et al. [27]. 4. Training satisfaction (post): we used a 5-point Likert scale based on the Training Evaluation Inventory [28], in which subscales included *subjective enjoyment, perceived usefulness, attitude towards training, and subjective knowledge gain.* 5.Training quality (post): we used a 5-point Likert scale with selected subscales from the Teacher Professional Development Monitor instrument [29]. We used the subscales *clarity and structure, practical relevance, and cognitive activation.*

### 3.4 Data Analysis

To analyse the data, we merged the datasets collected at different time points into a one data table using the students' unique codes. For the analysis, we constructed composite variables for all constructs as follows: From the pre- and post-questionnaire data, we created composite scores (by calculating means) as follows: (a) intended adoption; (b) self-efficacy; (c) teachers' digital competence: for each subscale and overall; (d) training satisfaction: for each subscale and combined; (e) training quality: for each subscale and combined. Additionally, we calculated gain for intended adoption, self-efficacy, and digital competence, including its subscales, based on the pre- and post-questionnaire results.

For first RQ, we used paired-samples and independent-samples t-tests to compare pre-and post-course data and difference of gain. To analyse differences between education programmes, we used repeated measures ANOVA. To answer the second research question, we used multiple linear regression analysis. In conducting the regression analysis, we used the stepwise method, in which independent variables are automatically added to and removed from the model based on their statistical significance. The inclusion and removal of variables were based on a predefined significance level of $p < 0.05$.

We also tested full regression models; however, none of the variables emerged as statistically significant predictors in these models. In presenting our research results, we report the coefficient of determination ($R^2$), regression coefficients ($\beta$), and significance levels (p) in the tables.

# 4 Results

## 4.1 Participant Perceived Usefulness and Overall Satisfaction

First, we compared participants' evaluations of the two course groups, focusing on overall training satisfaction and perceived training quality (Table 1), as well as their key subdimensions. Independent-samples t-tests showed a consistent pattern: participants in the more domain-specific course (Group 2, ECE) evaluated the training significantly more positively than participants in the more general course format (Group 1, SpE and TE). Specifically, the domain-specific course received higher ratings for overall training satisfaction, $t(75.79) = -3.27$, $p = .002$, and overall perceived training quality, $t(73.32) = -3.90$, $p < .001$.

At the level of training satisfaction subdimensions, the domain-specific course was rated significantly higher in subjective enjoyment, $t(73.91) = -3.18$, $p = .002$, perceived usefulness, $t(75.22) = -2.44$, $p = .017$, attitudes towards the training, $t(75.90) = -2.65$, $p = .010$, and subjective knowledge gain, $t(75.01) = -3.76$, $p < .001$. The strongest difference within this domain emerged for subjective knowledge gain, with participants in the domain-specific course reporting a substantially higher sense of learning ($M = 4.46$, $SD = 0.60$) than those in the more general course format ($M = 3.86$, $SD = 0.82$).

A similar pattern was observed for perceived training quality. Compared with the more general course format, the domain-specific course was rated significantly higher in clarity and structure, $t(70.87) = -3.98$, $p < .001$, practical relevance, $t(75.97) = -3.75$, $p < .001$, and cognitive activation, $t(75.93) = -2.43$, $p = .017$. These findings suggest that the more domain-specific course format was not only perceived as more useful, but also as more instructionally supportive and more relevant to participants' pedagogical practice. This pattern provides an important basis for interpreting later differences in course outcomes.

We also examined whether participants from the three teacher education programmes differed in their evaluations of the training. A Kruskal-Wallis test indicated statistically significant differences in overall training satisfaction across programmes, $\chi^2(2) = 10.26$, $p = .006$. ECE participants reported the highest satisfaction with the training ($M = 4.63$, $SD = 0.46$), whereas SpE participants reported the lowest satisfaction ($M = 4.10$, $SD = 0.74$). A similar pattern emerged for perceived training quality. Programme-level differences were also statistically significant, $\chi^2(2) = 13.99$, $p < .001$. Again, ECE participants reported the highest ratings for training quality ($M = 4.51$, $SD = 0.39$), whereas SpE participants reported the lowest ratings ($M = 3.89$, $SD = 0.69$). Thus, participants' immediate reactions to the course differed across programmes, with the most positive evaluations reported in the ECE programme.

**Table 1.** Training satisfaction and perceived quality between two groups

| Variable | Group 1 (general course) M (SD) | Group 2 (domain-specific course) M (SD) | $t$(df) | $p$ |
|---|---|---|---|---|
| Course satisfaction (combined) | 4.18 (0.74) | 4.63 (0.46) | −3.27 (75.79) | .002 |
| Subjective enjoyment | 4.37 (0.71) | 4.76 (0.39) | −3.18 (73.91) | .002 |
| Perceived usefulness | 4.35 (0.85) | 4.72 (0.50) | −2.44 (75.22) | .017 |
| Attitude towards the course | 4.15 (0.81) | 4.56 (0.55) | −2.65 (75.90) | .010 |
| Subjective knowledge gain | 3.86 (0.82) | 4.46 (0.60) | −3.76 (75.01) | < .001 |
| Perceived course quality (combined) | 4.02 (0.73) | 4.51 (0.39) | −3.90 (73.32) | < .001 |
| Clarity and structure | 4.09 (0.83) | 4.65 (0.40) | −3.98 (70.87) | < .001 |
| Practical relevance | 3.92 (0.84) | 4.52 (0.56) | −3.75 (75.97) | < .001 |
| Cognitive activation | 4.04 (0.76) | 4.38 (0.48) | −2.43 (75.93) | .017 |

## 4.2 Changes in Digital Competence across the Two Course Groups

Participants from both groups (Table 2) showed statistically significant gains in perceived PDC from pre- to post-course. In the full sample, perceived PDC increased from M = 2.79 (SD = 0.90) before the course to M = 3.71 (SD = 0.74) after the course, t(77) = −10.42, p < .001. A similar pattern was observed in both groups. In the more general course format (Group 1), perceived PDC increased significantly from M = 2.61 (SD = 0.95) to M = 3.65 (SD = 0.69), t(29) = −6.24, p < .001. In the more domain-specific course format (Group 2), it increased significantly from M = 2.82 (SD = 0.77) to M = 3.77 (SD = 0.65), t(30) = −8.03, p < .001. Thus, both course groups supported substantial growth in participants' perceived PDC.

Despite these within-group gains, the **two groups did not differ significantly in perceived PDC** at post-test. Participants in the more general course format reported a post-course mean of M = 3.67 (SD = 0.79), whereas participants in the more domain-specific course format reported a slightly higher mean of M = 3.77 (SD = 0.65), but this difference was not statistically significant, t(72.10) = −0.66, p = .513. To compare the **magnitude of change directly**, we also examined gain scores. The mean gain in perceived digital competence was comparable across the two course groups (Group 1: M = 0.90, SD = 0.86; Group 2: M = 0.96, SD = 0.66), t(73.94) = −0.33, $p$ = .744. **No statistically significant differences in gain were found** for any of the PDC sub-dimensions, including teaching and learning (t(71.98) = 0.04, $p$ = .971), empowering learners, (t(68.73) = 0.48, $p$ = .632) and facilitating learners' digital competence, (t(72.68) = −1.23, $p$ = .222). These findings suggest that both course groups were similarly effective in supporting broad PDC development.

**Table 2.** Training outcomes between two groups

| Variable | Group 1 (general course) M (SD) | Group 2 (domain-specific course) M (SD) | *t*(df) | *p* |
|---|---|---|---|---|
| Post PDC (global) | 3.67 (0.79) | 3.77 (0.65) | −0.66 (72.10) | .513 |
| Gain in PDC | 0.90 (0.86) | 0.96 (0.66) | −0.33 (73.94) | .744 |
| Gain in PDC: Teaching and learning | 0.89 (0.86) | 0.89 (0.72) | 0.04 (71.98) | .971 |
| Gain in PDC: Empowering learners | 1.02 (1.02) | 0.91 (0.92) | 0.48 (68.73) | .632 |
| Gain in PDC: Facilitating learners' digital competence | 0.79 (1.12) | 1.07 (0.91) | −1.23 (72.68) | .222 |
| Post SE for digital teaching | 5.90 (0.98) | 6.43 (0.63) | −2.91 (75.97) | .005 |
| Gain in SE for digital teaching | −0.02 (0.98) | 0.19 (0.67) | −1.15 (75.93) | .254 |
| Post course IA | 4.66 (0.87) | 5.37 (0.57) | −4.31 (76.00) | < .001 |
| Gain in IA | −0.14 (0.94) | 0.34 (0.91) | −2.21 (65.94) | 0.031 |

A somewhat different pattern emerged for **SE beliefs**. At post-test, participants in the more domain-specific course format reported **significantly higher SE for digital teaching** (M = 6.43, SD = 0.63) than those in the more general course format (M = 5.90, SD = 0.98), t(75.97) = −2.91, $p = .005$. However, the gain-score comparison did not indicate a significantly stronger increase in SE across the course (Group 1: M = −0.02, SD = 0.98; Group 2: M = 0.19, SD = 0.67), t(75.93) = −1.15, p = .254.

In contrast, the domain-specific group showed **higher post-course IA** of technology-enhanced teaching practices (M = 5.37, SD = 0.57) than the more general group (M = 4.66, SD = 0.87), t(76.00) = −4.31, p < .001, **and significantly stronger gains in IA** across the course (Group 1: M = −0.14, SD = 0.94; Group 2: M = 0.34, SD = 0.91), t(65.94) = −2.21, p = .031. Overall, the results suggest that both course groups supported broad competence development, but the more domain-specific format was experienced more positively and was particularly effective in strengthening teachers' IA of technology-enhanced teaching practices.

For observed differences between the two course groups is explained by differences between the underlying TE programmes, we conducted additional analyses across the three programme groups (ECE, SpE, and ST education). Paired-samples t-tests showed (Table 3) that participants in all three programmes reported statistically significant gains in **perceived PDC** from pre- to post-course. Learners across all programmes reported the strongest competence in empowering learners in technology-enhanced learning (TEL) environments, whereas more demanding aspects of technology integration, particularly personalized learning and technology-supported collaborative work, remained more challenging.

**Table 3.** Teachers' perceptions about PDC development, SE and IA across curricula and all educational programmes

| | | ECE | SpE | ST | Overall sample |
|---|---|---|---|---|---|
| PDC (scale 1–5) | $M^{B*}$ | 2.82 | 2.61 | 3.05 | 2.79 |
| | $M^{A**}$ | 3.77 | 3.65 | 3.69 | 3.71 |
| | *t* | – 8.025 | – 6.244 | – 3.850 | – 10.422 |
| | *p* | < .001 | < .001 | .001 | < .001 |
| SE (scale 1–6) | $M^{B}$ | 6.24 | 5.80 | 6.14 | 6.05 |
| | $M^{A}$ | 6.43 | 5.90 | 5.90 | 6.11 |
| | *t* | – 1.619 | – 0.518 | – 0.518 | – 0.649 |
| | *p* | .116 | .609 | 1.179 | .519 |
| IA (scale 1–7) | $M^{B}$ | 5.03 | 4.64 | 7.07 | 4.89 |
| | $M^{A}$ | 5.37 | 4.50 | 4.95 | 4.94 |
| | *t* | – 2.050 | .783 | .602 | – 0.475 |
| | *p* | .049 | .440 | .556 | .636 |

* $M^{B}$ – Before the training;
[a]$M^{A}$ – After the training

In the **teaching and learning** domain, participants across programmes rated after the training their ability to select technologies that add pedagogical value relatively highly (M = 3.99, SD = .614), while planning and implementing technology-supported group work remained (3.14, SD = 1.125) one of the weakest areas. In the **learner empowerment domain**, ECE students rated both anticipating and solving technical problems (M = 4.23, SD = .617) and enabling learners' active participation highly (M = 4.23, SD = .845), whereas students in SpE and ST education most strongly emphasised supporting learners' active participation (special education M = 4.13, SD = .900; subject teachers M = 3.88, SD = 1.054). Across all programmes, providing opportunities for personalised learning remained one of the most challenging aspects of technology integration (M = 3.59–4.07), which the students of the SpE value the most (M = 4.07, SD = .907). In the domain of **supporting learners' digital competence**, digital safety was rated as the strongest area across programmes (M = 3.96, SD = .932), while designing activities that support digitally mediated collaboration (M = 3.04, SD = 1.284) or digital content creation (M = 3.4, SD = 1.143) remained relatively weaker.

A similar descriptive pattern was observed for **SE for digital teaching** (Table 3). Mean SE increased in the overall sample as well as among ECE and SpE students, indicating greater confidence in using digital technology in teaching. In contrast, ST education students showed a slight decrease in SE. However, these changes were not statistically significant either within individual programmes or across the full sample.

For **IA of technology** (Table 3), mean scores increased in the overall sample and most clearly among ECE students, suggesting a stronger willingness to implement the learned practices in future teaching. In contrast, ST and SpE students showed slight decreases in IA. A statistically significant within-programme increase in IA was observed only among ECE students, which may reflect the stronger perceived relevance of the domain-specific course format for this group.

Importantly, however, one-way ANOVA comparisons of gain scores showed that the three programmes did not differ significantly in the magnitude of change in perceived **PDC**, $F(2, 75) = 1.17$, $p = .317$, **IA**, $F(2, 75) = 0.42$, $p = .661$, or **SE** for digital teaching, $F(2, 75) = 1.85$, $p = .165$. Thus, although descriptive differences between programmes were visible, these differences were not statistically robust at the level of overall change. Taken together, these findings suggest that the differences observed between the two course formats are unlikely to be explained simply by programme membership alone. Rather, they point more specifically to the importance of course design, domain specificity, and perceived relevance to participants' pedagogical context.

## 4.3 Teachers Training Experience Perceptions

As a second research question, we aimed to examine how training satisfaction and perceived quality predict teachers' IA, SE for digital teaching and the development of their PDC. The results indicate that both the subjective experience of the training and factors related to its quality play a role in teachers' intentions to implement technology and in the development of their competence.

**Table 4.** Predictors of teachers' SE for digital teaching and IA

| Criteria | | Self-efficacy for digital teaching | | Intended adoption | |
|---|---|---|---|---|---|
| | $R^2$ | .537 | | .622 | |
| | p | *< .001* | | *< .001* | |
| | Predictors | β | *p* | β | *p* |
| | *Constant* | 2.312 | *.000* | 1.211 | *.001* |
| Training satisfaction | Perceived usefulness | *.327* | *.012* | .457 | *.000* |
| | Subjective knowledge gain | *.447* | *.001* | | |
| Training quality | Practical relevance | | | .399 | *.000* |

The results of the regression analysis (Table 4) showed that teachers' **SE in using digital technology** is influenced by training satisfaction and quality. Perceived knowledge gain was a statistically significant predictor. This suggests that teachers who perceive their knowledge to have expanded as a result of the training (e.g., can later recall and apply) also rate their SE to use digital tools more highly.

**IA** after the training was statistically significantly influenced by perceived knowledge gain, indicating that the depth of the learning experience directly supports the adoption of technology. Practical relevance emerged as the most important predictor, significantly influencing teachers' IA after the training. This suggests that teachers who perceive the training content as closely connected to their everyday work (e.g., real practice examples and solving everyday professional problems) are more likely to adopt new technological solutions in their teaching. The development of **PDC** after the training is predicted (Table 5) by training quality indicators such as practical relevance and cognitive activation. Cognitive activation (e.g., opportunities to reflect, connect new knowledge with prior knowledge, and critically evaluate one's practices) significantly supports the teaching and learning domain of teachers' PDC, highlighting the importance of deeper learning in the development of digital competence.

A statistically significant positive effect on teachers' PDC is the practical relevance of the training, which supports teachers' skills in empowering learners, facilitating learners' digital competence, and digital competence overall. This indicates that when training is highly practical and closely connected to teachers' everyday work, it broadly supports the development of PDC.

**Table 5.** Predictors of Teachers' PDC

| Criteria | | | | | | Training quality | |
|---|---|---|---|---|---|---|---|
| | | $R^2$ | p | Predictors | *Constant* | Practical relevance | Cognitive activation |
| Teachers' PDC (after the training) | Teaching and learning | .105 | *.004* | β | 2.036 | | .325 |
| | | | | *p* | *< .001* | | *.004* |
| | Empowering learners | .124 | *.002* | β | 2.434 | .352 | |
| | | | | *p* | *< .001* | *.002* | |
| | Facilitating learners' digital competence | .229 | *< .001* | β | 1.407 | .478 | |
| | | | | *p* | *.004* | *< .001* | |
| | Teachers' Digital Competence (overall) | .186 | *< .001* | β | 2.044 | .432 | |
| | | | | *p* | *.000* | *.000* | |

The results indicate that teachers' intentions to adopt technology and the development of their diacrossgital competence are primarily influenced by perceived knowledge gain, positive attitudes towards the training and the practical relevance of the training. When designing effective training, it is important for teachers that the content is closely connected to everyday practice, supports deep learning and reflection. Based on teachers' self-report, such an approach creates the conditions for both the successful implementation of technology and the sustainable development of teachers' digital competence.

## 5 Discussion and Conclusions

The findings of this study suggest that the effects of PDC training in preservice teacher education depend not only on participation in the course, but also on how the course is designed and experienced. Both course formats supported significant gains in self-reported PDC, indicating that both general and more domain-specific training can contribute to broad competence development. This is consistent with prior research showing that professional development can strengthen teachers' PDC when it offers meaningful engagement with pedagogical uses of technology [4, 18].

At the same time, broader competence gains did not necessarily translate into stronger implementation-oriented outcomes. While both groups improved in perceived competence, the domain-specific course was evaluated more positively in terms of satisfaction and training quality, and it was associated with higher post-course SE and stronger IA of technology-integrated practices. This suggests that domain-specific and contextually relevant course designs may be particularly important for supporting preservice teachers' readiness to act, rather than only their general sense of competence. This interpretation aligns with research emphasizing that technology integration is inherently context-sensitive and depends on the alignment of digital tools with pedagogical goals and authentic teaching situations [6, 20, 22]. A plausible explanation is further supported by the regression analyses: practical relevance and perceived knowledge gain emerged as the strongest predictors of SE, IA, and several dimensions of PDC. In line with research on effective PD [4, 18, 19], this suggests that domain-specific course design may support stronger implementation-oriented outcomes not necessarily because it produces larger broad competence gains, but because it is experienced as more relevant, useful, and transferable. The study contributes to TEL research by showing that the effectiveness of PDC courses for preservice teachers should not be judged only by broad competence development, but also by implementation-oriented outcomes. In our study, domain-specific and practically relevant course design was especially important for outcomes that signal likely transfer into future teaching practice.

Several limitations should be acknowledged. The study relied on a non-random convenience sample. In addition, the sample was relatively small, all measures were based on self-report, and the study did not include behavioural or longitudinal evidence of actual transfer into practice. Therefore, the findings should be interpreted cautiously, especially regarding causal claims and long-term impact.

Overall, the study suggests that while general PDC courses may support broad competence development, domain-specific and practically relevant course designs appear particularly important for strengthening preservice teachers' confidence and willingness to adopt technology-integrated teaching practices. This highlights the need to evaluate PDC training not only in terms of what teachers learn, but also in terms of how well training prepares them to apply that learning in authentic pedagogical contexts.

## References

1. Olofsson, A.D., Lindberg, J.O.: A glimpse of a Nordic model? Policy and practice in the digitalisation of the K-12 school and teacher education in Denmark, Finland, Norway and Sweden: editorial introduction. Educ. Inq. **12**(4), 311–316 (2021)

2. Azevedo, R., Aleven, V.: International Handbook of Metacognition and Learning Technologies. Springer (2013)
3. Arstorp, A.T., Olofsson, A.D., Lindberg, J.O.: Professional digital competence in teacher education – where are we, where are we headed and how to get there? Teach. Teach. **30**(4), 395–399 (2024)
4. Darling-Hammond, L., Hyler, M.E., Gardner, M.: Effective Teacher Professional Development. Learning Policy Institute, Palo Alto, CA (2017) https://learningpolicyinstitute.org/product/teacher-prof-dev
5. Desimone, L.M.: Rethinking teacher PD: a focus on how to improve student learning. Prof. Dev. Educ. **49**(1), 1–3 (2023)
6. Tondeur, J., Howard, S.K., Yang, J.: One-size does not fit all : towards an adaptive model to develop preservice teachers' digital competencies. Comput. Hum. Behav. **116**, 106659 (2021)
7. Wang, F., Ni, X., Zhang, M., Zhang, J.: Educational digital inequality: a meta-analysis of the relationship between digital device use and academic performance in adolescents. Comput. Educ. **213**, 105003 (2024)
8. Radović, S., Seidel, N., Menze, D., Kasakowskij, R.: Investigating the effects of different levels of students' regulation support on learning process and outcome: in search of the optimal level of support for self-regulated learning. Comput. Educ. **215**, 105041 (2024)
9. Jin, S.H., Im, K., Yoo, M., et al.: Supporting students' self-regulated learning in online learning using artificial intelligence applications. Int. J. Educ. Technol. High. Educ. **20**, 37 (2023)
10. Yan, Z., Wu, Y.T., Mendoza, N.B., Zhan, Y.: Individual-level mechanisms of SRL in digital learning environments: motivational, metacognitive, and behavioural dynamics. Educ. Psychol., 341–349 (2026)
11. OECD: Technology Use at School and Students' Learning Outcomes: Exploring the Relationship with New Data from Germany. OECD Education Spotlights, No. 17. OECD Publishing (2024).
12. Moore, S., Eckstein, L., Kwon, C., Stamper, J.: Integrating generative AI into instructional design practice: effects on graduate student learning and self-efficacy. In: Tammets, K., Sosnovsky, S., Ferreira Mello, R., Pishtari, G., Nazaretsky, T. (eds.) Two Decades of TEL. from Lessons Learnt to Challenges Ahead. EC-TEL 2025 Lecture Notes in Computer Science, vol. 16063. Springer, Cham (2026)
13. Tondeur, J., Trevisan, O., Howard, S.K., van Braak, J.: Preparing preservice teachers to teach with digital technologies: an update of effective SQD-strategies. Comput. Educ. **232**, 105262 (2025). https://doi.org/10.1016/j.compedu.2025.105262
14. Chi, M.T.H., Wylie, R.: The ICAP framework: linking cognitive engagement to active learning outcomes. Educ. Psychol. **49**(4), 219–243 (2014)
15. Redecker, C., Punie, Y.: Digital Competence of Educators DigCompEdu (2017)
16. Hatlevik, O.E.: Examining the Relationship between Teachers' Self-Efficacy, their Digital Competence, Strategies to Evaluate Information, and use of ICT at School, 3831 (2017).
17. Mannila, L., Pears, A.: Digital Competence, Teacher Self-Efficacy and Training Needs (2026).
18. Desimone, L.M.: Improving Impact Studies of Teachers' Professional Development: toward Better Conceptualizations and Measures, pp. 181–199 (2009)
19. Sims, S., et al.: Effective teacher professional development: new theory and a meta-analytic test. Rev. Educ. Res. **95**(2), 213–254 (2025)
20. Lachner, A., Backfisch, I., Franke, U.: Towards an Integrated Perspective of Teachers' Technology Integration: A Preliminary Model and Future Research Directions, 12(1), 1–15 (2024).
21. Koehler, M., Mishra, P.: What is technological pedagogical content knowledge (TPACK)? Contemp. Issues Technol. Teach. Educ. **9**(1), 60–70 (2009)

22. Hatlevik, O.E.: Examining the relationship between teachers' self-efficacy, their digital competence, strategies to evaluate information, and use of ICT at school. Scand. J. Educ. Res. **61**(5), 555–567 (2017)
23. Karlen, Y., et al.: Research papers in education teachers matter: linking teachers and students' self-regulated learning. Res. Pap. Educ. **40**(3), 414–441 (2025)
24. Lachner, A., Russ, H., Hübner, N., Sibley, L., Scheiter, K.: When does learning by non - interactive teaching work? A large - scale analysis of learner characteristics in a classroom setting. Educ. Psychol. Rev. 37 (2025). Springer US.
25. Lucas, M., Bem-Haja, P., Siddiq, F., Moreira, A., Redecker, C.: The relation between in-service teachers' digital competence and personal and contextual factors: what matters most? Comput. Educ. **160**, 104052 (2021)
26. Van Acker, F., van Buuren, H., Kreijns, K., Vermeulen, M.: Why teachers use digital learning materials: the role of self-efficacy, subjective norm and attitude. Educ. Inf. Technol. **18**, 495–514 (2013)
27. Ley, T., et al.: Adopting technology in schools: modelling, measuring and supporting knowledge appropriation. Eur. J. Teach. Educ. **45**(4), 548–571 (2022)
28. Ritzmann, S., Hagemann, V., Kluge, A.: The training evaluation inventory (TEI)-evaluation of training design and measurement of training outcomes for predicting training success. Vocat. Learn. **7**(1), 41–73 (2014)
29. Richter, E., Richter, D.: Measuring the quality of teacher professional development: a large-scale validation study of an 18-item instrument for daily use. Stud. Educ. Eval. **81**, 101357 (2024)

# New Lenses on Learning Design: Course Types and Indicators from Large-Scale Moodle Data

Ekaterina Soroka(✉), Niels Seidel, Marcus Specht, and Kamila Misiejuk

CATALPA, FernUniversität in Hagen, 58097 Hagen, Germany
{ekaterina.soroka,niels.seidel,marcus.specht, kamila.misiejuk}@fernuni-hagen.de

**Abstract.** Although learning design (LD) plays a central role in shaping online courses, large-scale empirical evidence on how courses are actually structured remains scarce, and existing analytics work has characterised courses through student engagement with specific learning activities rather than through indicators of the design itself. This study addresses both gaps through an analysis of learning management system (LMS) data from 606 courses at a distance university. Using LMS data, we first applied dimensionality reduction and clustering to a structural variable set, from which three distinct LD types emerged empirically: *Compact*, *Expansive*, and *Interactive* and statistically characterised how their design elements differ across disciplines, activity load, and interfaces. Building on this typology, we derived three LD indicators, *activity-mode balance*, *structural clarity*, and *analytics readiness*, each combining multiple LMS-derived variables into higher-order constructs that target a different aspect of LD. All three indicators differentiated significantly across the LD types and added pedagogically meaningful dimensions for interpretation. These contributions advance the operationalisation of LD in technology-enhanced learning research by demonstrating that higher-order LD indicators can be derived directly from routinely collected LMS data, and offer empirical insight into how LD manifests at scale within a large distance university.

**Keywords:** learning design · learning analytics · learning management system data · indicators · design analytics · higher education

## 1 Introduction

How instructors design their courses shapes the conditions for student learning. The pathways they create, the activities they sequence, and the ways they balance content, assessment, and collaboration all structure the environment in which student engagement unfolds. These decisions are increasingly enacted through learning management systems (LMS), where course structure, activity


J. Weidlich et al. (Eds.): EC-TEL 2026, LNCS 16905, pp. 561–576, 2027.
https://doi.org/10.1007/978-3-032-37979-5_38

composition, and resource organisation are directly configurable by instructors. Particularly in fully online settings, these design decisions, collectively referred to as learning design (LD) [12], mediate nearly every interaction between students and content, peers, and instructors. Without understanding how student learning is structured, it is not possible to explain why the environment affords or constrains particular behaviours, which is a central concern for technology-enhanced learning (TEL) research [11].

This paper addresses that need through a large-scale analysis of LMS data from 606 courses at a large German distance university. We examine how recurring course structure patterns from LMS data can be identified as LD types, operationalised, and interpreted and how these insights can be used to develop meaningful LD indicators. In particular, we address the following research questions: **RQ1** What LD types characterise Moodle course designs at scale, and how do they differ in their characteristics? **RQ2** How can the LD indicators be derived from LMS course data, and how can derived LD indicators be used to characterize the LD types?

The contributions of this paper are fourfold: (1) a comprehensive large-scale analysis of course designs from Moodle data; (2) the identification of three distinct LD types from authentic institutional data using dimensionality reduction and clustering techniques; (3) a novel approach to derive LD indicators from both theoretical considerations and the analysis of LMS structural data; and (4) the introduction of three new LD indicators grounded in this approach.

**Background.** LD refers to the deliberate structuring of learning opportunities, encompassing decisions about activity types, sequencing, resources, and the social organisation of learning [18]. While LD encompasses a rich set of decisions including learning outcomes (LOs), intended task duration, or pedagogical strategy [13], LMS data provides a practical and scalable window into the enacted design, capturing the activity structures and resource configurations that instructors have made visible to students. Learning analytics (LA) offers the possibility of examining how these LD decisions play out in practice, by capturing and analysing traces of students' interactions with the learning environment [19]. [8] introduced *design analytics* as a distinct analytical perspective focused on the properties of a course as designed, rather than as experienced by students. Where learning analytics captures what students do, design analytics captures what instructors have put in place: goals, tasks, social configurations, temporal structures, and resource arrangements, as well as the design process, which can include task structure, workload balance, or implementation sustainability.

Empirical large-scale analyses of actual LDs remain scarce. The most substantial body of work comes from the Open University UK (OU UK), where the LDs of all university courses were coded and examined across seven faculties and multiple years [15]. [22] applied epistemic network analysis to 6,040 Moodle course offerings across four years and ten faculties to examine disciplinary differences in blended learning activity patterns. [14] similarly used epistemic network analysis on 102 courses over three years at a Norwegian university to examine how Canvas use profiles shifted in response to the COVID-19 pandemic.

The classification of learning activities into taxonomic categories has provided the dominant framework for characterising LD in LMS data. The most widely applied is the LD taxonomy developed at the OU UK, which distinguishes seven activity types: *assimilative*, *finding and handling information*, *communication*, *productive*, *experiential*, *interactive/adaptive*, and *assessment* [18]. In practice, LMS activities are mapped onto these categories, for example forums and chats are classified as communicative, assignments and quizzes as assessment, and pages and resources as assimilative [15]. This can be compared to a more granular taxonomy used by [8], further subdeviding these broad categories into six distinct learning activity types: *acquisition, inquiry, practice, production, discussion,* and *collaboration*. A similar categorisation approach was applied by [22], who grouped LMS activities into *administration*, *assessment*, *content*, and *engagement* categories, and by [14], who categorized LMS data to map *administrative*, *content*, and *activity* variables.

Beyond activity categorisation, other frameworks have proposed multilevel classifications distinguishing design decisions at the level of pedagogy, strategy, and individual task [13]. Across the design analytics space more broadly, indicator development has focused predominantly on the student behavioural layer: the Constructivist Learning Design and Learning Analytics model [4] maps LA indicators onto a seven-step constructivist design sequence, while other studies have mapped LMS activity logs onto LD taxonomy categories to examine student engagement patterns [1], or derived engagement indicators around constructs of workload and active learning [16]. In each case, indicators characterise how students interact with a course rather than properties of the design itself [8]. Computable indicators that go beyond activity categorisation, capturing higher-order properties of LD directly from LMS data remain underdeveloped. This study addresses this gap by demonstrating a systematic process for deriving a set of composite LD indicators from Moodle LMS data, providing a scalable way to surface design choices and support the deliberate, evidence-informed practice required when instructors act as designers of technology-enhanced learning [11].

## 2 Methods

Our dataset, exported from institutional Moodle, includes course LD data for all courses at a german large distance university that were active and visible to students in summer semester 2025 and winter semester 2025/2026. The dataset comprises 606 courses, with a mean of 7.3 sections ($SD = 5.7$) and a mean of 50.6 activities per course ($SD = 64.5$). The data include LD elements, but no user interaction logs. Basic preprocessing removed duplicate records, excluded courses that were not part of regular teaching, and dropped variables with substantial missing data or plugin-specific scope (Table 1).

To determine the LD types in our dataset, addressing RQ1, we applied principal component analysis (PCA), a dimensionality reduction technique. PCA

**Table 1.** Overview of variables derived from Moodle data.

| Variable | Definition |
|---|---|
| # of sections | Total number of sections in the course. |
| # of activities | Total number of activities in the course. |
| # of page items | Total number of page-type items in the course. |
| # of assessment activities | Total number of assessment-related activities. |
| # of receptive activities | Total number of activities focused on receptive learning |
| # of productive activities | Total number of activities focused on productive work. |
| # of unique activity types | Total number of distinct activity types present in a course. |
| assessment ratio | Proportion of graded activities out of all activities in a course. |
| nested surface ratio | Proportion of course-page activities that serve as containers linking to nested sub-pages or structures. |
| collaboration ratio | Proportion of collaborative activities out of all activities in a course. |
| LA block ratio | Proportion of LA-related blocks among all blocks present on course page. |
| mean orderliness | Mean regularity of activity-type sequencing within sections, averaged across sections (range: 0–1); computed as the ratio of distinct activity types to consecutive activity-type changes per section; higher values indicate more uniform, repetitive sequencing of activity types. |
| section density | Mean *# of activities* per section in a course. |
| SD activities | Standard deviation of *# of activities* per section in a course. |

was applied to the standardised variable set, given that LMS-derived variables are interdependent, with instructors' integrated design choices affecting multiple structural variables at once, generating systematic co-variation that PCA reveals as interpretable latent dimensions. PCA was preferred over direct k-means on the full variable space as it reduces noise from correlated variables and produces a lower-dimensional representation that is more stable for clustering. While Singular Value Decomposition offers a related dimensionality reduction, PCA was chosen because it explicitly maximizes explained variance in the standardized variable space and produces components that are more interpretable in terms of the original LMS variables. As robustness checks, we repeated k-means and compared this solution with the PCA-based clustering using the Adjusted Rand Index [9], and evaluated internal validity using average silhouette width, Calinski-Harabasz [5], and Davies-Bouldin indices [7].

After determining the LD types, we characterised their distribution across three contextual dimensions: **Discipline**, categorised according to the university's faculty classification *HASS* (Humanities and Social Sciences), *STEM*

(Mathematics and Computer Science), *Psychology*, *Commerce* (Business Administration and Economics), and *Law*. **Activity load**, operationalised as a three-level band based on the number of activities per course: *small* (fewer than 30), *medium* (30–79), and *large* (80 or more). This variable can serve as a proxy for the expected student workload and the granularity of course designs. **Interface**, encompassing three Moodle-native course-page formats: *one-topic*, a tabbed arrangement displaying one section at a time; *tiles*, a card-grid arrangement presenting sections as visual tiles with optional progress indicators; and *topics*, the default vertically stacked section arrangement. Although interface choice is not inherently pedagogical, it is fundamental to the pedagogical interpretability of the course, as the visual organization of content can either make the intended learning path explicit or obscure it [20,21].

For each dimension, we computed the proportional representation of each LD type and Fisher's exact test (FET) after Bonferroni correction [3,10]. In addition, we examined courses along three composite dimensions using scatter plots, and correlation within-type Pearson correlations between the two variables of each composite dimension to quantify the coherence of structural relationships per LD type. Additional ordinary least squares (OLS) regression lines were fitted within each LD type to visually characterise the direction and strength of these relationships in the scatter plots. PCA and k-means diagnostics are provided as supplementary information (SI) (https://figshare.com/s/4b5320308cbdeae1df9c).

To address RQ2, focusing on how LD indicators can be derived from LMS course data and how they can be used to characterise the LD types, we followed a two-stage process. First, we derived three categorical measures from simple LMS variables. Thresholds for each measure were determined iteratively through expert discussion and evaluated against the observed empirical distributions in the RQ1 data, in order to ensure that the resulting bands reflected meaningful breaks rather than arbitrary cut-offs. Second, these categorical measures were combined with additional LMS variables to define three LD indicators, each targeting a different aspect of course design.

The thresholds for the indicators were again set through expert discussion and validated against the empirical distributions of specific variables in the Moodle data. To characterise the LD types, the indicators were then applied to the full Moodle dataset and their distributions compared across types. Finally, to evaluate the indicator's ability to differentiate meaningfully across LD types, we tested each indicator's distribution using FET with Monte Carlo approximation ($B = 199,999$ resamples), which is appropriate for contingency tables containing small expected counts, and reported effect sizes as Cramér's V [10]. Pairwise comparisons between LD types were Bonferroni-corrected within each indicator to control the family-wise error rate [3].

## 3 Results

### 3.1 Identifying and Characterising LD Types in LMS Data

To identify recurring LD types within the LMS data (RQ1), we applied PCA to the standardised variable set, retaining the leading components explaining approximately 92 % of the total variance. We then ran k-means clustering with Euclidean distance on the PCA scores. To select an appropriate number of LD types, we first examined the elbow and silhouette plots across candidate $k$ values. Although the silhouette score for k=3 (0.19) was only somewhat lower than for k=2 (0.30), we retained three clusters because they yielded more interpretable and pedagogically distinct LD types. The moderate silhouette scores suggest that courses form a continuum rather than discrete clusters; the three-cluster solution thus represents a pragmatic segmentation rather than naturally bounded types. To inspect the structure of the three LD types, we projected courses onto the first two principal components and coloured points by LD type (SI Fig. 4, Fig. 6). PC1 and PC2 together explained approximately 52% of the variance (PC1: 34.7%, PC2: 17.2%), revealing three partially overlapping but clearly distinguishable clouds. PC1 functioned primarily as a course-scale axis, loading most strongly on total activities, number of sections, and page-based content. PC2 captured structural clarity and activity mix, combining positive loadings for orderliness, nested-surface ratio, and collaborative activities with negative loadings for section density and its variability. Thus, higher PC2 scores characterised more orderly and interaction-rich courses with more evenly distributed section layouts.

One LD type extended furthest along PC1, corresponding to larger, more activity-dense courses, while the remaining two types were differentiated primarily along PC2. The names assigned to each type reflect their defining characteristics as revealed by the PCA structure: **Expansive** LD type ($n$ = 425 courses) was characterised by high scores on PC1, reflecting courses with a large number of activities, many sections, and substantial page-based content. These are courses that cover broad ground through sheer volume of designed learning experiences. **Compact** LD type ($n$ = 135 courses) occupied a distinct region along PC2, distinguished by structural regularity and orderliness: courses with evenly distributed section layouts, a high nested-surface ratio, and low variability in section density. These are tightly organised courses that achieve coherence through deliberate structure rather than volume. **Interactive** LD type ($n$ = 46 courses) was set apart not by its activity load but by its activity composition. These courses show elevated collaborative activities and a higher proportion of interaction-oriented content, positioned at moderate PC1 scores but high on the PC2, the interaction-rich dimension.

Across all disciplines, *Expansive* courses were the dominant pattern, *Compact* courses formed a consistent secondary presence, and *Interactive* courses were comparatively rare (Fig. 1a). However, the degree of concentration varied meaningfully across disciplines. HASS, Commerce, and STEM, shared a broadly similar profile dominated by *Expansive* designs, ranging from approximately 75% in HASS to 86% in Commerce and STEM, with no significant differences among them after Bonferroni correction (Table 2). Psychology stood apart as the only discipline with a more balanced distribution and the only one in which *Interactive* courses formed a substantial minority (24.7%), differing significantly from all other disciplines (HASS: $p$ = .001; Commerce: $p$ = .001; STEM: $p$ = .001;

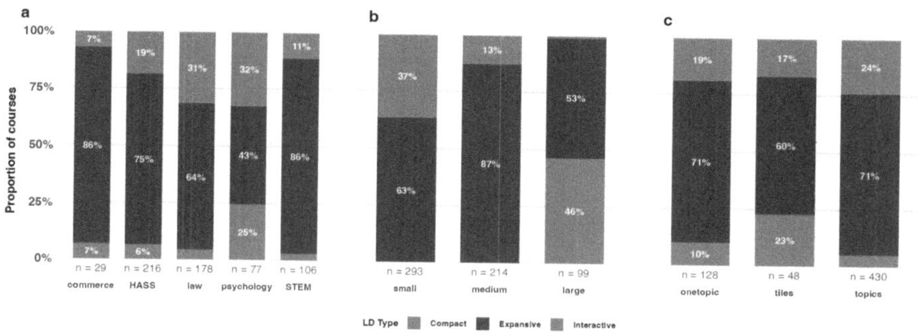


**Fig. 1.** Distribution of LD types by: (a) discipline, (b) activity load, (c) interface.

Law: $p = .001$). A further significant difference emerged between STEM and Law ($p = .002$), reflecting STEM's stronger concentration in *Expansive* designs relative to Law's larger share of *Compact* courses. Overall, FET confirmed that the distribution of LD types differed significantly across disciplines ($p < .001$, Cramér's $V = 0.24$).

Activity load was strongly related to LD type (Fig. 1b). Here, small, medium, and large refer to the scale of the Moodle course structure measured by num-

**Table 2.** Distribution of LD types by discipline, activity load, and interface, with FET results.

| | *Compact* | | *Expansive* | | *Interactive* | | |
|---|---|---|---|---|---|---|---|
| Category | $n$ | % | $n$ | % | $n$ | % | FET |
| *Discipline* | | | | | | | $p < .001$, $V = .24$ |
| HASS | 40 | 18.5 | 162 | 75.0 | 14 | 6.5 | |
| STEM | 12 | 11.3 | 91 | 85.8 | 3 | 2.8 | |
| Commerce | 2 | 6.9 | 25 | 86.2 | 2 | 6.9 | |
| Law | 56 | 31.5 | 114 | 64.0 | 8 | 4.5 | |
| Psychology | 25 | 32.5 | 33 | 42.9 | 19 | 24.7 | |
| *Activity load* | | | | | | | $p < .001$, $V = .50$ |
| Small | 107 | 36.5 | 186 | 63.5 | 0 | 0.0 | |
| Medium | 27 | 12.6 | 187 | 87.4 | 0 | 0.0 | |
| Large | 1 | 1.0 | 52 | 52.5 | 46 | 46.5 | |
| *Interface* | | | | | | | $p < .001$, $V = .13$ |
| One-topic | 24 | 18.8 | 91 | 71.1 | 13 | 10.2 | |
| Tiles | 8 | 16.7 | 29 | 60.4 | 11 | 22.9 | |
| Topics | 103 | 24.0 | 305 | 70.9 | 22 | 5.1 | |

ber of activities, not student enrolment. *Compact* LDs were almost exclusively small or medium in scale, with only a single course classified as large. *Expansive* LDs spanned the full range of activity loads, from small to large, reflecting their position as the dominant pattern across the dataset (Table 2). *Interactive* LDs, by contrast, were found exclusively among large courses, marking activity volume as a defining variable of this type. FET confirmed that LD types differed significantly in their distribution across activity load bands ($p < .001$, Cramér's $V = 0.50$, a large effect), and Bonferroni-corrected pairwise comparisons showed that all three pairs differed significantly ($p_{\text{adj}} < .001$).

The distribution of interfaces across the three LD types was broadly similar: all three types relied predominantly on the topics arrangement (around 60–80%), with smaller shares using one-topic and tiles (Table 2). FET indicated a statistically significant difference ($p < .001$, Cramér's $V = 0.13$), but the effect was small and the differences were modest in practical terms. The clearest distinction was that *Interactive* courses made comparatively greater use of the tiles arrangement than the other two LD types, and Bonferroni-corrected pairwise comparisons indicated that this difference was driven by the topics–tiles contrast ($p_{\text{adj}} < .001$), while one-topic did not differ significantly from either tiles ($p_{\text{adj}} = .334$) or topics ($p_{\text{adj}} = .253$). Overall, interface was a weaker discriminator of LD type than discipline or activity load.

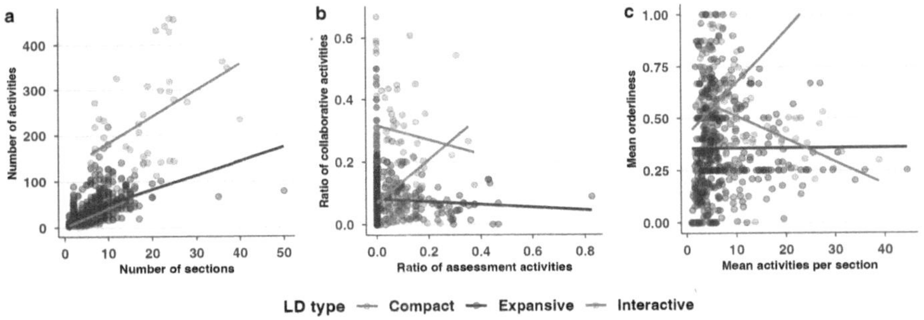


**Fig. 2.** Distribution of structural variables by LD type across three analytical dimensions: (a) *# of sections* × *# of activities*, (b) *assessment ratio* × *collaboration ratio*, and (c) *section density* × *mean orderliness*. Each point represents one course, coloured by LD type. Lines show within-type ordinary least squares (OLS) regression fits.

To examine how the three LD types differ beyond their cluster assignments, we visualised their distributions across three dimensions. The scatter plot of *number of sections* by the *number of activities* showed that *Compact* courses clustered compactly in the low-scale region, combining few sections with few activities (Fig. 2a). *Expansive* courses went beyond this dimension towards higher section and activity counts, while *Interactive* courses occupied a distinct position, combining few sections with substantially more activities per section. Within-type correlations between sections and activities were strongest for *Compact*

($r = .77$), and similarly moderate for both *Expansive* and *Interactive* ($r = .47$ each), though for structurally different reasons. The high correlation in *Compact* courses reflects their tight, proportional scaling: few sections and few activities co-vary closely within a narrow range. The moderate correlation in *Expansive*courses reflects greater heterogeneity across a wide scale range. For *Interactive* courses, the same moderate correlation masks a structurally distinct pattern: sections and activities do not scale together but are instead decoupled, with activity load concentrated into comparatively few sections.

In the scatter plot showing the relationship between *assessment ratio* and *collaboration ratio*, *Expansive* courses remained comparatively content-oriented, with lower shares of both activity types, reflecting their overall activity volume. *Compact* courses showed the highest ratio of collaborative activities, with minimal use of assessment activities (Fig. 2b). *Interactive* courses devoted a larger proportion of activities to collaborative and interactive elements, with moderate assessment use, suggesting a pedagogical orientation distinct from the other two types. Within-type correlations between assessment and collaboration ratios were moderate and positive for *Interactive* courses ($r = .48$), indicating that these courses tend to combine higher collaboration with higher assessment use simultaneously, and near zero for both *Compact* ($r = -.08$) and *Expansive* courses ($r = -.08$).

The *section density* by *mean orderliness* scatter plot revealed that *Compact* courses formed sparse but highly orderly layouts, combining low activity density per section with high structural consistency (Fig. 2c). *Expansive* courses occupied a broad intermediate band, showing moderate density and variable orderliness. *Interactive* courses tended toward denser sections with comparatively lower orderliness, suggesting that their activity concentration comes at the cost of structural regularity. Within-type correlations between mean activities per section and mean orderliness were weakly positive for *Compact* ($r = .27$), near zero for *Expansive* ($r = .00$), and moderately negative for *Interactive* courses ($r = -.48$), confirming that within this type, higher section density is associated with lower structural regularity and concentration of activities into fewer sections comes at a measurable cost to layout consistency.

### 3.2 Deriving and Evaluating LD Indicators Using LMS Data

To develop LD indicators from Moodle data (RQ2), we first operationalised three categorical measures that translated simple LMS variables into interpretable bands: *assessment diversity*, capturing the volume and variety of assessment activities; *section density*, classifying the mean number of activities per section; and *orderliness*, reflecting the structural regularity of section layouts (Table 3).

The indicators were designed to capture three aspects repeatedly identified as important in the LA and design analytics literature: the pedagogical balance of activities, the structural organisation of the course, and the readiness of the design for analytics [1,2]. Because no established cut-offs exist for these aspects [6], the thresholds themselves were determined iteratively through expert discussion and validation with empirical distributions. With the indicators and

**Table 3.** Derived categorical measures and LD indicators.

| Name | Thresholds |
|---|---|
| *Categorical measures* | |
| **Assessment diversity** | none: *# of assessment activities* $= 0$<br>1–3 items: $1 \leq$ *# of assessment activities* $\leq 3$<br>4–10 items: $4 \leq$ *# of assessment activities* $\leq 10$<br>11+ items: *# of assessment activities* $\geq 11$ |
| **Section density band** | low: *mean activities per section* $< 5$<br>medium: $5 \leq$ *mean activities per section* $< 15$<br>high: *mean activities per section* $\geq 15$ |
| **Orderliness band** | low: *mean orderliness* $< 0.33$<br>medium: $0.33 \leq$ *mean orderliness* $< 0.66$<br>high: *mean orderliness* $\geq 0.66$ |
| *LD indicators* | |
| **Activity-mode balance** | content-heavy: *collaboration ratio* $< 0.05$ & *assessment ratio* $< 0.05$<br>assessment-heavy: *assessment ratio* $\geq 0.30$ & *collaboration ratio* $< 0.10$<br>collaboration-heavy: *collaboration ratio* $\geq 0.20$ & *assessment ratio* $\geq 0.20$<br>mixed: all remaining combinations of collaboration ratio and assessment ratio |
| **Structural clarity** | clear: low/medium *section density band* + high *orderliness band*<br>cluttered: high *section density band* + low/medium *orderliness band*<br>mixed: all remaining combinations |
| **Analytics readiness** | low: *LA block ratio* $= 0$ & *number of nested items* $< 10$<br>moderate: *LA block ratio* $> 0$ or *number of nested items* $\geq 10$<br>high: *LA block ratio* $> 0$ & *number of nested items* $\geq 100$ |

thresholds defined, we applied them to the full Moodle dataset to characterise the three LD types in greater detail. To evaluate whether the indicators differentiated meaningfully across LD types, we additionally tested their distributions for statistical differences.

*Activity-Mode Balance* is an indicator that classifies courses into four profiles according to the relative weight of content, assessment, and collaborative activities. It captures the degree to which a course concentrates learning opportunities within a single activity mode or distributes them across multiple modes. The statistical analysis revealed that *activity-mode balance* differentiated significantly across the three LD types ($p < .001$, Cramér's $V = 0.26$), and Bonferroni-corrected pairwise comparisons confirmed that every pair of LD types was distinguishable (all $p_{\text{adj}} < .01$) (Table 4). The dominant pattern was the near-absence of content-heavy designs among *Compact* LDs (0.7%), in sharp contrast with *Expansive* (26.6%) and *Interactive* (13.0%) LDs (Fig. 3a). *Compact* LDs were characterised by a substantially higher share of collaboration-heavy designs (81.5%) compared with *Expansive* (4.0%) and *Interactive* (21.7%) LDs. Conversely, mixed designs dominated *Expansive* (66.1%) and *Interactive* LDs

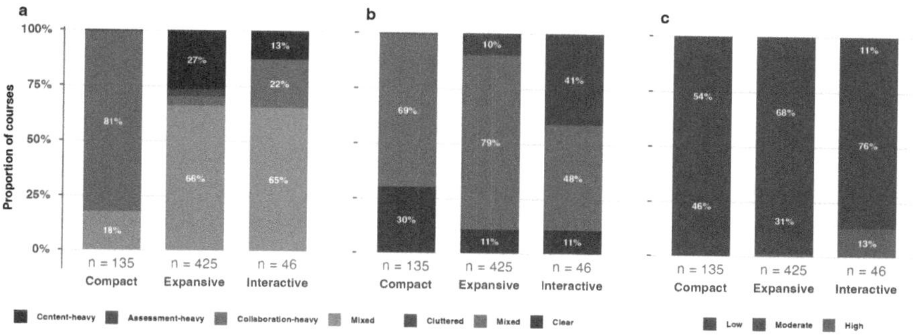


**Fig. 3.** Distribution of LD indicators by LD type for: (a) activity-mode balance, (b) structural clarity, (c) analytics readiness.

(65.2%), compared with only 17.8% in *Compact* LDs. The strongest pairwise separation was between *Compact* and *Expansive* ($V = 0.35$).

**Table 4.** LD indicators by LD type, with FET results.

| | *Compact* | | *Expansive* | | *Interactive* | | |
|---|---|---|---|---|---|---|---|
| Indicator | $n$ | % | $n$ | % | $n$ | % | FET |
| *Activity-mode balance* | | | | | | | $p < .001$, $V = 0.26$ |
| Content-heavy | 1 | 0.7 | 113 | 26.6 | 6 | 13.0 | |
| Assessment-heavy | 0 | 0.0 | 14 | 3.3 | 0 | 0.0 | |
| Mixed | 24 | 17.8 | 17 | 4.0 | 10 | 21.7 | |
| Collaboration-heavy | 110 | 81.5 | 281 | 66.1 | 30 | 65.2 | |
| *Structural clarity* | | | | | | | $p < .001$, $V = 0.27$ |
| Clear | 41 | 30.4 | 47 | 11.1 | 5 | 10.9 | |
| Mixed | 93 | 68.9 | 336 | 79.1 | 22 | 47.8 | |
| Cluttered | 1 | 0.7 | 42 | 9.9 | 19 | 41.3 | |
| *Analytics readiness* | | | | | | | $p < .001$, $V = 0.27$ |
| Low | 73 | 54.1 | 289 | 68.0 | 5 | 10.9 | |
| Moderate | 62 | 45.9 | 132 | 31.1 | 35 | 76.1 | |
| High | 0 | 0.0 | 4 | 0.9 | 6 | 13.0 | |

*Structural Clarity* combines section density and orderliness to characterise the course interface based on the relative weights. It reflects the extent to which the organisation of content into sections is consistent, predictable, and transparent to students. *Structural clarity* also differentiated significantly across the three LD types ($p < .001$, $V = 0.27$), with all pairwise comparisons remaining significant after Bonferroni correction (all $p_{\text{adj}} < .001$). The largest effect was observed between *Compact* and *Interactive* LDs ($V = 0.57$): *Compact* LDs were almost never cluttered (0.7%) and were the most likely to be classified as *clear* (30.4%), whereas *Interactive* LDs were cluttered in 41.3% of cases and clear in only 10.9%

(Fig. 3b). *Expansive* LDs sat between the two extremes, with the largest share of *mixed* designs (79.1%) and intermediate levels of both clear (11.1%) and cluttered (9.9%) structures.

Finally, *analytics readiness* reflects the degree to which a course is instrumented for analytics data collection. It operationalises the structural preconditions for generating meaningful interaction traces and supporting evidence-based monitoring of student engagement. For *analytics readiness*, significant differences were found across all three LD types ($p < .001$, $V = 0.27$; all pairwise $p_{\text{adj}} < .05$ after Bonferroni correction). The strongest separations involved *Interactive* LDs, which stood out with a *moderate* readiness level in 76.1% of cases and were the only type with a substantial share of *high* readiness (13.0%), compared with *Expansive* ($V = 0.40$) and *Compact* ($V = 0.46$) LDs (Fig. 3c). *Expansive* LDs were predominantly classified as *low* readiness (68.0%), while *Compact* LDs were more evenly split between *low* (54.1%) and *moderate* (45.9%) and contained no designs at the *high* level. The difference between *Compact* and *Expansive* was statistically significant but substantially smaller in magnitude ($V = 0.14$).

## 4 Discussions and Conclusion

This study examined how LD can be operationalised at scale from Moodle data, addressing two research questions: what LD types characterise Moodle course designs and how they differ in their characteristics and institutional distribution (RQ1), and how LD indicators can be derived from LMS course data to characterise these types (RQ2).

**What the Data Reveal About Moodle Course Designs.** The analysis identified three distinct LD types, *Compact*, *Expansive*, and *Interactive*, that differ systematically along two principal dimensions: activity load and the combination of structural clarity with interaction richness.

*Expansive* LDs dominate the dataset and are the predominant pattern across HASS, STEM, and Commerce, reflecting courses that cover broad ground through the sheer volume of designed learning experiences. An alternative explanation is that these courses share a similar default way of being configured in Moodle, a phenomenon also observed in large-scale analyses of university courses where a majority were found to follow a traditional, repository-like model [17]. *Expansive* courses are characterised by a large number of activities, many sections, and substantial page-based content, spread across a wide range of activity loads with variable orderliness, a finding consistent with large-scale institutional analyses that have also identified a dominant pattern of high-volume, content-focused course designs [18]. The indicator analysis corroborated and extended this picture: *Expansive* courses are the only type with a substantial share of content-heavy designs, and most of them show a mixed structural layout, neither clearly organised nor cluttered. They were also low in analytics readiness, a profile consistent with their high volume and broad coverage but one that points to a missed opportunity for data-informed course design at scale.

*Compact* LDs form a consistent secondary presence characterised by tight, proportional scaling between sections and activities and by high structural regularity, and are particularly common in Law and Psychology. The indicator analysis corroborated this by showing that *Compact* courses are almost never cluttered and are the most likely of any type to be classified as clear, while also revealing a subtler pattern: despite their limited scale, they contain a comparatively high share of collaboration-heavy designs. Concurrently, they were limited in analytics readiness, suggesting that structural clarity does not automatically translate into analytics readiness. These findings align with previous research on usability of mobile learning applications, which recommends that to improve usability, interfaces should be kept simple and compact, for instance by segmenting long pages into smaller, more manageable chunks to improve navigation [21].

*Interactive* LDs, though comparatively rare, form a distinctive group defined not by activity load but by activity composition, combining elevated collaboration and assessment use with denser, less orderly section layouts, and are concentrated almost exclusively in Psychology and in large courses. This aligns with disciplinary characteristics of Psychology as a discipline that has a strong tradition of active, discussion-based, and lab-oriented instruction [22]. The indicator analysis corroborated and extended this: *Interactive* courses were predominantly classified as mixed but with a substantial share of cluttered layouts, confirming that their activity concentration comes at a measurable cost to layout consistency, which highlights the critical need to interpret analytics within the context of the specific learning design to make sense of student behaviour [20]. As shown in previous research, interactive courses concentrate many activities into fewer sections, which makes them structurally denser but also more likely to appear cluttered and to require more careful structuring if they are meant to support students' course navigation and analytics support [20]. Despite this, they were the best instrumented for analytics and the only type with a substantial share of high-readiness designs, showing that analytics readiness can coexist with, and perhaps even follow from, more complex and interaction-dense course structures.

Importantly, the three types are not simply different points on a common continuum but reflect structurally distinct organising logics: *Compact* courses scale sections and activities in tight proportion, *Expansive* courses spread activities across many sections with variable orderliness, and *Interactive* courses decouple the two, concentrating activity load into comparatively few sections. This is reflected most sharply in the contrast between *Compact* and *Interactive* LDs, which showed the largest separation of the entire analysis on structural clarity, capturing the fundamentally different logic of small, tightly organised courses and large, mixed activity-mode ones. LD at scale, then, is not a single spectrum from "simple to complex", but a space of qualitatively different approaches that different disciplines adopt in different proportions.

**What LD Indicators from LMS Data Reveal About Course Designs.** Building on these findings, we introduced a novel, transparent approach to deriving LD indicators from LMS data, combining theoretical grounding with iterative, data-driven threshold setting. To our knowledge, this is also the first work to propose indicators for LD: rather than simply classifying individual activities by type, our indicators aggregate and combine multiple structural variables into higher-order constructs that capture how these variables interact. Three indicators were derived, targeting the pedagogical balance of activities (*activity-mode balance*), the structural organisation of the course (*structural clarity*), and the readiness of the design for analytics (*analytics readiness*). All three indicators differentiated significantly across the LD types, with every pair of types distinguishable on every indicator. Importantly, the indicators do not simply redescribe the clustering solution in a different form but add interpretable, pedagogically meaningful dimensions to it, most notably analytics readiness, which does not enter the clustering solution directly but proves to be a strong discriminator once introduced. This convergence between the raw LMS variables and the categorical indicators strengthens confidence in the robustness of the three LD types and offers a lightweight, scalable way to characterise them without manual coding.

**Pedagogical Impact and Future Directions.** That the introduced indicators can be derived from LMS data alone, without access to pedagogical intent, reinforces the argument that LMS data can serve as a proxy for underlying LD, providing a foundation for design analytics that focus on the properties of the course as designed [8]. However, LMS data captures only one layer of the picture: it shows how courses are organised, but not why particular choices were made. Furthermore, using a snapshot of course designs excludes their evolution over time and the connection to student activity and LOs. This limitation stems from the available data: student interaction logs were not included and LOs are not systematically captured in the LMS. Consequently, the analysis enables the description of course designs, but prevents conclusions about how the identified LD types affect student engagement or performance. A key avenue for future research is to link these LD types with student interaction data and LOs, ideally through longitudinal analysis, to examine their correlation with learner success. Defining thresholds for categorical measures and LD indicators through expert discussion and validation with empirical distributions represents an approach tailored to a specific institutional context, which may limit its generalizability. Future work should therefore test the robustness of the chosen thresholds through sensitivity analysis, validate the indicators across additional institutions, LMS platforms, and disciplines, and complement them with instructor rationales to move from characterising LD toward understanding the reasoning behind the specific design choices.

In conclusion, this study showed how LD can be operationalised at scale from Moodle data, contributing a large-scale empirical characterisation of 606 courses, the identification of three distinct LD types (*Compact*, *Expansive*, and *Interactive*), and a novel approach to deriving LD indicators directly from LMS data. The emergence of generative AI is reshaping what LD has to do: instructors are integrating new tools, rethinking assessment, and restructuring courses to assure the quality of student learning. These pressures place instructors more squarely than ever in the role of designers [11], yet the choices they make at the level of the course as a whole remain largely invisible at scale, leaving both researchers and institutions without a clear view of how course design is actually evolving under these demands. The approach introduced here begins to close that gap, offering a lightweight, scalable way to surface those choices and, in doing so, supporting instructors in their designer role. More broadly, the indicators developed here are a first step toward a more deliberate, evidence-informed conversation about what LD should look like in a rapidly changing educational landscape.

**Acknowledgments.** This research was supported by the project LEAD:FUH funded by the Stiftung Innovation in der Hochschullehre (1001-3223), and Center of Advanced Technology for Assisted Learning and Predictive Analytics (CATALPA) at FernUniversität in Hagen, Germany. We thank the Moodle team, particularly Daniel Poggenpohl, and the faculties' associate deans for enabling this analysis.

## References

1. Ahmad, A., et al.: Connecting the dots-a literature review on learning analytics indicators from a learning design perspective. JCAL **40**(6), 2432–2470 (2024)
2. Albó, L., Barria-Pineda, J., Brusilovsky, P., Hernández-Leo, D.: Knowledge-Based design analytics for authoring courses with smart learning content. IJAIED **32**(1), 4–27 (2022)
3. Armstrong, R.A.: When to use the b onferroni correction. Ophthalmic Physiol. Opt. **34**(5), 502–508 (2014)
4. Banihashem, S.K., Farrokhnia, M., Badali, M., Noroozi, O.: The impacts of constructivist learning design and learning analytics on students' engagement and self-regulation. IETI **59**(4), 442–452 (2022)
5. Caliński, T., Harabasz, J.: A dendrite method for cluster analysis. Commun. Stat. **3**(1), 1–27 (1974)
6. Claassen, A., Mirriahi, N., Kovanović, V., Dawson, S.: From data to design: integrating learning analytics into educational design for effective decision-making: from data to design. In: Proceedings of the 15th LAK Conference, pp. 558–567 (2025)
7. Davies, D.L., Bouldin, D.W.: A Cluster Separation Measure. IEEE Trans. Pattern Anal. Mach. Intell. PAMI **1**(2), 224–227 (1979)
8. Hernández-Leo, D., Martinez-Maldonado, R., Pardo, A., Muñoz-Cristóbal, J.A., Rodríguez-Triana, M.J.: Analytics for learning design: a layered framework and tools. BJET **50**(1), 139–152 (2019)
9. Hubert, L., Arabie, P.: Comparing partitions. J. Classif. **2**(1), 193–218 (1985)
10. Kim, H.Y.: Statistical notes for clinical researchers: chi-squared test and fisher's exact test. Restor. Dent. Endod. **42**(2), 152–155 (2017)
11. Kirschner, P.A.: Do we need teachers as designers of technology enhanced learning? Instr. Sci. **43**(2), 309–322 (2015)
12. Koper, R., Tattersall, C.: Learning design: a handbook on modelling and delivering networked education and training (2005)
13. Law, N., Liang, L.: A multilevel framework and method for learning analytics integrated learning design. JLA **7**(3), 98–117 (2020)

14. Misiejuk, K., Ness, I.J., Gray, R., Wasson, B.: Changes in online course designs: Before, during, and after the pandemic. Front. Educ. **7** (2023)
15. Nguyen, Q., Rienties, B., Toetenel, L.: Mixing and matching learning design and learning analytics. In: Proceedings of the LCT 2017, pp. 302–316. Springer (2017)
16. Ortiz-Beltrán, A., Hernández-Leo, D.: Extracting institutional analytics features from LMS data: towards bridging learning design analytics and learning analytics. In: Proceedings of the LASI Spain (2025)
17. Revuelta-Domínguez, F.I., Guerra-Antequera, J., González-Pérez, A., Arriazu-Muñoz, R.: Structural study of post-COVID-19 use based on LMS log data analysis from the university of Extremadura: a case study of learning analytics. Educ. Sci. **16**(2), 319 (2026)
18. Rienties, B., Nguyen, Q., Holmes, W., Reedy, K.: A review of ten years of implementation and research in aligning learning design with learning analytics at the Open University UK. IxD&A **33**, 134–154 (2017)
19. Schmitz, M., Van Limbeek, E., Greller, W., Sloep, P., Drachsler, H.: Opportunities and challenges in using learning analytics in learning design. In: Proceedings of the 12th EC-TEL Conference, pp. 209–223 (2017)
20. Shen, H., Liang, L., Law, N., Hemberg, E., O'Reilly, U.M.: Understanding learner behavior through learning design informed learning analytics. In: Proceedings of the 7th L@S Conference, pp. 135–145 (2020)
21. Tabuenca, B., Kalz, M., Drachsler, H., Specht, M.: Time will tell: the role of mobile learning analytics in self-regulated learning. Comput. Educ. **89**, 53–74 (2015)
22. Whitelock-Wainwright, A., et al.: Disciplinary differences in blended learning design: a network analytic study. In: Proceedings of the 10th LAK Conference, pp. 579–588 (2020)

# Are LLM-Based Chatbots Good Enough to Support Computer Science Students in Multiple-Choice Exercises?

Markos Stamatakis[1(✉)], Omkar Gavali[2,3], Joshua Berger[4], Christian Wartena[4], Anett Hoppe[1,2,3], and Ralph Ewerth[1,2,3,5]

[1] TIB – Leibniz Information Centre for Science and Technology, Hannover, Germany
markos.stamatakis@tib.eu
[2] University of Marburg, Marburg, Germany
[3] Hessian Center for AI (hessian.AI), Darmstadt/Marburg, Germany
[4] Hochschule Hannover – Data and H Institute for Applied Data Science, Hannover, Germany
[5] L3S Research Center – Leibniz University Hannover, Hannover, Germany

**Abstract.** Chatbots based on large language models (LLMs) are increasingly adopted for information retrieval, text generation, and writing assistance. In educational settings, their use is also rapidly increasing. Students leverage these systems to complete tasks, access information, and support learning. However, the role of LLM-based chatbots in supporting learning and assessment in university-level computer science education is still underexplored. To address this gap, we investigate the performance of several LLM-based chatbots in solving multiple-choice questions (MCQs) at the university level and evaluate their capabilities to assist student learning. We developed 70 MCQs for a university lecture on interactive visual data analysis and evaluated the chatbots' performance using different prompt designs. We further compared the results with students' performance. Finally, we conducted a user study in two lectures (interactive visual data analysis, computer vision) to investigate how chatbot-generated answers and explanations affect students' performance. The chatbot performance showed significant differences between smaller models and GPT-4o and GPT-5 models, which achieved the best results. The results of the user study show that presenting ChatGPT answers alongside an explanation does not yield a statistically significant improvement in students' performance, though the effect may vary with their prior knowledge.

**Keywords:** Multiple-Choice Tests · Multiple-Choice Questions · LLM-based Chatbots · Prompting · Computer Science · Education

## 1 Introduction

LLM-based chatbots such as ChatGPT [26] and DeepSeek [5] are increasingly used for everyday tasks and have proven effective for a wide range of applications,


J. Weidlich et al. (Eds.): EC-TEL 2026, LNCS 16905, pp. 577–592, 2027.
https://doi.org/10.1007/978-3-032-37979-5_39

including text generation, translation, and problem-solving [21]. In education, they are used to support both studying and teaching [28,37]. Initial research suggests potential learning benefits, with LLM-based systems improving knowledge gains compared to traditional textbooks, and supporting the generation of learning materials and assessment items at varying competency [2,18]. However, less is known about their accuracy in answering domain-specific questions and their influence on students' answers during test scenarios.

In this paper, we address this gap and investigate whether LLM-based chatbots can accurately answer multiple-choice questions (MCQs) in a university-level computer science (CS) lecture on interactive visual data analysis (IVDA). We manually created 70 MCQs based on course slides as our evaluation dataset. Specifically, we examine chatbot performance across different prompt variations using a structured prompting approach. Additionally, we report results of a user study conducted in the lectures on IVDA and computer vision (CV) that investigated whether GPT-generated answer suggestions influence student behavior during assessments. Drawing on the study results, we position the use of such systems within pedagogical and socio-technical perspectives. We focus on the following research questions:

**RQ1** To what extent can LLM-based chatbots generate accurate answers to MCQs derived from a university-level IVDA lecture?
**RQ2** How does prompt design affect the accuracy and reliability of LLM outputs on these MCQs?
**RQ3** How do LLM-based outputs compare to student responses on these MCQs?
**RQ4** How do GPT-generated answer suggestions influence student response patterns on MCQs in IVDA and CV?

This paper is structured as follows: Section 2 reviews related work on question generation, answering, and the use of LLM-based chatbots in education. Section 3 describes the experimental setup. Section 4 and 5 describe the evaluation of LLM performance on MCQs and the impact of GPT-generated outputs on student responses, respectively. Finally, Sect. 6 concludes and outlines future work.

## 2 Related Work

This section examines current research on automatic LLM-based question and answer generation (Sect. 2.1), and their use as a learning resource in educational contexts (Sect. 2.2) to highlight challenges in analyzing models' processing. Here, unlike direct LLM outputs, LLM-based chatbots add an interaction layer with personas, instructions, or conversation management that shape processing.

### 2.1 LLM-Based Question Generation and Answering

Prior work shows that models such as GPT-3.5 and GPT-4 can generate domain-specific questions and answers in zero-shot settings across fields like medicine, biology, and mathematics [4,8,31], highlighting their potential for assessment and learning support. However, limitations in quality and reliability are still reported. Generated questions and answers, especially MCQs, often require human verification due to duplicates or misaligned difficulty level [23,31]. Furthermore, LLM hallucinations are a well-known problem [1]. Such models can also be very sensitive to prompt formatting and phrasing [16,33]. Focusing more on errors of LLM-based models in education, Liu et al. [13] found moderate correlations between models' and students' misconceptions across subjects. Smaller models show a higher similarity to student mistakes, while larger ones do not necessarily align with student error patterns.

These studies provide insights into the performance of LLM-based question generation and answering, but overlook how prompting factors, such as persona, context, and response format, affect reliability. Different domains were analyzed, but higher-level CS education is not the main focus. We address this gap by evaluating 70 manually designed MCQs across different models (Sect. 4).

### 2.2 LLM-Based Chatbots for Learning

Common educational applications of LLM-based models include question generation, answer grading, code correction, and content explanation [9]. Integrating these into learning environments presents both technical and pedagogical challenges. Technical limitations include solving complex math problems and programming tasks [30], model costs, and adaptability [34]. Pedagogically, challenges include identifying LLM-generated work and guiding appropriate use [34]. Recent studies have begun to examine the impact of utilizing LLMs for learning. For instance, research in programming education suggests that extensive reliance on LLM-based assistance may reduce undergraduate students' final grades and problem-solving abilities [11]. In contrast, LLM-based models may deepen understanding of course content when used as teaching assistants rather than for answer retrieval [17]. In CS education, these systems have been explored for formative feedback like tutor-style feedback [29]. Additional generated explanations can improve transparency, interpretability, and trust. Still, it needs to be tailored to learners to support learning [12]. In student assessment, these systems raise ethical concerns such as cheating, data privacy, and fairness [7]. They are also classified as high-risk under the EU AI Act when used to evaluate learning [6].

Overall, the current research reflects that LLM-based models offer promising support for learning, but remain limited in deep understanding and problem-solving. In particular, it is not revealed how information from LLMs influences learners in test scenarios. We therefore investigate how the availability of LLM-generated output impacts learners in different test scenarios (Sect. 5).

## 3 Experimental Setup

This section describes our experimental approach. The code and experimental data are available in a GitHub repository[1]. Section 3.1 describes our MCQ

[1] https://github.com/markossta/mcq_llm_answer_paper.

dataset. We then introduce the investigated models (Sect. 3.2), our prompting strategy (Sect. 3.3), the user study design (Sect. 3.4), and our evaluation methods (Sect. 3.5).

### 3.1 Multiple-Choice Questions (MCQs)

To evaluate LLM-based models' performance on generating answers for MCQs, we created 70 MCQs based on a university-level CS lecture on IVDA. The lecture covers definitions, criteria, and visualization and analysis approaches for different data types, delivered through slide presentations [35] under a CC-BY-4.0 license. We manually composed up to nine questions per presentation to test content understanding. We selected IVDA as a less common CS topic, likely underrepresented in training data, to evaluate how well LLMs handle specialized content when answering MCQs in CS. To ensure quality, we applied a two-step validation process: one author created the questions, which were then reviewed and discussed with a second author. Each question includes four answer options with a varying number of correct answers to prevent consistent response patterns. Correct answers are distributed evenly across all answer positions, preventing participants from benefiting from systematic guessing. These questions were answered by up to 36 students throughout multiple lectures, with a fixed set of MCQs assigned to each lecture unit. Each set of MCQs referred to the topic of the previous week, encouraging students to revisit the material and enabling an assessment of their longer-term retention of the learned content. All student answers were collected anonymously with students' informed consent, using only a participant ID for tracking the points.

For the user study, we used two sets of questions across two independent lectures to allow a comparison across different CS topics. In the first lecture, the question set contains five of our created questions in the context of IVDA. The second lecture focused on computer vision (CV), for which we created eight additional CV-MCQs, extending the already created 70 IVDA-MCQs. These questions are based on Chap. 9 of *Foundations of Computer Vision* [36] (CC-BY-ND-NC license) and include content related to how the learning process is performed to train models for solving specific problems. We selected CV as a second scenario to examine how GPT-generated output of a more common topic affects student behavior and performance differently. Both question sets include questions that GPT did not answer correctly, allowing analysis of how student answer patterns are impacted by correct and incorrect chatbot-generated outputs.

### 3.2 Investigated Models

To compare models of different scales, we evaluated ChatGPT [26], DeepSeek-R1 [5], and Mistral-7B [10]. For ChatGPT, we used GPT-4o and GPT-5.2 via the API connection. For DeepSeek-R1 and Mistral-7B, we selected 7B-parameter variants to reflect more realistic deployment scenarios and to assess the performance of smaller-scale models. Specifically, we used *DeepSeek-R1-Distill-Qwen-7B* and *Mistral-7B-Instruct-v0.3*. For DeepSeek-R1, all responses are generated using a dedicated *think mode* allowing deeper reasoning. All models supported the required context windows. To improve reproducibility for the local models (DeepSeek-R1, Mistral-7B), we disabled sampling and used a fixed seed (1234).

### 3.3 Prompt Design

*Prompting Strategy:* Given the strong influence of prompt design on model performance [32], we employ a structured prompting strategy. Several approaches and extra information can be used to improve the processing of the models [32]. Additionally, there are formulation guidelines to improve LLMs' processing [3,27]. Drawing on these guidelines, we derived the following prompt components for our structured prompting strategy:

- **Defined Persona**: guides the model toward a specific perspective
- **Thematic Focus**: ensures that irrelevant content is excluded
- **Background Knowledge**: provides additional information on the topic so the model can better process the context
- **Level of Detail of the Response**: controls whether the model provides only answers or also explanations
- **Task**: explicitly defines what the model is required to do
- **Output Format**: specifies the format for an easier evaluation

We excluded other techniques, such as few-shot learning and chain-of-thought prompting, as they were not suited to our evaluation. Speech style, follow-up prompts, dialogue, explicit constraints, and key-term definitions were omitted to minimize stylistic and interaction-related biases. Audience specification was implicitly integrated through persona.

*Defined Prompts:* Each prompt is structured into four sections: *Persona*, *Task Definition*, *Output Format*, and *Background Knowledge*. To separate instructions from task content, the question and optional background knowledge were provided as a user prompt, while the instructions were given as a system prompt.

We evaluated three persona settings: *none*, *student*, and *professor* to evaluate their effect on model performance. Prior research has shown that the use of expert personas can influence outputs [25] We also included topic context to provide more details. For *none*, we skipped the persona section.

After the persona, the task is defined in detail to ensure correct processing. The general topic (IVDA) and the structure of the MCQs are clarified. Two output format settings were used: *answer-only* and *answer-with-explanation*, both enforcing a fixed format for consistency. To assess the impact of background knowledge, we compared prompts with and without slide-based context, manually extracted from the lecture slides of the current question.

The combination of all settings results in 12 distinct prompts, allowing analysis of optimal configurations and influencing factors. For the user study on the impact of LLM-generated suggestions on learners, we created a prompt that mirrors student prompting behavior. Students tend to ask procedural questions without completely structuring the prompt [22]. To approximate student-like requests, we limited the prompt to persona, task, and brief explanations.

### 3.4 User Study Design

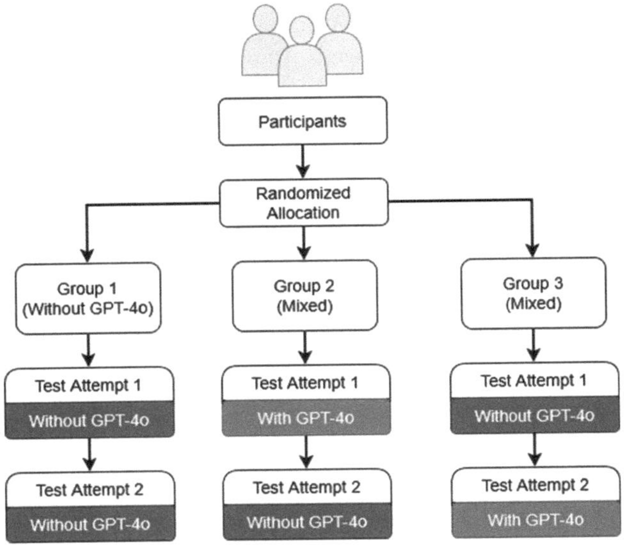


**Fig. 1.** User study design with three randomized groups. All participants had to complete two test attempts with identical tasks under different settings: with/out GPT-4o.

We conducted a user study to analyze how pre-computed GPT-4o output influences Master's students' behavior during an MCQ test. An overview of the user study design is given in Fig. 1. Participants were recruited from two specific Master-level lectures, IVDA and CV, at a German university. Both lectures were held in English. All students of the courses were informed about the experimental setting of the exercise and were free to choose whether to participate; approximately 30% of the students consented to take part. All data were fully anonymized using participant IDs to track attempts without identifying individuals. The study was designed to reflect the participants' level of acquired knowledge, such that the topics covered in the test had already been presented in the specific lecture. The user study scenarios were conducted independently for each lecture, involving different participants in each case. Participants were randomly assigned to one of three groups, while ensuring a balanced distribution across groups. They were instructed to complete two test attempts to assess potential changes in responses. Both attempts consisted of the same set of MCQs. Between the two attempts, participants were encouraged to take a break of one hour for reflection on their answers. The first group completed an MCQ test without GPT-4o output, the second group received the output for all questions on the first attempt, and the third group completed the test first without and then with the output. GPT-4o output included labels for each multiple-choice option (true/false) and provided explanations, enabling students to reflect and compare with their own knowledge. Additionally, a group-specific questionnaire assessed students' perceptions of LLMs and the test setting. It consisted of five sections: *general use of LLMs*, *personal perception*, *LLM usage during the test*, *acceptance of LLMs*, and *feedback* to assess subjective experiences and willingness to integrate LLMs into learning. Most questions used five-point Likert scales ranging from 1 (strongly disagree) to 5 (strongly agree) to assess students' views. The feedback question consists of an open-text response for further insights. Versions varied slightly by group to reflect the setting.

### 3.5 Evaluation Methods

We assessed model performance across all prompt variants using multiple metrics. For scoring, each MCQ comprised four answer options worth one point each, yielding a maximum score of four points per question. We report two complementary measures: the mean score (total points earned out of four) and the proportion of fully correct answers - that is, the percentage of MCQs for which a model selected all correct options. To compare model and student performance, we averaged scores per question and ranked questions by difficulty (i.e., the proportion of correct answers). We then examined whether models and students agreed on which questions were easiest and hardest by comparing the overlap in their top and bottom 10 % of questions. Finally, for each MCQ, we identified the most frequent incorrect option chosen by students and checked whether a model selected the same distractor, using a binary option-level similarity measure.

To statistically evaluate the user study results (see Sect. 5), we employed a linear mixed model (LMM), which is robust to unbalanced data and repeated measurements [14]. In our study, the experimental groups differed in the number of participants, resulting in an unbalanced dataset. As the dependent variable, we focused on each student's score per attempt. This forms the group, attempt, and interaction (group x attempt) as fixed effects. Participant identity was included as a random intercept to account for repeated measurements and inter-individual differences in baseline performance. The model structure is given in Eq. 1.

$$\text{Score} \sim \text{Group} * \text{Attempt} + (1 \mid \text{Participant}) \tag{1}$$

Based on this, the following null hypotheses were formulated:

**H1** Attempt Effect: Student performance does not differ between the first and the second test attempt.

**H2** Group Effect: Student performance does not differ between the experimental groups.

**H3** Interaction Effect: The change in student performance between the first and second attempt does not differ between the experimental groups.

Each of the hypotheses corresponds to a fixed effect in the linear mixed model, whose significance was assessed using likelihood-ratio tests (LRT). Wald $\chi^2$ tests can be unreliable on small samples [15]. Still, we reported the results of such tests for comparison. We used a conventional $\alpha = 0.05$ for evaluation.

**Table 1.** Results (%) for all models across prompt variations. The three-part setting code indicates persona (*None* = no persona, *Stud.* = student, *Prof.* = professor), requested justification (*Y*/*N*), and usage of slide context (*Y*/*N*). For example, *Prof.-Y-Y* denotes a professor persona with justification and slide context. *Acc.* is the mean score, *Corr.* the percentage of fully correct answers, and *Sim.* the similarity between the models' and students' most frequent incorrect answer.

| Setting | Models | | | | | | | | | | | |
|---|---|---|---|---|---|---|---|---|---|---|---|---|
| | Mistral-7B | | | DeepSeek-R1 | | | GPT-4o | | | GPT-5.2 | | |
| | Acc. | Corr. | Sim. | Acc. | Corr. | Sim. | Acc. | Corr. | Sim. | Acc. | Corr. | Sim. |
| None-N-N | **74.6** | 28.6 | 32.0 | 79.6 | 44.3 | 33.3 | 83.9 | 57.1 | 43.3 | 87.9 | 61.4 | 55.6 |
| None-N-Y | 63.9 | 17.1 | 12.1 | 72.1 | 32.9 | 21.3 | 90.0 | 67.1 | 52.2 | 94.6 | 84.3 | **72.7** |
| None-Y-N | 73.2 | 28.6 | 40.0 | 79.6 | 40.0 | 33.3 | 84.6 | 54.3 | 50.0 | 85.4 | 54.3 | 50.0 |
| None-Y-Y | 63.9 | 24.3 | 17.0 | 66.1 | 32.9 | 10.6 | **91.4** | 70.0 | 57.1 | 95.0 | 84.3 | 54.6 |
| Stud.-N-N | 72.9 | **31.4** | 25.0 | 75.4 | 35.7 | 33.3 | 82.5 | 50.0 | **60.0** | 87.9 | 50.0 | 46.4 |
| Stud.-N-Y | 67.5 | 25.7 | 11.5 | 73.2 | 40.0 | 14.3 | 89.6 | 68.6 | 54.6 | 95.7 | 84.3 | 63.6 |
| Stud.-Y-N | 73.2 | 28.6 | 30.0 | 80.0 | 42.9 | 37.5 | 84.3 | 55.7 | 54.8 | 88.6 | 61.4 | 51.9 |
| Stud.-Y-Y | 63.2 | 21.4 | 9.1 | 70.0 | 34.3 | 17.4 | 91.1 | **71.4** | 55.0 | **96.4** | **87.1** | 66.7 |
| Prof.-N-N | 73.9 | 30.0 | 32.7 | 79.3 | 38.6 | **44.2** | 83.2 | 52.9 | 51.5 | 88.6 | 65.7 | 41.7 |
| Prof.-N-Y | 68.6 | 25.7 | 13.5 | 74.3 | 38.6 | 20.9 | 91.1 | **71.4** | 45.0 | 95.0 | 85.7 | 60.0 |
| Prof.-Y-N | 73.2 | 28.6 | **42.0** | **81.8** | **45.7** | 39.5 | 82.5 | 51.4 | 50.0 | 85.7 | 55.7 | 48.4 |
| Prof.-Y-Y | 62.5 | 21.4 | 18.2 | 71.4 | 31.4 | 16.7 | 88.6 | 65.7 | 41.7 | 93.9 | 81.4 | 53.9 |
| **Avg.** | 69.2 | 26.0 | 23.6 | 75.2 | 38.1 | 26.9 | 86.9 | 61.3 | 51.3 | 91.2 | 71.3 | 55.5 |

## 4 LLM-Based Chatbot Performance on MCQs

*Performance Evaluation:* For each prompt variation, we tested the models on all 70 MCQs using the option-level accuracy, fully correct questions, and similarity to the average wrong student response. Table 1 reports the results.

For Mistral-7B, providing slide content consistently reduces accuracy to 62 – 69 %. Approaches without content reach over 70 %, suggesting larger input hinders identification of question-relevant information. Personas and requested explanations reduce accuracy by up to 1.7 %. The highest accuracy ($\approx$ 75 %) is achieved without personas, explanations, and slide context. Across all variants, about 70 %–80 % of questions were not answered fully correctly. The student error similarity varies, indicating differences in how the information is handled.

DeepSeek-R1 performs similar to Mistral-7B, but shows a performance advantage. The results differ across prompt variants without a clear systematic pattern. In contrast, the GPT models achieve higher accuracy and more fully correct responses. Performance improved when slide content was provided. In general, more than half of all questions are completely correct, indicating deeper processing, with GPT-5.2 outperforming GPT-4o. Although the similarity error varies and reaches up to 60 % (GPT-4o) and ≈ 73 % (GPT-5.2), it does not fully align with student error responses (**RQ3**). The smaller models achieve moderate performance, but select incorrect options for most questions. In contrast, GPT models perform better (**RQ1**). The consistently high proportion of partially correct answers and context sensitivity highlight limitations of smaller LLM-based chatbots in reliably solving IVDA-MCQs. Furthermore, prompting affects performance while persona effects remain inconsistent (**RQ2**).

**Table 2.** Top and bottom 10% of questions based on the average performance of models and students. Each entry lists the question ID and percentage of correct answers in parentheses. Questions in bold appear in both the student and model rankings.

| Rank | Average of Models | Average of Students |
|---|---|---|
| Top | Q66 (97.9), Q30 (97.9), Q2 (95.8) **Q50** (91.7), Q41 (89.6), **Q7** (87.5) Q4 (87.5) | Q69 (100.0), Q5 (97.1), Q25 (96.0) Q24 (95.8), **Q50** (94.7), **Q7** (92.3) Q31 (91.7) |
| Worst | Q62 (0.0), **Q40** (6.3), **Q47** (6.3) **Q63** (10.4), Q45 (12.5), Q48 (12.5) Q3 (16.7) | Q26 (0.0), Q27 (0.0), **Q63** (0.0) Q28 (4.2), **Q40** (14.3), **Q47** (14.3) Q61 (22.2) |

*Chatbot-User Comparison:* Table 2 shows limited consistency between the best- and worst-performing questions for models and students, with minimal overlap of questions. Considering the performance score, both exhibit comparable behavior: the best-performing questions achieve similarly accurate scores above 85 %, while the worst-performing ones often fall below 15 %. This indicates comparable difficulty distributions, reflecting similar average performance for top and worst questions rather than identical error characteristics (**RQ3**).

*Stability Evaluation:* We conducted a stability evaluation because the models are not fully deterministic. We focus on the smaller models, as they are more easily reproducible and configurable locally. Robustness to option ordering was tested by cyclically shifting MCQ options so that each option appeared once in every position. We further analyze the effect of randomness under enabled default sampling by running the identical prompt 10 times. For both models, we used the prompt with the highest accuracy to focus only on robustness. As shown in Table 3, option order slightly affects the score, indicating a minor position bias for both models. The error similarity also indicates that the models vary regarding the wrong answers, hinting at partial guessing. Repeating the same prompt without option permutation (last row) leads to slight score variation. Overall, accuracy and fully correct answers remain relatively stable. The error similarity varies like the permutation evaluation, indicating the same reason.

## 5 GPT Impact on Student Responses

*Test Results:* Only students completing both attempts were included to ensure comparability, resulting in varying group sizes. Table 4 summarizes results across groups, attempts, and GPT-4o. For IVDA-MCQs, GPT-4o generally outperforms an average student. Still, there are students with at least an equivalent score, especially in Group 2. Group 1 achieves the lowest average score across both attempts, while Group 3 aligns with Group 1 in the first attempt and Group 2 in the second. Group 2 performs slightly worse during the second attempt, implying uncertainty after seeing the questions without GPT-4o output. Similarities between student and GPT-4o solutions are also comparable to the test setting, indicating frequent use of solutions (**RQ4**).

**Table 3.** Results (%) for local models under option rotation (top) and 10 runs using sampling (bottom). *Acc.* denotes accuracy, *Corr.* fully correct answers, and *Sim.* the error similarity to the most frequently chosen incorrect answer by students.

| Setting | Mistral-7B | | | DeepSeek-R1 | | |
|---|---|---|---|---|---|---|
| | Acc. | Corr. | Sim. | Acc. | Corr. | Sim. |
| Permutation: 0123 | **74.6** | 28.6 | **32.0** | **81.8** | **45.7** | 39.5 |
| Permutation: 3012 | 69.6 | 25.7 | 23.0 | 77.9 | 37.1 | 36.4 |
| Permutation: 2301 | 70.7 | 25.7 | 19.2 | 75.7 | 40.0 | 42.5 |
| Permutation: 1230 | 72.9 | **32.9** | 25.5 | 78.6 | 37.1 | **43.2** |
| Std. | ±2.2 | ±3.4 | ±5.4 | ±2.5 | ±4.0 | ±3.1 |
| Std. (10 runs: 0123) | ±0.9 | ±2.4 | ±4.1 | ±1.6 | ±3.0 | ±4.0 |

In the CV scenario, the average student outperforms GPT in all attempts, with many achieving comparable or higher scores. The similarity to GPT-4o output is always over 80 %. Group 1 remains stable across attempts. Group 2 improves slightly, while Group 3 declines in the second attempt. This suggests that GPT-4o outputs may reduce performance when prior knowledge is higher, potentially introducing uncertainty rather than clarification (**RQ4**).

Table 5 summarizes changes between the two attempts. For IVDA-MCQs, 63.64 % of Group 3 improved, while 18.18 % performed worse. ≈ 80 % of students

**Table 4.** Comparison of participant groups and *GPT-4o*. *N* describes number of participants, *Min.*, *Max.* and *Avg.* refers to the points of the students, *Avg. %* denotes average performance, *Sim.* the similarity to *GPT-4o* outputs, and *Better/Same* the proportion of students outperforming or matching *GPT-4o*. *G*: group; *A*: attempt.

| Setting | Group | N | Min. | Max. | Avg. | Avg. % | Sim. | Better | Same | Worse |
|---|---|---|---|---|---|---|---|---|---|---|
| IVDA | G1-A1 | 15 | 14 | 19 | 15.86 | 79.29 | 64.76 | 4.67 | 9.52 | 85.81 |
| IVDA | G1-A2 | 15 | 14 | 19 | 16.13 | 80.67 | 65.00 | 6.67 | 13.33 | 80.00 |
| IVDA | G2-A1 | 10 | 15 | 18 | 17.00 | 85.00 | **87.50** | 0.00 | **50.00** | **50.00** |
| IVDA | G2-A2 | 10 | 14 | 18 | 16.70 | 83.50 | 79.50 | 0.00 | 40.00 | 60.00 |
| IVDA | G3-A1 | 11 | 12 | 19 | 16.18 | 80.90 | 64.09 | **9.09** | 0.00 | 90.91 |
| IVDA | G3-A2 | 11 | 15 | **20** | 17.09 | 85.46 | 80.91 | **9.09** | 18.18 | 72.73 |
| IVDA | GPT-4o | – | **18** | 18 | **18.00** | **90.00** | – | – | – | – |
| CV | G1-A1 | 16 | 23 | **32** | 29.25 | 91.41 | 82.03 | 87.50 | 0.00 | 12.50 |
| CV | G1-A2 | 16 | 22 | **32** | 29.38 | 91.80 | 81.64 | 87.50 | 0.00 | 12.50 |
| CV | G2-A1 | 9 | 21 | **32** | 27.56 | 86.11 | 85.76 | 55.56 | **11.11** | 33.33 |
| CV | G2-A2 | 9 | 25 | 31 | 28.78 | 89.93 | **91.67** | 66.67 | 2.22 | 31.11 |
| CV | G3-A1 | 9 | **29** | **32** | **30.33** | **94.79** | 86.81 | **100.00** | 0.00 | **0.00** |
| CV | G3-A2 | 9 | 27 | **32** | 30.00 | 93.75 | 90.63 | 89.88 | **11.11** | **0.00** |
| CV | GPT-4o | – | 27 | 27 | 27.00 | 84.38 | – | – | – | – |

in Group 1 and Group 2 show unchanged performance, indicating that the altered setting in Group 3 has an observable effect. Only a few students outperform GPT in both attempts, suggesting reliance on GPT and potential uncertainty (**RQ4**).

In the CV scenario, at least half of the students achieved identical scores across the groups. In Groups 1 and 3, over 80 % outperformed GPT-4o in both attempts. Group 2 shows the largest gain, possibly following an initial GPT-induced deficit. This suggests that GPT-generated outputs may influence students differently depending on prior knowledge (**RQ4**).

*Statistical Evaluation:* Table 6 shows the p-values of the statistical tests for both scenarios. Based on LRT, no fixed effects are significant at $\alpha = 0.05$, reflecting no evidence for attempt-dependent performance differences.

For IVDA-MCQs, the interaction effect (**H3**) only approaches significance ($p = 0.058$), indicating a tendency toward group-specific performance changes. Under the Wald $\chi^2$ tests, the interaction effect (**H3**) for IVDA-MCQs and the group effect (**H2**) for CV-MCQs are significant. However, these findings should be treated cautiously due to the sample size and non-significant LRT results.

Overall, no conclusive evidence is found for a significant impact of GPT-generated output on student performance. However, the tendency for **H3** in IVDA-MCQs and the limited sample size motivate larger studies (**RQ4**).

*Questionnaire Results:* Across both scenarios, students reported regular LLM use for studying and rated GPT output as understandable and helpful, often

**Table 5.** Change in student performance (%) between the first and second attempt of each group in both user study scenarios. $N$ describes the number of participants. *Improved*, *Unchanged*, and *Worsened* indicate performance changes; *Better than GPT* denotes participants outperforming GPT-4o in both attempts. $G$: group; $A$: attempt.

| Setting | Group | N | Improved | Unchanged | Worsened | Better than GPT |
|---|---|---|---|---|---|---|
| IVDA | G1 A1→A2 | 15 | 13.33 | **80.00** | 6.67 | 6.67 |
| IVDA | G2 A1→A2 | 10 | 20.00 | 60.00 | **20.00** | 0.00 |
| IVDA | G3 A1→A2 | 11 | **63.64** | 18.18 | 18.18 | **9.09** |
| CV | G1 A1→A2 | 16 | 25.00 | 50.00 | **25.00** | 81.25 |
| CV | G2 A1→A2 | 9 | **33.33** | 55.56 | 11.11 | 55.56 |
| CV | G3 A1→A2 | 9 | 0.00 | **77.78** | 22.22 | **88.89** |

**Table 6.** p-values of LRT and Wald tests for hypotheses (H) in both user study scenarios (IVDA and CV). Bold indicates significance at $\alpha = 0.05$.

| H | LRT (IVDA) | LRT (CV) | Wald (IVDA) | Wald (CV) |
|---|---|---|---|---|
| H1 | 0.229 | 0.438 | 0.650 | 0.814 |
| H2 | 0.449 | 0.145 | 0.277 | **0.041** |
| H3 | 0.058 | 0.285 | **0.046** | 0.272 |

increasing confidence and engagement. However, trust varied. For IVDA-MCQs, agreement was neutral to moderate, whereas for CV-MCQs, trust was more skeptical. This suggests that they see utility but do not unconditionally trust these systems. However, Table 4 shows that the answer similarity is quite high for all groups. Especially Group 2 and Group 3 indicate a tendency to follow GPT-generated answers despite students' reported critical perspective. The open-answer feedback shows that such models were perceived as helpful for simplifying concepts and improving learning efficiency, but problematic due to hallucinations, overconfidence, and inconsistencies. The IVDA-MCQs scenario highlighted risks of dependency and cognitive offloading, while the other scenario emphasized organizational benefits and answer uncertainty. Overall, students view these models as useful for learning but requiring critical use (**RQ4**).

*Pedagogical and Socio-Technical Aspects:* Pedagogically, our results indicate a first trend that LLM-generated output can serve as scaffolding for students with lower prior knowledge, as in the IVDA setting, who benefit more from structured guidance due to higher cognitive load [24]. These models can be seen as a technological layer linking pedagogical guidance and domain knowledge, which aligns with the TPACK framework [20]. However, results for CV-MCQs indicate that students with higher prior knowledge may have only limited benefits and increased cognitive offloading, i.e., relying on the output instead of reasoning. This may impair self-regulated learning (SRL), while metacognitive guidance can support SRL by encouraging their own reasoning about generated outputs [38].

From the socio-technical perspective, LLM-based chatbots enable interactive support by allowing learners to ask follow-up questions or request clarification. However, the questionnaire results indicate that students have limited trust compared to human support. Still, this aligns with the community of inquiry framework (CoI) [19], as aspects of teaching presence can be simulated.

## 6 Conclusions

In this paper, we have analyzed LLM-based outputs on university-level MCQs and their influence on student behavior. The smaller models performed worse in zero-shot MCQ answering. GPT-based models achieved higher accuracy, but errors remain (**RQ1**). Overall, models might benefit from course-specific fine-tuning (**RQ1**). Prompt design affects performance, smaller models performed worse with additional context, whereas GPT-based models benefited from it. Still, persona effects remain inconsistent (**RQ2**). Model and student responses show limited question-level alignment but comparable performance distributions, suggesting the use of student error patterns to train a difficulty-based question classification (**RQ3**). The study suggests a possible trend: chatbot output can either support or hinder student learning depending on domain, setup, and prior knowledge, with most support observed when prior knowledge is lower (RQ4).

However, these findings are limited by the dataset, the number of participants, and the performance evaluation on only IVDA-MCQS, limiting generalization. The study's small group sizes reduced interpretability, meaning potentially relevant group- or attempt-specific differences may have remained undetected.

Future work should focus on larger datasets and user studies across CS domains and difficulty levels to enable more reliable assessment. Long-term studies are relevant to examine how such models affect students' problem-solving skills, as cognitive offloading may reduce independent thinking over time.

**Acknowledgments.** This work has been financially supported by the Lower Saxony Ministry of Science and Culture with funds from the zukunft.niedersachsen program of the VolkswagenStiftung for the project "VidQA: Automated comprehension tests for learning videos".

**Disclosure of Interests.** The authors have no competing interests to declare that are relevant to the content of this article.

## References

1. Alansari, A., Luqman, H.: Large language models hallucination: a comprehensive survey. Comput. Sci. Rev. **61**, 100970 (2026). https://doi.org/10.1016/j.cosrev.2026.100970
2. Alnajjar, F., et al.: Exploring the pedagogical potential of large language models: A multimodal study on student learning outcomes. In: International Workshop on Artificial Intelligence and Education, WAIE 2024, Tokyo, Japan, 28–30 August 2024, pp. 93–96. IEEE (2024). https://doi.org/10.1109/WAIE63876.2024.00024

3. DAIR.AI: prompt engineering guide (2025). https://www.promptingguide.ai/. Accessed 17 Jan 2026
4. Das, D., et al.: Assessing the capability of chatgpt in answering first-and second-order knowledge questions on microbiology as per competency-based medical education curriculum. Cureus **15**(3), (2023). https://doi.org/10.7759/cureus.36034
5. DeepSeek-AI: Deepseek-r1: Incentivizing reasoning capability in llms via reinforcement learning. arXiv preprint arXiv:2501.12948 (2025). https://doi.org/10.48550/ARXIV.2501.12948
6. European parliament, council of the european union: regulation (eu) 2024/1689 laying down harmonised rules on artificial intelligence and amending regulations (2024). http://data.europa.eu/eli/reg/2024/1689/oj
7. Evangelista, E.D.L.: Ensuring academic integrity in the age of chatgpt: Rethinking exam design, assessment strategies, and ethical ai policies in higher education. Contemp. Educ. Technol. **17**(1), ep559 (2025). https://doi.org/10.30935/cedtech/15775
8. Gandolfi, A.: GPT-4 in education: evaluating aptness, reliability, and loss of coherence in solving calculus problems and grading submissions. Int. J. Artif. Intell. Educ. **35**(1), 367–397 (2025). https://doi.org/10.1007/S40593-024-00403-3
9. García-Méndez, S., de Arriba-Pérez, F., del Carmen Lopez-Perez, M.: A review on the use of large language models as virtual tutors. Sci. Educ. **34**, 877–892 (2025). https://doi.org/10.1007/s11191-024-00530-2
10. Jiang, A.Q., et al.: Mistral 7b. arXiv preprint arXiv:2310.06825 (2023). https://doi.org/10.48550/ARXIV.2310.06825
11. Jošt, G., Taneski, V., Karakatič, S.: The impact of large language models on programming education and student learning outcomes. Appl. Sci. **14**(10), 4115 (2024). https://doi.org/10.3390/app14104115
12. Khosravi, H., et al.: Explainable artificial intelligence in education. Comput. Educ. Artif. Intell. **3**, 100074 (2022). https://doi.org/10.1016/J.CAEAI.2022.100074
13. Liu, N., Sonkar, S., Baraniuk, R.G.: Do llms make mistakes like students? exploring natural alignments between language models and human error patterns. In: Artificial Intelligence in Education, AIED 2025, Palermo, Italy, 22–26 July 2025, pp. 364–377. Springer (2025). https://doi.org/10.1007/978-3-031-98459-4_26
14. Lovric, M.: Linear mixed models: an overview, pp. 1356–1374. Springer (2025). https://doi.org/10.1007/978-3-662-69359-9_328
15. Luke, S.G.: Evaluating significance in linear mixed-effects models in r. Behav. Res. Methods **49**, 1494–1502 (2016). https://api.semanticscholar.org/CorpusID:4367544
16. Lunardi, R., Mea, V.D., Mizzaro, S., Roitero, K.: On robustness and reliability of benchmark-based evaluation of llms. In: European Conference on Artificial Intelligence, ECAI 2025,Bologna, Italy, 25–30 October 2025, pp. 4603–4610. Frontiers in Artificial Intelligence and Applications, IOS Press (2025). https://doi.org/10.3233/FAIA251363
17. Maiti, P., Goel, A.K.: How do students interact with an llm-powered virtual teaching assistant in different educational settings? arXiv preprint arXiv:2407.17429 (2024). https://doi.org/10.48550/ARXIV.2407.17429
18. Maity, S., Deroy, A., Sarkar, S.: Can large language models meet the challenge of generating school-level questions? Computers and Education. Artif. Intell. **8**, 100370 (2025). https://doi.org/10.1016/J.CAEAI.2025.100370
19. Micsky, T., Foels, L.: Community of inquiry (coi): a framework for social work distance educators. J. Teach. Soc. Work **39**(4-5), 293–307 (2019). https://doi.org/10.1080/08841233.2019.1642976

20. Mishra, P., Koehler, M.J.: Technological pedagogical content knowledge: a framework for teacher knowledge. Teach. Coll. Rec. **108**(6), 1017–1054 (2006). https://doi.org/10.1111/j.1467-9620.2006.00684.x
21. Naveed, H., et al.: A comprehensive overview of large language models. ACM Trans. Intell. Syst. Technol. **16**(5), 106:1–106:72 (2025). https://doi.org/10.1145/3744746
22. Neagu, A., Messer, M., Johnson, P., Nelson, R.: "how do I...?": procedural questions predominate student-llm chatbot conversations. arXiv preprint arXiv:2602.18372 (2026). https://doi.org/10.48550/ARXIV.2602.18372
23. Ngo, A., Gupta, S., Perrine, O., Reddy, R., Ershadi, S., Remick, D.: Chatgpt 3.5 fails to write appropriate multiple choice practice exam questions. Acad. Pathol. **11**(1), 100099 (2024). https://doi.org/10.1016/j.acpath.2023.100099
24. Ngu, B.H., Phan, H.P., Usop, H., Hong, K.S.: Instructional efficiency: the role of prior knowledge and cognitive load. Appl. Cogn. Psychol. **37**(6), 1223–1237 (2023). https://doi.org/10.1002/acp.4117
25. Olea, C., et al.: Evaluating persona prompting for question answering tasks. In: International Conference on Artificial Intelligence and Soft Computing, AIS (2024), Sydney, Australia, 22–23 June 2024 (2024). https://doi.org/10.5121/csit.2024.141106
26. OpenAI: GPT-4 technical report. arXiv preprint arXiv:2303.08774 (2023). https://doi.org/10.48550/ARXIV.2303.08774
27. OpenAI: Openai prompt engineering guide (2025). https://platform.openai.com/docs/guides/prompt-engineering. Accessed 17 Jan 2026
28. Park, H., Ahn, D.: The promise and peril of chatgpt in higher education: opportunities, challenges, and design implications. In: Conference on Human Factors in Computing Systems, CHI 2024, Honolulu, HI, USA, 11–16 May 2024, pp. 271:1–271:21. ACM (2024). https://doi.org/10.1145/3613904.3642785
29. Phung, T., et al.: Automating human tutor-style programming feedback: Leveraging GPT-4 tutor model for hint generation and GPT-3.5 student model for hint validation. In: Learning Analytics and Knowledge Conference, LAK 2024, Kyoto, Japan, 18–22 March 2024, pp. 12–23. ACM (2024). https://doi.org/10.1145/3636555.3636846
30. Razafinirina, M.A., Dimbisoa, W.G., Mahatody, T.: Pedagogical alignment of large language models (llm) for personalized learning: a survey, trends and challenges. J. Intell. Learn. Syst. Appl. **16**(4), 448–480 (2024). https://doi.org/10.4236/jilsa.2024.164023
31. Rivera-Rosas, C.N., Calleja-López, J.T., Ruibal-Tavares, E., Villanueva-Neri, A., Flores-Felix, C.M., Trujillo-López, S.: Exploring the potential of chatgpt to create multiple-choice question exams. Educación Médica **25**(4), 100930 (2024). https://doi.org/10.1016/j.edumed.2024.100930
32. Sahoo, P., Singh, A.K., Saha, S., Jain, V., Mondal, S., Chadha, A.: A systematic survey of prompt engineering in large language models: techniques and applications. arXiv preprint arXiv:2402.07927 (2024). https://doi.org/10.48550/ARXIV.2402.07927
33. Seleznyov, M., Chaichuk, M., Ershov, G., Panchenko, A., Tutubalina, E., Somov, O.: When punctuation matters: a large-scale comparison of prompt robustness methods for llms. In: Conference on Empirical Methods in Natural Language Processing, EMNLP 2025, Suzhou, China, 4–9 November 2025, pp. 20370–20385. ACL (2025). https://doi.org/10.18653/v1/2025.findings-emnlp.1109

34. Shahzad, T., Mazhar, T., Tariq, M.U., Ahmad, W., Ouahada, K., Hamam, H.: A comprehensive review of large language models: issues and solutions in learning environments. Discov. Sustain. **6**(1), 27 (2025). https://doi.org/10.1007/s43621-025-00815-8
35. Tominski, C., Schumann, H.: Slides for interactive visual data analysis (2020). https://www.ivda-book.de/slides. Accessed 17 Jan 2026
36. Torralba, A., Isola, P., Freeman, W.T.: Introduction to learning. In: Foundations of Computer Vision, chap. 9. MIT Press (2024). https://visionbook.mit.edu/intro_to_learning.html, open-access edition. Accessed 17 Jan 2026
37. Wang, S., et al.: Large language models for education: a survey and outlook. IEEE Signal Process. Mag. **42**(6), 51–63 (2025). https://doi.org/10.1109/MSP.2025.3594309
38. Xu, X., Qiao, L., Cheng, N., Liu, H., Zhao, W.: Enhancing self-regulated learning and learning experience in generative ai environments: the critical role of metacognitive support. Br. J. Edu. Technol. **56**(5), 1842–1863 (2025). https://doi.org/10.1111/bjet.13599

# Not all Situation-Specific Skills Develop Alike: Professional Learning for Teachers' Perception, Interpretation, and Decision-Making in Technology-Enhanced Classrooms

Kairit Tammets(✉) and Jüri Kurvits

School of Digital Technologies, Tallinn University, Tallinn, Estonia
kairit.tammets@tlu.ee

**Abstract.** Teaching in technology-enhanced learning (TEL) environments requires to judge whether technology integration supports student learning. This places particular demands on teachers' situation-specific skills (SSS), here operationalised as their perception, interpretation, and decision-making (PID): the ability to perceive pedagogically relevant events, interpret them in relation to learning processes and make appropriate instructional decisions. Our quasi-experimental study compared three TEL-focused teacher training courses: a systematic PID-support condition with explicit and structured scaffolding; an implicit PID-support condition with reflective activities but less explicit support, and an assessment-only comparison condition in which SSS were assessed but not directly targeted. Teachers' SSS were measured using a scenario-based written assessment of perception, interpretation and decision-making in TEL environments. Results showed a dimension-specific developmental pattern: perception improved across all three conditions, whereas interpretation and decision-making showed significantly stronger gains only in the systematic PID-support condition. The findings suggest that SSS in TEL do not develop uniformly: repeated introduction of TEL classroom cases may support perception of pedagogically relevant cues, whereas stronger development in interpretation and decision-making requires more explicit support for analysing and justifying pedagogical responses.

## 1 Introduction

Teaching-learning situations are complex, dynamic environments in which teachers must continuously recognise, interpret and respond to events that influence student learning [1, 2]. This challenge becomes especially important in technology-enhanced learning (TEL) contexts, where teachers must make sense of students' actions and interactions, but also of digital tasks, artefacts and tool-mediated forms of participation. Research on professional vision and teacher competence suggests that **effective teaching depends** not only on what teachers know, but also on **their ability to apply this knowledge in context through situation-specific skills** (SSS), including perception, interpretation and decision-making (PID) [3, 4]. In the competence model proposed by Blömeke and colleagues [3], SSS functions as the mechanism linking teachers' dispositions, such as


J. Weidlich et al. (Eds.): EC-TEL 2026, LNCS 16905, pp. 593–605, 2027.
https://doi.org/10.1007/978-3-032-37979-5_40

professional knowledge and motivational-affective orientations to instructional performance. Thus, formal professional knowledge does not translate directly into teaching practice, but is mediated by teachers' ability to perceive pedagogically relevant cues, interpret them in relation to learning processes, and make context-sensitive decisions [3, 5, 6]

Existing research has often suggested **a relatively linear developmental logic of SSS,** whereby more experienced or more expert teachers demonstrate stronger perception, interpretation, or decision-making than novices [7, 8]. However, findings are not fully consistent. Some studies have shown that teachers with less classroom experience may outperform more experienced peers in specific aspects of professional vision, particularly when they have received more targeted or theoretically grounded teacher training [9]. These findings suggest that differences in SSS cannot be attributed to experience alone, but may also reflect the nature of teachers' preparation, the professional learning opportunities they experience and the ways in which these skills are assessed. Taken together, **this highlights the need for research that examines under what conditions situation-specific skills develop,** including how different forms of teacher preparation and professional learning may support or constrain their development.

Prior research on teachers' SSS and professional vision has mainly focused on general classroom situations [10], with only limited attention to technology-enhanced teaching contexts (e.g [11].). This gap is important because, in TEL, teachers must judge not only students' actions and interactions, but also whether digital tasks and tools meaningfully support learning. Visible activity in digital environments does not necessarily indicate cognitive engagement, and technology use may appear active without being instructionally aligned. TEL therefore broadens what becomes pedagogically relevant and may place different demands on perception, interpretation, and decision-making. Yet little is known about whether these dimensions develop similarly or differentially in TEL-focused professional learning, or whether more explicit support for perception, interpretation, and decision-making is particularly important for the higher-order dimensions.

To address this gap, our quasi-experimental study examined whether teachers' SSS showed different developmental patterns across three professional learning conditions with varying levels of explicit support for PID processes. Post-course adoption intentions were also examined as a complementary outcome to contextualise the PID findings. Specifically, the study addressed the following research questions: (1) To what extent do teachers' perception, interpretation, and decision-making skills change over the course of the intervention? (2) How do professional learning conditions with different levels of explicit PID support relate to teachers' growth in these dimensions, and how do adoption intentions help contextualise the observed patterns?

## 2 Theoretical Background

### 2.1 Situation-Specific Skills as a Core Component of Teacher Competence

Teachers' professional competence cannot be reduced to knowledge alone. In Blömeke and colleagues' continuum model [3], cognitive and affective-motivational dispositions form the foundation for performance, but are translated into observable instructional behaviour through SSS. From this perspective, competence must be understood not only in terms of what teachers know, but also through the processes by which this knowledge becomes actionable in practice (see Fig. 1) [3, 12].

Situation-specific skills are often understood through three PID processes: perception, interpretation, and decision-making [3, 10, 12]. In more concrete terms, **perception** refers to noticing and identifying what is pedagogically relevant in a classroom situation, such as salient features of students' and teachers' actions and interactions, without yet inferring their underlying meaning [13]. **Interpretation** involves making sense of these observations by drawing on professional knowledge for example, by considering what observed events may indicate about students' understanding, motivation, prior knowledge, or learning difficulties [12, 13] **Decision-making,** concerns selecting an appropriate course of action on the basis of this interpretation, such as whether to clarify a task, pose a follow-up question, adjust support, or redirect the lesson [13].

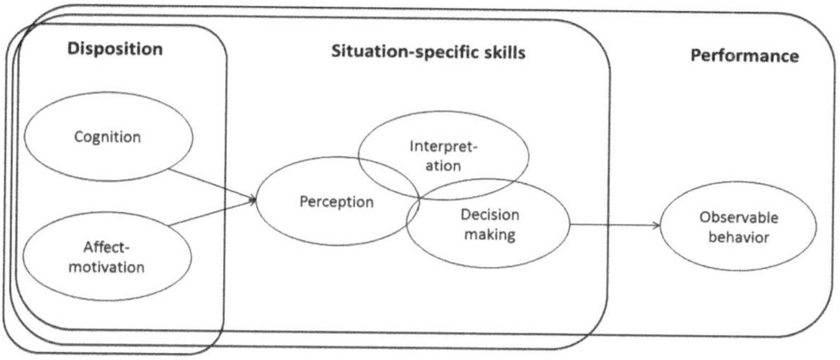


**Fig. 1.** Situation-specific skills as a mediating process between teachers' dispositions and instructional performance [3].

More broadly, this process-oriented perspective has been used to conceptualise how teachers apply professional knowledge in practice and to connect cognitive and situated views of teacher competence [3, 14]. Recent reviews also show that teacher noticing and professional vision are now understood as a broad and theoretically diverse field, within which perception, interpretation, and decision-making represent one influential way of operationalising teachers' situation-specific reasoning [15]. Unlike general professional knowledge, which refers to what teachers know, SSS reflect how this knowledge is enacted in concrete instructional situations. Teachers may possess relevant knowledge yet still differ in what they notice, how they interpret classroom events, and how they respond in the moment. In this sense, SSS capture the enacted, context-sensitive dimension of teacher competence [3].

A closely related line of research has conceptualised these in-the-moment abilities through the notion of professional vision [16]. In this tradition, teachers' professional vision refers to their ability to notice and interpret significant classroom interactions, especially in the very moments of instruction [1]. Research on professional vision distinguishes between description, explanation, and prediction, emphasising that teachers do not merely observe classroom events but interpret them in professionally informed ways

[4]. The present study adopts the competence-oriented framing of SSS, because it more directly conceptualises perception, interpretation and decision-making as the processes linking teachers' dispositions to instructional performance [3].

Accordingly, this study treats perception, interpretation, and decision-making as analytically distinct yet interrelated processes within teachers' situation-specific skills. If these processes mediate how professional knowledge becomes instructional action, a key question is how they can be supported through professional learning and whether they develop similarly or differently across professional learning initiatives.

## 2.2 Professional Learning for Developing Teachers' Situation-Specific Skills

Research in teacher education and professional development suggests that teachers' SSS can be supported through different professional learning designs. Most of this work has been conducted in pre-service teacher education, but this is not necessarily a limitation, as many of the underlying design principles may also be relevant for in-service professional learning. Across the literature, the development of SSS is not treated as a process that emerges automatically from experience alone. Rather, it is typically supported through structured opportunities to analyse practice, interpret classroom events and justify instructional decisions in relation to pedagogical goals.

A first recurring design feature is the use of **instructional case analysis tasks** that engage teachers with authentic or authentic-like classroom situations. Research on professional vision and teacher noticing has shown that teachers' situation-specific reasoning can be fostered when they analyse concrete classroom events rather than relying only on abstract theoretical instruction. For example, video-based approaches such as video clubs have demonstrated that teachers' noticing develops through repeated engagement with classroom episodes and systematic reflection on what is pedagogically relevant in practice [2, 17]. Similarly, lesson-analysis approaches have shown that competence develops when teachers are supported in examining how instructional situations unfold and how student learning can be interpreted within them [18, 19]. Thus, the development of SSS appears to depend in part on whether professional learning is grounded in classroom practice rather than remaining at the level of decontextualised knowledge.

A second design feature concerns the **explicit scaffolding of professional reasoning.** Prior research suggests that introduction to classroom situations alone is not sufficient: teachers benefit when their analysis is structured through worked examples, reflection or guided discussion formats that direct attention toward relevant pedagogical features and support interpretation. In technology-related teacher education, similar features have been used to support situation-specific technological pedagogical reasoning through case comparison, worked examples and structured analysis of technology-enhanced teaching situations [11]. More recent work has also noted that, although much is known about the outcomes of professional learning, less is understood about the learning processes through which professional vision and related SSS actually develop [20].

A third design feature is that the **development of SSS is often socially mediated**. Although perception, interpretation, and decision-making are frequently conceptualised as individual cognitive processes, research on video clubs and collaborative lesson analysis suggests that what counts as pedagogically relevant is often negotiated through shared discussion. Research on video clubs has shown that teachers learn to identify professionally relevant features through collective discussion, shared interpretive frames, and the development of a more precise professional language for analysing classroom events [2, 17]. From this perspective, the development of SSS can be understood not only as an individual increase in sensitivity to classroom cues, but also as participation in socially organised practices of interpreting teaching and learning.

In conclusion, prior research suggests that the development of teachers' SSS is most strongly supported when professional learning combines (1) engagement with authentic or authentic-like classroom situations, (2) explicit scaffolding of perception, interpretation, and decision-making, and (3) opportunities for socially shared analysis of practice.

## 3 Methodology

### 3.1 Research Design and the Sample

The study employed a quasi-experimental pre-post design comparing three professional learning settings that differed in the degree to which situation-specific skills were explicitly addressed in the course design.

**Group 1 - in the systematic PID training** condition, participants engaged in structured reflective activities in which perception, interpretation and decision-making were explicitly scaffolded, practiced and assessed. **Group 1** was the oldest cohort, with 46.2% aged 31–40 and 23.1% aged 41 or older, and included participants from **Educational Technology** (56.4%) and **Informatics Teacher Education** (43.6%).

**Group 2 - in the implicit PID support condition,** participants completed comparable activities and reflective tasks, but with less scaffolding and without expert-guided modelling of the reflection process. **Group 2** was younger overall, with 73.1% aged 30 or younger, and also drew participants from **Educational Technology** (76.9%) and **Informatics Teacher Education** (23.1%).

**Group 3 PID assessment-only condition** served as a comparison group in which SSS were assessed as part of the study but were not explicitly targeted within the course design. This group was the youngest overall, with 66.0% of participants aged 30 or younger, and consisted entirely of female participants enrolled in the Special Education curriculum (63.8%) and various subject teacher education programmes (36.2%).

As participants followed existing course structures, individual random assignment was not possible; therefore, age and study programme differences should be considered when interpreting group-level effects.

### 3.2 Design of the Systematic PID-Support Condition

In our study, the systematic PID-support condition was designed to operationalise three key design features identified in prior research on the development of SSS: (1) engagement with authentic-like classroom situations, (2) explicit scaffolding of perception, interpretation, and decision-making, and (3) opportunities for socially shared analysis of practice.

Although the analysed situations were simulated rather than drawn directly from participants' own classrooms, they were deliberately constructed as technology-enhanced classroom cases that reflected realistic pedagogical dilemmas. In these cases, participants were asked to identify classroom events, but also to judge whether students were cognitively engaged in TEL activities and whether the use of technology was pedagogically meaningful.

Importantly, technology played a dual role in this condition. First, it was the object of professional judgment: participants analysed whether digital tasks, tools and student activity supported meaningful learning based on the ICAP framework, which distinguishes passive, active, constructive, and interactive modes of cognitive engagement [21]. Second, it was the medium of professional learning: the Learning Amplify platform was used to structure the sequence of reflection, coordinate individual and collective analysis and make the learning process more visible to both participants and the instructor. In this sense, participants did not only discuss TEL as a topic, but also experienced how technology can structure and support reflective professional learning.

The development of PID was embedded as a recurring routine throughout the course. Participants repeatedly engaged with TEL-related classroom cases in which they were guided to separate what they noticed, how they interpreted the situation, and what they would do next. The PID framework was explicitly introduced as a model for analysing teaching-learning situations, supported by short conceptual input and contrasting examples that helped distinguish factual noticing from evaluative judgment and intuitive reactions from theory-informed interpretation. Classroom cases were then decomposed into sequential PID-aligned prompts (e.g., what do you identify as pedagogically relevant, how do you interpret it, what could be done differently), which scaffolded attention to each component before participants integrated them into a more complete analysis.

Interpretation was further connected to the theoretical basis of the course. Participants were asked to analyse classroom situations through specific conceptual lenses, such as self-regulated learning and cognitive engagement, in order to connect their judgments to models of cognitive engagement and learning. This was especially important in the TEL context, where participants were expected to evaluate not only visible student activity, but whether technology use supported deeper learning processes.

Finally, PID development was supported through technology-enabled pacing, shared discussion and structured expert feedback. The Learning Amplify platform helped maintain a shared pace and created pauses for collective interpretation before individual decision-making. Structured feedback further helped participants to develop an understanding of what counted as high-quality perception, interpretation and decision-making in technology-enhanced teaching situations. Overall, the systematic PID-support condition embedded PID as a repeated, theory-linked and socially mediated form of professional reasoning within a TEL-focused course.

In the implicit PID-support condition, participants engaged with comparable TEL-related classroom cases and reflective activities, but the PID framework was not explicitly introduced as a structured model for analysis. Case work remained more open-ended, with fewer stepwise prompts and without explicit decomposition of perception, interpretation, and decision-making or structured expert calibration of response quality. In the assessment-only comparison condition, participants completed the same pre- and post-assessments, but the course did not include explicit instructional activities targeting PID development. Thus, this condition allowed us to examine whether repeated assessment alone, without structured PID-focused support, was associated with change in SSS.

### 3.3 Data Collection

Teachers' SSS were assessed using an adapted **scenario-based written task** informed by the vignette approach described by Wekerle and Kollar [11] and drawing on the classroom scenario format used in prior research on professional vision in TEL. The assessment targeted three PID dimensions within teachers' SSS: perception, interpretation, and decision-making.

At pre-test, **a simplified version of the task was applied,** in which participants responded to one central classroom incident embedded in the scenario. Responses were scored using an analytic rubric across the three PID dimensions, giving a maximum of 7 points. At post-test, participants completed an extended version of the same scenario-based assessment, in which they responded to three classroom incidents. The same analytic scoring principles were applied across the three PID dimensions, with a maximum score of 21 points.

In addition to the PID measures, self-reported measures were collected after the course on perceived digital competence, self-efficacy for digital teaching and adoption intentions. Perceived digital competence was assessed using an adapted version of Lucas et al. [22] covering teaching and learning, empowering learners and facilitating learners' digital competence. Self-efficacy for digital teaching was measured with three items adapted from von Acker et al. [23] focusing on confidence in planning, implementing, and managing digital teaching. In addition, post-course adoption intentions regarding TEL practices were assessed with a five-item scale adapted from Ley et al. [24].

### 3.4 Data Analysis

Data analysis proceeded in four steps. First, descriptive statistics were calculated for all PID dimensions at pre- and post-test for each group. Because the pre- and post-assessments differed in the number of classroom incidents and maximum possible raw scores, all PID outcomes were transformed into proportional scores by dividing each participant's score by the maximum possible score for that dimension at each measurement occasion. This produced comparable values between 0 and 1 for perception, interpretation, and decision-making, which were used in all analyses. In addition, gain scores were computed for each PID dimension to provide a descriptive overview of change across the three professional learning conditions.

Second, baseline comparability between the three groups was examined using Welch's one-way ANOVAs on the pre-test scores for each PID dimension. To test overall pre–post change and whether developmental trajectories differed across groups, separate repeated-measures ANOVAs were then conducted for each PID dimension, with time as the within-subject factor and group as the between-subject factor.

Third, to clarify significant interaction effects, Welch's ANOVAs were conducted on the gain scores for each PID dimension, followed by post hoc pairwise comparisons.

Because significant baseline differences were observed for interpretation and decision-making, follow-up ANCOVAs were also conducted for these dimensions, using post-test scores as dependent variables, group as the fixed factor, and the corresponding pre-test score as a covariate, in order to examine whether post-test group differences remained after accounting for initial differences.

Finally, complementary analyses were conducted to contextualise the SSS findings. Group differences in self-efficacy for digital learning, perceived digital competence, and adoption intentions were examined using Welch's ANOVAs.

## 4 Results

### 4.1 Development of Situation-Specific Skills across Trainings

Across the three professional learning conditions, a differentiated pattern of SSS development emerged, with perception improving across conditions and interpretation and decision-making showing stronger and more selective growth when PID processes were more explicitly scaffolded (see Fig. 1).

Descriptively, teachers' **SSS changed across the intervention period**, but the pattern differed by dimension and by condition. **Perception** increased in all three groups. For **interpretation**, all groups also improved, but the increase was clearly largest in Group 1 (systematic PID scaffolding). A similar pattern emerged for **decision-making**: Group 1 showed the strongest improvement, Group 3 a more modest increase, whereas Group 2 showed little change overall and a slight negative mean gain.

To assess initial comparability, Welch's one-way ANOVAs were conducted on the pre-test scores. The groups **did not differ significantly in prior perception**, $F(2, 70.1) = 1.78$, $p = .176$. In contrast, **significant baseline differences emerged for interpretation**, $F(2, 65.4) = 7.35$, $p = .001$ and **decision-making**, $F(2, 67.0) = 3.26$, $p = .045$. Descriptively, Group 1 started from the lowest levels in both interpretation (M = .25, SD = .26) and decision-making (M = .48, SD = .26), whereas Groups 2 and 3 showed higher initial scores. Thus, the groups were comparable in perception at baseline, but not in the higher-order PID dimensions.

To examine changes over time, separate repeated-measures ANOVAs were conducted for the three SSS dimensions. For **perception**, there was a significant **main effect** of time, $F(1, 109) = 20.28$, $p < .001$, $\eta^2p = .157$, indicating overall improvement across the sample. However, changes in perception did not differ significantly across the three professional learning conditions $F(2, 109) = 0.95$, $p = .390$, $\eta^2p = .017$.

For **interpretation**, a strong **main effect** of time was found, $F(1, 109) = 215.76$, $p < .001$, $\eta^2p = .664$, qualified by **a significant time x group interaction,** $F(2, 109) = 9.93$, $p < .001$, $\eta^2p = .154$. Descriptively, the largest gain was observed in the **systematic PID training condition** (from M = .25 to M = .74), compared with smaller gains in the implicit PID support condition (from M = .42 to M = .53) and the assessment-only condition (from M = .48 to M = .64) (Fig. 2).

For **decision-making**, there was likewise **a significant main effect of time**, $F(1, 109) = 19.50$, $p < .001$, $\eta^2p = .152$, alongside a significant **time x group** interaction, $F(2, 109) = 10.70$, $p < .001$, $\eta^2p = .165$. Again, the systematic PID training condition

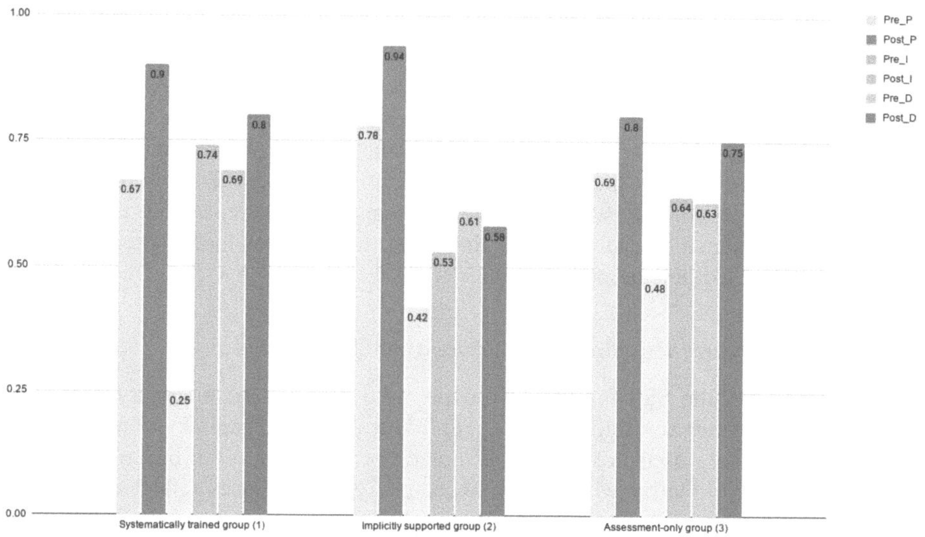


**Fig. 2.** PID scores in three conditions

showed the strongest increase (from $M = .69$ to $M = .86$), whereas the implicit PID support condition showed little change overall (from $M = .61$ to $M = .58$), and the assessment-only condition showed a smaller positive increase (from $M = .63$ to $M = .75$).

To clarify the direction of these interaction effects, **Welch's ANOVAs** were conducted on the gain scores. These showed no significant group differences in **perception gains**, $F(2, 71.5) = 0.77$, $p = .467$, but significant group differences in **interpretation**, $F(2, 64.3) = 13.61$, $p < .001$, and **decision-making gains**, $F(2, 66.7) = 11.98$, $p < .001$. Post hoc comparisons indicated that **Group 1** showed significantly larger gains in both interpretation and decision-making than **Group 2** and **Group 3** (all *ps* $\leq .003$), whereas Groups 2 and 3 did not differ significantly. This pattern suggests that an explicit and systematic emphasis on perception-interpretation-decision-making within professional learning was associated with stronger development in the more demanding SSS dimensions, whereas perception improved more generally across conditions.

Because significant baseline differences were observed for **interpretation** and **decision-making, follow-up ANCOVAs** were conducted to examine whether post-test group differences remained after controlling for pre-test performance. For interpretation, the preliminary group × pre-test interaction was not significant, $F(2, 106) = 0.66$, $p = .517$, supporting the use of ANCOVA. The final ANCOVA, with **post-test interpretation** as the dependent variable, **group** as the fixed factor and **pre-test interpretation** as the covariate, showed a significant effect of **group**, $F(2, 108) = 6.57$, $p = .002$, $\eta^2 p = .108$, whereas **pre-test interpretation** was not significant, $F(1, 108) = 0.35$, $p = .558$.

For **decision-making**, the final ANCOVA likewise showed a significant effect of **group**, $F(2, 108) = 10.02$, $p < .001$, $\eta^2 p = .157$, while **pre-test decision-making** was not significant, $F(1, 108) = 1.22$, $p = .272$. These baseline-adjusted analyses strengthen the interpretation that the systematically scaffolded condition was associated with stronger post-test performance in interpretation and decision-making beyond initial group differences in the corresponding PID scores.

In summary, we found that perception improved across all conditions, whereas interpretation and decision-making showed stronger and more differentiated development depending on the extent to which PID processes were explicitly scaffolded. Although the assessment-only condition also showed modest gains, these were substantially smaller than in the systematically scaffolded condition and stronger growth in higher-order SSS depends on more explicit support.

## 4.2 Complementary Outcomes and Contextual Conditions

To better interpret the SSS findings, we explored a set of complementary outcomes, including self-efficacy for digital learning, digital competence and adoption intentions. These analyses were used not as parallel outcomes of the training, but as contextual contrasts helping to clarify whether the observed SSS differences reflected a broader positive course effect or a more specific effect of explicit PID-oriented scaffolding.

First, no significant group differences were found in **gain in self-efficacy for digital learning**, $F(2, 55.4) = 0.97$, $p = .387$. This is important because it suggests that the stronger development of interpretation and decision-making in Group 1 was not simply accompanied by a more general increase in confidence. In other words, the differentiated SSS pattern cannot be reduced to a general sense of increased self-efficacy.

Second, significant group differences emerged for several perceived digital competence indicators. For **teaching and learning**, Welch's ANOVA was significant, $F(2, 67.7) = 13.58$, $p < .001$; the same applied to **empowerment of learners**, $F(2, 69.1) = 15.06$, $p < .001$, and **supporting students' digital competence**, $F(2, 70.6) = 10.56$, $p < .001$. Across these measures, Group 2 consistently reported lower competence perceptions than the other groups, whereas Groups 1 and 3 were generally similar. This suggests that the implicitly supported condition was associated with lower post-course perceptions of digital competence, alongside weaker gains in the higher-order SSS dimensions.

**Adoption intentions** differed significantly, $F(2, 65.5) = 4.55$, $p = .014$. Post hoc comparisons showed that both Group 1 and Group 2 reported significantly higher adoption intentions than Group 3, whereas Groups 1 and 2 did not differ. Descriptively, standardised adoption scores were 0.82 (Group 1), 0.84 (Group 2), and 0.73 (Group 3). This contrast is especially relevant for interpreting the main findings: both training conditions were seen as similarly adoptable, yet only the systematically scaffolded PID condition was associated with clearly stronger gains in interpretation and decision-making. Thus, positive adoption alone did not appear sufficient for stronger higher-order SSS development. Rather, the findings suggest that explicit support for perceiving relevant events, interpreting them, and justifying pedagogical responses may be necessary to translate favourable course perceptions into deeper professional learning outcomes.

These complementary analyses reinforce the interpretation of the study. The observed SSS differences do not appear to reflect a broad increase in confidence. Instead, the results point to a more specific pattern: while training conditions were perceived as adoptable, only the condition with stronger explicit PID scaffolding was associated with clearly stronger growth in the higher-order dimensions of interpretation and decision-making.

## 5 Conclusion

This quasi-experimental study showed a dimension-specific pattern in teachers' SSS in TEL contexts: while perception improved across all three conditions, stronger growth in interpretation and decision-making emerged only in the systematically scaffolded PID-support condition.

This interpretation aligns with prior research suggesting that professional vision and related situation-specific reasoning develop not only through individual exposure to classroom situations, but through socially organised and pedagogically structured forms of practice [2, 13, 17]. From this perspective, the stronger gains observed in the systematically scaffolded condition support the view that higher-order SSS are not simply individual cognitive skills, but are shaped through professional learning designs that make relevant cues visible, support theory-based interpretation and help teachers understand what counts as a pedagogically appropriate response.

A particularly important contribution of the study is the dimension-specific pattern of development. While perception improved more generally across conditions, interpretation and decision-making were more sensitive to differences in course design. This suggests that the three PID dimensions should not be treated as interchangeable indicators of teacher competence. Rather, the findings support a more differentiated view in which perception may be more readily influenced by engagement with classroom cases, whereas interpretation and decision-making represent more demanding forms of professional reasoning that require stronger conceptual and instructional support. This is theoretically important because it helps move beyond a general assumption that "SSS improved" and instead highlights that different dimensions may develop through different learning mechanisms.

The findings are particularly relevant for TEL contexts, where visible student activity in digital environments does not necessarily indicate meaningful learning. Teachers must evaluate not only what students are doing, but also whether technology use supports cognitive engagement and pedagogical goals. The results suggest that developing this kind of technology-related professional reasoning may require more explicit support than is typically provided through exposure to classroom cases alone. From a professional learning perspective, the findings suggest that supporting teachers' situation-specific skills may require more than repeated exposure to classroom cases. Professional learning designs may benefit from explicitly naming and separating perception, interpretation and decision-making, linking interpretations to learning theories, and providing opportunities for collective analysis and feedback. Such design features may be particularly important in TEL contexts, where teachers need to justify not only instructional decisions but also the pedagogical value of technology use.

Several limitations should be considered when interpreting the findings. First, because the study used a quasi-experimental design with baseline differences between groups, the results should be interpreted as evidence of differential associations rather than definitive causal effects. Second, the findings are based on written responses to simulated TEL classroom cases. Such vignette-based assessments are well suited for capturing teachers' professional reasoning, including what they notice, how they interpret classroom events, and how they justify instructional decisions. However, they do not capture the real-time demands of classroom interaction, where decisions must be enacted under constraints of time, uncertainty, and competing instructional goals. Future research should therefore examine whether similar patterns emerge in authentic classroom practice, across different assessment formats, and over longer time periods.

Despite these limitations, the findings suggest that not all situation-specific skills develop alike. While perception may improve through repeated engagement with classroom cases, interpretation and decision-making appear to require more explicit support for analysing and justifying pedagogical responses. Designing professional learning around these distinctions may be particularly important in TEL contexts, where effective teaching depends not only on using technology but on judging when and how it meaningfully supports learning.

**Acknowledgements.** This research was funded by the European Commission (grant number 101132603) and the Estonian Research Council (grant number PRG1634).

## References

1. Sherin, M.G., Russ, R.S., Sherin, B.L., Colestock, A.: Professional vision in action: an exploratory study. Issues Teach. Educ. **17**(2), 27–46 (2008)
2. van Es, E.A., Sherin, M.G.: Mathematics teachers' "learning to notice" in the context of a video club. Teach. Teach. Educ. **24**, 244–276 (2008)
3. Blömeke, S., Gustafsson, J.-E., Shavelson, R.J.: Beyond dichotomies: competence viewed as a continuum. Z. Psychol. **223**(1), 3–13 (2015)
4. Seidel, T., Stürmer, K.: Modeling and measuring the structure of professional vision in preservice teachers. Am. Educ. Res. J. **51**(4), 739–771 (2014)
5. Depaepe, F., Verschaffel, L., Star, J.: Expertise in developing students' expertise in mathematics: bridging teachers' professional knowledge and instructional quality. ZDM. **52**(2), 179–192 (2020)
6. Hill, H.C., Umland, K., Litke, E., Kapitula, L.R.: Teacher quality and quality teaching: examining the relationship of a teacher assessment to practice. Am. J. Educ. **118**(4), 489–519 (2012)
7. Kini, T., Podolsky, A.: Does Teaching Experience Increase Teacher Effectiveness? A review of the research. Learning Policy Institute, Palo Alto (2016)
8. Van der Lans, R.M., Van de Grift, W.J., van Veen, K.: Individual differences in teacher development: an exploration of the applicability of a stage model to assess individual teachers. Learn. Individ. Differ. **58**, 46–55 (2017)
9. Muhonen, H., Pakarinen, E., Lerkkanen, M.-K.: Do teachers' professional vision and teaching experience always go hand in hand? Examining knowledge-based reasoning of Finnish grade 1 teachers. Teach. Teach. Educ. **106**, 103458 (2021)
10. Müller, M.M., Gold, B.: Exploring profiles of pre-service teachers' situation-specific skills regarding classroom management. Eur. J. Teach. Educ. **1–19** (2026)
11. Wekerle, C., Kollar, I.: Fostering pre-service teachers' situation-specific technological pedagogical knowledge: does learning by mapping and learning from worked examples help? Comput. Hum. Behav. **115**, 106617 (2021)
12. Stahnke, R., Schueler, S., Roesken-Winter, B.: Teachers' perception, interpretation, and decision-making: a systematic review of empirical mathematics education research. ZDM. **48**(1), 1–27 (2016)

13. Santagata, R., Fuentes Acevedo, P., Kimmerling, C., Pelayo, R., Pantano, A., Tschönhens, F.: Fostering expansive noticing practices through video-based professional development in college mathematics. ZDM–mathematics. Education. **58**(1), 295–309 (2026)
14. Blömeke, S., Jentsch, A., Ross, N., Kaiser, G., König, J.: Opening up the black box: teacher competence, instructional quality, and students' learning progress. Learn. Instr. **79**, 101600 (2022)
15. König, J., Santagata, R., Scheiner, T., Adleff, A.K., Yang, X., Kaiser, G.: Teacher noticing: a systematic literature review of conceptualizations, research designs, and findings on learning to notice. Educ. Res. Rev. **36**, 100453 (2022)
16. Goodwin, C.: Professional vision. In: Aufmerksamkeit: Geschichte – Theorie – Empirie, pp. 387–425. Springer Fachmedien, Wiesbaden (2015)
17. Sherin, M.G., van Es, E.A.: Effects of video club participation on teachers' professional vision. J. Teach. Educ. **60**(1), 20–37 (2009)
18. Santagata, R., Zannoni, C., Stigler, J.W.: The role of lesson analysis in pre-service teacher education: an empirical investigation of teacher learning from a virtual video-based field experience. J. Math. Teach. Educ. **10**(2), 123–140 (2007)
19. Santagata, R., Yeh, C.: The role of perception, interpretation, and decision making in the development of beginning teachers' competence. ZDM. **48**(1), 153–165 (2016)
20. Oellers, M., Junker, R., Holodynski, M.: Individual learning paths mastering teachers' professional vision. Front. Educ. **9**, 1305073 (2024)
21. Chi, M.T., Wylie, R.: The ICAP framework: linking cognitive engagement to active learning outcomes. Educ. Psychol. **49**(4), 219–243 (2014)
22. Lucas, M., Bem-Haja, P., Siddiq, F., Moreira, A., Redecker, C.: The relation between in-service teachers' digital competence and personal and contextual factors: what matters most? Comput. Educ. **160**, 104052 (2021)
23. van Acker, F., van Buuren, H., Kreijns, K., Vermeulen, M.: Why teachers use digital learning materials: the role of self-efficacy, subjective norm and attitude. Educ. Inf. Technol. **18**, 495–514 (2013). https://doi.org/10.1007/s10639-011-9181-9
24. Ley, T., Tammets, K., Sarmiento-Márquez, E.M., Leoste, J., Hallik, M., Poom-Valickis, K.: Adopting technology in schools: modelling, measuring and supporting knowledge appropriation. Eur. J. Teach. Educ. **45**(4), 548–571 (2022)

# AI-Driven Assessment of Human Tutors: Linking Training Performance to Real-Life Practice

Danielle R. Thomas[1(✉)], Marie Cynthia Abijuru Kamikazi[1], Clara Brandt[1], Conrad Borchers[2], and Kenneth R. Koedinger[1]

[1] Carnegie Mellon University, Pittsburgh, PA, USA
{drthomas,koedinger}@cmu.edu, {mabijuru,clarabra}@andrew.cmu.edu
[2] Vanderbilt University, Nashville, TN, USA
c.borchers@vanderbilt.edu

**Abstract.** There exist numerous tutor training platforms. However, few provide AI-driven training and evaluation for human tutors based on real-life performance. We present an AI-driven system that assesses both open responses during training and authentic real-life tutoring. Unlike platforms that only assess learning through online training or simulations, our system utilizes Generative AI (Gemini-2.5-pro) to analyze transcriptions of authentic tutoring, measuring the transfer of tutor skills to real-life application. Human tutors instructing students remotely in math (N=86) completed six scenario-based lessons, averaging a significant 7.4% learning gain. Using mixed-effects models across 405 session-to-lesson pairs, we found that training performance significantly predicted real-life transcript scores with an effect size of 0.25 SD. Model comparison (AIC/BIC) indicated averaging open response and multiple choice performance during training predicted real-life tutor performance best, although open responses were comparatively more predictive. Exploratory analysis showed that after training, tutors were significantly more likely to encounter pedagogical opportunities to apply their skills (61.1% to 68.9%) and demonstrated higher execution quality within those opportunities (65.5% to 68.1%). Interrupted time series analysis suggested that these tutor improvements were part of a gradual trend over time rather than an immediate intervention effect of training. We illustrate an AI-driven method to link tutor training with real-life assessment. In doing so, we contribute open datasets, AI prompts, and scoring rubrics to support transparency and reproducibility.

**Keywords:** Tutor Training · Assessment · Large Language Models

## 1 Introduction

The demonstrated efficacy of tutoring has created a surging demand for effective human tutors [17]. Consequently, the need for trained human tutors is a priority within the technology-enhanced learning community [1]. To successfully


J. Weidlich et al. (Eds.): EC-TEL 2026, LNCS 16905, pp. 606–621, 2027.
https://doi.org/10.1007/978-3-032-37979-5_41

scale tutoring programs, ongoing and intensive human training is essential, particularly for volunteers, college students, and paraprofessionals who may lack pedagogical understanding and formal teaching experience [14]. Although existing AI-driven professional development (PD) and workforce training platforms offer training via simulations and AI-generated scenarios, they generally lack the ability to verify whether these skills transfer to real-world practice [20,25].

The inability to assess the transfer of new tutoring skills to real-life applications creates a disconnect between training environments and authentic tutoring interactions [29]. A key challenge in assessing transfer is that many pedagogical skills are opportunity-dependent: tutors can only demonstrate a given skill when a relevant moment arises. We refer to these moments as *pedagogical opportunities* and distinguish between the likelihood of encountering such opportunities and the quality of a tutor's move when they occur. Distinguishing both is important when determining whether costly and resource-intensive PD actually improves instructional quality and, therefore, student learning outcomes [11]. To date, little has been done to establish a robust process for validating the external validity and generalizability of human tutor training across diverse tutoring implementations. Additionally, predictive modeling is needed to reveal whether human tutor performance on open responses in training or multiple-choice questions (MCQs) is a stronger driver of behavioral transfer to real-life application [22]. Accordingly, we examine whether AI-driven assessments of tutor training can serve as a signal of real-life application of pedagogical skills. We aim to answer: **RQ1 (Learning):** Do tutors demonstrate significant learning gains on specific pedagogical skills ("tutor moves") within AI-enhanced lessons, as measured by pretest to posttest performance improvements? **RQ2 (Application & Prediction):** To what extent does performance in training predict the successful application and quality of those skills in real-life tutoring sessions? **RQ3 (Predictive Formats):** Does the open response or multiple-choice format provide a stronger predictor of behavioral transfer to real-life tutoring?

We introduce an AI-driven pipeline to link tutor performance in online lessons to real-life tutoring behaviors using generative AI. We contribute LLM prompts and pipelines to score tutor open responses and evaluate the application of tutor moves in real-life tutoring (Accessible in GitHub [9]). We provide datasets of human tutor training performance (Accessible in DataShop [8]).

### 1.1 AI-Driven Human Tutor Training and Evaluation System

Figure 1 illustrates the AI-driven system designed to link tutor training with the assessment of real-life performance. It begins with research-supported tutoring competencies, or **tutor moves** and practice via immersive **scenario-based tutor lessons**. The process transitions to **real-life application of tutor moves,** where LLMs evaluate the quality of tutor moves by determining if opportunities were present, and then evaluating within authentic tutoring transcriptions (e.g., audio, chat). If proficiency is not met, the system triggers a remediation loop of self-reflection or recommends the tutor take the lesson again.

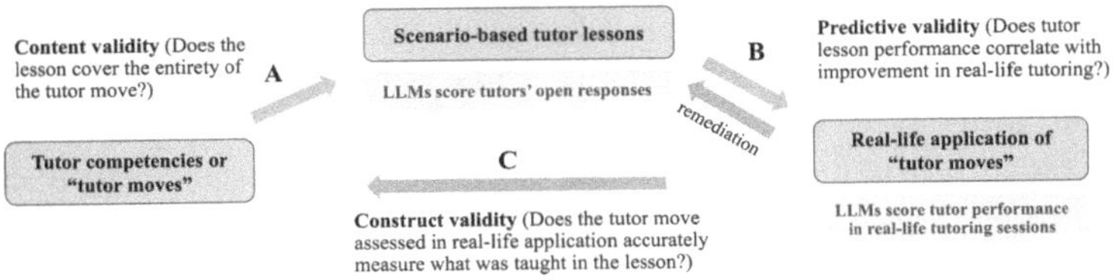


**Fig. 1.** AI-driven tutor training and real-life assessment system.

We map three validity types to stages of the system, drawing on standard methodology [26]. **Content validity (A)** is established via expert judgment to confirm lessons fully cover the "tutor move" construct. **Predictive validity (B)** assesses whether training success correlates with real-world application as measured by LLM transcript analysis. **Construct validity (C)** verifies that AI-driven scoring accurately reflects the intended theoretical pedagogical skills.

## 2 Related Work

### 2.1 Tutor Competencies and Scenario-Based Workforce Training

Tutor competencies, often termed "tutor moves," are categorized through various theoretical lenses. These include Accountable Talk Moves, which promote equitable classroom discourse [19]; dialogue act theory, which focuses on the structural mechanics of conversational turns [27]; and cognitive science, which distinguishes between knowledge-telling by tutors and the more effective tutor knowledge-building by prompting students [6]. Despite these frameworks, empirical evidence linking tutor professional development to real-life application is rare. Scenario-based learning facilitates rapid skill acquisition by embedding instruction in real-world, low-risk contexts [3,7,25]. Proven effective for teacher and tutor training, this "learning by doing" approach ensures skill transfer to authentic sessions [13,18,20]. Lessons often utilize a modified predict-observe-explain framework grounded in Gibbs' Reflective Cycle [12] to drive learning gains of ~20% [20,21]. While open-response questions are often assumed to foster deeper learning in these scenarios, recent research suggests that MCQs can be equally effective for tutor advocacy training while offering significantly greater efficiency, reducing the time required for tutors to reach proficiency by 30% [22].

### 2.2 LLMs in Workforce Training and Real-Life Application

**Open-Response Scoring using LLMs.** Recently, LLMs have demonstrated considerable potential in scoring open responses [21]. Previous automated short answer grading, such as those utilizing BERT or Sentence-BERT, often struggled with the linguistic nuances and complex semantics inherent in tutor-student interactions [10]. However, LLMs like GPT-4 have shown the ability to perform nuanced situational reasoning and automated scoring that rivals human-authored support [15]. In a study evaluating tutor advocacy training, researchers used GPT-4o and GPT-4-turbo to autograde open responses across scenario-based training similar to this present work [22]. Employing a few-shot prompting strategy, such as providing the model with a limited set of learner-sourced responses scored by human raters [5], the models performed moderately well. While these findings suggest that LLMs offer a viable pathway for scaling the evaluation of complex "tutor moves" [16], the researchers also identified limitations in highly subjective domains (e.g., advocacy training), where the models showed lower performance compared to simpler pedagogical tasks. These results highlight that while LLMs are effective for low-stakes assessment, further refinement in prompt engineering is required for highly nuanced contexts [21,30].

**LLM-driven Analysis of Real-life Application of Tutor Moves.** Little research exists on the use of AI-based methods to evaluate human tutors and teachers using transcription analysis of instructional interaction [4,23,28]. One notable example is M-Powering Teachers, an automated NLP-based tool developed by Demszky et al. [11] to provide teachers with feedback on their "uptake" of student contributions—a high-leverage dialogic teaching practice that makes students feel heard. In a randomized controlled trial (RCT) of M-Powering Teachers involving 1,136 instructors in an online computer science course, researchers evaluated the effectiveness of the tool. They found that the automated feedback improved instructors' uptake of student contributions by 13% [11]. These results demonstrate the promise of automated feedback tools to complement existing efforts in teachers' PD, particularly when coaching resources are limited.

## 3 Method

### 3.1 Tutor Participants, Study Design, and Data Collection

**Tutor Participants.** The study involved 86 undergraduate students from a Mid-Atlantic college in the U.S. who served as paid tutors. They provided semester-long remote tutoring to middle school students in math, and the tutor cohort was culturally and racially diverse. The students, although not research subjects in this present work, were middle school students receiving virtual tutoring during the school day from a dozen schools and five U.S. states. Approximately 80% of the students came from low-income communities. We prioritized maintaining the privacy and confidentiality of tutors and adhered to all Institutional Review Board (IRB) requirements.

**Study Design.** We utilized a within-subjects interrupted time series design across three phases (Fig. 2). **Phase 1** established baseline behavior prior to tutors completing online training. In **Phase 2,** tutors paused active tutoring to complete six AI-enhanced scenario-based lessons. In **Phase 3,** tutors resumed real-life tutoring sessions, where audio transcriptions and Zoom chat logs were collected to evaluate the frequency and quality of targeted tutor moves. Tutor lesson log data and transcript analysis allowed for the measurement of construct and predictive validity by comparing lesson performance and comparing baseline behavior to post-training performance. Data collection consisted of system-generated lesson logs and real-life remote tutoring session data. To generate comprehensive session transcripts, audio from Zoom recordings was processed using OpenAI's Whisper model and subsequently merged with the corresponding synchronized chat files. Following IRB protocols, all transcripts were deidentified to ensure participant privacy. Tutor lesson data are accessible in DataShop [8].

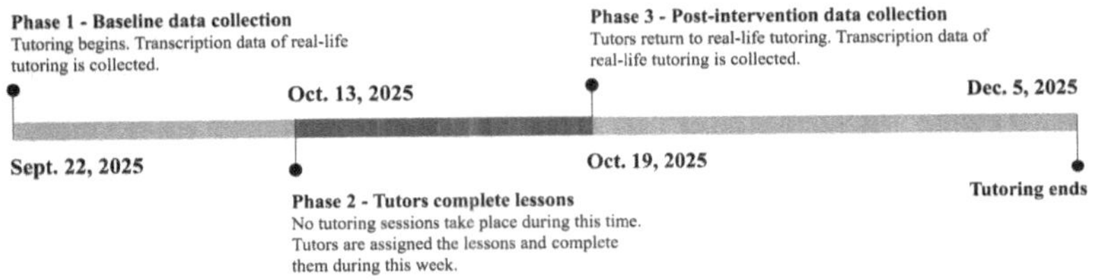


**Fig. 2.** Interrupted-time series research design.

### 3.2 Assessing Tutors' Scenario-Based Lesson Performance

The lessons focused on six research-supported tutor moves. Three of the lessons covered competencies for which construct validity (see Fig. 1) has been demonstrated previously [20]: 1) giving effective praise (GIVE_PRAISE); 2) reacting to errors (REACT_ERRORS); and 3) determining what students know (DETERMINE_KNOW) [20]. Three other lessons aligned with high-quality tutoring strategies identified by Tutor CoPilot, an AI-powered tutoring system that assists human tutors [28]: 4) affirming a correct attempt (AFFIRM_CORRECT); 5) asking questions to guide thinking (GUIDE_THINKING); and 6) prompting students to explain (PROMPT_EXPLAIN). Lessons were co-designed by learning scientists and tutor trainers using authentic, real-life scenarios to ensure face and construct validity (Fig. 1, step A).

As illustrated in Fig. 3, tutors completed a pretest and had to *predict* and *explain* optimal responses in both open responses and MCQs (1–4). After observing the research-based best approach (5–6), tutors performed a parallel transfer scenario as a posttest (7–10). Pretest and posttest scenarios were counterbalanced. Both tests totaled four points (two MCQs, two open-ended).

Learning gains were determined by subtracting pretest from posttest scores, providing a quantitative measure of skill gains [7,20,21]. While MCQs were automatically scored by the training platform, open responses were evaluated using Gemini-2.5-pro. The AI scoring process was driven by prompts derived directly from expert-validated human scoring rubrics and the process for establishing IRR was documented. Full documentation of the lesson content, human annotation rubrics, and LLM scoring prompts are available in the GitHub [9].

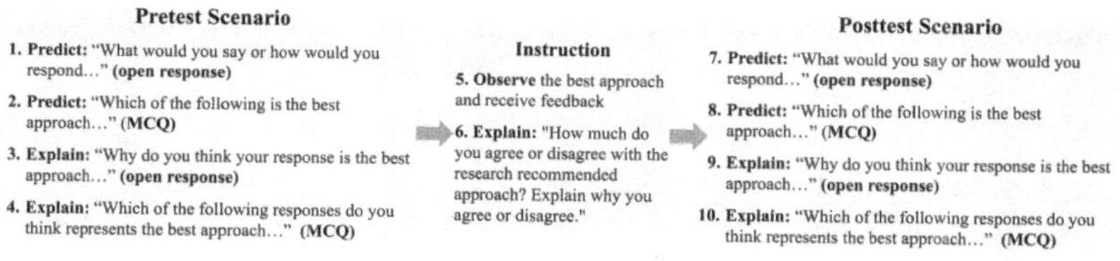


**Fig. 3.** Pretest-posttest instructional design.

**Inter-rater Reliability of Open Responses.** Inter-rater reliability (IRR) was established by comparing AI scores against a "human truth" gold standard. Two expert coders manually graded a subset of 40 responses per lesson (20 *predict* and 20 *explain* responses, see Fig. 3), reconciling disagreements to establish the ground truth. Cohen's Kappa ($\kappa$) was then calculated to measure the agreement between humans and Gemini-2.5 pro. Table 1 displays reliability results, which were heterogeneous across question types with $\kappa$ values ranging from 0.41 to 1.00 across different tutor moves and question types.

**Table 1.** IRR for Open Response Scoring

| Lesson | Human-to-human ($\kappa$) | | Human-to-LLM ($\kappa$) | |
|---|---|---|---|---|
| | Predict | Explain | Predict | Explain |
| GUIDE_THINKING | 0.78 | 0.57 | 0.78 | 0.41 |
| AFFIRM_CORRECT | 1.00 | 0.77 | 1.00 | 1.00 |
| DETERMINE_KNOW | 0.69 | 0.69 | 0.89 | 0.74 |
| GIVE_PRAISE | 0.64 | 1.00 | 0.41 | 0.76 |
| PROMPT_EXPLAIN | 1.00 | 0.67 | 1.00 | 0.53 |
| REACT_ERRORS | 1.00 | 0.89 | 0.69 | 0.67 |

### 3.3 Evaluating Real-Life Application of Tutor Moves

Regarding RQ2 and using a previously described method [23], we utilized Gemini-2.5-pro to identify and evaluate the six tutor moves within session transcripts. This automated assessment pipeline employed a two-stage prompting strategy: an "opportunity prompt" identified relevant moments where a tutor move was applicable (0/1), e.g., a student making a math error or a correct attempt; an "evaluation prompt" scored the quality of the tutor action following the same evidence-based best practices of the corresponding lesson (0-ineffective, 1-effective). Table 2 shows part of the prompts for the tutor move of reacting to a student error (REACT_ERRORS). By adapting prompts from validated human coding rubrics, the system provided a scalable measure of skill transfer. Correlation, linear mixed-effects models, and ITS analysis were used to answer RQ2.

Full documentation of the lesson content, human annotation rubrics, and full LLM scoring prompts are available in the GitHub [9].

**Table 2.** A segment of the two-stage LLM prompt for determining if there was an opportunity for a tutor to react to a student's math error and, if so, evaluating the tutor's response to it (REACT_ERROR).

| Stage 1: Opportunity Identification Prompt |
|---|
| Your task is to determine whether the following tutoring transcript contains a clear opportunity for a tutor to react to a student's math error. An **opportunity to react to a student's math error** exists when: A student makes a mistake while solving a math problem (e.g., The student incorrectly solves $118 + 18 = 126$).<br>—<br>**Scoring rules:**<br>**1:** If there was an opportunity for a tutor to react to a student's math error.<br>**0:** If there was NO opportunity for a tutor to react to a student's math error.<br>If the student and the tutor did not work on any math problem then there was no opportunity.<br>—<br>**Constraints:**<br>Focus only on students making math errors, not whether the tutor reacted effectively or ineffectively. |
| **Stage 2: Evaluation Prompt (If Opportunity = 1)** |
| Analyze the tutoring audio transcripts below and score the tutor on the following 6 binary (0 or 1) dimensions. For each dimension, return both a binary score (0 or 1) and a short evidence from the transcript under that dimension name.<br>—<br>**Rubric Dimensions (Return 0 or 1 for each)**<br>**1.** `REACT_ERROR:`<br>**0:** The student made a mistake and the tutor either gave the answer **OR** pointed out the error directly.<br>**1:** The tutor responded to a math error by asking the student to explain their thinking **OR** prompting them to think again. |

**Inter-rater Reliability of Transcription Scoring.** To validate the LLM-based assessment method, two experienced researchers annotated a subset of 10 transcripts across all six tutor moves for the "opportunity" and "evaluation" prompts shown in Table 2. In total, researchers evaluated 2,063 lines of transcript dialogue to identify pedagogical opportunities and score tutor execution quality. IRR between the human raters was calculated and shown in Table 3, and all disagreements were reconciled to establish a "ground truth" score. The model was then evaluated on these transcriptions to determine its alignment with expert judgment. Kappa scores for Gemini-2.5-pro compared to ground truth in the lessons ranged from 0.0 (when nearly all transcriptions lacked the given tutor move) to 1.00. However, these scores are rendered less representative of the

LLM ability due to the small number of transcripts analyzed, where even minor disagreements can have an outsized impact on the agreement measures.

**Table 3.** Inter-Rater Reliability (IRR) of Transcript Scoring

| Lesson | Opportunity Identification | | Tutor Evaluation | |
|---|---|---|---|---|
| | Human-Human ($\kappa$) | Human-LLM ($\kappa$) | Human-Human ($\kappa$) | Human-LLM ($\kappa$) |
| DETERMINE_KNOW | 0.73 | 0.38 | 0.80 | 0.35 |
| GIVE_PRAISE | 1.00 | 0.40 | 1.00 | 0.60 |
| REACT_ERRORS | 1.00 | 1.00 | 0.00* | 0.00* |
| AFFIRM_CORRECT | 1.00 | 0.74 | 1.00 | 0.74 |
| GUIDE_THINKING | 0.74 | 0.52 | 1.00 | 0.38 |
| PROMPT_EXPLAIN | 0.73 | 0.00* | 0.80 | 0.80 |

*Low $\kappa$ despite high agreement due to data imbalance.

### 3.4 Analytical Methods

To address **RQ1**, we measured learning gains from tutoring lessons by calculating the percentage increase from the average pre- to post-test score. We then ran univariate ANOVAs for individual lessons with time as a factor (post vs. pre) to test whether these gains were statistically significant.

For **RQ2**, we examined the relationship between tutor training performance and their real-life transcript performance using multiple complementary analyses. First, we computed descriptive Pearson correlations between tutor-level performance on individual lessons and corresponding transcript scores. Second, we estimated linear mixed-effects models predicting transcript scores for each lesson from tutors' training scores, with random effects to account for repeated measures within tutors. This approach allowed us to formally test whether an overall positive association existed between training performance and transcript outcomes while appropriately modeling within-tutor repeated measures.

To attend to **RQ3**, we evaluated whether specific types of training performance were more predictive of transcript scores. To do so, we estimated a series of analogous mixed-effects models that replaced overall lesson performance with predictors capturing (a) MCQ performance only, (b) open response performance only, (c) MCQs and *predict* responses, and (d) open responses and *predict* responses. We compared these models to the overall-performance model using AIC and BIC [2]. These criteria are used for model selection, where lower values indicate a better-fitting model. They work by balancing a model's goodness-of-fit against its complexity, effectively penalizing the inclusion of unnecessary parameters. This comparison enabled us to assess whether holistic measures of training performance better predict transcript outcomes than models focused solely on open responses, which may be viewed as more closely approximating authentic tutoring moves in practice. We similarly compared overall performance across pre- and post-test to pre- and post-training performance only.

# 4 Results

## 4.1 RQ1: Do Tutors Show Learning Gains in Lessons?

Table 4 shows tutor lesson performance. The results indicate significant learning gains for the three tutor moves with previously established construct validity REACT_ERRORS, achieving a 25.2% gain ($F$=30.10, $p$ < .001), followed by DETERMINE_KNOW (14.2% gain, $p$ = .006) and GIVE_PRAISE (8.1% gain, $p$ = .009). These findings reinforce the efficacy of these established lessons in driving tutor growth in learning. In contrast, the lessons inspired by Wang et al. [28], AFFIRM_CORRECT, GUIDE_THINKING, and PROMPT_EXPLAIN, did not yield statistically significant learning gains (ranging from 1.4% to 2.1%, all $p$>.05). This lack of significant growth is likely attributable to a ceiling effect; tutors exhibited exceptionally high baseline performance on these specific moves, with pretest scores already ranging from 0.92 to 0.98 out of 1.0. Despite the flat growth in these newer lessons, the aggregate analysis on all lessons (pooled) revealed a statistically significant learning gain of 7.4% ($F$=27.50, $p$ < .001), supporting overall content validity.

**Table 4.** Descriptive statistics and performance of tutors on lessons.

| Lesson | Tutors (n) | Pretest (SD) | Posttest (SD) | Score gain | F-statistic | p-value |
|---|---|---|---|---|---|---|
| DETERMINE_KNOW | 72 | 0.76 (0.29) | 0.87 (0.20) | 14.2% | 8.194 | 0.006* |
| GIVE_PRAISE | 70 | 0.86 (0.18) | 0.93 (0.14) | 8.1% | 7.305 | 0.009* |
| REACT_ERRORS | 66 | 0.70 (0.25) | 0.87 (0.21) | 25.2% | 30.096 | <.001* |
| AFFIRM_CORRECT | 75 | 0.98 (0.10) | 0.99 (0.06) | 1.4% | 1.00 | 0.321 |
| GUIDE_THINKING | 74 | 0.95 (0.17) | 0.97 (0.15) | 1.4% | 0.247 | 0.620 |
| PROMPT_EXPLAIN | 76 | 0.92 (0.22) | 0.94 (0.16) | 2.1% | 0.425 | 0.516 |
| All lessons (pooled) | 433 | 0.87 (0.23) | 0.93 (0.17) | 7.4% | 27.495 | <.001* |

*denotes statistical significance, $p$ < .05.

## 4.2 RQ2: Does Lesson Performance Predict Real-Life Application?

To examine predictive validity (RQ2), we assessed the relationship between tutors' lesson performance and their application of the corresponding tutor moves in tutoring sessions. Across tutor-lesson pairs with available transcript data where tutors had the opportunity to demonstrate skills (N = 405), mixed effects models indicated that one SD increase in overall lesson performance was associated with a 0.25 SD increase in transcript scores ($p$ < .001).

Within lessons, tutor-level correlations between tutor training and real-life performance captured from transcriptions ranged from -0.02 (REACT_ERRORS) to 0.28 (GIVE_PRAISE), though only GIVE_PRAISE ($p$ = .029) and AFFIRM_CORRECT ($p$ = .030) were statistically significant while others were not ($p > .211$). Figure 4 displays observed transcript scores as a function of lesson performance, with fitted linear trend lines and Pearson correlation coefficients. Across lessons, it is notable that transcript or lesson performance (or both) often exhibited a ceiling effect with high average scores. Therefore, evidence of transfer from lessons to practice was constrained by distributional limitations.

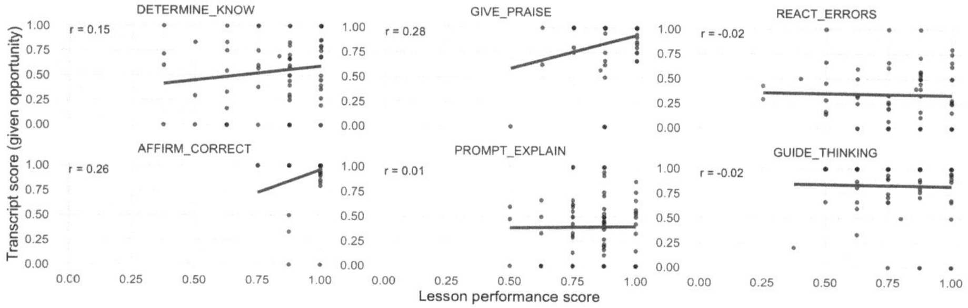


**Fig. 4.** Linear relationship between lesson performance and assessment of real-life execution, given tutors had the opportunity, by tutor move with correlations.

## 4.3 RQ3: Which Question Formats Are Stronger Predictors of Behavioral Transfer to Real-Life Tutoring?

Model comparisons showed that overall training performance provided the best fit to transcript scores (AIC = 1129.7, BIC = 1145.8), outperforming models based on open responses only (AIC = 1130.0, BIC = 1146.1), multiple-choice responses only (AIC = 1150.0, BIC = 1166.0), and models incorporating predicted responses (AICs $\geq$ 1139.2; BICs $\geq$ 1155.2). A model separating coefficients for MCQ and open-response scores did not improve fit (AIC = 1135.1, BIC = 1155.1). Overall, these results indicate that comprehensive measures of training performance yield stronger predictive validity for transcript outcomes than models focused on individual response types. Models estimating tutor training performance via pre- and post-training items did not clearly improve model fit relative to the overall-performance model, with the pre-training model yielding a lower AIC but comparable BIC (AIC = 1118.4, BIC = 1134.4) and the post-training model performing substantially worse (AIC = 1146.0, BIC = 1162.0). Models were fit on different sample sizes and should be interpreted cautiously.

## 4.4 Exploration of Tutor Opportunities and Quality Over Time

We observed significant improvements over time in both tutors' opportunities to respond and the quality of their responses. The probability of having an opportunity to execute a target tutoring move was higher post-training than pre-training (post: 68.9% vs. pre: 61.1%), a difference that was statistically significant (binomial test, $p < .001$). Conditional on having an opportunity, tutors' probability of successfully executing the target move also increased from pre- to post-training (65.5% to 68.1%; $p = .003$). Together, these results suggest modest but reliable gains in both opportunity and execution quality following training. This strengthens the validity link between scenario-based training performance and real-life transcript performance.

However, we did not gather evidence that changes in tutor quality pre-to-post training were attributable to the training itself. Instead, we observed that tutors generally improved as more weeks passed in the tutoring program. An interrupted time series analysis of average transcript score showed a small but significant linear trend over time ($\beta = 0.01, p = .022$), indicating gradual improvement in tutor quality independent of the training intervention. There was no evidence of an immediate level change at the intervention point (post: p = .246) or a change in slope following training (time × post: $p = .479$). Variation in transcript quality was largely attributable to stable differences between tutors (ICC = .27), with fixed effects explaining little variance (marginal $R^2 = .01$).

Tutors' limited post-training performance may reflect constraints in recognizing and capitalizing on opportunities to apply target skills; a competency that is not explicitly trained in the scenario-based intervention, which instead presents tutors with predefined opportunities. A logistic mixed-effects interrupted time series model predicting the likelihood of observing an opportunity to apply a target tutoring skill revealed a significant positive pre-training trend (odds ratio, OR = 1.07 per unit time, $p < .001$), indicating that opportunities were becoming increasingly frequent prior to training. At the intervention point, the estimated level change was negative, suggesting lower immediate odds of opportunity post-training, although this effect was not statistically significant (post OR = 0.63, $p = .111$). Moreover, the post-training slope was significantly attenuated relative to the pre-training trend (time × post OR = 0.99, $p = .028$), indicating a modest slowing in the growth of opportunities following training. Together, these patterns suggest that improvements in tutors' skill execution may have been constrained by reduced or limited opportunities to deploy those skills in practice (either by recognizing or being presented with relevant tutoring moments), with substantial heterogeneity across tutors and skills remaining (ICC = .35).

Finally, we examined if the linear improvements in tutor performance over time was dependent on them applying skills and learning from these opportunities. We fit a growth curve using a generalized linear mixed-effects model predicting the probability of successful execution conditional on opportunity. An opportunity was defined as a tutoring interaction in which the transcript provided enough context for a specific tutor move to be reasonably demonstrated, as identified by AI-based transcript analysis. The model included cumulative opportunity count, lesson completion (yes vs. no), and their interaction as fixed effects, with a random intercept for tutors. Results indicated no statistically significant effect of opportunity count on successful execution ($\beta = 0.06$, $p = .39$), suggesting limited evidence of improvement purely through repeated opportunities. The main effect of lesson completion showed a positive but non-significant trend ($\beta = 0.35$, $p = .098$), and the interaction between opportunity count and lesson completion was also not significant ($\beta = -0.07$, $p = .36$), indicating that training did not reliably alter the rate of improvement per opportunity.

## 5 Discussion and Future Work

While the results confirm the system's potential to measure and predict tutoring quality, the updated findings reveal a complex relationship between training interventions and real-world behavior.

**Tutor Open-Response Performance is a Significant Predictor of Real-Life Behavior.** A primary contribution of this work is the empirical evidence regarding training formats. Our model comparisons demonstrate that performance on open-response items is a stronger predictor of real-life behavioral transfer than MCQ performance. This suggests that the cognitive effort required to generate a pedagogical move, rather than simply recognizing a correct one, more closely mirrors the real-time demands of tutoring. In terms of technology-enhanced learning, this indicates that while MCQs are easier to automate, open responses are essential to validly assess "readiness" for authentic tutoring. Aligning with past work, LLM-based grading of open responses has been shown to be an effective method of scaling training containing open responses [22]. Still, models that combined open-response and selected-response performance yielded the strongest predictive fit, suggesting that incorporating both assessment formats may be optimal when resources permit. Overall predictive validity, however, was modest (0.25 SD) and varied substantially across lessons. In comparable domains such as medical simulation training, substantially stronger associations have been reported (correlations of approximately 0.6; [29]). One likely explanation for this discrepancy is that tutors in our context must not only execute high-quality pedagogical responses (e.g., following student errors) but also recognize when such responses are warranted—an ability not explicitly trained in the current scenario-based intervention. This limitation may also help explain lesson-level heterogeneity, as identifying opportunities to react to errors may be more straightforward than recognizing moments that call for prompting explanations or guiding thinking.

**Training Supports Gradual Tutor Growth.** Although tutors demonstrated significant learning gains within lessons (7.4%, $p < .001$) and measurable improvements in real-life quality (65.5% to 68.1%, $p = .003$), ITS analysis reveals a lack of a significant immediate performance change at the point of intervention, suggesting that tutoring skill is not acquired through single training events, such as lessons completed at a certain time. Instead, the small but significant linear trend over time ($\beta = 0.01$, $p = .022$) indicates that growth is a gradual longitudinal process. At the same time, we did not find evidence that opportunities to apply relevant skills explained this linear time trend. An explanation of this finding is that the tutors did not receive feedback on their real-life performance during the semester. Hence, continuous PD with feedback might enhance tutors' gradual improvement over time. One of the most encouraging findings is the significant increase in tutors' ability to encounter or create pedagogical opportunities (61.1% pre-training to 68.9% post-training, $p < .001$). This suggests that the training was effective in helping tutors identify moments where a student's error or success warranted a specific "tutor move." However, as mentioned, improvements in the quality of execution in those moments rose less strongly. This gap underscores the necessity for continuous feedback. If a tutor performs poorly on executing a "tutor move" in real-life, the system can recommend a tutor to complete the corresponding scenario-based lesson. An area of future work is to provide a library of scenarios that can be generated based on the level of difficulty, and is learnersourced from real-life tutoring interactions. The tutor lessons, inspired by [28], whereby these tutor moves previously demonstrated predictive validity linking to student learning in TutorCoPilot, did not demonstrate construct validity (see Fig. 1). A key reason for this is a content validity limitation regarding over-scaffolding in the newer lessons, particularly in `PROMPT_EXPLAIN`. The scenario-based practice questions evaluated tutors on *how* to prompt for self-explanation rather than *when* to do so. Because baseline pretest scores were high, tutors did not require further instruction on the mechanics of execution. However, despite the lack of active practice on identifying opportunities (*when* to prompt), field-based improvement was indeed demonstrated: post-training transcript analysis showed a significant increase in tutors encountering or creating pedagogical opportunities. This suggests that tutors benefit from passive learning via the explicit instruction, worked examples, and explanations embedded in these lessons, translating this knowledge to real-life practice even when over-scaffolded training questions failed to reflect that growth.

**Low Kappa Scores Reflect Statistical Artifacts of Small, Imbalanced Datasets, Not Poor Model Performance.** The human-to-human and human-to-LLM agreement on assessing tutor skills is challenging in practice. This is particularly evident in our transcript scoring results (Table 3), where several human-to-LLM $\kappa$ scores were low, some between 0.38 and 0.6. As noted, these low scores are often a consequence of two main factors. First, they are impacted by significant data imbalance; for instance, when an opportunity for a specific tutor move is rare, the high agreement on its absence (the majority class) is heavily penalized by the Kappa statistic, which corrects for chance agreement. Second, these IRR measures were calculated on a sample of 10 transcripts, where a single disagreement can have a disproportionate impact on the metric. While 10 transcripts represents a relatively small sample, the annotation was highly granular, requiring manual coding across 2,063 individual lines of dialogue. To illustrate this sensitivity, a change in just one coded label in our data could cause the $\kappa$ to swing from 0.38 (fair agreement) to 0.74 (substantial agreement), highlighting the volatility of the metric with small datasets. In line with recent calls to reframe IRR [24], future work will focus on the continuous refinement of our LLM prompts to better capture the nuance of these pedagogical moves. By automating data collection, we aim to calculate IRR on a much larger and more robust dataset to get a more representative measure of the system's performance.

**We Demonstrate Progress Towards an AI-Driven System of Training Tutors and Assessing Real-Life Application.** Referencing Fig. 1, we first established **content validity (A)** through the expert co-design of our scenario-based lessons, ensuring the lessons fully covered the intended "tutor move" constructs. We then established **predictive validity (B)**. Our mixed-effects model showed that a one SD increase in tutors' lesson performance predicted a 0.25 SD increase in their real-life transcript scores ($p < .001$). Progress was made towards **construct validity (C)** by developing and validating an AI-driven pipeline capable of identifying pedagogical opportunities and evaluating tutor execution within authentic tutoring transcripts.

## 6 Limitations and Conclusion

Despite the success of Gemini-2.5-pro in these evaluations, the wide range of IRR scores (as noted in Sect. 3.3) suggests that LLM prompts require continuous auditing. Furthermore, because tutors manually uploaded sessions, a selection bias may exist where more confident tutors submitted more data. Future iterations will focus on automated data collection and the refinement of "evaluation prompts" to better capture the nuance of effective moves. Finally, the study acknowledges that the use of LLMs to identify opportunities for tutor moves and evaluate performance is not a perfect process, as indicated by the wide range of IRR (See Table 3 and GitHub [9]).

In conclusion, we present a novel AI-driven system designed to train human tutors and assess the real-world application of their skills. The findings demonstrate that while scenario-based training can increase tutors' ability to identify pedagogical opportunities, ongoing, real-life feedback is crucial for improving the quality of their execution. By contributing datasets, AI prompts, and scoring rubrics, this work supports greater transparency and reproducibility, providing a strong foundation for future work on scaling high-quality human tutoring.

**Acknowledgments.** This work was made possible with the support of the Learning Engineering Virtual Institute. The opinions, findings, and conclusions are those of the authors.

## References

1. Aleven, V., et al.: Towards the future of ai-augmented human tutoring in math learning. In: AIED (2023)
2. Baker, R.S.: Big Data and Education. 9 edn. University of Pennsylvania (2025)
3. Bardach, L., Klassen, R.M., Durksen, T.L., Rushby, J.V., Bostwick, K.C., Sheridan, L.: The power of feedback and reflection: testing an online scenario-based learning intervention for student teachers. Comput. Educ. **169**, 104194 (2021)
4. Borchers, C., Gurung, A., Liu, Q., Thomas, D.R., Khalil, M., Koedinger, K.R.: Brief but impactful: how human tutoring interactions shape online learning (2026)

5. Brown, T., et al.: Language models are few-shot learners. Adv. Neural. Inf. Process. Syst. **33**, 1877–1901 (2020)
6. Chi, M.T., Siler, S.A., Jeong, H., Yamauchi, T., Hausmann, R.G.: Learning from human tutoring. Cogn. Sci. **25**(4), 471–533 (2001)
7. Chine, D.R., Chhabra, P., Adeniran, A., Gupta, S., Koedinger, K.R.: Development of scenario-based mentor lessons: an iterative design process for training at scale. In: Proceedings of the Ninth ACM Conference on Learning@ Scale (2022)
8. CMU/PLUS: Ai-driven assessment of human tutors: linking training performance to real-life practice, pslc datashop. https://pslcdatashop.web.cmu.edu/DatasetInfo?datasetId=6815 (2026)
9. CMU/PLUS: supplementary material: Ai-driven-assessment. https://github.com/CMU-PLUS/tutor_training_to_practice (2026)
10. Condor, A., Litster, M., Pardos, Z.: Automatic short answer grading with sbert on out-of-sample questions. Int. Educ. Data Min. Soc. (2021)
11. Demszky, D., Liu, J., Hill, H.C., Jurafsky, D., Piech, C.: Can automated feedback improve teachers' uptake of student ideas? Educ. Eval. Policy Anal. **46**(3), 483–505 (2024)
12. Gibbs, G.: Learning by doing: a guide to teaching and learning methods. Further Educ. Unit (1988)
13. Hursen, C., Fasli, F.G.: Investigating the efficiency of scenario based learning and reflective learning approaches in teacher education. Eur. J. Contemp. Educ. **6**(2), 264–279 (2017)
14. Kraft, M.A., Falken, G.T.: A blueprint for scaling tutoring and mentoring across public schools. Aera Open **7**, 23328584211042856 (2021)
15. Lee, G.G., Latif, E., Wu, X., Liu, N., Zhai, X.: Applying large language models and chain-of-thought for automatic scoring. Comput. Educ. Artif. Intell. **6**, 100213 (2024)
16. Lin, J., et al.: How can i improve? using gpt to highlight the desired and undesired parts of open-ended responses. arXiv preprint arXiv:2405.00291 (2024)
17. Nickow, A., Oreopoulos, P., Quan, V.: The impressive effects of tutoring on prek-12 learning: a systematic review of the experimental evidence (2020)
18. Schank, R.C., Berman, T.R., Macpherson, K.A.: Learning by doing. In: Instructional-Design Theories and Models, pp. 161–181. Routledge (2013)
19. Suresh, A., Jacobs, J., Harty, C., Perkoff, M., Martin, J.H., Sumner, T.: The talkmoves dataset: K-12 mathematics lesson transcripts annotated for teachers (2022)
20. Thomas, D., Yang, X., Gupta, S., Adeniran, A., Mclaughlin, E., Koedinger, K.: When the tutor becomes the student: Design and evaluation of efficient scenario-based lessons for tutors. In: LAK23: 13th International Learning Analytics and Knowledge Conference, pp. 250–261 (2023)
21. Thomas, D.R., Borchers, C., Bhushan, S., Gatz, E., Gupta, S., Koedinger, K.R.: Llm-generated feedback supports learning if learners choose to use it. In: ECTEL, pp. 489–503. Springer (2025)
22. Thomas, D.R., et al.: Does multiple choice have a future in the age of generative ai? a posttest-only rct, pp. 494–504. LAK (2025)
23. Thomas, D.R., et al.: Leveraging llms to assess tutor moves in real-life dialogues: a feasibility study. In: ECTEL, pp. 268–273. Springer (2025)
24. Thomas, D.R., Borchers, C., Vanacore, K.P., Koedinger, K.R., Kizilcec, R.F.: Modernizing ground truth: four shifts toward improving reliability and validity in ai in education. arXiv preprint arXiv:2603.29141 (2026)

25. Thompson, M., Owho-Ovuakporie, K., Robinson, K., Kim, Y.J., Slama, R., Reich, J.: Teacher moments: a digital simulation for preservice teachers to approximate parent-teacher conversations. J. of Digital Learn. Teach. Ed (2019)
26. Trochim, W.M., Donnelly, J.P., Arora, K.: Research methods: the essential knowledge base (2016)
27. Vail, A.K., Boyer, K.E.: Identifying effective moves in tutoring: On the refinement of dialogue act annotation. In: Conference on Intelligent Tutoring Systems (2014)
28. Wang, R.E., Ribeiro, A.T., Robinson, C.D., Loeb, S., Demszky, D.: Tutor copilot: a human-ai approach for scaling real-time expertise (2024)
29. Weersink, K., Hall, A.K., Rich, J., Szulewski, A., Dagnone, J.D.: Simulation versus real-world performance. Adv. Simul. **4**(1), 9 (2019)
30. Yun, J., Hicke, Y., Olson, M., Demszky, D.: Enhancing tutoring effectiveness through automated feedback: Preliminary findings from a pilot rct. In: L@S (2024)

# "I Think I Would Rather Decide What to Do": Students' Perception of Control in an AI-Infused Classroom

Martina Vincoli[1](✉), Niklas Scholz[2], and Tomohiro Nagashima[3]

[1] Department of Humanities, Social and Political Sciences, ETH Zürich, Zürich, Switzerland
martina.vincoli@gess.ethz.ch
[2] RWTH Aachen University, Aachen, Germany
niklas.scholz@rwth-aachen.de
[3] Saarland University, Saarland Informatics Campus, Saarbrücken, Germany
nagashima@cs.uni-saarland.de

**Abstract.** Artificial Intelligence (AI) has increasingly been integrated into school classrooms to optimize human learning. However, prior studies do not yet offer a complete understanding of students' experiences and preferences for learning with AI in the classroom, specifically regarding the desired degree of control as AI systems begin to automate important decision-making opportunities. We conducted a qualitative speed-dating study with 16 secondary-school students to investigate their preferences for control in an AI-augmented classroom. Our findings reveal that students' desire for control is not uniform; rather, it fluctuates based on the specific type of decision being made. Our work demonstrates the importance of understanding students' sense of control as a multi-dimensional concept and its dynamic nature involving how students view their teacher and AI, rather than a single-dimensional, static concept. Based on our findings, we provide design recommendations for future classroom AI systems.

**Keywords:** Intelligent Tutoring Systems · AI · Decision-making · Control · Design study

## 1 Introduction

Artificial intelligence (AI) is becoming an integral part of our everyday lives, and education is no exception. AI-based learning technologies, such as Intelligent Tutoring Systems (ITSs), offer adaptive support for students such that the system can provide the most optimal content, scaffolding, and feedback based on its understanding of each student's mastery and knowledge status [1–3]. While AI-based, intelligent learning software has been shown effective in enhancing learning [4], its efficacy does not necessarily guarantee ethical or meaningful use that meets stakeholders' needs and desires. Despite a rise in participatory design approaches in addressing stakeholder needs and desires [5], K-12 students remain largely excluded from the development of classroom AI, which typically prioritizes teachers as the primary user group [6–9]. This exclusion of students


J. Weidlich et al. (Eds.): EC-TEL 2026, LNCS 16905, pp. 622–635, 2027.
https://doi.org/10.1007/978-3-032-37979-5_42

is concerning, as students are central stakeholders whose perspectives on data privacy and control often diverge significantly from those of their teachers [5]. In particular, students' perspectives on how much control to exercise during learning with AI in the classroom environment have gained limited attention [10, 11].

In this work, we address the following research question: *What are students' preferred levels of control when learning with AI systems in the classroom?* We conducted a speed-dating study [6, 12] with 16 secondary-school students in Germany to address the question. Speed dating is a design method in which users react to a variety of stimuli, in this case hypothetical AI technology use in the classroom, to understand how participants react to possible technology use cases [12]. Our findings show that students prefer varying levels of control over different kinds of decisions when learning with AI in the classroom, revealing the multi-dimensional nature of their sense of control. We also found that these preferences are shaped by how students perceive other key decision makers in the classroom (i.e., teachers and AI), showing the importance of dynamic interactions among all agents in the learning environment. This work contributes to the field of technology-enhanced learning by offering empirical evidence that students' desired level of control cannot be understood as a single construct but rather as shifting negotiations across multiple dimensions in the complex classroom environment.

## 2 Related Work

Prior research on youth and AI has typically been conducted outside of school classrooms (e.g., voice assistants at home). This line of research highlights that youth often perceive AI as social beings, either scary or trustworthy, attributing human-like traits to conversational agents [13, 14]. While these studies show how to achieve effective youth-AI collaboration (e.g., through turn-taking and shared goals [15, 16]), classroom dynamics are more complex. Classroom interactions are mediated by peers and teachers who intervene in and influence the student-AI relationship [17–20]. Consequently, perceptions of control in other contexts may not directly transfer to the classroom environment.

In the context of K-12 school classrooms, studies have proposed and documented how AI could be used to enhance effective collaborations among stakeholders (i.e., students, teachers, and AI technologies as decision-making agents). For example, while early work on ITSs conducted classroom evaluations without paying particular attention to the teacher's role, the focus has shifted toward an *empowerment* view, emphasizing collaboration between humans and AI in supporting student learning [10, 11, 15, 21, 22]. In line with this shift, Molenaar's [22] framework illustrates varying levels of teacher-AI reliance in the classroom, such as "conditional automation," where AI would lead instruction while teachers would monitor it. This paradigm highlights how AI can complement human teaching rather than substitute for it [9, 23].

However, current *hybrid intelligence* (i.e., combining human intelligence and artificial intelligence) [22] or *humans in the loop* (e.g., incorporate people's viewpoints in the design and development of tools) [9] research in K-12 classrooms primarily focuses on teachers, leaving out students' perspectives [22]. While recent studies have captured students' perspectives towards AI, most of these studies are typically concerned with either higher education environments [11]. We consider K-12 classroom dynamics to be complex yet meaningful environments for AI interaction that warrant investigation, particularly as we currently lack a holistic view of the student experience [19]. Students and teachers frequently have diverging needs and privacy preferences regarding AI use [6, 19]. Addressing this literature gap in students' perspectives of AI use in K-12 classrooms is essential for designing systems that respect student desires and align design with their specific goals [10].

In particular, student control, which we refer to as the autonomy and decision-making power exercised during technology-enhanced learning, is a central factor in classroom AI adoption. While prior research often implicitly assumes that higher control yields better outcomes for students [24], empirical evidence is mixed; some studies found that higher decision-making control leads to improved learning, while others suggest restricted control can scaffold students well and produce higher gains despite lower engagement [11, 24]. Critically, students' decision-making control in these prior studies has primarily been simplified as a one-dimensional metric of *high vs. low* [25]. Following recent work by Vincoli [26], who proposed a multi-dimensional framework of student agency in classroom decision-making, we consider that student control spans multiple aspects of decision-making opportunities in the classroom. Specifically, beyond just choosing (or having AI choose) what to learn (Content Control) [26], students might decide on what data to share and with whom (Data Control) [10, 26, 27], when and with whom to collaborate in the classroom (Orchestration Control) [23, 26–28], and the level of assistance they receive in the classroom (Help & Feedback Control) [26, 29]. The mentioned dimensions of control are illustrated in Table 1. Past studies have not fully investigated students' views on these critical aspects of decision-making in the classroom environment. The multi-dimensional understanding of student-AI control is critical for identifying where standardized AI metrics may generate unfair and inappropriate decisions; AI systems that rely on one-size-fits-all quantitative indicators can oversimplify complex human behavior and penalize specific personality traits [11].

## 3 Methods

To better understand students' perspectives on decision-making control in the AI-supported classroom, we conducted a speed-dating study in Germany. Our research question (RQ) asks: *What are students' preferred levels of control when learning with AI systems in the classroom?*

### 3.1 Participants

We recruited 16 students from German secondary schools with a mean age of 14 years old (more details can be found in Table 2). We specifically targeted secondary-school students, as secondary schools are often a strong focus for digitalization initiatives in Germany.[1] Participants were recruited either through their school or through prior contacts in the lab. Participants were given the option to choose the language of participation (German or English). The study had been approved by the third author's university's ethical review board prior to data collection, and each participant was given an informed

[1] https://www.digitalpaktschule.de/de/digitalpakt-2-0-1874.html

consent, which their parents or legal guardian signed. Participation was fully voluntary. Participants were compensated with 12 euros upon completion of the study.

**Table 1.** Multi-dimensional student control in learning with AI in the classroom

| Control Dimension | Description | Example decision-making situation | |
|---|---|---|---|
| | | When a learner has more control | When an AI system has more control |
| Help & Feedback Control | Control on how much help (e.g., scaffolding) and feedback learners request/need/want vs. what AI provides during learning | A learner spontaneously asks for hints from an AI system when they want help. | An AI system provides feedback when it detects learners' consecutive incorrect attempts in the system. |
| Data Control | Control on how much learning data learners share with the AI system (vs. AI collects) and with whom (e.g., teacher) | A learner chooses not to share their learning data with their teacher. | An AI system automatically sends learners' data to their teacher without notifying learners. |
| Orchestration Control | Control on how much and with whom to work on collaborative activities in the classroom | A learner picks whom to work with on a collaborative learning task. | An AI system determines group assignments based on the performance of the learners. |
| Content Control | Control on what and how much content to work on in an AI-based learning system | A student chooses to work on problems that they have practiced already. | An AI system assigns a student a difficult problem based on its understanding of the student's mastery. |

### 3.2 Materials

With the goal of grounding stakeholder views in a specific context, we developed a set of materials to capture insights tailored to AI-supported classroom interactions. Specifically, we created eight storyboards (referred to as scenarios in this paper) depicting concrete interactions that may occur in classrooms that involve AI systems and teachers. To elicit student insights, we developed scenarios spanning four dimensions of control proposed by Vincoli [26], each instantiated through two extreme cases: *full student control* and *full AI control*. In total, we created eight scenarios (four dimensions × two versions). For each scenario, we then designed two possible endings: one positive and one negative (Figs. 1 and 2). For example, Fig. 1 illustrates two outcomes under full student control over homework assignment (Content Control): successful (positive) test preparation (4A) and insufficient (negative) preparation (4B), depending on the student's decision.

Similarly, Fig. 2 presents outcomes under full AI control over homework assignment: in 4A, the student is satisfied with an appropriate assignment (positive), whereas in 4B, students discuss a perceived unfair outcome (negative).

**Table 2.** Participants' demographics including reported AI tools they are familiar with. Google Services includes services such as Google Lens and Google Assistant. "-"indicates that the participant did not name any AI tool they had used before

| Participant ID | Age | Grade level | Known/Used AI Tools |
|---|---|---|---|
| P1 | 16 | 11th | ChatGPT, Dall-E |
| P2 | 16 | 10th | Siri, Alexa, Snapchat AI |
| P3 | 12 | 6th | ChatGPT, Bing AI, Crayon AI, Google Services |
| P4 | 14 | 8th | ChatGPT, Snapchat AI, |
| P5 | 12 | 6th | – |
| P6 | 14 | 7th | Translator |
| P7 | 13 | 7th | – |
| P8 | 17 | 11th | ChatGPT, Dall-E, |
| P9 | 12 | 6th | ChatGPT |
| P10 | 16 | 10th | ChatGPT, Translator |
| P11 | 13 | 8th | ChatGPT, Google Services |
| P12 | 12 | 7th | ChatGPT |
| P13 | 16 | 10th | ChatGPT |
| P14 | 18 | 12th | ChatGPT, Google Services |
| P15 | 12 | 6th | – |
| P16 | 14 | 8th | – |

These scenarios were selected and designed based on prior design-based studies using storyboards to investigate classroom AI use [6, 17] and empirical studies testing multiple control dimensions [29]. We used contrasting outcomes to capture how students' views vary based on the results of AI use (because showing only positive or negative endings would bias their views). We chose to provide such scaffolding materials since the use of AI-based tools and digital tools was still in a very early stage in German schools at the time of data collection (therefore, it would have been difficult for school-aged children to imagine what AI could do) [29, 30]. Prior work has used storyboards as an effective way to elicit deep insights into how teachers and students think about the use of AI technology in the classroom [6, 23]. All eight scenarios are available online.[2]

### 3.3 Procedure

Participants attended the study either online or in-person. In total, 13 participants chose the online option; the other three were interviewed at the university. Each session took

[2] https://tinyurl.com/ectelstudentscenarios

45–60 min. Two researchers joined each session, where one researcher facilitated the study and the second researcher took notes and asked further questions if needed. The eight scenarios were presented in a randomized order to minimize the order effect. They were presented in English or German, depending on the language of choice. All sessions were video recorded for later analysis, except for one where consent was given only for taking written notes.

To capture students' contextualized view toward agency when interacting with AI, we designed study materials that are aimed at eliciting their deep insights into the topic. Specifically, we designed an interview protocol where students would be introduced to the study comfortably, starting with warm-up questions about their school environment, and then onto the topic of AI, letting them freely express their thoughts as they wanted. We asked seven main questions in total (e.g., "What do you do when you don't understand something in class? and "Have you ever used an AI tool?," also see Table 2). We intentionally designed it as a semi-structured interview, as the main purpose was to help participants feel comfortable in sharing their honest thoughts in the session.

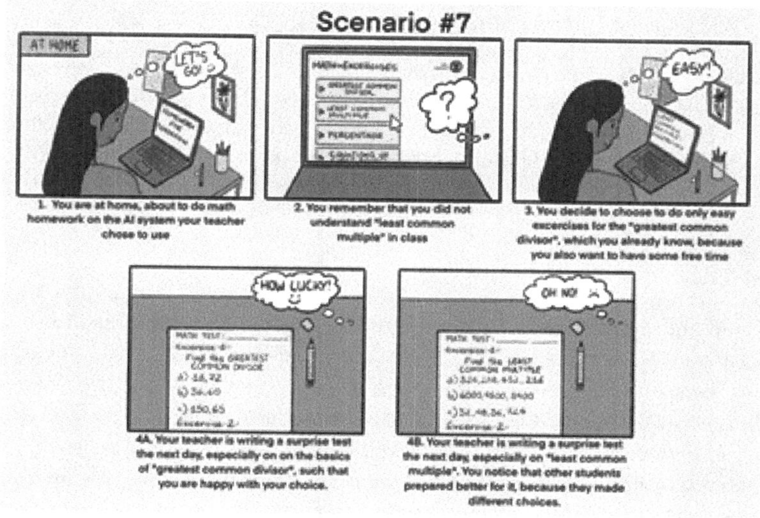


**Fig. 1.** Scenario with full student control over their homework assignment; the student chose to work on easy tasks they already know. A positive ending (4A) shows that the teacher assigns a test on the practiced topic, while a negative ending (4B) shows that their choice did not match what the teacher assigns (Content Control - full student control)

**Fig. 2.** Scenario with full AI control over assignment; the AI assigns students different homework based on each one's knowledge state. A positive ending (4A) shows that the assignment matched the student's level of understanding, a negative ending (4B) shows the student feeling unfairly treated due to such differences (Content Control – full AI control)

### 3.4 Analysis

We gathered and machine-transcribed approximately 14 h of video recordings, which, where necessary, were adjusted or translated from German into English. The transcribed interviews were first analyzed using a thematic analysis, following a hybrid deductive-inductive approach. Specifically, we utilized a coding rubric based on the four dimensions of control to deductively categorize the data. Researchers extracted segments from the transcripts into discrete codes (labels and short descriptive sentences), which were then synthesized using the Affinity Diagramming method [31]. Affinity Diagramming is a technique that allows researchers to collaboratively group codes into emergent themes. We iteratively refined our original assumptions to ensure that the analysis was both theoretically structured by Vincoli's framework [26] and flexible enough to capture bottom-up insights from the participants.

We first organized codes following the original study interview structure (Fig. 3 a). A total of 644 codes were developed using the deductive approach (described above), which were then placed onto the whiteboard (Fig. 3 b). Using the 644 initial codes, we first conducted Affinity Diagramming *horizontally* (i.e., finding common themes across participants within each topic, Fig. 3 c). Then, we performed Affinity Diagramming *vertically* (i.e., looking for common themes across different topics) to find common codes across the different sub-parts of the interview (Fig. 3 d). Finally, we re-organized resulting theme categories based on commonalities to formulate high-level themes.

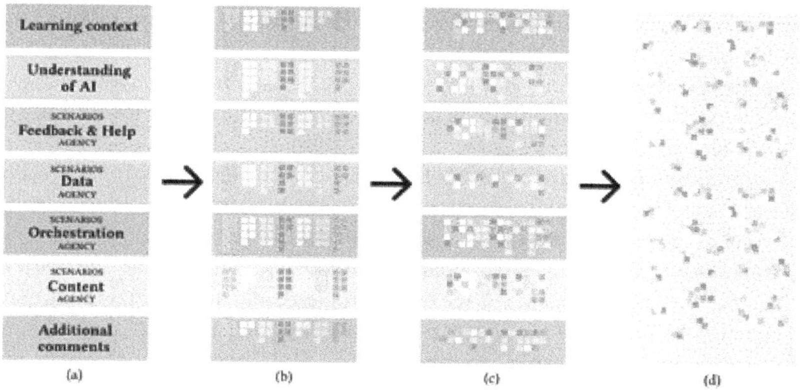


**Fig. 3.** Visualization of the analysis process: (a) shows the interview procedure that we followed (from top to bottom). We first structured codes following the interview procedure (b), then organized codes within each part of the study procedure (c). Then, we looked across the categories and formed themes across all categories (d)

# 4 Results

The Affinity Diagramming process produced a total of three high-level themes and 30 low-level themes. The three high-level themes are described in the following sections.

## 4.1 Students' Perceived Control in AI-Supported Learning Differs across Types of Learning Decisions

First, we found that students generally expressed a desire to retain control over learning decisions. This preference was particularly strong regarding Data Control, with some students viewing their learning data as a direct representation of themselves ("[The data] is what I am," P1). For most, it was important to establish clear boundaries around who could access this information ("[learning data] should be your opinion and you should not be forced to show [it to] everyone," P13). AI-driven data collection and monitoring were often perceived as unsettling or judgmental, with students describing feelings of anxiety and pressure ("I'd be more anxious about seeing the teacher on the next day," P14; "You always have this pressure in the back of your mind that you can't make a mistake," P8; "If you struggle on one task, [...] it ruins your complete stats, then you feel very bad about it," P1). As a result, many expressed reluctance toward extensive AI monitoring of their learning activities.

In contrast, students felt less confident in making decisions about content assignments (Content Control) and generally preferred these decisions to be made by a more knowledgeable agent. They believed that many students would choose easier tasks for convenience ("I can see a lot of students just picking the easier way just because they want more free time or something," P15), and therefore trusted either their teachers or AI systems to make more appropriate decisions. Many also recognized AI's ability to gradually adapt tasks to individual performance levels, and thus make better learning choices for them in the long run, showing a preference on delegating their decision-making control over to AI long-term ("If you get tasks adapted to your performance level, that is perfect, and if the topic is adapted to the performance level of the class, I think that is also great," P8).

The remaining control dimensions revealed more nuanced preferences. Regarding Help & Feedback Control, students expressed a balanced view of the appropriate level of AI involvement. Some students favored AI-driven control to overcome the limitations of human teachers, viewing AI as a personal tutor for every student ("We can learn a lot of things because the teacher can never see every problem, and an artificial intelligence can do this because AI is like for every student one teacher," P10). Others, however, viewed human teachers as irreplaceable, arguing that AI hints lack the contextual, nuanced understanding of a teacher's intuition ("When you talk with a person [...] they see if you're understanding it, and if not, they can help you and with this [AI-generated] hints, you just do not understand it really well," P13). Overall, students advocated for a collaborative approach in which AI-generated learning analytics empowers teachers to identify difficulties and provide targeted instruction ("if your data shows that this is a topic a lot of students struggle with, then the teacher can just help a lot more," P14; "I would share [with] my teacher [...] because they could help," P16).

For Orchestration Control, students generally appreciated AI's ability to manage organizational aspects of learning but considered that social dynamics among peers are complex, and an AI would not be able to capture them accurately. As one student summarized, "[AI] just doesn't get [interactions]," P13.

## 4.2 The Tension Between Students' Understanding of AI and their Trust in it

Beyond their desire for control, we found that students' views on AI varied depending on their experience with and knowledge of AI. Most viewed AI as a functional tool "for writing texts, for spell checking or [when] you need help with the structure of some texts," (P8) or that "[gives] answers quite quickly on the basis of information," (P13), or a tutor that "would kind of give you feedback on its own" (P14). Few offered slightly more technical definitions, describing it as "just a mathematical function" that "adapts and learns" (P1). The observed variation in students' understanding of AI likely reflects differences in their prior exposure to AI. It also seems that these differences, in turn, appeared to shape where students placed their trust. Although AI was generally perceived as beneficial, some students who lack a complete understanding of AI expressed concerns that relying on it too heavily could negatively affect their own learning ("Disadvantages are probably that you don't learn anything yourself," P4).

This variability in preferences for the appropriate level of control led to divergent views on automated personalization. While some viewed AI-based adaptation of task difficulty as "perfect," others expressed concerns about feeling "unfairly treated" (P8). Skepticism toward AI-assigned tasks often stemmed from concerns about "gaming the system" [11, 32], with students sharing that the absence of human oversight could encourage behaviors such as "just click[ing] on all the hints" (P1) rather than meaningfully engaging with the assigned tasks.

Also, students viewed teachers as irreplaceable sources of authority and oversight in an AI-infused classroom environment: "I think the teacher should always be there because AI won't be perfect" (P1). Regardless of AI-generated recommendations, students emphasized that teachers should retain final decision-making power, citing teachers' superior skill to understand students as individuals: "I think [the AI] is able to do this but I would give it to the teacher [...] because I think a human [...] knows you better" (P11). This strong trust in human teachers may reflect participants' limited experience with AI learning systems, but it nevertheless highlights the critical role teachers continue to play in students' perceptions of AI-supported instruction. For these students, the right level of control is one where the AI handles task generation, but the human teacher maintains the moral and pedagogical authority to validate the outcome.

### 4.3 Social Factors Influencing Safe and Effective AI Use in Learning

The study also provides an initial view of how classroom social dynamics may be influenced by the presence of a new intelligent agent, such as an AI-powered tutor. For instance, although students generally showed a positive view towards getting help from peers, they expressed contrasting thoughts when it comes to peer involvement in personal data, causing embarrassment: "if you don't understand something, you feel a little bit bad and the teacher goes to you [...] and you think that everybody is looking at you" (P11) and "When your grades aren't that good and you're embarrassed in front of your teacher or your parents" (P13). This suggests that AI-supported learning may intensify the social visibility of individual performance, with critical implications for students' emotion and privacy.

## 5 Discussion

### 5.1 Key Findings

Prior research rarely consults students on the optimal integration of AI into classroom learning, despite their unique and important perspectives as the primary users of AI systems. We conducted a design-based study with 16 German secondary-school students to investigate their views on AI use in school classrooms. Our study reveals that students' preferences for learner-AI control are highly situational; for instance, participants strongly preferred retaining Data Control, emphasizing ownership and autonomy over their data. On the other hand, they were more willing to delegate Content Control as they recognized the limitations of their own metacognitive decision-making skills and value AI's ability to personalize learning.

Beyond these dimension-specific preferences, the study also suggests dynamic interactions and control negotiations among students, AI systems, and teachers in making important decisions in the classroom. Students' trust in AI varied according to their familiarity with AI technologies, illustrating the individual differences in how much they could accept AI-driven personalization. At the same time, students consistently regarded teachers as the ultimate decision-makers in AI-supported classrooms. Participants valued teachers' skills in understanding students as individuals and providing oversight beyond AI capabilities. This finding reflects students' trust in teachers; students tended to view AI as a supportive assistant rather than an autonomous authority, whose recommendations should remain subject to teacher decisions.

These findings underscore that student-AI control in the unique classroom context cannot be reduced to a single high-vs.-low dimension. Instead, it needs to be understood as multi-dimensional and dynamic interactions between individual students, AI, and teachers. Based on these insights, we propose design recommendations for future AI-based TEL systems for classroom use.

### 5.2 Design Recommendations for Future Classroom AI Systems

Our findings suggest that a static approach to designing AI-based classroom systems would fail to account for the diverse and dynamic control preferences of students. We argue that future systems must transition from fixed automation to adaptive control interfaces that allow for granular user adjustment, thereby considering students as decision-makers in the classroom [19]. For example, rather than designing a system that assumes and determines the *appropriate* level of support, the interface could incorporate *scaffolded choices* inviting students to decide between receiving an answer, receiving a problem-solving hint, solving the problem independently, or asking their teacher for help. Such an explicit choice-making mechanism could help address the tension we observed between students' desire for efficiency and their concerns about "gaming the system" by allowing them to regulate their cognitive load and help-seeking behavior.

To further address the unsettling feelings that students would have toward AI surveillance and monitoring, future systems could integrate student-facing privacy dashboards. These dashboards would provide a transparent visualization of the data being tracked and clearly state which data are accessible to the teacher (and other stakeholders) [10, 33]. By making data-sharing settings explicit and adjustable, systems can transform the feeling of being watched into an experience of being supported, aligning with research that prioritizes student-led control in Open Learner Models [3, 34]. Also, these preferences may evolve with experience and growing technical fluency; therefore, systems should incorporate periodic preference reassessment cycles to accommodate changing needs.

Finally, while current participatory design practices for K-12 classroom AI tools predominantly focus on teachers, having students in the design process would reveal unique insights and inspire novel features, such as motivational virtual agents that explain system logic. Student-centered design processes ensure that classroom AI tools are not only effective but also safe, ethical, and meaningful [11].

### 5.3 Limitations

We acknowledge several limitations of the study. First, the small sample size, with a sparse age distribution, limits the generalizability of these findings. Second, the cultural context of the study, i.e., Germany/Europe, likely shaped participants' perspectives. Cultural norms regarding data privacy, institutional trust, and the role of automation in society vary significantly, and our findings may reflect a specific viewpoint on student-AI control negotiation. Also, given the voluntary nature of the study, the participants might not represent the general population of German K-12 students. Finally, even though the materials we used in the study (i.e., hypothetical scenarios of AI use) were designed based on prior work, the eight scenarios may not fully represent what would happen in German classrooms in the future.

### 5.4 Conclusion

Despite a growing interest in AI systems for classroom use, students' perspectives on student-AI interactions are not sufficiently represented in the literature. We conducted a qualitative study with 16 secondary-school students in Germany to understand their perspectives, focusing on how much control they would desire when learning with AI. Our findings showed the complexity of students' sense of control in AI-student interactions that encompass multiple dimensions of decision-making opportunities. We provide design recommendations for future classroom AI systems such that designers and researchers can meaningfully address and respect students' sense of control in their deign practice. Future studies can investigate how the insights we found might look different/similar in other contexts.

**Acknowledgments.** We thank all the students participating in the study.

## References

1. Wu, R., Yu, Z.: Do AI Chatbots improve students learning outcomes? Evidence from a meta-analysis. Br. J. Educ. Technol. **55**, 10–33 (2024). https://doi.org/10.1111/bjet.13334
2. Urban, M. et al.: ChatGPT improves creative problem-solving performance in university students: an experimental study. Comput. Educ. **215**, 105031 (2024). https://doi.org/10.1016/j.compedu.2024.105031
3. Khosravi, H. et al.: Explainable artificial intelligence in education. Comput. Educ. Artif. Intell. **3**, 100074 (2022). https://doi.org/10.1016/j.caeai.2022.100074
4. Holmes, W., Tuomi, I.: State of the art and practice in AI in education. Eur. J. Educ. **57**, 542–570 (2022). https://doi.org/10.1111/ejed.12533
5. Holstein, K., McLaren, B.M., Aleven, V.: Designing for complementarity: teacher and student needs for orchestration support in AI-enhanced classrooms. In: Isotani, S., Millán, E., Ogan, A., Hastings, P., McLaren, B., Luckin, R. (eds.) Artificial Intelligence in Education, pp. 157–171. Springer International Publishing, Cham (2019). https://doi.org/10.1007/978-3-030-23204-7_14
6. Holstein, K., McLaren, B.M., Aleven, V.: Co-designing a real-time classroom orchestration tool to support teacher–AI complementarity. J. Learn. Anal. **6**(2), 27–52 (2019). https://doi.org/10.18608/jla.2019.62.3
7. Lawrence, L., Echeverria, V., Yang, K., Aleven, V., Rummel, N.: How teachers conceptualise shared control with an AI co-orchestration tool: a multiyear teacher-Centred design process. Br. J. Educ. Technol. **55**, 823–844 (2024). https://doi.org/10.1111/bjet.13372
8. Bond, M. et al.: A meta systematic review of artificial intelligence in higher education: a call for increased ethics, collaboration, and rigour. Int. J. Educ. Technol. High. Educ. **21**, 4 (2024). https://doi.org/10.1186/s41239-023-00436-z

9. Cheah, Y.H., Lu, J., Kim, J.: Integrating generative artificial intelligence in K-12 education: examining teachers' preparedness, practices, and barriers. Comput. Educ. Artif. Intell. **8**, 100363 (2025). https://doi.org/10.1016/j.caeai.2025.100363
10. Toth, A., Roch, N., Zufferey, N., Zimmermann, V.: "I would share it, but..." exploring ways to optimize the privacy-personalization trade-off in intelligent tutoring systems. In: Cristea, A.I., Walker, E., Lu, Y., Santos, O.C., Isotani, S. (eds.) Artificial Intelligence in Education, pp. 68–76. Springer Nature, Switzerland, Cham (2025). https://doi.org/10.1007/978-3-031-98462-4_9
11. Han, B., Coghlan, S., Buchanan, G., McKay, D.: Who is helping whom? Student concerns about AI-teacher collaboration in higher education classrooms. Proc ACM Hum. Comput. Interact. **9, CSCW206: 1-CSCW206**, 32 (2025). https://doi.org/10.1145/3711104
12. Zimmerman, J., Forlizzi, J.: Speed dating: providing a menu of possible futures. She Ji J. Des. Econ. Innov. **3**, 30–50 (2017). https://doi.org/10.1016/j.sheji.2017.08.003
13. Williams, R., Park, H.W., Breazeal, C.: A is for artificial intelligence: the impact of artificial intelligence activities on young Children's perceptions of robots. In: Proceedings of the 2019 CHI Conference on Human Factors in Computing Systems, pp. 1–11. ACM, Glasgow Scotland Uk (2019). https://doi.org/10.1145/3290605.3300677
14. Li, Z., Thomas, T., Yu, C.-L., Xu, Y.: "I said Knight, not night!": Children's communication breakdowns and repairs with AI versus human partners. In: Proceedings of the 23rd Annual ACM Interaction Design and Children Conference, pp. 781–788. ACM, Delft Netherlands (2024). https://doi.org/10.1145/3628516.3659394
15. Chen, F. Human-AI Cooperation in Education:Human in Loop and Teaching as leadership. J. Educ. Technol. Innov. **2**(1) (2022). https://doi.org/10.61414/jeti.v2i1.34.
16. Zheng, Q., Tang, Y., Liu, Y., Liu, W., Huang, Y.: UX research on conversational human-AI interaction: a literature review of the ACM digital library. In: CHI Conference on Human Factors in Computing Systems, pp. 1–24. ACM, New Orleans LA USA (2022). https://doi.org/10.1145/3491102.3501855
17. Yang, K.B., Lawrence, L., Echeverria, V., Guo, B., Rummel, N., Aleven, V.: Surveying teachers' preferences and boundaries regarding human-AI control in dynamic pairing of students for collaborative learning. In: De Laet, T., Klemke, R., Alario-Hoyos, C., Hilliger, I., Ortega-Arranz, A. (eds.) Technology-Enhanced Learning for a Free, Safe, and Sustainable World, pp. 260–274. Springer International Publishing, Cham (2021). https://doi.org/10.1007/978-3-030-86436-1_20
18. Yip, J.C., Ello, F.M.T., Tsukiyama, F., Wairagade, A., Ahn, J.: "Money shouldn't be money!": an examination of financial literacy and Technology for Children through co-Design. In: Proceedings of the 22nd Annual ACM Interaction Design and Children Conference, pp. 82–93. ACM, Chicago IL USA (2023). https://doi.org/10.1145/3585088.3589355
19. Han, A. et al.: Teachers, parents, and students' perspectives on integrating generative AI into elementary literacy education. In: Proceedings of the 2024 CHI Conference on Human Factors in Computing Systems, pp. 1–17. Association for Computing Machinery, New York, NY, USA (2024). https://doi.org/10.1145/3613904.3642438
20. Luo, J.: How does GenAI affect trust in teacher-student relationships? Insights from students' assessment experiences. Teach. High. Educ. **30**, 991–1006 (2025). https://doi.org/10.1080/13562517.2024.2341005
21. Yan, L., Greiff, S., Teuber, Z., Gašević, D.: Promises and challenges of generative artificial intelligence for human learning. Nat. Hum. Behav. **8**, 1839–1850 (2024). https://doi.org/10.1038/s41562-024-02004-5
22. Molenaar, I.: Towards hybrid human-AI learning technologies. Eur. J. Educ. **57**, 632–645 (2022). https://doi.org/10.1111/ejed.12527

23. Yang, K.B. et al.: Pair-up: prototyping human-AI co-orchestration of dynamic transitions between individual and collaborative learning in the classroom. In: Proceedings of the 2023 CHI Conference on Human Factors in Computing Systems, pp. 1–17. Association for Computing Machinery, New York, NY, USA (2023). https://doi.org/10.1145/3544548.3581398
24. Snow, E.L., Allen, L.K., Jacovina, M.E., McNamara, D.S.: Does agency matter?: exploring the impact of controlled behaviors within a game-based environment. Comput. Educ. **82**, 378–392 (2015). https://doi.org/10.1016/j.compedu.2014.12.011
25. Guo, L., Wang, D., Gu, F., et al.: Evolution and trends in intelligent tutoring systems research: a multidisciplinary and scientometric view. Asia Pac. Educ. Rev. **22**, 441–461 (2021). https://doi.org/10.1007/s12564-021-09697-7
26. Vincoli, M., Scholz, N., Nagashima, T.: Multi-dimensional student Agency in Learning with AI: a conceptual framework and design implications. In: Cristea, A.I., Walker, E., Lu, Y., Santos, O.C., Isotani, S. (eds.) Artificial Intelligence in Education, pp. 218–232. Springer Nature, Switzerland, Cham (2025). https://doi.org/10.1007/978-3-031-98459-4_16
27. Holmes, W. et al.: Ethics of AI in education: towards a community-wide framework. Int. J. Artif. Intell. Educ. **32**, 504–526 (2022). https://doi.org/10.1007/s40593-021-00239-1
28. Lawrence, L.E.M. et al.: Co-designing AI-based orchestration tools to support dynamic transitions: design narratives through conjecture mapping. In: CSCL Proceedings -15th International Conference on Computer-Supported Collaborative Learning (CSCL) 2022, pp. 139–146. International Society of the Learning Sciences (2022)
29. Nagashima, T., Zheng, B., Tseng, S., Ling, E., Aleven, V.: Promoting students' self-regulated learning choices with diagrams in intelligent tutoring software. In: Blikstein, P., Van Aalst, J., Kizito, R., Brennan, K. (eds.) Proceedings of the 17th International Conference of the Learning Sciences-ICLS 2023, pp. 593–600. International Society of the Learning Sciences (2023)
30. The Children's Manifesto for the Future of AI. https://www.turing.ac.uk/news/publications/childrens-manifesto-future-ai. Accessed 14 June 2026
31. Rosala, M.: How to Analyze Qualitative Data from UX Research: Thematic Analysis. https://www.nngroup.com/articles/thematic-analysis/. Accessed 14 June 2026
32. Baker, R., Walonoski, J., Heffernan, N., Roll, I., Corbett, A., Koedinger, K.: Why students engage in "gaming the system" behavior in interactive learning environments. J. Interact. Learn. Res. **19**, 185–224 (2008)
33. Zimmermann, V. et al.: Let's get visual - testing visual analogies and metaphors for conveying privacy policies and data handling information. In: 2025 IEEE Symposium on Security and Privacy (SP), pp. 2303–2321 (2025) https://doi.org/10.1109/SP61157.2025.00240
34. Bodily, R. et al.: Open learner models and learning analytics dashboards: a systematic review. In: Proceedings of the 8th International Conference on Learning Analytics and Knowledge, pp. 41–50. ACM, Sydney New South Wales Australia (2018). https://doi.org/10.1145/3170358.3170409

# High and Low-Performing Groups in Collaborative VR Video-Based Learning: An Exploratory Study of Group Interaction and Experience

Lingkan Wang[1], Qianru Lyu[2], Yu Liu[3], and Qiao Jin[4](✉)

[1] Cyan Studio, Washington, USA
lingkanw@andrew.cmu.edu
[2] Carnegie Mellon University, Pittsburgh, USA
Qlyu@andrew.cmu.edu
[3] ByteDance, Los Angeles, USA
[4] North Carolina State University, Raleigh, USA
qjin4@ncsu.edu

**Abstract.** Virtual reality (VR) offers immersive opportunities for collaborative learning, yet little is known about how high- and low-performing groups differ in their collaborative processes and learning experiences. In this study, 54 students (18 groups) participated in a virtual field trip, collaboratively viewing a 360° video and creating a visitor map in VR. Group outcomes were assessed based on visitor map quality. We then selected the three highest- and three lowest-performing groups and compared their forms of interaction, note-taking behaviors, viewing patterns, and self-reported collaboration, satisfaction, and social presence. Interview data were used to contextualize these findings. Our results showed that high-performing groups displayed declaratory comments paired with more questioning and evaluative discourse, while low-performing groups focused on surface-level content sharing and activity planning without deeper elaboration. High-performing groups also tended to show lower view similarity and a preference for text-based note-taking. Interestingly, descriptive questionnaire results indicated that low-performing groups reported higher satisfaction, social presence, and collaborative experience than high-performing groups. Qualitative findings further contextualize these patterns and inform pedagogical and design implications for collaborative video-based learning in VR.

**Keywords:** VR · Collaborative Learning · Epistemic Network Analysis

## 1 Introduction

Video-based learning (VBL) allows self-paced and autonomous learning through videos, and is widely accepted as an e-learning trend due to the growing availability of online resources [21]. Collaborative VBL has been shown to increase


J. Weidlich et al. (Eds.): EC-TEL 2026, LNCS 16905, pp. 636–650, 2027.
https://doi.org/10.1007/978-3-032-37979-5_43

engagement, discussion, and knowledge construction compared with solitary viewing [16,20]. Recent work has extended this line of research to immersive virtual reality (VR), where learners view 360° videos together in a shared virtual space (hereafter referred to as VR videos). Compared with conventional 2D co-viewing, collaborative VR video-based learning (VR-VBL) offers new possibilities for shared attention, spatial reference, and coordination through features such as avatars, gaze cues, and shared annotations [11,13]. However, research on VR video-based learning (VR-VBL) has primarily focused on individual learning experiences [25], with relatively little attention to collaborative contexts. Existing collaborative VR-VBL studies [11,14] have often remained at the individual level or reported average trends across groups. For example, Jin et al. [11] examined collaborative learning in VR video environments but evaluated participants individually rather than analyzing group-level outcomes. Therefore, we still know little about why some groups produce stronger collaborative outcomes than others. This gap matters because group learning outcomes are rarely uniform. For instructors and system designers, the practical question is not only whether collaborative VR-VBL supports learning, but also what kinds of interactions are associated with stronger group performance. Prior research in non-VR collaborative learning suggests that high-performing (H) groups are more likely to engage in questioning, elaboration, and evaluation, whereas low-performing (L) groups more often remain at the level of surface coordination or limited knowledge building [32,33]. In collaborative VR-VBL, these differences may take new forms. Features such as synchronized viewing, shared gaze cues, avatars, and annotation tools may support coordination and awareness, but they may also shape how groups divide attention, interpret peers' actions, and build shared understanding [6,11]. Yet how these processes relate to differences in group performance remains underexplored.

To address this gap, we analyzed data from 18 groups of three (54 participants) using a collaborative VR system for VR video-based virtual field trips. Groups watched city-tour videos together and then created visitor maps in VR as a shared learning artifact. We compared high- and low-performing groups through a multi-layered analysis that combined Epistemic Network Analysis (ENA) of coded discourse, behavioral log analysis of notes and view similarity (i.e., the extent to which group members shared the same video context at the same time, an important indicator of collaborative attention [3]), questionnaires on collaboration experience, satisfaction, and social presence, and thematic analysis of interviews. Through this approach, we examine how group interaction, note-taking behavior, shared visual attention, and perceived experience differ across performance levels. This study addresses the following research questions:

(**RQ1**) How do forms of interaction differ between H and L groups during collaborative VR video-based learning?

(**RQ2**) How do note-taking behaviors and view similarities differ between H and L groups?

(**RQ3**) How do perceived user experiences, such as collaboration experience, satisfaction, and social presence, differ between H and L groups?

# 2 Methods

## 2.1 Participants and Settings

The study was conducted at a Midwestern U.S. university as part of a larger investigation of collaborative VR video tools. A total of 54 university students (age 19–31, $M = 22.5$, $SD = 2.65$) participated, forming 18 groups of three. The sample included 26 women, 27 men, and one participant who did not report gender. Groups were formed based on availability and participants' preference. Participants varied in teammate familiarity (26 knew none of their teammates, 18 knew one, and 10 knew both) and prior VR experience (14 extensive, 26 limited, and 14 none). The study took place in four adjacent campus rooms, with one participant in each room, to approximate an online learning setting. A researcher remained in a separate room as an in-VR technical facilitator. While physically separated, all entered the same shared virtual environment through Meta Quest 1 headsets. All procedures were approved by the university's IRB, and informed consent was obtained from all participants.

## 2.2 Artifacts and Learning Task

The collaborative VR video system used in this study was developed in prior work [11] and includes two connected components: a shared VR video viewing space (Fig. 1a) and a post-video virtual discussion room (Fig. 1bc). During video viewing, group members watched the same VR video with synchronized controls (e.g., play/pause and timeline jumps). The system also provided awareness cues, including peers' gaze boxes, pointing cursors, and 3D avatars, as well as shared note-taking tools such as screenshots, speech-to-text notes, and in-video annotations. All notes and annotations were visible to the group. After the video, participants entered a virtual discussion room where they could review the collected screenshots and notes and draw in 3D while collaboratively reflecting on the video content.

Participants were required to complete a virtual field trip task designed to promote cultural and historical understanding. The task was framed as: "Imagine a classmate missed today's lesson, your goal is to convey the video content to them in as much detail as possible and in a well-organized way." Each group collaboratively watched one narrated 360° city-tour video, during which they could discuss the content and use shared tools such as notes, annotations, and screenshots. After viewing, they entered the discussion room, where their collected materials were available for review, and collaboratively created a visitor map. The 18 groups were evenly assigned to one of three videos—Granada, Porto, or Seville—selected from the "One Day In" 360° travel video series.[1] Using multiple videos reduced stimulus-specific bias and made the task less dependent on any one video. The three videos were selected and reprocessed to be comparable in length, complexity, and narration style.

[1] "One Day In" 360° videos: https://www.youtube.com/playlist?list=PLHiCdB8YTO76Gv843e8rdcza-FJbYCYSj.

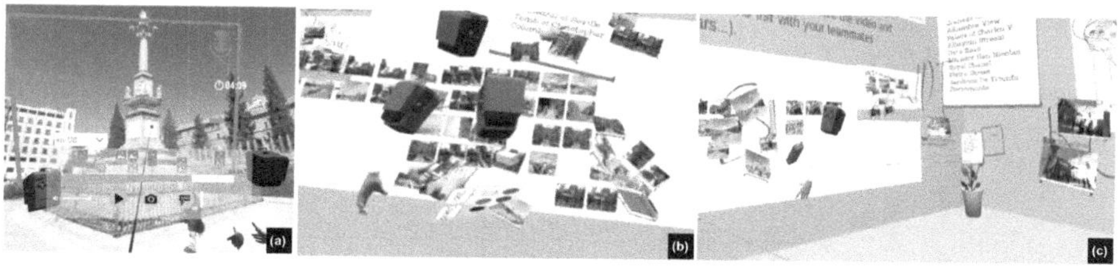


**Fig. 1.** (a) Shared VR video viewing space. (b) Example of a post-video virtual discussion room from a L group (Group 8). (c) Example of a post-video virtual discussion room from a H group (Group 18).

### 2.3 Procedure

The study began with a brief introductory discussion (~5 min), during which the three participants introduced themselves and shared their prior experiences with VR technology. Following this, researchers provided a concise briefing (~5 min) on the study's objectives, procedures, learning goals, and system functionalities. Participants then donned the VR headsets for a system tutorial, with training duration varying based on prior VR experience. A 5-min break followed to prevent motion discomfort. Once ready, participants entered the shared VR video viewing space, watching a 3.5-min video together and pausing, rewinding, or repositioning it as needed (up to 10 min). They then entered the post-video virtual discussion room, reviewed all materials collected during viewing (screenshots, speech-to-text notes, and annotations), and organized them into a visitor map. Afterward, participants completed self-reported questionnaires measuring collaboration experience [28], satisfaction [28] and social presence [17]. Finally, each participant completed a 15- to 20-min individual interview about their collaboration strategies, experiences, and perceptions of the system and its tools.

### 2.4 Data Collection and Analysis

We collected the following data: (1) post-video group visitor maps as the primary performance artifact; (2) recordings of group conversations during video viewing for interaction coding; (3) during-video system logs capturing note-taking, discussion duration, timestamps, and shared viewing (i.e., view similarity); (4) questionnaires measuring collaboration experience, satisfaction, and social presence, aggregated at the group level; and (5) individual interviews.

To evaluate group performance, we adapted De Sousa et al.'s rubric [4] for immersive video learning. The final rubric included four dimensions: Breadth of Net, Accuracy, Communication, and Layout and Structure (Table 2). Each dimension was rated on a 5-point scale, yielding a total score out of 20 for each visitor map. The rubric was iteratively developed by the research team based on the learning goals of the task. Two researchers independently rated all visitor maps, after which discrepancies were resolved through discussion until consensus was reached, with additional mediation from a third researcher when

**Table 1.** Coding scheme for collaborative VR video-based learning interactions.

| Main category | Sub category | Code | Coding rule | Example |
|---|---|---|---|---|
| Task-related interaction | Answer or comment | Declaratory comment | Agrees, states, repeats | "Okay. That sounds good." |
| | | Comment with explanation | Explains, justifies, clarifies | "Maybe just rewatch, cause we can discuss a little bit when revisit the content…" |
| | Question | Clarifying question | Clarifies previous question or asks for clarification | "What did you say about this building?" |
| | | New question | Brings new question into the discussion | "What's the year of this museum?" |
| | | Suggestion | States or suggests and waits for comments. | "You guys wanna watch the last few?" |
| | New knowledge | Content-based | Brings new topic based on the video content | "The Portuguese tiles are the bits of reference to the walls." |
| | | Experience-based | Brings new topic based on experience or opinion | "This was on the pre-questionnaire." |
| Group-related interaction | Socio-emotional expressions | Expressing cohesion | Helping, rewarding, acknowledging | "That's a good point. Very cool." |
| | | Accompanying | Expressing presence, mumbling | "...Moorish... fort… (repeat the video content)" |
| | | Decreasing tension | Laughing, joking | "Ah, Gothic oyster, that's close enough but I cannot eat. (laugh)" |
| | Coordination of group activities | Organizing ongoing activities | Planning and organising current group activities | "Ok, I'm gonna pause it and you take notes of the things she said about this." |
| | | Organizing upcoming activities | Planning and organising future group activities | "I don't know exactly where anybody wants to go but just skip back to someplace you need to review." |
| | | Technological issues | Technological challenges, use of technology | "I was trying to delete my notes because I realized that it did not interpret what I said at all." |
| | | Evaluating group work | Evaluating group work | "Our notes so far probably missed a good chunk of information." |
| | | Reporting current activities | Reporting, acknowledging current self-activities to group | "Um, I'm writing it down." |
| Off-task interaction | Off-task | Off-task | Topics that are not related to course content or group work. | "Wee I'm floating!" |

needed. Based on the final consensus scores, groups were categorized as low- (4–10), medium- (11–12), or high-performing (13–18). For targeted comparisons in discourse, log, and questionnaire analyses, we focused on the top three H and bottom three L groups to support an exploratory contrast between the most divergent cases.

To answer RQ1, the transcripts of group conversations from the extreme groups were segmented into speech turns and coded using an established interaction scheme for collaborative VR video learning (Table 1) [14]. Two researchers first jointly coded an initial subset of the data to refine shared interpretation of the coding categories and ensure consistent application of the scheme. They then independently coded the full transcript set and discussed every disagreement until they reached a single agreed code, so that, as with the artifact scoring, the final coding reflected complete agreement between the two researchers. The final coded discourse was analyzed with Epistemic Network Analysis (ENA) using the ENA Web Tool (version 1.7.0) [19]. Following prior work [14], each coded speech turn was treated as one code unit, and mean rotation normalization was applied to support comparison between H and L groups.

**Table 2.** Evaluation rubric for knowledge-map quality in collaborative VR video learning.

learnıng.

| **Dimension** | **Excellent (5)** | **Good (4)** | **Adequate (3)** | **Marginal (2)** | **Unacceptable (1)** |
|---|---|---|---|---|---|
| Breadth of Net *Did the knowledge map cover all key points from the video?* | Covers nearly all key landmarks, events, and cultural or architectural insights (90–100%) | Covers most key points (75–89%) | Includes a moderate number of key ideas (60–74%) | Includes few key points (40–59%) | Misses most key information; minimal coverage (<40%) |
| Accuracy *Are the facts, names, places, and sequence correct?* | All entries are factually accurate, in correct sequence, and precise | Minor inaccuracies; sequence mostly logical | Some incorrect facts or mixed-up sequences | Many inaccuracies or vague generalizations | Highly inaccurate or misleading content |
| Communication (Efficient Annotation) *Are annotations/labels used to communicate clearly?* | Annotations are clear, concise, and directly support understanding; visual labels aid comprehension | Mostly clear annotations; some could be better worded | Annotations somewhat helpful but inconsistent | Labels or annotations often vague or off-topic | Labels or annotations missing, irrelevant, or confusing |
| Layout and Structure (Hierarchy) *Is there a logical visual hierarchy or structure in the map?* | Excellent structure with logical flow, clear connections, and effective use of space; hierarchy enhances clarity | Mostly clear structure with visible relationships and good layout | Some structure present but connections are unclear or cluttered | Layout lacks clarity or logical progression | No recognizable structure; visually chaotic or disconnected |

For RQ2, log data were used to derive note-taking frequency and view similarity. View similarity was computed using the shared focus metric from prior collaborative VR analytics research [11]. Two participants' views were considered similar when the angle between their head orientations was no greater than 45° and the difference between their video timeline positions was less than 3 s. Group view similarity was then calculated as the proportion of total task time during which all three group members maintained similar views. Log measures were aggregated at the group level and compared descriptively between H and L groups.

For RQ3, questionnaire responses were averaged at the group level and compared descriptively between high- and low-performing groups. Interview transcripts were analyzed using thematic analysis [29]. Two researchers conducted open coding and iteratively grouped codes through constant comparison and affinity diagramming. Disagreements were resolved through team discussion, and the resulting themes were used to interpret the quantitative findings. Given the small sample size at the group level (N = 18) and the exploratory nature of the study, analyses for RQ2 and RQ3 focused on descriptive rather than inferential comparisons.

# 3 Results

We first report an overview of the group outcome, then summarize our quantitative results based on the research questions. Finally, we triangulate our quantitative results with qualitative findings to provide additional interpretive context.

## 3.1 Overview of Group Outcome

A total of 18 group visitor maps were rated in this study using a four-dimensional rubric (Breadth of Net, Accuracy, Communication, and Layout & Structure; 1–5 scale per dimension) as shown in Table 2. The summed scores ranged from 4 to 18 (M = 11.67, SD = 3). Top three groups were identified as high-performing (Group 13 = 16, Group 20 = 16, Group 18 = 18) and the last three as low-performing (Group 8 = 4, Group 5 = 8, Group 9 = 9). The remaining twelve groups fell in the medium range. For the main contrast we focused on a three-versus-three comparison of these extremes. Although a broader six-versus-six split (top six vs. bottom six) was also examined, the performance gap was considerably smaller in that case (top 6 M = 15.00 vs. bottom 6 M = 8.33; mean difference = 6.67) than in the extreme grouping (top 3 M = 16.67 vs. bottom 3 M = 7.00; mean difference = 9.67). Choosing the most divergent three-group sets reduced the sample size but preserved a clearer contrast between performance levels, which supported an exploratory comparison of our RQs.

## 3.2 Quantitative Results

**Forms of Interaction (RQ1).** Based on the fine-grained analysis of students' interactions during the collaborative VR video-based learning task, the ENA modeled the connections among the various interaction forms, producing weighted networks of co-occurrences for the H and L groups. Following normalization, singular value decomposition (SVD) was used to project the high-dimensional network data into a two-dimensional ENA space. The x-axis (SVD1) and y-axis (SVD2) represent the first two dimensions explaining the greatest variance in the network structures, accounting for 29.9% and 20.4% of the variance, respectively. In this projected space, each network is represented as a point, and the centroid indicates the mean location of all networks within a group. The comparison plot (Fig. 2) was output to highlight the differences in the co-occurrence patterns between the higher and lower-performing groups. The nodes represent the different interaction forms. The green rectangle represents the centroid of all networks in H groups, while the red rectangle represents that of the L groups. The thicker connection between nodes indicates the stronger co-occurrence pattern among the two interaction forms.

As Fig. 2 shows, the red connections between the nodes declaratory comment (e.g., "Yeah, I agree."), expressing cohesion (e.g., repeating or acknowledging others' output), organizing ongoing activities (e.g., "Let's move on."), and content-based (e.g., "There's a new building on the left.") show as stronger co-occurring patterns in the L groups. These connections indicate that students in the L

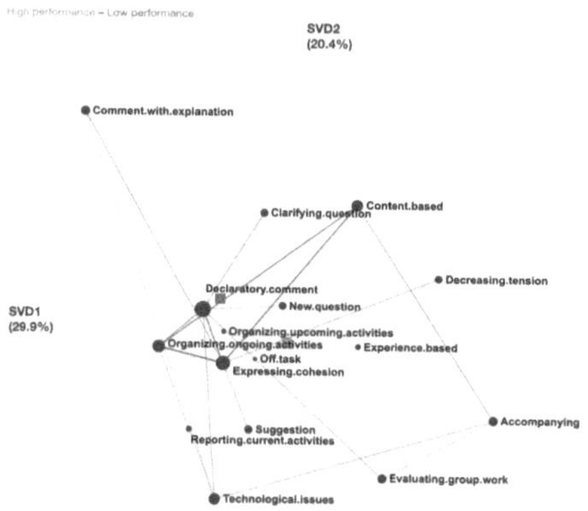


**Fig. 2.** ENA comparison of interaction patterns between three H and three L groups. Green lines show stronger co-occurrences in H groups; red lines show stronger co-occurrences in L groups. (Color figure online)

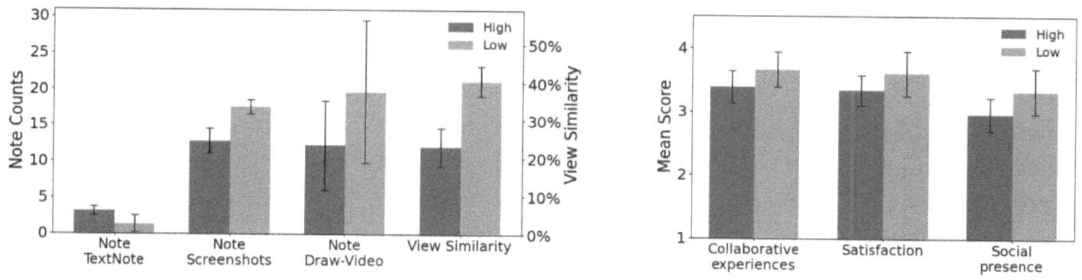


**Fig. 3.** Left: Note-taking behaviors and view similarity between the three H and three L groups. Right: User experience measures between the three H and three L groups. Error bars show 95% confidence intervals.

groups tended to make declaratory comments (agree with each other, simply repeat others' output) while expressing cohesion (rewording and acknowledging each other) and planning their current activities. They were also likely to mention much new content in the VR video (node content-based) without involving explanations or justifications at the same time. These connections represent a relatively superficial level of knowledge co-construction in which students mainly mention new knowledge and make declaratory comments without critical or in-depth elaboration or negotiation.

Some different co-occurrence patterns were identified in the H groups (see green connections). The declaratory comment played an important role in the higher-performing groups' network, similar to that in the lower-performing groups, but it connected with many different interaction forms: clarifying questions, new questions, and evaluating group work. These connections indicate that when students made declaratory comments (agree with each other or repeat each other's ideas), they tended to ask new questions, seek clarifications from each other, and reflectively self-evaluate their learning progress. Another node standing out in the higher-performing groups' network is technological issues, indicating that students were involved in many discussions about the technological affordances, functions, or difficulties in the VR video learning environments. In summary, both H and L groups consistently made declaratory comments during their collaborative VR video learning. The H groups engaged in more question-asking-answering and evaluative discourses while making declaratory comments than the L groups. The L groups, in comparison, tended to mention new content, express cohesion, and plan their activities without further elaborations or justifications.

**Note Taking and View Similarities (RQ2).** System log data captured note-taking actions and headset view overlaps during the video session, revealing different strategies between H and L groups (Fig. 3 left). Descriptively, H groups produced more text notes ($M = 3.11 \pm 1.07$) than L groups ($M = 1.33 \pm 2.03$), suggesting a stronger preference for precise, retrievable information capture. In contrast, L groups generated higher counts of screenshots ($M = 17.56 \pm 1.71$ vs. $12.78 \pm 2.99$) and drawing annotations ($M = 19.67 \pm 17.04$ vs. $12.22 \pm 10.77$). L groups also spent a larger proportion of task time in shared viewing (view similarity: $M = 0.404 \pm 0.068$) than H groups ($M = 0.228 \pm 0.088$), indicating greater reliance on synchronous navigation to maintain alignment. Taken together with the interview data, these patterns suggest that H groups more often used notes to support selective synthesis, whereas L groups more often combined multimodal note-taking with shared viewing to stay coordinated during the task.

**Collaborative Experiences, Satisfaction and Social Presence (RQ3).** Descriptively, the post-session questionnaires pointed to a similar contrast between the two performance levels. L groups reported slightly higher scores for collaborative experiences ($M = 3.67 \pm 0.47$ vs. $3.39 \pm 0.45$), satisfaction ($M = 3.61 \pm 0.61$ vs. $3.34 \pm 0.41$), and social presence ($M = 3.33 \pm 0.62$ vs. $2.96 \pm 0.46$). Despite their lower visitor-map quality, L participants consistently described feeling "more together" and valued the shared-view features that enabled constant coordination. In contrast, H groups intentionally limited synchronous controls to pursue independent observations, trading higher analytic depth for lower perceived social connection. This pattern may reflect a trade-off between social engagement and cognitive elaboration: stronger feelings of presence and satisfaction did not necessarily translate into higher task performance.

### 3.3 Qualitative Results

We conducted a thematic analysis and identified three themes that distinguished H and L groups in their user experiences (RQ3).

**Theme 1: H Groups Relied More on Text Notes, Whereas L Groups Used Drawing More Often.** While all participants recognized the value of note-taking tools, distinct usage patterns emerged between the groups. H groups frequently preferred text-based notes, avoiding drawing tools primarily due to usability issues. Participant 18A explicitly mentioned, "I definitely didn't use the drawing one." while Participant 13A focused on textual narratives, noting "I was like, kind of focusing on the narrative. " Conversely, L groups used drawing tools more frequently, often driven by enjoyment rather than effectiveness. Participant 8C stated, "Drawing something was very fun. The only complaint I have about that was because it was my first time using Like, drawing this way, I wasn't able to draw that well. So a lot of my handwriting turned to chicken scratch. " and Participant 8A remarked, "I think I just like to draw on the screen to take notes." This preference was corroborated by log data, reflecting higher drawing usage among low-scoring groups.

**Theme 2: L Groups Relied More on Shared Viewpoints, While H Groups Explored More Independently.** H groups showed a clearer preference for independent exploration, often perceiving synchronous viewing features such as shared timelines and view boxes as distracting or limiting. Participant 20C described the view box as "a little distracting" and suggested that discussion was more useful after the video than during note-taking. Participant 18C similarly noted that repeated backtracking made it hard to finish on time. To stay efficient, H groups tended to limit synchronous navigation and focus more on individual exploration. In contrast, L groups relied more on shared viewpoints even when they found shared control difficult. Participant 8C noted problems with "the person who kept restarting," yet these groups still used synchronous viewing frequently. Participant 8B explained this preference by saying, "I follow their view box to see what they're looking at," highlighting the value of staying synchronized. However, L groups often assumed teammates could infer their progress rather than actively communicating or integrating perspectives.

**Theme 3: H Groups Used Screenshots More Strategically, Whereas L Groups Treated Duplication as Acceptable.** H groups more actively reviewed and integrated others' screenshots to identify gaps and support discussion. Participant 20A described checking peers' captures to see whether they had "added details," while Participant 20B explained that looking at others' progress helped them decide "what areas that I should be focusing on." These groups used screenshots strategically to consolidate information and support synthesis. In contrast, L groups rarely reviewed peers' screenshots closely. Participant 8C admitted, "I don't think I paid much attention to the screenshots," and also described duplication as useful for "mak[ing] sure" shared observations were captured. Despite taking many screenshots, L groups often had difficulty recalling video details during discussion, which appeared to weaken discussion quality. While familiarity sometimes made communication feel easier, this comfort did not necessarily lead to more structured or in-depth analysis.

# 4 Discussion

This study addressed the three RQs by comparing H and L groups in collaborative VR video-based learning. For RQ1, our exploratory analysis suggested that H groups engaged in more elaborative interaction, whereas L groups more often remained at the level of content sharing and coordination. For RQ2, H groups used notes and screenshots more strategically and relied less on synchronous viewing, while L groups showed heavier use of screenshots and drawings together with higher view similarity. For RQ3, L groups reported more positive collaborative experiences, satisfaction, and social presence despite producing lower-quality visitor maps.

## 4.1 Interpreting the Mismatch Between Perceived Collaboration and Group Performance

Our findings extend prior work showing that H groups are more likely to engage in questioning, elaboration, and evaluation, whereas L groups often remain at the level of surface coordination or limited knowledge building [1,22,31]. In our study, this distinction also appeared in collaborative VR-VBL. H groups were more likely to connect declaratory comments with questioning and evaluation, while L groups more often paired content sharing with cohesion and activity planning. This suggests that the critical difference was not simply the amount of interaction, but whether interaction was used to deepen and refine understanding.

A possible explanation is that immersive awareness features supported the feeling of doing the task together without necessarily supporting deeper processing of the content. In our data, L groups relied more heavily on synchronous viewing and shared viewpoints, which appeared to strengthen alignment and togetherness, but also reduced opportunities for independent exploration and later integration. In contrast, H groups often limited synchronous viewing in order to inspect content more selectively and efficiently. This finding both aligns with and complicates prior work. Existing studies suggest that awareness cues and shared visual focus can support coordination in collaborative learning [5,15,27,30]. In this study, these benefits did not appear to translate directly into stronger group outcomes. Instead, social presence and coordination may sometimes coexist with relatively shallow knowledge construction. This interpretation is also consistent with prior work showing that immersive VR can increase presence and engagement without always improving learning [12,18,23]. Another possible explanation is that 360° VR environments place additional cognitive demands on learners, who must process rich visual scenes while also monitoring teammates' actions and presence [26]. Under such conditions, features that strengthen awareness may also compete with deeper analysis.

The same contrast appeared in note-taking and artifact use. H groups relied more on text notes and reviewed peers' screenshots more strategically, using shared materials to identify missing information and support synthesis. In contrast, L groups captured more screenshots, used drawing tools more often, and showed greater tolerance for redundancy. These patterns align with prior work suggesting that stronger groups use external artifacts in more organized and integrative ways [8]. At the same time, our results indicate that some VR note-taking affordances, particularly drawing, may encourage engagement without necessarily supporting clearer or more analytic collaboration. Prior work often links multimodal note-taking to stronger recall and engagement [7,9,10]. In our study, however, heavier use of drawings and screenshots was more characteristic of L groups. This suggests that the value of note-taking features depends not only on modality, but also on whether the tool supports precise, shareable, and discussion-ready representations. In this setting, drawing often appeared to function more as an enjoyable or low-precision activity than as a tool for elaboration.

### 4.2 Implications for Collaborative VR Learning Design and Pedagogy

These findings have implications for both pedagogy and system design. From an instructional perspective, simply placing learners in a shared VR environment is unlikely to be sufficient. Teachers may need to scaffold how groups interpret, compare, and justify what they observe. For example, groups could be assigned complementary observation roles, prompted to explain why a captured detail matters, or encouraged to pause shared viewing and shift into joint interpretation. Our results also suggest that awareness support should not be treated as uniformly beneficial. Groups that struggle with coordination may benefit from stronger synchronous support, whereas groups ready for deeper analysis may benefit from more room for independent exploration before regrouping.

From a system design perspective, the results highlight two priorities. First, awareness features should be adjustable rather than fixed. Shared viewpoints, cursors, and similar cues can support alignment, but may also constrain information seeking and interpretation. Systems should therefore allow groups or instructors to tune these features based on task demands and collaboration needs. Second, shared artifact tools should better support purposeful use. Because L groups often accumulated screenshots without integrating them, systems could support comparison, deduplication, and organization of captured materials. Improving drawing usability may also help. Greater precision, shape support, and clearer feedback [2,24] may make drawing more useful as a representational aid rather than only an engaging activity.

### 4.3 Limitations and Future Work

This study has several limitations that define the scope of our claims and suggest directions for future work. First, although the three VR city-tour videos were selected to be comparable in length, narration style, and overall difficulty, unavoidable differences in location and narrative may still have influenced group interaction and artifact quality. Second, this analysis focused on one condition within a broader study, so order or carryover effects may have shaped how participants engaged with the task and used the available tools. Third, because groups were assigned different videos, we cannot fully separate interaction effects from content effects. In addition, we only compared the three H and three L groups, so we report all results descriptively as an exploratory step. Future work should examine these patterns with larger samples, more controlled comparisons, and a wider range of collaborative tasks, and could further strengthen the analysis through methods such as automated discourse analysis or experimental manipulation of interface features.

## 5 Conclusion

This study explored differences between H and L groups in collaborative VR video-based learning. H groups tended to show more questioning and evaluative interaction, to use notes and screenshots more strategically, and to rely less on synchronous viewing. L groups tended to focus more on coordination, to use more screenshots and drawings, and to report higher social presence and satisfaction despite producing lower-quality group outcomes. These findings suggest that feeling more connected in collaborative VR does not necessarily align with deeper collaborative processing or stronger outcomes. Instead, performance differences appeared to depend not just on how much groups interacted, but on how they used interaction, shared attention, and external artifacts to interpret and organize information. As an exploratory analysis, this study offers an initial account of how these factors may relate to group performance in collaborative VR video-based learning, and future work should test these relationships with larger samples, more controlled designs, and a wider range of tasks.

## References

1. Chandler, C., et al.: Computational modeling of collaborative discourse to enable feedback and reflection in middle school classrooms. In: Proceedings of the 14th Learning Analytics and Knowledge Conference, pp. 576–586 (2024)
2. Chen, C., Yarmand, M., Xu, Z., Singh, V., Zhang, Y., Weibel, N.: Investigating input modality and task geometry on precision-first 3D drawing in virtual reality. In: 2022 IEEE International Symposium on Mixed and Augmented Reality (ISMAR), pp. 384–393. IEEE (2022)
3. Cordeil, M., Dwyer, T., Klein, K., Laha, B., Marriott, K., Thomas, B.H.: Immersive collaborative analysis of network connectivity: cave-style or head-mounted display? IEEE Trans. Visual Comput. Graphics **23**(1), 441–450 (2016)
4. De Sousa, L.O., Hay, E.A., Liebenberg, D.: Teachers' understanding of the interconnectedness of soil and climate change when developing a systems thinking concept map for teaching and learning. Int. Res. Geogr. Environ. Educ. **28**(4), 324–342 (2019)
5. Diederich, M., Kang, J., Kim, T., Lindgren, R.: Developing an in-application shared view metric to capture collaborative learning in a multi-platform astronomy simulation. In: LAK21: 11th International Learning Analytics and Knowledge Conference, pp. 173–183 (2021)

6. Drey, T., et al.: Towards collaborative learning in virtual reality: a comparison of co-located symmetric and asymmetric pair-learning. In: Proceedings of the 2022 CHI Conference on Human Factors in Computing Systems, pp. 1–19 (2022)
7. Fan, J.E., Bainbridge, W.A., Chamberlain, R., Wammes, J.D.: Drawing as a versatile cognitive tool. Nature Rev. Psychol. **2**(9), 556–568 (2023)
8. Fanguy, M., Baldwin, M., Shmeleva, E., Lee, K., Costley, J.: How collaboration influences the effect of note-taking on writing performance and recall of contents. Interact. Learn. Environ. **31**(7), 4057–4071 (2023)
9. Hefter, M.H.: Note-taking fosters distance video learning: smartphones as risk and intellectual values as protective factors. Sci. Rep. **14**(1), 16962 (2024)
10. Hu, D., Lee, S.W.: Scrapbook: screenshot-based bookmarks for effective digital resource curation across applications. In: Proceedings of the 35th Annual ACM Symposium on User Interface Software and Technology, pp. 1–13 (2022)
11. Jin, Q., et al.: Collaborative online learning with VR video: roles of collaborative tools and shared video control. In: Proceedings of the 2023 CHI Conference on Human Factors in Computing Systems, pp. 1–18 (2023)
12. Jin, Q., Liu, Y., Yarosh, S., Han, B., Qian, F.: How will VR enter university classrooms? Multi-stakeholders investigation of VR in higher education. In: Proceedings of the 2022 CHI Conference on Human factors in Computing Systems, pp. 1–17 (2022)
13. Jin, Q., Liu, Y., Yuan, Y., Han, B., Qian, F., Yarosh, S.: Virtual reality, real pedagogy: a contextual inquiry of instructor practices with VR video. In: Proceedings of the 2024 CHI Conference on Human Factors in Computing Systems, pp. 1–21 (2024)
14. Jin, Q., Sodhi, I., Chen, A., Yarosh, S.: Interaction forms of collaborative VR video learning: an exploratory study. In: Proceedings of the 17th International Conference on Computer-Supported Collaborative Learning-CSCL 2024, pp. 91-98. International Society of the Learning Sciences (2024)
15. de Jong, S., et al.: Assessing cognitive and social awareness among group members in AI-assisted collaboration. In: Proceedings of the International Conference on Mobile and Ubiquitous Multimedia, pp. 338–350 (2024)
16. Kay, R.H.: Exploring the use of video podcasts in education: a comprehensive review of the literature. Comput. Hum. Behav. **28**(3), 820–831 (2012)
17. Kreijns, K., Kirschner, P.A., Jochems, W., Van Buuren, H.: Measuring perceived social presence in distributed learning groups. Educ. Inf. Technol. **16**(4), 365–381 (2011)
18. Makransky, G., Terkildsen, T.S., Mayer, R.E.: Adding immersive virtual reality to a science lab simulation causes more presence but less learning. Learn. Instr. **60**, 225–236 (2019)
19. Marquart, C.L., Hinojosa, C., Swiecki, Z., Eagan, B., Shaffer, D.W.: Epistemic network analysis (version 1.7. 0)[software]. Available from app. epistemicnetwork. org (2018)
20. Morgado, M., Botelho, J., Machado, V., Mendes, J.J., Adesope, O., Proença, L.: Video-based approaches in health education: a systematic review and meta-analysis. Sci. Rep. **14**(1), 23651 (2024)
21. Muller, M.: Curiosity, creativity, and surprise as analytic tools: grounded theory method. In: Ways of Knowing in HCI, pp. 25–48. Springer (2014)
22. Park, S., Nixon, N., D'Mello, S., Shariff, D., Choi, J.: Understanding collaborative learning processes and outcomes through student discourse dynamics. In: Proceedings of the 15th International Learning Analytics and Knowledge Conference, pp. 938–943 (2025)

23. Parong, J., Mayer, R.E.: Learning science in immersive virtual reality. J. Educ. Psychol. **110**(6), 785 (2018)
24. Richard, G., Pietrzak, T., Argelaguet, F., Lécuyer, A., Casiez, G.: Studying the role of haptic feedback on virtual embodiment in a drawing task. Front. Virtual Reality **1**, 573167 (2021)
25. Rosendahl, P., Wagner, I.: 360 videos in education-a systematic literature review on application areas and future potentials. Educ. Inf. Technol. **29**(2), 1319–1355 (2024)
26. Sari, R.C., Pranesti, A., Solikhatun, I., Nurbaiti, N., Yuniarti, N.: Cognitive overload in immersive virtual reality in education: more presence but less learnt? Educ. Inf. Technol. **29**(10), 12887–12909 (2024)
27. Schneider, B., Sung, G., Hassan, J., Bhinder, H.: What matters most for learning from online videos, seeing the instructor's face or gaze? Impact on instructor-student synchrony. In: Proceedings of the 15th International Conference on Computer-Supported Collaborative Learning-CSCL 2022, pp. 3–10. International Society of the Learning Sciences (2022)
28. So, H.J., Brush, T.A.: Student perceptions of collaborative learning, social presence and satisfaction in a blended learning environment: Relationships and critical factors. Comput. Educ. **51**(1), 318–336 (2008)
29. Terry, G., Hayfield, N., Clarke, V., Braun, V., et al.: Thematic analysis. The SAGE Handbook of Qualitative Research in Psychology **2**(17–37), 25 (2017)
30. Xu, S., Hu, D., Zhang, X.: PeerEdu: bootstrapping online learning behaviors via asynchronous area of interest sharing from peer gaze. In: Proceedings of the 2025 CHI Conference on Human Factors in Computing Systems, pp. 1–14 (2025)
31. Yin, S.X., Liu, Z., Goh, D.H.L., Quek, C.L., Chen, N.F.: Scaling up collaborative dialogue analysis: an AI-driven approach to understanding dialogue patterns in computational thinking education. In: Proceedings of the 15th International Learning Analytics and Knowledge Conference, pp. 47–57 (2025)
32. Zhang, F., Possaghi, I., Sharma, K., Papavlasopoulou, S.: High-performing groups during children's collaborative coding activities: what can multimodal data tell us? In: Proceedings of the 23rd Annual ACM Interaction Design and Children Conference, pp. 533–559 (2024)
33. Zheng, L., Niu, J., Zhong, L., Gyasi, J.F.: Knowledge-building and metacognition matter: detecting differences between high-and low-performance groups in computer-supported collaborative learning. Innov. Educ. Teach. Int. **60**(1), 48–58 (2023)

# Whom to Help Next? Teachers' Self-Reported Real-Time Decisions in Analytics-Informed Classrooms

Luisa Wellert[1](✉) and Vincent Aleven[2]

[1] University of Tübingen, Tübingen, Germany
LUISA.WELLERT@UNI-TUEBINGEN.DE
[2] Carnegie Mellon University, Pittsburgh, USA

**Abstract.** Classroom orchestration in tech-rich, authentic classrooms requires teachers to quickly scan their classrooms and make rapid prioritization decisions. Mixed-Reality (MR) learning analytics tools were developed to support teachers' real-time awareness of students' learning. However, when multiple students working with math learning software need help simultaneously, how teachers prioritize their instructional decisions remains a critical but underexplored question. In this mixed-methods online survey study, we investigated $N = 112$ mathematics teachers' prioritization strategies when receiving information about their students' cognitive and behavioral states through a wearable MR learning analytics tool. Participants completed 21 dilemma scenarios and three card-sorting tasks, indicating how they would prioritize whom to help when multiple students required help simultaneously. Participants also elaborated on their reasoning for their decisions. Results showed that teachers consistently prioritized students who were unproductively struggling or misusing the learning software, while students who were recently doing well were typically deprioritized. Spatial proximity and students' prior knowledge influenced those decisions. Through qualitative content analysis, we identified six heuristics that reflect teachers' trade-offs between immediate support, student engagement, and potential learning gaps, highlighting the balance of maintaining classroom flow while preventing students from falling behind. Our results contribute to a detailed understanding of teachers' decision-making, informed by analytics tools and influenced by real-world factors. They extend theory by highlighting the importance of teacher-AI synergy in classroom orchestration. We further derive practical implications for the design of human-centered learning analytics tools, moving them from awareness to real-time decision support, thereby facilitating high-quality instruction in heterogeneous classrooms.

**Keywords:** Mixed Reality · Classroom Orchestration · Adaptive Teaching

## 1 Introduction

Imagine a teacher standing in front of her classroom, facing a group of students who, at that very moment, display very different support needs. The students are engaged in individual problem-solving activities with learning software, an increasingly common


J. Weidlich et al. (Eds.): EC-TEL 2026, LNCS 16905, pp. 651–665, 2027.
https://doi.org/10.1007/978-3-032-37979-5_44

scenario in K-12 education. Within seconds, the teacher must decide whom to help, which difficulty requires immediate attention, and how to provide support without disrupting the overall classroom flow. These rapid prioritization decisions shape not only individual students' learning processes but also the dynamics of the entire classroom. Although such decisions must be made quickly, they require high precision, as student support and classroom management, alongside cognitive activation, constitute core dimensions of instructional quality [1–3].

Digital tools have the potential to support teachers in these complex situations by increasing the visibility of students' cognitive and behavioral states [4, 5]. Learning analytics dashboards, for example, can provide aggregated, real-time information about students' progress and engagement [4, 6, 7], but also demand cognitive resources from teachers, as dashboard information must be interpreted and integrated into ongoing classroom management under time pressure [5].

Recent research has begun to explore tools that embed learning analytics directly into teachers' field of action. For example, wearable systems such as mixed-reality (MR) glasses can provide spatially embedded, real-time information about students as teachers move through the classroom [5, 8, 9]. In a study of the Lumilo system, Holstein et al. [5] showed that providing teachers with real-time analytics through MR glasses helped them allocate their time more strategically towards students with lower prior knowledge. As a result, disparities in learning outcomes between students with lower and higher prior knowledge were significantly reduced [10]. Prior work also shows that teachers tend to assist students who display overt behaviors, such as idleness, while paying less attention to less visible cognitive needs, regardless of whether they are supported by learning analytics dashboards [11] or not [12]. However, little is known about which student indicators teachers prioritize when multiple students simultaneously need help, why they prioritize certain indicators over others, and how analytics-informed insights shape these decision-making processes [11].

We address this gap by systematically examining teachers' prioritization of whom to help when they are informed by learning analytics about students' behavioral and cognitive states. We investigate how teachers make help-prioritization decisions in challenging classroom situations (i.e., more than one student requires help) and how these decisions are shaped by tools that provide spatially embedded real-time learning analytics. Specifically, we analyze (1) teachers' real-time, analytics-informed help prioritization, (2) the role of behavioral versus cognitive indicators, (3) the influence of contextual factors, and (4) teachers' heuristics for classroom orchestration. We explicitly address the underlying rationale behind teachers' decisions. Based on these insights, we derive design implications for real-time learning analytics tools, so they can provide meaningful support for classroom decision-making and orchestration.

## 2 Theoretical Background

### 2.1 Classroom Orchestration and Teachers' Help Prioritization Decisions

High-quality teaching requires teachers to continuously balance multiple instructional demands. Core dimensions such as classroom management, student support, and cognitive activation must be enacted simultaneously and in real time [1, 2]. With the increasing integration of digital technologies and generative AI into classrooms, coordinating these dimensions has become more complex while simultaneously offering new opportunities for technology-supported teaching [5, 13–16]. This complexity has been conceptualized as classroom orchestration, which describes how teachers coordinate learning activities, tools, and social configurations in the classroom [16]. From this perspective, teaching can be understood as a routine process of goal-oriented, contextually embedded, and continuous real-time decision-making in which teachers allocate their limited resources across competing classroom demands [17].

A central challenge within this orchestration process is prioritizing student support when multiple students require help simultaneously. These decisions are often guided by observable indicators in the classroom [11], and we distinguish between behavioral indicators, reflecting visible student actions such as idleness or software misuse, and cognitive indicators, reflecting struggles with learning content that often remain hidden without additional analytics-based support. Research shows that highly visible behaviors tend to attract teachers' attention more readily than less observable cognitive struggles, both in lessons supported by analytics dashboards and in settings without such tools [11, 12]. These decisions are influenced by situational factors such as time pressure and overall classroom dynamics [18]. While previous studies focused on which indicators attract teachers' attention, it remains unclear how teachers make real-time prioritization decisions when multiple students simultaneously need help.

## 2.2 Learning Analytics as Decision Support for Classroom Orchestration

Learning analytics dashboards aim to support teachers in these prioritization processes by making students' learning and behavioral states more visible through aggregated real-time information [4, 7, 19]. By making otherwise unobservable aspects of students' cognitive and behavioral states visible, analytics can complement the cues perceived by teachers and support more informed instructional decisions [6].

Learning analytics tools introduce additional indicators that may shape teachers' support. For example, Knoop-van Campen et al. [20] show that the type of feedback teachers provide differs depending on whether it is initiated by humans (teachers or students) or suggested by a learning analytics dashboard. The study found that dashboard-prompted feedback includes both task- and process-level feedback and leads to a more balanced distribution of feedback across students with different ability levels. However, teachers' willingness to rely on dashboard recommendations was found to depend on situational factors such as time pressure and classroom dynamics [18].

At the same time, accessing dashboards requires teachers to divide their attention between interpreting analytics and interacting with students, potentially increasing orchestration load and complicating real-time decision-making [5, 16]. Co-design studies, therefore, emphasize simple, actionable indicators that align with teachers' established classroom scanning practices and support rapid prioritization without constraining professional autonomy [5]. Yet, it remains unclear how teachers actually integrate these analytics indicators into their usual real-time prioritization decisions.

## 2.3 Mixed Reality and Spatially Embedded Real-Time Analytics

Recent research has explored wearable MR systems that embed learning analytics directly into teachers' field of view, providing spatially contextualized, real-time indicators of students' cognitive and behavioral states [5, 8, 9]. One prominent example is Lumilo, a wearable real-time learning analytics tool designed for classroom settings where students work with learning software. Lumilo visualizes students' cognitive and behavioral states through spatial indicators that appear above students' heads, allowing teachers to access analytic information without shifting their attention away from the classroom [5, 11, 14, 21].

By integrating analytics into the spatial environment, MR systems allow teachers to move through the classroom while receiving real-time indicators aligned with students' physical locations. This approach can reduce attentional switching between students and external displays and support real-time orchestration [5].

At the same time, the continuous availability of multiple indicators may increase the need for prioritization, as teachers must decide which indicators to act upon when several students simultaneously require support. MR therefore changes the classroom's indicator ecology by introducing spatially embedded information about students' learning processes. How the availability of these spatially embedded indicators shapes teachers' prioritization heuristics, however, remains largely unexplored.

## 2.4 Research Gap and Present Study

Existing research shows that teachers' support allocation is shaped by indicator visibility and efficiency considerations, often leading to a prioritization of behaviorally salient students [11, 12]. Learning analytics can make cognitive processes more visible [4, 6], and MR technologies embed such information directly into the classroom environment [5, 11]. However, little is known about how teachers make prioritization decisions, when multiple students require help simultaneously, and how the decisions are shaped by the availability of spatially embedded real-time analytics indicators.

In particular, it remains unclear which types of indicators teachers prioritize, how spatial proximity interacts with analytics-based indicators, how students' prior knowledge (not captured in the indicators because known to the teacher) influences these decisions, and which heuristics guide support allocation under conditions of limited resources. To address this gap, we addressed the following research questions:

*RQ 1: What do teachers say about whom they prioritize to help next when analytics-based indicators suggest multiple students simultaneously need help, and what individual differences shape these prioritization choices?*

*RQ 2: Do behavioral versus cognitive indicators affect teachers' self-reported prioritization decisions in different ways?*

*RQ 3: What factors outside of the analytics (i.e., teachers' distance from the to-be-helped student and teachers' knowledge about their students' prior knowledge) do teachers report as influencing their prioritization?*

*RQ 4: What are teachers' self-reported prioritization heuristics and reasons behind them?*

## 3 Methods

### 3.1 Study Design and Participants

We conducted a mixed-methods study to investigate teachers' real-time, analytics-supported prioritization decisions in MR-augmented classrooms. Data were collected via an online survey combining dilemma scenarios with single-choice items, card-sorting tasks, and open-ended questions. All participants received the same survey.

Participants were mainly recruited via the online platform Prolific, with additional invitations sent to teachers at a U.S. middle school, who had previously used the MR-system Lumilo. The final sample comprised $N = 112$ mathematics teachers from U.S. schools. Most participants reported 1–5 years of teaching experience ($n = 62$), followed by more than 10 years ($n = 25$), 6–10 years ($n = 19$), and less than one year ($n = 6$). A total of $n = 96$ teachers indicated prior experience with math tutoring software. All participants were 18 years or older and located in the United States.

### 3.2 Measures

**Dilemma-Based Decisions.** Our survey included 21 dilemma scenarios in which participants (i.e., teachers) were asked whom they would help first *(RQ1)*. Each scenario depicted a seatmap of a classroom with 24 students (coded A-X) arranged in three rows (near, medium, far from the teacher). The teacher was positioned at the front of the room. Students' learning status in a mathematics learning software was displayed by means of five different icons, which had been identified as relevant for teacher prioritization in previous extensive design-based research: misusing the software, unproductively struggling, struggling, idle, and recently doing very well [5]. For the purposes of this study *(RQ2)*, we grouped these analytics-based indicators into two categories: behavioral indicators (misusing the software and being idle) and cognitive indicators (struggling, unproductively struggling, and recently doing very well). In each scenario, multiple students might potentially need teacher support and were marked with one of these indicators (see Fig. 1). For each scenario, participants chose one of the 24 students to receive help first. Following prior research [5], student status and spatial position were systematically varied across the dilemmas while the classroom layout remained constant.

First, we modeled scenarios in which each of the five indicators appeared once, while all students displaying indicators were seated at the same distance from the teacher (all near or all far). Next, for each indicator, we systematically varied spatial distance from the teacher to examine how proximity influences prioritization. We also included scenarios with indicator clusters, that is, situations in which more than one student displayed the same indicator within a scenario. This design reflects prior findings that multiple students showing the same indicator attract more teacher attention [11]. In addition, we created two scenarios that included only a single indicator type across all three seating rows: one with only idle students and one with only unproductively struggling students. These scenarios allowed us to isolate the role of spatial proximity for two particularly relevant indicators when no competing indicator types were present. We focused on these two indicators because prior research has shown that teachers often prioritize idle students due to their high visibility in the classroom, even though students who are unproductively struggling may have more urgent but less visible needs [11, 12]. Finally, we included one scenario in which unproductive struggling students were seated near peers who were doing well. This scenario reflected a common classroom dynamic in which students who are doing well may support struggling students, potentially affecting teachers' prioritization decisions [22].

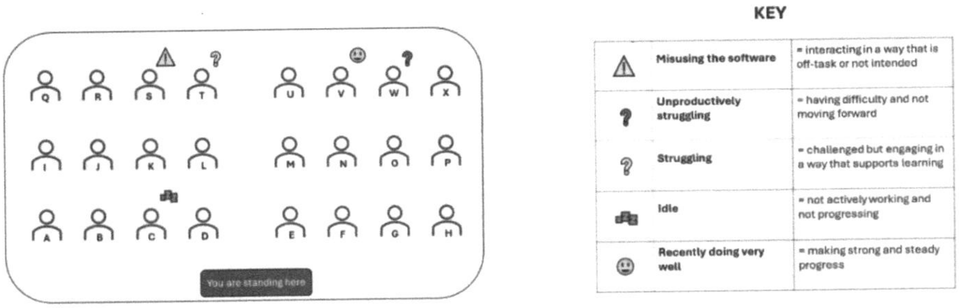


**Fig. 1.** Exemplary dilemma scenario with one idle student sitting in the front row and four students in the back row, showing indicators for misusing the software, struggling, recently doing very well, and unproductively struggling.

**Prioritization Decisions.** To further examine teachers' prioritization of help and how factors outside the analytics influence these decisions, we presented participants with three card-sorting tasks. In each task, participants were shown a set of cards and asked to sort them into the order in which they would provide help. The tasks differed in the information shown on the cards:

1. Analytics indicators (unproductive struggling, struggling, misusing the software, idle, doing very well) only (*RQ1*).
2. Analytics indicators and distance from the teacher (far vs. near, explicitly provided as part of the hypothetical scenario; *RQ3*).
3. Analytics indicators and students' prior knowledge (high vs. low, explicitly provided as part of the hypothetical scenario; *RQ3*).

The primary outcome measure was the priority rank assigned to each card (1 = highest priority). After each task, participants elaborated on their reasoning in open-text responses, providing qualitative data to explore self-reported prioritization heuristics and the factors influencing them (*RQ3, RQ4*).

### 3.3 Procedure

Participants accessed the online questionnaire on SoSci Survey (Version 3.8.00) via Prolific or via an email link, depending on the recruitment method. After providing informed consent and completing the demographic items, participants worked through the 21 dilemma scenarios presented in randomized order. For each scenario, they selected the student they would help first. Following the dilemma scenarios, participants completed the three card-sorting tasks and provided open-text explanations of their preferences. For all tasks, participants were instructed to imagine themselves standing at the front of the classroom, facing their students, and wearing MR glasses that displayed status indicators above some of the students' heads. The photos shown in Fig. 2 were presented to participants to help them better imagine the classroom situation. The survey was self-paced and took approximately 30–40 min to complete. Each participant received USD 15 as compensation for their time.

**Fig. 2.** Left: researcher wearing the Lumilo glasses. Right: student status indicators as seen through the Lumilo glasses [10].

### 3.4 Data Analysis

All quantitative and qualitative data and analysis scripts are publicly available on OSF: https://osf.io/rftud/overview?view_only=f05e6ca4af614f0595d7f4f67bcdf5e2

**Quantitative Analysis.** We analyzed participants' demographic and professional backgrounds descriptively to characterize the sample. To provide a descriptive overview of teachers' prioritization patterns, we calculated response frequencies and between-participant agreement ($\Sigma\, p^2$) for all 21 dilemma scenarios. This allowed us to examine which indicators participants most often prioritized and to visualize decision patterns. For analyses focusing on indicator-level prioritization, intraindividual stability, and teachers' experience (RQ1-RQ2), we restricted the dataset to the first nine dilemma scenarios, where each indicator appeared only once to ensure comparability.

To address *RQ1* we calculated response frequencies across all response options in the dilemma scenarios to determine which indicators participants prioritized first. We assessed between-participant consistency using the sum of squared response proportions ($\Sigma\, p^2$) for each dilemma. We calculated intraindividual stability as the maximum proportion of decisions allocated to a single indicator per participant, indicating consistency across scenarios. Teachers' experience level was examined by comparing relative frequencies of prioritized indicators across four experience groups (less than 1 year, 1–5 years, 6–10 years, more than 10 years). For *RQ2,* we compared the frequencies of behavioral and cognitive indicators across all 17 scenarios in which each indicator appeared at least once.

To complement these scenario-based analyses, we analyzed the three card-sorting tasks. We computed Kendall's coefficient of concordance ($W$) to assess overall agreement in indicator rankings across participants, and item-level absolute agreement ($\Sigma\ p^2$) to identify which indicators were most consistently prioritized.

To explore *RQ3*, we grouped students' seat positions into front, middle, and back rows. We then calculated response frequencies for each spatial group in the first nine dilemma scenarios. We conducted all analyses in R (version 4.5.1).

**Qualitative Analysis.** To address *RQ3* and *RQ4* we analyzed all open-text responses from the card-sorting tasks using verbal analysis [23]. We focused on teachers' explanations of their prioritization decisions. We conducted the coding at sentence level and developed categories iteratively following an inductive approach. The resulting categories captured factors that teachers reported influenced their prioritization (e.g., avoiding wasted learning time, preventing falling behind, influence of physical distance). For *RQ3*, we focused coding on mentions of factors outside the learning analytics indicators, such as teachers' physical distance from students or their knowledge of students' prior knowledge. To address RQ4, we aimed to capture teachers' reported prioritization heuristics and the reasons underlying these decisions. Two coders independently coded 20% of the dataset to assess reliability, achieving an agreement of $\kappa = .63$. The remaining data were coded by a single coder using the agreed-upon coding scheme. All qualitative analyses were conducted in MAXQDA (version 24.3.0).

# 4 Results

## 4.1 RQ1: Prioritization of which Student to Help Next

Frequency analyses revealed a consistent prioritization pattern across dilemmas. Unproductively struggling students and those misusing the software were most frequently selected as the first or second to receive help. See Table 1 for details.

This pattern was consistent across experience groups (<1 year to >10 years), with no systematic differences related to teaching experience. Mean intra-individual stability across teachers was .47 ($SD = .13$), indicating a moderate tendency to prioritize similar indicators across dilemmas, while still showing variation by scenario.

Absolute agreement across the 21 dilemma scenarios ranged from 0.21 (dilemma 16) to 0.40 (dilemma 20; scale: 0–1), reflecting that two randomly selected participants prioritize the same student (e.g., a value of 0.20 indicates a 20% chance that two teachers independently prioritize the same student). Scenario-specific chance agreement ranged from 0.17 to 0.33, depending on the number of indicators per scenario. This finding suggests that one-sixth to one-third of teacher pairs made the exact same decision in a given scenario. As expected, this number is lower than the agreement based solely on the indicators, but it is far above chance. Still, individual variation remained, including occasional prioritization of students not highlighted by indicators.

Absolute agreement on rankings in the three card-sorting tasks (i.e., agreement regarding the rank assigned to any status) was very low (Kendall's $W = 0.01$), indicating highly individualized rankings across participants. Frequency analyses showed that, although absolute agreement was generally low across most indicators (0.14–0.31),

**Table 1.** Response frequencies by indicator per dilemma (%)

| Dilemma | Misusing Software | Unprod. Struggling | Struggling | Idle | Doing Well |
|---|---|---|---|---|---|
| 1 | 29.5 | 40.2 | 13.4 | 11.6 | 0.9 |
| 2 | 43.8 | 35.7 | 7.1 | 6.2 | 1.8 |
| 3 | 33.0 | 44.6 | 7.1 | 8.9 | 1.8 |
| 4 | 41.1 | 34.8 | 5.4 | 12.5 | 2.7 |
| 5 | 23.2 | 49.1 | 11.6 | 9.8 | 1.8 |
| 6 | 26.8 | 49.1 | 7.1 | 9.8 | 1.8 |
| 7 | 31.2 | 34.8 | 21.4 | 6.2 | 0.9 |
| 8 | 32.1 | 28.6 | 8.9 | 25.9 | 0.9 |
| 9 | 57.1 | 21.4 | 4.5 | 7.1 | 0.9 |

*Note.* Percentages reflect the proportion of choices per dilemma. Only choices with assigned indicators are displayed in the table; therefore, the values do not sum to 100%.

participants consistently agreed on placing the card labeled "recently doing very well" last. Agreement scores for the indicator "recently doing very well" were 0.83 for Sorting Task 1 (indicators only), 0.61–0.65 for Sorting Task 2 (indicators combined with distance), and 0.43–0.53 for Sorting Task 3 (indicators combined with students' prior knowledge), suggesting that teachers generally did not consider students who are already doing well a priority when deciding whom to help next.

### 4.2 RQ2: Differences in Prioritization (Behavioral vs. Cognitive Indicators)

When comparing teachers' selections across behavioral (idle, misusing the software) and cognitive (struggling, unproductively struggling, recently doing very well) indicators in all 17 scenarios that included all indicators at least once, *unproductively struggling* students were most frequently prioritized (first in 9 scenarios, second in 8), followed closely by students *misusing the software* (first in 8 scenarios, second in 9). This suggests that teachers do not systematically differentiate between cognitive and behavioral indicators when deciding whom to help next. See Fig. 3 for an example.

### 4.3 RQ3: Influence of Context Factors (Distance and Prior Knowledge)

When examining choices across all selections, participants prioritized students in the front row most frequently (54%), followed by the back row (26%) and the middle row (20%). Across all selections, participants occasionally selected students without indicators, which did not provide information relevant for the decision. When restricting the analysis to students displaying indicators, participants showed a pronounced priority on front-row students (90%) over back-row students (10%).

Importantly, the distribution of indicators across scenarios was systematically balanced between front and back rows, suggesting that the observed preference for front-row students cannot be explained by differences in indicator placement alone. Although

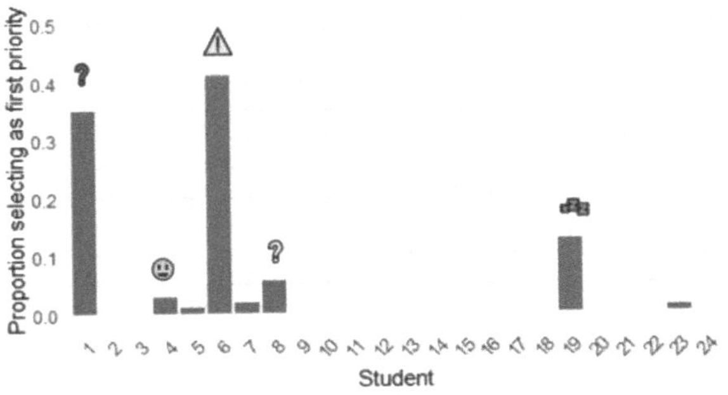


**Fig. 3.** Proportion of participants selecting each student as the first to receive help in an example scenario (Dilemma 4)

all 24 students were technically clickable, only those displaying indicators provided information relevant for the decision.

Open-text responses highlighted that teachers considered physical distance and students' prior knowledge, as provided in the hypothetical scenarios. For example, some teachers rank distant students lower because reaching them takes time (assuming that the teachers are initially standing at the front of the classroom), while others adjust prioritization based on their knowledge of students' learning history (e.g., "Prior knowledge matters because low knowledge students are less able to self-correct, while high knowledge students can often recover with minimal intervention").

## 4.4 RQ4: Teachers' Inferred Prioritization Heuristics and Reasons

We aggregated the reasons participants gave for their decision-making into heuristics that describe how teachers prioritize help in MR-augmented classrooms. These heuristics reflect recurring decision patterns and can co-occur within a single decision:

1. *Time matters:* Teachers ($n = 56$) reported that they prioritize students who are nearby or whose needs can be addressed quickly, such as idle students or those who can be nudged back on track. This reflects a time-efficiency heuristic when managing multiple help requests (e.g., "[…] far students are ranked lower because their distance means it will take longer to reach them.", ID01)
2. *Need over distance:* Teachers ($n = 70$) reported that spatial proximity can influence decisions of whom to help first, students' immediate cognitive needs take priority (e.g., "Students who are unproductively struggling are most urgent, with those nearby ranked slightly higher because I can help them immediately.", ID09).
3. *High knowledge, doing well, and struggling students wait longer:* Teachers ($n = 82$) reported that students capable of working independently are typically addressed later. Teachers frequently allow struggling students time for autonomous problem-solving, prioritizing them just before well-performing students, while assigning higher priority to students in more severe states of difficulty (e.g., "And struggling and recently doing very well rank low on my indicators […] because if they are struggling, they are engaged and working through it (as opposed to unproductively struggling) and if they are recently doing very well, then no assistance of mine is truly required")

4. *Maintaining classroom order:* Teachers ($n = 51$) reported that students misusing the software are addressed promptly to manage behavior and maintain classroom structure (e.g., "Students misusing the software come next because off-task behavior can quickly derail learning and affect the classroom environment if not addressed.", ID97).
5. *Preventing students from falling behind:* Teachers ($n = 81$) reported that they prioritize students who are at risk of falling behind in class to prevent long-term learning gaps. This indicated a concern with maintaining overall classroom flow (e.g., "[...] students who are struggling with low math knowledge were ranked the top of my list because they are more likely to fall behind in class.", ID48).
6. *Helping interested/engaged students first:* Some teachers ($n = 20$) reported prioritizing students they perceived as more interested or engaged. However, the provided indicators did not directly reflect students' interests or engagement; rather, teachers inferred these attributes from their own interpretations. For example, misusing the software was sometimes interpreted as a lack of interest. (e.g., "The mere effort they're making to grasp the learning material and understand the objectives makes them my first point of call.", ID71).

## 5 Discussion

In this study, we examined how teachers say they prioritize support when multiple students require help simultaneously while working with math learning software, and how analytics-informed insights might influence their decisions of whom to help next.

### 5.1 Prioritization Patterns and Indicator Relevance (RQ1 and RQ2)

Our quantitative results showed that teachers consistently, regardless of teaching experience, indicated they would prioritize students who misused the software or struggled unproductively. Students who were recently doing well were typically deprioritized because teachers say they assumed those students could continue working productively without immediate support. In open-text responses, teachers explained that they aim to maintain classroom flow by preventing off-task behavior while ensuring that students at risk of falling behind receive timely support. Notably, "misusing the software" was operationalized as interacting with the system in an off-task or unintended manner. Thus, teachers' prioritization of this indicator reflects their responses to deviations from the intended learning activity. Although the exact order in which students receive help can vary between teachers, overall prioritization heuristics were highly consistent, reflecting stable strategies for balancing behavioral and cognitive dimensions of instructional quality [1–3].

In contrast to earlier studies [11, 12], teachers in our study indicated that they would prioritize behavioral and cognitive indicators similarly. This may be because previous studies were not systematically designed to make all indicators equally visible in real time or to spatially embed them in the classroom. The imagined MR setup in our study allowed teachers to see cognitive and behavioral indicators simultaneously, and, for example, distinguish whether a student who was not working was simply idle or unproductively struggling. However, it should be noted that decisions were based on hypothetical scenarios rather than observed classroom behavior, which may have influenced how teachers reasoned about prioritization. Importantly, making cognitive difficulties visible did not shift teachers' attention away from maintaining classroom flow, instead, teachers said they aim to preserve behavioral and cognitive flow simultaneously. From a practical design perspective, our findings suggest that analytics-informed insights into students' cognitive and behavioral states can change teacher decision-making by making previously invisible indicators actionable in real time.

### 5.2 Integration of Context Factors Into the Decision Making (RQ3)

Our study shows that, as teachers move through the classroom, real-world factors, such as spatial proximity and students' prior knowledge, influence teachers' prioritization of help. Teachers say they typically address nearby students first due to natural movement patterns and efficiency considerations rather than perceived importance. They also mentioned in the open-ended responses that they generally deprioritize higher-knowledge students because they are more likely to resolve struggles independently. Overall, our findings indicate that teachers integrate analytics-informed insights with real-world factors when making in-the-moment prioritization decisions.

This interpretation also explains the apparent differences between the dilemma scenarios and the card-sorting tasks in our study. When required to select a single student to help next, teachers focused on the most urgent cases in the sense of the overall classroom flow, such as unproductive struggle or software misuse. However, when sequencing multiple interventions, teachers frequently described quickly nudging nearby students back on task as they moved toward more complex cases. These dynamic, movement-based prioritizations suggest that teachers adapt their decisions based on the classroom context rather than strictly following linear patterns.

In prior studies, teachers paid frequent attention to idle students [11, 12], likely reflecting these quick behavioral nudges rather than pedagogical priorities. Our results suggest that teachers address such low-effort interventions quickly on their way to help students who require more effortful support, reflecting teacher-AI synergy in analytics-informed and MR-supported classrooms.

### 5.3 Heuristics for Classroom Orchestration (RQ4)

Following teachers' elaborations on their prioritization decisions, they relied on shared heuristics balancing immediacy, risk, and engagement. The findings suggest that real-time learning analytics can meaningfully influence teachers' attention and prioritization while maintaining professional autonomy. By making previously invisible cognitive and behavioral indicators perceptible and actionable, analytics-informed indicators may change teachers' decision-making of whom to help next, enhancing support for students in heterogeneous classrooms. Designing tools that foster hybrid intelligence between teacher expertise and analytics insights is crucial for effective, high-quality instruction that balances classroom management with students' cognitive engagement [11, 16]. The identified heuristics also contribute to classroom orchestration theory by revealing how orchestration is enacted through real-time help prioritization under conditions of time pressure and contextual classroom constraints [16].

### 5.4 Limitations of the Study and Implications for Future Work

A key limitation of this self-report study is that participants were asked to imagine MR-augmented classrooms, yet only three teachers had prior experience with MR glasses. Consequently, the findings may be influenced by limited familiarity with the technology and challenges in accurately envisioning classroom dynamics. Nevertheless, the study provides important insights into teachers' prioritization patterns under conditions of equally visible cognitive and behavioral indicators, a condition that MR can uniquely support. Another limitation is that the study focused on learning with a mathematics learning software in secondary schools, which may limit the generalizability of the results to other subjects or educational levels. Future research could extend this work by investigating decision-making informed by analytics-based insights in real-world classrooms and across different subjects and grade levels.

Beyond these limitations, the findings carry broader implications for research, practice, and tool design. Grounding the design of analytics-informed insights in reasoning that resonates with teachers' professional judgment may support their interpretation and use in practice. Since teachers consistently prioritized unproductively struggling students and those misusing the software, MR displays should make these indicators particularly salient, for instance, through prominent visual alerts. In contrast, "recently doing very well" could be displayed less prominently to reduce cognitive load. The observed front-row bias, in which teachers prioritized front-row students substantially more often than back-row students, independent of their analytics indicators, further highlights a potential equity concern. Future studies should examine whether this bias replicates in teachers' actual behavior and how analytics-informed tools might help counteract such patterns. Finally, the prioritization heuristics identified in this study could serve as a basis for teacher professional development. Making these heuristics explicit may help teachers reflect on their decision-making. Future systems could additionally provide teachers with feedback on their own prioritization patterns to support reflection on their decision-making and deliberate adjustments in practice.

## 6 Conclusion

This study reveals that, even in complex classroom situations where multiple students simultaneously require help, teachers rely on consistent heuristics to prioritize support. These heuristics balance behavioral and cognitive indicators to maintain classroom flow and, if available, integrate analytics-informed indicators with contextual factors. From a theoretical perspective, these findings contribute to classroom orchestration research by illustrating how teachers enact decision-making through the integration of analytics-based information and real-time pedagogical judgment, reflecting teacher-AI synergy. From a practical and design perspective, our results highlight the potential of analytics-based MR tools to shift from supporting teachers' awareness toward real-time decision support. By making previously less visible indicators actionable, such tools can enhance instructional responsiveness and support high-quality instruction in heterogeneous classrooms.

## References

1. Klieme, E., Pauli, C., Reusser, K.: The Pythagoras study: investigating effects of teaching and learning in Swiss and German mathematics classrooms. In: Prenzel, M., Allolio-Näcke, L. (eds.) The Power of Video Studies in Investigating Teaching and Learning in the Classroom, pp. 137–160. Waxmann (2009)
2. Praetorius, A.-K., Klieme, E., Herbert, B., Pinger, P.: Generic dimensions of teaching quality: the german framework of three basic dimensions. ZDM. **50**, 407–426 (2018). https://doi.org/10.1007/s11858-018-0918-4
3. Seidel, T., Shavelson, R.J.: Teaching effectiveness research in the past decade: the role of theory and research design in disentangling meta-analysis results. Rev. Educ. Res. **77**, 454–499 (2007). https://doi.org/10.3102/0034654307310317
4. Aslan, S. et al.: Investigating the impact of a real-time, multimodal student engagement analytics technology in authentic classrooms. In: Proceedings of the 2019 CHI Conference on Human Factors in Computing Systems, pp. 1–12. Association for Computing Machinery (2019) https://doi.org/10.1145/3290605.3300534
5. Holstein, K., McLaren, B.M., Aleven, V.: Co-designing a real-time classroom orchestration tool to support teacher–AI complementarity. J. Learn. Anal. **6** (2019) https://doi.org/10.18608/jla.2019.62.3
6. Cukurova, M.: The interplay of learning, analytics and artificial intelligence in education: a vision for hybrid intelligence. Br. J. Educ. Technol. **56**, 469–488 (2025). https://doi.org/10.1111/bjet.13514
7. Lang, C., Siemens, G., Wise, A., Gasevic, D. (eds.): Handbook of learning analytics. Society for Learning Analytics Research (SoLAR) (2017). https://doi.org/10.18608/hla17
8. Chu, S.L., Garcia, B.M., Rani, N.: Research on wearable technologies for learning: a systematic review. Front. Educ. **8**, 1270389 (2023). https://doi.org/10.3389/feduc.2023.1270389
9. Hong, H., Dai, L., Zheng, X.: Advances in wearable sensors for learning analytics: trends, challenges, and prospects. Sensors. **25**, 2714 (2025). https://doi.org/10.3390/s25092714
10. Holstein, K., McLaren, B.M., Aleven, V.: Student learning benefits of a mixed-reality teacher awareness tool in AI-enhanced classrooms. In: Penstein Rosé, C., Martínez-Maldonado, R., Hoppe, H.U., Luckin, R., Mavrikis, M., Porayska-Pomsta, K., McLaren, B., Du Boulay, B. (eds.) Artificial Intelligence in Education, pp. 154–168. Springer International Publishing, Cham (2018). https://doi.org/10.1007/978-3-319-93843-1_12
11. Jin, Q., Borchers, C., Fancsali, S., Aleven, V.: Who to help? A time-slice analysis of K-12 teachers' decisions in classes with AI-supported tutoring. In: Conference on Educational Data Mining (2025)
12. Karumbaiah, S. et al.: A spatiotemporal analysis of teacher practices in supporting student learning and engagement in an AI-enabled classroom. In: Wang, N., Rebolledo-Mendez, G., Matsuda, N., Santos, O.C., Dimitrova, V. (eds.) Artificial Intelligence in Education, pp. 450–462. Springer Nature Switzerland, Cham (2023). https://doi.org/10.1007/978-3-031-36272-9_37
13. Alonso-Prieto, V., Dimitriadis, Y., Prieto, L.P., Zurita, G., Álvarez, C.: Towards capturing teacher agency manifestations within orchestration activities: a conceptual-analytical framework. In: Tammets, K., Sosnovsky, S., Ferreira Mello, R., Pishtari, G., Nazaretsky, T. (eds.) Two Decades of TEL. from Lessons Learnt to Challenges Ahead, pp. 107–112. Springer Nature, Switzerland, Cham (2026). https://doi.org/10.1007/978-3-032-03873-9_9

14. Holstein, K., Harpstead, E., Gulotta, R., Forlizzi, J.: Replay enactments: exploring possible futures through historical data. In: Proceedings of the 2020 ACM Designing Interactive Systems Conference, pp. 1607–1618. ACM, Eindhoven Netherlands (2020). https://doi.org/10.1145/3357236.3395427
15. Mishra, P., Warr, M., Islam, R.: TPACK in the age of ChatGPT and generative AI. J. Digit. Learn. Teach. Educ. **39**, 235–251 (2023). https://doi.org/10.1080/21532974.2023.2247480
16. Prieto, L.P., Dlab, M.H., Gutié, I., Rrez, N.A., Abdulwahed, M., Balid, W.: Orchestrating technology enhanced learning: a literature review and a conceptual framework. Int. J. Technol. Enhanced Learn. **3**, 583 (2011). https://doi.org/10.1504/IJTEL.2011.045449
17. Schoenfeld, A.H.: How We Think. Routledge (2010). https://doi.org/10.4324/9780203843000.
18. Van Leeuwen, A., Rummel, N.: The function of teacher dashboards depends on the amount of time pressure in the classroom situation: results from teacher interviews and an experimental study. Unterrichtswissenschaft. **50**, 561–588 (2022). https://doi.org/10.1007/s42010-022-00156-9
19. Xhakaj, F., Aleven, V., McLaren, B.M.: Effects of a teacher dashboard for an intelligent tutoring system on teacher knowledge, lesson planning, lessons and student learning. In: Lavoué, É., Drachsler, H., Verbert, K., Broisin, J., Pérez-Sanagustín, M. (eds.) Data Driven Approaches in Digital Education, pp. 315–329. Springer International Publishing, Cham (2017). https://doi.org/10.1007/978-3-319-66610-5_23
20. Knoop-van Campen, C.A.N., Wise, A., Molenaar, I.: The equalizing effect of teacher dashboards on feedback in K-12 classrooms. Interact. Learn. Environ. **31**, 3447–3463 (2023). https://doi.org/10.1080/10494820.2021.1931346
21. Holstein, K., Yu, Z., Sewall, J., Popescu, O., McLaren, B.M., Aleven, V.: Opening up an intelligent tutoring system development environment for extensible student modeling. In: Penstein Rosé, C., Martínez-Maldonado, R., Hoppe, H.U., Luckin, R., Mavrikis, M., Porayska-Pomsta, K., McLaren, B., du Boulay, B. (eds.) Artificial Intelligence in Education, pp. 169–183. Springer International Publishing, Cham (2018). https://doi.org/10.1007/978-3-319-93843-1_13
22. Yang, K.B. et al.: Exploring Policies for Dynamically Teaming up Students through Log Data Simulation. In, Proceedings of the International Conference on Educational Data Mining (2021)
23. Chi, M.T.H.: Quantifying qualitative analyses of verbal data: a practical guide. J. Learn. Sci. **6**(3), 271–315 (1997). https://doi.org/10.1207/s15327809jls0603_1

# Deep Learning Architectures for Predictive Tasks in Learning Analytics: A Systematic Mapping and Architectural Analysis

Alejandro Felipe Zárate Pérez[1,2](✉), Boris Escalante Ramírez[3], Idalia Flores de la Mota[3], and Jimena Olveres[3]

[1] Posgrado en Ciencia e Ingeniería de la Computación, Universidad Nacional Autónoma de México (UNAM), Mexico City, Mexico
alejandro.zarate@unam.mx

[2] Dirección General de Cómputo y de Tecnologías de Información y Comunicación (DGTIC), Universidad Nacional Autónoma de México (UNAM), Mexico City, Mexico

[3] Facultad de Ingeniería, Universidad Nacional Autónoma de México (UNAM), Mexico City, Mexico

**Abstract.** Learning Analytics (LA) and Educational Data Mining (EDM) have progressively incorporated deep learning techniques to address predictive tasks in digital educational environments, such as academic performance prediction and early detection of at-risk students. This study presents a systematic mapping of the literature on deep learning architectures applied to Learning Analytics and Educational Data Mining during the period 2015–2025. Following the PRISMA methodology, 33 empirical studies were identified and analyzed using an architectural taxonomy that considers aspects such as temporal modeling, data fusion strategies, modularity, and explainability. The results show a predominance of sequential architectures, particularly recurrent neural networks and attention-based models, while multimodal approaches, graph-based representations, and explicit interpretability mechanisms appear less frequently in literature. These findings reveal structural limitations in current predictive systems, which primarily capture observable behavioral patterns while overlooking social, collaborative, and contextual dimensions of learning. To address these identified research gaps, this paper conceptualizes a Multimodal Graph-Based Architecture with Explainability Modules. Integrating sequential, relational, and semantic components through attention-based fusion, the proposed approach captures the multidimensional nature of learning, cognitive, social, and behavioral, providing a conceptual foundation for more comprehensive, robust, and actionable educational decision-making systems.

**Keywords:** Learning Analytics · Deep Learning · Multimodal Learning · Graph Neural Networks · Explainable AI


J. Weidlich et al. (Eds.): EC-TEL 2026, LNCS 16905, pp. 666–680, 2027.
https://doi.org/10.1007/978-3-032-37979-5_45

## 1 Introduction

The increasing availability of educational data has driven the adoption of predictive models in Learning Analytics (LA) and Educational Data Mining (EDM), particularly for tasks such as student performance prediction, dropout detection, and knowledge tracing [4, 8]. In recent years, deep learning approaches have demonstrated strong capabilities in modeling complex and temporal patterns in educational data [6, 7].

Despite these advances, there is still a lack of structured understanding of how deep learning architectures are designed and applied in predictive tasks within LA. Limited attention has been given to architectural aspects such as temporal modeling, data fusion strategies, modularity, and explainability. To address this gap, this paper presents a systematic mapping study of deep learning architectures applied to predictive tasks in Learning Analytics and Educational Data Mining between 2015 and 2025. Following the PRISMA methodology [16], empirical studies are identified and analyzed to characterize architectural trends and identify current research limitations.

This work aims to characterize deep learning architectures used in predictive tasks within Learning Analytics, identify application trends, and uncover research gaps in the design of predictive systems.

The main contributions are threefold: (1) a systematic mapping of the literature on deep learning for predictive tasks in Learning Analytics; (2) a taxonomy of neural architectures considering temporal modeling, data fusion, modularity, and explainability; and (3) an analysis of research trends and gaps to guide the development of more robust and interpretable systems.

Accordingly, this study addresses the following research questions: (1) What types of deep learning architectures are used for predictive tasks in Learning Analytics? (2) How are the temporal dynamics of learning modeled? (3) What data integration strategies are employed? and (4) What architectural characteristics are present in terms of modularity and explainability?

## 2 Background and Related Work

Learning Analytics (LA) is defined as the measurement, collection, analysis, and reporting of data about learners and their contexts with the aim of understanding and optimizing learning processes [2, 4]. In parallel, Educational Data Mining (EDM) focuses on developing computational methods to discover patterns in large-scale educational data [9, 19, 21]. While both fields share similar goals, EDM has traditionally emphasized algorithmic development, whereas LA prioritizes the interpretation and application of insights to support educational decision-making [10].

Common applications include student performance prediction, dropout detection, early warning systems, and knowledge modeling, typically based on data from learning management systems and online platforms [8, 11, 12, 23, 24].

In recent years, deep learning has gained increasing attention in LA due to its ability to learn complex representations from large-scale educational data [23, 24]. Recurrent neural networks (RNN, LSTM, GRU) have been widely used to model temporal sequences of student interactions [20], while convolutional neural networks (CNN) have been applied to structured and multimodal data [22]. More recently, Transformer-based models have demonstrated strong performance in capturing long-term dependencies in learning sequences [18], and Graph Neural Networks (GNN) have been explored to model structural relationships between students, resources, and knowledge components [14].

Despite these advances, existing review studies have mainly focused on traditional machine learning approaches or specific applications such as performance prediction and dropout detection [8, 19, 21]. More recent works have highlighted the potential of deep learning in educational contexts [13, 24], but there is still a lack of systematic analyses that examine deep learning architectures from a structural and architectural perspective.

## 3 Methodology

This study follows a Systematic Mapping Study approach to identify and analyze research by applying deep learning architectures to predictive tasks in Learning Analytics and Educational Data Mining. To ensure transparency and reproducibility, the PRISMA (Preferred Reporting Items for Systematic Reviews and Meta-Analyses) framework was adopted [16], providing a structured process for identifying, screening, and selecting relevant studies.

The methodological process was organized into four main stages: search strategy, selection criteria, PRISMA-based filtering process, and data extraction.

### 3.1 Search Strategy

The literature search focused on studies published between 2015 and 2025, a period in which deep learning gained significant relevance in Learning Analytics. The search strategy combined three components: (i) Learning Analytics or Educational Data Mining, (ii) deep learning architectures, and (iii) predictive tasks.

A representative search string was defined as follows:

*("learning analytics" OR "educational data mining" OR "multimodal learning analytics") AND ("deep learning" OR "neural network" OR LSTM OR GRU OR CNN OR Transformer OR "graph neural network") AND (predict* OR "student performance" OR dropout OR "at-risk" OR engagement)*

The search was conducted across five major scientific databases: Scopus, Web of Science, IEEE Xplore, ACM Digital Library, and SpringerLink.

### 3.2 Inclusion and Exclusion Criteria

To ensure the relevance and quality of the selected studies, a set of inclusion and exclusion criteria was defined and applied during the filtering process.

**Inclusion Criteria.** Studies were included if they met the following conditions:

- The study is situated within the context of Learning Analytics or Educational Data Mining.

- The work employs deep learning architectures or neural networks.
- The study addresses predictive tasks related to learning (e.g., student performance, dropout, or engagement).
- The article describes model architecture or modeling pipeline.
- The study includes a quantitative evaluation of the proposed model.

**Exclusion Criteria.** Studies were excluded if they met any of the following conditions:

- The study is not related to Learning Analytics or Educational Data Mining.
- The work does not employ deep learning architectures.
- The study does not address predictive tasks.
- The study does not report experimental results or quantitative evaluation.
- The full text of the article is not available.

### 3.3 Study Selection Process

The study selection process was conducted following the phases defined in the PRISMA framework. Figure 1 summarizes the complete study selection process.

In the identification phase, a total of 215 potentially relevant records were retrieved through search queries. After removing 65 duplicate records, 150 unique studies remained.

During the screening phase, titles and abstracts were reviewed to assess their relevance according to the defined criteria, resulting in the exclusion of 85 studies.

In the eligibility phase, the full texts of the remaining articles were assessed for inclusion, leading to the exclusion of an additional 32 studies.

Finally, a total of 33 studies were included in the final corpus for analysis.

### 3.4 Data Extraction

To systematically analyze the selected studies, a structured data extraction process based on an analytical taxonomy was employed. Each article was reviewed and classified according to the educational problem addressed, the architectural characteristics of the proposed deep learning model, the data modeling strategy, and the evaluation approach. The extracted information was organized into a comparative analysis table using a pre-defined coding protocol. Extraction and classification were performed by the first author and subsequently reviewed by the co-authors, with any discrepancies resolved through discussion until consensus was reached.

**Definition of the Analysis Taxonomy**

To structure the analysis of the corpus, the selected studies were grouped according to the type of predictive task addressed. These categories were derived from the most recurrent themes in the Learning Analytics and Educational Data Mining literature (Romero & Ventura, 2010; Papamitsiou & Economides, 2014; Xiao, 2021).

The following categories were defined:

- **Knowledge Tracing.** Includes studies that model the evolution of students' knowledge over time, typically by predicting the probability of correctly answering future tasks. These approaches commonly rely on sequential interaction data and have been widely studied in Educational Data Mining [18, 20].
- **Dropout / Early Warning.** Encompasses studies aimed at identifying students at risk of dropping out or underperforming. These models typically analyze interaction patterns in educational platforms to generate early alerts [1, 5].
- **Performance Prediction.** Includes studies that predict overall academic performance, such as final grades or course completion. This is one of the most extensively studied problems in Learning Analytics and Educational Data Mining [8, 24].
- **NLP / Forum Prediction.** Covers studies that use textual data generated by students, such as forum posts or online discussions, to predict academic outcomes or engagement levels [11].
- **Multimodal Learning Analytics.** Refers to studies that integrate multiple sources of educational data, such as interaction logs, video, audio, or physiological signals, to obtain a more comprehensive view of the learning process [15].
- **Graph Neural Networks / Representation Learning.** Includes studies that model structural relationships in educational environments using graph-based representations, such as relationships between students, learning resources, or knowledge concepts [14].

This categorization enables the analysis of how different educational tasks influence the design of deep learning architectures.

**Architectural Analysis Variables**

In addition to the classification by predictive task, a set of variables was defined to analyze the architectural characteristics of the models. These variables constitute the taxonomy used for comparative analysis.

- **paper_id.** Identifier used to reference each study within the analysis table.
- **backbone.** Main neural architecture is employed in the model, such as RNN, CNN, Transformer, MLP, or Graph Neural Network.
- **temporal modeling.** Indicates whether the model incorporates mechanisms to capture temporal dependencies in the data.
- **data fusion.** Describes how the model integrates multiple sources of information or data modalities.
- **fusion level.** Specifies the stage at which data integration occurs within the model.
- **modularity.** Characterizes the architectural organization, distinguishing between monolithic, partially modular, and fully modular designs.
- **explainability.** Indicates whether the model includes mechanisms to support the interpretation of its predictions.

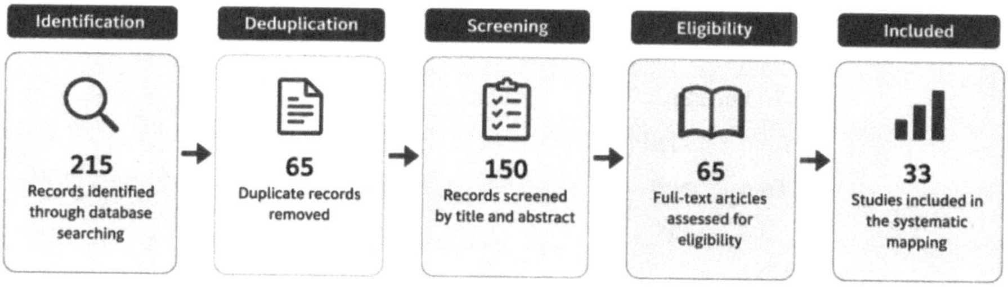


**Fig. 1.** PRISMA flow diagram

# 4 Results and Findings

The results are organized according to the four research questions defined in Sect. 1.

## 4.1 Overview of the Selected Studies

Following the PRISMA-based selection process, a total of 33 studies were included in the final corpus. These studies examine the application of deep learning architectures to predictive tasks within Learning Analytics (LA) and Educational Data Mining (EDM) over the period 2015–2025.

The identified studies cover a range of predictive tasks, including knowledge tracing, dropout prediction, performance prediction, text-based analysis, multimodal learning analytics, and graph-based modeling of educational relationships. Among these categories, knowledge tracing represents the largest proportion of the corpus, which is consistent with the strong alignment between this task and sequential modeling approaches in deep learning, particularly recurrent neural networks and attention-based architectures.

This distribution highlights the central role of sequential modeling in current predictive approaches within Learning Analytics, suggesting that most research conceptualizes learning as a temporal sequence of interactions rather than as a structured or multimodal process. As a result, alternative perspectives, such as relational or multimodal representations of learning, remain comparatively underexplored in literature.

## 4.2 Distribution of Neural Architectures (RQ1)

The analysis of the architectures used reveals a clear predominance of sequential models in the reviewed literature. Table 1 summarizes the distribution of neural architectures identified in the selected studies.

Overall, RNN-based and Transformer architectures account for 54.5% of the studies, indicating that most approaches model learning processes as temporal sequences of student interactions. This trend reflects a dominant paradigm in which learning is primarily conceptualized as a sequential and time-dependent process.

In contrast, Graph Neural Networks (GNNs) appear in a smaller portion of the literature (15.2%), suggesting that structural modeling of educational relationships, such as dependencies between concepts, activities, or learners, remains relatively underexplored. This imbalance indicates a potential limitation in current approaches, which tend to prioritize temporal dynamics over relational representations of learning.

**Table 1.** The distribution of neural architectures

| Architecture | Papers | Percentage |
|---|---|---|
| RNN / LSTM / GRU | 11 | 33.3% |
| Transformer | 7 | 21.2% |
| MLP / ANN | 5 | 15.2% |
| CNN | 4 | 12.1% |
| GNN | 5 | 15.2% |
| Hybrid architectures | 1 | 3.0% |

### 4.3 Temporal Modeling (RQ2)

Temporal modeling is a fundamental component in many predictive educational systems, particularly in tasks such as knowledge tracing and behavioral analysis in digital learning environments. Table 2 presents the distribution of studies according to the use of temporal modeling mechanisms.

**Table 2.** Distribution of temporal modeling in selected studies

| Temporal Modeling | Papers | Percentage |
|---|---|---|
| Yes | 21 | 63.6% |
| No | 12 | 36.4% |

Most studies explicitly incorporate the temporal dynamics of learning, typically through sequences of student interactions recorded in educational platforms. These approaches model learning as a sequence of student actions, such as problem-solving attempts, navigation through learning resources, or participation in online activities.

This prevalence reinforces the dominant reliance on sequential representations of learning processes, where temporal dependencies are treated as the primary source of predictive signal. However, the fact that over one-third of the studies do not incorporate temporal modeling suggests that a significant portion of the literature still relies on static or aggregated representations of student behavior, potentially overlooking the dynamic nature of learning.

### 4.4 Data Fusion Strategies (RQ3)

The integration of multiple data sources remains limited in the analyzed literature. In this study, early fusion refers to the integration of multiple data sources before feature extraction, late fusion combines the outputs of independent models at the decision level, and attention-based fusion dynamically assigns weights to different modalities according to their relevance for prediction. Table 3 summarizes the data fusion strategies adopted by the reviewed deep learning architectures.

**Table 3.** Data fusion strategies in deep learning architectures for learning analytics

| Data Fusion Strategy | Papers | Percentage |
|---|---|---|
| Single modality | 22 | 66.7% |
| Early fusion | 4 | 12.1% |
| Late fusion | 3 | 9.1% |
| Attention-based fusion | 4 | 12.1% |

Most studies rely on single data modality, typically interaction logs derived from Learning Management Systems (LMS) or intelligent tutoring systems.

Only a small number of works explore multimodal Learning Analytics, combining different sources of information such as behavioral logs, student-generated text, or signals from sensors and video data. This indicates that most current approaches operate under a limited view of the learning process, focusing on isolated data streams rather than integrating multiple dimensions of learner activity.

This imbalance suggests that multimodal data fusion remains an underdeveloped area, despite its potential to provide a more comprehensive and context-aware representation of learning processes. In particular, the low adoption of advanced fusion strategies, such as attention-based mechanisms, highlights an opportunity for developing models that can dynamically integrate heterogeneous data sources. This limitation may hinder the ability of predictive models to capture the full complexity of learning processes, which are inherently multimodal in nature.

## 4.5 Architectural Modularity (RQ4)

The organizational structure of neural architectures was also analyzed to assess the degree of modularity present in the models. Table 4 presents the degree of architectural modularity observed across the selected studies.

**Table 4.** Distribution of architectural modularity in deep learning models for LA

| Modularity | Papers | Percentage |
|---|---|---|
| Monolithic architectures | 23 | 69.7% |
| Partially modular architectures | 7 | 21.2% |
| Explicitly modular architectures | 3 | 9.1% |

The results show that most models adopt monolithic architecture, relying on a single neural network to process all available information without distinguishing between different educational subsystems.

Explicitly modular architecture remains relatively uncommon, despite their potential advantages. Modular designs can facilitate the integration of heterogeneous data sources and improve the interpretability of model behavior by separating distinct functional components.

This predominance of monolithic approaches suggests a limited exploration of architectural design principles in current research. As a result, opportunities to develop more flexible, extensible, and interpretable systems through modular design remain largely underexploited. This limitation may constrain the scalability and adaptability of predictive systems in complex educational environments.

### 4.6 Explainability (RQ4)

Explainability represents one of the main challenges in the application of deep learning to educational contexts. Table 5 summarizes the explainability mechanisms incorporated into the reviewed models.

**Table 5.** Distribution of explainability mechanisms in deep learning models for LA

| Explainability Type | Papers | Percentage |
|---|---|---|
| No explainability | 27 | 81.8% |
| Attention-based explainability | 5 | 15.2% |
| Post-hoc methods | 1 | 3.0% |

Most studies do not include explicit interpretability mechanisms, which may limit the adoption of these models in real educational settings, where transparency and trust are essential for instructors and decision-makers.

This lack of explainability highlights a critical gap between model performance and practical applicability. While deep learning models may achieve high predictive accuracy, their limited transparency can hinder their integration into educational decision-making processes, where understanding the rationale behind predictions is crucial. This suggests the need for the development of inherently interpretable or hybrid models that balance predictive performance with transparency.

### 4.7 Key Findings

The analysis reveals several important trends in the current literature:

1. **Dominance of sequential architectures.** A large proportion of the reviewed studies employ architectures designed to process sequential data, reflecting the temporal nature of many educational interactions captured in digital platforms. Recurrent models and attention-based architectures have become standard approaches for modeling the evolution of student knowledge and behavior over time, especially in tasks such as knowledge tracing [18, 20]. This trend reinforces a prevailing view of learning as a time-dependent process, often at the expense of alternative representations.

2. **Limited use of Graph Neural Networks.** Despite the inherently relational nature of educational environments, where interactions occur between students, content, concepts, and activities, the use of Graph Neural Networks remains relatively limited. This suggests that explicit modeling of complex educational structures is still an emerging research direction within Learning Analytics [14].
3. **Prevalence of monolithic architectures.** Most of the reviewed models rely on unified neural architectures that process all information within a single framework. While this simplifies model design, it may hinder interpretability and limit the integration of heterogeneous data sources within a coherent analytical structure.
4. **Low adoption of multimodal approaches.** Despite increasing interest in Multimodal Learning Analytics, most studies continue to rely on single data source, typically interaction logs from LMS platforms. This contrasts with the potential of integrating multiple signals, such as text, video, or sensor data, to achieve a more comprehensive understanding of learning processes [15]. This limitation suggests that current models may only capture a partial view of learner activity.
5. **Limited explainability.** Most studies focus on predictive performance, while mechanisms for interpreting model outputs receive comparatively little attention. This lack of explainability may hinder the adoption of deep learning-based systems in real educational settings, where transparency and trust are essential for instructors and institutional decision-makers [10].

Together, these findings point to structural limitations in current approaches, highlighting the need for more modular, multimodal, and interpretable architectures in Learning Analytics.

## 5 Research Gaps and Future Directions

The systematic mapping revealed limitations in current deep learning approaches for Learning Analytics, including limited multimodal data integration, scarce graph-based representations, monolithic architectures, and a lack of explainability mechanisms. To address these gaps, we outline a conceptual architectural approach to guide future research on predictive systems for Learning Analytics.

First, many approaches treat educational data as a homogeneous source processed by a single model, despite learning emerging from cognitive, behavioral, and social dimensions. These are reflected in diverse interactions such as platform activity, discussions, and peer communication. However, current architectures rarely distinguish these components explicitly, limiting their ability to capture the multidimensional nature of learning. This highlights the need for modular architectures that model different aspects of the educational process [10].

Second, most predictive models rely primarily on behavioral data (e.g., clicks, logs, submissions), providing only a partial view of learning. Social and discursive interactions, such as forum participation, offer meaningful insights into engagement and outcomes but remain underutilized in predictive architectures [11].

Third, the potential of multimodal learning analytics remains underexplored. Digital environments generate heterogeneous data (e.g., text, interaction logs, behavioral patterns), whose integration could enable richer representations of learning contexts and improve predictive performance [15].

Finally, interpretability remains a major challenge. Many models prioritize performance without explaining their predictions. In educational contexts, however, systems must support pedagogical decision-making, requiring models that clarify how behavioral, social, and contextual factors influence outcomes [25].

Taking together, these observations suggest that future research should move toward approaches that integrate multiple perspectives of the learning process. Combining behavioral, social, and discursive data may lead to more comprehensive and interpretable Learning Analytics systems.

Specifically, a Multimodal Graph-Based Architecture with Explainability Modules is proposed, structured into three components. First, a modular design incorporates specialized input branches: a sequential branch (Transformer-based) for temporal interaction patterns [18, 20], a relational branch (GNN-based) for modeling relationships between students, concepts, and social interactions [14], and a semantic branch (NLP-based) for analyzing discourse and inferring affective and cognitive states. Second, an attention-based fusion layer integrates these modalities by assigning adaptive weights to each data source, enabling context-aware predictions and mitigating sparse or missing data [15]. Finally, an explainability engine provides both predictive outputs and interpretable explanations (e.g., SHAP, LIME, or attention-based visualizations), supporting actionable insights for educators [25] (see Fig. 2).

Fig. 2 illustrates the conceptual architecture derived from the research gaps identified in the systematic mapping.

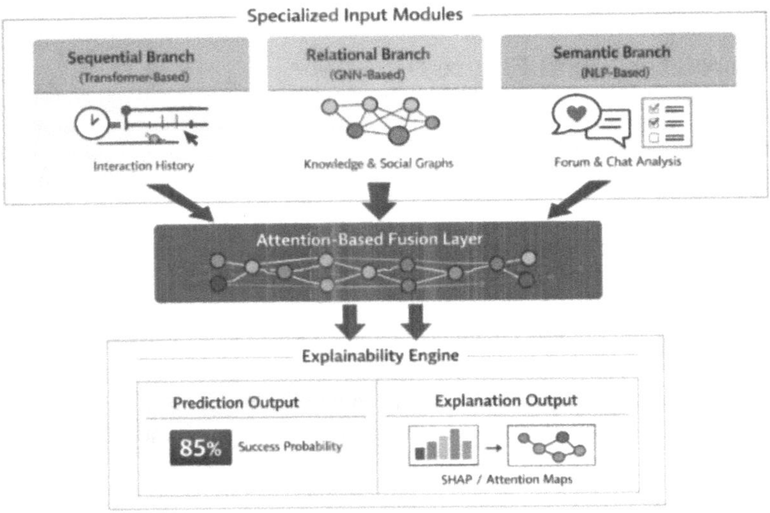


**Fig. 2.** Multimodal graph-based architecture with explainability modules

Overall, the proposed architecture captures the multidimensional nature of learning, cognitive, social, and behavioral, while improving robustness and interpretability. Although conceptual, it provides a foundation for future empirical validation.

## 6 Conclusions

This paper presented a Systematic Mapping Study on the use of deep learning architectures for predictive tasks in Learning Analytics between 2015 and 2025. Following the PRISMA framework, 33 empirical studies were analyzed using a taxonomy that considers architectural design, temporal modeling, data fusion strategies, modularity, and explainability.

The results reveal a clear predominance of sequential architectures, particularly recurrent and attention-based models, reflecting a dominant view of learning as a time-dependent process derived from interaction sequences. However, the analysis also identifies key structural limitations, including the limited adoption of graph-based approaches, the underutilization of multimodal data integration, and the lack of interpretability mechanisms.

These findings indicate that current approaches primarily capture observable behavioral patterns while overlooking social, collaborative, and contextual dimensions of learning. Addressing these limitations requires moving beyond monolithic and unimodal models toward architectures capable of representing the multidimensional nature of learning processes.

In response to these gaps, this work outlines a multimodal, modular, and explainable architectural direction, integrating sequential, relational, and semantic components through attention-based fusion and transparent output mechanisms. This approach provides a conceptual foundation for more comprehensive and actionable Learning Analytics systems.

Future research should focus on the empirical validation and implementation of such architectures, particularly in real-world educational settings. Advancing in this direction may not only improve predictive performance but also enhance interpretability and support informed pedagogical decision-making.

**Acknowledgments.** The authors acknowledge the support of the UNAM PAPIIT grants IN108624 and IT101624.

## Appendix - Extraction Tables

| ID | Study | Year | Venue |
|---|---|---|---|
| S1 | Piech et al. – Deep Knowledge Tracing | 2015 | NeurIPS |
| S2 | Fei & Yeung – Temporal Models for Predicting MOOC Dropout | 2015 | AAAI |
| S3 | Worsley & Blikstein – Multimodal Learning Analytics | 2015 | Journal of Learning Analytics |
| S4 | Joksimović et al. – Social Presence in Online Discussions | 2015 | Journal of Computer Assisted Learning |

(*continued*)

(*continued*)

| ID | Study | Year | Venue |
|---|---|---|---|
| S5 | Ochoa & Worsley – Augmenting Learning Analytics with Multimodal Data | 2016 | Journal of Learning Analytics |
| S6 | Bosch et al. – Detection of Learning-Centered Affective States | 2016 | ITS Conference |
| S7 | Gašević et al. – Learning Analytics Should Support Learning Design | 2016 | Journal of Learning Analytics |
| S8 | Whitehill et al. – Delving Deeper into MOOC Dropout Prediction | 2017 | LAK |
| S9 | Okubo et al. – Neural Network Approach for Predicting Student Performance | 2017 | LAK |
| S10 | Zhang et al. – Dynamic Key-Value Memory Networks for Knowledge Tracing | 2017 | WWW |
| S11 | Minn et al. – Deep Knowledge Tracing and Dynamic Student Modeling | 2018 | AIED |
| S12 | Okur et al. – Multimodal Approaches for Modeling Student Engagement | 2018 | EDM |
| S13 | Zhang & Rangwala – Deep Learning for Modeling Educational Processes | 2018 | EDM |
| S14 | Liu et al. – Neural Knowledge Tracing Machines | 2018 | AAAI |
| S15 | Pandey & Karypis – Self-Attentive Knowledge Tracing | 2019 | EDM |
| S16 | Nakagawa et al. – Graph-based Knowledge Tracing | 2019 | Web Intelligence |
| S17 | Xing & Du – Dropout Prediction in MOOCs Using Deep Learning | 2019 | EDM |
| S18 | Hernández-Blanco et al. – Deep Learning Approaches to Educational Data Mining | 2019 | IEEE Access |
| S19 | Tang et al. – Modeling Student Learning with Neural Networks | 2019 | EDM |
| S20 | Liu et al. – EKT: Exercise-Aware Knowledge Tracing | 2019 | AAAI |
| S21 | Choi et al. – SAINT: Self-Attentive Knowledge Tracing | 2020 | AIED |
| S22 | Tong et al. – Relation-Aware Knowledge Tracing | 2020 | CIKM |

(*continued*)

(*continued*)

| ID | Study | Year | Venue |
|---|---|---|---|
| S23 | Liu et al. – Deep Learning for Student Performance in Intelligent Tutoring Systems | 2020 | EDM |
| S24 | Ghosh et al. – Context-Aware Attentive Knowledge Tracing | 2020 | KDD |
| S25 | Veluri et al. – Deep Learning for Student Performance Prediction | 2021 | Materials Today Proceedings |
| S26 | Yang et al. – Transformer-based Knowledge Tracing | 2021 | EDM |
| S27 | Shen et al. – Graph Neural Networks for Student Representation Learning | 2021 | EDM |
| S28 | Wang & Pardos – BERT-based Student Performance Prediction | 2021 | EDM |
| S29 | Abdelrahman et al. – Graph-based Deep Learning for Educational Data Mining | 2021 | EDM |
| S30 | Liu et al. – Learning Process-Consistent Knowledge Tracing | 2021 | AAAI |
| S31 | Wang & Liu – Relation-Aware Graph Neural Networks for Knowledge Tracing | 2022 | AAAI |
| S32 | Li et al. – A multimodal deep learning framework for student engagement prediction | 2023 | IEEE Transactions on Learning Technologies |
| S33 | Wang et al. – A knowledge tracing approach with dual graph convolutional networks | 2025 | Computers & Education |

## References


1. Arnold, K.E., Pistilli, M.D.: Course signals at Purdue: using learning analytics to increase student success. In: Proceedings of the 2nd International Conference on Learning Analytics and Knowledge, pp. 267–270. ACM (2012)
2. Ferguson, R.: The State of Learning Analytics in 2012: a Review and Future Challenges. The Open University, Knowledge Media Institute (2012)
3. Siemens, G.: Learning analytics: the emergence of a discipline. Am. Behav. Sci. **57**(10), 1380–1400 (2013)
4. Siemens, G., Long, P.: Penetrating the fog: analytics in learning and education. EDUCAUSE Rev. **46**(5), 30–32 (2011)
5. Oliveira, C.F., Sobral, S.R., Ferreira, M.J., Moreira, F.: How does learning analytics contribute to prevent students' dropout in higher education: a systematic literature review. Big Data Cogn. Comput. **5**(4), 64 (2021)

6. Jamila, M., Lenar, G., Rustam, V., Mahyoub, M.: The application of artificial neural networks in learning analytics. In: 13th International Conference on Developments in eSystems Engineering (DeSE), pp. 1–6. IEEE (2020)
7. Borhani, A., Wong, R.T.K.: An artificial neural network for exploring the relationship between learning activities and students' performance. Decis. Anal. J. **9**, 100332 (2023)
8. Avella, J.T., Kebritchi, M., Nunn, S.G., Kanai, T.: Learning analytics methods, benefits, and challenges in higher education: a systematic literature review. Online Learn. **20**(2), 13–29 (2016)
9. Baker, R.S., Yacef, K.: The state of educational data mining in 2009: a review and future visions. J. Educ. Data Min. **1**(1), 3–17 (2009)
10. Gašević, D., Dawson, S., Siemens, G.: Let's not forget: learning analytics are about learning. TechTrends. **59**(1), 64–71 (2015)
11. Joksimović, S., Gašević, D., Kovanović, V., Riecke, B.E., Hatala, M.: Social presence in online discussions as a process predictor of academic performance. J. Comput. Assist. Learn. **31**(6), 638–654 (2015)
12. Khalil, M., Ebner, M.: What is learning analytics about? A survey of different methods used in 2013–2015. J. Learn. Analytics. **3**(2), 30–56 (2016)
13. Li, K.C., Wong, B.T.M., Liu, M.: A survey on predicting at-risk students through learning analytics. Int. J. Innov. Learn. **36**(5), 1–15 (2024)
14. Nakagawa, H., Iwasawa, Y., Matsuo, Y.: Graph-Based Knowledge Tracing: Modeling Student Proficiency Using Graph Neural Networks. In, IEEE/WIC/ACM International Conference on Web Intelligence (2019)
15. Ochoa, X., Worsley, M.: Augmenting learning analytics with multimodal sensory data. J. Learn. Analytics. **3**(2), 213–219 (2016)
16. Page, M.J., McKenzie, J.E., Bossuyt, P.M., et al.: The PRISMA 2020 statement: an updated guideline for reporting systematic reviews. BMJ. **372**, n71 (2021)
17. Page, M.J., Moher, D., Bossuyt, P.M., et al.: PRISMA 2020 explanation and elaboration: updated guidance and exemplars for reporting systematic reviews. BMJ. **372**, n160 (2021)
18. Pandey, S., Karypis, G.: A self-attentive model for knowledge tracing. In: Proceedings of the 12th International Conference on Educational Data Mining (EDM) (2019)
19. Papamitsiou, Z., Economides, A.A.: Learning analytics and educational data mining in practice: a systematic literature review of empirical evidence. Educ. Technol. Soc. **17**(4), 49–64 (2014)
20. Piech, C., Bassen, J., Huang, J., et al.: Deep knowledge tracing. Adv. Neural Inf. Proc. Syst. **28**, 505–513 (2015)
21. Romero, C., Ventura, S.: Educational data mining: a review of the state of the art. IEEE Trans. Syst. Man Cybern. Part C. **40**(6), 601–618 (2010)
22. Veluri, R.K., Patra, I., Naved, M., et al.: Learning analytics using deep learning techniques for efficiently predicting student performance. Mater. Today Proc. (2021)
23. Viberg, O., Hatakka, M., Balter, O., Mavroudi, A.: The current landscape of learning analytics in higher education. Comput. Hum. Behav. **89**, 98–110 (2018)
24. Xiao, Y.: A survey on educational data mining methods used for predicting students' performance. Eng. Rep. **3**(3), e12377 (2021)
25. Pardo, A., Siemens, G.: Ethical and privacy principles for learning analytics. Br. J. Educ. Technol. **45**(3), 438–450 (2014)

# Industry and Practitioner

# Co-designing GenAI Teacher-Focused Tools for Competency Annotation

Ivania Donoso-Guzmán[1,2,3](✉), Anna Verheyden[1,2], Shana V. F. Hazboun[1,2], Denis Parra[3], Xavier Ochoa[4], and Katrien Verbert[1,2]

[1] KU Leuven, Department of Computer Science, 3001 Leuven, Belgium
{ivania.donoso,anna.verheyden,shanavf.hazboun, katrien.verbert}@kuleuven.be

[2] Augment, an imec research group at KU Leuven, Leuven, Belgium

[3] Department of Computer Science, Pontificia Universidad Católica de Chile, Santiago, Chile

[4] Steinhardt School of Culture, Education, and Human Development, New York University (NYU), New York, USA

**Abstract.** Competency-based curricula are gaining traction in education, emphasising competencies over topic-specific knowledge. Teachers design assignments and activities (e.g., tests, exams) to support these competencies, yet documenting students' progress is difficult: competencies are numerous, often vaguely defined, and different across levels. We present a large language model (LLM) powered annotation tool that assists teachers in linking activities to competencies in the pre-instructional design phase. Using a human-in-the-loop approach, the system suggests relevant competencies while allowing teachers to review, validate, and refine annotations. Through co-design with teachers, we developed an interface that prioritises user needs, reducing annotation effort with recommendations and explanations. Our work contributes a case study in designing teacher-centred AI tools that move beyond prompt engineering, highlighting how co-design can reframe LLM integration in education and suggesting broader implications for AI-supported annotation in other domains.

**Keywords:** Large Language Models · Explainable AI · Competency-Based curriculum

## 1 Introduction

Large Language Models (LLMs) have become versatile tools for tasks ranging from writing assistance to data annotation [22,23,27]. However, designing effective interfaces remains a significant challenge. Most systems rely on prompt-based interactions that force users to translate intentions into model-specific syntax while navigating ambiguous outputs [10,19,25]. Such barriers, alongside


J. Weidlich et al. (Eds.): EC-TEL 2026, LNCS 16905, pp. 683–698, 2027.
https://doi.org/10.1007/978-3-032-37979-5_46

risks of overtrust [18] and information overload [15], highlight the need for interfaces that support human understanding rather than just automation.

In education, AI should enhance the teaching experience, yet many workload-reduction tools [3,7] neglect teachers' perspectives during design [8,11,17]. We address this gap by investigating how LLMs can assist teachers with competency annotation, the process of linking classroom activities to curriculum goals. Unlike prior automated approaches [12,24], we prioritised teacher agency through a co-design process with a partner school. This study is guided by the research question: **How can we design and refine an interface that integrates LLM recommendations and explanations to support teachers in competency annotation?**

Using a co-design methodology, we developed an interface that departs from the traditional prompt-based paradigm by providing organised, grounded recommendations. Teachers use these suggestions and accompanying explanations to maintain final authority over the annotation process. This work makes three primary contributions: (i) We present a teacher-centred, LLM-powered system that aligns classroom activities with competency-based curricula, (ii) We demonstrate that teachers engage with AI explanations as a "second opinion" to calibrate their reasoning, treating the interaction as a social process, (iii) We provide evidence that in interpretive domains, explanations promote reflection and sense-making, even when AI recommendations are incorrect or unexpected.

## 2 Related Work

Generative AI has been applied to various educational tasks like tutoring systems, assignment assessment and learning design [1]. In assessment tasks, we have seen that Hou et al. [7] and Davalos et al. [3] demonstrate how LLMs can provide automated and explainable assessments of student responses. Li et al. [12] and Xu et al. [24] showcase how LLMs can be used to link skills or course goals to students' assignments, thereby better understanding their learning progress and adapting courses. Collectively, these systems showcase the potential of generative AI when it comes to the reduction of educators' workload, which has been perceived as the most valuable contribution of current generative AI progress [16]. However, it is worth noting that prior work has primarily focused on the technical design and evaluation of systems, without systematically incorporating teachers' perspectives into the design process. In contrast, our work directly involves teachers through co-design sessions and iterative evaluations, ensuring the system aligns with their practices and needs without adding to their workload.

Research emphasises that the depth of stakeholder involvement directly determines the sustainability of AI systems in education. While co-design allows teachers to shape functionality, such as classroom awareness tools [6] or curriculum materials [13], success depends on balancing supportive features with professional constraints. Like stakeholders in other sectors [26], educators value tools that reflect their lived realities and reject designs that ignore their pedagogical expertise or add unnecessary workload. These dynamics illustrate that co-design is essential not only for usability but for building professional trust.

However, a significant gap remains in the design lifecycle. Systematic reviews show that while teachers are often consulted during exploratory stages, their influence typically diminishes during later development and evaluation [8, 11, 17]. Consequently, many resulting systems support basic awareness but fail to enable deeper reflection or sense-making with pedagogical data [21]. Transitioning from one-off consultations to sustained, iterative co-design is necessary to move beyond initial prototypes toward actionable, trustworthy tools that account for teacher agency throughout the entire development and deployment cycle.

## 3 Co-design Approach

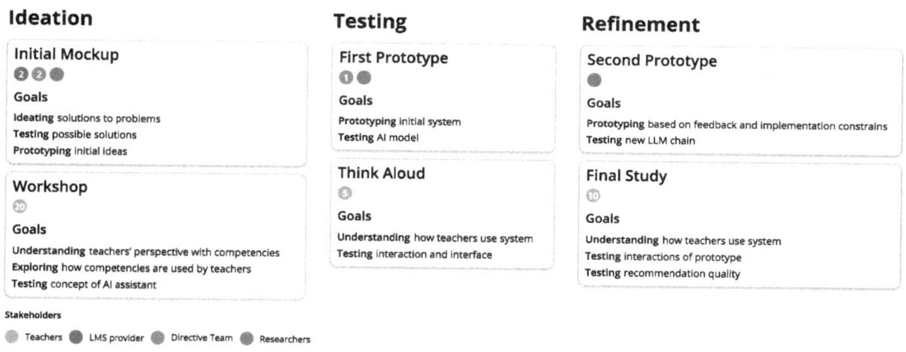


**Fig. 1. Co-Design process overview** with 3 research stages: Ideation, Testing and Refinement. Stakeholders' involvement is marked with ● for teachers, ● for the directive team, ● for the LMS provider, and ● for researchers.

The research context focuses on a secondary school in <text removed for peer review>, which serves 344 students and employs 71 teachers, offering 26 educational programs over six academic years. In response to a local government mandate to shift from content-based evaluations to competency-based qualifications, the school must adapt to the evolving competency frameworks for assessing student progress. This transition has been facilitated by an upgrade to the Learning Management System (LMS). However, teachers have reported that under a competency-based curriculum, their workload has increased, and the LMS workflow has not alleviated this burden, as it requires much manual work. The LMS supports only competencies linked to activities, not the individual exercises within those activities. For each activity in their courses, they must explicitly declare which competencies are being developed, i.e. link materials with curriculum objectives [12]. To illustrate the task, consider an activity where students analyse a short story about migration. The first competency they consider is part of *Literature*: "The students articulate their own experience and interpretation of literary texts". Since the story is about migration and the students have to analyse it, the teacher considers the *Citizenship* competency "The students explain how different forms of diversity are enriching and challenging for living together". Finally, since the students have to write their analysis, the competency from *Communication* is "The students purposefully summarise a written text in writing" will also be developed. When multiplied by 200+ available competencies and dozens of assignments per year, the manual 'linking' process becomes a significant source of workload. Our work focuses exclusively on supporting teachers in this linking process to alleviate their burden.

We followed the co-design approach of Kerr et al. [9]. We treated the co-design as a paradigm, rather than using specific methods to capture user feedback. Under this lens, we defined 3 research stages *Ideation*, *Testing* and *Refinement*, each with different interactions with multiple users as seen in Fig. 1. The first stage, **Ideation**, aimed to outline possible solutions. To achieve this, we created an initial Mock-Up that was used in a co-design workshop with 20 teachers with the goal of eliciting their views on the use of competencies and on the important aspects related to annotating competencies in materials. After these activities, we proceeded to a **Testing** stage, whose goal was to implement a functional prototype that could be assessed by teachers. Five teachers interacted with and tested the system, providing valuable feedback on its strengths and areas for improvement. These two stages defined the design goals used to update the prototype in the **Refinement phase**. This prototype utilised a multi-agent LLM to generate recommendations, provided competency recommendations for the teacher's materials, and provided explanations at the exercise level. This prototype was evaluated through a qualitative study with 10 secondary teachers. The study received ethical approval from the university's institutional review board, and all participants gave informed consent.

## 3.1 Ideation

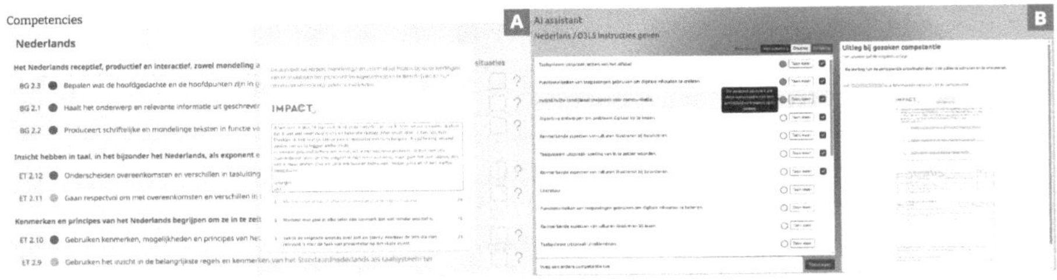


**Fig. 2.** Interface design in Ideation A and Testing B phases

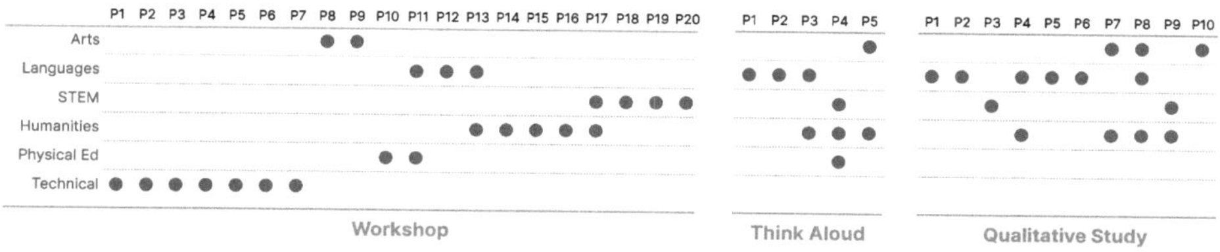


**Fig. 3.** Subjects of participating teachers at each of the co-design activities that involved them. Their subjects were grouped into six areas: Arts, Languages, STEM, Humanities, Physical Education, and Technical Education.

This stage aimed to sketch possible solutions and test these initial ideas with teachers to evaluate their applicability in the context of secondary education. The system's context was established within the **pre-instructional design phase**, the period when teachers plan activities and align them with curriculum standards. Consequently, we limited the system's input to activity descriptions and excluded student responses. This ensures that generated AI explanations justify why an activity is a suitable vehicle for a competency, regardless of individual student performance. We designed a **mockup** to reduce the burden of adding competencies to activities. We investigated the use of LLMs to automatically suggest relevant competencies for activities and tested it on a small set of sample activities. The interface (Fig. 2.A) displays a list of course-relevant competencies, each with a colour-coded uncertainty indicator. It enables users to search for competencies, providing the functionality to accept AI predictions or expand entries for detailed information. By clicking the explanation button, users view the activity document, which highlights specific quotes as supporting evidence, allowing them to validate the recommendations.

This solution was presented to the school principal and educational technologist. Their feedback was positive: they considered it a promising strategy for reducing workload. They emphasised that teachers were responsible for the accuracy of these links, which meant that the system could not automatically link competencies to materials. Additionally, they highlighted that teachers needed to understand why the system provided the specific recommendations, as sometimes the differences between competencies were subtle, making it difficult to distinguish when to apply one or the other.

Afterwards, twenty secondary teachers (Fig. 3) participated in a **workshop** and evaluated the mockup using the "I like, I wish, I wonder" method [9]. One researcher conducted the workshop while the other two took notes during the activity. After the workshop was completed, the teachers' and facilitators' post-its and notes were translated into English. We followed the *Affinity Diagramming* technique [5] to analyse the activity data and notes. To ensure a rigorous interpretation of the feedback, the three facilitators and an additional researcher performed the analysis. The four coders employed an iterative process of grouping notes and teacher feedback, reaching a consensus on thematic topics and representative teacher sentiments[1].

The initial responses were generally positive, though they revealed an opposition between teacher agency and workload. While participants appreciated the potential for automation to reduce labour, a significant portion expressed concern that the need to maintain "human-in-the-loop" control and remain responsible for final verification might counteract any intended time-saving benefits. Despite this, the system's ability to serve as a pedagogical oversight tool, helping teachers ensure they were covering the necessary curriculum standards from a list of over 200–300 possible competencies, was highly valued. While reactions varied by pedagogical approach, teachers who mapped competencies post-hoc found the tool particularly valuable for managing the complex selection process. One last finding from this iteration was the clarification of the teachers' pedagogical mental model: they conceptualised an "activity" not as a monolithic document, but as a set of exercises, each potentially contributing to different competencies, which contradicts the LMS's current competency model.

### 3.2 Testing

The system was updated with a multi-agent LLM pipeline that segments activities into exercises (see footnote 1), providing more granular, evidence-based recommendations. Key interface refinements (Fig. 2.B) include a persistent PDF viewer for constant context, competency filtering, and the ability to manually add competencies. The LLM pipeline outcomes were evaluated in an informal, blind review, with ChatGPT's reasoning capabilities preferred.

To evaluate the **first prototype**, we conducted a **think-aloud** study with five teachers, complemented with semi-structured interviews. The system presented recommendations for activities in teachers' courses to ensure they were familiar with the activities and competencies, and knew beforehand which competencies they wanted students to achieve. This allowed them to critically evaluate how the system works and assess its quality.

Participants expressed strong interest, specifically valuing the competency descriptions and search functionality. They particularly expressed interest in the Explanation section and appreciated that they could see the specific exercise(s) used by the system to infer the presence of a competency in the activity. However, the evidence was not always seen as sufficient; They wanted more information to understand *why the exercise or section of the activity could/could not develop the competency* to get deeper pedagogical rationales and noted that a simplified exercise list could occasionally replace the full PDF view. Ultimately, the prediction quality was deemed sufficient because the interface allowed for easy manual overrides, with teachers maintaining final authority over the results.

[1] Available in digital appendix.

### 3.3 Refinement

These two stages served to define the design goals for the assistant, as follows:

**(DG1) Reduce teacher workload while maintaining teachers' control and agency.** The system should automate the initial linking of competencies to activities to save teachers' time, while keeping the interaction lightweight. Teachers should only need to validate or reject recommendations rather than manually browse long lists of competencies. Teachers remain the final decision-makers.

**(DG2) Provide grounded and actionable explanations.** Explanations must be supported by exercises from the activity itself, as it is considered a unit of information. The explanations should provide reasons to help teachers understand why the competency could be achieved by the activity.

**(DG3) Visualize uncertainty transparently.** Recommendations should always be accompanied by an explicit confidence score, visually represented in an intuitive way. The system should clearly communicate when it is unsure, avoiding overconfidence.

**(DG4) Align with teachers' mental models.** Explanations and recommendations should reflect how teachers conceptualise activities: as collections of

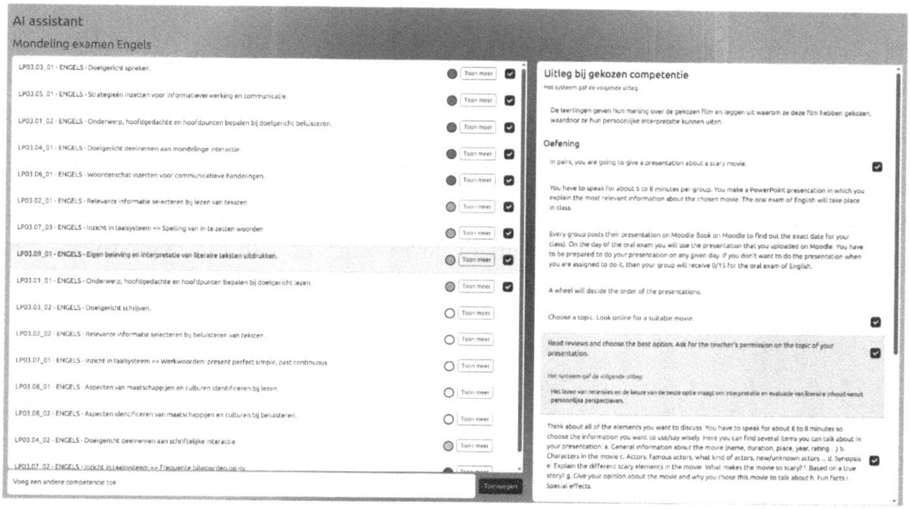


**Fig. 4.** System's Interface. It displays the activity name at the top, followed by two sections. The Competencies section displays course-related competencies. Each entry I includes title, code, and hierarchy details. The prediction area II contains the AI certainty score, Toon meer button, and decision checkbox. A dedicated form IV enables searching and manually adding new competencies. The Explanation view, accessed via Toon meer, provides an activity-level rationale IV alongside a list of exercises V ordered by the activity file VI. Checkboxes indicate competency development VII. Selecting an individual exercise VIII reveals its specific textual explanation IX.

exercises that may each contribute differently to competency development. Evidence must be presented at both the activity and exercise levels.

These goals helped to further *refine* the prototype, shown in Fig. 4, as follows:

**Competencies** To reduce workload while maintaining teacher agency (**DG1**), this section Competencies presents AI-driven recommendations for quick validation or rejection. It includes each course competency I and search functionality III. Section II displays the prediction and its certainty. The button Toon meer (Dutch for "show more") allows the user to view the explanation, and the checkbox enables the user to provide their decision, ensuring teachers remain the final decision-makers throughout the process.

**Uncertainty/Prediction:** To obtain the uncertainty score, we followed the guidance of Tian et al. [20] and directly asked the LLM agent in the final step to rate their confidence in its answer on a scale from 1 to 100. To visualise the score transparently (**DG3**), a divergent colour-coded circle II indicates both the prediction category and the confidence level. The visual indicator spans a spectrum where the left side denotes a high-certainty *competency-present* recommendation, the right side denotes a high-certainty *competency-not-present* recommendation, and the centre represents a low-certainty state where *no-recommendation-possible* . This visual cue alerts users to the reliability of each recommendation, preventing over-reliance on ambiguous AI outputs.

**Explanation:** Aligning with teachers' mental models (**DG4**), the Explanation section decomposes the activity into a list of constituent exercises V. It provides grounded explanations (**DG2**) at both the activity IV and exercise IX levels, allowing teachers to inspect specific textual rationales and evidence from the source material.

**AI Model:** The system utilizes a multi-agent chain (Fig. 5) combining `Gemini-2.0-flash-lite` for document processing and `GPT-4.1-mini` for reasoning. Gemini was chosen because it could process the PDFs directly and had a

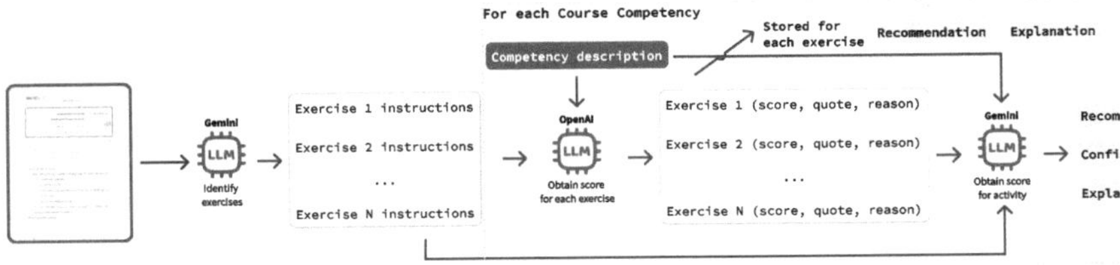


**Fig. 5.** The system follows a three-step chain of prompts to obtain the recommendation for each (`Competency, Activity`) tuple. First, an LLM agent identifies exercises from the PDF document. Afterwards, the system iterates over each competency. For each of them, it asks another agent to provide, for each activity's exercise, a score, a quote from the exercise that serves as evidence for the score, and a textual explanation for the score. Finally, these outputs are used to generate a (`Competency, Activity`) recommendation, along with a confidence score and a textual explanation.

larger input window. This pipeline generates the structured, exercise-level data required to provide the high-quality, verifiable feedback necessary for evaluation (**DG2**).

## 4 Refinement: Final Study

Building on previous iterations that validated the interface's core components, this final study focuses specifically on refining explanation quality. We employed a qualitative approach, combining the think-aloud protocol with semi-structured interviews, to assess the accuracy of recommendations and gain deeper insights into how teachers interact with the system.

The school's coordinator contacted teachers from the school, and 12 agreed to participate. One participant did not attend the interviews, and another participant requested that her data be removed after the study was completed. Table 1 displays the demographics of the 10 remaining participants, and Fig. 3 displays the subjects that these teachers taught at the school. The interviews were conducted in Dutch at the school over two days.

**Table 1.** Participant demographics and AI experience

| ID | Gender | Age | Comfort with digital tools | Experience Teaching | Experience LLMs |
|---|---|---|---|---|---|
| 1 | Female | 41 | Uncomfortable | 2.5 years | Brainstorming and interactivity |
| 2 | Male | 30 | Comfortable | 8.5 years | Question generation |
| 3 | Male | 32 | Comfortable | 10 years | Limited personal use; none for work |
| 4 | Female | 52 | Comfortable | 28 years | Examples and exercises |
| 5 | Female | 21 | Uncomfortable | <1 year | Inspiration and exercises |
| 6 | Female | 29 | Comfortable | 5 years | Lesson prep and fact-checking |
| 7 | Female | 32 | Comfortable | 10 years | Admin, assignments, and emails |
| 8 | Female | 31 | Comfortable | 7 years | Frequent use; created AI course |
| 9 | Male | 34 | Comfortable | 10 years | Sporadic material creation |
| 10 | Male | 59 | Comfortable | 28 years | No active use |

### 4.1 Study Protocol

The goal of this study was to gather feedback on the quality of recommendations and the information provided in the explanations. To do so, we selected aspects from the framework proposed by Donoso-Guzmán et al. [4] and supplemented them with additional concepts relevant to our context.

First, we focused on the informational quality of the explanations. We examined whether the provided reasons contained sufficient evidence to support a decision, defined as *Sufficiency*, while ensuring they did not overwhelm teachers with unnecessary details, thereby maintaining *Necessity*. To further assess whether participants could make sense of these reasons, we evaluated how effectively the explanations supported teachers' ability to internalise and interpret the Assistant's logic. This allowed us to measure *Understanding* based on how well they could meaningfully assimilate recommendations into their existing pedagogical knowledge.

Beyond informational quality, we assessed the perceived value of the explanations to teachers, focusing on *Usefulness* for the task and overall *Satisfaction* with the system. Since the system is intended to support teachers' decision-making, we additionally evaluated the *Confidence* they felt in their final choices, as this reflects how effectively the explanations strengthen decision support. In order to capture potential adoption, we considered the *Intention to Use* by observing whether participants could envision integrating the tool into their future practice. Finally, given the nature of generative models, we verified alignment with educational standards to ensure *Information Correctness*, confirming that the AI's rationales were factually sound and pedagogically appropriate rather than misleading.

During the audio-recorded session, teachers were asked to explore the system and evaluate whether the recommendations were correct and how relevant and useful the explanations were for a selected activity. Specifically, participants selected one activity from a predefined list and then used the interface to review and reflect on the competency recommendations generated by the system. While performing this task, they were encouraged to verbalise their thoughts, reasoning, and impressions aloud. After completing the think-aloud task, we conducted a semi-structured interview to evaluate the previously described properties (*Sufficiency, Necessity, Understanding, Usefulness, Confidence, Information Correctness*). For each property, we prepared 2–3 guiding questions to ensure coverage of all aspects (see footnote 1).

### 4.2 Results

We followed the steps described by Braun et al. [2] to analyse the data. To get *familiarised with the data*, the interviewer transcribed the audio and translated the interviews. The other two researchers read the interviews and discuss unclear translations and contextual information. The *initial codes* comprised the different explanation properties [4] we aimed to measure. To *search for themes*, the three researchers coded 1 interview together to understand the coding scheme and added codes that were not part of the properties. Afterwards, all coders independently coded two interviews to compare results; any differences were discussed and resolved in a single meeting. The remaining interviews were split among researchers. To *review themes*, the researchers discussed difficult or unclear sections in two further meetings. Afterwards, all researchers reviewed each of the codes together to ensure consistency. The main author *defined and named themes* while consulting with the other two researchers. The codebook is available as digital appendix (see footnote 1).

**Explanation Components.** Participants demonstrated varying levels of engagement with the three explanation components, prioritising high-level rationales and system confidence over granular connections. The **textual explanation** was the most utilised feature for understanding system logic (P2–4, P6–10), though some teachers (P3, P7) felt that "robotic" phrasing or vague vocabulary occasionally undermined its credibility. The **certainty indicator** was also widely valued for its transparency (P1, P3, P6-10). Finally, the competency-exercise link was the least mentioned component, likely because teachers conflated it with the broader textual rationales and focused their attention on the system's overall confidence scores instead.

**User Perception of Explanations.** The use of the explanation components influenced the teachers' attitudes toward the system. Figure 6 displays the summary of user perception of the explanations and the system usage. The explanations helped teachers to *understand* the recommendations (P2-P7, P9-10) while also increasing their *confidence* (P1-9). Most teachers found the system *useful* (P2-10) and the majority said they would *use the system* (P1-2, P4-8). Based on the individual analysis of each interview, we found relations between the aspects that teachers mentioned. These relations are shown in Fig. 7. In the following, we explain and provide evidence for each link.

*High Sufficiency Leads to High Understanding.* Textual explanations accompanying each exercise helped users understand the recommendations, especially in cases when the recommendation was not expected. As P6 states "...without the explanation, I sometimes had the feeling of... "Oh, why does it do something?" Or "why does it do that?" You really have to click on the text. Then it gives the explanation. And then I think it makes more sense why certain choices are made". The textual explanations provided were sufficient to clarify the system's reasoning and help teachers understand the system's choices.

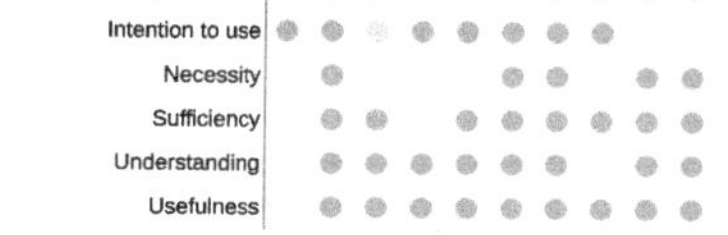


**Fig. 6.** User perception properties reported by teachers.

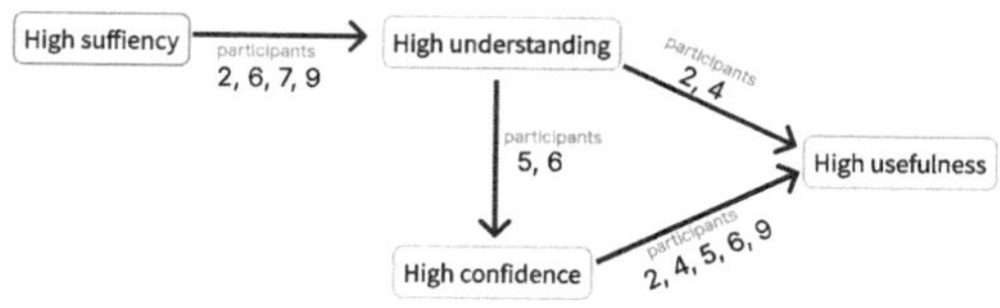


**Fig. 7. Connections between properties.** Based on the individual analysis of each interview, we found relations between the aspects that teachers mentioned.

*High Understanding Leads to High Usefulness.* Given the number of competencies, it is difficult for teachers to consider all of them when linking them to materials. Understanding why the system made specific recommendations enabled teachers to evaluate their relevance in context, thereby increasing perceived usefulness. As P2 explained, "I have a hard time sometimes making a link between this [materials] and that [competencies]. For example, I wouldn't indicate the first one [competency]. In itself, yes, but when I look at it [explanation], I would pick it.".

*High Understanding Leads to High Confidence.* Understanding the rationale behind recommendations increased teachers' confidence in their decisions. P6 explained that because it was easy to see and understand why some competencies were checked, she felt more confident. Overall, several teachers explained that they would initially "check" the system, but after using it for a while without too many errors, they would trust it more (P2, P7, P9). This pattern suggests that explainability not only supported comprehension but also calibrated trust, which could potentially make teachers rely on the system more confidently over time.

*High Confidence Leads to High Usefulness.* Across participants, confidence in their decisions was consistently high (P1-9). Explanations often acted as a "second opinion", reinforcing teachers' own judgments. As several teachers explained (P1, P3, P4), "The computer says it's like that, I think so too. Then you're already two [opinions]." This sense of validation was particularly valuable for teachers, like P4, who lacked peer collaboration: "Sometimes we [colleagues] are both unsure and then the question remains: is it correct now or not? [...] then that [the tool] could help, yes". Increased confidence, in turn, translated into greater perceived usefulness, with most teachers (P2–6, P8–10) expressing intentions to continue using the system.

**Wrong Recommendations and Understanding.** Teachers frequently disagreed with the density of AI suggestions, with some participants (P3, P8-9) preferring more "concrete" results than the system's broader selections. As P9 noted: "I think I would be more critical or cautious about indicating the competences than the tool is now.". However, disagreement did not equate to a lack of understanding; teachers often found unexpected links understandable after reading the textual rationale, even if they ultimately rejected the suggestion (P3, P9).

Furthermore, teachers were generally forgiving of incorrect recommendations (P2-5, P7, P9-10) when they could follow the underlying logic of the mistake, such as when the explanation itself reflected the ambiguity of a competency. This transparency reinforced the teachers' role as the final authority. Highlighting the shift from AI as an oracle to a support tool, P10 remarked: "Some see that [AI] as *the* tool, but that is *a* tool. In terms of content, there still has to be a check by someone who knows 'that it is right, that it is not right."'

**Competency Ambiguity.** Teachers noted that system "errors" often mirrored their own difficulties in defining broad or vaguely phrased competencies (P1–3, P5, P7–10). This ambiguity is compounded by the fact that the same exercise can target different competencies depending on whether the evaluation is oral or written. While some participants, like P4, acknowledged that even human colleagues "collectively" feel uncertain about certain links, others found the AI's presence helpful for clarification; P7 noted that having the system define the competency "made the process easier" because they often did not know exactly what a competency encompassed.

Conversely, P3 disagreed with the AI's broad definitions, preferring to only include competencies specifically targeted by their test. Despite these differences in interpretation, the system functioned as a valuable "brainstorming" tool. For instance, P4 suggested using the AI's suggestions to optimise assignments, identifying less frequent competencies so that a question could be "added or adapted to specifically test it".

## 5 Discussion

**Co-designing Task-Specific Interfaces.** To develop a tool that supports teachers in working with the competency-based curriculum, this study employed a co-design approach. Connecting with the teachers multiple times throughout the process helped us see the nuances, showing that the low adoption of competency annotation was not due to unwillingness, but often due to an inconvenient workflow and the cognitive load of navigating many new or vague competencies. By involving stakeholders early, including the school principal and educational technologist, we moved beyond generic chat interfaces to a task-specific design that reduced the design search space and cognitive load. Using the teachers' own course material in the interviews helped teachers imagine using it in their daily practices and to assess more easily whether the explanations made sense. It was thus an important design choice, as it allowed teachers to better and more concretely criticise the system's recommendations.

**Explanations as Collaborative Sensemaking.** The explanations transformed the AI from a simple classifier into a collaborative *second opinion*, supporting a social dialogue rather than one-way justification [14]. We observed a clear path from informational quality to perceived value: when participants perceived *Sufficiency* in the reasons provided, it led to higher *Understanding*, which in turn created *Confidence*. This was particularly evident when teachers forgave incorrect recommendations (P2-5, P7, P9-10) because they could follow the underlying logic. Beyond task completion, the system functioned as a *brainstorming* tool; for instance, P4 envisioned using AI suggestions to optimise assignments and identify less frequent competencies. This suggests that AI in pedagogical domains should prioritise user sensemaking over purely objective accuracy.

**The Role of AI in Ambiguous Contexts.** An important finding was that system errors often reflected the inherent ambiguity teachers felt toward the competency framework itself. Rather than being a drawback, these unexpected or *far-fetched* links (P3, P9) stimulated reflection. The explanations helped teachers re-evaluate their own interpretations of the curriculum, effectively acting as a professional companion. This reinforces the potential of explainable AI to support human learning within a domain, rather than merely explaining model outcomes.

**Trust Calibration and the Risk of Over-Reliance.** While explicit certainty scores helped mitigate over-reliance on low-confidence suggestions, they led to the opposite for high-confidence suggestions. The results suggest a shift from initial scepticism to reliance (P5-6), yet several teachers (P1, P7, P9) admitted they might eventually stop checking high-certainty links. This confirms risks identified in prior research [18], where *Confidence* in the system's logic might inadvertently encourage uncritical acceptance. While explainability supports *Understanding*, it does not automatically guarantee active engagement, underscoring the need to keep teachers in control (P10).

## 6 Conclusions

The development of this system exemplifies new interactions with AI in the era of large language models (LLMs). By adopting a co-design approach, we created a novel interface that supports teachers in the task of annotating competencies for activities. This methodology encouraged us to move away from the traditional prompt-refining and conversational paradigms, allowing us to tailor a system to the needs of the end user. The fact that the competencies were perceived as vague or ambiguous by the teachers made the explanations crucial to the acceptance of the recommendations and to perceptions of usefulness and confidence. Even when AI's suggestions were incorrect or unexpected, the explanations sparked reflection on the competency and activity. This suggests that in a subjective domain such as education, the AI assistant must not only provide definite answers, but can also serve as a brainstorming tool.

Our study has several limitations. The teachers were recruited from the same school, which may limit the generalizability of our findings. Moreover, while the explanations appeared to enable social-like negotiation between teachers and the system, this interaction was mediated by static text rather than genuine dialogue. Future systems could explore more interactive, conversational forms of explainability to support richer human–AI collaboration. Lastly, our study focused on short-term interactions; future research should investigate the long-term adoption of such tools, examining how teachers' trust, reliance, and usage patterns evolve over extended periods of real-world use.

We plan to evaluate the use of this system in a longitudinal study to gain a deeper understanding of the quality of the recommendations and explore ways to capture quality feedback from teachers to improve the recommendations of competencies. Finally, we aim to understand their constraints and identify potential workflow changes necessary to integrate this approach for real-time interaction.

**Acknowledgments.** This research was supported by the imec.icon CAPTURE project, with project support from VLAIO (Flanders Innovation & Entrepreneurship) (Grant No. HBC.2024.0220), the Flanders AI Research Program (FAIR), and **Smart Education @ Schools programme**. The research of Ivania Donoso-Guzmán was supported by the doctoral scholarship of ANID BECAS/DOCTORADO NACIONAL 21202228.

## References

1. Alkhasawneh, S.N., Lampropoulos, G., Hernández-Leo, D.: Generative ai in learning design: a systematic review. Presented at the (2025) Artificial Intelligence in Education
2. Braun, V., Clarke, V.: Using thematic analysis in psychology. Qual. Res. Psychol. **3**, 77–101 (2006)
3. Davalos, E., et al.: LLMs as educational analysts: transforming multimodal data traces into actionable reading assessment reports. In: Cristea, A.I., Walker, E., Lu, Y., Santos, O.C., Isotani, S. (eds.) Artificial Intelligence in Education, pp. 191–204. Springer Nature Switzerland (2025)
4. Donoso-Guzmán, I., Ooge, J., Parra, D., Verbert, K.: Towards a comprehensive human-centred evaluation framework for explainable AI. Presented at the (2023) Explainable Artificial Intelligence
5. Harboe, G., Huang, E.M.: Real-world affinity diagramming practices: bridging the paper-digital gap. In: Conference on Human Factors in Computing Systems - Proceedings. vol. 2015-April, pp. 95–104 (2015)
6. Holstein, K., McLaren, B.M., Aleven, V.: Co-designing a real-time classroom orchestration tool to support teacher-AI complementarity. J. Learn. Anal. **6**(2), 27–52 (2019)
7. Hou, X., et al.: An LLM-enhanced multi-agent architecture for conversation-based assessment. Presented at the (2025) Artificial Intelligence in Education
8. Kaliisa, R., Jivet, I., Prinsloo, P.: A checklist to guide the planning, designing, implementation, and evaluation of learning analytics dashboards. Int. J. Educ. Technol. High. Educ. **20**(1) (2023)
9. Kerr, J., Cheers, J., Gallegos, D., Blackler, A., Kelly, N.: The Art of Co-Design: A Guide to Creative Collaboration. BIS Publishers (2023)
10. Kraljic, T., Lahav, M.: From prompt engineering to collaborating: a human-centered approach to AI interfaces. Interactions **31**(3), 30–35 (2024)
11. Lang, C., Davis, L.: Learning analytics and stakeholder inclusion: what do we mean when we say "human-centered"? In: LAK23: 13th International Learning Analytics and Knowledge Conference, pp. 411–417. LAK2023 (2023)
12. Li, X., Henriksson, A., Duneld, M., Nouri, J., Wu, Y.: Supporting teaching-to-the-curriculum by linking diagnostic tests to curriculum goals: Using textbook content as context for retrieval-augmented generation with large language models. In: Olney, A.M., Chounta, I.A., Liu, Z., Santos, O.C., Bittencourt, I.I. (eds.) Artificial Intelligence in Education, pp. 118–132. Springer Nature Switzerland (2024)

13. Lin, P., Van Brummelen, J.: Engaging teachers to co-design integrated ai curriculum for k-12 classrooms. In: CHI '21: Proceedings of the 2021 CHI Conference on Human Factors in Computing Systems, pp. 1–12. ACM (2021)
14. Miller, T.: Explanation in artificial intelligence: insights from the social sciences. Artif. Intell. **267**, 1–38 (2019)
15. Muralidhar, D., Belloum, R., de Oliveira, K.M., Ashok, A., Mohammad, P.B.: The effect of progressive disclosure in the transparency of large language models. In: Communications in Computer and Information Science, pp. 269–288. Communications in computer and information science, Springer Nature Switzerland (2025)
16. Oh, S.Y., Ahn, Y.: Exploring teachers' perception of artificial intelligence: The socio-emotional deficiency as opportunities and challenges in human-AI complementarity in k-12 education. Presented at the (2024) Artificial Intelligence in Education
17. Sarmiento, J.P., Wise, A.F.: Participatory and co-design of learning analytics: an initial review of the literature. In: LAK22: 12th International Learning Analytics and Knowledge Conference, pp. 535–541. LAK22 (2022)
18. Schroeder, H., Roy, D., Kabbara, J.: Just put a human in the loop? Investigating LLM-assisted annotation for subjective tasks. In: Findings of the Association for Computational Linguistics: ACL 2025, pp. 25771–25795 (2025)
19. Subramonyam, H., Pea, R., Pondoc, C.L., Agrawala, M., Seifert, C.: Bridging the gulf of envisioning: cognitive challenges in prompt based interactions with LLMs. In: Conference on Human Factors in Computing Systems (2024)
20. Tian, K., et al.: Just Ask for Calibration: Strategies for Eliciting Calibrated Confidence Scores from Language Models Fine-Tuned with Human Feedback (2023)
21. Verbert, K., Duval, E., Klerkx, J., Govaerts, S., Santos, J.L.: Learning analytics dashboard applications. Am. Behav. Sci. **57**(10), 1500–1509 (2013)
22. Vujinović, A., Luburić, N., Slivka, J., Kovačević, A.: Using ChatGPT to annotate a dataset: a case study in intelligent tutoring systems. Mach. Learn. Appl. **16**, 100557 (2024)
23. Wang, S., Liu, Y., Xu, Y., Zhu, C., Zeng, M.: Want to reduce labeling cost? GPT-3 can help. In: Findings of the Association for Computational Linguistics: EMNLP 2021, pp. 4195–4205. Association for Computational Linguistics (2021)
24. Xu, Z., Li, X., Huan, Y., Minaya, V., Yu, R.: From course to skill: Evaluating large language model performance in curricular analytics. Presented at the (2025) Artificial Intelligence in Education
25. Zamfirescu-Pereira, J., Wong, R.Y., Hartmann, B., Yang, Q.: Why johnny can't prompt: How non-ai experts try (and fail) to design LLM prompts. In: Conference on Human Factors in Computing Systems. CHI '23, (2023)
26. Zhang, A., Boltz, A., Lynn, J., Wang, C., Lee, M.K.: Stakeholder-centered AI design: co-designing worker tools with gig workers through data probes. In: Conference on Human Factors in Computing Systems, pp. 1–19. ACM (2023)
27. Zhu, Y., Zhang, P., Haq, E.U., Hui, P., Tyson, G.: Can ChatGPT Reproduce Human-Generated Labels? A Study of Social Computing Tasks (2023)

# Data-Sovereign AI Avatars for Immersive Training: Lessons from 18 Months of Cloud–To–Offline Deployment

Robert Hillman(✉) and Tai Nyirenda

Metaverse-VR Ltd, Portsmouth, UK
{Robert.Hillman,Tai.Nyirenda}@metaverse-vr.co.uk

**Abstract.** Immersive virtual training can now host conversational virtual instructors that support dialogue, feedback, and learner guidance. However, integrating such systems into real-time mixed reality environments introduces challenges in latency, accuracy, data governance, and reliability. Existing approaches often rely on scripted interactions or cloud-dependent architectures, limiting institutional control and preventing deployment in network-constrained or compliance-sensitive contexts.

This paper presents the design, deployment, and evaluation of EnvisionAI, a modular virtual AI avatar platform developed through an 18-month Innovate UK funded project spanning public engagement, curriculum-aligned education, and defence-oriented training. The system evolved from a tightly coupled prototype to a microservice-based architecture enabling flexible deployment across cloud and offline environments. Three deployments are used to examine this progression: a public-facing space education avatar, a physics tutor, and an offline diving instructor for data-sovereign training contexts.

Across five system iterations, latency analysis identified conversational responsiveness as the primary design constraint for immersive AI instructors. Streaming-based orchestration reduced perceived end-to-end response time to approximately 1.3 s. Comparative evaluation of locally deployed models indicates that moderate-sized models, combined with retrieval-augmented generation, provide more effective real-time performance than larger reasoning-optimised models in training contexts. A small feasibility demonstration with four participants suggested practical usability for training and education contexts, while highlighting the need for larger studies before claims about learning effectiveness can be made.

The contribution of this paper is practical design knowledge for deploying conversational artificial intelligence instructors in immersive training systems. It shows how latency management, model selection, grounding, and deployment architecture jointly shape the feasibility of data-sovereign immersive learning applications.

**Keywords:** VR training · AI instructors · Data sovereignty · Immersive learning · LLM · RAG · Offline AI deployment


J. Weidlich et al. (Eds.): EC-TEL 2026, LNCS 16905, pp. 699–713, 2027.
https://doi.org/10.1007/978-3-032-37979-5_47

# 1 Introduction

Immersive virtual environments are increasingly used for training in domains where real-world instruction is expensive, hazardous, or difficult to scale, including defence, education, and technical skills development (Hamilton et al., 2021). However, many virtual training experiences still rely on scripted non-player characters or tightly constrained interaction flows, limiting responsiveness, adaptability, and the sense of authentic dialogue (Kuhail et al., 2023; Labadze et al., 2023). Recent advances in large language models (LLMs), speech recognition, and speech synthesis have created new opportunities for conversational virtual instructors that can answer questions, guide learners, and support more natural interaction. In practice, however, integrating these capabilities into real-time immersive systems remains difficult. Latency, response reliability, deployment complexity, and data governance constraints can all undermine the feasibility of AI immersive learning systems (Shaw et al., 2020; Seuren et al., 2021).

Despite these advances, conversational AI remains rare in operational immersive training deployments. In many contexts, the challenge is not only educational but also infrastructural. Even where conversational interaction appears promising, deployment can remain difficult in settings that require low latency, institutional control over data, or operation without reliable network connectivity. This paper therefore focuses on three practical constraints: conversational latency, data sovereignty, and offline capability. It is also guided by the following design question: how can conversational artificial intelligence avatars be architected and deployed in immersive learning environments while maintaining acceptable responsiveness, grounded responses, and institutional control over data and services?

This paper presents EnvisionAI, a modular AI-powered virtual avatar platform developed through an 18-month Innovate UK-funded project. Our contribution is practical design knowledge for educational technology practitioners and researchers seeking to deploy conversational artificial intelligence instructors in immersive training environments. Across this project, streaming-based orchestration reduced conversational delays, a provider-agnostic microservice architecture enabled both cloud and offline deployment modes, and retrieval-augmented generation supported the use of moderate-sized local models for domain-specific instruction. We examine these design choices through three real-world deployments representing distinct operational contexts: a public-facing space education avatar deployed at large exhibitions, a curriculum-aligned physics tutor on Apple Vision Pro, and an offline, environment-aware diving instructor for defence training. Together, these deployments illustrate how deployment requirements shifted across public engagement, educational, and regulated training scenarios. This work does not provide a comprehensive evaluation of pedagogical effectiveness, which remains important future work. Instead, its contribution is practical and demonstrates how infrastructure constraints can be addressed in ways that make conversational AI deployment feasible in immersive training contexts, while also creating more realistic conditions for future evaluation.

## 2 Background and Practical Context

Immersive extended reality (XR) training is increasingly used in domains where real-world practice is costly, risky, or difficult to scale. Its value lies in allowing learners to rehearse procedures and decisions in a safe, repeatable environment (Hamilton et al., 2021). However, many current XR training systems still rely on scripted dialogue trees or tightly authored branching interactions. These approaches can be reliable, but they are often inflexible when learners ask unexpected questions, deviate from ideal procedures, or require contextualised coaching. As a result, conversational virtual instructors are attractive for technology-enhanced learning, particularly where dialogue, explanation, and guided questioning are central to the learning experience. Educational chatbot research has shown clear potential for conversational support, but reviews also note limits in evidence quality, long-term deployment reporting, and grounded guidance for building trustworthy systems across diverse contexts (Kuhail et al., 2023; Labadze et al., 2023).

Recent advances in large language models (LLMs), speech recognition, and speech synthesis have made open-ended conversational agents increasingly feasible in XR. In practice, however, these capabilities introduce new implementation challenges. Responses must remain accurate and appropriately grounded, spoken interaction must feel responsive enough to preserve turn-taking, and the underlying system must remain robust across different deployment settings. Retrieval-augmented generation (RAG) is therefore important for improving factual grounding and traceability in training systems (Lewis et al., 2020), while deployment strategy becomes a core architectural decision: cloud services can accelerate development, but local or edge deployment may be preferable where privacy, or institutional control are critical (Zhou et al., 2019; Deng et al., 2020).

For immersive learning systems, responsiveness and governance are especially important. Studies of mediated conversation show that relatively small delays can disrupt turn-taking and weaken conversational flow, requiring participants to repair interaction timing (Shaw et al., 2020; Seuren et al., 2021). In immersive training contexts, this makes time-to-first-audio as important as final answer quality. At the same time, educational and training uses of AI are subject to growing expectations around data minimisation, auditability, and institutional control. The EU Artificial Intelligence Act classifies several education and vocational training uses as high-risk, and explicitly restricts certain forms of emotion inference in educational settings except in limited circumstances (European Parliament and Council, 2024). Alongside GDPR principles such as purpose limitation, data minimisation, security, and accountability (European Data Protection Board, n.d.), these developments make governance a practical system-design concern rather than a purely legal one. In this context, the challenge is not simply to build a capable conversational avatar, but to design one that can operate with acceptable latency, grounded responses, and an appropriate balance between cloud convenience and data-sovereign deployment.

## 3 Platform Evolution and Key Design Decisions

The EnvisionAI platform evolved in response to constraints encountered during real-world deployment. Rather than emerging from an upfront system architecture plan, the platform was repeatedly redesigned to address failures in responsiveness, provider flexibility, and deployment viability. The most significant shift was the transition from a tightly coupled prototype embedded directly in Unreal Engine to a modular microservice-based architecture.

### 3.1 From Prototype to Deployable Platform

The initial prototype was built to validate the feasibility of conversational AI avatars in immersive VR. Speech recognition, language model inference, and speech synthesis were accessed through direct API calls embedded within the Unreal Engine application using C++ and Blueprint scripting. This approach enabled rapid proof-of-concept development and supported the first public deployment of the Tim Peake avatar.

However, live deployment quickly exposed important limitations. During the Goodwood Festival deployment, high ambient noise substantially reduced speech-recognition accuracy. Changing providers required rebuilding and redeploying the full application, turning what should have been a configuration change into a disruptive live intervention. Dependence on cloud connectivity also reduced robustness under poor network conditions, and the architecture could not support offline deployment. This was a critical limitation for defense and education settings where data sovereignty and institutional control were important requirements.

To address these issues, the platform was redesigned as a set of containerised Python microservices orchestrated through Docker Compose. The redesigned system separated language model inference and RAG, speech services, safety checks, and API routing into distinct services exposed through a unified interface. An Unreal Engine plugin then provided Blueprint-accessible nodes, allowing game engine developers to use the system without managing backend service coordination directly. This redesign enabled cloud, local, and hybrid deployment modes, depending on the latency, governance, and operational needs of each use case.

### 3.2 Design Decisions that Proved Necessary in Practice

Several architectural decisions became essential across deployments. First, streaming response generation was necessary for acceptable conversational interaction. By allowing text-to-speech synthesis to begin before full response generation had completed, streaming reduced perceived response time and improved turn-taking even when total generation time remained similar.

Second, provider abstraction proved important for experimentation and resilience. Adapter-based interfaces allowed speech and language model providers to be swapped or compared without rebuilding the client application.

Third, acceptable local deployment depended on grounding and layered safeguards. RAG was critical for improving the reliability of local models, which otherwise produced generic or occasionally hallucinated responses. Safety was treated as a layered mitigation problem rather than a single-model solution: input classification, document-grounded generation, and output checks were combined to reduce the likelihood of unsafe or unsupported responses.

### 3.3 Capabilities Deprioritised for Production Use

Prior work on empathic pedagogical conversational agents highlights the potential value of affective feedback, learner perception, and emotionally responsive interaction in educational agents (Ortega-Ochoa et al., 2024). However, not all technically feasible capabilities were worth prioritising in production. A multimodal emotion-recognition prototype showed promise in controlled settings, but performance degraded substantially in real deployment conditions, particularly under variable lighting, ambient noise, and diverse user expression. Because false positives risked damaging user trust, this capability was not integrated into the main platform. Automatic lip synchronization was also explored but required significant calibration effort across phoneme pairs with avatar rigs while delivering limited practical benefits for training-focused interactions. In both cases, simpler and more robust alternatives proved more appropriate.

These decisions reflect a broader design principle that shaped the platform throughout the project, when advanced capabilities conflicted with operational constraints, we prioritized robustness, responsiveness, and deployment flexibility over maximal feature sophistication.

## 4 Deployments in Practice

To evaluate the platform across progressively more demanding contexts, EnvisionAI was deployed in three real-world scenarios spanning public engagement, curriculum-aligned education, and defence-oriented training. Together, these deployments provided practical progression from feasibility testing to offline, domain-grounded operation, and revealed how system requirements changed across contexts.

### 4.1 Tim Peake: Public-Facing Feasibility Deployment

The Tim Peake deployment served as the project's first large-scale proof of concept. It featured a high-fidelity virtual astronaut, implemented in Unreal Engine using the Metahuman SDK and deployed as an interactive public exhibition experience on a Meta Quest 3, designed to answer space-related questions through spoken interaction. This implementation was deployed at the Goodwood Festival of Speed and the Royal International Air Tattoo, environments that imposed challenging operational conditions, particularly high ambient noise, short interaction windows, and a broad audience with highly variable prior knowledge. As a result, the interaction design prioritised concise, accessible responses and robust conversational behaviour over depth or pedagogical sophistication (Figs. 1 and 2).

This deployment confirmed that users readily engaged with a conversational avatar as an informational guide, but it also exposed major architectural weaknesses. Speech

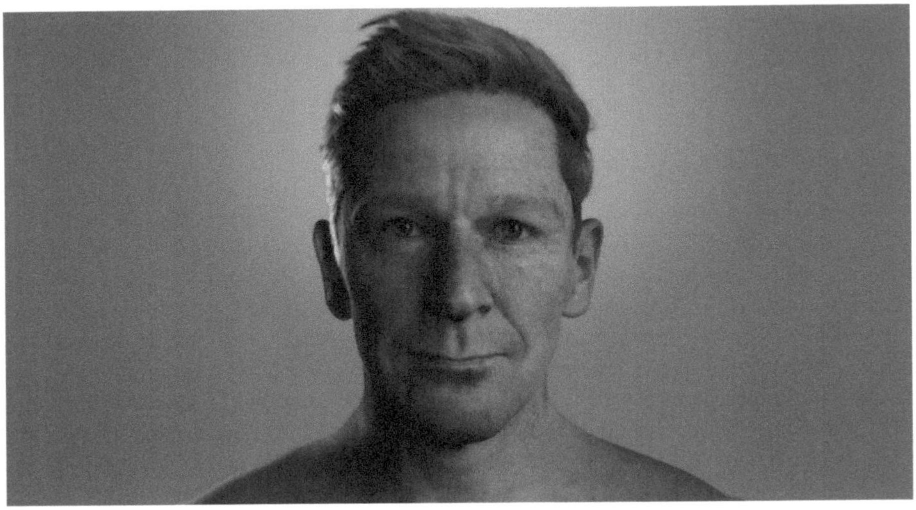

**Fig. 1.** A screenshot of the Tim Peake Metahuman avatar

recognition degraded under live exhibition conditions, provider changes were operationally difficult, and reliance on external cloud services limited robustness. In this sense, the Tim Peake deployment was valuable less as a mature learning system than as a practical feasibility test that revealed the constraints the platform would need to overcome.

### 4.2 Sir Isaac Newton: Curriculum-Aligned Educational Deployment

The Sir Isaac Newton deployment represented a more targeted educational use case. Unlike the broad public-facing Tim Peake scenario, the Newton avatar was designed to support structured question-and-answer interaction aligned with lower-secondary physics content for learners aged approximately 11–14. To improve consistency with expected terminology and conceptual framing, the underlying language model was fine-tuned using curriculum-relevant material. This demonstrated the importance of domain grounding for educational avatars intended to operate beyond general-purpose dialogue.

This deployment also played an important role in maturing the platform itself. It supported comparative use of multiple speech and language model providers, reinforcing the value of a provider-agnostic backend architecture. Deployment on Apple Vision Pro further demonstrated that the system could be adapted to emerging XR hardware and interaction models without fundamental backend redesign. Overall, the Newton deployment marked a transition from early feasibility work toward a more reusable instructional platform.

### 4.3 Dive Kit: Offline, Environment-Aware Deployment

The Dive Kit deployment brought the platform's core architectural aims together in a single integrated demonstration. Presented at DSEI as an Unreal Engine-based immersive training demonstrator, it featured a virtual Royal Navy diving instructor capable of answering questions about procedures and equipment while operating entirely offline. Responses were grounded in curated domain documentation, enabling the system to deliver factual, contextually appropriate answers without dependence on larger cloud models. This made the deployment particularly relevant to defence and other regulated settings where data sovereignty and operational resilience are essential.

**Fig. 2.** A screenshot of the Dive Kit Demo Environment

A key extension in this deployment was the incorporation of virtual-environment context into the interaction loop. The scene included multiple pieces of diving equipment, allowing the system to interpret references such as "What is this?" in relation to the object currently being viewed. This moved the platform beyond generic conversational response generation toward context-sensitive instructional interaction embedded in the training environment. Among the three deployments, Dive Kit provided the clearest demonstration that offline, domain-grounded conversational avatars can be practically deployed for immersive training when architecture, grounding strategy, and interaction design are aligned.

Across the three deployments, the platform evolved from a public-facing conversational prototype into a more robust and portable training system. The progression also clarified a recurring implementation pattern, as deployment contexts became more operationally demanding, architectural flexibility, domain grounding, and offline capability became more important than maximising general conversational sophistication.

# 5 Results & Findings

## 5.1 End-to-End Interaction Latency

To quantify and analyse latency sources, controlled experiments were conducted on the final EnvisionAI microservice architecture used for the Dive Kit deployment. The experiments examined speech-to-text, language model, and text-to-speech components individually, as well as their combined effect within an end-to-end spoken interaction pipeline. Each benchmark consisted of five repeated runs using representative diving-training prompts averaging 12–15 words in length. Speech input clips ranged from 3–5 s and reflected typical spoken user questions about equipment or procedures. The purpose of these benchmarks was not to compare providers exhaustively, but to identify latency constraints relevant to real-time avatar interaction.

Results (Tables 1, 2 and 3) showed that latency is introduced at multiple stages of the interaction pipeline, including request transmission, model inference, and response retrieval. Among these stages, LLM response generation and cloud-based STT processing were the dominant contributors. Experiments comparing non-streaming and streaming LLM response generation demonstrated that streaming significantly reduced perceived response time, particularly for longer responses. While total generation time remained similar, the time to first audio output was reduced by approximately 30% improving conversational flow

Further benchmarking across model providers revealed substantial variability in response times. Lightweight cloud-based models, particularly GPT-4.1-nano and the Gemini Flash variants, consistently outperformed slower alternatives in latency-sensitive scenarios, with the fastest models reducing average response time by roughly 75–78% relative to the slowest tested models. These findings informed subsequent model-selection strategies for avatar deployments prioritising real-time interaction.

When combined into an optimised end-to-end pipeline using the fastest-performing STT, LLM, and TTS components, average non-streaming response times were reduced to under two s, with streaming approaches further lowering perceived latency to approximately 1.3 s, seen in Table 4. These results demonstrate that conversational latency suitable for immersive avatar interaction is achievable through careful architectural and model-level optimisation.

Achieving approximately 1.3-s perceived response times is not only a technical optimisation but also a condition for usable instructional dialogue. Research on mediated conversation shows that delays can disrupt turn-taking, increase cognitive load and weaken conversational engagement. (Shaw et al., 2020; Seuren et al., 2021). In immersive training scenarios, where learners may ask follow-up questions while attending to objects, procedures, or instructions, conversational flow is important for maintaining attention and interaction quality. Latency optimisation therefore supports the practical conditions under which educational dialogue can occur.

## 5.2 Offline Model Performance and Accuracy Assessment

To evaluate the feasibility of offline deployment within the EnvisionAI platform, a comparative assessment of locally deployed language models was conducted, with a particular focus on response accuracy, and latency. These evaluations were performed on a machine with an Nvidia 5090 graphics card. Locally deployed models were run using quantised Ollama variants where available. The quantisation level followed the default distribution provided for each Ollama model tag, and no additional manual quantisation or layer-offloading configuration was applied.

**Table 1.** LLM latency results (seconds)

| Run | gpt-4.1-2025-04-14 | o4-mini-2025-04-16 | gpt-4.1-nano-2025-04-14 | gemini-2.0-flash-lite | gemini-2.0-flash | claude-3-7-sonnet-20250219 | claude-3-5-haiku-20241022 |
|---|---|---|---|---|---|---|---|
| 1 | 5.075 | 7.169 | 1.880 | 1.435 | 1.138 | 4.427 | 3.882 |
| 2 | 2.202 | 3.888 | 1.343 | 1.131 | 1.206 | 5.431 | 3.919 |
| 3 | 2.878 | 5.616 | 1.209 | 1.259 | 1.111 | 4.492 | 4.024 |
| 4 | 2.905 | 3.742 | 1.204 | 1.171 | 1.103 | 4.037 | 3.592 |
| 5 | 2.307 | 5.662 | 1.107 | 1.103 | 1.082 | 4.629 | 4.349 |
| **Av** | **3.074** | **5.216** | **1.348** | **1.220** | **1.128** | **4.603** | **3.953** |

**Table 2.** STT latency results (seconds)

| Run | gpt-4o-mini-transcribe | gpt-4o-transcribe | whisper-1 | scribe_v1 | scribe_v1_ experimental | nova-3 | slam-1 |
|---|---|---|---|---|---|---|---|
| 1 | 3.23 | 2.57 | 1.69 | 1.54 | 1.07 | 1.56 | 5.08 |
| 2 | 2.66 | 3.29 | 3.37 | 1.57 | 1.03 | 1.65 | 5.01 |
| 3 | 4.86 | 2.14 | 1.94 | 1.24 | 1.04 | 1.53 | 5.58 |
| 4 | 3.76 | 3.99 | 2.13 | 1.28 | 1.06 | 1.64 | 5.01 |
| 5 | 2.73 | 2.26 | 2.96 | 1.44 | 1.03 | 1.43 | 5.03 |
| **Av** | **3.45** | **2.85** | **2.42** | **1.41** | **1.05** | **1.56** | **5.14** |

**Table 3.** TTS latency results (seconds)

| | OpenAI | | | ElevenLabs | | | | |
|---|---|---|---|---|---|---|---|---|
| Run | gpt-4o-mini-tts | tts-1 | tts-1-hd | multilingual _v2 | flash_v2_5 | flash_v2 | turbo_v2_5 | turbo_v2 |
| 1 | 1.655 | 1.271 | 2.017 | 2.854 | 0.699 | 1.018 | 0.676 | 0.963 |
| 2 | 1.358 | 1.157 | 3.266 | 2.741 | 0.747 | 1.115 | 0.654 | 0.980 |
| 3 | 0.784 | 1.147 | 1.917 | 2.818 | 0.730 | 1.079 | 0.652 | 0.999 |
| 4 | 1.449 | 1.569 | 2.653 | 2.825 | 0.769 | 1.013 | 0.652 | 0.953 |
| 5 | 1.568 | 0.998 | 2.123 | 3.142 | 0.779 | 1.074 | 0.637 | 0.999 |
| **Av** | **1.363** | **1.228** | **2.395** | **2.876** | **0.745** | **1.060** | **0.654** | **0.979** |

**Table 4.** Streaming vs. non-streaming latency results (seconds)

| Run | Non-streaming Time (Seconds) | Streaming Time (Seconds) |
|---|---|---|
| 1 | 1.832 | 1.174 |
| 2 | 2.039 | 1.389 |
| 3 | 2.049 | 1.406 |
| 4 | 1.901 | 1.199 |
| 5 | 1.851 | 1.273 |
| **Average** | **1.934** | **1.288** |

Model performance was assessed using an "AI-as-a-judge" evaluation framework. For each test prompt, candidate model responses were scored by a judge model (GPT-4o) on a 1–10 scale for factual correctness against the provided domain material. All candidate models were evaluated under comparable conditions, using identical prompts and access to the same supporting documentation. Latency was measured alongside judged response quality to assess practical deployability within immersive systems.

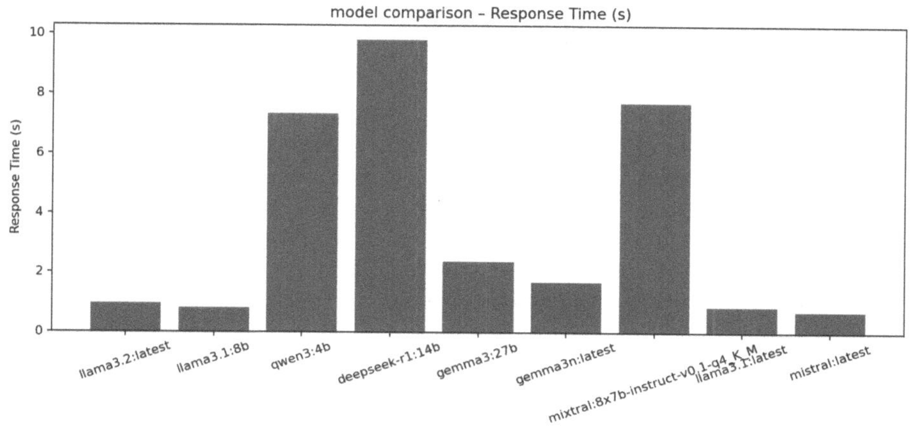


**Fig. 3.** A bar chart displaying average response times for local models

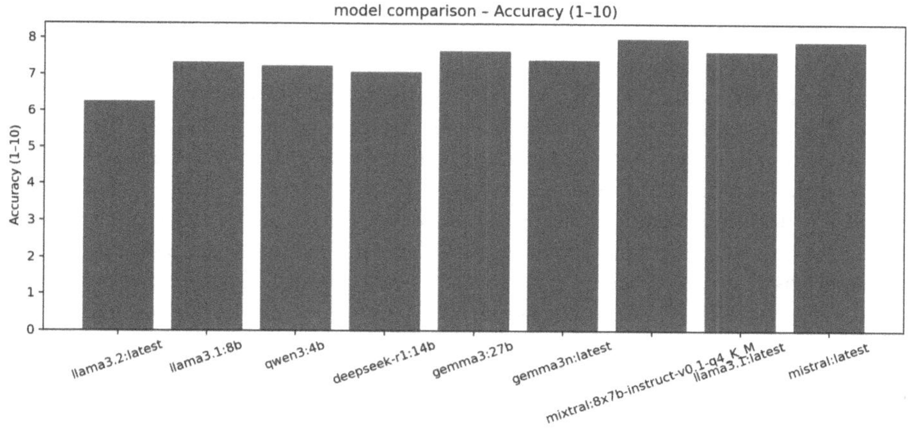


**Fig. 4.** A bar chart displaying average accuracy for local models

The results (Figs. 3 and 4) revealed a clear trade-off between reasoning capability and response latency. Models explicitly optimised for reasoning consistently produced more accurate and well-structured responses, however, these models also exhibited substantially higher response times. In practice, delays of several seconds disrupted dialogue flow and negatively impacted perceived responsiveness, rendering such models unsuitable for interactive avatar deployment despite their superior reasoning performance.

Several smaller local models, including Llama3:8B and Mistral:7B, performed similarly on accuracy and latency. Gemma 3 27B was selected as the preferred offline model because it provided the best practical balance observed in the project between response latency, factual adequacy, and conversational style. The assessment of conversational naturalness was based on internal review during deployment preparation rather than a formal user study, so this finding should be interpreted as a practitioner judgement rather than a validated user-experience result. Although Gemma 3 27B lacked the deeper reasoning capabilities of other models, it provided sufficiently accurate domain-specific answers while maintaining response times compatible with real-time use, making it a more suitable option for offline deployment in training scenarios

The viability of local model deployment with RAG has direct implications for educational technology adoption. Many sectors cannot use cloud-based AI due to data governance requirements. Demonstrating that local models with RAG can achieve acceptable accuracy for domain-specific instruction while maintaining complete data sovereignty removes a critical barrier to institutional adoption.

### 5.3 Preliminary Exploration of Learning Outcomes

To assess practical deployability, we conducted a small-scale usability and feasibility demonstration using the Dive Kit deployment. Four adult participants used the offline diving instructor avatar to learn equipment procedures, completed brief pre/post knowledge checks, and provided post-interaction feedback. This activity was designed to assess system use in a training-oriented context rather than pedagogical effectiveness, which would require larger samples, controls, validated instruments, and longitudinal study.

All participants completed the interaction without technical difficulty and reported the spoken dialogue format as intuitive and engaging. Knowledge check responses improved from baseline to post-interaction, although no generalisable learning claims can be made. The demonstration primarily confirmed deployment feasibility and highlighted key usability considerations: response latency, the avatar's formal tone reduced conversational naturalness, and environment-aware interaction using gaze-based object reference was positively received in equipment-based training. The system also remained robust throughout fully offline operation, with no crashes or interaction breakdowns. These findings support practical feasibility while identifying refinements needed before broader educational evaluation.

## 6 Discussion

The deployments and evaluations reported in this paper suggest that the practical success of AI-driven avatars in immersive training depends less on maximising model sophistication than on making appropriate architectural trade-offs for the target context. Returning to the design question posed in the introduction, the deployments suggest that conversational AI avatars for immersive training require architectural decisions that prioritise responsiveness, grounded interaction, deployment flexibility, and institutional control over data.

### 6.1 Optimise Responsiveness and Model Capability

A consistent finding across the project was that conversational latency governs perceived interaction quality more strongly than incremental gains in reasoning performance. In immersive spoken interaction, delays interrupt turn-taking, reduce perceived agency, and weaken presence (Shaw et al., 2020; Seuren et al., 2021). For this reason, optimisation should target end-to-end responsiveness, particularly time-to-first audio, rather than model quality in isolation. In our evaluations, streaming and careful model selection improved usability more than adopting the biggest or newest reasoning models.

## 6.2 Design for Portability, Grounding, and Governance

The project also showed that deployment architecture is not a secondary engineering concern but a primary design decision. Cloud services accelerated early prototyping, but local and hybrid deployment became necessary where offline resilience, data sovereignty, and predictable operational behaviour were required. Retrieval-augmented generation proved essential in these settings, improving factual accuracy and making moderate-sized local models viable for domain-specific instruction. Layered safeguards further reduced the likelihood of unsupported responses, although these should be understood as risk mitigations rather than guarantees.

## 6.3 Use Environment Context

The Dive Kit deployment suggested that interaction becomes more contextually useful when the system can incorporate information about the learner's current environment. Resolving references such as "this" through gaze or object focus made interaction more natural and more appropriate for procedural and equipment-based training. However, this capability introduces additional complexity in client sensing, context passing, and prompt construction, and should therefore be implemented where it directly supports the instructional task.

## 6.4 Deprioritise Features that Will Not Survive Deployment

Two capabilities explored during the project illustrate the importance of selective prioritisation. Multimodal emotion recognition showed promise in controlled settings but lacked sufficient robustness for deployment, while automatic lip synchronisation introduced substantial implementation complexity with limited benefit for training-focused interaction. In both cases, the more reliable design choice was to favour responsiveness, clarity, and robustness over technically impressive but operationally fragile features.

## 6.5 Limitations

This work has important limitations. User evaluation was small in scale, particularly in the Dive Kit usability demonstration, which limits the generalisability of the findings. Model evaluation focused on locally deployed language models under specific conditions. While latency and response quality were examined systematically, longer-term learning transfer, repeated use over time, and broader comparative pedagogical evaluation were outside the scope of the project. Most critically, this work does not provide rigorous evidence of educational effectiveness. The contribution is demonstrating technical feasibility and removing infrastructure barriers, not validating pedagogical impact. These results should therefore be interpreted as evidence of practical deployability and enabling capability rather than proof of learning outcomes.

## 7 Conclusion

This paper has reported on the design, deployment, and evaluation of EnvisionAI, a modular platform for conversational AI avatars in immersive training. Across three real-world deployments, the work showed that key barriers to deployment, particularly conversational latency, data sovereignty, and offline operation requirements, can be addressed through architectural design choices including streaming-based orchestration, provider-agnostic microservices, and retrieval-augmented generation.

These results establish practical feasibility rather than pedagogical proof. While the project demonstrated that conversational AI can be deployed across public engagement, educational, and defence-oriented training contexts, and that users can engage with such systems in training-oriented scenarios, rigorous evaluation of learning outcomes, transfer, and instructional effectiveness remains necessary future work. The contribution of this paper is therefore not to show that conversational AI improves learning in general, but to show that important infrastructure barriers to researching and deploying such systems can be reduced.

In response to the guiding design question, the main implication for practitioners is that immersive AI instructors depend less on maximising model sophistication than on designing architectures that support acceptable responsiveness, grounded interaction, deployment flexibility, and institutional control. As these technical barriers continue to fall, the next step is more rigorous educational research examining when, where, and how conversational AI can produce meaningful learning benefits in the immersive training contexts that are now becoming practically accessible.

**Acknowledgments.** This work was supported by Innovate UK. The authors, all employed by Metaverse-VR Ltd., led the technical development, deployment, and evaluation of the platform described in this paper. We thank Toby Everitt, Paul Pine, Tom Butler, and Claire Jones for leadership and stakeholder coordination. We also acknowledge and thank Robbie Ballie and Lewis Freeman for contributions to the wider project and evaluation activities.

**Disclosure of Interests..** The authors are employees of Metaverse-VR Ltd., the organisation that developed the EnvisionAI platform described in this paper. Robert Hillman's PhD research is funded by Metaverse-VR Ltd. and is in a related field. The authors led the technical development, deployment, and evaluation of the platform. The authors have no other competing interests to declare that are relevant to the content of this article.

## References

Deng, S., Zhao, H., Fang, W., Yin, J., Dustdar, S., Zomaya, A.Y.: Edge intelligence: the confluence of edge computing and artificial intelligence. IEEE Internet Things J. **7**(8), 7457–7469 (2020). https://doi.org/10.1109/JIOT.2020.2984887

European Data Protection Board: What are the basic processing principles under the GDPR? European Data Protection Board (n.d.). Retrieved from (2026). https://www.edpb.europa.eu/sme-data-protection-guide/faq-frequently-asked-questions/answer/what-are-basic-processing_en Accessed 11 June 2026

European Parliament and Council: Regulation (EU) 2024/1689 of the European Parliament and of the Council of 13 June 2024 laying down harmonised rules on artificial intelligence and amending certain Union legislative acts. Official Journal of the European Union, OJ L, 2024/1689, 12.7.2024 (2024).

Hamilton, D., McKechnie, J., Edgerton, E., Wilson, C.: Immersive virtual reality as a pedagogical tool in education: a systematic literature review of quantitative learning outcomes and experimental design. J. Comput. Educ. **8**, 1–32 (2021). https://doi.org/10.1007/s40692-020-00169-2

Kuhail, M.A., Alturki, N., Alramlawi, S., Alhejori, K.: Interacting with educational Chatbots: a systematic review. Educ. Inf. Technol. **28**, 973–1018 (2023). https://doi.org/10.1007/s10639-022-11177-3

Labadze, L., Grigolia, M., Machaidze, L.: Role of AI Chatbots in education: systematic literature review. Int. J. Educ. Technol. High. Educ. **20**, 56 (2023). https://doi.org/10.1186/s41239-023-00426-1

Lewis, P., et al.: Retrieval-augmented generation for knowledge-intensive NLP tasks. In: Advances in Neural Information Processing Systems, vol. 33, pp. 9459–9474 (2020)

Ortega-Ochoa, E., Arguedas, M., Daradoumis, T.: Empathic pedagogical conversational agents: a systematic literature review. Br. J. Educ. Technol. **55**(3), 886–909 (2024). https://doi.org/10.1111/bjet.13413

Seuren, L.M., Wherton, J., Greenhalgh, T., Shaw, S.E.: Whose turn is it anyway? Latency and the Organization of Turn-Taking in video-mediated interaction. J. Pragmat. **172**, 63–78 (2021). https://doi.org/10.1016/j.pragma.2020.11.005

Shaw, S.E., et al.: Video consultations between patients and clinicians in diabetes, cancer, and heart failure services: linguistic ethnographic study of video-mediated interaction. J. Med. Internet Res. **22**(5), e18378 (2020). https://doi.org/10.2196/18378

Zhou, Z., Chen, X., Li, E., Zeng, L., Luo, K., Zhang, J.: Edge intelligence: paving the last mile of artificial intelligence with edge computing. Proc. IEEE. **107**(8), 1738–1762 (2019). https://doi.org/10.1109/JPROC.2019.2918951

# SmarTest: AI Assisted Development of a Student Testing Framework

Ionuț Cristian Pistol(✉), Laura Cornei, Diana Trandabăț, and Mădălina Răschip

"Alexandru Ioan Cuza" University of Iași, 700506 Iași, Romania
{ionut.pistol,laura.cornei,diana.trandabat,madalina.raschip}@uaic.ro

**Abstract.** Integrating large language models into student software development raises questions beyond productivity: how do students learn to trust and evaluate AI outputs, and what happens when they study the same technology they use as a tool? This paper reports an empirical study involving 68 Computer Science teams aiming at building, assisted by LLMs (Large Language Models), an application to generate, answer, and evaluate Artificial Intelligence exam questions. All interactions were logged, yielding over four million words, plus tutor observations and team reflections. Based on lexical analysis and topic modelling of interaction data, evaluation data, and qualitative feedback, we examine three dimensions: the substitution–complementarity dynamic in LLM use, the development of trust calibration in AI setting, and the epistemological impact of using AI to learn about AI. Higher-performing teams engaged with LLMs differently (i.e. using more domain-specific language, revisiting topics in greater depth, and developing task-specific judgment about which tool to use) while neither the type nor number of agents used significantly affected grades. The experiment lead to a number of conclusions and ideas for future work, both discussed in the paper.

**Keywords:** Computer-managed instruction · Technology enhanced learning · Natural Language Processing

## 1 Introduction

The adoption of large language models (LLMs) within software development workflows has progressed at a rapid pace, with significant use among students alongside growing adoption by developers. Tools such as GitHub Copilot, Chat-GPT, and Gemini are now routinely used by Computer Science students to generate code, debug logic, and explore new concepts, often before institutions have defined clear pedagogical positions on their use. At the same time, higher education is grappling with a deeper question: not just whether students use these tools, but what kinds of learning, if any, results from that use. Jonassen's conception of mindtools [6] showed that the educationally valuable technology is one that makes the learner work harder cognitively, engaging them as designers


J. Weidlich et al. (Eds.): EC-TEL 2026, LNCS 16905, pp. 714–728, 2027.
https://doi.org/10.1007/978-3-032-37979-5_48

and constructors of knowledge rather than as passive recipients of it. Vygotsky's theory [21] of mediated learning raises a complementary question: whether a scaffold genuinely extends a learner toward independent competence, or does it merely replace the rigorous engagement that would have fostered such development? Large language models pose both questions at once and at unprecedented scale. As conversational systems that generate plausible answers learners may not yet be able to evaluate, they create a new mode of mediation: always available, endlessly patient, and indifferent to whether students truly understand or are merely satisfied. An expanding body of research investigates the productivity implications of LLM-assisted programming in educational contexts [5,9]. Initial empirical findings indicate that students can complete programming tasks faster and with fewer superficial errors when receiving generative support. Prevailing emphases on output quality and task completion leave a crucial dimension underexplored: how students negotiate epistemic and operational authority with an AI collaborator, how they decide when to accept, modify, or reject its output, and translate (or fail to translate) these interactions into durable conceptual understanding. Trust, defined as calibrated reliance on an automated system [10], has been extensively theorized in human factors and HCI (Human Computer Interaction), yet its dynamics in instructional and learning contexts remain comparatively under-specified.

The paper is structured as follows: the second section includes a review of related work in intelligent agents and AI assisted learning, organised around three dimensions. The following section describes the SmarTest project requirements that the student teams were tasked with. The fourth section describes the development process and the observed results, while the last section includes several project insights and conclusions for current and future AI assisted learning.

## 2 AI Assisted Learning

Recent advances in large language models have intensified research on their role in computer science education. In a few years, AI-assisted learning has moved from asking whether these tools can solve introductory programming exercises to examining what their success means for learning. While substantial literature exists, it focuses mainly on productivity, leaving two areas underexplored: how students learn to trust and evaluate LLM outputs, and what happens when the AI concepts students are learning are the same ones they ask LLMs to implement. This study sits at the intersection of these three dimensions.

### 2.1 LLMs in Computing Education: Productivity and Limits

Early work such as [4] showed that LLMs trained on large code corpora can generate code directly from natural language. Finnie-Ansley et al. [5] found that these models can outperform average introductory students on standard programming assessments. More recent studies have examined student use of these tools over longer periods. Lyu et al. [12] tracked students using an LLM assistant over a semester in introductory programming, finding increased productivity but highlighting the need for instructor guidance and raising concerns about impacts on critical thinking. Tanay et al. [19] observed a similar pattern with upper-level students in a semester-long software engineering project: students viewed LLMs as valuable for productivity, but recognized potential harm to knowledge retention.

The retention concern connects to a broader and more troubling pattern: over-reliance. Kazemitabaar et al. [9] found that novice learners given AI code generators completed tasks faster, but engaged less deeply with the underlying concepts than peers working without assistance – faster, but not better. Pirzado et al. [15] reviewed the behaviour of LLMs as coding assistants across the literature and documented recurring problems of correctness and reliability that students frequently failed to catch before accepting the tool's output. Lehman et al. [11] went further, showing that the effect of LLM access on learning depends entirely on how students use it: those who let the tool generate solutions learned less, while those who engaged with it conversationally—asking for explanations, reasoning through the responses, pushing back—actually improved their understanding. This distinction between substitution and complementarity also motivated CodeAid [8], an LLM-based assistant deliberately constrained to provide technically accurate guidance without disclosing complete solutions. Systematic reviews identify this productivity–comprehension tension as the central open problem in the field [16].

### 2.2 Trust and Calibration

A deeper issue behind over-reliance is one the computing education literature has mostly left implicit: trust. Lee and See [10] define appropriate trust in automation as calibrated reliance—a disposition aligned with the system's actual capabilities and limitations, rather than blanket acceptance or rejection. They distinguish over-trust, marked by automation bias and uncritical acceptance of outputs, from under-trust, marked by failure to use reliable assistance. When students over-trust an LLM, they do more than make a workflow error—they surrender the cognitive work the task is meant to evoke. The studies above show that over-trust is the more common novice failure, partly because limited domain knowledge impairs independent checks of output plausibility.

Beyond coding, LLMs now support varied tasks for Computer Science students. Agarwal et al. [1] evaluate several LLMs (ChatGPT 3.5, Microsoft Copilot, GitHub Copilot Chat, Google Bard) on code explanation, assignment solving, interview preparation, learning new concepts, and email writing. Performance varies by task and complexity; no model dominates across all cases. Thus, trust calibration in a multi-agent setting becomes a portfolio of task-specific judgments—a skill rarely taught or studied.

Argumentation is one mechanism by which trust recalibration may occur. Andriessen [2] shows that argumentative learning—confronting, evaluating, and responding to challenges to one's claims—is highly effective for deepening understanding. When an LLM produces hallucinated or inconsistent output, a student who critiques it, instead of simply accepting or rejecting it, is effectively engaging in argumentative learning: forming a position, testing it against the system's response, and revising. How often this pattern appears in real-world LLM use, and under what conditions, remains largely unstudied.

## 2.3 Reflexivity: Learning About NLP with AI

Few studies have examined LLM-assisted learning in project-based, team settings beyond individual coding tasks. Rasnayaka et al. [17] investigate LLM use by student teams in a software engineering project, analyzing AI-generated code, prompting strategies along with student perceptions. They find LLMs are most useful in early development stages and suggest a maturation effect in human–LLM collaboration: teams that first clarify their task before delegating to the LLM gain more value. Kasneci et al. [7] offer a broad theoretical framing, arguing that LLMs have real educational potential for personalization, engagement, and formative feedback, but only when embedded in deliberate pedagogical design rather than provided as unrestricted tools.

Existing work seems to not include experiments where the learning process has both as an teaching objective and as an educational tool Natural Language Processing (NLP) technologies. This reflexive setup changes how both learners and tools function epistemologically. When students use an AI enhanced dialog system, their capacity to judge and assimilate the LLM's answers depends directly on how well they understand the technologies being studied. Trust and comprehension, therefore, develop together in both directions. Their earliest uses, when their knowledge is weakest, are when they are most epistemically vulnerable. In this setting, Lehmann et al.'s [11] substitution–complementarity distinction becomes especially consequential: a student who lets the LLM do the reasoning without engaging the logic not only performs the task poorly, but also fails to learn the very content the task is meant to teach. When students use several LLMs, choosing different tools for different tasks or using them in sequence to check outputs, the reflexive complexity grows: they must calibrate trust across a portfolio of agents while also building the needed domain knowledge, a challenge not yet addressed.

## 2.4 Synthesis: the Gap This Study Addresses

These three dimensions expose a shared blind spot in current work. Productivity studies show that whether LLMs substitute for or complement human work shapes learning, but they do not ask what enables complementary use in practice. Trust research theorizes calibrated reliance but ignores learners whose domain knowledge and trust judgments co-develop. And the reflexive case - using AI to reason about AI - remains unstudied.

Based on the gaps identified in the literature, this study investigates the following research questions:

- How do students integrate LLMs into their problem-solving processes during a semester-long software development project?
- How does trust in LLM outputs evolve as students gain experience and domain knowledge?
- What learning dynamics emerge when students use AI systems to learn about the same AI technologies they are using as tools?

This paper tackles all three gaps in one naturalistic setting: an undergraduate AI course where student teams built an AI-powered exam tool using LLMs as collaborative coding assistants. All interactions were logged; the course content was the tool's domain; and grades and written feedback were collected. These data provide a rare view of human–LLM collaboration when trust has visible academic stakes, the task demands real conceptual reasoning, and AI is both subject and instrument.

## 3 The SmarTest Project

Natural Language Processing (NLP) is one of the major areas of research and development in Computer Science, the technologies developed in NLP leading to the emergence of the current AI agents. Extensive collections of NLP components, such as [20] or [18], and overview papers such as [13,14], show both the high level of complexity of the resources available, as well as the range of options available when building a project involving NLP components. The experiment, as introduced to the 3rd year Computer Science students, required the development, with the help of any available AI conversational assistants, of a NLP system capable of generating exam-style questions similar to those given in the "Artificial Intelligence" course exam, as well as evaluating received answers. Calls to AI agents could not be included in the actual projects being developed, they were to be used only as guides and support in the development process.

The SmarTest project was designed to achieve several interconnected learning objectives. Beyond producing a functional software system, students were expected to acquire technical knowledge and develop effective practices for collaborating with LLMs. More specifically, the project aimed to: (1) deepen students' understanding of the AI algorithms covered in the Artificial Intelligence course, (2) encourage them to learn and apply previously unfamiliar NLP techniques needed to implement the system, (3) develop effective practices for collaborating with LLMs during software development, and (4) learn how to use LLMs as tools for acquiring knowledge in an unfamiliar technical domain.

Briefly, the main requirements were:

- The system can generate a question by selecting an available question type or by randomly selecting from the available types. The question can be closed or open-ended.
- The system can evaluate an answer to a known question (previously generated) on a scale from 0% (completely wrong) to 100% (completely accurate).

- The system can generate an answer to a question provided by the user, if that question is recognized as being of a type known to the system.

Four types of questions were set as minimal requirements, and students were able to freely add additional types. The four mandatory were:

- For a given [Problem] and [Instance], suggest a search strategy from those included in the Artificial Intelligence course support. [Problem] can be one of the AI toy problems discussed with the tutors during courses and seminars (generalized Hanoi towers, n-queens, graph coloring, knight's tour), and [Instance] can be a randomly generated valid instance for that problem or one selected from a curated list.
- For a given game in a normal form representation, does a pure Nash equilibrium exist?
- Given a set of variables, domains, constraints and a partial assignment of values to a subset of variables, what solution would be obtained, if one exists, when using Backtracking with a specified [Optimization] to assign values to the remaining variables?
- For a given tree, what value will be obtained at the root, and how many leaf nodes will be visited when applying the MinMax strategy with Alpha-Beta pruning?

Technical requirements were set but are not directly relevant to the results reported here. Students worked in teams of up to five members and had 13 weeks to complete the project.

The key feature of the project was the mandatory, tutor-enforced use of AI agents to learn previously untaught text-generation and analysis techniques, and to design a general system architecture and workflow. This was intentional: by placing students in an area where they did not know the answers in advance, the project made the substitution–complementarity distinction consequential and ensured that purely passive LLM use would visibly fail.

Tutors monitored progress weekly and gave only general guidance and feedback. The explicit ban on direct implementation help was also deliberate. Tutors offered evaluative and directional comments—indicating that a solution was suboptimal or that better directions existed—but did not solve concrete technical issues. This constraint made critical engagement with LLM outputs the main problem-solving resource and was intended to foster argumentative learning.

The project required documentation of all AI interactions. This produced the dataset analysed in Sect. 4 and, pedagogically, aimed to make students more reflective about their LLM use, knowing their interactions would be read and assessed, and thus encouraging deliberate rather than casual engagement.

## 4 Results of the Experiment

During the 13 weeks of the semester, students and teachers provided feedback on the experiment using three main methods:

- Direct interaction between students and teachers, who monitored the progress of the teams and offered feedback and general guidance.
- Each team collected a data set on student interaction with AI Agents, relevant to the project objectives.
- At the end of the experiment, each team provided a brief written description of their experience developing a project with these particular requirements.

Taken together, these sources allow us to examine, with real data, how students negotiated authority with LLM collaborators when the task demanded genuine engagement with AI concepts they were simultaneously learning—the reflexive condition. The feedback is described in more details below, with the general conclusions of the experiment being included in the next section.

### 4.1 Direct Interaction

Although the feedback during the development weeks was extensive and varied, several key themes relevant to the experiment emerged. Tutor observations during the semester provide process-level evidence of how the three dimensions identified in Sect. 2 appeared in practice as students learned to work with LLMs on a technically and conceptually demanding task.

The main early observation was that most students initially underestimated the capabilities of available NLP technologies. Because the core AI-assisted learning objective was to enable them to choose and use suitable technologies for their projects, tutors gave extensive feedback to guide the students' interactions with the AI agents.

A second pattern in architectural decision-making mapped directly onto the substitution–complementarity distinction. Initially, all teams delegated too broadly—asking the LLM to design full architectures, generate whole components, or solve open-ended problems in one exchange. This reflected over-trust in Lee and See's [10] sense: students depended on the LLM beyond its actual competence and lacked the prior knowledge to calibrate that trust. Tutors steered them toward a more modular, flexible strategy. Because AI agents tend to mirror users' apparent expertise, tutors also urged students to ask more ambitious, wide-ranging questions. For example, many did not realize they could use multiple tools to compare texts semantically for answer validation. A similar pattern arose in code generation: useful code appeared only when students' requests were highly specific and atomic. As teams learned to prompt effectively, they simultaneously deepened their subject knowledge.

The third and most theoretically rich pattern emerged later in the project, as interactions became more specific and domain-grounded. As teams moved from architectural questions to implementation details—such as particular NLP components, algorithm behaviors, or edge-case handling—hallucinated or irrelevant responses increased. Rather than undermining the project, this produced what Andriessen [2] calls argumentative learning: students had to notice inconsistencies, investigate them, and construct more precise or better-evidenced positions. Though effortful and sometimes frustrating, teams that engaged in this process—instead of simply trying new prompts until something looked plausible—developed a deeper understanding of their problem. This pattern was not accidental; it arose from the project's constraint structure, which required students to document interactions and barred instructors from giving direct implementation guidance, making critical engagement with LLM outputs the only viable path forward.

After the final project presentation, all 68 teams were graded (on a scale from 1 to 10), with a general overview of the results shown in Table 1. Exactly 50% (34) of the teams got a good grade (8 or above), which indicates a successful solution covering all requirements. The failing teams (with grades below 5) did not meet the minimal requirements, i.e. to generate and answer the four question types mentioned in Sect. 3. A quantifiable evaluation of the AI agents impact on these grades is discussed in the next subsection.

**Table 1.** Evaluation of the implemented projects

| Evaluation | 3 | 4 | 5 | 6 | 7 | 8 | 9 | 10 |
|---|---|---|---|---|---|---|---|---|
| # of teams | 6 | 6 | 5 | 7 | 10 | 8 | 10 | 16 |
| Group | low | | medium | | | | | top |

### 4.2 Collected Logs

The collected logs highlighting the students' interaction with AI agents provided very useful (and quantifiable) reference data that could give us clues as to what works and what doesn't in the context of similar experiments. They included over 4 million words in 77 files (several teams provided multiple logs). The statistical data discussed below for all files is available at an anonymised repository[1].

**Vocabulary Data.** The collected logs allow for various lexical analyses to be performed, which, when correlated to the assigned grades for the corresponding teams, provide some interesting insights. By grouping the grades into three categories (top - 10, medium, and low - below 5), some rounded statistical lexical data about the logs was extracted, as highlighted in Table 2.

**Table 2.** Lexical data for the collected logs.

| grade range | words | distinct words | hapax | hapax token-ratio |
|---|---|---|---|---|
| low | 21705.00 | 2383.56 | 954.57 | 0.48 |
| medium | 35451.81 | 3188.29 | 1282.74 | 0.44 |
| top | 132291.22 | 6217.91 | 2418.13 | 0.43 |

[1] https://anonymous.4open.science/r/SmarTest-data-6C61/.

The data show that the teams that got better grades interacted much more with the AI agents (over four times as much compared to the low graded teams). Also, the vocabulary used was much more extensive, with a significantly increased number of distinct words. The hapax score (the number of single occurrence words) and the hapax token-ration (the probability of a word to have a single occurrence) show that the highest scoring teams used a more consolidated vocabulary (likely more technical lexicon), and that a higher proportion of their vocabulary included domain-specific terminology that recurred across multiple prompts. Thus, the depth of interaction with the AI agents was higher.

The lists of most frequently used words show other significant differences between the top teams and the lower graded ones (Table 3). The data confirms that the teams with the highest grades generally made more specific prompts, using AI Agents not only for a general guidance, but also down to implementation details. This is confirmed by the extracted collocations, where the lower graded teams used frequently expressions such as *'Algorithm selection'*, *'Architectural decisions'*, and *'Answer question'*. The collocations discovered in the logs of the higher graded teams usually refer to particular instances for the questions covered (*'20-Queens strategy limit'*), or to very specific implementation details (*'caF potkseD'*).

**Table 3.** Most frequently used words.

| grade range | Top 20 most frequently used words, excluding stopwords |
|---|---|
| low | function, keywords, return, write, scenario, generates, build, screen, choose, explanation, pruning, window, python, strategy, backtracking, random, answer, id, randomly, smartest |
| medium | tests, smartest, file, users, documents, nash, return, projects, read, phase, lines, question_types, csp, question, command, terminal, generation, python, files, templates |
| top | const, backend, question, problem, search, app, div, minimax, document, error, style, result, return, node, question, score, value, text, nash, length |

**Usage of AI Agents.** Figure 1 describes the types of employed AI agents, as well as their usage frequency across all teams. It is noticeable that only four types of agents were utilized: ChatGPT, Claude, GitHub Copilot, and Google Gemini. The most popular agent, used by 90.6% of the teams, was ChatGPT, followed by Google Gemini (75.0%), and GitHub Copilot (70.3%).

To assess whether the types of used AI agents had a significant impact over the final grades, for each type of agent, the grades received by the teams using it were collected and used to compute the mean and standard deviation for each sample. Students using the Claude AI agent obtained the highest average

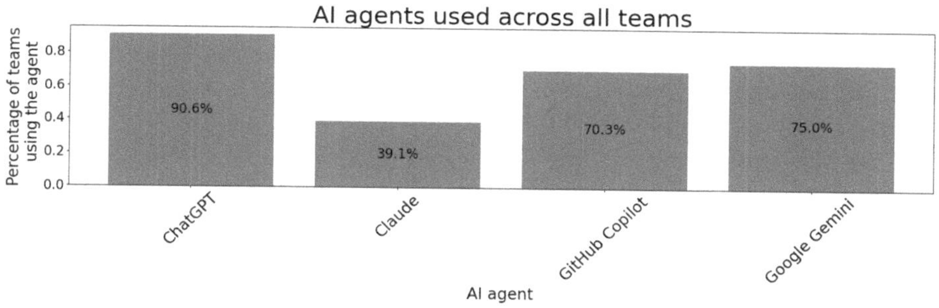


**Fig. 1.** Usage of AI agents across all teams.

grade (7.91), followed by students using GitHub Copilot (7.76), ChatGPT (7.68), and Gemini (7.61). Then, the Welch's t-test was applied on the grade samples associated to each pair of AI agents and the results indicated that all differences in the average grade values were not statistically significant. Therefore, the type of used AI agent(s) did not bring a substantial variation in the grades' values.

Figure 2 highlights the types of used AI agents for each team. Out of all teams, 64 of them reported using AI agents for completing the project. 18 teams integrated all four agents to address the given tasks, while of 15 them relied on a single AI agent.

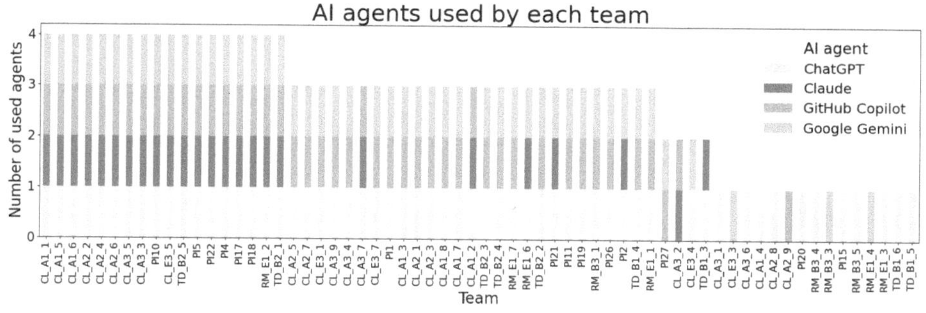


**Fig. 2.** Usage of AI agents per team.

To examine whether the number of used agents had an impact over the project grade, the grade values were grouped based on the number of employed AI agents by each team, and were further used to compute the means and standard deviations for each sample. The average project grade obtained by teams utilizing 3 or 4 agents (7.85 and 7.82, respectively) was higher than the ones obtained by the teams using 1 or 2 agents (7.04 and 6.62, respectively). However, when applying the Welch's t-test, we again observed that these differences in the average grade value were not statistically significant.

**Extracted Topics.** The Top2Vec [3] algorithm was used to extract relevant topics from the collected logs. Given the fact that analyzed logs were both in Romanian and in English, a multilingual embedding model was chosen as part of Top2Vec: paraphrase-multilingual-MiniLM-L12-v2. For this algorithm, the hyper-parameter *speed* was set to value $'deep-learn'$, to learn the best quality vectors. After multiple trials, the rest of the Top2Vec hyper-parameters were fixed as follows: $min\_cluster\_size = 5$, $min\_samples = 5$, $n\_neighbors = 25$, and $n\_components = 4$, to obtain visually qualitative results, considering both the size of the dataset and the number of expected topics.

Figure 3 illustrates the 2D visualisation of the primary topics identified in the log files associated to each team, when using the UMAP dimensionality reduction technique. The Top2Vec algorithm identified two major topics:

- One topic was associated to the question generation process. Since the project primarily focused on question generation, question answering, and evaluation, this topic was anticipated.
- The other topic was related to AI specific algorithms. The presence of this topic is justified by the fact that the generated questions were related to algorithms and models studied in the Artificial Intelligence course.

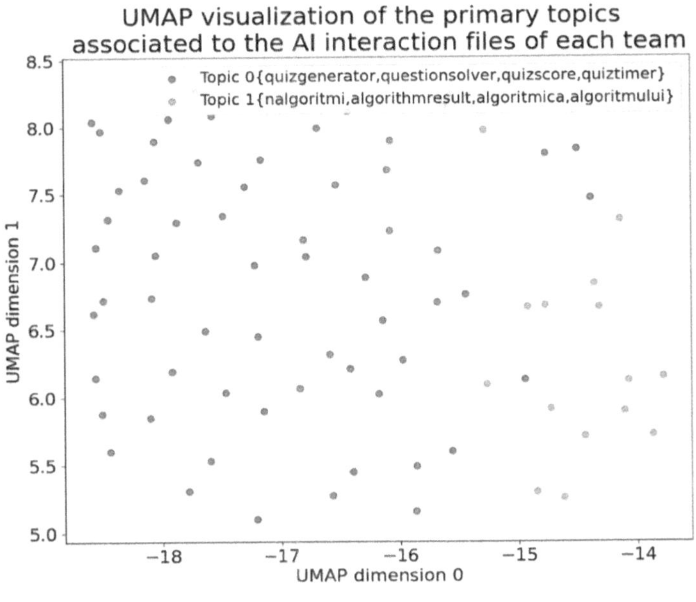


**Fig. 3.** UMAP visualization of the primary topics associated to the collected logs.

Figure 4 represents the word cloud associated to the question generation topic. As it can be seen, the word cloud includes two categories of tokens: one directly related to the question generation process (e.g., 'quiz generator', 'question score', 'quiz answers'), and the other related to the development of a web application associated to the project (e.g., 'quiz timer', 'quiz controller', 'question service', 'question plug-in', 'questions' cache').

The Top2Vec algorithm revealed that the two predominant topics from the AI interaction log files were related to the question generation process and to the employed AI algorithms. The question generation topic additionally included keywords referring to the development of a web application associated to the project, while the topic referring to algorithms had associated keywords corresponding to specific AI algorithms mentioned in the project specification. For more than three-quarters of the teams, the question generation topic appeared more frequently than the algorithm-based one, being identified as a primary topic for those teams. This phenomenon could be due to the fact that the requirements of the question generation task were broadly defined, which led the students to explore and learn various NLP techniques with AI assistance. In contrast, implementing AI algorithms required fewer interactions since those methods were already taught in the course, leaving little room for confusion. The topic distribution in the logs is therefore an empirical trace of the trust co-development dynamic from Sect. 2.3.

**Fig. 4.** Word cloud associated to the question generation topic.

### 4.3 Written Feedback

The written feedback collected from each team provided a series of insights into their experience, including some confirmed hypothesis and some novel ideas, as summarised below.

Across teams, the main theme was a recalibration of expectations. Students found the AI agents less useful and autonomous than expected, needing more critical guidance and iterative prompts to obtain relevant, usable answers. This shift from over-reliance to more calibrated use was both anticipated and beneficial, helping students move from general requirements to implementation details. At the same time, the AI did supply previously unknown information and generate basic code that reduced the development effort.

Another theme was using multiple agents strategically. Teams often started with one tool, then realized different LLMs had complementary strengths. For example, one team used ChatGPT to scope and plan, Claude Haiku to implement, GitHub Copilot to review code, and Claude Sonnet to test. This task-specific allocation of tools reflects different levels of trust in multiple agents and arose naturally because teams understood each tool's limits. The fact that several teams independently adopted this pattern, and that teams using three or four tools earned slightly higher grades on average, suggests it is a teachable heuristic rather than a random outcome.

Some teams used multiple agents to iteratively improve solutions: one generated an implementation, a second refined it, a third improved the revision, and so on. After several bootstrapping rounds, the final result was consistently better than any single agent's initial solution.

A final theme was the reflexive nature of the experience. Students realized that judging the LLM's answers on AI topics depended on their own developing understanding. Several teams said they only recognized errors in LLM-generated content about Minimax or constraint satisfaction after those lectures, and that revisiting earlier interactions with new knowledge felt disorienting. This reflects the trust–comprehension co-development dynamic from Sect. 2 and shows that the reflexive condition creates a distinct learning experience in which using the tool, learning the subject, and evaluating the tool's knowledge merge.

## 5 Conclusions

The SmarTest experiment studied human–LLM collaboration in realistic, high-stakes educational settings. Its main practical finding: performance depended more on how teams used the tool, rather than on which tool they used. Teams that broadly delegated—asking the LLM for answers, accepting outputs uncritically, and moving on—produced weaker implementations and shallower interactions. Teams that used the LLM to deepen their own problem solving skills—making specific requests, challenging inconsistencies, and revisiting concepts with increasing precision—produced stronger projects and richer logs. This showcases the substitution–complementarity distinction in a naturalistic, semester-long project with 68 teams in varied configurations.

Neither the type of used AI agent(s) nor the number of used agents led to statistically significant variations in the grade outcomes. This might indicate that the used technology, although helpful, could not be used as a substitute for human effort which made the actual difference in the results. Combining multiple agents, which appeared to posses varied degrees of competency in different tasks, or using them in a bootstrapping process, provided generally the better results.

Early in the project, over-trust dominated: students accepted the LLM's suggestions uncritically, wrote vague prompts that yielded plausible but inadequate outputs, and often missed errors in areas where they lacked independent knowledge. Calibration improved over time, not through explicit instruction, but because mandatory interaction logging, bans on direct implementation guidance, and tutor pressure for more specific engagement made passive LLM use untenable. AI agents performed best with precise, narrow specifications, requiring human supervision for overall development. Intentionally keeping project specifications less precise supports genuine learning for students and ensures competition between teams rather than between AI agents.

The contributions of the experiment extend to the technology-enhanced learning literature by presenting evidence for the substitution-complementarity distinction, offering insights on how design constraints can facilitate trust calibration, and introducing the concept of reflexive co-development.

However, limitations include the study's focus on a single course and institution, raising questions about generalizability across contexts. Future research can also include a longer period with two or more tasks to be developed one after the other, or including teams with different levels of knowledge regarding the technologies the project requires, thus identifying if certain topics, such as NLP, GUI or Machine Learning, are better suited for AI assisted learning.

The bootstrapping behaviour discovered independently by multiple teams—passing outputs iteratively between agents to improve quality—deserves investigation as a teachable strategy.

**Acknowledgments.** We would like to thank the 3rd year students at the Faculty of Computer Science, who worked on the actual experiment and provided valuable feedback during and after its completion.

## References

1. Agarwal, V., Garg, M.K., Dharmavaram, S., Kumar, D.: "which LLM should I use?": Evaluating LLMs for tasks performed by undergraduate computer science students. In: arXiv preprint arXiv:2402.01687 (2024)
2. Andriessen, J.: Arguing to learn. In: Sawyer, R.K. (ed.) The Cambridge Handbook of the Learning Sciences, pp. 443–460. Cambridge University Press (2006)
3. Angelov, D.: Top2Vec: Distributed representations of topics. In: arXiv preprint arXiv:2008.09470 (2020)
4. Chen, M., et al.: Evaluating large language models trained on code. In: arXiv preprint arXiv:2107.03374 (2021)
5. Finnie-Ansley, J., Denny, P., Becker, B.A., Luxton-Reilly, A., Prather, J.: The robots are coming: exploring the implications of OpenAI codex on introductory programming. In: Proceedings of the 24th Australasian Computing Education Conference, pp. 10–19 (2022)
6. Jonassen, D.H.: Computers in the classroom: Mindtools for critical thinking. In: Merrill/Prentice-Hall Monograph Series, Merrill/Prentice-Hall (1996)
7. Kasneci, E., et al.: ChatGPT for good? On opportunities and challenges of large language models for education. In: Learning and Individual Differences, vol. 103, pp. 102274 (2023)
8. Kazemitabaar, M., et al.: Studying the effect of AI code generators on supporting novice learners in introductory programming. In: Proceedings of the 2023 CHI Conference on Human Factors in Computing Systems, pp. 1–23 (2023)
9. Kazemitabaar, M., et al.: CodeAid: evaluating a classroom deployment of an LLM-based programming assistant that balances student and educator needs. In: Proceedings of the 2024 CHI Conference on Human Factors in Computing Systems, pp. 1–20 (2024)

10. Lee, J.D., See, K.A.: Trust in automation: designing for appropriate reliance. In: Human Factors: The Journal of the Human Factors and Ergonomics Society, vol. 46, pp. 50–80 (2004)
11. Lehmann, M., Cornelius, P.B., Sting, F.J.: AI meets the classroom: When does ChatGPT harm learning. In: arXiv preprint arXiv:2409.09047 (2024)
12. Lyu, W., Wang, Y., Chung, T., Sun, Y., Zhang, Y.: Evaluating the effectiveness of LLMs in introductory computer science education: a semester-long field study. In: Proceedings of the 11th ACM Conference on Learning @ Scale, pp. 63–74 (2024)
13. Min, B., et al.: Recent advances in natural language processing via large pre-trained language models: a survey. In: ACM Computing Surveys, vol. 56, pp. 1–40 (2023)
14. Patil, R., Boit, S., Gudivada, V., Nandigam, J.: A survey of text representation and embedding techniques in NLP. In: IEEE Access, vol. 11, pp. 36120–36146 (2023)
15. Pirzado, F.A., Ahmed, A., Mendoza-Urdiales, R.A., Terashima-Marin, H.: Navigating the pitfalls: analyzing the behavior of LLMs as a coding assistant for computer science students–a systematic review of the literature. In: IEEE Access, vol. 12, pp. 112605–112625 (2024)
16. Raihan, N., Siddiq, M.L., Santos, J.C., Zampieri, M.: Large language models in computer science education: a systematic literature review. In: Proceedings of the 56th ACM Technical Symposium on Computer Science Education, vol. 1, pp. 938–944 (2025)
17. Rasnayaka, S., Wang, G., Shariffdeen, R., Iyer, G.N.: An empirical study on usage and perceptions of LLMs in a software engineering project. In: Proceedings of the 1st International Workshop on Large Language Models for Code, pp. 111–118 (2024)
18. Shen, Y., Song, K., Tan, X., Li, D., Lu, W., Zhuang, Y.: HuggingGPT: solving AI tasks with ChatGPT and its friends in hugging face. In: Advances in Neural Information Processing Systems, vol. 36, pp. 38154–38180 (2023)
19. Tanay, B.A., Arinze, L., Joshi, S.S., Davis, K.A., Davis, J.C.: An exploratory study on upper-level computing students' use of large language models as tools in a semester-long project. In: arXiv preprint arXiv:2403.18679 (2024)
20. Vasiliev, Y.: Natural language processing with Python and spacy: A practical introduction. In: No Starch Press Technical Publications, No Starch Press (2020)
21. Vygotsky, L.S.: Mind in society: The development of higher psychological processes. In: Harvard University Press Monographs, Harvard University Press (1978)

# Author Index




J. Weidlich et al. (Eds.): EC-TEL 2026, LNCS 16905, pp. 729–731, 2027.
https://doi.org/10.1007/978-3-032-37979-5